ENCYCLOPEDIA OF

Violence, Peace, & Conflict

ENCYCLOPEDIA OF

Violence, Peace, & Conflict

VOLUME 3 Po – Z Index

ACADEMIC PRESS

SAN DIEGO   LONDON   BOSTON   NEW YORK   SYDNEY   TOKYO   TORONTO

This book is printed on acid-free paper.

Academic Press
A Harcourt Science and Technology Company
525 B Street, Suite 1900, San Diego, California 92101-4495, USA
http://www.apnet.com

Academic Press
24-28 Oval Road, London NW1 7DX, UK
http://www.hbuk.co.uk/ap/

Library of Congress Catalog Card Number: 99-60408

International Standard Book Number: 0-12-227010-X (set)
International Standard Book Number: 0-12-227011-8 (Volume 1)
International Standard Book Number: 0-12-227012-6 (Volume 2)
International Standard Book Number: 0-12-227013-4 (Volume 3)

PRINTED IN THE UNITED STATES OF AMERICA
99   00   01   02   03   04   MM   9   8   7   6   5   4   3   2   1

Contents

Contents of Other Volumes

Contents by Subject Area

Public Policy Studies

Sociological Studies

Warfare and Military Studies

Contributors

Mimi Ajzenstadt
Women, Violence Against
  Hebrew University
  Jerusalem, Israel

Peter Almquist
Economic Conversion
  US Arms Control and Disarmament Agency
  Washington, DC, USA

Randall Amster
Power and Deviance
  Arizona State University
  Tempe, Arizona, USA

Kristin L. Anderson
Child Abuse
  Drew University
  Madison, New Jersey, USA

Kauko Aromaa
Victimology
  National Research Institute of Legal Policy
  Helsinki, Finland

Sidney Axinn
Moral Judgments and Values
  Temple University
  Philadelphia, Pennsylvania, USA

Kerri Lynn Bates
Urban and Community Studies
  University of British Columbia
  Vancouver, British Columbia, Canada

Hugo Adam Bedau
Death Penalty
  Tufts University
  Medford, Massachusetts, USA

Nancy Bell
Power, Alternative Theories of
  University of Texas
  Austin, Texas, USA

Robert D. Benford
Peace Movements
  University of Nebraska
  Lincoln, Nebraska, USA

Chawki Benkelfat
Biochemical Factors
  McGill University
  Montreal, Quebec, Canada

Nachman Ben-Yehuda
Assassinations, Political
  Hebrew University
  Jerusalem, Israel

Jacob Bercovitch
Mediation and Negotiation Techniques
  University of Canterbury
  Christchurch, New Zealand

Leonard Berkowitz
Aggression, Psychology of
  University of Wisconsin
  Madison, Wisconsin, USA

Irwin S. Bernstein
Animal Behavior Studies, Primates
  University of Georgia
  Athens, Georgia, USA

Mike Berry
Communication Studies, Overview
  University of California, Santa Barbara
  Santa Barbara, California

Vincent Boudreau
Political Theories
  City University of New York
  New York, NY, USA

Elise Boulding
Peace Culture
  Dartmouth College (emerita)
  Hanover, New Hampshire, USA

Janet Welsh Brown
Environmental Issues and Politics
Nongovernmental Actors in International
  Politics
Trade and the Environment
  World Resources Institute
  Washington, DC, USA

Lisa Brown
Ethnicity and Identity Politics
   University of Florida
   Gainesville, Florida, USA

Arden Bucholz
Militarism
   State University of New York
   Brockport, New York, USA

James Burk
Military Culture
   Texas A&M University
   College Station, Texas, USA

Gabriella Cagliesi
Trade Wars (Disputes)
   Rutgers University
   Newark, New Jersey, USA

Deborah Cai
Interpersonal Conflict, History of
   University of Maryland
   College Park, Maryland, USA

James Calleja
Aged Population, Violence and Nonviolence
   toward
   International Institute on Aging
   United Nations, Malta

Jesus Casquette
Draft, Resistance and Evasion of
   Universidad del Pais Vasco
   Leioa, Spain

Victor D. Cha
Collective Security Systems
   Georgetown University
   Washington, DC, USA

Paul Chevigny
Police Brutality
   New York University Law School
   New York, NY, USA

Stephen J. Cimbala
Nuclear Weapons Policies
   Pennsylvania State University, Delaware County
   Media, Pennsylvania, USA

Murray Code
Reason and Violence
   University of Guelph
   Toronto, Ontario, Canada

Irwin Cohen
Torture (State)
   Simon Fraser University
   Burnaby, British Columbia, Canada

Noé Cornago-Prieto
Diplomacy
   University of the Basque Country
   Bilbao, Spain

Raymond R. Corrado
Torture (State)
   Simon Fraser University
   Burnaby, British Columbia, Canada

Alex E. Crosby
Public Health Models of Violence and Violence Prevention
   Centers for Disease Control
   Atlanta, Georgia, USA

S. Cumner
Peacekeeping
   Pearson Peacekeeping Centre
   Clementsport, Nova Scotia, Canada

G. David Curry
Gangs
Law and Violence
   University of Missouri, St. Louis
   St. Louis, Missouri, USA

Thomas C. Daffern
Peacemaking and Peacebuilding
   International Institute of Peace Studies
   London, UK

Linda L. Dahlberg
Public Health Models of Violence and Violence Prevention
   Centers for Disease Control
   Atlanta, Georgia, USA

James C. Davies
Human Nature, Views of
   University of Oregon (Emeritus)
   Eugene, Oregon, USA

Angela Davis
Crime and Punishment, Changing Attitudes toward
   University of California, Santa Cruz
   Santa Cruz, California, USA

Scott H. Decker
Gangs
   University of Missouri, St. Louis
   St. Louis, Missouri, USA

Paul F. Diehl
Territorial Disputes
   University of Illinois
   Urbana, Illinois, USA

Edward Donnerstein
Mass Media, General View
   University of California, Santa Barbara
   Santa Barbara, California, USA

William Donohue
Interpersonal Conflict, History of
   Michigan State University
   East Lansing, Michigan, USA

Steven Dubin
Peace and the Arts
   State University of New York
   Purchase, New York, USA

Antulio J. Echevarria
Warfare, Modern
    U.S. Army Training and Doctrine Command
    Fort Monroe, Virginia, USA

Riane Eisler
Family Structure and Family Violence and
    Nonviolence
    Carmel, California, USA

Robert Elias
Violence as Solution, Culture of
    University of San Francisco
    San Francisco, California, USA

Leonard D. Eron
Television Programming and Violence, U.S.
    University of Michigan
    Ann Arbor, Michigan, USA

Paul Lawrence Farber
Evolutionary Theory
    Oregon State University
    Corvallis, Oregon, USA

David N. Farnsworth
International Relations, Overview
    Wichita State University
    Wichita, Kansas, USA

Gordon Fellman
Enemy, Concept and Identity of
    Brandeis University
    Waltham, Massachusetts, USA

Juanita M. Firestone
Warfare and Military Studies, Overview
    University of Texas
    San Antonio, Texas, USA

Dietrich Fischer
Economics of War and Peace, Overview
    Pace University
    Pleasantville, New York, USA

Virginia Floresca-Cawages
Institutionalization of Nonviolence
    University of Alberta
    Edmonton, Alberta, Canada

Linda Rennie Forcey
Feminist and Peace Perspectives on Women
    Binghamton University
    Binghamton, New York, USA

Nicholas G. Fotion
Warfare, Trends in
    Emory University
    Atlanta, Georgia, USA

Karen Franklin
Homosexuals, Violence toward
    University of Washington
    Seattle, Washington, USA

Marvin D. Free
Minorities as Perpetrators and Victims
    of Crime
    University of Wisconsin
    Madison, Wisconsin, USA

David Noel Freedman
Religious Traditions, Violence and Nonviolence
    University of California, San Diego
    San Diego, California, USA

William C. French
Ecoethics
    Loyola University
    Chicago, Illinois, USA

Gregory Fried
Critiques of Violence
    Boston University
    Boston, Massachusetts, USA

Robert Friedmann
Policing and Society
    Georgia State University
    Atlanta, Georgia, USA

Douglas P. Fry
Aggression and Altruism
Peaceful Societies
    University of Abo
    Helsinki, Finland

Theodore Gabriel
Ethical and Religious Traditions, Eastern
    Cheltenham and Gloucester College
    Gloucester, UK

James Garbarino
Long-Term Effects of War on Children
    Cornell University
    Ithaca, New York, USA

William Gay
Language of War and Peace, The
    University of North Carolina
    Charlotte, North Carolina, USA

George Gerbner
Mass Media and Dissent
    Temple University
    Philadelphia, Pennsylvania, USA

Douglas M. Gibler
Alliance Systems
    Stanford University
    Stanford, California, USA

Howard Giles
Communication Studies, Overview
    University of California, Santa Barbara
    Santa Barbara, California, USA

William Gissy
Political Economy of Violence and Nonviolence
    Morehouse College
    Atlanta, Georgia, USA

Nils-Petter Gleditsch
Peace and Democracy
  International Peace Research Institute
  Oslo, Norway

Mark Gold
Drugs and Violence
  University of Florida College of Medicine
  Gainesville, Florida, USA

Ralph M. Goldman
Political Systems and Conflict Management
  San Francisco State University
  San Francisco, California, USA

Janine Goldman-Pach
Sexual Assault
  University of Arizona
  Tucson, Arizona, USA

Jeff Goodwin
Revolutions
  New York University
  New York, NY, USA

Deborah Gorman-Smith
Urban Violence, Youth
  University of Illinois
  Chicago, Illinois, USA

F. Lincoln Grahlfs
Veterans in the Political Culture
  National Association of Radiation Survivors
  St. Louis, Missouri, USA

Adam Green
Revolutions
  New York University
  New York, NY, USA

Allen D. Grimshaw
Genocide and Democide
  Indiana University
  Bloomington, Indiana, USA

Linda Groff
Religion and Peace, Inner-Outer Dimensions of
  California State University
  Dominguez Hills, California, USA

David Grossman
Behavioral Psychology
Psychological Effects of Combat
Weaponry, Evolution of
  Arkansas State University
  Jonesboro, Arkansas, USA

Barrie Gunter
Television Programming and Violence, International
  University of Sheffield
  Sheffield, UK

Brien Hallett
Just-War Criteria
  University of Hawaii
  Honolulu, Hawaii, USA

Fen Osler Hampson
Peace Agreements
  Carleton University
  Ottawa, Ontario, Canada

Michael Hanagan
Industrial vs. Preindustrial Forms of Violence
  New School for Social Research
  New York, NY, USA

Ian M. Harris
Peace Education: Colleges and Universities
  University of Wisconsin, Milwaukee
  Milwaukee, Wisconsin, USA

John Hartman
Psychoanalysis
  University of Michigan
  Ann Arbor, Michigan, USA

Akira Hattori
Economics of War and Peace, Overview
  Fukuoka University
  Fukuoka, Japan

Mark Haugaard
Power, Social and Political Theories of
  University College, Galway
  Galway City, Ireland

Ira Heilveil
Violence Prediction
  Ojai, California
  USA

Errol A. Henderson
Civil Wars
Ethnic Conflicts and Cooperation
  University of Florida
  Gainesville, Florida, USA

Gregory Herek
Homosexuals, Violence toward
  University of California, Davis
  Davis, California, USA

Marjorie Hogan
Popular Music
  Hennepin County Medical Center
  Minneapolis, Minnesota, USA

Gregory Hooks
Military-Industrial Complex, Organization and History
  Washington State University
  Pullman, Washington, USA

Brenda Horrigan
Security Studies
  Vineyard Haven, Massachusetts, USA

Michael W. Hovey
Conscientious Objection, Ethics of
  Iona College
  New Rochelle, New York, USA

L. Rowell Huesmann
Television Programming and Violence, U.S.
  Institute for Social Research, University of Michigan
  Ann Arbor, Michigan, USA

Paul K. Huth
Military Deterrence and Statecraft
    University of Michigan
    Ann Arbor, Michigan, USA

Larry W. Isaac
Class Conflict
    Florida State University
    Tallahassee, Florida, USA

James M. Jasper
Animals, Violence toward
    New York University
    New York, NY, USA

Ho-Won Jeong
Conflict Management and Resolution
Theories of Conflict
    George Mason University
    Fairfax, Virginia, USA

Hans Joas
Social Theorizing about War and Peace
    Free University of Berlin
    Berlin, Germany

Anthony James Joes
Guerrilla Warfare
    St. Joseph's University
    Philadelphia, Pennsylvania, USA

Hubert C. Johnson
Warfare, Strategies and Tactics of
    University of Saskatchewan
    Saskatoon, Saskatchewan, Canada

Theodore Karasik
Security Studies
    University of California, Los Angeles
    Los Angeles, California, USA

Robert W. Kentridge
Behavioral Psychology
    University of Durham
    Durham, UK

James R. Kerin, Jr.
Combat
    United States Military Academy
    West Point, New York, USA

Wolfgang Knöbl
Social Control and Violence
    Free University of Berlin
    Berlin, Germany

Edward Kolodziej
Arms Control
    University of Illinois
    Urbana, Illinois, USA

Fiona M. Kay
Urban and Community Studies
    University of British Columbia
    Vancouver, British Columbia, Canada

Mary Koss
Sexual Assault
    Arizona Prevention Center
    Tucson, Arizona, USA

Rajini Kothari
Institutionalization of Violence
    Center for the Study of Developing Societies
    Delhi, India

Louis Kriesberg
Conflict Transformation
    Syracuse University
    Syracuse, New York, USA

Mitsuru Kurosawa
Arms Control and Disarmament Treaties
    Osaka School of International Public Policy
    Osaka, Japan

John Kydd
Violence to Children, Definition and Prevention of
    Child VIP—Child Violence Identification and
    Prevention Project
    Seattle, Washington, USA

Christos N. Kyrou
Cultural Anthropology Studies of Conflict
    Syracuse, New York, USA
    Syracuse University

Linda Lantieri
Peace Education: Youth
    Educators for Social Responsibility
    New York, NY, USA

Pat Lauderdale
Power and Deviance
    Arizona State University
    Tempe, Arizona, USA

Colin Wayne Leach
Ethnicity and Identity Politics
    Swarthmore College
    Swarthmore, Pennsylvania, USA

David LeMarquand
Biochemical Factors
    McGill University
    Montreal, Quebec, Canada

David Lester
Suicide and Other Violence toward the Self
    Center for the Study of Suicide
    Blackwood, New Jersey, USA

Amy Leventhal
Urban Violence, Youth
    University of Illinois
    Chicago, Illinois, USA

Howard S. Levie
Chemical and Biological Warfare
War Crimes
    U.S. Naval War College
    Newport, Rhode Island, USA

Jack Levin
Hate Crimes
  Northeastern University
  Boston, Massachusetts, USA

Sheldon G. Levy
Conformity and Obedience
Cooperation, Competition, and Conflict
Mass Conflict and the Participants, Attitudes toward
  Wayne State University
  Detroit, Michigan, USA

Elliott Leyton
Serial and Mass Murderers
  Memorial University of Newfoundland
  St. John's, Newfoundland, Canada

Daniel G. Linz
Mass Media, General View
  University of California
  Santa Barbara, California, USA

David Loye
Evil, Concept of
  Center for Partnership Studies
  Carmel, California, USA

Derek F. Lynch
Balance of Power Relationships
  University of Huddersfield
  Queensgate, Yorkshire, UK

Graeme MacQueen
Spirituality and Peacemaking
  McMaster University
  Hamilton, Ontario, Canada

Esther Madriz
Criminology, Overview
  University of San Francisco
  San Francisco, California, USA

Sanja Magdalenic
Folklore
  Stockholm University
  Stockholm, Sweden

Kevin Magill
Justification for Violence
  University of Wolverhampton
  Dudley, UK

Neil Malamuth
Pornography
  University of California, Los Angeles
  Los Angeles, California, USA

Brian Martin
Technology, Violence, and Peace
  University of Wollongong
  Wollongong, Australia

Peter B. Mayer
Militarism and Development in Underdeveloped
  Societies
  University of Adelaide
  Adelaide, Australia

Alfred McAlister
International Variation in Attitudes toward Violence
  University of Texas
  Austin, Texas, USA

Laura Ann McCloskey
Family Structure and Family Violence and
  Nonviolence
  University of Arizona
  Tucson, Arizona, USA

Michael J. McClymond
Religious Traditions, Violence and Nonviolence
  University of California, San Diego
  San Diego, California, USA

Jack McDevitt
Hate Crimes
  Northeastern University
  Boston, Massachusetts, USA

Gregory McLauchlan
Military-Industrial Complex, Contemporary Significance
  University of Oregon
  Eugene, Oregon, USA

Eduardo Mendieta
Ethical Studies, Overview
  University of San Francisco
  San Francisco, California, USA

James A. Mercy
Public Health Models of Violence and Violence Prevention
  Centers for Disease Control
  Atlanta, Georgia, USA

Thomas Mieczkowski
Drug Control Policies
  University of South Florida
  St. Petersburg, Florida, USA

Dinshaw Mistry
Arms Control
  University of Illinois
  Urbana, Illinois, USA

Alex Morrison
Peacekeeping
  Pearson Peacekeeping Centre
  Clementsport, Nova Scotia, Canada

C. David Mortensen
Linguistic Constructions of Violence, Peace, and Conflict
  University of Wisconsin
  Madison, Wisconsin, USA

Kenneth R. Murray
Behavioral Psychology
  Armiger Police Training Institute
  Ottawa, Ontario, Canada

Hanna Newcombe
World Government
  Peace Research Institute
  Dundas, Ontario, Canada

Roderick Ogley
Conflict Theory
    University of Sussex
    Brighton, UK

Tamayo Okamoto
Means and Ends
    Hiroshima Prefectural College of Health
        and Welfare
    Hiroshima, Japan

Marie Olson
Arms Trade, Economics of
    Center for Peace and Conflict Studies
    Wayne State University
    Detroit, Michigan, USA

Keith F. Otterbein
Clan and Tribal Conflict
    State University of New York
    Buffalo, New York, USA

Jan Pakulski
Social Equality and Inequality
    University of Tasmania
    Hobart, Tasmania, Australia

Edward L. Palmer
Children, Impact of Television on
    Davidson College
    Davidson, North Carolina, USA

Martin Palous
Totalitarianism and Authoritarianism
    Charles University
    Prague, Czech Republic

Hanbin Park
Peacekeeping
    Pearson Peacekeeping Centre
    Clementsport, Nova Scotia, Canada

Janet Patti
Peace Education: Youth
    Hunter College of the City of New York
    New York, NY, USA

Frederic S. Pearson
Arms Trade, Economics of
    Center for Peace and Conflict Studies, Wayne State
    University
    Detroit, Michigan, USA

Jordan B. Peterson
Neuropsychology and Mythology of Motivation for Group
Aggression
    Harvard University
    Cambridge, Massachusetts, USA

Robert O. Pihl
Biochemical Factors
    McGill University
    Montreal, Quebec, Canada

Solomon W. Polachek
Trade, Conflict, and Cooperation among Nations
    State University of New York
    Binghamton, New York, USA

Kenneth Powell
Public Health Models of Violence and Violence Prevention
    Centers for Disease Control
    Atlanta, Georgia, USA

Jason Pribilsky
Cultural Anthropology Studies of Conflict
    Syracuse, New York, USA
    Syracuse University

Anatol Rapoport
Decision Theory and Game Theory
Peace, Definitions and Concepts of
    University of Toronto
    Toronto, Ontario, Canada

David C. Rapoport
Terrorism
    University of California, Los Angeles
    Los Angeles, California, USA

Alison Dundes Renteln
Human Rights
    University of Southern California
    Los Angeles, California, USA

Claire Renzetti
Criminal Behavior, Theories of
    St. Joseph's University
    Philadelphia, Pennsylvania, USA

Patricia Richards
Effects of War and Political Violence on Health Services
Health Consequences of War and Political Violence
    London School of Hygiene and Tropical Medicine
    London, UK

Marc Riedel
Homicide
    Southern Illinois University
    Carbondale, Illinois, USA

John Robst
Trade, Conflict, and Cooperation among
    Nations
    State University of New York
    Binghamton, New York, USA

Robert A. Rubinstein
Cultural Anthropology Studies of Conflict
    Syracuse University
    Syracuse, New York, USA

Gordon W. Russell
Sports
    University of Lethbridge
    Lethbridge, Alberta, Canada

Andrew Sanders
Warriors, Anthropology of
    University of Ulster
    Coleraine, Northern Ireland, UK

Joanna Santa Barbara
Childrearing, Violent and Nonviolent
    McMaster University
    Hamilton, Ontario, Canada

Robert K. Schaeffer
Secession and Separatism
San Jose State University
San Jose, California, USA

Thomas J. Scheff
Collective Emotions in Warfare
University of California, Santa Barbara
Santa Barbara, California, USA

Christian P. Scherrer
Structural Prevention and Conflict Management, Imperatives of
Copenhagen Peace Research Institute
Copenhagen, Denmark

Brigitte H. Schulz
Cold War
Trinity College
Hartford, Connecticut, USA

John Paul Scott
Animal Behavior Studies, Nonprimates
Bowling Green University
Bowling Green, Ohio, USA

Leslie Sebba
Punishment of Criminals
Hebrew Institute of Jerusalem
Jerusalem, Israel

Daniel M. Segesser
World War I
Universiy of Berne
Berne, Switzerland

Carlos Seiglie
Economic Costs and Consequences of War
Rutgers University
Newark, New Jersey, USA

Gene Sharp
Nonviolent Action
Albert Einstein Institution
Cambridge, Massachusetts, USA

Martin Shaw
Civil Society
University of Sussex
Brighton, UK

James F. Short, Jr.
Youth Violence
Washington State University
Pullman, Washington, USA

Bruce K. Siddle
Psychological Effects of Combat
Executive Director, PPCT Management
Millstadt, Illinois, USA

Thomas R. Simon
Public Health Models of Violence and Violence Prevention
Centers for Disease Control
Atlanta, Georgia, USA

J. David Singer
Correlates of War
University of Michigan
Ann Arbor, Michigan, USA

Simon I. Singer
Juvenile Crime
State University of New York
Buffalo, New York, USA

John Sislin
Arms Trade, Economics of
Center for International Studies, University of Missouri
St. Louis, Missouri, USA

Elisabeth Skons
Arms Production, Economics of
Stockholm International Peace Research Institute
Stockholm, Sweden

Jackie Smith
Transnational Organizations
State University of New York at Stony Brook
Stony Brook, NY, USA

Philip Smith
Cultural Studies, Overview
Ritual and Symbolic Behavior
University of Queensland
Queensland, Australia

Paul Smoker
Religion and Peace, Inner-Outer Dimensions of
Antioch College
Yellow Springs, Ohio, USA

H. F. (Rika) Snyman
Organized Crime
Technikon SA
Florida, South Africa

Metta Spencer
Sociological Studies, Overview
University of Toronto
Toronto, Ontario, Canada

Carolyn M. Stephenson
Peace Studies, Overview
University of Hawaii at Manoa
Honolulu, Hawaii, USA

Pamela J. Stewart
Anthropology of Violence and Conflict, Overview
University of Pittsburgh
Pittsburgh, Pennsylvania, USA

Victor C. Strasburger
Popular Music
University of New Mexico School of Medicine
Albuquerque, New Mexico

Andrew Strathern
Anthropology of Violence and Conflict, Overview
University of Pittsburgh
Pittsburgh, Pennsylvania, USA

Mira Sucharov
Collective Security
Georgetown University
Washington, DC, USA

Keith Suter
Peace Organizations, Nongovernmental
United Nations Association of Australia and Wesley
Mission
Sydney, Australia

Jukka-Pekka Takala
Evolutionary Factors
Victimology
National Research Institute of Legal Policy
Helsinki, Finland

Kenneth Tardiff
Mental Illness
Cornell University Medical School, New York Hospital
New York, NY, USA

Frank O. Taylor IV
Peace Movements
Dana College
Blair, Nebraska, USA

Bryan Teixeira
Nonviolence Theory and Practice
Camosun College
Victoria, British Columbia, Canada

Charles Thomas
World War II
U.S. Naval War College
Newport, Rhode Island, USA

David Tindall
Urban and Community Studies
University of British Columbia
Vancouver, British Columbia, Canada

Swee-Hin Toh
Institutionalization of Nonviolence
University of Alberta
Edmonton, Alberta, Canada

Patrick Tolan
Urban Violence, Youth
University of Illinois
Chicago, Illinois, USA

Jennifer Turpin
Women and War
University of San Francisco
San Francisco, California, USA

Bernard Udis
Economic Conversion
University of Colorado
Boulder, Colorado, USA

Antonio Ugalde
Effects of War and Political Violence on Health Services
Health Consequences of War and Political Violence
University of Texas
Austin, Texas, USA

Debra Umberson
Child Abuse
University of Texas
Austin, Texas, USA

Sheldon Ungar
Total War, Social Impact of
University of Toronto
Toronto, Ontario, Canada

Alonzo Valentine
Ethical and Religious Traditions, Western
Earlham College and School of Religion
Richmond, Indiana, USA

Peter van den Dungen
Peace Education: Peace Museums
Peace Prizes
University of Bradford
West Yorkshire, UK

Paul Viotti
Professional versus Citizen Soldiery
University of Denver
Denver, Colorado, USA

Joseph Vorrasi
Long-Term Effects of War on Children
Cornell University
Ithaca, New York, USA

Dierk Walter
Colonialism and Imperialism
University of Berne
Berne, Switzerland

Kathleen Maas Weigert
Structural Violence
University of Notre Dame
Notre Dame, Indiana, USA

Reinhilde Weidacher
Arms Production, Economics of
Stockholm International Peace Research Institute
Stockholm, Sweden

Peter Weiss
Legal Theories and Remedies
Center for Constitutional Rights
New York, NY, USA

Michael G. Wessells
Psychology, General View
Randolph-Macon College
Ashland, Virginia, USA

Dean A. Wilkening
Nuclear Warfare
Center for International Security and Cooperation
Stanford University
Stanford, California, USA

Angie Williams
Communication Studies, Overview
Cardiff University
Cardiff, Wales, UK

Franke Wilmer
Indigenous Peoples' Responses to Conquest
Montana State University
Bozeman, Montana, USA

Jon D. Wisman
Economic Causes of War and Peace
American University
Washington, DC, USA

Lynne Woehrle
Gender Studies
Wilson College
Chambersburg, Pennsylvania, USA

Gordon C. Zahn
Conscientious Objection, Ethics of
University of Wisconsin
Milwaukee, Wisconsin, USA

Kristeva A. Zoë
Peacekeeping
Pearson Peacekeeping Centre
Clementsport, Nova Scotia, Canada

Anthony Zwi
Effects of War and Political Violence on Health
Services
Health Consequences of War and Political Violence
London School of Hygiene and Tropical Medicine
London, UK

Guide to the Encyclopedia

The *Encyclopedia of Violence, Peace, and Conflict* is a complete source of information within the covers of a single unified work. It is the first reference book to address a full range of topics in the field of violence, peace, and conflict studies, with coverage of issues as disparate as peace education, trends in warfare, mental illness, and violence toward animals. It also includes many topics of concern to contemporary society, such as ethnic conflict, hate crimes, drug control policies, and child abuse.

The Encyclopedia consists of three volumes and includes 196 separate full-length articles, all prepared especially for this publication. It includes not only entries on the leading theories and concepts of violence, peace, and conflict, but also a vast selection of entries on applied topics in areas such as criminology, politics, economics, communications, and biomedicine. Each article provides a detailed overview of the selected topic to inform a broad spectrum of readers, from research professionals to students to the interested general public.

In order that you, the reader, will derive maximum benefit from your use of the Encyclopedia, we have provided this Guide. It explains how the work is organized and how the information within it can be located.

ORGANIZATION

The *Encyclopedia of Violence, Peace, and Conflict* is organized to provide the maximum ease of use for its readers. All of the articles are arranged in a single alphabetical sequence by title. So that they can be easily located, article titles generally begin with the key word or phrase indicating the topic, with any descriptive terms following. For example, "Criminal Behavior, Theories of" is the article title rather than "Theories of Criminal Behavior" because the specific phrase *criminal behavior* is the key term rather than the more general term *theories*.

Similarly, "Criminology, Overview" is the article title rather than "Overview of Criminology" and "Warfare, Trends in" is the title rather than "Trends in Warfare."

TABLE OF CONTENTS

A complete alphabetical table of contents for the Encyclopedia appears at the front of each volume of the set, beginning on page v of the Introduction. This list includes not only the articles that appear in that particular volume but also those in the other two volumes.

The list of article titles represents topics that have been carefully selected by the Editor-in-Chief, Prof. Lester Kurtz of the University of Texas, Austin, in collaboration with the members of the Editorial Board.

In addition to the alphabetical table of contents, the Encyclopedia also provides a second table of contents at the front of each volume, listing all the articles according to their subject area. The Encyclopedia provides coverage of 15 specific subject areas within the overall field of violence, peace, and conflict, as indicated below:

- **Anthropological Studies**
- **Biomedical Studies**
- **Communications**
- **Criminology**
- **Cultural Studies**
- **Economic Studies**
- **Ethical Studies**
- **Historical Studies**
- **International Relations**
- **Peace and Conflict Studies**
- **Political Studies**
- **Psychological Studies**
- **Public Policy Studies**
- **Sociological Studies**
- **Warfare and Military Studies**

OUTLINE

Each article in the Encyclopedia begins with an Outline that indicates the general content of the article. This outline serves two functions. First, it provides a brief preview of the article, so that the reader can get a sense of what is contained there without having to leaf through the pages. Second, it highlights important subtopics that are discussed within the article. For example, the article "Youth Violence" includes among its subtopics "The Age/Crime Connection" and "Understanding and Controlling Youth Violence."

The Outline is intended as an overview and thus it lists only the major headings of the article. In addition, extensive second-level and third-level headings will be found within the article.

GLOSSARY

The Glossary contains terms that are important to an understanding of the article and that may be unfamiliar to the reader, or that may need clarification as to their specific use in the article. Each term is defined in the context of the particular article in which it is used. Thus the same term may appear as a Glossary entry in two or more articles, with the details of the definition varying slightly from one article to another. The Encyclopedia includes more than 1,000 glossary entries.

The following example is a glossary entry that appears with the article "Aged Population."

Dementia An acquired, ongoing impairment of general intellectual abilities to such a degree as to seriously interfere with social and occupational functioning, including memory loss and failures of abstract thinking and judgment, as well as personality changes; an age-related condition and especially associated with Alzheimer's disease.

DEFINING STATEMENT

The text of each article in the Encyclopedia begins with a single introductory paragraph that defines the topic under discussion and summarizes the content of the article. For example, the article "Ecoethics" begins with the following statement:

ECOETHICS is an emerging discipline that in recent decades has been prompted by alarm about increasing environmental degradation and its impact on human and nonhuman life.

CROSS-REFERENCES

Virtually all of the articles in the Encyclopedia have cross-references to other articles. These cross-references appear at the end of the article, following the conclusion of the text. They indicate related articles that can be consulted for further information on the same topic, or for other information on a related topic. For example, the article "Guerrilla Warfare" contains cross references to the articles "Civil Wars," "Colonialism and Imperialism," "Revolutions," "Terrorism," "Warfare, Modern," and "Warfare, Strategies and Tactics of." The Encyclopedia contains about 1,150 cross-references in all.

BIBLIOGRAPHY

The Bibliography appears as the last element in an article. It lists recent secondary sources to aid the reader in locating more detailed or technical information. Review articles and research papers that are important to an understanding of the topic are also listed.

The bibliographies in this Encyclopedia are for the benefit of the reader, to provide references for further reading or research on the given topic. Thus they typically consist of a limited number of entries. They are not intended to represent a complete listing of all the materials consulted by the author in preparing the article.

INDEX

The Subject Index in Volume 3 contains more than 10,000 entries. The entries indicate the volume and page number where information on this topic will be found. The Index serves, along with the alphabetical Table of Contents, as the starting point for information on a subject of interest.

INTERNET RESOURCES

The *Encyclopedia of Violence, Peace, and Conflict* maintains its own editorial Web Page on the Internet at:

http://www.apnet.com/violence/

This site gives information about the Encyclopedia project. It also features a link to the Academic Press Reference Works home page, which has information about related titles, such as the *Encyclopedia of Applied Ethics* and the *Encyclopedia of Human Behavior.*

Preface

The problem of violence poses such a monumental challenge at the end of the 20th century that it is surprising we have addressed it so inadequately. We have not made much progress in learning how to cooperate with one another more effectively or how to conduct our conflicts more peacefully. Instead, we have increased the lethality of our combat through revolutions in weapons technology and military training. The *Encyclopedia of Violence, Peace, and Conflict* is designed to help us to take stock of our knowledge concerning these crucial phenomena.

Most people have a profound ambivalence about violence, a simultaneous abhorrence of and reliance upon it; consequently we engage what policy makers use to guide their discourse and decisions. The relationship between knowledge and practice is complex, of course; many Moderns seem to have something like an addiction to violent solutions that is much like any dependency and escapes rational analysis. Knowledge of dire consequences does not automatically promote constructive action or deter destructive behavior; like the smoker who wants to quit but cannot, we sometimes move ahead consciously along a destructive path. Many of the articles in this encyclopedia, while remaining rooted in academic research, attempt to explore the policy implications of those investigations.

The study of violence—especially war—is as ancient as our religious texts, from the reflective insights of the Mahabharata and Sun Tzu in the East to the Torah and Thucydides in the West, and has an overwhelming advantage over the study of peace when it comes to research funding. The conduct of war is so significant to those in power that its study has a privileged place in the production of knowledge. A large proportion of public expenditures on all research in both the natural and social sciences is, in fact, controlled by military establishments. In the United States, for example, the Army Research Bureau's annual budget exceeds the total combined funding for every other federally funded so-cial science research program including such agencies as the National Science Foundation, the National Institutes of Health, and the National Institute for Mental Health.

As a consequence of massive data-gathering we have, in recent decades, learned a great deal about a wide range of violent behaviors from war to patterns of crime. In these volumes readers can find summaries of those findings; e.g., David Singer's "Correlates of War" project, criminological investigations and cross-cultural anthropological studies of violence, psychological studies of combat and aggressive behavior, case studies of urban and youth violence, UN investigations of the causes of war, and so forth. We have gained a great deal of insight into specific types of violence and have some reasonable theories about what causes people to engage in them. We are still uncertain, however, about how to construct social institutions that provide secure neighborhoods and nations or how to nurture peaceful cultures.

The academic study of peace—a poor cousin to the science of war—is a relatively recent development. This encyclopedia encompasses both enterprises, along with an array of academic disciplines in neither camp that can deepen our understanding of violence. Most of the Enlightenment philosophers—in the same intellectual movement that gave birth to the modern encyclopedia—incorrectly speculated that war would gradually disappear as human society became more rational and civilized. It was not until the 20th century—in response to the horrors of modern warfare—that empirical research and systematic study oriented toward the construction of peace became a part of the academy. Indeed, the field called "peace studies" remains marginal to the academy despite its remarkable growth worldwide since the 1960s with formal programs in hundreds of universities and professional associations such as the International Peace Research Association, the Peace Studies Association, and the Consortium on Peace Research, Education, and Development (COPRED), as well as organized groups of conflict resolution professionals and sections devoted to peace studies in disciplinary societies.

The purpose of this encyclopedia is to bring together in one place a broad range of information and perspectives on violence, peace, and conflict in order to enhance our understanding of these crucial phenomena and to stimulate new research, insights, and better public policies. The encyclopedia's most significant contribution is its addressing the problem of intellectual compartmentalization by including scholarship from diverse disciplines from around the world, from military and peace sciences, to the social and biological sciences, as well as the humanities.

What Do We Know?

It is impossible to summarize briefly the information contained in these three volumes; I would, however, like to highlight some of the themes that emerge. First of all, it is salient that we do not even have a consensus on how to define these three concepts. Rather than impose one on the authors, we include a variety of approaches and a discussion of the debates. Some perceive conflict as a broader phenomenon that encompasses the other two: one can engage in either violent or peaceful conflict. Others perceive peace as something that reflects the absence of conflict. These conflicting definitions reflect salient domain assumptions and produce different theories and policies regarding how to manage the conflicts that seem to be an inevitable part of social life.

Similarly, violence is defined in several markedly different ways. Whereas some contend that the term should refer only to the deliberate infliction of physical harm, others insist that psychological harm must be included as well. Still others claim that we must include the injury caused by inequality (what Johan Galtung calls "structural violence") if the definition is to be sufficiently inclusive. Indeed, the holocaust-like deaths caused by contemporary malnutrition can scarcely be seen as anything but violent, especially by its victims, although usually not inflicted deliberately. UNICEF estimates that six million children under the age of five die annually from malnutrition—as many each year as were murdered in all the German death camps. How violence is defined is an issue with profound policy implications, as demonstrated in the elaborate taxonomy provided in the article "Violence to Children, Definition and Prevention of."

An adequate definition of peace seems almost as elusive as peace itself. The most basic concept, of course, is the absence of war, or more broadly the mitigation of violence. Some would insist, however, that one cannot have peace without justice. Whereas some, following Thomas Hobbes, view peace as something that must be imposed from the top, others claim that it will result only from the grassroots mobilization of common people demanding policy changes from the elites. Some contend that it is something that one must first find within oneself; for others, inner peace comes from living within a peaceful culture. As Linda Groff and Paul Smoker note, peace has many dimensions and understandings of it vary over time and across cultures.

Differing perceptions of peace within the academy reflect the participation of different groups involved in its study. Whereas scholars in the military sciences tend to see peace as primarily the absence of war, for example, many Third World students of peace will emphasize justice as a crucial component of peace; those in religious and cultural studies, as well as many psychologists, may include inner peace as a necessary condition for peace. We have included a range of these positions in this collection.

A second central theme that emerges in these volumes is that conflict has always been part of the human experience, but that the way in which it is carried out varies substantially across time and space, in different eras and cultures. Radical changes in our technologies and strategies of conflict in the 20th century, moreover, distinguish our conflicts from those of past eras. Because they are more destructive in their scale and scope, some age-old wisdom may become inappropriate, whereas other elements of our shared ethical and cultural heritage may be revived.

Conflict can be carried out in a variety of ways from war and violence on one end of the spectrum to nonviolent struggle on the other. In recent decades the means of violent conflict have changed so radically as to transform the very character of violence; dual revolutions in weapons technology and military training have made violence increasingly deadly in both interpersonal and large-scale conflicts. Warfare has been relatively limited until quite recently in scale and scope. Despite widespread destruction bordering on genocide reported in ancient scriptures, premodern combat was relatively inefficient compared to contemporary warfare, and it occurred infrequently. David Grossman observes that a significant majority of soldiers in World War II combat were reportedly not firing directly at the enemy. Modern training thus incorporates operant conditioning to help recruits to the military and police overcome what appears to be a natural resistance to killing.

A growing body of evidence suggests that violent television programs, movies, and interactive video games are providing the sort of psychological conditioning for violence previously reserved for the military and police, whose behavior is usually bounded by strict rules of discipline that are missing from the lay version of the process. Consequently, although it is too early to tell what the larger impact of video games might be on various cultures, the evidence suggests strongly that homicide rates and aggressive behavior—at least among males—increase with the introduction of violent entertainment media into a culture. What is less clear is the nature of human nature with regard to propensities to violence.

A final theme of this compilation is that our understanding of peace and of nonviolent conflict has undergone a revolution that (not accidentally) parallels the transformation of violent conflict in the 20th century. Whereas the change in combat is symbolized by the atomic bomb, the revolution in nonviolence is symbolized by Mahatma Gandhi, Martin Luther King, Jr., and the mobilization of nonviolent social movements. As with warfare, the basic strategies and tactics of nonviolent struggle have been used throughout human history but were transformed in scale and scope in the 20th century. People in many cultures have employed methods of nonviolent direct action and conflict resolution over the millennia, but their development and elaboration in recent decades is unprecedented. Nonviolent struggles are not always successful (nor are violent ones) but they have been remarkably effective in country after country, especially in toppling unpopular dictatorships through mass mobilization and nonviolent tactics of resistance from the people-power movements that toppled U.S.-backed dictatorships in the Philippines and Chile to the Velvet Revolution in Czechoslovakia and the Solidarity movement in Poland that overthrew Soviet-backed regimes.

Scholarly studies of both nonviolence and military combat converge in a surprising possibility, something perhaps never fully verifiable empirically but certainly suggested by the evidence: that human beings—like other species—have not only a capacity for aggression but also a natural resistance to killing their own kind. They may also inherit an inclination toward nonviolent behaviors such as cooperation, affection, and so forth. How else could one explain the remarkable successes of nonviolent social movements in recent decades and the resistance to killing in combat addressed by modern military training? Human genetics seem to provide relatively broad parameters for potential behavioral choices, allowing for a strong influence by culture. The question

of the inherent aggressiveness or tendency toward violence in human nature remains a key unanswered question at the turn of the century, one that has profound policy implications and poses complicated methodological dilemmas for students of violence.

Nature versus Nurture

Are humans inherently violent and condemned to periodic and increasingly destructive warfare? A review of our knowledge may produce more questions than answers. We do know that violent behavior is not universal among animal species (see J. P. Scott's article "Animal Behavior Studies, Nonprimates"). We also know that humans exhibit a wide range of behaviors and that their language and tool-making abilities set them somewhat apart from other species in their use of violence and the extent to which their lives are limited by biological parameters. Certainly some individuals and cultures engage in more violence than others; is that because of biological or cultural differences, or is the variation a result of some complex interaction between the two? Most of the violence caused by humans is carried out by the males of the species; is that a direct result of genetic differences or does it come from gender socialization that promotes the use of force by males in solving problems while females are taught to create less violent solutions?

Is war inevitable, given our biological makeup? This question was addressed recently at a conference organized by the Spanish office of the United Nations Educational, Social, and Cultural Organization (UNESCO). An interdisciplinary group of scientists participating from around the world endorsed "The Seville Statement of Violence" that calls into question much popular wisdom about the inherently violent nature of humanity. In their evaluation of the available scientific literature on violence they concluded that it is scientifically incorrect to say that:

- we have inherited a tendency to make war from our animal ancestors;
- war or any other violent behavior is genetically programmed into our human nature;
- in the course of human evolution there has been selection for aggressive behavior more than for other kinds of behavior;
- humans have a "violent brain";
- war is caused by "instinct" or any single motivation.

They conclude that "biology does not condemn humanity to war, and that humanity can be freed from the bondage of biological pessimism" that prevents it from seeking peace. "The same species that invented war," they contend, "is capable of inventing peace." Although the nature–nurture debate will probably not be solved, at least in the near future, one interesting development is recent attention—especially by UNESCO—to cultures of peace in human social organization.

Cultures vary dramatically in the extent to which they promote violent behavior; indeed, many societies can be characterized as having cultures of peace. An ongoing UNESCO project initiated in 1995 analyzes the elements of peaceful cultures in hopes that they might be incorporated elsewhere, such as in war-torn societies attempting to rebuild their civil societies. A pioneer in this field of peace culture, Elise Boulding, outlines some of those characteristics in her article "Peace Culture," noting that humans have a natural tendency to respond to other humans. They are capable of conducting their conflicts peacefully and developing cultures that nurture cooperation, democratic decision making, and nonviolent conflict. Comparative studies of conflict resolution demonstrate that human cultures can organize social life on a peaceful basis. In many communities, children are socialized to conduct their conflicts nonviolently, to cooperate with and respect others, and to create social environments that are not free of conflict but have relatively little coercion or violence.

If humans may not be genetically programmed for violence and war, but are capable of developing cultures of peace, why then is there so much carnage in human life? Although the evidence is far from conclusive, and there is clearly a biological component—especially in extreme sociopathic cases—current studies of violence seem to suggest that it is a consequence primarily of the way in which we instruct our youth, construct our values and beliefs about violence, and structure our options for carrying out conflict. In short, levels of violence probably have more to do with cultural values and social institutions than with the biological parameters within which we operate.

Violence, Culture, and Society

Many of the articles in this encyclopedia outline aspects of the way in which societies are organized within what Robert Elias calls a "culture of violent solutions." The underlying assumption in such a culture is that violence must be used to solve serious problems, including the problem of violence itself. Consequently, we often declare war upon those who commit acts of violence,

using "legitimate" violence to put an end to their "illegitimate" use of force. A great deal of time, energy, and money in modern societies and governments is invested in a sort of war over impression management, a struggle to gain the upper hand in how one's use of violence is defined so that ours is viewed as legitimate and necessary, whereas our adversary's is illegitimate and despicable.

This framing process often involves an effort to obtain hegemony in public discourse about violence, as states, social movements, and various interest groups all struggle to have the situation defined in their favor. The ruling ideas about violence in any given social context are, of course, profoundly influenced by the ideas of those who have the most power in that context. In cultures that emphasize the use of violence in their conflicts, the narratives used to differentiate between legitimate and illegitimate violence usually reflect the social structure: violence by the state and elites is considered legitimate. The poor and marginalized are scapegoated and blamed for the violence in their society even if they actually perpetrate a small proportion of it.

Even in societies where there is relatively free public discourse, a limited range of options for defining violence and its use are enforced, setting up boundaries around what is considered viable. This aspect of framing varies dramatically from culture to culture. In some societies the use of violence is so soundly condemned that it is seldom considered as a serious option for conflict management. In other contexts, the failure to use violence is condemned as weak and ineffective. Control over the narrative process defining these norms thus becomes crucial in determining whose violence is accepted and whose is rejected, which modes of conflict are considered useful and which ineffective. St. Augustine understood this when he laid the groundwork for Just War theory in the fourth century, just as did Clausewitz when he founded modern military science centuries later. The nature of those narratives and who controls them has varied widely over time and across cultures.

In most preagricultural and even preindustrial societies, religious elites and institutions tend to control the defining narratives. The legends and stories of oral traditions and sacred scriptures provide the standards by which particular acts of violence or modes of conflict are evaluated. From the Hebrew Torah to the Bhagavad Gita and the Qur'an, stories told around the campfire by village storytellers and recited in places of worship, people learn which styles of conflict are considered ethical with regard to the use of force. The violence of nature, as well as that of foreign peoples, is often explained as an "act of God," and remedies that can be applied to problematic situations are provided in the narratives.

In modern cultures, authoritative storytelling—like many other social functions—is wrested from religious institutions and given to the state in an effort to democratize political authority. Giving the state authority does offer some remedies to earlier abuses, but modern political elites claim a monopoly of violence for the state and use force so widely to back up their claims that state violence has caused an unprecedented number of deaths by war, genocide, and democide in the 20th century, as Alan Grimshaw observes.

Now a new force is moving to center stage, the commercialization of storytelling, so that the narratives that have the most impact on popular culture are written by professionals, told in the media of the age—television, movies, and interactive video games, etc.—and sponsored by multinational corporations.

These new myths and legends regarding the appropriate use of force continue to reflect the interests of those in power and have three major themes. First, we find the age-old maxim that force is often necessary for serious problem solving. This idea is presented repeatedly in narrative form in the popular media and recounted by people who discuss the latest television shows and movies: a crime is committed and the police track down the criminals and drag them off to jail. They are brought to trial, convicted, and justice prevails. In the international arena parallel narratives unfold as criminal heads of state and marginal groups lacking states are apprehended and brought to justice. Terrorists operating on behalf of a dictator or religious fanatic are hunted down and punished, and so on. We all know the stories and their various reincarnations—how security is threatened by criminals and then reestablished by proper authorities using necessary force within a framework of laws.

Embedded within these entertaining narratives are lessons to be drawn about how people are to solve their problems and to recognize the necessity for legitimate authorities to use violence, thus raising the second theme, i.e., that some violence is legitimate and other force is not. As with the first theme, a social problem emerges, a struggle ensues, and sooner or later the problem is solved by force. Erich Fromm once observed that when individuals behave like nations do, we put them in an institution, either a prison or a mental hospital. When states kill, maim, or appropriate property, we hear stories about the honor of such acts. When the same acts are committed by individuals or groups not sanctioned by the state, or by enemy states, they are condemned as horrific.

The difference between the two kinds of violence is determined, of course, by the power of those who use it. The mechanism by which the violence employed by those in power is defined as legitimate is the cultural process embedded in the narratives of the culture. The monopoly of legitimacy still lies with the state even in postmodern culture, but it is not taken for granted; even well-established and popular regimes must now hire professional storytellers to frame their use of violence as legitimate and to counter the critics of their war-fighting, crime-fighting policies.

These for-profit stories about the necessity of fighting bad violence with good are not the only frame provided by modern culture. The major alternative to the good-versus-bad-violence frame is the innovative idea of the industrial age that consumerism can be used to solve problems as well, as told explicitly in advertisements and more subtly in the story lines of other genres. The paradigm here appears in fast food advertisements: within a 60-second story an entire drama unfolds. A problem disrupts the routine of social life but is quickly and efficiently solved by having everyone buy fast food. Everyone sits around smiling and eating; conflicts are resolved and order is restored.

This example seems to have taken us far afield from the initial problem of violence. It is, however, extremely salient: the consumer alternative to brute force seems less violent, certainly, than the use of guns, and many claim that a peaceful future will result from world trade, the free market, and the creation of an affluent lifestyle for everyone. This vision, others argue, is only superficially benign. Hidden behind the smiling consumer faces, they claim, is a very elaborate story of structural violence and destruction. The apparently positive search for happiness through material consumption is globally seductive, the critics argue. It promises more than it delivers because the satisfaction it brings is elusive and temporary, and the process creates a global social system with the hidden violence of mass poverty held in place by a system of overt violence in the form of a military–industrial complex that protects the interests of the rich and powerful. This sort of violence is the object of more recent research, and we know little about its mechansims because it is subtle, complex, and global, and its investigation often marginalized or politicized.

A final set of narratives in the postmodern era is also examined in this encyclopedia: those of nonviolent resistance from Gandhi and the Indian Freedom Movement to Martin Luther King, Jr. and the U.S. civil rights movement, as well as the prodemocracy and other non-violent movements for social change that they inspired. These stories challenge much conventional wisdom but have their roots in ancient cultures and have taken their place in the dominant culture of the late 20th century, legitimating what Czech president Vaclav Havel calls the power of the powerless. From this perspective, violence accentuates and forces hierarchy and embellishes inequality, whereas nonviolence facilitates equality and empowers democratic movements.

We know much less about how to mobilize Gandhi-style nonviolent struggles than we do about training and employing military forces. After all, we have not been doing it very long. The strategies and tactics of nonviolent action have been examined historically and explicitly only in the 20th century and are summarized here by the most prominent student of modern nonviolent action, Gene Sharp, as well as in Bryan Teixeira's broader discussion of nonviolence in theory and practice. We know even less about how individuals, families, and nations might be organized nonviolently, but that too is a subject of analysis that will persist into the next century. The future of nonviolence remains problematic, of course, especially given the domain assumptions of prevailing realpolitik theories of conflict and current structures for militarizing international conflict, but some remarkable changes have occurred in recent decades that are explored in this encyclopedia. These volumes attempt to bring into clearer focus the options before us and the consequences of our collective choices, as we evaluate these debates and study our policies.

Our hope is that this work will provide us with a more comprehensive picture of our current state of knowledge about violence, peace, and conflict. This collection is broader in its coverage than any other currently available resource, but we cannot claim to raise all of the right questions, let alone provide the necessary answers to them. It is not as comprehensive as one might hope, however, and some caveats are in order.

First, despite our best efforts to broaden the authorship of the encyclopedia, the majority of the contributors are Western, notably North American. Although this does in some sense reflect the current state of scholarship (because of Western dominance and resources), it does not necessarily reveal our best knowledge.

Second, the very genre of the Encyclopedia—with its nonadversarial standpoint and objective tone—may ironically exclude some of our best insights into the subject matter. Indeed, articles by two people, each knowing more about violence and peace (in my opinion) than some entire university faculties put together, were not included because their articles were inappropriate for the genre because they were too argumentative. Another piece was edited substantially but in the end was deemed too pejorative in tone. One prominent Latin American scholar declined our invitation up front, suggesting that if we wanted an objective article on the topic we had asked the wrong person.

Finally, the publication of this sort of resource—which we hope will be relevant for some time—can give the misleading notion that knowledge about a topic is fixed and definitive. On the contrary, the truth about any topic—and especially our understanding of the truth—changes dramatically over time so that it can be misleading to interpret the contents of these volumes in a reified manner. Although this work reviews our current state of knowledge about violence, peace, and conflict, it is a snapshot of a rapidly changing area of inquiry into a constantly shifting set of phenomena.

Thank you for joining us in this ongoing investigation. I would be happy to hear from you if you have comments, criticisms, or information about ongoing research or perspectives that are not adequately represented here.

Lester R. Kurtz
University of Texas at Austin

Police Brutality

Paul G. Chevigny

New York University Law School

GLOSSARY

Corruption Conferring a benefit on an official, outside those benefits that are prescribed by law, to influence the action of the official. Also, the receipt of such a benefit.

Police An official body, organized at the local or national level, to keep civil order. Police are empowered to make arrests for violations of the criminal law, and to use force at least as a last resort to enforce their actions when lawful.

Polyarchy A term for a government that has its power diffused among several sources, branches, or institutions, as, for example, a pluralist democracy.

Vigilantism Punishment, performed outside the confines of the official legal process, for perceived wrong-doing or deviance.

THE TERM "POLICE BRUTALITY" is a phrase from common speech; thus its meaning is not well-defined. In general, it connotes the use of excessive force by the police against members of the public. It is accepted that many uses of force by the police cannot be labeled "police brutality" or "excessive," because the use of force is sometimes necessary in police work. It is in fact, as Egon Bittner has pointed out, part of the essence of the police role, which he says "... is best understood as a mechanism for the distribution of non-negotiably coercive force employed in accordance with the dictates of an intuitive grasp of situational emergencies" (Bittner, 1990: 131). Put another way, the police are the officials in modern society who commonly are called upon when the state has to use its ultimate power of coercion against its own citizens, either for reasons rooted in the enforcement of lawful orders or simply to keep order. Because the power to use force is an essential part of police work, Fyfe and Skolnick have made an important distinction, between the "unnecessary" use of force, which may be excessive because of poor training, negligence, or the misperception of a situation, and "police brutality," which they define as a "conscious and venal act." The term "brutality" does seem to imply a deliberately violent act. Nevertheless, in common parlance, the distinction is not usually made between force that is unnecessary under the circumstances, but is not deliberately so, and the deliberate use of excessive force. Force by the police that is viewed as excessive is commonly called "police brutality."

In addition, some people perceive very rude or racist verbal abuse by police as "brutal." Nevertheless, for purposes of definition here, it seems most useful to restrict the term to physical brutality of the sort described in the previous paragraph.

I. LIMITATIONS ON POLICE BRUTALITY BY LAW

A. International

The United Nations has established standards for the use of force by law enforcement officials (which include police). The UN Code of Conduct for Law Enforcement Officials (1979) states, in Art. 3, "Law enforcement officials may use force only when strictly necessary and to the extent required for the performance of their duty." The UN Basic Principles on the Use of Force and Firearms by Law Enforcement Officials (1991) expand the point in their principle 5, "Whenever the lawful use of force and firearms is unavoidable, law enforcement officials shall: (a) Exercise restraint in such use and act in proportion to the seriousness of the offence and the legitimate objective to be achieved." The Basic Principles go on in principle 9 to specify standards for the use of firearms, "Law enforcement officials shall not use firearms against persons except in self-defense or defense of others against the imminent threat of death or serious injury, to prevent the perpetration of a particularly serious crime involving grave threat to life, to arrest a person presenting such a danger and resisting their authority, or to prevent his or her escape, and only when less extreme means are insufficient to achieve these objectives. In any event, intentional lethal use of firearms may only be made when strictly unavoidable in order to protect life." While the Code of Conduct and the Basic Principles do not have the force of treaty law among nations, they are approved by United Nations bodies in elaboration of articles of the International Covenant on Civil and Political Rights (1966), a treaty adopted by more than 90 countries, including the United States, and they are thought to embody minimum standards for the use of force by police. They are widely adopted by police departments throughout the world. They express the general propositions that all use of force by the police must be proportional to the threat presented, and that deadly force, through firearms, may be used only as a last resort in a situation that threatens life; uses of force that violate these principles would commonly be called "police brutality."

In addition, international law condemns "cruel, inhuman or degrading treatment or punishment," both through the Covenant on Civil and Political Rights (Art. 7) and the UN Convention against Torture and Other Cruel, Inhuman or Degrading Treatment or Punishment (1985), when such acts are "committed by or at the instigation of or with the consent or acquiescence of a public official or other persons acting in an official capacity" (Art. 16). Similar norms are also recognized as part of customary international law, independent of treaty. These provisions forbid not only torture, as defined more fully below, but other cruel acts that do not rise to the level of torture, a standard that would include acts of police brutality, especially when performed knowingly or purposefully.

B. The United States

Legal doctrine in the United States has accepted standards for police brutality that are roughly parallel as a practical matter to those in the international community, but are cast in categories derived from the U.S. Constitution. If a fleeing suspect "threatens the officer with a weapon or there is probable cause to believe that he has committed a crime involving the infliction or threatened infliction of serious physical harm, deadly force may be used if necessary to prevent escape, and if, where feasible, some warning has been given." The decision in *Tennessee v. Garner* (1985) presented a case, formerly permissible under Anglo-American common law, that we would now call a case of police brutality; there a policeman in the city of Memphis, Tennessee, shot an unarmed Black teenager fleeing from a burglary. The U.S. Supreme Court held that the shooting was an "unreasonable seizure" of the person of the suspect under the Fourth Amendment to the U.S. Constitution. Similarly, beating a suspect unnecessarily during an arrest (short of the use of deadly force) has been held to be an "unreasonable seizure" of the person under the Fourth Amendment in *Graham v. Connor* (1989). The *Graham* case presented a rather typical instance of police brutality, in which Graham, a diabetic in search of orange juice to counteract the onset of an insulin reaction, was stopped by the police for investigation. When the police mistook Graham's reaction to the insulin for a state of drunkenness, Graham, a Black man, was arrested, his head was slammed against a car, and he was thrown head first into a police car, resulting in cuts, bruises, a broken foot, and ringing in his ears.

Beating a person already in custody for the purpose of punishment or of forcing the person to confess will be viewed as a violation of the due process clause either of the Fourteenth Amendment or the Fifth Amendment to the U.S. Constitution; if the person does confess, it will also be a violation of the right of a person under the Fifth Amendment not to be compelled to testify against himself.

II. TYPES OF POLICE BRUTALITY

Police brutality may be divided between brutality that occurs as part of the order-keeping and crime-prevention function of police, on the one hand, or brutality that occurs during the investigative function on the other. The former usually occurs in the street, and takes the form of a beating, or in the extreme, a shooting. The latter usually occurs inside a police facility or a vehicle, and takes the form of assaults of persons by beating or other violent means, for example by electric shock, for the purpose of coercing them to give information, or as a summary punishment, or both. The latter is a version of torture, defined by the UN Convention against Torture (Art. 1) as "any act by which severe pain or suffering, whether physical or mental, is intentionally inflicted on a person for such purposes as obtaining from him or a third person information or a confession, punishing him for an act he or a third person has committed or is suspected of having committed, or intimidating or coercing him or a third person, or for any reason based on discrimination of any kind, when such pain or suffering is inflicted by or at the instigation of or with the consent or acquiescence of a public official or other person acting in an official capacity. It does not include pain or suffering arising only from, inherent in or incidental to lawful sanctions."

A distinction may also be drawn between police brutality that is perpetrated for overtly political reasons, to maintain a regime in power, and brutality that occurs in the name of crime control or order-keeping. Thus political dissenters may be beaten or killed to deter them from protesting or to eliminate them; or they may be tortured to punish them and to force them to give information about plans against the regime. More commonly, suspects of ordinary crime may be similarly punished or forced to confess. The distinction is blurred, however, because in some cases regimes do not distinguish clearly between political agitation and ordinary crime. Both are viewed as threats to order and to the stability of the regime.

III. CAUSES AND OCCASIONS OF POLICE BRUTALITY

A. Arrogation of the Punishment Functions of the Criminal Justice System

Police brutality tends to occur in situations where the police take it upon themselves, or are encouraged, to act independently as if they were a governing body, bypassing other elements in the criminal justice system to administer punishment as they see fit. In repressive regimes, the police sometimes have discretion to act against opponents of the regime, to punish them or to torture them. While police under these regimes may

violate contemporary standards of international human rights, they do not act against any positive law of their own country because it is part of their job to repress opponents by violence, independent of the intervention of the courts or other institutions. In such states, which have become familiar at least since the time of the fascist regimes in Germany and Italy, it is useless to make complaints about police violence to domestic authorities. We refer to them as "police states," implying precisely that the police are an uncontrolled instrument of government.

In states such as contemporary polyarchies where the police are viewed as part of the system of justice the problem of police brutality arises through more ambiguous political causes. Even though police are subject to the rule of law, much of their work is carried out under circumstances where they necessarily exercise a great deal of discretion. Many police come to feel, and some political forces encourage the view, that they have an expertise that equips them to act directly to repress crime and disorder, in effect to govern in the streets. An extreme case of this may be seen in Sao Paulo, Brazil, where in the late 1980s and early 1990s the police took it upon themselves to control crime by violence, holding that other elements of the justice system were failing in their tasks. A similar spirit is to be found in the United States in agitation for increased police discretion and references to the rest of the justice system as, for example, a "revolving door." As a very specific example, after the notorious Dalton Avenue raid by the Los Angeles (City) police in 1988, the words "LAPD rules" were found painted on the walls of raided apartments.

To be sure, the police always have functions that go beyond "law enforcement," encompassing general order-keeping functions, such as breaking up crowds or keeping them moving, or checking persons who seem suspicious. These are gradually assimilated in police practice in some places to law enforcement jobs, so that what seems "out of order" may also be seen as a violation of law, and a threat to society. The identification between the police and criminal justice generally is memorialized in the United States in the popular usage that refers to the police as the "law," as well as in the familiar saying attributed to Alexander "Clubber" Williams of the New York City Police in the 19th century, "there is more law in a night stick than in all the statute books."

It is because of the identification between police, order-keeping, and criminal justice generally that so much conflict between police and citizens resulting in excessive use of force grows out of situations where people defy police orders. For example, drivers who refuse to stop their cars in response to a police command and thus provoke a vehicle pursuit are sometimes beaten, as in the famous case of Rodney King, beaten in 1991 by members of the Los Angeles Police Department after he had engaged in a vehicle pursuit. The outright, risky defiance of a police order is viewed as an antisocial act, equivalent to a crime, and one directed specifically at the police; thus it provokes summary punishment from the police. So also, disorderly persons, such as those in unruly crowds, or drunken individuals, may be beaten if they refuse to return to good order in response to a police command to disperse or be quiet. In societies where there is more police violence, such as Sao Paulo, Brazil, defiant drivers and even persons who defy the police by running away on foot may be shot.

When they are not tightly controlled, and do not adhere to lawful police regulations, police tend to react with violence against those who are outcasts, including those who are "out of order," as well as those outcast by reason of their status or behavior. So for example, much police brutality is directed against lower class persons, for several reasons. Much of the law-enforcement work of the police concerns crimes, such as robbery, burglary, and more minor offenses, that are primarily committed by poor persons. Furthermore, most routine police work, including order-keeping functions, is directed at poor persons; thus when police brutality is used for any reason other than political control, it tends to be used against the poor. Police brutality can be a way of reminding poor people where they stand in society, and of pushing them back into the social order when they get "out of place" by becoming disorderly, committing minor offenses, or sometimes just by being in the wrong neighborhood. In racially divided societies such as the United States and Brazil, a disproportionate amount of police activity is directed against minority people, because they are often poor, because the police sometimes find them "out of place," and because the police stereotype them as responsible for disorder. The number of Black persons shot by police is out of proportion to their numbers in the United States and Brazil. This creates constant friction between the police and minority people; acts of violence by the police are widely interpreted as instances of police brutality. In the United States, the police are suspected of discriminating against minorities, particularly against Blacks and Hispanics; acts of violence by the police have come to symbolize such discrimination and on several occasions have resulted in destructive rebellions in U.S. cities.

Police selection of outcast groups for aggressive action, including violence, varies with the culture. Thus in Central European countries where there are large populations of Roma (gypsies), such as Romania and Bulgaria, police violence has been directed against the Roma. To select a rather different example, where there is strong prejudice against homosexuals, overtly homosexual behavior in public may be viewed as contrary to order, provoking aggressive action by the police. This occurs in Latin America as well as in the United States, where it is less common than it was formerly; police violence has also been directed against derelicts and "hippies."

To take another example, where torture is practiced, it is traditionally directed against poor people, while people above the lowest class are protected from it. Torture is a way for the police to put the suspect in his place, to emphasize what an outcast he is in relation to others, including the police themselves. Furthermore, the refusal to answer questions in the way the interrogators want is in itself a form of defiance that tends to provoke violence. On the other hand, when torture is used for outright political reasons, then it is directed against all those suspected of opposition, regardless of their class.

One of the characteristics of police brutality used for political repression generally is that it may be directed against persons of all classes and not primarily against the poor and other outcasts. One reason is that those who subscribe to unacceptable political views or are opposed to the government are ipso facto considered out of order, outcast, and in some cases even criminal. Their opposition is a form of defiance that may provoke police violence.

Police react with violence perhaps most predictably when they confront people who are poor, or are outcast for other reasons, and who are at the same time opposed to the status quo, either political or economic or both. Thus it is that in Latin American countries, as well as elsewhere in the world, the police have dealt with peasants and laborers agitating against land tenure and working conditions by beating and killing them. The combination of outcast status with defiance of the existing order creates a strong temptation to reassert that order by violence.

B. Military Model of Policing

The police function is essentially different from that of the military; the term "police" in origin refers to the keeping of civil order rather than the use of violence, although violence is recognized as a legitimate instrument of police work when it is proportional to the threat. Furthermore, the police act or should act as civilian officials, drawn from their own population, selecting some people for sanctions for individualized reasons. An army, on the other hand, is engaged in the systematic use of violence, usually against a group of people defined as an enemy. Nevertheless, historically the police have developed out of local military organizations and have continued to maintain some military characteristics, such as a hierarchical command structure and uniforms to identify most of their members; they also are the civilian functionaries who are empowered to use violence. In some places, groups of police are more closely assimilated to the military, as *gens d'armes* (France), *carabineros* (Chile), or military police (Brazil). There is thus always a tendency on the part of the public and politicians to confuse police functions with those of the military.

The tendency is pronounced in places where military action has been taken against part of the domestic population as an internal enemy, usually because of supposed subversion of the government. This occurred, for example, in the dictatorships in Argentina and Brazil in the 1960s and 1970s, when a doctrine of "national security" was used to identify leftists and liberals as an internal enemy; it is significant that in both cases the domestic police were actually placed under military administration. The police and the military acted with great violence against all those identified with subversion as well as against those suspected of ordinary crimes. Similarly, it is common in colonial societies for the police to be organized along military lines, because there is a sense of systematic enmity between the colonizer and the colonized that preserves the military functions of the police.

But the tendency is not restricted to places where there is a history of colonial rule or military action against a perceived domestic enemy. The popular rhetoric of a "war on crime" embodies the notion that the police are called upon to act against crime, in some ill-defined way, as the military would do. The rhetoric is employed particularly when society is confronted with widespread fear of crime, which may be interpreted as a threat similar to that offered by an enemy. Governments, democratic as well as authoritarian, draw upon such fears as a way to mobilize their people and retain their support; thus such rhetoric is used frequently as a political tool. However justified the fear of crime may be in many cases, the analogy to military action is confusing because it encourages the police to ignore other parts of the criminal justice system, to use violence as a principal tool for control, and to search for an "enemy" among their own people, rather than to treat cases on an individualized basis. The semimilitary model emphasizes the tendency of police violence to dehumanize its victims, to conceive the person beaten, shot, or tortured as if in a special depersonalized category, like an enemy. In places where there is reliance on a semimilitary model as well as a war rhetoric for the police, there tends to be more police brutality. A notable recent example in the United States has been the police in the City and County of Los Angeles, California, who have long used the military model and rhetoric, and who have been accounted among the most violent urban police in the country. In varying degrees the military model of police, with accompanying violence, recurs throughout the United States and elsewhere in the world. It follows that where military forces are assigned actually to take over police functions, or even to act together with the police in domestic police functions, the level of official violence will rise, as has happened in Brazil, Jamaica, and Mexico.

C. Corruption

There is no necessary connection between corruption and police brutality; there are police who are violent without being corrupt. Nevertheless, police brutality is commonly tied to corruption in complex and varied ways. Most generally, corruption and brutality share a common set of attitudes: that the police are replacing the formal justice system with their own system, in which they decide who shall be rewarded, who punished, and how. The police show their power over their victims by extorting bribes from them as well as by administering summary punishment. The official Mollen Commission report on corruption in the New York City police in 1994 has been particularly insightful in pointing out the connection between corruption and brutality (Mollen Commission, 1994: 21):

> Corrupt officers usually raided drug locations for profit, but sometimes also to show who was in control of the crime-ridden streets of their precincts; sometimes to feel the power and thrill of their badges and uniforms; sometimes because they believed that vigilante justice was the only way to teach a lesson or punish those who might otherwise go unpunished.

One of the most extreme forms of such power is the coercion of a suspect by means that amount to torture. Such coercion may itself be used as an instrument of corruption, to force the suspect to tell where the proceeds of a property crime are hidden so that the police can take the property, or more directly so that the police can extract a bribe to stop the torture. Such corrupt uses of torture have occurred in recent years in Sao Paulo, Brazil, as well as in the United States at an earlier period.

Finally, corruption is a way of resisting accountability (discussed more fully below) for all breaches of police duty, including brutality. Police who have been corrupt, even in minor ways, find it almost impossible to report on the misconduct of other officers. Thus the "code of silence" about police misconduct is vastly strengthened by corruption. Conversely, as the Mollen Commission pointed out in 1994, brutality may smooth the way to corruption, serving as a "rite of passage to other forms of corruption and misconduct," by letting other police know that the perpetrator can be trusted not to report wrongdoing.

D. Vigilantism

Apart from those cases where police violence is used as an instrument of policy by the government, chiefly to intimidate its opponents, most police brutality functions as a form of vigilante justice. It is a case of the "police taking the law into their own hands," in the common phrase describing vigilantism. They are reproducing order and imposing punishment according to their own standards and without the intervention of other government agencies. It is a striking fact that police brutality, particularly the use of deadly force against suspects in the streets, is at its worst in societies, such as Brazil and Jamaica, where there is also vigilante justice by unofficial agents such as gunmen hired to eliminate undesirables. In such cases, the official and unofficial forms of vengeance feed one another; retired and off-duty policemen participate in the unofficial execution squads, notably in Brazil. The reciprocal relation exists because the police are, in effect, doing vigilante actions that private persons might carry out themselves, or of which they at least do not disapprove. By the same token, as private vengeance becomes unacceptable, police brutality also tends to become less serious.

The suppression of private vengeance has been one of the ways that governments show that they actually govern, that they have a monopoly of legitimate force, particularly in law enforcement. The available evidence suggests that during the long 19th century, up to the First World War, there was a general decline in urban violence in the West, not only by the state but among private persons as well. This civil pacification accompanied increased state control of the legitimate instruments of violence, as well as the processes of urbaniza-tion and the relative rationalization of government. It was in this period that modern urban police forces were developed and came to symbolize much of the pacification. The armed forces were hardly used anymore to control the domestic population.

Some of the spirit of the change is captured in Max Weber's ideal model of modern society, bureaucratized and rationalized. People are managed by government, rather than merely coerced; at the same time, the management becomes legitimate. The change is accompanied by the growth of modern law and the expectation of regularity and rights under the law. Present-day writers emphasize what Weber perhaps discounted, an increased demand for participation and citizenship; the satisfaction of the demand depends upon the recognition of civil rights and at least the appearance of dialogue with the government. The simmering class war between capital and labor begins to fade into a government-sponsored negotiation between organized labor and business. In penology, deterrence and the "correction" of offenders replaces punishment as the chief justification of criminal penalties.

Under contemporary conditions, the problem of police brutality is most pronounced where a government's legitimacy or its grip on the instruments of violence is weak—where there is rebellious activity or where there is a large amount of private vengeance, or both. Conversely, governments that claim to have a monopoly of legitimate force, and at least tell a story of peaceful urban government, have had less abuse of deadly force by the police. Where the rule of law is strong, and people expect officials to be bound by the law, the incidence of official abuse should be even more firmly under control. Where the rule of law is not strong, and a strong government rules, the police often control society through close surveillance of the people, and use the outright violence of police more sparingly and for purposes of controlling or eliminating political opposition. Thus it is that authoritarian governments do not necessarily have the most exigent problems with the use of extrajudicial killing in ordinary crime cases; in cases where such governments actually have control of the society, as in contemporary Cuba, for example, they do not use violence in such a haphazard way. In democratic societies where the government is weak, and private violence and respect for the rule of law are not strong, police violence in the streets may be much more serious. The abuse of deadly force is neither democratic nor authoritarian; it is used as an instrument of terror where control by the government is weak and where the poor are seen as outcast.

IV. ACCOUNTABILITY FOR AND CONTROL OF POLICE BRUTALITY

Police brutality is a perennial political issue in modern societies because it symbolizes the tension between violence and order. The threat and sometimes the imposition of violence is a strong impulse in the criminal law; the threat and the imposition of lawful punishment is supposed to strengthen the sense of order. And yet we recognize that violence is always in danger of escaping from the strictures of law, particularly when violence has to be used on the spur of the moment in the streets. For incidents of the use of violence by the police then, there frequently arises the question whether the action taken has been within the bounds of the law or outside it; whether the action was required by the situation or was gratuitous. And if the action should fall outside what is permitted, then the question is whether the police will at least be subject to the rule of law to the extent that they will be accountable for their action. The UN Basic Principles on the Use of Force and Firearms provide in principle 22 that governments must provide "effective reporting and review procedures" for incidents involving the use of force that result in injury.

Review of police actions after they have occurred, in the effort to determine whether they were lawful or not, presents a set of systemic problems. It is in the nature of police work that some police use of force is lawful, either in making arrests or in keeping order; the question in the vast majority of cases, then, is whether the force used was necessary, in the sense that it was, as the UN Code of Conduct for Law Enforcement Officials puts it, "proportional to the legitimate objective to be achieved." In most cases, the police will make a claim that no more force than necessary was used. When nondeadly force has been used by the police, the police will typically claim that the suspect resisted arrest, resulting in a pattern of criminal charges against the injured suspect of resisting arrest and assaulting a police person. When deadly force (usually shooting) has been used, the police will typically claim that the suspect was armed and threatened them or fired on them, or that they had reason to believe that the suspect was armed and threatening. This latter claim has sometimes resulted in charges that the police have planted weapons on suspects in the effort to justify their actions. In almost every case in which police brutality is alleged, then, there will be a difficult normative and factual question about whether the force was justified. The controversy tends to be similar under virtually all systems of review in every place, because all of them confront the basic propositions that some police violence is legally permissible and that the boundaries for justification are established roughly by the international standards for the use of force by law enforcement officials. Furthermore, it is widely reported that the police usually corroborate one another's account of the facts through a strong "code of silence." The effectiveness of every institution of accountability that is rooted in an inquiry about misconduct after the fact, then, whether pursued through administrative discipline or through the courts, is limited by the circumstances that the police personnel under review are usually able to offer an explanation to justify their actions and to explain the injuries received by the person complaining.

In the courts, the police may be prosecuted for crimes such as assault or homicide in all countries where extreme official abuses are viewed as crimes. In the United States, such a prosecution usually takes place in the state criminal courts; in some local jurisdictions, it has been difficult to persuade the authorities to initiate criminal cases against police, and it is always difficult to obtain convictions for the reasons described in the preceding paragraph. In addition, police personnel may be prosecuted by the federal government in the federal courts for violating or conspiring to violate the civil rights of the person injured (Title 18 U.S. Code secs 241; 242); the fact that there has been a prosecution in the state courts, whether successful or not, is no bar to a federal prosecution.

A private civil suit for damages due to the police action may also be brought by the person injured or his family. Restrictions on such suits vary from place to place. In some places where civil suits against the police have been studied, for example in Brazil and Jamaica, the damages have been found to be insufficient. On the other hand, in United States cities, while such suits have sometimes functioned as an effective way of obtaining damages for injuries, they have not functioned well in bringing about systemic reforms that reduce the amount of police violence. Political officials have not taken account of the civil suits in managing the police.

In the United States, such a civil suit may be brought in the state courts, or, again, in the federal courts alleging a deprivation of federal constitutional rights (Title 42 U.S. Code sec. 1983). Under limited circumstances, a private civil suit may also be brought to enjoin an official policy or practice that encourages police brutality. In addition, a 1994 federal law provides that the U.S. attorney general may bring a civil suit to enjoin local law enforcement officials from engaging in a pattern or practice that deprives people of constitutional or other federal rights (Title 42 U.S. Code sec. 14141).

Administrative discipline for police personnel accused of brutality presents its own problems. For at least the past 40 years, there has been a continuing controversy between those who claim that the police ought to discipline their own people and those who claim that police discipline ought to be handled by a body external to the police (commonly called "civilian review," which is a misnomer since the police, not being military, are themselves "civilians"). The call for external review has arisen just because of the ability of police personnel to offer justifications for their conduct; proponents of external review claim that the difficult normative and fact questions in police brutality charges should be resolved by parties outside the police. This argument has been increasingly accepted and such external review bodies have been established in many American cities as well as elsewhere in the English-speaking world. On the other side, responsible command officials have claimed that it is part of their job to discipline their own people and to set and enforce standards. The choice between internal and external review in many cases presents a dilemma. External review tends to rouse the opposition of police commanders as well as the rank and file; without some cooperation from within, then, it is nearly impossible for outsiders to investigate, and any policy recommendations they make are likely to be ignored. If the review is exclusively internal, it may become assimilated to existing mores among the police, and commanders may use it as a way to protect the police from criticism. Neither internal nor external systems of administrative review can entirely resolve the systemic problems of accountability for police actions after they have occurred. It is notable that under all systems of administrative review, the number of citizen complaints that are found substantiated is small.

Where police and other officials are genuinely committed to controlling unnecessary police violence, there is no doubt that the most successful controls are instituted as a way of avoiding confrontations before they occur, so that questions of fact concerning the justifications for violence will not arise. This may be done through training to minimize violence in confrontations and also through regulations that will minimize occasions to use force, especially deadly force. Thus since the 1970s, police departments in the United States have had stringent regulations limiting the use of firearms; where they are enforced systematically through record-keeping, they have reduced the use of such force. Similarly, confrontations after vehicle pursuits can be re-

duced by limiting the circumstances in which pursuits are authorized. "Early-warning" systems that track police who have been accused of violence may prevent its recurrence and improve the work of the officers. Even where there is a will to end police brutality, however, there will remain cases in which it occurs and even more in which it is claimed. Thus methods of review after the fact must always be combined with management controls before the fact.

Furthermore, there are police forces in the United States and elsewhere in which incidents of brutality are concealed or whitewashed with the connivance or the indifference of commanding officers. In those cases, the methods of review of police violence after the fact, including administrative discipline and court actions, are absolutely essential. In cases where these institutions prove ineffective, it is possible to seek redress through international agencies. In countries that have signed the protocol to the International Covenant on Civil and Political Rights that permits individual claims, complaints about police brutality may be made to the UN Human Rights Committee. In the Americas, complaints may be made to the Inter American Commission on Human Rights, and in Europe, to the European Commission on Human Rights. The commissions have power to decide such cases, and may refer them to regional human rights courts in Costa Rica or in Strasbourg, respectively, in instances where the government complained of has accepted the jurisdiction of the court (the United States has accepted the jurisdiction of the Inter American Commission but has not accepted the jurisdiction of the court in Costa Rica). In all cases, the remedies in the nation complained of must be exhausted or shown to be ineffective before a claim can be made to an international agency.

V. PREVALENCE OF POLICE BRUTALITY

Reliable statistics concerning the incidence of police brutality are in all places difficult to obtain. In places where brutality is most serious, the systems of accountability are so inadequate that the police have virtual impunity, so that the frequency of the use of brutality can only be inferred. Even where the problem is not so serious, furthermore, almost all charges of police brutality are contested, because, as noted above, it is usually possible for the police to offer a plausible justification for their action. It is in the nature of the problem that its incidence is hard to determine. Nevertheless, we can get a sense of the relative prevalence of police brutality from place to place and over time.

A. The United States

Most police in the United States are organized on a local level, into many thousands of departments, and most of the localities do not collect statistics on excessive force. At the time of this writing, national statistics of police misconduct are not reported, although there is a 1994 federal statute that requires the federal attorney general to collect and report data on "excessive force by law enforcement officers" (Title 42 U.S. Code sec. 14142). It is not clear how such statistics can be collected or how reliable they would be.

We have reliable data concerning the use of firearms in many cities, and we can determine at least how frequently deadly force has been used. The overwhelming majority of such shootings are not acts of police brutality so far as we know because they are legally justified under the standards of the U.S Constitution and local police regulations. Nevertheless, it is clear that the incidence of excessive force in shootings has declined, because the number of all police shootings in big cities in the United States has declined by about half in the 20 years before 1990. It is clear also that the use of coercion against suspects to force them to confess has declined in the last 75 years, to the point where even vigorous critics of the police do not often charge that suspects have been coerced, although there have been scandals about the use of torture in New York City and in Chicago in the 1980s and 1990s.

In the United States, police brutality even of a lesser sort, such as unnecessary force against a suspect, has to be a statistically rare event. Studies show that force, whether legally appropriate or not, is used in less than 10% of arrests, which are themselves a small part of all police-citizen encounters. The absolute number of cases that are experienced by citizens as police brutality may still be large, and where such cases are contested and receive public notice, the number may seem larger. Among Black males, moreover, a large proportion of whom have contact with the criminal justice system, a substantial number of people can be expected to believe either that they themselves have encountered police brutality or that they have heard an account of it directly from a victim.

B. Outside the United States

It may be that police brutality is common enough in some parts of the world outside the United States so that a large proportion at least of poor people will encounter it. In Brazilian cities, for example, the police conduct sweeps of entire neighborhoods ("blitzes") from time to time in search of suspects, and may abuse a number of people in full view of others. In the 1980s it was said to be so common to beat up persons who were arrested in Sao Paulo that when an arrestee was brought into the station house unscathed, other suspects in the jail suspected him of being an informer.

The U.S. Department of State publishes an annual report on the condition of human rights throughout the world outside the United States. A survey of any recent volume of these *Country Reports on Human Rights Practices* will give the reader a general idea, not of the numbers of cases, but of how frequently a police abuse is reported for the countries of the world. As an example, we draw here on the volume of reports for 1995, published in 1996. It should be noted that these counts are not meant to be exhaustive, but only suggestive of the scope of the problems; there may well be similar abuses in other countries that have simply escaped the notice of those who report to the U.S. State Department. If we were to choose another recent year, we would obtain similar but slightly different counts for the countries.

Torture of suspects to force them to confess is very widely reported throughout the world. In Africa, forced confessions or torture were reported from 18 of 37 significant countries. In Latin America and the Caribbean, such reports come from 17 of 33 countries, in East Asia and the Pacific, from 9 of 18 countries, in Europe from 12 of 38 countries, in the Near East from 9 of 13 countries, and in South Asia from all 3 countries reporting. Thus coercion of suspects is probably used in more than half the countries of the world; in the majority of cases, it is used against ordinary suspects rather than for political reasons against supposed enemies of the government.

The abuse of deadly force—shooting and often killing persons without sufficient justification—is apparently less widespread. In Africa, such reports come from 14 of 37 significant countries, in Latin America and the Caribbean, from 7 of 33 countries, in Asia and the Pacific from 2 of 18 countries, in Europe from 4 of 38 countries, in the Near East from 3 of 13 countries, and in South Asia from 2 out of the 3 countries. In Europe, police brutality of a lesser sort, such as beating up suspects, is more common, being reported in 13 of 38 countries. The great majority of acts of brutality reported are apparently used against ordinary suspects, rather than against political opponents of the government. It is striking that vigilantism by private parties is reported as accompanying deadly police violence in 8 countries in Africa, in 4 countries in Latin America and the Caribbean, and in a few cases in Europe and

Asia. In some cases in Africa and Latin America, the State Department notes that widespread police corruption accompanies the violations of human rights. These reports are consistent with the Causes and Occasions of Police Brutality described above.

VI. POLICE BRUTALITY AND THE PROBLEM OF PUBLIC SAFETY

The persistence of police brutality as a governmental problem, at least in democratic states, raises the question why the authorities have not taken effective measures in more countries and cities to minimize police use of violence and thus to avoid claims of police brutality. A widespread sense that there is impunity for unlawful acts has resulted, for example, in the demand for external review of charges of police misconduct (see above), yet police commanders in many places do not undertake systematic management actions to control violence. Part of the reason is that senior police officials often minimize the problem; they do not admit even to themselves how many cases of unlawful violence there may be and how important is the public perceptions of such cases. Where there is corruption among the police the problem is compounded, as noted above, because all those who are tainted by corruption are obliged to keep silent about all problems, including problems of violence, in order to avoid being accused themselves. Most important, however, is a sense that violence may be an effective way to repress crime. In some places, such as Argentina, Jamaica, and Brazil, officials privately believe that criminals sometimes have to be eliminated when the courts cannot deal with them. Even where such views are not accepted, a belief persists that a reputation for being "tough," in the sense of being violent, has a deterrent effect. As a result some police administrators are reluctant to try to ensure that violence is minimized. Former police chiefs in Los Angeles have expressed opinions that are consistent with this belief, and police in Sao Paulo and Rio de Janeiro, Brazil, have supported the view.

The belief that violence on the part of the police has a deterrent effect on crime is extremely difficult to test empirically. Although some scholars have supported the proposition and others have attacked it as improbable, it is difficult to make a conclusive decision because we have no general way of determining how violent a police department is, nor of relating its violent activities to the crime rate. In the case of the use of deadly force, however, researchers have found ways to test the question whether the use of more deadly force may make for more effective crime control. We do have official counts in some U.S. cities of the number of persons shot by police, as well as of the number of police shot; these can be combined with studies of the arrest rate across time and across localities. James Fyfe has shown for New York City that after the number of police shootings dropped in the early 1970s, the crime rate, the arrest rate, and the safety of officers were not adversely affected. More pointedly, comparing the cities of Memphis, Tenn., and New York in the 1970s, Fyfe was able to show that although Memphis police had a higher rate of use of deadly force, they were not more effective in making felony arrests than the New York police. These studies suggest that increased official violence does not make cities safer.

Also See the Following Articles

ENEMY, CONCEPT AND IDENTITY OF • INSTITUTIONALIZATION OF VIOLENCE • JUSTIFICATIONS FOR VIOLENCE • MINORITIES AS PERPETRATORS AND VICTIMS OF CRIME • POLICING AND SOCIETY • TORTURE • URBAN VIOLENCE, YOUTH

Bibliography

Avery, M., Rudovsky, D., & Blum, K. (1996). *Police misconduct: Law and litigation* (3d. Ed.). Deerfield, Il: Clark, Boardman Callaghan.

Bittner, E. (1990). *Aspects of police work*. Boston, MA: Northeastern U. Press.

Chevigny, P. (1995). *Edge of the knife: Police violence in the Americas*. New York: New Press.

Fyfe, J. (1979). Administrative interventions in police shootings: An empirical examination. *Journal of Criminal Justice, 7*, 309.

Fyfe, J. (1982). Blind justice: Police shootings in Memphis. *Journal of Criminal Law and Criminology, 73*, 707.

Geller, W., & Scott, M. (1992). *Deadly force: What we know*. Washington, DC: Police Executive Research Forum.

Geller, W., & Toch, H. (1995). And justice for all: Understanding and controlling police abuse of force. Washington, DC: Police Executive Research Forum.

Mollen Commission (1994). *Commission report*. New York: Commission to Investigate Allegations of Police Corruption and the Anti-Corruption Procedures of the Police Department.

Skolnick, J., & Fyfe, J. (1993). *Above the law: Police and the excessive use of force*. New York: Free Press.

United Nations Basic Principles on the Use of Force and Firearms (1991). New York: United Nations.

United Nations Code of Conduct for Law Enforcement Officials (1979). New York: United Nations.

United States Department of State (annual). Country Reports on Human Rights Practices. Washington, DC: U.S. Gov't Printing Office.

Walker, S. (1995). *Citizen review resource manual*. Washington, DC: Police Executive Research Forum.

Policing and Society

Robert R. Friedmann
Georgia State University

GLOSSARY

Community Policing A new approach to policing developed in the early 1980s to open up the police for improved collaboration with the community to better combat crime.

Crime Control Traditional view of policing as a crime control agent; a view that does not necessarily match realities of policing to reduce crime.

Crime Prevention A host of programs and approaches attempting to reduce crime through education, information sharing, and target hardening.

Proactive Policing One of the key elements of community policing that views the police and the community as entrepreneurial in changing the conditions under which crime emerges.

Reactive Policing The traditional and pervasive policing approach that reacts to crime after it happens.

Sir Robert Peel Founder of the London Metropolitan Police.

THIS ARTICLE EXAMINES POLICING as a formal social control institution in society. It explores the history of and development of policing and identifies some of the major phases in the policing movement. Attention is given to the role of policing as a traditionally reactive societal force; reference is also made for viewing police as a proactive element that not merely reacts to crime but actively seeks to reduce crime causing conditions. Policing is examined in several countries and historical developments serve as a basis for offering future prospects for policing.

I. HISTORY

Policing roots are often traced back to 11th-century England. However, the first known direct reference to police officers can be found in Deuteronomy 16:18: "Judges and police officers shalt thou make thee in all thy gates." Gates were posited in the wall that typically surrounded the city. The Hebrew word (used to date) for police officers has the same root as the word "government."[1] Officers played mostly a regulatory role enforcing trade and commerce laws (such as measuring and verifying proper weight and content of merchandise and overseeing monetary exchange). City gates provided strategic points to control the in-and-out traffic of people and merchandise and to allow the apprehension of perpetrators and their on-the-spot trials.

Following the Norman Conquest of 1066, the "frank-pledge" was established, based on a community model where groups of people (a tything) formed the earliest version of community-based (nonpaid) policing. One hundred tythings were directed by a constable who reported to the shire reeve (sheriff). This system disintegrated by the 13th century when the role of the Justice of the Peace was introduced over the sheriff. In 17th- and 18th-century colonial America, the government system of control followed the English system where the sheriff (paid position) collected taxes, the mayor was the chief law enforcement officer, and constables and marshals served warrants and made arrests. The period was characterized by growing decentralization—where each colony developed its own law enforcement system—coupled with increased puritanism (emanating out of New England) where strong emphasis was placed and enforced on conformity to laws and the state.

The Industrial Revolution was characterized by a loss of formal control. As cities expanded and populations grew (mostly under, and creating, difficult conditions for needy population masses) crime increased. Against growing urbanization the old community-based system was no longer sufficient or effective. Following calls for the establishment of a police force composed of persons who would dedicate their time to preventing crime, the London Metropolitan Police Act resulted in the establishment of the first modern police force. Police, known as "bobbies," were highly centralized and were considered civil servants. American policing modeled itself after the London police. Following serious social unrest and rioting in the Northeastern industrial cities, the early "independent" police jurisdictions were established where each city had its own police system run by its mayor and police positions were filled by appointments highly dependent on political patronage.

American policing grew rapidly between 1860 and 1890. Officers were not paid well, had little job security, and high turnover occurred with every new elected

official, who would rush to get rid of the officers in place and appoint his own. Police work was unsupervised and there was large-scale corruption as police often looked the other way as long as they got to share in the criminals' profits. In some instances police officers initiated criminal acts, such as burglarizing residences, to supplement their low income. During the period of 1890–1920, the reform movement at the time demanded shifting more power from the mayor to the chief; hiring better selected, better trained, and more disciplined officers; and giving up activities unrelated to crime. The focus of police activities changed somewhat and the overall quality of officers improved, but it is safe to say that to date, political power is still in the hands of the mayors and it is only a matter of degrees of independence and exercise of control, depending on leadership style, personalities, or the possibility of rivalry, that determines mayor–chief relations.

A second reform movement shaped up between 1920 and 1960. The two best known reformers of this period were Richard Sylvester, the President of the International Association of Chiefs of Police, who identified the need for professionalism and called to separate police from politics and to make police professional as any other occupation and to accept technology. The second reformer, August Vollmer, the chief of police of Berkeley, California, developed college level police education programs and the first forensic laboratory for crime investigations. During this time the chief acquired more power and authority but to date remains a political appointee. Technology in the form of two-way radio and the patrol car enhanced both supervision and officers' response time.

The 1960s were times of civil disturbance and unrest. The population increased as WWII "baby boomers" matured along with an increase in crime that police could not keep up with. The period was characterized by increasing police brutality along with police being ordered to suppress civil rights demonstrations. Following the shooting death of a Black teenager by a White police officer in New York, on July 16, 1964, Black leaders demanded justice and marched to precinct headquarters and rioting broke out. President Johnson appointed the Kerner Commission (The National Advisory Commission on Civil Disorders), which concluded that police conduct was brutal, abusive, and racist; that training and supervision were inadequate; and that police–community relations were at an all-time low.

These turbulent times set up the next 30 years of policing. However, increased police professionalism distanced and alienated police from administrative staff, police were still not trusted by communities, police

---

[1] Police officer in Hebrew is *shoter*. The root of the word *shoter* (*shin.tet.resh*) is also the root of the terms government/order/regime/administration (*mishtar*) and police (*mishtara*)

officers nurtured a culture of "us against them," and with the increase in crime police were blamed for not handling it well. Increasing social unrest resulted in some of the worst rioting occurring in countries such as England and Israel. In England, for example, the Brixton riots were assessed in the Scarman Report with conclusions similar to those of the Kerner Commission.

II. CURRENT STATE OF POLICING IN THE UNITED STATES

The police professionalism model created several problems for police. The preoccupation with management has led to a decline in handling the serious crime problems of a community. Agencies became so concerned with management that officers were often not adequately trained to understand current crime problems and trends. This was coupled with a general lack of awareness by police of conditions and needs of the community. Despite the police mandate to offer preventive patrol, most policing has been reactive and not very successful at preventing crime. The switch to and growing dependence on the patrol car and improved radio communication eliminated the foot patrol and has spurred reactive policing in many western countries. The professional policing model values responding to every call as fast as possible, with police departments following this to date. The introduction of and the promotion and emphasis on 911 has increased the reactive responses from police as well as its load and ability (or lack of) to be as responsive to the public as expected.

Reactive policing tended to ignore the community despite its potential as being a helping resource to the police. Against this backdrop and with increasing administrative demands, workloads, and decreasing budgets, policing in several countries (particularly Canada, England, and the U.S.) returned to Sir Robert Peel's notion that people need to police themselves not only in formal ways (foot patrol) but in informal ways as well. Proponents of the emergent community policing model argued that cities need to possess a greater sense of community and that if a community allows itself to deteriorate, residents will reduce efforts to maintain homes and control unruly conduct, which could then result in more serious crime and further decay.

While it was recognized and understood that police must improve relations with poor and minority groups in the community, focus was also placed on the ineffective use of rank-and-file officers who are managed without much flexibility of judgement and operation. Many

officers complained that police management ignores individual talents and intelligence. For changes to occur in policing adjustments in organizational structure and in policies must be made. Despite the growing saliency of community policing, officers' performances are still often rated on number of arrests, ticket writing, and the number of calls they handle. Police leadership needs to reward the proactive and preventative actions of officers as well and construct coherent plans that are implemented departmentwide.

Herman Goldstein, a key proponent of community policing, argued that the professional model allows for officers to handle incidents efficiently. However, he perceives these incidents as symptoms of a larger problem. Therefore the underlying solution of "problem-oriented policing" involves moving beyond just handling incidents and actually taking into consideration its precursors or underlying factors such as location, persons involved, crime committed, and general community behavior. Goldstein maintains that frequently reoccurring incidents in a community take up the majority of police time and become "substantive problems." Therefore, problem-oriented policing is a major change in policing because it shifts the focus from internal police management to effectively dealing with substantive problems. It also increases proactive responses as officers are not just responding after the incident has been reported but actively trying to remedy substantive problems. Problem-oriented policing calls for developing the skills, procedures, and research techniques to analyze problems and to evaluate police effectiveness as an integral continuing part of management. For example, problem-oriented policing programs implemented in Baltimore and Virginia led to a decrease in residents' fear of crime.

III. COMMUNITY-ORIENTED POLICING AND COMMUNITY POLICING

Another key proponent of community policing, Robert Trojanowicz, argued that "Community Policing requires a department-wide philosophical commitment to involve citizens as partners in the process of reducing and controlling the contemporary problems of crime, drugs, fear of crime and neighborhood decay; and in efforts to improve the overall quality of life in the community." His work acknowledges that all community policing incorporates problem-oriented policing but not all problem-oriented policing is community policing. Community policing has also the added dimension of decentralization and greater involvement of community members. A key component in community policing is that the power is shared inside the police force. Strong hierarchical management techniques are put aside in favor of incorporating more from the police officers on the street who actually know and handle the "substantive problems." It offers more personalized policing as well as diminishes notorious bureaucracy.

The key differences between community policing and traditional policing evolve around random patrol, rapid response, and follow-up investigation, which characterize traditional reactive policing, while community policing involves a philosophy that aims to bring police and community closer, to decrease community fear of crime, and to increase the sense of community and community cohesion. Community policing is, therefore, proactive. Some even "fortify" the concept of community policing by promoting "total community policing," which is characterized more by (citizen-based) informal social control and less by (police-based) formal social control. The assumptions of this approach are that crime is ultimately controlled by the public and that therefore a mere increase of police presence in neighborhoods that lack a sense of community will produce only a marginal decrease in crime. Informal crime control can be created through the use of community boundaries. Police can implicitly or explicitly define community boundaries by interacting with communities. Once boundaries have been formed, increased community cohesiveness is possible. Police should assist, then, in creating neighborhood crime prevention groups, as these informal social control networks will result in long term declines in community crime and disorder. A strong community is expected to deflect crime from outsiders who will see a decrease in criminal opportunity. The problem with this expectation is that it neglects the often "home-grown" criminals and the fact that many communities lack a sense of community and cohesiveness and those characteristics provide the backdrop against which crime is produced and nurtured. It is appropriate to mention that an implicit assumption of policing (traditional or community) is that it handles street and/or violent crime; white collar crime or political crime (often with more far reaching consequences in damage to property and life) are rarely addressed.

A. Types of Community Policing and Its Precursors

1. Team Policing

The first form of community policing was tried in the late 1960s with team policing units assigned to long-term beats, guided by the need to get closer to the community and become more effective. However, due to ineffective implementation, team policing never worked as suggested and was discredited by the end of the 1970s and considered a failed strategy.

2. Foot Patrol

This is clearly among the most popular and common forms of community policing. Foot patrol aims to bring back the beat cop so that increased, personalized police presence and visibility in the community will decrease community fear of crime and improve police–community relations. Officers are not only responsible for monitoring the community but are also expected to attend community meetings, identify problems, and make referrals to social service agencies. Extensive research on foot patrol indicates that the most positive change that foot patrol brings about is in the community's perception of crime. However, in most instances it did not significantly decrease incidents of criminal activity.

3. Ministations and Community Centers

Ministations are decentralized police stations in shopping malls and other visible and accessible places in the community. With the help of local volunteers ministations are mostly used to assist walk-in clients, hold crime prevention meetings, and respond to policing needs for that specific community. Detroit developed 52 ministations in neighborhoods throughout the city. Although formal research has not been conducted, the Detroit ministations were known to have had implementation problems associated with decentralization and officers were labeled as social workers and not police. In Houston, storefront community centers were found to have decreased residents fear of personal crime and their perceptions of the amount of crime in the area.

4. Bicycle Patrol

An increasingly popularized mode is found in many U.S. city police departments, campus police departments, and in countries such as Canada, England, and Israel and on the European continent. The different transportation means offer officers greater visibility and accessibility which is often accompanied with more "friendly" uniform and it enhances positive interaction with the public.

B. Issues in Community Policing

1. Legitimation

Without legitimacy police cannot be effective. Community policing provides advantages in "opening doors" to gain support from the public for police actions. Legitimization is an important part in social control especially in times when relations between minorities and police have a lot to be desired. Through community policing, police are able to improve relations with residents and further legitimize their purpose for being in the community.

2. Change in Control

For community policing to succeed there must be a change of police control from city hall to precinct stations and community meeting halls along with an expanding decentralization process that must be supported from the top of elected officials through appointed officers to community members. City leaders who understand the complex problems in a neighborhood are more likely to make police address various crime-relevant issues of the community. Elected officials who believe all communities are the same are more likely to keep police officers in their traditional roles. However, decentralization cannot happen without the change in political powers and policies. A strong commitment from all involved must occur to change the level of control in the police force and in the community.

3. Deployment

Programs must be started that link the police to the community. Community policing tactics such as foot patrol and bike patrol are geared to decrease crime and fear of crime. Officers must not be assessed merely on number of arrests but also on the number of households visited, community meetings attended, and overall proactive initiatives in a neighborhood.

4. Implementation

Several problems can arise when trying to implement community policing programs. Police departments are highly complex, and gaining the consensus needed to start community policing is difficult. Community policing incorporates fundamental changes in policing design, and whole precinct consent to the program is unlikely without significant preparatory work. Choosing a method of community policing can be difficult, therefore research done with the community (clients) and street officers (service providers) enhances the understanding of what they recommend for the community as well as the likelihood of incorporating their input. Oftentimes, shortages in resources can derail a community policing program or not even put it on track. A measurement for success should be clearly defined so that the community can clearly understand the impact the new policing has on the neighborhood. In this sense, organizing community residents is a key component, as without community support the idea of community policing is impossible to implement. While this seems to be self evident, the "community" part is typically missing in the community policing equation as it is more convenient and comfortable to focus on the traditional known elements of reactive police work, which are more easily measurable.

Internal police changes conducive to successful implementation of community policing include breaking down the barriers in the police department so that change can be discussed and promoted, educating the leaders and rank-and-file officers on community policing and its augmenting advantages on traditional policing, reassuring officers that community policing is not something that the higher political forces are demanding but an improvement of programs already in place, and providing on-going training in an attempt to reduce the fears of change. Once the program has been chosen, clearly defining the new police roles is mandatory so there is no confusion throughout the transformation to community policing; keeping the officers consistently updated with the progress of change is essential for success. Finally, an often-mentioned but less-often-upheld key component is the development of partnerships.

C. Possible Negative Consequences of Community Policing

There are several potential risks and negative consequences with community policing. For example, highly organized communities with little crime get little policing. There is also the separation of police officers into "community police" and "incident-handling police." As communities are more likely to look down upon incident-handling police this can increase tension between police officers. In their corner, incident handling police do not consider community police as "real officers." This could further create conflict in the community as well as in the precincts. While community policing may have been underimplemented it also has been oversold as every city wants it to perform miracles for crime reduction and when the results are not occurring fast enough, cities are giving up.

The development of community policing in the west is by no means automatically replicated or copied in other parts of the world. It would therefore be helpful to examine several countries that represent different traditions, structures, and approaches to policing to evidence the complexity of policing.

IV. POLICING IN CHINA

From the 1920s until the emergence of the Chinese Communist Party (CCP) and the communist regime in the late 1940s, the country was ruled by the Nationalist Government (Guodindang), which operated the police force. Police were corrupt and local governments had inconsistent laws and enforcement practices. Each town could have a separate set of laws depending on what the Nationalist's regime determined. In large cities like Shanghai, the government lost control and a high crime rate existed. Crimes such as gambling, prostitution, and murder were commonplace and the offenders usually got away with their crimes without punishment.

After the Communist Revolution in 1949, the People's Republic abolished all Nationalist laws. From 1954 to 1957, police in China went through a similar professionalization process as police in the United States. The People's Liberation Army (PLA) aided local governments in gaining control in cities. Courts, police, and laws became more uniform and less corrupt with an emphasis on constitutional procedure. The CCP wanted police to be highly trained and educated in the communist laws to serve as control agents in the local communities and as enforcers of the communist ideology. The Cultural Revolution's (1966–1976) supporters rioted and demonstrated, claiming that new law enforcement and the PLA were too controlled by the state.

Following Mao Tse Tung's death (in 1976) the professional police model shifted the police role from teaching communism to maintaining public order. The police and the PLA had similar uniforms and police were seen as a direct product of the state. In 1984, policing in China changed with the establishment of the Ministry of Public Security, which was a division of the Ministry of State Security. It was led by Ruan Chongwu, who believed the role of the Ministry was to be in charge of law and order, traffic safety, and fire control. Twenty-five divisions of the PLA were transferred to the Ministry of Public Security and by 1996 the Chinese police force was composed of 1.2 million security personnel and 600,000 armed policemen with a police : population ratio of 1.7 police for every 1000 citizens.

The Chinese leadership under Deng Xiaoping and Ruan Chongwu emphasized the importance of education and initiated plans to have all law enforcement college educated. The Ministry has an emphasis on chains of command, is run by the State Council, and controls the Social Security Bureau, which trains officers in criminal investigations and forensic science. Each city has Social Security Bureau representatives who train local Public Security Bureaus, which, in turn, run the local police departments.

The huge size of China (about 7% of the world's land), its huge population (about 20% of the world's population), its ethnic structure (many languages, dialects), and its peasant/rural character (about 80% of the population are peasants) place a formidable challenge on policing and social control. While the Chinese governmental and police hierarchies are still intact there has been a recent change in command and China is attempting to open its doors to trade with the outside world. Yet the likelihood of developing anything that resembles community policing as it is espoused and practiced in the west is not likely as long as a dictatorial regime is in place that exerts strong centralized control over the country.

V. POLICING IN INDIA

Prior to 1609, India had two distinct types of police systems. Traditional rural village-based policing dates back to the first days of Indian civilization and has remained constant throughout history. The headman in the village was responsible for policing and he could hire a special police helper to assist him. The headman was responsible for the village security as well as the detection and capture of villagers who committed crimes in other villages. The headman was also responsible for paying the other village the damages from any act by a member of his village. However, a dominant landowner would stand above the headman and the two would work together in securing the village. The second type of policing was that carried out by the Imperial power of the time, which was responsible for policing the large cities. The villages were considered self-sufficient and rarely experience pressure from the Imperial power as to how to police a village.

The western influence in India is several centuries old and was brought into India by the British. Given that much of western policing emerged from or was heavily influenced by the British model of policing and given that the British exported their policing system to their colonies and mandatory territories, the impact of the British approach should not be underestimated. Captain Hawkins brought England to India in 1609; in 1792, Lord Cornwallis changed policing there. Under the Darogha system an appointed British official (Darogha) would replace the headman in the village. The Darogha would be responsible for overseeing the headman and the village. This system was inefficient due to the centuries of tradition in the villages. The citizens were not very cooperative with the new police. In the 19th century the British attempted to police India like England. Due to cultural, environmental, and geographic differences, the use of England's criminal law code was destined to fail.

The Indian Police Act of 1861 is still the basic mandate for the Indian police. The Indian police follow the hierarchical patterns of British police. The police exist under the Royal Irish Constabulary, which is under an Inspector General of Police, who answers to the state government and is responsible for the internal administration in local police departments. The existence of armed and unarmed police also developed in this time. Unlike in the United States, where police are always armed, or in England, where police are never armed, the Indian police have armed officers who go to those situations that are known to be violent and unarmed officers take care of any nonviolent policing needs.

At midnight, August 14, 1947, India was no longer under British rule and became an independent nation. The first Home Minister of India, Sardar Vallahbai Patel, did nothing to change the 1861 Indian Police Act. The police did change its name to the Indian Police Service (IPS), yet despite the change in name and the replacement of British police by Indian police the basic structure of the British policing model remained in place. In 1979, the Indian Police Act was updated with the introduction of 12 responsibilities (under police mandate) such as public safety, investigations of crimes, apprehension of criminals, stopping crime before it happens, usage of crime preventative patrols, increasing the sense of security in the community, providing appropriate services to the community (including relief in distress situations), and resolving conflicts.

In modern-day India crime is of utmost importance yet police are highly underpaid and do not have the skills or equipment to properly apprehend criminals. Also no legislation to modernize the police system has existed since the end of British rule. The Indian police force is fraught with corruption and inefficiency and is overly controlled by the state. Calls for police reform in India focus on the reduction of state control, increasing the strength of the unarmed and civilian police, and, most importantly, modernizing the police policies with respect to technology and management.

VI. POLICING IN ENGLAND

England is transitioning from its traditional model of policing, which looked more like what the U.S. is now striving to achieve, into the modern model, which is more of what the U.S. has. Under the traditional model few police have great control due to community support and police are close to the community and have general consent from the public. The public, in turn, dictates what it wants in policing as expressed in changes in social attitudes. The public supports police because they are not oppressive and that allows police to maintain social control without force and excess policing staff. Police do not have more legal powers than a regular citizen although this was challenged in the 1950s (also known as the Golden Era of policing) when police were at the peak of their popularity.

Under the modern model, and due mostly to increased crime, not to systematically and carefully planned public policy, police are no longer low in numbers. Police have more legal powers now, as the Public Order Act of 1986 gave police more powers in search, seizure, arrest, and detention. Since the Police Act of 1964, police governance is divided among local police, chief constables, and the Home Secretary. Local police have the responsibility of maintaining control, the chief constables organize and oversee the local police, and the Home Secretary is a higher power that has "shareholders" authority, as the Home Office controls 51% of the constabularies budget. Public consent for police declined steadily in the 1980s. Much like in the United States, policing in England has become very bureaucratic with a complex hierarchy. Despite the recommendations found in the Scarman Report, England still has a disproportionate amount of minority police; this was not very conducive for an efficient handling of racial tensions between the Afro-Caribbeans and predominately White police. English police are currently moving toward specialized units, which includes police work in the community.

VII. POLICING IN FRANCE

Under an authoritarian model, police are controlled by executive power and are heavily involved in the political arena. France also experienced a professionalism movement, which started in 1941 at the *Ecole Nationale Superieure de Police*. In 1967, the police were centralized and became officers of the state. France has a national civilian police, which is responsible for policing the cities, and the National Constabulary, a military force responsible for policing rural areas. In addition, France has separate specialized forces for different crimes. Paris police are an exception, as they are grouped under a single authority associated with the city and not with the state.

France experiences problems with centralized policing as the gap between civilians and police is wide. The strongly centralized structure of the French police is prohibitive to the introduction of decentralized community policing, which urges a nonauthoritarian command.

VIII. POLICING IN ISRAEL

Despite its small size, Israel provides a social laboratory to students of policing. Upon its establishment in 1948 the country adopted British policing and British law and through the years it modified both. As of 1974 Israel is looking more at legal precedents in the U.S. than relying on British rulings. Israel's police system is centralized and its policing system makes sense for the smallness of the country. In Israel the key responsibility of the police is security and public order and it gives terrorist threat and postincident management the highest priority over "traditional" crime. However, unlike France, centralization has advantages. In the mid-1990s a decision was made to adapt community policing forcewide and extensive efforts are made at the station and community levels to implement this strategy. Considering various organizational changes it remains to be seen whether such plans will survive routine leadership changes.

IX. POLICING IN THE FORMER SOVIET BLOC

One of the most fascinating policing transitions is currently taking place in the former Soviet bloc countries as they move from a continental and communist police model to postcommunist policing. The continental model was influenced by the German idea of *rechtsstaat* (rule-of-law state). With the expansion of the Soviet entity the colonial model was introduced as a way to enforce the law of the state in the Eastern bloc, Yugoslavia, and Bulgaria. The Soviet colonial method was different from the Anglo-Saxon method in that the Soviet colonial police were operated from Moscow, whereas in England the colonial police were operated from outside the home country. The Soviet militia in the new colonies were responsible for maintaining social and political control and were instructed to arrest anyone who defied the new authority. Traditional customs to those areas were outlawed and punishable by law yet

police corruption was rampant and the law often favored the Soviets over the native people.

The communist model was a combination of colonial and continental policing and its role was to enforce the laws of the state. Under communist rule, the state had authority over religious beliefs, private property, and every action of the citizens in enforcing the communist ideology. Under postcommunist policing a more careful balance in controlling the rule of law and criminal behavior is being struck. Until some stabilization is reached in the new capitalist economy, the role of the police will be in constant flux. It is already apparent that the postcommunist police officer has lost much of his or her power and authority, which paradoxically makes it more difficult for him or her to carry out what has become a more limited crime control approach of policing. Some interesting developments, such as the abolition of the death penalty in Hungary as unconstitutional, provide almost a contradictory approach to that of the U.S., particularly in times when crime is rampant in the former Soviet bloc countries and when police departments are expected to adhere to smaller budgets with increasing demands. Despite the narrowing of the police mandate to control crime police appear to be weaker and less well equipped to provide an adequate professional and legal response to the rising crime problem.

Professional police developments are increasingly characterized by a cooperative initiative with the west. The Dutch–Hungarian partnership, the Swiss assistance to the Hungarian police, and the establishment in Budapest of the FBI's International Law Enforcement Academy to serve as a regional training facility to the former Soviet bloc countries are but a few prominent examples.

X. CONCLUDING REMARKS

Policing has undergone several major transitions and despite some tendencies to view community policing today as closing a full circle by returning to the old days of the beat officer, the fact remains that the policing movement has not truly completed a full circle but is progressing in a "linear" fashion. It has not really ever returned to where it was because the innovations in technology, organizational, and political power and the division of labor have not allowed that to happen. It may be easier to accept community policing innovations by stating that "we have always done that," but being a foot patrol officer 100 years ago had very little to do with the principles and applications of community policing today that are geared toward developing partnerships, utilizing community resources, and solving problems in a concerted, proactive effort to reduce the level of crime production.

Traditionally, the key role of policing in society has been crime control and the provision of formal social control. Yet despite the spurious attribution of that responsibility to police and police being blamed for increases in crime (or taking the blame when it increases), the fact remains that police are not the crime producers in society. They are at best street administrators and managers of crime statistics. This is not to say that it is not possible for police to manipulate some crime statistics up or down. The point is that for crime statistics to show a significant shift they must reflect a corresponding shift in crime causing conditions. That element was missing from traditional, reactive policing and it became part and parcel of the latest development in the policing movement, namely, community policing. Hence there needs to be a better understanding among police (and other social service delivery agencies as well as the policy-making bodies) of what affects crime and to recognize the limitations of formal control and reactive policing.

Despite the advent of community policing, for over a decade since the emergence of modern community policing there was no definition provided for it. There were the 10 guiding principles originally proposed by John Alderson in England and the 10 principles offered by Trojanowicz and Bucqueroux in the U.S. In 1992 Friedmann suggested the following comprehensive definition:

> *Community policing* is a policy and a strategy aimed at achieving more effective and efficient crime control, reduced fear of crime, improved quality of life, improved police services and police legitimacy, through a *proactive reliance* on community resources that seeks to change crime-causing conditions. It assumes a need for greater accountability of police, greater public share in decision-making, and greater concern for civil rights and liberties.

According to this definition, for community policing to be effective as a social control mechanism in any society, it needs to be much larger in scope than the definition and mandate that traditional reactive policing has allowed for. Therefore, to obtain successful implementation of community policing, several organizational changes are required.

A. Intraagency Organizational Change

The organizational structure of police departments needs to be decentralized and community policing adapted forcewide and not into (or by) specialized units only. Emphasis is to be placed on flattening rank structure and increasing civilianization and civilian involvement. Communications need to be improved not only as two-way radios are employed between officers and command/control centers, but also among officers so they are more aware of the dynamics of the community they serve. Supervision requires increased interaction between officer and supervisor and between the officer and the community. Officers are limited in exercising their power and mandate and in many departments an arrest cannot be made without a supervisor's presence; hence, officers' discretion needs to be widened, officers need to feel empowered, and departments should encourage more operational flexibility.

Many would-be officers apply for positions in law enforcement because of thrill-seeking and adventurism and many departments screen in these action-oriented personnel. Community policing requires that police recruitment emphasize mediation and defusion of conflict over action, that it recognize interpersonal skills, and that departments seek to increase the level of education of their personnel. Training needs to expand on community-oriented elements as well as on interpersonal skills. At the same time officers' performances need to be assessed on the basis of being community oriented, on being measurable, on having quality in the nonlaw enforcement aspects of job performance, and on matching expectations with standards and agency values. With that comes the provision of a matching reward signifying to officers that if they do what is expected they will be appropriately rewarded. Hence rewarding proactive activities and providing tangible raises and promotions as well as intangible recognition are of key importance. *The New York Times Magazine* featured a story on officer Kevin Jett, who found that his community policing assignment was at a dead-end in terms of promotion and raises.

B. Interagency Change

Even if police undergo a complete transition toward community policing it is still impossible for it to control crime alone. A neglected aspect of traditional policing is the formation of partnerships and improved coordination (and prevention of duplication) with other social services. Interaction with other agencies needs to be flattened, increased in scope, and to encourage interagency planning and cooperation. Different agencies have different responsibilities, roles, and needs and so do the professionals that are employed by them. Therefore, understanding working definitions and professional expectations can make a difference in life-saving situations, in criminal prosecution, or in caring for needy groups. Agencies also have different needs and resources and therefore understanding them is crucial for functioning in a cooperative environment. Yet, the shift from defined (and closed) to ambiguous (and more open) organizational/agency boundaries will not take place without some anticipated resistance to change. Hence agencies should assess potential problem areas for friction and conflict as well as identify potential (and actual) sources of support in an increasingly inter-dependent world. Agencies should reward cross-agency cooperation and reassess the existing division of labor. Agencies should provide incentives for cross-boundary (departmental) cooperation and encourage comprehensive cooperation. Police and other public service agencies as well as private organizations and civic groups should establish a coordinating body (such as the Super-Agency, as suggested by Friedmann, 1992) to oversee the identification of problems in the community and the extent to which adequate solutions are provided in a timely manner.

C. Mapping the Community: Taking Inventory

The most neglected element in traditional policing, and to some extent also in community policing, is that of the community itself. Often officers are very familiar with their beats (streets, shops, citizens) but much less often are they aware of the problems and needs of the community as is reflected by official data and by citizens perceptions. Even the picture of crime is not commonly distributed to residents or even police officers. An increasing effort is evident in many police departments to provide crime analysis by using crime mapping and more of it needs to be done in an on-going comprehensive fashion. This applies not only to mapping crime trends but also in profiling neighborhood and community characteristics and identifying the social networks that underline a given community. This will allow the identification of real and perceived problems as well as the identification of the resources and leadership to manage them in cooperation with the police. Police agencies need to enhance proactive planning and facilitate comprehensive solutions. This can be achieved if the key element of community policing, that of building partnerships, is done. Therefore, creating and enhanc-

ing a climate conducive to partnership and encouraging broad-based community activities is highly relevant. The partnership with the community is part of the increase of and internalization of informal social control mechanisms. These could be best facilitated by giving a more prominent role to the family, school, church, civic associations, private and public advocacy groups, and volunteers. Finally, two elements of technology ought to be considered: the mass media should disseminate positive stories about community policing and the increase of Internet usage has the potential of enhancing communication and knowledge among various partners (agencies and individual residents alike) in this effort.

Community policing cannot and should not be considered a panacea to the crime problem. Yet it offers (if implemented well) the best hope that along with (the necessary) reactive policing it could have an impact on the production (and minimization) of crime in the community. Some preliminary evidence of success is reported in cities such as Boston and Chicago. The irony of community policing is that with the decentralization of policing, it risks the return to the political sphere from which police have never fully shied away. Also, given the tendency to come up with new names ("total community policing" is already available), that rather than investing in a long-range strategy, police (and other agencies) may fall into the trap of reinventing the wheel.

Also See the Following Articles

CRIME AND PUNISHMENT, CHANGING ATTITUDES TOWARD • CRIMINOLOGY, OVERVIEW • LAW AND VIOLENCE • SOCIAL CONTROL AND VIOLENCE

Bibliography

Alderson, J. C. (1979). *Policing freedom: A commentary on the dilemmas of policing in western democracies.* Estover, Plymouth, UK: Macdonald & Evans.

Bayley, D. (1969). *The police and political development in India.* Princeton, NJ: Princeton University Press.

Bailey, W. G. (1989). *The encyclopedia of police science.* New York/ London: Garland.

Braiden, C. (1992). Community Policing: Nothing new under the sun. In *Community oriented policing and problem solving* (pp. 17–22). Sacramento, CA: Crime Prevention Center, Office of the Attorney General.

Brewer, J. D., Guelke, A., Hume, I., Moxon-Browne, E., & Wilford, R. (1996). *The Police, Public Order, and the State.* New York, NY: St. Martin's Press, Inc.

Burns, I. M. (1995). Perspectives on the British model of policing in an open Europe. In J.-P. Brodeur (Ed.), *Comparisons in policing: An international perspective* (pp. 166–175). Brookfield, VT: Avebury.

Curry, J. C. (1977). *The indian police.* New Delhi, India: Manu.

Das, D. (1993). *Policing in six countries around the world.* Chicago, IL: The University of Illinois at Chicago, Office of International Criminal Justice.

Deakin, T. J. (1988). *Police professionalism: The renaissance of American law enforcement.* Springfield, IL: Charles C. Thomas.

Diaz, S. M. (1994). Police in India. In D. Das (Ed.), *Police practices: An international review,* Metuchen, NJ: The Scarecrow Press.

Dunham, R., & Alpert, G. (Eds.) (1989). *Critical issues in policing: Contemporary readings.* Prospect Heights, IL: Waveland.

Eck, J. (1993). Alternative futures for policing. In D. Weisburd & C. Uchida (Eds.), *Police innovation and control of the police: Problems of law, order, and community,* (pp. 59–79). New York: Springer-Verlag.

Evans, R. (1993). *Deng Xiaoping and the making of modern China.* New York: Viking.

Fielding, N. (1991). *The police and social conflict: Rhetoric and reality.* Atlantic Highlands, NJ: Athlone.

Fijnaut, C. (1995). International policing in Europe: It's present situation and future. In J.-P. Brodeur (Ed.), *Comparisons in policing: An international perspective* (pp. 115–135). Brookfield, VT: Avebury.

Friedmann, R. (1992). *Community policing: Comparative perspectives and prospects.* New York: St. Martin's Press.

Funk, A. (1995). The German police system in a European context. In J.-P. Brodeur (Ed.), *Comparisons in policing: An international perspective* (pp. 69–86). Brookfield, VT: Avebury.

Goldstein, H. (1990). *Problem-oriented policing.* Philadelphia, PA: Temple University Press.

Horton, C. (1995). *Policing policy in France.* London, UK: Policy Studies Institute.

Jackson, P. (1989). *Minority group threat, Crime and policing.* New York: Praeger.

Kappeler, V. E. (Ed.) (1995). *The police & society.* Prospect Heights, IL: Waveland.

Kratcoski, P., & Dukes, D. (Eds.) (1995). *Issues in community policing.* Highland Heights, KY: ACJS/Anderson Monograph Series.

Lasley, J., Vernon, R., Robert, R., & Dery, G. M., III (1995). Operation Cul-de-Sac: LAPD's "Total Community" Policing Program. In P. C. Kratcoski & D. Dukes (Eds.), *Issues in Community Policing* (pp. 51–69). Highland Heights, KY: ACJS/Anderson Monograph Series.

Manning, P. K. (1989). Community policing. In R. G. Dunham & G. P. Alpert (Eds.), *Critical issues in policing: Contemporary readings* (pp. 395–406). Prospect Heights, IL: Waveland.

Mastrofski, S. (1993). Eyeing the doughnut: Community policing and progressive reform. *American Journal of Police, 12,* 1–17.

Monjardet, D. (1995). The French model of policing. In J.-P. Brodeur (Ed.), *Comparisons in policing: An international perspective* (pp. 49–69). Brookfield, VT: Avebury.

Nalla, M., & Newman, G. (1994). Is white collar policing, policing? *Policing and society, 3,* 303–318.

Normandeau, A., & Leighton, B. (Eds.) (1991). Police and society in Canada. *Canadian Journal of Criminology, 33,* 241–585.

Rawlings, P. (1995). The idea of policing: A history. *Policing and Society, 5,* 129–149.

Reiner, R. (1995). Community policing in England and Wales. In J.-P. Brodeur (Ed.), *Comparisons in policing: An international perspective.* Brookfield, VT: Avebury.

Rosenbaum, D. P., & Lurigio, A. J. (1994). An inside look at community policing reform: Definitions, organizational changes and evaluation findings. *Crime and Delinquency, 40,* 299–314.

Ruan, C. (1986). Minister on social order in China. *Beijing Review, 29,* 34.

Saville, G. (1994). *Crime problems, community solutions: Environmental criminology as a developing prevention strategy.* Port Moody, British Columbia: AAG.

Shelley, L. (1994). The sources of Soviet policing. *Police studies, 17,* 49–65.

Silverman, E. (1995). Community policing: The implementation gap. In P. C. Kratcoski & D. Dukes (Eds.), *Issues in Community policing* (pp. 35–49). Highland Heights, KY: ACJS/Anderson Monograph Series.

Skogan, W. G. (1995). Community policing in the United States. In J.-P. Brodeur (Ed.), *Comparisons in policing: An international perspective* (pp. 86–112). Brookfield, VT: Avebury.

Smith, D. (1991). The origins of Black hostility to the police. *Policing and Society, 1,* 1–15.

Sparrow, M., Moore, M. H., & Kennedy, D. M. (1990). *Beyond 911: A new era for policing.* New York: Basic Books.

Tonry, M., & Morris, N. (1992). *Modern policing.* Chicago, IL: University of Chicago Press.

Trojanowicz, R. C. (1990). Community policing is not police community relations. *FBI Law Enforcement Bulletin, 59*(10), 6–11.

Trojanowicz, R. C., & Bucqueroux, B. (1990). *Community policing: A contemporary perspective.* Cincinnati, Ohio: Anderson.

Trojanowicz, R. C. (1994). *Community policing: How to get started.* Cincinnati, OH: Anderson.

Wakeman, F. R. (1995). *Policing Shanghai 1927–1937.* Berkeley, CA: University of California Press.

Ward, R., & Bracey, D. H. (1985). Police training and professionalism in the People's Republic of China. *Police Chief, 52,* 36–38.

Weisburd, D., & Uchida, C. (1993). *Police innovation and control of the police: Problems of law, order and community.* New York: Springer Verlag.

Political Economy of Violence and Nonviolence

William Gissy

Morehouse College

THIS ARTICLE compares economic views on conflict and violence, with the focus on war, with views from other social disciplines.

GLOSSARY

Economics The study of resource allocation and the production and distribution of goods and services.

Economic Liberalism The belief that individuals are the best judge of their own welfare and should be free to pursue their own interests.

Economic Nationalism The belief that government policies should be designed to promote national welfare at the expense of other nations and individuals.

Economic Pacifism The belief that individuals and nations will learn to coexist peacefully as their economic interdependence increases.

Economic Rationality The notion that an individual's behavior is consistent with his or her stated goals and assumptions.

Political Economy The approach to economics that takes a more interdisciplinary view and incorporates normative consideration.

I. VIOLENCE AS A TOPIC OF POLITICAL ECONOMY

Over the course of recorded history, violence and its ultimate manifestation, war, has been an important topic of inquiry. Scholars from a variety of fields have endeavored to understand the nature of violence, constructing theories of its causes, consequences, and prevention. Such investigations are of great importance, for once generally accepted theories have a way of influencing individual and societal behavior, thus becoming self-filling prophecies. Aware of this profound influence on human lives, theorists generally incorporate a strong normative element into their writing. Violence may be analyzed from one of several academic perspectives, the most common being political, sociological, and historical. The various approaches result in contrasting points of interest as well as differences in the analytical technique. However, due to the complex nature of violence, most theories of violence become a mix of perspectives. This article examines the concepts of violence and conflict within the framework of political economy. Political economy, as used in this article, is an essentially Western discipline, albeit imported as are other Western intellectual traditions. This is not to imply that a political economy based on Hindu, Islamic, African, or other cultural traditions cannot be developed or examined. Such an effort, however, would be the basis of a separate article. The reader should simply bear in mind that the Western tradition of a political economy is merely one of several ways to link economics with the concepts of conflict and violence.

A. Violence and War

Although this article deals with violence in general, a substantial portion focuses on violence within the context of war. The reasons are twofold. First, much of the early studies on violence concentrated on war, later expanding the inquiry to other forms of violence. Second, the concept of war itself has been broadened from its 19th century usage. Writers in the 19th century generally viewed war as an instrument of foreign policy employed to compel an opponent to succumb to the other's will. Contemporary military definitions generally classify war as any armed conflict among political units. This extended the concept of war beyond formally declared conflicts between nations-states to include civil wars, but still excluded other forms of armed conflict between groups. Additionally, military definitions usually required that the two sides be equally sufficient in terms of military power, as to render an uncertain outcome. In a more generic sense "war" could be taken to include conflicts between powerful and primitive states, often referred to as military interventions or military expeditions. Although a broader concept of war fails to include all forms of violence, it serves as a basis to understand violence in general. Factors that motivate nations to enact armed conflicts may well be, albeit on a smaller scale, the same fundamental influences that lead individuals to commit violent crimes or acts of terrorism.

B. Political Economy and Violence

Political economy, in its initial usage, was the term applied to what we now call economics. Economics itself is the study of how individuals and societies choose to allocate scarce resources for the production and distribution of goods and services. Today the term political economy is used in reference to any inquiry within the context of economics, that is often interdisciplinary and generally interwoven with normative considerations. What then does violence have to do with economics or political economy? From a purely economic perspective the impact of expenditures designed to produce violence, including peacetime military ex-

penditures, is a question of efficient resource allocations. Likewise, the costs of violence, in terms of destruction of resources or infrastructure as well as the loss of human life, are matters that fall under the domain of economic analysis. However, economics is about decision making, so the decisions to engage in violence are, themselves, an economic consideration. Indeed a burgeoning literature has emerged examining various forms of violence from an economic perspective. In addition to war, revolution, terrorism, and crime represent areas where economics has extended its views since violence represents the extreme form of conflict response. Economists have also extended the story to cover alliances, the formulation of law and methods of nonviolent conflict resolution. The political economy of violence, therefore, represents an attempt to interweave the economic approach, choice based on cost-benefit analysis, with other social disciplines. Contrary to pure economics, the focus is more holistic, interweaving the economic forces with social, political, and psychological influences.

II. PHILOSOPHICAL ORIGINS

As stated earlier, the investigations into violence in general have their origins in the inquiries into the nature and consequences of wars. World War I is often cited as a turning point in the theory of war, in economics as well as other disciplines because of the extensive nature of the conflict. Modern peace economics and the focus on nonviolent conflict resolution were influenced, in part, by the view that war had become economically irrational. Unlike the controlled conflicts, which were the focus of much of the 19th century theory, war had grown to encompass the total mobilization of a nation's social, economic, and technological resources, resulting in enormous losses of life and material resources. This view, however, is somewhat simplistic. As we shall see in the next section, the economic theory of war is actually five distinct theories, each owing to one of three particular philosophical traditions. What is now referred to as modern peace economics is, to a great extent, an offshoot of one of these prevailing theories that existed prior to World War I. This section is concerned with the three principal philosophical traditions that gave rise to various economic theories of war. These traditions are liberalism, nationalism, and socialism.

A. Liberalism

Economic liberalism is often dated with the publication of Adam Smith's classic book, *An Inquiry into the Nature and Causes of the Wealth of Nations* in 1776. Smith's views, however, were influenced by numerous thinkers from the 17th and 18th centuries, such as Francois Quesney, Richard Cantillion, and David Hume. As were the theorists of political liberalism, such as John Locke, Jean Jacques Rousseau, and Charles de Secondat de Montesquieu, the proponents of economic liberalism were inspired by scientific revolution. Additionally, economic liberalism was influenced by the emerging industrial revolution.

1. Background

The revolution in science, associated with Isaac Newton, had two major impacts that influenced thought in other areas. First, the rejection of the belief that knowledge could be derived from reason alone. The scientific method, with its reliance on experimental evidence, gave importance to experience and measurement as sources of knowledge and understanding. In 1776, as the industrial revolution was beginning, England stood as the most efficient and powerful country in the world. Yet, the significant growth of manufacturing and inventions occurring during this period caused political economists to rethink the nature of wealth and growth and to rethink the proper role of the state in economic affairs. An increasing number of entrepreneurs and a growing supply of factory labor created a natural condition to keep costs down. The need for government rules on trade and commerce were increasingly viewed as antiquated.

2. Major Tenets

Economic liberalism is based on the principles of personal liberty, private property, and limited government interference. The term "liberalism" should be understood in its historical context. Classical liberalism emphasized liberty from government regulation. In the economic context this would include the elimination of restriction on the choice of occupations or transfers of land. Liberalism accents that self-interest is a basic component of human nature. In the economic arena, producers provide us with goods, not out of concern for our well-being, but due to their desire to make a profit. Likewise, workers sell their labor and buy the producer's goods as a means of satisfying their own wants. This leads to the belief in a natural harmony of interests. By each individual pursuing their own interest the best interest of society are served. The forces of a free competitive market economy would guide production, exchange, and distribution in a manner that no government could improve upon. The government's role,

therefore, is limited to the enforcement of property rights, providing public goods, and maintaining internal and external security.

B. Nationalism

Economic nationalism preceded liberalism as an aspect of mercantilist thought. It also served as a key component of the postclassical German economists as well as early American political economists. Economic nationalism is closely tied to sociopolitical philosophies that view the state as the center of our social lives. Economic nationalism places great emphasis on government intervention in economic affairs, holding that society has interests of its own that differ substantially from those of any individual. It is the responsibility of the state to foster industry and transportation, to establish colonies to supply the nation with needed raw materials, and to protect the course of international commerce. To hold colonies and dominate trade routes the state must develop a powerful military. The interests of the state, and therefore the individual, are best served by a highly regulated economy. The principals of individualism and free enterprise are viewed as perversions. If everything ultimately reflects on the state then the state has a vested interest in not only what is produced but the quality of the product as well. The government must protect society and the reputation of the state from poor workmanship and low quality materials. Uniform standards of quality can only be guaranteed by a strong central government.

C. Socialism

The industrial revolution did more than alter the structure of the agricultural-handicraft economy. Innovation reduced the need for agricultural workers and mass production displaced the craftsman. These displaced workers now sought to make a living by working in one of the numerous new factories that emerged. They tended to reside in the vicinity of the factory, creating neighborhoods riddled with crime, disease, and poverty. Misery was a way of life with wages low and no compensation if injured in an industrial accident. From this backdrop, a variety of reform movements were initiated; these are commonly labeled as socialist. Although the various advocates disagreed with each other as to the particular type of socialism, that is, utopian, guild, Christian, Marxism, or state, there are certain common tenets associated with socialist thought. First, there is a universal rejection of the notion of harmony of interest. In its place, socialists offer a view of society composed of distinct classes whose interests were generally in conflict. This leads us to a second common theme in socialism, the rejection of laissez-faire. With some exceptions, socialists viewed government as a potential representative of working-class interests. A third common belief is that capitalism is often subject to periods of crisis or stagnation. These periods merely heightened the general misery of the workers, as capitalists take measures to preserve their wealth. The next common aspect of socialist thought is the rejection of self-interested behavior. Such behavior, as it is observed, is not the natural state of man, rather it is a product of the capitalist system. The emphasis capitalism places on making profits and accumulating wealth forces individuals to look out for their welfare at the expense of others. Placed in a different environment, self-interested individuals would expose their nobler virtues, and sharing and cooperation would become the norm. The last common aspect of socialist thought is the belief in collective action and public ownership of enterprise. This collective behavior is necessary to alleviate the conditions of poverty that ravage the working class in a capitalist system. Although socialists, with the exception of anarchists, believed in a strong government with a central role in economic activity, one must not confuse them with the nationalists. In nationalism, the individual functions to serve the state, whereas in socialism the state exists to serve the interests of the individual.

III. ECONOMIC THEORIES OF WAR

From a historical perspective, World War I marks the turning point in the economic approach to conflict and peace. For the first time industrial nations pooled their technological and economic resources to mobilize mass armies outfitted with sophisticated weapons. The enormous losses in life and materials, as well as the global economic and financial breakdown, proved that war is economically irrational. However, these views can be found in the earliest writings on the economics of conflict. This view, that war was irrational, was only one of five prevailing approaches prior to World War I, each of which was influenced by one of three prevailing attitudes: liberalism, nationalism, and socialism.

A. Philosophical Origins and Conflict

1. Liberalism

Economic liberals viewed war as a ruinous exercise for all participants. This view was based on the immense costs associated with violent conflict, either explicit (depopulation, reduced trade, destruction of capital and infrastructure) or implicit (lost production, lost investment expenditure, lost education expenditure). In addition to their revulsion to war, they opposed the concept of the armed peace, since the consequence of such military expenditures would be increased taxation or debt, either of which would be harmful to national welfare. In order to secure peace, nations should embark on a course of free trade, which in turn, will result in an increase in national wealth, international communication, thus leading to peaceful coexistence of nations guided by the harmony of interests. Freed from the ambitions of the monarch or industry clique expecting gains from conflict, the "invisible hand" of the free market will lead to international peace and prosperity.

2. Nationalism

On the other hand, economic nationalists distinguish between victors and losers in war. War can be profitable to the successful participant since the resulting territorial expansion provides new markets, resources, and commercial supremacy, all of which enhance the nation's industrial production possibilities. Nationalists view the world as being divided into competing national entities. Trade, the key to global harmony of interests in liberal thought, is viewed as a disadvantage to less developed countries. Such countries lack the means to provide for their security and will be dependent on the established defense industries of the more developed nations. If industrialization is the key to national economic welfare, then nations are better served by pursuing a course of protectionism and military power.

3. Socialism

Socialists view war and military buildup as a moral evil resulting from the decay of the capitalist economic and social order. The foundations of this decadent order are private property and the class system. Although the ruling classes may reap benefits from war, the total balance is negative. The burden of the negative balance is passed on to the masses. To secure a lasting peace it is necessary to transform the existing social and economic basis of the existing political system. By eliminating private property and competition, socialist communities will rid themselves of the principal sources of conflict, corruption, and exploitation. By forming a global federation of such communities the causes of war and the idea of war itself will disappear.

B. Five Schools of Economics and Conflict

The pre-World War I era was dominated by the traditional views discussed in the previous section. Additionally, the lower degree of specialization in the social sciences resulted in extensive discussion that transcended the purely economic literature. This results in a classification scheme for the political economy of conflict, war, and peace that can be broadened into five schools of thought, although each of these schools draw extensively from one of the three traditional economic schools of thought.

1. Economic Pacifism

Economic pacifism is based on classical liberal thought and is the purest representation of economic liberalism. Its principal view is that the costs of weapons are too high for militarism to serve as a rational means to national welfare. A militarily victorious nation cannot increase its wealth by territorial expansion or weakening another country's commerce. In the former case, those residing in newly gained territory now apply their trades in competition with the citizens of the occupying nation, as members of a single customs area, taking advantage of country-specific know-how. In the later case, destruction of an opponent's property reduced their ability to produce and consume. Therefore, the victorious nation may well lose an important customer. War reparations, cited as a gain to the victorious, may actually benefit the paying nation. Reparation payments represent a massive inflow of money into the winning nation, resulting in domestic demand increasing at a faster rate than production. This in turn results in upward pressure on the prices of goods in the victorious nation, creating a trade advantage to the paying nation. War can also lead to a lack of monetary discipline as governments, in order to reduce the burdens of taxation or debt, seek to pay for their expenses by creating more money, "monetization" with the same effect on domestic prices. If enough nations embark on such an undisciplined course, a total breakdown of international finance and investment could occur, a problem that would confront all nations, even those that emerge "victorious." A final concern of economic pacifists is the net economic loss resulting from massive casualties on both sides. "Improvements" in military technology lead to the development of weapons that result in the mass slaughters of armed forces. Those mobilized for war are diverted from domestic production for the duration of their service and those who die in war are diverted from domestic production permanently. War is not the only concern for economic pacifists. The burdens of defensive military expenditures are an additional point of focus. Arms buildups result in increased debt and subsequently, higher taxes and interest rates. The net effect of such expenditures is the crowding out of private capital investment and social expenditure that then promote the social conditions that stimulate the rise of socialism and anarchy. Another consideration is that military power does not generate the benefits of economic power. Weapons expenditure generates less benefit to a society than capital expenditure and renders a country to a disadvantage in trade with less taxed nonmilitarized nations. If war and military expenditure are not beneficial to a nation's wealth, what explains their existence? The short-run increase in expenditures is due to special interests that derive benefits from public expenditures on weaponry or the acquisition of new territory. The legitimate function of protecting a citizen's interest overseas is altered to become interventionism and aggression. Over time, however, improved distributional justice and increased democratization will result in an informed electorate countering the influence of the economic special interests. Those concerned with the costs will outnumber those who derive the benefits of war. In time, due to growth and an increased understanding of mutual economic interest, war will cease to serve as a tool of foreign policy.

2. Economic Limitationalists

A second school accepts the view that war is economically irrational. However, this group of thinkers does not accept the optimism of the economic pacifists and their conclusion that the forces of global commerce and growth will eliminate the desire for conflict. Instead, this group believes that diplomacy is needed to negotiate a freeze on weapons procurement, followed by a gradual reduction of arms levels. The goal is threefold: decrease the probability of war, protect nations from the bankruptcy associated with military expenditures, and initiate limitations to the scope of actual warfare through the implementation of international laws minimizing the involvement of civilians, thus avoiding unnecessary suffering. Additionally, restrictions in weapons technology may be considered if such innovations would clash with the interests of neutral nations. Thus, this group does not believe that ending wars will come about as a result of global economic development. Arms reductions and the humanization of war can only be achieved through arbitration and international law. The key belief of the ecolimitationalists is that a nation arming itself for defensive purposes is actually arming itself for the next war. Additionally, they generally reject the notion that a nation in the presence of persistent innovation can ever be "prepared" militarily. Military obsolescence reenforces the armament procurement cycle.

3. Economic Deterrence

While the first two schools draw a logical link between war and arms accumulation, a third school of thought sees them as separate and distinct. While accepting the view that the costs of actual war are unbearable, thus rendering war economically irrational, this school advocated increased levels of weapons procurement. The reason for their position was to heighten the economic folly of war by increasing the expected cost of military conflict. In their view the best guarantee for peace is the preparation for war with all means available, preferably with weapons that could totally destroy an adversary. Ideally, military superiority should lie with those nations that are less likely to be aggressive. A second reason for this school's preference for weapons accumulation is the improvement in commercial security it affords. Although this school accepted the nationalist view on the importance of naval superiority for protecting the flow of commerce between nations, they further argue that military power might be viewed as a form of insurance for national independence, thus securing a degree of credit worthiness and serving as an incentive for foreign investment. In this manner, weapons are indirectly productive. Additionally, military budgets are viewed as instruments for combating economic slumps due to underconsumption. The consequences of the business cycle can be softened by an appropriate manipulation to the public budget. Such manipulations can be implemented by varying the rate of arms accumulation in response to changes in the state of private demand.

4. Economic Chauvinists

While the first three schools argue over how to avoid war, the fourth changes direction by not only advocating the preparation of war but supporting the notion that warfare itself is beneficial. As an essential element of the dynamics of civilization, war is a necessary condition to combat decadence and moral decline, reflecting the cyclical rise and fall of nations. War is viewed as a positive economic activity despite the losses of life and capital, higher taxes, and debt. Economic chauvinists argue that war will lead to higher overall consumption since a soldier's needs exceed equivalent civilian consumption in peacetime. War enables a nation to mobilize idle workers, thus reducing unemployment. Additionally, casualties will lead to higher per-capita wealth provided the loss of life exceeds the degree of capital

destruction. As such, social welfare will be improved, which in turn enhances domestic tranquility. By achieving victory in war, a nation expands its territory and takes over the overseas trade of the enemy. A nation's self-sufficiency in the provision of raw materials is improved, enhancing its prospects for the next war. By expropriating the enemy's land, additional labor for the industrial sector can be developed and internal good production is increased. Finally, territorial expansion enhances the strategic location of troops for future ventures. In essence, war is the central engine of economic development. The massive demand for goods to provide for military forces is a stimulus to technological advances, which in turn filter down to the level of civilian production. War promotes the spirit of competition and initiative, two prerequisites for a modern capitalist economy. Thus, despite the short-run destruction that occurs, war promotes the economic growth of a victorious nation.

5. Economic Fatalism

Although this last group was critical of arms buildups and opposed war as ethically wrong and economically irrational, they viewed war as an inevitable result of a world system based on capitalism. Imperialist expansion is a necessary step in societal development. Once the expansion of colonial powers has reached the limits of physical boundaries, this drive to expand will result in an all-out conflict of capitalist powers. Military expansion is a consequence of financial interests. A rising accumulation of capital due to insufficient demand by the impoverished masses at home generates a need to invest abroad. As a hedge against risk, investors urge governments to expand their legal authority over relevant territories. Given that a broader population, due to colonization, will generate more tax revenue for the central government, the military venture is essentially paid for. Public sentiment in favor of the action is generated by the press, raising public concerns over foreign enemies, which gives a degree of legitimacy to the imperialism. In short, war is a natural process of economic development. The growing need for infrastructure due to the division of labor and grants places countries in conflict over limited resources. The ultimate result of global economic competition is military conflict.

IV. RELATION TO NONECONOMIC THEORIES

If we view political economy as economics with a mixture of normative valuation and external influences from outside disciplines, we should not be surprised to observe some striking similarities between some of the economic theories of war and various noneconomic theories. Those noneconomic explanations for conflict can be divided into two principal groups: those that use innate biological or psychological traits to explain aggressive behavior and those that focus on the role of social and political institutions. Generally, these two broad "schools" include both optimistic and pessimistic views on the nature of aggression and conflict, as do the various economic theories.

A. Innate Behavior Theories

1. Ethological Theory

Ethologists study animal behavior in an attempt to explain human behavior. They believe that the study of animal conflict may lead to a better understanding of human warfare. For example, some similarities exist between the behavior of monkeys and apes in captivity and small children. Aggressive behavior, leading to conflict and violence, results from several innate drives: rivalry for possession, intrusion by an outsider, and interference with activity. The major conflict situations among animals involve the control of territory. Two subjects of general interest to ethologists are the effects of overcrowding and behavior regarding territory. Although studies on overcrowding are far from complete, preliminary findings indicate that normal behavior patterns break down in such situations and aggressive behavior becomes a prominent display. Additionally, animal behavior is often characterized by a strong display of territorial imperative. The analogies between animal and human behavior are severely questioned by many social researchers. Attempts to draw parallels between animal and human behavior must be checked by actual studies of human behavior. Given that human behavior is not fixed to the extent animal behavior is, the ethological approach represents little more than an interesting set of hypotheses that have little support in terms of empirical foundation. The notion that humans have an innate tendency toward aggression and conflict, while it might explain the motives behind economic chauvinism and its views on territorial expansion, is at best tenuous. A central problem in drawing such an analogy is the confusion between animal territory and nation-states. Although animals have a subjective notion about the limits of their territory, such boundaries are unknown to other members of the species. Intrusions are often by accident and result in an expression of signals to warn the intruder rather than physical conflict. This hardly conforms to the human experience of deliberate

invasions met with violent defense tactics. Although animals exhibit a tendency to defend territory, evidence is lacking to show an innate desire to invade.

2. Psychological Theory

Rather than innate biological impulses, proponents of psychological theory suggest that the major cause of conflict is the psychological nature of humans. Modern researchers utilizing the psychological approach emphasize the importance of emotional maladjustment or complexes. Additionally, generally accepted stereotypes add to the individual's distrust and tendency toward aggressive behavior. At the level of the nation-state, the stereotypes may be projected to the people residing in another country or their leaders. Although some psychologists argue that the tendency toward aggression is innate, others focus their attention on the role of public opinion in influencing an individual's attitudes, hence their aggressive behavior on others.

B. Institutional Influence Theories

Although psychological theories of conflict appear to contain much that is valid, they are insufficient explanations because humans behave differently in different settings. Therefore, many researchers have focused on the role of institutions and organizations. In the case of war, the emphasis includes the international order within which various states operate. The institutional approach to conflict and war has received contributions from each of the social sciences aside from economics, many of which parallel one of the economic theories previously discussed.

1. Political Thought

A multitude of theories exist that attribute conflict and war to the nature of the political structure, the state. These theories fall into two broad categories that may be loosely labeled liberal or socialist.

a. Liberal Approach

As stated earlier in the article, classical liberals of the 18th and 19th centuries formulated a political philosophy based on three elements: individuals, society, and the state. The latter is viewed as an outgrowth of the interaction between the two former elements. Classical liberals assume that society is self-resulting and that the socioeconomic system is capable of running smoothly with minimal interference from the state. Their main concerns, therefore, were decentralization and freedom from governmental control. They acknowledged the necessity of maintaining a defense but held that the natural harmony of interest among states would minimize the incidence of war, just as the natural harmony of interests among members of a society would work to minimize domestic forms of conflict. In the international setting, economic cooperation would result from free trade and the international division of labor. Commerce would become the rational substitute for war. However, classical liberals had to explain why wars did, in fact, occur and they offered a variety of explanations. A primary point of emphasis was the influence of autocratic governments, which were presumed to wage war despite the intentions of their citizens. Thus, a major tenet of classical liberal political philosophy was that war could be eliminated by introducing universal suffrage, allowing people to vote out of office any belligerently inclined individual. The focus on minimal government in domestic affairs led to a belief that peaceful coexistence among nations could be achieved with a minimum of international organization. The use of force would be limited to repelling aggression, those tendencies being minimized by public opinion and democratically elected governments, and an appeal to rational conflict resolutions. After World War I, however, classical liberals began to accept the conclusion that an unregulated international structure did not automatically tend toward peace and advocated international organization as a corrective element.

b. Socialist Approach

The socialist approach, with its roots in the works of Karl Marx, views the state as a tool of the ruling capitalist class. The state engages in war because the ruling class is driven by the growing needs of a capitalist economic system: raw materials, markets, and a source of cheap labor. Therefore, they disagree with the classical liberals on the importance of suffrage as the source of war's elimination. As long as the capitalists control the state, the tendencies for aggression will continue. The only solution to war, and conflict in general, is to abolish the class system by replacing capitalism with socialism. With the demise of the class structure will come the decline of the state, since the sole purpose of the state is to support the ruling class of capitalists. In the absence of states, the world order will be marked by an international solidarity of the proletariat. However, just as it disproved the liberal theory of unregulated international harmony, World War I showed the notion of international worker solidarity to be nothing more than a myth. Although working-class parties originally pressured their respective governments to avoid war, once the conflict erupted each party sided with its government and participated in the war effort, claiming

that its government was merely fighting a defensive war. After the war, socialists in the West turned to revisionist interpretations of Marxism and began to focus on internal socioeconomic reforms within the constitutional process. In the Soviet Union, the socialist theory of war underwent refinement and modification as Soviet theoreticians responded to changing circumstances. New socialist theory identified three types of war: intracapitalist, capitalist-socialist, and colonial liberation. Intracapitalist wars are supposed to result from capitalist competition and imperialist rivalries. This, in essence, is the original socialist theory that relates to the theory of economic fatalism. However, Soviet theoreticians added a twist by arguing that such wars were desirable since they served to weaken capitalist states. Capitalist-socialist wars are the ultimate expression of the class struggle. The existence of thriving socialist states threatened the ruling class of capitalist nations since they serve as models to the oppressed in other nations. Aside from their growing economic needs, capitalist states will seek to wage war against socialist societies for no other reason than to destroy their influence. The third kind of war also involves capitalist states, since it is their chains that the subjugated peoples of the colony seek to break. In essence, this kind of war is a response to oppression of colonial masters who exploit the people and their resources for the benefit of the ruling class in the home country. The weakness of Soviet socialist theory is twofold. First, two types of war, the intracapitalist and the capitalist-socialist, do not occur as often as theoreticians predict. Second, the theory ignores two alternative war types, neither of which is motivated by a capitalist ruling class.

One possibility is the intrasocialist conflict. While Soviet theoreticians could not conceive of two socialist states going to war, tensions have existed between various socialist nations. Only a preponderance of Soviet troops prevented full-scale war from erupting in Hungary in 1956 and Czechoslovakia in 1968. The other ignored source of conflict and war is the fight for liberation from socialist oppressors, such as Afghanistan in 1979. In short, the socialist view that war is the product of governments who only serve the interests of the capitalist ruling class is generally unfounded.

2. Historical Theory

Many theorists argue that wars result from the allegiance of men to nations and from an intimate connection between nations and states. Whereas state refers to a political entity, nation has a much broader meaning, generally referring to ethnic or cultural similarities among people. As historians note, the ideal of the nation-state, a political unit containing all members of a particular cultural or ethnic group and excluding all others, is never fully achieved. In no historical case does one find all members of a particular group gathered within the border of a single state. Conversely, most states include national minorities. This historical pattern of failing to match nations and states is a constant source of conflict. Examples would be the policies of assimilation conducted by Eastern European states during the interwar period as well as Nazi Germany's conquest of German-populated Austria and Sudetenland. Sometimes conflicts emerge as national minorities seek to establish independence and self-determination, such as the attempt to carve the state of Biafra out of Nigeria and the separation of Bangladesh from Pakistan. More recent examples of how conflict arises from a mismatch of nation and state are Eriteria in Ethiopia and the Bosnian conflict involving Muslims, Serbs, and Croats. While historians are correct to point out the numerous conflicts and wars resulting from nonconformity between nation and state, this explanation cannot serve as a general theory of conflict and war since far more wars do not involve the struggle for national self-determination.

3. Sociological Theory

Many of the theories discussed so far have regarded the state as an undifferentiated whole. The sociological approach focuses on the roles played within the state by various special interest groups. These theories make a distinction between the general population and those groups that have influence over the government. The general assumption is that those in the former group are for the most part peaceful and highly preoccupied with their daily lives. Since some governments are more prone to engage in war, researchers are curious as to which kinds of special interest groups place the greatest pressure on the government to engage in conflict. The most obvious special interest group is the military. In peacetime, the military establishment is less important, which results in a reduction of resources. Military service during peacetime does not convey the same image to voters, so those seeking subsequent political power find no advantage to their military career. However, war not only allows the military to obtain more resources but serves to satisfy status-seeking and may help to serve future political aspirations. Critics of this view point out that military leaders are more aware of the potential dangers to its members and the state. Although they desire to maintain a high state of military preparedness, the military establishment may be more cautious than civilian leaders when it comes to armed

conflict. However, a commonly held view is that high levels of military preparedness are viewed by neighboring states as quasi-aggressive and may lead to increased tension, and may ultimately lead to an armed conflict. Aside from the military, those groups who stand to profit from war may also exert influence on the government. This view is shared by both the socialists and the liberals, each stressing the importance of curbing the influence of a country's military-industrial complex. A classic example of this view would be the Spanish-American War, where support for Cuban rebels against Spain was fostered by an American media on behalf of those with threatened business ventures in Cuba. On the other hand, some contemporary theorists question the degree to which industrialists can influence democratic governments. Although they may lobby on behalf of armament levels with some degree of success, it is another matter to assume that they can influence the actual decision to engage in some form of armed conflict. A final group that may exert undo influence on a government is the scientific community. Although this group is heterogeneous in specialization, if they are involved in defense work they share the military's interest in the level of resources devoted to weapons development. Although military applications helped the pace of research in the arms of nuclear power and space exploration, war does not enhance the status of scientists. Additionally, military researchers often seek peaceful applications for their research, albeit with limited success. On the whole, while scientists do depend on military contracts for much of their research, they do not have a vested interest in war itself. In fact, many scientists are concerned with the mass destruction associated with their discoveries and participate in international peace movements.

4. Anthropological Theory

The increased importance of multinational enterprises (MNE) in the global flow of goods and capital might cause one to believe that economic pacifism is finally coming into play. However, the diminished role of the state as a central economic entity is not resulting in a single economically integrated world as some might believe. Although institutional development beyond the nation-state has occurred in the form of organizations like the International Securities Markets Association, World Trade Organization, and the Bank of International Settlements, other tendencies tend to subdivide the world at a greater scale than the nation-state. According to anthropologist Samuel Huntington, the new global divisiveness is neither ideological nor economic. Instead, the world order will be replaced by groups of nations divided along cultural lines. In the future, global politics will be dominated by a class of civilizations. A civilization is the broadest cultural grouping of a people based on the common objective element of language, history, religion, customs, and institutions. While there are cultural differences between southern and northern Italy, or Italy and Germany, they both relate to the common heritage of Western civilization. The future of conflict and violence at the global level will be shaped by the interactions of eight major civilizations: Western, Confucian, Japanese, Islamic, Hindu, Slavic, Latin American, and African. The most important conflicts will occur a long cultural fault line separating these civilizations such as the conflicts in the Balkans and the Caucasus. The fault lines between civilizations will replace the political and ideological boundaries of the past as the flash points for conflicts and violence. These conflicts will occur at two levels. Microlevel conflicts will occur between adjacent groups for control of territory as in the case of Bosnia. Macrolevel conflicts will involve struggles for the control of international organizations and the promotion of particular cultural values. Most conflicts will occur between the West and the remaining civilizations, driven, primarily, by a response to the diffusion of Western values. This rejection of Western values, with its return-to-your-roots emphasis is referred to as the Kin-Country Syndrome. One consequence of this syndrome is the breakdown of economic globalization into economic regionalism. The European community is based on the shared foundations of European culture and Western Christianity . The connection of Confucian civilization facilitates the expanding economic relations between Taiwan, Singapore, and Chinese communities in other Asian countries. It is also evident in the formation of the Economic Cooperation Organization, which is an association of 10 non-Arab Muslim countries. Economic pacifism, with its origins in classical liberal philosophy, stresses the role of harmony of interests in the eventual elimination of conflict between individuals and nations. The new anthropological view argues that civilizational differences interfere with the process resulting in economic regionalism that accepts the concept of common interests within a civilizational region, but serves as a source of conflict between civilizational groups.

V. POLITICAL ECONOMY AND OTHER FORMS OF VIOLENCE

Aside from war, which could include rebellions and insurrections, violence is more prevalent in the form of violent crimes such as assaults and murder. As with war, alternative forms of violence have been a topic of interest across numerous disciplines and a contemporary social view often represents an interweaving of ideas from different social disciplines. If we view war in a narrow sense as a conflict between two states, then rebellion and insurrection appear to be different forms of violence. The economic rationale of rebellion against external rulers or an overthrow of a domestic government are clearly related to one or more of the economic theories of war.

A. Rebellion

One source of conflict, often addressed by socialists, is the exploitation of colonies for the benefit of capitalists in the home country. The social and political institutions in the colony are not for the benefit of the indigenous population but for their exploiters. Resentment over the injustices perpetuated by the capitalist foreigners builds over time until the people erupt in a violent backlash in an attempt to regain control over their destiny. Often the reaction to the economic injustice is shrouded by a call to national unity and identity that overwhelms the demands for economic justice. Africa was beset by numerous confrontations between the indigenous peoples and their colonial exploiters from the United Kingdom, France, and Belgium. Two of the more noted uprisings in Africa were the Zulu uprising and the Mau Mau rebellion. One should also consider the various rebellions of Latin America. Ironically, it may not be the indigenous population that generates the rebellion. On occasion the colonist population begins to resent the external rule of their home country, especially after the passing of a generation or two when few of the colonist population feel any strong ties to the home country. They tend to see the colony as their home country and resent the degree to which the fruit of their labor goes to serve their foreign rulers. The most obvious example in this case is the United States. In this case, the indigenous population may fight on behalf of the foreign ruler, who at least acknowledges their status as an outsider. Thus, Native American nations fought on behalf of England, believing that uncontrolled colonists would prove to be a greater threat with less regard to the inherent rights of the native population. The only shortcoming of the socialist view is their belief that colonial exploitation and the resulting rebellion is the privy of capitalism. External economic exploitation will create an atmosphere of resentment and mistrust regardless of the prevailing economic system. Hungary in 1956 and Czechoslovakia in 1968 are examples of rebellion against the external rule of the Soviet Union, as was the uprising in Afghanistan in 1979.

B. Insurrection

Bleak economic conditions, especially at the hands of an authoritarian ruler, can result in a violent overthrow of the government. However, the economic forces creating the foundation for violent insurrections goes beyond the economic conditions at the time of revolt. Postcolonialism often results in the creation of states that have little relation to the concept of nation. Consider the colonial participation of Africa resulting from a conflict between the economic interests of various European nations. Often these colonies were drawn up with no regard to the traditional boundaries between tribes. Postcolonial independence results in states with conflicting ethnic groups, each struggling for a share of power that often translates into economic welfare. This represents a smaller scale of the civilizational fault lines discussed by anthropologists. Contemporary insurrections in the Third World could easily be characterized as continuations of the colonial rebellion process. Inhabitants of a region controlled by a colonial power react against the system that rewards the foreign ruler but neglects the local population. The struggle is for political and economic justice.

C. Intranational Conflict

Independence, however, finds a state with conflicting ethnic groups and undeveloped political and economic systems. The state or nation is often defined in terms of the dominant ethnic or religious group. Rewards remain few and accrue to those who now hold the political power. Resources that could be used to improve general economic conditions are often allocated to sustaining the political power of the ruling party. When fighting breaks out, the infrastructure development that did occur is often destroyed, as in Sudan's 10-year civil war, which destroyed most of the country's schools and hospitals. This increases the internal economic stress and contributes to further political instability. Although ethnic tensions resulting in violent reaction by the state have occurred throughout modern times, there is an increased level of such outbreaks in the era of the new world order. The lack of legitimate input into the political process often creates a desire for a local autonomy by the minority. Such expressions represent a threat to the national interests and are responded to with the use of force. The failed attempt at

creating a separate state of Biafra in the late 1960s was crushed by the ruling forces in Nigeria. The past 15 years have been marked by such outbreaks in Bosnia, Rwanda, Afghanistan, Sri Lanka, India, and the Sudan. The political institutions comprising the state are controlled by the dominant group who, in turn, define the nation and state as one. Members of ethnic or religious minorities are "outsiders" who provide service to the national welfare but are not afforded access to the political process. Both autonomy and shared power represent threats to the interests of the state and are treated in the same manner as threats from foreign nations.

D. Crime

The most common form of violence confronting people in politically stable nations is crime. Assault and murder take us beyond the realm of macroviolence to the more individualistic microviolence. The economic theory of crime is itself related to the several social theories that attempt to explain violent acts between two individuals.

1. Social Theories of Violent Crime

The four major social theories of violent crime have as their root cause the frustration over economic inequality. Often wedded to the socialist view that capitalism brutalizes the poor and demoralizes them in their struggle to succeed, these theories tend to focus on violence as an action of the poor. One theory, however, attempts to explain why those who are not in financial or economic distress nevertheless engage in violent behavior.

a. Strain Theory

Strain theory starts with the proposition that people are inherently good and ambitious. Some, however, are confronted with inequality of opportunity resulting in economic deprivation. The deprivation and the ensuing inability to care for one's family results in frustration, which then leads an individual to respond violently to any further confrontations.

b. Anomic Theory

Similar to strain theory, anomic theory differs in that frustration arises, not from an inability to meet basic needs but a culturally imposed sense of success. In this case the view of economic deprivation is relative. An individual may be able to feed and clothe his or her family but the level of existence is viewed as inferior. Lacking legitimate opportunities to pursue a higher level of material success consistent with societal standards, the individual develops patterns of resentment and aggression similar to those in the strain theory.

c. Social Reaction Theory

Unlike strain theory and anomic theory, social reaction theory does not view violent crime as a reaction against poverty or material deprivation. Rather, it is a reaction toward society's views and treatment of the poor. Society marginalizes the poor, often viewing them with contempt. They are thought of as lazy and dishonest, and are subjected to outlandish treatment by the criminal justice system. They are the victims of unjust searches and investigations, which creates a strong sense of mistrust in the poor community. Resentment toward the political injustice eventually erupts when an individual is yet again confronted by "outsiders" who represents the system that continually frustrates the member of the poor community.

d. Control Theory

While the first three theories seek to explain violence as it exists in economically deprived communities, control theory seeks to explain violence by those who are economically well-off. The control argument is that economic success and affluence develops a low sense of attachment to others in the community. With wealth comes power and a desire to exercise more power. This drive for power becomes an obsession that eventually pushes some over the limit as they seek to exert their power over individuals in areas outside the home or workplace. Violent acts against others is little more than an exercise in power, which serves as a luxury good for the economically well-off.

2. Rational Choice Theory: The Economic View

While economists recognize the social influences that come into play, they are quick to point out that most poor do not commit crimes in general, much less violent crimes. Additionally, low-income neighborhoods in small towns have, as a rule, much lower crime rates than urban neighborhoods with equally low incomes. As is generally the case in economics, crime, even violent crime, is viewed from a cost-benefit perspective. Individuals are assumed to be economically rational so that an action is undertaken when the benefit exceeds the cost. While the costs of committing a crime are often viewed in terms of time, costs to get to and from the location of the activity, or the costs associated with getting caught, costs can also include lack of standing within the family or community. Where family and community structures are weak, there are fewer moral barriers to engaging in criminal activity including vio-

lent behavior. Where violent behavior is viewed as a source of pride, community response switches from being a cost to being a benefit. The utility derived from enhanced social standing raises the likelihood that the benefit of a violent action outweighs the cost. The individual has a rational incentive to prey on others.

VI. CONCLUSION: THE POLITICAL ECONOMY OF NONVIOLENCE

The reasons for violent behavior, be it war or crime, are numerous. Unfortunately, economists have done little in the way of developing theories of nonviolence. Although there is a substantial body of literature concerning conflict resolution, the models generally deal with nonviolent forms of conflict, such as price bargaining or contract negotiation. The only economic theory that could be viewed as a theory of nonviolence is economic pacifism. When people find it mutually beneficial to coexist in a nonviolent manner, they will. However, control theory would argue that individuals who derive satisfaction from exerting power over others will do so if the satisfaction from the display of power is greater than the benefit of peaceful coexistence. If individuals and nations are not motivated by a natural harmony of interest, the general solution would be to structure an institutional framework that would generate incentives for abstaining from violent behavior. In pure economic terms this would imply either reducing the benefits or increasing the costs of violent behavior. This approach would require case-by-case analysis rather than the development of a general theory of promoting nonviolent behavior. One current example would be violent crime related to the drug industry. Many economists today advocate the legalization of drugs, which would reduce the profit levels of drug suppliers as competition increases. With less profit associated with the industry, and the rights of competitors protected by the legal system, the benefit of violent response is dramatically reduced. Even the simple task of economic stabilization can work to reduce the level of violent crime. Studies in Poland, Wales, and the United Kingdom show a correlation between economic contractions, a slowdown in economic activity associated with higher unemployment and lower job security, and levels of alcohol abuse. A novel twist on the research is that it is more often those that have not yet lost their jobs who exhibit the increased alcohol consumption. There is also evidence to indicate that violent crimes are correlated with alcohol abuse. It is important to note that the argument centers on stress rather than economic deprivation. In this sense the argument differs from standard sociological assertions that economic deprivation is the cause of crime. As people become more fearful of their job situation they seek to relieve the pressure by partaking in a legal, socially accepted drug. This substance, however, lowers inhibitions and impairs judgment, which then causes some to strike out violently when faced with a conflict situation. By stabilizing economic activity, the psychological forces leading one to abuse alcohol will be diminished. The obvious result is that lower levels of alcohol abuse will, in turn, result in a decrease in alcohol-related acts of violence. In short, economists can offer solutions to reduce violence in certain cases, but they do not offer a panacea to eliminate violence. Since so much conflict is due to ideological and cultural differences, the vision set out by economic pacifism becomes clouded. Yet, as many economists see it, the dropping of differences and developing an appreciation for the concept of mutual benefit is the only sure way to a nonviolent world. Unfortunately, there is no clear economic solution to the problems of ideological and cultural hatred.

Also See the Following Articles

AGGRESSION, PSYCHOLOGY OF • ANIMAL BEHAVIOR STUDIES, PRIMATES • ECONOMIC CAUSES OF WAR AND PEACE • ECONOMIC COSTS AND CONSEQUENCES OF WAR • MILITARISM • PEACE AND DEMOCRACY • WORLD WAR I

Bibliography

Anderton, C., & Anderton, R. (1997). The economics of conflict, production and exchange. In J. Brauer & W. Gissy (Eds.), *Economics of conflict and peace*, pp. 54–82. Aldershot, UK: Avebury Press.

Hofstede, G. (1980). *Culture's consequences: International differences in work-related values*, Beverly Hills: Sage Press.

Huntington, S. (1993). The clash of civilizations. *Foreign Affairs, 72*, 22–49.

Jutte, R. (1996). *Poverty and deviance in early modern Europe.* Cambridge UK: Cambridge University Press.

Ohmae, K. (1993). The rise of the region state. *Foreign Affairs, 72*, 78–88.

Porter, M. (1990). *The comparative advantage of nations.* New York: Freedom Press.

Rotte, R. (1997). Economics and peace theory on the eve of World War I. In J. Brauer & W. Gissy (Eds.). *Economics of conflict and peace.* pp. 7–30. Aldershot, UK: Avery Press.

Schelling, T. (1960). *The strategy of conflict.* Cambridge: Harvard University Press.

Schelling, T., & Halperin, M. (1961). *Strategy of arms control,* New York: 20th Century Fund.

Short, J. (1980). *An investigation of the relationship between crime and the business cycle.* New York: Arno Press.

Sumner, W. G. (1911). War. In A. Galloway (Ed.), *The collected essays of William Graham Sumner,* pp. 136–173. New Haven: Yale University Press.

Tinbergen, J. (1991). *World Security and equity.* Brookfield: Gower.

Tinbergen, J., & Fischer, D. (1987). *Warfare and welfare: Integrating security policy into socioeconomic policy,* Brighton: Wheatsheaf.

Political Systems and Conflict Management

Ralph M. Goldman

Center for Party Development San Francisco State University

GLOSSARY

Black Box In systems theory, a device, for example, a thermostat, that an operator cannot open, but whose inputs he or she is able to control in order to produce desired outputs.

Conflict A social interaction between two or more parties in which the actions are intense, adversarial, and likely to produce an organizational or institutional disequilibrium for an unspecified period of time.

Conflict Process A sequence of conflict cycles that produces socialization, formalization, or investiture outcomes that further the structural development of an institution.

Critical Transition A historical period when transactions between the leaders of certain institutions elevate political parties to a degree of influence that makes parties the institutional alternative to warfare.

Formalization A conflict process outcome that modifies the set of task expectations that comprise a particular organizational or institutional position or office.

Institutional Integration A sequence of events whereby two or more actors form a new actor.

Institutionalized Trust Those repeated mutually profitable currency exchanges that promote attitudes of trust between transactors.

Investiture A conflict process outcome that modifies the circumstances endowing particular persons with incumbency; in particular, organizational or institutional positions.

Political Currencies Categories of those empirically observable objects, actions, or conditions, for example, incumbencies in offices, shares of decision-making, and material commodities, valued by a set of transacting persons and capable of being exchanged between them.

Socialization A conflict process outcome that modifies the characteristic role behavior of a person within an organizational or institutional context.

Systems Theory A mode of analysis that examines the dynamic relationship between a whole and its parts and seeks to discover how a system's inputs produce desired outputs.

Trust An anticipatory attitude in which the expectation is that one person's probable behavior will have favorable consequences for another person.

POLITICAL SYSTEMS, when viewed as black boxes, handle conflict inputs in ways that produce outputs that affect attitudes of trust as well as the structural aspects of institutions. The black box itself acts as a marketplace for transactions in political currencies. There is historical evidence that certain patterns of transaction promote transitions from warfare to less-violent institutional arrangements, particularly by strengthening competitive political party systems. The system's transactions may also, through structural changes, advance institutional integration by socializing members, formalizing offices, or modifying circumstances of incumbency.

I. ORIGINS OF CONCEPTS OF POLITICAL CONFLICT

Human conflict has been perceived as *systematic* by those men of thought and science for at least 2500 years. The Iranian philosopher/poet Zarathustra (600–583 B.C.) described conflict as a continuous struggle between the "powers of Light" and the "powers of Darkness" around and within each human individual. Violence was seen as a consequence of conflict, as evidenced by the prehistoric skulls found in Chinese soil, shattered by special artifacts.

Greek poets and political thinkers were among the first to be concerned with the institutional consequences of conflicts. Plato viewed war as an inevitable expression of politics, seeking to define a place for certain of its principal actors—the guardians—and a *system* for controlling them. Aristotle condoned war as a means to the end of imposing governmental institutions upon men. Machiavelli, writing in an age of disintegrating empires, emergent nations, and seasonal warfare, reasserted the Aristotelian view that war was one of the Prince's means for preserving his sovereign powers. Hobbes believed that struggle was universal, driving men, out of necessity, into compacts with monarchs as a means for preventing violence and maintaining order among themselves; these compacts remained valid only so long as the monarchs fulfilled their responsibility for keeping the peace. Karl Marx, adapting Hegel's dialectical system, interpreted human history as a "class struggle" whose "final" outcome would be communism. By the 19th century, liberal laissez-faire economists, following the theory of Adam Smith, held economic competition—believed to be a distinctive, nonviolent kind of conflict—to be the most desirable method for achieving peace as well as the greatest prosperity for the greatest number.

Among the first to offer an explicit and comprehensive theory of conflict was the sociologist Georg Simmel, who argued that conflict is best studied as a form of intense social interaction producing socialization and civilization. Social conflict, he declared, is a process in which accumulated social tensions are liquidated and through which, as a consequence, new and more complex forms of social organization are established. Simmel saw conflict as *a systematic process that had institutional consequences.*

Conflict as the central concern of *political* systems was probably given its most succinct and influential formulation by E. E. Schattschneider in his 1957 presidential address to the American Political Science Association.

If politics is the management of conflict, it is necessary first to get rid of some simplistic concepts of conflict. Political conflict is not primarily or usually a matter of head-on collisions or tests of strength, for a good reason: intelligent people prefer to avoid tests of strength, about matters more serious than sports, unless they are sure to win.

Nor is political conflict like an inter-collegiate debate in which the opponents agree in advance on the definition of the issues. The definition of alternatives is the supreme instrument of power; the antagonists can rarely agree on what the issues are because power is involved in the definition. He who determines what politics is about runs the country because the definition of the alternatives is the choice of conflicts, and the choice of conflicts allocates power.

… The grand strategy of politics deals with public policy concerning conflict. This is the policy of policies, the sovereign policy—what to do about conflict.

Views such as this place conflict within the framework of human institutions and self-government, that is, within a framework of implicit cooperation. In behavioral theory, the organizational and institutional consequences of the relationship between conflict and cooperation, while often inadequately delineated, are widely recognized. In general, behavioral research on systems and conflicts has gained its greatest contemporary prominence in the United States and Europe where wars have been endemic, particularly during the 20th century. The connections among conflict, cooperation, and institutional development paved the way for systems theory.

II. A DEFINITION OF CONFLICT

Contemporary approaches to the study of conflict were greatly facilitated by an early literature survey conducted by Mack and Snyder, a sociologist and a political scientist, respectively. While their survey may be biased in the direction of confrontation, it nonetheless provided a summary of previous literature and became the basis for the approach of most political scientists.

A. The Mack–Snyder Propositional Inventory

Some fifty propositions were drawn as a sample from a much larger inventory of propositions. Mack and Snyder concluded that the distinctions between conflict and nonconflict were fuzzy at best and, at worst, not made at all. Without attempting a formal definition of conflict, the two behavioral scientists did derive from the theoretical literature a set of properties and empirical conditions for characterizing conflict phenomena and situations.

First, social conflict requires at least *two analytically distinct entities* or units, such as persons, groups, or organizations. Conflict implies a minimal degree of visibility, contact, and interaction (not necessarily face-to-face) between the two or more parties. Since at least two persons are also needed to enter a cooperative relationship, it is often difficult to discern whether the individuals or entities are engaged in a conflict or a cooperative relationship.

Second, according to Mack and Snyder, conflict arises from at least two kinds of scarcity: *position scarcity* and *resources scarcity*. Position scarcity is a condition that results from the fact that an object cannot occupy two places at the same time, serve two different functions simultaneously, or perform two or more roles simultaneously. Resource scarcity is a condition in which the supply of desired objects is limited so that parties cannot have all they are demanding.

A third feature of conflict behavior is the parties' *presumed intent to destroy, injure, thwart, or otherwise diminish each other*. In this characterization, a conflict relationship is conceived as one in which the parties can gain, relatively, only at each other's expense—a kind of zero-sum game. It is this aspect that often leads to violence. At other times it leads to heightened social tension.

Fourth, conflict requires *interaction among the parties* during which actions and counteractions are mutually opposed. Conflict does not exist without action. The action must presumably embody the pursuit of mutu-

ally exclusive or incompatible goals or values. However, as indicated above, it is sometimes difficult to know when and to what degree particular actions are "opposed," that is, in conflict.

Fifth, conflict relationships involve attempts to influence behavior in certain directions. These attempts are aimed at *acquiring or exercising power*, that is, control over decisions regarding the disposition of scarce positions and resources. Since power is used reciprocally between or among parties, the conflict process will reflect power strains during which opposed actions are directed toward changing or preserving existing power relations.

Sixth, conflict relations are a fundamental *action process* going on through time and having important dynamic and developmental consequences. Conflict processes represent temporary tendencies toward disjunction (disequilibrium, in the idiom of systems theory) in the interaction flow between parties. Conflict relations do not necessarily represent a breakdown in the cooperative or regulated conduct of the parties, but rather a shift in their governing norms and expectations. In other words, conflict may proceed within the framework of a cooperative relationship. Alternatively, conflict may become violent.

In sum, a conflict situation, as generally perceived among political scientists and illustrated by their applications of game theory, is a social relationship between two or more parties in which at least one of the parties perceives the other as an adversary engaging in behaviors designed to destroy, injure, thwart, or gain scarce resources at the expense of the perceiver. Yet, others see conflict behaviors as involving some degree of cooperation and may often be so subtle or indirect that even the target party may not know he has a disagreement or a fight on his hands. It may not take two parties to start a fight, but it necessarily takes at least two to sustain it.

B. Contemporary Approaches to Conflict and Violence

The Schattschneider analysis and the Mack–Snyder propositional inventory were followed by a substantial output of political and sociological research dealing with conflict in its many manifestations and, with the exception of studies of international conflicts, taking on a western-oriented body of data and illustration. By the 1970s and later, several books and compendiums of articles summarized the new approaches, theories, and empirical findings. Very few hinted at the relevance of systems theory. Most focused on the incidence, components, and correlates of conflict and violence. Political scientists were particularly interested in applying a special form of conflict theory—the theory of games of strategy—to the analysis of international politics and defense policy.

An early impulse was to explore the feasibility of quantitative research techniques. For example, taking advantage of the work of Taylor and Hudson in gathering comparative data for 108 countries, Douglas Hibbs, assuming confrontation and violence, sought to operationalize variables, create indexes, and factor analyze conflict phenomena. Six event variables were operationally defined: riots, armed attacks, political strikes, assassinations, deaths from political violence, and antigovernment demonstrations. Linear relationships among the variables were sought by factor analysis. A Collective Protest index was derived from associations among riots, antigovernment demonstrations, and political strikes. An Internal War index was based upon relationships among deaths from political violence, armed attacks, and assassinations. Each index was correlated with rates of population and economic growth.

Hibb's data demonstrated that violence tended to occur in nations with the highest rates of population growth and relatively low rates of economic development. Similar associations were examined for ethnic and linguistic differences, degrees of oppression by governing elites, democratic versus totalitarian regimes, and types of related institutions. Although discovering indexes and correlations made important contributions to the description of conflict relationships, they did not describe systematic processes nor predict ways of achieving nonviolent outcomes.

In 1980, the state of the field was surveyed by contributors to a volume edited by Ted Robert Gurr. Gurr's *Handbook* focused upon four general themes: individual participation in conflict, conflict within nations, international conflict, and the practical implications of conflict research. Building on the Mack–Snyder inventory, the authors reported investigations of political riots, insurrections, revolutions, and wars among nations. Reliance on quantification continued as raw data were developed and often applied to models by such pioneers as Louis F. Richardson, Pitrim Sorokin, Quincy Wright, Jessie Bernard, Lewis A. Coser, Ralf Dahrendorf, Johan Galtung, Kurt Lewin, Kenneth Boulding, and Anatol Rapoport.

Another source on the state of the field was Ekkart Zimmermann's review of the relevant literature, published in English in 1983. Zimmermann examined about 2400 items, most published since 1960. He found that the primary objective of most of the research at this time was understanding the causes of conflict and political violence. There was a proliferation of causal models and classifications of conflicts.

In his evaluation of the body of research on political conflict and violence, Sheldon Levy repeats the observation that many contemporary studies employ quantifiable data and methods. Among the prevalent types of research he found were: studies of the frequency and intensity of wars, particularly with respect to casualties, alliances, and mediated resolutions; internation events manifesting hostility or friendship; and categories of domestic violence which included riots, demonstrations, boycotts, arrests, governmental action against specific groups, sabotage, martial law, coups d'etat, revolts, guerrilla warfare, assassinations, executions, and civil war. Again, the results were primarily descriptive, although numerous hypotheses were generated.

Overall, the research sought causal variables and their relationship to each other, descriptive categories of political violence, and the resolution of particular violent conflicts. There was still relatively little investigation of *the way conflict is processed by political systems*, particularly in cases where violence gives way to the development of political institutions capable of substituting and sustaining nonviolence.

III. SYSTEMS THEORY AND POLITICAL SYSTEMS

How does a political system deal with political conflict? First, a brief description of systems theory.

A. Systems Theory

In 1948, Norbert Wiener coined the term cybernetics, which he derived from the Greek word *kubernetes*, or "steerman." Cybernetics deals with the systems characteristics that produce the "steering" or control mechanisms for the purpose assigned to them. Cybernetics was readily accepted in the fields of communications engineering and mechanics. By 1950, viewing people and society as systems amendable to cybernetic study, Wiener wrote *The Human Use of Human Beings*.

The analogy between persons and machines began with the fact that every instrument created by scientific instrument makers is in some respect a sense organ constructed to record readings remotely through the medium of some appropriate electrical apparatus. These instruments not only sense incoming information, but also send out messages that act on the external world. The photoelectric automatic door-opener is a familiar example. When a message created by the interruption of a beam of light is sent to the apparatus, the message opens the door, usually so that a person may go through.

On the basis of this applied theory, engineers built large and complex automatic machines. These mechanisms receive an *input*, that is, message data, to which they respond with an *output*, or action upon some element in the outer world. If past data is stored in the machine, at some time to be combined with new incoming data, as in the case of the computer or guided missiles, the mechanism is said to have a *memory*. As the machine performs in response to messages from the environment, the effects of that performance produce further information, that is, *feedback*, from the environment. For example, a thermostat switches on a furnace when its thermometer "reads" the surrounding temperature as falling lower than some preset level. The same thermostat also "reads" as feedback the consequent rise in temperature, enabling it to switch off the furnace at some preset maximum temperature. In this way, the cybernetics engineer is able to control mechanical tendencies toward disequilibrium, guiding the machine's responses back to the desired state, or *equilibrium*. The mechanism is able to counter or reverse the disequilibrium, that is, control the tendencies toward entropy.

Several problems arose with the development of systems theory and cybernetics. How do we make the distinction between a system and its environment? How do we differentiate between closed systems that do not make exchanges with their environments and open systems that do? What is the nature of the interaction between a system and its environment, as in the case of a guided missile that changes the environment by exploding its target and is itself destroyed in the process? How do we describe the conditions of stationary equilibrium wherein components are held constant and dynamic equilibrium wherein there is constant activity and change?

In 1953, David Easton recommended that empirical political scientists begin to use systems analysis, particularly its notion of equilibrium, in their studies. Within a few years, the systems approach, or aspects of it, found their way into a wide range of political writing. Easton's concern with systems theory reflected a revived interest in the relationship of parts to wholes and the integration of parts into wholes. Entire political structures, the dynamic interaction of their parts, and their contributions to the functioning of the system as a whole therefore warranted examination.

A second motivation for behavioral interest in systems theory came from its emphasis upon homeostatic systems and the analysis of informational feedback. The most relevant portrayal of systems theory was that which viewed systems as *convertors* of inputs into outputs. In emphasizing the conversion of inputs into outputs, the system model drew an analogy to the *black box*, a device borrowed directly from electrical engineering.

The operator has before him a black box that cannot be opened. It has various input switches that he may move up or down, terminals to which he may apply potentials, photoelectric cells onto which he may shine lights, and so on. The box also has various output terminals on which a potential may be measured, lights that may flash, pointers that may move over a graduated scale, and so on. The operator is supposed to estimate what the outputs of the black box will be. He does this from his knowledge of how to manipulate the switches and levers controlling the inputs or how the black box will respond on the input side to various feedback information it receives.

B. Political Systems

Easton considered the black box, input–output analytic approach as appropriate to the study of political systems. His argument was as follows:

The study of politics is concerned with understanding how authoritative decisions are made and executed for a society. We can try to understand political life by viewing each of its aspects piecemeal. We can examine the operation of such institutions as political parties, interest groups, government, and voting; we can study the nature and consequences of such political practices as manipulation, propaganda, and violence; we can seek to reveal the structure within which these practices occur. By combining the results we can obtain a rough picture of what happens in any self-contained political unit.

In seeking a model of the political community that would help him discover the sources of political instability and failure, Easton described certain elements of the political system as *political actions*. The boundary of a political system is determined by all those actions more or less directly related to the making of binding decisions for a society. Among the actions are the *inputs* into the political system. Inputs are of two kinds: *demands* and *supports*. A political group in the community will, for example, make a demand for, say, reduced taxes. It may support this demand with lobbying efforts at the legislature and with campaign contributions to friendly candidates for office. The *conversion institutions* (notice that all are decision-making institutions)—legislature, executive, courts, and so on—lie within the black box and process the demands, producing *outputs* in the form of decisions, policies, programs as promulgated in laws, executive orders, decrees, judicial decisions, and so on.

These outputs lead to various consequences for the group making the demand as well as for others. These consequences produce *feedback* (expressions of satisfaction or dissatisfaction, suggestions for change, public demonstrations, etc.) to the input side of the system. The feedback may give rise to new demands (by the original group or others), new demonstrations of political clout, and the next round of inputs into the system. All these activities are presumably intended to move the entire system (read: political community) toward its goals of, say, liberty, equality, justice, and prosperity. All this was represented in a diagrammatic model (Fig. 1).

The internal factors (endogenous variables) in the Easton model are the demand and support inputs, the conversion institutions, and the outputs in the form of decisions and acts. The factors outside the boundary of the political system (exogenous variables) are the goals, the environment, and the feedback.

The model may help answer such questions as: How well does the system perform? Does the system provide outputs that approximate what people demand so that the system remains stable and in fair equilibrium? Can the system receive inputs of conflict and violence and produce outputs that modify the relevant institution and return it to equilibrium?

Political scientists have applied the Easton model in various ways. Democratic systems have been considered to be open systems, whereas totalitarian systems are closed systems. Political scientists have tended to view the geographical boundaries of a particular community as separating the political system from its environment, e.g., a city's boundary is the limit of an urban political system, a nation's boundaries limit that nation's political system.

Feedback has been recognized as significant in maintaining system equilibrium. Feedback consists of those messages from the political environment that become

new inputs entering the system. The new inputs start up a new cycle which further modifies previous outputs. In making public policy, for example, U.S. government economists watch such feedback indicators as Cost-of-Living Index, Gross Domestic Product, unemployment rate, and similar economic information to aid the president and federal agencies in arriving at their spending, interest rate, and related economic decisions. The economic feedback from the American economy further affects inputs in order to maintain a general state of economic and political equilibrium.

However, politics has few precise "desired states" or goals. Political systems cannot remain on course in the same sense as a guided missile. Specificity of political goals or targets is either uncertain or missing. Some political goals may *seem* quite specific, e.g., the maintenance of a 3% rate of growth in Gross Domestic Product or the maintenance of full employment to within three or four percentage points of the total labor force. These, however, have the presumed quantitative precision of such economic units as dollars or employed persons. Most political goals are hardly as specific or quantifiable, e.g., "equal opportunity" or "free speech." Some political systems do nonetheless give the impression of being guided missiles locked in on political targets. Nazi Germany, in its declared thousand-year goal of world domination, certainly had the appearance of a goal-oriented system. On the other hand, open political systems such as the United States or the European Union *seem* at times to be without goals, unguided, and constantly in disequilibrium.

One example of an input–output analysis in political science was the Simulmatics Project employed in the campaign of John F. Kennedy against Richard M. Nixon in 1960. In a predominantly Protestant nation, Kennedy was the second Catholic to be nominated for the presidency by a major party. To obtain the best possible advice regarding campaign issues, particularly the religious one, the Kennedy staff turned to the Simulmatics Corporation for information based upon the latter's model of the U.S. electorate, the first ever such model.

The Simulmatics Project built a computer model of the U.S. electorate from polling data gathered in 66

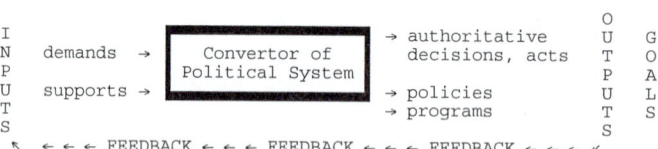

FIGURE 1 Easton's political system model.

nationwide opinion surveys between 1952 and 1960. This represented a total of more than 100,000 interviews with eligible voters in scientifically drawn national samples. The average interview consisted of some 50–60 items. In all, over 6,000,000 pieces of information were consolidated into computer storage. This information included data about past voting behavior, record of turnout at the polls, and attitudes and opinions on as many as 50 issues such as civil rights, the H-bomb, and Catholicism, not to mention various kinds of demographic information about each respondent.

The object was to determine how different voter-types might respond to different intensities of the issues, particularly the possible embitterment of the religious issue. The model was designed to present the issues in changing ways to 480 voter-types found in the 100,000 interviews. Examples of voter-types include: Eastern-rural-affluent-Protestant-male; Midwestern-small-town-poor-Catholic-female; Western-metropolitan-Jewish-male. Between five and eight variables identified each of the 480 groups in the model. The model then proceeded to simulate strong and weak presentations of the issues. These were inputs that could be increased or decreased as the Project sought to identify different levels of output.

The outputs of the Simulmatics computer simulation were stated as the probable Kennedy vote in percentiles, regionally, and on a state-by-state basis resulting from the "embitterment of the religious issue." By changing the input variables (the polling data) in order to achieve different outputs (voter behavior), the results suggested that exacerbation of the religious issue after August, 1960 would probably not damage Kennedy any more than he had already been damaged once his nomination was assured. The report gave the regional vote for Kennedy in the following percentages.

Region	Results of preconvention polls	Religious issue simulation results
East	53	51
Border	55	49
South	70	47
Midwest	52	45
West	54	46

The report on the outputs of the study went on to say: "... Kennedy today has lost the bulk of the votes he would lose if the election campaign were to be embittered by the issue of anti-Catholicism. The net worst has been done. If the campaign becomes embittered, he will lose a few more reluctant Protestant votes to Nixon, but will gain Catholic and minority group votes. Bitter anti-Catholicism in the campaign would bring a reaction against prejudice and for Kennedy from Catholics and others who would resent overt prejudice."

IV. POLITICAL SUBSYSTEMS OF CONFLICT MANAGEMENT

As the systems model was more widely adopted, it was applied to subsystems within the larger whole, e.g., the legislative system within the context of the entire U.S. political system. A. Lee Brown offered a diagrammatic model of political systems in general that enabled researchers to consider political subsystems as conflict management systems.

According to the generic formulation of Fig. 2, political conflicts are of two kinds: those that demand a change in the present distribution of goods and values and those that wish to leave matters alone. Demanders and supporters select strategies for bringing their wishes to the attention of appropriate policy makers (judges in courts, administrators in bureaucracies, representatives in legislatures, etc.). Their demand inputs are conveyed to the black box conversion process through some combination of any one or all of three communication strategies: by individual participation, through organized group activity, or by influencing political parties. The outputs may be changes in one or more decrees, mores, laws, policies, or commands. Once the new policies are implemented, there is feedback to the input sources.

To illustrate the usefulness of the model, let us apply it to one of the goals of a political system. From Plato to the present, political philosophers have argued that one of the principal goals of any political system is the education of its citizens, thus making them wise and virtuous. With this goal in mind, a pro-education interest group *demands* greater allocation of public resources (tax dollars) to schools (a valued institution). The group *supports* its demand by forming voting blocs in legislative districts, hoping to reward with reelection those legislators who favor its objectives or retiring those who oppose. The group's input goes into a *convertor* (the legislative process) where it is rejected or converted into *outputs* (statutes and appropriations) intended to satisfy the demand. Hostile *feedback* from, for example, childless families may make the case that these families object to paying taxes to support the education of other people's children. These objectors

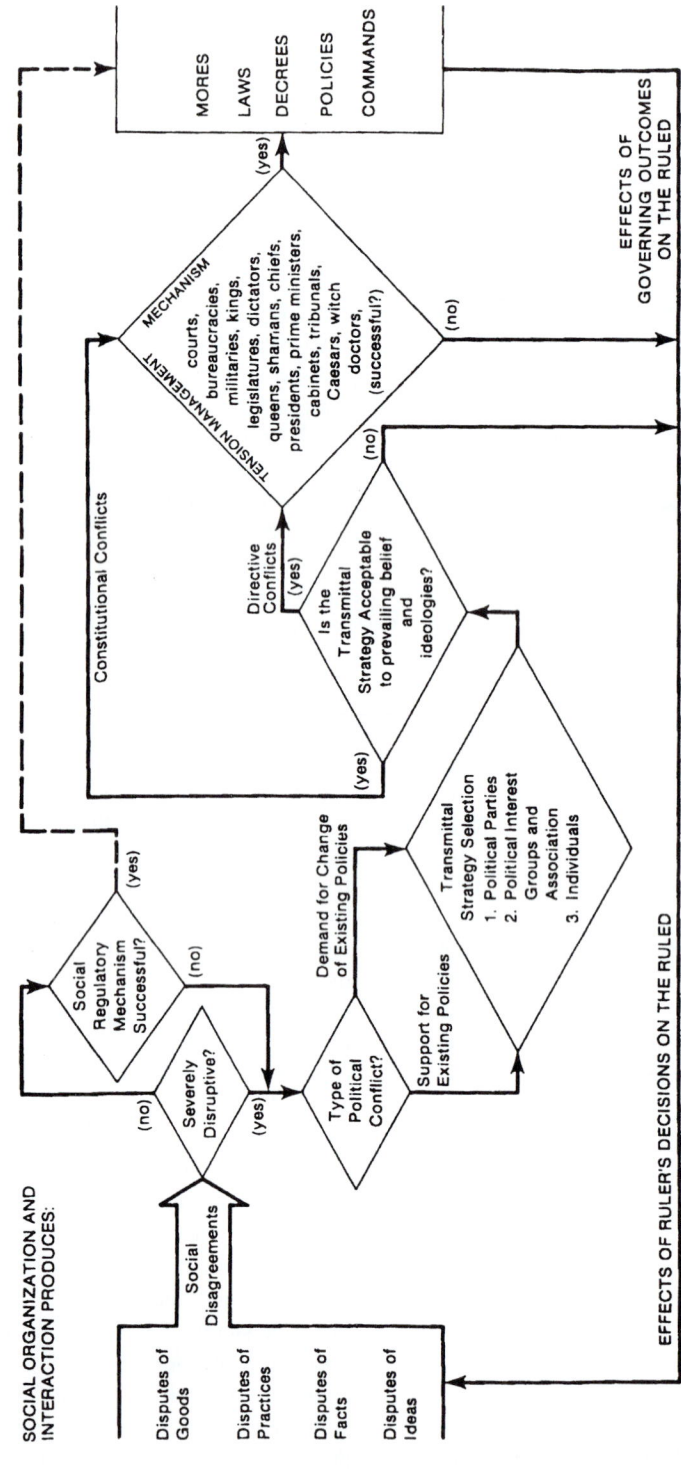

FIGURE 2 Brown's expanded model of the political system. (From *Rules and Conflict* by Brown, © 1981. Reprinted by permission of Prentice-Hall, Inc., Upper Saddle River, NJ)

form their own pressure group. Their demands now become new inputs into the system. The cycle begins again.

The primary goal of democratic constitutional systems is to discover, define, and preserve basic agreements about the procedures and content of human disagreements. To reduce this broad goal to a more manageable size, constitutions tend to create as many subsystems as feasible to cope with different types of disagreement, e.g., federal systems. In short, the democratic society takes constructive account of political conflict and develops contracts, that is, constitutions, setting out rules for how its subsystems will handle different disagreements. In stark contrast, totalitarian and authoritarian systems, based upon ideological certainties or dictatorial authority, are inflexible; they neither perceive nor tolerate serious disagreement. This, of course, makes it more difficult for totalitarian and authoritarian systems to make pragmatic "trajectory corrections" in pursuing their goals.

There are several specialized subsystems common to most democratic constitutions. Each classifies and processes conflicts of a different kind. Legislative subsystems deal mainly with conflicts about the content of laws. Political party subsystems handle contests for positions of official leadership and the mandates regarding the values of the society. Electoral subsystems make for competitive popular participation in self-governance. Executive bureaucracies, including the military and other security forces, cope with disputes about implementation of the laws. Private associations demand the allocation of resources supportive of particular policies. Public universities and public schools teach the citizenry how to compete in skills and in knowledge.

V. NEGOTIATING INCREMENTS OF INSTITUTIONALIZATION

Each subsystem develops its own input–output procedures for receiving, converting, and resolving conflicts or producing institutional change. As each input–output cycle is successfully completed, the adversaries involved acquire confidence that "the system works" and that it can be "trusted" to bring at least partial satisfaction to the participants. This outcome may be referred to as *institutionalized trust*, that is, confidence that the expected rules for conflict resolution will be implemented and be profitable (see below) to an acceptable extent for all the parties.

A. Currencies, Transactions, and Trust

To examine whether the system works, it is necessary to look inside the black box. This is where input–output conversions are accomplished. The black box contains the mechanisms that facilitate the exchanges of political currencies, maintain the marketplaces for these transactions, promote institutionalize trust, and create the changes in the decision-making structure that lead to institutional integration.

The process of institutional integration almost invariably begins with a conflict, followed by negotiated outcomes. The transactions that accompany negotiations lead to institutional consequences. Various tactics of influence, such as violence, argumentation, or vote-taking, are the tactical weapons of political transactions. These transactions, when consummated, establish new or altered patterns of organization and institutionalized behavior. One important additional consequence of successful transactions, particularly those which seem to *profit* each party to the conflict, is the enhancement of *attitudes of trust* among the transactors. As trust grows, it becomes institutionalized and may serve as the basis for the next transaction.

Transactional explanations of political behavior have great antiquity. Plato, discussing the essential activities of the inhabitants of a state, observed that "they exchange with one another, and one gives and another receives, each under the idea that the exchange will be for his own good." Aristotle's conception of distributive justice viewed the distribution of the offices and rights of a community as a transaction in which each citizen receives these goods in proportion to his contribution to the goals of the state.

In traditional usage, a transaction involves the giving up of goods by one party contingent upon receipt of goods from a second party. A transaction is an exchange, along with the attendant negotiation and bargaining. George Homans added a social dimension by defining all social behavior as a form of exchange that is more or less rewarding or costly to each actor. Each actor's *activity* includes, according to Homans' usage, not only the transfer of objects and materials, but also the emission of *sentiments* by one party toward the other, e.g., deference in exchange for advice. Each party nets a *social profit* if his or her perceived reward from the exchange exceeds the perceived personal cost. Each person evaluates rewards and costs in an entirely subjective way.

Homans' conception of activity as the content of an exchange may be designated as *social currencies*. A currency may be defined as any empirically observable object, action, or condition valued by a set of transacting persons and capable of being transferred by one to the other. Social currencies are of three general types: *positional*, *decisional*, and *material*, comparable to the Mack–Snyder categories of position and resource scarcity.

Positional currencies include such familiar phenomena as jobs, positions, offices, and certain associated attributes of each, such as job titles and task expectations. For example, when an employer offers an employee a higher wage (material currency) for taking on additional job duties (task expectations as an attribute of positional currency), this is an exchange of social currencies: material for positional.

Decisional currencies are shares of prerogative derived from participation in the decision making of a collectivity. For example, each member of a legislature such as Congress can exercise one vote as his or her share of the total collective prerogative (435 in the House of Representatives, 100 in the Senate, and one in the White House) for making legislative decisions.

Material currencies, because they make up much of our daily economic lives, are perhaps more familiar than the previous two. Material currencies refer to the goods and services (or their surrogate, money) that are commonly exchanged, most visibly as commercial transactions.

Political currencies are versions of social currencies. *Incumbencies* are a kind of positional currency, *shares* are a decisional currency, and *commodities* a material currency. The classification of political currencies tends to bring into the framework of political analysis matters that are usually omitted or believed to be unrelated to each other. The concept of political currency facilitates the description of classes of negotiated political "deals." An appointive government job (incumbency) as payoff for election campaign services (commodity) is a well-known political transaction. The apportionment of seats in a legislature, wherein negotiators are party leaders, distributes *shares* of the community's collective decision prerogative (sovereignty) to particular districts or groups.

Political exchanges are carried on regularly in a number of "marketplaces" and over different time periods. Shopping centers, stock markets, auctions, and commodity markets, for example, are familiar commercial marketplaces. Legislatures, political party conventions, courts, diplomatic conferences, regional and world organizations, and similar political institutions are also marketplaces, although not normally described as such.

There is a temporal aspect to transactions. Transactions may occur within at least two principal types of time period: *simultaneously*, e.g., $200 given immediately in payment for a bicycle delivered immediately, and *delayed-exchanges* wherein time passes before an exchange is completed, if ever, e.g., an automobile purchased on the installment plan. When transfers take place at different times, as is often the case in political transactions, anticipation and *trust* become significant elements in the exchange.

Trust and distrust are terms that may be best understood as polar extremes of a particular attitude. The attitude is anticipatory, that is, an expectation about the *future consequences for oneself* of another's *probable behavior*. If Person A anticipates that Person B will reliably act as expected, with positive consequences for A's interests, A's attitude toward B will tend to be a trusting one. If there is substantial doubt about the predictability of B's behavior and/or if the consequences for A are expected by A to be negative, A will be inclined to distrust B.

A familiar example of delayed exchange occurs when a home purchaser applies for a mortgage at a bank where he or she may be a total stranger. The bank's officers must decide whether to trust the prospective borrower. A system goes into operation. The loan officer proceeds to gather evidence about two factors (inputs): (1) the applicant's credit rating, that is, past behavior as a borrower and (2) the applicant's future income prospects, that is, job status, income from investments, and the like. Having determined that the applicant's past borrowing behavior is good and that he or she is likely to have the ability to repay the loan, the loan officer approves the loan (output), nevertheless retaining legal title to the dwelling as collateral until the mortgage is fully paid. If the borrower fails to make payments on schedule, he or she may lose all accumulated equity in the property. Given this system, the bank earns a profit from making the loan and the borrower profits by acquiring a residence immediately. With each party profiting, the system begets institutionalized trust.

Transactions negotiated by political adversaries are usually of the delayed-exchange type. Present compromises and exchanges create future obligations. Those obligations that are fulfilled are likely to promote trust and provide a basis for further mutually profitable exchanges. A series of mutually profitable transactions and their associated increases in mutual trust are likely to lead to the institutionalization of the transaction process itself. Conversely, institutionalization will fail if obligations are unmet. Exchanges will diminish or cease. Distrust will be reignited. The adversaries will regress to conflict and possibly violent tactics.

Institutionalized trust in politics is the kind that enables long-time allies such as Great Britain and the United States to disagree strenuously on some matters, yet not resort to warfare or other violence. Institutionalized trust arises from a series of mutually profitable transactions that make it unlikely that democracies will war against each other.

Although less overt than those for mortgage loans, deals between politicians tend to be equally binding. In the field of diplomacy, treaties are, in a general sense, the equivalent of the mortgage contract. Treaties are published records of delayed-exchange expectations associated with particular international transactions. A treaty that is circumvented or broken is a breach of trustworthiness, hence the guilty party is a candidate for punitive measures initiated by the aggrieved party, e.g., war, economic boycott, withdrawal of diplomatic recognition. When international institutions are unavailable or unable to review and adjudicate the complaint of an aggrieved nation, *institutional insufficiency* is likely to lead the aggrieved party to resort to violent tactics and, at worst, make war. Conversely, after a plethora of arms control treaties and successful peacekeeping operations, as Goldman and Hardman point out, former adversaries such as Russia and the United States have learned to trust each other regarding these critical matters.

B. The English Settlement of 1689

The English Settlement of 1689, which concluded the Glorious Revolution in Great Britain, is a classic example of a conflicted political system that produced a significant contractual document as the result of a process of negotiation, transaction, and trust.

The Settlement was preceded by a period in which Oliver Cromwell's Model Army became the enforcer of the Cromwellian dictatorship. The Model Army was eventually brought under Parliament's control because of its military defeat and its ultimate dependence upon Parliament's financial appropriations.

However, the reinstated king was still able to recruit forces of his own apart from Parliament's. The contest for power between Parliament and the royal family evolved to the point where the principal adversaries in the Glorious Revolution were a Parliamentary coalition of English nobles versus King James II. After a few minor military engagements, the king found that he could not rouse popular support for his cause. He fled the country, leaving the field to the coalition of nobles and their parliamentary allies. Parliament declared the throne vacant by abdication.

By this time the English political system had developed to the point that Parliament could not function constitutionally without a king. The black box and the input–output mechanisms were fairly well in place. Parliament therefore invited Mary, the daughter of James II, and her husband, William of Orange (The Netherlands), to assume the throne as joint sovereigns. This transaction consisted essentially of a delayed exchange: an *incumbency* (joint kingship) for *shares* of prerogative (increased prerogatives for Parliament). The transaction was eventually confirmed by The Settlement of 1689, that is, formal exchanges of political currencies between Parliament and the new sovereigns.

1. Parliament and the coalition of nobles swore allegiance to William and Mary as *de facto* sovereigns (legitimizing their incumbency) in exchange for the royal promise that no Roman Catholic would ever wear the crown (a negative attribute of incumbency).

2. English laws would be promulgated or altered only if a statute were passed by both houses of Parliament (increased shares of national sovereignty) and received the consent of the monarchs (reduced share of national sovereignty).

3. To end the royal prerogative of arbitrary removal of judges, often exercised by earlier kings, it was agreed that judges would have tenure (reduced share) during good behavior (a condition of incumbency). This affirmed the importance of an independent judiciary (increased shares of prerogative).

4. Royal prerogative was further limited by the requirement that the army would be financed (commodities) for only one year at a time. Additionally, the army could not be mobilized by the monarch unilaterally (reduced share). This affirmed the principle of civilian supremacy over the military, although the principle was frequently tested during the decades to come.

The Settlement, in small part presented here, was a contract. It recorded a major political transaction among the leaders of several institutions: Parliament, the royal household, the Church of England, and the military. This sharing of national sovereignty was expected to compel communication, negotiation, and political transactions among these leaders—a process necessary for establishing institutionalized trust. Any attempt by the monarch or Parliament to enact laws in ways other than those prescribed would promptly be recognized as a breach of contract and trust, hence, unconstitutional and subject to substantial punitive responses, even civil war. The requirements of the Settlement were in many ways a model for the system designed by the Founding Fathers in America—a system that dispersed components of sovereignty.

As this example illustrates, a classification of political currencies and a system of political transactions enable the observer to assess otherwise unnoticed or poorly understood data about the circumstances of institutional development and integration, particularly with respect to the content of political negotiations. The content is made more recognizable, explicit, and comprehensive, and enables us to track the process of *critical transition* from warfare to nonviolent institutional development more readily and on a sounder comparative basis.

The Settlement was one in a long series of British political transactions over the course of most of the 17th century. After the Settlement, the role of the military changed significantly. The armed forces were no longer the servants of oppression, but instead the guarantors of internal peace as well as protectors against foreign attack. In the 18th century, following the critical transition, British elites carried on their contests nonviolently, that is, through political parties, in Parliament, and in the electorate. Thus ended a millennium of English civil wars.

VI. TRANSITIONS FROM WARFARE TO PARTY SYSTEMS

Putting together several of the concepts discussed above—institutional insufficiency, trust, the tactics of violence, words and numbers, political currencies, and transactions, the author examined institutional developments in Great Britain, the United States, Mexico, and the European Community. What were the dynamics and processes that enabled these nations to make transitions from recurrent civil wars to a period when internal warfare no longer occurred despite the fact that serious political tensions and conflicts continued?

The political subsystems examined were those most centrally involved in conflict and violence, namely, the military, the representative assembly, and the party system. The period most proximate to the transition from warfare to nonviolent competition was called the *critical transition*. In the three political systems, what were the inputs that were converted to nonviolent outputs? Were the patterns of transition similar?

In each of the four case studies, issues in conflict over centuries and decades were identified, transactions in political currencies were traced, and the institutional consequences (outputs) noted. Surprisingly, similar patterns of currency transaction and institutional development were found within and among the three political subsystems. Warring military forces became nationalized and unified as the result of at least one of three events: battlefield victories, negotiated political alliances, and/or negotiated employment arrangements for the military. The representative institution, usually a legislative assembly, expanded to the point of including almost all constituencies demanding participation. A political party system, previously absent or weak, emerged as a new actor and became stabilized and influential. As a consequence, the hierarchical status among the three subsystems reversed itself.

Prior to the critical transition, the military was senior in influence and resources, whereas parties were either nonexistent or at the bottom of the institutional hierarchy. By the time the critical transition was traversed, the parties were senior in influence and control of resources. The military was subordinated to both party system and representative institution. The process shifted elite conflict from tactics of violence (warfare) to those that were numerical and verbal (party politics). The before-and-after rankings are illustrated in Fig. 3.

The subsystem hierarchy *before* the period of critical transition was as follows.

Superior: Military organizations (many)
Intermediate: Representative assembly (exclusionary)
Subordinate: Political parties (weak or none)

The rank order of influence *after* the critical transitions was reversed, as illustrated above in the English Settlement of 1689.

Superior: Political parties (stable and competitive)
Intermediate: Representative assembly (comprehensively inclusive)
Subordinate: Military organization (centralized, professional, and dependent)

The reversal was a consequence of (a) political transactions consummated by adversary leaders during the critical transition and (b) the arrival of a new political

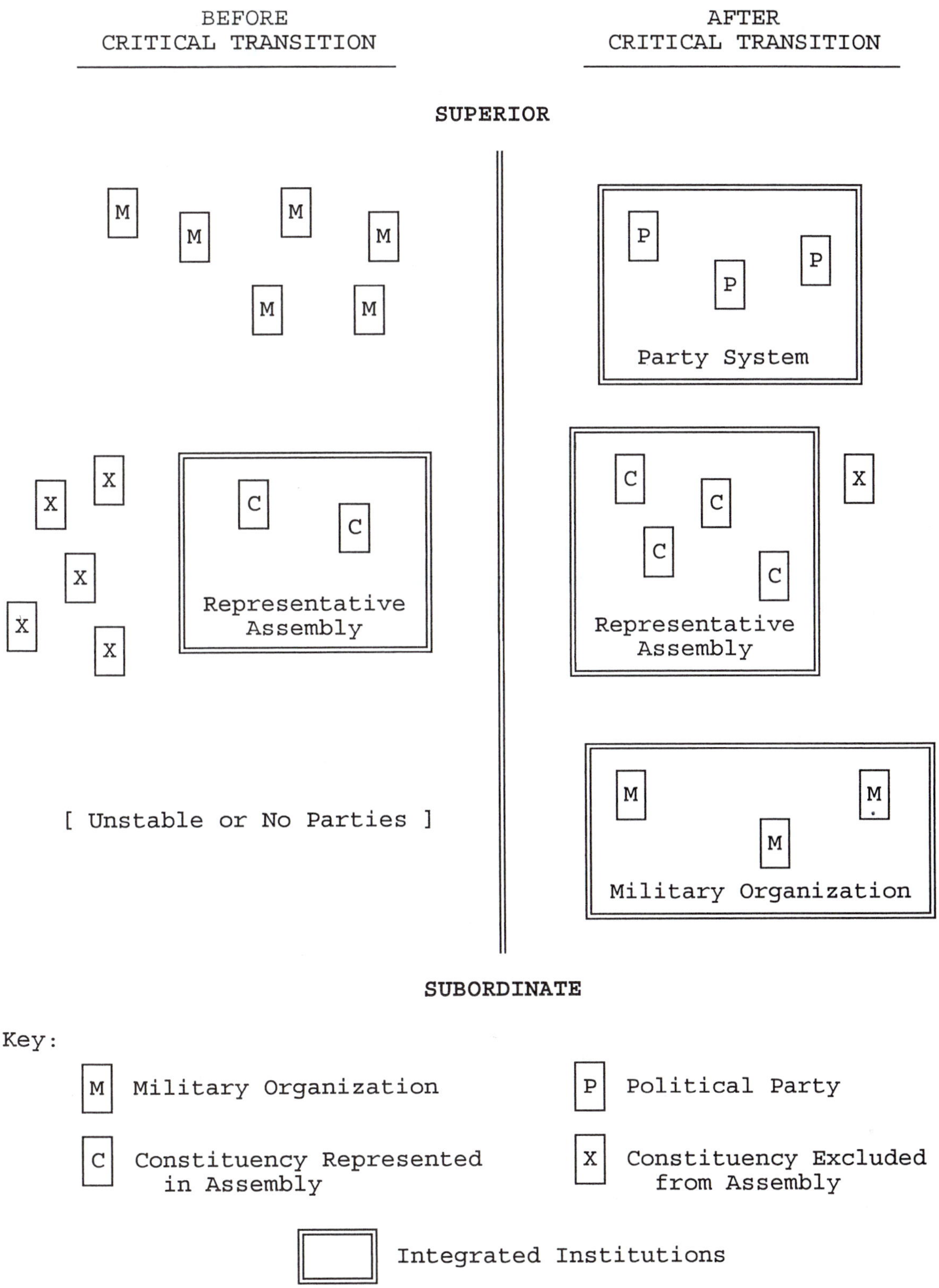
BEFORE
CRITICAL TRANSITION
AFTER
CRITICAL TRANSITION
SUPERIOR
M
M
M
M
M
M
P
P
P
Party System
X
X
X
X
X
C
C
Representative Assembly
C
C
C
C
X
Representative Assembly
[Unstable or No Parties]
M
M
M
Military Organization
SUBORDINATE
Key:
M Military Organization
P Political Party
C Constituency Represented in Assembly
X Constituency Excluded from Assembly
Integrated Institutions

FIGURE 3 The critical transition model.

actor, namely, competing political party organizations (or competing factions within a single party). In addition, during the critical transition, (c) numerous military organizations (usually independent armies) became integrated into a single force and (d) the representative body was expanded to include major constituencies previously unrepresented. *Instead of competing with armies and warfare, as before the critical transition, adversary elites continued to carry on their competition mainly through political parties.* The military was no longer the principal institution of conflict within the community. Instead, the military became the agent of internal order under the control of the civilian representative body, which in turn came under the control of the political parties. In the language of systems theory, the political system produced outputs that gave civilians (in parties and in legislatures) supremacy over the military. Elite conflicts were managed by the political parties.

The posttransition relationship among the three institutions came to be sufficiently well-established to allow for strenuous competition among adversary leaders. This promoted political trust, progressively reduced or eliminated the prospect of violence among them, and facilitated the political integration of the nation or region. Civil war was no longer a reasonable or profitable approach to political conflict. Conversely, when the period of critical transition was *not* successfully traversed, as in Mexico for 300 years, regression to warfare ensued.

The findings of this study were hypothetically extrapolated to the development of regional and global institutions. Thus, the United Nations Secretariat and Security Council, with their evolving peacemaking and peacekeeping functions, were deemed prospective global military institutions, possibly building on an expansion of the North Atlantic Treaty Organization or the Organization of Security and Cooperation in Europe. The U.N. General Assembly, possibly after reforms making it more representative of the world's peoples, was a potential world legislature. It was anticipated that the current transnational political party system— Socialist, Christian Democrat, Liberal, Conservative, Green, and other internationals—would become stronger, more stable, and more influential. These prospective outputs would presumably be negotiated by elites manipulating the global black box and experiencing profitable transactions in political currencies. If and when this critical transition occurs, the transnational party system would become what party systems have been in the national cases just reviewed, namely, the institutional alternative to international warfare.

VII. CONFLICT PROCESSES AND INSTITUTIONAL INTEGRATION

Another set of outputs of political systems are those that have consequences for organizational and institutional structures, that is, socializes their members, formalizes their positions, or determines who is incumbent in which position.

A. Socialization, Formalization, and Investiture

The system inputs are conflicts about such matters as (a) personal role behavior, (b) the tasks prescribed for particular positions, or (c) the circumstances that endow particular persons with incumbency in particular positions. These are different aspects of the same structural unit, namely, a person holding a position in a group, organization, or institution. For example, John (a person) has a job as a postman (a position) in the postal service (an organization). Disputes may arise over how well John performs his job, how clearly the duties of postman are described, or whether John should be fired from the job or reassigned. The disputes take time and conflict activity to resolve, hence, it becomes a process. If John learns to modify his role behavior, the output of the process could be called *socialization*. If the tasks descriptive of the job are changed, it is a *formalization process*. If John is separated from the job, it is an *investiture process*.

In dealing with the conflicts of an organization, according to Goldman (1966), it is appropriate to examine the conflicts in their structural as well as their functional aspects, that is, as organizational *members*, as organizational *positions*, or as indications of *incumbency* that recognize which particular members occupy and are responsible for fulfilling the tasks expected of particular positions.

As many politicians understand, substantive issues such as taxation, health care, and so on often conceal underlying efforts to change institutional structure. For example, a conflict cycle may deal substantively with a tax issue, but relate implicitly to the *role behavior* of particular institutional officers (Does the tax collector treat taxpayers imperiously or with hostility?). Whatever the solution to the tax issue, the outputs may also have consequences for the officers' behavior and, if so, is an output of the socialization process. If the substantive issue relates primarily to the *task expectations* (e.g., job description) that are associated with a particular position, the relevant output may be a phase in the formalization process. If the conflict has to do with the *circumstances of incumbency* that endow a particular person with a particular position, this may be referred to as an investiture process.

A role behavior is an observable, repeated pattern of conduct performed by a person who believes that this pattern of activity is appropriate for the organizational position in which he or she is incumbent. Each role performance associated with a position is only one of many roles that make up the personality of the individual. For example, the person performing as secretary-general of the United Nations is undoubtedly also a spouse, a parent, a friend, a church member, a political party member, and so on. Extra-organizational roles may overlap or conflict with organizational ones; a person may prefer to spend his weekends as spouse and parent than as secretary-general. Disputes may arise from different assessments of how the incumbent in a position is actually behaving and whether the behavior matches the organization's task expectations. If one of the adversaries in the dispute over role behavior prevails, he will presumably have taught the incumbent "a lesson" in "proper" behavior.

A task expectation is a prescription of the conduct expected of an individual in order to implement an organizational goal. Task expectations are regularly associated with a named position in the organization. They are usually set forth in constitutions, regulations, job descriptions, speeches, and other declarations by organized groups or their leaders. When bundled together in an enduring way, sets of task expectations become the job descriptions of particular positions or offices. For example, Articles 97 to 101 of Chapter XV of the United Nations Charter specifies in broad terms the set of tasks expected to be performed by the secretary-general. Disputes over task expectations arise when leaders or factions in an organization have different interpretations of the job specifications, different expectations regarding the relevance of the tasks for the goals being sought, or, for other reasons, wish to change the expectations. These differences become the inputs of a conflict cycle.

An incumbency is the result of an explicit consensus among the members of an organization that a particular person is to be held accountable for the performance of the task expectations making up a particular position. Usually the beginning or the conclusion of an incumbency is crowned by such familiar events as an election, an appointment, an installation ceremony, or a removal procedure. Disputes over incumbency issues (inputs) may lead to divesting the incumbent of the office or changing the conditions of incumbency in general (out-

puts). A relevant hypothesis, for example, is that incumbency issues are most likely to generate wars, as was World War II to remove Hitler, Mussolini, and their associates from the leadership offices of their governments.

Illustrations may be drawn from the early history of the United Nations. Take the case of Secretary-General Trygvie Lie. The former Soviet Union, as a member of the Security Council, objected to the way Lie performed his duties in that he acted as a political broker among major powers rather than as a civil servant taking orders from the major powers. The Soviets demanded that Lie change his ways (become socialized) or be removed (divested) from office. The Soviet Union called on its Third World allies for support of its input demand. Had the conflict led to a modification in Lie's role behavior, the conflict cycle would be a phase in a socialization process. If the Security Council had adopted a resolution changing the duties (task expectations) of the secretary-general, this output would have constituted a phase in the formalization process. If the rules for selecting or installing a secretary-general had been changed, or if Lie had been removed from office, these would be outputs of an investiture process.

For reasons of analytical simplicity, conflict processes are often treated episodically, that is, as time-limited cycles or phases of input–output events. Conflicts limited to cycles help reduce the scope of analysis and, in the real world, may facilitate at least limited resolution of conflicts. Legal conflicts in courts, for example, have formal beginnings and endings signaling when inputs are received and outputs emerge; the issues in conflict may continue to be disputed in a different venue. Wars begin and end, although the dispute between the nations involved may not. Election contests appear to start with the opening of a campaign and end on election day, yet adversary parties will continue to debate the meaning of the popular mandate.

As the course of a conflict proceeds, tactics—whether *violent*, *verbal*, or *numerical*—vary. Violent tactics employ means intended to destroy or disrupt life, property, or the normal activities of the adversary. Verbal tactics employ linguistic actions or devices, e.g., verbal threats, name calling, arguments, resolutions, propaganda, legalistic concepts, and definitions. Numerical tactics endeavor to frame the argument in quantitative terms, such as a vote in an official body, the exercise of a special voting prerogative, e.g., the veto, or some other demonstration of quantifiable influence.

During a conflict cycle, each party usually pays greatest attention to the more immediate and visible substantive issue—who gets what, when, and how—rather than to the far less visible elements of institutional structure, that is, person, position, and incumbency, or the contents of the black box, such as the currencies transacted or the decision-making procedure. However, astute managers of organizations, particularly when dealing with conflict, are likely to resolve conflicts by retraining the person(s), rewriting the job description for the position(s), or making changes related to incumbency(ies). In short, they manipulate the socialization, formalization, and investiture processes.

Conflict cycles usually conclude when the adversaries assess their respective conflict costs in order to determine how much they are willing to expend to achieve their preferred outputs. They decide privately and subjectively whether they have expended enough or more than enough. They may then decide to negotiate or otherwise communicate with each other, directly or indirectly, about the conditions necessary to resolve or ameliorate the conflict.

B. Institutional Integration

In input–output analysis, the political system's black box contains different methods of decision making, currency transaction, tactics of influence, and degrees of institutional integration. These are the elements with which policy makers deal if and when they alter the contents of the black box. If the alterations are successful, the consequence is likely to be further integration of the institution. If they fail, the institution will decline or terminate.

Decision-making lies at the core of the black box. Decisions to negotiate are probably the most difficult to make, for they may signal weakness or they may be so subtle as to be indiscernible. Should the desire to negotiate be viewed as rhetoric, propaganda, or deception? Is the move to negotiate essentially tactical? Is negotiation about specific or general substantive or organizational issues? If a conclusion to the conflict cycle is imminent, will the parties be willing to announce their agreement together with enough ceremony to certify publicly an end to the conflict and perhaps reveal an inclination toward future cooperation? The answer to this last question may become a first step in a process of integration.

If conflict processes produce positive changes in institutional structure, they are also likely to affect the decision-making mechanism in the black box. This may alter the manner in which the organization is integrated. Galtung's definition of integration applies. Galtung defines *integration* as a sequence of events whereby two or more actors form a new actor, that is, a new decision maker. For example, during the Second Continental Congress, colonial leaders wrote the Articles of Confederation and formed a new actor—a national government—superseding the original 13 colonial actors.

To the extent that the outcomes of each of the three conflict processes alter the organizational structure, they are also likely to modify the contents of the black box, that is, the decision structure and rules under which new actors are expected to operate. To this extent, the conflict process outputs have a direct bearing upon the manner of integration experienced by the organization. Institutionalized trust in an integrating organization is likely to help outweigh the forces for conflict, particularly those that are violent.

VIII. RESEARCH AND POLICIES

The application of systems theory to the study of the politics of conflict has been minimal. There is little empirical research that elucidates how political systems foster change from recurring warfare to enduring nonviolent institutions. The theory sketches offered here and the evidence supporting them provide insights that may help fill the gap. For example, the critical transition model, already modestly tested in the case studies of Britain, the United States, Mexico, and the European Community, could be applied to the many contemporary transitions from civil war to party politics: El Salvador, Nicaragua, Mozambique, and numerous other cases.

A scientific payoff for conflict process theory would presumably be achieved if the analytical framework revealed relationships among (a) particular types of tactics, (b) particular structural outcomes, and (c) specific manifestations of organizational integration. For example, empirical findings could possibly reveal that conflicts about task expectations, more than other structural issues, tend to conclude with decisions promotive of organizational integration. Or research findings might reveal that a higher incidence of violent tactics is associated with role behavior than with task expectations or incumbencies. The findings could give conflict managers a more strongly confirmed basis for developing their strategies and choosing their tactics. In general, the managers of the political system would be able to improve their input-output analyses.

As the body of knowledge regarding conflict and political violence expands, government policies should do likewise. Policy-makers should debate the underlying assumptions and consequences of policies regarding disagreement, conflict, and violence. In doing so, a first principle should be that conflict is inevitable in all social systems. Violence is not and should be diminished. However, ironically, the *capacity* for violence, if substantial enough, can serve as a deterrent to violence. This is the basic rationale for powerful defense and police forces.

In addition, several forms of conflict may be creative, constructive, and integrative and should be institutionalized. The profitability of political violence, particularly in the contemporary context, should be recognized as short term and ultimately destructive of trust as well as resources.

Finally, communication and negotiation are the *sine qua non* of conflict management and must be pursued relentlessly. Without communication and negotiation, parties will ultimately become frustrated and regress to violent tactics.

These principles, if they can be called principles, are likely to facilitate the development of political systems capable of diminishing political violence and harnessing nonviolent conflict to the positive and peaceful goals of the community.

Also See the Following Articles

CONFLICT THEORY • COOPERATION, COMPETITION, AND CONFLICT • DECISION THEORY AND GAME THEORY • POLITICAL THEORIES • POWER, SOCIAL AND POLITICAL THEORIES OF

Bibliography

Blau, P. M. (1964). *Exchange and power in social life.* New York: Wiley.

Brown, A. L., Jr. (1981). *Rules and conflict.* Englewood Cliffs, NJ: Prentice-Hall.

Buckley, W. (Ed.) (1968). *Modern systems research for the behavioral scientist.* Chicago, IL: Aldine.

Cook, K. S. (Ed.) (1987). *Social exchange theory.* Beverly Hills, CA: Sage.

Easton, D. (1971). *The political system,* 2nd ed. New York: Knopf.

Galtung, J. (1968). A structural theory of integration. *Journal of Peace Research,* 475–395.

Goldman, R. M. (1966). A theory of conflict process and organizational offices. *Journal of Conflict Resolution, 10,* 328–343.

Goldman, R. M. (1969). A transactional theory of political integration and arms control. *American Political Science Review, 62,* 719–733.

Goldman, R. M. (1990). *From warfare to party politics: The critical transition to civilian control.* Syracuse, NY: Syracuse University Press.

Goldman, R. M., & Hardman, W. M. (1997). *Building trust: An introduction to peacekeeping and arms control.* Brookfield, VT: Ashgate.

Gurr, T. R. (Ed.) (1980). *Handbook of political conflict: Theory and research.* New York: The Free Press.

Hibbs, D. A., Jr. (1973). *Mass political violence: A cross-national causal analysis.* New York: Wiley.

Homans, G. C. (1961). *Social behavior: Its elementary forms.* Boston: Harcourt, Brace & World.

Creamer, R. M., & Tyler, T. R. (Eds.) (1996). *Trust in organization: Frontiers of theory and research.* Thousand Oaks, CA: Sage.

Levy, S. G. (1981). Political violence: A critical evaluation. In S. L. Long (Ed.), *Handbook of political behavior,* Vol. 2, ch. 3. New York: Plenum.

Mack, R. W., & Snyder, R. C. (1957). The analysis of social conflict—Toward an overview and synthesis. *Journal of Conflict Resolution, 1,* 212–248.

North, R. C., et al. (1960). The integrative functions of conflict. *Journal of Conflict Resolution, 4,* 355–374.

Pool, I. de S., Abelson, R. P., & Popkin, S. (1965). *Candidates, issues, and strategies: A computer simulation of the 1960 and 1964 presidential elections.* Cambridge, MA: MIT Press.

Schattschneider, E. E. (1957). Intensity, visibility, direction and scope. *American Political Science Review, 51,* 933–942.

Simmel, G. (1955). *Conflict.* K. H. Wolff (trans.). Glencoe, ILL: Free Press.

Singer, K. (1949). *The idea of conflict.* Melbourne: Melbourne University Press.

Strauss, A. (1978). *Negotiations.* San Francisco, CA: Jossey–Bass.

Wiener, N. (1950). *The human use of human beings.* Boston, MA: Houghton–Mifflin.

Zimmermann, E. (1983). *Political violence, crises, and revolutions: Theories and research.* Cambridge, MA: Schenkman.

Political Theories

Vincent G. Boudreau

The City College of New York

GLOSSARY

Bureaucratic Authoritarian Model School of analysis influential in the study of Latin American dictatorships that explains state repression in terms of coup coalitions formed among international and domestic capitalists, the military, and technocrats in response to economic crisis.

Claim-Makers Individuals engaged in protest, demonstration, or resistance.

Collective Repertoire The contentious forms (i.e., strikes, building occupations, demonstrations) that are available to claim makers at sociocultural conjuncture.

Cycle of Protest Clusters of political mobilization, protest, and rebellion launched at roughly the same time by different networks and associations.

Free Rider From collective behavior theory, individuals who enjoy the benefits of collective activity without participating in that activity.

Game Theory An approach that formally models the interactions of two or more actors under specified constraints, usually assuming actor rationality.

Mesomobilization Mobilization that takes place as a result of coalitions among or cooperation between social movement organizations.

Micromobilization Context Social and organizational connections, often of a face-to-face variety, which produce nascent solidarities instrumental in mobilizing solidarity and participation in collective action.

New Social Movements A concept of primarily European origin developed to characterize movements organized around concepts of peace, gender, race identity, and youth; such movements are viewed as replacing older class-based movements in contemporary society.

Relative Deprivation The feeling of deprivation relative to others, which some theorists link to the onset of rebellion.

Security Dilemma Any state's attempts to increase its own security through the acquisition of arms threatens neighboring states, which then also acquire weapons, touching off a new cycle of insecurity and arms acquisitions.

Transnational Ties Connections that link one society to another across international borders.

World Systems Theory A theory associated with dependency analysis that analyzes social, political, and economic phenomena produced by the world capitalist system conceived as the smallest possible unit of analysis.

I. INTRODUCTION

For years the study of political violence, peace, and conflict approached the subject from widely different points of origin. In the 1960s and 1970s collective violence received great attention in light of urban unrest across America and Southern Europe. Others at that time regarded violence *per se* as less important than the larger social phenomena in which it occurred, i.e., nationalism, protest, or revolutions. Different literatures developed to explain the violence of states, of armies, of societies and of ethnicities. Writings about international and domestic violence and conflict seldom spoke to one another. Moreover, authors addressed themselves to these various topics with approaches ranging from the structural to the psychological.

Over the past decade or two, however, areas of dialogue within and among these literatures have expanded. In one seminal project underway at this writing, Doug McAdam, Sidney Tarrow, and Charles Tilly have set out to develop a unified approach to the study of contentious politics. But apart from this and other explicitly synthetic efforts, more autonomous theory building has brought previously segregated perspectives into closer interaction. Theorists have increasingly stopped making analytical distinctions between state violence and the violence of thieves, extortionists, and bandits. James Scott has successfully argued against the distinction between political and prepolitical modes of resistance. A wealth of work has explored the connection between protest and the formation of foreign policy or international pressure and the rise of domestic contention. Distinctions between domestic and international conflict, while still significant, have worn away before the general trend toward globalism and the specific emergence of transnational social movements. In discussing the literature on violence, peace, and conflict, this article takes account of these various moves toward broader theoretical dialogue.

This theoretical convergence is possible largely because most analysts of conflict, violence, and peace ask some version or combination of three questions. First, when and among what populations is conflict in *interests or values* likely to become manifest in terms of conflictual or contentious *behavior*? Second, when mobilization does occur, what forces regulate its forms and scope? Third, is it possible to describe patterns according to which different types of contention rise and fall, succeed or fail? The next section takes up questions of political mobilization, while the second half of the article addresses questions of conflict's form and pattern. Each section takes up issues of international and domestic conflict separately, while at the same time noting areas of overlap and contrast between the two literatures.

II. MOBILIZATION AND THE OUTBREAK OF WAR

Efforts to explain mobilization have long preoccupied those who write about contention. Some regard conflict as an inherent aspect of human nature, while others argue that it depends on external stimulus. T. R. Gurr explained violence in terms of actors' dispositions or emotions, while other theorists, such as Kenneth Waltz or Theda Skocpol, developed explanations based on political structures. Interestingly, students of international relations (IR) and comparative politics initially advanced sharply opposed visions of contention. The realist school of IR assumed that states normally advance their interests through force and threat and were compelled to exercise restraint only by counteractions and power balances. Conversely, systems theory, developed by the political scientist David Easton, persuaded many postwar comparativists to expect governments efficiently to respond to social demands with appropriate policies, which made extrainstitutional conflict seem irrational or dysfunctional. Over the past 20 years, both perspectives faced sustained challenge, and much innovation in conflict studies sprang from this critical scrutiny.

A. Realist Answers to Why War Occurs

After the convulsions of two world wars seemed finally to dispatch the internationalist aspirations of IR's idealist school, political realism quickly consolidated its position as the field's dominant paradigm. The theory owed much to earlier writings of the Greek historian Thucydides and the English philosopher Thomas Hobbes. In his classic realist formulation, Hans Morgenthau argued that states act to maximize their interest, defined as power; moreover, Morgenthau argued that states were both unified rational actors and the only theoretically significant players in international relations. Realism was both normative and predictive: state leaders were both advised and expected to act to maximize the national interest. Recent work by neorealists and others have modified these initial principles. Neorealists such as Robert Koehane argue that states seek security rather than unbridled power or, like Richard Ashley, define the national interest as long-term security rather than immediate conquest. Others concede that, while power relations set the basic rules of the international system, those rules acquire limited power of their own that may act autonomously of power relations in limited ways. Still, for most members of the realist school warfare represented a constant threat, and only under special conditions would hostility give way to more stable peace.

The precise character of these conditions, however, remained in question among realists. Some have acquired the name volunterists, because they argue that maintaining stable power balances in the international system requires careful statecraft. For volunterists, political realism constitutes a set of principles to guide such efforts. Structuralists, in contrast, explain war in terms of systemic attributes, like the distribution of power resources. A famous debate among these structuralists, in fact, tries to settle which international structure is most stable. Singer and Deutsch maintained that multipolar structures provide states with multiple balancing options and inhibit differences or rivalries from becoming rigid and deepening animosities and so promote stability. Kenneth Waltz countered that bipolar structures reduce uncertainty by allowing great powers to focus on one or two principal adversaries; this focus diminishes the chance that surprise or uncertainty will lead to an inadvertent war. This debate acquired renewed vigor when the Soviet Union's collapse pushed the exiting bipolar structure toward a more multipolar arrangement.

One of the major efforts of the time made central contributions to realist theory by developing important qualitative measures for abstract concepts such as state power. The correlates of war project, directed by David Singer and based at the University of Michigan, produced many inductive correlations between social, political, and geographic variables and the likelihood of war. While the project never itself produced any definitive empirical evidence of what precisely causes war, it has developed important statistical data bases which are widely used by social scientists in the study of international conflict.

Realists assume that states act rationally. For most, rationality forms the conceptual glue attaching state activity to the system's opportunities and constraints: the former is deductively read from the latter. Waltz perhaps most strongly insists on weeding from the analysis explanations based on the character of individual states, societies, or decision-makers. Yet Waltz's aggressive disregard for subsystemic features underscores that the rationality assumption requires us to think about states and decision-makers as basically similar to one another. The outbreak of peace or violence has nothing to do with the character of any involved state, nation, or leader, for all are assumed to act similarly under similar conditions. All are, in a sense, generic players in a particular game.

B. Comparative Politics, Systems Theory, and Domestic Contention

In contrast with international relations theory, postwar comparativists often depicted conflict as involving particular players in generic games. One of the great innovations to accompany systems theory was the structural–functionalist approach to comparison; this approach argued that all governments fulfilled similar functions (albeit through different structures) and responded to social demands and supports with appropriate policy. Yet in this "normal" interplay between state and society, there was insufficient basis to explain contention and conflict. If state policy was merely a response to social demand, why would normal individuals resort to unconventional or disruptive activities? Initially, the answer was that, under normal circumstances, they should not. Conflict was treated as social dysfunction or deviance: In the late 1940s, Roethlisberger described conflict as a "social disease," while Warner viewed it as a pathological obstacle to the normally integrative pulls that communities exert.

Others soon found more systemic answers to the question and viewed conflict as rooted in larger breakdown. From an individualist perspective, T. R. Gurr argued that the feeling of deprivation relative to others rather than poverty itself made people rebel. A greatly unequal society would be less stable than one with broadly shared poverty because inequity breeds frustration, and frustration begets aggression. Others linked conflict to rapid social change. Huntington's breakdown theory is a variant of Gurr's relative deprivation approach, although political objectives, rather than economic, are the object of social frustration: modernizing society places increased demands on political institutions that outstrip capacities and cause social breakdown. Ultimately, such works shared a common analytic principle: to explain why systems don't function as they ought and to examine actors' orientations and emotions.

Hence, by the early 1970s, research on conflict remained sharply divided. Between states, one expected warfare and power struggles and predicted war or peace according to the structural balance of forces. Within states, one expected more civil relations and regarded conflict as the symptom of some breakdown. From this point, however, both fields began to change. In IR, liberal theory challenged many of realism's basic assumptions, while comparativists began to look at collective action as more reasonable responses to social and political circumstances. As the IR field began more to appreciate actor-based explanations of political activity, comparativists began to explore the relationship between actors and broader social and political structures.

C. Liberalism and the Question of International War

Liberal IR theory took shape as a critique of realism's foundation claims that states were unified rational actors striving to amass power. Some argued that states share vast and relatively stable areas of common interest, that world politics consists largely in expanding connections between societies and governments, and that both encourage peaceful relations. Koehane and Nye maintained that close ties between some states create areas of complex interdependence within which security no longer dominates international relations, and states cannot use force against one another. Even within the realist tradition some writers set out to redefine national interest to incorporate an understanding for the mutual concerns that enable cooperation: trade, development, environmental conservation, and health care. Game theorists like Kenneth Oye argued that iterated relations moved states to value those agreements themselves and to support norms and regimes that reduced uncertainty and lowered the transaction costs of international relations. Michael Doyle, building on Kant's expectation that republican governments would carve out a "separate peace" with one another, notes that for almost 200 years, no two liberal democracies have gone to war against one another. Such ideas, compared to earlier realist writings, depict the international realm as containing a more developed society, with elements that suggest congenial and stable relations.

That the structure of international relations could promote cooperative and peaceful relations also moved IR theorists increasingly to regard warfare in terms of breakdowns and crises. Decision-making theorists used psychological arguments to challenge realism's rationality assumption. Richard Ned Lebow and Ole Holsti both argue that in times of international crisis, state leaders likely make suboptimal decisions designed more to alleviate stress than to promote national interests. Others identified domestic organizational or bureaucratic breakdowns as destabilizing influences that drove states toward war. Allison's classic work on the Cuban missile crisis placed the influence of bureaucratic politics and organizational routines on the research agenda for a whole generation of analysts.

Some newer work seeks to enrich, rather than displace, structuralism. Jervis's spiral model of the arms race—essentially an accelerating security dilemma—identifies both the material build-up of forces and actors' perceptions of their neighbors' acquisitions at the contest's core. Jervis combines perceptual factors with an analysis of technological capacities. State leaders, he argues, react differently to one another's arms program, depending on whether offensive or defensive weapons are judged to possess a battlefield advantage. Increasingly, those who take political structures seriously have answered Jervis's question, "Do perceptions matter?" in the affirmative.

D. Resource Mobilization, Political Process, and Domestic Contention

As new IR theory looked beyond structuralism, literatures on protest and revolution began to discover the benefits of the approach. In 1966, Barrington Moore argued that misery predicts peasant rebellion less accurately than community resources at rebels' disposal. Charles Tilly contended that a curvilinear relationship existed between rebellion and claim makers' access to institutional avenues of power: populations with no access to the polity and those with unrestricted access will both be unlikely to rebel—the former because they lack resources and the latter because they lack cause. Somewhere between, where populations have both substantial grievances and some resources, rebellion is more likely. Theda Skocpol posed a telling challenge to relative deprivation theory: if rebellion is accurately predicted by changes in actors' conditions (i.e., increased poverty, disempowerment, or the *perception* of relative deprivation), then analysts must assume relative social satisfaction in cases where rebellion does not occur—something she rejects out of hand. James Scott's work on everyday resistance builds on this theme, arguing that a broad range of apparently unpolitical activities, from theft to gossip, are acts of resistance staged under conditions of great power disparity. Importantly, all of these approaches assume that most societies contain aggrieved populations and so something beyond grievance stimulates contention.

Yet scholars disagreed about what elements of the social environment could reliably predict mobilization. Beginning with Mancur Olson's pioneering work on collective behavior in 1965, analysts began to construct an interpretation based on the costs and benefits associated with mobilization. This resource mobilization (RM) approach stressed that participation in collective action drew people away from daily routines and did so in relation to the interplay of costs and benefits surrounding participation—including the conspicuous possibility of nonparticipating free riders or collective failure. As the perspective developed scholars began to regard the interplay between organized and unorganized participants as a decisive influence over the distribution of costs, benefits, and participatory incentives. Some pointed to interactions between long-standing movement "entrepreneurs" (activists and social movement organizations, or SMOs) and a rising or falling tide of mass activism. Accordingly, entrepreneurs with long-term interests sifted through society like salesmen looking for new markets and the right sales pitch to sell their political project. Others placed entrepreneurs in different organizational settings—Garner and Zald wrote of social movement "sectors," while McCarthey and Zald described the interrelations of beneficiary and conscience constituencies.

As the RM paradigm was under construction, Charles Tilly and his collaborators developed the collective action (CA, later the political process, or PP) approach to social movements, which argued that contention occurred when political outsiders gained greater resources or access to the polity. In this perspective, the generation of movement power and capacity was not an inherent organizational problem, but contingent on the movement's political and social context. Organization and social connection constituted important elements of this context, but so did the array of allies and adversaries. McAdam's 1982 work on the civil rights movement in the U.S. argued that southern Black churches provided micromobilization contexts that helped recruit activists and define collective action; these churches served many of the functions that RM assigned to political entrepreneurs. Others describe protest produced by SMO organizations in coalition with one another as "mesomobilization"; in such events, SMOs mount demonstrations by pooling their organized resources and depend less on discovering and directing spontaneous discontent. Tarrow's 1994 work describes the growth of lighter "externalized" movement organizations in response to the 1960s expansion of the electronic media, which vitiated the need for a large SMO apparatus and explains how more or less spontaneous protest has been able to achieve broad scope over the past several decades. Yet, for questions of mobilization, nothing was more central to the PP model than external factors collectively referred to as the political opportunity structure (POS).

What is a POS and how does it influence movement politics? Researchers disagree. For some, the POS refers to stable arrangement of state institutions and social networks; following de Tocqueville's comparison of the French and American states, authors like Peter Eisinger and Herbert Kitschelt argue that differences in state structures influence patterns of contention. In contrast, other analysts focus on volatile elements of the political opportunity structure and associate mobilization with either expanding opportunities or increased threats. Sidney Tarrow's descriptions of volatile elements of the POS has attracted broad support: "... the opening up of access to participation, shifts in ruling alignments, the availability of influential allies, and cleavages within and among elites" (1994, p. 86). In the end, most analysts agree that both elements of the POS are in some way significant. Stable aspects of the POS may well help determine the sorts of collective action likely to emerge in any setting, while volatile aspects influence mobilization's scope and timing.

E. State Violence and State Building

As the contentions politics literature developed its structural approach to social mobilization, a related literature, often rooted in Marxist ideas, produced its own structural models. The approach set out to explain state activities, first by examining the state's task of mediating between classes (and acquiring the resources to accomplish that mediation) and second by analyzing the tools and techniques that the state had at its disposal. A great deal of the argumentation directed attention at the social basis of state activity, the reciprocal relationship between the construction of state institutions, and the exercise of the state's coercive powers. Some explained state violence in terms of even larger processes. Barrington Moore's account of the transition from agrarian to industrial society contains a deeply pessimistic political message: the transition seems invariably to require violence, usually state violence. Even his ostensible comparison between the peaceful British and violent French transitions boils down to differences between the quiet violence of the English enclosures as against the public violence of the French revolution. Perry Anderson called attention to organizational innovations, such as the invention of the standing army or the national tax-collecting bureaucracy as milestones in establishing the state's absolutist powers. Charles Tilly links the most significant advances in state capacities to war-making efforts.

Others find explanations for state violence in the conjunction of social alignments and economic capacities. One prominent thesis links states' willingness to use coercion with the timing of industrialization. Gershenkron argues that states striving to catch up with international competitors, in a context where advanced technology is available, often resort to a combination of internal violence and external expansion to generate the resources necessary for that modernizing push. Guillermo O'Donnell's bureaucratic authoritarian model, so influential for the study of Latin American dictatorships, requires both analysis of a particular stage in capitalist development (the end of the easy period of import-substitution) and a coalition of domestic and international forces. Those associated with Immanuel Wallerstein's world systems school of analysis link any one state's ability or willingness to use violence to requirements of the world capitalist system; accordingly, in countries that contribute cheap labor to the production process, one would expect to find a great deal of oppression against labor movements.

III. THE NATURE OF CONFLICT

International relations theorists asked about the character of warfare long before those interested in domestic conflict began to ask analogous questions. The participation of the state in wars, and the prominence of security functions among state responsibilities, made it logical for both IR analysts and policy-makers to ask what war might look like and what military strategies would likely succeed. In the domestic realm, the initial inclination to regard contention as deviance forestalled any effort to trace the activity's logic. Research has often treated collective violence as the abandonment of rational activity, and for years, *all* contentious politics was regarded as essentially violent. Recently, however, the search to define and explain collective repertoires in terms of both cultural patterns and social-structural realities have captured the attention of social movements theorists no less than that of IR scholars.

A. Tactics, Technology, and International Relations

Almost from the beginning of sustained interest in international relations, analysts have attempted to describe war between states, to explain victories and defeats, and to prescribe how state leaders might achieve the former and avoid the latter. It is possible to read both Thucydides's *History of the Peloponnesian War* and portions of Machiavelli's *The Prince* as pioneering efforts

in this vein. Clauzwitz's great, though unfinished *On War* enjoins us to think about war as the continuation of politics by other means—but also warns military planners to include calculations of "friction" in their designs. Perhaps the most famous global work on warfare, Sun-Tzu's *The Art of War* stresses the need to subjugate an enemy politically if possible and militarily only if necessary. The era of anti-imperialist struggles produced new works that elaborated guerrilla strategies for application to the physical and sociological terrains of third world countries; Jose Maria Sison's *Philippine Society and Revolution,* for example, develops Mao Tse Tung's peasant revolutionary line, itself a seminal innovation, for application to an archipelagic setting.

In these explorations—especially when undertaken by political realists or military practitioners—four questions attracted most attention. First, what are the physical attributes of the principle contestants and over what terrain is war likely to be waged? Second, how do the prevailing technologies of war influence battle and how are these technologies distributed among contestants? Third, what tactics are most effective in such contests? Finally, how does the international structure shape warfare?

While individual authors may emphasize one or another of the above questions, the field's most important contributions often demonstrate their interrelationship. Robert Jervis argued in 1978 that technology and geography interact, and while inventions like the cavalry, the railroad, the airplane or the nuclear missile certainly shaped warfare in their own right, they had different influences on states with different geographical attributes. Hence the rise of naval technology corresponded with the ascent of geographically small oceanic states like the Netherlands and Great Britain, while rail power provided a similar boost to landlocked countries like Germany. Similarly, new technologies interact with and force revisions in military and political tactics. Before World War II, establishing a deterrent capacity often moved state leaders to shield their populations from enemy attack; in contrast, as Thomas Schelling argued in *Arms and Influence,* leaders of nuclear powers strove toward a deterrent balance partly by assuaging adversaries' fears: demonstrating, that is, their own population's abiding vulnerability. Christianson and Snyder, in a 1990 article, show that perceptions of how military technology will work—and especially of whether offensive or defensive weaponry will have the advantage—influence alliance politics and mobilization processes. Writing on the subject of war duration in 1996, Bennet and Stam consider interactions between terrain, strategy, and contestant capacity.

Explanations of why warfare changes from one period to another frequently focus on exogenous changes in either technology or international structure. Because global structure and technology undergo periodic shifts, major moments of innovation in the study and execution of inter-state conflict often follow either structural changes or important technological innovations. Either sort of shift may reverse the fortunes of states possessing newly favored geographic characteristics or resource reserves; most also compel revisions in strategic and tactical orthodoxies. Weapons innovation has at different moments changed fundamental aspects of how people wage war. Changes in the international structure often alter the costs of confrontation by influencing the number and types of players most likely to participate in conflict.

B. Two Challenges: Nuclear Weapons and the End of the Cold War

The past 40 years have shown two outstanding challenges to theorists interested in forms of warfare: one centering on the impact of new weapons technology that altered both the power and range of modern arms, and the second emerging from structural changes accompanying the Cold War's end. The invention and proliferation of nuclear weapons has in many ways changed the character of international conflict. Robert Jervis's 1989 *The Meaning of the Nuclear Revolution* argues that the tremendous destructiveness of nuclear weapons forced fundamentally new calculations onto state leaders. In Jervis's view, these weapons compelled nuclear powers to work toward mutual security rather than unilateral interest in their interactions. In his 1990 article "Nuclear Myths and Political Realities," Kenneth Waltz reasons to similar conclusions based on his recognition that states cannot defend themselves entirely from nuclear weapons. This technologically imposed vulnerability shifts the emphasis of conflict away from war fighting—severing any possible connection between military and political objectives—and pushes states to work toward mutual security. More broadly, John Mueller's *Retreat from Doomsday* argues that tremendous increases in warfare's destructive force over the past 100 years so raised the costs of major war as to make it obsolete.

The invention of nuclear weapons, however, did not alone shape conflict during the Cold War; equally decisive was the distribution of those weapons between relatively evenly matched bipolar camps. Since this structural distribution began to change in 1989, however, international relations theorists have struggled to understand how this shift will influence inter-state conflict. Their assessments range from the pessimistic to the hopeful. John Gaddis has described the Cold War as the "long peace" and argues that its most important confrontations—the Cuban missile crisis, the U2 incident, and the Berlin crisis—all occurred before the mid-1960s, when both Soviet and American forces were groping to learn basic rules of the nuclear stand-off. Having deciphered one another's strategic orientation following these confrontations, the Cold War rivals interacted in ways at once more regular and less antagonistic. For Gaddis, the new international structure promises uncertainty and so danger. K. J. Holsti's *The State, War, and the State of War* expects the new multipolar context to accelerate the emergence of new conflict forms: what he calls wars of a third kind. Distinct from the limited wars of the 18th century and the total wars of the early 20th, wars of the third kind are typically internal struggles for unification, liberation, or succession: drawn-out wars of attrition that make little distinction between combatants and civilians. Kumar Rupesinghe also argues that conflicts over identity, race, and ideology will proliferate in a post-Cold War era. Without the support of Cold War sponsors, weak states presiding over contentious nations will cease to have a monopoly over coercive force—producing new forms of insecurity.

On balance, however, there has been at least as much optimism at the end of the Cold War as pessimism. On the one hand, those who celebrate the stability of the Cold War often do not acknowledge the tremendous human costs of proxy conflicts in the third world. George Kahin's *Intervention* and Walter Lefever's *Inevitable Revolutions* are particularly outstanding examples of a large body of scholarly work demonstrating that superpowers regarded third world civil struggles as appropriate proxies for the larger ideological contest, often to devastating effect. Such work makes too sanguine an assessment of Cold War peace rather difficult to sustain. On the other hand, many welcome the new political possibilities of the post-Cold War period. The contributors to *Beyond Confrontation: Learning Conflict Resolution in the Post-Cold War Era* regard the new global arrangement as a moment of opportunity during which methods of nonviolent conflict resolution might more successfully come into play than previously. *Beyond Westphalia: State Sovereignty and International Intervention* contains several chapters that argue for the expanded possibility of international cooperation to secure human rights and environmental protection.

For analysts outside the realist tradition, the passing of the Cold War accelerated an existing movement to undertake a more fundamental, and often hopeful, reexamination of inter-state conflict. Scholars increasingly question the centrality of power resources to the development or management of conflict. In an important new anthology, for example, Peter Katzenstein and his collaborators examine cultural dimensions of security norms. Johan Galtung, among the most prominent writers in the field of peace studies, has defined peace as a context in which conflicts can be resolved without violence—a definition that focuses attention on methods of intersubjective conflict resolution. In his 1996 volume *Peace by Peaceful Means: Peace and Conflict, Development and Civilization*, Galtung urges a critical stance toward the cultural categories that transform issues of conflict into violent conflict. Others elaborate this critical theory in international relations. In the anthology *On Security*, Ole Waever's chapter argues that security cannot be viewed in empirical terms, but rather must be regarded as a speech act of state leaders. In defining interest, threat, and security, state leaders and analysts—including academic proponents of realist theories of conflict—create and legitimate conflictual behavior. Hence, a more critical examination of these speech acts might allow populations to redefine security in ways that do not threaten conflict.

Despite the variety of these perspectives, perhaps one notion ties them together, however loosely: analysts seem more convinced that processes of conflict resolution, diplomacy, and learning among international actors can reduce the intensity and frequency of conflict between states. Galtung's work rests almost entirely on the premise that we can discover methods of interacting that will diffuse tension between states. Even Gaddis's nostalgia for the Cold War depends on his observation that major world powers had learned how to work within that system—this conviction holds the possibility that we can also learn to work within the arrangement currently unfolding. Work on the process of diplomacy also relies a great deal on accumulated knowledge: George and Craig's diplomatic history *Force and Statecraft* argues that state leaders should strive to limit conflict by introducing pauses in hostilities to give contestants the opportunity to negotiate settlements or reverse military escalations. Some of the most important policy debates, not the least of which sparked by then-UN Secretary-General Bhutros-Ghali's *An Agenda for Peace*, set forth positions on methods of preventive diplomacy, dispute resolution, and establishing global rights and interests. Perhaps more people than ever before seem convinced that such goals now lie within our grasp.

C. Domestic Contention, the Collective Repertoire, and Protest Cycles

Until recently, comparativists treated revolutions, riots, crime waves, and social movements as separate phenomena, each with its own literature. The study of conflict thus developed an internal segregation separating different forms of struggle from one another. Few asked what forces shaped contention. Why, for example, did discontent produce revolution in one setting and protest in others? Why do once-common practices like tarring and feathering pass into disuse? Instead of explaining the historical relationship between modes of struggle, scholars once opted to design their studies around single contentious form—peasant revolt (as in the work of James Scott) or crowd violence (as in that of George Rude)—set clearly apart from others. Someone who wrote about revolution might consequently ignore periods of protest that failed to reach a state-shaking climax. Theda Skocpol's 1979 work carefully distinguishes social revolutions from purely political transitions and then delineates conditions under which revolutions occur (though she does examine some negative cases for comparative perspective). Defined as separate phenomena from the outset, her cases thus appear almost congenitally revolutionary. Similarly, students of social movements once commonly assumed that their subjects had little interest in or capacity for seizing state power; work on protest often assumed that movement participants seek more limited goals of reform or voice in existing political systems.

Yet in defining cases in terms of contentious form, analysts often missed an essential dynamic at the heart of conflict. In the process of asserting power over an adversary or recruiting support, claim-makers readjust and redefine their activities. The process of contention requires participants to negotiate a fit between a constituency's demands and political opportunities, a process shaped by social structures and the exigencies of struggle. Moreover, forms of struggle are themselves a product of prevailing cultures and models of struggle, forms which themselves change over the years. Unfortunately, much early scholarship had relatively little to contribute toward an understanding of how forms of struggle operate socially or politically, either in the long term or during a single episode of protest.

More recently, however, forms of struggle have themselves attracted scholarly attention. A broadening circle of analysts have set out to describe both long- and short-term influences on contentious forms. In this new scholarship, modes of struggle emerge as expressions of the larger contest for power, and understanding what claim-makers do collectively has become as important a research goal as understanding when and in what numbers they act. Writing from the standpoint of broad historical shifts, some scholars link the evolution of collective forms to macrochanges in human society—processes of state building, centralization, deindustrialization, and the expansion of communication and transportation networks. Others examine shorter-term influences on forms of collective action and try to express how interactions between different actors involved in a specific struggle shape the process of contention.

Ideas about which long-term forces mold contentious expressions developed differently on either side of the Atlantic. Beginning in the United States (but with significant adherents in Latin America) analysts adopted the idea of the collective repertoire to describe the forms of action at any historicocultural moment that both engaged existing social and political structures and resonated with existing cultural forms. Charles Tilly, whose 1986 book *The Contentious French* introduced the concept of the collective repertoire, later argued that the British invented political demonstrations in the 18th century, more or less apace with the growing role of national parliament. Yet the practice of demonstration also reproduced itself culturally: as more people made claims via demonstrations, they grew less likely to seize bread stores or to tar and feather tax collectors. Lynne Hunt focuses on this cultural aspect of conflict. Her seminal 1984 work described the image of Hercules as capturing the character of the French spirit of resistance. "The repertoire," Sidney Tarrow underscores in his 1994 *Power in Movement,* "is at once a structural and cultural concept."

As the contentious repertoire developed into an accepted concept in the United States, European analysts refined the concept of the new social movement. Writers like Alberto Melucci and Ruud Koopmans claimed that new aspects of modern society produced forms of social movements that differed sharply from what had come before. New forms of oppression (or perhaps a new recognition of old forms) produced "new social movements" organized around issues of peace and identity that joined more established class-based movements. Theorists in this school argued that postindustrial society replaced what had been a single dominant locus of oppression (between capital and labor) with multiple oppressive loci including that between men and women, state and civil society, the young and old, and between different racial communities. New forms of movement organization (nonhierarchical) and decision-making (consensual) developed in new social

movements as well so that the methodology of protest came to reflect issues of collective concern.

Yet other perspectives on long-term influences over protest emerged from outside the West. T. K. Oomen cautions readers against the too-facile application of Western theory to places like India. In Oomen's view, Western perspectives on social movements contain two important biases: one emphasizes individual participant interests and the other assumes firm boundaries between states, markets, and civil societies. Western protest forms typically involve individuals within civil society making claims against states and economic authorities. In contrast, non-Western and ex-socialist states often themselves attempt to create and control basic elements of the market and society. The polity's central role in these institutions prevents one from assuming that movements will emerge from the society to make claims against the polity or the market. Rather, the location of claim-makers and the direction of their antagonism will be more fluid. One must expect as many struggles to take place between social groups as between society and the state and indeed society itself will be hotly contested terrain. Conversely, social movements may also emerge from within the state or the market, and in most cases, social networks rather than individual decisions will most strongly influence participation. Others writing in the southern hemisphere stress other points of departure for a distinctly non-Western analysis of social movements. For Ponna Wignaraja, social movements in the global South reflect the failure of anticolonial and mainstream development models to meet human needs. As the inadequacies of both models grew clearer, new paradigms for social change emerged around ideas of popular participation in policy-making, decentralization of authority, and microorganizational forms.

Other work attempts to indicate the forces at work within specific episodes of protest and resistance. Two main concerns animate the inquiry into protest's shorter-term dynamic. The first focuses on the dynamic of movement activity at different points in the mobilization curve and examines the relationship between authorities, claim-makers, and the broader society. The second concerns interactions between different movements and countermovements mobilizing at roughly the same time and influencing one another's fortunes in what has come to be called a cycle of protest.

Protest and conflict are extraordinary phenomena that pull participants away from established routines and individual economic activity. Contention compels participants to set aside activities like tending crops, going to work, or preparing for exams. Indeed, the economic costs of such participation, and the variable ability of different populations to shoulder those costs, have long been considered important influences on contentious behavior, as Edelman argues in *Proletarian Peasants: The Revolution of 1905 in Russia's Southwest*. For the study of individual moments of contention, the implications of the point are clear: individual movements have a notoriously difficult time sustaining the upward thrust of mobilization. Initially, claim-makers respond to opportunities by presenting an interpretation, or collective frame, of grievances that assign blame and formulate an appeal for redress. The movement may capture popular imagination or take the state by surprise; political allies inside the polity may promote the movement's efforts—but often in ways narrowly circumscribed by the overlap between elite and claim-makers' interests.

The moments of powerful and spontaneous mobilization produced by expanding political opportunities, however, are typically fleeting. Hence a good deal of movement activity aims to compensate for changes in political opportunity, faltering external alliances, weakening participant support, or fading popular interest. But in the face of these inherent pressures toward demobilization, how do movements typically respond? Some move toward greater organization, but this effort often diverts energy away from collective action, a point argued first and most clearly by Piven and Cloward in their 1977 book *Poor People's Movements*. Some radicalize, adopting tactics that raise the stakes, heighten conflict, and require smaller numbers of more devoted activists than would massed demonstrations (see della Porta and Tarrow's 1986 article, "Unwanted Children: Political Violence and the Cycle of Protest in Italy, 1966–73"). Other movements institutionalize, either by accepting state offers to work in cooperation with government leaders or by converting movement organizations geared toward external advocacy to more stable public interest groups or service organizations—what Jane Mansbridge describes as "professionalization" in her 1986 book *Why We Lost the ERA*. Other movements replace extroverted struggles against adversaries with internal efforts to provide for participant needs; Boudreau's 1996 "Of Motorcades and Masses" links the rise of Philippine nongovernmental organizations in the late 1980s to movement activists' efforts to retain a mass base by providing concrete services. Tarrow's 1994 work provides a good summation of the puzzle in the arguments that the choice between radicalization and institutionalization constitutes a primary dilemma for demobilizing movements. In either case, changes in movement politics are triggered by decreasing resources and opportunities.

A different perspective emerges from those who take a longer view of protest by concentrating on "cycles of protest" composed of several different movements rising at roughly the same time. Such clustering, of course, should not be surprising, for if contention rises in response to external opportunities or pressures, then more than one movement might surely rise in response to openings or changes in that structure. Goldstone's 1991 *Rebellions and Revolutions in the Early Modern World*, for example, associated global clusterings of protest and state breakdowns in the 17th and 18th centuries with broadly synchronous increases in population pressure on existing institutions. Yet scholars concerned with cycles of protest, Sidney Tarrow again most prominent among them, also worry about the interactions between different movements within the cycle. For Tarrow, the cycle's most important dynamic is that its early risers expand political opportunities, and this encourages subsequent mobilization by other groups. Others, such as David Meyer and Suzanne Staggenborg, examine dynamics between movement and countermovements in cycles of protest. Reflecting on the apparently denser and more rapid spread of contention in the modern era, Valerie Bunce and Dennis Chong noted the speed with which contentious strategies and perspectives spread from one country to another.

It is in the convergence between studies of protest cycles and of evolving repertoires where we find the most provocative perspectives on the evolution of contention in the contemporary world. As scholars acquired a broader understanding of the interaction at the heart of protest cycles, they also noted the increasing speed and density of those interactions over the past decades. Transnational connections between states have intensified external pressures on the state and provided more channels along which movement politics might diffuse from one group to others. At least a partial consequence of this increased international connection to domestic politics is a denser and more fully-supported organizational fabric in many societies. In *Turbulence in World Politics*, James Rosneau argues that associations and movement organizations are becoming at once more connected to one another transnationally and more autonomous from their national states—something that he links to increases in protest and contention worldwide. Tarrow ends *Power in Movement* with the question of whether changes in political institutions are currently creating "movement societies" in which mobilization and contention will be more widespread and common. In the work of people like Tarrow and Rosneau, the anticipation of deeper and broader conflict emerges from an understanding both of how modern structural changes are influencing the pattern of protest and of how denser associational life will produce more complicated interactions, and so larger cycles, of protest.

IV. CONCLUSION

The first half of this article described a convergence in the study of violence, peace, and conflict and the growth of more common perspectives between analysts in the respective schools of international relations and comparative politics. Indeed, a fair amount of cross-pollination has already taken place between theories of international relations and domestic contention. Early work on contention often proceeded from either a purely structural or agent-centered perspective—but this no longer is the case. Culturalists now increasingly look to explain patterns of interaction by looking for their structural wellsprings, even as structuralists have increasingly read actors' interpretations of structural opportunities and threats in terms that incorporate cultural perspectives. Questions of rationality, national interest, and movement objective have been recast in ways that break down older divisions in the literature and yield a more nuanced interpretation of conflict, peace, and violence.

Similarly, analysts' expectations of how contemporary changes will influence the shape of conflict draw considerable mutual support across disciplinary divisions between comparative politics and international relations. Many of the changes that influence the shape of conflict have roots in important developments in human society. As webs of cross-border connection grow between states and societies, conflict and contention will require increasingly transnational frames of analysis. Following the Cold War, many anticipated more frequently negotiated solutions to international conflicts—though others anticipate increased Northern indifference to global poverty and conflict. Alongside developments in the international realm, increasing connections between and within societies suggest that claim-makers may now have at their disposal stronger and more integrated vehicles for the expression of dissent and the generation of solidarity than ever before—and the balance between states and societies may resolutely be shifting toward social empowerment. As international relations analysts increasingly argue that major wars are less likely—as they develop prescriptions that allow state-makers to avoid such con-

flicts—many nonetheless fear the rise of new forms of domestic conflict: Holsti's "wars of a third kind" or Rupesinghe's fears over identity conflicts within states. The fear is echoed among analysts of domestic political contention. Movement perspectives and issues diffuse more quickly now than before. Given current technology of mass communication and transportation, the organizational links between communities separated by great physical distance and what seems the relative decline (at least in some parts of the world) of state authority, the power at the hands of social movements is potentially staggering.

International relations theorists have long been so concerned with great power conflict that the prospect of smaller wars, no matter their eventual cost, seemed a relief, particularly given the specter of nuclear annihilation that hovered throughout the Cold War. Yet domestic explosions can be just as bloody, and not a whit more tractable, as major wars. It is, perhaps, a lesson we are learning in the 1990s—the decade of the Los Angeles riots, genocide in Rwanda, and ethnic civil war in the former Yugoslavia—that small confrontations between neighbors and communities waged over issues as personal as identity or dignity can be as compelling and devastating as any between great powers over grand ideals. And if many analysts fear the generalization of conflict in the decades to come, then it is perhaps also appropriate to recall that the expansion and diffusion of conflict have accompanied—indeed even partially defined—the 1989 revolutions in Eastern Europe and the wave of prodemocracy movements that moved through Latin America and that are now sweeping East and Southeast Asia.

Also See the Following Articles

CONFLICT THEORY • COOPERATION, COMPETITION, AND CONFLICT • DECISION THEORY AND GAME THEORY • INTERNATIONAL RELATIONS, OVERVIEW • MILITARISM AND DEVELOPMENT IN UNDERDEVELOPED SOCIETIES • NUCLEAR WARFARE • PEACE AND DEMOCRACY • POLITICAL SYSTEMS AND CONFLICT MANAGEMENT • POWER, SOCIAL AND POLITICAL THEORIES OF

Bibliography

Ashley, R. (1981). Political realism and human interests. *International Studies Quarterly*, 25(2) 204–236.
Galtung, J. (1996). *Peace by peaceful means: Peace and conflict, development and civilization*. Oslo: Peace Research Institute of Oslo Press.
Gurr, T. R. (1971). *Why men rebel*. Princeton, NJ: Princeton University Press.
Jervis, R. (1976). *Perception and misperception in international politics*. Princeton, NJ: Princeton University Press.
Katzenstein, P. (Ed.) (1996). *The culture of national security: Norms*

and identity in world politics. New York: Columbia University Press.

Lyons, G., & Mastenduno, M. (Eds.) (1995). *Beyond Westphalia? State sovereignty and international intervention.* Baltimore: Johns Hopkins University Press.

McAdam, D., Tarrow, D., & Tilly, C. (1996). To map contentious politics. *Mobilization, An International Journal, 1*(1), 17–34.

McAdam, D., Tarrow, D., & Tilly, C. (1982). *The political process and the development of black insurgency.* Chicago: University of Chicago Press.

Meyer, D. S. (1990). *A winter of discontent: The nuclear freeze and American politics.* New York: Praeger.

Moore, B. (1966). *Social origins of dictatorship and democracy: Peasant and lord in the making of the modern world.* Cambridge, MA: Harvard University Press.

Morgenthau, H. (1978). *Politics among nations: The struggle for power and peace.* New York: Knopf.

O'Donnell, G. (1973). *Modernization and bureaucratic authoritarianism: Studies in South American politics.* Berkeley: Institute for International Studies, University of California.

Skocpol, T. (1979). *States and social revolutions: A comparative analysis of France, Russia and China.* Princeton, NJ: Princeton University Press.

Tarrow, S. (1994). *Power in movement.* New York: Cambridge.

Tilly, C. (1993). Contentious repertoires in Britain, 1758–1843. *Social Science History, 17,* 253–280.

Tilly, C. (1978). *From mobilization to revolution.* Reading, MA: Addison–Wesley.

Waltz, K. (1979). *Theory of international politics.* Reading, MA: Addison–Wesley.

Popular Music

Marjorie J. Hogan
Hennepin County Medical Center

Victor C. Strasburger
University of New Mexico

GLOSSARY

Rock Music Music currently preferred by adolescents and preadolescents; also called popular music.

Music Television (MTV) Comprises performance music videos (in which a singer or group of musicians sings a song), concept music videos (in which a story is added to the song), regular programming, and advertising.

Music Videos This medium pairs a musical number with visual images.

POPULAR MUSIC refers to music currently preferred by preadolescents or adolescents. In this context, popular music is synonymous with rock music and includes such subtypes as hard rock, soft rock, rap, heavy metal, new wave, punk, hip-hop, salsa, soul, and traditional rock 'n' roll.

I. INTRODUCTION

Throughout the ages, music has provided entertainment, identity, education, and emotion to cultures and peoples. Music celebrates, mourns, incites, and calms; it can profoundly affect attitudes, moods, and emotions. Music has sent soldiers to war to the sound of fife and drum. During the Vietnam War years, antiwar themes in popular songs unified American adolescents and young adults and echoed the growing fervor for peace. Today, background music to entice or lull the listener is common in stores and offices. As stated in the *Anthology of Music* by A.P. Merriam: "The importance of music, as judged by the sheer ubiquity of its presence is enormous ... there is probably no other human cultural activity which is so all pervasive and which reaches into, shapes and often controls so much of human behavior."

The purpose of this article is to examine and to attempt to understand the impact of popular music, especially rock music, on violence, peace, and conflict.

II. HISTORY

With the inception of rock 'n' roll in America in the 1950s, popular music has been synonymous with music enjoyed by adolescents. And, ever since parents and other adults first expressed concern over suggestive rock 'n' roll lyrics and Elvis Presley's pelvic gyrations, popular music themes have continued to evolve, becoming increasingly graphic and provocative.

Music that is popular with the preadolescent and adolescent subculture is often symbolic, a marker of identity during the tumultuous teen years, that features themes of rebellion and risk. Popular music must be controversial, antiestablishment, and disliked by adults in order to allow young people to define themselves. When adolescents move into adulthood, they often bring their popular music along (perhaps reluctant to relinquish important markers of youth); as a result, rock music must evolve and mutate in order to remain meaningful to the next generation of teenagers. And, if popular music is co-opted by adults in society (e.g., using the Beatles' controversial hit "Revolution" to sell everyday products) youth music must become more outrageous and more controversial to be symbolically independent and antiestablishment.

Historically, some parents and advocacy groups have attempted unsuccessfully to regulate or censor bothersome popular songs. In 1985, the Parent Music Resource Center, a nonprofit citizens' group, prompted public discussions on objectionable lyrics, leading to Senate hearings on the issue. The PMRC called for labeling of music with notices alerting parents to violent or sexually explicit lyrics. Today, religious, medical, and political groups have added voices to the growing concern about explicit music lyrics that convey negative and possibly harmful health messages for adolescents. Even judges have heard arguments about the risks posed by popular music, specifically in cases when violent adolescent behavior was blamed on rock music lyrics and themes. In several separate instances, parents have attempted to bring suit against heavy metal performers, blaming suggestive lyrics for the death of their teenagers by suicide. On the basis of constitutionally guaranteed free speech rights, Ozzie Osborne, Judas Priest, and CBS were acquitted in high-profile cases, but public debate continues about the influence of rock music lyrics and music artists on young listeners.

Although the concerns are not new, today the stakes are higher for adolescents, and the lyrics and images are far more graphic. The American Academy of Pediatrics' 1996 position statement reports: "Such lyrics are of special concern in today's environment, which poses unprecedented threats to the health and well-being of adolescents. Pregnancy, drug use, acquired immune deficiency syndrome (and other sexually transmitted diseases), injuries, homicide and suicide have all become part of the landscape of everyday life for many American teens." An analysis of selected harmful themes in current rock music includes:

1. Glamorizing of drugs and alcohol;
2. Suicide presented as alternative or solution;
3. Graphic violence;
4. Preoccupation with the occult;
5. Unhealthy, disrespectful, or violent sex.

Understanding the history of popular music and the legacy of concern engendered by lyrics and the influence of performers is important in focusing the debate at the turn of the century. Does consumption of popular music have a behavioral impact on young people? Is the enjoyment of rock music merely characteristic of the adolescent subculture or does it incite teenagers to riot? Does the adolescent's environment, including his or her consumption of popular music, play a role in the subsequent development of harmful behaviors, including involvement in or approval of violence?

III. ADOLESCENT DEVELOPMENT

A. Tasks of Adolescence

Adolescence, which is often a time of stress for young people, marks the transition from childhood to adulthood. Many skills are learned, and many tasks negotiated. Tasks include the consolidation of personal and sexual identities, the acceptance of independence and autonomy, the forging of a moral value system, and the adoption of appropriate standards of adult behavior (see Table I). Physically, socially, emotionally, and cognitively, the adolescent is evolving through profound and critical changes. Although most youths ultimately complete the journey to adulthood, coping skills and strong, positive role models are necessary tools for their safe travel.

B. Mass Media as Teacher

During these years, adolescents may learn life's lessons and coping skills from parents and other important

---

TABLE I

Adolescent Developmental Tasks

1. Consolidation of personal and sexual identities.
2. Acceptance of independence and autonomy.
3. Forging of a moral value system.
4. Adoption of appropriate standards of adult behavior.

adults; however, the mass media are also sources of information. In fact, adolescents tend to learn about controversial issues through television, music, or movies, rather than from parents or school. Whatever the medium, adolescents learn attitudes and adult behavior standards by observing the attractive adult role model. Communications research shows conclusively that television is a powerful cultural storyteller, as well as one that places heavy viewers at risk for aggressive or antisocial behavior, desensitization to violence, and an altered worldview.

Additionally, heavy adolescent users of the mass media, including television, radio, music, and magazines, demonstrate an increased incidence of risky behaviors. Media portrayals may provide scripts of behavior that are accessible to adolescents, particularly scripts that involve violent, sexual, or other risky behavior. Whether toddler or teen, learning occurs through observation, imitation, and incorporation of modeled behavior. As hours spent watching television decrease with age, the hours spent listening to music increase rapidly, usually at around age 9 or 10 years. In fact, for both sexes, listening to music is first choice both as a leisure activity and a coping strategy.

C. Why Do Adolescents Listen to Music?

Music is very important to preadolescents and adolescents; for 81%, music is a central facet in their lives. As a popular leisure activity, listening to music occupies many hours and fills many needs for young people, including socialization and identity formation (see Table II). Popular music, with its antiestablishment and rebellious themes, forges strong bonds between teens, reinforces the identity of the peer group, and draws a clear boundary between the adult and the teen worlds. Music lyrics and music videos may symbolize crucial

TABLE II
Adolescent Needs Met Through Popular Music

1. Relaxation.
2. Mood regulation.
3. Social or entertainment—friends, parties.
4. Silence-filling.
5. Expressive—identification with group, performer, subculture.
6. Socialization, identity formation.
7. Information or education.
8. Symbolic—independence, autonomy.
9. Loneliness or boredom.

adolescent themes of independence and autonomy. Music is also entertainment and encourages movement, dancing, and expressiveness. Music may create, alter, or intensify a mood, and for some youths, it may fill a void of loneliness or boredom. In many homes, music is on all day, acting as silence filler against a backdrop of studying or socializing. The role music plays varies between individual adolescents and groups of adolescents. Listening to music may be a solitary activity in one's bedroom or a group activity with friends at a rock concert or party. Music has also become ubiquitous. From the earlier days of heavy, unwieldy radios has emerged the modern-day miniature, portable headphone—adolescents can surround themselves with their favorite music, carrying it along on their life journey.

Teens may identify strongly with a particular genre of popular music, for instance, rap or heavy metal, leading to instant rapport and understanding with a larger group of fans. Clothing choices, speech patterns, attitudes, and interests may be dictated by allegiance to a music subtype. Studies have found adolescents who function poorly in school may feel alienated and negative about academic pursuits, and so, may be drawn toward music with themes of alienation or anger. In this way, disenfranchised youths may seek an identity with a group of like adolescents through music choice. Studies have shown that school achievement dictates music choice, and not the reverse. Also, very young adolescent fans of rock music tend to be influenced more by peers than by their parents.

Music performers also play important roles in adolescents' lives. They are role models and may provide "scripts" for adult behavior, life and death, and define success and happiness for many young fans. For these reasons, egregious on-stage (or on-video) antics by music artists, featuring violence or graphic sexuality, make profound, imitable impressions on adolescents. On a positive note, studies note that heavy metal fans not uncommonly pick up guitars themselves to make music.

Music also exerts influence over adolescents as consumers, as when corporate America sells goods or services by using popular music themes or attractive musical performers. Understanding adolescent developmental realities and the importance of music for youth, it is likely that the symbolism of popular music with its themes of rebellion and angst, the compelling and unique rhythms, and the appeal of the musical artists are more important than the specific messages in rock music lyrics or the images in music videos.

IV. ROCK MUSIC LYRICS

A. Definitions

Societal concerns about music lyrics and negative influence exerted by performers commonly are centered on heavy metal and rap music. The former, including such groups as Metallica, Black Sabbath, Megadeath, and Slayer, and typified by loud, pulsating rhythms, reliance on bass guitars and drums, and themes of violence, hate, death, the occult, and dominance over women, has become increasingly popular. Once a fringe subtype of popular music, heavy metal has become a lucrative industry, largely through sales of recordings and tickets to well-attended concerts.

Rooted in the African-American culture, rap music is best described as talking or chanting to a driving musical beat. Rap is often replete with angry, violent, and misogynistic themes, but may also feature prosocial themes of drug abuse prevention, nurturing, or positive relationships. A controversial song called "Cop Killer" by Ice-T with lyrics of "I'm 'bout to bust some shots off / I'm 'bout to dust some cops off" and a chant of "Die, Die, Die, Pig, Die!" led to police organizations demanding the recall of the track and a general outcry about the dangerous messages in the song. Although rap is quite popular with African American youth, there is significant crossover with adolescents of other ethnic and racial backgrounds.

Other genres of popular music also feature distinctive beats, instrumentation, and themes and tend to be more mainstream in the values espoused in the lyrics. Although adolescents of different ethnic, racial, or cultural backgrounds, as well as different gender, may be more attracted to a particular form of popular music, there is clearly crossover. Musical preferences may reflect developmental struggles faced by distinct subgroups of adolescents during their lives. Young females often confront different challenges than do males, and at the same time, struggles confronting youths of color may be at times similar, but at times very different, from those facing other youths. Music choices may reflect or symbolize these struggles.

B. Consumption

Paralleling a decrease in the number of hours spent viewing television, time spent listening to popular music continues to increase through the preadolescent and adolescent years. Klein's study of more than 2700 adolescents found them listening to popular music an aver-age of 40 hours per week; in late adolescence, television viewing added to time spent listening to music averaged between 4 and 5 hours daily. Often, adolescents listen to music while engaged in other activities—studying, socializing, driving the car, or eating meals. In sum, between 7th and 12th grades, adolescents listen to an average of more than 10,500 hours of popular music; this nearly equals the number of hours spent in school from kindergarten through high school.

Studies have shown that heavy users of media, including music, have more academic problems in school. Low school achievement leads to alienation from school for some students; immersion in the rock music culture may be an adaptation to school failure through identification with a music subculture. Students with positive attitudes about school and a history of school achievement tend to prefer music that is more mainstream.

C. Comprehension of Music Lyrics

Adults' concern about the graphic, negative nature of popular music lyrics is not new, although unquestionably, the recent deterioration of lyrics demands societal attention. Even if there is no evidence to prove that rock music lyrics can encourage aberrant behavior in young listeners, "objections to sexually explicit or violent lyrics CAN exist on common sense, philosophical, aesthetic, humanistic, or public health grounds as well as on scientific grounds."

Research indicates that most young adolescents do not know or understand the lyrics to their favorite songs. In one study, only 30% of teens generally, and only 40% of heavy metal fans, were aware of lyrics. Furthermore, even knowing the lyrics did not ensure comprehension of a song's meaning for adolescents. Only 10% of 4th graders understood the theme behind Madonna's "Like a Virgin," and only 50% of college students correctly interpreted Bruce Springsteen's "Born in the USA" as a song about alienation, not patriotism.

In general, the ability to interpret the lyrics of songs increases with age, consonant with adolescents moving from a concrete to a more abstract stage of cognitive development. The ability to recognize and interpret lyrics to rock songs varies with an individual adolescent's motivation, experience, and knowledge. Notably, adults and adolescents interpret lyrics differently. Even when adults hear references to explicit sexuality or graphic violence, young people may tend to report themes of love, friendship, growing up, and life's struggles. Not only do many preadolescents and adolescents lack life experience about controversial issues, but they may lack the cognitive ability to understand complex or metaphorical messages. Thus, when a teenager listens to a "favorite song", he or she may enjoy the rhythm and beat, the aura of the musical artist, the comfort of an identity, or a symbolism inherent in startling adults with rock music. In a study from Southern California, teenage subjects were unable to identify any theme in their favorite songs 37% of the time, and themes of sex, violence, or drugs were identified in only 7% of songs. Even then, the interpretations tended to be literal and naive. Songs with violent content may be particularly unintelligible because of a characteristic driving, loud, fast beat, and therefore, may lack significant impact on young listeners.

D. Behavioral Impact of Rock Music Lyrics

The scientific literature is replete with studies documenting the effects of television on young minds—that debate is over. Heavy viewers of violent television not only may manifest antisocial and aggressive behavior as a result of social learning in front of the screen, but also become desensitized to violence and view the world as a hostile, sinister place. While not the sole, or most important root cause of violence in society, televised violence plays a critical role in teaching youngsters dangerous lessons about the world, relationships, and the premier role of violence in modern life.

We know less about the other forms of the mass media, but extrapolating from knowledge about television violence because of its ubiquity, we fear the lessons and messages from violence in video games, on the Internet, on the movie screen, and from music lyrics and images may be equally dangerous. The research into these other forms of mass media is in its infancy, and because confounding factors are difficult to control, much is inferred rather than clearly documented.

Although adolescents spend a great deal of their waking hours listening to rock music, and lyrics are graphic in terms of violence, explicit sex, and other controversial issues, there is no firm evidence that these lyrics and messages translate into violent or harmful behavior by listeners.

Adolescents are active participants in listening to and enjoying their favorite music; song choices are self-censored and may be replayed or fast-forwarded at the listener's whim. Once a teen chooses to listen to certain music to satisfy a need, whether for entertainment, mood enhancing, or filling silence, the message of the music is interpreted by that individual and assimilated accordingly. The interpretation of lyrics and specific needs of the listener are modifiers between the exact

message in the lyrics and any effect on behavior the lyrics might have. Thus, the effect of music lyrics on adolescents is elusive—there are too many variables, among individuals and within one individual at given times.

Some studies have documented worrisome behavior in adolescents choosing heavy metal music as their preferred genre of rock music. Wass showed that 87% of adolescent heavy metal fans knew the lyrics to favorite songs with prominent messages of alienation, suicide, violence, and pessimism. These "metalheads" identified strongly with the artists and identified with the music. In a follow-up study, a relationship was found between youthful offenders' preference for heavy metal music and destructive, antisocial behavior. The dark themes present in heavy metal may trigger harmful behavior in some high-risk youths. In a well-known study of disturbed adolescents, King found that 60% of chemically dependent youth chose heavy metal as their music of choice and the "musical expression of forces at work in their lives," including violence. Three-fourths of the chemically dependent heavy metal fans in this study were involved in violent activity. The conclusion was that a clear-cut cause-and-effect relationship could not be established between heavy metal music and violent, negative behavior. However, a preference for heavy metal music may be an important marker for alienation or antisocial behavior. A summary of five studies suggesting that heavy metal may be associated with alienation, substance abuse, suicide, risk-taking behaviors, or psychiatric disorders is shown in Table III.

Other studies of the heavy metal subculture find that music may serve to purge alienated youth of anger, in fact, decreasing risk of violent or angry behavior. Heavy metal music was found not to specifically cause recklessness; rather adolescents seeking sensation were attracted to both heavy metal music and to reckless behav-

TABLE III

Studies of Heavy Metal Music as Marker for Risk

1. 87% heavy metal fans knew lyrics, identified with destructive themes and artists, felt music would not negatively affect behavior (Wass, et al.).
2. 60% chemically dependent inpatient youths preferred heavy metal; 74% of these patients involved in violence (King).
3. Preference for rock/heavy metal music and feeling worse after listening may indicate vulnerability to suicide (Martin, et al.).
4. Heavy use of media, including music, is associated with multiple risk-taking behaviors (Klein, et al.).
5. Greater the strength of the heavy metal subculture, the higher the youth suicide rate (Stack, et al.)

TABLE IV

Adolescents' Lack of Comprehension of Lyrics

1. Only 30% of adolescents know lyrics to their favorite songs
2. Even if they know the lyrics, children and young adolescents may not comprehend the meaning
3. Comprehension of lyrics increases with age
4. Adults and children or adolescents interpret lyrics differently; this is based on cognitive development
5. Motivation, knowledge, and experience and important factors in ability to comprehend lyrics

ior. If a feeling of alienation leads a youngster to the heavy metal subculture, rather than a heavy metal preference causing alienation, societal concern about the influence of lyrics or performers seems misdirected. Indeed, immersion of a teenager in the heavy metal world may typify not only adolescent alienation, but may also reflect his or her perception of adult society with all its moral and ethical shortcomings.

Healthy, well-adjusted teens may be minimally affected by explicit rock music lyrics. The lack of behavioral effects is likely a combination of lack of comprehension of lyrics and misinterpretation of lyrics, as well as simply not knowing the lyrics. Lyrics are not as important to most adolescent popular music fans as is the beat or rhythm, the persona of the musical artist, or the symbolism of themes of independence and rebellion (see Table IV). A strong family with strongly felt and modeled values, and positive relationships, may well buffer an adolescent from potential negative, harmful media messages. For secure, media literate adolescents, their own value systems influence the evaluation of the meaning of music lyrics, as opposed to messages from music changing the adolescent's own values and beliefs.

V. MUSIC VIDEOS AND MTV

A. Introductions and Definitions

Music videos are viewed in millions of homes around the world by a growing number of preadolescents and adolescents. The concept of the music video has rejuvenated popular music with increased sales of accessories, music, and concert tickets. Popular music now goes far beyond mere music and lyrics to capture the visual senses. Music videos are used by television producers to increase the viewing audience and by record producers to sell music.

There are two types of music videos: performance and concept. Music television includes both types of music videos, as well as advertising and regular programming. Performance videos feature a performer or a musical group singing a song in a studio or at a concert. A concept video adds a storyline or plot to the music selection. The latter type has engendered much of the criticism for images of explicit sex, violence, or a combination of both. In one oft-quoted content analysis, more than 50% of concept videos contain violence or violent themes and more than 75% feature sexual imagery. Even more troublesome, sex and violence are frequently juxtaposed into graphic depictions of violence against women; in violent videos, 81% also included sexual images. In a world where rape and sexual assault are horrifyingly common, sexually violent scenes in the context of entertainment seem unjustifiable and dangerous. Typically, music videos have been male-oriented. Themes in concept music videos include:

1. Visual abstraction or special effects;
2. Sex;
3. Dance;
4. Violence and/or crime.

Images are nihilistic 44% of the time, including themes of death, destruction, aggression against authority, and ridicule of social institutions. Violence may be shown as unconnected segments to maximize shock effect—this emphasizes violence as random and meaningless and may serve to desensitize viewers to the impact of violence.

B. Consumption

With more than 70% of American homes receiving cable service, MTV and VH-1 are available to millions of teenagers and younger children. Tens of millions of homes in more than 40 countries worldwide have access to these images. Nearly half of all teenagers watch music television, viewing between 30 and 120 minutes of music television daily. Music television is also highly profitable, with profits near $100 million yearly, and the effects of the advertising content are considerable. Given the purchasing power of adolescents, MTV uses its powerful, compelling images to urge this market to be influential consumers. Musical performers and tantalizing images are used to sell everything from shoes to beer.

Music television is used differently than either television or radio by adolescents. The former is commonly viewed with peers; the latter is often used as background music. On the other hand, MTV is watched actively, rather than passively, and MTV is chosen for its entertainment value, not as a mood enhancer or social lubricant.

C. Comprehension

In a way that is similar to their comprehension of rock music lyrics, adolescents differ in their ability to understand and interpret messages from music videos. Studies show that viewers differ in their interpretations of music videos based on gender, age, and race, cognitive development, and social background.

Music videos are more than merely television accompanied by music. Teenagers who may not hear or comprehend rock lyrics cannot avoid the vivid visual images on MTV. With their compelling images and themes, videos are self-reinforcing. After an adolescent has viewed a music video, subsequent renditions of the song lead to immediate flashback to the images in the video. When simply listening to a song, the young person supplies his or her own images or meaning of the song. With a music video, that creativity is precluded by the vivid visual cues on the screen.

Studies demonstrate that seeing music videos may decrease a viewer's creativity and inhibit imaginative thinking about a song. Listeners felt that hearing a song alone is more meaningful than seeing an accompanying music video; the song alone engendered greater emotional response from the listener.

D. Behavioral Impact of Music Videos

Although there is no firm evidence of a cause and effect relationship between explicit or violent music lyrics and subsequent negative behavior by listeners, the power of a combination of television images and explicit or violent music is compelling. Youthful viewers of music television report that violent and sexual images heighten the enjoyment but not the appreciation of a performance. Seeing a powerful image on a screen in conjunction with a dangerous, repetitive musical message is likely to be synergistic and reinforcing, enhancing learning and recall.

There are no cause and effect studies linking adolescent behavior with viewing MTV, but this medium certainly seems capable of modeling adult behavior for young viewers. By extrapolating knowledge about the impact of viewing violent television, there is reason to be concerned about the deleterious messages in music videos, including violence, explicit sex, disrespect, and substance use being modeled for and learned by young viewers. Negative behaviors are often validated by attractive, imitable models. Studies show that heavy viewers of television violence have an increased risk of aggressive behavior, an altered worldview, and desensitization to violence. In addition, advertising on television influences smoking and alcohol consumption and sexually explicit television programming distorts young viewers' impressions of healthy sexuality. All these potentially harmful behaviors are heavily represented on music television. Also worrisome is the violent and sexually demeaning world of MTV in which women are unequal, disrespected, and used for gratification only. Will heavy viewers of music television see this as the real world and alter their perceptions and behaviors accordingly? Clearly, more studies are needed.

Information regarding the power of music videos to affect behavior comes from a few studies and several anecdotal events reported in the media. One study suggested that watching violent music videos leads to desensitization of young viewers to violence, both on a short-term and a long-term basis. Greater approval of premarital sex after viewing an hour of MTV was noted in adolescent males; the older subset of these boys also showed less disapproval of violence. Three groups of young African American males viewed violent rap videos, nonviolent rap videos, or no videos. Those viewing the violent videos were more likely to condone violence in general and violence against women, and both groups viewing the rap videos were less likely to approve of high academic aspirations. The first group also reported a higher probability of engaging in violence in the future. In a study eliminating MTV from the wards of a maximum-security forensic hospital for a trial period, a significant decrease in the frequency of violent behavior was noted. In this setting, MTV was felt to be a source of situational cues for violent arousal for patients and provided activation of primitive thought processes via themes of aggression and sexuality. These research studies, albeit few in number, parallel the large body of research in other media.

Theoretically, and anecdotally, music videos can graphically model harmful behavior for young, impressionable viewers. MTV's *Beavis and Butthead* show, not a music video but a cartoon that often refers to music videos, was reported to have modeled arson for a young boy who set fire to his home, killing his infant sister. This incident followed a similar episode involving three girls in Ohio; they started a fire by imitating a scene from the cartoon. Some rap critics have suggested that some episodes of violence among African American youths could be linked to exposure to violent rap music videos. An example is a case of a young rapper listening to Tupac Shakur's violent "2pocalyse Now" before shooting a policeman. Compelling visual images, set to popular music, could theoretically provide scripts of violent or inappropriate behaviors for high risk youths or catalyze antisocial behavior.

With the large and impressive body of existing literature on the effects of television violence on children and adolescents, these few studies pique concern. However, far more research is needed. Despite concerns and the studies, most adolescents seem to watch music videos for the enjoyment, to see "what's hot" or who's popular. "Music video has become a pervasive and influential form of consumer culture and has altered the television viewing, music listening, and record buying habits of the people who constitute its audience."

VI. PROSOCIAL EFFECTS

From ancient times until today, music has been used for its soothing and healing properties. Today, in America, more than 4000 music therapists work with people of all ages who are cognitively impaired, psychiatrically disordered, or physically handicapped. For these individuals, music may allow physical and emotional self-expression.

Research into music therapy suggests positive, therapeutic uses for music in the lives of adolescents. In a juvenile detention center, playing a musical instrument (e.g., guitar, drums, or piano) or singing encouraged self-expression and stress reduction. As a result, these incarcerated youths had fewer acting-out behaviors; an opportunity to demonstrate competence through music was a strong motivator. In a study of young people in a mental health ward, increased aggression was observed while hard rock music was played; however, fewer aggressive acts were noted with the playing of classical romantic music, suggesting a relationship between behavior and music. Music can also be a therapeutic bridge for troubled adolescents, helping them move out of a depressed, hostile, or uncommunicative state. More research is needed on prosocial and therapeutic uses of music.

Many would argue that community-building and cross-cultural understanding may be enhanced through music. The American antiwar movement in the late 1960s and early 1970s was galvanized and defined by the popular music of the era; Woodstock is remembered as the symbol of a place and time celebrating peace and unity. The songs and themes of specific musical groups, including folk singers (such as the Weavers or Peter, Paul and Mary), the Beatles, and even the Grateful Dead

often invoked powerful, yet comforting emotions of harmony, hopefulness, and accord. More recently, well-promoted songs (*We are the World*) have emphasized unity and have appealed to listener empathy. However, as we near the end of the 20th century, the bulk of currently popular music does not promise the same positive impact; the laudable themes of peace and unity are notably absent.

Without a doubt, the possible prosocial contributions of popular music have been largely untapped. That human emotions are susceptible to the lyrics, melodies, and suggestions of musical offerings is not in question—witness the soaring of the spirit of appreciative opera buffs or the audience at a Beethoven symphony. Similarly, popular music writers and artists could focus their considerable creative energies in a positive way, encouraging feelings of cooperation, compassion, and hopefulness in young listeners.

VII. RESPONSE

Further research should be funded and conducted to better understand the influence of music lyrics and music videos on adolescents. Longitudinal, controlled, correlational studies using two groups of adolescents could provide vital information: Which adolescents are at risk? Which music is problematic? What factors provide resilience so that young people can resist harmful messages?

The benefits and costs of parent advisory labels on music products have been debated and continue to be a contentious issue. Record companies have been labeling products (records, tapes, compact discs) voluntarily since 1985, if judged to be violent, sexually explicit, or potentially offensive: the label reads "parent advisory, explicit lyrics." Alternatively, the lyrics could be printed on the cover of the product. Studies suggesting young people do not know lyrics to their favorite songs lead some experts to downplay the importance of labeling. Affixing an advisory label could enhance the appeal of a particular selection to adolescents ("forbidden fruit"), or publishing distasteful lyrics could make them accessible to impressionable youths. In one study evaluating the impact of advisory labels, adolescents liked the labeled music less, but the impact was limited. As experience predicts, teens ultimately responded to the music rather than to the lyrics. In its 1996 policy statement on "The Impact of Music Lyrics and Music Videos on Children and Youth," the American Academy of Pediatrics acknowledges the conflict about labeling popular music; however, it does recommend voluntary descriptive labeling of music content to enhance the awareness of parents and the public. Categories could include: violence, explicit sex, drugs, and offensive language.

Record companies, television producers, and music artists should be encouraged to use the power of their media to broadcast prosocial and health messages for adolescents. With attractive performers, exciting beats and rhythms, and a captive audience, the potential for positive influence is great but untapped. Potential themes and messages could include: relationships, abstinence, pregnancy prevention, STD prevention, racial harmony, drug avoidance, nonviolence, and conflict resolution.

Parents and professionals have important roles to play in promoting media literacy and media education—the only intuitive, creative means of making sense of mass media influences. Media education takes many forms, including encouragment of critical listening and viewing of music lyrics and music videos, parental involvement in selection and discussion about music choices, and provision of alternative activities for adolescents.

Parents and professionals, including pediatricians, should be cognizant of risk factors related to music preference. Adolescents deeply immersed in the rock music subculture with total identification with group or performer may be at risk for harmful lifestyle choices or poor developmental outcomes. Similarly, heavy metal preference may be a marker for alienation. Most often parents should be reassured that music preferences of a well-adjusted, secure adolescent are not indicative of deep pathology, but that communication should be open, honest, and supportive. Parent interest and involvement in an adolescent's life and choices are critical protective factors. While understanding the normal, healthy need for a teenager to express independence and autonomy, parents must transmit their own values and concerns in a nonjudgmental, caring fashion. Parents can also expose children and adolescents to a wide variety of musical styles and they can model interest in all the world of music has to offer.

If parents have concerns about destructive or potentially harmful behavior in their adolescents, including isolation, depression, drug use, school failure, or suicidal ideation, professional help through a primary care physician or mental health worker is essential. Parents and professionals can be important voices in the debate about media and adolescents, holding producers and artists to a higher standard and working with coalition groups to improve the mass media. Censorship is not a legal or reasonable option. Encouragement of media literacy holds the most promise as a response to societal concerns about the content of music lyrics and music videos.

VIII. SUMMARY

Despite the sufficiently small body of existing research, concern about the effects of rock music lyrics and music videos on young people seems warranted when we extrapolate from other media studies. Unfortunately, causal relationships between popular music choices and adolescent behavior and attitudes cannot be shown from currently available information. In all likelihood, music lyrics and music videos only recreate and reaffirm adolescent behavior and attitudes, rather than creating or causing them primarily. Healthy adolescents who are secure in their own families and with their own values, can safely negotiate the minefield of adolescent popular music messages. Although a clear cause and effect relationship is elusive, for a certain subset of vulnerable adolescents, rock music may reinforce harmful behaviors or destructive ideation. The questions: Which adolescents? Which music? What are the risk factors? must be answered with further research. And, while we await answers to these questions, objections to media images and messages to children and adolescents can also exist on "purely aesthetic, humanistic, and philosophical grounds" even if available studies are not unanimous in their conclusions.

Also See the Following Articles

DRUGS AND VIOLENCE • FOLKLORE • JUVENILE CRIME • MASS MEDIA AND DISSENT • MASS MEDIA, GENERAL VIEW • TELEVISION PROGRAMMING AND VIOLENCE

Bibliography

American Academy of Pediatrics, Committee on Communications (1996). Impact of music lyrics and music videos on children and youth. *Pediatrics, 98,* 1219–1221.
Brown, E. F., & Hendee, W. R. (1989). Adolescents and their music: insights into the health of adolescents. *JAMA, 262,* 1659–1663.
Christenson, P. G., & Roberts, D. F. (1990). *Popular music in early adolescence.* Washington, DC: Carnegie Council on Adolescent Medicine.
Hendren, R. L., & Strasburger, V. C. (1993). Rock music and music videos. *Adolescent Medicine: State of the Art Reviews, 4,* 577–587.
Strasburger. V. C. (1995). Rock music and music videos. In *Adolescents and the media: Medical and psychological impact.* Thousand Oaks, CA: Sage.

Pornography

Neil M. Malamuth

University of California, Los Angeles

GLOSSARY

Erotica The word is derived from the name of the Greek god *Eros* and refers to "sexual love." It is typically defined as materials intended to arouse sexual feelings that portray mutually consenting, pleasurable acts. Some writers have emphasized that such materials contain no sexist or violent connotations.

Evolutionary Psychology Scientific approach that applies current knowledge of evolutionary processes to understanding the human mind and behavior.

Obscenity The word is derived from the Latin "*ob*," meaning "to," and the term *caenum*, meaning "filth." It is a legal term that is based on offense to accepted standards of decency or sexual morality. Most states use a definition provided by the U.S. Supreme Court in *Miller v. California,* which considers three criteria. They include considerations of whether the material, taken as a whole, appeals to the prurient interest (i.e., characterized by or lascivious or lustful thoughts or desires), depicts sex in a patently offensive way, and lacks serious literary, artistic, political, or scientific value.

Pornography Derived from the Greek *porne,* meaning "whore," and *graphein,* meaning to write. Pornography literally means the "writing of harlots" or "depictions of acts of prostitutes." It has come to mean materials intended to arouse sexual feelings that may include sexist or violent elements.

Prurient Characterized by lascivious or lustful thoughts or desires.

A VERY LARGE MASS MEDIA INDUSTRY exists throughout the world that produces sexually explicit movies, magazines, books, videos, and various images on the worldwide Internet. Although reliable data regarding this industry are sometimes difficult to obtain, estimated profits are extremely high and indicate that this is a multibillion dollar mass media industry. Not only is this industry a large and important segment of the mass media, but it has often generated a great deal of controversy, rhetoric, and acrimonious debate. One of the major areas of concern in debates about pornography has been the possibility that certain types of portrayals, particularly those referred to as sexually violent ones, may affect some men's attitudinal and other responses to "real world" sexual violence and thereby possibly affect their aggressive behaviors.

This article's focus on the topic of pornography can be meaningfully divided into two major parts. The first describes theory and research regarding the effects of pornography whereas the second part focuses on an evolutionary-based explanation of gender differences in consumption of sexually explicit media.

Numerous efforts have been made to define pornography and distinguish it from other terms, such as erotica. A consensus regarding definitions of terms such as "pornography" or "erotica" does not exist among laypersons, policymakers, or the legal system. A consensus, too, is lacking among researchers. Scientists have approached the issue largely guided by three ideological/theoretical perspectives, including the moralist, feminist, and liberalist approaches. These differ in framing the importance of this topic as primarily about issues such as moral decay, sexuality, oppression of women, free speech, and so on. Each of these theories makes assumptions about human nature. Research has often addressed separate questions raised by each of the three perspectives and has seldom pitted the predictions of one theory against the others. While the moralist perspective focuses on the negative influence of pornography on individuals and social structures, the liberalist perspective generally considers pornography to have negligible and sometimes even beneficial effects. The radical feminist perspective emphasizes the negative effects on women and the power structure between men and women. Each perspective has some findings in support of its position and it is not feasible at this stage to conclude that any one of these theories has been clearly supported while the others have been falsified. It may be that each has some merit under differing conditions.

One thing that is apparent is that there are large gender differences in the consumption of different types of sexually explicit media. Evolutionary psychology provides an explanation for such sex differences based on the evolved sexual strategies that were naturally selected in ancestral environments. Although evolutionary approaches emphasize the possible interactive role of socialization differences as well, explanations based on socialization or cultural differences alone must be better developed if they are to account for the observed differences.

I. DEFINING THE CONCEPTS OF PORNOGRAPHY AND OBSCENITY

Pornography and obscenity have been difficult concepts to define. Supreme Court Justice Potter Stewart even admitted, although he could not define pornography, "he knew it when he saw it" (*Jacobellis v. Ohio*, 1964). Through this infamous admission, he implied that most observers, upon inspection of certain materials would agree whether or not they were pornographic.

There is, however, little agreement among laypersons and policymakers about the definition of pornography. Various commissions have acknowledged the difficulties associated with this concept. Members of the 1970 President's Commission of Obscenity and Pornography complained that attempts to draw conclusions about the effects of pornography have been "marked by enormous confusion over terminology." In addition, the Attorney General's Commission on Pornography (1986) noted that "the range of materials to which people are likely to affix the designation 'pornographic' seems to mean in practice any discussion or depiction of sex to which the person using the word objects" (Attorney General's Commission, 1986, p. 227).

The search for a workable definition is illuminated by understanding of the etiology of the terms pornography and obscenity. One should consider what terms have come to mean in both the legal system and in practice. It is important to distinguish between "conceptual" and "operational" definitions used by communication researchers who have investigated the effects of pornography. Finally, it is important to consider categories of stimuli used by researchers to aid in the definition of terminology.

The three terms most often used in this area are erotica, obscenity, and pornography. The following is a brief summary of the origin of these terms and their definitions:

1. *Erotica.* The word is derived from the name of the Greek god *Eros* and refers to "sexual love." It is typically defined as materials intended to arouse sexual feelings that portray mutually consenting, pleasurable acts. Some writers, such as the noted feminist writer Gloria Steinem, have emphasized that such materials contain no sexist or violent connotations.

2. *Obscenity.* The word is derived from the Latin "*ob*," meaning "to," and the term *caenum,* meaning "filth." It is a legal term that is based on offense to accepted standards of decency or sexual morality. As described below, most American states use a definition provided by the U.S. Supreme Court.

3. *Pornography.* Derived from the Greek *porne,* meaning "whore," and *graphein* meaning to write. Pornography literally means the "writing of harlots" or "depictions of acts of prostitutes." For writers such as Gloria Steinem and others, it has come to mean materials intended to arouse sexual feelings that include sexist or violent elements.

A. Legal Definition

In the legal system, the term obscenity has been used in the evaluation of sexual materials. What is pornographic to the law is not necessarily obscene. *Playboy* and *Penthouse* magazines, for example, might be considered pornographic by some, but they would not be considered legally obscene in most states. In practice, the term obscenity has come to mean those materials, within the broader set of pornographic depictions, that have been adjudicated "obscene" by the courts.

Most states use the 1973 U.S. Supreme Court decision in *Miller v. California* as the legal definition of pornography. To summarize the Court's decision, the material would be judged obscene if the following apply: (a) the average person, applying contemporary community standards, would find that the work, taken as a whole, appeals to the prurient interest; (b) the work depicts sexual conduct in a patently offensive way; and (c) the work, taken as a whole, lacks serious literary, artistic, political, or scientific value.

B. Scientific Definitions

For social scientists studying pornography and its effects, defining this concept has also been problematic. Because the term has been applied loosely to many depictions of human sexuality, inconsistent use of the term pornography has made it difficult to compare results of different studies.

Early research on what is now known as the effects of "pornography" frequently used the term "erotica." The Effects Panel of the 1970 Commission's Report, for example, was titled "The Impact of Erotica." Pornography later became the favored term. For both social scientists and the general public, the term erotica has now come to mean "mutually consenting and pleasurable, sexual expression between adults." Incompatible or contradictory terms such as "aggressive erotica," have unfortunately become part of the research terminology, further complicating research efforts.

1. Conceptual and Operational Definitions

Not only is it important to understand the legal and scientific definitions of pornography, but it is also important to understand pornography both on a conceptual and operational level. Conceptual definitions characterize concepts or classes of phenomena by relating them to other concepts, whereas operational definitions assign meaning to a construct or variable by specifying the activities or "operations" used to measure it. A conceptual definition of "violent pornography" might be material that depicts coercion in a sexually explicit context. An operational definition of this term might involve showing subjects a short film about rape in which a young woman is tied up, stripped, and raped by men.

Prior to the experiment, samples of individuals could be asked to report their perceptions of the intended manipulations (e.g., degree of coercion, sexual explicitness, etc.) or experimental subjects might be asked to respond to validity assessment scales. Research in this area can benefit by greater emphasis on more consistency among researchers in conceptual and operational definitions and more frequent systematic attempts to validate the researcher's distinctions among concepts with ratings by independent observers.

2. Classification of Stimuli and Materials

To reduce the confusion among terms, some researchers have used multicategory classification systems and have validated them with empirical support. For example, in one study the researchers differentiated between erotica, "nonviolent pornography," and violent pornography:

(i) Erotica, which was defined as sexual ". . . images that have as their focus the depiction of mutually pleasurable sexual expression between people who have enough power to be there by positive choice. . . . They have no sexist or violent connotations and are hinged on equal power dynamics between individuals as well as between the model(s) and the camera/photographer." (Senn & Radtke, 1990, p. 144).

(ii) "Nonviolent pornography," which was defined as sexual "images that have no explicitly violent content but may imply acts of submission or violence by the positioning of the models or the use of props. They may also imply unequal power relationships by differential dress, costuming, positioning. . ., or by setting up the viewer as voyeur (the model is engaged in some solitary activity and seems totally unaware or very surprised to find someone looking at her)" (Senn & Radtke, 1990, p. 144). (It should be emphasized that the use of the term "nonviolent" by these investigators and in this chapter differs somewhat from the way it is often used in other areas of this encyclopedia and the literature. The term "nonviolent pornography" is therefore placed in quotation marks throughout this chapter.)

(iii) Violent pornography, which was defined as sexual ". . . images that portray explicit violence of varying degrees perpetrated against one individual by another" (Senn & Radtke, 1990, p. 144).

Using these categories in research, Senn and Radtke found that their subjects, female Canadian undergraduates, could reliably differentiate between these categories of materials. For the stimuli used (depictions taken from *Playboy*, *Penthouse*, and *Hustler*) there was considerable agreement among subjects on about 75% of the materials, but considerable disagreement on about 25% of the materials. Findings also showed exposure to different categories of materials has different effects on subjects. For example, violent and nonviolent pornography were negatively evaluated. Erotica, on the other hand, was positively evaluated. In addition, subjects exposed to violent and nonviolent pornography had increased mood disturbance, while those exposed to erotica or a control condition did not experience these negative effects, suggesting that different types of material have different effects.

II. IDEOLOGICAL/THEORETICAL PERSPECTIVES AS ORGANIZING FRAMEWORKS FOR RESEARCH

The overwhelming role that researchers' ideological stance has on their evaluation of research findings in this area is shown by the widely divergent conclusions that reviewers of the literature have come to. Some reviewers, such as Diana Russell, conclude that the data clearly show strong and consistent effects in a wide variety of areas. Some, such as the Attorney General's Commission on Pornography conclude that there are data that are quite convincing for negative effects of some types of pornography (e.g., violent pornography) but not for other stimuli. Yet others, such as Paul Abramson, believe that the findings are not convincing of negative effects and that considerable evidence actually supports largely beneficial effects of pornography.

It is also important to consider the ethical and practical constraints placed on research studying these complex processes. For example, from a methodological perspective, the ideal study investigating the effects of sexually violent media (which includes violent pornography and other stimuli that combine sex and violence) on children might include having youngsters randomly assigned to view, over several years, sexually violent media. Since for obvious ethical reasons such "ideal" research cannot occur, the studies available typically involve considerable compromises to the limits imposed by various constraints.

In keeping with a book published by Daniel Linz and Neil Malamuth, this article will consider the topic of pornography within three major ideological and theoretical perspectives. These differ in framing the importance of this topic as primarily about issues such as moral decay, sexuality, oppression of women, free speech, and so on. The theories are (1) Conservative-Moralist; (2) Liberal; and (3) Feminist. It will be shown that each of these theories makes assumptions about human nature. These assumptions, in turn, lead to definitions of what is pornographic and predictions about pornography's impact on both individuals and society as a whole. Specific legal and policy decisions about pornography are often based on these predictions. These social/legal policies and their underlying assumptions have also guided the formation of scientific research on the effects of pornography. Specifically, they have influenced the formation of hypotheses and the selection of dependent variables by investigators from among the vast array of outcomes that could be measured. These policies have also influenced the interpretation of ambiguous or inconsistent research results. Finally, the findings from scientific investigations, have, in turn, often been used by policy and lawmakers who operate within each of the perspectives to bolster their notions of what should or should not be done about pornography.

These three theories have explicitly or implicitly been the primary guiding forces underlying pornography research. Such work has often addressed separate questions raised by each of the three perspectives and has seldom pitted the predictions of one theory against the others. Each perspective has some findings in support of its position and it is not feasible at this stage to conclude that any one of these theories has been clearly supported while the others have been falsified. It may be that each has some merit under differing conditions. Rather than attempt to directly contrast these approaches, the presentation below will present examples of supportive research for each of these three theoretical approaches.

A. The Moralist Perspective

1. Explication of the Conservative-Moralist Perspective

Derived from Judeo/Christian theology, the moralist perspective argues that man's creation in the image of God enables him, unlike animals, to choose between good and evil. Although people are viewed as having a certain degree of "free will" or choice, the social environment created in a given culture plays a significant role in the choices made. A society that does not have control over messages portraying undesirable behavior can encourage such behavior among its members. Humans, therefore, have the potential to behave in evil ways when exposed to "tempting social environments."

According to the moralist perspective, sex is a private act engaged in by consenting married adults, primarily for the purpose of procreation. Pornography, therefore, is viewed by moralists as offensive as well as a negative influence on society. Not only does it encourage sexual acts outside the boundaries of private behavior among married adults, but it also publicly displays sex. Through these public displays of sex, pornography sexually arouses consumers in ways that might encourage unacceptable sexual behavior. Some pornography communicates positive messages about adultery, homosexuality, and bestiality, which according to the moralist perspective are unacceptable and undesirable behaviors. Through its emphasis on the importance of sex and sexual gratification, pornography encourages illicit fantasies and acts, degrading sex and marriage.

Not only does exposure to pornography have the power to affect individuals' behavior, but it also has the power to affect the moral climate of a society. Pornography's message of permissiveness can result in sexual promiscuity and a moral climate of laxness. Pornography, therefore can lead to a decrease in authority and can influence other moral institutions. Exposure to pornography, according to the moralist view, has the potential to undermine important social connections and moral judgments, specifically sexual monogamy and the traditional family structure.

2. Research Supporting the Moralist Position

Dolf Zillmann and Jennings Bryant argue that pornography is causally related to the general decline of basic American values. In their research, they tested the moralist assumption that pornography fosters a lack of respect for, and belief in, traditional institutions such as marriage, relations between men and women, and traditional roles for women. With exposure to pornography, viewers may accept "sex crimes," alter perceptions and evaluations of marriage, spawn distrust among intimate partners, inspire claims for "sexual freedom," and even diminish the desire to have children.

Dolf Zillmann and his colleagues argue that exposure to "nonviolent pornography" (a term used in this chapter to refer to pornography that does not contain explicitly violent content) can foster distorted beliefs. Viewers may believe that nontraditional sex acts occur frequently. Furthermore, viewers may believe that women are generally promiscuous, so promiscuous that they will even tolerate rape.

To test whether exposure to pornography resulted in a greater acceptance of nontraditional sex acts and whether perpetrators of rape are punished less severely following exposure to pornography, Dolf Zillmann and

Jennings Bryant exposed 80 unmarried male and 80 unmarried female college students to depictions of heterosexual activities. Subjects viewed "Swedish Erotica" films that depicted heterosexual activities, mainly fellatio, cunnilingus, coitus, and anal intercourse. Subjects received one of four exposures: "massive exposure" (six sexually explicit films per session, approximately 48 minutes, one session per week for 6 weeks, for a total of 4 hours and 48 minutes); "intermediate exposure" (3 films a week for 6 weeks, for a total of 2 hours and 24 minutes) "no exposure" (36 nonerotic films); and a no-treatment control condition where subjects showed up for a session in the final week of the experiment to complete questionnaires only.

After viewing the last film, subjects were assessed on several dependent variables, including estimates of the percentage of American adults that perform common and uncommon sexual acts and recommended prison sentence (in years) for a man described in a newspaper account as a rapist. In addition, subjects completed the sexual callousness toward women scale. Findings showed males and female subjects in the massive exposure condition not only estimated higher percentages of persons involved in uncommon sex acts such as fellatio, cunnilingus, anal intercourse, group sex, sadomasochism, and bestiality. Subjects with this intense exposure were also more lenient in their punishment of the rapist. Furthermore, massive exposure to pornography significantly increased males' sexual callousness toward women.

These investigators have also investigated the effects of prolonged exposure to pornography on marriage and family. Under the assumption that the nuclear family plays a significant role for societal welfare, they note the values expressed in pornography obviously clash with the traditional family concept, and potentially undermine the traditional values that favor marriage, family, and children. They tested the implications of prolonged pornography exposure on perceptions and attitudes concerning sexually intimate relationships, marriage, and the family as essential societal institutions. Male and female subjects were exposed to either "nonviolent pornography" or "control materials" in hourly sessions over a 6-week period. One week after the exposure treatment, subjects participated in an unrelated project on the "American family and aspects of personal happiness." To measure attitudes and perceptions, the "Value of Marriage," and " Indiana Inventory of Personal Happiness" surveys were then administered to subjects.

Results showed that prolonged exposure to pornography fostered greater acceptance of pre- and extramarital relations. Those exposed to pornography also showed significant effects on evaluations regarding the desirability of marriage and the desire to have children when compared to the control group. Only 39% of the subjects in the treatment condition viewed marriage as an essential institution compared to 60% of those in the control group. Finally, subjects exposed to pornography wanted fewer children than did control subjects. These results led the investigators to conclude that prolonged exposure to pornography diminishes the value of marriage as an essential institution.

B. The Liberal Perspective

1. Explication of the Liberal Perspective

In the liberal perspective, the concepts of "good" versus "evil" are viewed as culturally defined and therefore arbitrary. Human adults who are given free access to the full range of messages and information are able to make rational choices about what is appropriate behavior in their culture. This view is based on political theorists such as John Locke and John Stuart, who asserted that individuals have the basic human right to free expression of ideas. They further argued that the state should not restrict such a right because the free exchange of ideas leads to an effective government. Restricting the rights of one individual should only be considered if his or her actions infringe on the rights of another person. Pornography is considered an expression of ideas regarding women, men, and sex. According to the liberal perspective, adults should be given complete freedom to use pornography for their personal pleasures, such as sexual fantasy or as a sex stimulant in interactions with other consenting adults.

Four assertions made by supporters of the liberal theory help to understand pornography research guided by this perspective: (1) Most pornography merely triggers sexual *thoughts* that are not acted out. Unless these thoughts result in harmful actions against others, pornography should be considered "harmless." (2) Pornography may even be a socially beneficial form of communication that allows for self-expression of sexual interests. (3) The state should not restrict individuals' basic human right to free expression of ideas. As long as the recipient restricts his behavior to private actions such as sexual arousal, fantasy or use of pornography with consenting partners, society has no right to interfere. (4) While pornography is generally not harmful, consumers who are particularly susceptible to it and cannot behave rationally may require some form of message restriction once they have acted illegally.

2. Research Supporting the Liberal Perspective

Social scientists researching the effects of pornography using the liberal framework have examined dependent measures that address the possibility of direct or demonstrable physical harms following exposure to pornography. These measures include actual physical aggression or crime. Guided by such a perspective in 1970 a commission appointed by the president of the United States concluded that "On the basis of the available data . . . it is not possible to conclude that erotic material is a significant cause of crime" (*Presidential Commission on Obscenity and Pornography*, 1970, p. 243).

Several researchers, who had originally conducted research for this commission, continued for many years to investigate the relationship between pornography and criminal sexual behavior such as rape. In particular, Berl Kutchinsky examined the incidence of rape and aggravated assault in several different societies where pornography had become readily available, such as Denmark, Sweden, West Germany, and the United States. This study was similar to an earlier study conducted by the 1970 commission, but this time he examined data from a longer time period, 1964 to 1984. With 20 years of crime data, he could be assured that a substantial number of people had been exposed to pornography as part of a general trend in greater availability of sexually explicit materials of all forms.

Although the countries studied experienced a large increase in availability of pornography, results showed that rape did not increase more than nonsexual violent crimes. In fact, in three countries, Denmark, Sweden and West Germany, rape increased less than nonsexual assault. In some Western countries that had not similarly changed their pornography laws during this period, rape and nonsexual assault followed the same pattern. Consistent with the liberal theory, these results led the investigator to conclude that there is no causal connection between rape and pornography.

The liberal perspective also assumes that pornography may be beneficial. By allowing an individual to create a fantasy world built around sexual interests, pornography can provide a way of releasing strong sexual urges without harming others. The 1970 commission administered public opinion surveys to test the assumption regarding the beneficial effects of pornography. To determine whether Americans thought the availability of erotic materials was a social problem, the Commission surveyed 2486 adults (aged 21 and up) and 769 young persons (aged 15–20). These individuals were asked about the effects of exposure to erotic materials. Results of the survey showed individuals were more likely to list effects the commission termed "socially desirable" than socially undesirable ones. "Socially desirable" responses included pornography gave individuals information about sex and it improved their sexual relations. Virtually none of those surveyed reported that it led them to commit rape or made them "sex crazy," effects considered socially undesirable, although many people believed that it could have such an effect on some other people.

In addition to public opinion surveys, findings from sexual arousal studies conducted by the 1970 Commission suggested that pornography had little, if any negative effects. Commission researchers found that individuals became less "excited" and more "bored" after continuous exposure to sexually explicit materials. In their study, men were first shown a sexually explicit film and for the following 3 weeks viewed sexually explicit materials for 90 minutes a day, 5 days a week. Five and eight weeks after the initial exposure, the men were shown the original sexually explicit film. Over the period of the study, the men were less physiologically responsive to sexual materials and showed less interest in the materials (as measured by time spent viewing them). In addition, the men exposed to massive pornography became more "liberal" in their attitudes toward pornography. Not only did they believe that pornography would not harm adults or stable adolescents, but they were also less inclined to place restrictions on sales and distribution of pornography. Based on these findings, Howard and colleagues concluded that "exposure to pornography was a relatively innocuous stimulus without lasting or detrimental effect on the individual or his behavior" (Howard, Reifler, & Liptzin, 1971, p. 97).

The 1970 Commission also demonstrated that exposure to pornography did not significantly change patterns of sexual behavior. Subjects who were sexually active before exposure remained so afterward, and those inactive before exposure remained so afterward. Commission researchers did not find changes in antisocial sexual behavior after short- or long-term exposure to erotica. Following exposure to erotica, married couples experienced a temporary increase in sexual activity (up to 24 hours after exposure), then returned to normal levels. For people not currently involved in a sexual relationship, results showed no increase of heterosexual activity. Generally, any increase in heterosexual activity following exposure to pornography depended upon the presence of a consenting partner with whom the participant was already sexually involved. In addition, results showed an increase in masturbation in a minority of the subjects (up to 30%) who already had a history of frequent masturbation.

Research for the Commission also studied the influence of erotica on "low-frequency" sexual activity such as homosexuality, anal sex, group sex, and sadomasochism. Studies with both short-term (one exposure) and a long-term exposure (4-week exposure) showed no evidence of increases in sexual activity immediately or within 6 months after exposure to materials that included depictions of these activities.

After reviewing the findings of these studies, the panel reached the following conclusion regarding the relationship between exposure to erotica and sexual arousal and sexual behavior: "The findings of the available research cast considerable doubt on the thesis that erotica is a determinant of either the extent or nature of individuals' habitual sexual behavior. Such behavioral effects as were observed were short-lived, and consisted virtually exclusively of transitory increase in masturbation or coitus among persons who habitually engage in these activities" (*President's Commission on Obscenity and Pornography,* 1970, p. 194).

C. The Radical Feminist Perspective

1. Explication of the Radical Feminist Perspective

Within the feminist movement there are a variety of perspectives on the subject of pornography that will not be discussed here. Instead, only the radical feminist position will be discussed and whenever the term feminist is used it will refer to this position and it should be kept in mind that it is by no means representative of the feminist community generally. Feminists such as Andrea Dworkin and Catharine MacKinnon, who have often referred to themselves as "radical feminists," have been particularly outspoken on this subject and have challenged both the conservative and liberal perspectives. According to this feminist theory, concepts such as good and evil should not only be considered as culturally determined, but also, human perception itself and knowledge are socially constructed and represent the interests of those "doing the construction." Our perception of good and bad, of women, and the act of sex between men and women is a product of social relations. Feminists therefore challenge the belief in objectivity in analyses of relations between men and women, scientific research, conception of desirable versus undesirable sexual behavior, or of social relation generally. All of these are perceived to be shaped by cultural values and norms.

Radical feminists view social relations in terms of power dynamics. In our society, men hold considerable power over women. Sex, these feminists contend, is the primary means by which men exert power over women. Through this unequal distribution of power, men have been able to force their notions of appropriate sexual relations between men and women as well as shape how women perceive themselves. Men "possess" and use women through the sexualization of intimate intrusion. Sexual access to women is a central feature of women's definition of inferior and of feminine. According to this feminist perspective, pornography is a form of "hate literature." It is visual and verbal intrusion, access, and possession of women by men. Because pornography plays a significant role in defining and hurting women, feminists argue that women should be able to claim damages resulting from pornography's harmful effects.

The feminist theory is critical of both moralist and liberal theories. Moralists' objections to pornography on the basis of its appeal to prurient interests differs radically from the feminists' concern on pornography's effects on women. Liberals' concerns for freedom of speech fail to recognize that men are the ones who control political speech and that women are often left "speechless" due to lack of access to means of power. The liberal view that all forms of speech should go unregulated does not recognize that the power men have over women to define them in pornography has silenced women's voices. As exemplified in the following quote, unlike the moralist and liberal theories, the feminist approach focuses on the effects of pornography on attitudes about women and various behaviors toward women, including but by no means limited to physical harms.

> Pornography is a systematic practice of exploitation and subordination based on sex that differentially harms women.... The bigotry and contempt pornography promotes, with the acts of aggression it fosters, diminish opportunities for equality of rights in employment, education, property, public accommodations, and public services...." (Dworkin & MacKinnon, 1988, p. 33).

2. Research Supporting the Feminist Perspective

Some of the research testing the feminist theory has examined the effects of certain types of pornography on attitudes that justify violence toward women. These attitudes not only undermine viewer sensitivity to female victims of rape and violence, but also may increase discriminatory and sexually aggressive behavior. In addition to examining direct behavior effects, researchers

testing this perspective have examined widespread effects of pornography such as endorsement of limiting sex roles, beliefs in rape myths, and increased acceptance of violence and discrimination against women.

Neil Malamuth and his colleagues have conducted studies relevant to the feminists' contentions. They examined the effects of exposure to media sexual violence on attitudes and perceptions. Studies have generally taken the following form: Male subjects were either exposed to depictions of mutually consenting sex, rape in which the female victim eventually became aroused, or rape abhorred by the victim. Afterwards the subjects were shown a rape depiction and asked about their perception of the act and the victim. Results show that subjects exposed to the "positive" rape portrayal perceived the second rape as less negative and more normative than those first exposed to the other depictions. The effect of portrayal was particularly apparent in men with higher self-reported inclination to aggress against women. In addition, some research subjects asked men to report their beliefs about how women in general would react to being victimized by sexual violence. Those first exposed to a "positive rape portrayal" believed that a higher percentage of women would derive pleasure from being sexually assaulted.

Another study examined the effects of different portrayals in a "naturalistic" environment. In this study, male and female college students received free tickets to view feature-length films on two different evenings. Subjects were randomly assigned to one of two exposures. One group saw films that portrayed aggression against women in a positive light. The other group saw films that did not contain portrayals of aggression against women. The films used were R-rated, uncut, feature-length films.

A survey was administered to both the experimental and the control group a few days after viewing the films. The survey examined subjects' attitudes and beliefs with the following scales (1) Acceptance of Interpersonal Violence (AIV) against women (e.g. acceptance of sexual aggression and wife battering); (2) Rape Myth Acceptance (RMA) (e.g., the belief that women desire to be raped); and (3) Adversarial Sexual Beliefs (ASB) (e.g., the notion that women are sly and manipulating when out to attract a man). In addition, the survey measured irrelevant items in order to disguise the purpose of the survey. Subjects did not know that the survey was connected to the earlier phase of the research in which films had been viewed.

Male subjects exposed to "positive" portrayals of aggression against women showed a significant increase on the acceptance of violence against women scale (i.e., the AIV). There was a similar effect that approached significance on the Rape Myth Acceptance (RMA) scale. There were no effects on the ASB scale for men nor were there any significant effects on any of the scales for women. The results therefore showed that media messages that portray violence against women in a favorable light can affect men's attitudes about violence against women. These results were recently replicated by other investigators.

In another recent study conducted by Neil Malamuth and his associates, the investigators examined the association between sexual aggression against women and exposure to pornography. Researchers in an earlier study had developed a model that identified risk factors correlated with sexual aggression. In this follow-up study, the researchers conducted a series of risk analyses using these risk factors as well as the variable pornography consumption, which was operationally defined as the degree of exposure to sexually explicit magazines, the most widely consumed medium of the sexually explicit industry.

Results showed pornography consumption was significantly correlated with sexually aggressive behavior. However, further analyses conducted by these investigators indicated that for most men, this correlation could be due to the overlap between pornography consumption and other risk factors. Interestingly, however, the analyses also showed that for those men most at risk, the added factor of pornography consumption put them at even higher risk for sexually aggressive behavior. Additional results suggest that these findings are not consistent with a "general deviancy" explanation, which suggests that pornography consumption is simply an indicator of some general extremity or deviance. For example, the investigators also examined nonsexual aggression (e.g., yelling, hitting, in a nonsexual context). Using the same risk factors they found that pornography consumption did not increase risk for this type of aggression. However, they did find that alcohol consumption was a contributor to the risk for nonsexual aggression. Correspondingly, levels of alcohol consumption were not found to contribute to the risk for sexual aggression in the context of the other risk factors.

It is important to emphasize that these data do not enable any causal conclusions, but might only be useful as risk "markers" or indicators. However, they are consistent with some earlier experimental research showing that men who are at relatively high risk for sexual aggression are more likely to be attracted to and aroused by sexually violent media and may be more likely to be influenced by them. This bidirectional relationship (i.e., higher proclivity to aggress resulting in more expo-

sure to certain media, which in turn contributes to higher risk for aggression) is also consistent with some research on media violence, such as that recently reported by Brad Bushman. Furthermore, it provides support for assertions made some time ago by Neil Malamuth and Victoria Billings regarding the importance of certain differences in individuals' backgrounds, personality characteristics, cultural milieu, and situational factors as moderators of the impact of pornography. These writers had emphasized that studies focusing only on quantity of exposure (e.g., who consumes more or less pornography) may be an oversimplified approach. Sexually explicit media's degree of influence on a person may largely depend on how that exposure interacts with other influences. For example, people raised with little education about sexuality or in families where sex was treated as "taboo," may be more susceptible to the influences of explicit media than those reared with considerable education about sex. Those with other sources of sex information may more accurately assess the myths about women and sexuality portrayed in some pornography. However, those without much sex education might be more apt to use explicit media as a primary source of information. Similarly, the effects of exposure to pornography are likely to be moderated not only by the different types of pornography but also by individuals' circumstances. Important factors may include the availability of sexual partners, the types of social relationships a person is in, their personal thresholds for engaging in various behaviors (including coercive acts) and other important situational factors. Earlier laboratory research on the relationship between exposure to pornography and aggressive behavior also supports the emphasis on individual and situational moderators.

III. GENDER DIFFERENCES IN PORNOGRAPHY CONSUMPTION

Although the research findings illustrated above do not reveal a general consensus about the effects of pornography, one thing that is apparent is that there are large sex differences in the consumption of different types of sexually explicit media. Evolutionary psychology provides an explanation for such sex differences based on the evolved sexual strategies that were naturally selected in ancestral environments. Although evolutionary approaches emphasize the possible interactive role of socialization differences as well, as emphasized below, explanations based on socialization or cultural differences alone must be better developed if they are to attempt to account for the observed differences.

A. What Is Evolutionary Psychology?

Evolutionary psychology is a growing scientific discipline that applies current knowledge of evolutionary processes to understand the human mind and behavior. Charles Darwin's evolutionary theory postulates that living organisms are formed by natural selection. Through evolution, a continuous process of differential reproductive success (or fitness), certain design differences are passed on to subsequent generations.

The evolutionary paradigm allows one to understand features of the human mind that are not likely to be understood without asking the question, Why would that design have been selected rather than the other one?. Adaptations are characteristics that were naturally selected in the evolutionary history of our species because they contributed to fitness. Because a behavior may have been adaptive in evolutionary environments and thus contributed to the current structure of the mind, this does not indicate that such a behavior contributes to reproductive success in current environments. Further, this does not suggest that the behavior is desirable, moral, or inevitable.

A comprehensive theory needs to incorporate the "design" of the mind, as formed by evolutionary processes, and its interaction with the physical and social environment, including the cultures created by human minds. According to evolutionary psychology, to understand the human mind today it is essential to analyze the "mental organs" or psychological mechanisms (i.e., information processing algorithms or decision rules) which evolved in ancestral environments and which have been inherited by us today. These mechanisms are a part of all of us and guide our emotions, thoughts, and behaviors. They process relevant environmental information and can result in highly flexible behavior which is responsive to environmental variability. It is therefore important to realize the psychologically relevant traits that we inherit are not behaviors per se, but the mental organs which can result in various behaviors.

The mind is composed of many "domain specific" psychological mechanisms rather than general mechanisms relevant to many domains. While the mind was designed by natural selection processes operating in ancestral environments to promote fitness, people are not presumed to consciously strive to achieve the goal of fitness. In other words, people do not consciously "choose" their actions in order to promote fitness. Rather, the types of mind mechanisms which evolved in ancestral environments and which can be "activated" in current environments were naturally selected because in those earlier environments they had fitness-favoring consequences.

B. Understanding Sex Differences Within the Evolutionary Paradigm

As David Buss has emphasized, unlike other sex differences theories, evolutionary metatheory provides a framework of testable predictions allowing one to predict when gender differences are or are not expected, the direction of the differences, and why these differences are predicted. Males and females are expected to have the same psychological mechanisms in those domains where natural selection has favored the same solutions to adaptive problems for all humans. In some domains however, males and females faced different problems in evolutionary history. Therefore, different mechanisms to solve these problems evolved between the sexes.

Sexuality is predicted to be one of the domains for which exists sex differences in evolved mechanisms. In this domain, the differing natural selection processes for males and females resulted in differing sexual strategies for males and females. As Robert Trivers noted in his now classic article, different mating strategies among males and females may be traced to the minimum parental investment required to produce an offspring. In humans, females require more parental investment to produce offspring than do males (e.g., 9 months vs. 9 minutes). Carefully selecting a mate with successful characteristics, who will play a significant role in the raising of the offspring, is a better investment for female reproductive success than seeking sex with a large number of males. In comparison, males' reproductive success may be relatively correlated with having intercourse with a larger number of fertile partners since in ancestral environments contraceptive devices were not available, and the upper limit for males siring offspring is in the thousands. Even totally uninvited sex may therefore have favorable reproductive consequences under some circumstances.

As noted by Bruce Ellis and Don Symons and more recently elaborated on by Neil Malamuth, the consumption of sexually explicit media, appears to be the result of inherited evolved sexuality mechanisms interacting with environmental factors. Differences in the types of sexually explicit media heavily consumed by males and females is reflective of differences in their sexual strategies. While males consume sexually explicit media containing elements related to short-term mating strategy, females consume media that reflect the relatively long-term aspect of their mating strategy.

In current environments, the expression of sexual strategies is expected to be moderated by their interaction with other mechanisms that place limitations on sexuality mechanisms. Some constraints faced by males, including the fear of venereal diseases, reputation damage, or rejection by females, a need to find a suitable compromise with female sexual strategy in order to attract and retain a desired woman, competition and threats from other men, and/or limited resources, may result in fewer sexual encounters with fertile women. Although sexual behavior may be constrained by certain mechanisms, attraction to sexually explicit media is not constrained to the same degree by compromises imposed by other mechanisms. As well, it should be noted that males' and females' choices of long-term opposite-sex partners (e.g., marital partners) are not exclusively based on sexuality mechanisms alone but reflect the powerful influence of many other mechanisms (e.g., attachment, friendship, etc.). It is therefore not surprising that males and females have actually been found to be very similar in their criteria for choosing long-term partners while differing in the inclination to and criteria used for short-term sexual partners.

C. Sexually Explicit Media and Gender Differences

Survey studies conducted over the past 4 decades consistently show large gender differences in the uses of and gratifications derived from sexual media. Table 1 summarizes the findings of these studies and various related gender differences documented by other researchers and presents a summary of an evolutionary-based model's explanations for these differences.

D. Adaptive Evolutionary Problems and the Content of Sexual Media

Another source of information about the relevance of the evolutionary analysis to understanding gender differences in consumption of pornography is revealed in examining the correspondence between the content of sex strategies and the recurring formulas of sexually explicit media. In a recent article by Neil Malamuth it was concluded that there is an excellent fit between the content of today's sexually explicit media geared primarily to male consumers and the major adaptive problems that according to evolutionary psychologists led to the evolution of a male short-term sexual strategy.

For example, the adaptive problems underlying such a male strategy included how to gain sexual access to as many fertile females as possible while minimizing the commitment and investment in any single woman. Today's sexually explicit media geared to males portray primarily casual sex with numerous, accessible women who display fertility cues through their age, body shape, and so on.

Similarly, this analysis also showed very clear correspondence between the content of female-oriented sexual media (i.e., romance novels) and the adaptive problems that led to an evolved female long-term sexual strategy. Females' adaptive problems included identifying and securing commitment from a man who had the ability (e.g., relatively high status) and willingness to successfully invest in her and their offspring. In addition, a man who could provide physical protection particularly during the period of increased vulnerability associated with pregnancy and child rearing was also an important characteristic for females' mates. Finally, it was important to solve the problem of identifying a man who possessed good parental abilities and skill. Men with such attributes as kindness and sensitivity, potentially possessed these abilities. Content analyses of the very large media industry of romance novels (in which there is considerable portrayal of sexuality) show that they typically portray a woman securing a relationship with a high-status, physically protective male who also possessed parenting skills and the ability and willingness to invest time in a single female and her offspring.

E. Cultural Socialization as an Explanation for Gender Differences

The gender differences described here are often explained by the socialization of our cultural roles and institutions that create differing social environments for females and males. These environments could include messages from parents, peers, media, and other cultural institutions, including messages about the dangers inherent for girls in sexuality. They could also include cultural barriers, such as laws and norms that channel males and females into differing careers, lifestyles, or behavioral patterns. Although such cultural factors are obviously important in explaining many gender differences and may indeed have considerable relevance to explaining differences in consumption of pornography and other sexual media, such a model would need to consider the reasons that certain roles, norms, and laws emerge or are enacted. Using culture to explain may

TABLE I

Summary of Sex Differences in Reactions to Sexually Explicit Media and Evolutionary Model's Explanation

(1) Sex Differences in Content That Is Appealing

In comparison to women, men consume more regularly, are more sexually aroused by, have more favorable attitudes, and react with less negative affect to portrayals featuring nudity of the opposite sex and/or sexual acts devoid of relationship context. Such differences have consistently been found in survey studies focusing on various media, including magazines, movies and on the computer internet and in laboratory studies presenting subjects with stimuli. In contrast, men are less likely than women to consume sexually explicit media that emphasize "sexual communion" and romance.

Evolutionary Model's Explanation: In general, the underlying algorithms for male and female sexual strategies differ. Male algorithms are designed to be less selective and cautious in short-term mating opportunities and to prime more frequent short-term acts (i.e., the threshold is lower for eliciting behavior). Consequently, the availability of an attractive nude female displaying sexual availability may constitute a sufficient condition to activate an "associative network" of responses (e.g., arousal, attitudes, positive affect) designed to elicit "approach" responses likely to lead to sexual acts. Female algorithms are designed to be more cautious in short-term mating situations and to evaluate more carefully the desirability of their potential mate. The availability of an attractive nude male displaying sexual availability is less likely to constitute a sufficient condition to elicit sexual behavior and may be "counteracted" by mechanisms designed to "put the brakes" (e.g., negative affect). Added "contextual" information, such as the desirability of the man and his trustworthiness, her familiarity with him, and his desire and other feelings for the woman, are important ingredients contributing to women's arousal and comfort levels. It is possible to provide such contextual information in portraying a "casual" sexual encounter.

(2) Sex Differences in Reactions to Novelty

Men become more aroused sexually than women by films showing novelty consisting of different actors but less aroused by the same actors performing different acts.

Evolutionary Model's Explanation: Novelty of sexual partners is a more powerful stimulant to male sexual strategy, since the opportunity to mate with a larger number of partners was more likely in ancestral environments to have contributed to male reproductive success than to female reproductive success.

(3) Sex Differences in Reactions to Form

Men are generally more aroused than women by visual portrayals, even when content has been "controlled" for. Women are much more likely to be the consumers of stories (e.g., novels) that incorporate sexuality within a much broader context than magazines or movies featuring visual sexual displays.

Evolutionary Model's Explanation: Men's evolved strategies prime them to be more visually attracted and aroused sexually, since such a "medium of communication" is likely to occur with many persons, including strangers (e.g., seeing from a distance) and to elicit sexual arousal frequently, resulting in greater likelihood of short-term mating. Women's arousal mechanisms, in contrast, are designed to be less likely to be easily aroused simply by the sight of an attractive stranger since that might prime women to "careless" decisions regarding sex.

(4) Sex Differences Functions and Approach/Avoidance Behavior

Men are more likely to seek out opportunities to be exposed to sexually explicit media, even when alone or with a same sex friend. They are more likely to use such stimuli as an end for themselves, reporting purposes such as "seeing great bodies," "releasing sexual frustrations," and as a stimulant for masturbation. Women are less likely to volunteer for studies involving sexually explicit media, regardless of whether they are described as hard- or soft-core. Among men, there do not appear to be differences between those who volunteer for erotica studies as compared to those who volunteer for nonsexual studies. In women, in comparison to those volunteering for non-sexual studies, volunteers for erotica research are more erotophilic (i.e., they have more favorable reactions to sexually explicit media) and have less negative affect to sexual films. Even when levels of sexual arousal in response to a sexual film are the same among men and women, men are much more likely than women to indicate that they would participate in a similar experiment in the future.

Evolutionary Model's Explanation: Female sexual strategy results in greater caution in placing oneself in sexual situations. Mediated by the "associative network" of responses and their underlying algorithms, females are more likely to avoid situations involving the display of sex per se. Men's sexual strategy makes them more responsive to sexual display that is not contextualized. Therefore, becoming sexually aroused can be gratifying even in a context that does not stimulate other feelings connecting the experience to a desire for another person. Such experiences are more likely to elicit negative affect in females when presented in a potentially "unsuitable" context.

---

move the level of analysis from the individual to that of the group but it is not an adequate endpoint of an explanatory model. It does not address the question of why humans have recurrently developed certain types of cultures, including ones in which the social environments differ for males and females.

Also, there are close similarities between findings in the area of gender differences in sexually explicit media and data in other areas (e.g., self-generated sexual fantasies, visits to strip shows, fetishes, sexual jealousy, etc.) that seem to provide a wealth of data on gender dimorphism in sexuality mechanisms. Whether informed by an evolutionary paradigm or not, researchers arguing against sexual dimorphism need to provide a comprehensive model that explains such consistent findings across various domains.

F. The Evolutionary Approach and Effects of Exposure

Evolutionary-based perspectives can provide a framework for integrating the other perspectives on pornography and they can provide us with a relatively clear model regarding the functions of sexually explicit media (e.g., Why do they exist in content and form?) but they do not necessarily provide clear predictions regarding the effects of exposure to sexually explicit media. Some evolutionary-based models may argue that the desire for various types of male-oriented pornography and female-oriented romance novels is simply a reflection of sexuality mechanisms in males and females; therefore, exposure to pornography has no significant impact on subsequent responses. Others may argue that even when understood as reflecting sexuality mechanisms, the content of such media exposure can have powerful effects. Our mechanisms for discriminating fantasy versus reality may not be sufficiently sharp to totally avoid any long-term impact of exposure on our feelings, thoughts, and behavior.

Also See the Following Articles

EVOLUTIONARY FACTORS • GENDER STUDIES • SEXUAL ASSAULT • TELEVISION PROGRAMMING AND VIOLENCE • WOMEN, VIOLENCE AGAINST

Bibliography

Attorney General's Commission on Pornography: Final Report. (1986, July).Washington, DC: U.S. Department of Justice.

Buss, D. M., & Schmitt, D. P. (1993). Sexual strategies theory: An evolutionary perspective on human mating. *Psychological Review, 100,* 204–232.

Dworkin, A., & MacKinnon, C. A. (1988). *Pornography and civil rights.* Minneapolis, MN: Organizing Against Pornography.

Ellis, B., & Symons, D. (1989) Sex differences in sexual fantasy. *Journal of Sex Research, 27,* 527–555.

Howard, J. L., Reifler, C. B., & Liptzin. M. B. (1971). Effects of exposure to pornography. In *Technical report of The Commission on Obscenity and Pornography* (Vol. 8, pp. 97–132). Washington, DC: U.S. Government Printing Office.

Jacobellis v Ohio, 378 U.S. 184 (1964).

Kutchinsky, B. (1970a). Pornography in Denmark: Pieces of a jigsaw puzzle collected around New Year 1970. In *Technical reports of the Commission on Obscenity and Pornography* (Vol. 4). Washington, DC: U.S. Government Printing Office.

Kutchinsky, B (1991). Pornography and rape: Theory and practice? Evidence from crime data in four countries where pornography is easily available. *International Journal of Law and Psychiatry, 14,* 147–64.

Linz, D., & Malamuth, N. M. (1993). *Pornography.* Newbury Park, CA: Sage.

Malamuth, N. (1996). Sexually explicit media, gender differences and evolutionary theory. *Journal of Communication, 46*(3), 8–31.

Malamuth, N., & Check, J. (1981). The effects of mass media exposure on acceptance of violence against women: A field experiment. *Journal of Research in Personality, 15,* 436–446.

Miller v. California, 413 U.S. 15 (1973).

President's Commission on Obscenity and Pornography. (1970). *The report of the Commission on Obscenity and Pornography.* Washington, DC: U.S. Government Printing Office.

Senn, C. Y., & Radtke, H. L. (1990). Women's evaluations of and affective reactions to mainstream violent pornography, nonviolent erotica, and erotica. *Violence and Victims, 5,* 143–155.

Symons, D. (1979). *The evolution of human sexuality.* Oxford: Oxford University Press.

Trivers, R. L. (1972). Parental investment and sexual selection. In B. Campbell (Ed.), *Sexual selection and the descent of man.* (pp. 1871–1971). Chicago: Aldine.

Zillmann, D., & Bryant, J. (1982). Pornography, sexual callousness, and the trivialization of rape. *Journal of Communication, 32,* 10–21.

Zillmann, D., & Bryant, J. (1988). Effects of prolonged consumption of pornography on family values. *Journal of Family Issues, 9,* 518–544.

Power and Deviance

Pat Lauderdale and Randall Amster

Arizona State University

I. Classical Perspectives on Deviance and Power
II. Intent and Consequences
III. The Roots of Power and Deviance
IV. Contemporary Analyses of Power and Deviance

GLOSSARY

Deviance Departure from social norms; traditionally defined by sociologists and psychologists as the violation or transgression of norms and expectations.

Hegemony The predominance in society of a shared cultural sense of ideas, values, and ethics during a particular historical period; hegemony comprises the "things that go without saying," and the complex sources of this unspoken cultural predominance typically are beyond the control and awareness of the society's members.

Interest Anything in which a right, claim, or share is held or pursued, and in the case of deviance it often acts to promote solidarity, hierarchies and statuses, and collective and individual identities.

Political Deviance Departure from social norms or expectations that is viewed as having positive intent and/or consequences for society.

Power The ability or capacity to exercise social control; often conceived as the ability to define, categorize, or label; operates macroscopically as structural or systemic control and the preservation of interests and statuses, and microcosmically as resistance to existing power relations in society.

POWER AND DEVIANCE have been frequent subjects of analysis by sociologists, and there is a significant legacy of work analyzing the concurrent operation of both phenomena in a variety of settings and from an array of perspectives. In "Two Laws of Penal Evolution," Emile Durkheim, for example, suggested in the late 1800s the relevance of the relation between power and deviance in his analysis of sanctioning, in which he posited that increases in the consolidation of power in society will lead to proportional increases in the repressive sanctioning of people who are defined as the most deviant (i.e., criminal). Indeed, any discussion of deviance that ignores the role of power relations in society in creating, maintaining, and adjusting the moral boundaries of "deviant" behavior runs the risk of presenting an incomplete or even inaccurate picture of the processes by which certain conduct is defined as deviant and the implicit or explicit agendas of social control agents (from individuals to institutions) in propounding such definitions or categorizations. Thus, the power and deviance approach does not focus upon why people engage in deviant behavior, for example, as a prostitute or thief. Instead, the approach centers on questions such as: (1) What processes of power lead to the formation of such labels, categories, and definitions? (2) What arrangements of power lead to arguments over what constitutes "deviance" such as prostitution or thievery? and (3) Under what conditions are people defined as a particular type of deviant once the hegemonic category is established and used in any particular culture?

I. CLASSICAL PERSPECTIVES ON DEVIANCE AND POWER

The primary classical perspectives on deviance—such as anomie by Merton, subculture by Cohen, differential association by Sutherland and Cressy, conflict by Quinney, and their derivatives—contain three basic assumptions. First, they all assume the preexistence of a deviant category or definition; second, the individual deviant is viewed by the rest of society as violating an established norm or value; third, particular actors within society (e.g., social control agents) will react to the perceived violator by negatively sanctioning the deviant behavior. While the latter two assumptions are theoretically and empirically informed (see Durkheim on the functional theory of social control, and Becker on labeling), assuming the preexistence of a deviant category is highly problematic. It pronounces "deviance" as a fixed category with unchanging parameters throughout history and across different cultures.

Definitions of appropriate and inappropriate social conduct are subject to a variety of dynamic elements and shifting historical conditions, some examples of which have been examined theoretically by Gusfield and Erikson; to assume otherwise—that definitions of appropriate social behavior somehow preexist and are lodged permanently within society—is to fundamentally misapprehend the parameters of deviance and power. In the earlier part of this century the Chicago school of sociology firmly opened the door for this analysis of the relevance of the power to define via W. I. Thomas's observation that if people define situations as real, then they are real in their consequences. Moreover, research from the Chicago school noted the transition zone where more recent immigrant groups would find themselves more likely to be defined as deviant as they struggled to become more fully integrated into mainstream society. The research noted explicitly the conflict of power for immigrants and revealed implicitly the roles of the market economy, which often restricted access to the mainstream, and the clash of social classes.

At a more explicit level, social class entered as a variable into the sociological study of deviance via Merton's anomie theory. He argued that the social class distribution of crime was a key problem. Merton explained this distribution by examining the social stresses that might lead to different forms of individual deviant behavior. Burglary, for example, might be motivated by a desire for material success and an inability to achieve those institutionalized goals through legitimate means of occupational roles. The fact that this condition was statistically more frequent among the unemployed and marginally employed accounted for the observed (or assumed) relationships between burglary and social class. Merton explicated the power of societal norms in influencing individuals to seek high status which he referred to as one of the institutionalized goals of society.

The relationship between deviance and social class was also critical for subsequent researchers, such as Sutherland and Cressy. The emerging theory of differential association, however, began with a different view of the social class distribution of deviance. This theory suggested that deviance is common among all social classes and that the process of differential association creates a bias against those members of society with little power. Subsequent studies of white-collar crime demonstrated, for example, that becoming a price fixer involved the same basic learning and social support processes that led to becoming a burglar. What is interesting, from the power and deviance approach, is that this study raised serious questions about the political issues of definition. Why is it the case that offenses committed by higher status members of society typically are lightly sanctioned (e.g., corporate offenses often are adjudicated under civil rather than criminal law), while offenses committed by lower class individuals receive not only a harsher (criminal) sanction but in many instances a sanction vastly disproportionate to the relative harm of the offense?

This concern with explaining society's reaction to deviance rather than the motivation of the actor was addressed more thoroughly by the labeling theory of the 1960s. Many sociologists suggested that the critical factor needing attention was the reaction to deviance. This reorientation, in turn, resulted in the rebirth of the sociology of law. The labeling theorists remained partially tied to the traditional concern with motivation, despite their revolution in perspective. In particular, most of them sought to demonstrate how sanctioning and the associated stigma serve to reinforce and stabilize the deviant behavior of the individual. Labeling theorists tended to take as their central mission the exorcism of explanations of deviance in terms of individual characteristics. It was believed by these theorists that deviance is a property conferred on rather than inherent in the actor. However, in fighting this war with their predecessors and focusing on the consequences of stigma, labeling theorists often overlooked the sources of the deviant labels being imposed by powerful agencies, the ways in which such labels changed, and especially the explicit processes of power underlying the development and imposition of labels.

Many of the factors that may contribute to changes in the definition of acts or actors have been touched upon by a variety of labeling theorists. Among these theories are those that discuss the methods used by the deviants, and the status of the definers (labelers) and the defined. The focus of the labeling approach, however, has been somewhat misdirected. As an illustration, it may be instructive to compare these developments with contemporary developments in the sociological field called stratification. The research in stratification has taken the direction of emphasizing individual motivational issues at the expense of political and structural questions. The field became consumed with the process of status attainment by individuals, tracing out the career trajectories of individuals in the occupational structure, and with the rather precise estimation of the role of actual performance versus unearned progress in an individual's career development—but failed to account for impediments to the attainment of status, for example, as a result of inequities in power.

Some ideologies present a system of thought that offers what could be considered a pragmatist's view of deviance and social control. Rather than attempting to explain, define, or alter how deviance is viewed, these explanations simply accept that deviance exists and must be controlled. Related to this idea is the concept of pluralism. Pluralism appeared to many as a working feature of the political system that allowed for at least minimal fulfillment of the needs of all groups in society. While it is accepted that there are competing power elites, it is believed that by the nature of their competing interests no group is able to wield an inordinate amount of control or power over another. Based on these perspectives, there can be some similarities in interpretations of political reality between those in power and those subjected to that power. Politics, as the ongoing discussion of means and ends, seemed to subside since what was meaningful for the rulers appeared meaningful for the ruled as well. These pluralistic perspectives fell by the wayside during the politicality of the late 1960s.

The history of the sociology of deviance is also replete with debates concerning the relative importance of legal and extralegal factors in society's reaction to deviancy. The notion that societal reaction is the most fundamental process of deviance is an established observation. The literature to date reveals that society nearly always *reacts* to deviancy, so continued efforts to estimate the relative impact of legal and extralegal factors are no longer particularly fruitful. The attendant body of knowledge currently consists of a number of competing and divergent arguments, and while each has some merit and potential in explaining the process of the reaction to deviant behavior, they appear, as Sumner demonstrates, incapable of being reconciled with one another, and moreover fail to address the role of power by which behavior comes to be defined as deviant. A power and deviance approach specifies and then seeks to elaborate the conditions under which amorphous behavior becomes *defined* as deviant, or behavior that was once characterized as deviant becomes *redefined* as some kind of nondeviant conduct or attribute, as in the case, for example, when the medical or psychiatric communities redefine a deviant behavior as a physiological malady or cognitive abnormality (i.e., "sickness").

II. INTENT AND CONSEQUENCES

The preceding material provides only a partial understanding of the definitional processes involved in deviance. Determining the intent of the actors and the consequences of their behavior is part of a more complex picture. Many scholars fail to recognize that intent is socially negotiated. Although some have looked at deviance per se, they do not give adequate attention to the role of other relevant factors. These factors include relevant social movements, public opinion, and the role of agents of social control in determining social perception of the deviants' actions and their consequences. To thoroughly understand social definitions, we must cast aside the preoccupation with strictly studying the intent and consequences of behavior. We must also look at other means by which behavior is defined as deviant or "normal."

Through a variety of societal mechanisms, most individual diversity is categorized as normal variation, a small fraction as apolitical deviance, and an even smaller fraction as political deviance. As Ben-Yehuda has noted, the principal area of inquiry is how the boundaries of these categories are drawn and what determines the placement of specific actors and acts within any given category. The creation of categories and the placement of individuals within these categories are viewed as two basic processes of social definition that are found to be outcomes of political variables. Any in-depth analysis of the social organization of the definition of deviance requires a look at how criminal or political intent is socially negotiated and how objectively harmful social actions are frequently relabeled as socially acceptable—perhaps even necessary. A logical question at this point is: under what conditions would deviance be acceptable or necessary in society? One reason society defines individuals as deviant is to shape and control how people within a society are expected to act. A certain amount of deviant behavior is to be expected within the society, and if not typically encouraged, it is tolerated; that is, if there were no deviance, there would be no normality.

The intent of the actor is a central ingredient in the construction of deviant definitions. An emphasis on the role of intent, however, has the unintended negative consequence of injecting into sociological analysis all the uncertainties associated with applying the *mens rea* criteria of crime in the law. Note, for example, the legal controversy surrounding one exemption from *mens rea,* the insanity defense. Actor A shooting and killing Victim B may not be a crime because Actor A was incapable of telling right from wrong and/or was driven by an uncontrollable impulse. An uncontrolled impulse may be momentary, making it extremely difficult to distinguish between sane and temporarily insane actors. The net result is that the insanity plea has turned into a bargaining device, the status of sanity being something to be negotiated.

Deviance cannot be determined solely by an examination of an actor's intent, because intent is socially negotiated. Reliance on the individual's own interpretations places a heavy burden of proof upon observers to determine whether the actor's justifications are legitimate or simply intended to mitigate the perceived severity of their actions. Even if observers are able to discern with some certainty the underlying motives behind the words, we are still left with a partial analysis of deviance. Attribution of intent is an important variable in the creation of deviance, but it is not sufficient in and of itself.

A second common conception of deviance conceives of the actions of the deviants as intrinsically political or apolitical. Related to this position is the view that deviance is generally a property inherent in the act. The argument maintains that certain acts are inherently criminal or deviant depending on the magnitude of harm they cause. The seriousness of "real crimes," for example, exploitation, sexism, racism, imperialism, and consumer fraud, can be objectively defined by their harmful consequences. These positions would seem to suggest that the distinction between apolitical and political deviance should be made in terms of the objective consequences of the action. If the action (for example, a collective disturbance) has "positive" social consequences, then it is revolutionary or political; otherwise, it is deviant.

III. THE ROOTS OF POWER AND DEVIANCE

The present field of power and deviance is primarily a product of a succession of theories. In order to understand its orientation, it is necessary to examine how the field evolved and how most perspectives have been influenced by their predecessors.

Aristotelian philosophy associated deviance with punishment inflicted on individuals by the power of the gods. Under this deterministic view, logic revealed that the gods defined some individuals as deviant. A subsequent approach was the *Medieval Scholastic,* which was based on the belief that deviance was created by the power of the devil (or similar religious or spiritual entity). Rather than look at deviance as a "punishment" inflicted by the gods, the deviant individual was thought to be possessed with an evil, demonic spirit that manipulated the deviant for its own ends. Another theory is the *Physiological,* which, rather than attribute deviance to external power, tied deviance to the physical (exterior) characteristics of the individual, regardless of whether the researcher thought the cause was biological or psychological. Physiognomy, craniology, cranioscopy, phrenology, or a general conception of ugliness served as the frame of reference. The next theory of deviance, the *Biological,* was also based on the physiology of the individual. Under this theory, deviance was thought to be rooted in the biochemistry of the person; the emphasis was on the inner characteristics (interior) of individuals. The *Economic* theory, which still has its supporters today, equates the force of economic conditions with deviance. For example, drunkenness was associated with prosperity and burglary with depression. A more recent theory is the *Psychological.* Deviance was initially viewed as a consequence of events in the individual's biography, be it situational frustration or an arrested stage of psychosexual development. Recent views propose a modified frustration-aggression perspective, a series of reinforcement theories, or a modeling explanation of deviance.

In essence, the development of the study of deviance has traditionally been psychologically based, centered on attempting to explain the problematic behavior of the isolated individual. Since the problem of deviance was essentially dictated by a research tradition that took individual personality as the unit of analysis, the role of power and social organizations in separating deviance from normality was not seen as an important issue. Each new set of researchers was content to modify the psychological tradition in the study of deviance without considering how the behavior being studied first came to be defined as deviant.

The assumptions that deviance is a property of acts or actors, and that it has individualistic, identifiable causes, not only have a long history but are still popular today. Recently, low blood sugar or XYY chromosomal arrangements have been proposed to cause some forms of deviant behavior; and an explanation of the Salem witchcraft episode contends that bread contaminated with a parasitic fungus induced hallucinations in the young women who were labeled as witches. It is unclear which, if any, of these causal factors may ultimately be shown to cause variations in behavior that is labeled deviant. Regardless, none of these investigations can tell us why such behaviors are first defined as deviant. Furthermore, looking at deviance as an individual phenomenon creates a myopia that has prevented and continues to prevent sociologists from considering how social and political power can affect the definitions of deviant behavior.

Even when sociologists eventually began to study the relationship between power and deviance, they retained key assumptions from the psychologistic approaches. The commitment to explaining individual motivation caused sociologists to ignore definitional issues related to social phenomena, despite using such variables as social stratification, hierarchy, and subculture in their studies.

IV. CONTEMPORARY ANALYSES OF POWER AND DEVIANCE

Several different routes were taken to arrive at the notion that processes of power are inherent in deviance. The absence of a single theory of social structure—or even a clearly articulated set of alternative theories of social structure—resulted in a consensus on the significance of these processes but a conflict over approaches, theories, and paradigms from which to view the phenomenon. Concern with the moral and political character of deviance control has been pursued recently in various conflict and critical forms. A well-known argument contained within most of these works contends that the most salient item in the study of deviance and crime should not be the deviations of lower class individuals, but should instead include broader problems such as economic advantages and disadvantages, civil rights and race, and bias in gender and ethnicity.

It should be noted that essentially this position was presented more than 50 years ago in a penetrating article by C. Wright Mills.

Power is central to any analysis of deviance since *all forms of deviance have a political dimension*. As Schur has noted, the deviant definition is created, maintained, and revised through processes of power in which the manipulation of political symbols is used for the control of public opinion. Accordingly, a power and deviance perspective focuses upon: (1) how the definition of behavior as deviant is initially created; (2) the actors intimately involved with the creation of the definition; (3) how the definition is maintained or adjusted over time; and (4) the effects of that definition. It also is important to consider the following factors: (a) the status of the definer (e.g., is the actor doing the defining a well-respected opinion leader or a criminal?); (b) the historical period during which the debate emerges (e.g., someone who is labeled as deviant during a period of social unrest may not be considered deviant during a period of strong social cohesion); and (c) the ideological differences between the conflicting parties (i.e., is the content of the actors' behavior strictly related to the power of the defining agent?). By exploring each of these areas one can derive a perspective on how definitions are created and applied. These concerns highlight the primacy of precipitating factors of power in the creation of deviance that can and should be distinguished from structural conditions of deviant behavior, raising important questions concerning the role of the state, mass media, and information networks in constructing and perpetuating definitions of deviant behavior.

Prevailing views on the nature of deviance have historically been created by studying the overt political conflicts between economic groups, status groups, interest groups, and professions. Empirical studies surrounding such phenomena have focused on specific historical instances of conflict. A limiting factor of these studies, however, is that they involve mostly victimless crimes. This one-sided approach does not offer a comprehensive understanding of power and deviance, but instead provides a lopsided theory of social definition of victimless crime. While the often clearly defined political nature of victimless crimes provide a convenient basis for study, the end result is that forms of deviance that historically have no political connections (e.g., assault, homicide) tend to be overlooked.

Deviance is socially defined and as such is created, maintained, and changed through the interaction of a variety of societal factors. Thus, the power and deviance approach seeks to understand and explain the recurrent definitional transformations. Consider that in recent years a major goal has been to discover how a form of action comes to be defined as deviant or conversely redefined as normal. This change in emphasis is largely based on a broader historical and comparative view that recognizes the variability in social definitions of deviance. Evidence of this variability can be found in studies tracing the development (i.e., enactment and/or enforcement) of particular laws. The more subtle role of political power and its relationship to rule-making is presented at other levels of analysis by Heitzeg (extending the seminal analyses of Garfinkel and Goffman). Such recognition comes mainly in the form of historical case studies that in themselves are mere curiosities. Hence, the power and deviance character of deviance is most clearly demonstrated when new categories of deviance are being created or old categories are being transformed. For example, under the Fugitive Slave Laws of the 1850s, aiding and abetting an escaped slave was a crime, but with the passage of the Fourteenth Amendment less than a decade later slavery itself was the crime. And in 1800, the organization of a labor union was a crime (conspiracy in restraint of trade), yet by 1940 not only were unions legal, but employers were required by law to engage in collective bargaining. Through the political process, then, an accepted and socialized form of activity can become delegitimized, or vice versa. The power and deviance approach examines the processes that maintain, create, and change the definition of certain behaviors as deviant.

While most prior research in the area of deviance has focused primarily upon the distinctive characteristics of deviance (e.g., substance addiction, sexual perversion, social pathology), the processes of power in creating definitions of deviance typically have been ignored or overlooked. Who benefits from the designation of certain forms of harmful (or harmless) behavior as deviant when other forms of behavior are treated as "normal"? Pfohl responds generally to this query with the suggestion that defining particular acts as deviance is one method of suppressing the resistance of those who threaten power arrangements. As Downes and Rock intimate, this raises at least two possible perspectives on power and deviance, one a macroscopic view focusing on the nature of power relations in the larger society and the ability of certain forces to label or categorize behavior as deviant, and the other viewing deviance as a means of asserting power in resistance to such encompassing forces.

Thus, on the one hand, conceptions of deviance often become embedded within the social structure and are in this sense institutionalized, much in the same way that, for example, gender discrimination is a regular feature of social life in Western society. Institutionalized deviant categories are typically beyond the immediate control of special interest groups and moral entrepreneurs, although their efforts at redefinition may at some point alter significantly an institutionalized characterization. On the other hand, however, since conceptions of deviance are pliable under certain conditions, they can subsequently be altered or manipulated to serve the varied interests of individuals, organizations and institutions. The study of the history of the medicalization of a variety of deviant categories, for example by Conrad and Schneider, lucidly reveals the process of redefinition of noninstitutionalized characterizations, with the concomitant effect of depoliticizing the original deviant characterizations. These observations beg concern over whose interests are being served by the defining and labeling of social behaviors. The definition or redefinition of certain acts, concepts and disputes can be a very effective technique in creating and maintaining social (in)equalities and hierarchies. In other words, maintaining the social order and its existing power relations is an essential aim of certain social control agents, and the processes by which moral boundaries and deviant categories are generated and modified are a principal part of the maintenance of these power relations.

Attempts at altering social inequality, whether by moral entrepreneurs, social movements, professional organizations, or the state, have not been the focus of the sociology of deviance but have instead been relegated to the area of social mobility. In essence, the study of power and social mobility can reveal elements central to the process by which definitions are created, maintained, and changed. In this context, analyses of power and social mobility and the definition of deviance are tied inextricably to the study of status hierarchies and stratification. This definitional process is perhaps the most important dynamic to examine in the deviance phenomenon. Pfuhl and Henry present a nascent perspective on this relation between power and deviance while others such as Ben-Yehuda, following Erikson, tend to focus on societal factors such as realignment of power that move the moral boundaries between deviant and normal definitions of conduct.

A. Political Trials

An interesting and important example of the intersection between power and deviance is the study of political trials. The advocacy system of justice provides for due process under law, protecting the legal rights of the defendant against the overwhelming power of the state. Individual rights have the latent function of depoliticizing courtroom trials, making it virtually impossible for individuals placed in the roles of defendants to redefine their action as beyond incrimination. Only by breaking out of the role of "defendant" is it possible for the accused to establish himself or herself as a political actor. Studies reveal that this is very difficult to accomplish in liberal capitalist states because adherence to due process legitimizes the criminalization of deviants. The legitimacy of the trial makes it an ideal weapon of repression, for by charging political "troublemakers" with crimes the state can tie them down with extensive litigation, contrary to traditional approaches to political criminality based on the notion that certain crimes are unambiguously political in nature. The distinction between the criminal trial and the political trial is a product of a negotiating process that is dependent on a number of interrelated factors, including the articulations of the defendants, the expertise of legal counsel, and the presence or absence of an external support movement. Future work regarding the symbolic definition of defendants as political or criminal should explicitly consider variations in structures of the legal system (e.g., adversarial versus inquisitorial procedures) and levels of social support external to the courtroom. In short, political crimes ought not to be considered a separate species of phenomenon, tucked away in an obscure corner of typologies of deviant behavior, but rather should be viewed as a crack in the hegemonic facade of social order and control.

Although the area of political trials is troublesome because the research is typically based upon secondary data and explanations, the study of social movements is problematic because much of the social reality of the movements is created by the selective data presented via the mass media, organizational linkages, and other information networks. Defendants in the antiwar trials of the 1960s in the United States were in unusual situations not only because support for their political articulations was created by an ongoing social movement but also because the movement's activities were brought before the courts and public via the mass media. An important question is to what extent actors who attempt to articulate political aims are ignored because they lack the support of a movement or media coverage of the movement. Following Gamson, it becomes especially relevant to examine the actions of the stably unrepresented—that is, the unorganized, unmobilized, and typically undefined mass. The boundaries between movement and "normal" politics have become hazy since the tactics of the two appear, on closer analysis, to be strikingly similar, in that both normal political organizations (institutionalized movements) and emerging movements engage in rational decision making, operate on the scheme of means to ends, create useful ideologies, and calculate consequences. Therefore, it becomes increasingly clear that social movements are simply politics by other means. The task remains to determine the explicit role of structural conduciveness in the emergence and possible institutionalization of nascent movements. Although some of the factors have been implicitly explored, the explicit role of conduciveness has only begun to be examined.

B. Hegemony and Interest

Another important concept related to the study of changing definitions is *hegemony*. Hegemony refers to the predominance of a shared system of ideas, values, and ethics within a society or community during a particular historical period. The concept is concerned with the process by which the majority of society comes to believe that societal norms are made to benefit each member more or less equally, leading to widespread agreement on and assent to these norms. This "consensus reality" includes a shared notion of the relative seriousness of deviant acts. Based on this perspective, viewing deviance as unrelated to power cannot be defined as simply "false consciousness" or the result of the machinations of the "ruling class," but rather as denoting a situation in which the ruling class is aware of its interests while the working class remains ignorant of its conflicting interests. This characterization perhaps is not adequate for modern, complex societies. The problem, as noted by Lauderdale and Amster in 1997, is in accounting for the pervasiveness of hegemony in modern societies. Unraveling this issue is essential to understanding the related areas of rule-making, law, and the legal system.

Similarly, the concept of *interest* and its relationship to deviance designation is ambiguous in the current literature. First, the identification of interest and its relationship to stigmatizing does not necessarily yield an adequate explanation. The concept of hegemony is essential to an understanding of the role of structural factors that affect stigmatizing. Second, we must clarify the concept of interest. Third, we must consider the circumstances under which relationships can be empirically investigated. As is clear from current research by Oliverio, the crisis situation (for example where a "national disaster" captures media headlines, such as the Oklahoma City bombing or the explosion of TWA Flight 800 near Long Island) appears particularly heuristic in gaining a relatively clear picture of hegemony and interests. This strategy is leading to theory and research not only on the definition of deviance but on related processes of social definition as well. Relevant studies include those on moral panics by Goode and Ben-Yehuda, radical ecology by Merchant, business and professional deviance by Farrell and Case, deviance in media by Ericson, Baranek, and Chan, and conflict management by Black. Recent analyses also include research in such areas as the activities of police by Marx, psychiatric manipulation of dissent by Crelinsten and Schmid, and terrorism by Oliverio. Such work embraces a wider range of phenomena including labor relations, ethnic cleavages, global resources, and the collective recognition of social harm.

In conjunction with an analysis of hegemony, recent studies by Garland and by Lauderdale and Cruit suggest that where power is increasingly concentrated or consolidated, the hegemonic forces that *pre*scribe rules and laws, and *pro*scribe certain conduct as deviant, play a concomitantly greater role in the promotion, revision, and maintenance of demonizing categories and labels. As a corollary, where power is more diffuse, deviance may still persist but is more likely to be construed positively, as with the work of certain geniuses, artists, musicians, scientists, or leaders. And where power approaches complete diffusion, deviance often comes to be seen as "diversity" and not as abnormal, immoral, or unlawful. Thus, the consolidation of power and the persistence of categories of deviance correspond in a manner that highlights the utility of an approach that incorporates analyses of the contours of both power and deviance.

Also See the Following Articles

CRIMINAL BEHAVIOR, THEORIES OF • POLITICAL ECONOMY OF VIOLENCE AND NONVIOLENCE • POWER, SOCIAL AND POLITICAL THEORIES OF • SOCIAL CONTROL AND VIOLENCE • SOCIAL EQUALITY AND INEQUALITY

Bioliography

Becker, H. S. (1963). *Outsiders: Studies in the sociology of deviance.* New York: Free Press.

Ben-Yehuda, N. (1985). *Deviance and moral boundaries.* Chicago: University of Chicago Press.

Black, D. (1993). *The social structure of right and wrong.* San Diego: Academic Press.

Cohen, A. K. (1955). *Delinquent boys.* Glencoe, IL: Free Press.

Crelinsten, R. D., & Schmid, A. P. (Eds.). (1995). *The politics of pain: Torturers and their masters.* Boulder, CO: Westview Press.

Downes, D., & Rock, P. (1988). *Understanding deviance* (2nd. ed.). Oxford: Clarendon Press.

Durkheim, E. (1899/1973). Two laws of penal evolution (T. A. Jones & A. Scull, Trans.). *Economy and Society, 2,* 285–308.

Ericson, R. V., Baranek, P. M., & Chan, J. B. (1991). *Representing order: Crime, law, and justice in the news media.* Toronto: University of Toronto Press.

Erikson, K. T. (1966). *Wayward Puritans: A study in the sociology of deviance.* New York: John Wiley.

Farrell, R. A., & Case, C. (1995). *The black book and the Mob: The untold story of the control of Nevada's casinos.* Madison, WI: University of Wisconsin Press.

Gamson, W. A. (1975). *The strategy of social protest.* Homewood, IL: Dorsey Press.

Garfinkel, H. (1956). Conditions of successful degradation ceremonies. *American Journal of Sociology, 61,* 420–424.

Garland, D. (1990). *Punishment and modern society.* Oxford: University of Chicago Press.

Goddman, E. (1963). *Stigma.* Englewood Cliffs, NJ: Prentice-Hall.

Goode, E., & Ben-Yehuda, N. (1994). *Moral panics: The social construction of deviance.* Cambridge, MA: Blackwell.

Gusfield, J. R. (1963). *Symbolic crusade: Status politics and the American temperance movement.* Urbana, IL: University of Illinois Press.

Heitzeg, N. A. (1996). *Deviance: Rulemakers & rulebreakers.* New York: West.

Lauderdale, P., & Amster, R. (Eds.). (1997). *Lives in the balance: Perspectives on global injustice and inequality.* New York: Brill.

Lauderdale, P., & Cruit, M. (1993). *The struggle for control: A study of law, disputes, and deviance.* Albany, NY: SUNY Press.

Marx, G. (1988). *Undercover: Police surveillance in America.* Berkeley, CA: University of California Press.

Merchant, C. (1992). *Radical ecology: The search for a livable world.* New York: Routledge.

Merton, R. K. (1938). Social structure and anomie. *American Sociological Review, 3,* 672–682.

Mills, C. W. (1942). The professional ideology of social pathologists. *American Journal of Sociology, 49,* 165–180.

Oliverio, A. (1998). *The state of terror.* New York: SUNY Press.

Pfohl, S. J. (1994). *Images of deviance and social control: A sociological history.* New York: McGraw-Hill.

Pfuhl, E. H., Jr., & Henry, S. (1994). *The deviance process* (2nd ed.). Belmont, CA: Wadsworth.

Quinney, R. P. (1977). *Class, state and crime: On the theory and practice of criminal justice.* New York: David McKay.

Schur, E. M. (1980). *The politics of deviance.* Englewood Cliffs, NJ: Prentice-Hall.

Sumner, C. (1994). *The sociology of deviance: An obituary.* Buckingham, UK: Open University Press.

Sutherland, E. H., & Cressey, D.R. (1966). *Principles of criminology* (7th ed). Philadelphia: J. P. Lippincott.

Power, Alternative Theories of

Nancy Bell

The University of Texas at Austin

I. Broad Definitions of Power
II. Power as a Relational and Communal Phenomenon
III. Focus on the Weak
IV. New Forms of Expressing Power
V. Power and Violence

GLOSSARY

Alternative Structures New social structures that exist alongside and challenge the legitimacy of previously established structures.

Nonadherence One potential response of the "weak" in traditional power relations in which the demands of the "powerful" are denied.

One Up/One Down Relationships Interactions based on the assumption that when two people come together, one must occupy a superior position, while the other must play a subordinate role.

Power Over The traditional definition of power that focuses on power as domination, generally maintained through authority, force, or coercion.

Power To An alternative definition of power that focuses on power as "empowerment," ability, competence.

Zero-Sum A situation or relationship in which a gain for one side entails a corresponding loss for the other side.

THE CONCEPT OF POWER is fundamental to discussions of politics, and it has been explored extensively by social and political theorists as well as by philosophers for literally centuries. While there is little agreement on a single, correct definition of power, the majority of available discourses on the topic are remarkably similar in that most authors treat power as if it were a thing to possess for the purpose of achieving one's will over others. Defined as a form of domination, power is generally discussed in the context of its effects on others.

Using this basic definition, the questions in which most theorists have been interested focus on the mechanics of obtaining and maintaining dominance in the public arena: Who rules whom? What are the various forms of domination? What resources are required to maintain a position of dominance and how are they most effectively used? What political strategies arise out of the efforts of those who have power in a society to control their subjects? What differentiates legitimate power over others from more tyrannical and unacceptable forms? And, more recently, how are international relations affected by the actions of various national leaders? What all of these questions have in common is: first, an assumption that the most important issues to be addressed in discussions of power focus on power in the form of domination; second, that the primary subject that warrants attention is the behavior of those who dominate; and third, that the most important demonstrations of power take place in the political (or at least the public) arena.

While these foci are undoubtedly important, traditional theories of power have been criticized in recent years for being too narrow and for not attending to the broader range of power relations that exists in all societies. Some social and political scientists have begun to formulate new theories about power that address some of these additional concerns. While quite divergent in their approaches, many of the authors of this new body of theory have developed their ideas along similar lines, and some common themes can be identified in their work. It is the task of this article to identify several of these themes and to discuss some of the implications of alternative theories of power for our understanding of the broader issues of social violence, peace, and conflict.

I. BROAD DEFINITIONS OF POWER

The starting point for nearly all alternative theories of power is to broaden the definition of the basic concept to include more than the traditional relationship between the "powerful" (few) and the (many) "weak." Many theorists make a distinction between "power over," characterized by domination, and "power to," which expands the concept to include multiple forms of individual and communal empowerment. In this way, power in general is clearly distinguished from force, coercion, and control and is associated with characteristics such as ability, capacity, competence, and potentiality. This fundamental shift broadens the subject matter of inquiries into the dynamics of power relations to include not only those who possess power over others, but also those who have been labeled "powerless" and therefore excluded as primary subjects to be considered in the study of power.

This change of focus is partially due to the social position of those who are questioning more traditional assumptions about power. For instance, in many cases, these alternative theorists are women (feminists as well as nonfeminists), and their theories are guided by their social experiences as women. As many feminist theorists have pointed out, the experience of being male or female in a gendered society fundamentally shapes one's worldview and his or her ideas about what is important and valuable. The general assumption here is that traditional theories of power have focused on questions and issues more salient to the experience of men and, in particular, white men (i.e., those who have historically been in positions of dominance over other segments of the population).

One result of this situation is that the specific experiences of those defined as the "weak" in society have received much less attention or have been left out of discussions of power altogether. In order to give voice to their subjective experiences with power, women have provided a primary source of alternative theories, as have members of other groups such as people of color, those whose countries have been colonized, and those interested in the dynamics of nonviolent direct action. The contributions of these new theorists have broadened the context in which power is studied, as well as the very definition of power itself. It is also understood that power relations exist in the private sphere of the family and in intimate relations as well as in the public domain of politics and international relations, and that these two levels of power relations are interconnected in important ways.

In alternative views, power is not understood as a "zero-sum" quantity to be possessed by some at the expense of others. The zero-sum approach is based on a scarcity model and assumes that there is a limited amount of power available for distribution. Therefore, if one party's power increases, another's must necessarily decrease. This sets up a whole series of either/or dichotomous categories around which traditional theories of power are organized (e.g., the ruler and the ruled, the powerful and the powerless, the state and the masses, oppressors and the oppressed, colonizers and the colonized, etc.). Stated somewhat differently, this can be thought of as a "one-up/one-down" dynamic of interaction, complete with norms for behavior on each side of the relationship.

In contrast, empowerment theories emphasize power relationships based on the assumption that the availability of power (as ability, competence, energy) is unlimited and that the dynamics of power relationships can be of the "both/and" or "win/win" variety. In other words, power is potentially exercised by all people involved in an interaction, and an increase of power on one side does not necessarily lead to a lessening of power on the other. This is possible because power is not defined as a "thing" to be possessed and hoarded, but rather as a "capacity" to be developed and shared. In discussing alternative definitions of power, Marilyn French has noted that the syntax available in the English language for talking about power is actually very misleading because it is "in fact false to speak of 'having power.'" This observation indicates that efforts to reconceptualize power as a process or an interactive dynamic can be aided by a reconsideration of the very vocabulary we use to describe power.

Empowerment theorists do not deny the presence or

significance of "power over" in social interaction—they simply state that this is not the only type of power exercised. Again, this is related to the subjective experiences of many of those who propose alternative theories of power. If they limited their perspective to incorporate only those definitions of power operative in more traditional theories, then the only descriptions available to describe their position would be those of "weak" or "powerless," and these labels do not adequately describe their life experiences. So the development of alternative theories of power is not based on denial or naiveté, but rather on the desire to create more inclusive theories that incorporate the experiences of *all* people involved in power relationships. It is important to note that empowerment can be practiced by the "weak" in relationships characterized by dominance and submission, and when it is, this inevitably presents a challenge to the authority of the "powerful" in such interactions. We return to this point in a later section.

II. POWER AS A RELATIONAL AND COMMUNAL PHENOMENON

When power is defined as an attribute, then the "powerful" (or those who have this attribute) can be studied totally independently of those who do not possess it. Indeed, this has been the approach in numerous studies of the social and political "elite" and in some classic analyses of political parties and leaders. One important insight of alternative theories of power is that while such an approach provides a great deal of important information, it is incomplete. This critique is based on an understanding of the fact that power is not simply an attribute, but always and inherently involves a relationship between individuals and groups in an interactive social context. In other words, power is a *relational* phenomenon—it cannot be exercised by one person in isolation from others.

This basic insight has implications for examining the relationships both among those individuals labeled "weak" in traditional theories of power and between "rulers" and the "ruled." As mentioned above, alternative theorists frequently suggest that power (defined as "power to") is a *communal* phenomenon rather than an individual attribute. In defining power, Hannah Arendt goes so far as to say that power cannot be exercised except in situations where people are "acting in concert" (otherwise, it is strength, force, authority, or violence—each of which is specifically distinguishable from power). Power, then, is seen as a product of co-operation, not control. This assumption constitutes a major break with traditional theories focused on domination.

The concept of community becomes important, then, in many alternative theories of power. People in communities are held together by common interests, which serve as the catalyst for the exercise of "power from below." Power in this context is not seen as limited in quantity, but is rather a regenerative phenomenon—it increases as it is shared. Neither is it something to be feared as a source of corruption (as Lord Acton's famous statement implies) because it is governed by the morals of the community. Nancy Hartsock has suggested that "power fundamentally structures community"—it is the motivation for the formation of community as well as the glue that holds it together. In her book on Black feminist thought, Patricia Hill Collins stresses the historical importance of community for racially oppressed groups in the United States. According to Collins, the community has traditionally served as a "potential sanctuary" and a source of nurturance for Black men and women and as a source of empowerment and support to help them face external oppression. Certain feminist groups have been characterized in a similar way. None of these views of community as a source of power really make sense within the context of a perspective that views power as domination and as an individual attribute, but they are fundamental to theories that define power as ability, capacity, and energy.

In looking at the relationship between the "powerful" and the "weak," alternative theorists recognize that domination is not a unidirectional phenomenon. While it may appear that the source of the energy exchange in interactions between the powerful and the weak is always "from above," this is not the case. In writing about power interactions in the early 1900s, Georg Simmel noted that there is an "exchange of influences" in any interaction, whether or not this exchange is immediately apparent to the observer. According to Simmel, acknowledging the multidimensional nature of power interactions transforms what appears to be "absolute influence, on the one side, and an absolute being-influenced, on the other," into a "sociological form," which inherently embodies an exchange of influences originating from *both* sides of the interaction. The implication here is that one cannot understand power over others without considering the role played by the "others." One result of emphasizing this relational dimension of power is that the frequently dismissed "weak" are redefined as an important part of power interactions and their role becomes a primary focus of interest in alternative theories.

III. FOCUS ON THE WEAK

While traditional theories of power focus primarily on those who dominate, the forms this domination takes, and how power as domination is most successfully exercised, many alternative theories are more interested in the other side of the equation—those who are "dominated." This is perhaps the most important contribution of these theories both for understanding power as an abstract concept as well as the ways in which it is manifested as concrete, political action. Michel Foucault observed that the "concrete nature of power" (i.e., the way it is specifically exercised) can be most clearly seen in the daily struggles that take place at the grassroots level—that is, the powers wielded by that group of people in society traditionally defined as "weak." He criticized political analysts for their limited focus on the state and other social institutions designed to create and sustain power from above because they had failed to address the "mechanics of power in themselves." In many cases, the forms of power enacted by the "weak" remain largely invisible in traditional studies of power. James C. Scott uses the notion of "hidden transcripts of power" to explore these externally invisible "infra-politics of the powerless," and his analysis of various "powerless" groups provides important insight into how power is exercised at various levels.

The key to analyzing the "weak" is in recognizing that they are not truly weak. The primary reason that this is true relates back to the idea that power is relational. While power as domination appears to be immutable, in actuality the position of those who use power to control others is ultimately quite unstable, even tenuous. This is because their continued success is utterly dependent upon the consent of those whom they attempt to govern. In other words, for the "dominator's" role in a power relationship to work, there must be those willing to fulfill the requirements of being the "dominated" on the opposite side of the interaction. This is not necessarily something that can be insured by force or coercion alone, although these manifestations of power may delay, for a certain time, rebellious responses from the governed. Even Machiavelli acknowledged the dependence of the ruler on the goodwill of his subjects and concluded in *The Prince* that although violent coercion may insure adherence, it can never do so permanently.

The danger to those who attempt to dominate others is that they may encounter significant resistance to their right or ability to rule. This resistance can take many forms—violent or nonviolent, verbal or nonverbal, sub-tle or overt—but it always presents a threat. Many of those working on alternative theories of power have pointed out that, ultimately, to insure successful long-term domination, the person or regime attempting to rule must be granted a certain degree of legitimacy from those under their control. Refusing to grant this legitimacy may be the most effective manifestation of "power to." There is an interesting curiosity in this basic insight: if domination were truly the most effective form of power, why is it that those who practice it in its most extreme forms are often the most paranoid about losing their position of control? And why is it that the most repressive regimes are often the most likely to fail? One will not find the answers to these questions by focusing on those who dominate in isolation from their relationships with those whom they attempt to control.

In his writings on nonviolent action, Gene Sharp offers numerous historical examples of the power of nonadherence on the part of those who refuse to grant legitimacy to the dictates of those in positions of dominance. This form of power is often manifested in the most repressive of situations. Gandhi understood its full potential in the struggle for India's independence, as did Martin Luther King, Jr. in his campaign for civil rights in the United States. Citizens in various countries also successfully challenged Hitler during World War II by denying the legitimacy of the Nazi occupation forces. More recently, the nonviolent revolutions in the Philippines, in eastern Europe, the former Soviet states, and in Russia itself provide examples of the potential impact of the withdrawal of consent by the governed.

Theoretically, the most important point here is that noncooperation, withdrawal of consent, and other forms of resistance to domination are not just *responses* to power, they are, in and of themselves, alternative *forms* of power. Thus, some alternative theorists have focused very specifically on what Elizabeth Janeway calls the "powers of the weak." The first power of the weak that she discusses is also perhaps the most important: the power to "disbelieve." If those who exercise power over others have the power to define, they must face the possibility that the definitions of the power relationship that they create may be disbelieved and rejected by the supposedly powerless people whose reality they attempt to shape. This is the ultimate expression of the denial of legitimacy that is required for power over to be effective.

A second power of the weak is the power to organize and to work collectively toward achieving social change. This form of power relates back to the importance of community empowerment discussed above. Communities provide not only a site for strategizing and communicating common interests, but also the strength of sheer numbers for the purpose of challenging those attempting to maintain "power over." Some theorists have emphasized that "power to" must be enacted collectively—in part, to increase the likelihood of its success, but also because of the very definition of this form of power. As was previously stated, "power to" is not an individual attribute, but a communal phenomenon; it cannot exist except in the context of people acting collectively.

Finally, it should be noted that the enactment of power by the weak does not always take such agreeable forms. Berenice Carroll discusses the possibility that oppressed people may exhibit "disintegrative power" as a way of defying the "law and order" established by the ruling regime. These actions may take violent forms such as rioting, vandalism, and the destruction of public property and services. They are most often enacted by large groups of people who lack a long-term agenda for social improvement and are simply venting their frustrations. In spite of the fact that manifested disintegrative power is generally in the form of a "short-term burst," it can be very destructive and can effectively disrupt or break down existing social, economic, and political structures. Carroll states that this kind of power is, in the long run, capable of "destroying great empires" and must be recognized and dealt with in developing more inclusive theories of power.

Whether the "weak" manifest their power in positive or negative, violent or nonviolent forms, the important thing to recognize is that they are fully capable of presenting a very real challenge to the coercive power of domination. While some traditional power theorists admit that the power of resistance must not be overlooked, they often continue to focus their attention on how to "control" this form of power to increase the likelihood that power over will prevail. Many alternative theorists, on the other hand, celebrate the power of the weak and frequently turn their attention toward trying to foster its growth. This may be due, at least in part, to the subjective experiences and worldviews of those who theorize about power, a point discussed above in Section I. In either case, what seems clear is that an adequate theory of social and political power must be broad enough to include consideration of types of power that have traditionally been deemphasized.

IV. NEW FORMS OF EXPRESSING POWER

Expanding the focus of studies of power to include the "weak" necessitates the consideration of alternative methods of expressing power, and this has been another theme in developing alternative theories of power. "Power over" is generally communicated in a hierarchical manner and, in its more extreme forms, through the use of force to insure the compliance of the weak. There is an emphasis on the use of rational argument to achieve this goal, and the tone of such communication is quite often authoritarian and/or coercive—especially if any challenge to the authority of the powerful is perceived to be present. These are forms of expression that logically match the goals of obtaining and maintaining dominance over others. They do not, however, fit as well with efforts to create and sustain the type of power being described here as "power to" or empowerment.

Because empowerment is not a zero-sum or limited quantity, one need not be concerned with losing it in the process of communicating with others. This removes the necessity of taking a defensive stance and opens up the possibility for additional forms of expression. Some of these forms may not seem "rational" according to traditional definitions, but they can be very effective, and they reflect the affective elements often present in alternative forms of power. Numerous illustrations of this type of expression of power can be found in the literature on nonviolent direct action.

Gandhi, for instance, and Martin Luther King, Jr. after him, understood very well the value of combining affective and cognitive elements in communicating power "from below." The rhetoric of nonviolence often takes on a moral or religious tone in the midst of secular struggles. Both Gandhi and King emphasized the necessity of love and forgiveness in their liberation movements, and Adam Michnik, a leader in the Solidarity movement, noted the strong "religious background" of the antitotalitarian struggle in Poland. In a similar way, women peace activists have frequently expressed their power in apparently illogical but ultimately effective ways. Female activists have surrounded the Pentagon in the United States with ribbons and attached colored ribbons and children's pictures to the fence surrounding the missile base at Grenham Common in England. These are not responses of powerless people but rather creative expressions of alternative forms of power. It might be added that this form of expressing power is increasingly effective in the modern age because of the ability to quickly and globally communicate visual images through television, computers, and other media forms.

Innovative and alternative expressions of power can also be found in efforts to redefine the internal structure of various organizations. Both bell hooks and Nancy Hartsock have noted efforts by feminists in the United

States to develop new strategies within existing organizations to facilitate the expression of power by all members of a particular group. By adopting strategies such as consensus decision-making, rotating tasks, and internal democracy, those previously defined as powerless are working to build increasingly nonhierarchical organizations that nullify the dichotomous vision of powerful/powerless.

Another nontraditional form of expressing power is through the construction of alternative or "parallel" structures. Sustaining domination-based power relations generally involves the maintenance of existing social structures and the institutions that support them. Conversely, challenges from below can be expressed by creating new structures and patterns of interaction that make the supposedly powerless less dependent upon the requirements and rules of those trying to dominate them. The establishment of parallel structures does not deny the existence of repressive structures, it simply denies their legitimacy and the forms of power they promote.

An example of this type of expression of power is Gandhi's emphasis on doing "constructive work" to build a free India without waiting for the British to leave. For instance, he created an alternative to Indian dependence on imported textiles by not only initiating a boycott of British cloth, but then challenging Indians to spin and weave their own cloth. In so doing, they created an alternative, coexisting structure to meet their needs without promoting dependence on those who had colonized their country. In addition, Václav Havel, the famous dissident-now-President of the Czech Republic, has written of the importance of the development of a strong alternative press in Czechoslovakia and other eastern European countries prior to the departure of the Soviets in 1989–1990. While emphatically outlawed by the "powerful" in these countries, these thriving alternative structures provided a valuable means of communication of power "from below." All of these examples of new forms of expressing power require a certain level of creativity and a commitment to the sort of expansive view of power emphasized by the alternative theorists being discussed here.

V. POWER AND VIOLENCE

What, if any, insights do alternative theories of power offer concerning the relationship between power and violence? When conceived as domination, acting out power inherently involves a hierarchical relationship, where conflict ultimately leads to one person or group "winning out" over the other. Violence (or at least the threat of violence) is a common feature of this type of competitive interaction, and the chance of violence being employed seems to increase as the level of conflict escalates. Several of the theorists whose ideas have been discussed here suggest that practicing alternative forms of power may reduce the likelihood of violence. The justification for this claim is rooted in the assumption that when power is reconceptualized, the means and desired results of conflict are also framed differently; conflictual relationships are not guided by a "one-up/one-down" mentality, but rather by the notion of empowerment as a common goal.

Viewed in this way, it is neither possible nor desirable to get rid of conflict in human interactions. Conflict is inevitable; what is *not* inevitable is resorting to violence as a means of resolving conflict. The goal is to transform destructive conflict into what has been called "constructive" or "productive" conflict. Rather than presenting a threat, conflict can be an effective tool in the process of achieving desired social change. Thus, Gandhi used the term "constructive work" to describe the nonviolent resistance to domination that he advocated and believed that it was through engaging in this form of constructive conflict that people came to realize their "true power." Riane Eisler argues in her book *The Chalice and the Blade* that there is a strong historical precedence for resolving conflict in this way and that it is associated with alternative definitions of power that have been proposed by women for centuries. Gene Sharp also provides numerous concrete examples of the effects of nonviolent direct action as a form of power. The conclusion to be drawn from these and other alternative theories of power is that there is a direct correlation between framing power as dominance and the use of violence. It follows, then, that adopting new definitions of power that are not focused on domination is a necessary step in achieving the goal of reducing violence.

Hannah Arendt's analysis of power also offers important insights into the relationship between power and violence. Arendt defines power as the ability of people not only to act, but to act in concert. In stating this definition, she is very specifically contrasting the concept of power with that of violence. What distinguishes power and violence, for Arendt, is the fact that while power is a human ability, violence is instrumental in character (i.e., it requires implements and is never an end in itself as power can be). This leads her to several conclusions about the relationship between power and violence. First, although violence and power are frequently found together, they are in fact opposites; where one rules absolutely, the other does not appear. Second, power is the "glue" that holds community together, while violence destroys community. Third, and perhaps most important in the present context, whereas violence can defeat power, it can never create it.

Violence tends to be used when power is being lost, but since power cannot be created or recreated by violent acts, it can be overcome later by power. As an example of this, Arendt offers the case of the Soviet invasion of Czechoslovakia in 1968: the Soviets' strong display of violence was temporarily effective, but it never did become power. Writing in 1969, she did not know that power in Czechoslovakia would ultimately prevail over violence, but she might have logically predicted this outcome. According to Arendt's definitions of violence and power, to speak of "nonviolent power" is actually redundant—power can never be violent because these are oppositional terms. When carried to its logical conclusion, Arendt's argument leads to the idea that, ultimately, in order to *reduce violence*, we must *empower people*. This insight runs counter to the assumption behind numerous social policies that are designed to reduce violence by controlling (or disempowering) people.

Traditional definitions of power as domination are pervasive in the existing literature on violence as well as in peace studies. In her review of the development of peace research in 1972, Berenice Carroll argued that scholars in the field of peace research had failed to "challenge the prevailing conception of power as dominance" and were therefore unwittingly promoting a view of the world that ran counter to their stated intention of reducing global and domestic violence. By choosing to focus on persons, groups, and institutions conceived as powerful according to traditional definitions, even those interested in promoting peace have frequently produced theoretical and empirical research that is most useful to those who seek to establish and maintain power over others. To overcome this problem, Carroll proposed a fundamental shift in the field of peace research that would begin with redefining power and lead to the systematic study of "the powers of the powerless."

Breaking out of what Carroll calls the "mental straightjacket of the cult of power" is extremely difficult. It is *always* extremely difficult to get outside of conceptual definitions that have become the unconscious components of one's generalized worldview. This, however, is precisely what alternative theorists of power believe is required. What all of these theories have in common is the idea that power is intricately linked to violence and that reconceptualizing power is a first and necessary step toward understanding and ultimately reducing violence.

Also See the Following Articles

POWER AND DEVIANCE • POWER, SOCIAL AND POLITICAL THEORIES OF

Bibliography

Arendt, H. (1972). *Crises of the republic.* New York: Harcourt Brace Jovanovich.

Carroll, B. A. (1972). Peace research: The cult of power. *Journal of Conflict Resolution, 16*(4), 585–616.

Collins, P. H. (1991). *Black feminist thought: Knowledge, consciousness, and the politics of empowerment.* New York: Routledge.

Eisler, R. (1987). *The chalice and the blade.* San Francisco: Harper and Row.

Foucault, M. (1980). *Power/knowledge.* New York: Pantheon.

French, M. (1985). *Beyond power: On women, men, and morals.* New York: Ballantine.

Gandhi, M. K. (1967). *The mind of Mahatma Gandhi* Ahmedabad, India: Navajivan.

Hartsock, N. C. M. (1983). *Money, sex, and power.* Boston: Northeastern University Press.

Havel, V. (1978/1990). The power of the powerless. *Without force or lies: Voices from the revolution of central Europe in 1989–90* (W. M. Brinton & A. Rinzler, Eds.) (pp. 43–127). San Francisco: Mercury House.

hooks, b. (1984). *Feminist theory: From margin to center.* Boston: South End Press.

Janeway, E. (1980). *Powers of the weak.* New York: Alfred A. Knopf.

King, M. L., Jr. (1986). *A testament of hope: The essential writings of Martin Luther King, Jr.* San Francisco: HarperCollins.

Machiavelli, N. (1514/1961). *The prince.* New York: Penguin Books.

Schaef, A. W. (1981). *Women's reality.* San Francisco: Harper & Row.

Scott, J. C. (1990). *Domination and the arts of resistance.* New Haven, CT: Yale University Press.

Sharp, G. (1973). *Power and struggle, part one of the politics of nonviolent action.* Boston: Porter Sargent.

Simmel, G. (1908/1950). *The sociology of Georg Simmel.* New York: The Free Press.

Smith, D. E. (1990). *The conceptual practices of power.* Boston: Northeastern University Press.

Power, Social and Political Theories of

Mark Haugaard

National University of Ireland, Galway

GLOSSARY

False consciousness A set of beliefs that sustain relationships of power and powerlessness between actors.

Genealogy The second phase of Foucault's work where he analyzed the constitution of the relationship between power, knowledge, and truth.

Nondecision-Making The decision to set an agenda.

Power

Coercive: social power with a threat attached.

Consensual: power that is in the subjectively perceived interests of all the social actors in an interaction.

Conflictual: power that is contrary to the perceived interests of the social actor over whom it is exercised.

Exercise of: A exercises power over B to the extent to which A can get B to do something that B would not otherwise do.

Resources: potential power that exists prior to the exercise of power, including allocative and authoritative sources of power.

Scope of: the issues over which power is exercised.

Social: as opposed to physical power, social power is structurally and systemically mediated.

Structure The fundamental unit of social order.

System An assembled set of mutually referring structures.

Violence Unmediated physical power between agents.

AT THE MOST GENERAL LEVEL, most social and political theorists conceive of the study of power as both the analysis of the capacity of individuals to make others do things that they would not otherwise do and as the study of the social relationships that sustain that capacity.

I. THE CONCEPT OF POWER

In this analysis of power we shall make a number of conceptual moves beginning with a general analysis of the concept of power. This will be followed by an analysis of two contemporary debates concerning power in modern social and in political theory that gives us a background framework within which to analyze the relationship between power and other closely related social phenomena, such as violence, peace, and conflict.

Machiavelli was the first of many to argue that the study of power is the main object of political analysis and, yet, to date there is no single agreed definition of power. One of the reasons for this lack of agreement on the definition of power is that it is what Wittgenstein termed a "family resemblance" concept. In much the same way as members of a family resemble each other without there being one single characteristic that they all have in common, a family resemblance concept is a word that has an overlapping set of meanings without the existence of a single core essence to link all usages. While there are many characteristics shared by "the power of love," the power of money," "the president's power," "electric power," "A exercises power over B," "the power of paranoid delusions should not be underestimated," yet there is no obvious single characteristic that links them together. Even if one were to be found, it would always be possible to imagine a further usage, not in this list, that would not share this essence.

The fact that a word is a family resemblance concept does not necessarily entail that it is vague. One of the characteristics of family resemblance concepts is that they frequently have relatively stable usage within a "language game." A language game is a system of thoughts or ideas with an internal logic that generates specific interrelated usages of words. The logical relations of a system of ideas create relatively stable usages of words that refer to each other in a systemic way. The language of political analysis constitutes a separate language game from the one that is reproduced by those who concern themselves with the generation of electricity or writing romantic tales of love and affection. Consequently, "the power of love," in the context of romantic fiction, and "electric power" belong to different language games than "the power of the president," and those of us working in the academic fields of politics or sociology need not concern ourselves with the former usages of the word.

A language game is self-referential to the extent to which a system of specific usages has internal consistency. Unless the purpose of a specific language game is purely the clarification of everyday speech, the usages of words will be inherently local to, and determined by, the system of ideas being developed. In other words, there will be specific usages that are more confined and more rigid than everyday speech.

In the case of this particular analysis of social and political theories of power we shall develop a local language game where terms are used in a specific way that is determined by our theoretical understanding of social relations. The purpose of this usage is not pedantic, nor is it to clarify "mistakes" in everyday speech.

Rather, it is a means that enables us to understand the workings of power relations at the level of social and political theory. Consequently, the usage of language within this entry is specific to a particular, essentially Western, tradition of theory. In this context, it should be noted that in Eastern philosophy there is also a highly sophisticated literature on power that, because it is shaped by a different system of ideas, embodies a different language game and, consequently, a different conceptualization of power than is analyzed here.

Even within the confines of the tradition of Western social and political thought there is no one single social and political theory of power that everyone accepts as the only true and valid one. In the first half of our analysis we shall examine two of the big theories of power: the three-dimensional power debate and Foucault's perception of power. This will be followed by an overview position bringing together these perceptions of power in combination with insights from the work of Max Weber, Anthony Giddens, Stewart Clegg, Barry Barnes, and Mark Haugaard among others. In this analysis every effort will be made to clarify not only the workings of power but also the relationship between power and other related concepts, such as, violence, coercion, and peace.

II. THE ORIGINS OF THE DEBATE

Contemporary debates on power began in the fifties in the United States. At that time C. Wright Mills—in his influential book, *The Power Elite*—and community power theorists—most notably Floyd Hunter, in *Community Power Structure*—were highly critical of American democracy. Put simply, they argued that power was distributed unequally and, as a consequence, existing democratic political procedures were ineffective. Instead of a true democracy involving the equal distribution of power, the United States was characterized by an essentially pyramidal system of social stratification dominated by a small power elite. In response to these criticisms Robert Dahl tried to defend the workings of the system by developing a model of democracy that he termed polyarchy. Central to this model was a new vocabulary of power that is still, in part, with us today.

Dahl had a conflictual view of power which was influenced by Max Weber's famous definition of power, whereby "Power is the probability that one actor within a social relationship will be in a position to carry out his will despite resistance, regardless of the basis on which this probability rests." (Weber, 1978: 53). Dahl also distinguished power from *power resources*. Within his framework, power is identified with *the exercise of power* where one actor makes another actor do something which they would not otherwise have done: "A has power over B to the extent that he can get B to do something that B would not otherwise have done" (Dahl, 1957: 202–203). For Dahl power entails a direct causal relationship between actors and, as such, is an interactive and non-subjective phenomenon. As he observes:

> Suppose I stand on a corner and say to myself, "I command all automobile drivers on this street to drive on the right side of the road"; suppose further that all the drivers actually do as I "command" them to do; still, most people will regard me as mentally ill if I insist that I have enough power over automobile drivers to compel them to use the right side of the road. On the other hand, suppose a policeman is standing in the middle of an intersection at which most ordinary traffic moves ahead; he orders all traffic to turn right or left; the traffic moves as he orders it to do. Then it accords with what I conceive to be the bedrock idea of power to say that the policeman acting in this particular role evidently has the power to make automobile drivers turn right or left rather than go ahead. (Dahl, 1957: 202).

In contrast to this cause and effect identification of power, power resources are a form of *potential* power. While it is the case that, for instance, wealth is a power resource that is unequally distributed, it may be the case that one wealthy man chooses to collect paintings while another may collect politicians. It is only the latter wealthy person who exercises power and, as a consequence, influences the democratic process. Hence, the identification of power resources should not automatically be equated with actual power.

In evaluating the distribution of power it is important to remember that resources are not a generalized capacity for action. Resources are limited to certain issues, which he referred to as the *scope* of power. So, for instance, Dahl's resources as University Professor at Yale gave him a scope of power that included control over what students of politics read, whereas the power of the local traffic police included where they parked their cars but not what they read. The scope of power of Dahl and the police concerned different issues areas even if some of the individuals over whom it could be exercised were the same. Importantly for his defense of American democracy, power resources of different scope are frequently nonmutually-cumulative or non-

combinable—it is hard to imagine a single power elite having both the power resources of university professor and the police.

Power resources are not only potential in the sense that they need to be exercised in order to influence the political process but they are also potential in the deeper sense that their effective mobilization presupposes *skill* and *motivation*. A highly motivated and skilled individual or group of people may well be able to mobilize relatively few resources to great effect. To take the instance of labor, employees can organize successfully against their employers through the use of skill and motivation. Similarly, highly motivated, relatively resourceless groups—such as environmental lobbies—frequently exercise more power than less motivated and disunited millionaires.

In addition to this Dahl also introduces several other terms including the *domain* of power, which refers to those over whom power is exercised, and the *intensity* of power, which refers to the amount of power exercised. In power relations those who exercise power of great domain frequently have power of low intensity, and vice versa. Politicians frequently exercise power of great domain but of low intensity whereas, comparatively, employers usually exercise power of great intensity but of a small domain.

Using this sophisticated set of theoretical distinctions, Dahl argued that Mills and community power theorists had demonstrated that there was an unequal distribution of potential power but not actual power in American society. Put simply, while he was willing to accept that there were many millionaires and heads of corporations who had great potential power this was not the same as showing that they exercised power in a manner which subverted the democratic process. In order to analyze actual power, Dahl argued that one should analyze actual political decision-making, not simply the distribution of resources, which is what Mills and the community power theorists had done. In *Who Governs?* (1961), Dahl analyzed who initiated and who vetoed important decisions in New Haven and concluded that there was no single power elite. New Haven was made up of many competing elites. The aggregate consequence of these disunited elites was polyarchy, a process whereby there is unequal distribution of potential power but, in the long run, the difference between potential and actual power ensures that the system is relatively democratic.

While most theorists accept the distinction between the exercise of power and power resources, and make reference to skill, scope, domain, and intensity of power, few today, including Dahl himself, would accept that America is a perfectly functioning polyarchy. Part of the flaw of the model is that power and democracy are purely identified with decision-making.

Bachrach and Baratz argued that Dahl failed to take account of the biases of the system within which decisions were made. In two articles, "The Two Faces of Power" (1962), and "Decision and Nondecision" (1963), they argued that nondecision making was as important as decision-making. Nondecision-making is described as the second "face" of power whereby institutional biases are reproduced. Quoting Schattshneider, they argued that: "All forms of political organization have a bias in favour of the exploitation of some kinds of conflict and the suppression of others because *organization is the mobilization of bias*. Some issues are organized into politics while others are organized out" (Bachrach and Baratz, 1962: 949). In short, by focusing solely on public decision-making, Dahl failed to take account of the possibility that there were institutional biases built into the system that were so constructed that the interests of the relatively powerless never reached the decision-making stage. Interestingly, like Dahl, Bachrach and Baratz insisted that the creation of bias should be described as an exercise of power which is attributable to individual decisionmakers or, more accurately in this context, nondecisionmakers.

Aside from expanding the concept of power to include institutional bias, Bachrach and Baratz included some further conceptual clarifications to the language of power. While most of these have not remained in usage, and as a consequence shall not concern us, they drew a distinction between power and force that is theoretically significant. They argued that power is an essentially social and relational act whereas force is an unmediated direct physical act. Power involves communication and the reproduction of social relations whereas force is unmediated and, as such, takes place without a dependence upon reproduction of the norms of political society. We shall come to this distinction again, in greater detail, when discussing power and violence.

In *Power: A Radical View* (1974) Lukes joined the debate by arguing that, from the perspective of democratic theory, Bachrach and Baratz did not go far enough in their critique of Dahl. Lukes argued that structural biases are not only attributable to nondecisionmakers but are the product of general structural biases. Furthermore, he also argued that the ultimate and most insidious exercise of power is the control of the thoughts and desires of social actors. Lukes renamed Dahl's decision-making perspective the "first dimension of power," Bachrach and Baratz's nondecision-making

the "second dimension of power" and his more radical perception of power the "third dimension of power." The third dimension of power combines both a critique of the individualist focus of the first two dimensions of power with the concept of "false consciousness." The latter has its historical origins in Marxism where it is used to explain the prevalence of nonrevolutionary, and sometimes conservative, aspirations among the working classes.

The extension of the concept of power to cover false consciousness entailed a reformulation of the concept of power in terms of interests. According to this reformulation "... A exercises power over B when A affects B in a manner contrary to B's interests" (Lukes, 1974: 23). Following from this the first dimension of power is where A and B both know their interests and engage in overt conflict based upon those interests. In the second dimension of power B's interests are prevented from reaching the decision-making stage by nondecision-making and, in the third dimension of power, B cannot realize their interests either because of systemic structural biases and/or because they do not know what their true interests are.

While the third dimension of power undoubtedly radicalized the power debate it also rendered it problematic on two levels. First, the concept of structural biases entailed that it was necessary to divorce power from identified actors A exercising power over B, which had the potential of widening the concept of power to include all forms of systemic bias. Realizing this, Lukes wavered between a wide concept of power and a narrower conception that was specifically attributable to agents consistent with the agent A and B definition of power. A second, and arguably greater, problem for Lukes was the issue of false consciousness. Who is to decide what are the true and false interests of social actors? To take an instance: to those of Western culture the biases and beliefs of non-Western societies may appear as false consciousness, yet, describing them as such will almost invariably appear ethnocentric. However, despite these drawbacks, Lukes is obviously correct to point out that structures and beliefs are central to the maintenance of relations of domination.

During the late seventies and early eighties the three-dimensional power debate became stalled and, gradually, many of the issues raised in it became subsumed by other debates and, in so doing, became altered and clarified. In particular, the perceived link between power and knowledge has been theorized very differently by Michel Foucault and the relationship between power and structure has been central to the agent-structure debate, especially to the work of Anthony Giddens.

III. FOUCAULT, POWER/KNOWLEDGE

Foucault's concept of power is substantially more diffuse and, as a consequence, qualitatively different from that found in the three dimensional power debate. In Foucault, power is not the property of individual actors (in the direct A and B sense) although it is individuals who are the subjects of power. Even though power is directly linked to knowledge, it is not tied to a distinction between true or false interests. In order to understand how this works we must look at his position more generally.

Foucault's work can be divided into three distinct phases: the archaeology, the genealogy, and the "care of the self." The archaeology includes, among others, *The Order of Things* (1970); the genealogy, *Discipline and Punish* (1979), *Power/Knowledge* (1980), and *History of Sexuality*, Volume 1 (1981); and "the care of the self," the other two volumes of *History of Sexuality*. In the archaeology his theory of power is more implicit than explicit—he never actually mentions the concept in archaeology but later asserted that the archaeological works were about power even though he had not been aware of it at the time. The genealogical works are where his theory of power is most developed. The "care of the self" is not about power and, as a consequence, shall not concern us.

Genealogy is a logical development of archaeology. Central to both is the idea of writing a "history of the present." In writing a history of the present, Foucault wanted to understand how it is that we have come see the world in the way we do. He wished to explore the tacit and taken-for-granted that enable us to order things in the way we do. *The Order of Things* begins with a list of animals quoted from an ancient Chinese encyclopedia that included, among other things: "(a) belonging to the emperor, (b) embalmed, (c) tame, (d) suckling pigs, (d) sirens, (f) fabulous, (g) stray dogs, (h) included in the presents classification, (i) frenzied, . . ." (Foucault, 1970: xv). To us this appears an arbitrary classification, in the sense that, it is virtually impossible to imagine what type of mind could possibly see this as an ordered list. The reason we cannot make sense of the list is that the tacit knowledge, or what he termed the *episteme*, which informs this perception of the world is missing. We do not know what it must have been like to order the world in this way.

In writing a history of the present, Foucault tries to make us conscious of our episteme, or our tacit knowledge, which enables us to order the world the way we do and, in so doing, he makes us question everything that we take for granted. The object of this exercise is a form of radical social critique for the purpose of undermining the relations of domination that are reinforced by these take-for-granted beliefs.

Epistemes are shared systems of knowledge that have a layered historical existence. It is this layering that makes archaeology different from traditional history. In the latter there is continuous development across time whereas in archaeology there are self-contained systems of thought that, just as on an archaeological site, are situated horizontally relative to each other. Foucault argued that modern European history is characterized by three separate systems of thought. They extend approximately as follows: the Renaissance from about 1450 to 1650, the classical period from 1650 to 1800, and the modern period from 1800 to before or after the present. The moment of transition from one episteme to other he characterized as a *discontinuity* of world view.

In the Renaissance period knowledge was sought in the resemblances between things. The world was seen as mirroring unto itself. So, for instance, the human face mirrors the sky—the seven orifices mirror the seven planets. There were debates that to our ears sound as absurd as the Chinese encyclopedia, such as the debate between those who argued that plants mirrored animals except that they were upside-down (the roots corresponding to the mouth) whereas others argued that they were right-side up (the flower corresponding to the face).

In the classical period the whole pursuit of resemblances became perceived as a source of error. In its place there emerged elaborate systems of classifications. Classificatory tables were compiled—tables of different plant types and language were compiled as classificatory systems. Interestingly, man, the compiler of these tables, was missing from the system of classification (please note, that Foucault used "man" to signify both man and woman, and we will follow in the use of this, admittedly, gender-biased word purely for the purpose of analyzing his work, otherwise gender-neutral terms will be used. As the reader may have noted, in general, quotes are also left in their original gendered form).

For Foucault a key element in the transition to the modern period was introduction of man as an object of knowledge. From being entirely absent in the classical period, in the modern period man became a key source of knowledge and with that event the sciences of man were born. Truth was not found in either resemblance or tables but in humans as living beings.

This perception of man as a source of truth resulted in new forms of domination and power. All of a sudden a model of judgmental normality emerged. Certain behavioral patterns became classified as mad or delinquent, an exercise that was reinforced and legitimated by the human sciences proclaiming these classifications as scientifically true. A new class of social deviants was created to be studied, judged on their abnormality and ultimately resocialized. This judgment became central to modern power.

One of the characteristics of Foucault's archaeology was an inability to theorize social change between epistemes. In genealogy social change became tied to power. He argued that power is not a thing and is not situated anywhere but it is always exercised at the level of local strategy and struggle. Reversing Clausewitz's view that war is politics by other means, in *Power/Knowledge* (1980: 90) Foucault argued that politics is war by other means. The opposite of war is peace and peace does not represent the absence of war but, rather, represents the reinscription of the rules of war through the creation of rules of power. In this sense power is a form of pacification that works by codifying and taming war though the imposition of rules which create order. War is violence and violence, in turn, represents the absence of power.

In Lukes we saw that power was tied to the false perception of interests; in Foucault this is reversed and power is tied to truth. Power is located at the level of truth production. Truth is what reinforces certain worldviews and, as a consequence, is intrinsically tied up with ordering of the world. Epistemes do not simply happen but are, rather, reinforced through local power struggles at the level of truth production.

Foucault argues that social life is characterized by two levels of power conflict. There are the local struggles that take place within a regime of truth production and the deeper struggles that take place over the regime of truth production. The best image to explain this distinction between levels might be in terms of the image of a game. In an ongoing game of chess there is conflict between players. At this level the conflict is controlled and managed according to the rules of the game. According to Foucault, this is a relatively contained conflict compared to the situation where the rules of procedure are contested. In real life, as distinct from in games of chess, the rules of the game are continually contested and it is this that characterizes deep power conflict.

Epistemes and systems of thought are ways of ordering the world that constrain and limit action. Within the Renaissance episteme the conflict between those who regarded a plant as a right-side-up animal and those who regarded it as upside-down, was a constrained power conflict within a specific order. More significantly, in the modern period the study of social agents as objects of knowledge contributes to a set of rules of the game that characterize a new mode of power and domination.

Perceptions of the world are not considered arbitrary social constructs by those who reproduce them but are, rather, deemed to be anchored in truth. In this context, truth performs a legitimating function that reinforces tacit knowledge and, as a consequence, deep power struggles are a struggle over truth. As Foucault argued in *Power/Knowledge* (1980: 66) among other works, what interested him concerning truth was not the search for philosophical certainty but, rather, to show what function truth performed. A function that is to reinforce the rules of ordering the world and, as a consequence, to inscribe particular power relations.

The rules of ordering the world are not neutral between interests but favor certain relations of domination over others. The modern system of knowledge, with social actors as objects of knowledge, reinforces relations of domination where experts normalize those whose behavioral patterns do not accord with the scientifically established norm. Notice, the norm is "scientifically" established, the deviant is not deviant because their behavior does not conform relative to some subjective criteria but because it is deemed deviant relative to truth—scientific truth. As a consequence, the resistance in which deviants engage is both a resistance to truth and a resistance to a particular regime of power, and it is because their resistance has this dual aspect that they are inherently less powerful than those who have truth on their side.

Tacit knowledge is not only a way of ordering the world, but is also quite explicitly a way of reinforcing relations of domination. If power is bound up with struggle over perceptions, then power and truth are functional to each other, not dysfunctional. Where you have power, you will always have truth and where you have power and truth, you will always have resistance.

Power is not solely a negative that simply says no, as we tend to assume, but is inextricably bound up with the production of reality: "power produces; it produces reality; it produces domains of objects and rituals of truth" (Foucault, 1979: 194). The idea that power always says no, is negative, is functional to the workings of power. Because of the expectation that it is negative we are blind to it in its positive constituting mode.

In *History of Sexuality,* Volume 1, Foucault begins with the common perception of the history of sexuality. According to this view sexuality was repressed during the Victorian era and liberated in this century. According to this view, the Victorians could not talk about sexuality, yet, according to Foucault, if one looks at it another way they did nothing but talk about sexuality. In fact through their regime of suppression they produced a whole system of classifying deviant sexualities. To take the instance of child masturbation, the other side of the suppression of child masturbation was of course the creation of child masturbation as an object of knowledge. There was a science surrounding the discourse of masturbation and, with that, children became subjects of power and knowledge in a manner in which they had never previously. In short, power had produced something new, the child whose sexuality has to be monitored and controlled. Yet, this productive aspect of power is generally not visible to social critics because of our focus on the suppressive story.

The contrast between negative and productive power is central to Foucault's analysis of the modern prison system. In *Discipline and Punish* (1979) Foucault argues that there are two models of power. There is the premodern sovereign model of power, which is purely negative in its functioning, and there is the modern productive model of power.

The premodern system of punishment is based upon the idea of a sovereign situated at the apex of a power pyramid that is made up of powerless individuals at its base. The sovereign model of punishment represents a top-down and negative view of power. Interestingly, in this model of punishment violence is common. However, with the modern system of punishment, of which the prison is a paradigm example, the object of punishment is no longer physical abuse but, rather, discipline. This contrast is graphically illustrated in the opening pages of *Discipline and Punish,* which begins with a mid-eighteenth century description of a person being hanged, drawn, and quartered, which is then followed by a time-table of prison discipline dating from a mere 80 years later. The reason for the transition from one system of punishment to the other is not, as people generally assume, that society had become more civilized and humanitarian. What had happened was a transition to a new system of knowledge. As stated earlier, as a living being the individual was not an object of knowledge in premodern systems of knowledge whereas they are in the modern. The person to be disciplined is a person whose social functions have to be changed in accordance with a specific perception of normality. This perception of normality is not an arbitrary thing, it is the product of a new set of sciences—the sciences of man (the social sciences, criminology, and psychology, etc.). As sciences they are linked to truth and to a given perception of reality. This perception of reality is an academic discipline that produces new objects of knowledge (deviant individuals) who in turn have to be disciplined in accordance with the dictates of the discipline itself. In short, a perfect self-reproducing cycle of power is created.

Foucault's emphasis on power as constituting reality has been enormously influential in new social movements concerned with sexual identity and, similarly, in the feminist movement where his ideas are used to analyze the construction of "female" identity and gender as a mode of domination—for an interesting example of a feminist analysis of gender identity and power relations, see Judith Butler's *Gender Trouble* (1990).

IV. THE EXERCISE OF POWER

While there are differences between the concept of power central to the three-dimensional power debate and Foucault's analysis of power, they do have substantially more in common than is apparent at first sight. They address common elements of power and domination that may be teased out with the help of contemporary social and political theory.

What is clear from both debates is that relations of domination have three broad levels of analysis with different extents of visibility. At the first level there are the immediate and visibly obvious exercises of power that take place between individual actors in decision-making. This is the exercise of power that was central to Dahl's analysis but also, to a certain extent, part of the individual life experience of the subjects of power as theorized by Foucault. The second level is the structural context within which the exercise of power takes place. This includes not only the biases of the system that are visible in nondecision-making but, also, Lukes' analysis of structural bias and Foucault's rules of power. At a third level we have the social consciousness of social actors, which include both false consciousness and epistemes. In what follows we shall analyse these three levels.

With regard to the first level, Dahl is correct in arguing that we have to distinguish between the exercise of power from the standing conditions that make that exercise of power possible. However, in so doing we must be quite clear about the fact that the standing conditions within which the exercise of power takes place determine the relative distribution of power resources. In other words, the identification of power with the exercise of power should not entail trivialization of the conditions which the exercise of power presuppose, as it did for Dahl.

With regard to the second level, structures and institutions are what give order to a social or political system. They are the basic units of social order. As units of social order, structures and institutions are broadly similar. What distinguishes them is that we will use the concept of institutions to refer to obviously deliberately created units of order whereas structures are more unintentionally created. Political systems and organizations contain institutions whereas language and broader ordered social interaction is structural.

As has convincingly been argued by Giddens in his theory of structuration in *The Constitution of Society* (1984), structures do not exist in the world in a manner that is external to the actions of the individuals who reproduce society. Social structures are reproduced in the moment of action by social agents interacting in an ordered way. For the actors reproducing them, these structures exist as rules of procedure which enable them to act competently. If an act is ordered according to shared social rules the act in question is a structured act. Rules make the actions of others predictable and this enabling facet of social structure gives actors an ability to do things with others that they could not otherwise do if it were not for the existence of these social structures. In short, structure facilitates agency through the creation of social power.

Social structures do not exist in isolation from each other but relate to each other in a mutually reinforcing way. There is not a single social order in social life but many systems that interrelate and interpenetrate. What distinguishes one system from another is that the structures within a particular system are mutually relating. So, to take an instance, a political system is composed of structures and political institutions that gain meaning from mutual relations. For instance, in democratic systems the acts of voting and standing for election are both structured acts that gain meaning from each other.

Within a system, structures and institutions facilitate the exercise of power. In a democracy political parties desire mutually excluding outcomes—each wants to form a government (or be part of one, in the case of coalitions) and yet, simultaneously, not all can win. In a stable democracy the winner prevails over the loser by procedural means. The winner does not physically confront the loser but, rather, both parties subscribe to a set of structural principles that enables one party to prevail over the other because of mutual constraint.

The structured institutions of political systems are substantially more overt or more obvious than the structures of less well-defined social systems. However the same logic still prevails so, for instance, Foucault is correct to observe that a modern system of domination presupposes a modern way of ordering or structuring the world. The power relations that permeate organizations such as the school, the factory, or the prison all presuppose a structuring of the world that entails giving power resources to certain individuals (teachers, doctors, and prison officers) and disempowering others (students, patients, and prisoners). The ordering of society that a particular group of individuals subscribes to within a social system creates standing conditions of empowerment and disempowerment between them. As Stewart Clegg has argued in his book, *Frameworks of Power* (1989), the exercise of power (which he termed "episodic power") presupposes rules of the game, or structures of domination (which he called "dispositional power"), which are, in turn, reproduced through the routine exercise of power.

Giddens' famous "duality of structure" is based on the idea that structures enable actors to do things that they could not otherwise be able to do while simultaneously constraining them. The democratic system is an assembled set of social structures that both facilitate certain exercises of power while simultaneously constraining others. As Foucault argued, it is undoubtedly the case that the modern ordering of society facilitates exercises of power that were inconceivable in premodern societies and this is accomplished through the imposition of a shared regime of structural constraints.

This theorization of a shared structural basis of power converges with observations of so-called consensual power theorists. The first exponent of this position was Talcott Parsons who, in "On the Concept of Political Power" (1963), argued that power has its basis in a shared symbolic medium that is akin to money. While many have had problems with the money analogy, the more general point of the article is still accepted, which is: that in modern society social power is tied to the reproduction of systemic structural properties. More recently, in *The Nature of Power* (1988), Barry Barnes has also argued that the basis of social power is a shared commitment to the reproduction of social order.

The theorization of power within a context of structure naturally leads us to the analysis of the social consciousness of social actors. As we have just argued, the reproduction of social order is premised on the beliefs and perceptions of the social actors who reproduce social systems. The structured context of an exercise of power is not external to the lives of social actors, it is part of their social consciousness. Following Giddens, our social consciousness is divided into discursive consciousness knowledge and practical consciousness knowledge. Discursive consciousness knowledge is knowledge that we can easily put into words whereas practical consciousness is tacit knowledge which enables us to "go on" as socially competent agents. Obvious examples of practical consciousness knowledge include the rules of language and Foucault's analysis of epistemes. When Foucault argues that it is possible to order the world differently, or that in the classical period the world was ordered differently, he is making a claim about the incommensurable content of practical consciousness knowledges in different historical epochs.

The collective practical consciousness knowledge of a group of people is what we term their "culture." Culture is a collective repository of shared practical consciousness knowledge that ensures that a group of people will reproduce systems of relatively ordered interaction. In theoretical terms culture and episteme correspond. The main difference is that an episteme is a shared practical consciousness knowledge that is different across time whereas, in most usages, the difference between cultures is a consequence of a geographical move across space. The most common use of culture is in distinguishing between, for instance, French and Spanish culture, but it is obviously true that we can contrast modern Italian and ancient Roman culture, in which case it is a difference of time, not space, that is involved.

Our tacit beliefs allow us to reproduce certain forms of structured interaction in an unquestioning way and, consequently, the practical consciousness knowledge into which actors have been socialized is inextricably bound up with what type of structurally dependent power they find it dispositionally easy to reproduce. The success of structural power is dependent on the practical consciousness knowledge of social actors and as a consequence, for instance, a woman who has internalized structural patterns that are part of a patriarchal system of domination is likely to be a relatively reliable subject in exercises of power involving the reproduction of patriarchal social structures. Although it is inherently controversial to argue in terms of true and false consciousness, Lukes is correct in pointing out that the social consciousness of actors is central to power relations within a given society. Furthermore, even if we do not accept the empirical accuracy of Foucault's characterization of history, similarly, he is correct to point out that the ordered reproduction of social life is sustained and reproduced as a consequence of the tacit beliefs of social actors. Similarly, culture is central to the creation of the structured conditions of cer-

tain exercises of power that characterize particular societies.

In short, analyzing the exercise of power presupposes a context within which the exercise of power takes place. This is a context of ordered or structured interaction. In turn, these structures do not exist externally to social actors but are based upon tacit, or practical consciousness, knowledge of social life.

V. POWER, VIOLENCE, AND COERCION

In the previous section we concentrated on the power relations within structural context. Another way for A to make B do something that they would not otherwise do is for A physically to force B to do something. If this is done outside a structured context this can be considered "primitive" in the sense that it does not depend on any form of social or political procedure. This is what Bachrach and Baratz had in mind when they argued that force is not relational and what lay behind Foucault's distinction between war and politics. The exercise of power in social life, especially politics, presupposes an ordered mode of interaction, which violence does not. In its pure form, violence is a form of natural power, as distinct from social power and represents the absence of a shared set of structures and institutions that can be used to encode or contain conflict.

The distinction between violence and power is also to be found in the work of Hannah Arendt who, in *On Violence* (1970), argued that violence and power are opposites. Building on this we would say that the exercise of social and political power should be distinguished from direct physical confrontation, which is a form of *physical* power. In its pure form, physical power usually indicates the failure of social power. To take a couple of instances, when the United States and its allies went to war with Iraq, they did so because could not prevail over Iraq through political channels, such as, the United Nations and, similarly, when a parent hits a child or the police physically overpower people, these are events that signal a failure in the exercise of institutionally or structurally mediated social power.

It is important to remember that the contrast between structural power relations and violence is only an ideal type. In its pure form violence is a relatively rare occurrence. Structurally based power and violence should be considered as opposite ends of a continuous scale. On the structural side we have a system where routine exercise of power takes place totally efficiently through an appeal to the rules of structural reproduction and, in the case of pure violence, we have nothing other than physical confrontation. Between these two extremes lies the hybrid of social and physical, which is what we shall refer to as 'coercion'.

In modern systems of domination coercion is both structurally ordered and, simultaneously, carries with it the threat of violence or some other form of deprivation. In the middle of the scale, compliance both arises from the structures that are reproduced and from a threat that has been artificially linked to the course of action. We say that it is artificially linked because the course of action in itself does not lead to the undesirable consequences in question. "If you do not sow, you will not reap" is an intrinsic relationship whereas, in contrast, "if you do not pay your taxes you will go to jail" is coercive—there is no intrinsic cause and effect relationship between taxes and jail.

Modern political systems have, or aspire to, a monopoly of violence. They control the army and police. The illegality of private armies or police is a relatively modern phenomenon. In the feudal system armies were privately owned in a pyramidal structure. The consequence of this was that social life was substantially more violent. In contrast to this, modern states aspire to the monopoly of violence. Interestingly, as the historical sociologist Norbert Elias has argued in his study of the origins of the modern state, states do not do this in order to inflict violence on their subjects but in order to pacify society—in order to remove violence from society. While a modern state has an exclusive control of the resources of violence (a control that a feudal monarch would both have envied and considered impossible) this control has resulted in an increase in structural power.

In modern democracies, the purpose of coercion is to ensure that people prevail over each other through the reproduction of the power structures of society rather than through violence or coercion. Coercion is an external threat to individuals interacting which exists as a reinforcer to the exercise of power within established structured relations of domination. At this level state coercion is in total contrast, for instance, to a robber threatening a person with a knife. State coercive resources exist precisely in order to make that form of private coercion impossible.

In our discussion of Foucault's *Discipline and Punish* we have already seen that the purpose of institutions, such as the prison, is not simply to inflict physical suffering. The object of punishment is not violence in itself, as in the sovereign model of power. Even if someone is physically restrained, the purpose of the prison is to resocialize individuals through the practice of dis-

cipline. The object of discipline is to teach recalcitrant individuals how to reproduce social order. In contrast to this, in the sovereign model of power the purpose of hanging, drawing, and quartering is to use violence in order to instill fear in the rest of the population. The object of public execution is to coerce people other than the subject of punishment into reproducing structured power relations. In contrast, in the modern prison the aim is to teach the prisoner—the person being punished—how to reproduce social order. The purpose of prison discipline is to make them willing reproducers of structured relations of domination. The social deviant is a threat precisely because they have not internalized into their practical consciousness the "rules of the game" that are necessary for the routine exercise of power. The purpose of resocialization is to create a social being who willingly reproduces the existing structured system and, as such, is a reliable subject of the structured exercise of power. Again, violence and coercion are in aid of the establishment of routinizable, structural, social, power relations.

VI. POWER RESOURCES

As we have argued, power resources are potential power. With the notable exception of the means of violence, power resources are not the same across social systems. What constitutes a power resource in one system may not be a power resource in another. Resources are created by social systems as social constructs with the consequence that what is a resource in one system may not be a resource in another. In Western capitalist society we take for granted that, for instance, private property is a power resource. As Michael Mann has argued in *The Sources of Social Power* (1987), when we consider the thousands of years when societies were nomadic, it is evident that private property is a relatively new concept that is particular to modern relations of domination. In fact, even today, Western concepts of private property are contested by many, such as, the Inuit in Canada and the aboriginal population in Australia.

As Giddens has analysed at length in *Contemporary Critique of Historical Materialism* (1981), there are two important classes of power resources: *allocative* and *authoritative* resources. Allocative resources are material resources. In a capitalist mode of production these include raw materials, the means of production (such as machines), finished products, and money (a symbolic medium which is used to secure the previously mentioned resources). Authoritative resources are those resources that give individuals control over others by virtue of occupying a specific social role with symbolic content. Authoritative resources derive from the social system and are delegated to individuals by virtue of their membership of that system. To take an instance, the authoritative resources of a police officer are delegated to an individual by virtue of their capacity to fulfill a particular socially defined role. What it is to be a police officer is a systemic phenomenon that gives certain individuals a capacity for action by virtue of their integration into the social system as police officers. The authoritative power of a police officer is very clearly defined; however, many authoritative resources are more diffuse. Part of Foucault's critique of modern society consists precisely in pointing out that experts have authoritative resources of which we are not fully aware and, consequently, do not scrutinize sufficiently.

Both allocative and authoritative resources are limited in scope. The limits of these resources are particularly obvious in the interaction of allocative and authoritative resources. One of the principles of liberal democracy is the separation of the public and private spheres. Consistent with this, those who have publicly authoritative power, such as police officers, are not empowered to use these authoritative resources to secure compliance for personal gain. In contrast, allocative resources are regularly employed for personal advantage. Both allocative and authoritative resources are non-zero-sum. A gain in resources by one individual is not necessarily premised upon an equal loss of resources by another. This is in contrast to a zero-sum situation where one person's gain is another's loss. Power resources are not zero-sum because there is not a fixed quantity of resources in the system. If we use the image of a cake, a cake is zero-sum—if I get a bigger piece this is, of necessity, your loss. Social systems are unlike cakes in that they can expand or contract the number of resources that they contain. As Parsons was at great pains to emphasize in his article "On the Concept of Political Power" (1963), it is frequently the case that an increase in authoritative power has the consequence of increasing the total amount of authoritative resources in the system as a whole. The paradigmatic instance of this is where popular leaders are given increased authoritative resources in response to their perceived effectiveness at achieving shared social goals. This increase in authoritative power is not only a personal affair for the leaders in question but represents an increase in authoritative power resources in the system as a whole. The opposite can equally happen: if leaders with authoritative power are seen to use their power resources outside its legitimate scope, those over whom authoritative power is exercised may become less compliant and withdraw authoritative power. Typically, this will represent both a decrease in power for the person in authority and for the total authoritative resources in the system as a whole.

One of the most famous analyses of authoritative resources is Weber's classification of modes of authoritative domination. For Weber there are three important types of authoritative domination: legal, traditional, and charismatic domination. Each of these modes of authority rests on different rationalities of legitimation. Legal authoritative resources rest on a "belief in the legality of enacted rules and the right of those elevated to authority under such rules to issue commands. . .," traditional authority rests "on an established belief in the sanctity of immemorial traditions and the legitimacy of those exercising authority under them. . .," while charismatic authority rests "on devotion to the exceptional sanctity, heroism or exemplary character of an individual person, and of the normative patterns or order revealed or ordained by him. . ." (Weber, 1978: 215).

Both traditional and legal authority are relatively stable modes of authority that correspond to specific historically constituted modes of ordering social life. Traditional authority is predominant in traditional societies where continuity with the past and the virtue of age-old rules is seen as a form of legitimation. Legal domination is associated with the type of modern social organization that began to emerge in Europe with the Reformation in the 16th century and the rise of capitalism in the following centuries. Legal authority is associated with bureaucratic organizations. While ancient Egypt, China, and the medieval Catholic church were bureaucratic in organization, they did not embody the same principles as modern bureaucracy and, as a consequence, were not associated with legal authority. In a modern bureaucracy, staff are appointed according to qualifications and there is a clearly defined hierarchy of offices with an impersonal bond between officials based on the duty of office. Officials are appointed, rather than elected or in receipt of their position in any other manner. Officials are paid and the official does not own any part of the bureaucracy that they administer. There exists a clearly defined career structure and all organization takes place according to rationally established norms, deemed rational with regard to some relatively utilitarian means-ends criteria of efficiency. The person who has legal authority has at their disposal this bureaucracy that carries out orders efficiently without questioning the objectives pursued. This latter characteristic is particularly dangerous if legal authority falls into the wrong hands—the willingness of the Nazi bureaucracy to obey orders is a notorious example of this phenomenon.

Charismatic authority is not epoch specific in the manner in which traditional and legal authority are. Charismatic authority is by definition an exceptional mode of domination and, as such, is sharply opposed to the rationality of legal and traditional authority. While legal authority is specifically rational in the sense of being analyzable according to specific rules and traditional authority has its rationality defined by precedents handed down from the past, charismatic authority repudiates both established rules and the past. The charismatic leader frequently has a "mission," "call," or "spiritual duty" that legitimates this break from traditional or modern modes of justification. Charismatic leadership is by definition revolutionary and is legitimated by reference to some extraordinary qualities that the charismatic leader is claimed to possess. Because of these characteristics, charismatic authority is exceptional as a dominant mode form of social organization and, as a consequence, in order to stablize the social relations instituted by a charismatic leader it is necessary to convert the charismatic basis of legitimacy into traditional or legal authority. However, as a subordinate mode of organization, charismatic authority is frequently, and relatively stably, found within political systems that are either predominantly traditional or bureaucratically legal overall. Possibly the most obvious example of this is the use of parliament as a forum for charismatic display (on these forms of domination see Weber, 1978: 212–271).

Materialist theories of history, most typically Marxism, are in large part the story of the increase of allocative resources. The transition from feudalism to capitalism was not simply a change of social organization but was, more significantly, a change that was brought about by an increase of allocative resources. Above all else, capitalism represented a virtual revolution in the means of production. However, following Weber, many contemporary theorists, including Giddens and Bourdieu, have argued that the advent of Western capitalism was equally attributable to a dramatic increase in authoritative resources. The great increases in allocative resources associated with the process of industrialisation would have been inconceivable without a revolutionary change in the extent of authoritative resources.

In the feudal mode of production, relatively powerless peasants had control over their working day. In contrast, in capitalism the sale of labor time entailed a loss of control over the working day by the proletariat. This loss of control gave a new form of authoritative control to the capitalist class that was absent in the feudal system. As Giddens puts it, capitalism was as much due to the invention of the clock as it was to the steam engine. In this regard, Foucault's study of discipline is in part the study of the creation and increase of modern authoritative resources. The study of man as an object of knowledge was inextricably bound up with the creation of new authoritative resources that characterize modernity. Foucault's critique of social life is, partly, precisely an attempt to deconstruct these forms of authoritative resources. In this context, it is interesting to note that, in contemporary society, these forms of authoritative power are being circumscribed and decreased in total quantity with the advent of increased worker control over the production process as is exemplified by phenomena such as increased worker control of production and flexitime.

In his multivolume work (1986 and 1993—volumes 3 and 4 are still to be published) on the history of power sources Michael Mann uses a vocabulary of power that is slightly different from the one used here. He argues that there are four sources (what we term "resources") of power: ideological, economic, military, and political. To simplify slightly: economic power sources correspond to what we have been calling allocative resources, political power to authoritative power resources, and military power to coercive physical power. According to Mann, ideological power resources are derived from control over three bases: perceptions of meaning, norms, and aesthetic/ritual practices. Central to Mann's analysis of the history of power is the idea that each of the sources of power develops at a different rate during different historical epochs and that, by and large, advances in one power source are usually dependent on, or interrelated with, advances in other power resources. As we have already seen, the rise of capitalism is associated with advances in authoritative resources. However, additionally, Mann argues that the advance of capitalism was associated with ideological changes, which included, not only, protestantism (as argued by Weber) but earlier, in the medieval period and even before, by the establishment of shared systems of norms and expectations as a consequence of the process of christianization. Using the same model, Mann also argues that the success of the Roman empire was, in part, attributable to mutually reinforcing relations between military and economic resources.

Mann's use of the concept of ideological resources has strong echoes of Lukes' concept of false consciousness, Foucault's analysis of micropractices of power, Giddens' theory of structuration, and Clegg's analysis of circuits of power. On the one hand, religious belief can be used to shape individual aspirations—as argued by Lukes. On the other hand, Mann's wide use of the concept of ideology to include meanings and norms is broadly similar to what we mean by structural practices and practical consciousness (tacit knowledge) as presented here—under the influence of Giddens and Foucault—and is also largely consistent with Clegg's analysis of power whereby he argues that the exercise of power (episodic power) presupposes rules of the game, structures of domination and meaning (dispositional power) as bases for the exercise of power.

VII. CONFLICT, CONSENSUS INTERNATIONAL RELATIONS, AND DEMOCRATIC POLITICS

In our analysis of Lukes, we saw that he redefined power relative to interests. This reflected a view of power whereby it is purely a conflictual phenomenon exercised over people. However, Parsons, Barnes, Giddens, and Foucault, as we saw, have argued for a less negative view of power. As Barnes put it in *The Nature of Power* (1988), we regard physical power as the capacity for action that individuals derive from physical objects, so, similarly, we should conceptualize social power as any form of capacity for action that actors gain from their membership of society irrespective of interests. A capacity for action may be used either in conflict with others or it may equally be used collaboratively. Furthermore, even in the case of conflict, it is not necessarily the case that conflict goes all the way down. As we saw in our analysis of Foucault, conflict may occur within the rules of the game (consensus on structural reproduction) as opposed to deep conflict that is over the rules of the game.

In *The Nature of Power* Barnes analyses the way in which actors gain social power from social order. The central concept is the idea that social order facilitates coordination between individuals by making their behavior predictable and, in so doing, gives social agents a capacity to make things happen. In other words, social order is the basis of social power. Much as we have argued here, Barnes also maintains that violence represents the limit of social power and that one of the important functions of coercion is the maintenance of social order.

Power may be perceived of both in a negative or positive light. A powerful individual A may exercise power that is either in the interests or contrary to the interests of B. In a consensual exercise of power those who obey may consider the outcome involved inher-

ently desirable or, alternatively, they may comply because they agree with the structures or institutions being reproduced. In a democracy the ability of one party to prevail over the other is premised on the commitment of the loser to the rules of the democratic game and, in a traditional society, social elders may command obedience from a respect for the structures of tradition.

Legitimacy is a central concept in this context. The legitimacy of power structures makes possible the management of conflict by reinforcing social relations. Legitimacy performs the function of ensuring that individuals will reproduce the rules of the game even if it is not in their immediate short-term interest to do so.

Social relations may be legitimated in many ways that include not only legality and tradition, as was argued by Weber, but also the use of truth. As argued by Foucault, in modern modes of domination truth reinforces expert discourses and, simultaneously, legitimate structures of domination. Part of the deep conflict over how to constitute the rules of the game is a fight for truth. Truth makes certain rules of the game legitimate and, in so doing, facilitates the routinized reproduction of modern power relations. With regard to consciousness, truth legitimizes certain perceptions of the world and, thus, reinforces the power relations that go with these perceptions.

Finding legitimate structures that facilitate power conflict without coercion is central to modern liberal political theory. In procedural liberalism the guiding principle is the search for a set of procedures, or social structures, which are neutral between competing perceptions of the good life. For instance, the great liberal theorist John Rawls describes a set of structural procedures for resolving conflict in a pluralist society, which he calls the "original position." The original position is considered legitimate by all parties as a consequence of a shared commitment to fairness. In essence, the original position is a set of social structures that makes the management of conflict possible.

The idea of managing conflict takes us back to Foucault's distinction between levels of conflict. A deep conflict is a conflict where there are no procedures or structures to which the parties involved in a conflict can appeal. A more superficial conflict is one where these shared structures exist. In terms of conflict resolution, the first step to resolving a conflict is to ensure that the conflict can be made shallow by the creation of structured, as opposed to unstructured, conflict. Once this has been done, compromise between conflicting groups is, at least potentially, possible because structural consensus can be used to convert violence into structurally based exercises of power. Politics is the encoding of war in the sense that it is the management of conflict within rules and procedures.

The reliance on structural power also carries with it its opposite—a new type of resistance. The nonviolent direct action of people like Gandhi and the growth of popular grass-root movements are the other side of the same coin. The reproduction of social systems presupposes the participation of those over whom power is exercised. If this participation is withdrawn, then the system is not reproduced. For those controlling the monopoly of violence this creates a dilemma when structural power fails: do they send in the tanks? (violence)—as was ultimately the case in Tiananmen Square—or do they withdraw?—as was finally so in the case of the British in India. The levels of coercion necessary to maintain order in a society are in directly inverse proportion to the structural consensus of that society. Hence, in a strange way the continual use of coercion and violence represents an indication of an absence of social and political power. This is what Arendt meant when she argued that "rule by sheer violence comes into play where power is being lost" (Arendt, 1970: 53).

It is important to remember that structural consensus and legitimacy are not simply a feature of political institutions but are central to the maintenance of both allocative and authoritative resources. Not only do the authoritative resources of political leaders and experts rest on structural consensus but the effectiveness of allocative resources are similarly attributable to the existence of structural norms. As stated in our analysis of allocative resources, the concept of private property is a unique historical phenomenon that depends on contemporary capitalist structured relations. It is precisely because the Inuit of Canada and the aboriginal population of Australia do not accept these structures as inherently legitimate that there is conflict between them and their respective governments. With regard to Foucault's image of deep and shallow conflict, these are deep conflicts.

Because of their dependence on structural reproduction, allocative and authoritative resources are systemic qualities. This is precisely why they tend to break down in conflicts between different social systems. As we have already noted, violence is not systemically mediated. So, in the case of deep conflict (where there is no structural consensus to build on), it is more than likely that the conflict will become violent. This is particularly relevant to the analysis of international politics. In international politics there is no world government that can be compared to the state. In the absence of shared procedures there is a tendency for relations to be violent

even if the states in question are largely run internally through structural power. In many respects the establishment of international organizations, such as the United Nations or the European Union, is an attempt to extend the basis for structural consensus from the national to the international arena and, in so doing, to prevent deep conflicts (wars) from taking place.

As we have already noted, structural consensus does not only take the form of explicit rules as exemplified by political institutions but also exists as practical consciousness knowledge. When we reproduce the structures pertaining to private property, or behave in a disciplined way, we are not usually discursively conscious of the social structures being reproduced. This knowledge is not only part of our individual practical consciousness knowledge but part of our greater collective practical consciousness or culture. Tacit knowledge is central to the reproduction of structures within a system and, as a consequence, to the routine exercise of power. This has particular implications for conflict between different cultural groups. For instance, as a result of cultural difference, many societies are reluctant to reproduce relations of domination that Westerners take for granted as "the natural order of things." This absence of shared culture is particularly evident in international relations where it is sometimes counterbalanced by shared socialization among diplomats and political elites.

In international relations theory the concept of "ordered anarchy" partly refers to a shared practical consciousness knowledge existing between states. International politics is anarchic in the sense that there exists no world government and, yet it is ordered because there exists a fairly complex tacit shared practical consciousness knowledge on which states can draw in order to manage conflict using social structural power rather than violence and war.

With regard to democracy, as a system for managing conflict, it not only presupposes a certain cultural context but its continued functioning is also premised on the relative fairness of outcomes. In democratic pluralist societies all interest groups should have the possibility of exercising power at some point in time so that losers will accept democratic defeat. If this is the case, democratic structures and institutions can be relied on to contain conflict at the level of structural power. However, in a sharply divided society, where there are fixed winners and losers, conflict will tend to degenerate into violent confrontation. To take the instance of Northern Ireland, which is a society divided into two stable groups of unequal size, the Nationalists representing one-third of the population and Unionists with two-thirds: because the democratic system was largely one of majority rule prior to 1998, the actual functioning of the democratic process entailed certain, and continual, defeat for the nationalist minority. Such a situation invariably undermines the willingness of some members of the defeated group to accept the rules of the game. This has the consequence of undermining civic culture and, as a further consequence, routinized and democratically based structural exercises of political power become partly replaced with violence and coercion.

Democracy is premised on the containment of political conflict through the constraints of political structures and institutions. These political processes presuppose a shared practical consciousness knowledge or culture. As de Alexis de Tocqueville noted in his analysis of American democracy, a democratic system presupposes a shared civic culture; it is not simply the product of structures and institutions existing in isolation. It is for this reason that Western-type democracy does not always flourish in all cultures and also, conversely, why there are few instances of democracies dissolving themselves once they have been established for more than 20 years. A fact that is possibly as good a guide as any to the amount of time that it takes to create sufficiently strong shared political culture so that political conflict takes place through structural social power rather than violence.

Bibliography

Arendt, H. (1970). *On violence.* London: Allen Lane The Penguin Press.

Bachrach, P., & Baratz, M. S. (1962). The two faces of power. *American Political Science Review*, vol. 56.

Bachrach, P., & Baratz, M. S. (1963). Decisions and nondecisions. *American Political Science Review*, 57.

Barnes, B. (1988). *The nature of power.* Cambridge: Polity Press.

Butler, J. (1990). *Gender trouble: Feminism and the subversion of identity.* New York: Routledge.

Clegg, S. R. (1989). *Frameworks of power*, London: Sage.

Dahl, R. A. (1957). The concept of power. *Behavioural Science*, 2.

Dahl, R. A. (1961). *Who governs? Democracy and power in an American city*, New Haven: Yale University Press.

Dahl, R. A. (1968). Power. In D. L. Shills (Ed.), *International Encyclopedia of the Social Sciences*, Vol. 12.

Foucault, M. (1970). *The order of things*, London: Routledge.

Foucault, M. (1979). *Discipline and punish: The birth of the prison.* Harmondsworth: Penguin.

Foucault, M. (1980). *Power/knowledge: Selected interviews and other writings 1972–1977*, C. Gordon, (Ed.). Brighton: Harvester Press.

Foucault, M. (1981). *The history of sexuality: Vol. 1. An introduction*, Harmondsworth: Penguin.

Giddens, A. (1981). *A contemporary critique of historical materialism: Vol. I. Power, property and the state.* London: Macmillan.

Giddens, A. (1984). *The constitution of society*, Cambridge: Polity Press.

Haugaard, M. (1997). *The constitution of power: A theoretical analysis of power, knowledge and structure*, Manchester: Manchester University Press.

Hunter, Floyed (1953). *Community Power*, North Carolina Press, Chapel Hill.

Lukes, S. (1974). *Power: A radical view.* London: Macmillan.

Mann M. (1986). *The sources of social power: Vol. 1., A history of power from the beginning to A.D. 1760.* Cambridge: Cambridge University Press.

Mann M. (1993). *The sources of social power: Vol. 2. The rise of classes and nation-States. 1760–1914.* Cambridge: Cambridge University Press.

Mills, C. Wright (1951). *The Power Elite*, Oxford University Press, Oxford.

Morriss, P. (1987). *Power: A philosophical analysis.* Manchester: Manchester University Press.

Parsons (1963). On the concept of political power. *Proceedings of the American Philosophical Society*, 107.

Weber, M. (1978). *Economy and society: An outline of interpretive sociology*, G. Roth & C. Wittich (Eds.). Berkeley, Los Angeles: University of California Press.

Professional versus Citizen Soldiery

Paul R. Viotti

University of Denver

I. INTRODUCTION

Consistent with Samuel Huntington's separatist thesis in *Soldier and the State,* the *military professional* is one who pursues expertise in combat in service to a country's or society's defense. In this separatist view, such service does not require the solider to be fully integrated with civil society. Professional soldiers in a democratic society also have as part of their organizational ethos a strong disinclination to intervene in politics. Indeed, one finds professional militaries in the United States, the United Kingdom, and elsewhere imbued with this separatist, professional ethic but at the same time committed as professionals to respecting constitutional government, institutions, and political processes.

On the other hand, the logic of the late Morris Janowitz's integrationist thesis in *The Professional Soldier* is compelling. Maintaining a positive balance in civil–military relations that supports democratic institutions and processes is never automatic, even in countries with long-standing traditions against military intervention in politics. It is a problem that requires continuing

attention at any time and is an ongoing challenge for policy-makers who seek to prevent the isolation of military establishments.

Are separatist norms against intervention in politics sufficient to dissuade military establishments from doing so, not just when things are going well, but also in times of adversity? From this more-skeptical perspective, the norms internalized by military professionals are important, but not enough. Greatest assurance occurs when these professionals are fully a part of their societies. They are the *citizens* who just happen to be in uniform.

Establishing this concept of professionalism that eschews intervention in politics has proven to be particularly problematic in newly industrializing and economically less-developed societies in which the miltary is often times one of the strongest institutions. The problem is exacerbated in those societies in which the armed forces not only have an established historical pattern of political intervention, but also see this as a legitimate role as self-proclaimed protectors of society, its culture, and even its "Constitution."

When in power, civilian leadership elites in these countries often do not attempt to integrate these military elements within society, preferring to buy off, marginalize, or relegate them to the sidelines rather than to make them a viable part of the societal mainstream. As the historical record shows, this approach runs a very real risk that civil society will yet again become victim to military *coup* (or *golpe* as the phenomenon is known in many Latin American countries).

By contrast, the Swiss and Swedish approach is to integrate soldiers and society as fully as practicable for their military purpose. A relatively small number of full-time professionals are complemented by trained reservists drawn from those able to serve within the society. Although women, children, and senior citizens are largely excluded and alternative-service provisions are made for at least some conscientious objectors to military service, the militaries in these countries are so constructed that one is hard pressed to draw any meaningful distinction between the citizen and the soldier.

In such societies it is difficult to imagine how the military would intervene in politics or be a threat to society since they are already so much a part of it as individuals in their daily lives. Military service for such *citizen soldiers* is just one more additional duty or responsibility that goes with citizenship in a civil society.

II. DEMOCRATIC CIVIL–MILITARY SOCIETY

Consistent with Max Weber's understanding, construction of an ideal or pure type gives us a benchmark or standard against which real-world cases can be compared. As such, a pure type of democratic civil–military society cannot, in fact, exist anywhere. The empirical can only approximate the ideal; the ideal or pure type is a limiting case. Using pure types also gives us a degree of definitional precision in the use of concepts; constructing an ideal type of democratic civil–military society forces us to specify the attributes of such a society.

The first attribute is that the armed forces in a democratic society are composed of full citizens who also are completely integrated with other citizens in the society. Citizens in uniform have neither more nor fewer rights than those not in uniform. They have equal protection of the laws and other benefits; they have the same obligations or duties. Military service is merely an activity the citizen may volunteer (or be called upon) to perform. It does not change his or her status as citizen. The military member is merely the citizen who happens to be in uniform.

Second, the armed forces in such a democratic society are representative of the people as a whole, *not drawn exclusively or disproportionately from particular socioeconomic classes; racial, ethnic, tribal, or other cultural segments; gender; or other categories of peoples.* The armed forces are as diverse—as heterogeneous (or homogeneous)—as society is as a whole. Values held by military members also reflect the same degree of diversity found in society.

Third, the military as corporate group is separated from others in society only to the extent that is functionally necessary to perform military tasks. Combat effectiveness does require unit training and *esprit de corps* established within military units separated from those who are not part of these units. Military necessity, however, is narrowly construed as the effort is not to separate but to integrate fully the military within society. Separation from the rest of society is limited as much as possible by this narrow construction of military necessity. Some degree of separateness, of course, is true of any group even nonmilitary citizens form to perform tasks in civil society. Pluralist, democratic societies are composed of groups, but these separate identities do not challenge democratic society so long as members of these groups remain integrated within society as a whole.

Finally, in democratic societies the military is subordinated politically to civil authorities who represent the people in society as a whole. Authority is delegated to military commanders who must carry out their assigned tasks, but military personnel are always accountable to civil authorities who retain ultimate responsibility and authority for the armed forces. The Clausewitzian view of the military as a means or instrumentality to policy ends, not as an end in itself, applies as much to democratic as it does to nondemocratic societies. Military inputs are part of the political or policy process just as inputs are made by other citizens with expertise on issues facing policy-makers. Society is inclusive of its military, which is not isolated from political or bureaucratic processes, but integrated within society as a whole and subordinated to civil authorities.

There is, of course, no society (nor will there be) that fits this pure type perfectly. Nevertheless, these attributes provide a standard, however ideal, for measuring and comparing empirical cases. By way of example, we turn now to the historical, cultural, and legal tradition that underlies the concept of democratic civil–military society in the United States.

III. THE CITIZEN-SOLDIER MODEL IN THE AMERICAN TRADITION

Standing armies or armed forces in peacetime were so feared by most of the 18th-century Constitutional framers that they put explicit provision in the U.S.

Constitution against (or at least to constrain) them.[1] The framers were reacting to the role the British army had played in abusing citizen rights in the colonial period. These offenses were listed in the Declaration of Independence (July 4, 1776).[2] The experience of the 17th-century English civil war also influenced their thinking. Whether soldiers were subject to king or Cromwell, they could be used to threaten citizen rights and liberties.

Washington reaffirmed military subordination to civil authority immediately after the Revolutionary War. He was no Cromwell willing to use the army as a power base. He certainly had an opportunity to do so when disaffected soldiers, frustrated in their efforts to secure due compensation from Congress for their contributions to the war effort, wanted General Washington to use the army to seize public lands in the west for redistribution to the troops in lieu of back pay, some even advocating he subsequently become king! Washington completely rejected any such idea. He told the soldiers: "If you have any regard for yourself or posterity, or respect for me, to banish these thoughts from your mind, and never communicate, as from yourself or anyone else, a sentiment of the like nature" (MacDonald, pp. 24 and 27).

To guard against any military abuse of private property rights, the third amendment to the Constitution states that "no soldier shall, in time of peace be quartered in any house, without the consent of the owner, nor in time of war, but in a manner to be prescribed by law." Beyond that protection, the second amendment also upholds "the right of the people to keep and bear arms" as essential to "a well regulated militia" tasked with maintaining "the security of a free State."

Indeed, primary reliance was to be on the organized militia within the states (or what is now the national guard) in large part because of their proximity to the people and their peacetime control by the states. Standing forces were to be avoided or minimized. Article I, Section 8.12 empowers Congress "to raise and support armies" but provides that "no appropriation of money to that use shall be for a longer term than two years."[3] In other words, not only is Congress the authority that funds the armed forces, but also each new Congress is in a constitutional position to reverse prior decisions on the existence and size of any standing army.

When standing armies are necessary, the framers separate authority over them lest either executive or legislative branch use the military as an exclusive power base. The logic is explained in Federalist Paper No. 51 as setting branch against branch to check or balance each other. Similarly, the federalism explained in Federalist Paper No. 10 gives states and localities the independence or autonomy they seek from central direction or control.

In Article II, Section 2, the framers vest the President as chief executive with the foreign policy power "to make treaties" and to "be commander in chief of the army and navy of the United States, and of the militia of the several States, when called into the actual service of the United States." Concerning treaties, his power is limited by the requirement that he act "by and with the advice and consent of the Senate," securing concurrence by at least "two thirds of the senators present."

After all, each state has equal representation in the Senate and the states were not about to relinquish complete authority over foreign policy or security matters that had previously been their responsibility. Moreover, the states, acting through the Senate, would retain by majority vote a check on Executive appointments of all "ambassadors, other public ministers and consuls . . . and all other officers of the United States."

The historical and continuing experience with the dispute between the executive and the legislature over war powers was, perhaps, an intended consequence of the framers' decision to separate powers over the armed forces. Supporters of executive authority have argued that even though only Congress may *declare* war, the President as commander-in-chief of the armed forces has the Constitutional authority to *make* war. Presidents since Franklin Roosevelt have tended to have a more expansive interpretation of executive authority conveyed by this "commander-in-chief" function, particu-

---

[1] In Federalist Paper No. 8, Alexander Hamilton argued that "the continual necessity for their services enhances the importance for the soldier, and proportionately degrades the condition of the citizen. The military state becomes elevated above the civil." Hamilton sees a remedy in the proposed union of states that will strengthen their security and reduce the need for large armies among them.

[2] Referring to the British sovereign, the document asserts: "He has kept among us, in times of peace, Standing Armies without the Consent of our legislature; he has affected to render the Military independent of and superior to the Civil Power . . .; For quartering large bodies of armed troops among us: For protecting them, by a mock Trial, from Punishment; For any Murders which they should commit on the Inhabitants of these States."

[3] In Federalist Paper No. 41, James Madison observes that "the best possible precaution against danger from standing armies is a limitation of the term for which revenue may be appropriated to their support."

larly concerning war-*making* powers, than historically has been the case.

Congressional claims to the war-*declaring* power under Article I, Section 8.11 challenge these executive claims to authority. Moreover, it is the Congress that has the authority under the same article to appropriate money "to raise and support armies" and "to provide and maintain a navy." In this split between executive and legislative authority over the armed forces, the framers seemed to tip the balance in favor of the latter by a broad grant of authority "to make rules for the government and regulation of the land and naval forces"—functions normally one might expect to be performed by an executive authority.

The framers in effect conceded that to be effective the armed forces need the unity of command provided by the executive; however, their fear of standing armies led them to establish checks by the states, acting through the Senate and by the people, acting through the Congress as a whole, but particularly the House of Representatives—the more democratic chamber elected directly *by* the people.

It is Congress that has this authority "to make rules for the government and regulation of the land and naval forces." Of the two branches, it is Congress that thus has the larger claim to formal, legal authority. In a narrow construction that may well have been intended by the Constitutional framers, executive power is formally limited to command—preserving the military's functional necessity of unity of command, while reserving other prerogatives to Congress.

Even command of the militia by the President is subject to Congressional authority. It is the legislature under Article I, Section 8 that has authority "for calling forth the militia to execute the laws of the Union, suppress insurrections and repel invasions." Congress also retains the authority "to provide for organizing, arming, and disciplining the militia, and for governing such part of them as may be employed in the service of the United States, reserving to the States respectively, the appointment of the officers, and the authority of training the militia according to the discipline prescribed by Congress."

There is a preference in the Anglo-American democratic tradition for smaller militaries—particularly smaller numbers of standing forces.[4] The 18th-century framers of the U.S. Constitution certainly thought so and Alexis de Tocqueville later allocated several chapters in his *Democracy in America* to this topic, noting that "a large army amidst a democratic people will always be a source of great danger." Consistent with these worries, standing forces in peacetime were kept small throughout the century-and-a-half prior to World War II. By contrast, the large peacetime standing forces maintained by the U.S. during the Cold War represent a historical aberration made necessary by national security concerns.

Although a small military may be desirable in a democratic society, an isolated one decidedly is not. The ideal for the military member in a democratic society, then, is to be seen (and to be) a citizen like any other, but one who happens to be in uniform in direct service to the country. It was de Tocqueville who saw the importance in a "democratic army" of "the love of freedom and the respect of rights" as being "in common with their fellow-citizens."

The emphasis is on the citizen-soldier who is first and foremost the citizen. This was the model George Washington attempted to convey both as army general and later as commander-in-chief.[5] To Washington, it is the citizen who responds to military necessity, but later returns to civil pursuits:

> As to the fatal, but necessary operations of war, *when we assumed the soldier, we did not lay aside the citizen* [emphasis added]; and we shall most sincerely rejoice ... when the establishment of American liberty, on the most firm and solid foundations, shall enable us to return to our private stations.... (Schwartz, 1987)[6]

He anticipated the end of the Revolutionary War when he would be "translated into a private citizen"—able "to sink into sweet retirement, and the full enjoyment of that peace and happiness, which will accompany a domestic life" (Ford, 1902). This was the spirit in which Washington finally bade farewell to his officers and resigned his commission in December, 1783, thus taking "leave of all the employments of public life"

---

[4] In Federalist Paper No. 8, Alexander Hamilton states: "The smallness of the army renders the natural strength of the community an overmatch for it.... The army ... will be unable to enforce encroachments against the united efforts of the great body of the people."

[5] Huntington (1964) observes: "Washington obeyed the Continental Congress not as a soldier but as a citizen." He also notes that "Washington and Hamilton were indeed the antitheses of the professional type, moving with ease from military to political office and back again."

[6] Early discussions with Normal Provizer underscored the importance of Washington's views on the citizen soldier.

(Schwartz, 1987). Washington saw himself as the citizen who happened to be in uniform.

Notwithstanding the 18th-century tradition of a military integrated with society, the American military in the 19th and 20th centuries has, in fact, followed more of a separatist path during the longer periods of peace between major wars. Reliance has been on smaller, professional standing armies backed up by the national guard and reservists except in major wars when military ranks swell with both conscripts and volunteers. Only since World War II, spurred by national security concerns during the Cold War, have large standing armies, navies, and air forces been maintained in peacetime.

Large forces that draw heavily from society, particularly in the enlisted and noncommissioned officer ranks, tend by their nature to become somewhat more integrated than smaller professional militaries that run the risk of becoming isolated from the societal mainstream. Be that as it may, whether large or small, the degree of integration of standing professional forces that can or should be sought has remained a difficult and often contentious issue for the society and its policymakers.

IV. INTEGRATING PROFESSIONAL SOLDIERS IN CIVIL SOCIETY

Participation in societal activities to include its politics is one approach to military integration. The American tradition will not likely allow the degree of political participation engaged in by present-day German military members who are allowed to participate in partisan activities and even run for office. This highly participative model of civil–military relations (referred to as *Innerefuehrung*) is the pattern in which post-World War II German military members make themselves fully a part of, while not threatening, society's political processes. There is in concept an inner discipline that keeps the soldier a citizen who is not a threat to civil society.

Adopting this participative model is, in fact, an effort since the 1950s to correct the prewar separatist and militarist orientation of the German armed forces that never really had been integrated with (and was, in fact, more of a threat to) the Weimar democracy in the interwar period. Adopting so participative a model was a bold attempt to establish through daily practice a new democratic form of citizen-soldier to replace the separatist model that had been so problematic in the past. Universal conscription into a citizen army underscored this orientation.

Innerefuehrung contrasts sharply with the less-participative expectations for the military in the American political culture. Subordination to civil authority by American military members has taken the form of minimizing political participation. Even though military members are encouraged to vote, most do not. This may reflect, in part, the survival of an earlier, nonvoting tradition in which military professionals as public servants avoided even this minimal form of political participation lest they encroach (or be seen as encroaching) on civil authorities.

Volunteer forces tend to be less representative of the population as a whole than conscript armies drawn from across the socioeconomic spectrum in a given society. Merely having a draft, of course, does not assure representativeness. Accompanied by elimination of most grounds for deferment, conscription by lottery finally was introduced during the Vietnam War. The earlier draft had been more permissive, allowing many, particularly those in the middle and upper socioeconomic strata, to find legal exemptions and thus avoid military service. As a result, much of the wartime burden fell on those in lower socioeconomic levels. This had not been the case in World War II when the armed forces were broadly representative of American society.

The United States quickly retreated in the early 1970s from the lottery draft to all-volunteer forces. Taking the long view, the end of peacetime conscription was a return to customary practice. Just as standing armies were minimized in the American experience, a peacetime draft was virtually unheard of prior to the Cold War. In any event, historically strong sentiments against conscription, except in times of national emergency, have returned. This is distinctly different from the continental European tradition and those influenced by that tradition in other parts of the world. Conscription, though not usually any more popular politically than taxation, nevertheless has a legitimacy in these countries it does not have in the United States (or most other English-speaking countries for that matter). The Anglo-liberal tradition of voluntary military service is deeply rooted not just in the United States, but also in other countries that came under British influence. Favorable geopolitical circumstances (islands or continents separated by bodies of water) also made large standing armies unnecessary in many of these English-speaking countries.

The problem, of course, is that keeping the armed forces broadly representative of society is more difficult when resort to conscription is a political nonstarter. Although the quality of the American armed forces, in fact, has become quite high, the self-selection process does not produce the same representative cross section as a randomized draft. That the armed forces tend to overrepresent both rural and inner-city populations—underrepresenting other segments of American society—is not a new observation.

Nor is this social unrepresentativeness necessarily troublesome so long as military members share values and become integrated in other respects with the whole of society. Morris Janowitz observed the benefit to democratic society of a representative officer corps: "If the officer corps were a representative cross section, they would hardly harbor intentions to upset the political balance" (Janowitz, p. 80). In an earlier, pre-World War II period, however, "instead of a representative social background" reliance was on an officer corps "that would have many of the characteristics of the business and political elite" (Janowitz, p. 81). Janowitz notes that "traditionally, the military community has been more sharply segregated from civilian life in the United States than in the major nations of Western Europe" (pp. 175–176). He was concerned, however, lest "an all-volunteer force" produce an even greater "separation of the civilian and military sectors" (p. ix). Downsizing in the post-Cold War period makes this issue more salient now than in the 1970s, when Janowitz and others dealt with it.

Greater reliance on reserves or national guard units is another way of achieving integration. Lateral entry to active-duty ranks from reserve units and from professions and others with needed expertise is another such mechanism. Driven by national security needs, policymakers concerned with this issue seek an effective balance between full-time professionals and citizen-soldiers who join the uniformed ranks when needed.

Substantial progress on integrating minority racial and ethnic groups has been made in the U.S. and other armed forces, particularly in the last half-century. The problem is not just one of numbers, but also the opportunities to enter and advance within both enlisted and officer ranks. Equal treatment is the core concern. Militaries that reflect the degree of diversity of the countries of which they are a part contribute substantially to the viability of democratic civil–military society.

Similarly, another challenge is greater integration and equal treatment of women if militaries are in fact to be representative of the societies they defend. Modern technologies of warfare that put greater emphasis on cognitive and motor skills than on brute strength have opened more avenues functionally to both men and women. Whether for combat or noncombat tasks, setting standards that are gender neutral is a social goal favored by many in the United States. By contrast, most other societies have exhibited much less interest in moving from a traditional, almost exclusive, reliance on males for combat service.

On gender, race, ethnicity, sexual orientation, and other social issues, criticism is sometimes directed against those who would force their militaries to engage in what they refer to as "social experimentation" that could undermine combat capabilities. The argument in this essay, however, is that while combat capabilities are the central focus in recruiting, organizing, training, and equipping armed forces, making militaries more representative and compatible with the societies they defend is also central to sustaining a democratic civil–military society. Applying combat-based standards of conduct and realistic criteria for recruitment that are neutral in relation to race, ethnicity, gender, sexual orientation or any other social matter is the approach recommended by those who see militaries as open to and broadly representative of the citizenry as a whole.

It was Machiavelli who observed that "good laws and good armies" are "the principal foundations of all states." In this regard, he advocated reliance on "citizen armies" as the most effective form of defense for state and society. Those who share this view seek to approximate as many of the tenets of democratic civil–military society as are politically feasible. From their perspective, citizens who happen to be in uniform are the most reliable contributers to national security.

Also See the Following Articles

COLD WAR • DRAFT, RESISTANCE AND EVASION OF • MILITARISM • MILITARISM AND DEVELOPMENT IN UNDERDEVELOPED SOCIETIES • MILITARY CULTURE • MILITARY-INDUSTRIAL COMPLEX • PEACE AND DEMOCRACY • WARRIORS, ANTHROPOLOGY OF

Bibliography

Diamond, L., & Plattner, M. F. (1996). *Civil–military relations and democracy.* Baltimore, MD: Johns Hopkins University Press.

Fallows, J. (1981). *National defense.* New York: Random House.

Ford, P. L. (1902). *The true George Washington,* p. 291. Philadelphia, PA: J. B. Lippincott.

Hendrickson, D. C. (1988). *Reforming defense: The state of American civil–military relations.* Baltimore, MD: Johns Hopkins University Press.

Huntington, S. (1964). *The soldier and the state.* New York: Vintage Books.

Janowitz, M. (1960/1971). *The professional soldier.* New York: The Free Press.

Janowitz, M. (1964). *The military in the political development of new nations.* Chicago: University of Chicago Press.

Kelleher, C. M. (1982/1989/1994). In D. J. Murray & P. R. Viotti

(Eds.), *The defense policy of nations*. Baltimore, MD: The Johns Hopkins University Press.

MacDonald, W. (1973). *George Washington: A brief biography* (originally published in *Encyclopedia Britannica*, 11th ed. 1911). Mt. Vernon, VA.

Millett, A. R. (1979). *The American political system and civil control of the military*. Columbus: Ohio State University.

Moskos, C. C. (1988). *A call to civic service*. New York: The Free Press.

Sarkesian, S. C., Williams, J. A., & Bryant, F. B. (1995). *Soldiers, society, and national security*. Boulder, CO: Lynne Rienner.

Schwartz, B. (1987). *George Washington: The making of an American symbol*, p. 132. Ithaca, NY: Cornell University Press.

Simon, S. W. (Ed.) (1978). *The military and security in the third world*. Boulder, CO: Westview Press.

von Clausewitz, C. (1976). *On war* (edited and translated by M. Howard and P. Paret). Princeton, NJ: Princeton University Press.

Weber, M. (1949). *The methodology of the social sciences* (translated by E. A. Shils and H. A. Finch). New York: The Free Press.

Yarmolinsky, A. (1971). *The military establishment*. New York: Harper Colophon Books.

Psychoanalysis

John J. Hartman
University of Michigan

GLOSSARY

Death Instinct Freud's controversial assumption of a gene-determined, biological substrate that manifests itself in destructive actions toward the environment, the self, or both.

Identification Freud's term for the first relationship with an object in which aspects of that object are taken in as part of the self-representation.

Identity Erikson's term for the relatively enduring experience of oneself as a unique, coherent entity over time in consonance with others' views of oneself.

Instinctual Drive The endogenously derived motivational force that provides the psychic energy necessary for the work of the mind. Freud postulated sexual and aggressive forms of this drive energy.

Narcissism of Minor Differences A term mentioned by Freud denoting the way in which minor differences between individuals and groups can come to assume

great significance in self-esteem regulation and identity maintenance.

Object Relations That part of psychoanalytic theory which emphasizes the psychic representations of the experience of the self and others.

Paranoid Elaboration of Mourning Fornari's term for a defense utilized by individuals or shared in a group by which depressive and persecutory feelings are dealt with by the construction of a paranoid view involving the identification of enemies and a wish to annihilate them.

Paranoid Process Meissner's term for a process in individuals and in groups in which core identifications of the individual are projected and then elaborated in a paranoid cognitive structure. This often involves fantasies of an enemy and primitive defensive operations in the maintenance of the paranoid construction.

Projection The process by which the ego attributes an unacceptable impulse, idea, or representation to the external world.

Stranger Anxiety The distress experienced by the infant between 6 and 8 months at experiencing the unfamiliar, particularly a strange person.

Suitable Target for Externalization Volkan's term for objects, animate or inanimate, which serve as recipients for positive (idealized) and negative (denigrated) projections. These projections serve to regulate the individual's self esteem and identity. In groups these targets also serve to regulate group identity, particularly in times of stress.

Track II Diplomacy Diplomat Joseph Montville's term for unofficial diplomacy in which informal interaction between influential members of opposing groups takes place to lay a foundation for formal negotiations.

PSYCHOANALYSIS is a theory of the mind, a method of investigation, and a treatment procedure for individuals that posits the interacting effects of endogenous emotional experiences, psychological development in childhood, and relations with the environment in the production of mental conflicts. Application of this theory to group psychology describes the role of these unconscious forces in the dynamics of small and large groups. Specifically, the contribution of psychoanalysis to the study of group violence involves evidence of psychological conflict, often unconscious, in the constant tension between peace and war in intergroup behavior.

I. INTRODUCTION

At the end of 1997, according to the Center for Defense Information, a Washington, DC think tank, there were 68 active conflict areas around the world. This is double the number in 1989. Since 1989 it is estimated that 4 million men, women, and children have died in these conflicts, and millions more are refugees. There were 21 wars still active in 1997.

In 1931, the International Institute of Intellectual Co-operation was instructed by the Permanent Committee for Literature and the Arts of the League of Nations to arrange for an exchange of letters between prominent intellectuals. Albert Einstein was one person chosen by the committee, and he in turn chose Sigmund Freud, the founder of psychoanalysis, as his correspondent. His topic: the causes of war. The exchange of letters was published in March of 1933 simultaneously in German, French, and English under the title, *Why War?* It was, however, banned in Germany where Adolph Hitler had just assumed power.

It is the purpose of this article to describe the contribution of psychoanalysis to the understanding of the causes of war and ethnic violence and to outline the efforts of psychoanalysts to apply their knowledge of human psychology to specific efforts to reduce intergroup tensions and their violent outcomes. The chapter begins with a review of Freud's views on war which appeared in a number of different writings in addition to his exchange with Einstein.

Freud was personally affected by the wars that ravaged Europe during his life. His three sons served in the military in World War I. One was wounded and decorated, and all survived. In March of 1938, 5 years after the publication of *Why War?*, the Germans took over Austria. Freud was 82 and dying of cancer. As a Jew, Freud and his family were in great danger of being sent to concentration camps. His children had all managed to leave Austria except Anna, who was caring for her father. Anna was detained by the Gestapo, and the Freud household was besieged by the Nazis. Diplomatic efforts by several governments and payment of large sums of money by Princess Marie Bonaparte, a psychoanalytic student of Freud, enabled him and his family to go to England to "die in freedom" as he had wished. However, his three living sisters perished, two at Auschwitz-Birkenau and one at Theresienstadt.

World War II and the Holocaust occurred after Freud's death and spurred a number of psychoanalytic studies on the effects of war and violence on individual children and adults. Freud's daughter, Anna, ran a nursery in England for orphans and children who had been separated from their parents by the war. Psychoanalysts were prominent in treating survivors of the Holocaust and in identifying psychic trauma and its role in personality development and pathology. The "survivor syndrome" was identified as well as the intergenerational transmission of psychic trauma to the children of survivors. This work with survivors and their children has resulted in a greater appreciation of the complex role trauma plays in human life and a greater attention to its effects in posttraumatic syndromes. One result has been the development of programs for immediate intervention to reduce the pathological effects of trauma in war, disasters, and other psychologically overwhelming events.

During the Cold War, a few psychoanalysts were involved with other mental health professionals in trying to understand and reduce the psychological barriers to peaceful relations between the two main nuclear powers, the U.S. and the USSR. With the break-up of the former Soviet Union and the end of the Cold War, ethnic strife in a number of areas, either dormant or unnoticed, has become more prominent and deadly, accounting for the statistics cited at the beginning of this chapter. Psychoanalysts, using theory which has evolved in conceptual breadth, have written about the causes of war and ethnic violence, extending Freud's work toward a more comprehensive psychoanalytic large group psychology.

Prominent in these efforts have been Erik Erikson, Franco Fornari, William Meissner, and Vamik Volkan.

Section III details these efforts. The result has been not only a more comprehensive view of the role of psychology in international relations but the ability to apply this understanding to the reduction of group conflict in particular situations. Analogous to psychoanalytic therapists helping their patients to use insights about themselves to make meaningful changes in their lives, psychoanalytically informed interdisciplinary teams intervene in conflict areas to reduce tension and violence. Part IV describes these contributions in some detail.

War and ethnic violence are conducted by individual human beings, although they do so in groups and in the name of groups. It is the purpose of this chapter to describe the ways in which knowledge about the individual gained in the course of clinical psychoanalysis has contributed to the understanding of collective activities in war. The application of psychoanalytic knowledge to large group psychology and practical experience derived from this knowledge are instrumental to this endeavor.

II. SIGMUND FREUD'S EXPLANATION OF WAR AND VIOLENCE

Freud derived much of his understanding of the mind from his own self-analysis, and it is clear now that his own personal experiences influenced his theorizing. According to his letters, Freud began World War I as an enthusiastic Austrian patriot. However, after a few months his enthusiasm cooled and was replaced by a disillusioned view of that war and of all wars.

Freud published *Thoughts for the Times on War and Death* in 1915 from the standpoint of a bystander seeking to understand war. At this time he had been formulating a major theoretical work on unconscious mental functioning and the nature of what he called instinctual drives (*trieb*). He applied his thinking about unconscious drives to his questions about war. In this paper he expressed the idea that judged by our unconscious wishful impulses, human beings are "a gang of murderers." These impulses exist in a repressed state most of the time but can be released depending on the circumstances, internal and external. A counterweight to these destructive impulses, the intellect, was thought by Freud to be "feeble" and dependent on the drives for the psychic energy necessary to do its work. He hoped that forces of reason and rationality could outweigh the forces of drive. Freud concluded, however, that war could not be abolished as long as the conditions among nations were so different. By this he meant the economic

struggle between the haves and the have-nots set up conditions for inevitable competition and strife which caused the release of the repressed drives.

This condition fit his earlier notions described in *Totem and Taboo* about the beginning of civilization in the small human horde. He speculated that a group of brothers collectively killed their father-ruler, ate him, and out of remorse, erected a totem representation of him which they worshipped. Freud's group psychology, then, was based upon his thinking about the male Oedipus complex and his theory of the destructive wishful drives. He was pessimistic about mankind's ability to tame these inner impulses and to undo the outer inequalities.

Some 17 years later, on the eve of Hitler's accession to power, Freud's reply to Einstein's letter was a bit more hopeful. Freud agreed with Einstein's suggestion that a stronger international body with power to mediate disputes between states was needed to prevent these disputes from turning into wars. Freud also emphasized the positive emotional ties between members of a group which could be a source of unity among states. Freud had investigated these emotional ties between members of a group, which he called identifications, in his earlier book, *Group Psychology and the Analysis of the Ego*. He saw identifications as a form of love, the first emotional tie to another person. He had, by the time of the Einstein letter, consolidated his thinking about a dual drive theory, the destructive aggressive drive and the libidinal, loving, and unifying drive. Peace and war thus became for Freud the outcome of the tension between the tendency toward unity and the tendency toward destruction.

In analogy to his psychoanalytic work with patients, Freud told Einstein that he hoped that political leaders could be taught to "subordinate their instinctual life to the dictatorship of reason." In contrast to his previous enthusiasm for Austrian patriotism, Freud called himself a pacifist and a pacifist by nature. He elaborated for Einstein his theory that civilization was a process, evolving toward ethical and aesthetic ideals but opposed by the strength of the individual's instinctual drives. By this time he had also formulated his tripartite view of the functional "agencies" of the mind—the instinctual id, the executive ego, and the evaluating superego. The healthy individual could integrate and accommodate these conflicting tendencies in the mind and experience relative harmony and inner peace. When these conflicts could not be integrated, the mind was at war with itself.

Freud analogized from the view of the individual to that of the large group. Anything that fosters the strength of civilization, the force of growth and unity, works against war, destruction, and death. The strength of intellectual life with its reason, rationality, and the renunciation of the destructive instinct fostered civilization.

Freud had elaborated this theory a few years earlier in *Civilization and Its Discontents*, published in 1930. In this work he described mankind as struggling with the irremediable conflict between the demands of instinct and the restrictions of civilization. Here we can see war as a pathological destructiveness, freed from the restraints of conscience and of civilization.

Freud postulated the sources of mankind's suffering as the power of nature, the feebleness of our bodies, and the inadequacy of the regulations which mediate human relations in the family, the state, and society at large. Freud felt that mankind seeks a certain protection from this suffering through a "delusional remolding of reality" shared by large numbers of people in common. One such delusion was religion which he explained at some length in his *Future of an Illusion*, published in 1927. Delusional thinking can also be applied to aspects of the political process particularly when it comes to identifying enemies and going to war.

Freud considered the step taken to replace the individual's power with that of the community as a decisive one for civilization. He compared that step to character formation and the sublimation of the drives in individuals. In this connection he considered the realistic prospects for the ideal of loving one's neighbor as oneself, surely an antidote to war and violence. He made the observation that it was certainly possible to band together a large number of people in communal love as long as there were other people left over to receive the destructiveness that needed an outlet as well. Civilization, though he equated it with the quest for unity and life, was in constant conflict with the tendency toward destruction and death. He added that perhaps one day, someone would begin a study of the pathology of communities. Freud died in 1939 on the eve of World War II and the Holocaust, the results of which have made the study of the pathology of communities mandatory for subsequent generations of psychoanalysts.

In summary, Freud's view of war, a social phenomenon, was based primarily on his understanding of the psychology of the individual mind and, in addition, on his not-fully-developed large-group psychology. This understanding rested heavily on his concept of the instinctual drives, particularly the aggressive one, and on the conflict between the drives and the civilizing effects of the ego and superego. His theory of large group psychology rested on his theory of male psychosexual development in the Oedipal phase of child development and on the concept of the beginning of civilization in the primal horde. His notions about the identifications between members of the group taking the leader as their ideal was also an important part of his group psychology.

III. POST-FREUDIAN PSYCHOANALYTIC EXPLANATIONS OF WAR AND VIOLENCE

The intention of this section is to describe those post-Freudian contributions to the study of war and violence which built upon and extended Freud's work. World War II had a very disruptive effect on psychoanalysis in Europe, causing the displacement of most European psychoanalysts to the Americas or to Great Britain. After the war interest in psychoanalysis accelerated, particularly in the United States, and a period of extremely productive theoretical and clinical work ensued.

Psychoanalysis turned its attention to the study of the ego, those functions of the mind dealing with adaptation and the management of conflict. It also turned to the study of "object relations," the mental representations of the sense of self and of the significant others crucial to growth and development. In addition, the role of the mother in the early development of the child's personality was given greater emphasis. Finally, the kind of patients treated with psychoanalytic therapy widened, allowing greater appreciation of the earliest pre-Oedipal periods of development where more primitive mechanisms of defense are so influential. All of this had a powerful influence on extending Freud's initial views of group psychology, war, and ethnic conflict.

The pilot of the plane that dropped the first atomic bomb on Hiroshima named the plane after his mother, Enola Gay. The announcement from the director of the Manhattan Project which developed the bomb announced this success to President Truman in code: "Baby is born." Psychoanalysts see importance in these kind of details in which a weapon of mass destruction is associated with mothers, babies, and the procreative function. Explaining this kind of association became the province of the next generation of psychoanalytic theorists of war.

Erik Erikson, a refugee from Europe, extended Freud's concept of the psychosexual stages of child development, oral–anal–phallic/oedipal, by postulating corresponding psychosocial stages and extending these stages beyond the age of 6 to school-age, adolescence, and so on throughout the life cycle. Erikson called these stages crises with polar alternatives: trust versus mistrust, autonomy versus shame and guilt, initiative versus guilt, industry versus inferiority, identity versus identity diffusion, intimacy versus isolation, and ego integrity versus despair. Tilting toward the positive pole at each stage denotes healthy adaptation.

Erikson's work is significant for extending the individual psychology of Freud to the interpersonal, cultural, historical, and sociological context in which the individual develops. While Erikson did not specifically devote any single work to the question of the causes of war and violence, his theory, by emphasizing the relationship of the individual to the group and the influence of the historical and the cultural process on the individual psyche, extended the psychoanalytic conceptualization of social phenomena.

Erikson's stage of identity versus identity diffusion, which rests heavily on his clinical experiences with very disturbed hospitalized adolescents as well as his own personal history of identity diffusion, is perhaps his most influential single concept. Identity, he emphasized, is more than the accumulation of identifications; it is an integrated sense of oneself which is confirmed by one's surrounding interpersonal and cultural environment. This extended psychoanalytic attention from mankind's instinctual nature to one of mutual interaction between biology, interpersonal relations, culture, and history.

Erikson illustrated his theories in his studies of historical figures like Hitler, Luther, Gandhi, and Jefferson. These works are not only a further contribution to a psychoanalytic large group psychology, they also have become the intellectual source of the fields of psychohistory and political psychology. In his psychobiographical studies, Erikson emphasized the role of identity formation in the adolescent as a crucial factor in the kind of charismatic leadership these men were to provide for their groups. His emphasis was on the mutual interaction between the leader and the group.

Identity is a concept bridging both the individual and the social. It can be applied to social groups so that societies can be seen to suffer from identity diffusion. In his work *Gandhi's Truth*, for example, Erikson explored the psychosocial determinants of nonviolence just as he did in exploring the role of hatred in Hitler's life. The leadership of both men was analyzed also in terms of the psychosocial needs of their respective societies at the time they offered leadership.

This integration of the psychological and the social led others to apply these concepts to historical conflicts. Psychoanalyst and historian Peter Loewenberg studied the influence of social forces on the generation of youth

that became Hitler's *Freikorps*. Loewenberg has also examined the vicissitudes of nationalism from the standpoint of identity. Inspired by Eriksonian theory and methodology, the psychiatrist Robert Jay Lifton has explored the effects of totalism and brainwashing, the effects of the Hiroshima bombing, Nazi doctors, and the genocidal mentality.

Erikson's work demonstrated the extension of theory from the study of the drives to the study of the ego and the self. Other theorists sought to extend Freud's work into the earliest stages of the infant's interaction with the mother. Most notably the work of Melanie Klein and her followers has been most influential in this respect. In more recent years, the work of Otto Kernberg and Heinz Kohut called attention to early object relations and the psychology of the self, particularly in the treatment of more disturbed patients with a borderline or narcissistic diagnosis. Application of this paradigmatic extension of Freud's work was made to group psychology and to the motives for war.

In his analysis of war the Italian psychoanalyst Franco Fornari (1966) utilized Melanie Klein's thinking about the conflicts generated in the earliest months of the infant's life. In contrast to Freud, who saw war as the product of mankind's aggressive drive overwhelming civilizing influences, Fornari postulates an adaptive, if not therapeutic, motive for war. He sees war as an institution which serves to deal with the primitive anxieties stemming from the individual's earliest years and which are endemic to group psychology. These psychological causes of war are necessary but not sufficient explanations; it takes particular economic, political, and historical events to mobilize or activate war.

Fornari advances the notion of war as a "paranoid elaboration of mourning" by which he means specific processes aimed at avoiding the "profound human suffering" associated with mourning loss, real and fantasized, from infancy. In Klein's view the infant goes through a paranoid developmental phase in which images of the self and mother are split into all-good or all-bad, a phase which is succeeded by the depressive phase in which the infant feels ambivalent about the mother, loving and hating at the same time, and capable of integrating resultant good–bad images of both the mother-object and the self. The depressive phase marks a crucial integration of the sense of self and other. In Fornari's view, the motive for war involves the externalization of the individual's unresolved capacity to mourn and involves the return to the paranoid solutions of splitting into good–bad images. In this way an enemy is created, identified, and attacked as the solution to the inability to mourn. It is in this sense that Fornari believes war is adaptive and an attempt to heal the archaic conflicts around loss and mourning.

Since the late 1980s, roughly coinciding with the break-up of the Soviet Union, several American psychoanalysts have renewed interest in the explanation of war and ethnic violence in terms of the analogy between the earliest relations of the child with mother and those of the individual to the large group.

William Meissner, both a psychoanalyst and a Jesuit priest, elaborates the idea of the paranoid process. Based on his work with clinically paranoid individuals, Meissner postulates a more general process in which cognitive mechanisms associated with early development and clinical paranoia are employed to identify an enemy. These mechanisms include the kind of all-good, all-bad thinking described by Fornari, primitive idealization, introjection, and projection. Projection, the attributing of unwanted sexual or aggressive impulses onto the other, who is in turn feared, is a hallmark of clinical paranoia and a basic mechanism of the paranoid process.

Meissner applies the notion of the paranoid process to group psychology and to intergroup hostility in his analysis of prejudice and violence. Paranoia is a defense, in his view, against feelings of helplessness and worthlessness. These feelings are experienced as an inner enemy which may in turn be externalized outward onto the recipient of these unwanted feelings. The inner enemy is now an external enemy. War against the external enemy is waged in order to defeat the inner enemy and to relieve the individual's powerless and helpless feelings. Meissner conceptualizes these dynamics in his concept of the cult, a group dynamic version of the paranoid process, in which everything that is good is seen as residing within the cultic group and everything that is bad is outside of the cult's boundaries. In this way the all-bad out-group is also dehumanized, rendering it worthy of destruction. Meissner thus attempts to create a group psychology, based on and consonant with, individual psychology on a primitive level.

Vamik Volkan, a Turkish Cypriot-American psychoanalyst, has elaborated an integrated theory of the motive for war and ethnic conflict, utilizing much of the previously described work. His viewpoint owes much to his own experiences growing up in Cyprus, where ethnic violence has been especially bitter and long-lasting, as well as on his extensive experience in treating and theorizing about very disturbed psychotic patients. He calls the motive for war the need for enemies and allies.

In his book *The Need to Have Enemies and Allies*, Volkan first traces the need to have enemies back to the stranger anxiety of 9 months of age and extends this no-

tion to a more inclusive theory of the development of the concept of enemy throughout childhood. He calls this process finding "suitable targets for externalization," something which can be of a positive (ally) or negative (enemy) type. Also, these targets can be animate or inanimate. He is especially interested in those examples of externalization of the primitive unwanted impulses described by Klein, Fornari, Meissner, and many others onto ethnic identity by which conflicts can be perpetuated for hundreds of years by the institutionalization of the enemy concept.

In another book, *Bloodlines*, Volkan gives some examples of these ethnic blood feuds which have lasted centuries. The ethnic conflicts in the former Yugoslavia harks back to Serbian feelings about their defeat by the Ottoman Empire in the battle of Kosovo, which occurred in 1389. Current discussions of disputes in Bosnia reveal that grievances from centuries ago are alive in the thinking of the antagonists today. Volkan observes that these grievances have been transmitted from generation to generation, keeping alive potential conflict and a readiness for war along these ancient ethnic lines.

His analysis follows along several psychoanalytic paths already mentioned but elaborates into a more coherent, easily comprehended, and practical theory. He describes as relevant Freud's mention of the narcissism of minor differences, the idea that small differences between individuals or groups can be greatly accentuated to enhance self-esteem and maintain identity. The process may easily turn into the identification of targets of externalization and thus the identification of enemies and allies along rigid lines which can be passed from generation to generation without resolution. Volkan acknowledges Freud's views on man's aggressiveness and destructiveness as well as the primitive mechanisms outlined by Fornari. He also posits the failure to properly mourn on the part of antagonistic groups which keeps the conflicts brewing without resolution. Revenge is the antidote to feelings of helplessness, powerlessness, and loss. Suitable mourning and rational solutions to grievances are avoided in favor of the perpetuation of the need for an enemy which has to be fought and destroyed.

In summary, post-Freudian theorizing about motives for war has emphasized war's adaptive function in dealing with primitive anxieties by exploiting paranoid, externalizing identification of a dehumanized enemy and the fantasy that destruction of this enemy is a solution to this individual and group distress. Pre-Oedipal issues, primitive defenses, and object relations have extended Freud's original theorizing. Identifying the atom bomb as a baby may now be seen to be consonant with psychoanalytic theories about the unresolved nature of the infant's persecutory and depressive distress and the rageful solution to this distress. It represents a kind of reaction formation in which awareness of the massive destructiveness of the weapon is defended against by naming it for its opposite—procreation and life. It also points to conflicts generated by the early mother–child relationship as the source of fantasies justifying and promoting war.

IV. PSYCHOANALYTIC CONTRIBUTIONS TO REDUCING VIOLENT SOCIAL CONFLICTS

Because psychoanalysis is also a treatment of mental disorders, psychoanalysts have been involved in the treatment of those who have been adversely affected by war and ethnic violence. Psychoanalysts treated "war neuroses" during and after World Wars I and II. Anna Freud ran a nursery for children orphaned or displaced from their families by World War II and provided detailed reports on the effects of this dislocation on the children's development. Psychoanalysts were also in the forefront of treating Holocaust survivors and subsequently the children of these survivors. The role of trauma in the survivor syndrome aided in the concept of posttraumatic stress disorders involving the negative effects of traumatic events. This understanding led to new interventions and programs. Most of this work was done with individuals within the general nature of psychoanalytic practice.

In the many writings cited above, the psychoanalysts writing about war have made some recommendations aimed at ameliorating the conditions leading to war, and a few even were able to have their ideas heard at governmental levels. The English analyst Edward Glover, for example, made several recommendations dealing with his thesis of the role of sadism in motives for war. He was advisor to the British government in evaluating future leadership for post-war Germany. The American psychoanalyst Stephen Sonnenberg began an extensive collaboration with an arms control expert in order to explore the psychological implications of arms control negotiations during the Cold War.

Vamik Volkan has been involved for a number of years in trying to apply his notions of the need for enemies and allies to a series of interventions aimed at reducing conflicts between enemy states. He has worked with Joseph Montville, an American diplomat who developed the notion of informal or Track II diplomacy, and other experienced diplomats. Volkan's efforts are

worth noting because the interventions involve a practical, yet psychoanalytically informed, process which can be replicated in different conflict settings.

The method involves face-to-face meetings in small and large groups of influential diplomatic and political figures from both enemy camps along with a "neutral" team of diplomats and mental health professionals. This group experience becomes a microcosm of the larger dispute facing the antagonistic states—a reexperiencing of the conflicts that are involved in the dispute which can then be helped by the interventions of the neutral team.

In trying to solve their intergroup conflicts, participants in Volkan's interventions come upon emotional snags that make it difficult to resolve the dispute in the first place. With the helpful intervention of members of the neutral team, the group forces responsible for the maintenance of the need for enemies lessen, and a more humane, rational, and problem-solving spirit can prevail. If this indeed becomes the case, these influential leaders on both sides can return to their respective communities and act as agents of peaceful change and compromise in future, more formal, negotiations. In *Blood Lines*, Volkan discusses some of the interventions he has been involved with: the Greek Cypriot–Turkish Cypriot conflict, the Israeli–Palestinian conflict, and the conflict between the Baltic countries and the Soviet Union over Baltic independence.

The neutral team attempts to allow a full airing of the grievances but also attempts to prevent further dehumanization of the enemy. Usually the failure to acknowledge enemy suffering and mourning and a complicated difficulty in mourning losses from one's own group are often found to be the psychological basis of the impasses standing in the way of further discussion and resolution. Very much in accord with Fornari's earlier views, if mourning of this kind can be achieved, paranoid fears and projections and the accompanying dehumanization of the enemy recede, and a better feeling, sometimes temporarily euphoric, holds sway.

Based on these experiences, Volkan has founded the Center for the Study of Mind and Interaction at the University of Virginia. The Center sponsors interdisciplinary research, scholarship, and interventions of the type just described. Diplomats, scholars, psychoanalysts, and other mental health professions make up the interdisciplinary teams. Projects are underway dealing with the Baltic states, Kuwait, racism and violence in the United States, and the cultic leader–follower relationship.

As an example of this work, the Center has been engaged for 3 years in a project in Estonia to resolve disputes between Estonia, Russia and the Russian speaking residents of Estonia. This project cost $3 million, there has been no bloodshed, and the basis for an on-going dialogue between the competing groups has been established. Volkan argues that though this type of preventative work is expensive, the cost of war in lives lost and people displaced and traumatized is far larger.

V. CONCLUSION

In *Civilization and Its Discontents*, Freud expressed the hope that someday someone would begin a study of the pathology of communities. In his letter to Einstein he had hoped that political leaders could be taught to subordinate their aggressive drives to reason. When Anwar Sadat addressed the Israeli Knesset in 1977, he described the psychological barriers that separated the enemies Egypt and Israel. He estimated that psychological factors were 70% of the problem. This article has described the ways in which psychoanalysts have sought to fulfill Freud's unfinished mission to identify the pathology of communities when going to war with each other and to help to break down the psychological walls to which Sadat referred.

Also See the Following Articles

AGGRESSION, PSYCHOLOGY OF • BEHAVIORAL PSYCHOLOGY • ENEMY, CONCEPT AND IDENTITY OF • ETHNICITY AND IDENTITY POLITICS • HUMAN NATURE, VIEWS OF • PSYCHOLOGY, A GENERAL VIEW • WORLD WAR II

Bibliography

Fornari, F. (1966). *The psychoanalysis of war.* (A. Pfeifer, trans.). Bloomington: University of Indiana Press.

Freud, S. (1915). *Thoughts for the times on war and death.* (pp. 275–300). London: Hogarth.

Freud, S. (1930). *Civilization and its discontents.* (pp. 59–145). London: Hogarth.

Freud, S. (1932). *Why war?* (pp. 197–215). London: Hogarth.

Erikson, E. H. (1950). *Childhood and society.* New York: W. W. Norton.

Erikson, E. H. (1969). *Gandhi's truth: On the origins of militant non-violence.* New York: W. W. Norton.

Glover, E. (1946). *War, sadism, and pacifism.* London: Allen and Unwin.

Meissner, W. W. (1978). *The paranoid process.* New York: Jason Aronson.

Volkan, V. D. (1988). *The need to have enemies and allies: From clinical practice to international relationships.* Northvale, NJ: Jason Aronson.

Volkan, V. D. (1997). *Bloodlines: From ethnic pride to ethnic terrorism.* New York: Farrar, Straus and Giroux.

Winnik, H. Z., Moses, R., & Ostow, M. (1973). *Psychological bases of war.* New York: Quadrangle Books.

Psychological Effects of Combat

Dave Grossman
Arkansas State University

Bruce K. Siddle
PPCT Management Systems

GLOSSARY

Evacuation Syndrome The paradox of combat psychiatry. Psychiatric casualties must be treated, but if soldiers begin to realize that psychiatric casualties are being evacuated, the number of psychiatric casualties will increase dramatically.

Fear A cognitive or emotional label for nonspecific physiological arousal in response to a threat.

Midbrain Sometimes referred to as the mammalian brain, it is the primitive part of the brain that is generally indistinguishable from that of any other mammal. During times of extreme stress cognition tends to localize in this portion of the brain.

Operant Conditioning Training that prepares an organism to react to a specific stimulus with a specific voluntary motor response. Operant conditioning is highly effective in preparing individuals to respond with desired actions in highly stressful circumstances.

Parasympathetic Nervous System The branch of the autonomic nervous system that is responsible for the body's digestive and recuperative processes.

Post-Traumatic Stress Disorder (PTSD) A psychological disorder resulting from a traumatic event. PTSD manifests itself in persistent reexperiencing of the traumatic event, numbing of emotional responsiveness, and persistent symptoms of increased arousal, resulting in clinically significant distress or impairment in social and occupational functioning. There is often a long delay time between the traumatic event and the manifestation of PTSD. PTSD has been strongly linked with greatly increased divorce rates, increased suicide rates, and increased incidence of alcohol and drug abuse.

Psychiatric Casualty A combatant who is no longer able to participate in combat due to mental (as opposed to physical) debilitation.

Purification Ritual A set of symbolic social mechanisms that help returning veterans to come to terms with their actions in combat and successfully integrate back into peacetime society.

Sympathetic Nervous System (SNS): The branch of the autonomic nervous system that mobilizes and directs the body's energy resources for action.

THE PSYCHOLOGICAL EFFECTS OF COMBAT is a concept which encompasses a wide variety of processes and negative impacts, all of which must be taken into consideration in any assessment of the immediate and long term costs of war. This entry will address the wide spectrum psychological effects of combat, to include psychiatric casualties suffered during combat, physiological arousal and fear, the physiology of close combat, the price of killing, and Post-Traumatic Stress Disorder (PTSD).

I. INTRODUCTION: A LEGACY OF LIES

An examination of the psychological effects of combat must begin by acknowledging that there are some positive aspects to combat. Throughout recorded history these positive aspects have been emphasized and exaggerated in order to protect the self-image of combatants, to honor the memory of the fallen and rationalize their deaths, to aggrandize and glorify political leaders and military commanders, and to manipulate populations into supporting war and sending their sons to their deaths. But the fact that these positive aspects have been manipulated and exploited does not deny their existence. There is a reason for the powerful attraction of combat over the centuries, and there is no value in going from the dysfunctional extreme of glorifying war to the equally dysfunctional extreme of denying its attraction.

The ability to recognize and confront danger, the powerful group bonding that occurs in times of stress, the awe-inspiring spectacle of a nation focused and aligned to achieve a single aim, selfless dedication to abstract concepts and goals, and the ability to overcome the powerful imperatives of the survival instinct and willingly die for others: these common aspects of war represent both important survival traits and a potentially positive comment on basic human nature. But if war does have a capacity for reflecting some usually hidden, positive aspects of humanity, it irrefutably does so at a great and tragic cost.

One obvious and tragic price of war is the toll of death and destruction. But there is an additional cost, a psychological cost borne by the *survivors* of combat, and a full understanding of this cost has been too long repressed by a legacy of self-deception and intentional misrepresentation. After peeling away this "legacy of lies" that has perpetuated and glorified warfare there is no escaping the conclusion that combat, and the killing that lies at the heart of combat, is an extraordinarily traumatic and psychologically costly endeavor that profoundly impacts all who participate in it.

This psychological cost of war is most readily observable and measurable at the individual level. At the national level, a country at war can anticipate a small but statistically significant increase in the domestic murder rate, probably due to the glorification of violence and the resultant reduction in the level of "repression" of natural aggressive instincts which Freud held to be essential to the existence of civilization. At the group level, even the most elite unit is usually psychologically destroyed when between 50 and 60% casualties have been inflicted, and the integration of the individual into the group is so strong that this destruction often leads to depression and suicide. However, the nation (if not eliminated by the war) is generally resilient, and the group (if not destroyed) is inevitably disbanded. But the individual who survives combat may well end up paying a profound psychological cost for a lifetime. The cumulative impact of these effects on hundreds of thousands of veterans is pervasive, with significant potential to have a profound effect on society at large.

II. PSYCHIATRIC CASUALTIES IN WAR

Richard Gabriel has noted that: "Nations customarily measure the 'costs of war' in dollars, lost production, or the number of soldiers killed or wounded." But, "rarely do military establishments attempt to measure the costs of war in terms of individual suffering. Psychiatric breakdown remains one of the most costly items of war when expressed in human terms." Indeed, for the combatants in every major war fought in this century, there has been a greater probability of becoming a psychiatric casualty than of being killed by enemy fire.

A psychiatric casualty is a combatant who is no longer able to participate in combat due to mental (as opposed to physical) debilitation. Psychiatric casualties seldom represent a permanent debilitation, and with proper care they can be rotated back into the line. (However, Israeli research has demonstrated that, after combat, psychiatric casualties are strongly predisposed toward the more long-term and more permanently debilitating manifestation of Post-Traumatic Stress Disorder.)

The actual casualty can manifest itself in many ways, ranging from affective disorders to somatoform disorders, but the treatment for the many manifestations of combat stress involves simply removing the soldier from the combat environment. But the problem is that the military does not want to simply return the psychiatric casualties to normal life, it wants to return them to combat. And these casualties are understandably reluctant to do so.

The evacuation syndrome is the paradox of combat psychiatry. A nation must care for its psychiatric casualties, since they are of no value on the battlefield (indeed, their presence in combat can have a negative impact on the morale of other combatants) and they can still be used again as valuable seasoned replacements once they have recovered from combat stress. But if combatants begin to realize that insane combatants are being evacuated, the number of psychiatric casualties will increase dramatically.

Continued "proximity" to the battlefield (through forward treatment, usually within enemy artillery range) combined with an "expectancy" of rapid return to combat, are the principles developed to overcome the paradox of the evacuation syndrome. These principles of proximity and expectancy have proven themselves quite effective since World War I. They permit the psychiatric casualty to get the rest that is the only current cure for his problem, while not giving a message to still healthy comrades that insanity is a ticket away from the madness of the battlefield.

But even with the careful application of the principles of proximity and expectancy the incidence of psychiatric casualties is still enormous. During World War II, 504,000 men were lost from America's combat forces due to psychiatric collapse—enough to man 50 divisions. The United States suffered this loss despite efforts to weed out those mentally and emotionally unfit for combat by classifying more than 800,000 men 4-F (unfit for military service) due to psychiatric reasons. At one point in World War II, psychiatric casualties were being discharged from the U.S. Army faster than new recruits were being drafted in.

Swank and Marchand's World War II study of U.S. Army combatants on the beaches of Normandy found that after 60 days of continuous combat, 98% of the surviving soldiers had become psychiatric casualties. And the remaining 2% were identified as "aggressive psychopathic personalities." Thus it is not too far from the mark to observe that there is something about continuous, inescapable combat which will drive 98% of all men insane, and the other 2% were crazy when they got there. Figure 1 presents a schematic representation of the effects of continuous combat.

It must be understood that the kind of continuous, protracted combat that produces such high psychiatric casualty rates is largely a product of 20th-century warfare. The Battle of Waterloo lasted only a day. Gettysburg lasted only three days—and they took the nights off. It was only in World War I that armies began to experience months of 24-hour combat, and it is in World War I that vast numbers of psychiatric casualties were first observed.

The democratic nations of this century have been better than most at admitting and dealing with their combat psychiatric casualties, and information from non-Western sources is extremely limited, but we now know that America's World War II experience is repre-

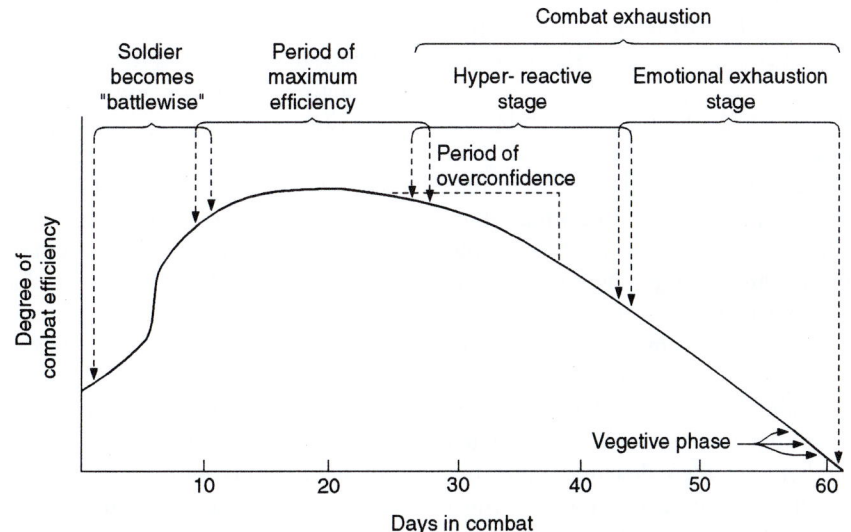

FIGURE 1 Effects of continuous combat.

sentative of a universal cost of modern, protracted warfare. Armies around the world have experienced similar mass psychiatric casualties, but many have simply driven these casualties into battle at bayonet point, shooting those who refused or were unable to continue. Japanese units in World War II employed a unique set of powerful cultural and group processes to delay psychiatric breakdown, but they only succeeded in temporarily delaying the cost of combat, a cost that eventually manifested itself in mass suicide. Ultimately the toll of modern combat is truly fearful, and no nation or culture has been able to escape it.

III. PHYSIOLOGICAL AROUSAL AND FEAR

The soldier in combat endures many indignities. Among these can be endless months and years of exposure to desert heat, sweltering jungle, torrential rains, or frozen mountains and tundras. Usually the soldier lives amidst swarming vermin. Very often there is lack of food, lack of sleep, and the constant uncertainty that eats away at the combatants' sense of control over their lives and their environment. But, bad as they are, all of these stressors can be found in many cultural, geographic, or social circumstances, and when the ingredient of war is removed individuals exposed to these circumstances do not suffer mass psychiatric casualties.

To fully comprehend the intensity of the stress of combat, we must keep these other stressors in mind while understanding the body's physiological response to combat, as manifested in the sympathetic nervous system's mobilization of resources. And then we must understand the impact of the parasympathetic nervous system "backlash" that occurs as a result of the demands placed upon it.

The sympathetic nervous system (SNS) mobilizes and directs the body's energy resources for action. It is the physiological equivalent of the body's front-line soldiers who actually do the fighting in a military unit.

The parasympathetic nervous system is responsible for the body's digestive and recuperative processes. It is the physiological equivalent of the body's cooks, mechanics, and clerks who sustain a military unit over an extended period of time.

Usually the body maintains itself in a state of homeostasis, which ensures that these two nervous systems maintain a balance between their demands upon the body's resources. But during extremely stressful circumstances the "fight-or-flight" response kicks in and the SNS mobilizes all available energy for survival. This is the physiological equivalent of throwing the cooks, mechanics, and clerks into the battle. This process is so intense that soldiers very often suffer stress diarrhea due to redirecting of energies from nonessential parasympathetic processes, and it is not at all uncommon to lose control of urination and defecation as the body literally "blows its ballast" and redirects all available energy in an attempt to provide the resources required to ensure survival. This is reflected in World War II surveys in which a quarter of combat veterans admitted that they urinated in their pants in combat, and a quarter admitted that they defecated in their pants in combat.

A combatant must pay a physiological price for an enervating process so intense. The "price" that the body pays is an equally powerful "backlash" when the neglected demands of the parasympathetic nervous system become ascendant. This parasympathetic backlash occurs as soon as the danger and the excitement is over, and it takes the form of an incredibly powerful weariness and sleepiness on the part of the soldier.

Napoleon stated that the moment of greatest danger was the instant immediately after victory, and in saying so he demonstrated a powerful understanding of the way in which soldiers become physiologically and psychologically incapacitated by the parasympathetic backlash that occurs as soon as the momentum of the attack has halted and the soldier briefly believes himself to be safe. During this period of vulnerability a counterattack by fresh troops can have an effect completely out of proportion to the number of troops attacking.

It is basically for this reason that the maintenance of a "unblown" reserve has historically been essential in combat, with battles often revolving around which side can hold out and deploy their reserves last. Clausewitz understood the danger of reserve forces becoming prematurely enervated and exhausted (and he provides insight into the root cause of the enervation) when he cautioned that the reserves should always be maintained out of sight of the battle.

In continuous combat the soldier roller-coasters through a seemingly endless series of these surges of adrenaline and their subsequent backlashes, and the body's natural, useful, and appropriate response to danger ultimately becomes extremely counterproductive. Unable to flee, and unable to overcome the danger through a brief burst of fighting, posturing, or submission, the bodies of modern soldiers in sustained combat exhaust their capacity to enervate and slide into a state of profound physical and emotional exhaustion of such a magnitude that it appears to be almost impossible to communicate it to those who have not experienced it.

Most observers of combat lump the impact of this physiological arousal process under the general heading of "fear," but fear is really a cognitive or emotional label for nonspecific physiological arousal in response to a threat. The impact of fear and its attendant physiological arousal is significant, but it must be understood that fear is just a symptom and not the disease, it is an effect but not the cause. To truly understand the psychological effects of combat, we must understand exactly what it is that causes this intense fear response in individuals, and it has become increasingly clear that there are two key, core stressors causing the psychological toll associated with combat. These stressors are: the trauma associated with being the victim of close-range, interpersonal aggression; and the trauma associated with the responsibility to kill a fellow human being at close range.

IV. THE TRAUMA OF CLOSE-RANGE, INTERPERSONAL AGGRESSION

During World War II the carnage and destruction caused by months of continuous German bombing in England, and years of Allied bombing in Germany, was systematically inflicted in order to create psychological casualties among civilian populations. Day and night, in an intentionally unpredictable pattern, for months and even years on end, civilians, relatives and friends were mutilated and killed, and homes were destroyed. These civilian populations suffered fear and horror of a magnitude that few humans will ever experience.

This unpredictable, uncontrollable reign of shock, horror, and terror is exactly what psychiatrists and psychologists prior to World War II believed to be responsible for the vast numbers of psychiatric casualties suffered by soldiers in World War I. And yet, incredibly, the Rand Corporation's Strategic Bombing Study published in 1949 found that there was only a very slight increase in the psychological disorders in these populations as compared to peacetime rates and that these occurred primarily among individuals already predisposed to psychiatric illness. These bombings, which were intended to break the will of the population, appear to have served primarily to harden the hearts and increase the determination to fight among those who endured them.

The impact of fear, physiological arousal, horror, and physical deprivation in combat should never be underestimated, but it has become clear that other factors are responsible for psychiatric casualties among combatants. One of those factors is the impact of close-range, interpersonal, aggressive confrontation.

Through roller coasters, action and horror movies, drugs, rock climbing, whitewater rafting, scuba diving, parachuting, hunting, contact sports, and a hundred other means, modern society pursues fear. Fear in and of itself is seldom a cause of trauma in everyday peacetime existence, but facing close-range interpersonal aggression and hatred from fellow citizens is a horrifying experience of an entirely different magnitude.

The ultimate fear and horror in most modern lives is to be raped, tortured, or beaten; to be physically degraded in front of loved ones or to have the sanctity of the home invaded by aggressive and hateful intruders. The *Diagnostic and Statistical Manual* of the American Psychiatric Association affirms this when it notes that Post-Traumatic Stress Disorder (PTSD) "... may be especially severe or longer lasting when the stressor is of human design." PTSD resulting from natural disasters such as tornadoes, floods, and hurricanes is comparatively rare and mild, but acute cases of PTSD will consistently result from torture or rape. Ultimately, like tornadoes, floods, and hurricanes, bombs from 20,000 feet are simply not "personal" and are significantly less traumatic—to both the victim and aggressor.

Death or debilitation is statistically far more likely to occur by disease or accident than by malicious action, but statistics have nothing to do with fear. Statistically speaking, cigarette smoking is an extraordinarily dangerous activity that annually inflicts slow, hideous deaths upon millions of individuals worldwide, but this fact does not dissuade millions of individuals from smoking, and around the globe few nations are motivated to pass laws to protect their citizens from this threat. But the presence of one serial rapist in a large city can change the behavior of hundreds of thousands of individuals, and there is a broad tradition of laws designed to protect citizens from rape, assault, and murder.

When snakes, heights, or darkness cause an intense fear reaction in an individual it is considered a phobia, a dysfunction, an abnormality. But it is very natural and normal to respond to an attacking, aggressive fellow human being with a phobic-scale response. This is a universal human phobia. More than anything else in life, it is intentional, overt, *human* hostility and aggression that assaults the self-image, sense of control and, ultimately, the mental and physical health of human beings.

The soldier in combat is inserted straight into the inescapable midst of this most psychologically traumatic of environments. Ultimately, if the combatant is unable get some respite from the trauma of combat, and if not injured or killed, the only escape available is the psychological escape of becoming a psychiatric casualty and mentally fleeing the battlefield.

V. THE PHYSIOLOGY OF CLOSE COMBAT

An understanding of the stress of close combat begins with an understanding of the physiological response to close-range interpersonal aggression. The traditional view of combat stress is most often associated with combat fatigue and Post-Traumatic Stress Disorder, which are actually manifestations that occur after, and as a result of, combat stress. Bruce Siddle has defined combat stress as the perception of an imminent threat of serious personal injury or death, or when tasked with the responsibility to protect another party from imminent serious injury or death, under conditions where response time is minimal.

The debilitating effects of combat stress have been recognized for centuries. Phenomenon such as tunnel vision, auditory exclusion, the loss of fine and complex motor control, irrational behavior, and the inability to think clearly have all been observed as byproducts of combat stress. Even though these phenomena have been observed and documented for hundreds of years, very little research has been conducted to understand why combat stress deteriorates performance.

The key characteristic which distinguishes combat stress is the activation of the SNS. The SNS is activated when the brain perceives a threat to survival, resulting in a immediate discharge of stress hormones. This "mass discharge" is designed to prepare the body for fight or flight. The response is characterized by increasing arterial pressure and blood flow to large muscle mass (resulting in increased strength capabilities and enhanced gross motor skills—such as running from or charging into an opponent), vasoconstriction of minor blood vessels at the end of appendages (which serves to reduce bleeding from wounds), pupil dilation, cessation of digestive processes, and muscle tremors. Figure 2 presents a schematic representation of the effects of hormonal induced heart rate increase resulting from SNS activation.

The activation of the SNS is automatic and virtually uncontrollable. It is a reflex triggered by the perception of a threat. Once initiated, the SNS will dominate all voluntary and involuntary systems until the perceived threat has been eliminated or escaped, performance

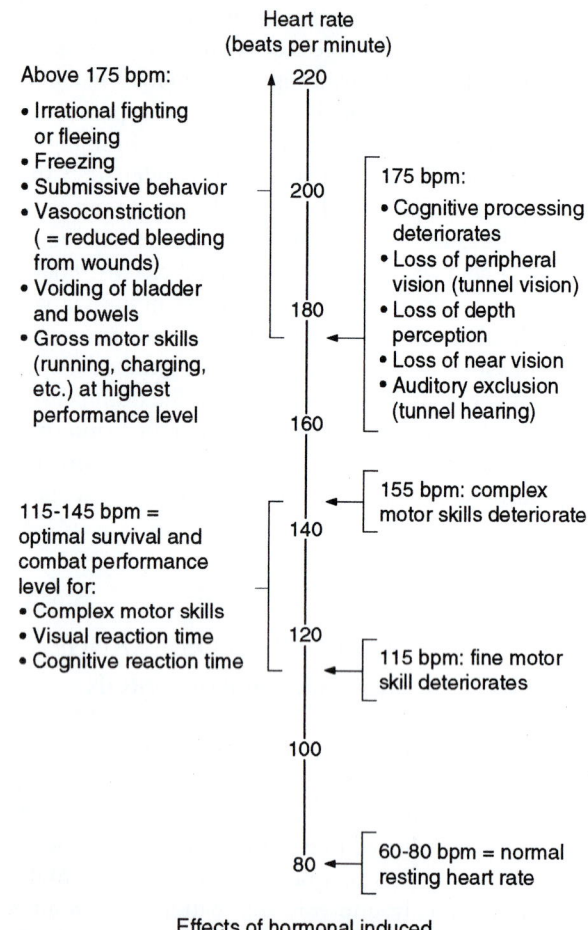

FIGURE 2 Effects of hormonal induced heart rate increase.

deteriorates, or the parasympathetic nervous system activates to reestablish homeostasis.

The degree of SNS activation centers around the level of perceived threat. For example, low-level SNS activation may result from the anticipation of combat. This is especially common with police officers or soldiers minutes before they make a tactical assault into a potential deadly force environment. Under these conditions combatants will generally experience increases in heart rates and respiration, muscle tremors, and a psychological sense of anxiety.

In contrast, high-level SNS activation occurs when combatants are confronted with an unanticipated deadly force threat and the time to respond is minimal. Under these conditions the extreme effects of the SNS will cause catastrophic failure of the visual, cognitive, and motor control systems. Although there are endless variables that may trigger the SNS, there are six key variables that have an immediate impact of the level of SNS activation. These are the degree of malevolent, human intent behind the threat; the perceived level of threat, ranging from risk of injury to the potential for death; the time available to response; the level of confidence in personal skills and training; the level of experience in dealing with the specific threat; and the degree of physical fatigue that is combined with the anxiety.

Once activated, the SNS causes immediate physiological changes, of which the most noticeable and easily monitored is increased heart rate. SNS activation will drive the heart rate from an average of 70 beats per minute (BPM) to more than 200 BPM in less than a second. And as combat stress increases, heart rate and respiration will increase until catastrophic failure, or until the parasympathetic nervous system is triggered.

In 1950, S.L.A. Marshall's *The Soldier's Load and the Mobility of a Nation* was one of the first studies to identify how combat performance deteriorates when soldiers are exposed to combat stress. Marshall concluded that we must reject "... the superstition that under danger men can be expected to have more than their normal powers, and that they will outdo their best efforts simply because their lives are in danger." Indeed, in many ways, the reality is just the opposite and individuals under stress are far less capable of doing anything other than blindly running from or charging toward a threat. Humans have three primary survival systems: vision, cognitive processing, and motor skill performance. Under stress, all three break down.

Bruce K. Siddle's landmark research at PPCT involved monitoring the heart rate responses of law-enforcement officers in interpersonal conflict simulations using paintball-type simulation weapons. This research has consistently recorded heart rate increases to well over 200 beats per minute, with some peak heart rates of up to 300 beats per minute. These were simulations in which the combatants knew that their life was not in danger. The combatant in a true, life-and-death situation (whether soldier or law enforcement officer), faces the ultimate, universal human phobia of interpersonal aggression, and will certainly experience a physiological reaction even greater than that of Siddle's subjects. The fundamental truth of modern combat is that the stress of facing close-range interpersonal aggression is so great that, if endured for months on end without any other means of respite or escape, the combatant will inevitably become a psychiatric casualty.

But even greater than the resistance to being the *victim* of close-range aggression, is the combatant's powerful aversion to *inflicting* aggression on fellow human beings. And at the heart of this dread is the average, healthy person's resistance to killing one's own kind.

VI. A RESISTANCE TO KILLING

There is a notable reduction in the kind of psychiatric casualties usually identified with long-term exposure to combat among medical personnel, chaplains, officers, and soldiers on reconnaissance patrols behind enemy lines. The key factor that is not present in each of these situations is that, although they are in the front lines and the enemy may attempt to kill them, they have no direct responsibility to participate personally in close-range killing activities. Even when there is equal or even greater danger of dying, combat is much less stressful if you do not have to kill.

The existence of a resistance to killing lies at the heart of this dichotomy between killers and nonkillers. This is an additional, final stressor that the combatant must face. To truly understand the nature of this resistance of killing we must first recognize that most participants in close combat are literally "frightened out of their wits." Once the bullets start flying, combatants stop thinking with the forebrain, which is the part of the brain which makes us human, and start thinking with the midbrain, or mammalian brain, which is the primitive part of the brain that is generally indistinguishable from that of an animal.

In conflict situations this primitive, midbrain processing can be observed in the existence of a powerful resistance to killing one's own kind. During territorial and mating battles, animals with antlers and horns slam together in a relatively harmless head-to-head fashion, rattlesnakes wrestle each other, and piranha fight their own kind with flicks of the tail, but against any other species these creatures unleash their horns, fangs, and teeth without restraint. This is an essential survival mechanism that prevents a species from destroying itself during territorial and mating rituals.

One major modern revelation in the field of military psychology is the observation that this resistance to killing one's own species is also a key factor in human combat. Brigadier General S.L.A. Marshall first observed this during his work as the official U.S. historian of the European Theater of Operations in World War II. Based on his postcombat interviews, Marshall concluded in his landmark book, *Men Against Fire*, that only 15 to 20% of the individual riflemen in World War II fired their weapons at an exposed enemy soldier. Specialized weapons, such as a flamethrower, usually were fired. Crew-served weapons, such as a machine gun, almost always were fired. And firing would increase greatly if a nearby leader demanded that the soldier fire. But, when left to their own devices, the great majority of individual combatants throughout history appear to have been unable or unwilling to kill.

Marshall's findings have been somewhat controversial. Faced with scholarly concern about a researcher's methodology and conclusions, the scientific method involves replicating the research. In Marshall's case, every available, parallel, scholarly study validates his basic findings. Ardant du Picq's surveys of French officers in the 1860s and his observations on ancient battles, Keegan and Holmes' numerous accounts of ineffectual firing throughout history, Richard Holmes' assessment of Argentine firing rates in the Falklands War, Paddy Griffith's data on the extraordinarily low killing rate among Napoleonic and American Civil War regiments, the British Army's laser reenactments of historical battles, the FBI's studies of nonfiring rates among law enforcement officers in the 1950s and 1960s, and countless other individual and anecdotal observations, all confirm Marshall's fundamental conclusion that man is not, by nature, a killer.

The exception to this resistance can be observed in sociopaths who, by definition, feel no empathy or remorse for their fellow human beings. Pit bull dogs have been selectively bred for sociopathy, bred for the absence of the resistance to killing one's of kind in order to ensure that they will perform the unnatural act of killing another dog in battle. Similarly, human sociopaths represent Swank and Marchand's 2% who did not become psychiatric casualties after months of continuous combat, since they were not disturbed by the requirement to kill. But sociopaths would be a flawed tool that is impossible to control in peacetime, and social dynamics make it very difficult for humans to breed themselves for such a trait. However, humans are very adept at finding mechanical means to overcome natural limitations. Humans were born without the physical ability to fly, so we found mechanisms that overcame this limitation and enabled flight. Humans also were born without the psychological ability to kill our fellow humans, and so, throughout history, we have devoted great effort to finding a way to overcome this resistance. From a psychological perspective, the history of warfare can be viewed as a series of successively

more effective tactical and mechanical mechanisms to enable or force combatants to overcome their resistance to killing.

VII. OVERCOMING THE RESISTANCE TO KILLING

By 1946 the U.S. Army had accepted Marshall's conclusions, and the Human Resources Research Office of the U.S. Army subsequently pioneered a revolution in combat training that eventually replaced firing at bullseye targets with deeply ingrained "conditioning" using realistic, man-shaped, pop-up targets that fall when hit. Psychologists know that this kind of powerful "operant conditioning" is the only technique that will reliably influence the primitive, midbrain processing of a frightened human being, just as fire drills condition terrified school children to respond properly during a fire, and repetitious, "stimulus-response" conditioning in flight simulators enables frightened pilots to respond reflexively to emergency situations.

Throughout history the ingredients of groups, leadership, and distance have been manipulated to enable and force combatants to kill, but the introduction of conditioning in modern training was a true revolution. The application and perfection of these basic conditioning techniques increased the rate of fire from near 20% in World War II to approximately 55% in Korea and around 95% in Vietnam. Similar high rates of fire resulting from modern conditioning techniques can be seen in FBI data on law enforcement firing rates since the nationwide introduction of modern conditioning techniques in the late 1960s. Figure 3 presents a schematic representation of the interaction between the killing enabling factors that have been manipulated throughout history, including the key, modern ingredient of conditioning.

One of the most dramatic examples of the value and power of this modern, psychological revolution in training can be seen in Richard Holmes' observations of the 1982 Falklands War. The superbly trained (i.e., "conditioned") British forces were without air or artillery superiority and consistently outnumbered three-to-one while attacking the poorly trained but well-equipped and carefully dug-in Argentine defenders. Superior British firing rates (which Holmes estimates to be well over 90%), resulting from modern training techniques, has been credited as a key factor in the series of British victories in that brief but bloody war. Any future army that attempts to go into battle without

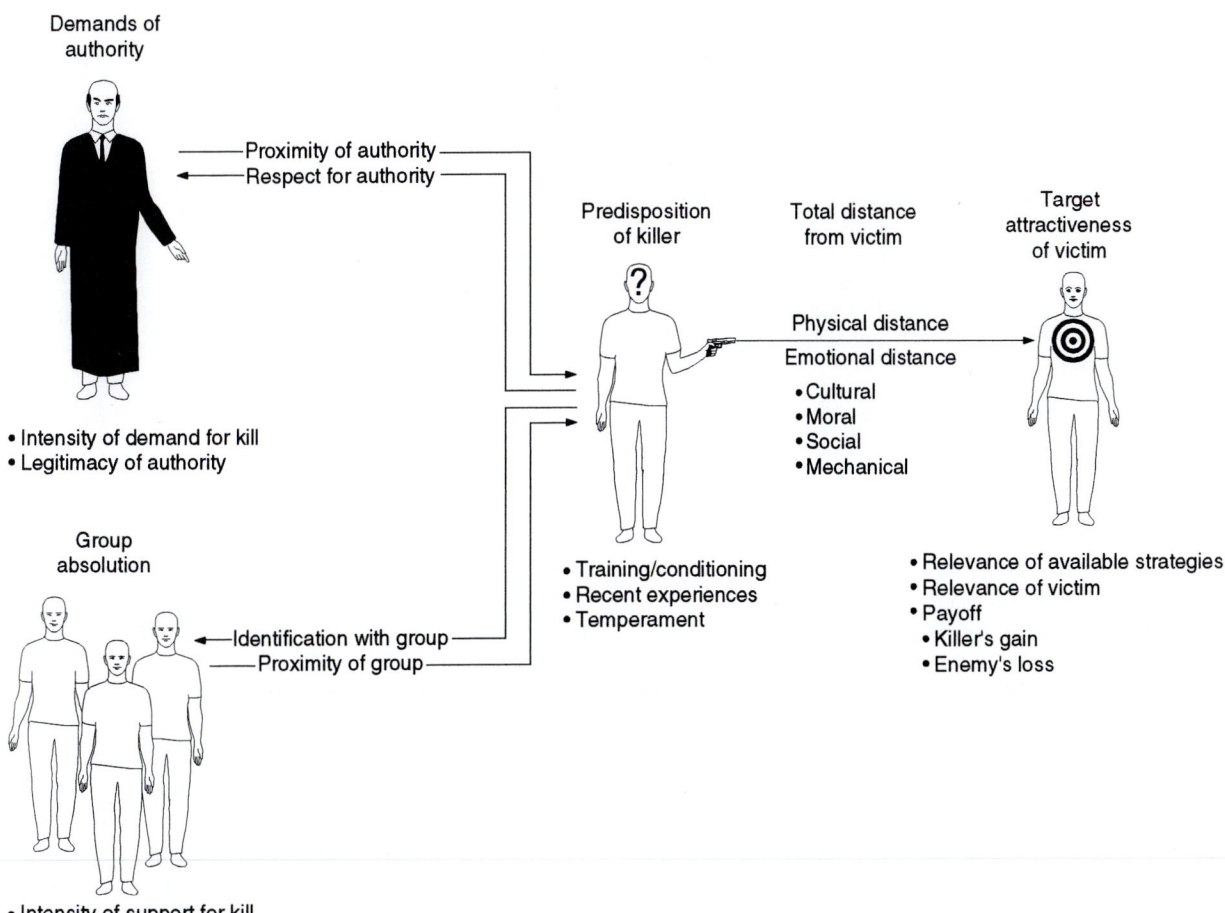

FIGURE 3   Killing enabling factors.

similar psychological preparation is likely to meet a fate similar to that of the Argentines.

VIII. THE PRICE OF OVERCOMING THE RESISTANCE TO KILLING

The extraordinarily high firing rate resulting from modern conditioning processes was a key factor in America's ability to claim that U.S. ground forces never lost a major engagement in Vietnam. But conditioning that overrides such a powerful, innate resistance carries with it enormous potential for psychological backlash. Every warrior society has a "purification ritual" to help returning warriors deal with their "blood guilt" and to reassure them that what they did in combat was "good."

In primitive tribes this generally involves ritual bathing, ritual separation (which serves as a cooling-off and "group therapy" session), and a ceremony embracing the veteran back into the tribe. Modern Western rituals traditionally involve long periods while marching or sailing home, parades, monuments, and the unconditional acceptance of society and family.

Table I outlines some of the key factors in the killing experience rationalization and acceptance processes, using the example of U.S. troops in Vietnam as a case study of an extreme circumstance in which the purification rituals broke down. For example, combatants do not do what they do in combat for medals, they are motivated largely by a concern for their comrades; but after the battle medals serve as a kind of "Get Out of Jail Free Card": a powerful talisman that proclaims to them and to others that what the combatant did was

TABLE I

Killing Experience Rationalization and Acceptance Processes
A Comparative Study

Process	Past wars	Vietnam
Praise from peers and superiors (medals, citations)	Yes	Yes (not worn)
The presence of mature, older comrades	Yes	No (Reduced)
Circumstances limiting civilian kills/atrocities	Yes	No (Reduced)
Rear lines and safe areas	Yes	No
Presence of close, trusted friends throughout the war	Yes	No
Cool-down period with comrades while returning home	Yes	No
Knowledge of victory, gain, and accomplishments	Yes	No
Parades and monuments	Yes	No (Delayed)
Reunions and continued commo with comrades after the war	Yes	No
Acceptance and praise from friends, family, and society	Yes	No (Mixed)
Support to veteran from religious and political systems	Yes	No (Mixed)

honorable and acceptable. Although medals were issued in Vietnam, the social environment was such that veterans could not wear the medals or their uniforms in public. Similarly, the young combatant needs the presence of mature, older comrades to seek guidance and support from, but in Vietnam the average age of the combatant was 19, as opposed to 26 in World War II. Other key factors unique to the American experience in Vietnam include the absence of any truly safe, secure area in-country; the individual replacement system that hampered bonding and ensured that soldiers often arrived and left as strangers; and the use of aircraft to immediately return veterans to America, without the usual cool-down, group therapy period experienced for thousands of years as veterans sailed or marched home.

For America's Vietnam veterans the purification ritual was largely denied, and a host of studies have demonstrated that one of the the most significant causal factors in Post-Traumatic Stress Disorder is the lack of support structure after the traumatic event, which in this case occurred when the returning veteran was attacked and condemned in an unprecedented manner. The traditional horrors of combat were magnified by modern conditioning techniques, and this combined with the nature of the war and an unprecedented degree of societal condemnation to create a circumstance which resulted in between 0.5 and 1.5 million cases (the results of studies vary greatly) of Post-Traumatic Stress Disorder (PTSD) among the 3.5 million U.S. veterans of Southeast Asia. This mass incidence of psychiatric disorders among Vietnam veterans resulted in the "discovery" of PTSD, a condition that we now know has always occurred as a result of warfare, but never before in this quantity. Armies around the world have integrated these lessons from Vietnam, and in Britain's

Falklands War, Israel's 1982 Lebanon incursion, and in the U.S.'s Gulf War the lessons of Vietnam and the need for the purification ritual have been closely and carefully considered and applied. In the former U.S.S.R.'s Afghanistan War this need was again ignored, and the resulting social turmoil was a one of the factors that eventually led to the collapse of that nation. Indeed, the Weinberger Doctrine, later referred to as the Powell Doctrine, which holds that the United States will not engage in a war without strong societal support, is a reflection of the tragic lessons learned from the psychological effects of combat in Vietnam.

PTSD is a psychological disorder resulting from a traumatic event. PTSD manifests itself in persistent reexperiencing of the traumatic event, numbing of emotional responsiveness, and persistent symptoms of increased arousal, resulting in clinically significant distress or impairment in social and occupational functioning. There is often a long delay between the traumatic event and the manifestation of PTSD. Among Vietnam veterans in the United States, PTSD has been strongly linked with greatly increased divorce rates, increased incidence of alcohol and drug abuse, and increased suicide rates. Indeed, Veterans Administration data indicate that, as of 1996, three times more Vietnam veterans have died from suicide after the war than died from enemy action during the war, and this number is increasing every year.

But PTSD seldom results in violent criminal acts, and U.S. Bureau of Justice Statistics research indicates that veterans, including Vietnam veterans, are statistically less likely to be incarcerated than a nonveteran of the same age. The key safeguard in this process appears to be the deeply ingrained discipline which the soldier internalizes with military training. However, with the advent of interactive "point-and-shoot" arcade and video games there is significant concern that society is aping military conditioning, but without the vital safeguard of discipline. There is strong evidence to indicate that the indiscriminate civilian application of combat conditioning techniques as entertainment may be a key factor in worldwide, skyrocketing violent crime rates, including a seven-fold increase in per capita aggravated assaults in America since 1956. Thus, the psychological effects of combat can increasingly be observed on the streets of nations around the world.

IX. CONCLUSION: A CULTURAL CONSPIRACY

It is essential to acknowledge that good ends have been and will continue to be accomplished through combat. Many democracies owe their very existence to successful combat. Few individuals will deny the need for combat against Nazi Germany and Imperial Japan in World War II. And around the world the price of civilization is paid every day by military units on peacekeeping operations and domestic police forces who are forced to engage in close combat. There have been and will continue to be times and places where combat is unavoidable, but when a society requires its police and armed forces to participate in combat it is essential to fully comprehend the magnitude of the inevitable psychological toll.

It is often said that "All's fair in love and war," and this expression provides a valuable insight into the human psyche, since these twin, taboo fields of sexuality and aggression represent the two realms in which most individuals will consistently deceive both themselves and others. Our psychological and societal inability to confront the truth about the effects of combat is the foundation for the cultural conspiracy of repression, deception, and denial that has helped to perpetuate and propagate war throughout recorded history.

In the field of developmental psychology a mature adult is sometimes defined as someone who has attained a degree of insight and self-control in the two areas of sexuality and aggression. This is also a useful definition of maturity in civilizations. Thus two important and reassuring trends in recent years have been the development of the science of human sexuality, which has been termed "sexology," and a parallel development of the science of human aggression, which D. Grossman has termed "killology." There is universal consensus that continued research in this previously taboo realm of human aggression is vital to the future development, and perhaps to the very existence, of our civilization.

Also See the Following Articles

BEHAVIORAL PSYCHOLOGY • MILITARY CULTURE • VETERANS IN THE POLITICAL CULTURE • WEAPONRY, EVOLUTION OF

Bibliography

Gabriel, R. A. (1987). *No more Heroes: Madness and psychiatry in war.* New York: Hill and Wang.

Greene, B. (1989). *Homecoming.* New York: G. P. Putnam's Sons.

Griffith, P. (1989). *Battle tactics of the (American) civil war.* London.

Grossman, D. (1995, 1996). *On killing: The psychological cost of learning to kill in war and society.* New York: Little, Brown, and Co.

Holmes, R. (1985). *Acts of war: the behavior of men in battle.* New York: The Free Press.

Keegan, J. (1976). *The face of battle.* Harmondsworth, England: The Chaucer Press.

Keegan, J., & Holmes, R. (1985). *Soldiers.* London: Hamish Hamilton.

Marshal, S. L. A. (1978). *Men against fire.* Gloucester, MA: Peter Smith.

Siddle, B. K. (1995). *Sharpening the warrior's edge: The psychology and science of training.* Millstadt, IL: PPCT Management Systems.

Swank, R. L., & Marchand, W. E. (1946). Combat neuroses: development of combat exhaustion. *Archives of Neurology and Psychology,* 55, 236–247.

Psychology, General View

Michael Wessells

Randolph-Macon College

GLOSSARY

Biological Determinism The view that behavior is caused by genetic, biological factors.

Cognitive Scripts Learned patterns and expectations about violence and conflict and about how conflicts develop, escalate, and get resolved.

Dehumanization The mental process of stripping away the human qualities of the Other.

Desensitization Diminished emotional responsiveness to violent events due to repeated exposure to or witnessing of violent acts.

Empathy Taking the perspective of another person or group in an effort to learn their perceptions, feelings, values, and motives.

Enemy Images Exaggerated representations of the Other as thoroughly diabolical, aggressive, and untrustworthy.

Ethnocentrism Dynamic of intergroup conflict in which the perspective of one's own group is placed at the center, yielding in-group favoritism and out-group derogation.

Misperception The distorted perception of events, motives, or behavior, due typically to biasing effects of prior expectations or fear.

Post-traumatic Stress Disorder Trauma-induced disorder associated with flashbacks, reduced responsiveness, avoidant behavior and hypervigilance.

Structural Violence Indirect violence through social injustice, inequity, and failure to meet basic human needs for items such as food and shelter.

Sublimation The channeling of socially unacceptable impulses such as aggressive urges into socially acceptable forms of behavior such as playing sports.

Superordinate Goals Goals that lie within the interests of each group in a conflict but that can be attained only through inter-group cooperation, which reduces tensions and destructive conflict.

MOST PSYCHOLOGISTS view violent and peaceful behavior as the product of interaction between biological and social processes. Significant debate, however, occurs over the extent of biological determination and the preventability of violence, particularly organized armed conflict. Conflict pervades all social levels, from the family to the international. Although conflict can be constructive, it often becomes destructive through excessive competition, inappropriate use of power and contentious tactics, and the creation of systems that privilege some groups over others. Destructive conflict creates emotional and social wounds that may hurt more than physical wounds, and the psychological damage can contribute to cycles of ongoing violence. Between groups, destructive conflict is fueled not by innate human aggressive impulses but by processes such as ethnocentrism, enemy imaging, social identity processes, discrimination, and processes of conformity and obedience. As evident in current ethnopolitical conflicts, powerful survival fears stir nationalistic impulses and quest for positive social identity, animating highly aggressive behavior. To build peace, it is necessary to meet basic human needs and to address the deep fears, negative images, and malignant social processes that stimulate violence. Numerous psychological methods and tools are available for reducing destructive conflict, preventing violence, and building peace. These themes are developed within the framework of peace psychology, which recognizes that psychological processes always operate in a complex political, economic, social, and cultural milieu; that individual behavior is conditioned by the wider social context; and that psychology is only one element in what ought to be a multidisciplinary, analytic framework.

I. PSYCHOLOGICAL STUDIES, CULTURE, AND HUMAN NATURE

The psychological study of violence, peace, and conflict has been dominated by Western perspectives, and this global hegemony of Western psychology introduces values and biases that color research on the psychological roots of violence, peace, and conflict. Broadly, these values honor science over traditional knowledge and practice, men over women, individualism over collectivism, and materialism over spiritualism. Overwhelmingly, the psychological study of violence, peace, and conflict has failed to draw upon diverse cosmologies, to bring forward the voices of women, to recognize the value of local wisdom and cultural diversity, or to be sufficiently aware and self-critical of its own biases and limitations. Although this article cannot escape these limitations, it attempts to reduce them by calling attention to biases where they exist and by drawing to the extent possible on excellent psychological work being conducted in different parts of the world.

Issues of culture have figured prominently in psychologists' analyses of human nature. Whereas biologi-cally oriented theories have held that humans are violent by nature, other theories have contended that violence is socially constructed, a product of culture and the social system in which one lives. These diverging views and the current state of psychological knowledge pertaining to them are outlined below.

A. Biological Determinism

Historically, influential psychological analysts such as Sigmund Freud viewed human aggression and violence as having instinctive roots and as motivated by unconscious processes. Some theorists have posited that the organization and direction of innate, individual impulses toward violence is the basis of war. In this view, war is biologically determined and inevitable, with politics providing the conditions that unleash destructive forces buried deep within the human psyche. Freud himself, however, believed that war might be prevented through processes such as sublimation, wherein socially undesirable impulses are channeled into socially acceptable forms of behavior. For example, aggressive impulses that could lead to violence might be channeled into socially acceptable sports such as football or hockey. More broadly, Freud viewed civilization as the product of a dialectic between instinctive tendencies and societally instilled social restraints. At the individual level, this dialectic involved ongoing conflict between the instinctive impulses (id) and internalized social restraints (superego), with the mediation of this conflict by ego being one of the main venues of personal development.

Hard biological determinism asserts that humans are wired genetically for violence and war—the best that culture and government can do is to restrain primordial impulses. Proponents of this approach have pointed to evidence that in prisons, one is more likely to find males who have an abnormal XYY chromosomal pattern (rather than the XY pattern typical for men), suggesting that chromosomal abnormality produced heightened aggression. In addition, XYY males are four times as likely as XY males to have a criminal record. Critics, however, have noted that most of the arrests were for nonviolent crimes, that XYY males show no increased rate of committing violent crimes, and that the XYY syndrome may be correlated with lower intelligence and education levels. Biological determinists also point to longitudinal evidence showing that boys who are highly aggressive at age 9 are likely to be highly aggressive and to have arrest records for violent crime later in life. Still others note the higher correlations between aggressive behavior of identical twins than for fraternal twins. Yet the data are far from conclusive. Long-term patterns of individual aggression may reflect patterns of upbringing. More similar behavioral outcomes for identical twins than for fraternal twins does not imply genetic inevitability, as high levels of heritability in one environment may not hold up when the environment is changed. In light of the uncertainties remaining on these issues, one ought to resist social policies predicated on the idea that some groups of people are naturally more violent than others and that the best society can hope to do with such people is to use harsh law-and-order methods and imprisonment as means of protecting public safety.

A softer form of biological determinism is the frustration-aggression theory, which states that frustration or exposure to unpleasant events increases the likelihood of aggression or violence. While this idea is familiar to anyone who has ever pounded a drink machine that accepted one's coins but delivered no drink, contemporary versions of the theory do not reduce all human violence to frustration. Nor do these theories hold that frustration invariably leads to aggression—people can learn to cope with frustration and to respond to it in diverse ways, and fear of punishment can inhibit an outburst of frustration-induced rage. According to this theory, biology predisposes people toward violence much as people are predisposed toward use of language.

Another version of the predisposition theory asserts that humans have an innate ethnocentric tendency to categorize people into in-groups, which are viewed favorably, and out-groups, which are viewed negatively. This tendency to categorize into a preferred "us" and a less valued "them" appears in many different societies. In the laboratory, this in-group preference shows up in minimal group experiments after people have divided themselves into groups according to seemingly inconsequential criteria such as preference for particular paintings over others. Some analysts have speculated that the ethnocentric tendency is rooted in ancestral patterns of living in kin groups that competed with rival clans and kin groups for scarce resources. These conditions may make it advantageous to distinguish sharply between one's own group and others, giving preference to one's own group while regarding others less favorably. It has also been argued that this tendency to distinguish "us" from "them" makes it easier for people to mistreat the out-group or to fight them when contentious political or economic circumstances arise. These interpretations remain controversial, however, as a large gap separates preference ratings from acts of mistreatment and physical violence. In addition, in-group preferences may be learned, generalized patterns of categorization

that reflect upbringing in societies that have widespread norms for carving up the social world and valuing people, aside from any biological mandate.

B. Cultural Constructionism

Theories of cultural constructionism contend that violence and war are predominantly the products of culture, that is, culturally constructed. Cultural constructionists such as the authors of the Seville Statement on Violence have pointed out glaring problems of biological determinism. First, among preindustrial societies that are not part of the dominant international system, more than 20% do not engage in war and have no history of war fighting. No compelling evidence exists that these societies have developed highly effective means of sublimating or displacing violent urges. Second, nations such as Switzerland and Sweden that had engaged in war frequently in earlier times have now altered their policies and gone generations without fighting wars. Third, there is remarkable variety in the war-fighting behavior of countries and peoples who do wage war. Whereas some fight using ritualized behaviors and simple technologies having low casualty rates, others fight with high-technology weapons, including weapons of mass destruction, that inflict very high casualty rates. Biological determinism predicts, incorrectly, greater universality of war among cultures and higher degrees of uniformity in modes of war fighting.

In addition, biological determinists have often argued across categories of behavior and levels of analysis in inappropriate ways. For example, some have argued that fighting and killing are widespread in the animal kingdom and that humans have inherited from their proto-human ancestors a tendency to fight and make war. In fact, however, the vast majority of killing in the animal kingdom occurs across species, as in predator-prey relations. Although struggles for dominance, territory, and mating rights are common among males of many species and occasion extensive fighting and some deaths, the fighting behavior in these contests tends to be highly stereotyped and to have relatively low levels of lethality. In many cases, the fighting males fail to use their most lethal weapons, and fixed signals of submission are often used to end a violent exchange. Humans are unique in their propensity to kill members of their own species in large numbers. Furthermore, when humans' ancestors hunted, they killed members of other species. No convincing evidence exists that those who hunt other species are more likely to be systematic killers of their own kind. Hunters may be less likely to kill their own kind by virtue of the cooperation and interdependence inherent in the hunt. Proponents of strong determinism have seldom noted that nonhumans exhibit a wide range of methods of reducing tension and violence.

Moreover, the link between individual fighting and organized violence is tenuous. Unlike individual acts of violence, war involves organized fighting between groups containing large numbers of trained combatants and high levels of communication and coordination. Military training does not simply organize and channel existing impulses toward violence, as soldiers are deliberately taught to follow orders to kill. Whereas many homicides are impulsive, military activity is quite the opposite, and training is frequently required to overcome impulsivity. To explain military fighting, one must analyze how groups and states organize armies, how they train and equip soldiers, why decisions are made about whether to go to war, which strategies and tactics to use, and so on. Answering these questions requires analysis of political, social, and cultural systems.

Learning theory also supports cultural constructionism. B. F. Skinner, the prominent behaviorist, argued that both violent and peaceful behavior are learned through interaction with a social community that applies contingencies of reinforcement and punishment. Through positive reinforcement, behavior that has positive consequences is strengthened and becomes more likely to occur in the future. For example, if two young boys both wanted to ride a bike and the larger boy pushed the smaller boy out of the way and took the bike, this consequence would increase the likelihood of similar bullying behavior in the future for the larger boy. Similarly, negative reinforcement strengthens behavior through the removal of an unpleasant or aversive stimulus following a response. Assume, for example, that person A threatened person B. If person B then punched person A, removing the noxious threat, this would increase the likelihood that person B would engage in aggressive hitting behavior in similar circumstances in the future. In contrast to positive and negative reinforcement, both of which strengthen a response, punishment weakens a response or decreases its frequency of occurrence. For example, if a 12-year-old girl hit a boy and was ostracized by her peer group, this might decrease the likelihood that she would engage in hitting behavior under similar conditions in the future. According to Skinner, it is the consequences of behavior—primarily one's history of reinforcement by one's parents, teachers, and peers—that shape and maintain violent or peaceful behavior.

Skinner's vision of a utopian community, outlined in *Walden Two*, suggested that if contingencies were arranged properly, it would be possible to eliminate violent behavior and build peace. Critics have denounced Skinner's envisioned social engineering as totalitarian, politically naive, and antithetical to free will. Although the cognitive revolution in psychology has relegated behaviorism to the sidelines, Skinner's approach remains rather widely used today in behavior modification programs.

Taking a more cognitive approach, Albert Bandura argued that children observe and imitate the behavior of adults, evaluate whether a particular model deserves emulation, assess whether an imitated behavior is likely to be rewarded, and internalize rules used in self-regulation. Through social learning, children may become highly aggressive, or they may become cooperative and nonviolent. In this view, socialization practices, mediated by individual cognition, determine aggression and peaceful behavior. Violence, like peace, is based on learned patterns of belief, value, and behavior.

C. Interactionism

Both biological determinism and cultural constructionism are too reductionistic. Most psychologists recognize that human behavior has multiple causes. As psychology has matured, most researchers have come to support an interactionist position. Human biological capacity admits a vast range of behaviors, and the capacities for learning, consciousness, foresight, social identity, and morality enable diverse forms of culture, social organization, and behavior. Some cultures and social systems encourage aggressive behavior, violence, war preparations, and war, while others do not. From this standpoint, it is illegitimate to say that war is in the genes or that peace is in the genes. Humans have the biological capacity for both, and it is culture and social systems that shape political, economic, and social life and that determine the likelihood of war. Biological influences, undeniably important, are always expressed in a cultural context that has a powerful influence. In building peace, it pays to be skeptical of ideologies that either tacitly or explicitly condone simplistic views of human nature.

II. CONSTRUCTIVE AND DESTRUCTIVE CONFLICT

Social conflict is an inescapable part of life, but it is not always undesirable and antithetical to peace. Whether conflict is constructive or destructive depends in no small part on how one deals with it. Building peace requires the creation of social processes that encourage the constructive handling of conflict.

Personality is one of many factors that influence how people will handle conflict. Impulsivity, for example, correlates with aggressiveness, as people with hostile dispositions are likely to respond to disagreements with anger and rage. In addition, people who exhibit sociopathic tendencies may derive pleasure from dominating and controlling others, and they typically have little empathy or concern for the damage they cause. Following the interactionist view presented earlier, personality develops in part through one's life experiences. People who have observed violence repeatedly and who have been reared in a social context that tacitly or explicitly normalizes and approves violence are at risk of becoming perpetrators of violence. Similarly, people who have learned effective skills of nonviolent conflict resolution may be less likely to use violence as the method of first resort. Often it is experience that produces the inclinations, individual differences, and durable patterns of behavior that are grouped under the label "personality."

Morton Deutsch has established the importance of motivational orientation. A cooperative orientation entails a positive interest in the well-being of the other as well as one's own. A competitive orientation entails an interest in outperforming the other and in doing as well as possible for oneself. A cooperative orientation encourages a positive, win-win approach to handling conflict, whereas a competitive orientation encourages a win-lose approach that often leads to conflict escalation and destructive effects. Situational factors often determine which orientation comes into play.

Situational factors are also evident in the power of social context to define and shape the course of a conflict. A seemingly minor issue such as seating patterns on buses can assume major importance if it symbolizes larger patterns of racism and injustice. A small transgression such as the refusal of a boss to meet with a worker can be a major source of conflict if it occurs against a background of mistreatment, pay inequity, and labor-management hostility. Disagreement over where to hold a peace conference may seem trivial if viewed against the lives that will be lost through continued fighting, but the issue can be highly significant if the outcome tilts the balance of power in ways that favor one party over the other. To understand conflict, one must understand the psychological significances and meanings of the issues to the parties, and one must situate the conflict in the wider relationship between the parties.

A. Constructive Aspects of Conflict

At the personal level, conflict can contribute much to growth and development. Artists have argued that inner conflict fuels creativity, and Freud argued that growth often occurs when the ego, the reality-based component of the personality, develops strategies of satisfying unconscious urges (id impulses) through the socially acceptable means demanded by the superego. Through conflict and choice, individuals define their personal identity and actualize the capacities for self-awareness, consciousness, and moral responsibility that are distinctively human.

Socially, as well as personally, conflict can be psychologically beneficial. In interpersonal relationships, conflict can stimulate new learning and growth. Marital conflict, if handled well, can lead partners to express their feelings, talk problems through, and solve issues in a mutually satisfying way that strengthens the long-term relationship. In fact, counselors and psychotherapists often use conflict as such an opportunity for growth and relational development. Between groups, too, conflict provides discernible benefits. Intense conflict typically promotes in-group cohesion that is psychologically satisfying and contributes to improved communication, cooperation, and performance by the group.

At the societal and international levels, conflict is often the engine for constructive social change. In the United States, conflict between African Americans and supporters of civil rights on one hand and segregationists and White supremacists on the other led to civil rights reforms that promoted greater social equity. Even where violence has been used as a principal means of pursuing a conflict, constructive changes can and have occurred. In apartheid South Africa, armed conflict between opponents and supporters of the apartheid regime heightened fears that the country would be plunged into all-out civil war, and these fears animated the quest for nonviolent options, the end of apartheid, and the transition to democracy. Under some circumstances, then, conflict may promote social justice. At the international level, too, conflict can promote positive social change. In India and throughout Africa, conflict between nationals and colonial regimes has been instrumental in ending unjust systems of domination. To say that violence has produced positive social change in selected cases, however, implies neither that armed conflict is typically beneficial and justified nor that violence was the only route to positive change.

B. Destructive Aspects of Conflict

Although conflict often entails physical damage, some of the most harmful kinds and impacts of violence are psychological. Interpersonally, hurtful things that are said can produce deep emotional wounds that persist much longer than most physical wounds. In unhealthy relationships, psychological violence may become part of a persistent pattern in which one partner controls, degrades, and psychologically abuses and manipulates the other, corroding love, trust, and self-esteem.

At the intergroup and international levels, too, psychological violence is often woven into systems of oppression and injustice. During the Cultural Revolution in China, for example, intellectuals, among many others, were subjected repeatedly to psychologically brutal "criticism" sessions, and the damage and sustained pressure from peers resulted in many suicides. In situations where there is great inequity and divisions along lines of ethnicity, gender, or social class, deep emotional wounds can result from racial epithets, refusal to provide service, or being mistreated through a demeaning attitude. People of minority groups comment frequently that the emotional damage from small daily slights is very great and that physical wounds heal more easily than psychological wounds.

Even in the absence of overt violence, destructive conflict fuels social psychological changes that promote subsequent violence. As conflict between ethnic groups or political factions escalates, for example, members of each group become fearful and suspicious of the other group, and the groups tend to become polarized and socially isolated from each other. These changes may encourage negative behavior toward the out-group, giving impetus to spiral processes of conflict escalation, which can lead to violence. Aside from physical fighting, international conflict can produce trade wars, so-called cold wars, and tensions that animate arms races and military practices perceived as threatening by fearful adversaries. These tensions and perceptions are not mere by-products of hostile interaction—under the appropriate conditions, they actively contribute to violence. When violence does occur, it can have tremendously damaging psychological effects, as outlined below.

III. PSYCHOSOCIAL IMPACTS OF VIOLENCE

The emotional damage caused by violence contributes to additional violence. Since victims of violence have had their views of a secure world shattered, they live in a heightened state of fear and are at risk of becoming perpetrators of violence. This pattern of circular causation is conspicuous in conflicts such as those in Bosnia, Afghanistan, and Rwanda, where collective trauma planted the seeds of future mass violence.

In analyzing the impact of violence, it is important to adopt a systems analytic framework and to look beyond individual behavior. Even where violence is not organized, circular causation generates violence across different social levels and can erode the fabric of civility, undermine law and order, and make violence the norm. For example, children who are abused at home may become more aggressive at school or on the streets. Conversely, violence in the community can induce problems of aggressiveness or rebellion against authority that then gets acted out in the family. In war zones and inner-city areas that are virtual combat zones, violence frequently becomes a self-sustaining system, a subculture of violence, in which violence permeates the fabric of daily life. When violence is normalized and large numbers of people have been affected by violence, it becomes difficult to arrange education, economic development, political reconstruction, and other steps toward peace.

The psychological effects of violence depend on factors such as the intensity and kind of violence, whether one is a witness or a direct victim of violence, whether the violence is a one-time event or chronic in nature, the victim's coping resources, developmental level, and social support systems, among others. Significant individual differences exist in resilience and responses to stress and violence, cautioning against assumptions that exposure to a violent event invariably produces trauma. The effects of victimization depend also on the cumulative stress impacting the victim. A beating or rape is likely to be more damaging psychologically if the victim is already affected by stressors such as physical illness, poverty, or uprooting. The effects of additional stressors are exponential, as an increase from two to three stressors can produce a 10-fold increase in the psychological impact. The impact of violence depends strongly on the social context—the cultural meanings attributed to it, the presence of others who provide emotional support, the living conditions in the community, and so on. Because individual mental and emotional functioning is closely connected with the social context, the impacts of violence are best thought of in psychosocial terms.

This section reviews selectively some of the main psychological effects of violence at different levels, and it examines the systemic impacts of violence in regard to situations of armed conflict. Although relatively effective psychological interventions exist for addressing the damaging impacts of violence, the greatest help is in the form of prevention.

A. Family Violence

In many countries, women are often victims of beatings, rape, and homicide in their own homes. Spouse abuse produces fear, trauma, and denial in the short run and anxiety, depression, and reduced self-esteem over the long run. These problems amplify and are in turn amplified by difficulties battered women often face in finding alternative living quarters, supporting themselves economically, and providing a safe environment for themselves and their children. Cultural factors often influence motives behind and patterns of spouse abuse. For example, in India, significant numbers of women are killed in dowry deaths associated with men's desire to remarry as a means of obtaining additional dowry money. Practices such as this contribute to women's sense of devaluation and oppression. Also within the family, the physical abuse of children, including sexual abuse, damages the sense of trust and impairs the formation of healthy social relationships. Children who are victims of family violence are at much greater risk of subsequently abusing their own children than are those who are not victims of family violence—cycles of violence often begin in the family.

B. Community Violence

At the community level, sexual harassment in schools or the workplace creates an atmosphere of fear and intimidation and induces psychological problems such as anxiety, depression, and stress-related somatic problems. In regard to rape, the psychological impact is profound. Typically motivated by power or hate, rape produces a powerful sense of insecurity and of personal violation. Normal reactions include trauma, a marked sense of discontinuity in experience that is associated with intrusive reexperiencing in the form of flashbacks or nightmares that can lead to sleep problems and impair daily functioning. Rape victims often exhibit avoidant behavior that reduces exposure to any stimuli that might evoke memories of the horrible event. Rape victims frequently experience anxiety, reduced self-esteem, and long-term depression. In the aftermath of rape, women asked to recount their experience as part of a police report or criminal trial may experience retraumatization and require professional support.

Also at the community level, people may be impacted by gang violence, homicide, and violent crime. In many urban areas, children grow up seeing dead bodies, shootings and muggings, and drug use. Chronic exposure to community violence normalizes violence and can encourage the view that killing and violent handling of conflict is an ordinary, inevitable part of life. In gang-controlled areas, young people see older role models engage in violence on a daily basis, and youth may be attracted to gangs by desire for power and reputation, wealth, affiliation, and avoidance of victimization. With homicide as the leading cause of death among African American men between the ages of 16 and 26 years, however, many youth experience a sense of futurelessness, which encourages recklessness and inattention to the consequences of one's behavior. While involved with gangs, many young people develop expensive physical and psychological dependencies on drugs, and the need to buy expensive drugs fuels crime and violence.

C. Societal Violence

At the societal level, media such as television are among the primary definers of social reality, and they may give millions of viewers a heavy diet of violence. The psychological impact of watching violence on TV depends on the kind and frequency of violence, the viewers' interpretation of the violence and whether it was justified, whether the perpetrator is perceived to be someone worthy of emulation, whether the violence had positive or negative consequences, and whether the viewers had critical viewing skills, among others. Looking across hundreds of studies in a literature studded with controversy, several patterns emerge clearly. First, through desensitization, televised violence blunts viewers' emotional responsiveness to violence and reduces their willingness to assist victims in violent situations. Second, watching large amounts of violence on television helps to teach viewers cognitive scripts of violence, learned patterns of how conflict escalates and is dealt with or resolved through violence. Third, televised violence can encourage the view of a mean world that is saturated with violence and dangerous at best. Particularly among senior citizens who seldom go out and for whom television is a primary agent in the social construction of reality, this view can encourage excessive fear and social isolation. In addition, watching violence on television can produce observational learning or imitation of violent behavior. On the other hand, the effects of TV violence are intricate. There is great individual variation, and effects that appear to result from exposure to TV violence are attributable in fact to peer pressure, observation in the home, or exposure to violence in other media.

On the societal level, structural violence, an inherent feature of all systems marked by oppression and social injustice, have profound psychological impact. As Gandhi once said, poverty is the greatest violence. More than one billion people, mostly in developing countries, live in dire poverty, having fewer than 2150 calories daily and earning under $500 annually. More than two billion people suffer from deficiencies of micro-nutrients such as iron, vitamin A, and iodine. These deficiencies and chronic malnutrition are known to cause extensive mental retardation and cognitive deficits. More than 100 million children, mostly girls, are not in school.

Forms of structural violence such as poverty, racism, and sexism induce powerful psychological reactions such as stress, frustration, anger, reduced self-esteem, and helplessness. Psychological violence inheres in the loss of human dignity and the internalization of the view of oneself as inferior. But structural violence also enables physical violence and psychological impacts thereof by stimulating interactions between other levels. For example, patriarchal systems that treat women as property and as inferior enable violence in the home and domination-oriented crimes such as rape. Similarly, poverty-induced economic stresses may lead parents to use excessive, harsh discipline with their children. In addition to producing psychological scars and damaged family relationships, this can lead young people to become disaffected and to spend more time on the streets, where they are influenced by gangs and exposed to community violence. Alternatively, exposures to racist remarks in the community or to ethnic tensions in schools can lead to a sense of reputational or image damage that induces frustration, anger, and aggressive behavior in the home. Although it is not explicitly planned, social systems often create violent subsystems in which violence in homes, schools, and workplaces interact in mutually supportive ways.

D. State Terrorism and Torture

Turning next to organized violence, repressive military regimes around the world rule through methods of state terrorism, which thrive by making citizens feel fearful, confused, powerless, distrustful, helpless, and bereft of meaning and legitimated social identity. Chronic fear, unpredictability, and stress are created by threats of job loss, disappearance, or torture. Through control over the public media, the government uses disinformation, plants seeds of doubt (as in messages such as "one never knows" or "no one can be trusted"), silences dissent, and provides rationalizations for the necessity of the violence (e.g., "terrorists must be stopped"). The disruption of daily patterns of communication, meeting, and dialogue, coupled with state control over political and religious beliefs and practices, undermines established systems of meaning that ordinarily give people a sense of stability, structure, and control over their lives. The disruption of patterns of meaning can create uncertainty about who one really is, how one should feel and act, and whether one is responsible for one's own suffering. Above all, state terrorism creates high levels of fear and obedience to authority that paralyze the population and encourage a strong sense of helplessness and inability to resist.

People who live in these circumstances often experience depression, high levels of stress, guilt, and self-blame for the suffering that occur, and a pervasive feeling of the senselessness and unreality of what goes on around them. Unable to express and test their own feelings publicly, some people experience extreme confusion and wonder whether they are going mad. Ultimately, state terrorism constructs a false reality and destroys the social contract of trust that binds individual and social community, making it impossible to talk meaningfully about "mental health."

Since torture is one of the primary instruments of state terrorism, it is not surprising that it induces, indeed exploits, many of the factors identified above. Torture victims frequently develop posttraumatic stress disorder with its associated problems of intrusive reexperiencing, numbing of responsiveness, and social avoidance. Victims may also experience problems of depression, stigmatization, reduced self-esteem, chronic anxiety, somatic disorders, helplessness, and despair. Since torturers often use methods designed to destroy the victim's sense of identity and meaning, many victims experience long-term problems in reconstructing a coherent identity and a sense of meaning in life. There may also be problems of guilt and self-blame for what happened or in regard to the fact that one survived while family and friends did not. Suicidal ideation and self-injury, including suicide, are not uncommon. Like the state terrorism that it supports, torture undermines trust, making it difficult to rebuild healthy relationships and a psychologically viable contract between person and society.

E. War

In World War I, extensive combat exposure led to clinical problems such as panic, confusion, exhaustion, and psychosomatic disorders. Psychiatrists and psychologists used the concept of "shell-shock" to relate these symptoms to experiences such as exposure to heavy shelling. In World War II, combat experience frequently led to exhaustion, apathy, confusion, and anxiety, and psychologists spoke of "combat fatigue" rather than shell-shock. Followup studies of former soldiers from World War II revealed problems such as intrusive dreams, noise hypersensitivity, sleep disturbances, and depression. It was the Vietnam War, however, that led to the systematic description of these potentially long-term symptoms into the diagnostic category of posttraumatic stress disorder (PTSD). The definition of PTSD is evolving but centers mainly around exposure to a stressor outside the range of normal human experience, the reexperiencing of the traumatic episode, persistent avoidance of stimuli associated with the trauma, and symptoms of increased arousal. Of combatants in the Vietnam War, approximately one-third developed the full symptom pattern characteristic of PTSD at some point in their lives, and half exhibited symptoms associated with war-related stress. In addition, drug use was relatively common in the Vietnam War, many veterans of which experience problems of substance abuse.

Culture exerts a strong influence on psychological reactions to combat. Although the diagnostic PTSD has been used in many cultures, it was constructed and validated in Western, highly industrialized society, and there are many questions regarding its applicability to non-Western societies. What counts as stress is itself culturally constructed and dependent upon cosmology or worldview. In Angola, for example, some of the greatest war-related stresses are believed to be spiritual, as a soldier who kills may believe he is haunted by the unavenged spirits of those killed. Western diagnostics typically underplay or fail to take into account such dimensions of stress. In addition, differences in social context make it risky to use concepts such as "trauma" in the intercommunal wars now fought in many developing nations. In a country such as Angola or Sudan, exposure to shelling typically occurs against a background of multiple, chronic stressors such as poverty, hunger, community destruction, and displacement. It cannot be assumed that Western concepts of trauma (or interventions for addressing trauma) apply directly to these situations.

Noncombatants also experience significant stress in times of war. During the Gulf War of 1991, when Israel was under threat of attack by chemical weapons and Israeli families sealed themselves into single rooms for protection, several stress-related deaths occurred even though there was no evidence of actual exposure to chemical weapons. Palestinian families, who had not been issued gas masks, also experienced very high stress

levels. Furthermore, high levels of stress occur in families of combatants, who experience not only separation but also great uncertainty, fear, and problems of adjustment when the soldiers return.

F. Fears of Nuclear War

The Cold War, with its attendant threat of nuclear war, either accidental or intentional, created significant public concerns, which had some grounding in events such as the Cuban Missile Crisis. In the 1980s, a large literature indicated that people, particularly adolescents, in the United States, the Soviet Union, and many other countries, feared or worried about the threat of a nuclear war during their lifetime. Clinicians reported a small number of cases in which young people presented symptoms such as depression and lack of a positive future orientation, ostensibly as a result of fears of nuclear war. In addition, although children were often aware of the nuclear threat, U. S. families seldom had open, constructive discussions about the problem, leaving many children alone with their concerns. Some researchers expressed concern that nuclear fears would lead to psychological problems such as a "live for today" attitude or suicidal tendencies.

Research eventually created a more nuanced picture, as there turned out to be very large individual differences in response to the nuclear threat. Moreover, numerous studies showed that youths who worry about nuclear war showed greater optimism about preventing nuclear war and had a greater sense of their own effectiveness, whereas those who did not worry were more pessimistic about the future. Studies also showed that whereas some individuals appraised the nuclear threat as significant, others did not. Among those for whom the nuclear threat was highly salient and personally felt, the level of anxiety or worry experienced depended on the individual's mode of coping. Those who engaged in nuclear war prevention efforts and who experienced high levels of perceived personal efficacy tended not to develop destructive patterns of behavior or worry. The end of the Cold War diminished public concerns over the nuclear threat and related concerns over the well-being of children in the nuclear age. This reduction of public concern is ironic since the long-term threats associated with the proliferation of nuclear weapons remain quite high.

G. War Preparations

Most societies have created extensive military systems for purposes such as defense, domination, and internal control. These systems often consume vast amounts of economic resources, as it is not uncommon for developing nations to spend as much as 40% of their gross domestic product on defense. The United States, by far the world leader in military spending, spends approximately $250 billion annually on defense. This level of spending is nearly as high as that which occurred during the Cold War. Psychological studies of U. S. policy leaders and people in the defense establishment suggest that support for high levels of defense spending make many people feel safer, even if the same people recognize that no pressing external threat mandates such extensive spending. Critics point out that such large expenditures reduce the amount of funding available for programs of mental health, violence prevention, and education. In this sense, war preparations and military-industrial complexes have indirect but powerful psychological effects.

Systems of war preparation also have a variety of more direct effects. For example, in the United States, there are approximately 250,000 atomic veterans, soldiers who were exposed to ionizing radiation from the above-ground program of testing nuclear weapons from 1945 to 1962. These veterans and their families experience high levels of stress associated with recurrent health problems, the long delay between exposure and the appearance of symptoms, transgenerational effects, and the silence and denial of the government regarding their problems. Among civilians, toxic releases associated with nuclear weapons development has exposed entire communities ("downwinders") in southern Utah to high levels of stress and severe health problems. Typically, these problems stir significant fears about the health and future of one's family. Within the nuclear weapons complex, significant stresses occur due to concerns about the harmful effects of one's activity and powerful economic and personal pressures to avoid whistle-blowing when wrongdoing is discovered. Indeed, members of the weapons community often live according to a code of silence.

H. The Impact of Armed Conflict on Children

On a global scale, armed conflict has powerful emotional and social effects on children, defined as anyone under 18 years of age. In some cases, the psychological impacts come through children's direct war experiences, while in others, psychological damage occurs through living in the aftermath of an armed conflict that has shattered social trust, amplified poverty and environmental destruction, and torn apart many of the child's social support systems. Either way, the damage owes not only to the frequency of bitter, intrastate wars such as those in Bosnia, Afghanistan, Rwanda, Angola, and Sudan but also to the changed nature of war. Early in the 20th century, approximately 80% of war-related casualties were combatants, but now the figure has been reversed, as over 80% of the casualties are noncombatants, mostly women and children. In contemporary conflicts, no well-defined battlefields exist, civilian populations are primary instruments of war, and community destruction amplifies ongoing problems of poverty, hunger, environmental degradation, and infrastructure erosion.

As documented by the United Nations Study on the Impact of Armed Conflict on Children, which was presented by Ms. Graça Machel November 8, 1996, children face unprecedented, holistic threats. There are approximately 300,000 child soldiers, who, owing to the wide availability of lightweight weapons such as the AK-47 assault rifle, provide a ready source of military power. Many have been forcibly recruited; others are drawn by poverty, ideology, promise of wealth, excitement, or desire for protection. Drugs have often been used to induce children to kill and to accept the most dangerous missions. Girl soldiers are often victims of sexual abuse. Child soldiers have missed important educational activities, had war experiences that induce significant guilt, fear, and trauma, and have often been rejected by their communities. Even after a ceasefire has been signed, young people who have become accustomed to lives as fighters may use violence and banditry as a means of meeting their needs, and they may find it difficult to reenter their communities and return to civilian life.

Among children who are not soldiers, there are large individual differences in response to the stresses imposed by war. During and after armed conflict, children face problems of uprooting, loss, sexual violence, exposure to attack, and disease. Millions of children have been displaced by armed conflict, and many live outside their home country as refugees. Particularly vulnerable are unaccompanied children, who lack the emotional, social, and physical support typically provided by parents. Large numbers of girls and women are exposed to gender-based violence, including mass rapes and other terror tactics. Sexual exploitation, often in the form of prostitution, permeates zones of armed conflict due to poverty and desperation. Many thousands of children are disfigured or made into amputees by nearly 60 million land mines worldwide. Long after the fighting stops, land mines continue to threaten children, and they make it impossible to resume agriculture and normal community life. Imposition of sanctions often damages children by depriving them of food and other necessities.

These multiple stressors may lead to psychological problems such as flashbacks, nightmares, sleep disorders, social isolation, heightened aggression, depression, and diminished future orientation. Normally, education serves as a means of reducing the impact of these stressors, as education provides a sense of stability and continuity, exposure to emotionally supportive adults, and a pathway to a more positive future. But armed conflict disrupts education for millions of children and destroys the schools and communities that are vital parts of any educational system. Children's responses to situations of armed conflict depend on culture. For example, in Bantu areas of Africa, a displaced child whose mother had been killed in an attack from which the child escaped would suffer emotionally over the loss of her mother. But significant stress may also be associated with the inability to perform the culturally appropriate burial ritual, as it is believed that the mother's spirit lingers in a troubled state, causing problems for both the child and the community. Being predominantly Western and a relatively young discipline, psychology has hardly begun to analyze thoroughly these cultural influences.

IV. PSYCHOLOGICAL DETERMINANTS OF ORGANIZED VIOLENCE

The upsurge in intrastate conflict has heightened attention to psychological origins of armed conflict. In Bosnia, Rwanda, and the Middle East, the brutal fighting of former neighbors, the scale of the atrocities, and the use of horrifying methods such as mass rape provide poignant reminders of the political as well as emotional power of fear and hate.

The prevention of such horrible events in the future requires careful analysis of the causes of organized violence. To do this, two common pitfalls must be avoided. The first is the temptation to reduce complex conflicts to a single cause, using terms such as "ethnic conflict" or related terms such as "tribal violence" and "ancient hatreds." More often than not, these terms suspend careful analysis, play on fears of the primitive Other, induce hopeless by implying that the conflicts are unpreventable, and fail to recognize that human conflict typically has multiple causes. Related concerns mitigate against attempts to reduce conflicts to strictly psychological causes. The second is the tendency to assume that violence at all levels has identical causes. While

similarities exist between gang violence and war, for example, the latter brings into play new factors such as bureaucracies for preparing for and fighting wars; complex multi-agency processes of setting foreign policy and deciding when to fight; and international norms and institutions of diplomacy, negotiation, and treaty making that lack exact parallels at the level of gangs. In analyzing causes of violence, one must recognize that different levels of social complexity have emergent properties, and this cautions against the search for a universal theory of violence.

A. Realistic Competition

Resource scarcity contributes to organized violence. In Rwanda, for example, land is a highly precious commodity for Hutus and Tutsis, who are predominantly cultivators and pastoralists, respectively. Tensions between the groups escalated in part due to a tripling of population between 1954 and 1993. Arable land had always been in extremely short supply, but the population explosion, coupled with erosion of the hillsides used for cultivation, created intense desperation for land. Competition for diverse economic resources occurred due to soaring inflation in the late 1980s and the crippling effects of a collapse in the international price of coffee, Rwanda's main export. The soaring external debt and the plunge of the gross domestic product led to an economic crisis that interacted with problems of refugees, historic patterns of inequity and impunity for mass violence, the scars of colonialism, and the culture of fear created by the Habyarimana regime, enabling the 1994 genocide in which nearly 800,000 Tutsis and their supporters were brutally murdered.

In international conflicts, too, competition for scarce resources contributes to tension and violence. The struggle for control over Middle East oil reserves has sparked extensive conflict, including confrontation between the superpowers during the Cold War. Disputes over land animate hostility between Israel and Syria, India and Pakistan, and Armenia and Azerbaijan, among many others. Competition for land is an important part of the resurgent nationalism that has sparked much conflict and led to changes in political geography following the Cold War.

The psychological dynamics of realistic competition are evident in the Cold War, during which the superpowers competed economically, politically, and militarily. This entailed a spiral process of conflict escalation in which actions taken on one side evoked tension and hostile reactions on the other side, which in turn led to additional tension and hostile reactions by the first side, and so on. This conflict escalation dynamic, which was saturated with mutual suspicions, fear, and distrust, was conspicuous in the nuclear arms race, as weapons built by one side threatened the other, leading them to build additional weapons and in turn threatening the first side, and so on. Each side feared falling behind the other out of concern that clear superiority by the other side might encourage it to attack. In addition, each side feared that the failure to keep up would be regarded as a weakness that might encourage other enemies to attack. Creating the perception of strength and resolve was a very high priority, leading both sides to build many more weapons than they objectively were likely to have used. Indeed, both superpowers claimed at various points in time that they had climbed so far up the ladder of tension and nuclear weapons escalation precisely to make war unthinkable.

The spiral model of escalation, however, overemphasizes the action-reaction process and fails to take into account the internal psychological, social, and political changes that fuel the conflict. In the United States, for example, the Cold War spawned a huge military-industrial complex that encouraged weapons production quite apart from tit-for-tat interactions with the Soviets. It also led to the formation of large agencies such as the CIA that were predicated on the idea of Soviet enmity and oriented toward spying and covert activity that themselves increased Soviets' fears and suspicions. In many parts of the United States, communist-bashing became quite popular, anticommunist groups cropped up, and large numbers of people got swept up in the anticommunist hysteria of the McCarthy era. New norms evolved that gauged patriotism by loathing of communism, and popular sentiments led aspiring political leaders to take a hard position against the Soviets. Leaders and ordinary citizens subscribed increasingly to a worldview that depicted Soviet communism as inherently expansionist, evil, and necessary to resist. Although many people opposed such simplistic stereotypes, they were often labeled unpatriotic, naive, and soft on communism. As anticommunism became part of American political culture, there was steady internal pressure for building more weapons and expanding U. S. political, military, and economic influence. Mirror-image processes occurred in the Soviet Union.

It is possible to integrate these two approaches by noting that in competition, action-reaction spiral processes do occur, increasing tension, fear, and hostility and encouraging polarization and segregation. The social, psychological, and political isolation of each side enables a host of internal changes motivated by fear of the other side. These include relatively militant leadership, the rise of enemy-hating groups, shifts in public attitudes and media representations of the other, extensive military preparations, and altered patterns of socialization for entry into a political culture that opposes the enemy. These internal changes may encourage policies and behaviors regarded as negative and threatening by the other side, ratcheting tensions up even further. Thus when competition begins over realistic divergences of interest, competition brings into play psychological processes that serve to fuel conflict. Conflict escalates through the interaction of objective and subjective factors.

B. Survival Fears and Enemy Images

Just how powerful subjective factors can be in conflict is evident in the role of survival fears and the demonic images of the Other. In intense conflicts such as those between Serbs and Muslims, Hutus and Tutsis, or Arabs and Jews, each group may develop such profound fear of the other that they literally fear for their survival and come to believe that nothing less than the total destruction or removal of the enemy is necessary. These fears are so powerful that they can be used, albeit inappropriately, to justify and rationalize practically any form of violence. Since the fears may be in part the product of actual or perceived personal mistreatment and victimization at the hands of the other group, the fears acquire a deep personal significance, become integrated into one's identity, and motivate exceptional levels of hostility and fighting. This very personal element of survival fears is an essential reason why ethnopolitical wars are fought in such a savage manner.

Although fears often have a basis in reality, their highly subjective nature becomes most conspicuous in enemy images, mental representations, images, or beliefs that portray the Other as thoroughly diabolical, untrustworthy, and evil. These images are the cognitive extension of fear, and they have powerful motivational effects. By amplifying fear and negative attitudes toward the out-group, enemy images create a simplistic view in which of the good "Us" opposing the evil "Them." In extreme cases, enemy images entail the dehumanization, the stripping away of all human qualities of the Other. Extreme enemies often create mirror images of each other as demons or bloodthirsty killers, and these images spread through political rhetoric and graphic media such as posters and political cartoons. As shown by Ralph K. White in regard to the Cold War, enemy images encourage bad behavior toward the out-group, and they pose significant obstacles to peace by impeding empathy and communication while strengthening the view that the adversary can be dealt with only through violence and military threat.

Enemy images play a significant role in genocide. Hitler used enemy images of Jews as a means of fomenting violence against them and enabling the Holocaust. By portraying Jews as subhuman and as a pestilence, Hitler created a rationalization, albeit horribly incorrect, for the destruction of the Jews, and he also removed moral qualms about killing. Through a process of moral exclusion, enemy imaging enables killing without remorse, as those who are killed are no longer part of the moral universe. Enemy imaging played a prominent role in the 1994 Rwandan genocide, which was enabled by the spread of demonic images of Tutsis by radio and other means.

Enemy images are also part of the psychological engine of war. Leaders often use them to arouse public support for war, and military trainers have used enemy images to prepare troops for killing. Skillful manipulation of enemy images is typically part of propaganda and disinformation campaigns, and leaders have not uncommonly used this tactic to divert public attention away from domestic problems. Even without organized manipulation of public opinion, enemy images often become vital parts of political culture and heighten tensions and hostility at the community level.

C. Social Identity

People exhibit a strong tendency to form groups and to define their identity and sense of place in the world relative to these groups. Around the world, people form ethnic groups, culturally defined communities that share such distinctive cultural elements as language, religion, social institutions, and origin myths. Although these are "imagined communities" (Benedict Anderson's term) in that they are subjectively constructed, their power is very real, as they exercise strong emotional and social influences. The extended community or perceived "nation" may be regarded as a family, the language spoken as the "mother tongue," and the felt allegiance may be as deep as psychological ties to one's family. During socialization, internalization of collectively defined values and views forges an intimate connection between self and community develops. The individual defines himself or herself by reference to the larger group (e.g., "I am a Turk" or "I am an American"), and individual self-esteem rises and falls according to the fate and status of the collective group with which one identifies. Through culturally distinctive practices and the use of symbols, myths, and rituals, collective

consciousness and sense of unity is strengthened and passed on to succeeding generations. This sense of unity and collective consciousness, often associated with longing for and attachment to a homeland, can lead to separatist desire for an independent national state.

Social identity processes fuel conflict in several ways. Henri Tajfel and others have emphasized that even in the absence of competition for scarce resources, people tend to form categories of in-group and out-group. In addition, people derive self-esteem, positive status, and a sense of positive self-identity from identification with the in-group. While they tend to favor and to judge positively members of the in-group, they tend to derogate and judge negatively members of the out-group, a phenomenon called ethnocentrism. Status competition helps to fuel this process, as positive evaluation of one's own group and negative evaluation of the other group elevate one's own sense of status and self-esteem.

In heated conflict, social identity processes interact with processes of enmification. As conflict between groups escalates, each group typically experiences an increased sense of cohesion and unity within the group—nothing unites like having an enemy. Increased in-group cohesion is associated with a heightened sense of difference from the out-group. The resulting polarization contributes to self- and group-imposed isolation from members of the other group, making it easier to maintain dehumanized stereotypes of the other group. Furthermore, in violent conflicts such as that between Hutus and Tutsis in Rwanda, people tend to define their identity in part through extreme opposition to the out-group. To be Hutu is to be opposed to Tutsis and vice-versa. The fusion of enmity and social identity enables scapegoating, mistreatment, and oppression, and the process is circular, as mistreatment and oppression strengthens enmity and identity differences between groups. Eventually, the rival groups may come to believe that coexistence is impossible, heightening nationalistic impulses to form one's own homeland that provides security, that gives expression to one's identity and quest for meaning, and that confers legitimacy by making one's identity group an equal player in a world of nations.

By fueling nationalism, social identity processes contribute significantly to the conflicts that rack the post-Cold War world. During the Cold War, it was in the interests of the superpowers to restrain many intranational conflicts. Within the Soviet Union and the Warsaw Pact nations, ethnic groups having distinctive language, religion, and culture cultivated their own identity and sought, often at great human expense, their independence so that they could translate their imagined community into a national homeland. The end of the Cold War removed the superpower restraints on collective self-identity, unleashing nationalistic impulses. It also destroyed old structures for defining meaning and social identity, created a power vacuum in diverse regions where rival groups eyed each other warily, and brought great urgency to the need for meaning and positive social identity in a rapidly changing world. These needs add strength to the grip of ideology, which provides clarity of meaning, identity, and direction and which animated orgies of violence in the regimes of Hitler and Stalin.

It would be a mistake to view social identity processes themselves as primary causes of violence, as there are multiethnic societies in which the identity needs of different groups are met peacefully. Social identity processes never act in a vacuum and always interact with other potential factors that encourage violence. The subjective significance of ethnic identity and the sense of extreme opposition to an Other, for example, increase under external threat and also under conditions of social and economic injustice. Social identity processes may become sources of conflict when they contain the aspect of victimhood. People who see themselves as victims are likely to lash out against the perceived sources of the injustices done to them. Further, when victimhood is part of one's identity, one perceives transgressions or atrocities committed against members of one's own group on a deep, personal level, building connections between group trauma and individual trauma. Communities often construct powerful collective memories of victimization, which are transmitted across generations, and are honored publicly in rituals and memorials. In the former Yugoslavia, Serbs remembered their victimization by the Croat Ustasha during World War II, providing Slobodan Milosevic with a powerful tool to exploit. In apartheid South Africa, oppression and collective memories of mistreatment helped to fuel Black consciousness, which contributed to violence against the apartheid regime. In Israel, searing Jewish memories of their history of global persecution and Hitler's attempt to exterminate them became woven into their collective identity, creating a "never again" mindset that helped to fuel the already heated conflict between Jews and Arabs. Identity, then, is inextricably interwoven with social context, memory, and perception.

D. Cognitive Biases

Although humans have extensive capacity for rational thought and behavior, there are severe limits on human rationality. Particularly in situations pervaded by fear, strong biases in perception, judgment, and memory undermine strictly rational behavior and contribute to destructive conflict.

Ralph K. White has emphasized that fear is the dominant motive behind war fighting in the 20th century and that fear leads to misperceptions that fuel destructive conflict. During the Cold War, for example, both superpowers exhibited high levels of fear, which in turn inclined each side to misperceive the other's motives as more hostile than they may actually have been. If the Soviets built a new missile system, the U. S. leadership, under the influence of diabolical enemy images of the Soviets, attributed this act to offensive motives, overlooking the possibility that the Soviets might have been building the missiles for defensive purposes, as the United States often did. American misperceptions of Soviet motives strengthened the prevailing subjective view of Soviets-as-enemies and may have led the United States to take more strident actions toward the Soviet Union as a result. The converse process is also likely to have occurred, as the Soviets held mirror-image perceptions of the United States as enemy. A serious risk in the superpower nuclear arms race was that crisis-induced misperceptions of the actions and motives on the other side would lead to belligerent behavior, triggering belligerent behavior from the other. Critics of deterrence policy pointed out that the result could be a hostile spiral process which, if it got out of control, might precipitate an accidental (i.e., unintended) nuclear war.

In addition to encouraging negative behavior in a particular situation, perceptual biases can become woven into the fabric of a relationship of enmity. When the subjective impression of the Other-as-enemy is very strong, adversaries may see the other side inaccurately, and they tend to remember mainly the negative actions undertaken by the other. This selective perception and memory strengthens enemy images, makes them highly resistant to change, and encourages mutual negative behavior, creating a self-fulfilling prophecy. Although objective conflict and divergences of interest are real, subjective elements of the conflict make enemies appear bigger than life and animate much destructive behavior.

In situations in which there are high levels of fear and threat, the complexity of thought tends to decline. People tend to be cognitive misers who limit potential burdens on their mental resources by adopting simplified views of the world. In violent conflict, groups tend to adopt black-white views of the Good Us versus the Bad Them, with each group typically deemphasizing the diversity of views that may in fact exist among the members of the opposition. Leaders, too, show a marked propensity to simplify when under stress. In analyzing the complexity of leaders' speeches and writing before and during crises, Philip Tetlock has established that in the heat of a crisis, leaders show less tolerance of ambiguity, tend not to explore diverse arguments regarding the crisis, and tend to overlook differences that exist among the opposition. The net result can be oversimplification and misguided action.

Facing a complex situation involving much uncertainty, people use, without conscious planning, fallible heuristics or shortcuts for making difficult decisions. Leaders, for example, may judge a current threatening situation by its similarity to the patterns of conflict that are most available in memory. If the Hitler-at-Munich pattern is highly salient and available in memory, then leaders may judge attempts at negotiation as inappropriate since attempts to negotiate with or to appease Hitler had disastrous consequences. In addition, leaders show strong loss-avoidance tendencies and are often willing to avoid losses by taking risks much greater than those they would take to obtain a goal they had not previously achieved.

E. Social Influence: Conformity and Obedience

In popular movements and revolutions, inclination toward violence can come through conformity pressures applied by peers. Pressures for conformity in thought and action also operate in elite groups whose decisions may affect millions of people. Irving Janis has established that flawed decisions such as the Kennedy administration's decision to launch the Bay of Pigs invasion, which turned out to be a total fiasco, arise in part from groupthink, the tendency to reach consensus prematurely and with inadequate moral deliberation, information collection, contingency planning, and foresight of the likely negative consequences of mission failure. Groupthink is particularly likely to occur in groups that are highly cohesive, that have a highly charismatic leader, and that have members who act as self-appointed mindguards to bring potential dissenters into line with the group thinking. One cannot assume that groupthink is at work whenever a small group renders a bad decision, as other factors such as competing political agendas and quest for personal gain may be at work. In some cases, however, small-group processes themselves bias decision making and contribute to violence.

One of the most significant causes of organized violence, particularly in situations of tyranny, is obedience to authority. While some have assumed that only a very small percentage of people—mostly psychopaths and moral indigents—would carry out unwarranted commands to inflict harm or to kill, the evidence indicates otherwise. In classic experiments by Stanley Milgram, adults hired through newspaper ads were paid to serve as "teachers" in a study ostensibly of the effects of punishment on learning at prestigious Yale University. The teachers administered electric shocks to "learners" whenever they made mistakes, and each mistake led to a higher intensity of shock. Surprisingly, two-thirds of the "teachers," urged on by an experimenter who wore a white lab coat and said the experiment must continue, were willing to deliver the most severe shocks. Although no shocks were actually administered, the subjects believed they were delivering real shocks, including ones that were life-threatening. A key psychological dynamic was the abdication of responsibility, as the subjects attributed to the experimenter the moral responsibility for any harm done.

In real life, the tendency to obey authorities can be very strong. Government officials such as presidents often serve to define social reality, and their actions and commands carry the weight of official state sanction and legitimacy. In a Muslim society, it may be seen as a high imperative to follow the commands of religious leaders, who actions are seen as having divine sanction. Through political socialization, people learn to obey leaders' commands, and the inculcation of political ideology and values may strengthen this inclination to obey. In preparation for the 1994 Rwandan genocide, President Habyarimana created an extremist militia, the Interahamwe, into which youth were attracted and then indoctrinated with messages that Tutsis were foreigners and threats who must be killed. In official military establishments around the world, soldiers regularly receive training to follow superiors' commands. The power of obedience is indicated by tragic events such as the My Lai massacre in which U. S. troops followed the unjustifiable orders of their commander to slaughter more than 200 unarmed people, including women and children. Obedience to authority may become particularly powerful in situations of tyranny, where there are few limits on the behavior of the head of state and where terror tactics are used to ensure compliance.

F. Personality

Many accounts of acts of mass violence have emphasized leaders' personalities, particularly in undemocratic governments where few checks exist on leaders' behavior. It has been argued that Hitler, for example, was a megalomaniac whose narcissistic, infantile needs for power were unrestrained and whose thinking became progressively detached from reality. Much has also been written about the paranoia of Stalin, who killed millions of his countrymen and condemned more to labor camps. Hitler and Stalin, like more recent tyrants such as Saddam Hussein, encouraged personality cults that glorified them to the masses and enabled acceptance of their brutality. While leader personality is important, one should recognize the problems of doing clinical interpretation at a distance and of excessive attributions of individual causation of large-scale events. Extra caution is needed in regard to most cases of "mad leader" theories of organized violence. Psychopathology may occur in someone already in power, but it must be recognized that true psychosis is rare, and psychotic individuals are unlikely to have the political acumen required to rise to power. "Mad leader" theories are attractive in part because events such as the Holocaust are so horrifying and strain one's capacity for rational explanation. There is safety in attributing terrible deeds to the acts of a handful of madmen, as this removes the burden of responsibility from the shoulders of ordinary people. In reality, however, leaders such as Hitler arose out of the fear and desperation of millions of ordinary people living in situations of economic deprivation and political instability. Furthermore, leaders' actions are almost always a product of interaction between person and situation, making it inappropriate to assign personality the full explanatory burden.

Further, as this section has emphasized, many powerful factors other than personality compel organized violence. For masses of people caught up in acts of killing and genocide, it is not negative personality traits but processes such as obedience to authority, adherence to ideology, pressures for conformity, and influence of socially constructed identity and ideas of enmity that are at work. Even when leader behavior seems irrational or where a gap exists between perceptions and reality, it is seldom psychopathology that is responsible. Saddam Hussein appeared irrational to many Westerners, but his objectionable behavior becomes more understandable in light of his desire to gain honor and avoid loss of face by standing up to West and his need to use external enemies and affairs to draw attention from Iraq's pressing internal problems. A similar point applies to most misperceptions, which are not the product of psychosis but fall within the normal range of human response to fear and threat. Indeed, it is the very normality of these responses that makes them so widely influential and potentially dangerous.

V. NONVIOLENT RESOLUTION AND PREVENTION OF DESTRUCTIVE CONFLICT

Psychological processes play a powerful role in the construction of peace. Traditionally, peace has been viewed as the absence of war and as an outcome reached through means such as negotiated treaties. An alternate view, however, is that the signing of treaties and the economic and political reforms thereby made possible must be complemented by changes in collectively held beliefs, perceptions, attitudes, and behaviors. The signing of a treaty will not bring peace if powerful fears and searing memories of abuse and mistreatment remain deeply entrenched in rival communities. To achieve peace, fears and hostilities must be addressed, perceptions must be altered, and processes must be put in place for the nonviolent handling of conflict. Otherwise, as is seen in ethnopolitical conflicts around the world, the likely pattern is cyclical violence, the wounds inflicted in each round of which plant the seeds for additional violence. Breaking cycles of violence requires intervention and the use of effective tools for building peace.

Psychological processes may also enable political and economic steps for building peace. As illustrated by the Oslo Accords in the Middle East peace process and the sudden dismantlement of apartheid and movement toward a democratic South Africa, movement toward peace sometimes entails sudden psychological breakthroughs that reframe or transform old conflicts, allowing political and economic changes to occur and to take root. In addition, it is through psychological processes that peace often becomes possible at the darkest hour of a conflict. In protracted conflict, a hurting stalemate may arise and animate movement toward peace. Having experienced heavy losses, spent precious resources, lost social support and positive self-esteem, and failed to achieve their goals through fighting, both sides may acquire a sense of futility about fighting and view continued war as unacceptable. These feelings of futility can create loss of internal support for the war effort and lead parties to seek peace or at least get to the bargaining table. When this occurs, nonviolent means of handling the conflict may become more feasible. This section outlines some of the main psychological tools and processes that may contribute to building peace.

A. Negotiation

Negotiation consists of an attempt to resolve a conflict through bargaining by the parties. Among diverse methods of negotiation, one of the most widely used is hard positional bargaining, an adversarial approach used frequently by wary opponents. In hard bargaining, each party seeks victory; asserts its position; uses contentious tactics such as threats, arguments, and harsh criticism of the other party to try to obtain what it wants; demands concessions from the other; withholds information about its own bottom line; and applies pressure to induce the other side to accede to its demands. Typically, participants in this process view the negotiation as a contest of will, each works hard to avoid any appearance of weakness, and each hires professional lawyers or negotiators to press its case.

Peace psychologists, who realize the importance of process, have been quick to point out the limits of hard positional bargaining. By emphasizing contentious tactics, hard bargaining encourages contentious behavior and hostility, which may create a conflict spiral in which the negative behavior of one party increases the negative behavior of the other party. As opponents issue threats or criticize the other harshly, they may damage the relationship and create a negative emotional residue that persists over long periods of time. Since the emphasis is on winning and on holding one's ground, there is little emphasis on empathizing with the other side and generating options that may satisfy the needs of both sides. Even when a negotiated settlement occurs, it may be flawed since it does not address adequately the needs of all parties, and it may not be adhered to if one of the parties feels abused by the opposition or short-changed by the agreement. On the other hand, hard positional bargaining is often the best alternative available in dealing with a hardened adversary, particularly when there are relatively high levels of fear and distrust and political pressures on both sides that make it necessary to maintain an image of toughness. In this sense, no all-perfect method of negotiation exists—the method used must be tailored to fit the situation.

A preferred method of negotiation, principled negotiation, treats conflict not as a win-lose struggle but as an opportunity for joint problem-solving leading to mutually beneficial outcomes. In principled negotiation, the emphasis is on win-win approaches to meeting the interests or needs of all the parties. The key elements of the process include treating the other parties with dignity and respect; focusing not on stated positions but on the underlying interests that motivate the positions; encouraging empathy so that each party thoroughly understands what the other parties really want; separating the people from the problem, avoiding criticism of people while engaging in hard-nosed analysis of the problem at hand; sharing information openly; generating multiple options that yield mutual gains; and using objective criteria or principles to judge which option meets the needs of all parties in the fairest, most effective manner. This process tends to generate creative exploration of options, less positional fixity, and improved relationship through mutual learning and cooperative solving of the problem. Each time a problem is solved cooperatively, there is increased trust in the other and increased hope that the relationship is sufficiently strong to meet future challenges.

Unfortunately, numerous psychological obstacles can impede effective negotiation. Norms and styles of negotiation vary widely across cultures, and cultural differences can create problems of misperception and incompatibility. In Japan, for example, "No" messages were traditionally given indirectly, whereas U. S. negotiators typically prefer a direct, matter-of-fact approach. Typically, Western culture emphasizes effective time utilization. But in other cultures, there may be much less inclination to live by the clock, and the premium may be on building a relationship before beginning a negotiation. These differences can create divergent perceptions of the other side's willingness to negotiate a deal. Aside from cultural differences, parties to heated conflicts typically lack readiness to engage in principled negotiation, particularly if they harbor strong enemy images and doubt the other's integrity and trustworthiness. Under extreme circumstances, they may be unable to negotiate at all out of fear that coming to the bargaining table will be interpreted as a sign of weakness and used against them. To circumvent this problem, it is useful to involve a third party, as in mediation.

B. Mediation

Mediation consists of assisted negotiation in which a third party enables and helps the parties negotiate a settlement. Mediation is used widely at local levels for purposes such as handling child custody disputes or labor-management disputes, and it is used very frequently in the international arena, where heads of state and U.N. officials use their prestige and the trust vested in them to help warring parties achieve a peaceful agreement. Although effective mediators do not have to be neutral, they do have to be trusted by the parties to the conflict and perceived as being able to help reach an appropriate agreement.

Effective mediators change the psychological field

and alter the motivation, perceptions, patterns of communication and problem solving, and relationship between the conflicting parties. Amidst hostility and distrust between warring parties that are reluctant to negotiate, a mediator can use leverage in the form of rewards and punishments (often referred to as "carrots" and "sticks") to increase the parties' motivation to begin talks and to move toward a negotiated settlement. When, for example, U. S. President Jimmy Carter brokered a peace agreement between Egypt and Israel at Camp David in 1979, he used promises of large amounts of military and economic aid to each party as a means of increasing its willingness to reach an agreement. When the talks stalled, he motivated forward movement by threatening to withdraw U. S. support and by criticizing recalcitrant leaders as responsible for the wars their people would have to endure if peace talks failed.

At the same time, Carter allowed the wary adversaries to save face by suggesting options that they themselves could not have raised out of fear of appearing weak or willing to make excessive concessions. For example, at Camp David, Carter proposed and managed to win the agreement of Israeli leader Menachim Begin to withdraw settlements from the Sinai, a step that Begin had been unwilling to propose himself and that he knew would be opposed by many of his right-wing constituents. Carter's action enabled Israel to save face by creating the perception that it was the mediator who suggested this concession. Face-saving is one of the most powerful psychological dynamics in mediation, particularly when adversaries are fearful, have outside pressures to maintain a hard line, or view concession making as dishonorable or as a sign of weakness. Ultimately, though, it was Carter's personal approach that enabled a psychological breakthrough and the signing of the Camp David Accord. With the talks having stalled and Sadat having packed his bags to leave, Carter followed his secretary's suggestion to give each leader a signed photograph as a souvenir. When Carter signed the photograph while talking with Begin, they began talking about Begin's grandchildren and their future if the conflict continued. This conversation led Begin to make key concessions, breaking the impasse and allowing the talks to proceed.

Effective mediators also structure interactions and enable positive communication, which can be very valuable if the parties have no formal relations or have been refusing to talk. When levels of hostility are extremely high, the mediator may keep the parties separate out of concern that damaging things might be said or done in face-to-face meetings. Even when parties do agree to meet, issues such as the meeting site, the agenda, and the participant list all take on great symbolic importance, and skilled mediators play a key role in addressing these issues. Once the meetings are underway, the mediator may manage the communications process, arranging some face-to-face meetings and some written exchanges. Typically, mediators work to keep the lid on heated exchanges, to separate the parties when it is clear that tensions are too severe, and to promote constructive dialogue and empathy. By reframing ideas, mediators may help to create perceptions of common ground, building hope that a mutually satisfactory agreement is possible. In most cases, the mediator asks the parties to achieve a written agreement both for purposes of clarity and of building commitment.

At its best, mediation improves the relationship between parties by encouraging positive perceptions of the other, undermining old patterns of distrust and hostility, and building hope for a future in which conflicts can be handled constructively. In building peace, the nonviolent resolution of a particular conflict is an immediate goal, but the longer term goal is to transform the relationship between conflicting parties so that new conflicts that arise in the future can be handled nonviolently. Mediation, however, is no panacea. During conflict escalation and in situations of impassioned fighting and before a hurting stalemate has evolved, mediation may not work due to the parties' lack of readiness to work for peace. The failure of a mediation often becomes an occasion for mutual blame and recrimination, and these accusations of intransigence and bad faith themselves inflame conflict. In addition, excessive reliance on mediation could encourage dependency by reducing the parties' faith in their own ability to handle conflicts themselves.

Furthermore, since mediated agreements may result in part from leverage applied by the mediator, the agreements can produce suspicions about whose interests were served. While the United States hailed the Camp David Accords as a breakthrough for peace, many Arab leaders perceived it as an attempt to divide the Arab world, to dodge the wider issues in the Arab-Israeli conflict, to expand the sphere of U. S. influence in the Middle East, giving the United States the oil it wanted. As this example illustrates, what counts as an effective, appropriate peace agreement is partly subjective.

C. Interactive Problem-Solving Workshops

Official negotiation and mediation, although important and useful, suffer numerous limits. Warring parties may have great difficulty negotiating officially due to profound fears and hatreds and deeply entrenched patterns of isolation and destructive communication. The public attention associated with official diplomacy ignites powerful psychological pressures, as occurs, for example, when right-wing constituencies decry negotiations as unwise or as playing into the hands of the enemy. The act of coming to the negotiating table publicly can produce image loss or carry implications disliked by one or both of the parties. Once engaged in formal negotiations, the parties may behave in a fearful, rigid manner that limits the flexible problem solving needed to address complex issues. Most important, formal agreements alone do not build peace, which consists of an ongoing process. In intrastate wars, this process is blocked by the persistence of communal fears, grievances, and enemy images. Even after peace treaties have been signed, many complex implementation issues remain, and conflict over these need to be addressed constructively if the peace process is to move ahead.

Interactive problem solving is a set of tools for addressing these problems. For example, the interactive problem-solving workshop has been useful in addressing identity, existential conflicts. As developed by Herbert Kelman in the context of the Israeli-Palestinian conflict, a typical workshop brings together three to six respected members of the Israeli and Palestinian communities for two-and-a-half days of intensive dialogue. The dialogue, facilitated by a small group of social scientists, is nonbinding, and the parties are not official representatives of their respective communities. To encourage truth seeking and flexible exploration of ideas, the workshops convene in a private academic setting, and no records are kept. At the small group level, the workshops aim to stimulate new learning between formerly isolated adversaries, to open a more flexible discourse about the conflict, and to stimulate creative thinking about options for dealing with the conflict constructively. The workshops, however, also seek to induce changes in the wider political communities from which the participants are drawn. Accordingly, the participants consist of political influentials such as respected policy analysts, academicians, and advisers who are free to explore ideas since they hold no official positions and who can infuse the insights from their new learning back into their respective communities.

The workshop begins with each party stating the conflict as it sees it and with the other side acknowledging what the initial party had said. This process helps to build empathy and to move each side beyond its stereotypical understandings of the other's position. The heart of the workshop is analytic, problem-solving discussion in which the participants analyze the main

issues at stake in the conflict, explore their main concerns and fears, and identify possible solutions and steps that could be taken to overcome the psychological and political barriers on both sides. In these discussions, each side learns to see the other as thoughtful, problem oriented, pursuing articulated concerns, and, above all, willing to consider new options. By making observations, limiting unproductive lines of discussion, and asking well-timed questions, the third party works to help each party understand the other's needs and priorities and to stimulate creative "what-if" thinking on particular issues.

Although the workshops are difficult to evaluate, they have been instrumental in establishing positive communication and empathy, altering dehumanizing stereotypes of the other, and stimulating constructive dialogue about various options for building peace. By altering the perceptual world of the participants, the workshops puncture the view of the other as irretrievably hostile and disinterested in peace. The workshops make a long-term contribution by building more positive relationships that advance the peace process. In the near term, they also help set the stage for official negotiations and for official back-channel, secret meetings such as those that led to the Oslo Accords. Over several decades, participants in the workshops have taken their new learning about the other side back into their communities, beginning the arduous process of community transformation that is essential for resolving and preventing intercommunal conflict. As Kelman points out, changing conflicts in healthy ways requires changing the societies in which the conflict is rooted.

D. Contact and Cooperation

To reduce destructive conflict, numerous analysts have suggested the contact hypothesis that bringing members of conflicting groups into contact with each other reduces conflict by allowing each side to encounter the humanity of the other and to develop more positive attitudes toward them. This hypothesis helped to guide the integration of schools in countries such as Northern Ireland and the United States. Early evidence suggested that contact, to be beneficial, needed to be supported by authority figures and to occur under pleasant social conditions, on a voluntary basis, and in a situation of equal status between groups.

The contact hypothesis, however, has encountered numerous problems. Contact may provide the occasion for insults, slights, or damaging actions, all of which escalate conflict. In addition, short-term contact has rather small effects. Even when contact is sustained, changes may occur more at the interpersonal level than at the intergroup level. For example, favorable contact between a Sinhalese and a Tamil member of Sri Lankan society might produce positive attitudes in both people. But the positively viewed individuals may be seen as exceptions, leaving intact the idea that the other group is threatening or undesirable. The effects of favorable contact with a member of the out-group generalize best when that person is perceived categorically, that is, as a representative member of the out-group. Furthermore, since positive contact does not alter basic power relations between groups, it is unrealistic to expect contact alone to produce positive social transformation. Structural changes may be needed in order for contact to succeed.

Following the work of Muzafer Sherif, extensive research indicates that it is more constructive to encourage cooperation between conflicting groups on superordinate goals, which by definition lie within the interests of each group but which cannot be reached by either group acting alone. In labor-management disputes, cooperation toward the achievement of superordinate goals has stimulated improved attitudes, perceptions of common ground across group lines, and belief that the other group can deal with problems in a constructive manner and that future conflicts can be settled without violence. The aftermath of intercommunal conflict presents many opportunities for cooperation. Israelis and Palestinians, for example, worked together to address community security threats and to set up effective local police arrangements following the signing of the Oslo Accords.

In the international arena, too, cooperation on superordinate goals helps to reduce conflict. For example, relations between Russia and the United States have benefitted from the Cooperative Threat Reduction program in which U. S. funding supports the dismantlement and safe disposal of nuclear warheads in the former Soviet Union. This disarmament is in the interests of both countries, and neither could have achieved it by acting alone. Similarly, the European Community, with its emphasis on cooperation toward the achievement of shared economic goals, is an arrangement that builds positive relationships and contributes to peace. Cooperation can also enable structural change, as the creation of equal-partner cooperative arrangements can help to shift power, and arrangements implemented on a societal scale can have impact at the macrosocial level. For these reasons, the UNESCO Cultures of Peace Programme has made the superordinate goals method central to its work.

E. Unilateral Initiatives

Contact and cooperation require a willingness to meet and talk, but this willingness may not exist in severe conflict. Nevertheless, tensions can be reduced through unilateral initiatives, steps taken by one side in an effort to signal peaceful intent and to deescalate the conflict. The best-known strategy, called GRIT for "graduated and reciprocated initiatives in tension reduction," was designed by Charles Osgood in regard to the U.S.–Soviet nuclear arms race. It entailed taking a step (e.g., a verifiable reduction in arms) or series of steps unilaterally, announcing the intent to build peace and inviting the other side to reciprocate. If positive reciprocation occurs, then additional steps are taken. To protect oneself, the steps taken should not be so large as to alter the military balance of power, and the steps should be discontinued if the other side uses contentious tactics. Although some have regarded unilateral initiatives as unrealistic or even dangerous, numerous international events indicate their efficacy in undermining old perceptions of enmity and enabling positive change. Among these events is Egyptian President Sadat's 1977 visit to Jerusalem, a breakthrough that helped set the stage for negotiations leading to the Camp David Accords. At the peak of U. S.–Soviet tensions, shortly following the 1962 nuclear confrontation in the Cuban Missile Crisis, American President Kennedy announced in 1963 that the United States was stopping all atmospheric nuclear tests and would resume them only if some other country conducted atmospheric nuclear tests. This symbolic gesture led to Soviet reciprocation, enabling the signing of the Partial Test Ban Treaty in 1963.

As these examples illustrate, symbolism and perceptual changes can enable changes in official policy. As is true of all the psychological approaches discussed above, psychological changes alone are not sufficient for the nonviolent resolution of destructive conflict, but they can enable political and structural changes that might not have been possible otherwise. To transform a conflict, it is essential to change its subjective elements.

VI. BUILDING CULTURES OF PEACE

The larger task of everyone concerned about peace is to convert social systems that nourish violence and war into cultures of peace, that is, systems that nourish social justice, nonviolence, and sustainable development. Building cultures of peace requires a mixture of reactive and proactive work of a psychological nature.

In the wake of a deadly conflict, there is need of interventions that address traumas and fears that plant seeds of future wars. Too often, however, attention is focused on the most horrible war or immediate crises, and little attention is devoted to violence prevention. If the world is to have peace, it must focus much more intensively on proactive approaches to preventing violence at all levels, to build positive human relationships that enable groups to handle conflict nonviolently, and to create social structures and processes that meet basic human needs and encourage social and gender equity and justice. This section identifies some psychological approaches to this long-term project. Although the emphasis is on large-scale, organized violence, many of the points developed below apply equally to inner-city combat zones and other areas saturated by violence that is not organized on a large scale.

A. Reconstructing War-Torn Societies

The reconstruction of war-torn societies for peace and social justice is a high priority for which few blueprints exist. Societal reconstruction is inherently multidisciplinary and must involve communities, nongovernmental organizations (NGOs), governments, international relief and development agencies, and many others. Since war damages social trust, creates deep fears and grievances, and leaves large numbers of people in high degrees of psychological and social distress that invites additional violence, psychological interventions are necessary. Because stress and trauma impede education and economic development and amplify health problems that may already exist on a massive scale, psychological intervention must be more than an afterthought. Ideally, psychological interventions are not made in isolation but are integrated into and coordinated with wider efforts to meet basic physical needs and to effect political and economic reforms.

Intercommunal war typically leaves thousands of people with emotional damage or difficulties associated with multiple stresses such as shelling, loss, uprooting, and sexual violence. One immediate task is to assist war-affected people with the emotional tasks of mourning and coming to terms with their war experiences. It is a great challenge to intervene on a scale that will make a difference, particularly since there is economic ruin and a scarcity of trained psychologists. Although Western-trained psychologists may be sent in, they may lack a full understanding of the culture, the situation, and the mental health processes and resources that had been used traditionally by the affected communities. A second challenge, then, is to intervene in

culturally appropriate ways that utilize and build local capacities.

Although much remains to be learned about psychosocial reconstruction, it is possible to make effective interventions. As one example, Christian Children's Fund, a U.S.-based NGO, developed a program for war-affected adults and children in Angola, where warring factions had fought for over two decades. Heading the project is a national team of Angolans who know the language, culture, situation, and traditions and who understand the psychological impact of war and how to assist war-affected children and adults. To intervene on a national scale, the project employs a training-of-trainers methodology in which the national team trains a team of trainers in each of seven provinces, and the province-based teams then train adults who work with children in local communities.

Each seminar runs for one week and engages approximately 20 adults in trainings on children's psychological needs, on children's war experiences, and on how to assist children who show problems such as flashbacks, social isolation, or excessive aggression. In the seminars, adults discuss and process their own war experiences, and this is significant since children typically rely on adults for emotional support. The seminars teach how to help children to express their war experiences and associated feeling through media such as drawing, which complements traditional African media for expression such as song, dance, and storytelling. The seminars, however, are also an occasion for joint learning and dialogue. The participants discuss their community's traditional ceremonies and healing rituals used in situations involving death and mourning. They also discuss how to tailor Western approaches to their own situation. The participants then take this combination of Western and traditional approaches back to the community, where they help to apply what they have learned in helping children at the local level. They might, for example, help children to draw pictures, to arrange community mourning rituals, or to engage children in structured play and educational activities that reduce isolation. Evidence indicates that this intervention reduces the frequency of children's flashbacks, isolation, and aggressive behavior. It also communalizes grieving processes and helps to mobilize the community around the needs of children. By drawing upon local traditions and working with local communities, the project has encouraged culturally appropriate interventions. Many communities have begun development projects such as school construction, and the physical rebuilding has contributed to community healing and hope.

To break cycles of violence, many other kinds of psychological work are also needed. For example, methods of nonviolent conflict resolution need to be taught and instituted at a variety of levels, creating new social norms for handling conflict. People at all levels need to learn values and practices that support tolerance. Former soldiers, including child soldiers, need to be demobilized and reintegrated back into civilian communities. This entails developing prosocial behavior and values in the former soldiers, preparing local communities to accept former combatants, training combatants for jobs or entry into school, among other tasks. Communities that are isolated and mutually fearful need to develop positive means of communicating and problem solving by using methods such as the problem-solving workshops and superordinate goals method discussed above. Since violence prevention is by definition a long-term, ongoing task, these methods need to be institutionalized.

B. Peacebuilding and Conflict Prevention

Building peace requires attention to both structure and process. Peace does not exist when there is structural violence such as dire poverty, large social class distinctions, or systematic discrimination against a category of people within a society. To achieve peace, a society must include institutions that ensure equity, social justice, and sustainability. Psychologically, a useful way to gauge whether social structures and institutions contribute to peace is to ask to what extent they enable the satisfaction of human needs, including not only biological needs for food, water, and shelter but also socially constructed needs for group identity and collective positive esteem. When basic needs go unmet, as occurs when large numbers of people are hungry or when particular identity groups are privileged over others, the result is widespread frustration, sense of victimization, and social unrest, all of which can encourage resort to violence. To build peace, unjust structures must be changed so that basic human needs are met.

Changing these structures, however, requires many changes in human process. If intergroup tensions exist, for example, there may be an inclination for the more powerful group to exclude the out-group and to create discriminatory laws or norms. Hostile social processes encourage patterns of privileging that enable oppressive structures and institutions. Similarly, if groups are relatively polarized and isolated, it will be challenging to create structures that contribute to an multiethnic, peaceful society. Ultimately, social institutions and structures are rooted in communally shared beliefs, practices, and patterns of living.

This social and psychological interconnection of structure and process has powerful implications for building peace and preventing destructive conflict. One must work simultaneously on promoting structural changes such as equitable political and economic policies and practices but also on building processes at all levels of society that support nonviolence. At the individual and family levels, peacebuilding efforts should encourage beliefs such as that in human interdependence, prosocial attitudes and values such as tolerance and respect for human dignity and justice, and behavior patterns such as skills and habits of cooperation, communication, and nonviolent conflict resolution. In communities, in venues such as schools, workplaces, and houses of worship, there must be processes that encourage tolerance, enable dialogue and learning across group lines, and encourage the nonviolent handling of conflict. At the societal level, there must be norms of civility, respect, and equity, respect for gender and social justice, and communally shared commitment to nonviolent conflict resolution. Women play a particularly important role in peacebuilding as they are often at the center of local efforts to build positive, caring relationships and processes of nonviolence and sustainability. It is only when these processes have been institutionalized and woven into patterns of living that cultures of peace may evolve. To build structural peace, there must be a psychological infrastructure of peace.

1. Education for Peace

Violent societies teach people through informal and formal means that violence is acceptable, normal, and necessary. In many societies, children often learn at an early age that violence is an acceptable response to conflict, and they may learn particular methods of violence by observing parents, peers, and people in the community. Similarly, they may learn in school that particular other groups or nations are threatening or wicked, and in the community, having been mistreated by members of an out-group, they may learn to affiliate with members of their own group and to fight against and to devalue the out-group. Through media such as television, they may learn gender stereotypes that devalue women or negative images of other groups that encourage isolation, segregation, and human rights abuses.

To build cultures of peace, it is essential to educate for peace using both formal and informal means. Since patterns of responding to conflict are often established through early family experience, families should promote a healthy awareness of conflict, encourage norms of equity and tolerance, and cultivate nonviolent methods. If parents settle a conflict through nonviolent means, they provide an occasion for observational learning of peaceful behavior for their children. Parents may also encourage cooperative games and nonviolent forms of play in their children. Where violence is widespread, as on television or in the use of war toys, parents can engage children in a dialogue about the harmful effects of violence, about why TV producers tend to show such graphic violence, and about the motives of toy manufacturers and TV producers. In this way, critical viewing skills may be developed to promote peace.

As vehicles of formal education, schools have much to contribute to peace. Historical experience has shown that an educated, informed citizenry is one of the best means of preventing tyranny and ending or preventing unjustified wars. Curricula can help to teach conflict analysis, basic values such as tolerance and human interdependence, skills of mediation and nonviolent conflict resolution. With regard to particular conflicts in the society, education can help people to understand why the parties to a conflict have divergent perceptions and constructed histories and to identify various options for responding to the conflict. Peaceful values and behavior may also be encouraged through the use of teaching pedagogies such as cooperative learning, in which students do not compete individually for grades but rather work cooperatively in teams to accomplish shared goals. Evidence indicates that cooperative learning generates high levels of motivation and learning, reduces destructive competition, and encourages attitudes and skills conducive to cooperation. Outside the classroom, the use of peer-mediation programs for handling conflicts can provide options to violence and to traditional, disciplinary methods of responding to conflict. If carefully constructed and supported by appropriate steps to train teachers and administrators, peer mediation programs may help to develop norms of handling conflict nonviolently. In some programs, the achievement of a peer-mediated settlement culminates with a public apology by all parties to the conflict, and this apology allows both reconciliation and face-saving.

Education for peace, however, must reach well beyond school walls and family boundaries. In communities, there need to be mediation centers such as those in Japan that not only assist in mediation but educate people about how to resolve conflict nonviolently. Houses of worship may be very helpful in arranging summer camps and exchanges that bring together youths from conflicting groups for dialogue and collab-

oration. Local businesses may help set standards of nondiscrimination and educate their employees about the importance of protecting human rights and avoiding sexual harassment. Public media such as television can arrange programs that show less violence and honor nonviolence. Work on no single level can succeed in violence prevention, and successful prevention requires concerted effort at all these levels.

2. Participation

Building cultures of peace is a process of societal transformation that is best accomplished through a mixture of bottom-up and top-down efforts. As shown in this essay, violence is systemic, and this means that efforts to build cultures of peace must be equally systemic and must engage identity groups, communities, families, and individuals. To build cultures of peace, it is essential to encourage participation at all levels of society—the process itself should embody nonviolent values of equal voices for all.

Violence prevention requires high levels of local participation. In addition to knowing what local needs are, people in local communities are in the best position to create programs that are sustainable by virtue of their compatibility with local structures and cultural beliefs, values, and practices. When international donors have Western psychologists create and implement violence prevention programs in non-Western cultures, the likely result is a misapplication of tools that yields limited benefits. The more damaging result, however, is that the process of designing and conducting the intervention becomes a form of cultural imperialism that marginalizes local communities, continuing historic patterns of structural violence. Effective psychological work toward cultures of peace will be culturally relevant, undertaken in partnership with people in local communities, and enriched by the ideas and values of different cultures.

Also See the Following Articles

AGGRESSION, PSYCHOLOGY OF • ANIMAL BEHAVIOR STUDIES • BEHAVIORAL PSYCHOLOGY • BIOCHEMICAL FACTORS • CONFLICT MANAGEMENT AND RESOLUTION • CRIMINOLOGY, OVERVIEW • ENEMY, CONCEPT AND IDENTITY OF • ETHNICITY AND IDENTITY POLITICS • EVOLUTIONARY FACTORS • MILITARY CULTURES • PEACEMAKING AND PEACEBUILDING

Bibliography

Berkowitz, L. (1993). Aggression: Its causes, consequences, and control. New York: McGraw-Hill.

Blumberg, H., & French, C. (Eds.). (1992). *Peace: Abstracts of the psychological and behavioral literature.* Washington, DC: American Psychological Association.

Cairns, E. (1996). *Children and political violence.* Oxford: Blackwell.

Crocker, C., Hampson, F. O., Aall, P. (Eds.). (1996). *Managing global chaos: Sources of and responses to international conflict.* Washington, DC: U. S. Institute of Peace.

Deutsch, M. (1973). *The resolution of conflict: Constructive and destructive processes.* New Haven: Yale University Press.

Eron, L. D., Gentry, J. H., & Schlegel, P. (Eds.). (1994). *Reason to hope: A psychosocial perspective on violence & youth.* Washington, DC: American Psychological Association.

Freud, S. (1933). *New introductory lectures on psychoanalysis.* New York: Norton.

Kelman, H. C. (1965). *International behavior: A social psychological analysis.* New York: Holt, Rinehart & Winston, .

Marsella, A., Friedman, M., Gerrity, E., & Scurfield, R. (1996). *Ethnocultural aspects of posttraumatic stress disorder: Issues, research, and clinical applications.* Washington, DC: American Psychological Association.

Martín-Baró, I. (1994). *Writings for a liberation psychology: Ignacio Martín-Baró.* (A. Aron & S. Core, Eds.). Cambridge, MA: Harvard University Press.

Montville, J. V. (Ed.). (1991). *Conflict and peacemaking in multiethnic societies.* Lexington, MA: D. C. Heath.

Pruitt, D., & Carnevale, P. J. (1993). *Negotiation in social conflict.* Pacific Grove, CA: Brooks/Cole.

Renshon, S. A. (Ed.). (1979). *Political psychology.* Oxford: Blackwell.

Rubin, J., Pruitt, D., & Kim, S. (1994). *Social conflict: Escalation, stalemate, and settlement,* (2nd ed.). New York: McGraw-Hill.

Schwebel, M. (Ed.). (1995). *Peace and conflict: Journal of peace psychology. Mahwah, NJ: Erlbaum.*

Sivard, R. (1996). *World military and social expenditures 1996.* Washington, DC: World Priorities.

Skinner, B. F. (1953). Science and human behavior. New York: Free Press.

Staub, E. (1989). *The roots of evil: The origins of genocide and other group violence.* New York Cambridge University Press.

Tedeschi, J., and Felson, R. (1994). *Violence, aggression, & coercive actions.* Washington, DC: American Psychological Association.

White, R. K. (1984). *Fearful warriors: A psychological profile of U.S.–Soviet relations. New York: Free Press.*

White, R. K. (Ed.). (1986). Psychology and the prevention of nuclear war. New York: New York University.

Public Health Models of Violence and Violence Prevention

Kenneth E. Powell, James A. Mercy, Alex E. Crosby,
Linda L. Dahlberg, and Thomas R. Simon
Centers for Disease Control and Prevention

GLOSSARY

Epidemiology The study of the distribution and determinants of health-related conditions and events in populations, and the application of this study to control health problems.

Interventions Specific, targeted activities designed to prevent violent events.

Programs Combinations of interventions.

Public Health Focuses on health issues in populations. It emphasizes prevention, is based on scientific and technical knowledge, and addresses those problems through collective or social action.

I. BACKGROUND

A. Models

The purpose of this article is to describe several models used by public health scientists to guide the description, understanding, and prevention of violence. Violence is a complex problem with many causes and manifestations. Models are useful for simplifying reality and for organizing information and guiding understanding of a problem. The models described in this article fall into three general categories: (1) models to describe the occurrence and characteristics of violent events, (2) models to guide thinking about causes and types of prevention, and (3) models to guide thinking about prevention activities. Examples are used throughout the article to orient the reader to the various models and the public health approach to violence. This article concerns personal violence as opposed to war or other types of organized or institutional violence.

B. Public Health and Violence

Violence is a public health issue because violence causes large numbers of injuries, disabilities, and deaths; because violence can be prevented; and because the prevention of violence requires collective action.

Self-directed and interpersonal violence are leading causes of injury, disability, and death. In 1990, self-directed and interpersonal violence caused an estimated 2.7% of the worldwide burden from disability, and that percentage is expected to increase to 4.2% by 2020. In the United States in 1994 suicide and homicide were the 9th and 11th most common causes of death and the 7th and 6th leading causes of premature death, respectively (Fig. 1).

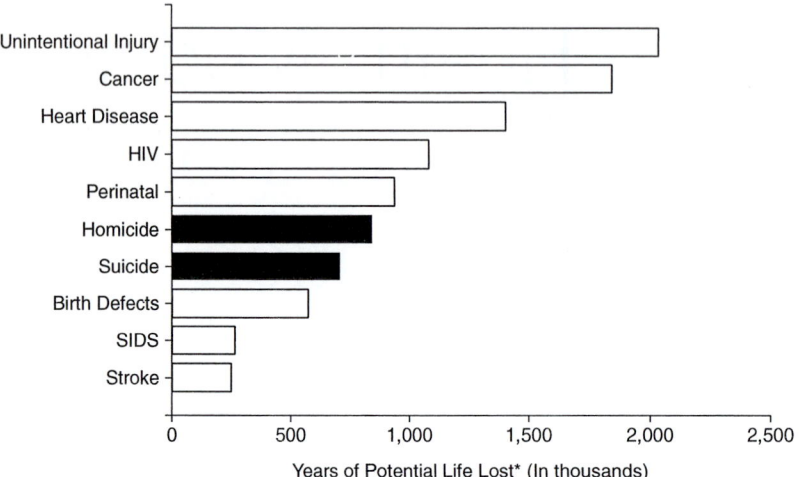

FIGURE 1 Top 10 causes of premature death in the U.S.A (1994). * Difference between age 65 and age at death.

Violence is a learned behavior, and much of the existing evidence indicates that violence can be prevented. Differing rates among nations and within a single nation over time indicate that violence is a product of complex but modifiable social and environmental factors.

Modification of these factors generally requires collective action. For example, the type, amount, and quality of educational, social, judicial, or health services, all systems that influence the frequency and severity of violent injuries, are determined by cooperative efforts rather than by individual action.

C. Core Functions of Public Health

Public health, in contrast to personal medical services, is concerned with the well being of the population as a whole, addressing problems that require collective action as opposed to individual action. Public health activities also exhibit a firm commitment to prevention and a foundation in empirical science. The core functions of public health include:

- Assessment—the systematic collection, analysis, interpretation, and dissemination of information about the health and health needs of the community.
- Policy development—the development of public health policy designed to achieve agreed-upon goals and based upon scientific information.
- Assurance—making sure that goals are achieved either by encouraging others to act, by requiring action through regulation, or by providing services directly. The assurance function requires valid information (assessment) to determine if the policies are achieving the goals, thereby linking the three core functions of public health in a continuous cycle.

D. The Public Health Approach to Science-Based Policy

Public health often is concerned with problems large or threatening enough to require an immediate response while more information is being obtained. As a result, identifying and influencing modifiable causes of diseases and injuries are more important than building precise theoretical models or completely understanding an underlying mechanism. Methods to prevent scurvy, smallpox, and scrotal cancer, for example, each were known and used more than a century before the causative molecular or infectious agents were identified. In similar fashion, public health describes and studies violence to prevent its adverse effects rather than to provide a complete understanding of it.

II. DESCRIBING THE PROBLEM OF VIOLENCE

A. Definitions and Types of Violence

The definition of personal violence commonly used in public health provides a general description of violence (Fig. 2). Several methods are used to subdivide violent events into separate categories; many of these methods

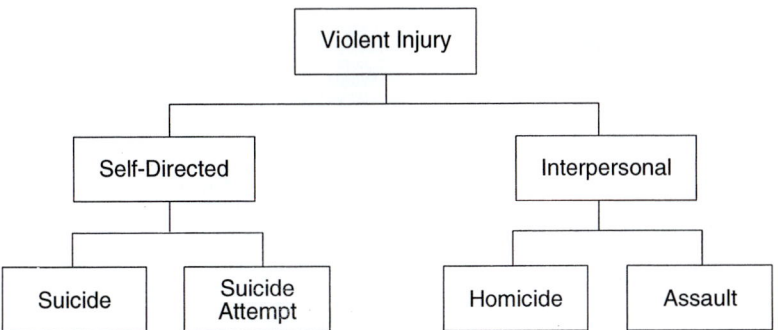

FIGURE 2 Violence is the intentional use of physical force against another person or against oneself which results in or has a high likelihood of resulting in injury or death.

are useful but none serves all purposes. One scheme (Fig. 2) separates violent events into self-directed and interpersonal events, and each of those into fatal and nonfatal events. Other schemes categorize events by type of violence (child abuse, intimate partner abuse, elder abuse, or youth violence) or by the presumptive intentions of the perpetrator such as predatory (robberies, gang killings) or emotional (barroom fights, lovers' triangles). To demonstrate public health models, we begin with data subdivided only into suicide and homicide.

B. Model: Time, Place, Person

This model portrays events according to their time and place of occurrence and the characteristics of the vic-tims. In so doing, important changes over time, differences in setting or geographic location, and useful characteristics of people most and least likely to be victims are uncovered. The systematic examination of health data according to these three simple parameters, first alone and then in combination, provides clear and revealing information about important characteristics of the problem.

1. Time

Data can be grouped by year, day of week, hour of day, or other time periods. As an example, the homicide rate in the United States nearly doubled between 1965 and 1975, with subsequent and higher undulations peaking about 1980 and 1990 (Fig. 3). In contrast, the suicide rate has ranged more narrowly. The time trend

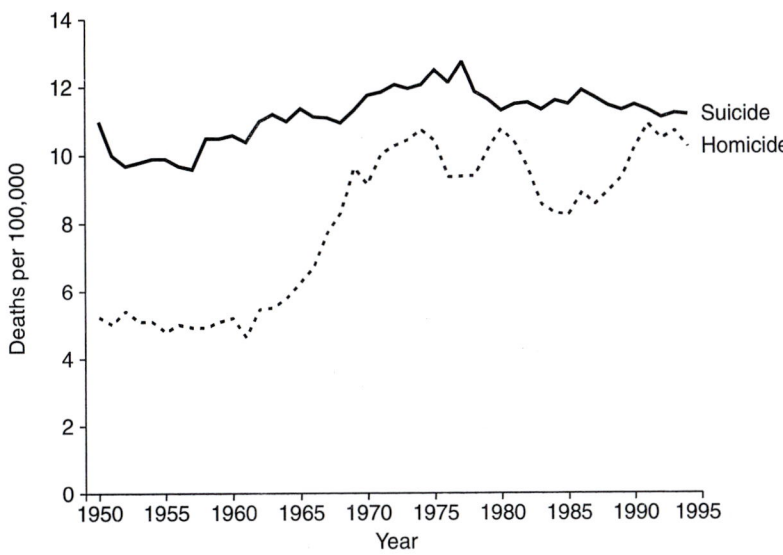

FIGURE 3 Age-adjusted suicide and homicide rates in the U.S. (1950–1994).

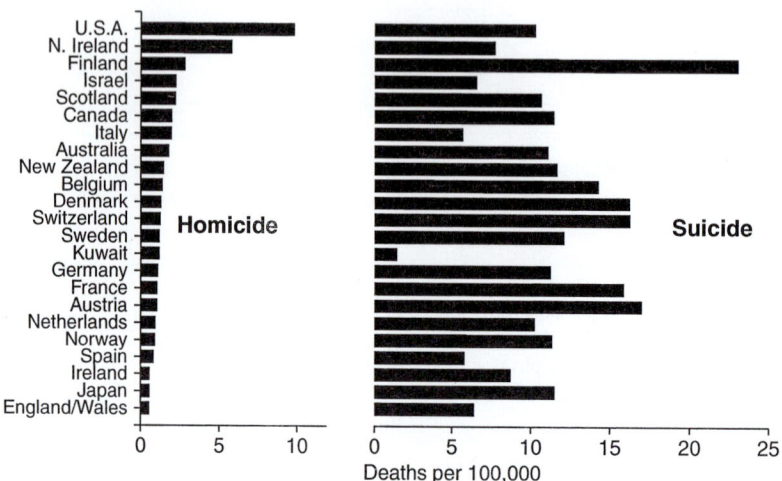

FIGURE 4   Age-adjusted homicide and suicide rates in 23 high-income countries (1994 or most recent year available).

data indicate that the incidence of homicide and suicide change over time, presumably in response to societal or environmental changes.

These data indicate that homicide and suicide rates differ markedly among countries, presumably due to different societal and environmental conditions.

2. Place

The location of events can be examined by spot maps of individual events, comparison of rates by geographic location (e.g., by state, by country), by type of location (e.g., urban, rural), or other characteristics of "place." As an example, the homicide rate in the United States is higher than in any other high-income country (Fig. 4), whereas the suicide rate in the United States is near the middle.

3. Person

Victims of violence can be grouped by sex, age, race or ethnicity, socioeconomic status, educational achievement, marital status, religion, occupation, or other characteristics of persons. For example, both homicide and suicide are more common among males than females; but while homicide rates are appreciably higher among young adults, the reverse is true for suicide (Fig. 5).

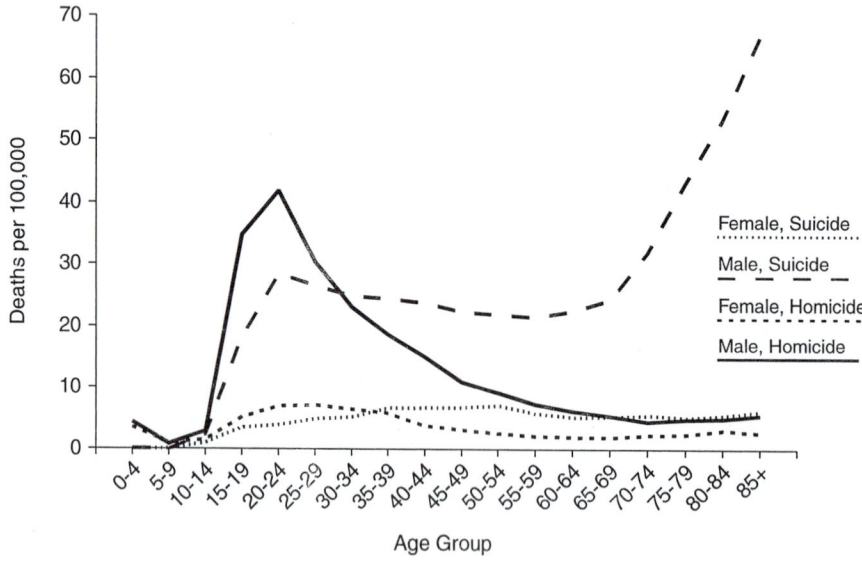

FIGURE 5   Age-specific homicide and suicide rates by sex in the U.S.A. (1994).

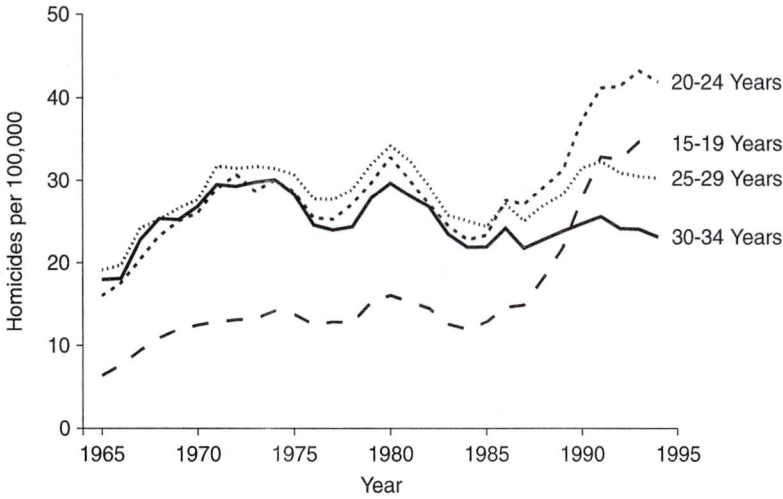

FIGURE 6 Male homicide rates by age group in the U.S.A. (1965–1994).

4. Time, Place, and Person Combined

Time, place, and person can be combined in many ways to further describe important characteristics of violent events. For example, the homicide rates since 1965 (time), in the United States (place), among young males (person) indicate striking changes in pattern since 1985, most notably a surge in homicide rates among 15- to 19-year-old males compared to the next three higher age groups (Fig. 6).

Examining the incidence of violent events according to the parameters *time, place,* and *person,* individually and in combination, provides considerable information about the magnitude and trends of these events. Summarizing data in this fashion generally is the first step in a public health assessment of a problem. These parameters focus on the victim and, as a result, provide no information about other factors relevant to the understanding and ultimate prevention of violence. The next model, the epidemiologic triangle, calls attention to several of these other factors.

C. Model: Epidemiologic Triangle

A consideration of only time, place, and person is inadequate for describing most, if not all, public health problems. Public health scientists and practitioners have adopted the epidemiologic triangle (*host, agent, environment*) as a model for providing a more complete description of public health problems. This model was originally designed to assist in the description of infectious diseases but, with minor adjustments, has also been applied to the problem of injuries. We have further

modified the terminology and form of this model to highlight the components of violent events, the points of the pyramid now being *victim, perpetrator, weapon or method used,* and *environment* (Fig. 7). Highlighting these important aspects calls attention to the complexity of violent events, provides a structure and orientation for analysis, and indicates that preventive actions may address any of the components. Because it is a conceptual rather than a predictive model, the triangle presupposes no set relationships among the components.

The characteristics of victims has been discussed above under characteristics of persons; perpetrators can be described similarly. Important characteristics of weapons or method include not only the type such as firearms, medications, knives, or ropes but also the

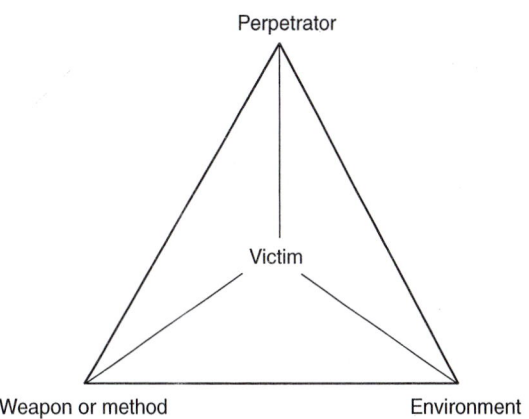

FIGURE 7 The epidemiologic triangle as applied to violent events.

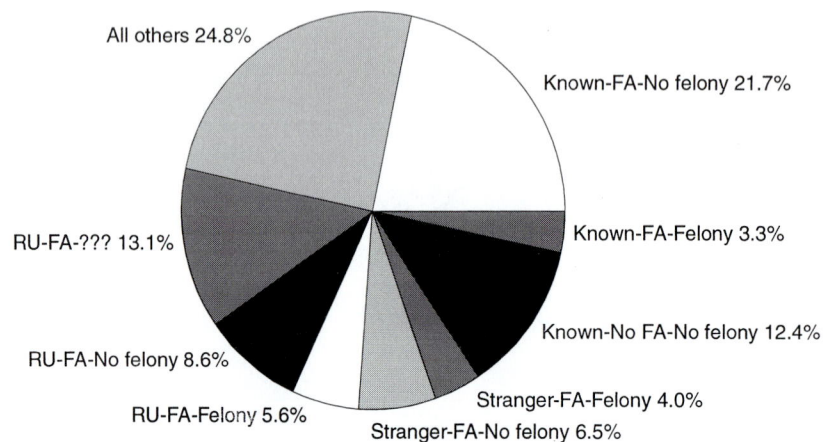

Relationship: Known=victim and perpetrator known to each other. Stranger=victim and perpetrator were strangers. RU=relationship undetermined.
Weapon: FA=firearm. No FA=weapon other than firearm.
Circumstance: Felony=felony in addition to the homicide. No felony=no felony other than the homicide. ???=not known if associated felony.

FIGURE 8 The victim–perpetrator relationship, weapon, and circumstance of homicides in the U.S. (1985–1994).

owner of the weapon and how the weapon came to be involved in the violent event. The environment for injuries or deaths from violence encompasses a vast array of factors, including the social environment (e.g., norms regarding suicide and aggression), the immediate physical environment (e.g., availability of weapons), and the historical environment (e.g., public riots, political assassinations).

After the components are considered individually, they are considered in pairs, threesomes, or all four together. For example, victims and perpetrators are often of the same sex, age, and race or ethnicity; also, the most common set of conditions for homicides includes victims and perpetrators who know each other, firearms as the weapon, and no other felonious crime, such as a robbery, involved (Fig. 8).

The epidemiologic triangle builds upon the simple analyses of time, place, and person and provides a richer and more complete description of violent events. It does not, however, provide guidance about how the various factors interact to cause a violent event.

III. UNDERSTANDING THE CAUSES OF VIOLENT EVENTS

Violence is a complex event that is caused by the effects and interactions among a range of social, psychological, and biological factors. Models help conceptualize the complicated combinations of causes that produce complex phenomena such as violence. The following models for thinking about causality have been applied to many public health issues but are particularly useful for violence, given its mulitifaceted origins.

A. Model: Causal Pies

The causal pie model, sometimes referred to as the sufficient/component cause model, indicates that an event occurs when a sufficient set of component causes are present. A fundamental principle of the model is that no event has but a single cause. Instead, events occur in response to a collection of component causes. A partial list of component causes for interpersonal and self-directed violence is provided (Box 1). The model is often named "causal pies" because it is commonly described utilizing pie slices to depict component causes and whole pies as sufficient causes (Fig. 9). A violent event occurs when all slices (component causes) of a whole pie (sufficient cause) are present. The removal of one component cause will make incomplete, and thereby render inoperative, any sufficient cause of which it is a part. For example, during a strike by Finnish liquor store workers in 1972, the incidence of assault and battery declined 20–25%. This suggests that in Finland something related to purchasing alcohol from a state liquor store, be that drinking the alcohol or the social groupings and behavioral patterns associated

Box 1

Selected component causes of interpersonal
violence
    Exposure to violence
    Poor social skills
    Low academic achievement
    Poor parenting skills
    Concentrated poverty
    Bystander encouragement
    Media violence
    Cultural acceptance

Selected component causes of self-directed
violence
    Depression
    Bipolar disorder
    Alcoholism
    Emotional loss
    Social isolation

which can be changed. For complex events such as
violence, full knowledge of a sufficient cause is rare, if
not impossible. Therefore, while it is important to keep
expanding our knowledge of causes, preventive action
can be taken with the knowledge at hand. This willingness to take action when full understanding is lacking
is characteristic of public health.

Implicit in the causal pie model is the possibility
that a factor may be present in many violent events
but a component cause in only some of them because
component causes vary among individuals. For example, about 60% of suicides involve firearms but the
number of suicides that would not have occurred if a
firearm had not been present is unknown. Preventing
access to a firearm will prevent some people who would
have suicided from doing so. For them, access to a
firearm is a component of their sufficient cause for
suicide. For others, who would use another method,
access to a firearm is not a component of their sufficient cause.

The component/sufficient cause model suggests that
many component causes must come together into one
sufficient cause before a violent event occurs. It also
demonstrates that some component causes (e.g., in Fig.
9, exposure to violence, X1, and X2) contribute to more
than one sufficient cause and that the removal of one
component cause may prevent more than one sufficient
cause from occurring. In so doing, the model brings
clarity and improved understanding to discussions

with buying and drinking alcohol, was a component
cause in about one-quarter of cases of assault and battery but was not a component cause for the other three-
quarters. Thus, it is not necessary to know all the components of a sufficient cause to prevent a violent event,
it is only necessary to know one component cause

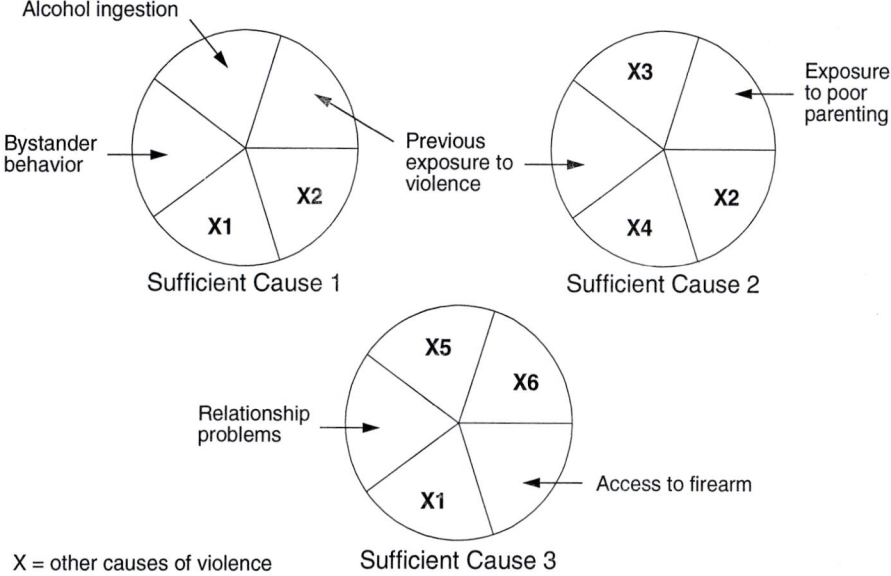

FIGURE 9 Hypothetical sufficient causes for violent events.

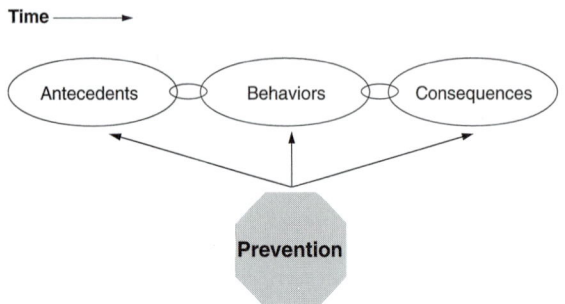

FIGURE 10 The causal chain—multiple opportunities to prevent injuries or death.

about the causes of violence and provides guidance for its prevention. The model, however, does not provide much information about how or when the component causes that compose a sufficient cause come together.

B. Model: Causal Chain

The causal chain emphasizes that any health outcome, such as an injury from a violent event, results from a temporal sequence of factors or conditions, commonly grouped into antecedents, behaviors, and consequences (Fig. 10). For example, nicotine addiction, social custom, or peer pressure are antecedents (component causes) of cigarette smoking, a behavior, that causes lung cancer, a health consequence. A parallel example for interpersonal violence might be as follows: being a victim of child abuse, watching many hours of violent movies and television, having poor social skills, or being goaded by bystanders are antecedents of physical fights (behaviors) which may cause injuries or deaths (consequences). The model emphasizes that the adverse health outcome can be prevented at several different points in time, including influencing experiences in childhood or at school, changing the immediate environment of the violent event such as bystander behavior or access to lethal weapons, and providing rapid and increasingly more sophisticated medical care after an injury has been inflicted.

C. Criteria for Causation

Identifying modifiable causes of violence is challenging. Experimental study designs often are impractical because the outcomes are rare (e.g., suicide, homicide) or because random assignment is unethical or impossible (e.g., use of illegal substances). As a result, other types of research designs are necessary. These methods entail collecting information from or about individuals whose

exposures and outcomes are determined by their personal experiences and choices rather than by experimental design. Public health workers commonly refer to these as observational studies because the exposures and outcomes have been observed rather than manipulated.

Because public health is concerned frequently with problems for which observational studies constitute a major portion of research, guidelines for making decisions about causality based upon observational studies have been developed (Box 2). Not all six of the criteria must be satisfied, and only one, an appropriate sequence, is essential. Taken as a group, they provide a framework for assessing the persuasiveness of scientific observations.

The public health need to study rare events using observational methods also has led to the refinement of case-control studies. Unlike longitudinal, or cohort, studies in which subjects with known experiences are followed for the subsequent development of the condition(s) of interest, case-control studies begin with individuals who have and others who do not have the condition and collecting information about their exposures. Case-control studies are better suited for rare outcomes, such as homicide or suicide, because they require no

---

Box 2

Criteria for causation

- Consistency: an association is repeatedly observed in different populations and circumstances
- Strength: strong associations are more likely causal than weak ones
- Appropriately sequenced: the cause must precede the effect
- Biologic gradient: larger or more intense exposures should be more strongly associated with the outcome of interest, producing a dose-response relationship
- Plausible and coherent: the relationship between the presumptive cause and the observed effect should be consistent with other knowledge
- Experimental evidence: findings from observational studies should be consistent with findings from experimental studies, if any are available

follow-up period and fewer subjects than cohort studies. They are also better suited to explore a broad spectrum of possible exposures than are cohort studies. Because of the retrospective nature of case-control studies, special care must be taken. Most importantly, unbiased information about the exposures and experiences that preceded the event must be obtained. In addition, both cases and controls should come from the same defined population, controls must have been at risk for the condition, and the selection of both cases and controls must be done without regard to their exposures or experiences prior to the event. In spite of these problems associated with retrospective data, the sophisticated use and understanding of case-control studies is an outstanding development of modern public health science.

These models of causation use the results from causal research to facilitate understanding about how component causes contribute to violent events. They remind us that the causal factors accumulate over time and can be prevented at multiple stages. The models do not provide guidance about how to assemble prevention activities into coordinated prevention programs.

IV. PLANNING SCIENCE-BASED PREVENTION ACTIVITIES

The descriptive models guide our understanding about the magnitude, trends, victims, perpetrators, weapons, and circumstances of violent events. The causal models help us understand that component causes accumulate over time and can be prevented at multiple stages. Descriptive and causal models, however, do not provide guidance about how to assemble prevention activities into coordinated prevention programs. Decisions must be made concerning the selection of groups to be targeted for intervention activities, the strategies that can be selected to address different types of causal factors, and the settings in which prevention programs are implemented.

A. High-Risk and Population Approaches

One of the first decisions in assembling a prevention program concerns the factors or behaviors that need to be changed and the group or groups who need to be influenced to bring about that change. Prevention programs often focus on a specific population subgroup that has been identified as being at high risk for the problem, in this case either as perpetrators or as victims of violence. Sometimes it is preferable to direct attention to the entire population, other times to use both approaches simultaneously. In the case of violence, many people have observed that a relatively small number of people are responsible for the majority of serious violent events that occur in our society. Others argue that, despite the existence of high-risk groups for perpetrating violence, the roots of the problem extend through the entire population and that the actions of many people contribute to the behaviors of a few. The choice of whether to target high-risk groups or the entire population in violence prevention has profound implications for the policies adopted to address the problem.

1. High-Risk Approach

The high-risk approach seeks to identify those individuals who are at higher risk, to understand the causes that elevate their risk, and to reduce their risk. High-risk approaches toward violence prevention would include counseling for individuals who have already attempted suicide or special training for aggressive youths. The high-risk approach is appealing because it focuses scarce resources on the individuals with the highest probability of causing or receiving violent injuries. Service providers are well motivated because the objectives of their efforts are clearly focused. The high-risk approach works best when the target group is accurately and inexpensively identified and known to be the source of many if not most new events. A deficiency of the high-risk approach is that it fails to reduce the flow of new individuals into the high-risk group.

2. Population Approach

The population approach directs the preventive efforts toward the entire population regardless of individual risk. The population approach to violence prevention would include universal preschool training, school-based cognitive-behavioral training, and efforts to reduce prejudicial behavior based solely on ethnicity, sex, religion, or other demographic characteristics. Methods and messages are tailored for different groups; all groups are addressed but not necessarily with identical strategies. The population approach is appealing because it provides an opportunity to prevent people from becoming high risk and further reduces the risk of violence among those at lower risk. The main disadvantage of the population approach is that, despite population-wide improvement, individuals perceive little benefit to themselves. As a result, support for such programs may be small.

The population approach is appropriate in four situations. First, it is appropriate when everyone in the population is at roughly equivalent risk. Second, the popula-

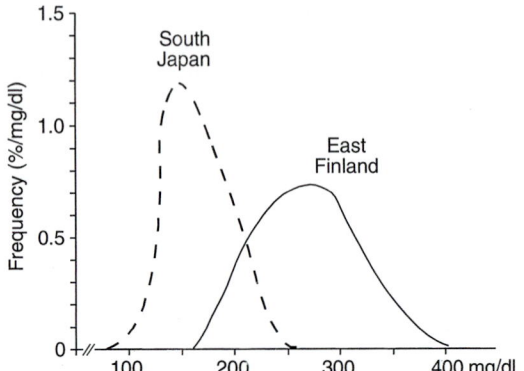

FIGURE 11 Cultural differences in serum-cholesterol levels. After Blackburn, H. Diet and mass hyperlipidemia: A public health view. In: Levy, R. *et al.* (eds.), *Nutrition, lipids and coronary heart disease,* New York, Raven Press, 1979(4); reproduced with permission.

tion approach works well when the intervention is inexpensive and harmless even though only some in the population are at risk. Third, it is appropriate when the actions of many people contribute to the problems in a few. Fourth, the population approach is appropriate when the entire population is at elevated risk even though certain individuals within the population can be identified as having the highest risk. An example of the last situation is coronary heart disease (CHD) due to hypercholesterolemia. Coronary heart disease mortality in Finland is considerably higher than in Japan, due largely to the markedly different blood cholesterol con-

centrations in those two countries (Fig. 11). Individuals in Finland with the highest cholesterol levels can be identified and treated, but that would have little effect on the elevated risk of CHD for the Finnish population as a whole. Reduction in blood cholesterol concentration for the entire population is in order.

A similar situation likely exists for violent injuries in the United States. Although we lack a simple measure for risk of violence, a distribution exists and it can be schematically represented (Fig. 12A). Given that the homicide rate in the United States exceeds that of other high-income countries severalfold, the risk of being a victim or a perpetrator of violence is higher for many people in the United States than in other countries, such as Canada (Fig. 12B). Efforts affecting only those at the highest risk do not appreciably change the elevated risk for the majority of the population (Fig. 12C). Therefore, reducing the likelihood of violent behavior of all U.S. citizens is necessary to bring the risk of violent injuries in the United States in line with other high-income countries (Fig. 12D). Reducing the likelihood of violent behavior of all U.S. citizens does not mean providing the same violence prevention programs to everyone. Instead, programs appropriate for different groups are designed and implemented.

Many prevention programs, particularly those pertaining to complex conditions such as violence, employ both the high-risk and the population approaches. Conceptualizing both approaches directs attention to the full spectrum of important causes of violence and re-

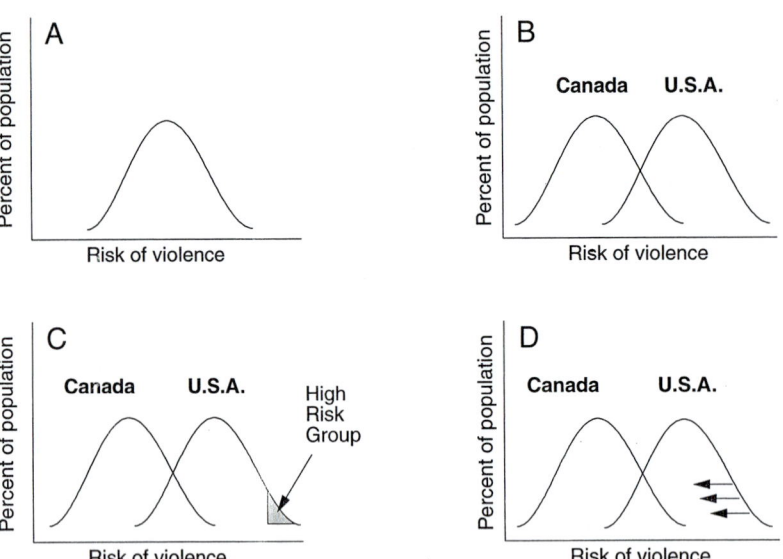

FIGURE 12 Hypothetical risk for being a victim or perpetrator of a violent event.

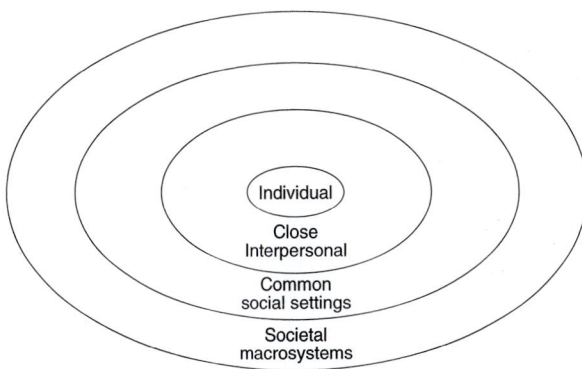

FIGURE 13   Circles of influence on violent behavior.

duces the likelihood of a preventive approach that is too narrowly focused.

B. Model: Circles of Influence

The circles of influence model calls attention to the diversity of causes and potential sites for prevention activities. Similar to the causal chain, which arrays events in temporal sequence, the circles of influence model arrays causes according to their social proximity to targeted individuals, beginning with the individuals themselves and moving outward to the whole society (Fig. 13). Although the circles of influence model can be used to conceptualize the causes of violence, it is most commonly used in discussions about interventions.

- *Individual*-level interventions are directed specifically toward members of the target group themselves. They often are designed to affect an individual's social and cognitive skills and behavioral practices. Examples include classroom training or mentoring.
- *Close interpersonal*-level interventions are directed toward people with close interpersonal contact with the target group, primarily family, and peers. These interventions often are designed to improve parenting practices or to modify the nature of peer group interactions.
- *Common social setting*-level interventions are directed toward the social groups or organizations with which the target group has frequent contact, such as schools, churches, work sites, or neighborhoods. They are designed to improve the attitudes, training skills, and interpersonal skills of those who work in those settings and to modify the climate of the settings themselves.

- *Societal macrosystem*-level interventions are directed at characteristics of the general society, such as economic opportunity, firearm availability, or media exposure. Such interventions generally involve the concerted efforts of multiple groups to educate both the general population and policy-makers about the necessity for change.

A major value of the circles of influence model is the attention it calls to causes and interventions that are not focused on individuals. Much violence prevention research has focused on individual-level interventions because individual-level research is more easily and cheaply conducted. Interventions at other levels may be equally or more effective but have been less frequently studied.

C. Model: Violence Prevention Cube

The violence prevention cube illustrates that every intervention has three elements (Fig. 14). The first is a target group for activities. Target groups may be children or youths, young parents, male batterers, or the entire population. The second element is the strategy to bring about the desired change in the target group. Strategies encompass information dissemination to individuals or groups; skill building for individuals, parents, or others; and legislative, regulatory, environmental, and technological change. The third element of a prevention activity is the setting, or location, at which the strategy is applied to the target group. Settings may be homes, schools, work sites, medical care facilities, and other places within the community. The target group, strategy, and setting define the focus of any prevention activity.

Second, the violence prevention cube shows many different violence prevention activities are possible. There are many target groups, strategies, and settings; and each intersection of these three elements is a potential intervention. This message is consistent with the causal pies, causal chain, and circles of influence, all of which suggest that there are multiple foci at which progress toward a violent event can be prevented.

Third, the more intersections at which violence prevention activities occur the more likely is the overall reduction in violent events. Public health efforts in other spheres, such as smoking cessation, adolescent drug use, and dietary change, indicate that the greater the number and variety of interventions the more successful the program. The same will be true for violence prevention. The augmented violence reduction results from both additive and complementary effects. If differ-

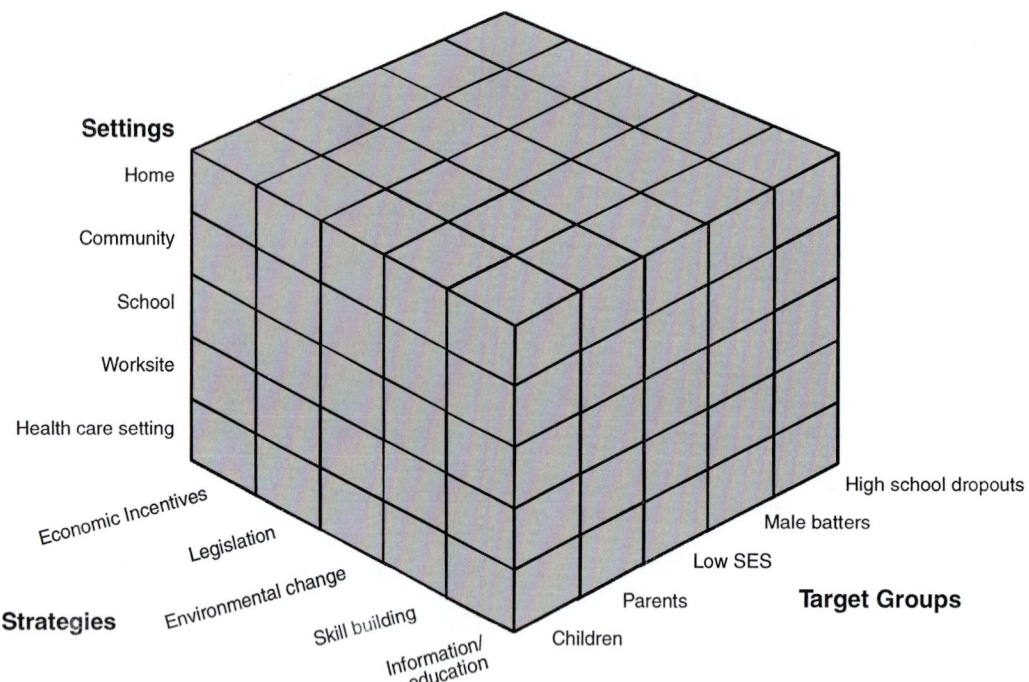

FIGURE 14 Violence prevention cube.

ent activities address different component causes, and those component causes do not coincide in a sufficient cause, the effects will be additive. When different activities address the same component cause the likelihood of violence reduction is improved if the activities complement and reinforce the same messages, thereby increasing the probability of behavior change.

Finally, the violence prevention cube cautions against a narrow prevention focus, such as targeting a single risk factor in only one way. Presentations in the media about violence and violence prevention efforts often oversimplify the situation. For example, recent newspaper articles have attributed the decline in firearm homicides among youths in Boston to increased cooperation between police and parole officers and to increased pressure on the illegal firearm market. These activities may be important in the decline of firearm homicides in Boston. The media accounts, however, have ignored the efforts of schools, hospitals, churches, and others over the past several years to provide young people with the justification and skills to avoid violence, which may also have played a role. In most real-world situations the relative importance of any specific activity rarely, if ever, is known. For complex events such as violence, it is likely that multiple activities have contributed, and it is imprudent to attribute reductions in violence to solitary efforts.

V. SUMMARY AND CONCLUSION

The above discussion has focused on models, or tools, used by public health workers to describe and understand the problem of violence and to develop prevention activities for violence. The first models (i.e., time–place–person, epidemiologic triangle) provide fundamental descriptions of violent events. The second set of models (i.e., causal pies, causal chain) helps us understand how the many complex factors that contribute to violence interact to produce violence and to understand which factors are necessary for violence to occur. The latter models (i.e., high-risk and population approaches, circles of influence, violence prevention cube) help to reassemble the simpler pieces into effective prevention programs. The latter models emphasize the selection of target groups, the range of personal and social factors that contribute to the component causes, and the importance of multifaceted and reinforcing interventions.

At present, the knowledge of the magnitude, causes, and effective prevention actions varies for different types of violence. As a result, models appropriate for one type of violence may be less useful for another. For example, suitable definitions and measurement methods are just now being developed for the abusive, nonfatal violence that occurs within the home, such as in intimate partner, child, and elder abuse. Data to describe those events according to time, place, and person and the epidemiologic triangle should be forthcoming over the next several years. The descriptions should enable public health workers and others to progress to more-focused causal research and preventive work. In contrast, we know more about the magnitude and causes of interpersonal youth violence. As a result, prevention models are more useful than they are for violence within families and between intimate partners. Research has shown and prevention efforts have taken note that some component causes of interpersonal youth violence occur at an early age (causal chain), that violent behavior is influenced by family, friends, and community conditions as well as individual factors (high-risk and population approaches, circles of influence), and that reinforcing messages need to be delivered (violence prevention cube). Preliminary results from evaluations of these projects suggest that school-based cognitive-behavioral training and skillbuilding programs are likely to be helpful, as are early interventions such as home visits, parent training, and quality preschool.

Also See the Following Articles

CHILD ABUSE • HEALTH CONSEQUENCES OF WAR AND POLITICAL VIOLENCE • HOMICIDE • PUBLIC HEALTH STRATEGIES • VIOLENCE PREDICTION

Bibliography

Committee for the Study of the Future of Public Health (1988). *The future of public health.* Washington, DC: Institute of Medicine, National Academy Press.

Crowell, N. A., & Burgess, A. W. (Eds.) (1996). *Understanding violence against women.* Washington, DC: National Research Council, National Academy Press.

Goldfried, M. R., & Davidson, S. I. (1976). *Clinical behavior therapy.* New York: Holt, Rinehart, and Winston.

Kachur, S. P., Potter, L. B., James, S. P., & Powell, K. E. (1995). *Suicide in the United States. 1980–1992: Violence Surveillance Summary Series, No. 1.* Atlanta, GA: Centers for Disease Control and Prevention, National Center for Injury Prevention and Control.

Kellermann, A. L., Rivara, F. P., Somes, G., Reay, D. T., Francisco, J., Banton, J. G., Prodzinski, J., Fligner, C., and Hackman, B. B. (1992). Suicide in the home in relation to gun ownership. *New England Journal of Medicine, 327,* 467–472.

Makela, K. (1980). Differential effects of restricting the supply of alcohol: Studies of a strike in Finnish liquor stores. *Journal of Drug Issues, 10,* 131–144.

Mercy, J. A., Rosenberg, M. L., Powell, K. E., Broome, C. V., & Roper, W. L. (1993). Public health policy for preventing violence. Health Affairs, 12(4), 7–29.

Potter, L., Powell, K. E., & Kachur, S. P. (1995). Suicide prevention from a public health perspective. *Suicide & Life-Threatening, Behavior, 25,* 82–91.

Powell, K. E., & Hawkins, D. F. (editors) (1996). Youth violence prevention: Descriptions and baseline data from 13 evaluation projects. *American Journal of Preventative Medicine, 12(5)(Suppl.),* pp. 1–134.

Reiss, A. J., & Roth, J. A. (Eds.) (1993). *Understanding and preventing violence: Panel on the understanding and control of violent behavior.* Washington DC: Committee on Law and Justice, Commission on Behavioral and Social Sciences and Education, National Research Council, National Academy Press.

Robertson, L. S. (1992). *Injury epidemiology.* New York: Oxford University Press.

Rose, G. (1985). Sick individuals and sick populations. *International Journal of Epidemiology, 14,* 32–38.

Rothman, K. J. (1976). Causes. *American Journal of Epidemiology, 104,* 587–592.

Rothman, K. J. (1986). *Modern epidemiology.* Boston/Toronto: Little, Brown.

Silverman, M. M., & Maris, R. W. (1995). The prevention of suicide behaviors: An overview. Suicide & Life Threatening, Behaviors 25, 10–21.

Tolan, P., & Guerra, N. (1994). *What works in reducing adolescent violence: An empirical review of the field.* Boulder, CO: Center for the Study and Prevention of Violence.

Widom, C. S. (1989). The cycle of violence. *Science, 244,* 160–166.

Punishment of Criminals

Leslie Sebba

Institute of Criminology, Faculty of Law, Hebrew University of Jerusalem*

GLOSSARY

Boot Camps Form of punishment for young offenders modeled on military camp.

Borstal Penal institutions with educational and training orientation for young offenders in Britain.

Bridewells Institutions established in 16th-century England for the punishment and occupation of deviants (also: "houses of correction").

Consequentialist Intended to achieve a practical goal.

Decarceration Reduction of the size of the prison population.

Deontological Based on ethical principle(s).

Family Conferencing Alternative framework for dealing with young offenders whereby a proposal for the disposition of the case is brought before an informal meeting involving the offender's family, the victim and a law enforcement representative.

Good Time Laws Laws providing for a reduction of prison terms for good behavior.

Mandatory Minimum Sentencing provision obligating the court to impose a penalty (usually of imprisonment) no less than that specified.

Moral Panic Outbreak of public concern over issue perceived as threatening consensual values.

Power–Knowledge Paradigm Concept developed by Michel Foucault emphasizing the relationship between knowledge and the exercise of power and control (as, for example, in the case of files on prisoners held by the prison administration).

Prison Hulks Ships used in 18th-century England to house convicted offenders, especially when transportation routes closed.

Shock Incarceration Short period of imprisonment followed by discretionary early release, usually with supervision.

Social Defense Movement in penology emphasising treatment measures adopted toward offenders perceived as dangerous for the protection of society.

Three Strikes Law Law providing for lengthy prison sentence (usually life imprisonment) for the third offense of a specified type.

I. INTRODUCTION

Punishment (in the context of this article) may be defined as pain or suffering inflicted by agents of the state and in the name of the state on (generally) a citizen

---

* This article was written while the author was Visiting Fellow, Centre for Socio-Legal Studies, Wolfson College, Oxford

of that state, following a breach of the criminal law committed by that citizen and in the course of a legal process. This being a rather extreme form of (coercive) social intervention, a wide-ranging literature has developed regarding its justifications and the forms it should assume. Interest in this topic is further stimulated by the fact that the forms that punishments may assume have varied over time and from society to society. Moreover, the fact that a variety of punishments are available at any one time—even for a particular person committing a particular act—also serves to generate interest in this topic.

Other factors have pushed this topic into the popular as well as the academic limelight. In the light of continuing high crime rates punishment is perceived as being ineffective, while at the same time the penal system has become an economic burden—Nils Christie has referred to "crime control as industry." Academics see politicians and policy-makers as driven by populism and "moral panics." "Like the crime it is supposed to deal with," observes David Garland, "punishment is nowadays seen as a chronic social problem."

Academic writing on punishment does not, however, focus exclusively on contemporary crises. The topic is analyzed in the literature from different perspectives—notably those of political philosophy, social theory, and psychology. Clearly, punishment practices raise profound questions regarding the role of the state, the structure of society, and the analysis of personality. Since such study may be more objectively pursued outside one's own society, historians, too, have been occupied with this topic, particularly in recent times. Jurists have also contributed to the literature on punishment, not only in their expositions of the relevant legal provisions, but also by the invocation of human rights issues. Criminologists and penologists, whose eclectic approaches may embrace all of the aforementioned disciplines, have in some cases integrated theories of punishment with the study of the etiology of crime.

Finally, while most of the above disciplines have been concerned primarily with analyzing and evaluating the policies and practices that have been adopted and considering their effects as well as their rationale, others have endeavored—in the light of such evaluations and of the political debates referred to above—to contribute themselves to the formulation of policy.

II. DEFINITIONAL ISSUES

Some of the ideological and practical issues relating to punishment arise in connection with the definition of the subject matter. "Punishment" was defined above as the infliction of pain or suffering by agents of the state following a breach of the law and in the course of a legal process. Clearly, however, the ambit of this article must include sanctions which arguably do not involve "pain or suffering," such as treatment orders or restitution payments, or what continental jurists would refer to as "measures" rather than penalties.

The "legal process" typically involves a judicial proceeding and the conviction of the accused as a precondition to the imposition of the punishment. Some measures, however, such as probation orders, may in some jurisdictions be imposed without registering a formal conviction. Moreover, first-offenders charged with relatively trivial offences will often be "diverted" out of the system at the stage of the police investigation or by the exercise of prosecutorial discretion. Such a disposition may involve a minor sanction. Is this a "punishment"? Such practices are particularly frequent for juveniles—for whom the word "crime" is in the American lexicon replaced by the term "delinquency." While jurists may have a problem regarding such sanctioning as punishment in the absence of a judicial finding of guilt, the decisions are part of the official response network to breaches of the criminal law and are thus of interest in considering punishment as a social phenomenon. The same is true of the informal alternative sanctioning processes, such as mediation, which are considered below. Conversely, violations of minor traffic provisions may be of less interest—although complying with the legal criteria for punishment.

Another grey area in this context is the treatment of the infringement of fiscal, environmental, commercial, and other "regulatory" provisions as administrative or civil offences resulting in processing by administrative tribunals or civil courts. The sanctions, in monetary and professional terms, may be severe, but physical punishments are excluded (except, e.g., for contempt), and constitutional guarantees provided to criminal defendants are not observed. Such practices gave rise to a historic debate between the sociologist Edwin Sutherland, who "discovered" such "white-collar crime" (as he termed it), and the jurist Paul Tappan, who argued that without a criminal process the acts could not properly be designated "crime"—and by implication there could be no punishment. The issue remains pertinent: Ken Mann and others have described a proliferation of legal techniques in recent years for the nonpenal control of white-collar deviance.

Finally, some researchers have drawn attention to internal sanctioning systems operating in particular sections of the community. Examples would be the disciplinary systems operating in schools and other educational establishments, in religious institutions, within professions, and in the military; Stuart Henry has researched such practices in the workplace. Such proceedings are traditionally perceived as being less formal than the criminal justice system and outside that system. It should be noted, however, that the sanctions imposed by these systems may be meaningful (and involve "pain and suffering"), while in the modern state they may in fact draw their authority—including the power to impose sanctions—from the state, under legislation, albeit not explicitly penal. Indeed, this may apply even to parental powers within the family.

Not only do these systems resemble the "punishment of criminals," but they also interact with the official criminal justice system. Thus, while the focus of the ensuing discussion will be on the official system, the alternative systems cannot analytically be excluded. For this reason some analysts of this area prefer to relate to "social control" rather than "punishment." That expression being too encompassing, however, David Garland has coined the term "penality."

III. HISTORICAL OVERVIEW

The penal systems of ancient societies have been studied not only to learn about these societies but also to seek patterns and parallels in penal developments. Thus A. S. Diamond noted the connection between the political and economic organizations of these societies and the level of sophistication of their penal systems and found parallels in the development of early English history. The pioneering sociologist Emile Durkheim formulated "laws of penal evolution," the most notable of which posited that society developed historically from an emphasis on *repressive* law to an emphasis on *restitutive* sanctions. This analysis has been challenged by some writers who have pointed out that the more punitive sanctions (generally corporal) exacted in the name of the King or other political ruler were preceded by systems in which the initiative lay with the victim and the emphasis was on restitution or some other form of mutual accommodation.

The latter view is illustrated in the XII Tables of early Roman law, which declared that "if the parties reach no accommodation, there shall be '*talio*.'" This talionic principal was an echo of the "eye for an eye" prescript found both in the Bible and in the earlier Hammurabic code and gave rise to an interpretative literature as to how far this principle was to be implemented: (a) literally, (b) symbolically (e.g., amputa-

tion of the limb used for theft), or (c) as a residual or maximum penalty, as suggested by Maimonides in the context of Jewish law and reflected in the XII Tables.

The retributive penalties of early law also had a deterrent aspect (cf., the biblical exhortation "so that they should see and be fearful"), and in this they were echoed by the penalties that developed in feudal and post-feudal Europe. As populations were released from feudal bondage and became increasingly urban and mobile, they were perceived as a potential threat to social order. New laws (e.g., against vagrancy) and new penalties were developed of a public and corporal character: amputation of limbs, branding, the stocks, and so on. From the 16th century, however, more sophisticated solutions were advanced. Sentences to the death penalty would be commuted on condition that the offender agreed to serve in the army or on the galley ships or to be transported to the newly founded colonies (the galleys and transportation subsequently became independent sanctions). For Georg Rusche and Otto Kirchheimer, radical German social theorists of the 1930s, these developments show how the penal system may be manipulated to serve political and, in particular, economic interests.

An even more significant development from a historical perspective was the establishment in mid-16th century England of the Bridewells and at the end of that century in Holland of the Houses of Correction. These institutions, in which young delinquents, as well as other marginal populations such as vagrants and prostitutes, were to apply themselves to hard work and prayer, may be considered the precursors of the 19th-century prison and later correctional institutions. Such experiments were of limited application ("bridewells," although mandated by legislation in all counties, came to resemble local jails), and while the transportation systems flourished in colonial countries, the penal systems of the 17th and 18th centuries were generally characterized by public cruelty—as described in detail in Michel Foucault's *Discipline and Punishment*—and by arbitrary implementation, reflecting the absence of a rule of law in contemporary regimes.

A detailed account of the penal institutions, both in Britain and in the rest of Europe, was published (the first edition in 1777) by John Howard of Bedfordshire, who became familiar with this topic as a result of his responsibilities as sheriff. This followed a period during which the legal systems of Europe had been subjected to severe criticism on the part of the French philosophers of the enlightenment, which had, in turn, inspired the Italian nobleman Cesare Beccaria to publish his short monograph *Of Crimes and Punishments*. This document is regarded as the authoritative statement of the "classic school" as to the optimal structure of a rational legal system based upon the rule of law and the need for predictability of both procedures and punishments. The system presumes the rationality of potential offenders, who will be deterred by even moderate penalties, so long as these increase in proportion to the seriousness of the offence, and apprehension will result in the certainty of their imposition. In principle the death penalty formed no part of Beccaria's penal scheme.

The publication of these enlightend proposals and of John Howard's expose of the existing institutions coincided with the American Revolution and as a result the transportation option was denied to the English authorities. A public commission (of which Howard was a member) offered a blueprint for a new system of penitentiary, based upon labor, penitence, and responsible management. The new model was not adopted at this time: the English housed the awaiting convicts in "prison hulks," and the problem was resolved with the discovery of Australia in 1789, beginning a new era in transportation. The penitentiary was, however, adopted with enthusiasm by the new American republic, where public debate pitted the Pennsylvania model (of the Eastern Penitentiary) of segregated prisoners in separate cells against New York's Auburn model based on a regime of silence. By the middle of the 19th century the concept of the penitentiary had been reimported into England and was also being imitated in other European countries. This was the era in which large institutions were seen as the solution for marginal populations, whether criminals (the prison), the mentally ill (the asylum), or the unemployed (the workhouse). Moreover, while traditional accounts described the development of the prison in terms of human progress (sometimes mistaken, but always paved with good intentions), the "revisionist" critiques by David Rothman, Foucault, and others saw the prison as part of a state-maintained industrial complex imposing regimentation on a marginal population. Foucault also emphasised the power–knowledge paradigm as the basis of the discipline (or surveillance) imposed on the prisoner and saw such punishment as operating on the *souls* of the offenders, whereas earlier (corporal) punishments had focused on their *bodies*.

The second half of the 19th century saw the rise of the positivist school, which viewed human behavior as being determined by extraneous causes rather than as freely willed. Punishment, according to this school, should be adapted to the requirements of the offender rather than being determined by the seriousness of the offence. The American Prison Congress of 1870 called for indeterminate sentences and the "progressive stage" system, whereby prisoners progressed from one stage to the next (culminating in their conditional release subject to supervision), a system that had been pioneered in Ireland in the 1850s. As the treatment professions developed and a "medical model" adopted (i.e., diagnosis, prognosis, and treatment), punishment was increasingly individualized according to the perceived needs of the offender. The probation order and the suspended sentence were the products of this era as was the reformatory for younger offenders. At the turn of the century (1899) the juvenile court was established, with a gamut of associated treatments.

The rehabilitation model, as the above came to be known, was undoubtedly the dominating trend from the end of the 19th century until the 1960s. Developments during this period were mostly concerned with varieties in treatment approaches, sometimes reflecting new theories of crime causation. One variant of this model, however, was the school of social defence, which laid emphasis on the need to protect society: the treatment of the nondangerous might be unnecessary, while the dangerous should be restrained pending their treatment (this philosophy was articulated mainly in Europe, but was reflected also in American legislation). It should also be noted that while the rehabilitation model dominated the American criminal justice system as reflected by the indeterminate sentence, it was more marginal in European systems where institutions such as probation orders and presentence reports operated in the margins of a more "classic" system.

The 1960s saw the awakening of doubts with regard to the validity of the treatment model as then operating. The labeling school (e.g., Edwin Lemert and Edwin Schur) held that stigmatizing deviants by their punishment might itself be a cause of their subsequent criminality. This gave rise to a movement in favor of minimizing punitive (including treatment) interventions and of the so-called "de"s—deinstitutionalization, decarceration, decentralization (of correctional policies), decriminalization (of "victimless" crimes and juvenile "status" offences such as truancy), and diversion (from the official processes). This was not necessarily inconsistent with rehabilitation as an objective, but the means of achieving this goal had clearly been radically altered.

The 1970s witnessed the beginning of a frontal attack on the primacy of the rehabilitative model in sentencing. The reasons for this, and for the model's demise (albeit not complete), is considered in the next section.

IV. THE PURPOSES OF PUNISHMENT

The philosophical literature on the aims of or justifications for punishment differentiates between two types of justification: (a) the deontological, where the justification is based upon some ethical principle, and (b) the consequentialist, according to which punishment is intended to achieve some practical outcome. (This is often referred to as utilitarian, but this term more properly describes a particular school of consequentialism.) The first category is backward-looking in that the suitability of the punishment in a particular case may be determined merely by a consideration of the offense that was perpetrated: the main example of this type of objective is retribution. The second category is forward-looking in that the appropriateness of the sentence can only be determined (if at all) by monitoring its outcome. The main examples falling in this category are rehabilitation, deterrence (both general and special), and incapacitation.

Two qualifications should be added to the above classification. First, some aims attributed to punishment cut across the two categories. Thus the denunciatory principle sees punishment as an expression—or even a measure—of society's condemnation of the injurious act, suggestive of (backward-looking) retribution but also as the delivery of a warning to others to refrain from such behavior (and hence is also forward-looking). This duality certainly operates in the analysis proffered by Durkheim, who saw the punishment for crime as a means of strengthening social solidarity around the legal norms.

Second, two or more justifications may be attributed to punishment simultaneously, including a combination of the deontological and the consequentialist. Thus Ted Honderich (in his *Punishment: The Supposed Justifications*) elaborated a combination of criteria that a punishment would have to meet to gain legitimacy. This type of approach was further developed by the legal philosopher H. L. A. Hart, who argued that controversies regarding the purposes of punishment had failed to differentiate between two distinct questions: (a) what was the general justifying aim of the punishment system as a whole and (b) what were the principles of distribution according to which punishments should be allocated in particular cases. Thus while the general justifying principle of punishment might be general deterrence, retributivist principles should be invoked in the course of sentencing. Hart is thus identified with "mixed theories" of punishment.

We now consider, in turn, the main aims of punishment traditionally cited in the literature. Since the revival of deontological theories in modern times has resulted in large measure from disillusion with the consequentialist approaches, we consider the latter first.

A. Rehabilitation

As noted above, the rehabilitative ideal dominated penological thinking from the rise of the positivist school in the late 19th century until recent times. This approach was shared by academic penologists and correctional personnel alike. New, allegedly more effective treatments were constantly being proposed (and adopted) and the treatment professions, in particular social workers, psychiatrists, and psychologists, set the tone for correctional policies. The criminal justice system was characterized by the exercise of wide discretionary powers at all stages so that the sentence could be adjusted to the offender's perceived treatment needs at all stages of the process. Insofar as problems were encountered and correctional programs appeared to be failing, appropriate formulas were adopted to explain these, e.g., inadequate funding. (This theme has been developed in Stanley Cohen's analysis of social control policies). Not only was the rehabilitative ideal perceived as being humane and progressive by contrast with the retrogressive nature of the alternative theories, it was also seen as the means whereby offenders would be dissuaded from recidivism, would internalize prosocial values, and would be reintegrated into the community as useful citizens. So what were the forces that led to the demise of this ideal since the 1970s?

Criticisms of the rehabilitative ideal came from many quarters, reflecting diverse ideologies. Liberals and civil libertarians decried the poor conditions of so-called rehabilitative regimes (reflected in Jessica Mitford's *Kind and Usual Punishment*). A Quaker monograph (and the Quakers had been a major influence in establishing the prison system in the early 19th century) pointed to the arbitrariness of the decisions reached; disparities in sentencing and parole were the order of the day, and the variations in disposition appeared to lack any rational foundation. Often decision-making would reflect the value system of the decision-maker, so that inmates might be punished for their preferences and lifestyles rather than for their crimes. Marxists and other radicals identified with this complaint; indeed, they saw the whole correctional apparatus as a technique for repression by empowered socioeconomic interests, whereby oppressed persons were coerced to a form of "good citizenship" to which they did not adhere.

Moreover, white-collar offenders were seen as slipping through the correctional net.

On the other side of the political spectrum, conservatives viewed the system of individualized sentencing as a means of "going soft" on criminals, for in some cases perpetrators of serious crimes might get probation or early parole. The "law and order" slogan provided a basis for limiting discretion and mandating harsher and more uniform penalties. This approach was fueled by the burgeoning victim movement, which objected to the overriding focus in the rehabilitative discourse on the offender's needs, while ignoring the needs of the victims. Some (although by no means all) of the spokespersons of this movement translated this complaint into an insistence on the imposition of harsher measures on the offender and the adoption of a system that would insure that the sentence would reflect the gravity of the offence.

All these criticisms were further fueled by the findings of empirical researchers to which attention was being drawn at this time. Early evaluations of the effectiveness of rehabilitation methods were generally simplistic, but by the second half of the 20th century statistical techniques (including the employment of control groups) had become more sophisticated, while use of the computer enabled researchers to engage in multivariate analyses with much greater facility. Researchers were thus enabled to determine the specific contribution of individual variables, including the treatment or punishment variable, to the outcome being monitored (usually recidivism). In other words the research would indicate whether a particular intervention—a sanction or treatment applied in an institution or in the community—had actually affected the recidivism rate by producing a result different from that expected for similar offenders not exposed to the same intervention.

The publication of such research findings in the academic journals did not attract a great deal of attention. However, in the 1970s a research team commissioned in New York conducted a meta-survey of this literature and concluded that no one correctional or treatment intervention could be said to have been shown to be consistently effective. Robert Martinson published their preliminary findings in *The Public Interest* under the title "What Works—Questions and Answers about Prison Reform" in 1974 and in effect concluded that *"nothing works."* This conclusion was seized upon with some enthusiasm by the various critics of the rehabilitative model referred to above. The ideological criticisms leveled at this model from these diverse sources were now lacking any counterweight support of claims as to its effectiveness in reducing criminality.

As noted, these developments led substantially to the demise of the rehabilitative model, both as an ideology and in terms of prevailing sentencing structures. Nevertheless, residual support for the model has remained on the part of persons unconvinced by the alternative ideologies, and in the light of findings which have challenged Martinson's negative conclusions.

B. Individual Deterrence

This refers to the use of punishment to intimidate the offender into refraining from further crime by dint of fear of the unpleasant consequences. This objective (also referred to as *special* or *specific* deterrence) is sometimes reflected in the language of sentencing judges who use such expressions as "teaching the offender a lesson."

While many types of sentence could be imposed with such a purpose in mind, the sanction most closely identified with this objective is the suspended sentence of imprisonment, whereby the court designates a term of imprisonment, but specifies that the offender will not be required to serve this term unless he or she commits another offence (usually of a certain type or types) within a specified period of time. The offender then has this "sword of Damocles" hanging over him or her to be exercised in the case of failure to abide by the condition. This also applies to an offender qualifying under a "three strikes" law, who has been convicted of the first two qualifying offences. Other types of sentence which have been perceived as having a specific deterrence component include corporal punishment (see below) and lengthy prison terms.

It is hard to determine the degree to which the deterrent component of such sentences is effective, since it may be difficult to separate the deterrent effect from other effects operating simultaneously: a relatively low recidivism rate following one of the above-mentioned sanctions might reflect a rehabilitative rather than a deterrent effect or it might equally reflect some negative effects occurring within the control groups. As to *corporal punishment,* studies of whipping in the United States, when this form of punishment was still used, indicated high recidivism rates, while in Britain the use of a caning as a discipline for young offenders absconding from an institution was found to be effective. The use of corporal punishments is, however, today generally proscribed in western societies, but is practiced in some Islamic countries. (A return to some form of corporal punishment has been advocated in recent times by Graeme Newman.)

The effects of *long-term imprisonment* were included in Martinson's review and were found to produce recidivism rates similar to or higher than those following shorter terms. The main test of the deterrent effects of *suspended sentences* is whether the sentence has to be activated because of the commission of further offences while the prison term is pending; activation rates have been found to be low in Israel, Japan, and the Netherlands, but high in England and Wales.

An informal study undertaken several decades ago by W. H. Hammond found that first-time prisoners were in a state of shock during the first weeks of their sentence, but subsequently adjusted to prison conditions. This would support a policy of a "short, sharp shock" in a penal institution followed by a return to the community. This type of policy was adopted in some U.S. jurisdictions in the form of "shock probation" and "shock parole." English detention centers for young offenders were operated on a similar principle, as are the more recently established "boot camps," also known as "shock incarceration." Studies have shown recidivist rates for these sanctions to be similar to those of the alternatives.

C. General Deterrence

This refers to policies or practices intended to deter the general public from committing offences. As with the other penal objectives being considered here, such policies and practices may emanate from the legislature, from the courts, or from other decision-making bodies such as parole boards. Unlike the other objectives, however, there is an assumption here that information regarding the policies and practices adopted, or decisions made, will filter down to the general population (or that section of it contemplating the behavior in question).

Although invocation of general deterrence as an objective of punishment dates back to the codes of ancient times, it is highly problematical in terms of *justice,* at least for the purpose of the allocation of penalties (cf., the Hart distinction referred to above). Punishment is being determined in this context not according to the seriousness of the offence, nor the needs of the offender, but according to what is thought to be necessary to influence others. It may also be affected by the frequency of the type of offence it is being sought to deter at the time when the sentence is imposed; again, a factor unrelated to the defendant.

At the least, therefore, it must be shown that sentences imposed in the name of deterrence will be effective in their objective. For centuries the evidence was anecdotal, judges being generally convinced of the de-

terrent value of the punishments they meted out, while skeptics pointed to the activity of pickpockets at the public hangings of their copractitioners. Since the 1970s, however, there has been a plethora of empirical studies in this area. These have adopted a variety of techniques. They have focused on legislative policy, judicial sentencing, or law enforcement bodies. They have been concerned with either severity of sentence or probability of enforcement (or both). They have used geographical comparisons (cross-sectional studies) or comparisons over time (longitudinal studies). Dramatic policy changes or "crackdowns" have in particular provided fuel for research.

While space does not permit an analysis of the manifold, complex, and often contradictory findings, it may be noted that severity of punishment has not generally been found to lead to lower crime rates. This even applies (in spite of one study indicating the contrary) to the death penalty. Indeed, in terms of U.S. sentencing patterns across the states, severe sentencing is statistically associated with high crime rates, although extraneous factors (e.g., a culture of violence) may explain both these phenomena. Nor does the introduction of mandatory sanctions appear generally to reduce crime rates.

Some studies (in particular the comparisons among states) indicate, however, that a high probability of apprehension, or of receiving some penalty, may be related to lower crime rates. There is thus support for Beccaria's claim of more than 200 years ago that the *certainty* of punishment is more important for deterring crime than the *severity* of punishment.

D. Incapacitation

This refers to policies designed to protect the public by isolating the offender or otherwise neutralizing his or her potential to commit crimes. Historically this was achieved by the death penalty, transportation, amputation, or castration; but in the 20th century it is achieved mainly by prolonged incarceration. (The risk of offences being committed against other inmates is not generally weighed.) Statutory examples of this policy were the English institutions of "preventive detention" and "extended sentences" and provisions in the U.S. for habitual offenders, dangerous offenders, psychopaths, and so on. Some of these provisions have required incarceration in closed treatment institutions, often for indeterminate periods; such provisions bear a strong resemblance to civil commitment procedures for psychiatric patients who are perceived as being dangerous.

Although this type of objective was regarded by the

"social defence" school as an appropriate basis for the penal system, such policies are fraught with difficulties. First, penal policy is oriented here not to what offenders have done, but to the acts attributed to them at a future time. This, of course, is in direct conflict with the retributive approach, which focuses on the act committed. (It may also be inconsistent with the other objectives which have been considered here.) Second, it assumes that knowledge is available as to which are the offenders (on the assumption that the policy will only be applied to proven offenders) to whom future dangerousness should be attributed. While studies of criminal careers provide data bases for estimates of this type, it is disputed whether such knowledge can provide a prediction of future conduct sufficiently accurate for the purposes of penal decision-making.

Two methods of prediction are discussed in the literature. Clinical prediction is based on an evaluation of the individual case on the basis of reports and personal impressions. This is the method used by psychiatrists for the purposes of hospital commitments and also by decision-makers in the criminal justice system for the purposes of sentencing and parole decisions. Evaluations of predictions of this type have shown them to have a low degree of validity, often no better than would be produced by the random allocation of subjects. Statistical prediction, achieved by translating research findings based on samples previously processed by the system into predictive formulas, have sometimes reached a high degree of validity. Examples are the pioneering Mannheim and Wilkins Borstal prediction study and the parole prediction formula used in recent years in Britain as an aid to decision-making.

A weakness of such formulas for practical purposes is that they predict in terms of *probabilities* of the relevant outcome (recidivism), and for large proportions of the samples the probability may be near to 50%. Moreover, even if the probability of a particular result is very high, e.g., a 95% probability of further offending, there remains a 5% probability that this will not be the case. This raises the possibility of mistakenly designating a person as a risk ("false positives") or mistakenly designating him (her) as not being a risk ("false negatives"). Additional problems relate to the time frame within which the further offence is predicted and its seriousness. The prediction rate is often higher for petty offences than for serious ones. If not controlled for, a prediction of "dangerousness" may relate to a minor offence.

Legislation oriented toward incapacitation does not generally rely directly on either of the above predictive methods, but is generally based on assumptions that the accumulation of a number of past offences of certain types (or which have attracted certain penalties) is an indicator of future dangerousness and warrants the imposition of preventative sentences. While previous convictions are indeed a predictor of future offences, these will not necessarily be serious. Moreover, the degree of seriousness of the qualifying offences themselves may be in doubt. Surveys of prison populations in the preventive detention wings in Britain earlier in the century were found to comprise mainly petty offenders. Criticisms of this type are now being directed at some of the offenders caught by contemporary "three strikes" laws.

E. Retribution

This ancient concept may take many forms. In ancient societies punishment was often associated with expiation and appeasing the gods. The notion of an imbalance, and of the need to "right the wrong," however, continued independent of the religious associations. Thus the philosopher Immanuel Kant regarded the punishment of criminals as a "categorical" moral imperative—to be undertaken irrespective of any practical considerations—and even if society was about to disband. Hegel regarded punishment as the right of the criminal, and more recent retributivist thinkers have referred to the need to prevent or neutralize the unfair advantage that would accrue to the offender.

While retributivism has always had its adherents, it was for a long time overshadowed in the penological literature by the rehabilitationist ideal and other consequentialist objectives. Supporters of the rehabilitation model in particular tended to decry the idea of retributivism, which was perceived as an expression of public vengeance—primitive, cruel, and, above all, ineffective. Foremost among the critics were the psychoanalysts, who explained the "urge to punish" in terms of guilt and anger at those who apparently failed to repress their id (although criminality was also sometimes explained in terms of guilt deriving from too strong a superego). So what was the source of the revival of the retributivist approach in the 1970s?

The seeds of this revival were found in the disillusionment with the rehabilitation model prevailing at this time and the lack of convincing evidence in favor of other consequentialist objectives, as indicated by Martinson and his colleagues, and in the comprehensive reports subsequently published by the National Academy of Sciences. In 1976 a landmark volume was published by Andrew von Hirsch in the name of a committee which reviewed prevailing practices under the title *Doing Justice: The Choice of Punishments*. Citing the criticisms of the existing models, von Hirsch proposed a scheme of fixed sentences, proportional to the seriousness of the offence. This bore a strong resemblance to the classic model of Beccaria; but the rationale here was not deterrence but a moderate form of retribution, which came to be known as the justice, the desert, or the just deserts model.

As noted, the concept of proportionate sentencing was strongly supported by the "law-and-order lobby" on the political right, and there was a movement in favor of the restriction of sentencing discretion and the abolition of parole. New sentencing policies were developed, not only in the United States, but also in Britain, Sweden, and other countries, laying greater emphasis on the seriousness of the offence. There has been much debate as to the optimal method of achieving this, whether by restrictive legislative provisions, by the establishment of sentencing guidelines, or through the mechanism of tighter control of the appeal courts. The U.S. Congress established a Sentencing Commission for the development of sentencing guidelines, which substantially limit the sentencing powers of the federal criminal courts. Courts must state reasons for departure from the guidelines, and these are reviewable on appeal.

"Dessert" principles involve two concepts of proportionality, "ordinal" proportionality, whereby relatively more serious offences attract relatively harsher penalties, and "cardinal" proportionality, whereby the severity of the punishment is in some sense "equivalent" to the gravity of the offence. Von Hirsch laid greater emphasis on the former, stating that 5–6 years imprisonment would be sufficient for the worst crimes (other than homicide), while less serious crimes would attract proportionately lower penalties. Unlike Von Hirsch, however, legislators (and sentencing commissioners) have opted for relatively severe sentencing scales, as well as mandatory minima for selected offences, perhaps also seeking to achieve general deterrence. Moreover, they have tended to adopt lengthy sentences for repeat offenders, notably under the well-known "three strikes and you're out" provisions, whereby three convictions for certain offences may result in life sentences. These sentences suggest policies of incapacitation and individual (as well as general) deterrence, rather than merely "looking back" to the gravity of the offence. Thus desert principles have provided a framework for the promotion of other, after populist, objectives.

V. OTHER RECENT TRENDS

In addition to the tensions among the main (traditional) aims of punishment referred to above, other ideological trends may be discerned. While they are sometimes difficult to define precisely, three significant themes seem worthy of mention here.

A. Restorative Justice

This theme has given rise to a prolific literature and a very active reforming movement. It refers primarily to the concept of persuading the offender to recognize the wrong that he or she has inflicted and to take steps to right this wrong vis-à-vis the victim or the general community. The procedures involved may either replace the orthodox criminal process or be additional to it. Where there is a personal victim, a meeting may take place between the parties in order to achieve reconciliation.

Restorative justice in the above sense has been pioneered by religious writers and activists, predominantly those appertaining to minority groups such as the Menonites. Inspiration for this movement has been derived from other sources (via the writings of anthropologists on settlement dispute in primitive societies), and there are many subthemes and related ideologies. One is the concept of restitutive justice, fostered in particular by Burt Galaway, Joe Hudson, and their colleagues in Minnesota. Here there is a somewhat greater emphasis on financial reparation as the primary sanction. The criminal process thus gives rise to essentially civil remedies described by some adherents as a "civilizing" process.

Restitution advocates initially emphasized the potential of restitution for the rehabilitation of the offender; reparation to the victim would be a step toward the offender's socialization. Increasingly, however, this group has come to recognize the potential of such sanctions as remedies for the victim, and victim advocates are now among its vocal supporters. On the other hand, victim advocates have also sought the availability of restitution as a sanction within the traditional criminal process, and this is now reflected in many jurisdictions that require sentencing courts to consider restitution orders as part of the sentence. This, however, is only marginally related to the restorative–restitutive movement.

Yet another related concept is that of *community*. The community is seen as the appropriate framework for the resolution of conflicts. While this term has become a buzzword for the promotion of many of the ideas referred to here (as well as others to be considered below), it has also been the basis of more sophisticated political theory. John Braithwait and Philip Pettit's "republican" theory of justice falls into this category. The authors' restorative approach forms a part of a more comprehensive political philosophy and builds on

Braithwaite's earlier proposals for "reintegrative shaming." This, in turn, has given rise to experimentation in the field of criminal justice, particularly in New Zealand and Australia, in the context of "family conferencing."

B. "Managerialism"

This concept is rather the antithesis of an ideology. It purports to describe the criminal justice system in societies dominated by market economics in which no serious attempt is any longer being made to achieve any meaningful form of "justice," individualized treatment, or other consequentialist objectives. Offenders are merely warehoused and processed as cheaply as possible. This approach, which is also perceived as including a component of repression of the underclass, has been referred to by Malcolm Feeley and Jonathan Simon as the "new penology." Garland links this approach to a policy of the British conservative governments of the 1980s and 1990s of divesting the government of responsibility for crime control and placing it in the hands of the community (private policing, neighborhood watch, etc.).

C. Human Rights

While the preceding developments (certainly the last) suggest the contrary, there has been some movement in recent years to enhance the status of human rights in the penal system (as well as in other areas). A number of countries have been undergoing increasing constitutionalization in recent years. Examples are Canada, South Africa, Germany, and Israel. Further, there is a very wide adherence, at least formally, to the various international human rights instruments, with their prohibition of torture and other inhumane forms of punishment and treatment. While the fora for the enforcement of these standards are generally limited, Europe has an active Commission and Court of Human Rights. Moreover, efforts have increased lately to have war crimes prosecuted by international tribunals.

VI. CURRENT ISSUES

This section focuses on a number of issues which appear to merit separate consideration.

A. Capital Punishment

Since ancient times the death penalty has symbolized the ultimate expression of societal response to criminality. Since the 18th century, however, it has been challenged by Beccaria, among others, as both inhumane and ineffective as a deterrent. A significant movement in favor of abolition developed during the course of the 20th century (notably, in recent times, by Amnesty International). While attempts to secure an international prohibition on the part of the United Nations have not yet proven successful, states adhering to Protocol 6 of the European Convention on Human Rights undertake its abolition.

Nevertheless, following a brief interlude between 1972 and 1976 during which the U.S. Supreme Court held that this penalty, as then administered, was in violation of the Eighth and Fourteenth Amendments to the Constitution, it has undergone a revival in this country and operates in most states. The Court does, however, insist that certain procedures be adopted prior to its implementation and that the crime for which it is being imposed should be of sufficient heinousness (in effect restricting it to murder).

A related issue, faced particularly by abolitionist states, is the constitutionality of life imprisonment without the possibility of early release. Leon Sheleff has argued that for some this punishment may be as inhumane as death, and jurisdictions retaining such life sentences should offer defendants the option of capital punishment.

B. Prisons

Reference was made earlier to the disillusionment with the prison system as an agency of rehabilitation. It has come to be seen as an environment which socializes toward criminality and one in which violence flourishes. Yet recent years have witnessed a burgeoning prison population, especially in the United States, where it is well in excess of 1 million excluding local jails, and in Britain, where, while not reaching such dimensions, it has exceeded the rate of 100 prisoners per 100,000 inhabitants, which is perceived as high by European standards. While some observers explain these rates partly in terms of high rates of serious crime, exploding prison populations are generally perceived primarily as a reflection of more punitive policies and, in particular, of the sentencing reforms abolishing parole, limiting judicial discretion, and introducing "mandatory minimums."

Against this background, there is a virtual consensus in seeking to deal with acute problems of prisoner overcrowding. Even supporters of punitive policies, generally fiscal conservatives, are reluctant to bear the financial burdens involved. Thus the search for alternatives to imprisonment, promoted for many decades mainly by rehabilitationists, has gained widespread support.

C. Alternatives to Imprisonment

The main alternatives to imprisonment developed since the end of the past century have been the suspended sentence and probation. These were additional to the fine, the other alternatives of corporal punishment and transportation having fallen into desuetude. In recent decades, a host of new alternatives has developed: community service, halfway houses, boot camps, home confinement, electronic tagging, day reporting, and intensive probation, as well as diversion programs, restitution, and informal dispute resolution. Additionally, alternatives have been sought (including some of the above) for parole to facilitate the early release of prisoners, e.g., "good time" laws, administrative release, and the use of hostels for prisoners. In some countries legislation is invoked to coerce courts into using alternatives, e.g., by restrictions on the use of short-term prison terms. These developments have raised a number of issues, some of them central to penological discourse.

The main theoretical debate has related to the social analysis of the above developments. For while policymakers purported to be following a policy of decarceration (compared by Andrew Scull to the deinstitutionalization of mental patients taking place contemporaneously), some skeptics, such as Stanley Cohen, claimed that the alternative measures were *supplementing* the traditional punishments. There was thus a widening of the net of social control, akin to Foucault's "dispersal of discipline," giving rise to the creation of a "punitive society."

This debate has an empirical aspect. "Net-widening" takes place only insofar as the alternative measures are being used for offenders who were not actually candidates for prison. In this case offenders who would have been released or have received nominal sentences are now being subjected to more controlling measures. Most empirical studies show that while most alternatives are used for some offenders who would have been sentenced to imprisonment, they are also used for offenders who would not. Moreover, many of these offenders may now actually be incarcerated as a result of noncompliance with the conditions of their "alternative" sentence. Thus, paradoxically, the introduction of the suspended sentence in Britain gave rise to an *increase* in the use of imprisonment.

Another empirical issue arising here is the relative effectiveness of the alternatives in terms of rates of recidivism. Wide differences are not generally found, although where they exist they tend to favor the noncustodial alternative. (Such an effect was found in a recent evaluation of "service work" in Israel, where sentenced "prisoners" are allowed to remain at home and work for the community.) Finally, the relative costs of the various alternatives has also been the focus of interest.

By contrast, two further ideological issues may also be referred to. The first relates to the degree of severity to be attributed to noncustodial penalties and the extent to which they should be differentiated in this respect. Thus writers such as Norval Morris and Michael Tonry have decried the failure to discriminate between simple probation and the more controlling sanctions, arguing that the latter should be perceived as *intermediate* sanctions. Such analysis is crucial insofar as the sentencing system purports to be structured and proportionate, thus requiring a concept of a tariff of penalties.

The other issue relates to the concept of *community*. This term has been widely used both to designate specific dispositions, such as community service orders, and to describe a collectivity of sentencing alternatives: "community corrections." Some writers, notably David Nelken, have questioned these uses of the term and have pointed to its ambiguities as well as to the lack of meaningful community identities in most contemporary western societies. Others have linked the concept to prevailing communitarian ideas, as in the case of Pettit and Braithwaite's "republican theory" of justice referred to earlier.

D. Fines

This sanction has a unique combination of two characteristics: (a) it is undoubtedly the most widely used sanction in western societies and (b) it is also almost certainly the least researched and least analyzed of all the main sentencing alternatives. It has the attraction of generating income to the state rather imposing a burden, except in the cases in which enforcement processes are costlier than the payment or where the offender is imprisoned in default of payment.

The main problem with the fine, however, has undoubtedly been on the issue of fairness; that is, how far the amount of the fine levied should be adjusted to the economic standing of the offender and how this should be achieved. This issue has become more acute in the age of "desert" sentencing, for which reason the fine was omitted from the sentencing options advocated in *Doing Justice*. Following a model developed in Sweden and Germany, experimentation is now proceeding in New York with the day fine, whereby the fine is imposed by designating a number of "days" appropriate in terms of the gravity of the offence, the value of each day being subsequently determined for each offender according to his or her financial situation.

E. Sentencing Structures and Socioeconomic Variables

The problem of discriminatory sentencing, hinted at in the context of the fine (a wealthy offender is unlikely to receive imprisonment for default on payment), has been endemic to criminal justice. The problem arises both in the legislative and judicial contexts. Thus white-collar offenses, such as corporate frauds and breaches of antitrust laws, are more likely to be dealt with by noncriminal sanctions or noncustodial penalties. The highly individualized sentencing and parole processes characteristic of the rehabilitation model were also seen as giving rise to disparities, sometimes resulting from the personalities of individual judges, but frequently also operating systematically against racial minorities; and a body of research supports this view. Females, too, have been perceived as receiving differential treatment, benefiting on the one hand from "chivalrous" law enforcement, but penalized, on the other, for perceived immorality.

Structured sentencing models such as the sentencing guidelines were intended to reduce (indeed, eliminate) such discrimination. Discrimination may, however, be incorporated into the official norms, as illustrated by the severe penalties designated by the federal sentencing guidelines for the possession of crack cocaine (used primarily by minorities and the poor) as compared with the relatively low penalties for powder cocaine used by the professional and business classes. Moreover, other forms of discrimination may infiltrate the system at "low visibility" decision-making points in the system, such as prosecutors' charging decisions, which, given a fixed penalty system, will largely determine the sentence ultimately imposed upon the offender.

It may be noted in this context that in the *McCleskey* case (1987) the U.S. Supreme Court held that statistical evidence of systematic discrimination in the imposition of the death penalty would not amount to constitutional grounds for a challenge to its use in particular cases. (There is evidence of a higher probability of its imposition on the murderer of a White victim than a murderer of a Black victim.)

F. Punishment and the Victim

The victim's role in the penal system has been muted in western societies since the development of the con-cept of "King's Peace" and the clear differentiation between criminal and civil justice. The recent revival of interest in the victim has been reflected not only in the movement for restorative justice and the restitution programs referred to above, but also in pressures for a greater input in the criminal justice system. These are now reflected in the Victims' Bills of Rights and constitutional amendments adopted in most states of the U.S. and other reforms elsewhere.

One such reform is the Victim Impact Statement, whereby the effect of the crime on the victim is made known to the sentencing judge or jury. The views of the victim may also be made known, whether by means of a Victim Statement of Opinion or otherwise. Such procedures, while enhancing the victim's sense of involvement in the process, have the potential to reintroduce disparities in sentencing, since some of the victim-related input will be subjective; and some victims are vengeful, while others are not. Moreover, there is no uniformity as to when such information is to be made available. The enormous significance of this topic was evidenced in the case of *Payne v. Tennessee* (1991) in which the U.S. Supreme Court (overturning its earlier decisions) held that victim-related evidence was legitimately placed before the jury in a capital sentencing hearing—resulting in a death sentence.

VII. CONCLUSION

The desert ideology which replaced the rehabilitation model in the 1980s has to some extent been hijacked by incapacitation and other crime-control ideologies, as illustrated by the "three strikes" laws. The victim movement may give rise to a further reorientation of the system, whether by reinforcing the "law and order" emphasis but rendering this idiosyncratic, reflecting the variegated nature of victim responses, or possibly by moving the system in the direction of a restorative or community-oriented model. The latter may, in turn, rekindle the ashes of the rehabilitation model, which are periodically warmed by researchers claiming that some treatments do in fact work and by liberals pointing to the harshness of current retributive policies. Finally, the excesses of all of such orientations may be tempered by the pressures of human rights activists, relying on guarantees and protections enshrined in both national and international legal norms.

Also See the Following Articles

CHILDREARING, VIOLENT AND NONVIOLENT • CRIME AND PUNISHMENT, CHANGING ATTITUDES TOWARD • CRIMINAL

BEHAVIOR, THEORIES OF • CRIMINOLOGY, OVERVIEW •
DEATH PENALTY

Bibliography

Baithwaite J. & Pettit P. (1990). *Not just deserts: The Republican theory of justice.* Oxford: Oxford University Press.

Cavadino M. & Dignan, J. (1997). *The penal system: An introduction,* 2nd ed. London: Sage Publications.

Cohen, S. (1985). *Visions of social control.* Cambridge: Polity Press.

Durham A. M. III (1994). *Crisis and reform: Current issues in American punishment.* Boston: Little Brown.

Feeley M. & Simon, J. (1992). The new penology: Emerging strategy of corrections and its implications. *Criminology, 30,* 449–474.

Garland D. (1990). *Punishment and modern society.* Oxford: Clarendon Press.

Hood R. (1996). *The death penalty: A world-wide perspective,* rev. ed. Oxford: Clarendon Press.

Lacey N. (1988). *State punishment: Political principles and community values.* Routledge: London.

Morris N. & Tonry, M. (1990). *Between prison and probation.* New York: Oxford University Press.

Morris N. & Rothman, D. J. (eds.) (1995). *Oxford history of the prison.* New York: Oxford University Press.

Primoratz I. (1989). *Justifying legal punishment.* New Jersey: Humanities Press International.

Tonry M. (1996). *Sentencing matters.* New York: Oxford University Press.

von Hirsch A. (1976). *Doing justice: The choice of punishments.* New York: Hill and Wang.

Reason and Violence

Murray Code

University of Guelph

I. INTRODUCTION

An inquiry into the relation between reason and violence must inevitably confront anomalies that throw doubt upon the common assumption that reason is "sweet"—that reason generally functions to promote peace, prevent violence, and resolve conflicts. This sanguine view is belied by indications that reason is under the spell of a dangerously narrow conception of rationality. Alluding to this narrowness, the logician/mathematician/philosopher A. N. Whitehead observes (in *Process and Reality*): "it is said that 'men are rational.' This is palpably false: they are only intermittently rational—merely liable to rationality." His scientifically informed scepticism derives largely from the failure of modern thinkers to examine critically their most fundamental metaphysical assumptions about nature, a critical failure that contemporary socio-cultural, environmentally concerned critics argue applies to the whole of Western culture, or better nature-culture. Their wide-ranging critiques of modernity indicate that reason has a hidden, self-destructive side. The recently coined term

ecocide sums up the charge that an acritical Reason theorized under the aegis of modern science is mainly responsible for a spreading violence that threatens the long-term health of the whole planet. Science is accused in particular of promoting quasi-religious beliefs that legitimate a new form of Western imperialism that "denatures" nature, destabilizes "other" cultures, and destroys ecological equilibriums.

An overweening desire for domination and control is identified as the driving force behind a hegemonic Western Reason that both feeds into and upon a proliferating "techno-science." This desire infuses the problematic of reason and violence with an air of paradox. Despite the common belief that we live in an Age of Enlightenment, the more science acquires control over the symbolic order the more urgent becomes the question whether reason can be trusted to give a just, accurate, and detached account of itself. In other words, the reasonableness of reason may be one of the first victim's of reason's dark side. This supervening anomaly of reason suggests that anthropological studies of Western ideas and ideals of reason are as important as historical studies of their development, if not more so.

More specifically, dominant conceptions of reason and rationality may be in thrall to a powerful, intrinsically violent myth, which might be called the grand myth of scientific superrationality since scientific methods of inquiry are widely upheld as exemplifying the quintessence of rational thought. Science is moreover championed as the principal bastion against superstitious or irrational beliefs on account of its unrelenting critical gaze. Yet its interpreters and apologists rarely direct this gaze onto their most fundamental assumptions about rationality itself (which often need to be inferred from the type of imagery that is privileged in would-be rational discourse).

To address the problematic of reason and violence is thus ultimately to engage with the question whether and if so how a flawed culture enslaved to a "bad" myth can heal itself. At issue is how myth and metaphor enter into rational thought. Myths can be viewed as incorporating a society's general beliefs about how it should conduct its various activities of self-constitution, a view that is supported, ironically enough, by the overweening power of the myth of scientific superrationality which underwrites modes of thought that work to turn living organisms into machines and render entire cultures subservient to the economic powers of multinational corporations. This myth at the same time encourages denials of the centrality of myths and metaphors in knowledge-making. Yet inasmuch as the governing myths and guiding imagery, or metaphorics, of a society both reflect and are reflected by the kind and quality of the movements of reason that are deemed good and legitimate, these two "literary" aspects of thought are pivotal in the construction of knowledge. If this is so, the problematic of reason and violence needs to be framed in a context that acknowledges the role of imagination in world-making. A form of cultural therapy designed to overcome the longstanding repression of imagination that characterizes Western metaphysics may even be an essential first step to developing a more pacific or "artful" reason, as well as a more "delicate," non-violent scientific empiricism.

II. RAPACIOUS REASON

The belief that violence is foreign to good reasoning is implicit in uncritical references to Western "civilization" which tacitly assume its leading position in whatever progressive and uplifting currents run through the world. This view is reinforced by the remarkable successes of Western science that promise unlimited powers of penetration into the secrets of natural processes. But in an era in which the names of Hiroshima and Nagasaki have become inextricably linked to the idea of progress in understanding, it is far from obvious that progressive refinements in the reach, subtlety, and precision of formal methods of reasoning signify advances in civilization. Neither do such refinements manifestly produce sounder understandings of reason

itself, or attest to a positive direction in the evolution of rational thought.

Indeed, G. J. Warnock begins his article "Reason" in *The Encyclopaedia of Philosophy* by noting that "the word 'reason' has long had, and still has, a wide variety of senses and uses, related to one another in ways that are often complicated and often not clear." Furthermore, attempts to come to grips with the question "What can reason do?" raise almost every problem of philosophy. One definition—which informs much Anglo-American philosophy—is that it is the function of reason to identify, analyze, and symbolically organize the necessary aspects of thought. Although this approach strives toward an ideally pure and logical language in which unambiguous bivalent propositions about clearly individuated objects are amenable to precise, mechanical treatments, it is plagued by an endemic vagueness. This is because to reason rightly about worldly matters presupposes a sound basis of fundamental general concepts, most of which, however, are extremely vague. Thus reason is intrinsically rough: it has neither a definite meaning nor a clear place to stand. Nor has it the capacity to show whether, or how, it can be purified of such allegedly irrational elements as poetic imagination, ephemeral emotions, and vague intuitions.

Rather than viewing reason, then, as an abstract faculty or capacity of individual minds that can be systematically studied and purified, an account of reason's faults and virtues must start from the idea of a mental activity involving a variety of more or less homogeneous and harmonious movements of mind. Some of these movements may be rough in a violent sense.

In their introduction to *Reason and Violence*, an exposition of three key works of Jean-Paul Sartre, R. D. Laing, and D. G. Cooper, it is suggested that reason in the analytic mode is a constant source of violence since it characteristically attempts to knead concrete experience into a shape with which analytic-positive methods can cope. This violence is intimately bound up with rape. Not only do these self-consciously rational theories disconnect subject from object, mind from body, and intellect from emotion, they distort the very self-constitution of Western culture. Analytic reason promotes theories that divorce behavior from experience, individuals from society, societies from individuals, and persons or societies from the material world. According to Cooper, the link between the objectivizations of analytic-instrumental language and the violence done perceptually and conceptually to human reality in its full concrete being is illustrated in Sartre's account of the life history of Jean Genet. The original and life-forming crisis of Genet stemmed from the childhood experience of being treated as an object. This treatment was not, in Sartre's view, merely analogous to a rape; it was rape.

The aptness of the metaphor of rape for characterizing Western scientific thought is urged by some feminists who tie this trope to the stress placed on power and control in the pursuit of scientific understanding. The authors of the *Rape of the Wild*, for example, maintain that hate, and especially misogyny, as well as a lust for control over all the "lesser" or weaker creatures of nature, is endemic in science. Even those sciences that explicitly aim to improve the health and future well-being of life on this planet cannot be exempted from the charge of fostering a domineering attitude of disgust/contempt for nature, animals, and women. Much research in biology is based on the routine use and "sacrifice" of experimental animals on a massive scale. The assumption that the nonhuman world can be limitlessly exploited to serve male-centered interpretations of human needs and purposes is thus termed "androcentric biophobia." This summary description applies not only to overt interventionist and "objectivist" practices but also to the transformative techniques of biotechnology and genetic engineering that threaten drastic consequences for future ecosystems.

The metaphor of rape is most appropriate for modes of investigation where subjectivity is systematically violated; for acts of rape are not merely assaults on physical bodies, they are gross denials or violations of the subjectivity of their victims. Hence scientific methodology mimics rape wherever it effects an objectification of nature and its creatures. According to many feminists, negations or suppressions of subjectivity have defined modern science from its very birth. Maintaining that "the most far-reaching effect of the Scientific Revolution is the death of nature," Carolyn Merchant argues that the main import of this revolution lies not in the introduction of a new methodology but rather in a reconceptualization of reality. This reorientation pivots on a replacement of the metaphor of living organism as the metaphorical key to understanding nature by that of controllable machine. Renouncing the image of nature as an active, nurturing mother, the "new" scientists promoted instead mechanistic metaphors linked to a conception of matter as passive and composed of immutable entities subject only to the laws of locomotion. With desires for domination and mastery thus freed from scruples concerning the propriety of certain interventions into natural processes, aggressive methods of inquiry were given free license (p. 193). It was urged that Nature be treated as an inferior "other" whose secrets could be wrested from "her" by violent means

(e.g., by intrusive mining techniques and heat induced chemical reactions). Although such practices did not contrast sharply with the manipulations of medieval scientists, the attitudes of mind involved underwent a definite shift. The quest of alchemists, magi, or natural magicians for knowledge of the powers inherent in nature, which led them to manipulate natural objects, were governed by the belief that, as helpmates of nature, they were aping and assisting her natural, living processes. Hence their practices were subject to overriding ethical strictures.

That it is no accident that the first scientific "rapists" granted the power to treat nature as a female object were predominantly male is implicit in Genevieve Lloyd's study of *The Man of Reason*. This historical account of the symbolisms associated with the ideas and ideals of reason of Western thought is based on the claim that metaphors are not merely decorative literary devices. Lloyd argues that the metaphor of the "maleness" of reason functions in various more or less subtle ways in the reasonings of many of Western civilization's most illustrious and influential philosophers (such as Aristotle, Plato, Hegel, Rousseau, Descartes, and Kant). Denying the frequently reiterated claim that, in the words of Augustine, the mind has no sex, Lloyd argues that "maleness" has consistently been "associated with a clear, determinate mode of thought, femaleness with the vague and indeterminate" (p. 3). Even Rousseau and Descartes, who explicitly maintain that male and female minds have an equal capacity to grasp truths, align the Reason–non-Reason distinction with the male–female distinction. Indeed, Descartes firmly ties the latter distinction to the mind–body dichotomy and thus ultimately reinforces the sexual division of mental labour.

Briefly then, good knowing and reasoning has consistently been associated at the symbolic level with disciplined and dispassionate, transcendent "masculine" minds. By contrast, "feminine" minds are subservient to the body or inferior senses and are thus subject to "wild and uncontrolled" impulses and irrational emotions, not to mention "soft" ideas. Yet "softness" generally connotes vagueness and ambiguity which are characteristics of words common to all natural languages. Nonetheless 20th century positivists have tended to view vagueness and ambiguity as the principal enemies of rational ("hard") thinking. Like Descartes such thinkers are inspired by the alleged purity and certainty of mathematical knowledge and yearn for a rigorous scientific and philosophic discourse modeled on the precise symbolisms of logico-mathematical systems. The influential philosopher-logician Gottlob Frege, for example, explicitly urges a logistic interpretation of the function of reason, holding that one of the chief merits of logic is its ability "to break the power of the word over the human mind" (Nye, 1990). Illustrating thereby the close affinity in the modern mind between knowledge and power, Frege also indicates the kind of violence that modern reason is inclined to commit upon itself. Not only does it repress the problematic aspects of its favorite metaphors and tropes (which, in the case of Frege, depict an allegedly impartial logic acting coercively like a hammer), it tends to deny altogether that tropes and metaphors play a significant role in rational discourse.

The idea that extremely vague general concepts (such as reason itself) should be amenable to precise, systematic, logistic analyses indicates that many self-proclaimed rigorous thinkers are victims of a "formal" mystification. Referring to this possibility, Sandra Harding holds that the restrictive, secretive nature of dominant Western conceptions of rigorous scientific methods recall mystical belief systems with no grounding in explicit assumptions. She traces these mystifications to the assumptions that structure the policies and practices of Western social institutions, assumptions that posit as necessary and/or as facts the dichotomies—culture/nature, rational mind/prerational body and irrational emotions and values, public/private, objectivity/subjectivity—where men and masculinity are linked to the first half and women and femininity to the second half. The problems created by such dichotomies, she argues, run so deep that they cannot be resolved merely by removing obstacles to including women in science.

For Harding, then, the Woman Question in science must be kept distinct from the *Science Question in Feminism*: the problem of how to conceive other, different ways of knowledge-making less inimical to feminist ideals. Claiming that the proper way to do science ought to be the chief concern of feminist critics of science, Harding notes that gender metaphors (involving rape and torture of a female Nature) can be as fruitful (pragmatically, methodologically, metaphysically) as mechanistic metaphors (p. 113). She suggests moreover that it might be more illuminating and honest to refer to "Newton's mechanics" as "Newton's rape manual." Harding's critique thus leads to a question similar to the one Frege prompts: should the choice of imagery and tropes be a focus of concern in evaluating Western conceptions of rationality?

But the very idea that reason is ultimately governed by privileged metaphors and tropes meets strong resistance in analytic thinkers for whom such devices serve merely to decorate texts. Since nonsystematic imagina-tion is involved in choosing tropes, the legitimacy, or otherwise, of this sort of creative activity bears directly on the question whether there is an ineradicable ideological dimension to all rational discourse. Vigorous denials of just this possibility have fueled the "Science Wars," where critics of science argue that it is a socially constructed and sociologically peculiar practice—a claim firmly rejected by many defenders of science who accuse the "culturists" (feminists, anthropologists, historians, and other "science studies" scholars) of promoting antienlightenment prejudices that foster the spread of unreason. A special issue of *Social Text* reveals the range of issues involved. These issues stretch from technological ethics through the cultural consequences of scientific expansion to the effects on individual lives of scientific constructions of sex and gender.

Defending their dispassionate objectivity with passionate fervor, many defenders of scientific rationality confirm Donna Haraway's suspicion that denial of fears and desires is characteristic of the *Modest Witness*. This figure, an ideal agent-spectator who emerged as an invisible amasser of truths with the advent of the "new" science, poses as a completely neutral recorder of nature's own disclosures. Yet betraying at least a tropic taste for rape, the modest witness has pursued explanatory goals, Haraway argues, that are neither modest nor ideologically innocent. Modern biology, which elevates the gene (or DNA) to the status of "master molecule" capable of underwriting all interpretations of the organic world, shows that the modest witness is as much culture-producing as a cultural product. Against an exclusive physicochemical interpretation of gene and genome, Haraway argues that biology as an all-embracing discourse needs to be engaged at many levels: "technically, semiotically, morally, economically, institutionally" (p. 104). Hence the transformation of a "material-semiotic entity" into a guarantor of life bespeaks a kind of "gene fetishism." She thus prompts the question: how could a fetish acquire wide-ranging (albeit unacknowledged) powers as a natural, cultural, and political agent?

That the answer involves the need for liberation from a certain monopolistic hold over choice of fundamental metaphysical concepts is suggested by the geneticist Richard Lewontin. In his account of *Biology As Ideology*, Lewontin stresses that the ascription of causal agency to genes is completely without empirical foundation. Nonetheless influential proponents of molecular genetic theory maintain that the development of individual physical or mental traits is determined by the configuration of nucleotide sequences in DNA molecules. Yet genes, Lewontin points out, only influence what may or may not be realized under given environmental conditions. The story of the role of genes in the dynamic processes of organic development is far more complex than is generally acknowledged, for "a living organism at any moment in its life is the unique consequence of a developmental history that results from the interaction of and determination by internal and external forces" (p. 118).

Lewontin's concerns go far beyond the merely intellectual since interpretations of causality influence how life itself is generally viewed. Only a powerful cultural force seems capable of sustaining an acritical metaphysical belief in the causal agency of genes which presupposes the prevalence of simple unitary causes in nature, a metaphysical presupposition that quantum physics, for example, has thoroughly undermined. Yet acritical deterministic interpretations of causality are commonly presupposed by the proponents of the neo-Darwinian interpretation of evolution, a situation that illustrates the power of a scientific theory (whose simplicity is championed as one of its chief virtues) to render invisible the very complexity of existence. Lewontin thus draws attention to an important, perhaps vital consideration: organic existence always and everywhere exemplifies complex dynamic tensions involving internal and external forces.

Yet biological determinism, as Lewontin notes, is not only the mainstream commitment of biologists, it underwrites sociobiological attempts to ascribe racial and gendered differences in intellectual ability to identifiable gene sequences. Hence biological determinism is far from ideologically innocent, as is indicated by its extension to sociobiology where it is applied "without a shred of evidence and in contradiction to every principle of biology and genetics" (p. 26). The ideological foundation of this doctrine is also illustrated by the Human Genome project which is premised on the claim that all we want to know about human beings is contained in the sequence of their DNA. This globally ambitious undertaking has spawned an industry, in whose expensive technology many leading biologists have a personal financial stake, that reflects and supports an individualistic economical and political ideology which aims to maintain "a society of inequality" (p. 37).

Lewontin sums up the excursions of sociobiology into the cultural sphere (where it is even proposed that there are genes for religiosity) as "the latest and most mystified attempt to convince people that human life is pretty much what it has to be and perhaps even ought to be" (p. 89). He thereby adds fuel to the suspicion that the violence of scientific reason is intimately bound up with mystifications inherent in prevailing scientific language. This lack of transparency is typical of quasi-

religious belief systems. Indeed, Lewontin claims that science in the 20th century has supplanted religion as the principal institution of social legitimation. His critique thus intensifies the cultural puzzle to which Harding and Harroway allude: who, or better, could be responsible for the mystifications and fetishes that underpin scientistic beliefs and projects? What cultural force might have sufficient power to invest science, as the dominant institution of social legitimation, with the authority to dictate instead of argue for beliefs that govern how we think and live?

III. RATIONALITY OR RATIONALITIES?

There is good reason to view rationality as a fundamental human concern, especially if, as Robert Nozick maintains, the intellectual health of this society is at stake. In *The Nature of Rationality*, Nozick describes rational thought as the human capacity that gives its bearers a special status in the universe. Maintaining that it is necessary to become familiar with its scientific or technical aspects, he describes his own approach to rationality as "awash in technical details"—e.g., of decision theory, game theory, probability theory, and theories of statistical inference. Although Nozick acknowledges that a concentration on scientific theories renders debates on rationality inaccessible to large portions of even a well-educated population, there is, in his view, no alternative. The peculiar scientific climate of the present era sets it radically apart from previous eras in which such discussions were accessible to any intelligent people willing to make the effort. But it is no longer possible to understand and think about society or people or the universe at large without becoming immersed in scientific theories. Furthermore, not only is a grasp of technical knowledge necessary for participation in the most fruitful and interesting lines of inquiry into rationality, says Nozick, the very terms for evaluating rationality itself have also become technical.

The critics of science indicate, however, that the scientific approach to evaluation simply begs the question of the meaning of rationality. Short of denying that there is an ideological dimension to science and reason, the would-be rational actor must first address the problem of choice of perspective. That a scientific perspective can never be made ideologically innocent becomes increasingly evident as the boundary between nature and culture becomes ever more indistinct. Haraway's account of OncoMouse, the first patented laboratory animal (genetically engineered to develop breast cancer), dramatically illustrates the point. This technoscientific "object" belongs as much to the category of marketable commodities as to the category of natural creatures. Haraway's general claim that technoscience is both a cultural practice and a practical culture thus translates into the observation that what a culture makes is a sign of what it is making of itself. And OncoMouse, who dwells in the hazy borderland between nature and culture, is a "monster" whose very existence holds up a mirror to the technoscientific perspective. Thus Haraway poignantly sums up the problem of evaluation when she asks: "what counts as nature, for whom, and at what cost?" (p. 75).

That the costs of the Western technoscientific perspective are as morally and spiritually high as they are globally far-reaching is argued by a number of Indian writers. They note that the most powerful upholders of the propriety of dispassionate, precise scientific methods tend to be white, European, male, and affluent. Collected under the provocative title of *Science, Hegemony and Violence*, their essays focus in particular on the destructive impact of modern scientific techniques on "little cultures." Some of these authors contend that the violence institutionalized on a world-wide scale in the name of scientific values (e.g., efficiency, cost-effectiveness, and economy of effort) is, in effect, the product of a distorted, if not pathological, culture. According to Vandana Shiva (in "Reductionist Science as Epistemological Violence") a necessarily violent reductionism is behind the destructive effects of monocultural practices in farming and forestry and the spread of health problems that accompany the displacement of natural products by synthetic drugs. These practices base their legitimacy on the twin myths of progress (i.e., material prosperity) and superior rationality. Other authors note that people are remarkably willing to make enormous sacrifices in the name of Western scientific values, which suggests that powerful myths are indeed involved in the spread of Western civilization. For these exercises of reason tend not only to weaken local cultures, they render whole populations powerless by undemocratic manipulations.

Sir Karl Popper's influential interpretation of rationality is another indication that Western conceptions of good reasoning valorize heroic aggression and competition at the expense of nondestructive or cooperative ways of living in the world. He deploys a martial rhetoric which enlists a neo-Darwinistic interpretation of evolution with its emphasis on the doctrine of the survival of the fittest. Popper claims, for instance, that a decisive feature of science is that scientists vigorously criticize their own theories with the aim of "killing them off." The cost of failure here is immense, he says, since a believer—whether animal or human—perishes with his false beliefs. The critical work of scientists, then, is directed toward making their own and other theories die in their stead, so that the art of argument is imaged as a peculiar form of the art of fighting—with words instead of swords.

Concerned about the global costs of this neo-Darwinian interpretation of rationality, Paul Feyerabend (Popper's former student) maintains that Popper's "critical rationalism" trivializes both reason and knowledge. In *Farewell to Reason*, Feyerabend argues for a distinction between Reason and reason, where the capitalized term refers to pure thought based on abstract categories. "Reason" and "Rationality," says Feyerabend, have acquired enormous and unwarranted beatifying power that can make almost any idea or procedure intellectually respectable. These "words of power" are especially effective in the steady expansion of Western civilization into all areas of the world and particularly in the pursuit of "developmental" projects that claim impartiality. While Feyerabend is equivocal about whether the power exercised in the name of science warrants the label "pathological," he observes that "Western science has now infected the whole world like a contagious disease" (p. 297).

Objecting that the idea of a monolithic Science is both dishonest and distorting, Feyerabend defends a form of relativism. Yet any claim that knowledge is dependent in part on the times and places of its articulations evokes the objection that standards of rationality are under threat. Nonetheless, argues Feyerabend, there *is* no universal standpoint from which all knowledge claims and reasonings *can* be judged. Hence rather than pursuing the dream of a unified Science or universal Reason, the honest rational enquirer ought in the first instance to acknowledge the plurality of the sciences. Such an admission, Feyerabend maintains, would be consonant with empirical principles anyway, since the events and results that constitute the sciences evidence no common unifying structure.

Thus Feyerabend insists that his "farewell to reason" neither amounts to a renunciation of reasoning and argument nor to an invitation to "irrational" (e.g., mystical, nihilistic, or superstitious) modes of thought. Although he advocates "epistemological anarchy," this is not tantamount to saying "anything goes," that there is no need to be concerned about the nature of the objective world. Rather, "epistemological anarchy" heralds the end of modes of thought that destroy or suppress the regionalism of natural and social phenomena. Feyerabend's critique of Reason and Science thus meshes with feminist and other critiques that emphasize (in

Haraway's term) the "situatedness" of all knowledge-making. The upshot is a general call for a radical revision of rationality, one that envisions not one dominant universal Rationality but rather a commonwealth of local rationalities.

IV. REASON, NATURE, AND CULTURE

If would-be rational thought is infected by dubious but hidden assumptions then further exploration of the problematic of rationality requires some rough conception of a rational actor. Such a creature is as much a child of nature as of whatever culture he/she inhabits, for all human beings are raised and trained in the midst of natural forces and cultural influences. Furthermore, there is no way for a communicating creature to discourse about the events of his/her life and environment without drawing upon the expressive resources of some culture. These elementary observations indicate that since nature, society, and discourse always come intimately bound together, no movement of reason in this world is ever pure, but is always a reflection of the nature-culture in which it is embedded.

Here an anomaly arises, since to take science even a little seriously is tacitly to acknowledge the everlasting relevance of nature, that shadowy presence that is both called forth only to be left waiting in the wings of many modern stories about science. Nature is curiously missing even from the writings of philosophers of science who style themselves "naturalists," although "the laws of nature" are objects of frequent reference. W. V. Quine, for instance, urges that philosophy be viewed as naturalism which he claims is continuous with science—for science tells us "how reality 'really' is" (Code, 1995). According to this view science provides philosophers both with the proper objects of investigation and with the framework within which investigations are to be conducted.

This "denatured" naturalism, which conflates science with nature while promoting a willful ignorance of metaphysics, is endemic to modern thought. As E. A. Burtt shows in his classic study of *The Metaphysical Foundations of Modern Science*, a combination of wishful thinking and early successes in the use of mathematical methods led early modern "naturalists" to refuse to face the anomalies in their metaphysical beliefs. Instead, they strove to ascribe ultimate reality and causal efficacy to mathematics. And they found it easier to get ahead in reducing nature to a system of mathematical equations by assuming that nothing exists outside the human mind that was not so reducible. Hence a successful

method transformed itself into a metaphysics, and all distractions, such as the qualitative characteristics of events, simply vanished from the world.

But when a reductive method becomes a metaphysics that downgrades, where it does not actually abolish, salient aspects of ordinary experience, vital metaphysical, social, political, and moral factors are also suppressed or repressed. This violence is so subtle and pervasive that it infects even the strongest critics of the "denaturalization" of nature. Burtt himself plays down the "ethico-social" implications of "progress," "control," and the like, claiming that "in the last analysis it is the ultimate picture which an age forms of the nature of its world that is its most fundamental possession. It is the final controlling factor in all thinking whatever" (p. 17).

However, the problem that Burtt raises (why is the main current of modern thought what it is?) requires a very broad perspective that cuts across both nature and culture, especially since denials and negations of ordinary experience accompany claims that the hallmark of science, the epitome of modern thinking, is the readiness of its practitioners to take experience seriously and to engage critically with fundamental beliefs. The remarkable tolerance of modern Western thought for this contradiction is especially evident in the popularity of science writers who emphasize the superiority of the scientific critical gaze for exposing superstitions and pseudoscience (as in, for example, Carl Sagan's *The Demon-Haunted World: Science as a Candle in the Dark*).

A mode of thought that insists on its own skeptical stance and empirical methods while exempting its fundamental assumptions from criticism invites, at the very least, a charge of hypocrisy. But not even those who level this charge, or who accuse science of fostering oppressive, imperialistic, ecocidal, and globally threatening policies and practices, accuse it of promoting a worldwide conspiracy based on conscious lies and cynical deceptions. Defensive, often unconscious, propaganda, Bryan Appleyard suggests, is the means by which Western science promotes and protects its burgeoning powers and destructive tendencies. Yet despite "the appalling spiritual damage" science has done and is continuing to do, Appleyard stops short of ascribing evil intentions to the propagandists of science. Rather, willful ignorance has led science to a point where it is incapable of coexisting with nature.

Or would it be better to say that an unconscious cultural *telos* with roots buried deep in the past is required to explain pervasive unconscious repressions and suppressions? The trouble is, repressed ontological-epistemological factors are not any easier to identify and classify than ideological, psychoanalytical, or spiritual ones. Furthermore, inasmuch as propaganda, too, amounts to a subtle form of violence (as Simone Weil, for instance, maintains), its power is not unlike that of the almost-invisible myths and mystifications referred to by many critics of modern science. Harding, for example, describes science's story about itself as a kind of "origins myth" which invests the ideology of science with an aura of sacredness, thus absolving it from having to submit its creations to close critical scrutiny. Indeed, the effectiveness of propaganda suggests that it is a debased form of myth, which indicates that myth itself may provide a key to understanding the contorted relations between Reason and the self-constitution of modern Western culture.

Addressing the empirical question of the actual processes of this self-constitution, Bruno Latour bases his critique of modern thought on anthropological studies of how technoscience is fashioned in the laboratory. Latour suggests that modernity is characterized throughout by an attempt totally to separate nature, culture, and discourse. This concerted effort to establish a "Great Divide" (i.e., a sharp boundary between humans and nonhumans) is legitimized by an unspoken Constitution that enshrines a contradiction. For the modern Constitution allows for "the expanded proliferation of the hybrids whose existence, whose very possibility, it denies" (p. 34). The term "hybrid" refers to an amalgamation of elements drawn from the three fundamental critical resources of nature, culture, and discourse; examples of which are a nuclear power plant, a hole in the ozone layer, or a map of the human genome. Thus despite overt claims to be engaged in works of purification, modern thought is, on the contrary, empowered by a hidden Constitution to create increasingly complex and problematic "quasi-objects" that trace both forms of nature and forms of society. Yet this work of mediation is "invisible, unthinkable, unrepresentable" (p. 34).

Latour's account of how networks of hybrids proliferate evokes an image of this planet becoming increasingly covered by ever more finely spun "networks of power" that concentrate its exercise in the hands of a privileged few. For the networks of hybrids are analogous to the maps drawn by the original cartographers of the European empire-builders, which radiated their exercises of power from "centers of accumulation" (e.g., of information). Such maps provided their makers with the means to act at a distance. Likewise, networks of technoscientific hybrids provide modern Reason with the means to extend its domains of influence indefinitely.

The great successes of hegemonic Reason, in sum, do not stem from a superior Rationality but rather from superior techniques for making and extending these networks of power. But these successes come at a high cost—a self-contradictory mode of thought that betrays Enlightenment ideals even as it promotes the virtues of reason. Thus Latour's comparative anthropology of science elicits a need not only for a parallel anthropology of reason to explain how Western Rationality has achieved its dominance over that of other, "weaker" cultures, but also a need for something like a psycho (cultural) analysis. For the fears, denials, contradictions, and repressions that are integral to modernity's ability to silence other voices (since whatever cannot be connected to the web of Reason is doomed to remain mute) are also instrumental in concealing its underlying contradictions.

Some tricky epistemological-ontological questions emerge at this point. Even if, as Latour maintains, the technoscientific hybrids created under the aegis of the modern Constitution are neither purely scientific nor purely social constructions, but always impure amalgams of nature-culture, the nature factor implies they are not "free-floating." What then keeps them from drifting off into the blue? If one grants that science has established *some* objective (albeit very vague and general) "facts" about nature with near certainty—for instance, that nature is evolutionary from bottom to top, from the microcosmos to the macrocosmos—the material aspects of hybrids means they are tied "below" by natural forces (e.g., gravity), however loosely. In addition, the myths of the culture "above" appear to provide a ceiling for the more volatile (e.g., speculative) products of the movements of reason. Hence these myths may explain the character and quality of the movements themselves.

V. WORDS WITH POWER

For the moderns, the phrase "science tells us..." conveys great power. But this power, the critics of modernity suggest, owes more to myth than to reason. Indeed, they can be read as asking what else except a grand myth—the myth of scientific superrationality—could render almost invisible so important a figure as nature while "naturalizing" the idea that science is uniquely capable of telling objective truths about it? And what else could sustain the belief that science is, without prejudice, capable of deciding what comes within the purview of rational inquiry? Or lend such widespread credence to the view that science is not only autonomous and self-justifying but also warranted in intervening, often violently, in all natural processes both on or off the earth? This grand myth colors not only our understanding of the esoteric deliverances of science; it exerts an influence in places where reason is generally thought to move independently of science. To take just one example (cited by Haraway, 1997, p. 90): in 1980 the U.S. Supreme Court affirmed the patentability of a living organism (a genetically modified oil-eating bacterium) on the ground that it was a "composition of matter." Yet "matter" refers to nature and hence (since it is an extremely vague fundamental idea) is susceptible to different metaphysical interpretations, a fact that the myth of scientific superrationality helps to conceal.

Hence the importance of myths and how they work. Myths are quite unlike scientific or logical propositions that can be classified as either true or false. Myths can only be evaluated roughly as more or less reliable guides to, say, life-enhancing beliefs and customs, responsible institutions, or fruitful theorizing about some aspect of nature-culture. Although some myths look like fictional stories, their real significance pertains to the social dynamics of their culture, according to Northrop Frye. No society, says Frye, can be understood without attending to its dominant myths since they encode what that society is trying to make of itself, for better or for worse. Furthermore, ideologies always presuppose myths and not the other way around. This order of precedence is crucial since "the mythology, good or bad, creates the ideology, good or bad" (p. 25).

In Frye's view there are two, only roughly distinguishable, orders of myth—primary and secondary—whose differences reflect the distinction between primary and secondary concerns. Secondary concerns underwrite dominant ideologies. But ideologies arise from attempts to realize ideals inspired by more primary concerns; those relating to health and illness, happiness and misery, life and death. Primary myths thus bear more directly on everyday existence; that is, on the places where human creatures experience their most intimate contacts with nature. Thus Frye opens a way to understand modern reason's highly ambivalent, often violent relations with nature, for the axioms of primary concern—such as that life is better than death—are forever at risk of being subverted by secondary concerns. As an example of the subversive power of secondary myths, Frye cites declarations of war, an example that (as will be seen later) resonates with interpretations of the current ecological crisis that also enlist the imagery of war.

Although he does not describe his thoughts in these terms, secondary myths are the principal theme of Ro-

land Barthes's celebrated article "Myth Today." But rather than distinguishing between orders of myth, Barthes describes myth *tout court* as a type of speech that works to "naturalize" ideologically motivated ideas and values. Inserting themselves silently into language, myths institute the uncriticized ideas and beliefs of the currently powerful. Thus myths fulfill their principle which is, says Barthes, to transform history into nature.

One of Barthes's examples is therefore particularly suggestive. He reads the subterranean text implicit in a photograph of a Black soldier in the act of saluting the French flag as an alibi for French imperialism. That is to say, this phototext "naturalizes" a history of colonialist aggression, suppression, and exploitation by invoking the hallowed figure of patriotism. The myth of scientific superrationality seems to work in a similar way, concealing a history of aggressive, imperialistic methods and aims behind a banner of universal and impersonal objective truth, all the while rendering ineffectual or invisible local modes of reasoning and experiencing. Barthes also holds that myth can reach everything, corrupt everything; a charge that resonates with Latour's image of duplicitous modernity endlessly creating and extending its uncriticizable networks of power. For myth in Barthes's view stubbornly resists criticism from the inside. It is not as if myth were invisible, for myth must make its presence felt in order to be influential. Like Harding's origins myth that surrounds science with an aura of the sacred, or like Latour's modern Constitution, myth is invincible.

Yet Barthes himself shows that myth is not absolutely uncriticizable—that sarcasm or irony is not the only mode of discourse open to the "mythologist." As Frye observes, irony cannot make its point as irony without pointing beyond itself. Hence questions of better or worse haunt every use of the word "myth." Although a good many secondary myths are, in Barthes's terms, "falsely obvious," not all myths are obviously false. The real difficulty in criticizing a myth is to determine whether it underwrites imperatives and intentions that are, on the whole, good; that is, whether they contribute to, say, what Frye calls "life in more abundance."

While few deny that science has produced a cornucopia of material benefits, such as the life-enhancing technical devices of medical science (but see the essay of Kothari and Mehta in Nandy, 1988), the adjective "material" is a reminder that social and spiritual costs are equally plentiful. As for what some of these costs are, Barthes's observation that myths exert an insidious, irresistible pressure on ordinary language, provides a hint. If Whitehead is right and "the souls of men are the gift from language to mankind" (p. 41), then the charge that myth distorts language by corrupting historically constituted linguistic meanings through instituting narrow, life-constricting formal meanings is serious. That the myth of scientific superrationality is guilty of betraying a sacred trust is in effect the gist of protests, for example, that the notion of local or psychological time is "flattened" or impoverished whenever it is modeled using the linear mathematical continuum. This reductive move, which replaces complexity by mere complicatedness (to use a distinction of Frye's) does a kind of violence to past, present, and future human experience, for time is integral to how human beings shape and live their worlds.

Philosopher of science Michel Serres is especially concerned with the violence that science does to the meaning of temporality by forcing time to flow in a linear fashion. Strongly influenced by Simone Weil, whom he reads as the first philosopher to speak of violence in all its dimensions. Serres examines how Western thought treats the large themes of time and passage, history and language, nature and culture. In *The Natural Contract*, Serres specifically ties science to the human animal's disrespectful attitude toward nature, even claiming that ours is a culture that "abhors the world" (p. 3). The pollution of the environment is not merely the accidental result of involuntary acts; rather, it reveals deep intentions and a primary motivation. In their references to the environment that surrounds them human beings betray the assumption that they are at the center of the system of nature. Driven by a desire for mastery and possession their behavior more closely resembles that of a parasite, which pursues its own interests exclusively (taking everything and giving nothing back), thus destroying equilibria and ultimately killing its host.

According to Serres, then, the term "pollution" should not be reserved exclusively for nature. Growing industrial activities and technological prowess bear witness to the hegemony of three contemporary powers—scientists, administrators, and journalists. These powers are wielded by "men of the short-term" who have inflicted a cultural pollution on long-term thoughts: "those guardians of the Earth, of humanity, and of things themselves." The upshot is an eradication of "long-term memory, the thousand-year-old traditions, the experience accumulated by cultures that have just died or that these powers are killing" (pp. 30–31). Since myths (following Frye) are the chief guardians of long-term thoughts, Serres adds weight to the charge that modern conceptions of reason and rationality are thoroughly infected by pernicious secondary myths. Indeed, he specifically alludes to (and denies) one of the major

components of the grand myth of scientific superrationality—that science has abolished all need for myth. On the contrary, says Serres, there is only one pure myth: that of a science purified of all myths.

An image thus emerges of humanity and nature facing each other across a deepening chasm. Modern science, says Serres, has helped push humanity to a place unique in its history. Attempting to convey the urgency of the situation, Serres proffers a more dynamic image, of a world transformed by Western civilization into a ship heading toward a rocky bar. It is not enough, in his view, to legislate environmental protection laws, replant devastated forests, and so on. A complete change of course is necessary. What is needed to stop the spreading violence is, in brief, a new myth—a Natural Contract. Only such a contract can rescue nature from its lowly position as victim and acknowledge its status as a subject with inviolable rights. Serres models his Natural Contract on the legendary Social Contract usually depicted as marking the beginning of societies: the decision of human beings to live together, join forces, and acknowledge their mutual interdependence, often for the express purpose of keeping violence in check. It is not a valid objection that the Social Contract is only a myth. It is a good myth, Serres suggests, in that it promotes a concern for others based on respect, attention, and reciprocity instead of a drive for mastery or control.

But a Natural Contract proffers only a hope; namely, that would-be rational thought is capable of achieving a more just and pacific relationship with nature. Whether this hope can be fulfilled is bound up with questions such as: why think a seriously ill, perhaps self-destructive, civilization could be cured by a new mythology? Can a new, healthier myth of rationality be willed or negotiated into existence? How could such a long-term enterprise be undertaken by short-term means (if the three contemporary powers that have entrenched current conceptions of rationality have, as Serres believes, no counterpowers)?

The outlook for cultural change through mythology is not bright if myths, as Barthes maintains, generally act "as a prohibition for man inventing himself" (p. 170). Indeed, it appears that one and only one act of self-invention is permissible under the aegis of the myth of scientific superrationality—the one in which the human animal convinces itself that it is, as Richard Dawkins (professor of Public Understanding of Science at Oxford University) puts it, nothing but "a survival machine." Cognitive scientists reinforce this neo-Darwinistic view of life (which is, so Dawkins argues in many books, nothing but a stream of genes transmitting encoded information from one generation to the next) by promoting the doctrine that thought is a by-product of information-processing brains that can be imaged as "organic machines."

The causally oriented, mechanistic imagery of popular scientific storytelling militates against a humble acknowledgment of the mysterious connection between subjects and objects. Yet only scientific faith in a future final clarification stands in the way of acknowledging that every account of perception must sooner or later privilege some type of imagery for treating what is probably an intrinsically blurry relationship. In other words, how one chooses to bridge the gulf between subjects and objects, and between human agents and nature, depends as much, if not more, on imagination and myth as on systematic investigations. Serres implies as much in calling for a global act of self-invention in which human beings will give back to the word "nature" its original meaning, "our natal and native conditions, the conditions in which we are born—or ought to be reborn tomorrow" (p. 44). At the personal level an act of self-invention is clearly impossible without imagination. But together with feelings and intuitions, imagination is alien to modern thought which valorizes explanations and descriptions based on mechanistic imagery. Few ideas can be more foreign to a machine than that of an imaginative insight.

VI. IMAGINING A MORE PACIFIC REASON

Harding's question thus goes to the heart of the matter—whether we can "imagine what a scientific mode of knowledge-seeking would look like that was not concerned to distinguish between objectivity and subjectivity, reason and the emotions" (p. 24). Along with many other feminists, she is skeptical as to whether there is anything morally and politically worth redeeming or reforming in the scientific worldview (a skepticism that extends from its underlying epistemology to the practices this legitimates). Indeed, insofar as this worldview depends at bottom on an imagery that both underwrites and derives from a violent reason, something far more radical than reform is required.

According to John Sallis, a repression of imagination is characteristic of the self-constitution of Western metaphysics. The history of Western philosophy records a strange dynamic between reason and imagination in which metaphysics both appropriates imagination and excludes it. Many "continental" philosophers have thoroughly exposed and criticized the covert uses of imagination in Western metaphysics. However their arguments for "the end of metaphysics" do not, according to Sallis, entail an end in the sense of showing the intrinsic impossibility of this mode of inquiry. Postmodern critiques of metaphysics only undermine a traditional view of metaphysics as a "drive to pure presence" wherein the truth will stand revealed without the intervention either of reason or imagination. In short, then, pronouncements of "the end of metaphysics" only announce the end of a prolonged conflict between reason and imagination: they herald a "return of the repressed—a release of imagination into the entire field" (p. 15).

It is possible to mention here only a few of the implications for a nonviolent reason of this dramatic "return." One line of thought, already present in the philosophical writings of S. T. Coleridge, postulates a primitive form of imagination which is necessary to explain the interactions between subjectivity and objectivity. He claims, in effect, that Kant was initially and insightfully right in the first edition of his *Critique of Pure Reason* when he proposed that the necessary synthesis of the sensible and the intelligible in acts of cognition depended upon a faculty of imagination (which he described as "a blind but indispensable function of the soul"). Despite Kant's subsequent retreat from the radical implications of this claim (that free, or creative, imagination is involved in the constitution of experience) and despite his ingenious efforts to subsume imagination under explicit rules of the understanding, an intrinsically untameable "primary imagination" (to use Coleridge's term) may be the *sine qua non* both for knowledge and reason.

Since Kant's *Critique of Pure Reason* is a pivotal text in the history of Western metaphysics, a reversal of his retreat from a productive or creative imagination might induce a revolutionary change in conceptions of reason and rationality. But Kant was not the first philosopher to broach the idea of a primitive form of imagination as constitutive of experience. According to psychoanalyst–philosopher Cornelius Castoriadis, 23 centuries ago Aristotle introduced two completely different meanings for *phantasia*, one of which—prime or primary imagination—is the source of both perceptual *quale* and logical forms (Castoriadis, 1994). This idea had little influence in the development of Western philosophy, no doubt because it goes completely against the grain of modern thought. For "radical imagination" (to use Castoriadis's term) implies that the concepts of experience and reality are as intimately related as *psyche* and *soma* in the constitution of individual embodied experiences. Indeed, Castoriadis claims that "it is because the radical imagination exists that 'reality' exists *for us*—exists *tout court*—and exists *as* it exists" (p. 138). But if this is so, reality–experience must be viewed as a bipolarity whose two poles, although distinguishable for the purposes of thought, are essentially inseparable. A bridging of this and related bipolarities (such as subjectivity–objectivity) thus suggest the need for a complex interweaving of different types of imagination—primary, metaphysical, mathematical, poetical, and social.

The working of a social or collective imagination in the emergence of distinct cultures is implied by the notion of a "radical social instituting imaginary," which Castoriadis maintains is the indispensable public or social counterweight to the privacy of individual acts of radical imagination. Yet the social instituting imaginary has, he says, been completely ignored in Western philosophy. Nonetheless, such an imaginary is needed to account for the social significations that dominate and shape a society just because these significations also shape the psyches of individuals. That is to say, a social instituting imaginary guides the meaning-making and evaluative judging that evolve into distinctive sciences, art forms, rituals, ceremonies, political organizations, and so on. Hence emerges the peculiar character of a nature-culture, for every society is self-creating within certain constraints, not all of which are material (i.e., biological, geographical, historical).

Such ideas resonate with Frye's observation that myths control both what a society *is* making and what it *can* make of itself. The above observations also suggest answers to the crucial questions prompted by Lewontin, Latour, and Haraway: what legitimates this technoscientific culture's institutions of social legitimation? What underwrites a modern Constitution that allows a proliferation of what it forbids? What warrants the creation of "monsters" such as OncoMouse? One answer implicit in the notion of a "social imaginary signification" is that insofar as reason can only move *inside* established imaginaries it is ultimately constrained by the myths that legitimize those imaginaries. As Frye indicates, there are no powers more potent than myths that *could* control the construction of dominant social imaginary significations. Such significations are good and/or healthy (as well as unlikely to encourage violent tendencies and monstrous practices) just to the extent that they are capable of fostering harmonious and balanced relations within and between human societies and between cultures and nature. That is to say, just to the extent that they are under the control of "good" myths.

It is difficult, however, to overestimate the number of problems to which the notion of a "good" myth gives

rise. Consider Serres's idea of a Natural Contract and the question it prompts: whether a seriously ill, even a self-destructive, civilization could be cured by a new mythology. Perhaps nothing less than a cultural-analytic (modeled on a psychoanalytic) therapy is required before a more balanced mythology could take root in Western civilization. Even then, there is no reason to think a cultural therapy would be significantly different from a personal therapy where, rather than a complete cure, only a better grasp of debilitating "sicknesses of the understanding" (to adopt Ludwig Wittgenstein's phase) can be hoped for.

Supposing that such a therapy were successful, what sort of conception of reason might emerge? Feyerabend's critique of monolithic Science suggests that reason is essentially an art; indeed, one art among many. More specifically, reason must find a way to include myth and the poetic imagination, "which grasps human life as a whole and gives it meaning" (Feyerabend, 1987, 91). Thus his distinction between Reason and reason points toward good reasoning as an activity requiring a subtle blend of poetic creativity and critical acuity, which aims at a certain "artful rightness." Such a view at least promises a reduction of the violence of modern Reason. No art seems able to sustain itself for long as art by violent means, although some current forms of art exploit shock and provoke anger in order to draw attention to unwelcome or unpopular ideas.

An "artful" reason could, moreover, accommodate feelings and emotions which are no more foreign to good reasoning than they are to the making of good art. The objection that emotions have no place in reason merely raises the therapeutic question whether these uneliminable aspects of concrete experience share (with imagination, intuitions and insights) in the systemic repressions, denials, and disconnections endemic to modernity's view of reason. Once the role of emotions in reason is acknowledged, nothing stands in the way of pursuing scientific and philosophical understandings along lines suggested by Nobel prize-winning Barbara McClintock in the field of plant genetics. Eschewing the objectifying methods of orthodox science, McClintock treated her plant "subjects" as subjects in the ordinary sense of the word; that is, as individuated creatures endowed with distinctive "personal" traits. *A Feeling for the Organism*, Evelyn Fox Keller's title for her account of McClintock's work, indicates that the feelings that McClintock developed for her experimental "subjects" were conductive to her remarkable achievements. She herself suggests that imagination is indispensable to performing (to use Goethe's term) a "delicate empiricism," wherein the investigator strives to make himself/

herself identical with the object of investigation. Although such a delicate empiricism, when conjoined with an artful, truly modest reason, may require closing off certain avenues of investigation as morally indefensible, McClintock shows in effect that scientists need not on this account fear a drastic curtailing of their domain of inquiry. In her own words (as quoted by Fox Keller in *Reflections on Gender and Science*), "nature is characterized by an a priori complexity that vastly exceeds the capacities of the human imagination."

But to stress the role of imagination in good reasoning undoubtedly problematizes the very idea of rational inquiry. Not the least of the difficulties is the fact, abundantly evidenced in this century alone, that imagination can serve evil ends. Yet insofar as reason is at least partially an imaginative movement of mind that aims generally to produce, improve, and "fix" beliefs, an ineradicable element of risk is unavoidable in deciding what beliefs *are* worth validating. The Kantian project of drawing a definite boundary between beliefs established in the domains of speculative reason and practical reason, respectively, evaporates like a dream. And there is no way to resolve once and for all the enigma of reason: the puzzle of how reason *ought* to move so as to establish its own legitimacy, never mind its purity and innocence. Once allow creative imagination into world-making and reason is plunged into a morass of moral and ethical problems that show that questions of responsibility are deeply involved in questions about who counts as a truly rational actor.

Nonetheless, this account of the violence of modern reason can still end on a positive, if not a completely optimistic, note. The possibility of a nonreductive, morally responsible, nonviolent reason is indicated by process philosophers such as A. N. Whitehead, W. James, C. S. Peirce, H. Bergson, and C. Hartshorne. Reacting against the modernist tendency to conflate science with a "denatured" nature, their postmodern (or better, nonmodern) "constructionist" approaches attempt to do justice to concrete experiences (which include imagination and feelings) as well as the deliverances of modern science. Whitehead's interpretation of the Function of Reason (in a book of the same name) also proffers a positive alternative to modernist interpretations of reason, one that resonates with Merchant's account of the humbler, more ethical and respectful attitudes toward nature of premodern thinkers. The principal aim of reason, Whitehead claims, is to promote the art of life. This assertion does not hold out a promise of an end to all violence in reason, let alone in the world, for he is well aware that there is no escape from the moral problems that attend every human intervention in the world. Life itself depends on robbery since all living creatures ensure their survival qua organisms at the expense of the lives of other organisms. Yet if reason can indeed be understood as an art devoted to promoting the greater art of life, the robbery that life entails can be evaluated for the responsibilities it also entails, and perhaps even distinguished—morally and epistemologically—from the robbery of subjectivity that characterizes modes of thought that invite the charge of rape.

It is thus worth emphasizing that Whitehead's principal aim in metaphysics is consonant with a total rejection of the violence of analytic reason. In his view, the elements of fundamental conceptual dyads such as subjectivity–objectivity and nature–culture (which are necessary for abstract thought) do not exemplify clear and distinct ideas but rather poles of indissociable contrasts. As such their reconciliations require subtle mediations and negotiations rather than sharp separations. Especially concerned with the inescapably blurry relationship between knowers and known, which quantum physics confirms, Whitehead's philosophy of organism shows one way in which the inevitable tensions in the interplay between reality and experience can be respected. His resurrection of the ancient link between nature and organism thus promises an antidote for imperialistic devaluations of the realities experienced by "other cultures," attitudes that are also bound up with Western civilization's arrogant, warlike attitudes toward nature and its "weaker" creatures. Lastly, but far from least if the centrality of myth and metaphor in rational thought is granted, Whitehead's philosophic method explicitly features the choice of guiding metaphors as an essential first step in the fashioning of a metaphysical language. And his own choice of a governing metaphorics demonstrates that there is a wisdom lying dormant in certain words which can be brought to the light by the gentle means of imagination. He thus shows that an essentially pacific metaphysical language conducive to an artful reason unequivocally on the side of peace and harmony is not merely a fond hope.

Also See the Following Articles

LANGUAGE OF WAR AND PEACE • STRUCTURAL VIOLENCE

Bibliography

Appleyard, B. (1992). *Understanding the present: Science and the soul of modern man.* London: Picador.

Barthes, R. (1957). *Mythologies* (trans. A. Lavers, 1973). London: Paladin.

Burtt, E. A. (1954). *The metaphysical foundations of modern science.* Garden City, NY: Doubleday.

Castoriadis, C. (1994). Radical imagination and the social instituting imaginary. In (G. Robinson and J. Rundell, Eds), *Rethinking imagination: Culture and creativity.* London: Routledge.

Code, M. (1995). *Myths of reason: Vagueness, rationality, and the lure of logic.* Atlantic Highlands, NJ: Humanities Press International.

Collard, A., & Contrucci, J. (1989). *Rape of the wild: Man's violence against animals and the earth.* Bloomington: Indiana University Press.

Feyerabend, P. (1987). *Farewell to reason.* London: Verso.

Frye, N. (1992). *Words with power: Being a second study of the bible and literature.* London: Penguin.

Griffin, D. (Ed.) (1993). *Founders of constructive postmodern philosophy: Peirce, James, Bergson, Whitehead, and Hartshorne.* Albany, NY: State University of New York Press.

Haraway, D. (1997) *Modest_Witness@Second_Millenium.FemaleMan©_Meets_OncoMouse™.* New York: Routledge.

Harding, S. (1986). *The science question in feminism.* Ithaca, NY: Cornell University Press.

Keller, E. Fox. (1983). *A feeling for the organism: The life and work of Barbara McClintock.* New York: W. H. Freeman.

Laing, R. D., & Cooper, D. G. (1964). *Reason and violence: A decade of Sartre's philosophy 1950–1960.* London: Tavistock.

Latour, B. (1991). *We have never been modern* (trans. C. Porter, 1995). Cambridge, MA: Harvard University Press.

Lewontin, R. C. (1993). *The doctrine of DNA: Biology as ideology.* London: Penguin.

Lloyd, G. (1994). *The man of reason: 'Male' and 'female' in western philosophy,* 2d. ed. Minneapolis: University of Minnesota Press.

Merchant, C. (1983). *The death of nature: Women, ecology, and the scientific revolution.* New York: Harper and Row.

Nandy, A. (Ed.) (1988). *Science, hegemony and violence: A requiem for modernity.* Delhi: Oxford University Press.

Nozick, R. (1993). *The nature of rationality.* Princeton, NJ: Princeton University Press.

Nye, A. (1990). *Words of power: A feminist reading of the history of logic.* New York: Routledge.

Sallis, J. (1995). *Delimitations: Phenomenology and the end of metaphysics,* 2nd ed. Bloomington: Indiana University Press.

Serres, M. (1992). *The natural contract* (trans. E. MacArthur & W. Paulson, 1995). Ann Arbor: University of Michigan Press.

Whitehead, A. N. (1968). *Modes of thought.* New York: Free Press.

Religion and Peace, Inner–Outer Dimensions of

Linda Groff

California State University at Dominguez Hills

Paul Smoker

Antioch College

I. INTRODUCTION

If a man sings of God and hears of Him, And lets love of God sprout within him, All his sorrows shall vanish, And in his mind, God will bestow abiding peace.

Sikhism

A Muslim is one who surrenders to the will of Allah and is an establisher of peace (while Islam means establishment of peace, Muslim means one who establishes peace through his actions and conduct).

Islam

The Lord lives in the heart of every creature. He turns them round and round upon the wheel of Maya. Take refuge utterly in Him. By his grace you will find supreme peace, and the state which is beyond all change.

Hinduism

The whole of the Torah is for the purpose of promoting peace.

Judaism

To be in harmony with others, you must be at peace with yourself.

Buddhism

All things exist for world peace.

Perfect Liberty Kyodan

Blessed are the peacemakers for they shall be called sons of God.

Christianity

Peace ... comes within the souls of men when they realize their relationship, their oneness, with the universe and all its powers and when they realize that at the center of the universe dwells Wakan-Tanka, and that this center is really everywhere, it is within each of us.

From *The Sacred Pipe* by Black Elk, Lakota
Sioux Medicine Man

The Great Peace towards which people of good will throughout the centuries have inclined their hearts, of which seers and poets for countless generations have expressed their vision, and for which from age to age the sacred scriptures of mankind have constantly held the promise, is now at long last within the reach of the nations.

Bahai

This article explores the inner and outer aspects of religion, as well as the inner and outer aspects of peace, and how these relate to each other and the implications of both for future generations. As the above quotations indicate, almost all of the world's religions, in their own sacred writings and scriptures, say that they support "peace." Yet it is a known fact that war and violence have often been undertaken historically, as well as at present, in the name of religion. Yet religions profess to want peace. So what is "peace"? And how have religions historically helped to promote peace and how might they help create a more peaceful world in the 21st century? These are a few of the questions that this article attempts to explore.

Traditionally many people focus on how wars and conflicts are seemingly undertaken for religious reasons or at least undertaken in the name of religion. Indeed, it is not difficult to find data and statistics in support of this hypothesis. Quincy Wright, in his monumental study *A Study of War*, documents numerous wars and armed conflicts that involve a direct or indirect religious component, as does Lewis Richardson in his statistical treatise *Statistics of Deadly Quarrels*. As the Cold War has ended and interethnic conflicts and internal wars have reemerged in many parts of the world, it has indeed been a popular thesis of different writers to argue that these interethnic conflicts often have a religious component. A few examples of such recent writing include: Samuel Huntington's "The Clash of Civilizations" in *Foreign Affairs*, Daniel Patrick Moynihan's *Pandaemonium: Ethnicity in International Politics*, and R. Scott Appleby's *Religious Fundamentalisms and Global Conflict*.

While much literature focuses on how religions have contributed to conflict, violence, and war, others are exploring how religions can work together for greater peace, understanding, and cooperation in the world. Examples include UNESCO's two conferences on The Contributions of Religions to a Culture of Peace (Barcelona, Spain, April, 1993 and December, 1994) and other interreligious and interfaith dialogues that are occurring in a serious way around the planet, including: the Parliament of World Religions, Chicago, August, 1993; the ongoing work of the World Council on Religion and Peace; and the United Religions Initiative, which is leading toward a United Religions Charter in 2000. In this spirit, this article also focuses on how religious and spiritual traditions can contribute to creating a more peaceful world via an exploration of the foundations for both inner and outer peace in the 21st century.

This article has three parts as follows.

The first part, "Exoteric/Outer and Esoteric/Inner Aspects of Religions," begins by providing a framework for looking at all the world's religions as having a potential spectrum of perspectives, including: the internal, mystical, direct spiritual experience or esoteric part and the external, socially learned, cultural or exoteric part, which includes both organized religion, as well as fundamentalism. Concerning the internal or esoteric aspect of religion, all the world's religions began with someone who had a mystical enlightenment or revelatory experience, which they then tried, as best they could, to share with others, leading often to the formation of new religions—even though this was not often the intention of the original founder. The exoteric or socially learned part of religion includes different religious organizations, rituals, and beliefs, which are passed down from one generation to the next. Here understanding and valuing of diversity can be taught. Fundamentalism or religious extremism or fanaticism—when religions claim their version of religion or truth is the only one—are seen as an extreme form of the socially learned aspect of religion and one not conducive to creating world peace. The second half of this part looks at the implications for future generations of this spectrum of possible, and often actual, perspectives within any given religion.

The second part, "Inner and Outer Aspects of Peace (Paralleling Esoteric and Exoteric Aspects of Religion)," traces the evolution of the concept of "peace" within Western and global peace research, including the recent development of more holistic definitions of peace. The conceptual shift involved in moving from peace as absence of war through peace as absence of large-scale physical and structural violence (negative and positive peace respectively) to more holistic definitions of peace—that apply across all levels and include both inner and outer dimensions—represents a substantial broadening of the peace concept in Western and global peace research. The second half of this part considers the implications for future generations of the broadening of the peace concept to include holistic paradigms that link inner and outer aspects of peace.

The third part, "The Need to Focus on Both Inner and Outer Aspects of Religion and Peace," examines some linkages between inner and outer peace—including mythology, spiritually based nonviolence, prayer, and meditation. It also looks at tendencies of Eastern and Western religions and cultures traditionally to focus more on either inner or outer aspects of peace, respectively, while noting that both are needed if peace is to be achieved. An East–West dialogue is needed, and it has begun.

II. ESOTERIC/INNER AND EXOTERIC/OUTER ASPECTS OF RELIGIONS

A. Mystical Experience, Organized Religion, and Fundamentalism: A Framework for Looking at All the World's Religions

In looking at external and internal aspects of religion, it is important to note that within any religion, there is a potential spectrum of possible perspectives on the teachings of that particular religious or spiritual tradition, including how those teachings relate to world peace. First, at one end of the spectrum, are mystical traditions which are based on direct inner spiritual experiences. Here, such mystical, revelatory, or enlightenment experiences by someone are the true precursors behind the later creation of different world religions. Such spiritual experiences have also occurred in mystics from all the world's religions throughout the ages. Indeed, the founders of the world's religions were themselves usually mystics, i.e., people who had revelatory or enlightenment experiences which they then tried to

share, as best they could, with others—even though they were often not trying to establish a new religion at the time (which was often left to their followers to do).

Next, there is religion as socially learned behavior, i.e., as part of culture—what can be called "organized religion." Here religious beliefs, rituals, and institutions are learned and passed down from one generation to the next, and religious institutions play an integral role in the teaching and transmission of those beliefs, rituals, and practices.

When religious beliefs take the form of rigid dogma, and the believers' beliefs and behavior are known to be right, while those of nonbelievers, or other religions—or even different variants within one's own religion—are known to be wrong, this leads into what has been variously called "fundamentalism" or "fanaticism" or "extremism"—a global trend in almost all of the world's religions today.

Given these considerations, it is possible to look at any religion as having a potential spectrum of different perspectives within it (Fig. 1).

B. Implications for Future Generations of the Spectrum of Possible Perspectives within Any Religion

It is interesting that mystics of all religions can usually communicate with each other and appreciate the spiritual or God force operating within each other—no matter what religious tradition other mystics come from. Organized religions have not always been tolerant of different religious traditions historically, but are more so today, as seen in ecumenical movements around the world, but there can still be misunderstanding between religions based on differing beliefs and practices. These misunderstandings can be lessened by educational programs focusing on the appreciation and understanding of cultural and religious diversity, as well as by interreligious and interfaith dialogue, which is definitely increasing in the world today. But fundamentalism often

```
MYSTICAL/SPIRITUAL___ORGANIZED RELIGION____FUNDAMENTALISM
     TRADITIONS              AND BELIEFS           OR EXTREMISM

   (Direct Inner           (Part of Social       (My dogma/beliefs
    experience)            learning and          are right and yours
                             culture)             are wrong; also
                                                   social learning
                                                   and culture)
```

FIGURE 1 Spectrum of potential perspectives within any religion.

stresses how one particular interpretation—of religion, scripture, and religious practice—is correct and other interpretations are wrong. This difficulty of fundamentalist from any religion, in dealing with diversity in a tolerant manner, presents a major problem for peaceful relations and understanding between religions and cultures and hinders the creation of a global culture of peace for future generations.

If the whole world were mystics—who tend to honor the mystical experience in people from all the world's religions—world peace would be easier to achieve in the future. But mystics are a small percentage of the world's population and so misunderstandings, conflicts, and wars have often resulted historically, in part at least, over different religious interpretations of what constitutes proper beliefs, practices, rituals, and organizational forms, i.e., over the socially learned aspects of religion. Nonetheless, interest in mysticism is increasing in the West and has always been a more fundamental aspect of spirituality in the East. Interreligious dialogue is also increasing as are intercultural and diversity trainings worldwide. All this bodes well for the future and for future generations. If we can come to see and experience a common spirituality underlying all the diversity of outer forms of religion through which that spirituality expresses itself, that will also greatly help humanity and future generations to see our underlying unity behind our outer diversity, which can then be valued and appreciated for the different insights and wisdom which religious diversity can provide.

Having now looked at inner and outer aspects of religion, it is now important to look at inner and outer aspects of peace.

III. EVOLUTION OF THE PEACE CONCEPT INCLUDING INNER–OUTER DIMENSIONS OF PEACE

A. Evolution of the Peace Concept

This part looks at the evolution of seven types of peace within peace research and how each type builds on the previous types leading toward a more holistic view of peace. It describes seven different ways of thinking about peace (grouped into three broad categories) that have evolved in peace research since the mid-1940s (since the end of World War II). The first five or six types of peace come primarily out of Western peace research and focus on creating peace in the external world, while the last one or two types come more from non-Western, including Eastern, cultural frameworks, which are now being incorporated into Western and global peace thinking. The fact that our ideas of peace have evolved does not mean that all scholars once thought one way and now think another, nor that the majority of peace researchers now adopt the later, holistic types of peace thinking. Rather it argues that overall there has been a trend in peace thinking away from the traditional idea that peace is simply the absence of war toward a more holistic view (see Fig. 2). Please also note that each new type of peace builds on the previous one, adding some new element or dimension to peace that was not there before, while still retaining the previous elements, thus leading ultimately toward a more holistic, multidimensional, multileveled view of peace.

Figure 2 summarizes seven ways of thinking about peace in terms of the levels of analysis and substantive

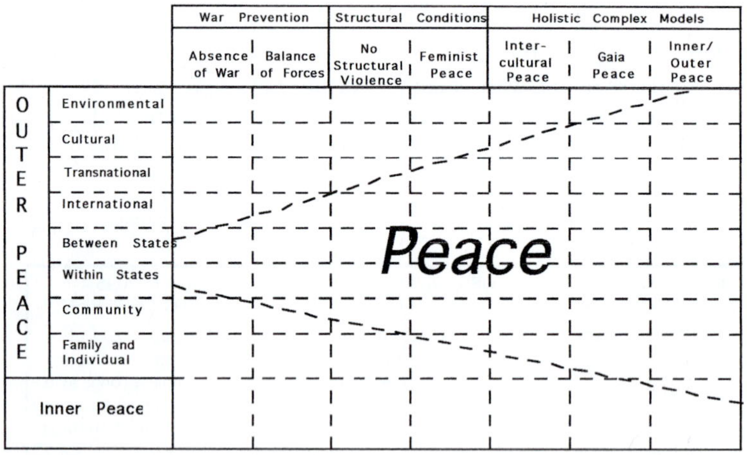

FIGURE 2 Seven concepts in the evolution of peace thinking.

focus that each includes. These stages in the evolution of the peace concept include the following.

1. Peace Thinking That Stresses War Prevention

The first two types of peace both deal with war and how to prevent it and the need to do so if any peace is to be possible in the world.

Peace as Absence of War

The first perspective, peace as the absence of war, focuses on avoiding violent conflict between and within states—war and civil war. This view of peace is still widely held among general populations and politicians in most countries, and there are good reasons why this is so. Everyone knows the ravages of World War I and World War II, as well as those occurring during the so-called "Cold War," where superpowers often intervened in local conflicts, such as Vietnam and Afghanistan. Wars, mostly of the internal or civil type, continue to rage around the globe, and the lives of millions of people are daily threatened by the specter of war. Under these circumstances, peace is seen as the absence of war—at least until the killing stops and it is possible to ask for more out of life than avoiding death in war. In fact, all seven definitions of peace discussed here include absence of war in their definition of peace, but only this first view defines peace as just the absence of war.

Peace as Balance of Forces in the International System

Quincy Wright modified this absence of war idea to suggest that peace was a dynamic balance involving political, social, cultural, and technological factors and that war occurred when this balance broke down in the international system. Wright defined the international system in terms of the overall pattern of relationships between states and International Governmental Organizations (IGOs). Wright also discussed the role of domestic public opinion within a state—the community level of analysis. His model assumed that any significant change in one of the factors involved in the peace balance would require corresponding changes in other factors to restore the balance. For example, Robert Oppenheimer, the much-misunderstood "father of the atomic bomb," adopted Wright's view when he insisted on continuing to develop the bomb so that a global political institution, the United Nations, would have to be created to help control the new global military technology.

2. Peace Thinking That Stresses Eliminating Macro and/or Micro Physical and Structural Violence

The next two types of peace each focus on adding social-structural dimensions of peace—including at macro international and transnational levels and at micro community, family, and individual levels.

Peace as Negative Peace (No War) and Positive Peace (No Structural Violence) on Macro Levels

Galtung further modified Wright's view using the categories "negative peace" and "positive peace" that Wright had first put forward some 28 years earlier. Galtung argued that negative peace was the absence of war and that positive peace was the absence of "structural violence," a concept defined in terms of the numbers of avoidable deaths caused simply by the way large-scale social, economic, and political structures were organized. Thus if people starve to death when there is food to feed them somewhere in the world or die from sickness when there is medicine to cure them, then structural violence exists since alternative structures could, in theory, prevent such deaths. Peace under this rubric involves both positive peace and negative peace being present. Galtung's model (in addition to the community, within states, between states, and international levels of analysis) includes the transnational level of analysis, such as the global economy, which is influenced by nonstate actors, such as International Nongovernmental Organizations (INGOs) and multinational corporations (MNCs).

Feminist Peace: Eliminating Physical and Structural Violence on Both Macro and Micro (Community, Family, and Individual) Levels

During the 1970s and 1980s, a fourth perspective was ushered in by feminist peace researchers, who extended both negative peace and positive peace to include eliminating both physical and structural violence down to the individual level. The new definition of peace then included not only abolishing macro-level organized violence, such as war, but also eliminating micro-level unorganized violence, such as rape in war or in the home. The concept of structural violence was similarly expanded to include personal micro- and macro-level structures that harm or discriminate against particular individuals, ethnic communities, or groups. This feminist peace model came to include the elimination of all types of violence (physical and structural) at all levels, from the individual and family up to the transnational level, as a necessary condition for a peaceful planet.

3. Peace Thinking That Stresses Holistic, Complex Systems

The last three types of peace all deal with holistic, complex systems that include a lot of diversity and that see diversity as a strength. Intercultural peace celebrates the diverse cultural forms human beings exhibit on this planet, and Gaia peace honors the diversity of life forms and their interdependencies in the single living system Earth. These two types of holistic peace focus on the external world. The last type of peace adds inner peace to all the forms of outer peace and is thus the most holistic, complex definition of peace.

Intercultural Peace: Peace between Peoples

The interaction between cultures has accelerated dramatically during recent centuries and decades, and too often the militarily stronger or economically more powerful culture has subdued or eliminated the militarily weaker or economically poorer one. While cultural violence has become a global phenomenon and a focus for peace researchers such as Galtung in his analysis of cultural violence, as well as mainstream scholars such as Samuel Huntington in his "Clash of Civilizations," relations between cultures can also be reframed from negative (cultural violence, cultural wars) to positive conceptions, such as "intercultural peace"—between different ethnic, racial, cultural, and religious groups. This stresses not only what we want to eliminate, but also what we want to create in a positive sense. Thus, intercultural peace requires the positive coevolution of cultures at both the macro and micro levels. As the great macro-historian Arnold Toynbee noted: "We shall, however, have to do more than just understand each other's cultural heritages, and more even than appreciate them. We shall have to value them and love them as being parts of Mankind's common treasure..." (Toynbee, 1972, p. 47). The whole diverse global cultural mix is seen as a cause of strength for humanity, in the same way that the rich diversity of plants and living creatures are seen as a strength for the ecosystem.

Holistic Gaia Peace: Peace with the World and the Environment

In addition to the earlier types of peace, holistic Gaia peace, peace with the environment, also sees the Earth as a complex living system, of which humans are a part, and places all forms of peace between people in that context. Holistic Gaia peace therefore requires peace between people at all levels of analysis—from the indi-

vidual and family levels to the global cultural level. In addition, Gaia peace places a very high value on the relationship of humans to bioenvironmental systems—the environmental level of analysis. Peace with the environment and responsible stewardship of the earth are seen as central to this type of holistic peace, where human beings are seen as one of many species inhabiting the earth, and the fate of the planet is seen as the most important goal.

In some cases, the Gaia concept is interpreted scientifically, in terms of a complex biochemical, energy system. When this is the case, Gaia peace is primarily concerned with physical aspects of the environment and reality, outlined in the first six types of peace. In other cases, the inner, spiritual aspects of Gaia are also seen as essential, and Gaia or Earth is also seen as a sacred, living being, or Goddess.

Holistic Inner and Outer Peace

This last type of peace includes all of the outer aspects of peace (covered above), as well as adding inner peace as an essential component and precondition for a peaceful world. Spiritually based peace theory stresses the centrality of inner peace, believing that all aspects of outer peace, from the individual to the environmental levels, must be based on inner peace. This spiritual dimension is expressed in different ways, depending on one's cultural context. As in Fritjov Capra's The Tao of Physics, where new paradigms in physics parallel worldviews found in Eastern mysticism, this new paradigm in peace research resonates with much thinking in world spiritual and religions traditions. Peace has truly become indivisible.

Just as peace researchers—especially in the West—have elaborated six different dimensions of peace in the external world, so also must they now begin to elaborate on the different dimensions and levels of consciousness related to inner peace. To do this, they will have to draw on centuries of experience by spiritual masters from the East, indigenous cultures, and from some more ancient Western cultures, where such traditions of inner experience are much older, more developed, and honored than in modern Western culture. Even in the West, however, there is now much greater interest in such topics, including a greater openness to exploring such inner dimensions of consciousness and peace.

4. Summary on Evolution of the Peace Concept

The above discussion illustrates a number of important changes in the peace concept in peace research since the mid-1940s. First, the idea that peace can be defined in terms of a single factor, "absence of war," has been replaced in subsequent peace research by multifactored theories. While the absence of war remains a necessary precondition for all peace definitions, it is no longer a sufficient one in most formulations of peace. Second, there has been a shift from including just the state level of analysis, in absence-of-war definitions, to peace theories that include (for outer peace) multiple levels of analysis—from the individual to environmental levels. Multifactor, multilevel concepts of peace are, as a consequence, considerably more complex than simple, absence-of-war theories. Finally, peace has come to be defined not only in negative terms (focusing on what to eliminate, such as physical or structural violence), but increasingly in holistic, positive terms (focusing on what a peaceful world would look like in a positive sense). The latter is also essential, not just the former, if effective change is to occur. (See Paul Smoker's 1981 article in *The Journal of Peace Research* on this point as well as the work of Elise Boulding, based on her translation of Fred Polak's book *The Image of the Future* and her "Imaging a Peaceful World" Workshops, as examples of the latter view in peace research. In future studies, people like R. Buckminster Fuller, Barbara Marx Hubbard, Jeanne Houston, and others have strongly noted the need to focus on the positive potentials and futures we want to create, if a more positive future world is to be created.)

The emergence of more holistic peace paradigms in peace research—whether intercultural, environmental, and/or spiritual—has included an increasing emphasis on positive conceptions of peace. In part, this is because of our realization that, whatever our nationality, culture, or religious tradition, we are all interconnected and interdependent. Viewed from space, planet Earth is a beautiful blue-green sphere without national borders but with land, water, ice caps, deserts forests, and clouds visible. The Earth is clearly a whole complex system, perhaps even a living being. We as individuals and groups are but a part of the planet, as the planet itself is a part of the solar system, galaxy, and universe. This whole systems mindset enables an appreciation of the interdependence of species in the global ecosystem, of particular cultural meanings in the context of the total global cultural system, and of particular faiths in the rich diversity of global religions—all contributing to the tapestry of the whole. The whole is more than the sum of the parts, and the greater the variety of the parts, the richer the expression of the global whole.

B. Implications for Future Generations

Some of the things that future generations will want to know when they look back on the world of the late 20th century are:

1. How much progress have we made in each of the seven areas of peace?
2. While good ideas were finally emerging on the different dimensions and levels of peace, why did 20th-century people not leave the world in better shape for future generations?

All of these are valid questions that responsible people today need to better address.

1. How Much Progress Have We Made in Each of the Seven Areas of Peace?

A few observations follow.

Peace as Absence of War

The danger of an all-out nuclear war between the United States and the Soviet Union (now Russia), which the whole world lived in fear of during the Cold War, is now gone, but the danger of nuclear terrorism or accidental nuclear war is still very much with us. So is the danger of chemical and biological warfare. While the frequency of wars between states has greatly declined, internal civil wars—especially between different racial/ethnic/cultural/religious groups—have greatly increased since the end of the Cold War. These can be just as deadly and terrifying for those effected—including the homeless, imprisoned, or families whose relatives have been killed. Eliminating the physical ravages of war still remains the essential prerequisite for all the other types of peace to be possible.

Peace as Balance of Forces in the International System

Today a multifaceted, interactive world system has emerged involving political, social, economic, cultural, technological, and other areas. State governments are no longer the only actors in the international system. The United Nations, though still limited in its powers, is at least begrudgingly recognized as a necessary global forum by most sane people. There has also been a growth in the number of other global, nonstate actors, including International Governmental Organizations (IGOs), International Nongovernmental Organizations, cultural and ethnic groups, multinational corporations, and transnational corporations (TNCs). For example, in 1996, McDonald's Hamburgers established an outlet in its 100th country, and as it happens, no two countries that both have a McDonald's have fought a war against each other. Another new global actor is the Internet, which is linking together increasing numbers of people across national boundaries. The global, transnational system will probably become even bigger and more complex in the future and, as a result, inter-state wars will probably be far less frequent in the 21st century.

Peace as Negative Peace (No War) and Positive Peace (No Structural Violence) on Macro Levels

If there is enough food in the world to feed everyone (which most people agree is true today), but people are starving (which they are today), then structural violence exists (which it does today). Why can't we do better in eliminating structural violence? Inadequate delivery systems to get food to those needing it, civil wars, and corruption of governments—all human factors that could be avoided—are reasons. The increasingly complex global system (noted above) may help control wars between states (positive), but it may also continue to increase gaps between rich and poor, not only between states, but also within states (negative). The effects of such structural violence are severe. For example, some 13 million children die each year through poverty and starvation, and this situation appears to be worsening. In order to reverse this trend and reduce the level of structural violence, there must be changes in lifestyles in developed countries, better food delivery systems to feed the hungry, and a reduction in global military expenditures—which will free up billions of dollars that can be used for constructive purposes, a reduction in the gap between rich and poor, and an increased awareness worldwide of our responsibilities to each other in an interdependent world. In this regard, the increased visibility of international citizens groups, such as Oxfam, Save the Children, and Amnesty International, is a positive trend that serves the interests of future generations.

Feminist Peace: Eliminating Physical and Structural Violence on Macro and Micro (Community, Family, and Individual) Levels

While such violence has existed for centuries and is only now getting greater attention, much still remains to be done here. Violence against women and children is a global fact of everyday life, as is street violence in every major city in the world. In addition, political, social, and economic structures at the local, national, and global levels systematically discriminate against women and minorities. Replacing patriarchal value sys-

tems with greater equality of opportunity in all areas and mutual respect between the sexes is one essential ingredient necessary for this type of peace to be achieved globally. This will not happen overnight: cultural values often change more slowly, but education is critical here, as well as social and political action to highlight and change such inequities. Small bank loans to women in developing countries have also been very effective in providing economic opportunities for women.

Intercultural Peace: Peace Between Peoples

The racial, ethnic, cultural, and religious diversity between peoples, who are increasingly interacting with each other today, means that intercultural wars and conflicts—especially in the form of internal civil wars and conflicts—are on the rise today, as noted above. With the relative weakening of the power of the state in the global system today, with the advent of other global actors (as outlined above), cultural and ethnic identity have become more important. "Racism"—my race is superior to yours; "nationalism"—my nation (or culture or group) is superior to yours; and "fundamentalism"—my religion, or interpretation of my religion, is right and yours is wrong, have become potent forces at all level of society worldwide. The world still needs to discover that diversity is a strength, not a problem or weakness, but to do this, we must recontextualize how we view and value relations with others from backgrounds different than our own. Many people are now doing "intercultural" and "diversity" trainings and workshops, but much work still remains to be done. Not only a change in attitude, but also a change in heart, are necessary within people, toward those of differing backgrounds.

Holistic Gaia Peace: Peace with the World and the Environment

There was a global environmental movement in the 1970s, and it has reemerged in the 1990s, as evidenced by the huge number of global participants at the United Nations Earth Summit in Rio in 1992. Non-Western cultures have always had a value and worldview of seeing themselves as part of nature, not separate from it, as compared to Western cultures, which focus more on individualism and thus see themselves as separate from nature, leading to a desire for control over nature. The industrial revolution has also wreaked havoc on environments all over the world, Western and non-Western. Rapid industrialization by governments from the top down has undercut traditional non-Western cultural values of living in harmony with nature. We must reclaim our relationship with nature and our stewardship of the earth—both as individuals and as national groups—if this type of peace is to be reestablished.

Holistic Inner and Outer Peace

Methods to find inner peace have been seen as necessary preconditions and cornerstones for establishing world peace for centuries in non-Western, including Eastern, cultures and religions (for example, Hinduism, Buddhism, and indigenous people's religions). This is a much newer idea in Western peace research and, indeed, in Western cultures in general, although there have always been selected individuals in the West who focused on inner peace and meditation. Traditionally, Eastern cultures focused more on inner mastery and peace, as the vehicle for a more peaceful world, while Western cultures focused more on inner mastery and changing aspects of the external world as a basis for creating a more peaceful world. Now, as both Eastern and Western cultures and religions increasingly interact, it is becoming increasingly apparent that both inner peace and work in the world for social justice, the elimination of poverty, democratic rights, and environmental preservation, are necessary, if a more peaceful 21st century world is to be possible. Eastern cultures are learning "social engagement" in the world, while Western cultures are learning Eastern meditation techniques. If this process continues, both Eastern and Western cultures will be more in balance, and the prospects for peace in the 21st century will be enhanced.

2. Why Did 20th-Century People Not Leave the World in Better Shape for Future Generations?

This is, of course, the ultimate question to ask people today from the perspective of future generations. Violence has existed throughout history, but so have efforts toward cooperation, nonviolence, and peace. In some ways, one can always look at the world or one's cup as being half full or half empty regarding how much peace there is. But violence is still part of life, and with modern weapons and technology, the damage done from violence and aggression can be more extensive and destructive to all life. Now that the Cold War is over, global nuclear war between the superpowers is no longer a real danger at present, though accidental nuclear war and nuclear terrorism remain definite dangers. While war between nations is greatly reduced, internal civil wars within countries have increased.

In other respects, some progress toward peace has been made. Indeed, it is only since the end of World War II (only 50 years) that these seven different types of peace have emerged as distinct types of peace—to be articulated and to be acted upon. Progress in each of these areas varies and there is clearly a great deal still to be done—as outlined above. But as more people become informed on these different types of peace and how each plays an essential role in the development towards holistic conceptions of peace and as more people become involved in activities in support of these different types of peace—including through NGOs and INGOs—one can at least hope that progress will continue to be made (no doubt with periodic setbacks) in each of these areas of peace so that in the 21st century the situation for future generations will continue to improve. Since different forms of inner and outer peace tend to work synergistically together (as elaborated below), progress in any area of peace also helps create conditions for progress in other areas of peace.

IV. THE NEED TO FOCUS ON BOTH INNER AND OUTER ASPECTS OF RELIGION AND PEACE

A. Some Linkages between Inner and Outer Peace

While various aspects of inner and outer peace have been explored in this article (especially outer peace, which is a more developed concept in Western peace research), it is also useful to ask what the possible linkages or bridges are between inner and outer peace in our lives. At least two suggestions can be made in this regard. First, authors such as Joseph Campbell and Jean Houston note how myths and archetypal hero figures of different cultures can provide road maps for individuals to show how their everyday life in the world can be linked to the inner life of the spirit. Second, spiritually based nonviolence, such as that practiced by Mahatma Gandhi and Martin Luther King, Jr. (i.e., nonviolence which is part of a whole philosophical way of life, based on spiritual principles, as opposed to nonviolence as a temporary tactic when it is expedient) provides a model of how one can turn to inner spiritual guidance—through meditation or prayer—to seek inner help and confirmation before embarking on action for social justice and social change in the world. Combining these two suggestions, we can thus see two distinct ways to connect inner and outer peace—one (mythology) leading from outer to inner peace and the other (spiritually based nonviolence) leading from inner to outer peace in the world, as seen in Figure 3 below.

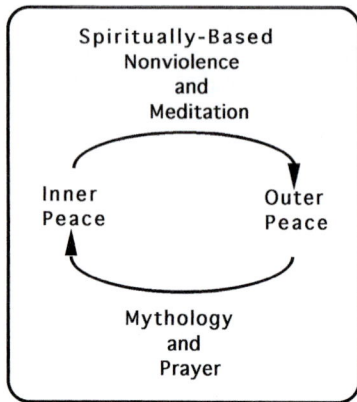

FIGURE 3 Some linkages between inner and outer peace.

Two other fundamental linkages between inner and outer peace are obviously prayer and meditation. Indeed, prayer is often seen as asking God or spirit for something, i.e., thus going from our outer life in the world to our inner life of the spirit, while meditation is clearing the mind and also listening to God or spirit for an answer, i.e., thus going from our inner life to our outer life in the world. While this sounds like a clear-cut distinction, in reality the two things—prayer and meditation—are often interconnected and part of a larger whole. In any case, both prayer and meditation are important and essential dimensions of the inner–outer peace relationship, as noted in Fig. 3.

B. Tendencies of Eastern and Western Religions and Cultures to Focus Traditionally More on Either Inner or Outer Aspects of Peace, Respectively, While Both Are Needed Today

1. Eastern Religions and Cultures (Hinduism, Buddhism): Tendency to Focus More on Inner Peace as a Precondition for World Peace

It is interesting that Eastern religions and cultures, including Hinduism and Buddhism, have a tendency—because of their focus more (though not exclusively) on the esoteric aspects of their religions—to focus more on inner peace as a precondition for peace in the world. They also have less of a tradition historically of concern with social justice questions, which are so important to the West. Nonetheless, it is noteworthy that the link between inner peace (based on a spiritual life) and outer peace (or action in the world for social justice) was

most clearly made for the first time in the world in any collective societal way by Mahatma Gandhi, who was born in India and came out of a Hindu background, but who also studied in England.

2. Western Religions and Cultures (Judaism, Christianity, and Islam): Tendency to Focus More on Outer Peace, Including Social Justice Questions, as a Precondition for World Peace

Western religions and cultures, including Judaism, Christianity, and Islam have had a tendency—because of their focus more (though not exclusively) on the exoteric aspects of their religions, at least in their every-day activities—to focus more on aspects of outer peace, including social justice questions, as a precondition for peace in the world. There are nonetheless esoteric, mystical traditions in the West, which though less dominant, were nonetheless the foundation for the original spiritual enlightenment experienced by the founders of all the world's great religions, including the three dominant Western religions—Judaism, Christianity, and Islam. These can take the form of the Kaballah (in Judaism), Gnostic Christianity (in Christianity), and Sufism (in Islam), as examples, although there have always been some mystics in the mainstream forms of all the Western religions as well.

3. World Peace Requires Attention to Both Inner and Outer Peace

If one focuses only on outer peace and creating social justice in the world, but not on inner peace, then people's unresolved inner conflicts can be projected out onto the world, creating scapegoating, prejudices, and conflicts, therefore making it more difficult to create social justice and peace in the world (the ostensible goal).

If one focuses only on inner peace, then social injustices and structural violence in the world, which are not addressed by society and people, will tend to make it difficult for many people to transcend their outer conditions of life, thus making it more difficult for them to attain inner peace (the ostensible goal).

Clearly there is a dynamic and synergistic relationship between inner and outer peace: by focusing on both aspects of peace, each aspect of peace—i.e., inner or outer—increases the probability that more people will also be able to attain the other aspect of peace. In this regard, interreligious and interfaith dialogue occurring around the world today between different religions is leading to Western religions learning about

Eastern meditation techniques and Eastern religions learning about Western social engagement in the world. This cross-fertilization between religions is helping create a more holistic and solid foundation for peace in the 21st century.

V. CONCLUSION

This article has developed the theme that peace requires a dynamic balance between different "opposites" or "extremes," including exoteric and esoteric forms of the religious experience, and between inner and outer aspects of peace, in such a way that peace action and research include both an inner component, such as meditation or prayer, and an outer component that deals with action in the world for peace and social justice. We have stressed the need to avoid "either/or" formulations and instead to seek paths that include "both/and" perspectives that include both poles and their dynamic interdependence. In helping the world to find such a balance, as a foundation for peace in the 21st century, the ongoing ecumenical dialogue and sharing of religious practices and concerns between Eastern and Western spiritual and religious traditions will play a critical role. This can only benefit future generations.

Also See the Following Articles

ENVIRONMENTAL ISSUES AND POLITICS • ETHICAL AND RELIGIOUS TRADITIONS, EASTERN • ETHICAL AND RELIGIOUS TRADITIONS, WESTERN • NONVIOLENCE THEORY AND PRACTICE • PEACE CULTURE • RELIGIOUS TRADITIONS, VIOLENCE AND NONVIOLENCE • SPIRITUALITY AND PEACEMAKING

Bibliography

Al-Dajani, A. S. (1993). The causes of religious extremism (fundamentalism) in the Arab countries. Arab Thought Forum, The Arab-European Dialogue V, Amman (September 1–2, 1993).

Appleby, R. S. (1994). *Religious fundamentalisms and global conflict.* New York: Foreign Policy Association.

Badiner, A. H. (1990). *Dharma Gaia: A harvest of essays in Buddhism and ecology.* Berkeley, CA: Parallax Press.

Boulding, K. (1990). Foreword. In N. Myers (Ed.), *The Gaia atlas of future worlds.* New York: Anchor Books.

Boulding, E. (1992). *The underside of history: A view of women through time* (Vols. 1 and 2). Newbury Park, CA: Sage.

Brock-Utne, B. (1989). *Feminist perspectives on peace and peace education.* Oxford: Pergamon Press.

Capra, F. (1991). *The Tao of physics: An exploration of the parallels between modern physics and eastern mysticism* (3rd ed.). Boston: Shambhala.

Clark, P. B. (Ed.) (1993). *The world's religions: Understanding the living faiths.* Pleasantville, NY: Reader's Digest.

His Holiness, The Dalai Lama of Tibet (1994). *The way to freedom: Core teachings of Tibetan Buddhism.* San Francisco: Harper.

Dreher, D. (1991). *The Tao of inner peace.* New York: Harper Perennial.

Dumoulin, H. (1993). *Understanding Buddhism: Key themes* (translated and adapted from the German by J. S. O'Leary). New York: Weatherhill.

Eliade, M. (1959). *The sacred and the profane: The nature of religion.* Orlando, FL: Harcourt, Brace, Jovanovich.

Eliade, M. (Ed.) (1986). *Encyclopedia of religion.* New York: Macmillan.

Galtung, J. (1969). Violence, peace and peace research. *Journal of Peace Research, 3.*

Gawain, S. (1993). *The path of transformation: How healing ourselves can change the world.* Mill Valley, CA: Nataraj.

A global ethic: The declaration of the parliament of the world's religions. New York: Continuum.

Groff, L., Smoker, P. (1996). Spirituality, religion, culture, and peace: Exploring the foundations for inner–outer peace in the 21st century. *International Journal of Peace Studies, 1*(1), 57–113.

Groff, L. (1991). Global unity & diversity: Creating tolerance for cultural, religious, & national diversity in an interdependent world. Paper presented at Third International Conference on Building Understanding and Respect Between People of Diverse Religions or Beliefs, New Delhi, India, January, 1991.

Groff, L. (1993). On the values of cultural and ecological diversity and their importance to an effectively functioning world—Including the UN & UNESCO. Paper and testimony, U.S. Commission on Improving the Effectiveness of the UN, Los Angeles, California, February, 1993.

Huntington, S. (1993). The clash of civilizations? *Foreign Affairs,* Summer, pp. 21–49.

Hurtak, J. J. (1987). *The book of knowledge: The keys of Enoch* (3rd ed.). Los Gatos, CA: The Academy of Future Science.

(1972). *Japanese religion: A survey by the agency for cultural affairs.* Tokyo/New York: Kodansha International.

Johnston, W. (1970). *The still point: Reflections on Zen and Christian mysticism.* New York: Fordham University Press.

Lao-tzu (1991). *Tao te ching.* New York: Harper Perennial.

Lovelock, J. E. (1991). *Gaia: A new look at life on Earth* (5th ed.). Oxford: Oxford University Press.

Marsden, G. M. (1986). Evangelical and fundamental Christianity. In *Encyclopedia of religion.* New York: Macmillan.

Mische, P. M. (1989). Ecological security in an interdependent world. *Breakthrough News, 10*(4), 7–17.

Mische, P. M. (1997). Religion and world order: How are they related? *Breakthrough News,* 1–4.

Moynihan, D. P. (1994). *Pandaemonium: Ethnicity in international politics.* New York: Oxford University Press.

O'Gorman, A. (Ed.) (1990). *The universe bends toward justice: A reader on Christian nonviolence in the U.S.* Philadelphia/Santa Cruz: New Society.

Ono, S., in collaboration with Woodard, W. P. (1962). *Shinto: The Kami way.* Rutland, VT/Tokyo: Charles E. Tuttle.

Panikkar, R. (1989). Epistula de pace: Response to: Philosophia pacis. In *Homenaje a Raimon Panikkar.* Madrid: Simbolo Editorial.

Richardson, L. F. (1960). *Statistics of deadly quarrels.* Chicago, IL: Quadrangle Books.

Schmidt, H. (1968). Politics and peace research. *Journal of Peace Research, 5*(3), ?

Schuon, F. (1984). *The transcendent unity of religions*. Wheaton, IL: The Theosophical Publishing House. 1984.

Shaw, I. (1964). *The Sufis*. Garden City, NY: Doubleday.

Smith, H. (1976). *Forgotten truth: The common vision of the world's religions*. San Francisco: Harper.

Smith, H. (1991). *The world's religions: Our great wisdom traditions*. San Francisco: Harper.

Smoker, P. (1981). Small peace. *Journal of Peace Research*.

Smoker, P. (1984). Exploding nuclear myths: Evidence from conflict research. *Coexistence, 21*, 93–106.

Smoker, P. (1991). Towards a new definition of global security. *Ritsumeikan Review, ?*

Smoker, P., & Groff, L. (1996). Spirituality, religion, culture, and peace: Exploring the foundations for inner–outer peace in the 21st century. *International Journal of Peace Studies, 1*(1), 57–113.

Suzuki, D. T. (1959). *Zen and Japanese culture*. Rutland, VT/Tokyo: Charles E. Tuttle.

Thich N. H. (1991). *Peace is every step: The path of mindfulness in everyday life*. New York: Bantam.

West, J. A. (1979). *Serpent in the sky: The high wisdom of ancient Egypt*. San Francisco, CA: Harper & Row.

Whitworth, E. E. (1980). *The nine faces of Christ: Quest of the true initiate*. San Francisco, CA: Great Western University Press.

(1991). *World scripture: A comparative anthology of sacred texts*. New York: Paragon House.

——————— (December 28, 1992). What does science tell us about God? *Time Magazine*, 140(26), pp. 38–44.

Wright, Q. (1941). *A study of war*. Chicago, IL: University of Chicago Press.

Yogananda, P. (1975). *Autobiography of a yogi*. Los Angeles, CA: Self-realization Fellowship.

Religious Traditions, Violence, and Nonviolence

David Noel Freedman
University of California, San Diego

Michael J. McClymond
Saint Louis University

GLOSSARY

Ahimsa From Sanskrit, "nonharm." A religious prohibition against killing animals or humans as found to differing degrees in the religions originating in India (e.g., Hinduism, Buddhism, Jainism).

Eschatology From Greek, "study of the last things." Religious teachings about the end of the world and the dawn of eternity, including such matters as the second coming of Jesus; a millennial age of peace and prosperity on earth; heaven; purgatory; hell; and so on.

Inquisition(s) Special tribunals created in medieval and early modern Europe to combat the spread of heresies. While the Roman Inquisition was under the direction of the Papacy, some tribunals (e.g., the Spanish Inquisition) were led by specific nations or rulers.

Jihad From Arabic, meaning "exertion," also djihad. An Islamic term often translated as "holy war," but also having a broader meaning that includes all exertions made by Muslims on behalf of the true faith. Certain writers, especially Shi'ite Muslims, distinguish between a "lesser *jihad*," involving physical conflict, and a "greater *jihad*" that is purely spiritual in nature and consists in a battle to attain moral and religious perfection.

Just War In the Christian (and especially Roman Catholic) tradition, a war that is morally justified because it meets a number of specific criteria, e.g., it is defensive and not imperialistic, does not involve undue use of force, does not injure noncombatants, and so on.

Martyr From Greek, meaning "witness." A religious person who has died for the faith, bearing witness to the truth of his or her beliefs.

Pacifism A moral or religious viewpoint of total opposition to violence in any and all circumstances, thus connected with a refusal to fight, bear arms, or assist in armed conflicts.

Shalom A Hebrew term meaning "to have or be at peace," with further connotations of completeness, wholeness, security, and prosperity.

IF ONE DEFINES "RELIGION" as the human preoccupation with God, transcendent reality, or the sacred, and "violence" as the use of physical force to inflict injury on human beings, then the question arises as to whether and how religion provides justification for violence or for nonviolence. Here we can provide only a general outline of some major trends in the varied relationships among religion, violence, and nonviolence.

I. DEFINITION AND OVERVIEW OF RELIGIOUS VIOLENCE

A. Definition of Religious Violence

The topics of religion, violence, and nonviolence are complex and manysided, in part because religion never exists as an autonomous entity apart from politics, economics, sexuality, and the other fundamental springs of human action. Violence is easy enough to recognize when and where it occurs, and yet the same is not always true of religion. For this reason informed observers may disagree on the appropriate application of the phrase "religious violence." An act of interpretation is involved: How is one to determine which acts of violence are *religious* and which are not? If a political leader such as Adolf Hitler or Pol Pot invokes the name of God as a sanction for killing, then does this imply that the violence in question is religious in character? What if the violence is supported by religious leaders as well as political leaders? What if it is opposed by religious leaders and/or laypersons? What if there is disagreement on violence between different religious groups in a given society? The subtlety of the notion of "religious violence" becomes readily apparent.

Those who, like Karl Marx, see religion as largely subservient to the interests of rulers and ruling classes are likely to see so-called religious violence as merely one instance of generalized class conflict. Social strife for Marx was rooted in economics, not beliefs about God. Those who, like Mircea Eliade, see religion as an element of human existence that cannot be reduced to any other denominator—political, economic, sexual, and so on—will probably interpret some acts of violence (or repudiations of violence) as arising from specifically religious motives. For the purposes of this article it is not necessary to decide the question as to whether religion is essentially a product of nonreligious cultural factors or whether nonreligious cultural factors are themselves often the products of religious motives and impulses. The working definition of "religious violence" here is violence that is somehow directly sanctioned by religious authorities—leaders or councils, rituals, myths, symbols, or sacred texts.

B. Historical Examples

As this article should make clear, the major world religions vary in their approaches and attitudes toward violence. A widespread perception exists that the monotheistic traditions of Judaism, Christianity, and Islam are more warlike than the religions of South and East Asia. Islam is typically thought to be the most militant and militaristic contemporary faith. Buddhism, conversely, is often viewed as the most peaceable of the major religions. Along these lines Schwartz (1997) has argued that biblical monotheism has brought a "violent legacy" to Western societies, and has encouraged a tendency for social groups to define themselves in oppositional fashion, e.g., Israelites versus Canaanites. Certainly the notion of holy war seems to be stronger in the monotheistic religions than in Hinduism, Buddhism, Chinese religions, or indigenous religions. On the other hand, the recent studies of Hindu–Buddhist and Hindu–Muslim conflicts by Tambiah (1992) and Kakar (1996) demonstrate that a simple dichotomy between Western violence and non-Western nonviolence is too simplistic. Mohandas Gandhi was killed by a militant Hindu in 1948, and the prime minister of Sri Lanka was assassinated by a Buddhist monk in 1959. It is best therefore to begin from the assumption that virtually all religious traditions are capable of promoting violence in certain instances, but that the conditions, nature, and extent of the violence differ greatly from tradition to tradition and from case to case.

Many historical instances of religious violence can be cited. Archaic societies in various parts of the globe, and some modern groups, have regularly practiced human sacrifice. The voluntary or coercive burning of Hindu widows in India—known as *sati*—is one instance of human sacrifice in recent times. The conquest and displacement of the Canaanites of Palestine by the Israelites is described in the Hebrew Bible or Old Testament as specifically commanded by God. Another example of religious violence from ancient times is the persecution and execution of Jews who refused to eat pork or otherwise renounce their Judaic practices under the Seleucid ruler, Antiochus IV, during the decade of the 160s B.C.E. The enormous geographical expansion of Islam in the 7th century C.E. was linked to wars of conquest stretching from Spain to Central Asia. In 11th-century Persia, a secret society of the Isma'ili Muslims, known as the "assassins," tried to exert social control through murdering their adversaries. Pope Urban II in 1095 declared a crusade to regain control of the Holy Land. "God wills it [*Deus vult*]!" became the rallying cry of soldiers who sought to win back control of Jerusalem and other holy sites from the Muslims. Subsequently the popes extended the war on infidels and heretics with an expanding network of special courts, known as the Inquisition, which possessed extraordinary powers (not allowed in most later judicial systems) to compel witnesses, secure confessions, and inflict penalties. Following the Protestant Reformation of the early

16th century, there was a century of bloodshed (ca. 1550–1650) between Protestant and Catholic rulers while a small minority of Anabaptists and others adopted a pacifist stance and unconditionally refused to participate in the warfare.

All through the modern period, and especially in the present century, violent communal conflicts have erupted in South Asia between Hindus and Muslims (in North India and Pakistan) and between Hindus and Buddhists (in Sri Lanka). Another communal conflict at the present time, with strong religious undertones, is that between Jews and Arabs in Israel–Palestine. Also worthy of mention is the often unreported persecution of Christian leaders and laypersons in contemporary communist and Islamic countries such as China, Iran, Egypt, Vietnam, and elsewhere. Moreover the Baha'is, who live in Iran, have suffered persecution since the very beginnings of their movement under Bab-ud-Din and Baha'u'llah in the 1850s.

Perhaps the most infamous instances of religious violence in recent times are the acts of terrorist groups that abuse or kill innocent persons in order to destabilize governments and dramatize a kind of cosmic battle between good and evil. When the Ayatollah Khomeini declared in the aftermath of the 1979 Iranian revolution that "America is the Great Satan," he gave voice to a notion of religious combat that has served as a justification for acts of violence. Sometimes terrorists act according to a grim logic of retaliation, nurturing the memory of injustices and atrocities suffered by the communities to which they belong. Religious ritual and symbolism can become a means for keeping alive the memory of past sufferings and an inducement to aggression and retaliation. In other instances terrorists act in response to a perceived threat of annihilation by enemy forces. The extreme circumstances are thought to demand extreme measures. Once again, religious language and symbolism can serve to demonize the adversaries, polarize the rival groups, and conceal their common humanity. Paul Mojzes and Michael Sells have described an "ethnoreligiosity" that fueled the bloodshed of the 1990s in the former Yugoslavia.

C. Violence in Religious Symbolism

The major religions are connected with violence not only in their histories but also in their central symbols. One could begin with the images and narratives of the gods and goddesses themselves. Both the monotheistic faiths and the religions of Asia present violent as well as peaceful images of the divine. "The Lord is a warrior," declares Exodus 15:3. The scriptural texts of Hinduism and Buddhism are rife with descriptions of war between humans and among the gods themselves. Like almost all ancient texts, these writings extol the military virtues of courage before adversaries and fierceness in battle. The best-loved and best-known Sanskrit text of all, *The Bhagavad Gita*, takes the form of a conversation that occurs while two opposing armies are frozen in their battle lines, on the verge of charging against each other. When the conversation ends, the warfare begins. The most familiar emblems of Islam and Sikhism are swords, and the central symbol of Christianity is an execution device, namely, the cross.

In the Roman Catholic tradition, the bleeding and dying Savior is often portrayed in graphic detail. In Protestant Christianity, the violence is conveyed in words rather than through physical images, as worshipers sing familiar hymns regarding "the old rugged cross" and "the blood of Jesus." The hymns of the German pietist Nicholas Zinzendorf (1700–1760) are especially noted for their constant references to Jesus' blood. One of the two central rituals of Christianity is the eucharist (or Lord's Supper, or communion, or Mass) that symbolically represents the broken body of Jesus on the cross (the divided bread) and the shed blood (the outpoured wine) followed by the consumption of these elements by the worshipers. In Roman Catholicism, the doctrine of transubstantiation stipulates that the consecrated bread and wine are transformed in their very substance into the body and blood of Christ while still retaining the outward appearance of bread and wine. Likewise the Catholic doctrine of the "sacrifice of the Mass" has often been taken to mean Jesus is sacrificed afresh on each occasion that the eucharist is celebrated. Shi'ite Muslims commemorate the brutal killings of Husain and his son, regarded as the legitimate spiritual leaders following Muhammed and Muhammed's cousin and son-in-law Ali. Their deaths are the subject of an annual festival during the month of Muharram, often with a passion play (*ta'ziya*) that reenacts this tragedy. As in the Christian preoccupation with Jesus' death, so in Shi'ite Islam an unjust death becomes a focus of veneration and an example to be emulated by later martyrs of the faith.

II. VARIETIES OF AND SANCTIONS FOR VIOLENCE

A. Varieties of Violence

Violence in world religions falls into multiple categories, including the following: sacrifice, persecution, martyrdom, inquisition, witchhunt, and holy war (or *jihad* in Arabic). All the above words have links both with violence and with religion. Other terms suggest violent activities that may in certain instances derive from religious motives: revolution, riot, assault, and terrorism. One of the most important categories of religious violence is sacrifice, which is among the most ubiquitous of religious activities and the most mysterious. The word "sacrifice" derives from a Latin verb "to make sacred" and may be defined as a ritual offering in the form of a presentation to (or exchange with) divine beings, sacred powers, or ancestors. Sacrifice involves the voluntary giving or giving up of a valued substance or object, usually requiring the destruction of the life or essence of the offering. The intention is to establish communication with the gods, an orderly relationship in the cosmos, and/or certain tangible benefits on behalf of an individual or community.

Even those religious traditions that affirm the importance of protecting and preserving life have often mandated the intentional killing of animals and/or humans in sacrifice. Theories of sacrifice have tried to explain this seeming paradox in a variety of ways. E. B. Tylor held that sacrifice among primitive peoples is simply a way of bribing the gods, according to the Latin maxim: *Do ut des* ("I give [to you], that you may give [to me]"). Then, as religion evolved, sacrifice became internalized in the form of self-renunciation. W. Robertson Smith, in his study of the ancient Semites, concluded that sacrifice is primarily significant as a covenantal meal in which the participants join themselves to one another and to spiritual powers through consuming the body of the victim. Sigmund Freud, in his evocative and controversial book *Totem and Taboo* (1913), developed a theory of sacrifice based on the Oedipal myth of the son who sexually desires the mother and hence must eliminate the father. Freud postulates a primordial killing of the father by a horde of sons who subsequently seize the father's power and the women previously under his control. In the wake of Freud, a controverted question is whether sacrificial violence is simply an expression of violent impulses endemic to human nature or rather is a means of shielding society from violence by focalizing it in a ritual context. René Girard provides an interesting variant on Freud's hypothesis when he suggests that rituals of violence evoke and thus release the hostilities among the members of a given society toward one another. The death of a scapegoated individual becomes the necessary price to be paid for harmony among the others.

The religious persecutions of world history and the sufferings of the martyrs are vivid illustrations of a widespread belief that God, true religion, or salvation are worth dying for and are sometimes worth killing for. Beginning with the Maccabean revolt of the 2nd century B.C.E., the Jewish tradition had its martyrs—perhaps the first documented instance in world history of persons killed solely because of their religious beliefs and practices. By the time of the apocryphal book of Fourth Maccabees (first century C.E.), the blood of the martyrs was thought to have the power to expiate sin, to overcome tyranny, and to renew the observance of the Jewish law (1:11, 6:28–29, 17:21, 18:4). This set of ideas is analogous to the New Testament doctrine that Jesus' death is an atonement that brings sinners back into a right relationship with God (Mark 10:45). Later, when Roman authorities persecuted the early church, the Christian tradition underwent a development not unlike that reflected in Fourth Maccabees: the dying martyrs were thought to have special power or merit, and their words of absolution could remove the stain of sin from those upon whom they pronounced them. This belief in the merit of the martyrs laid the foundation for the later cult of the saints in medieval and modern Christianity.

During the late medieval and early modern period in the West, the Crusades, the Inquisition, and the witchhunts were all related in complex ways. The Crusade represented a form of religious violence that was directed against perceived *external* enemies, in this case the "infidel" Muslims who controlled the holy sites connected with Jesus and other biblical characters. The Inquisition and the witchhunts in contrast were directed against perceived *internal* enemies, the heretics and diabolical agents who threatened to subvert Christian society from the inside. The practice of holy war in Christianity and Islam, and the general circumstances and conduct of the inquisition of the Middle Ages, are discussed below.

B. Sanctions for Violence

Sociologist Mark Juergensmeyer has researched and written extensively on the subject of violence and nonviolence in world religions and much of what follows is a summary of his conclusions.

In the Vedic period (1500–500 B.C.E.), the warriors of ancient India called upon the gods to participate in their struggles. As in the Greek *Iliad* and *Odyssey*, the realms of the human and the divine were unified, and earthly battle was part of a larger conflict between divine and/or cosmic powers. Reflecting the later development of Hinduism, *The Bhagavad Gita* provides arguments for the legitimacy of killing, including the teaching that the soul in its essential nature is deathless and immortal: "He who thinks this self a killer and he who thinks it is killed, both fail to understand; it does not kill, nor is it killed" (2.19). Moreover, killing is a duty (*dharma*) for Arjuna, the protagonist of the *Gita*, since he belongs to the warrior caste of the *kshatriya*: "If you fail to wage this war of sacred duty, you will abandon your own duty and fame only to gain evil" (2.33). Here we encounter a set of ideas common to many traditional cultures: society is composed of interdependent parts, and while some must hunt or farm, others must pray or meditate, and still others must fight on behalf of all. The ancient Hindu warrior, like the medieval Christian knight, was the divinely appointed protector of the social order. The modern Indian leader Mohandas K. Gandhi (1869–1948), who promoted a nonviolent approach to social conflict, interpreted the warfare of *The Bhagavad Gita* as allegorical. Yet even he allowed an exception to the general rule in the special case where a small, strategic act of violence could obviate a much greater danger. Other modern Hindus, especially those devoted to the dark goddess Kali, were more militant and felt a moral obligation to use force for the cause of Mother India.

Guru Nanak (1469–1538), the founder of the Sikh religion in Northern India, was known as a gentle soul, and yet the religious movement soon came under the leadership of a militant tribal group, the Jats. Throughout history the Sikhs have periodically clashed with the Moghuls, the British, and the other rulers of India. During the 1980s, a movement for Sikh automony gained momentum through the fiery preachings of J. S. Bhindranwale, who died in 1984 along with some 2000 others in fighting that occurred when the Indian government sent troops into the Golden Temple at Amritsar, the holiest site of the Sikh religion. The core of the Sikh community is known as "the army of the faithful" (*dal khalsa*), and their symbol is the double-edged sword. Violence is justified by the Sikh doctrine of *miripiri*—the idea that religion is to be victorious in both the spiritual and the worldly realms.

In the case of Buddhism, it is difficult to find specific sanctions for violence, and hence the topic of violence is better treated as an exception to the general rule of nonviolence (see Section III,B). On the other hand, some modern Buddhists in South and East Asia have joined together religion and political militancy in ways that seem to overturn the religion's well-known injunctions of nonviolence. In Southeast Asia, insurgent Buddhist groups have sometimes invoked *Maitreya*, a futuristic Buddha whose coming signifies the overthrow of evil forces and the beginning of a golden age. Eschatological ideas, or religious teachings regarding the end of the world and the dawning of eternity, have often motivated religious activism and sometimes even religious revolution. More often the appeal to eschatology has occurred in the monotheistic religions of Judaism, Christianity, and Islam, but sometimes in Buddhist contexts as well.

Despite the influence of Buddhism in East Asia, other religious teachings in this region have justified violence for the sake of maintaining social order or for expanding the empire. Starting in the 11th century C.E., the Japanese samurai tradition merged Confucian ideals of restraint and self-discipline with a militaristic ethic to produce *bushido*, a chivalrous code of conduct that placed honor above life itself. The ultimate sacrifice was an act of ritual suicide (*seppuku*) in which the samurai disemboweled himself with a sword and then was decapitated by an assistant. This self-sacrifice was done for reasons of shame, as an atonement for an error, or to protest an act of injustice.

In Jewish as well as in Hindu tradition, some of the earliest layers of the tradition are also the most violent. The Hebrew Bible describes scenes of desolation caused by God's acts of judgement against the unrighteous— fire and brimstone rained from heaven upon the cities of Sodom and Gomorrah (Genesis 19); a deadly plague upon the firstborn of the Egyptians (Exodus 12); and many other episodes of plague, famine, drought, and other natural calamities. When the Israelites are commanded to enter and conquer the land of Canaan, their adversaries are depicted as God's own enemies. The author of Deuteronomy declares that "we captured all his towns, and in each town we utterly destroyed men, women, and children. We left not a single survivor" (Deuteronomy 2:34). In this divinely mandated war of annihilation, only the plunder of the Canaanite cities— livestock and movable goods—were to be preserved intact by the conquering armies. Throughout Western history, the biblical texts regarding holy war have been invoked repeatedly and often with chilling results—by Christian crusaders in the Middle Ages, by European colonialists conquering indigenous peoples around the globe, and by today's religious radicals seeking justification for acts of violence.

Despite the armed conflicts between the Jews and their Gentile rulers in the Maccabean Revolt (166–164 B.C.E.), the Jewish War against the Romans (66–73 C.E.), and the Bar-Kochba Revolt (132–135 C.E.), the normative Jewish tradition as reflected in the rabbinical writings is basically nonviolent. The rabbis drew a contrast between religious war and war for political expediency. Only the former was strictly obligatory as a means of protecting the faith or defeating the enemies of the

Lord. The latter was always optional and a matter of statecraft. Yet since the emergence of Zionism in the early 20th century, certain radical individuals and groups have taken a militant stance regarding Jewish claims in Palestine. Up until his assassination in 1990, Rabbi Meir Kahane was widely known for his controversial claim that God has given the land of Israel to the Jews and that Arabs therefore have no rightful claim to reside there. Gershon Salomon has led symbolic marches at the Temple Mount in Jerusalem (sometimes resulting in bloodshed) to reclaim the site for Jews rather than Muslims. A group known as Gush Emunim, also convinced of Jewish claims to the land, encourages the expansion of settlements by Jews on the West Bank of the Jordan River.

From early in its history, there has been disagreement in the Christian church over the legitimacy of violence. Some have insisted that Christians must follow Jesus' example of selfless love: "Love your enemies and pray for those who persecute you" (Matthew 5:44). Others have cited biblical texts that speak of the civil state as bearing the "sword" (Romans 13:1–4) and thus claiming a legitimate use of force. The earliest Christians seem to have been consistently pacifistic, rejecting the use of violence under any and all circumstances. Among the early Christian authors, Tertullian (ca. 160–225) and Origen (ca. 185–254) asserted that Christians were not allowed to take human life, a principle that barred Christians from serving in the military. Modern pacifist groups include the Mennonites and the Quakers (see Section III,B below). Once Christianity had become the state religion of the Roman Empire in the early 4th century, there was a movement away from pacifism and in time Ambrose (ca. 339–397) and Augustine (354–430) adopted and developed the doctrine of the "just war" (first formulated by Cicero). According to this doctrine, war was permissible (though never desirable) if certain strict criteria were met, such as an inability to resolve the conflict by peaceful means, a use of force no greater than that needed to conclude the conflict, and a refusal to bring injury on civilians or noncombatants.

Since the 1960s, some Roman Catholic theologians have adapted the theory of the just war under the impact of liberation theology, arguing that the church that supports a just war could in principle also endorse a just revolution. The American Protestant theologian Reinhold Niebuhr (1891–1971), who began his career as a pacifist, later argued that Christians should not be pacifists because the pervasiveness of sin in the world sometimes makes it necessary to subdue evil with righteous force. The German Protestant Dietrich Bonhoeffer (1906–1945) is another instance of a Christian pacifist who had second thoughts. At first supporting pacifism in the 1930s, the rise of Adolf Hitler and the Third Reich convinced him that violent force was needed to overthrow the regime and avert a far greater evil. Bonhoeffer's life was ended in a Nazi camp, where he was executed for his involvement in a plot to assassinate Hitler.

In addition to war, another kind of violence in Christendom has been religious persecution, perhaps best exemplified by the Inquisition of the Middle Ages. When confronted by the breakaway Christian sect of the Donatists, Augustine reasoned that coercion was allowable in certain cases (*compelle intrahere*, "force them to come in," Luke 14:23), and this principle became enshrined in the imperial legislation of Theodosius (5th century) and Justinian (6th century). Yet until the 12th or 13th centuries, the Christian Church was not involved in most cases of execution of purported heretics by mobs or lay rulers. While the Church wished to curtail heresy and brings heretics to repentance, it did not in principle condone their execution. The high Middle Ages brought a change. The cultural metamorphosis that brought a new sense of spiritual unity throughout 12th- and 13th-century Europe, a renewal of learning, and a revival of monasticism, also brought a growing fear and antipathy to "outsiders" within the body politic. Anti-Semitism increased, heretics were hounded and punished, and holy war was declared in the Crusades against the Muslims in Palestine.

A series of church councils in the middle 1100s prescribed the penalties of excommunication, confiscation of property, and imprisonment for heresy, yet still did not recognize death as a proper penalty. The fierce battle against the heretical Cathars in southern France led Emperor Frederick II to decree that in Lombardy relapsed heretics (i.e., repeat offenders) were to be burned at the stake. Because Catharism had not been uprooted but only driven underground, Pope Gregory IX established a tribunal in 1233 at Toulouse, and the later popes of the 13th century extended the power of the Inquisition. Pope Innocent IV, in his bull *Ad extirpanda* (1252), stipulated that heretics handed over to the secular arm should be executed within 5 days and that torture could be used to elicit information from the accused.

By the beginning of the 14th century, the Inquisition had developed a systematic plan of operation. A place reputed to harbor heretics was visited by an inquisitor who, in a sermon that all were required to attend, preached on the wrongfulness of heresy and invited anyone who might have heretical tendencies, or knew of those with such tendencies, to appear before him. The suspect was presented with depositions from accusers but was not informed of their identities. Only two accusers were necessary, and the accused could only exonerate himself if he were able to discover the identity of his accusers and to demonstrate to the inquisitor's satisfaction that they acted from enmity. Otherwise, the accused had either to admit heresy or to deny it. If he admitted it, a penalty was inflicted. If he denied it, he was returned to prison, and often torture was applied to secure a confession. Suspects who refused to confess to heresy, and those confessed heretics who were thought to have lapsed again into falsehood, were liable to be handed over to the secular authorities for punishment at the stake. Heretics who recanted their errors while being led off to die were sent to lifelong imprisonment if their conversion seemed to be genuine. If not, their pleas were ignored.

While the heresy of the Cathars declined in France by the late 1200s, the Inquisition continued to develop in other parts of Europe along the lines already established. Under papal leadership it spread to Eastern Europe and Germany, though in the latter region the local bishops sometimes resisted papal interference. England never accepted the Inquisition at all. In Castile and Aragon it became an integral element in the political machinery of the Spanish monarchs Ferdinand and Isabella, who, with the help of the Grand Inquisitor Tomás de Torquemada (1420–1498), used it against the Moors (Muslims) and Marranos (Christianized Jews and Muslims). In the 14th century, groups such as the Brethren of the Free Spirit, the Béguines, and the Spiritual Franciscans were investigated and prosecuted. By the late 1400s an ominous new aspect appeared with a rising tide of accusations against witches and sorcerers, best illustrated in the witch-hunters' handbook of 1486, the *Malleus maleficarum*. By the close of the 17th century, perhaps a million women and men were hanged or burned at the stake on the charge of witchcraft.

Within the Muslim community, violence is justified and even required for subduing the enemies of the faith and insuring that the true religion of Islam has ample opportunity to spread itself into new territory and there take root. Islam divides the world into *dar al Islam* ("the house of Islam") and *dar al harb* ("the house of warfare")—the latter being that territory where Islam does not yet exist. Conflict on behalf of Islam is known as *jihad* (or *djihad*), a term that literally means "exertion" yet carries militant connotations. Some authors, especially Shi'ites, distinguish between a "lesser *jihad*" of physical conflict and a "greater *jihad*" that is spiritual

and consists in a battle to attain moral and religious perfection. Another distinction is between a nonviolent "*jihad* of tongue or pen" (see *Qur'an*, 16:125) and a violent "*jihad* of the sword" (*Qur'an*, 2:193). In light of the wide semantic range of the term, it is not accurate simply to equate *jihad* with "holy war," though conversely it is not accurate to say (as some recent Muslim apologists have said) that the term has no association with violence. In about two-thirds of the instances where the verb *jahada* or its derivatives occur in the *Qur'an*, it denotes warfare. *Jihad* is a collective duty that requires a sufficient number of persons to engage in conflict and so fulfill the community's obligation. In Islamic tradition, those killed in *jihad* are called martyrs; their sins are forgiven and they go immediately to paradise.

Jihad is based on the conception of Islam as universal, and hence it is always conceived as a battle between Muslims and non-Muslims. Conflicts between Muslim groups thus cannot be classified as *jihad*, at least according to the general Sunni opinion. According to some Shi'ite authorities, however, refusal to subscribe to their tenets may be considered as equivalent to unbelief and thus may elicit a call for *jihad*. According to both Muslim and secular scholars, *The Qur'an* shows varied emphases in its teaching on *jihad*. Some texts enjoin defensive warfare to ward off aggression (2:190, 9:13). Other passages seem to encourage an initiatory attack, provided it does not occur during the 4 sacred months (5:9). Still other texts stress peaceful persuasion, and hence there is a principle that *jihad* is never to be conducted unless the people opposed have first been invited to join the house of Islam.

Among scholars of Islam there is disagreement as to whether *jihad* includes only self-defense by Muslims or rather implies the right of offensive attack against unbelievers. Muslim authorities have argued that the "sword" verses in the *Qur'an* (e.g., 5:9) came later in time and thus "abrogated" the more peaceable teachings (2:190) and thus that Muslims have a standing order to engage in *jihad* against unbelievers. Others contest this and hold that there must be provocation from non-Muslims prior to attack. In either case, the doctrine of *jihad* has often been used to justify the expansion of Muslim states into non-Islamic regions. Strictly speaking, Muslim law does not allow *jihad* to be used as a means of forcible conversion to Islam. The only valid conversions are those that occur voluntarily and involve a genuine change of heart. In recent decades, some Muslim political activists have employed the notion of *jihad* to sanction violent acts. According to the Egyptian author Abd Al-Salam Faraj, *jihad* is every Muslim's "neglected duty" to defend the faith in the social and political spheres.

As James Turner Johnson points out in his writings on holy war, modern Westerners and Islamic traditionalists have fundamentally and perhaps irreconcilably divergent viewpoints on the proper relationship between religion and war. In the post-Enlightenment era, Westerners have adhered to a secular theory of the state that makes war for religion a thing of the past. Within the framework of traditional Islam, however, war for religion is associated with continuous striving for God in heart, word, and deed. It also reflects a deeply rooted understanding of religion as properly integral to the political order—a conception radically at odds with the modern West's separation of church and state. It comes as no surprise that today's radical Muslims (or Islamists) commonly regard the very notion of a secular state as a repudiation of Islamic principles and that communication between non-Muslims and Muslims is often stymied by profound mutual misunderstanding.

Mark Juergensmeyer, in his wide-ranging analysis of contemporary societies, sees in the Islamic world and elsewhere an increasing trend for peoplehood and nationhood to be defined in religious terms. The secular conception of the state may be on the decline. Sikhs seek a separate state of their own, Hindu fundamentalists lobby for India to be declared a Hindu state, Iran seeks to render itself fully Islamic, and Orthodox Christian Bosnians battle Muslim Bosnians in the name of God. In the coming era, religion may prove to be even stronger than nationalism as a constructive force in human affairs or, alternatively, as a destructive power of murder and mayhem.

III. VARIETIES OF AND SANCTIONS FOR NONVIOLENCE

A. Varieties of Nonviolence

Almost all religious traditions, both ancient and modern, Western and non-Western, have imperatives against taking human life. The Hebrew Bible teaches that "you shall not murder" (Exodus 20:13), and similar injunctions are found in the New Testament and in the Qur'an which states: "Slay not the life that God has made sacred" (6:152). In Buddhism, the commandment not to kill is the first of the Five Precepts, while the sacred writings of Jainism state that "if someone kills living things … his sin increases" (*Sutrakrtanga* 1.1) and those of Hinduism say that "the killing of living beings is not conducive to heaven" (*Manusmrti* 5.48).

Notwithstanding these imperatives, the general principle of "nonviolence" is something other than the mere commandment not to take life. The term "nonviolence" is a literal translation of the Sanskrit word *ahimsa* (lit. "nonharm") and it came into English usage only in the 20th century through its association with Mohandas Gandhi and his approach to resolving conflicts.

Mark Juergensmeyer distinguishes three aspects of nonviolence in world religions. The first is an inner state or attitude of nondestructiveness and reverence for life, especially as it exists in Jain, Hindu, and Buddhist traditions, in certain African and Native American tribal societies, and in certain Christian groups such as the Quakers. The second aspect is an ideal of social harmony and peaceful living with others, associated with the Hebrew term *shalom* and the Arabic word *salaam*, and often visualized as a perfect state to be achieved at the end of the world. A similar ideal is also found in ancient Greece where the deities Demeter and Apollo were embodiments of peace and harmony. The third aspect is an approach to social conflicts that repudiates violence and calls for a readiness to undergo suffering and even death rather than to inflict injury on others. This last aspect brings together the Jewish conception of martyrdom with the Christian notion of self-sacrificial love and a practical strategy for conducting and concluding conflicts in a nonviolent fashion.

B. Sanctions for Nonviolence

During the Vedic period in India (ca. 1500–500 B.C.E.), the concept of nonviolence was virtually unknown, inasmuch as the culture was permeated with military values and animals were used for food and sacrifice. Moreover, the Hindu texts from this period present the gods and goddesses as engaged in acts of violence, vengeance, and warfare. Nonviolence is first mentioned as a moral virtue in the *Chandogya Upanishad* (3.17.4), where the word *ahimsa* implies self-sacrifice and restraint. Somewhat later nonviolence becomes a prerequisite for those engaged in yogic practices, and in time it becomes a part of Hindu notions of *karma* that stipulate that each person reaps in future lives what he or she has sown in the present life. Acts and attitudes destructive to life are thought to be especially harmful to one's *karma*. The notion of *ahimsa* came to occupy a central place in the teachings of the great heterodox teachers of India during the 6th century B.C.E., namely Mahavira, the founder of the Jains, and Siddhartha Gautama, the Buddha. In the religions originating in India (viz., Hinduism, Jainism, and Buddhism), it is not feasible to separate the issue of human killing from animal killing, since humans and animals (and also gods and demons) are all inextricably linked in a immense cycle of death and rebirth with constant transitions from one of these forms of life to another. Hence our discussion of nonviolence in Asian religions will refer to animal as well as human killing.

The Jain ideal of nonviolence was extraordinarily strict, since even an accidental association with killing of any sort was thought to block one's advance toward karmic purity. Consequently many Jains wear masks over their faces to prevent breathing in and thus destroying tiny insects, and for the same reason they carry small brooms when traveling to brush the ground ahead before they step on it. Needless to say, the Jains are also vegetarians.

Within Buddhism the ideal of *ahimsa* has never been quite so strict as in Jainism, since there is a stress on motives as well as acts, and the guilt of killing applies only to persons who knowingly and intentionally bring about the death of some living thing. Some Buddhists will eat meat so long as they have not themselves been involved in the act of slaughtering. Even defensive warfare—though not war for political expansion—has been justified by some Buddhists on the grounds that such violence has the nature of a response and not an intent to harm. The great Buddhist emperor Ashoka (3rd century B.C.E.) instituted nonviolence as his official state policy, and yet did so only after he had greatly extended his territory through bloody wars of conquest. In modern Buddhist societies such as Thailand, kingship has a religious as well as a political dimension, and this introduces a certain tension between the principle of nonviolence and the demands of secular rule. In such countries as China and Japan, wherein Budddhism is closely intertwined with indigenous religious traditions such as Taoism, Confucianism, and Shinto, the stringent Buddhist principles of nonviolence are maintained only by the monks. Moreover the rulers of East Asia typically justify violence by appeal to non-Buddhist teachings from Confucianism and Shinto. Taoism, however, fits well with Buddhist nonviolence through its own principle of *wu-wei* ("non-action" or "non-striving"), which teaches that one must live peacefully and noncoercively by allowing things to follow their natural course.

In modern times, it was Mohandas Gandhi who brought the concept of nonviolence into the political sphere. By combining the notion of nonviolence with the general strike, Gandhi was able to make mass movements of nonviolent noncooperation into powerful forces for political change. He used the term *satyagraha* ("soul force") to describe his novel method of conflict resolution, suggesting that the spiritual realm had powers no less effective than those of the material realm. Gandhi applied this word both to his campaign for India's independence and to his way of resolving everyday disputes. While he insisted on nonviolence as a general rule, he made minor exceptions for the violence required to stop snipers or rapists as they attacked, and he permitted the killing of pests and wild animals that threatened his rural commune.

The Hebrew Bible, as we have already seen, contains militant and militaristic elements, yet presents aspects of nonviolence as well. Some of the psalms exalt the ideal of peace and disparage the practice of warfare (Psalms 20, 33, 120). "Too long have I had my dwelling among those who hate peace. I am for peace; but when I speak, they are for war" (Psalm 120:6–7). King David, who had waged many wars during his reign, was not allowed to build the Temple in Jerusalem because he had shed blood (1 Chronicles 28:2–3). The building was left to his son Solomon, whose very name is related to the word for peace—*shalom*. The ideal of *shalom*, which grows in importance in such later books as Isaiah and Jeremiah, includes not only an absence of warfare but also a more general sense of completeness, wholeness, security, and prosperity. *Shalom* thus includes many of the aspects of *ahimsa*, especially the absence of the desire to harm.

In later Judaism, the concept of martyrdom is central to a tradition of nonviolent resistance. The term *kiddush ha-Shem*, or "sanctifying the [divine] name," suggests that those who revere God must be perseveringly loyal to him, even at the cost of their lives. A rabbinical council of the 2nd century C.E. specified three offenses that a Jew is not to commit even under threat of death: idolatry, sexual immorality, and murder. It is better to die than to deny God through committing one of these acts. In times of political oppression, the ideal of *kiddush ha-Shem* inspired acts of courage and resistance even at the risk of life. The Spanish Inquisition resulted in the deaths of many Jews as martyrs. In the days of the Third Reich, many Orthodox Jews faced their Nazi opponents with dignity and composure, determined to avoid compromising their practice of Judaism even if this brought them to their deaths.

Nonviolence finds its clearest expression in Christianity in pacifist groups that renounce the use of violence under any and all circumstances. Among the Christian pacifists are the early Church (perhaps most Christians prior to the 4th century), the Waldensians (beginning in 1170), St. Francis of Assisi (1181–1226) and the Franciscans, the Lollards of 15th-century England, the Hussites and Taborites in the Czech Republic and their Moravian successors, the Anabaptists of Switzerland and the Netherlands in the 16th century (including Menno Simon and the Mennonites), and the Quakers or Society of Friends. In a sad and ironic twist of fate, many Anabaptist and Quaker pacifists of the 1500s and 1600s met their deaths at the hands of fellow Protestant and Catholic Christians. The Quakers' pacifism owed something to the doctrine of the "inner Christ," which led them to recognize God's presence in all whom they encountered. The Quakers became known for their respect for the Native Americans and for their vigorous opposition to slavery. Beginning in 11th-century Europe, the Truce of God (*pax Dei*) movement was an attempt to control violent behavior by members of the nobility and knightly classes—a kind of limited pacifism. It sought to prohibit bloodshed on the Lord's Day, or more precisely between Saturday evening and Monday morning. Later the church seasons of Advent and Lent were also brought within the truce.

Many pacifist movements of the 20th century, such as the Jehovah's Witnesses, are closely akin to their predecessors. Others have been influenced by Western humanist and Asian pacifism, most notably the ideas of Gandhi. Gandhi was himself influenced by Christian pacifists such as Leo Tolstoy (1829–1910) and the teaching on non-retaliation against evil in the Sermon on the Mount (Matthew 5–7). In the 20th-century United States, pacifist ideas played a major role in Martin Luther King, Jr.'s nonviolent struggle for racial justice, in the protest movements against the Vietnam War, and in the campaign for nuclear disarmament. Some recent Christian leaders and thinkers have been "nuclear pacifists" who believe that while some wars might be just, nuclear war—because of its wanton destruction of whole civilian populations—can never be just.

While the concept of nonviolence is not as well developed in Islam as in many other religions, the notion of *salaam*—etymologically related to the Hebrew *shalom*—offers a vision of a harmonious social order free from violence and conflict. Some Muslim mystics, known as Sufis, reject the traditional notion of *jihad* and replace it with an ideal of inner struggle, a "greater *jihad*," that is the battle of truth with falsehood in the heart and mind of every individual. A few overtly pacifist sects exist in Islam, such as the Maziyariyah and Ahmadiyah movements. When confronted by oppressive regimes, Muslims have sometimes responded with noncooperation and nonretaliation toward evil, meeting their end as martyrs in a fashion much like those in the Jewish and Christian traditions.

C. Ultimate Nonviolence: The Eschatological Hope

One cannot fully understand the religious sanctions for nonviolence without giving due attention to eschatology, or religious teachings regarding the end of the world. A key element in biblical eschatology is the vision of universal peace among the nations as classically expressed by the prophet Isaiah (2:1–4, New Revised Standard Version):

In days to come the mountain of the Lord's house shall be established as the highest of the mountains, and shall be raised above the hills; and all the nations shall stream to it. Many peoples shall come and say, "Come, let us go up to the mountain of the Lord, to the house of the God of Jacob; that he may teach us his ways and that we may walk in his paths." For out of Zion shall go forth instruction, and the word of the Lord from Jerusalem. He shall judge between the nations, and shall arbitrate for many peoples; they shall beat their swords into plowshares, and their spears into pruning hooks; nation shall not lift up sword against nation, and neither shall they learn war any more.

The nations will be in harmony, the passage seems to imply, only if and when they live under God's direction. The concluding phrases, inscribed on the facade of the United Nations Building in New York City, sum up an aspiration toward peace that is common to the great religions of the world, but frequently contradicted by the persecutions and holy wars conducted within these very same religions.

Also See the Following Articles

Bibliography

Armstrong, K. (1991). *Holy war: The crusades and their impact on today's world*. New York: Anchor Books/Doubleday Press.

Bainton, R. H. (1960). *Christian attitudes toward war and peace*. Nashville, TN: Abingdon Press.

Candland, C. (Ed.) (1992). *The spirit of violence: An interdisciplinary bibliography of religion and violence*. New York: Harry Frank Guggenheim Foundation.

Craigie, P. C. (1978). *The problem of war in the old testament.* Grand Rapids, MI: Eerdmans Press.

Finucane, R. C. (1987). The Inquisition. In M. Eliade (Ed.), *The encyclopedia of religion.* New York: Macmillan.

Frend, W. H. C. (1967). *Martyrdom and persecution in the early church: A study of a conflict from the Maccabees to Donatus.* New York: New York University Press.

Girard, R. (1977). *Violence and the sacred.* Baltimore, MD: Johns Hopkins University Press.

Hawley, J. S. (Ed.) (1994). *Sati, the blessing and the curse: The burning of wives in India.* New York: Oxford University Press.

Johnson, J. T. (1997). *The holy war idea in western and Islamic traditions.* University Park, PA: Pennsylvania State University Press.

Juergensmeyer, M. (1993). *The new cold war?: Religious nationalism confronts the secular state.* Berkeley: University of California Press.

Juergensmeyer, M. (1987). Nonviolence. In M. Eliade (Ed.), *The encyclopedia of religion.* New York: Macmillan.

Juergensmeyer, M. (1995). Violence and religion. In J. Z. Smith (Ed.), *The HarperCollins encyclopedia of religion.* San Francisco: HarperCollins.

Kakar, S. (1996). *The colors of violence: Cultural identities, religion, and conflict.* Chicago: University of Chicago Press.

Lea, H. C. (1963). *The inquisition of the middle ages: Its organization and operation.* London: Eyre and Spottiswoode.

Lewy, G. (1974). *Religion and revolution.* New York: Oxford University Press.

Mojzes, P. (1994). *Yugoslavian inferno: Ethnoreligious warfare in the Balkans.* New York: Continuum.

Murphy, T. P. (Ed.) (1976). *The holy war; Fifth conference on medieval and renaissance studies.* Columbus, OH: Ohio State University Press.

Nardin, T. (Ed.) (1996). *The ethics of war and peace: Religious and secular perspectives.* Princeton, NJ: Princeton University Press.

Schwartz, R. (1997). *The curse of Cain: The violent legacy of monotheism.* Chicago: University of Chicago Press.

Sells, M. (1996). *The bridge betrayed: Religion and genocide in Bosnia.* Berkeley: University of California.

Shea, N. (1997). *In the lion's den: A shocking account of persecution and martyrdom of christians today and how we should respond.* Nashville, TN: Broadman and Holman.

Tambiah, S. J. (1992). *Buddhism betrayed? Religion, politics, and violence in Sri Lanka.* Chicago: University of Chicago Press.

Revolutions

Jeff Goodwin and Adam Green

New York University

GLOSSARY

Coup d'etat The swift overthrow of a government or political regime, sometimes through violent means, by political elites and/or state officials, often led by military officers. (Also called a "palace revolution.") Coups may become "revolutions from above" if their leaders enact radical political and/or socioeconomic reforms.

Infrastructural Power A state's capacity to control and to enforce its will, including extant laws, upon the population that it claims to govern. Revolutions typically require, and follow upon, the contraction of such power and often result in the vast expansion of such power.

Rebellion or Insurrection A linked series of collective actions, typically organized by one or more popularly supported groups or parties, which are explicitly aimed at overthrowing a state or some territorial component thereof, but which do not necessarily succeed in doing so. (Also called a "revolutionary movement.")

Revolution The overthrow and resulting transformation of a state or political regime, usually through violent means, by a rebellion or insurrection, albeit sometimes with the assistance of former or extant state officials or personnel. (Also called a "political revolution.")

Revolutionary Situation The existence of two or more political blocs (including, typically, extant state officials and their allies) which are making competing claims for exclusive control of a state or some territorial component thereof. (Also called "dual power" or "multiple sovereignty" when there are two or three or more such contending blocs, respectively.)

Social Revolution A revolution, as defined above, that is accompanied by, facilitates, or brings about fundamental social, economic, and/or cultural change. (Also called a "great revolution.")

REVOLUTIONS entail the overthrow and transformation of states or political regimes, typically by violent means, by popular rebellions or insurrections. The new regimes that result from revolutions also often transform the regional or even global balance of power among states. Some revolutions, moreover, not only bring about new regimes or states, but also produce or facilitate more or less fundamental social, economic, and/or cultural changes among the populations governed by those states, sometimes through the use of coercion and often despite violent resistance from groups that oppose such changes. Accordingly, revolutions rival inter-state wars, which often help to cause and/or result from revolutions, as the most consequential and (frequently) violent form of political conflict in human history.

I. THE CONCEPT OF REVOLUTION

In common parlance, "revolution" has come to mean virtually any fundamental change. Thus, alterations in ways of thinking, artistic expression, technologies, fashions, and even consumer goods are often described as "revolutionary." Social scientists, however, tend to define revolution in one of two ways. For some, revolution refers broadly to any extralegal overthrow and reconstitution of a state or political regime by a popularly supported group, party, or movement. (Although some state officials may support revolutionaries, a revolution differs from a coup d'etat, which refers to the overthrow of a government by political elites, often led by military officers, with little if any popular support or active participation.) Others define revolutions more narrowly as only those instances in which the overthrow of a state is accompanied by or facilitates fundamental social, economic, and/or cultural change among the population ruled by that state. This latter type of revolution is often called a "social revolution" (or "great revolution") in order to distinguish it from those revolutions (or "political revolutions") that entail new political orders, but little, if any, social, economic, or cultural change. However, exactly what constitutes the "fundamental" change that social revolutions bring about is subject to debate. For some, including Marxists, revolutions necessarily involve a substantial redistribution of property or the creation of a new type of economy or "mode of production." Yet other analysts argue that revolutions may radically alter everyday life for millions of people—through political and cultural change, for example—without entailing much economic change. However defined, most social scientists agree that social revolutions have been relatively rare, if momentous, occurrences; by most counts, fewer than two dozen major social revolutions have taken place during the past 2 centuries (see Table I).

Prior to the French Revolution of 1789, the word "revolution" was generally applied to political affairs in its literal sense; the word referred, that is, to a return to some prior state of affairs. "Revolution" was thus synonymous with "restoration." With the French Revolution, however, the word itself was revolutionized. It no longer suggested a cyclical return to the *status quo ante*, but rather a linear progression to a radically different (and presumably superior) type of society.

After the French Revolution, "revolution" became

TABLE I

Major Social Revolutions, 1789–1989

Country	Year
France	1789
Mexico	1910
Russia	1917
Yugoslavia	1945
Vietnam	1945
China	1949
Bolivia	1952
Cuba	1959
Algeria	1962
Ethiopia	1974
Angola	1975
Mozambique	1975
Cambodia	1975
Laos	1975
Iran	1979
Nicaragua	1979
Eastern Europe	1989

Note. The listed dates are conventional markers, usually referring to the year in which revolutionaries overthrew extant political authorities. Revolutions, however, are best conceptualized not as events, but as processes that typically span many years or even decades.

not just a popular term and a social science concept, but also a moral ideal and even imperative for many millions of people. Myriad rebellions and insurgencies have occurred over the past 2 centuries with the explicit aim of deposing political authorities and, often, remaking the social order from top to bottom. When such rebellions obtain substantial popular support, one may speak of the existence of a "revolutionary situation." There have been hundreds if not thousands of revolutionary situations around the globe during the past 2 centuries. Most popular rebellions or insurgencies, however, do not succeed in overthrowing the state. If the state's armed forces remain strong and cohesive, rebellions are typically defeated or confined to some peripheral region within the national territory. Most revolutionary situations, in other words, do not result in political, let alone social, revolutions. A revolution typically requires the prior weakening or collapse of the state's "infrastructural power"; the state's capacity, that is, to enforce its will upon the society that it claims to govern (see Mann, 1993). While revolutionary movements themselves sometimes incapacitate states, such movements just as frequently overthrow states that have already been fatally weakened by inter-state wars, economic and fiscal crises, and/or elite conflicts.

If revolutions refashion states and, sometimes, the societies governed by those states, then revolutions simply could not occur on a large scale prior to the emergence of a system of consolidated national states; that is, before the past 2 centuries or so. Until the modern era, there existed no institution—with the possible exception of the Catholic Church—with the capacity to routinely enforce its will upon substantial populations inhabiting contiguous territories. Once political authorities developed this sort of infrastructural power, revolution became both possible and, for many people, desirable. Thus, while political conflict may be as old as humanity itself, the possibility of radically transforming a "society," "nation," or "people"—meaning the economic, political and/or cultural arrangements of a large population—is coeval with the modern state system as it originated in Europe and was then imposed and imitated around the globe. Unlike certain forms of political conflict, in sum, revolution is a distinctively modern phenomenon.

Many social scientists view violence as an essential characteristic of revolutions, and many if not most revolutions have in fact involved considerable violence among the parties contending for state power. Foreign states, moreover, have often intervened militarily in revolutionary conflicts or attacked newly installed revolutionary governments. Some revolutionary regimes, furthermore, have perpetrated genocides or mass murders or have attacked neighboring countries. Still, the extent of violence in revolutions is quite variable, and some have occurred with very little bloodshed. Some social scientists, furthermore, have detected a trend in recent decades toward nonviolent revolutions, which we discuss below. For these reasons, violence is best viewed as a potential and variable component of revolution, not as one of its defining characteristics. "Nonviolent revolution" is not an oxymoron.

Whether one employs the broader or narrower definition of revolution, the concept clearly stands apart analytically from such kindred forms of political conflict as wars, rebellions, social movements, riots, and coups d'etat. Historically, however, these latter forms of conflict have often been closely connected with revolutions or revolutionary situations. As noted, inter-state wars often help to cause revolutions by weakening states, as well as by inflaming popular grievances, including perceived threats to nationhood or national identity; in turn, revolutions often result in wars, usually because foreign powers seek to destroy those revolutionary

movements or regimes that they perceive as threats. For their part, rebellions create revolutionary situations if they obtain popular support, and they lead to revolutions if they successfully seize state power. Similarly, social movements that initially seek reforms within the existing political system become revolutionary movements if they attempt to overthrow the state, which often happens when the political order breaks down or when the state adamantly refuses to implement the reforms desired by such movements. Spontaneous riots, furthermore, may help to precipitate revolutions, and they have occurred frequently during the chaos that often accompanies revolutionary situations. Finally, coups may become "revolutions from above" if their leaders implement radical political or socioeconomic changes. In sum, while revolutions and especially social revolutions are a distinctive and comparatively rare form of political conflict, they are often connected, whether as cause or consequence, with other and more frequently occurring types of political contention.

II. A BRIEF HISTORY OF REVOLUTIONS

Like wars, social movements, and other forms of political conflict, rebellions and revolutions tend to occur in waves or cycles that spill across multiple national boundaries. This is so for several reasons. First, the socioeconomic processes that sometimes weaken existing states and/or encourage popular rebellions often operate on a transnational scale. Second, inter-state wars, which tend to weaken states (especially the losers in such wars) and to generate widespread grievances, may affect a great many countries simultaneously. Third, revolutions have a "demonstration effect" for other countries; their ideology, strategy, and tactics may be imitated by others. Finally, revolutionary movements, especially those that have successfully seized state power, may be able to assist other such movements materially and militarily. However, not all or even most revolutionary movements in any given wave are successful, and attempts to "export" revolution from one country to another have failed more often than they have succeeded. The so-called "domino effect," whereby revolution in one country leads to revolutions in adjacent countries, is a relatively rare phenomenon.

There were four major waves of rebellion and revolution prior to the Second World War. The first great revolutionary wave, which stretches from the 1630s through the 1660s, includes rebellions in Ireland and Scotland against the English crown; the English Civil

War; a series of rebellions known as the Fronde in France; and revolts in Catalonia, southern Italy, and Portugal against the Spanish kingdom of Castile. The second revolutionary cycle, which lasted from the 1770s through the 1840s, has been called "the age of revolutions." It encompasses the American war of independence against Great Britain, the French Revolution of 1789, the Irish rebellion against British rule, the revolt in the French colony of San Domingo (which established the independent state of Haiti), the multiple wars of independence against Spanish and Portuguese rule in what we now call Latin America, and the Greek revolt against Ottoman rule. It also includes the French Revolution of 1830 and the so-called "springtime of peoples" in Europe in 1848, including popular and nationalist rebellions in France, Italy, Switzerland, Austria, Hungary, Germany, Bohemia, and Romania. The general ideological thrust of these first two waves of rebellion and revolution was antifeudal, antimonarchical, democratic, and often nationalist.

A third cycle of revolutionary conflict (1905–1921) straddles the First World War. On the eve of the war, popular movements in Russia, Iran, Mexico, and China—generally led and supported by middle classes, albeit with substantial popular support—challenged autocracy and/or foreign domination, with decidedly mixed results. The ideological orientation of these movements was democratic and/or anti-imperialist. More rebellions occurred in Europe and in Turkey during and immediately after the war, beginning with the 1916 Easter Rising in Ireland against British rule; after a brief guerrilla war, most of Ireland attained effective independence in 1921, although six counties in Ulster province remained British. The Russian Revolution was the epicenter of this wave, but the hope of the victorious Bolshevik (later renamed Communist) Party that similar socialist revolutions would triumph across Europe was not to be. Left-wing revolutionary movements were defeated in Germany, Slovakia, Hungary, and Italy. Still, workers and artisans played a more central role in this wave than previously, and socialist ideology competed with liberal and nationalist currents.

The fourth and final revolutionary wave prior to the Second World War encompasses those fascist and right-wing movements, eventually triumphant in Italy, Germany, and Spain, which arose during the 1920s and 1930s, partly in response to the left-wing movements of the previous cycle. Fascism, which found support in both the lower-middle class and sectors of the working class, was profoundly antidemocratic, antisocialist, and nationalistic. Although fascism is generally viewed as non- or counterrevolutionary by both its Marxist and liberal foes, triumphant fascist movements were profoundly revolutionary in terms of the dramatic political, geopolitical, and cultural transformations that they brought about, not to mention the genocide perpetrated against European Jewry by Germany's Nazi regime.

There were four more revolutionary waves following the Second World War. Indeed, the Cold War era (1945–1991) probably witnessed more revolutionary situations, and certainly more social revolutions (see Table I), than any comparable period in history. The first three cycles of revolution of this era occurred primarily in the so-called third world and reflected a strong Marxist and socialist orientation. The first of these (1945–1949) was intimately connected to the disruptions and privations of the war itself. Communist-led revolutionary movements, which had gained considerable legitimacy during the war as resistance forces to occupation armies, seized power in Yugoslavia, Albania, North Korea, Vietnam, and China. A nationalist revolution also triumphed in Indonesia at this time. Strong revolutionary movements, ultimately defeated or contained, also arose during this period in Greece, Malaya, Burma, and the Philippines. Finally, the Soviet Union imposed Communist "revolutions from above" in those areas of Eastern Europe which it effectively controlled following the war.

The second cycle of postwar revolutionary movements (1959–1968) began with the Cuban Revolution, and encompasses the Algerian Revolution (1962) and the beginnings of the revolutionary conflict in South Vietnam (1960–1975). In Latin America, a number of attempts were made to replicate the Cuban Revolution, sometimes with Cuban assistance, but these failed in Venezuela, Guatemala, Colombia, Peru, and Bolivia. However, a third cycle of generally successful revolutionary movements (1974–1980) dates from the withdrawal of U.S. troops from Vietnam. Revolutionaries seized power during this period in Ethiopia, Cambodia, South Vietnam itself, Laos, Portugal's African colonies (Guinea-Bissau, Angola, and Mozambique), Iran, Grenada, and Nicaragua. Strong revolutionary movements also emerged or reemerged during this time in the Philippines, Colombia, Peru, El Salvador, and Guatemala. With the end of the Cold War, the movements in El Salvador and Guatemala negotiated peace accords with government authorities, which resulted in their disarmament and reconstitution as legal political parties.

Unlike the first three postwar waves, the last revolutionary cycle of the Cold War era (1989–1991), which encompasses the "collapse of Communism" in Eastern Europe, the Balkans, and the former Soviet Union, was decidedly antisocialist and at least rhetorically democratic. Nationalist opposition to Soviet (or Russian) and Yugoslavian (or Serbian) domination was also an important factor in this wave. Nonviolent popular movements quickly toppled Communist regimes in a number of countries (and Soviet republics), especially after Gorbachev, the Soviet leader, made it clear that Soviet tanks would not rescue unpopular rulers. Movements against Communism, however, were not uniformly successful during this wave; nonviolent protest was violently suppressed in China in 1989 and was barely evident in Cuba, Vietnam, and North Korea.

III. THEORIES OF REVOLUTION

Social scientists examine rebellions and revolutions from a variety of perspectives, employing the full range of competing analytic frameworks that inform the social sciences more generally. Three analytic frameworks in particular figure prominently in the recent literature on revolutions: Marxist (and neo-Marxist) perspectives, cultural approaches, and state-centered theories. After briefly reviewing these frameworks, we also examine the importance of "moral outrage" for revolutions, as well as the political contexts that create and channel it into revolutionary movements.

A. Marxist and Neo-Marxist Perspectives

Marxist and neo-Marxist theories of revolution identify the material or economic organization of a given society—i.e., the forces and relations of production—as the principle context determining revolutionary conflicts, which are understood as struggles between social classes. For Marxists, revolutions are the result of class struggles between dominant "ruling" classes, on the one hand, and "rising" or revolutionary classes, on the other. Revolutionary situations are understood to arise during those historical periods when the progressive development of the forces of production (technology, skills, the division of labor) comes into conflict with the existing relations of production, or class relations, which are based on the ownership or control of productive property. During these crisis periods, the existing social system is paralyzed, as it were, and social development requires a fundamental reorganization of the economy or mode of production, as well as of the state, by the revolutionary class. In short, objective structural conditions are seen to induce growing class antagonisms that culminate in the overthrow of the existing state and social order. (The state itself is seen by Marxists largely as an instrument of the dominant class, and politicians and bureaucrats are attributed little autonomy as independent political agents.) Under feudalism, the revolutionary class was the bourgeois or capitalist class; under capitalism, the revolutionary class is the proletariat or working class. Marx believed that capitalism would inevitably compel the working class to seize state power, destroy capitalism, and create a socialist society.

Since Marx first formulated his materialist approach to revolutions, many derivative explanatory models of revolution have emerged, often modifying components of his original formulations. What makes more recent neo-Marxist approaches definitively "Marxist" is the emphasis that they all place on class struggle as the key expression and determinant of revolutionary situations and outcomes. One such neo-Marxist approach identifies the rural peasantry as a potentially insurgent force and agent of socialist revolution. According to this approach, the commercialization of agriculture often leads to the radicalization of the peasantry. More generally, variations in the dynamics of the commercialization of agriculture produce variations in rural class conflict. In one version of this approach (Paige, 1975), the more landowners and cultivators become tied to global capital and markets, the greater their respective tactical mobility in political struggles; conversely, the more dependent landowners and cultivators remain on the land for income (as opposed to capital or wages), the less tactical mobility each is thought to have. The least revolutionary conditions are thought to exist where landowners draw income from their capital investments and peasants draw income from the land. Conversely, the conditions most conducive to revolution are allegedly found where landowners are dependent for income on the land and peasants draw their income from wages (i.e., sharecropping and migratory labor systems).

The fundamental weakness of Marxist and neo-Marxist theories of revolution can be simply stated: Class exploitation, even during periods of economic crisis, does not necessarily result in the development of class consciousness among the exploited, let alone actual rebellion. Members of exploited classes—including peasants, sharecroppers, and urban workers—may view their problems as the result of their own personal failures or as the result of impersonal (and perhaps other-worldly) forces that are beyond anyone's control. In order to understand how class exploitation and other "objective" realities come to be collectively perceived as unjust and alterable, some scholars have turned to modes of analysis that place greater weight than does Marxism on cultural and ideological factors, on the one hand, and state policies, on the other.

B. Cultural Approaches

Cultural theorists of revolution argue that Marxist and state-centered approaches conflate cultural and ideological factors with class struggle and state-building, respectively. In the latter approaches, culture and ideology are often equated with the conscious attitudes and choices of individual revolutionary actors and are understood as inconsequential for explaining the origins and outcomes of revolution. By contrast, those who emphasize the cultural determinants of revolution understand normative and ideological commitments to play an important causal role in catalyzing and shaping revolutionary struggles. In these accounts, cultural forces are seen not as a mere epiphenomenal product of material or political structures, but, on the contrary, as autonomous and transpersonal forces shaping social relations and the larger political field of action within which revolutions unfold. Revolutions may indeed arise in the context of particular structural, economic, and political conditions; yet analysts also need to treat seriously culture and ideology, both as motivating forces and as constitutive elements of collective identities.

Cultural analysts of revolutions also generally suggest that ideologies do not take shape at the individual level, but instead are "transpersonal." They are understood to constitute an "anonymous" structure in the sense that they are never wholly created nor present in the consciousness of any single actor; rather, ideologies and cultural frameworks are shared to a greater or lesser extent by groups or networks of connected individuals. This approach is further distinguished from Marxist and state-centered theories by its refusal to view ideology either as a simple "reflex" of class relations or as the ideas of revolutionary leaders. Instead, the social order itself is understood to be shaped and indeed constituted by ideological structures. In this complex conception of ideology, institutional structures, class relations, and the attitudes and predispositions of a given group are each shaped and organized by various ideologies and cultural frameworks.

Other cultural analyses focus on the cultural construction of revolutions as unitary political events—the "revolutionary script"—as it arises from within existing linguistic and symbolic fields. Similarly, conceptions of group identity and interest are resituated from the seemingly "objective" realm of a preexisting social reality to the realm of symbolic and meaning creation. Here, a full understanding of revolutionary processes demands that we look to the symbolic realm and the ways in which social events, interests, the identities of relevant social groups, and the nature of their claims are constructed and acted upon within historically specific fields of meanings. In this perspective, ideas and social action are inextricably bound together and must be incorporated into analyses of revolutionary conflicts.

C. State-Centered Theories

State-centered theories of revolutions are distinguished by their emphasis on the primacy of the state as an autonomous administrative and coercive organization. In marked contrast to Marxist theories of revolution, state-centered approaches identify the state as a potentially self-interested political actor, or set of actors, which cannot be analytically collapsed into the dominant class nor understood as a mere tool of its interests. Moreover, whereas Marxists focus on the purposive actions of the revolutionary class, state-centered theory shifts the explanatory focus from the domain of revolutionary motivations and intentions to an analysis of the structural conditions that make rebellions and revolutions possible and likely. Of greatest consequence here are both the state's external relationships with other states and its internal relationships with its subjects or citizens. While revolution is understood to require mass mobilization, its ultimate causes and outcomes will depend far less on the motivations and activities of revolutionary actors and far more on the weakening or even collapse of the state under certain circumstances, especially when states are caught in the crossfire of external and internal pressures. State crises, then, are not the result of revolutionary conflicts nor simply derivative of class struggles but instead provide the very conditions under which rebellions and revolutions are made possible. As Wendell Phillips once quipped, "Revolutions are not made; they come."

Looking to the unfolding of political history in revolutionary France, China, and Russia, Skocpol (1979)—perhaps the single most influential state-centered theorist—identifies fiscal and military crises to be particularly crucial factors contributing to the exacerbation of class conflicts and to the diminution of the prestige and coercive power of the state machinery. For example, in the case of the French Revolution, the War of Austrian Succession (1740–1748) and the Seven Years War (1756–1763) weakened the Old Regime, diminishing its capacity to raise much-needed revenue and impairing its ability to promote national economic development to maintain tax advantages and financial opportunities for the upper classes and to secure military stability and conquest. Under these historical conditions, the state incited and grew vulnerable to class contention and the subsequent formation of broad revolutionary coalitions.

Revolution would ultimately come to France when the fiscal crisis of 1787–1788 sharply increased the antagonisms among the peasantry, landed elites, and the Old Regime and forced the monarchy to call the Estates-General. In this account, revolution occurred as a consequence of the monarchy's competing interests with the landed elite and the subsequent exacerbation of class antagonisms and a state fiscal crisis in the context of international competition with other states. In the cases of France, Russia, and China alike, international conflict served to exacerbate class conflicts and increase the vulnerability of the state by weakening and delegitimating its coercive and administrative apparatus—the decisive structural conditions under which revolutions become likely.

D. Moral Outrage and the State

However helpful, state-centered approaches clearly do not provide a sufficient or exhaustive explanation of revolutions. For example, although states may strongly influence the forms of popular organization that factor into revolutions, they do not strictly determine these. Nor do state actions entirely explain the grievances or moral outrage that motivates revolutions. Nonetheless, state policies do help to explain how such grievances and outrage are sometimes channeled into revolutionary movements. Revolutionary movements prosper, for example, if the state sponsors or defends economic and social arrangements that are widely regarded as unjust. In certain societies, economic and social arrangements may be widely viewed as unjust (that is, as not simply unfortunate or inevitable), yet unless state officials are seen to sponsor or protect those arrangements—through legal codes, taxation, conscription, and, ultimately, force—*revolutionary* collective action aimed at overthrowing the state is unlikely. People may angrily blame their particular superiors or employers for their plight, for example, or even whole classes of superiors, yet the state itself may not be challenged unless there exists a widely shared perception that it stands behind those elites.

Revolutionaries also fare well, other things being equal, when the state legally or forcibly excludes aggrieved groups from state power or resources. Even if such groups do come to direct their claims at the state, they are unlikely to seek its overthrow if they manage to attain some fair share—or believe they *can* attain such a share—of state power or influence. Even if such groups view their political influence as unjustly limited,

their access to state resources or inclusion in policy-making deliberations will likely prevent them from becoming radicalized. In fact, the "incorporation" of mobilized groups—including the putatively revolutionary proletariat of Marxist theory—into parliamentary and other political institutions has typically served to deradicalize them. Such groups often view this sort of inclusion as the first step in the accumulation of greater influence and resources; as a result, they are unlikely to jeopardize their relatively low-cost access to the state by engaging in "disloyal" or illegal revolutionary activities. For this reason, among others, no popular revolutionary movement has ever violently overthrown a consolidated democratic regime.

Exclusionary authoritarian regimes, by contrast, tend to "incubate" radical forms of political contention: Those who call for revolution tend to prosper under such regimes, because they come to be viewed by many people as more realistic and potentially effective than political moderates and reformists. Virtually every powerful revolutionary movement has mobilized popular support against an exclusionary regime, including the Bolsheviks in Russia, the Communists in China and Vietnam, Castro's 26th of July Movement in Cuba, the broad coalition that opposed the Shah in Iran, and the guerrilla movements of Central America, among many others.

Indiscriminate, but not overwhelming, state violence against mobilized groups and oppositional political figures also unintentionally helps revolutionaries. For reasons of simple self-defense, people who are literally targeted by the state may arm themselves or join groups that have access to arms. People whose families or friends have been victimized by the state may also join or support revolutionaries in order to seek revenge against the perpetrators. Indiscriminate state violence may also be viewed by the general population as illegitimate or unjust, especially if the targets of this violence are making demands or claims that are widely perceived to be just or at least worthy of recognition.

Unless state violence is directed at unpopular groups or is simply overwhelming, then, indiscriminate coercion often backfires, producing an ever-growing popular mobilization, typically led by armed movements, and an even larger body of indignant sympathizers. Revolutionary movements may thus prosper not so much because of their ideology per se, but simply because they can offer people some sort of protection from authoritarian states. Political groups and parties have generally turned to militant strategies or armed struggle only after their previous efforts to secure change through legal means were violently repressed. Under repressive conditions, ordinary people are likely to view armed struggle as a legitimate and reasonable means of political contestation.

Finally, like political exclusion, indiscriminate state violence also reinforces the plausibility and legitimacy of revolutionary ideologies, that is, ideologies that (1) proclaim the existing order to be fundamentally unjust and (2) envisage a radical reorganization of the political system and perhaps of society as well. In other words, violent, exclusionary regimes often unintentionally bolster the popularity of their most radical social critics—religious zealots, socialist militants, and radical nationalists, for example, who view society as more or less totally corrupt, incapable of reform, and thus requiring a thorough and (if need be) violent reconstruction.

Certain sorts of states, in sum, unintentionally facilitate the development of powerful revolutionary movements by generating or reinforcing popular grievances, contributing to widespread feelings of moral outrage, focusing those feelings on the state, foreclosing possibilities for peaceful reform, enhancing the plausibility and legitimacy of revolutionary ideologies, and (often) compelling people to take up arms in order to defend themselves and to pursue effectively their collective interests and ideals.

IV. THE FUTURE OF REVOLUTIONS

A. Nonviolent Revolutions

Following the third postwar wave of revolutions (1974–1980) described above, there have occurred a growing number of nonviolent or at least unarmed popular insurgencies against authoritarian states. In fact, one of the most important revolutions of this third wave and one of the major social revolutions of the century, namely, the Iranian Revolution of 1978–1979, was largely unarmed, although a great deal of bloodshed resulted from government attacks on nonviolent demonstrations. During the 1980s and 1990s, there occurred more than a dozen major instances of unarmed antigovernment protests (see Table II). Most of these protest movements were repressed by government authorities, sometimes quite violently, but others succeeded in directly overthrowing authoritarian regimes (as in the Philippines, South Korea, and Eastern Europe) and still others contributed indirectly to democratic transitions (as in South Africa, Chile, and Haiti). Of course, nonviolent protest, including protest aimed at overthrowing or fundamentally reshaping political regimes, is hardly new. The nationalist movement

TABLE II

Major Unarmed Antigovernment Protests, 1978–1998

Country	Years
Iran	1978–1979
Poland	1980–1981
South Africa	1982–1985
Chile	1983–1986
Sudan	1985
Haiti	1985
Philippines	1986
South Korea	1987
Burma	1987–1988
West Bank and Gaza	1987–1993
Tibet	1987–1989
China	1989
Eastern Europe	1989
Mali	1990–1991
Kenya	1990–?
Madagascar	1991–1993
Kosova (Serbia)	1991–1997
Nigeria	1993–1995
Indonesia	1998–?

Note. Dates are approximate and refer to the peak year(s) of protest. (Adapted from Zunes, 1994.)

against British rule in India, protest by Black South Africans during the 1950s, and the civil rights movement in the United States all employed nonviolent strategies of protest. Still, there does seem to be a trend toward nonviolent or unarmed antigovernment protest during the final decades of the 20th century.

What might account for this trend? Analysts have pointed to several factors that may explain the growing appeal of nonviolent protest. Compared to armed struggle, for example, nonviolent protest often allows for greater popular mobilization, which need not be confined to peripheral or thinly populated regions where the state's infrastructural power is weak. There may also be a growing recognition that state violence against unarmed protesters, while compelling some of them to take up arms, may also swell the ranks of nonviolent movements, especially if such violence is only erratically and haphazardly employed. Indeed, the use of force against nonviolent protesters may create dissension and divisions among the state's armed forces, which may in turn facilitate revolutions. There has also occurred an international diffusion of the ideological principles of nonviolent protest, especially in the writings of Gandhi and Martin Luther King, Jr.

Perhaps the central reason for the increasing prevalence of nonviolent or unarmed protest, however, is the general expansion of most states' infrastructural power during the 20th century. New military, transportation, and surveillance technologies have made it extremely difficult for would-be revolutionaries to defeat a regular army by force of arms, unless that army has been weakened in war or by political dissension within its ranks. The latter type of schisms, however, may be generated by extensive nonviolent protest as well as by armed struggle. Indeed, few armed revolutionary movements that have seized state power actually defeated regular armies on the battlefield. More often, armed revolutionaries have triumphed when the armies that they have confronted broke apart during wartime (as in Russia), were very deeply divided along political lines (as in Bolivia), or ultimately refused to fight (as in Cuba). In colonial situations, moreover, armed revolutionaries have usually triumphed by gradually eroding the political will of the colonial power to maintain its rule, typically by waging guerrilla warfare and carrying out economic sabotage over many years or even decades. In these cases, armed revolutionaries eventually won by not losing. But this sort of "prolonged popular warfare" is enormously costly and is usually only adopted as a last resort. Nonviolent protest, if and when it proves effective, is generally preferred by protesters, whether they seek to overthrow the state or not.

B. Revolutions, Globalization, and Democratization

Will there be more nonviolent revolutions in coming decades? Indeed, what does the future hold for revolutions, violent or nonviolent, during the 21st century? Does either "globalization" (i.e., the increasingly transnational character and integration of capitalism) or the crisis of socialism brought on by the demise of the Soviet bloc herald the end of revolution as a distinctive mode of political conflict and change?

Some have suggested that economic "globalization" has destroyed the very rationale for revolutions. According to this perspective, state power—the traditional prize of revolutionaries—has been dramatically eroded by the growing power of multinational corporations and by the increasingly rapid and uncontrollable movements of commodities, people, and especially capital across national borders. These transnational movements allegedly undermine the autonomy of states by making it extraordinarily difficult for any single state to conduct a separate economic or military policy; accordingly, the former political advantages of controlling the institutions of national states have declined. In other words, as globalization increasingly diminishes and hollows out state power, the less compelling becomes any political project aimed at capturing state power, including revolution.

Rather than uniformly diminishing states, however, globalization has been just as likely to spur attempts to employ and, if necessary, expand state power for purposes of enhancing global economic competitiveness. Historically, in fact, there has been a strong correlation between a country's exposure to external economic competition and the size of its public sector. To a significant extent, globalization is itself a project of strong states in economically advanced societies. Popular support for revolutionaries, at any rate, is not usually based on estimations of their likely success in enhancing the autonomy of a state's fiscal policy or a country's global competitiveness. Ordinary folk have typically supported revolutionaries because they've spoken up for them when no one else would, protected them from state violence, provided for their subsistence, and defended their traditional rights. There seems little reason to believe that in the future people will accept the depredations of authoritarian regimes on the grounds that the autonomy of any subsequent regime would be limited due to globalization. However, while globalization per se has not made rebellions and political revolutions less likely, it has undoubtedly made social—and especially socialist—revolutions more difficult. At the very least, any government that attempted to create a socialist economy would be effectively shut off from transnational flows of capital and commerce.

Another common argument for the declining prospects for future socialist revolutions is the crisis of socialism linked to the collapse of the Soviet bloc. Many revolutionaries of the Cold War era, especially in poorer countries, were certainly emboldened by the existence of a powerful noncapitalist industrial society, one that was itself dependent and "backward" in the not-too-distant past. The appeal of the Soviet model was all the greater because the Soviets were the self-proclaimed foes of the capitalist powers (above all the U.S.) which often provided aid and comfort—in the name of anti-Communism—to brutal and authoritarian regimes. Yet it was, in the first instance, precisely the brutality and authoritarianism of so many states during the Cold War era—including the Soviet-backed regimes in Eastern Europe—that provided the seedbed for widespread revolutionary conflicts. For much of the Cold War era, vast tracts of the globe suffered more or less violent and exclusionary forms of colonial rule, imperial domination, military occupation, or postcolonial despotism. In these political contexts, popular rebellions, usually armed and necessarily violent, were often the only practical repertoire of political struggle for the attainment of the most elementary popular demands. Moderates and reformists, by contrast, seemed utopian or even suicidal in such contexts.

Today, however, this seedbed for revolution is virtually desiccated: Colonialism is all but dead; Soviet domination of Eastern Europe is no more; and U.S. hegemony in the third world—even in its Central American "backyard"—is increasingly challenged by rival powers. Most importantly, and partly because of these very developments, a transnational "wave" of democratization has swept across large parts of East Asia, Eastern Europe, Latin America, and (to a lesser extent) Africa over the past decade or two. While there were precious few democratic regimes in South America in 1980, for example, transitions to democracy were underway virtually everywhere on that continent just 15 years later. Thanks in large part to revolutionary movements themselves, moreover, democratic transitions are now also underway in Central America; but with democracy, of course, has also come the pacification of the revolutionaries.

If coming decades are unlikely to exhibit the same scale of revolutionary conflict as the Cold War era, it will be precisely because of this vast political transformation. The likelihood of future revolutions, that is rests in large part upon the future of democracy. For there can be no doubt that democracy is a potent counterrevolutionary force. As noted no popular revolutionary movement has ever overthrown a consolidated democratic regime. The great revolutions of the Cold War era, for example, toppled exclusionary colonial regimes (as in Vietnam and Algeria), personalist dictatorships (as in Cuba, Iran, and Nicaragua), and the Soviet-imposed regimes of Eastern Europe. But none overthrew a regime that even remotely resembled a democracy.

Why exactly is democracy so inhospitable to revolutionaries? First and foremost, democracy largely pacifies and institutionalizes—but hardly does away with—many forms of social conflict. Elections have been aptly described as a "democratic translation of the class struggle." Democracy "translates" and channels a variety of social conflicts—including, but not limited to, class conflicts—into party competition for votes and the lobbying of representatives by "interest groups." The temptation to rebel against the state, which is rarely seized without trepidation under any circumstances, given its life-or-death consequences, is generally quelled under

democratic regimes by the knowledge that new elections are but a few years off—and with them the chance to punish unpopular incumbent rulers. In addition, democracies have generally provided a context in which popular protest can win concessions from economic and political elites, although this often requires a good deal of disruption, if not violence. But armed struggles that are aimed at overthrowing fairly elected governments rarely win much popular support, unless such governments (or the armies that they putatively command) effectively push people into the armed opposition by indiscriminately repressing suspected rebel sympathizers. But by and large, the ballot box is the coffin of revolutionaries.

Does this mean that political radicalism and militancy go unrewarded in democratic societies? Hardly. Democracy, to repeat, by no means eliminates social conflict; in fact, in many ways democracy encourages a veritable flowering of social conflict by providing the "political space" with which those groups outside ruling circles can make claims on political authorities and economic elites. Not just political parties, then, but a whole range of interest groups, trade unions, professional associations, and social movements become the main organizational vehicles of political life in democratic polities. These institutions of "civil society," however, are generally just that—civil. Their repertoires of collective action include electoral campaigns, lobbying, strikes, boycotts, peaceful demonstrations, and civil disobedience—forms of collective action that may be undertaken with great passion and militancy, and sometimes for quite radical ends, but which are not aimed at bringing down the state.

Democracy, then, dramatically reduces the likelihood of revolutionary change, but not because it necessarily brings about social justice. Formal democracy is fully compatible with widespread poverty, inequality, and grievances of all sorts. This is why extraparliamentary movements for social justice so often arise in democratic contexts. But, again, these movements almost always view the state as an instrument to be pressured and influenced, not as something to be seized or smashed. Revolutionary movements, for their part, develop not simply because people are angry or aggrieved, but because the state under which they live provides no other mechanism for social change, violently repressing those who peacefully seek incremental reforms.

If the recent wave of global democratization, accordingly, should continue, then the future of revolution, or at least of widespread revolutionary conflict, looks bleak. To be sure, revolutionary movements will continue to thrive in those peripheral regions that lie beyond the reach of infrastructurally weak authoritarian regimes, as for example in contemporary Mexico, Colombia, Peru, Algeria, Kosova (a province of Serbia), East Timor, and Kurdistan (Southeastern Turkey and Northern Iraq). And more cycles of revolutionary conflict will undoubtedly occur if the nascent democracies in Eastern Europe, East Asia, Latin America, and Africa are replaced by violent, authoritarian regimes.

Past waves of democratization, alas, have in fact been regularly followed by antidemocratic waves. Yet this should give relatively little comfort to revolutionaries, for the vast majority of past transitions from democracy were not the result of popular rebellions, but of military coups or of "executive coups" in which democratically elected heads of state ended democracy by concentrating power in their own hands. Only a very few of the resulting authoritarian regimes, furthermore, were toppled by revolutions. As noted above, revolutionary movements, even those with extensive popular support, rarely succeed in seizing power unless the authoritarian regimes that they confront are very weak or suddenly weakened (through war, for example). That said, only the continued spread of democracy will render revolution passé as a form of political struggle. The future of revolutions is thus inextricably tied to the future of democracy.

Also See The Following Articles

CIVIL WARS • CLASS CONFLICTS • COLD WAR • COLONIALISM AND IMPERIALISM • LAW AND VIOLENCE • PEACE AND DEMOCRACY • SOCIAL CONTROL AND VIOLENCE

Bibliography

Foran, J. (Ed.) (1997). *Theorizing revolutions*. London: Routledge.

Goldstone, J. A. (1991). *Revolution and rebellion in the early modern world*. Berkeley/Los Angeles: University of California Press.

Goodwin, J. (2000). *No other way out: States and revolutionary movements, 1945–1991*. Cambridge, UK: Cambridge University Press.

Hobsbawm, E. J. (1962). *The age of revolution, 1789–1848*. New York: Mentor.

Mann, M. (1993). *The sources of social power: The rise of classes and nation-states, 1760–1914*, Vol. 2. Cambridge, UK: Cambridge University Press.

McDaniel, T. (1991). *Autocracy, modernization, and revolution in Russia and Iran*. Princeton, NJ: Princeton University Press.

Moore, B. Jr. (1966). *Social origins of dictatorship and democracy: Lord and peasant in the making of the modern world*. Boston: Beacon Press.

Paige, J. M. (1975). *Agrarian revolution: Social movements and export agriculture in the underdeveloped world*. New York: Free Press.

Selbin, E. (1993). *Modern Latin American revolutions*. Boulder, CO: Westview.

Sewell, W. H., Jr. (1985). Ideologies and social revolutions: Reflections on the French case. *Journal of Modern History, 57*, 57–85.

Skocpol, T. (1979). *States and social revolutions: A comparative analysis of France, Russia, and China*. Cambridge, UK: Cambridge University Press.

Skocpol, T. (1994). *Social revolutions in the modern world*. Cambridge, UK: Cambridge University Press.

Tilly, C. (1978). *From mobilization to revolution*. Reading, MA: Addison-Wesley.

Tilly, C. (1993). *European revolutions, 1492–1992*. Oxford, UK: Blackwell.

Walt, S. M. (1996). *Revolution and war*. Ithaca, NY: Cornell University Press.

Wickham-Crowley, T. P. (1992). *Guerrillas and revolution in Latin America: A comparative study of insurgents and regimes since 1956*. Princeton, NJ: Princeton University Press.

Zunes, S. (1994). Unarmed insurrections against authoritarian governments in the Third World: A new kind of revolution. *Third World Quarterly, 15*, 403–426.

Ritual and Symbolic Behavior

Philip Smith

University of Queensland

GLOSSARY

Ritual Forms of associative human activity organized around symbolic sets denoting the sacred and profane. Can also be used to denote repetitive, conventionalized forms of human activity and/or forms of human action which lack an obvious practical utility.

Symbolic Behavior Activities organized around a process of communication, usually involving the transmission and reception of information. Can also be used to describe deeds that have a normative or cultural component which is expressed in the action itself. The concept of symbolic behavior is often contrasted with ideas of purely rational or utilitarian action.

STUDIES OF RITUAL and symbolic behavior look at the signifying practices and expressive actions that underpin both peace and violence. An emphasis is therefore placed on symbols and communication practices and the contexts within which they operate. Two broad theoretical traditions can be identified, one rooted in evolutionary biology and the other in cultural theory. In this entry, greater attention is given to elucidating this cultural strand, with biological understandings used as a counterpoint.

I. CONCEPTS OF RITUAL AND SYMBOLIC BEHAVIOR

It has long been noted that many violent behaviors of both humans and animals cannot be accommodated within commonsense understandings of "real" violence and "rational" action. Observers have pointed to play, pretense, and mock violence and to elaborate preparations and displays that appear to have no obvious utility for the conduct of battle or to social norms which replace bloody combat with elaborate but harmless games. These sorts of disparate phenomena tend to be accounted for in terms of ideas of symbolic and ritual behavior, which to some extent operate as catch-all residual categories for explaining the apparently inexplicable. In the biological sciences understandings of symbolic behaviors are framed within the discourse of evolutionary biology and, in particular, game theory. This gives rise to a mechanistic and strategic model of action, with animals seen as engaging in expressive actions in order to obtain an evolutionary advantage. In the social sciences a greater emphasis is placed on culture and the imaginative faculties of the human species. Here the preferred vocabulary is one of symbolic

action rather than behavior. There is usually a greater emphasis placed on voluntarism and reflexivity, seeing symbolic systems as a resource with which humans construct meaningful worlds. Notwithstanding these divergent roots, both traditions give a central place to processes of communication and to describing the roles which participants take up.

II. RITUAL AND SYMBOLIC BEHAVIOR AMONG ANIMALS

The seminal text in the study of ritualistic violence in animal populations is Konrad Lorenz's (1966) *On Aggression*. In this work Lorenz pointed to the tendency of many animal species to engage in ritualized, nonlethal displays of aggression, especially in the context of mate selection. There may also be ceremonial displays of dominance and deference which animals conduct through the careful production and reading of the signs that are exchanged. Among African wild dogs, for example, a defeated combatant will signal when it is bested by posturing in submission and will usually be allowed to escape unharmed. Lorenz argued that such activities carried evolutionary advantages. They provided a harmless outlet for violent instincts, allowed superior specimens to locate mating partners (thus improving the gene pool), and provided a means of strengthening group bonds in social animals such as geese and rats.

More recent work argues that Lorenz wrongly specifies the level at which natural selection works. Instead of looking for benefits at the level of the species or even the individual, we should see natural selection operating at the level of the gene. Consequently ritualized combat behaviors should be seen as a manifestation of ruthless, genetically programmed competition between gene carrying organisms of the same species rather than as a more or less cooperative adaptation that allows a species to compete with other species. A fundamental problem for this sort of tooth-and-claw view of the animal world has been to explain why animals do not kill their opponents once they have defeated them in a ritual encounter. The current orthodoxy is to suggest that escalated fighting carries a risk of serious injury even for a dominant animal. Natural selection will favor genes that prevent animals from engaging in this activity too frequently.

Accompanying the shift to the gene level of analysis has been the rise of game theory as a means of explaining animal behavior. Using mathematical models it is possible to interpret and numerically represent displays of ritualistic behavior as a form of competition in which players (genes carried in organisms) engage in competition with other players. Strategies (escalation, bluff, submission, flight, etc.) are determined by the costs (e.g., time, energy), benefits (e.g., potential access to mates, food), and risks (e.g., danger of injury) of particular lines of action.

It is generally argued that ritualized displays of aggression are common in the animal world because they provide players with a low-cost, low-risk means of attaining benefits. Dominant animals can assert their power, and weaker animals can challenge, without either risking fatal injury. And both can obtain objective information about their position in the pecking order and their odds of future success.

Because such a system will eventually work to the benefit of participants, ensuring the survival of their genes, evolutionary process will work to effect a gradual improvement in the transfer efficiency of signals between actors and reactors, leading to sophisticated mechanisms for signaling "intentions" and future lines of action. With communication replacing (or at least augmenting) real force, possibilities arise for organisms to obtain an evolutionary advantage over other members of their species through specializing in or manipulating ritualized communication systems. It has been suggested this might account for hypertrophied display organs, such as the peacock's tail, which are in other respects possibly cumbersome and dysfunctional for survival. Such an analysis can also help interpret bluffing behaviors. For example, a bird might signal to its flock the arrival of a predator in order to have exclusive access to a food resource. In the case of ritual aggression, a skilled mimic could sound or look like a bigger animal or could fake the "intention" of being willing to fight to the death.

To sum up, current research on ritualized aggression and symbolic behaviors in animal populations is driven by evolutionary biology and game theory. Emphasis is given to the selective advantage that accrues to genes from participation in this kind of encounter rather than in escalated fighting. While the language of game theory speaks of the "strategies" and "ploys" that might be involved in a symbolic conflict, it is important to remember that these are linguistic conventions that assist in the application of a rationalistic game theory to a behaviorist context. Most biologists see animal behavior as a blind product of genetic programming. By contrast, social scientific understandings of ritualistic aggression in humans tend to point toward the culturally meaningful nature of such forms of conflict. The broad consensus is to see them as products of broader social values and specific human choices rather than as the expression of a utilitarian survival function. Despite these divergent paradigms there are some important areas of overlap. Sociobiologists like Edward O. Wilson, Lionel Tiger, and Konrad Lorenz have suggested that the resources of biology might be of use in explaining ritualized violence in areas like human territoriality, male bonding, and group cohesion. Other scholars exploring more microlevel issues of body language, emotions, and facial expressions have also tried to draw analogies from animal behavior to human experience.

Symbolic interactionists have also, albeit rarely, looked to animal studies in developing a broader understanding of routinized and ritualistic aspects of face-to-face human interactions. For example, although he was attentive to the creative, meaning-making qualities of human actors, Erving Goffman's work in areas like frame analysis and interaction ritual evinced an awareness of ethology. This is reflected in some of his terminology (e.g., deference and demeanor, grooming talk) and in the influence of Gregory Bateson's work on the metacontexts that frame the interpretation of behavior among animals. Despite these linkages, the dominant stream in cultural anthropology has been profoundly antithetical to biological understandings of ritualized encounters and violence, seeing them as deterministic and as insufficiently attuned to the complexities of human symbolic systems. This article now turns to this more cultural tradition.

III. RITUAL AND SYMBOLIC BEHAVIOR AMONG PEOPLE

One of the most significant findings across the anthropological and sociological record has been the centrality of symbolic and ritual behavior to forms of violence. In traditional societies war is often regarded as a ritual activity as much as a utilitarian activity for gaining political or economic power, with violence strongly linked to the attainment of manhood. Indeed one commentator sees it as "a rough male sport for underemployed hunters, with the kinds of damage-limiting rules that all competitive sports have" (Dyer, 1985). Conflicts are often small scale with tribes agreeing to limit the force that is used. In parts of Highland New Guinea, for example, wars are called off when someone is wounded and warriors use inaccurate arrows without feather flights. Among the Native Americans of the Great Plains, the highest honor came from "counting coup," not killing. This involved approaching an enemy without carrying weapons and touching him.

Comparative studies of war and violence across civi-

lizations, like that of Quincy Wright, suggest that the shift to more utilitarian, rationalized and unrestrained forms of violence organized around conquest and domination emerged with agriculture and large scale civilizations. In hunting and gathering societies there was no fixed wealth worth taking and people could easily run away. With the shift to agriculture people had to stand and fight if they wished to eat. Along with agriculture there also came larger population densities and complex hierarchies, the emergence of military specialists, and full scale wars associated with imperial expansion. These trends reached their logical conclusion in the militaristic empires of antiquity (Egypt, Rome, etc.), with their planned, "pragmatic" approach to violence. This saw mass killing replace the ritualized killing of small-scale societies, with defeated populations often put to the sword. The shift toward more "rational" and secular but also larger-scale forms of violence has continued up to the present day. Indeed, the rise of industrial capitalism and modernity in the West has seen the process accelerate thanks to a growing reliance on advanced technology and systems of coordination and control that operate at a distance from the points of battle.

This move from symbolic and ritual violence toward norms advocating a rational and utilitarian organization of combat is in degree rather than in kind. Throughout history we can identify ritualistic elements in fighting styles and ethics. Noted examples include the combat codes of European knights and Japanese samurai and the individualistic flair demonstrated by Cossacks and cavaliers. While contemporary combat styles have been rationalized by technowar, many scholars argue that conflict and violence is still underpinned by nonrational factors at levels from those of everyday life to full scale war. Moreover, normative constraints often play a role in limiting the intensity of violence. To a certain extent, then, contemporary violence can be still considered a form of symbolic action, even if its ritualistic qualities are sometimes latent rather than manifest. Consider the following examples from everyday life:

• Anthropological research shows that casual barroom brawls tend to follow a ritualistic sequence of threats and blows, with informal rules preventing fighters from using weapons like knives.
• Anthropologists and sociologists studying sport have pointed to the symbolic and ritualistic qualities of violence in sports like boxing, wrestling, cockfighting, and bull fighting.
• Crimes against women like domestic violence and rape are often interpreted as expressive acts

which dramatize male power and resentment and which are often underpinned by an irrational culture of machismo.

• Studies of urban gangs have pointed to the value system that leads young men to risk their lives and to kill to protect their territory and gang colors.

And the following examples from war:

• Ethnic, racist, and/or nationalist beliefs have played a role in every war this century. Today ethnonationalist beliefs remain important in arenas like Bosnia, Rwanda, and Kurdistan.

• Many states voluntarily subscribe to the Geneva Convention, a document that provides minimum rights for those involved in war. This might be seen as an endorsement of the idea of that war should be limited and constrained by human values.

• Religious beliefs and motivations remain important factors behind war (e.g., in the Middle East). It could also be argued that apparently secular beliefs in democracy, reason, and equality that underpin some prowar rhetoric amount to a civil religion.

• Extreme acts of atrocity, such as genocide or the mass destruction of cities, are difficult to interpret as rational actions that contribute much to winning a war. Indeed, they often divert vital resources from more important tasks. They can be better understood as dramatizations of power and hatred.

• The most technologically advanced war to date (the 1991 Gulf War) was supported by quasi-mythological themes such as the demonization of Saddam/Bush, apocalyptic narratives about the end of civilization, and surreal video game imagery.

Few commentators would claim that contemporary war is directly analogous to its more ritualistic counterparts. Like other major social processes it has been bureaucratized and its conduct is usually rational and strategic—in intention if not in enactment. However, it is important to realize that ritualistic and symbolic beliefs provide for its legitimacy in wider society and offer an important source of motivation for participants.

IV. RITUAL AND CONFLICT

So far this article has discussed the symbolic and ritualistic dimensions of violence in animals and humans. These have been described as the ways in which conflict is patterned, generated, or limited by meanings embodied in codes, signs, and symbols. This last section looks at theories of ritual itself and the ways in which theories of ritual have been used to explain peace, war, and violence.

The contemporary study of ritual in the social sciences has its foundational moment in Emile Durkheim's masterwork *The Elementary Forms of Religious Life*. Here Durkheim drew upon Australian Aboriginal ethnography to argue that societies must periodically come together to renew their bonds. He claimed they achieved this through rituals characterized by physical proximity and the manipulation of the symbols of the sacred and the profane. In his understanding these rituals worked to generate social stability and harmony. The broad thrust of Durkheim's work, then, is to suggest that ritual activity is important for allowing peaceful coexistence within groups.

Despite his data being drawn from a small-scale society, Durkheim claimed that his theory had a more general applicability. He argued, for instance, that the flags of modern nations were analogous to Aboriginal totems. Important arguments to this effect have come from scholars like Lloyd Warner and Edward Shils. Drawing upon ethnographic data from a small Massachusetts town, Warner suggested that Memorial Day ceremonies dedicated to fallen soldiers constituted a kind of cult of the dead that united citizens. Shils made a similar point about the 1952 coronation of Britain's Queen Elizabeth, arguing that it enabled the nation to come together. These kinds of claims are now generally perceived to be simplistic. In a seminal article, Steven Lukes suggested that we need to explore the relationship between rituals and social conflict. Pointing to sectarian Orange Day parades in Northern Ireland, Lukes maintained that rituals are often used to divide as well as to unite communities. He also argued for ideas of agency and strategic action to be included in thinking about rituals as a replacement for the vague and systemic causal attributions of the Durkheimian functionalists. Over the past 20 years the kind of agenda instantiated by Lukes has come to predominate in ritual studies. Functionalist models that locate ritual causality in "social needs" for harmony have been replaced by studies attentive to power, inequality, and interests. Here an emphasis is placed on the ways that rituals and ritual exchanges legitimate and reproduce structures of power and inequality. Important contributions within this critical tradition have come from scholars like Marc Auge and Pierre Bourdieu. Another significant feature of contemporary research has been inputs from structuralist and poststructuralist theories. These have enabled ideas of discourse, narrative, and semiotics to be incorporated into an understanding of the ritual dynamics, providing for a more sophisticated understanding of the ways culture works. Early contributions from Mary Douglas on purity and pollution and Victor Turner's processualist analyses of liminality remain important sources of inspiration. Also significant are borrowings from Levi-Strauss on cultural codes and Bakhtin on the carnivalesque. While also vital to critical understandings of ritual, this line of cultural elaboration has provided the basis for a recent revival in neo-Durkheimian scholarship. This research seeks to hold on to what is best in Durkheim's *Elementary Forms* (such as ideas about the autonomy of culture, solidarity, and emotion) while jettisoning what no longer seems viable (the assumption of social consensus, functionalism). This emerging research tradition also draws upon the critical theories discussed above so as to be able to put forward a more hard headed and empirically grounded understanding of ritual dynamics.

At present links between ritual studies and peace studies remain underdeveloped. Scholars in the ritual studies area often use phenomena like nationalist and military parades as sources of data, but do not have issues of peace and violence at the center of their research agenda. They are often more interested in theoretical issues concerning with the structure and process of rituals themselves. To be sure, ideas about domination, conflict, and exclusion can be found, but rarely are these translated into a central preoccupation with issues of physical violence or peaceful coexistence. On the other hand, scholars in the peace studies area often refer to the ritualistic qualities of violence (e.g., when discussing the kinds of themes listed in Section III above), but do so in passing and without reference to core theory in the ritual studies area. The result has been two literatures that have passed each other like ships in the night. This is unfortunate as the core issues of ritual theory, such as the dynamics of solidarity and exclusion, the importance of sacrifice, and the roles of quasi-religious symbolic codes and the collective memory in the legitimation of the social order, are obviously of very direct relevance to understanding peace and conflict. Nevertheless in recent years a number of studies have begun to think through these latent and potential connections. Important characteristics of the literature include an interdisciplinary theoretical input centering on the textuality of social life, the idea of ritual as an arena of struggle and violence as well as consensus, a concern with the autonomy of culture as a "variable" that makes possible violent and nonviolent outcomes, and, finally, a concern with the need for historically and culturally specific, process driven explanation. Perhaps the best way to get a feel for this expanding, interdisciplinary literature is to briefly review some representative examples.

• In her book entitled *The Moro Morality Play* Robin Wagner-Pacifici looked at the 1978 kidnapping and murder by the Red Brigades of Italian Prime Minister Aldo Moro. Drawing upon the work of Victor Turner and narrative theorists like Northrop Frye and Hayden White, she decodes the various texts that shaped the episode such as newspaper reports, political speeches, and photographs. Wagner-Pacifici interprets the event as a social drama; a kind of quasi-ritual theater in which various parties attempted to influence interpretations by proposing contending narratives and aesthetic frames. She argues that outcomes characterized by violence and discord emerged due to the triumph of simplistic melodramatic frames over those that emphasized human tragedy and, consequently, the need for reconciliation.

• In a study of capital punishment Philip Smith takes up the kinds of themes explored by Wagner-Pacifici but (somewhat unusually for studies of ritual) relates them to symbolic action at the level of the individual as well as of the group. Executions are seen as rituals in which the state makes efforts to project a morality play narrative. Individual victims, by contrast, are more interested in making a worthy presentation of self. These efforts at identity assertion typically shift the narrative projected by the ritual. When victims appear to be pious and humble, they can become the objects of pity and the state the object of popular discontent. When victims wish to project an unrepentant deviant identity, perhaps by displaying defiance or bravado, the event can turn into a farce or a celebration of the antihero. By looking at documents relating to procedural reform of capital punishment, Smith was able to show how the end of public executions and attempts to routinize procedure can be accounted for as an attempt by the state to regain control over the semiotics of capital punishment.

• Bruce Lincoln's explorations of ritual and violence are rooted in critical theory. Lincoln makes use of Roland Barthes and Maurice Bloch in developing a model of social life that sees symbolic and ritual activity as closely associated with the reproduction of, and challenges to, structures of power. In Lincoln's view social integration through ritual always benefits some groups more than others. This is evinced in his discussion of the Swazi Ncwala, an annual ritual ostensibly celebrating harvest, death and rebirth, and kingship. Lincoln shows how a covert subtext of the ritual was a sustained, but coded, critique of colonial domination. This affirmation of a universal Swazi identity worked, however, to reinforce the power of the Swazi king over his subjects by symbolically trumping internal conflicts between factions within the Swazi nation. So a ritual constructing solidarity in the face of one form of domination ended up reproducing another.

• The work of David Kertzer shares with Lincoln's an interest in the use of ritual as a political tool. Kertzer, however, believes that acting together is more important than building and sharing a symbolic code. Kertzer argues that rituals work not because they produce common beliefs, cultural codes, and cognitive orientations but simply because they generate collective emotion. Taking a somewhat anti-idealist position he argues that rituals are often useful precisely because they can work despite fundamental differences in belief and outlook. Participation allows people to feel sentiments of solidarity and belonging that take the sting out of more fundamental cultural and social cleavages. Kertzer sees rituals as diverse as Brazilian military parades and soccer games, Klu Klux Klan activity, and horseracing in Sienna (Italy) as politically charged attempts to generate enthusiasm, mobilization, and solidarity in the face of deeper differences in interests and worldview.

• In his comparative work on nationalism, militarism, and collective memory in Australia and Sri Lanka, Bruce Kapferer explored the intersection between mythologies of violence and ritual action. His discussion of the Australian data, for example, considered the role of the Gallipoli invasion in World War I in constituting a blood sacrifice around which the emerging nation could forge a collective identity. Kapferer looked to the annual Australia and New Zealand Army Corps parades as a site where this foundational mythology was renewed and linked to wider value patterns such as egalitarianism and mateship. According to Kapferer, this nexus between ritual, myth, and violence is central to understanding contemporary nationalism.

V. RITUAL, SYMBOLIC ACTION, AND BUILDING PEACE

Ethological studies belong to an intellectual field which borders on the morally dubious territories of Social Darwinism and eugenics. In the wrong hands, such as those of Adolf Hitler, such theories can be used to question the belief that peace is either possible or good. To the contrary, they can be taken to lead to the conclusion that conflict is not only inevitable, but also an ennobling duty. Through military triumph over the weak and through programs of "ethnic cleansing," the strong can claim their birthright and purify and refine their bloodstock thus fulfilling some kind of "racial destiny."

Fortunately it is possible to derive a more constructive lesson from the ethological literature once it is realized that there is no inevitable connection between scientific knowledge derived from observations of animal behavior and a pseudo-Darwinistic moral philosophy. Humans are different from animals, and one of the most important differences is their ability to construct moral codes and institutional arrangements which modify or transcend the effects of nature. An important argument along these lines is William James's essay on *The Moral Equivalent of War*. James recognizes the existence of martial traits in modern people that have arisen as a result of thousands of years of war but suggests that these can be channelled into nonviolent avenues such as public service. In this way, he argues, society could retain the constructive "character building" qualities of military service but avoid bloodshed. In a similar vein the biologist Richard Dawkins (1976) has denied that his analysis of the "selfish gene" is a justification for selfish, free-market individualism as some of his critics have suggested. Rather, he contends, scientific knowledge allows us to be aware of the operation of genetic conditioning and, consequently, to be able sit down and discuss rational strategies for thwarting genes and nurturing genuine altruism. In this way we can "rebel against the tyranny of the selfish replicators" (p. 215).

So knowledge about ethology allows for reflexivity and an awareness of the negative traits of our species—the instinctual and selfish behaviors which are to be avoided. We can also look to the ethological corpus for more positive suggestions for constructing peace. Two potential themes stand out. The first of these is that the literature can be used as a resource for strategy analysts who are attracted to rational choice and game theory. It might be possible to locate in the animal kingdom and the adaptive behaviors of its members exemplars for constructing distributions of resources, threats, and balances of power that encourage ritualistic rather than escalated fighting. The attraction (and also weakness) of these kinds of solutions is that they do not require changing people's minds. Rather they permit peaceful coexistence to be built into situations where human competition remains every bit as fierce as it is between genomes. An example of such a situation (which, thanks to its Dr. Strangelovesque absurdity perhaps undercuts the validity of the suggestion I am making here) was the doctrine of Mutually Assured Destruction, which underpinned the nuclear deterrence strategies of the United States and the Soviet Union in the post-World War II period. The idea here was that the costs of full scale nuclear war, such as global destruction and nuclear winter, would be too high for either side. Consequently, expressions of their mutual hostility were limited to regional wars (e.g., Nicaragua, Vietnam) and symbolic and diplomatic skirmishing. This is perhaps analogous to the deescalated violence we find in animal combats, where threat of death or serious injury prevents even dominant contestants from using full force.

A second possibility afforded by animal studies is that they can be creatively misread to serve as a kind of moral exemplar. While animal behaviors might be selfish from the perspective of science, they can often appear to be altruistic or moral to common sense. The shift toward postmodernity is seeing nature resacralised in contemporary popular culture as a zone of purity and symbiosis. This provides a fertile setting for distributing positive imagery that sees ritualistic, restrained violence in animals as a role-model for morally aware human action. We can already see signs of this kind of discourse emerging in popular advocacy for animals like dolphins, whales, and gorillas. Such animals are often attributed an almost spiritual ability to live in peace and harmony with their environment and each other.

The diversity of human cultures equally provides a rich resource with which to think creatively about building a peace culture. The literature on small-scale societies can be studied for ideas about how to replace a culture that valorizes escalated violence with one that recognizes the superiority of low-harm alternatives. An enhanced understanding of the ritual and symbolic foundations of contemporary violence can lead to greater reflexivity about existing practices and promote the search for nonviolent alternatives. By the same token, we can look in a pragmatic way for forms of symbolic action that seem to offer more positive alternatives. In the case of ritual, for example, the weight of academic research suggests that militaristic parades do

little to build peace and understanding. By contrast, forms of carnivalesque ritual seem to work well in terms of breaking down barriers and building community solidarity. Events such as Sydney's Gay and Lesbian Mardi Gras, the New Orleans Mardi Gras, and London's Notting Hill Carnival have all fostered the causes of multiculturalism, sexual tolerance, and diversity at local levels. By looking to these kinds of success stories, and through analyzing their symbolic and ritual foundations for generalizable principles, peace activists can start to construct lines of action that might make a difference.

Also See the Following Articles

AGGRESSION AND ALTRUISM • ANIMAL BEHAVIOR STUDIES • CLAN AND TRIBAL CONFLICT • CULTURAL STUDIES, OVERVIEW • DECISION THEORY AND GAME THEORY • ETHNICITY AND IDENTITY POLITICS • EVOLUTIONARY FACTORS • FOLKLORE • GENDER STUDIES • LANGUAGE OF WAR AND PEACE, THE • SPORTS • WARRIORS, ANTHROPOLOGY OF

Bibliography

Barnard, C. J. (1983). *Animal behaviour*. London. Croom Helm.

Dawkins, R. (1976). *The selfish gene*. Oxford, UK: Oxford University Press.

Durkheim, E. (1915). *The elementary forms of religious life*. London: Allen and Unwin.

Dyer, G. (1985). *War*. New York: Crown.

James, W. (1942). The moral equivalent of war. In *Essays on Faith and Morals*, pp. 311–328. New York: Meridian.

Kapferer, B. (1988). *Legends of the people, myths of state*. Washington, DC: Smithsonian Institute Press.

Kertzer, D. (1988). *Ritual, politics and power*. London: Yale University Press.

Lincoln, B. (1987). Ritual, rebellion, resistance. *Man, 22*, 132–156.

Lorenz, K. (1966). *On aggression*. London: Methuen.

Lukes, S. (1975). Political ritual and social integration. *Sociology, 9*(2), 289–308.

Smith, P. (1996). Executing executions. *Theory and Society, 25*, 235–261.

Smith, P. & Jeffrey, A. (1996). Durkheim's religious revival. *American Journal of Sociology, 102*(2) 585–592.

Sperber, D. (1975). *Rethinking symbolism*. Cambridge, UK: Cambridge University Press.

Wagner-Pacifici, R. (1986). *The Moro morality play*. Chicago: University of Chicago Press.

Wright, Q. (1965). *A study of war*. Chicago: University of Chicago Press.

Secession and Separatism

Robert K. Schaeffer

San Jose State University

GLOSSARY

Decolonization The withdrawal of imperial authority from colonial territories and the creation of independent states, usually republics.

Empire A polity where a supreme authority, a government or monarch, rules over people in other territories or colonies, treating them as subjects, not co-equals.

Interstate System The global set of political relations among sovereign, independent states.

Republic An independent state where sovereignty is vested in the people and exercised through representative institutions according to constitutional principles and laws.

Self-Determination The opportunity to secede from an established polity and practice self-government in an independent state.

THROUGHOUT THIS CENTURY, movements around the world have demanded self-determination, the opportunity to secede from an established polity, obtain an independent state, and practice self-government. For most, self-government has meant the creation of a constitutional republic, where sovereignty is vested in the people and exercised through representative institutions according to constitutional principles and laws. For anticolonial movements, independence could only be achieved by seceding from European or Asian empires. Widespread decolonization after World War II made self-determination possible for many movements, expanding the number of republican states belonging to the United Nations. But because many ethnic groups were denied the opportunity to obtain states of their own and were assigned to states they did not choose, or were discriminated against by the new republics, movements demanding self-determination for ethnic minorities emerged in some postcolonial states. After years of trying, some separatist movements seceded in the early 1990s, increasing the number of states and encouraging widespread emulation. Unfortunately, struggles over state power have frequently triggered conflict among ethnic groups and war between separated states. Recognizing this, some ethnic movements have modified their demand for self-determination. Instead of demanding a state of their own, or resigning themselves to minority status in a state controlled by others, some minorities have adopted "Commonwealth" or "Sovereignty-Association" as their goal, proposing these political arrangements as a way both to divide and share power with majorities. If these hybrid institutions are freely chosen and they establish equitable relations between minority and majority, they may provide an alternative to ethnic violence and uncivil war.

I. SELF-DETERMINATION AND ANTICOLONIAL MOVEMENTS

In the late 19th and early 20th century, movements demanding self-determination organized in European, Asian and American colonies. The Indian National Congress (founded in 1885), the Zionist movement (1896), Sinn Fein in Ireland (1905), the All-India Muslim League (1906), and the Arab National Congress (1913) were among the first. They were joined, after World War I, by noncommunist anticolonial movements in Korea (1919), China (1922), and Indonesia (1927), and by communist parties in Korea (1919), Indonesia (1920), China (1921), and Indochina (1925).

Initially, these movements demanded reform, a greater say in colonial government. But they soon demanded something more: "Home Rule" in Ireland, "*swaraj*" (national freedom) in India, and "*doc lap*" (the right to stand alone) in Indochina. Eventually, they argued that they should be allowed "self-determination," the opportunity to secede from empire and create self-governing states of their own.

Although revolutionaries in the United States, France and Latin America had demanded independence during the late 18th and early 19th centuries, the idea of self-determination was first advanced in 1896 by the Second International, a socialist organization founded by Karl Marx. It was soon adopted by many anti-colonial movements and endorsed by Russian revolutionary Vladimir Lenin and by U.S. President Woodrow Wilson. Lenin argued that self-determination "means the political separation of these [colonial] nations from alien national bodies [and] the formation of an independent national state." Wilson agreed that "All nations have a right to self-determination." For Soviet and U.S. leaders, and for anticolonial movements, self-determination meant that they should be allowed to secede from empire and create independent states where they could practice self-government.

The political and social character of anticolonial movements was extremely diverse, ranging from capitalist to communist, religious to secular, peaceful to violent. But diverse movements were joined by their common demand for self-determination and by their singular determination to create constitutional republics, where sovereignty is vested in the people, not in a monarchy, and is exercised through representative institutions according to constitutional law. Indian, Muslim, Arab, Zionist, nationalist, and communist parties in many colonies all sent delegates to party congresses, consciously modeled after the U.S. Congress,

where they deliberated policy and discussed how best to achieve self-determination. Whatever their social character or political orientation, they were all republican.

Although anticolonial movements and their supporters in the great republics—the United States and, after 1917, the Soviet Union—insisted on the right to secede from empire, they did not believe that the right of self-determination extended to peoples within independent, self-governing states. Lenin had only endorsed separation from an *alien* nation. But neither Lenin, Wilson, nor the League of Nations endorsed the right of a minority to secede from an independent state. As one League Commission wrote in 1921, "To concede to minorities either of language or religion . . . the right of withdrawing from the community to which they belong . . . would be to destroy order and stability within states, to inaugurate anarchy in international life. It would be to uphold a theory incompatible with the very idea of the state as a territorial and political entity." In this context, self-determination was synonymous with decolonization, the transfer of imperial power to indigenous movements in independent republics. But by encouraging the first (separation from empire), it would later be hard to deny the second (secession from republic).

After World War I, a few movements were allowed to separate from empires and establish states of their own. The overthrow of the Russian empire led to the creation of independent states in Latvia, Lithuania, and Estonia. The dissolution of the Austro-Hungarian empire produced new states in Austria, Hungary, Poland, Czechoslovakia, and Yugoslavia. But postwar decolonization was fairly limited in meaning and scope. Great Britain, for instance, allowed only Ireland to depart from the empire. But Irish independence was compromised by partition and restricted by treaty, which assigned to Britain important residual rights in the Irish Free State. No anticolonial movement outside Europe won their independence, despite Britain's wartime promises for a Jewish homeland in Palestine and eventual self-government in India. And the breakup of the Ottoman empire, which resulted in the transfer of Ottoman territories in the Middle East to British and French authority, actually expanded the size of their respective empires.

Although anticolonial movements continued to press for independence in the interwar period, they met with little success. Their lack of progress was due to several factors. The isolationist policies adopted by the United States and Soviet Union after the war deprived anticolonial movements of political support from powerful republics. (Of course, while the Union of Soviet

Socialist *Republics* was formally a republic, it was in fact also a dictatorship.) The European empires firmly resisted calls for self-determination in the colonies, arguing, as one British minister did, that "it may take generations, or even centuries, for the peoples in some parts of the Colonial Empire to achieve self-government." In some colonies, imperial authorities sponsored reforms designed to placate anticolonial movements, though movements generally greeted reform with hostility. As Muslim League president Sir Sayed Wazir Khan said of 1935 British reforms in India, "A constitution is literally being forced on us by the British Parliament which nobody likes, which no one approves of. After several years of Commissions, Reports, Conferences and Committees a monstrosity has been invented...." And the anticolonial movements were themselves fairly small, often divided between competing movements (Indian National Congress v. Muslim League, Chinese nationalists v. Chinese communists), and frequently unable to mobilize mass support in the difficult economic circumstances that accompanied global depression in the 1930s. Some movements in China, India, Indochina, Korea, and Palestine nonetheless organized demonstrations, riots, and minor rebellions or waged small-scale guerrilla wars that kept their demands in public and imperial view.

Anticolonial movements were further undermined by the expansion of Japanese, Italian, and German empires in the 1930s. Japan's 1931 invasion of China, Italy's 1935 war against Ethiopia, and Germany's annexation of Czech lands in 1938 expanded these empires. Germany's subsequent invasions of Poland and later the Soviet Union, Italy's invasion of Albania and then Greece, and Japan's attacks on U.S., British, Dutch, French and Portuguese possessions in Pacific Asia triggered world war. The initial success of Axis empires came at the expense of rival European empires, small republics (Czechoslovakia and Poland) and then great republics (the Soviet Union and the United States), and independence movements in the colonies, particularly in Asia. The war was bad for anticolonial movements not only in expanding Axis empires, but also in the empires of European states allied with the United States and Soviet Union. When the Indian National Congress objected to Britain's unilateral declaration of war on India's behalf, and in 1942 launched a nonviolent campaign to persuade Britain to "Quit India," its leaders were thrown in jail. Events in 1942 perhaps marked the nadir of anticolonial movement fortunes in this century. But their prospects would soon improve. For in that same year, U.S. and Soviet forces halted the expansion of Axis empires, prepared to reverse them, and began planning ways to dissolve Axis and then Allied empires after the war.

II. THE SUPERPOWERS AND DECOLONIZATION

During World War II, U.S. anticolonialism, which had lain dormant during the interwar period, revived. Roosevelt believed that colonialism contributed both to the Great Depression and world war. "The colonial system means war," Roosevelt said. And he told British Prime Minister Winston Churchill, "I can't believe that we can fight a war against fascist slavery, and at the same time not work to free people all over the world from a backward colonial policy." As an alternative, U.S. policymakers proposed that the old imperial interstate system be dissolved and a new one based on self-governing republics be established in its place. With the 1941 Atlantic Charter as a template, U.S. officials organized a series of summit meetings during and after the war to promote a new interstate system, which found institutional expression in the United Nations. The Soviet Union joined U.S. efforts to create a new interstate system during the war. The Soviets supported decolonization as a way to weaken its imperial adversaries and to promote communist revolution in the colonial world. With a few exceptions, only self-governing states were admitted as members of the new United Nations. By limiting membership to independent states and controlling the admission process, U.S. and Soviet officials created an organization in which republican states outnumbered imperial states by a two-to-one margin. And because they insisted that self-determination and decolonization be adopted as central principles of the new organization, U.S. and Soviet superpowers were in a position to press for widespread decolonization after the war, a process that would swell the number of anticolonial republics in the United Nations during the next two decades. As French leader Charles De Gaulle complained, "Roosevelt expected that the crowd of small nations would assault the position of the colonial power and assure the United States of an enormous political and economic clientele."

After the war, the United States and the United Nations moved quickly to decolonize Axis empires. They detached Austria and Czechoslovakia from Germany, ceding German territories to neighboring France and Poland; removed Tunisia, Libya, Somalia, Eritrea, and Ethiopia from Italy; and separated Formosa, Manchuria, and Korea from Japan. The United Nations then turned its attention to the empires of U.S. and Soviet allies, authorizing special commissions to investigate colonial conditions and accept petitions from indigenous populations, and forcing empires to submit political information and fix "time-tables" for eventual independence. Although Churchill had said he would never "consent to forty or fifty nations thrusting interfering fingers into the life's existence of the British empire," the republican members of the United Nations began to do just that.

But postwar decolonization was complicated by U.S. and Soviet determination to reserve spheres of influence for themselves. U.S. officials did so to preserve Monroe Doctrine privileges, which allowed the United States to intervene in Latin America, and they extended this policy to western Europe; Soviet leaders did so to consolidate gains made by occupying armies in eastern Europe. They agreed to recognize each other's spheres at wartime summits and inserted articles in the UN charter that allowed them to create political and military blocs outside of the organization. But while they agreed in principle to create spheres of influence, which would be used to justify superpower interventions and prevent countries from exiting their assigned spheres, the United State and Soviet Union did not carefully demarcate the boundaries. As a result, disputes over sphere borders soon led to a series of U.S.–Soviet disagreements and conflicts around the world, known collectively as the Cold War.

In some cases, U.S. and Soviet leaders settled Cold War differences by partitioning borderline countries between competing independence movements and assigning separate states to different spheres of influence, as they did in Korea, China, Vietnam, and Germany. But partition frequently led to conflict within and war between divided states, creating crises for the superpowers that had divided these countries. And to police sphere boundaries and consolidate political support for superpower policy in countries within their spheres, the Soviet Union and the United States often created or supported dictatorship in allied states. Dictatorship took hold quickly in many of the new republics. Communist dictatorships were soon established in Eastern Europe and East Asia, while capitalist dictatorships survived in Spain and Portugal, took hold in East Asia, and spread throughout much of Latin America, Africa, and the Middle East. The United States provided more than $70 billion in military aid to allied regimes in the 30 years after the war; the Soviets provided nearly $30 billion in military aid to client dictators.

But throughout the Cold War, despite serious disagreements and periodic crises, the two superpowers never abandoned their rhetorical support for self-determination, commitment to decolonization, or support for the United Nations as an institution. Indeed, UN membership grew throughout the Cold War, largely as a result of decolonization.

Decolonization was a difficult and protracted process. It began slowly in the late 1940s, with the British withdrawal from much of South Asia and the Middle East, the Dutch departure from Indonesia, and, in the early 1950s, the French retreat from defeat in Indochina. Then after the British and French failed to wrest control of the Suez Canal from Egypt in 1956, decolonization accelerated: 26 countries in Africa won their independence from British, French, and Belgian rule, along with Cyprus and Malaysia, between 1956 and 1965. And by 1965, with minor exceptions, most of the world had been decolonized. Many of these new republics refused or resisted assignment to either U.S. or Soviet spheres upon independence, and participated in the movement of "nonaligned states," which grew from 25 members in 1961 to 85 members in 1976.

European empires did not easily surrender their colonies. By and large they were forced to do so as a result of pressure from above and below. The United States and Soviet Union used economic, political, and military leverage, the United Nations and other international institutions such as the World Bank, and propaganda campaigns to pressure European empires to decolonize. In the colonies, meanwhile, independence movements organized from below. Movements in Indonesia, Malaysia, Vietnam, Palestine, Kenya, and Algeria took up arms against European rulers, waging irregular guerrilla wars to pry empire from colony. In India, independence movement leaders organized mass protests or "direct action" campaigns that often led to riots and contributed to an atmosphere of impending violence. "We have forged a pistol and are now in a position to use it," Muslim leader Ali Jinnah said of his movement's direct action campaign. Although not all leaders forged or fired mass-movement pistols in this period, imperial authorities came to regard anticolonial movements everywhere as potentially armed and dangerous.

Superpower pressure and colonial protest eventually persuaded European empires to withdraw, resulting in self-governing republics in Africa, Asia, and the Middle East. But while widespread decolonization made self-determination a reality, it also created new problems for some people in postcolonial settings.

One problem was that the new republics inherited territories defined by imperial powers. Some states contested or rejected imperial cartography and tried to redraw maps and create a new political landscape. So, after winning their independence, the leaders of some new states invaded or annexed territories and peoples not assigned to them by imperial powers or the United Nations.

For example, in the 1948 war that accompanied partition in Palestine, Israel acquired territories not assigned to it by the United Nations, and later incorporated additional territories and people after the 1967 Six Day War. Communist China in 1950 invaded and annexed Tibet. Indonesia invaded and annexed western New Guinea in 1962 and subsequently invaded East Timor in 1975 and 1976. India forcibly incorporated princely states like Hyderbad and Kashmir, which triggered war with Pakistan, and invaded Portuguese Goa, Daman, and Dieu in 1961. And Ethiopia incorporated Eritrea in 1962. The expansion of new republics was not unprecedented, since both the U.S. and Soviet republics had grown larger by invading or annexing adjacent territories. The Soviet Union, for example, had incorporated independent Baltic states at the outset of World War II, refusing to relinquish them after the war. But while it was not unprecedented, the expansion of postcolonial republics often antagonized people who had been incorporated into these states without their consent, leading to subsequent demands for self-determination and secession.

A second problem was that officials in postcolonial republics often adopted policies that favored some groups and disadvantaged others. They did so in part because imperial governments typically granted political favors to some ethnic minorities as part of their divide-and-rule colonial policies. So, for example, the British gave privileges to Karens in Burma, Sikhs in India, and Ibos in Nigeria that they did not extend generally. And they rewarded minority Protestants in Ireland, Muslims in India, and Jews in Palestine for supporting the empire during the world war, while punishing majority groups that opposed the British war effort. Of course these practices antagonized majority groups, which resented imperial favoritism. And when majorities took power in postcolonial states, they often demoted minority groups that had been privileged by imperial authorities. Because minority groups experienced these policies as discriminatory, they often organized movements demanding states of their own. The governments of postcolonial states rationalized their policies as part of a "nation-building" process, the creation of a singular, common identity for all of a state's inhabitants. The Italian patriot Massimo d'Azeglio gave expression to this idea when he argued, after the unification of Italy in 1860, "We have made Italy, now we must make Italians." In a similar vein, leaders of the new republics set out to make Indians, Pakistanis, or Nigerians.

In their determination to build nations, officials in many new republics used language, education, and military policies to great singular identities. They elevated one language over others, provided some groups with access to higher education and civil or military service, and used electoral systems to provide disproportionate representation to some groups. Because they did so in multiethnic states, the selection of one national language or elevation of one faith as the official religion disadvantaged groups that spoke other languages or professed other faiths. By making Urdu the official language of Pakistan, for example, despite the fact that only 7% of the population spoke it, authorities antagonized non-Urdu speakers throughout the country, but particularly in Bengali-speaking East Pakistan, where riots erupted.

Where states defined self-determination as the right to invade their neighbors or to discriminate against their compatriots, new movements often emerged to demand self-determination for themselves.

III. SELF-DETERMINATION AND ETHNIC MINORITIES

Although decolonization had resulted in self-determination for anti-colonial movements, new movements demanding self-determination emerged in many postcolonial settings. They sometimes also appeared in post-imperial states, such as Belgium, where Flemings demanded the kind of rights being given to Africans in the Belgian Congo, Rwanda, and Burundi. By demanding self-determination, ethnic minorities echoed demands previously made by anticolonial majorities. But while both demanded the opportunity to separate from an existing polity and establish self-governing states of their own, the meaning of self-determination was different for each. For anticolonial majorities, self-determination meant secession from *empire*. For ethnic minorities, it meant seceding from an independent *republic*. Because movements used the same term to mean different things, use of the term often resulted in considerable confusion. This was particularly true when a movement representing the first view (the Indian National Congress) confronted movements taking the second view (Kashmiris, Sikhs in the Punjab). These two meanings were sometimes further complicated by the fact that ethnic minorities often portrayed republics as empires, as the Sikhs have of India. The rhetoric of self-determination can be understood if one can determine whether a movement seeks to separate from empire or secede from republic. But this is sometimes difficult to do because republics can act like empires, annexing adjacent territories not assigned to them, and treat incorporated territories like colonies.

Like their anticolonial predecessors, separatist minorities are extremely diverse in social and political terms. Karen in Burma; Kurds in Turkey, Iraq, Iran, and Syria; Eritreans in Ethiopia; Biafrans in Nigeria; Moros in the Philippines; Tamils in Sri Lanka; and, more recently, Palestinians in Israel not only profess different religions and speak different languages, they also practice different politics and pursue different strategies. In the Baltics, Estonians, Latvians and Lithuanians adopted nonviolent Gandhian tactics to press their demands for separation from the Soviet Union, while in Yugoslavia, Slovenians, Croats, and Serbs took up arms and waged uncivil wars to achieve separate political ends. But despite these differences, they share some common social and political features. They generally represent ethnic groups that are minorities in the states where they reside. And they typically use "ethnic," or linguistic, religious, and racial identities to organize multiclass support for mass-based political parties. These parties argue that ethnic minorities be allowed to exercise their self-determination or to be "masters in their own house," a slogan commonly used by different movements.

While their anticolonial predecessors made common cause and participated in international political organizations—the socialist or communist internationals before World War II, the nonaligned movement after it—ethnic minorities have not created a separatist international or a global movement for peoples without states. Ethnic minorities may not make common cause because the great powers, who act as gate keepers for UN membership, are generally hostile to collective, international organizations such as the nonaligned movement or the Organization of Petroleum Exporting Countries. Ethnic minorities may also fear that their claim to representing a distinctive nation, which deserves a state because it is *unlike* any other, would be undermined by a collaboration with others: cooperation would make them seem commonplace, not unique. And groups that acquire states of their own become indifferent to the demands of similar groups in other states because they fear that this might encourage domestic minorities to echo these demands.

Although ethnic minorities do not make political alliances with other separatists, most count on support from emigre communities in nearby or distant states. They regard ethnic emigres as members of the nation, whatever their legal status. So, for example, the Palestine Liberation Organization regards Palestinians living not only in the West Bank and Gaza, but also in neighboring Arab states and throughout the world, as members of the Palestinian nation and citizens of an eventual Palestinian state. In this regard, separatist movements are generally indifferent to the fact that emigres may be citizens of another state. When the Baltic states seceded from the Soviet Union, they extended citizenship to ethnic emigres, even those in foreign countries, and gave them rights not available to some resident groups, particularly ethnic Russians.

More generally, ethnic minorities emerged to address problems associated with decolonization and to redeem promises implicit in the interstate system. All of these movements, and many others, were assigned to or incorporated by states they did not make or choose. And they were subjected to discriminatory policies and practices by state officials and co-residential majorities. As a result, they organized movements to protest these developments and to secure the substantial rewards given groups that obtain state power. They realized that if they could obtain a state and secure admission to the United Nations, they could receive real benefits: UN protection against aggression, economic aid from the World Bank, access to trade with member nations, and the opportunity to participate as equals in international conventions and Olympic games. Because the United Nations had adopted self-determination as a principle and extended real benefits to its members, ethnic minorities organized to demand states and claim rewards.

Even where their demands for self-determination may have had considerable historical merit, ethnic minorities had little success separating from republics between 1945 and 1990. The Biafran attempt to secede from Nigeria ended in disaster and more than one million died from conflict and famine. The Karen, Eritreans and Moros fought for decades, and the Tamils for more than 10 years without seceding. And the Kurds languished despite promises made in the 1920 Treaty of Sevres to create an independent Kurdistan. Only one movement, the Awami League, managed to secede from a postcolonial republic—Pakistan—and in 1971 create a state of its own: Bangladesh. But this was the exception, not the rule, in part because East Pakistan (Bangladesh) was already physically separated from West Pakistan, in part because the Awami League represented a *majority* of people in the country as a whole, in part because it received military assistance from neighboring India.

Separatist movements were generally unsuccessful in this period because they received little support from other states. The superpowers did not intervene on their behalf because U.S. and Soviet leaders believed that self-determination applied only to colonies, not to minorities in republics. UN members were reluctant to interfere in what they regarded as the internal affairs of other sovereign states. Members of the Organization of African Unity, for example, pledged not to change political boundaries drawn by European empires and to accept colonial borders as sacrosanct. And state officials and ethnic majorities in the new republics adamantly refused to surrender power or territory to indigenous minorities.

But while ethnic minorities rarely achieved state power, they were not often defeated. Except for Biafra, separatist movements were not conclusively defeated because they were assisted by indigenous minorities, who were subjected to discrimination and violence by state authorities and ethnic majorities. They could also draw on economic support from emigre communities and sometimes political support from neighboring states. For example, Tamils in India provided economic aid and refuge for Tamils in Sri Lanka, while the Indian government for a time provided diplomatic and even military support.

All this changed after 1990, when a number of ethnic movements seceded from established republics and acquired states of their own. The successful ones all benefited from political changes originating in the Soviet Union.

During the 1980s, Mikhail Gorbachev returned Soviet troops from Afghanistan and withdrew military support for allied dictatorships in Ethiopia and Eastern Europe as part of a comprehensive effort to reduce Soviet military spending and to address a series of economic, social, and political crises in the Soviet Union. The withdrawal of Soviet military support crippled dictatorship in Ethiopia, where the government had battled Eritrean separatists for years, and regimes in Eastern Europe, where rulers confronted serious economic crises of their own. As a result, in 1991, Eritrean rebels defeated the Ethiopian army and later held a referendum ratifying Eritrean secession and independence. In Eastern Europe, the collapse of communist regimes in 1989 and 1990 led to democratization but also to division in Yugoslavia, where ethnic movements based in the country's constituent republics seceded, a development that triggered partition and war in 1991, and in Czechoslovakia, where the government agreed to Slovak demands for a separate state and divided the country in 1992. And in the Soviet Union itself, the ongoing crisis encouraged the development of ethnic movements based in the constituent republics and triggered a coup, which led to the secession first of Baltic republics and then to the breakup of the Soviet Union.

The success of these separatist movements in the early 1990s encouraged widespread emulation, and ethnic movements have revived or formed in countries all over the world. Even in Latin America, where common languages and ethnic identities for many years inhibited formation of separatist groups, movements demanding self-determination for ethnic minorities have recently emerged. Just how many ethnic movements now exist around the world is hard to determine. There are probably hundreds, perhaps more. Political scientist Ted Gurr estimated in 1993 that there were 233 "politically active communal groups," numbering "some 900 million people." Others scholars have identified between 3000 and 5000 ethnic communities or "nations" that might demand power in independent states.

Secession and the partition of states into 2 or more successors (two each in Czechoslovakia and Ethiopia, 5 in Yugoslavia, 15 and perhaps more in the Soviet Union) created a series of problems, much as decolonization had earlier. Partition has led to disruptive migrations, as ethnic groups cross newly created borders to find refuge from real or potential violence and discrimination. The officials of new states often adopt laws discriminating against residual minorities. These developments, and disputes over borders and the sovereign powers of divided states, can trigger ethnic conflict within and war between successor states.

Contemporary separatism has also raised questions for republican governments generally, even the governments of separatist states, because it has called into question constitutional principles and practices. Can constitutional government be dissolved by ethnic or other minorities alone? What role does the majority play in the process? And what does this mean for constitutional government and the principle of majority rule? At issue is the answer to Abraham Lincoln's question, asked on the eve of civil war: "Why may not any portion of the confederacy a year or two hence arbitrarily secede again, precisely as portions of the present Union now claim to secede from it?"

And separatism has created problems for the republican interstate system as a whole. Should the United Nations intervene in these conflicts? If so, what principles should guide its response? (During the postwar period, the United Nations has frequently inserted itself between contending states, as it has for years in the Kashmir and Cyprus, and more recently in Yugoslavia, but its capacity to do so is limited.) Can the United Nations accommodate a growing number of members? And if so, how might that be peacefully accomplished given the disparity between the existing number of states (more than 184) and the number of ethnic groups in the world (hundreds or thousands)? As former U.S. Secretary of State Warren Christopher told Congress, "If we don't find some way that different ethnic groups can live together in a country, how many countries will we have? We'll have 5,000 countries rather than the hundred plus we now have."

IV. ALTERNATIVES TO SELF-DETERMINATION

Because contemporary separatism has been associated with conflict and violence, some ethnic movements have modified their demands for self-determination. Instead of demanding a state of their own, or resigning themselves to minority status in a state controlled by others, some minorities have adopted "commonwealth" or "sovereignty-association" as their goal. These alternative arrangements might provide a way for minorities to divide and share political power with majorities.

In Puerto Rico, for example, the electorate voted in a 1993 referendum to retain the island's commonwealth status, rejecting a proposal to apply for statehood in the United States by a small margin and a proposal for independence by a large margin. Commonwealth was initially established by the United States in the early 1950s as a way to transfer some political power to the inhabitants. But Puerto Ricans nonetheless support commonwealth because they believe it is tailored to suit their century-long relationship with the United States. In practical terms, it provides hybrid forms of sovereignty and of citizenship. The island's legislature possesses some powers that other U.S. states do not have, Puerto Rico enjoys UN recognition as an "autonomous political entity," and it participates in the Olympics under its own flag. But security, trade, and law enforcement policies are all controlled by the U.S. Congress, which admits only a non-voting delegate from Puerto Rico.

Just as commonwealth provides a hybrid form of sovereignty, it provides for a hybrid kind of citizenship. Island residents are given U.S. citizenship, may be drafted into the U.S. army, may migrate freely to the United States, as tens of thousands have done, and receive many social benefits. But they cannot vote in Puerto Rico for president, and their rights as citizens may be revoked by Congress. Proponents of Commonwealth argue that U.S.–Puerto Rican relations should be redefined and a "Compact of Association" adopted to reflect contemporary change, and they maintain that political power in any new relation be divided and shared by both parties.

In Hawaii, movements of ethnic Hawaiians, the *Kanaka Maoli*, have argued that solutions to the problems created by U.S. conquest in 1893 and admission as a state in 1959 be developed with this history and contemporary realities in mind. "Every Hawaiian in his heart would like to be independent," argues Mililani Trask, a leader of *Kalahui Hawaii* (Hawaiian Nation). "But we owe it to our people to be realistic. There is no mechanism for seceding from the Union. Secession doesn't do anything for the native people."

As an alternative, Hawaiian movements have proposed some form of "sovereignty-association," though they debate the precise meaning of the term. In a special 1996 plebiscite, native Hawaiians agreed that they should "elect delegates to propose a Native Hawaiian government" by a 3 to 1 majority. For many of them, sovereignty-association might provide for a restored Hawaiian monarchy, while also creating secular, representative political institutions for the indigenous minority. And these institutions would acquire and share specified powers with the state and federal governments.

In Canada, the movement of French-speaking Quebecois also describes its aim as sovereignty-association, though they do not attach to sovereignty any royalist meaning. For them, sovereignty-association would allow the state to protect the linguistic and cultural identity of Quebecois, while retaining important economic relations with Canada and trade relations with the United States. But its precise meaning has not been spelled out, and it is unclear whether Canada would consent to political and economic relations on Quebecois terms. What is more, while the Quebecois demand the right to develop a new political relation, they are unwilling to extend this same right to indigenous groups, particularly Indians in lands previously ceded to Quebec by Canada. The proposal for sovereignty-association was narrowly defeated in a 1995 referendum, the second of its kind in recent years, though its proponents vowed to raise the issue again.

To some extent, commonwealth and sovereignty-associate resemble the political institutions developed by imperial reformers during the interwar period. The British, for instance, introduced commonwealth in 1931 as a way to share some power with some colonies, chiefly those with large, White-settler populations. While commonwealth provided for shared rights and responsibilities, it was drafted by imperial authorities, not drawn up by subject colonies, and it was not made widely available to peoples throughout the colonies. Nonetheless, commonwealth survived the breakup of the British empire, and today counts as members many former colonies. By contrast, contemporary forms of commonwealth—in Puerto Rico or in the Commonwealth of Independent States—are to a great extent made or chosen by autonomous states and indigenous residents.

These hybrid arrangements may in some cases provide an alternative to self-determination and secession from republican states, but they are not without difficulty. While referendums and plebiscites have been used to gauge support for political alternatives, the process of determining choice is unclear and sometimes contentious. In the Puerto Rican referendum, there was intense debate about whether Puerto Ricans living in the United States could participate, and it was decided they could not, despite their stake in the outcome. In Hawaii, nonnative groups sued to void the plebiscite because it prohibited participation by nonnative residents. If the process of determining choice is seen as unfair, the results may be treated as illegitimate.

A second problem is that whatever the process or outcome of referendums, conventions or treaties designed to create alternative political relations, they may not be durable. In Puerto Rico and Quebec, the losers of recent referendum have vowed to try again, giving rise to ongoing debate about fundamental, constitutional issues. If decisions made are not regarded as permanent or binding, they may contribute to instability. The Israeli–Palestinian peace accords provided for new relations based on hybrid political institutions, which permitted greater Palestinian autonomy but also provided for residual Israeli authority in the West Bank and Gaza. But these accords are widely regarded as temporary, a way station to something else, probably the creation of a sovereign Palestinian state. Uncertainty about the temporal status of these agreements and disagreement about the eventual outcome has led to renewed conflict.

And finally, these political alternatives depart from political norms established after World War II. The postwar interstate system was based on a relatively homogeneous political form: the nation-state republic. Although the United Nations made some provision for heterogeneous forms that dated from the previous imperial system—dominions, colonies, mandated territories, monarchies, and religious enclaves like the Vatican—it has not provided easy accommodation for contemporary alternatives. Unless accommodation is made for polities that depart from the conventional political norm, it may be difficult for them to survive.

Still, to the extent that hybrid political institutions like commonwealth and sovereignty-association are freely chosen and establish equitable relations between minority and majority, they may provide an alternative to ethnic violence and uncivil war.

Also See the Following Articles

COLD WAR • COLONIALISM AND IMPERIALISM • ETHNIC CONFLICTS AND COOPERATION • ETHNICITY AND IDENTITY POLITICS • TERRITORIAL DISPUTES

Bibliography

Anderson, B. (1991). *Imagined communities: Reflections on the origin and spread of nationalism.* London: Verso.

Brown, M. E. (1993). *Ethnic conflict and international security.* Princeton: Princeton University Press.

Buchannan, A. (1991). *Secession: The morality of political divorce from Fort Sumter to Lithuania and Quebec.* Boulder: Westview Press.

Cultural Survival. (1987). *Southeast Asian tribal groups and ethnic minorities: Prospects for the eighties and beyond.* Cambridge, MA: Cultural Survival.

Dahbour, O., Ishay, M. R. (1995). *The nationalism reader.* Atlantic Highlands, NJ: Humanities Press.

Dunlap. J. (1993). *The rise and the fall of the Soviet Empire.* Princeton: Princeton University Press.

Gurr, T. R. (1993). *Minorities at risk: A global view of ethnopolitical conflicts.* Washington, DC: U.S. Institute of Peace Press.

Hannum, H. (1990). *Autonomy, sovereignty and self-determination: The accommodation of conflicting Rights.* Philadelphia: University of Pennsylvania Press.

Holland, R. F. (1985). *European decolonization, 1918–1981.* New York: St. Martin's Press.

Horowitz, D. D. (1985). *Ethnic groups in conflict.* Berkeley: University of California Press.

Louis, R. W. (1978). *Imperialism at bay.* New York: Oxford University Press.

Schaeffer, R. (1990). *Warpaths: The politics of partition.* New York: Hill and Wang.

Schaeffer, R. (1997). *Power to the people: Democratization around the world.* Boulder, CO: Westview Press.

Security Studies

Brenda L. Horrigan
Independent Scholar

Theodore Karasik
University of California at Los Angeles

GLOSSARY

Anarchy In security studies, a view of the world as having no ultimate authority to resolve inevitably conflicts between nation-states. Realists believe that anarchy is the basic, immutable characteristic of the world system.

Cold War The period between the end of World War II and approximately 1990 during which the United States and the Soviet Union were generally hostile to one another but did not engage in direct military conflict because both feared that such a conflict would escalate into a devastating exchange of nuclear weapons.

Collective Security Establishment, or efforts to establish, peace between nations based on legal standards that are enforced collectively by the nations of the world through a variety of means, including diplomatic pressure and military force. The United Nations is an example of an organization founded to achieve collective security.

Grand Strategy A nation-state's theory on how to achieve a state of security through various means, including diplomacy and military power.

Idealist A school of thought in international relations that considers the world from a holistic, global point of view. Much idealist thinking is based on abstract principles. Idealists tend to have an optimistic view of human nature and believe ways can be found for human beings to establish a world order and eliminate most conflicts and war. Tools favored by idealists include international norms, legal codes, and the use of collective international pressure for the adoption of agreed moral–ethical values by all nations.

National Interest Refers to those elements that make up a state's most vital needs and requirements, such as territorial integrity, political and cultural independence, military security, and economic health. Pursuit of national interests presumably guides the behavior of national decision-makers. Common national interests include self-preservation, independence, territorial integrity, and economic well-being.

National Security A term subject to considerable debate. One widely accepted definition considers national security to be a subjective sense of freedom from threats to a nation's territorial integrity and its citizens' quality of life. The leaders of nation-states endeavor to achieve national security through pursuit of their national interests.

Nongovernmental Organization (NGO) Also referred to as transnational organizations. A private group acting in the international arena that seeks to extend cooperation among nations, often on a particular set of issues, be they social, cultural, or technical.

Realist A school of thought in international relations that is based on fundamentally empirical and pragmatic concerns. A realist sees the world as being in a state of anarchy with no supreme authority to regulate and resolve conflicts between nation states. For a realist, who typically has a pessimistic view of human nature, conflict between states is virtually inevitable. Key scholars in the realist tradition include Hans Morgenthau and E. H. Carr.

Security Dilemma The problem that nation-states face regarding how to achieve security in a world characterized by anarchy. Related to this are such questions as whether complete security is attainable or always desirable.

State (or Nation-State) The primary unit of the international community defined as a social group occupying a particular territory and organized by shared political institutions. States are considered legal when their existence is acknowledged and recognized by other states.

SECURITY STUDIES is the subfield of *international relations* concerned with the issue of how nation-states handle threats to their territorial integrity and quality of life. This subfield is most highly developed in the United States and the end of the Cold War has spawned an increased interest in the field among U.S. scholars. This heightened interest, though, has been accompanied by demands for a redefinition of the field's concerns to include a broader range of issues related to human security.

I. ORIGINS OF THE SECURITY STUDIES FIELD

The subfield of security studies developed after the end of World War II and at the start of the nuclear age. Prior to this time, the study of military issues—use of force, weapons balances, security-based alliances, intelligence methods, and exploitation—was the domain of the professional military. Scholars confined themselves to the study of military or diplomatic history. With the development of nuclear power and the rise of tensions between the United States and the Soviet Union, the U.S. defense community expanded rapidly and more civilian professionals became involved in the study of such issues as the use of nuclear weapons as instruments of policy, the balance of forces between nation-states, arms control prospects, targeting alternatives, and the use of conventional forces. This expansion of civilian

involvement in security policy raised a demand for university courses on such subjects and by the mid-1960s security studies programs were established in about a dozen universities, with many more offering elective courses on security issues.

The field in its early "Golden Age" was dominated by the realist school of thought and by the specific issue of U.S.–Soviet relations in the nuclear era. The realist point of view considers conflict between nation-states inevitable, given an anarchic world system in which there is no supreme authority to resolve inter-state disputes without violence. Realists generally employed the rational actor model, which saw each state as a unitary actor guided by rational calculation of risks and benefits and supplied with perfect information on situations. United States security studies programs emphasized the study of deterrence theory and "containment" of presumed Soviet desires to expand its control through Europe and the Third World.

The field suffered a temporary decline in the late 1960s for several reasons. First, the field's narrow focus on military sources of international tensions coupled with the dominance of the realist theoretical model—which considered the nation-state as a unitary, rational actor—had limited explanatory value on many issues. Second, the unpopularity of the U.S. war in Vietnam both raised doubts about the explanatory value of security studies theory and also made it unfashionable at universities to study military issues. The period in the early 1970s of lessened tensions between the United States and the Soviet Union also undermined interest in the subfield of security studies.

Security studies enjoyed a renaissance after the mid-1970s, after the U.S. involvement in Vietnam ended and after détente collapsed. The Ford Foundation's funding of several academic centers for security affairs plus the founding of a new journal called *International Security* also raised interest in the field. During the 1970s there was a new emphasis on producing policy-relevant theory as well as an increased use of history, particularly use of the comparative case study method. The realist school's dominance of the field ended, with more scholars taking an idealist point of view that sought solution to international problems through collective security regimes and related methods. The 1970s and 1980s were also a period of "behavioral revolution," which introduced methods from other fields—like psychology, sociology, anthropology—to the study of politics. This period, therefore, can be viewed as one in which the field opened up to a variety of theories, points of view, and methods, although the realist interpretation of security continued to be pervasive.

By the late 1980s, security studies was a well-established field of international relations, particularly at U.S. universities. The end of U.S.–Soviet tensions, however, has compelled many to demand a redefinition of both the concept of security and of the subject matter addressed by those in the field.

II. CONTEMPORARY DEFINITION AND SCOPE OF SECURITY STUDIES

A. Traditional Definition and Scope

A precise and universally accepted definition of "security," and thus of security studies, has proved elusive. Some consider security to mean freedom from war or threat of war. Others define it as a nation-state's ability to pursue its interests without sacrificing core values. The *Oxford Companion to Politics of the World* acknowledges security to be an ambiguous term, but considers its fundamental meaning to be a subjective sense of freedom from threats or danger. Some scholars today want to expand dramatically the definition of security to include freedom from a range of threats, including economic deprivation and environmental degradation.

Central to most definitions of security is the concept of threat. Security studies has traditionally been defined as "the study of the threat, use, and control of military force, with the emphasis being on examining the causes, consequences, and cures for war. . . ." (Mandel, 1994). Key concerns in security studies include how a nation-state limits threats from other nation-states and projects its forces to achieve national interests. Thus, security studies scholars traditionally have focused on issues related to diplomacy, crisis management, and arms control.

B. Pressures for Redefinition of Definition and Scope

Prior to the end of the Cold War, some scholars recognized a need to redefine both the concept of security and the subject matter of security studies. These scholars believed it essential to recognize that a nation-state's relationship with other countries stemmed not only from its military power and influence but also from its economic health, the nature of its political system and leadership, its political and social cohesion, and its access to vital technology and natural resources.

Some scholars consider security studies to be in a period of crisis. They blame security specialists who failed to anticipate the collapse of the Soviet Union and the end of the Cold War. Kolodziej blames these failings on the field's overemphasis on the U.S.–Soviet balance of military forces in Europe. This narrow focus caused specialists to underestimate the effect of the Soviet-instigated reform of the central planning system and system of internal political control.

C. The Post-Cold War Reshaping of Security Studies

In the debate over the definition of "security" and "security studies," various scholars have proposed new approaches. Some wish to retain the traditional emphasis on military power and military threats. Yet, they explain, the end of the Cold War—and the accompanying decline in superpower control over the actions of smaller nations—has expanded the issues of concern to security studies scholars to include issues of regional conflict; separatist or nationalist conflict; irredentist conflict; ethnic, religious, or tribal power struggles; fundamentalist struggles; and prodemocracy movements. Conflict over access to vital resources necessary for weapons production would also be considered a key concern of neotraditionalist thinking. This approach, advocates claim, provides a definite focus while allowing for an interdisciplinary approach that incorporates the insights and methods of political science, sociology, history, philosophy, economics, and psychology.

In contrast, idealists in the security studies field feel the time is ripe to reconstruct the concept of security. Generally, they propose a global perspective that begins with the idea of a world community and emphasize the need to understand how these individuals—grouped in various cultural or social entities—can pursue fulfillment of their goals and protect their values simultaneously. The most extreme within this school of thought want a new emphasis on the security of the individual. The end of the U.S.–Soviet standoff, they argue, means the opportunity has arisen to consider all aspects of security: freedom from military threats is crucial, but so are issues of economic deprivation, environmentally caused health hazards, cultural integrity, oppression of women and racial minorities, and religious freedom. Nation-states cannot be secure if their citizens are not secure. International security, therefore, is unattainable as long as billions lack access to food and clean water or suffer from any sort of oppression.

Dissenting voices on the idealist-oriented suggestions for redefinition generally argue that conceiving security to include issues of pollution, poverty, AIDS, and so on would destroy the intellectual cohesion of the field. The new dilemma for the security studies field, as Mandel asserts, is how to broaden the field's concerns to deal with a new, wider range of issues without turning "security" into "a worthless, 'it-means-anything-you-wish' notion" (Mandel, 1994).

Middle-of-the-road proposals support an expansion of both the concept of security and the subject matter of security studies while retaining a traditional air. That is, security is to continue to be viewed as the freedom from direct, primarily foreign, threats to a nation-state's territory or citizens. The key player is to be considered the national government, although a range of nonstate actors is also recognized. Even with this rather conservative definition, advocates argue, the field can easily accommodate those interested in issues related to economic security, resource/environmental, and political/cultural security as well as military security. All four subsectors are acknowledged as legitimate components of security by a substantial number of students and scholars in the field, although many find it difficult to distinguish precisely the domain of each subsector.

III. SUBSTANTIVE AREAS OF SECURITY STUDIES

A. Military Security

For many decades, the term "security" was understood to mean *military* security. Despite the end of the Cold War—and subsequent pressures to rethink the concept of security—most agree that military issues continue to be an important concern for security studies.

The serious consequences of the threat or use of military force means that issues of military security typically receive the greatest attention by scholars and other experts. Military security threats come in a variety of forms. They can include the threat of attack, seizure of territory, blockades, or bombings. A primary security goal for most nation-states, therefore, is to discourage others from attacking. Most states' leaders accomplish this by seeking to obtain what they consider to be a sufficient amount and type of weaponry and trained military personnel to ensure victory should an armed conflict occur. There are exceptions; Costa Rica, for instance, does not keep armed forces. Some nation-states might also seek military power sufficient to intimidate other nation-states into acting in a desired fashion.

Many security studies scholars have noted that the end of the Cold War era has also meant the end of many patron–client relations between the superpowers

and smaller nations (such as the Soviet Union and Cuba or Nicaragua). Theorizing that such relationships had a stabilizing effect on smaller nations, these scholars believe the post-Cold War world will see a growth in the number of conflicts. These might include more clashes between nations, terrorism, internal ethnic, or religious unrest. These scholars cite the war in the former Yugoslavia, Iraq's attack on Kuwait, and fundamentalist-backed terrorism in Egypt as examples. The military security consequence, they believe, is that nations will need to acquire the ability to respond to a far broader range of threats. Nation-states will now need to acquire the military capabilities that allow them to react swiftly to this variety of threats. That is, military security requirements in the post-Cold War world now emphasize the need for more flexible, rapidly deployable, conventional weapons systems rather than the nuclear forces that were considered so vital during the Cold War.

Operations short of war are increasingly consuming the attention and resources of the world's military forces. The most stressing of these operations are collective responses to international crises and conflicts, such as Bosnia, Somalia, Haiti, Rwanda, and Kuwait. These situations have, especially for some specialized capabilities, stressed the forces to exhaustion or failure. More generally, they have encroached upon the training and readiness of the forces, leading to a debate as to whether such assignments are a "proper" use of military power. As a contribution to this debate, security studies scholars are now studying operations short of war and how those stresses affect organization, training, and equipment.

Recent technological developments are also posing new problems for military security scholars to solve. The development and proliferation of advanced information and communications technology, for example, is a growing concern. Concepts like "cyberwar" (use of information-based military operations to disrupt enemies) and "netwar" (low-intensity conflict in which the enemy employs networks for control and communication) are central to this developing area of military security studies.

One positive development of the end of the U.S.–Soviet Cold War rivalry is that there is greater potential for nation-states, particularly the two superpowers, to cooperate in keeping the peace. Interest is rising among national leaders in possibilities for collective security regimes and arms control.

As noted above, since the end of the Cold War, the security studies field has expanded to allow theoretical perspectives beyond realist perspectives. Two major thrusts have emerged in discussions of military security.

Realists continue to emphasize the causes of conflict and war, but idealists now are enjoying a rebirth of broad interest in arms control and collective peacekeeping. As the growing literature on "defensive" defense shows, identification of the sources of peace and cooperation, rather than simply the study of causes of conflict and war, is now a key part of the research program of security studies.

A key concern to all in security studies is weapons proliferation. The spread of modern weaponry—conventional, chemical/biological, and nuclear—threatens an escalation in the scale and intensity of wars. (It also increases the chance that a nation-state will have the resources for, and find value in, preemptive strikes.) How best to establish and enforce multilateral arms control treaties and regimes will be a key issue for the field of security studies. Other considerations will be how to manage the flow of advanced weapons technology and how to improve detection and inspection methods to prevent secret stockpiling by potential aggressor nations. Keeping military technology out of the hands of terrorists is also a concern.

The restructuring of the world order brought about by the end of the Cold War means that all scholars concerned with military security issues will face a new range of broad questions. During the Cold War scholars were preoccupied with containment of the Soviet Union and nuclear weapons deterrence. Today military security experts must grapple with a completely new situation. They face such difficult questions as whether the collapse of the Soviet Union inevitably means there will be an explosion of conflicts within former members of the Soviet bloc or whether regional powers, freed from the restraint of their Cold War patrons, will become more aggressive in pursuing their national interests. In addition, they must also address completely new areas, such as advanced information technology and its effect on the security situation. The field of security studies is certainly expanding beyond its traditional military-oriented areas of concern, but, nonetheless, scholars who stay focused on the field's traditional concerns will have much to do.

B. Economic Security

If military security is the longest established substantive area for security studies, then economic security is the most widely accepted *new* substantive area. Since at least the oil shocks of the 1970s most security studies experts have acknowledged the importance of economics to a nation-state's well-being and that of its citizens.

The collapse of Soviet-style communism and spread of market-based economic systems around the world has raised the saliency of this area in the post-Cold War era.

On the other hand, what constitutes an economic-based security threat is not easy to define. As Buzan showed in 1991, defining economic security is a tricky matter, considering that the central characteristic of a market economic system is *insecurity*. Market economies function best when there is widespread competition and the ever-present threat of failure. To seek economic security, therefore, seems at odds with support for a global economy based on market mechanisms like free trade and competition.

Another difficulty is that many things that harm a state's economic health—inept leadership, price or interest rate manipulation, foreign import competition—are not actually threats to a state's security (meaning that nation-state's physical integrity, ideology, institutions). For that reason, Buzan recommends that members of the security studies field confine their attention to economic threats that are linked to other security sectors—for example, economic threats that might damage a state's military industrial base or undermine domestic political stability.

One general definition of economic security might be the ability of a nation-state to obtain through production or fair trade those goods and services it needs to preserve its national security. Studies of economic security policy would focus, therefore, on how a state uses economic mechanisms to maintain territorial integrity, meet citizen demands for goods and services, preserve political and cultural independence, and achieve freedom from threat of foreign military assault.

Not surprisingly, realists and idealists interpret the general economic security goals for nation-states differently. Realists tend to stress the goal of national economic self-sufficiency and control; idealists tend to focus on how to achieve greater international economic efficiency through cooperation.

Contemporary economic security issues of concern to both schools of thought include the balance of trade among nation-states, the impact of foreign investment on a nation's economy, and the establishment of links between government and industry to carry out research and development crucial to national security. Evolving regional economic blocs and alliances and potential vulnerabilities in supplies of raw materials or access to markets are also of concern to students of economic security issues. Scholars of military security and economic security issues share a concern over how to best manage the flow of weapons technology under expanding free market conditions.

C. Resource/Environmental Security

Some of the most interesting research and debates in security studies since the end of the Cold War revolve around issues of security and the natural world. The term "environmental security," though, is a term that often confuses more than it clarifies this area of security studies. It is important here, therefore, to review the various meanings the term has within security studies before moving on to current issues of concern.

There are two aspects to resource/environmental security, both of which are based on threats posed to nation-states and citizens by the natural world. The first concerns access to natural resources; the second involves human-made environmentally based threats.

The essence of a state's security is its ability to protect and defend its territory and the resources—timber, fossil fuels, water, strategic minerals, and so on—it contains. Few if any states, though, have within their borders all the natural resources that government believes essential. Access to natural resources, therefore, is a long-standing security issue. Typically, states try to trade or establish treaties in order to acquire what they need. Yet military history is replete with cases of states going to war to defend, or acquire, access to natural resources deemed vital by a government: The 1991 Persian Gulf War—fought to ensure western states' access to oil—is one such example.

Even the most traditional and conservative members of the security studies field would accept a resource-oriented definition of environmental security. Because access to natural resources is so widely seen as a valid security issue, those advocating a broadening of the concept of security often prefer to refer to "resource/environmental security" rather than just "environmental security."

Beyond natural resource access issues, the field becomes more divisive. Some scholars now argue that those studying resource/environmental security should include threats that emanate from nature itself. This idea is controversial; for decades natural threats—floods, droughts, earthquakes, typhoons—were not considered valid subjects of study in the security studies field. Natural phenomena were random "acts of God" and not subject for study or debate. In recent years, though, environmentalists have pointed out humans' impact on the natural world. Human activity has expanded and humankind's impact on the natural world—in the form of greenhouse gases, acid rain, ozone depletion, toxic waste, and water pollution—is now seen by some as a political problem.

Major environmental threats, like global climate change, are not confined to one state's territory. A nation's pollution does not stay within its own boundaries. Therefore, the threat of major environmental degradation is a real source of conflict today, especially when the pollution is caused by one state's efforts to produce material goods for consumption or foreign trade. There is a crucial trade-off, Mandel shows, between production–consumption efforts and protection of the natural environment. Conflict is likely between developed and developing nations. The former are most focused on acquiring or attaining access to nonrenewable resources; they want poorer, developing nations to control their population. The developing nations, though, are pressed with feeding their growing citizenry and keeping their food and water sources clean; they want richer, developed nations to share the world's natural resources more equitably.

Environmental threats that go beyond traditional resource access issues, these scholars argue, pose a crucial new area for research. If national security means protecting one's territory and other national interests from outside threats, then the security studies field must recognize a wider range of threats. Among the specific subjects proposed for study are environmental degradation that affects a nation-state's economy or sociopolitical cohesion.

Scholars with an idealist orientation often pursue even broader courses of study. These academics—who define security in the broadest terms, with an eye to the health and well-being of each individual citizen—dominate this area of security studies. For them, the key security goal is not simply national access to strategic materials but the individual citizen's quality of life as it relates to the environment. One area of concern for them is how to establish practices that would prevent, for instance, environmental accidents or unintended environmental degradation as the result of war.

While resource/environmental problems mean an increase in security threats to the nation-states of the world, there is one positive aspect. Most human-made environmental problems are shared by many nation-states. There can be no zero-sum thinking in this area, for no nation benefits from environmental hazards. One state's pollution problem quite easily becomes the problem of all its neighbors. The shared nature of the problem provides an opportunity for collective solutions and an increase in leaders' and citizens' recognition for greater global cooperation to solve world problems. Major environmental hazards—such as the ozone hole discovered over Antarctica in 1985—can never be solved without broad international cooperation. Battles over scarce resources will likely continue to be a cause for conflict and even war between nation-states. Other environmental threats, though, offer prospects for greater collective security-seeking among states.

D. Political/Cultural Security

In the post-Cold War era, the field of security studies has been under pressure to adapt to new international conditions. While this has opened up the field to many new and useful ideas, it has also brought up for question the domain of the field and its intellectual purpose. Many argue that broadening the definition of security too far will undermine the intellectual integrity of the field. If the subject of security studies is everything in the natural world, then scholars will be able to focus on nothing.

The difficulties facing security studies in the post-Cold War era are nowhere more apparent than in discussions over issues of political and cultural security. This might be surprising, for political security is a traditional concern of security studies. In fact, there was for many years a tight link between the ideas of military and political security. Military threats to a nation-state were viewed in tandem with threats to a nation-state's ability to govern authoritatively within its borders.

Events in the late 20th century—especially the spread of democratic standards and market economy ideals—have called into question traditionally accepted ideas such as a government's rights over its citizens. In recent years, scholars have tried to separate issues of military security from issues of political security. In doing so, many have found political security issues in the post Cold War era to be closely related to issues of culture.

Mandel says that political/cultural security is best defined by two measures: The first is security related to a state government's authority and control within a nation; the second is the cohesion of a state's cultural identity. The security goal in the political/cultural issue area, scholars say, centers on the ability of a nation-state to preserve its basic political and cultural character, despite changing conditions or potential or actual threats. Preservation of the government structure, the national ideology, and the nation's distinctive culture are key goals.

Traditionally, security studies scholars focused on direct threats to the sovereignty of the government, domestic order, and central national control. Threats can rise from separatist movements or from huge inflows of persons from other states, such as immigrants or refugees. An influx of new, foreign ideas can also threaten a state's political and cultural cohesion. For example, rising expectations among citizens may result from the spread of democratic notions and market-based capitalism. (The affect of western ideas on the citizens of the Soviet Union is well-known. Simply put, when the Soviet government found it impossible to control the influx of democratic ideas—and modern consumerism—it essentially lost its ability to retain centralized control of that vast sociopolitical system.) In the modern world—with so many methods of mass transport and communication and such extensive trade of commodities and ideas—halting such processes can be a difficult task.

It can be difficult to separate such "threats" as cultural imports (EuroDisney) from threats to a nation-state's internal cultural or political cohesion. Yet such a distinction is essential, some scholars argue, for security studies to retain its focus. Seeing McDonalds restaurants in downtown Munich may be annoying, they say, but it hardly means the end of Bavarian culture. One solution, offered by Buzan, is to focus on cultural imports that lead to or intensify actual conflict between states.

There is a considerable difference in how idealists and realists treat political/cultural security issues. Generally, realists retain a traditional focus, dealing with threats to a state's political sovereignty, its ability to maintain domestic order through central control, and the maintenance of a unitary governmental authority. Idealists, on the other hand, have embraced the call in the post-Cold War era for a new approach. These scholars seem to care far less for the health of the nation-state's central government than for the individual citizen. They focus more on threats to individual political freedom and interpret security situations in terms of tolerance for diversity and the ability of interest groups and citizens to affect national policy.

Good examples of how realists and idealists differ are cases involving national suppression of minorities or subcultures within a state. In the name of national security, some states have suppressed the cultural identity or separatist ambitions of minority cultures. This does create, typically, a stronger and more viable state. Such suppression, in the name of national cohesion, is often applauded by realists. But just as often it is not. Certainly few in the west approved the "Russification" of large groups (Georgians, Ukrainians, Balts) during the Soviet regime. The interpretation of such suppression, though, is highly subjective. Western leaders have protested Iraqi assaults on the Kurds within Iraq's borders but said little about Russia's post-Cold War battle with Chechen separatists in the Russian Federation. Cultural suppression in the name of nation-state survival, Buzan suggests, might be a necessary evil, one of the "awful contradictions" of national security logic. Central to all these discussions is the issue of perception. A state's leaders, if they were highly xenophobic, might perceive threats where there are none. Some interpret Iraq's treatment of the Kurdish people as out of all proportion to that minority's threat to the central government. Russia's treatment of the Chechens, on the other hand, was interpreted by some as an unfortunately necessary step to prevent the splintering of the multiethnic state.

Those studying political/cultural security have a full plate before them. Much work still needs to be done on clarifying the precise subject matter in this issue area. The disruption of the Cold War international order, though, offers a variety of cases to study for those interested in the relationship between cultural and political security and for those focusing on specific types of political or cultural threats to national security.

IV. CONCLUSIONS

The subfield of security studies is undergoing a redefinition in the scholarly community. The basic boundaries of the field remain intact: security studies scholars continue to be concerned with the underlying root causes of peace, violence, and conflict. Equally important is the study of how nation-states pursue their national interests and how they handle threats to their territorial integrity and their citizens' quality of life. The end of the Cold War in the early 1990s, though, called into question the field's traditional emphasis on *military* threats.

Today many scholars are demanding that the concepts of threat and security be broadened. Areas of study now include threats related to the economic, resource/environmental, and political/cultural security of a nation-state (and its citizens). Some protest this expansion, arguing that if the field tries to study everything that might threaten an individual and his or her society,

the field will lose its intellectual cohesion. The debate over the proper areas of concern in the security studies field is one that will not be settled soon. In all probability, a final redefinition of the field's subject matter will rely on the fruits of current research in new areas. Regardless, security studies will remain a dynamic subfield of international relations.

Also See the Following Articles

COLD WAR • ENVIRONMENTAL ISSUES • MILITARY DETERRENCE AND STATECRAFT • NONGOVERNMENTAL ACTORS IN INTERNATIONAL POLITICS

Bibliography

Allison, G., & Treverton, G. F. (Eds.) (1992). *Rethinking America's security: Beyond Cold War to new world order.* New York: W. W. Norton & Co.

Arquilla, J., & Ronfeldt, D. (1996). *The advent of Netwar.* Santa Monica, CA: RAND.

Builder, C. H., & Karasik, T. W. (1995). *Organizing, training, and equipping the Air Force for crises and lesser conflicts.* Santa Monica, CA: RAND.

Buzan, B. (1991). *People, states & fear: An agenda for international security studies in the post-Cold War era.* (2nd ed.). Boulder, CO: Lynne Rienner.

Critchley, W. H., & Terriff, T. (1994). Environment and security. In R. Shultz, R. Godson, & T. Greenwood (Eds.), *Security studies for the 1990s.* Brassey's (US), Washington, DC.

Deudney, D. (1990). The case against linking environmental degradation and national security. *Millennium, 19*(3), 461–476.

George, A. L., & Smoke, R. (1974). *Deterrence in American foreign policy: Theory and practice.* New York: Columbia University Press.

Kakonen, J. (Ed.) (1992). *Perspectives on environmental conflict and international relations.* London/New York: Pinter.

Kapstein, E. (1992). *The political economy of national security.* New York: McGraw–Hill.

Klare, M. T. (Ed.) (1994). *Peace & world security studies: A curriculum guide* (6th ed.). Boulder, CO: Lynne Rienner.

Mandel, R. (1994). *The changing face of national security: A conceptual analysis.* Westport, CT: Greenwood Press.

Shultz, R., Godson, R., & Greenwood, T. (Eds.) (1993). *Security studies for the 1990s.* Washington, DC: Brassey's.

Walt, S. M. (1991). The renaissance of security studies. *International Studies Quarterly, 35,* 211–239.

Serial and Mass Murderers

Elliott Leyton

Memorial University of Newfoundland

GLOSSARY

Homicide The killing of another human being. A homicide is considered a "murder" when there are no exonerating circumstances to the killing, such as "self-defense."

Moral Panic Refers to the inappropriate public hysteria generated by media focus on a specific fear, such as "ritual murder."

Misogyny The fear and hatred of women, which is a fundamental principle of radical feminist analysis of the male ideology "justifying" the oppression of women.

Patriarchy This refers to the structure of male-dominated societies that permits the oppression and control of women.

Recidivism The likelihood that an offender, once released from prison, will repeat the offense.

MURDER refers to the unlawful killing of another human being. In both academic and police usage, the two forms of multiple murder usually refer to the slaughter of three or more persons, most often with "a common motive, method, and/or type of victim" (Lunde, 1979: 47). *Serial* murder refers to killings spread over time, often with a sexual component, as in the notorious Theodore Bundy case. *Mass* murder refers to killings that take place all at once, as in the case of the "McDonald's Massacre" in California, for motives that are as likely to be personal as political (as they were in the bombing of the federal building in Oklahoma City).

Both these terms are essentially descriptive, not analytic, and they are simply used to distinguish between the various forms of multiple murder. Extravagant claims have occasionally been advanced regarding the invention and the development of these terms, but they have in fact been drawn from common parlance and have been in use in one form or another throughout much of this century. Mass murder has been largely ignored by analysts, perhaps because the perpetrator is usually dead at the end of his spree and impossible to interview. Thus the detection of the identity and the ultimate capture of a mass killer is rarely difficult, provoking the comment from one senior police investigator that "mass murderers are a social problem, not a police problem." As for serial murder, the concept—"if not the exact term"—has been in use throughout the century (Wakefield was writing about 'serial-murder' as early as 1936 [1936: 9]), even if "systematic descriptions and analyses" did not begin until the 1980s (Jenkins, 1994: 8). In fact, there is now a substantial body of research and publication on serial killers.

Although many commentators give slightly varying definitions, they all refer to the same statistically rare and particular form of multiple homicide—often, but by no means always, of strangers. Such killings often *appear* to be motiveless and senseless, but on closer examination are usually found to have a warped logic of their own. Most commentators prefer simply to limit the definition to a minimum number of victims, usually three or four, sometimes five, without reference to motive.

I. THE FIELD OF STUDY

Few phenomena better illustrate the yawning chasm between popular and scholarly interests than that of serial and mass murder; and few subjects have so captured the public imagination yet have been so systematically ignored by academics. This neglect appears to be a consequence of several points of view: on the one hand, there are those who regard the study of such "sensational" criminal behavior as ultimately serving the interests of conservative "law-and-order" political pressure groups; and on the other hand, some regard the subject as too vulgar, even pornographic, for legitimate scholarly examination.

In fact, it was only in the aftermath of what has come to be called the great serial killer panic of the early 1980s that academics began to treat multiple murder as a social phenomenon worthy of separate analysis. After that, a series of books and articles appeared in rapid succession (for example, Levin & Fox, 1985; Leyton, 1986; Cameron & Frazer, 1987), and created an entirely new field of inquiry. Despite the recent attention, however, it remains what Egger (1990) called "an elusive phenomenon": the most basic definitions are hardly agreed upon, and a truly reliable comparative international and historical database has yet to be constructed (a problem that is universal in the study of violence). Typical work in the field still either concentrates in microscopic detail on a small number of cases, deriving tentative but sometimes unwarranted conclusions from this unrepresentative sample; or it consists of a myriad of unanalyzed cases haphazardly collected in an "encyclopedia"; or, more rarely, it discusses general patterns based on data of varying degrees of reliability. Typically too, scholars argue narrowly to advance their own specialties and theoretical prejudices— sociology, biopsychology, or feminism, for example— and make minimal reference to each other's insights.

As with many of the subjects covered in this encyclopedia of violence, peace, and conflict, the paucity of useful data radically narrows the descriptive and analytic possibilities open to the researcher: nonpolice researchers usually find it difficult or impossible to obtain the necessary official permission to interview individual offenders, and useful statistical data must be constructed and tabulated afresh for each new inquiry. These flaws are compounded by the fact that because virtually all descriptive and statistical data are from modern industrial nations, we know almost nothing about the phenomenon in the developing world. Given these limitations, the purpose of this entry is to outline what insights have so far been offered; to begin the integration of some of these primary insights; and to suggest directions for future research.

II. THE THEORETICAL BACKGROUND

A. Multiple and Single Murder Compared

Several fundamental characteristics distinguish serial and mass murder from conventional single murder. One is the social relationship between killer and victim. In the majority of homicides, there is some form of relationship prior to the event—family, acquaintances, associates, or lovers. Although historically significant, the murder of strangers is relatively rare in most modern societies. In one famous study of homicide in 1958 in Philadelphia, for example, only 12.2% of the killings were between strangers (Wolfgang, 1975: 207); although that figure has risen considerably in recent years in the United States. In multiple murder, however, except in the obvious case of familicides, the victims are more likely to be relative or complete strangers.

A second difference is that the perpetrators of single murder tend to be overwhelmingly drawn from the least successful strata of society—undereducated, chronically unemployed, living on state benefits, and with chronic drug and/or alcohol problems. Palmer (1972: 40) was one of many to note that it is "the poor, the uneducated, those without legitimate opportunities, [who] respond to their institutionalized oppression with outward explosions of aggression." On the other hand, multiple murderers are drawn from a greater range of social niches, and seem less likely to be from the ranks of the truly oppressed. Indeed, they are often gainfully employed, and, sometimes have reasonable expectations of conventional futures. Their problem is more likely to be internal: as Bolitho observed a half century ago, multiple murderers "very commonly construct for themselves a life-romance, a personal myth in which they are the maltreated hero," and which allows the murderer to engage in a fantasy of "social war, in which his hand is against society" (1926: 7–8, 274).

What follows is a review of the primary perspectives that have so far been brought to bear on multiple murder. Note that each theoretical tradition narrowly operates on the working assumption that its variables are the primary—or only—causes of the phenomenon. Note also that while other types of multiple murderers—say, for example, assassins—are assumed to be adequately explained by their degree of political commitment, this is thought to be an insufficient explanation for serial and mass murderers.

B. Typologies of Serial and Mass Murder

Many scholars believe that categorizing the varieties of a phenomenon—the construction of types, or typologies—is the necessary first step toward understanding it.

1. Mass Murder

Levin and Fox's initial work in 1985 distinguished three types of mass murder on the basis of the killers' motivations, goals, and self-justifications: these included family slayings, murders for profit or expediency, and sexual serial killing. However, in their more recent work they followed what had become general practice and treated serial killings as a separate phenomenon. In order to avoid the previous classificatory confusion between the killers' motives and the victim–offender relationships, their revised typology focuses purely on motivation.

They now distinguish four motives, then compare them with the relationships between victims and offenders, the forethought given to the killings, and the "state of mind of the perpetrator." They agree with most current commentators that the motive behind the majority of mass killings is revenge—"either against specific individuals, particular categories or groups of individuals or society at large." The largest single category of these revenge massacres includes husbands who murder their estranged wives and children; and alienated employees who avenge themselves on their boss or fellow employees. In the 1986 murder of 14 postal employees in Oklahoma by a disgruntled fellow worker, for example, Levin and Fox argue that the killer was "in a sense trying 'to kill the post office,' much like the estranged husband/father might attempt 'to kill the family.'" The victims in such massacres are not randomly selected: they are chosen because they are mem-

bers of a category of person—racial, familial, economic, or communal—who the killer feels are responsible for his unhappiness. "He seeks to get even, not with specific people whom he knows, but with anyone who fits his single criterion for hate" (Levin and Fox, 1996: 65).

Nevertheless, some mass murders are motivated by what Levin and Fox call a form of "love," wherein a depressed father massacres his family to spare them the suffering that life entails. Finally, some mass murders are motivated purely by profit, as when a family is murdered for an inheritance; or in a gangland operation, as in the robbery and execution of 13 guests at the Wah Mee Club in Seattle in 1983.

2. Serial Murder

Holmes and De Burger (1988) based their typology on 110 cases. Drawing on ideas that had emerged from the FBI Academy, they developed their typology of the "dominant motives" of serial murderers. They first distinguished serial murder from the two other traditionally accepted types of what they call "criminal multicide"—*mass murder*, in which "several people, in the same general area, at the same time, are slain by a lone assailant"; and *spree murder*, in which "several victims are murdered, typically over a period of hours or weeks, by a relatively reckless, impulsive killer."

Holmes and De Burger reject purely "social" explanations: for them, poverty, poor neighborhoods, unstable families, and a subculture of violence cannot be the cause of serial murder, since few who are exposed to such social stresses become serial killers. Because few serial murderers are thought to be from the most disenfranchised strata of society, they conclude that the explanation for the behavior must lie elsewhere—in psychological factors, that is, "in the psyche of the killer." Their categories include the *Visionary Type*, whose killings are "committed in response to 'voices' or 'visions' that demand that a person or category of persons be destroyed"; the *Mission-Oriented Type*, who typically decides to "go on a 'mission' to rid the world of a category of people" he has defined as beneath contempt (e.g., prostitutes); the *Hedonistic Type*, who is killing for thrills, seeking only "pleasure or a sense of well-being." Moreover, they have devised three subcategories of the hedonistic type: the *thrill-seeking* killers who "derive pleasure directly from the murder event"; the *creature comforts* killers who kill, for example, to find "the perfect lover, or the good life;" and the *lust murderer*, to whom "sexual arousal and gratification" are central. Their final major category is the *Power/Control-Oriented Type*, whose primary satisfaction comes from his complete domination over the life and death of the victim.

Gresswell and Hollin (1994) have criticized these typologies on three levels. First, the categories' lack of mutual exclusivity makes it difficult to distinguish visionary from missionary types except on the basis of the former's alleged insanity. Second, the categories are not exhaustive: for example, they do not include contract killers because their motivation is financial and is therefore deemed "extrinsic." On the other hand, the categories *do* include killing for insurance, or to eliminate the witness to a sexual assault, which are also extrinsically motivated. Finally, the categories are insensitive to "interactions between the killer, the victims, and the environment," and do not account for killers whose motivations may change over time (for example, from killing to mutilation, or to ensuring extensive coverage in the media). Gresswell and Hollin conclude with a call for typologies that are sufficiently flexible to accommodate "both psychological and environmental variables, and which also recognize that there is a process to multiple murder."

C. Psychobiological Perspectives

The psychobiological tradition assumes that the causes of human behavior, normal and pathological, are rooted in human biology. In the realm of criminal behavior, it has its origins in the work of the 19th-century Italian criminalist, Lombroso, and in the more modern work by the Gluecks (1956) that studied the relationship between body type, temperament and criminality.

Several primary paths can be discerned in contemporary research. Evolutionary psychology has had nothing to say about multiple murder per se, but it has postulated a general adaptive evolutionary advantage for male aggression. The work underlines the fact that most homicide worldwide is between males, and emphasizes the survival value of male aggression. Archer, for example, writes that the characteristic behavior of young human males, including "the willingness to accept a challenge, to take risks, and sexual jealousy" are just those confrontational qualities that can lead to a homicide. A willingness to kill was not necessarily an evolutionary advantage, but these qualities were adaptive because they were instrumental "in obtaining status and resources and keeping exclusive sexual access to a partner." This argument seems plausible, but recent primate studies cast doubt on the reproductive advantages of male aggressivity, and suggest not only that Alpha males are not the most aggressive ones, but also

that highly aggressive males tend to be expelled from the group.

Another major tradition looks to specific biological/chemical/neurological incapacities—operating alone or synergetically—as a possible explanation. One illustration was the XYY chromosome research that Fox criticized for "premature speculation and, consequently, much confusion": in fact, upon closer examination, only 3% of incarcerated populations were found to have the extra Y chromosome, and these actually "displayed, in their criminal behaviour, *less* violence against persons than did control patients." To date, XYY has only be decisively correlated with non-aggressive characteristics—mild retardation, tallness, and resistance to corrective training.

There are also many scattered and inconclusive case studies. Kraus, for example, studied a 45-year-old serial killer's medical history and found a paralyzed leg, a skull fracture and concussion, a "military" injury suffered in Vietnam, a psychological test diagnostic of antisocial personality disorder, and elevated levels of urinary kryptopyrroles. This combination of "genetic, biochemical, neurological and psychiatric impairments," Kraus thought, could "at least partially explain the 'actual inner workings' of this serial killer." Although this may be true in this case, there is no evidence that such factors are present in other killers.

Although few scientific researchers would argue that biological differences solely account for murder, some biological factors are being looked at as "vulnerability factors" that might well contribute to an increased susceptibility to violent behavior. Especially suggestive at this time is recent research on testosterone and serotonin. M. Leyton (personal communication) notes that in animal studies, reduced serotonin neurotransmission increases aggression "and decreased the behaviorally inhibiting effects of novelty and punishment," while elevated serotonin levels produce the opposite. Very preliminary work in humans has produced provocative results, finding indices of low serotonin function "in the majority of subjects with a history of impulsive violent behavior," as well as in the majority of depressed patients who have attempted suicide (Leyton *et al.*, 1997). Still, as one researcher remarked, "the circumstantial evidence may be considerable, but the smoking gun has yet to be found."

D. Psychiatric/Psychological Perspectives

The assumption in this field is that the origins of behavior lie in the internal psychological make-up of each individual, although authorities differ on whether this constitution is learned or inherited (the ancient, and so-far quite unresolved, nature/nurture debate).

The benchmark in psychiatric studies of multiple murder remains Lunde's classic *Murder and Madness*, first published in 1975. Lunde concluded that unlike single murders who may kill strangers or those with whom they have relationships, the victims of multiple murderers are more likely to be *slightly* known to the killer. Moreover, such multiple killers "are almost always insane"; and their insanity takes the form of selecting as victims those who have "certain attributes which torment him." The victims themselves "are unaware of their psychological or symbolic significance to the killer," which may include the killer's belief that they send telepathic messages to him.

Lunde hypothesizes that the insanity of these multiple killers takes two primary forms. One is a hostile paranoid schizophrenia, the causes of which lie in a combination of "genetic, metabolic, and psychological" factors, and the symptoms of which include hallucinations, "delusions of grandiosity or persecution, [and] bizarre religious ideas." The other is sexual sadism, in which the killer only achieves sexual fulfillment through "torture and/or killing and mutilation." The origins of sexual sadism, he believes, lie in the fusion in early childhood of "sexual and violent aggressive impulses." Unlike schizophrenia, which is treatable, the development of sexual sadism is likely to be derailed only by intervention during childhood.

Mainstream psychiatry continues to produce useful case studies of individual killers. Abrahamsen's study of one killer, David Berkowitz, develops the theme that the "Son of Sam" was the victim of a "death wish," which he turned "directly against others" by killing, and "indirectly against himself" by ensuring that he would be captured and punished. Abrahamsen thought the killer's rage had developed after discovering that he had been rejected by his natural parents and put out for adoption: his vengeful killing spree, according to the psychiatrist, was "rooted in his fantasies about killing his mother and half sister." Such work is interesting and important, but tells us nothing about why only a handful of adoptees should react with such violence.

In the years since all this pioneering work, however, the psychiatric and psychological sciences have largely shifted their attention away from the essentially *legal* category of "insanity". This move has been accompanied by an increasing awareness among professionals that, as Gaylin was one of the first to remark: "Most of us are aware how trivial, ephemeral, descriptive, and meaningless are psychiatric diagnoses." Perhaps the most widely accepted contemporary concept is that of psychopathy (sometimes called sociopathy, or antisocial personality disorder), which describes a remorseless and unfeeling personality that cannot respond to the humanity in other people. Hare and his colleagues, among others, have written extensively of the "common core of attributes" of psychopathy. These include "pathological lying," "impulsivity," "a lack of remorse, guilt and shame; [and an] inability to experience empathy or concern for others," or even to establish affectionate relationships.

Giannangelo's 1996 volume, *The Psychopathology of Serial Murder*, tries to strike a balanced perspective in the application of textbook psychiatric notions of pathology to serial murderers. While he concedes that "labels" such as antisocial and psychopath may be relevant to these killers, and that symptoms such as dissociation and post-traumatic stress disorder are often seen in them, he suggests that a history of "physical, sexual, or mental abuse" is perhaps the most important trait shared by "most" serial killers. As a result of their abusive childhoods, serial killers have developed "a pervasive lost sense of self and intimacy, an inadequacy of identity, [and] a feeling of no control." These deficits manifest themselves in what may be "the ultimate act of control," the murder of many people. Giannangelo's explanation tries to resolve the nature/nurture debate by dealing with both biological and environmental pressures. While maintaining that the abusive histories of serial killers constitute the "extreme psychological trauma" that is the environmental trigger, it would not be expressed as serial killing without a "biological ingredient that makes the mix an explosive one." His "serial killer diagnosis," then, sees a person who will commit predatory murders as having congenital or trauma-induced physiological anomalies, a personal life history of severe abuse, an early display of antisocial and/or criminal behavior, evidence of pervasive sexual deviance, and a tendency to live in a state of fantasy.

If the concept of psychopathy is now widely used in criminal psychiatry and psychology, it has several flaws which have been extensively criticized. Although it accurately describes many of the behavioral characteristics associated with multiple murderers, it does not explain why many who have these qualities do not kill. Indeed, psychiatrist J. Reid Meloy has written that such a diagnosis is "too descriptive, inclusive, criminally based, and socioeconomically skewed to be of much clinical or research use." In a similar critical vein, psychologist David Canter considers psychopath and sociopath to be "curious terms that imply a medical, pathogenic origin yet in fact describe someone for whom no obvious organic or psychotic diagnosis can be made."

Therefore, he argues, the terms are "more an admission of ignorance than an effective description" of a medical condition. Egger concludes that if the notion of psychopathy has proved to be a most useful label and category, its inability to predict whether a victim will be a remorseless killer or a corporate executive merely reminds us "that we in fact don't know why these people act as they do."

Yet it is David Canter's *Criminal Shadows* (1994: 240 ff) that linked the "secret" inner life of serial killers to their remorseless, psychopathological, use and abuse of other people. He observes that the majority of such killers are relatively *unaggressive* in day-to-day life, and that their outbursts of criminal violence are only a part of their life story. Focusing on the "discernible structure" of the killer's inner life, Canter examines the use of internal narratives, or autobiographical stories people "tell" themselves in the construction of their identities. All human beings half-consciously develop a story of their lives—"drawn from the culture and society in which we live"—with the self as the central character responding to a variety of situations. The narrative of the average person is a largely "public story of successes and failures," of family, friends, and career. A serial killer has also developed a story of his life, but in his personal narrative all other characters are assigned a subsidiary role as consumable objects, not persons. Canter concludes that such offenders lack the ability "to create private dramas in which others share centre-stage"; and this in turn makes it impossible for them to feel empathy for others. If we are all the central characters in our own dramas, the personal narratives of violent offenders distort the "themes of intimacy and appropriate use of power," deny empathy and self-respect, and portray others as less than human. Thus their victims can become mere "objects of anger or desire, vehicles to satisfy the perpetrator, possessions that are jealously guarded, targets for him to act upon." Such a life story denies the fundamental qualities of a healthy personality in a civil society—the ability to feel compassion for others while maintaining a sense of self-respect.

E. Feminist Issues and Perspectives

A basic assumption of radical feminist thought is that far from being a perversion of the male sexual impulse, rape and sexual murder can most accurately be seen as the *essence* of male sexuality and male culture. This is entirely compatible with beliefs that modern gender relations constitute a form of the oppressive patriarchal "war against women," and that serial murder is merely the control of women through their organized international execution. In the most influential feminist text on the subject to date, Cameron and Frazer review previous scientific attempts to explain such sex murder. They believe that the murderer has always been inaccurately portrayed by male science as somehow defective, as "deviant from male sexuality"—as biologically or psychologically deficient, or warped by a violent culture. In fact, they argue, there is a second discourse in our civilization; a sustained cultural statement in which the killer "is a hero, at the centre of literary and philosophical celebration." Revelations of feminist thought in the preceding decades have made it apparent that male violence is the "law of misogyny": indeed, some radical feminists claim unilaterally that regardless of whether the victims of a sex murderer are female or male, the one thing they all share is that the killer is *always* male. Thus they argue that in any patriarchal society, women are mere objects to be consumed by men, used by men for their "self-affirmation" and the fullest expression of their masculinity. Moreover, "it is under the banner of masculinity that all the main themes of sexual killing come together: misogyny, transcendence, sadistic sexuality, the basic ingredients of the lust to kill." In this view, then, the rape and murder of women becomes the *natural*, not deformed, path through which men transcend their narrow identities and liberate themselves from the constraints of conventional life.

However, Hickey's extensive 1991 database suggested that if the *motivation* of serial killers (for example, sexual gratification) is ignored, and analysis focused simply on the number of victims—three or more—then fully 17% of serial killers are female. He does not argue that serial killer Jane Toppan's motives were in any way typical when she claimed that her ambition was to "have killed more people—more helpless people—than any man or woman who has ever killed." Indeed, he found that the motives of female serial killers seemed more likely to involve material or social gain (as with women who serially murder their children, husbands, or tenants to collect their life insurance) than to satisfy an obviously perverted sexuality. While a quarter of the female offenders in his sample killed only members of their families, those who killed strangers preyed primarily on the most vulnerable—patients in hospitals and nursing homes, or young boys and girls. Still, he notes that in these cases "we cannot [always] be sure that money was actually the primary motive." In addition, he records the consistent increase in the number of female offenders, particularly since 1970. Not only did Hickey make it clear that serial killing is not exclusively a male crime against women, but he also stated that a very substantial minority of the victims were men: while more than one-third of male serial killers preyed exclusively on women, just under one-half killed both males and females, and one-fifth killed only males.

In his 1994 volume on the social construction of serial homicide, Jenkins criticizes the radical feminist theory that serial murder is both "the ultimate manifestation" of male sexual abuse of women and "a powerful weapon in the political suppression of women." He notes that such a belief "places the blame for the offense firmly on masculine characteristics" and "the structure of a male-dominated society," thereby transforming the fear of serial murder into an "ideological weapon" against patriarchal society. Moreover, he argues that the feminist analysis of serial murder is based on "questionable assumptions," not the least of which is that serial killers are invariably men preying on women: "cases involving women offenders were all but ignored." Cameron and Frazer's bald statement that there has never been a female equivalent of the Yorkshire Ripper must therefore "be examined critically in light of the undoubted existence of numerous women through history who have murdered repeatedly."

Jenkins adds that in order to maximize their political and emotional impact, hard-line radical "feminists have stuck to the original grossly inflated and long-discredited [U.S.] Department of Justice estimates of the number of serial killers and victims," when in fact women "are by far the *least likely* segment of the population to fall victim to homicide." Indeed, in contemporary America, Black men have a 1 in 21 life chance of falling victim to homicide, the chances for Black women are 1 in 104, while White men have a 1 in 131 chance, and White women only 1 in 369. However, Jenkins judiciously concludes, if the radical feminist analysis is lacking in "scholarly merit," the theories have been a significant rhetorical device for sensitizing the population to the injustices inflicted upon women, and in emphasizing that women have sustained terrible abuse, comparable in every way to that inflicted on other "relatively powerless groups."

Julie Cluff and her colleagues honor feminist theory for its illumination of society's demeaning "objectification of individuals" and "the glorification and normalization of violence within patriarchy." Nevertheless, while maintaining that feminist analysis has enormous potential for enriching our understanding of serial murder, Cluff and colleagues also criticize the narrowness of much feminist theorizing—especially in its insistence that only males can be serial killers, and in utterly "ignoring issues of class and race." They also express

concern about the consistent use of "narrow definitional criteria" and an unfortunate "emphasis on ideology and sensationalism." In their review of the literature, they laud feminist theory for pointing "the analysis of serial murder in an important direction," but state that it has been entirely self-limiting for feminists narrowly to study only male sexual predators and dismiss even "the possibility that women could be serial killers." They conclude that these "shortcomings demand an expansion and improvement of feminist analysis to account for the diversity in serial murderers and their differing modus operandi," and suggest this should begin with the serious study of the female serial killer.

Candice Skrapec pursued a central issue when she questioned the common assumption that the motivations of male and female serial killers *must* be quite different. Her 1996 essay, which expanded on the implications of Hickey's data, reminded us that since a significant minority of serial killers are female, a deformed sexuality might not be entirely a masculine preserve. She notes that psychiatry has often been insensitive to "the subtle emotional dynamics" that can be associated with female sexuality: thus if male perversions "tend to be more overtly sexual," female sexual perversions "are manifestly more subtle, involving symbolic acts centred on emotional dramas of abandonment, separation and loss." Yet, she adds significantly, "these differences serve to mask the more substantive underlying similarities between male and female multiple murderers," and she calls for a sustained and delicate exploration of the similarities and differences in the sexuality of the two genders.

F. Social Perspectives

The primary and recurring theme remains the vexing and unresolved question of causation. What could cause a person to take the life of a number of innocent human beings, often people of whom he has neither prior knowledge nor personal hatred? What are the social forces that might determine, underlie, or shape the production of such a remorseless killer? Do certain types of cultures or specific historical epochs incubate or encourage such violence?

1. Mass Murderers

Mass killers have still received little attention in the literature. Leyton's 1986 volume postulated that although mass and serial killers are quite different, they are similar in some important ways—especially in that their acts are personalized social protest, and they are neither politically revolutionary nor mentally deranged.

Arguing from an extremely limited sample, he speculated that mass killers were much more likely than serial killers to come from relatively stable middle-class family backgrounds. Moreover, rather than using their killings as a catapult to international celebrity (as so many serial killers do), the majority wished to avenge themselves in one sustained burst, and then *die*, "knowing that the social statement that is their killings will give them a form of immortality." The origins of their vengeful fantasy, Leyton thought, lay in their early and intense recognition of the impossibility of bettering their social condition—their jobs, their status, their persona. Starkweather experienced poverty and stigmatization throughout his brief life; Essex did not feel it until he left the warmth of his family and community for the racist embrace of the Navy: regardless, their confrontation with the social abyss rendered their lives unbearable. Compulsively, they chose to die in an explosion of violence directed at the group they felt oppressed, threatened, or excluded them. Thus in the McDonald's massacre, Huberty murdered the Hispanics he thought had usurped his social position—"society's had their chance," he told his wife; Starkweather murdered the middle classes whom he felt despised him as the garbageman who had himself been transmuted into "garbage"; and Essex murdered Whites who humiliated and unmanned him. Yet they made their final commitment to the killings not for others, but for themselves; not for lofty ideology, but seemingly because they could not come to terms with the "lowly" status offered them by society—as garbageman, as apartment security guard, and as repairman of vending machines.

A decade later, Levin and Fox refined these matters, and include the more common familicides into their definition of mass murder. Thus episodes such as the McDonald's massacre of complete strangers by definition become the exception to the rule. While concurring that "a majority of mass killers have clear-cut motives—such as profit or revenge," they insist that for the majority of such killings, the "victims are specially chosen," not just unfortunate individuals caught in "the wrong place at the wrong time." Levin and Fox construct a sequence of factors that contribute to the development of a mass murderer. *Predisposers* are long-established traits of the developing killer's personality and history, especially a depressive cast of mind, "failures at work, [the] military and [at] home," a "diminishing ability to cope" with life, and a chronic "tendency to blame others for problems" and disappointments. *Precipitants* are "short-term and acute triggers," that is, catalysts provoking the actual decision to kill and die, such as sud-

den unemployment or the ending of a marriage. *Facilitators* are circumstances "which increase the likelihood of a violent outburst," including the "social or psychological isolation" of the killer, and "access to [a] weapon of mass destruction." Thus the emerging mass killer is typically a middle-aged man whose life has been steeped in a deep sense of frustration, failure, and disappointment. The aggression generated by that lifelong frustration is turned outward if he has the kind of mentality that sees himself as the victim, and blames others for his own problems.

Levin and Fox also argue, perhaps less convincingly, that the overrepresentation of males in mass murder is due to "the fact that men are more likely to suffer the kind of catastrophic losses" that are the precipitants to mass murder: after a marital breakup, for example, it is the male who is more likely to be "ousted from the family home." Additionally, because men assess their own worth narrowly in terms of occupational status and income, they are more likely than women to suffer profoundly when they suddenly lose their jobs. These are provocative ideas and deserve further study alongside an assessment of male culture's apparent devotion to aggressivity.

2. Serial Murderers

If there is little material on mass killers, there is a rapidly expanding literature on serial murder. Levin and Fox opened the debate in 1985 with a critique of what they called "the psychiatric mistake": they argued that while psychiatric case studies often made for "engrossing reading," such analyses were bedeviled by unwarranted generalizations, and their validity was restricted to an unrepresentative handful of cases. Moreover, psychiatric diagnoses, with their emphasis on troubled childhoods, tended toward lists of symptoms—such as bed-wetting, fire-setting, and cruelty to animals—rather than explanatory discussions of cause.

Instead, quoting one serial rapist who maintained that "the rape wasn't really the important part, it was the dominance," Levin and Fox argue that the pleasure given the serial killer by his murders comes from the "absolute control" he exercises over his victims. The individuals who come to serial murder feel rejected, abused, and marginalized, and the intense frustration so engendered leads to various forms of aggressive behavior—designed to cure their feeling of impotence through "controlling, manipulating, or eliminating" others. Moreover, such personalities "have failed to internalize a moral code for the treatment of others": thus they are not victims of mental illness, not participants in another reality, but remorseless men "incapable of experiencing normal amounts of love and empathy."

Leyton (1986) developed a political, cultural, and historical overview. He argued that multiple murders aim at more than just the gratification of base appetites, but rather a kind of deformed campaign against the *political* order—"deformed," since its protest is not on behalf of others, only themselves; because their anguish is trivial, not profound; and since they punish the innocent, not the guilty. Like African witches, the serial killer reverses all social values to make "a demonstration to the authorities" (as one killer put it) in a manner that he thinks will force them to consider his legitimacy. Leyton's *cultural* argument is that modern civilization is one that both dehumanizes people and legitimizes violence as an acceptable, even praiseworthy, response to frustration. Moreover, through mass media and other pornography of violence, the civilization offers the killer advertising proclaiming the "joy" of sadism, and allows the killer to "grasp the 'manly' identity of pirate and avenger." Leyton also offered a *historical* argument, speculating that killers in each epoch were being drawn from the most "threatened" social class—the aristocracy in the pre-industrial era after their thousand-year feudal reign was challenged by a newly rebellious peasantry; the new middle classes created by the industrial revolution, insecure and rigid in their new-found roles, punishing the prostitutes and itinerants whose existence seemed to challenge their own legitimacy; and, in the modern era, the discontented ranks of the working class, preying on the middle class figures who had usurped their social position.

In *The Aesthetics of Murder*, Joel Black mounted an ambitious attempt to trace the connection between serial killers' treatment in literature and film and the manner in which the killers conceive and perceive their own actions. In this elegant study of the mirrors that reflect life and art, Black dwelt on the fact that "the most spectacular displays by the mass media are scenes of violence," and speculated on why art is "able to provide such cogent and compelling models for sociopathic behavior." He added the fundamental cultural question of why fictional creations are "able to engage impressionable and even critically sophisticated readers and viewers in a way that real-life human beings cannot?"

Also in 1991, Hickey fielded what he called a trauma-control model: here he argued what is now widely accepted—that regardless of predisposing biological, psychological, or social factors, an individual who will become a serial killer is invariably the product of severe childhood trauma. These trauma include "unstable home life, death of parents, divorce, corporal punish-ments, sexual abuse," and other wounding events. Thus the rejected child "feels a deep sense of anxiety, mistrust and confusion when psychologically or physically abused by an adult." Millions of people are exposed to such trauma, and learn to handle rejection constructively and nonaggressively. Those who will be serial killers, however, have never learned to cope with these trauma; and some begin destructively to act out their rage—against animals or objects, "or assaulting a spouse, a friend, or a relative." This aggression is an effort on the part of the destabilized child/adolescent to regain the internal equilibrium that has been taken away from him "by people in authority"; and Hickey speculates that this may be the process of becoming a "psychopath."

Curiously, the purely *sexual* component of serial murder has been relatively neglected—usually described, but rarely examined. Skrapec observes that the previous scholarly emphasis on the motivating factors of power and control have led to something resembling the "total sublimation of sex" in the literature; and she reminds us that serial killing is about sex as much as it is about murder. She distinguishes between the "expressive" quality of the murders (most especially the "rage" evident in the savage nature of the killing), and the "instrumentality" of murder for sexual pleasure or financial gain, and the way the two qualities can reinforce each other. When a killer preys on prostitutes, who may be symbols "of something that arouses tremendous hatred (or conflict) within him," then he acts out his desire to "punish or destroy them." If the initial reward of sexual pleasure from the killing may be subordinate to the hatred that drove him to kill, "he did, nonetheless, experience the arousal," and this flush of sexual pleasure may be a primary factor in any repetition of such murders—since the killing both relieved his hatred and was sexually gratifying. Moreover, Skrapec sees the ability of the killer to "objectify" the victim as not only a testament to the "power of the offender's emotions" but also an obvious marker of his pathological inability to feel empathy: if it is impossible to "put oneself in the emotional position of an object," then the serial killer is psychologically and morally "immune to his murders," as indeed he so often appears to be.

In "Ideological Homicide," R.S. Ratner offers an interpretation of serial murder that brings us closer to an understanding of the *social* origins of psychopathy. Ratner notes that historical periods of economic instability—either rising or declining affluence—are also usually times when cultural controls begin to crumble; and he observes that the two waves of multiple murder in the United States (1910–1930, and 1970–1996) were also periods of "massive economic destabilization." During such periods of social upheaval, of sudden hardship or affluence, "cultural codes harmonizing class goals and individual aspirations are no longer efficiently transmitted through weakened family units." Vulnerable individuals then become more likely to seek solutions to their predicaments through a vindictive "individual fantasy" that is "bereft of scruples." Ratner's hypothesized socio-economic path for the formation of serial killers is as follows:

1. Economic destabilization and cultural collapse increase the tension that results from social inequality.

2. This tends to destabilize all interpersonal relations, especially for the children of "dysfunctioning families, who suffer flagrant abuse and neglect."

3. This abuse "is partially eroticized by the child as the only available means of rationalizing maltreatment and maintaining some form of necessary emotional contact."

4. Because the abuse and pain cannot be comprehended by the victim, they must be "anaesthetized" if the pain is to be reduced: but the resulting "deadening of emotion" is precisely what produces sociopathy in the child.

5. Even when the pain is deadened and compartmentalized, inevitably it will later be expressed: "Scripted eroticized violence" becomes the means for fulfilling these fantasies, in the course of which the powerlessness of the child is "symbolically neutralized and avenged." In an orgy of serial murder, Ratner concludes, victims are ritually captured, possessed, defiled, and disposed of, affording the killer "brief vengeance against the rejecting family/society."

If Ratner's assumption is correct and these serial killers do indeed come from savagely abusive families (and this assumption is shared by other specialists, including Ressler and colleagues), then it still leaves unresolved the question of why some victims of abuse react by committing their own atrocities while others resolve their rage in alternative ways—such as alcoholism, drug addiction, or the excesses of religious or political fundamentalism.

III. TOWARD AN INTEGRATED EXPLANATION

In his magisterial work, *Europe and the People Without History*, Eric Wolf remarked that the primary intellectual achievement of the 20th century was also its greatest weakness. Science divided human behavior and experience into manageable "bits" such as history, biology, economy, psychology, society, and so on; but then, lost in these arbitrary distinctions, made no comparable attempt to reassemble what had been so artificially dismembered. Indeed, we are only at the beginning of our understanding of human behavior—healthy or otherwise; and a true and deepened comprehension of pathological aggression is unlikely to emerge until the insights from each discipline are integrated in a meaningful and balanced way.

The basic dilemmas remain unchanged: the social sciences have charted the cultural and structural pressures that ultimately create pathological behavior; yet they are unable to explain why the majority of people exposed to these social pressures do not kill. The psychological sciences have dissected a part of the psychological and biological vulnerability to aggressive behavior in any individual; yet they are unable to explain why there are such massive differences between societies (and genders, and social classes) in the likelihood that its most vulnerable individuals will commit murder. Everywhere in the world, physical violence is overwhelmingly (but by no means exclusively) a male domain; yet feminist analysis is not yet able to explicate the cause of the differences between men and women. Certain biological factors may well prove to be necessary to produce psychopaths, but they cannot do it alone without encouragement in one form or another from the environment.

One of the most intriguing possibilities at the moment is the proper integration of the levels of understanding offered by the various academic disciplines. Thus the social and economic forces that create so many violent and "dysfunctional" families could soon be brought together with the psychological mechanisms that severely abused children develop to cope with their obliteration. These socioeconomic and psychological factors would, in cases of individuals with biological/chemical deficits that mitigate against impulse control, create individuals "programmed" to revel in the display of vengeful savagery. If this is true, Skrapec may have over-stated her conclusion that individuals each take quite different paths to become serial killers, that some are biologically or psychologically disposed to their crimes, while others "are impelled by circumstance." Nevertheless, she is certainly correct that such behaviour appears to be part of the human condition and is "not, therefore, readily accessible by summary enquiry."

IV. FREQUENCY OF MULTIPLE MURDER

No one can yet confidently state how many multiple murderers there have been. It seems clear that such murderers exist in varying proportions in most, if not all, countries. Reported cases are especially concentrated in the United States, but some American commentators insist that this merely somehow reflects America's large population and much higher homicide rates. Despite a decade of serious research, no firm conclusions have yet been reached; nor is there much consensus among scholars about even the most general patterns, since the absence of any authoritative agency collecting reliable international information means each writer has access to different—but inevitably flawed—data.

A. Statistical Outline of Mass Murder

In their 1996 article, Levin and Fox laid the foundation for the quantitative study of mass murder. They note that mass murder has received considerably less attention from both scholars and journalists than has serial killing, perhaps because of its less sensational character. They were able to examine 329 such massacres (defined as having four or more victims) that had occurred in the United States between 1976 and 1989: perpetrated by more than 400 offenders, the murderers claimed almost 1500 victims. The data revealed that an average of two mass murders took place every month in the United States, producing an annual total of over 100 victims. To Levin and Fox, this suggested that mass murder, "although hardly of epidemic proportions, is not the rare occurrence that it is sometimes assumed to be."

They found no evidence of any recent increase in the rates of these offences, and noted that unlike single-victim crimes, which are quintessentially urban, "mass murders do not tend to cluster in large cities." The most striking differences are regional ones, they found: the Southern states, known for their high overall murder rates, "witness very few mass killings;" while states with high transient populations—especially Texas, Florida, Alaska and California—"have had more than their share."

Unlike serial killers, who generally avoid the use of firearms—probably because they are too impersonal—mass killers prefer the firearm, presumably for its obvious ability to kill the largest number in the shortest possible time. Because Levin and Fox include *familicides* (which constitute nearly 40% of massacres) in their classification of mass murder, they find that the majority of mass murderers do not "attack strangers who just happen to be in the wrong place at the wrong time." The incorporation of familicides also explains the relative youth and high proportion of females among the victims because the statistically "typical mass killing involves the breadwinner of the household who wipes out the whole family—his wife and his children."

B. Statistical Outline of Serial Murder

There are so many imponderables in the collection of statistics on serial murder that Egger's earlier comments still apply: the actual extent and prevalence of serial murder "is as yet unknown." In their first book, Levin and Fox (1985) initially thought commentators might even have "grossly underestimated" the number of multiple murderers active in the United States, and they speculated that "many of the more than five thousand unsolved homicides in the nation" each year might be the work of "a few very effective killers." In a similar vein, Leyton referred to the "remarkable increase" in multiple murder since the mid-1960s; Holmes and De Burger estimated that between 3500 and 5000 people might be murdered each year in the United States by serial killers; and Hickey, whose data showed that between 1795 and 1988, 34 women and 169 men in the United States were responsible for approximately 2000 homicides, noted a "ten-fold increase in the number of cases during the past 20 years in comparison to the previous 174 years" and suggested that "35–100 may be active in a given year."

Jenkins argument is more complex: he found only 25 officially recognized cases of serial murder in England and Wales in the period between 1880 and 1990—a time when the United States produced a minimum of 600 or 700 such killers. Moreover, serial murder was "common" between 1919 and the 1940s in other industrialized nations such as France and Germany. While there are now more *known* cases of serial killing in England and Wales than in the past, "the increase has been gradual and the 1980s produced about the same number of cases [as] the 1940s or 1960s." Serial murder in the United States takes a similar cyclical pattern, and its history falls into three periods: a rather high rate until 1940, when there were at least 24 "extreme" serial killers who killed a minimum of 10; "a time of relative tranquility in the mid century;" and a renewed "murder wave" that has continued from the mid-1960s to the present. Thus the increase of serial killing since 1965 was not "a wholly new phenomenon," but merely "a return to earlier historical patterns."

Jenkins argues further that the widely promulgated

idea of American "uniqueness" may be exaggerated. The number of U.S. serial killers may seem relatively high because its overall homicide rate is so much higher than other developed nations (10 times higher, for example, than England and Wales), when in the United States as in England, the *proportion* of all murders that are serial murders hovers around 1%. Moreover, the tighter libel laws in England and Wales make it impossible to attribute additional suspected murders to killers who have "only" been convicted of two or three: they would not therefore show up as serial killers in most databases, which usually stipulate a minimum of four or five victims. In addition, British police are less likely than their American counterparts to publicize sensational murders. Indeed, Jenkins believes it is even conceivable that with all these factors considered, the nations of the old British Commonwealth could have a proportionately "*higher* incidence of serial murder" than the United States.

Canter and colleagues' 1996 paper, "Are Serial Killers Special?" contains the preliminary results of the most ambitious international survey to date, one that elicited 3532 serial killers from over 30 countries between 1860 and the present. Their figures show a real increase in the fourth quarter of the 20th century, but "this increase directly reflects the growth in the number of homicides overall in that period," and they conclude that the allegedly worldwide pattern is "a by-product of an increasingly violent society." The bulk (2617) of these killers come from the United States, and they concur with Hickey's findings that "the great majority of US serial killers have come into being in the last 25 years." Canter and his colleagues identified 164 serial killers in the UK since 1860, 144 in France and 165 in Germany: all four countries showed a recent increase, and they estimate that as many as five killers are "active" each year in Britain, France and Germany. This conflicts with Greswell and Hollin's review, which finds "little empirical support" for the idea of such a dramatic postwar increase in Britain.

In the light of all this contradictory and tentative information, we can only echo Egger's conclusion that scholarship has so far provided "no decisive answers." Our data are weak, and quite unsupported by reliable official statistics at any national—let alone international—level. However, Egger adds ominously that murder by unknowns or strangers continues to increase in the United States: the proportion of killings that take place within the intimate circle of the family (a proportion that is always high in nations with low frequencies of homicide) has fallen in the high-homicide U.S. from 31% in 1965 to only 12% in 1992. The real quandary remains, as Kiger cautioned in 1990, that until we have developed a truly reliable international data base, we not only "will be unable to develop informed typologies, theories and policy decisions," but we also "run the risk of creating a social problem, the magnitude of which may be greatly exaggerated."

V. IMPACT ON SOCIETY OF MULTIPLE MURDER

In our civilization, the serial killer has assumed the symbolic mantle once worn by "monsters, demons, ghouls, vampires, werewolves and zombies": they occupy the same central position in our nightmares; and their role appears to be to embody, display, and define all evil. In *Sole Survivor*, Leyton reminded us of the impact such acts can have; and how such killings reverberate through the entire society. Indeed, any murder destroys far more than one person: it damages the spirit of the parents of the victim, the grandparents, siblings, lovers, and friends. Moreover, the fear it generates "erodes the social fabric, transforms public life from the joyous communal experience it might be to a savage zero-sum encounter; and demeans the humanity of all."

Multiple murder also has many political ramifications, far beyond its routine use by politicians to generate hostility toward criminals to strengthen conservative law-and-order political platforms. In the 1980s, serial killing became the basis for a widespread "moral panic," when an inappropriate amount (given their rarity) of deep-rooted anxiety was focused upon them. In Britain and America, unfounded beliefs became entrenched that there were now so many serial killers that they had become a significant threat to women and children. In fact, in the climate of fear generated by the issue, serial killers became part of many political struggles, as well as "weapons in the rhetoric of sexual politics." Indeed, the fear of serial killers was used by a variety of professional, social, and ideological groups pursuing their own quite separate political agendas—police forces such as the FBI, which saw it as a means to increase their visibility, funding and power; radical African American activists "who viewed it as part of systematic racial exploitation"; radical feminists who interpreted serial femicide as "a component of the larger problem of violence against women; children's rights activists concerned with missing and exploited children; as well as religious and other advocates of a ritual murder threat."

Ratner is especially critical of the exploitative role often taken by the media, and wondered to what extent "media depictions of women as available sex objects encourage serial killers to believe that women exist solely in order to gratify their bizarre fantasies?" He is concerned that the media's glorification of serial killers endlessly rehearses "the confusion between normal and pathological currents in mass culture." Moreover, Ratner argues that it is an error to dismiss "as mere commercialism" items such as serial killer trading cards, which he feels intensify "the association of serial murder with youthful recreation" and subtly encourage similar acts. He emphasizes that the significance of serial murder should not be in providing the media with further opportunities for degrading, titillating, and frightening the public: rather, the phenomenon should force modern society into a merciless self-examination. In doing so, he urges us to pay special attention to the modern family (an institution now "ill-suited to our social structure" and too disposed to the creation of pathology), and mount a "dispassionate analysis of the cause of split families, the scale of domestic violence and the effects of abuse and neglect."

VI. MULTIPLE MURDER AND JUSTICE

There is a widespread anxiety that notorious multiple murderers might one day be released from prison. This fear is fanned by the fact that in many jurisdictions—in the United States, Canada and elsewhere—the law requires that all convicted murderers automatically be at least *considered* for parole after serving a specified period of time in prison. Thus each time this usually perfunctory and legally mandated process is to be performed with notorious killers—say, with Myra Hindley in Britain, with Charles Manson in the United States, or with Clifford Olson in Canada—there is almost universal media and public hysteria that these killers might actually be paroled.

However, the facts do not justify this concern. It is true that Mary Bell who, as a pre-adolescent, murdered two small boys in England, was released and given a new identity after serving several decades in prison. Inexplicably, so was Denis Lortie—who murdered several people in Quebec's government buildings—after serving less than a decade. Caril Ann Fugate, who was convicted of being an accomplice at the age of 14 to Charles Starkweather's murderous rampage across Nebraska, was paroled after 18 years in prison (Starkweather was executed).

Yet these are rare exceptions. Despite public fears, multiple murderers do not normally receive parole. It is true that single murderers are usually released, and so many of them should be since their recidivism rate is very low (well below 1% in Canada). However, most courts implicitly recognize that multiple murderers have built their entire identities on the basis of their killings; and that consequently they are a continuing threat to society. Most politicians understand that to release such killers would be to corrode all sense of popular justice, as well as irrevocably weaken their own chances of reelection. According to Levin and Fox, most U.S. states specifically prohibit the release of serial and mass murderers, and employ either the death sentence or life imprisonment without parole to deal with such cases. In Hickey's U.S. sample of 157 male serial killers, one-fifth had been executed, another 14% were awaiting execution, a few had committed suicide or been killed in prison, and the remainder will be incarcerated for the rest of their lives.

Also See the Following Articles

BIOCHEMICAL FACTORS • CHILD ABUSE • HOMICIDE • MENTAL ILLNESS • TELEVISION PROGRAMMING AND VIOLENCE • WOMEN, VIOLENCE AGAINST

Acknowledgments

This entry is based partly on my own three books on homicide. I am grateful to my Canadian publishers, McClelland and Stewart, for permission to use material from previous work; and to the FBI Academy, New Scotland Yard, and the South Yorkshire Police for invaluable assistance.

I regret that space constraints have made it impossible for me to explore the considerable body of work that has emerged from the FBI Academy, the University of Liverpool, and elsewhere, regarding the "profiling" of serial offenders.

Bibliography

Abrahamsen, D. (1985). *Confessions of Son of Sam*. New York: Columbia University Press.

Archer, J. (1995). What can ethology offer the psychological study of human aggression?" *Aggressive Behavior 21*, 243–255.

Black, J. (1991). *The aesthetics of murder: A study in romantic literature and contemporary culture*. Baltimore: The Johns Hopkins University Press.

Bolitho, W. (1926). *Murder for profit*. New York: Garden City.

Canter, D. (1994). *Criminal shadows: Inside the mind of the serial killer*. London: HarperCollins.

Canter, D, Missen, C., & Hodge, S. (1996, April). Are serial killers special? *Policing Today*, 22–28.

Cameron, D. & Frazer, E. (1987). *The lust to kill: A feminist investigation of sexual murder*. New York: New York University Press.

Cluff, J., Hunter, A., & Hinch, R. (1997). Feminist perspectives on serial murder: A critical analysis. *Homicide Studies, 1*, (3), 291–308.

Egger, S. A. (Ed.). (1990). *Serial murder: An elusive phenomenon*. New York: Praeger.

Egger, S. A. (1998). *The killers among us: An examination of serial murder and its investigation.* Upper Saddle River, NJ: Prentice-Hall.

Fox, R. G. (1971). The XYY offender: A modern myth? *Journal of Criminal Law, Criminology and Police Science, 62*(1), 59–73.

Gaylin, W. (1983). *The killing of Bonnie Garland: A question of justice.* New York: Penguin.

Giannangelo, S. J. (1996). *The psychopathology of serial murder: A theory of violence.* Westport, CT: Praeger.

Glueck, S., & Glueck, E. (1956). *Physique and delinquency.* New York: Harper.

Gresswell, D. M. & Hollin, C. R. (1994). Multiple murder: A review. *British Journal of Criminology, 34,* 1–14.

Hare, R. D. (n.d.). Psychopathy and crime. In L. Otten (Ed.), *Colloquium on the correlates of crime and the determinants of criminal behavior.* Mitre.

Hazelwood, R. R., & Douglas, J. E. (1980, April). The lust murderer. *FBI Law Enforcement Bulletin,* 1–5

Hickey, E. W. (1991). *Serial murderers and their victims.* Pacific Grove, CA: Brooks/Cole.

Holmes, R. M., & De Burger, J. (1988). *Serial murder.* Beverly Hills, CA: Sage.

Jenkins, P. (1992). *Intimate enemies: Moral panics in contemporary Great Britain.* Hawthorne, NY: Aldine de Gruyter.

Jenkins, P. (1994). *Using murder: The social construction of serial homicide.* New York: Aldine de Gruyter.

Kiger, K. (1991). The Darker Figure of Crime: The Serial Murder Enigma. In S. A. Egger (Ed).

Kraus, R. T. (1995). An enigmatic personality: Case report of a serial killer. *Journal of Orthomolecular Medicine, 10*(1), 11–24.

Levin, J., & Fox, J. A. (1985). *Mass murder: America's growing menace.* New York: Plenum.

Levin, J., & Fox, J. A. (1996). A psycho-social analysis of mass murder. In T. O'Reilly-Fleming (Ed).

Leyton, E. (1986). *Compulsive killers: The story of modern multiple murder.* New York: New York University Press. Published simultaneously in Canada as *Hunting humans: The rise of the modern multiple murderer.* Toronto: McClelland and Stewart.

Leyton, E. (1991). *Sole survivor: Children who murder their families.* London: Penguin.

Leyton, E. (1996). *Men of Blood: Murder in Modern England.* London: Penguin.

Leyton, M., Diksic, M., Young, S. N., Okazawa, H., Nishizawa, S., Paris, J., Mzengeza, S., & Benkelfat, C. (1997). PET study of brain 5HT synthesis in borderline personality disorder. *Biological Psychiatry* (Abstract), *41*(7S), 17S.

Lunde, D. T. (1975). *Murder and madness.* New York: W.W. Norton.

Meloy, J. R. (1988). *The psychopathic mind: Origins, dynamics, and treatment.* Northvale, NJ: Jason Aronson.

O'Reilly-Fleming, T. (Ed.). (1996). *Serial and mass murder: Theory, research and policy.* Toronto: Canadian Scholars' Press.

Ratner, R. S. (1996). Ideological Homicide. In T. O'Reilly-Fleming (Ed).

Ressler, R. K., Burgess, A. W., Douglas, J. R., Hartman, C. R., & D'Agostino, R. B. (1986). Sexual killers and their victims. *Journal of Interpersonal Violence, 1,* 288–308.

Ressler, R. K., Burgess, A. W., & Douglas, J. E. (1988). *Sexual homicide: Patterns and motives.* Lexington, KY: Lexington Books.

Skrapec, C. (1996). The Sexual Component of Serial Murder. In T. O'Reilly-Fleming (Ed.).

Wakefield, H. R. (1936). "Landru: A real life bluebeard," in J. M. Parrish and John R. Crossland (Eds.). *The fifty most amazing crimes of the last 100 years.* London: Odhams Press.

Sexual Assault

Janine Goldman-Pach and Mary Koss

University of Arizona

I. INTRODUCTION

Sexual assault is both a crime and a public health concern. Rape violates the individual against whom it is perpetrated and impacts long-term health negatively. The National Women's Study, a longitudinal survey of a national probability sample of 4008 American women published by the National Victim Center and the Crime Victims Research and Treatment Center in 1992, found that 13% of women surveyed had been the victims of at least one completed rape in their lifetime. Extrapolating based on the United States Census and the National Women's Study, approximately 12.1 million American women have been forcibly raped in their lifetimes, which equates to 683,000 forcible rapes per year. The National Women's Study also found that rape victims are several times more likely than nonvictims of crime to develop Posttraumatic Stress Disorder, to experience a major depressive episode, to make a suicide attempt, and to have drug- and alcohol-related problems.

The trauma of rape exacts a very high toll. According to *The Extent and Costs of Crime Victimization: A New Look*, a National Institutes of Justice Research Preview published in January, 1996, "rape is the costliest crime ... a higher price than murder." Of $450 billion lost annually to crime, including short-term and long-term costs and losses, $127 billion is a result of rape. Continued monitoring of sexual assault trends is necessary to reduce the incidence and harmful effects of sexual assault. This article discusses the advantages and disadvantages of several methods of sexual assault data collection. Descriptions of methodology, recent findings, and critical assessments of criminal justice statistics, victimization surveys, service provider surveys, and perpetrator self-report surveys are provided.

II. SEXUAL ASSAULT DATA COLLECTION METHODS

Current government efforts at counting crime include official criminal justice statistics, victimization surveys, and surveys of service providers. Others have attempted to measure crime through self-report surveys. The advantages and disadvantages of each method of counting sexual assaults are summarized in Table I and detailed below.

III. OFFICIAL CRIMINAL JUSTICE STATISTICS

Official police statistics document how many sexual assaults have been reported to the police. In the United

TABLE I
Comparison of Sexual Assault Data Collection Methods

Property	Criminal justice	Victimization surveys	Perpetrator surveys	Service providers
Geographic area(s)	National, state, local	National, local	Local	National, state, local
Respondents	Criminal justice	Population	Population	Health, social services
Organizational level	Organization	Individual	Individual	Organization, individual
Cost	High	High	High	Medium
Validity	Low	Medium	Medium	Medium
Reliability	Low	Medium	Medium	Medium
Confidentiality	Low	High	High	High

States, forcible rape is an index crime collected by the Federal Bureau of Investigations (FBI) through the Uniform Crime Reporting (UCR) Program and published annually in Crime in the United States. Seven crime categories—murder and nonnegligent manslaughter, forcible rape, robbery, aggravated assault, burglary, larceny-theft, and motor vehicle theft—are collectively known as the Crime Index. The official purpose of tracking the Crime Index is to "measure the trend and distribution of crime in the United States" (Maguire and Pastore, 1996, p. 325).

According to the *Sourcebook of Criminal and Justice Statistics 1995*, it is estimated that 102,096 forcible rapes, 39.2 per 100,000 population, were known to the police in the United States in 1994. In 1994, 29,791 people, or 14.3 per 100,000 population, were arrested for forcible rape in the United States. In 1994, 178 defendants were convicted of rape in U.S. District Courts, 87.1% of whom were sentenced to prison with an average sentence length of 68.4 months. (Please note that most sexual assaults are prosecuted at the state level.) As of December 31, 1994, 430 prisoners in the custody of U.S. military authorities had been convicted of rape. These statistics are produced from a process that includes establishing a definition of rape, obtaining individual reports of rape, and aggregating these reports in a national system of data collection.

The first problem encountered in using official police statistics to track the incidence of sexual assault is the definition that the FBI requests that police departments follow in reporting. Forcible rape is defined as, "The carnal knowledge of a female forcibly and against her will. Included are rapes by force and attempts or assaults to rape. Statutory offenses (no force used—victim under age of consent) are excluded" (Maguire and Pastore 1996, p. 644). This definition includes only rape involving the penetration of a woman's vagina by a man's penis. Penetration of other orifices by other body parts or objects is excluded, as is penetration of a man. Most sexual assault statutes in the United States under which perpetrators can be arrested are both more general than forcible rape, including penetration of any orifice of a man or a woman by any object and gender neutral. For example, sexual assault is defined under the Arizona Revised Statutes Criminal Code, Chapter 14, Section 13–1406 as, "A person commits sexual assault by intentionally or knowingly engaging in sexual intercourse or oral sexual contact with any person without consent of such person," where sexual intercourse is, "penetration into the penis, vulva or anus by any part of the body or by any object or masturbatory contact with the penis or the vulva." Thus, sexual assault need not involve penetration. Whether the sexual assault of an adult woman is counted as a forcible rape depends on precisely how the assault was committed. Under the FBI definition, many severe sexual assaults are not counted as index crimes because they do not involve penetration.

The sex of the victim and perpetrator also influence whether a sexual assault is officially counted. The FBI definition of forcible rape excludes men as victims and women as perpetrators. Although both of these types of sexual assault are relatively rare because approximately 90 percent of victims are women and approximately 99 percent of perpetrators are male, excluding them does exacerbate the undercounting of sexual assault.

The estimated rate of sexual assault is more severely affected than the frequency by the biased manner in which men are included in forcible rape rates. Although the definition of forcible rape excludes men as victims (the numerator of the official forcible rape rate), men are included in the general population (the denominator of the calculation). Because the population is approximately half women and half men and because women constitute the majority of the rape victims, the rate of forcible rape among adult women is twice as large as the rate of forcible rape currently published.

Another bias contributing to the underestimation of sexual assault is inconsistent use of age. The definitions of forcible rape and sexual assault are not limited by age. Nonetheless, sexual assaults of children are generally classified by local police agencies as child molestation and not reported to the FBI as forcible rapes.

The aggregate statistics reported to the UCR Program for forcible rape depend largely on the training and availability of local police department staff. Those departments with staff and resources devoted to statistical record-keeping can afford to take the time to distinguish cases of forcible rape from cases of sexual assault. Others do not have as many resources to devote to data collection and reporting and report sexual assaults as forcible rapes. Reporting sexual assaults as forcible rapes overreports the number of forcible rapes.

Unfortunately, not all reports reach the stage where one must make the distinction between sexual assault and rape as defined by the FBI. The largest source of unreliability of police statistics as an indicator of the incidence of sexual assault is underreporting. Rape is one of the most underreported of all the index crimes. According to the National Crime Victimization Survey, only 32% of victims of rape or sexual assault reported to a law enforcement agency in 1994 and 1995. The most common reason for reporting to the police is to prevent further crimes by the perpetrator. However, most victims are reluctant to report assaults to the police for a number of reasons, often because they consider it a personal matter. Other reasons for not reporting to the police include believing that they were responsible for the assault, being afraid of the social consequences of identifying oneself as a rape victim, believing that the police will be ineffectual in investigating the crime, and not wanting to become involved in what they believe will be a long and complicated legal process. All of these reasons reduce the likelihood that a sexual assault will be reported to the police. A victim may also not report to the police because they believe that they simply had a bad sexual experience without recognizing that their sexual experience may fit the definition of rape.

Men are far less likely to report a sexual assault than women are. Cultural stereotypes discourage reporting. The standard answer we have received when inquiring of police departments as to how male rape is counted was to call the prisons. It is not surprising that men are much less likely to report sexual victimization when they are stigmatized as victims through the perception that they are homosexual and/or criminal if they were raped.

Another issue is the lag between incident and reporting. The 1-year reference period of the UCR statis-

tics does not reflect the reality that victims may delay seeking treatment and/or require treatment for a long period of time. For example, approximately 50% of the clients seeking treatment at the Tucson Rape Crisis Center are adults molested as children. The UCR statistics do not address the longitudinal nature of reporting and treating sexual assault. Many years may pass between when a sexual assault occurs and when the victim is emotionally ready to reveal it to anyone, making it unlikely that a rape will be reported in the year in which it occurred. The National Women's Study found that 84% of rape victims do not report to law enforcement.

Reporting a rape to the police does not guarantee that it will be included in the statistics. The number of rapes is underestimated because an incidence of a crime is generally classified by the most serious offense. For example, crimes involving victims who were both raped and murdered will be classified as murders. In addition, only founded reports are counted in the UCR Program. Once a crime has come to the attention of the police by being reported or by an officer seeing the crime occur, the report must be considered founded. Reports considered by an officer to be suspicious or impossible to prove are judged unfounded and will not be officially counted. The number of rapes occurring in the community can easily be an order of magnitude or more larger than the number officially known to the police. Conservatively, the National Crime Victimization Survey recorded more than 3 times as many reports of sexual assault as the number of forcible rapes reported in the Uniform Crime Reports in 1994. In addition, in the state of Arizona, the number of calls received by rape crisis hotlines is about 10 times the number of sexual assaults known to the police.

When the theoretical definition of a concept and its operationalization largely diverge, the estimates generated are grossly biased. Definitions of sexual assault that differ by agency and do not conform to established practice produce estimates of low reliability and validity. They are confusing and create an additional data collection and reporting burden on local police departments. The current implementation of the UCR Program collects only aggregate data from police departments around the country. The National Incident-Based Reporting System (NIBRS) is being piloted in several states. The NIBRS will provide more detailed crime incident-based data as it is phased in. Some preliminary data are available. However, many states are not scheduled to be included at this time.

The major advantage of using the UCR Program as a source of sexual assault surveillance data is its relatively low cost to users. The UCR program is a criminal justice program generating public data that will continue to be funded for the foreseeable future. The only financial costs incurred in accessing this data are personnel wages and telephone bills. However, the data obtained are most reliable as indicators of the functioning of law enforcement, they are not suitable as surveillance data.

IV. VICTIMIZATION SURVEYS

Victimization surveys have the potential for being the most accurate source of data on the incidence of sexual assault. They attempt to bypass the underreporting problem by contacting a sample of the population rather than by relying on victims to report to an authority. Surveys also collect data about the circumstances of the assault more systematically than the Uniform Crime Reports. The only longitudinal national survey of United States residents is the National Crime Victimization Survey. Other survey efforts include the National Women's Study conducted by the National Victim Center and the Crime Victim Research and Treatment Center and published in 1992 and the Behavioral Risk Factor Survey administered by the Centers for Disease Control and Prevention.

The National Crime Victimization Survey (NCVS) is conducted by the U.S. Bureau of the Census in cooperation with the Bureau of Justice Statistics and the U.S. Department of Justice. The NCVS polls over 50,000 households, totaling over 100,000 individuals, in the United States annually using a multistage sample of housing units. Individuals over 12 years old in selected households are interviewed every 6 months for about 3 years.

The first interview is conducted face-to-face and only used to bound the responses. Further interviews are conducted over the telephone. Unfortunately, this procedure produces an uncertain context for the interview. When interviews are conducted over the telephone, other household members may be present making the subject unlikely to respond. The privacy needed to maximize reporting is not assured by the interview protocol of the NCVS.

The redesign of the NCVS in 1992 produced sexual assault rate estimates about four times higher than were previously reported for rape by the NCVS. Table II summarizes more recent selected sexual assault statistics from the National Crime Victimization Survey. In 1994, the NCVS estimated that 433,000 rapes were experienced in the United States. The rape rates were

TABLE II

Selected National Crime Victimization Survey Statistics

Year	Description	Percentage
1994	Rapes officially known to police (UCR)/rapes reported to NCVS	31
1994	NCVS respondents reporting sexual assault to law enforcement	32
1994	Annual female rape rate	0.4
1994	Annual male rape rate	0.02
1994	Female victims	91
1994	Male single-victim perpetrators	99
1993	Occurring between 6 P.M. and 6 A.M.	66
1993	Own home or non-stranger home	60
1993	Within 1 mile of victim's home	> 50
1993	Single offender	91
1993	Firearm present	6
1993	No weapon	84
1993	Stranger perpetrator	24
1993	Perpetrator <21	25
1993	Self-protective measures taken	72
1993	Self-protective measures helpful	> 50
1993	Self-protective measures harmful	20
1993	Rape victims/Victims of violence	4
1993	Rapes requiring medical attention/incidents requiring medical attention	6

Source: Greenfeld, 1997.

1 rape for every 270 female residents and 1 rape for every 5000 male residents 12 years or older. Rape rates were highest among those 16 to 19 years of age, low-income residents, and urban residents. Rape rates did not differ significantly among racial groups. Ninety-one percent of rape victims were female. Ninety-nine percent of single-victim incidents involved male perpetrators. Approximately 32% were reported to a law enforcement agency.

In 1993, two-thirds of rapes occurred between 6 P.M. and 6 A.M. Almost 60% of the incidents took place in the home of the victim or the home of a friend, relative, or neighbor. Over 50% occurred within one mile of the victim's home. Ninety-one percent of rapes involved single offenders. Only 24% of incidents involved strangers. Victims reported that approximately 25% of perpetrators were under 21 years of age and 40% were 30 years of age or older.

Seventy-two percent of victims reported taking self-protective measures during the rape. Nineteen percent resisted or captured the offender. Eleven percent scared or warned the offender. Eleven percent persuaded or appeased the offender. Other self-protective measures include running away or hiding, attacking the offender, screaming, and getting help or giving alarm. A majority of those who took self-protective measures felt they helped the situation. However, about 20% felt they made the situation worse.

In 1993, rape or sexual assault victims accounted for 4% of victims of violence. Rapes accounted for 6% of the incidents in which medical assistance was obtained. Less than 10% of rape victims reported suffering a short-term economic loss. The average reported loss was approximately $200. Seven percent of victims reported losing time from work.

Rape is the most severe personal crime measured by the NCVS according to *Criminal Victimization in the United States, 1989: A National Crime Survey Report by the United States Bureau of Justice Statistics*. The definition of rape used by the NCVS is "Carnal knowledge through the use of force or threat of force, including attempts. Statutory rape (without force) is excluded. Both heterosexual and homosexual rape are included" (U.S. Bureau of Justice Statistics, 1991, p. 141). Rapes and sexual assaults are ascertained through three questions in the NCVS-1 Basic Screen Questionnaire. Question 41a asks, "(Other than any incident already mentioned) has anyone attacked or threatened you in any of these ways (exclude telephone threats) ... (e) Any rape, attempted rape or other type of sexual attack?" Question 42a asks, "People often don't think of incidents committed by someone they know. (Other than any incidents already mentioned) did you have something stolen from you OR were you attacked or threatened by (exclude telephone threats) (a) Someone at work or at school, (b) A neighbor or friend, (c) A relative or family member, OR (d) Any other person you've met or known?" Question 43a asks, "Incidents involving forced or unwanted sexual acts are often difficult to talk about. (Other than any incidents already mentioned) have you been forced or coerced to engage in unwanted sexual activity by (a) Someone you didn't know before, (b) A casual acquaintance, OR (c) Someone you know well?" Followed by question 43b, "Did any incidents of this type happen to you" and question 43c, "How many times?" In the NCVS-2 Crime Incident Report, Question 29 asks, "How were you attacked? Any other way?" Possible responses to question 29 include raped, tried to rape, and sexual assault other than rape or attempted rape. Question 31 asks, "What were the injuries you suffered, if any? Anything else?" Possible responses to question 31 include raped, attempted rape, and sexual assault other than rape or attempted rape. If the response to question 29 is raped or the response to question 31 is raped and the response to question 29 is not raped, the field representative is instructed to ask, "Do you mean forced or coerced sexual inter-

course?" Similarly, if the response to question 29 is tried to rape, or the response to question 31 is attempted rape and the response to question 29 is not tried to rape, the field representative is instructed to ask, "Do you mean attempted forced or coerced sexual intercourse?" If no is the response to either of the two preceding questions, they are to ask, "What do you mean?"

Although the NCVS is more effective than the UCR program at uncovering the incidence of rape at the national level, it has several disadvantages. The quality and quantity of information obtained by a survey is very sensitive to how questions are asked. The definition of sexual assault or rape is not clear in these questions. Unless the subject requests clarification, sexual assault is not defined during the interview. On the one hand, the initial question asks about any sexual attack. On the other hand, the definition provided if requested is coerced sexual intercourse. The former is too vague and the latter is too restrictive without being explicit about what is being asked.

The National Women's Study provides clear questions that do not leave the definition of sexual assault to the subjects imagination. "Women do not always report such experiences to police or discuss them with family or friends. The person making the advances isn't always a stranger, but can be a friend, boyfriend, or even a family member. Such experiences can occur anytime in a woman's life—even as a child. Regardless of how long ago it happened or who made the advances. ... Has a man or boy ever made you have sex by using force or threatening to harm you or someone close to you? Just so there is no mistake, by sex we mean putting a penis in your vagina. ... Has anyone ever made you have oral sex by force or threat of harm? Just so there is no mistake, by oral sex, we mean that a man or boy put his penis in your mouth or somebody penetrated your vagina or anus with his mouth or tongue. ... Has anyone ever made you have anal sex by force or threat of harm? ... Has anyone ever put fingers or objects in your vagina or anus against your will by using force or threat?" (*Rape in America: A report to the nation*, April 23, 1992, p.15). Although these questions limit the sex of the perpetrator to male, they improve on the National Crime Victimization Survey questions by defining the acts that are under consideration and not limiting the time frame of when the acts may have occurred. The National Crime Victimization Survey uses a short bounding period, 6 months, to ensure that the dates of crimes are accurately reported. For most crimes, this is reasonable. However, the low annual incidence of sexual assault makes 6 months a biased bounding period for this particular crime.

Without clear questions, the context of the questions can be misleading. In the National Crime Victimization Survey, the questions about rape are put into a violent crime context that is not associated with the typical rape. For example, the National Women's Study found that 70% of women sustained no physical injuries during rape. Asking about sexual assault in the context of crime reinforces the misconception that the interviewer is asking about violent assaults by strangers. Respondents are less likely to reveal incidents of sexual assault because they are misdirected in what types of interactions are being sought.

The major disadvantage of victimization surveys is that they are extremely expensive. Although the number of women raped at some point in their life is large, just a fraction of these rapes occurs in a given year. Amassing a sample of recent rapes requires screening a large sample, which makes victimization surveys very expensive. The problem of low yearly rates is compounded in the NCVS by the low rate of identification of sexual assault cases. The small number of rapes recorded in the National Crime Victimization Survey does not allow reliable estimation of rape rates at the national level, much less at the state or local levels. In fact, many of the statistics about sexual assault are based on 10 or fewer cases. Therefore, they neither reliable nor valuable as a source of local service planning.

The Behavioral Risk Factor Survey, a national public health survey program in which states can opt to participate, attempts to provide information that is useful at the state level. Unfortunately, the survey and modules presenting questions concerning intimate violence are optional. Many states do not participate in the survey and fewer include intimate violence questions in their administration of the Behavioral Risk Factor Survey. Resources available for conducting basic research limit the usefulness of surveys in determining the incidence of sexual assault. The existing resources could be better used, but few resources are available for these studies outside of the funding already in place.

V. PERPETRATOR SURVEYS

Perpetrator self-report surveys use the same methodology as victimization surveys. Participants are recruited using a sampling scheme, then interviewed by telephone, written questionnaires, or face-to-face. The major differences are that the respondents are perpetrators or potential perpetrators rather than victims or potential victims and that the respondent's behavior is the subject of inquiry rather than what has happened to the subject.

TABLE III

Selected Findings of Perpetrator Self-Report Surveys

Subjects	Rape	Percent	Source
Naval recruits	Attempted	3.5	Merrill *et al.* (1997)
	Completed	11.3	
College students	Attempted	4.0	Walker *et al.* (1993)
	Completed	4.5	
College students	Attempted	3.3	Koss and Dinero (1987)
	Completed	4.4	

Walker *et al.* and Koss and Dinero found in perpetrator surveys of college students that about 4% of males have attempted rape and about 4% have completed rape. New data from naval recruits gathered by Merrill *et al.* show a much higher incidence of completed rape at 11.3% (Table III).

Perpetrator self-report surveys have the advantage of providing another perspective on the question of the incidence of rape. However, perpetrator self-reports are sensitive to how questions are asked. The same errors in judgement and self-serving perceptions that lead to a rape in the first place can cause a perpetrator to fail to self-identify as a rapist. The legal definition of rape includes penetration, use of force, and lack of consent. The perception of two of these criteria can differ greatly between parties involved in an incident. Men and women differ in what they consider use of force. What is normal aggressive behavior to a man may be a strong use of force to a woman. It is also not unusual for men and women to disagree on whether consent has been given. Unfortunately, sexual signals can be ambiguous or misread. Even when a woman has said no, some men interpret this as signaling consent.

Like victimization surveys, perpetrator surveys are extremely expensive. Conducting a national perpetrator survey is probably not financially feasible. Furthermore, a perpetrator survey is not politically feasible. Ensuring the confidentiality of respondents while protecting victims or potential victims is extremely difficult. In addition, perpetrator surveys are seen as threatening to the status quo. Garnering the political support necessary to fund a national perpetrator survey is unlikely to be achieved.

VI. SURVEYS OF SERVICE PROVIDERS

An alternative to collecting information from those directly affected is collecting information from those who provide services to primary victims. A major advantage of gathering information from service providers is that they provide services at a variety of levels of victimization and prevention. Service providers gather information on secondary victims, those who are affected because their friends or loved ones were sexually assaulted, as well as primary victims. Service providers also work at many levels of prevention. Rape prevention education programs provide primary prevention by attempting to stop rapes from occurring. Sexual assault nurse examiners programs and crisis call services provide secondary prevention attempting to prevention negative short-term and long-term consequences by intervening shortly after the sexual assault has occurred. Hotlines and other counseling services act as tertiary prevention by attempting to minimize the long-term impact of sexual assault. Service providers encounter potential victims, recent victims, and those who have been dealing with the effects of sexual assault for a long time. Service providers may also encounter perpetrators. Service providers have the potential for contacting almost as broad a segment of the population as surveys. However, they are most likely to encounter those who are victims or perpetrators. In addition, it is difficult to maintain unduplicated data across or within counseling, crisis, and educational services. For example, multiple calls to a hotline by one person may be related to one assault or may be the result of multiple victimizations.

Ideally, sexual assault cases could be tracked nationally the way major infectious and chronic diseases are because the long-term impact on victims' quality life can be as severe as diseases such as AIDS, hepatitis, or cancer. However, there is currently no confidential national registry of sexual assault victims. Unlike many diseases, victims may actively avoid revealing that they have been sexually assaulted and sexual assault does not compel service-seeking. For example, an AIDS patient may try to hide their HIV status, but illnesses are likely to compel the patient to seek services. Some states are beginning to attempt unified individual level tracking of sexual assault cases. Some states have state coalitions collecting aggregate statistics from service providers. Establishing a national sexual assault surveillance system would provide a better basis for sexual assault services planning throughout the United States.

The sexual assault surveillance system currently implemented in Arizona is a limited example of surveying service providers for sexual assault surveillance information. The data for the annual *Violent and Abusive Behavior Data Report* is collected by the Arizona Rape and Sexual Assault Surveillance Project by contacting programs funded through the Arizona Department of Health Services to provide rape prevention education.

These include the largest rape crisis programs in the state. In addition, efforts are made to contact other service providers as well, such as Victim Witness organizations and rape crisis programs that have not been funded. Questions asked include the number of people provided rape-related counseling, the number of people attending rape prevention education, the number of law enforcement personnel trained in response to rape and sexual assault, and the number of hotline calls received.

Table IV summarizes selected state sexual assault statistics. In Arizona in 1994–1995, 974 women reported rape or attempted rape to law enforcement in the areas serviced by the service providers included in the report, 559 people were provided rape-related counseling, 82 law enforcement personnel were trained in response to rape and sexual assault, and 5966 rape hotline calls were received.

About half as many people as reported rapes to law enforcement were provided counseling in person, but about six times as many people called the rape hotlines as reported to law enforcement. Approximately twice as many people called rape hotlines as reported rapes to the National Crime Victimization Survey. Although hotline calls may be for nonrecent events as well as crisis, we can infer that many more people are disclosing sexual assaults to service providers than to the NCVS or law enforcement.

Much of the 1995–1996 *Violent and Abusive Behavior Data Report* was dedicated to pointing out the limitations of the data as it is currently collected. As a vehicle for accounting for how funds are spent, aggregate-level data collection efforts are adequate. However, as an attempt to collect data that may help to ameliorate the problem of sexual assault, there are limitations. First,

TABLE IV

1994–1995 Violent and Abusive Behavior Data for Arizona

Data Item	Number	Reporting period
Rapes reported to law enforcement	974	1/1/95—12/31/95
Women provided rape-related counseling	559	7/1/94—6/30/95
People attending rape prevention education	21110	7/1/94—6/30/95
Law enforcement personnel trained	82	7/1/94—6/30/95
Rape hotline calls received	5966	7/1/94—6/30/95

Source: Arizona Rape and Sexual Assault Surveillance Project: 1995–1996 Violent and Abusive Behavior Data, http://www.u.arizona.edu/~sexasslt/.

data reported by participating providers should be standardized. For example, hotline calls should be disaggregated into crisis, information, and referral calls and counseling services should be reported by type, e.g., psychological or advocacy. Second, more providers should be included. Many service providers throughout the state, including all of the tribal lands, were not included in last year's report. An inclusive surveillance system should contact as much of the population as possible geographically and socially.

VII. CONCLUSION

Each sexual assault surveillance method provides a particular perspective. The *Uniform Crime Reports* are not a very valid or reliable source of health-relevant data, but they are institutionalized in a well-funded branch of government and a reasonable snapshot of crimes known to police. As the National Incident Based Reporting System is introduced, this source of data will become more valid. However, it will never overcome the underreporting problem. Victimization and perpetrator surveys have the potential to produce the most accurate information about the largest population. However, the cost of longitudinal surveys is prohibitive and specific implementations need to continue to improve the quality of the questions presented and context effects may not be overcome. Gathering information from service providers can produce valid data with the cooperation of agencies and their clients. Service provider data is helpful in predicting service needs, but it suffers from the underreporting problem making it less useful for basic research on the causes of sexual assault. The development of sexual assault surveillance based on public health models is the most likely source of economical data useful for planning services. We must continue to evaluate the amount of resources devoted to data collection and use the results of that evaluation to guide the implementation of future data collection systems.

Also See the Following Articles

FEMINIST AND PEACE PERSPECTIVES ON WOMEN • GENDER STUDIES • POWER AND DEVIANCE • SOCIAL CONTROL AND VIOLENCE • VIOLENCE TO CHILDREN, DEFINITION AND PREVENTION OF

Bibliography

Greenfeld, L. A. (February 1997). *Sex offenses and offenders: An analysis of data on rape and sexual assault.* Washington, DC:U.S. Department of Justice, Office of Justice Programs, Bureau of Justice Statistics, NCJ-163392.

Koss, M. (1992). The measurement of rape victimization in crime surveys. *Criminal Justice and Behavior, 23*(1), 55–69.

Koss, M. (1992). The underdetection of rape: Methodological choices influence incidence estimates. *Journal of Social Issues, 48*(1), 61–75.

Koss, M. (1993). Detecting the scope of rape: A review of prevalence research methods. *Journal of Interpersonal Violence, 8*(2), 198–222.

Koss, M. (1997). Our guys and gals: Pre-enlistment sexual assault victimization and perpetration among naval recruits. Annual meeting of the American Psychological Association, August 15, Chicago, Illinois.

Koss, M. & Dinero, T. E. (1987). Predictors of sexual aggression among a national sample of male college students. *Annals of the New York Academy of Sciences, 528,* 133–147.

Maguire, K. & A. L. Pastore, (1996). *Sourcebook of criminal and justice statistics 1995.* Washington, DC: U.S. Government Printing Office, U.S. Department of Justice, Bureau of Justice Statistics.

National Victim Center and Crime Victim Research and Treatment Center (1992). *Rape in America: A report to the nation.* Washington DC: National Victim Center.

United States Bureau of Justice Statistics (June, 1991). *Criminal victimization in the United States, 1989: A national crime survey report.* Washington, DC: U.S. Government Printing Office.

Walker, W. D., Rowe, R. C., & V. L. Quinsey, (1993). Authoritarianism and sexual aggression. *Journal of Personality and Social Psychology, 65*(5), 1036–1045.

Social Control and Violence

Wolfgang Knöbl

Freie Universität Berlin

GLOSSARY

Discipline A permanent psychological attitude toward
a rational and unquestionable implementation of
orders.
Repression The subjugation of individuals or groups
by violent or nonviolent means.

SOCIAL CONTROL is a central concept in sociology
and social history. This article presents an overview of
the history of the concept and discusses its analytical
power concerning the explanation of individual and
collective violence.

I. THE CONCEPT OF SOCIAL CONTROL AND ITS EARLY HISTORY

As coined in the earliest phases of American sociology,
the meaning of the term "social control" was a very
broad one, insofar as it seemed to be useful to describe
and explain a whole variety of social facts and problems.
Edward A. Ross introduced the term into sociological
discourse in 1896 to analyze processes of fast social
change that took place at that time—immigration, industrialization, urbanization. Ross, whose views on that
point were not too different from those of other contemporary social scientists, believed societies to be on an
evolutionary path from archaic and simple to complex
and modern forms. In those modern societies of the
Western world, the question of order and harmony
becomes a very pressing one because—according to
Ross—"natural," unconscious, and unplanned mechanisms for the integration of societies have been lost in
the course of history. Therefore new forms of "social
control" are required to guarantee the stability of the
new and conflict-ridden industrial market societies. For
Ross, who sympathized with the ideas of American reformers in the Progressive Era, the meaning of social
control was closely connected with a rational society
that uses certain means such as public opinion, education, law, religion, art, and ceremonies to counter the
destructive consequences of modernization. It is important to note that Ross and others who used the concept
(see, for example, G. H. Mead) usually did *not* have in
mind repressive or even violent means when they aimed
to establish a "controlled" society. On the contrary, as
they believed in a rational and democratic order and
in planned social change they argued on the basis of
value positions that were intended to end human misery
and to reduce repression. Therefore the meaning of
social control was quite the opposite of mechanisms

that could be grouped under the heading of "coercive control." Social control focused on processes that guaranteed a more or less harmonious and successful integration of individuals and groups into society.

Under this theoretical perspective, which was typical for the so-called Chicago School of Sociology, crime and deviancy were usually explained as an effect of the loss of social control and of disorganized social structures. The social upheaval resulting from the growth of big cities was seen as one of the decisive causes for delinquent behavior, as a couple of ethnographic studies tried to prove. But although physical violence and violent crime were not neglected in those works of Chicago Sociology, it is fair to say that they did not play a very prominent role either. Researchers usually investigated gangs, hobos, and whores as exotic and deviant phenomena of city life. But it was not violence in itself that was the particular focus of this kind of research—neither the violent behavior of "criminals" nor the violence that was used by agents of the state (policemen, soldiers, etc.).

For two reasons at least the concept of social control lost its central position in sociological theory in the decades before World War II. First, insofar as it has always been a concept with a very broad and not very specified meaning, sociologists began to lose faith in its usefulness for sociological analysis. Second, sociologists no longer needed the concept as some of its basic ideas were taken over by functionalist reasoning, which began to be elaborated by Talcott Parsons at that time. Parsons, who traced back the most fruitful origins of sociology predominantly to European and not American thinkers, was heavily influenced by Emile Durkheim, whose themes converged with those of the original meaning of social control. But as Durkheim did not use the term "social control," because he described and explained the integration of societies and the "socialization" of individuals using different terminology, there was no need for Parsons and his followers to revive the concept of social control. Rather, it was Durkheim's concept of anomie that began to instruct theoretical and empirical research on deviancy, although one has to keep in mind that most functionalists did not regard violence and other conflictual relationships as central themes of sociological discourse.

II. THE NEW SOCIOLOGY OF SOCIAL CONTROL

It was not until the 1960s that the term "social control" came back into widespread use in sociology and social history. But this revival was accompanied by a rather far-reaching change in the meaning of the concept. Whereas in the early 20th century connotations of repression, force, and brute power relationships were absent when sociologists used the concept of social control, the term now became almost synonymous with those phenomena. Social control seemed to be an appropriate terminological instrument to analyze all social relationships in which institutions, groups, or classes use repressive means (whether violent or not) to stabilize social and political inequalities. The roots of that sharp semantic change are to be found in the historical background of the time. When the social and political stability of the 1950s vanished and social movements began to challenge old conventions and power structures, sociological thinking was affected as well. Parsonian functionalism increasingly came under attack as it seemed to be based on an "oversocialized conception of man," so that it was unable to explain processes of fast social change and it seemed to neglect power relationships and conflicts. Sociologists began to replace an apparently inadequate Parsonian consensus theory with theories that stressed the fluidity of social structures and the importance of power. This theoretical change also led to a change of subjects. Sociologists and historians increasingly focused on social conflicts that seemed to have been neglected by social scientists for far too long. Phenomena such as crime, deviancy, rebellions, and rioting became more and more interesting for those who were convinced that the former consensus theorists had painted much too peaceful and harmonious a picture of modern societies. In addition, according to the conviction that structured inequalities are an enduring feature especially of capitalist societies, researchers began to ask how the state and powerful groups and classes were and are able to stabilize those inequalities. What were and still are the instruments that keep underprivileged groups and classes from rebelling? How do privileged classes or the state succeed in socially and politically dominating the working class? In short, what are the mechanisms of repression, coercion, and discipline? How does social control—and this became the synonym for repression and discipline—really work?

Thus, a "New Sociology of Social Control" emerged, which analyzed institutions such as prisons, asylums, hospitals, and poor houses that apparently contributed to an increasing potential of social control in modern societies. As Andrew T. Scull made clear, this New Sociology of Social Control focused on the impact of state, economy, and ideology on social control, on the ways in which actions and actors become subject to social control, on the means with which modern institutions control "deviants," and on the interrelationships of power and knowledge in general.

But as this huge and rather heterogeneous list of subjects that all should have been explored and explained by the concept of social control already indicates: the meaning of the term was as "flabby" as the one which Ross had used more than 60 years earlier. Nearly every institution seemed to function as an instrument of social control so that the explanatory use of the concept could be questioned—especially if researchers did not sufficiently distinguish between coercive and merely ideological forms of social control. The reason for this poor terminological precision and explanatory power of the concept is not difficult to discover. The whole idea of this kind of repressive social control rested on rather incongruous theoretical ideas; moreover, these ideas have been developed for quite different explanatory contexts. Sociologists (and social historians) within this New Sociology of Social Control have built their research strategies at least on four theoretical traditions. In all of these theories the term "discipline" played a prominent role.

1. "Discipline" is a term that was coined at the beginning of our century to describe important aspects in the formation of early modern states. It was the German sociologist Max Weber who pointed out that "rational discipline" is a force that is sharply opposed to all individual and charismatic action and that historically can be traced back to the Middle Ages, when mass armies began to replace the hitherto predominant armies of knights with their highly individualized style of fighting. Mass armies and new weapons that began to be used at that time required new forms of coordination to guarantee military success. The time of the heroic warrior was gone. Instead, the army had to function as a machine and the parts of the army—the soldiers—had to be adapted to the working process of the machine. Discipline was the instrument and means to fulfill those requirements. As Weber explained: "Discipline" is the rational, planned, precise implementation of orders and a permanently positive psychological attitude toward such a purpose. Modern armies were the first institutions to create such attitudes among their members, among the common soldiers. But as Weber was quick to point out, discipline obviously did not remain enclosed in the military but spread out to other societal spheres, for example, the bureaucracy, which Weber called the "most rational child of discipline."

Although Weber explicitly stated that modern capitalist enterprises also incorporated the idea of discipline, and although he stressed the close organizational relationship between modern armies and big corporations, it was not he who stimulated research on the disciplinary aspects of modern industrial capitalism and the disciplinary subjection of workers and the working classes.

2. Rather, it was the British historian Edward P. Thompson whose famous essay, "Time, Work-discipline and Industrial Capitalism" (originally published in 1967), gave incentives for more research on that topic. In his essay Thompson described how behavioral patterns and subjective attitudes toward time rapidly (but not without resistance) changed within the English working-classes and how this change was caused by discipline as enforced in the modern capitalist factory. According to Thompson, discipline was a necessary means to subjugate a wild and often uncontrollable popular culture, a culture that was opposed to the rationality of capitalist production. In this perspective discipline was an instrument in the struggle between culturally, socially, and politically opposed classes, the capitalists and the working classes. Thompson's ideas became the starting point for a variety of Marxist sociologists who argued that institutions of social control and techniques of discipline came into being as functional necessities of capitalism.

3. The French social scientist Michel Foucault probably did more than anyone else to disseminate the term "discipline" and to popularize the idea of social control. Whereas Weber and Thompson looked for discipline in discrete institutions (e.g., the army, the bureaucracy, the capitalist enterprise) and clearly distinguished between those who became disciplined and those who controlled, Foucault's theory-building strategy pointed to a different direction (cf. especially his book *Discipline and Punish*, originally published in 1975). He developed a theory of power that interpreted modern societies as entities that were overwhelmed by disciplinary mechanisms in all their spheres. As Foucault decentered the concept of power—according to him power had not a special place or location like the state or the factory—and as he closely linked it to knowledge, it followed that nearly all aspects of everyday life (not only institutions such as the prison, the hospital, and the asylum, but also sexuality, the family, etc.) seemed to be an expression of power relationships and discipline. From this perspective it was clear that discipline had an extremely broad meaning as the theory did not re-

ally distinguish between different forms and effects of discipline—and sometimes not even between the oppressors and the oppressed. Foucault painted a picture of modernity in which successful resistance can only be interpreted as an exceptional occurrence and in which liberation from power relationships seems nearly impossible as knowledge, power, and action are always intertwined.

4. Finally, it was Norbert Elias who significantly contributed to the new social control paradigm. In *The Civilizing Process* (originally published in 1937/ 39) Elias, whose work began to be rediscovered in the late 1960s and the 1970s, analyzed the early phase of state-building in France when military competition between small feudal duchies led to larger political territories and—in the end—to a centralized and absolutist monarchy. This process of centralization—so Elias' fascinating story goes—was accompanied by a fundamental change in the behavioral patterns of political elites that lived at the King's Court in Paris. The close contact between those elites required increasingly peaceful and "courteous" manners that at the beginning had to be enforced by sanctions. But in the end this courteous behavior became an integral part of psychological life, and sanctions or external constraints were transformed into self-restraint. This kind of self control, Elias argued, did not remain enclosed in the upper stratum of society. Manners and self-controlled behavioral patterns spread out and reached the middle and lower classes as well.

Elias generalized his ideas and formulated a theory of the "civilizing process" that states that not only French history but also the history of most Western societies were characterized by long-term changes in the balance between societal sanctions and external restraint on the one hand and self-restraint on the other. External constraints would be increasingly replaced by self-control.

All four theories that influenced the New Sociology of Social Control stressed increasing levels of discipline carried through by a variety of institutions and organizations. They described the mechanisms leading to a different psychological constitution of citizens in modern societies and, in consequence, to a disciplined and controlled society. But none of the four theories is very helpful in illuminating the links between discipline, social control, and *violence*. Only the works of Max Weber and Norbert Elias give at least some hints in that particular direction. Weber's theory of modern bureaucracies and his definition of the state characterized

by the legitimate monopoly of the means of violence suggests that with the increasing activity of the state and the accelerating penetration of society by bureaucratic measures one might expect diminishing scope for members of society to use violence in everyday life. Elias' diagnosis is on the whole quite the same although his theoretical arguments differ. As he stressed the changing balance between self-restraint and "external constraints" in the civilizing process, it follows that *spontaneous* violence in the long run will be replaced by more *rational* (either individual or bureaucratic) forms of violence. But all in all, even the statements of those theorists concerning the role and development of violence in civil society are not very polished or concrete.

Whatever the reasons for that *theoretical* neglect, it is not surprising that *empirical* research into the social control paradigm did not and still does not touch on violence very much either. When Stanley Cohen argued that most of these historians and sociologists believe in a particular form of social change that is characterized by the "increasing involvement of the state in the business of deviancy control," by the "increasing differentiation and classification of deviant and dependent groups into separate types and categories," by the "increased segregation of deviants," and by the "decline of punishment involving the public infliction of physical pain" (Cohen, 1985, 13–14), it is clear that they are not particularly focusing on the *effects* of social control *in* society—a problem that obviously haunted many of the works that have been written in this theoretical tradition. Works within that paradigm rarely tried to specify how and how much the (peaceful or violent) behavior of ordinary people really changed by the growth of all those disciplinary institutions. Did the population really become less wild, less rebellious, less violent, more docile by the establishment of a controlled society? These questions were rarely addressed. Quite a few researchers focused only on the discourses expressing the intent to control without investigating whether the plans were really implemented and—further on—whether the enforced measures were really effective. A rigorous testing of the effects of disciplinary mechanisms, for example by the use of the comparative method, was rarely tried.

As a whole, neither works written in the tradition of the so-called Chicago School of Sociology nor the research in the New Sociology of Social Control are very helpful in analyzing the relationship between social control and violence. To throw light on this connection, it is therefore reasonable to concentrate only on those theoretical statements and hypotheses that explicitly approach the problem (1) and to focus on those institutions that have been created with a clearly recognizable intent to "control" *violent* behavior (2).

1. Not all research into violence has been done under the heading of social control. But at least there is an "old" theoretical question that addresses the phenomenon of violence in connection with the term "social control." Since Edward A. Ross' original use of the term and especially since Durkheim's book, *Suicide* (originally published in 1897), which explained a special type of suicide by the existence of anomic and disorganized societal structures, it has been a common theme for social scientists to look for the consequences of modernization as this process seems to be accompanied by a weakening of the means of social control: disorganized societal structures which are to be expected in periods of fast social change—so the hypothesis goes—could lead to higher levels of violence. The growth of cities, the development of huge metropolitan areas, rapid economic change, and migration processes could weaken social ties, could weaken social control, and thus could increase the chance of violent behavior.

2. As it is not clear how institutions such as the capitalist enterprise, the asylum, or the hospital function together to control the (violent) behavior of people outside the institutional setting one should focus on those institutions that have been created with a clear disciplinary purpose particularly in relation to violence such as the police (the military and the courts), which seem to embody Max Weber's strange "monopoly of the means of violence." *One* of the tasks—besides a whole array of others, of course—of police officers (soldiers, judges) is the containment or even elimination of violent behavior in civil society. By focusing especially on those institutions the question of the relationship between violence and social control becomes manageable: How did the emergence or the growth of the police (or the existence of the military or the decisions of the courts) affect violent behavior in society? Is there an observable deterrent effect with regard to the frequency of violent phenomena? Focusing on criminal justice systems as well as on historical and sociological research on violent crime and protest could help to answer these specific questions.

Thus, the relationship between violence and social control will be examined under two perspectives. In the next section we investigate whether the process of modernization caused disorganized social structures and a weakening of social control, which in turn changes the frequency of violent phenomena; in Section IV we ask whether, and if so to what degree, the police and other elements in the criminal justice system are able to influence the level of violence in society.

III. MODERNIZATION, SOCIAL CONTROL, AND VIOLENCE: HYPOTHESES AND TRENDS

Historically, the process of modernization quite often meant rapid change for traditional communities and dislocation that affected prevailing norms of behavior and forms of social control. Violent behavior could have been one of the consequences. As it has happened since the early phase of industrialization, migration from rural to urban areas seems to prepare the breeding ground for deviancy. It is always a difficult task to leave behind social ties and to try to make a living without much money or wealth in an unfamiliar city, and so it seems reasonable to assume a close connection between urbanization/industrialization on the one hand and deviancy and violent behavior on the other. Urbanization/industrialization—according to the hypothetical argument—will decrease the effectiveness of norms, weaken patterns of informal social control, and therefore increase crime and violence.

This hypothesis is probably wrong—at least with regard to its alleged universality. As historical and sociological research has shown, there has been *no* secular trend of rising violence since the beginning of modernity. Industrialization and urbanization were not the most decisive factors in violent crime. The reason simply is that life in traditional rural communities is not as peaceful as is normally assumed. Violent conflicts have always been a part of country life, which too often is romanticized by novelists and critics of modernity. And, on the other hand, most of the time life in big cities is not as anomic and disorganized as most people believe. It is definitely not true that the move from a traditional community to a metropolis is always accompanied by the loss of personal relations and thus by the loss of social control. Migration still is a process in which groups played a decisive role. It has very rarely been a purely individual enterprise, as the existence of homogenous ethnic neighborhoods and districts indicates.

So it is not really surprising that research into the history of violent crime has actually unearthed a *decreasing* trend in violent crime in the long process of modernization. For example, data on the English county of Kent shows that the regional homicide rate declined from a high of 4.6 per 100,000 population in the 16th century to a very low 0.7 per 100,000 in 1980. It was not a smooth decline without ups and downs, but a secular decrease nonetheless. What is more surprising, a continuous decline could even be observed in that period that witnessed the full impact of industrialization and urbanization, the period from the turn of the 19th century to the present day! Whatever the causes for that secular decline in violent behavior, it seems obvious that urbanization and industrialization did not lead automatically to a weakening of social control and, as a consequence, to an increase of individual violence. This claim can be confirmed by a couple of other studies and data that focus more closely than the aforementioned study on the period between the 19th and the 20th centuries: Swedish vital statistics demonstrate a remarkable and nearly continuous decline of the homicide rate from 1875 till the 1950s. Research in Germany has shown that it was not always the fast-growing and industrializing cities that experienced the highest levels of crime; on the contrary. Some rural areas were plagued by a much higher rate of violent crime than many of the growing towns. The difference, then, in the rate of violent crime between rural and urban regions and between different cities cannot be explained by a general state of urban anomie and by supposedly weaker mechanisms of social control in urban areas. Instead, it is reasonable to assume that economic hardships and specific ethnic conflicts were the decisive variables that account for the different levels of violence in particular regions. But it was not Europe alone that experienced a decline in the rate of violent behavior. Historical research in American cities revealed a very similar trend. Although cities like Boston or Philadelphia saw a rise in violent crime beginning in the 1830s, this did not continue into the second half of the 19th century. In the 1870s and 1880s violence in fact began to decline again—a period that was characterized by an enormous influx of European immigrants. Thus, even the undoubtedly serious societal effects of immigration did not lead to a loss of social control and to a consequential rise in violence—a historical experience that also was made in different civilizations under similar circumstances. Tokyo, which has seen an impressive population growth since the beginning of this century, could even see a decline in its rate of violent crime—at least till the 1950s. And Calcutta, India, had the same experience of a decreasing trend of violent crime in the 19th century, as did most of the cities in the West.

Even though it might be true that, for a variety of reasons, there is some relationship between violent crime and urbanization and industrialization, one cannot assume that these processes of modernization in themselves cause something like a loss of social control. Of course, comparative research has shown that the rate of violent crime in modern cities and metropolises is usually higher than in rural areas. Nevertheless, there is no linear relationship between the growth of cities and violent crime. The number of inhabitants in a city does *not* correlate with the frequency of violent crime. As comparative cross-national research has sufficiently shown, different cities do indeed have completely different levels of violence.

If all that is true, then the growth of big cities is definitely not automatically accompanied by a weakening of social control and, as a consequence, by an increase in violent behavior. People in modern societies are *not* more violent than their predecessors, as the aforementioned secular *decline* in violent behavior has shown. However, the reasons for such a decline are not clear and different interpretations and explanations can be found. Some researchers pointed out that since the beginning of modernity the concept of honor has lost its prevalence in society. Conflicts within elites were increasingly "solved" without the violent ritual of the duel. However, the "taming" of violent emotions—as Elias would have argued—affected not only the elites. Nonviolent means of conflict solution disseminated into wider society and reduced the overall level of violence. Other researchers stressed the argument that the European and American Enlightenment stigmatized the use of interpersonal violence, which then indeed affected the actual behavior of people. And still others indicated that, as violent crime is quite often commited among close acquaintances and relatives, it was even the much criticized anonymity of big cities that actually accounted for the decrease of violent crime.

At the moment it is not yet possible to decide the explanatory power of all these theories. But it seems reasonable to assume that all three interpretations account for at least part of the aforementioned secular decline in violent behavior, especially as these interpretations are not mutually exclusive.

Although there is—as indicated—no definite explanation even for the trends of the past, it is not completely useless to speculate about the future. And indeed, social scientists have raised the question of whether the conditions that led to such a decline in violent behavior will endure in future. Some doubts have been expressed, as in some European countries and in the United States of America in particular the hope for a more or less "peaceful" future has been shattered by the sharply rising rates of violent crime since the end of the 1960s. Of course, it still can be argued that this dramatic increase is just one of the temporal ups that will be followed by downs again. The secular trend of decreasing violence in the last few centuries has never been a very smooth one. But there are some arguments that claim that the trend as a whole could be reversed. As Western societies go through a period of fast economic change, and as those societies move from an industrial to a postindustrial phase, the past patterns of social control might lose their strengths with all the consequences concerning violent behavior. The historical form of industrial society as it was established in the 19th century created economic conditions that made stable social relationships and social networks at least possible. Huge numbers of migrants (from rural areas to urban regions; from Europe to America, etc.) could be integrated into society as large industrial factories provided sufficient jobs for most people. Although high rates of poverty apparently were virulent especially in the early phases of the industrial revolution, the emerging industrial centers often were surrounded by neighborhoods with stable structures. Networks of friends, associations, and political organizations obviously prevented a high level of violence. In addition, continuous work in industrial factories—as E. P. Thompson could have argued—seemed to have had some disciplinary effects that suppressed violent impulses and thus tended to influence the behavior of people outside the workplace. For example, Roger Lane has shown that in the context of American industrialization only those groups fully integrated into industrial society were characterized by a comparatively "peaceful" behavior. Groups that have been excluded from the economic and social structures of industrial society—Lane especially points to African Americans who never succeeded in getting steady jobs in industry—seemed to be more prone to use violence as a means of conflict solution.

If these observations are correct, then we can ask the following question: What happens right now and what will happen in the future if traditional structures of industrial society slowly but continuously dissolve, if high levels of unemployment will not vanish, if the number of people in the so-called underclass grows further, if traditional milieux and residential patterns that seem to have been the guarantee for a more or less peaceful civil society disappear? The huge rise in the rates of violent crime in certain quarters of American (and some European) cities might be interpreted as an indicator that the secular trend of decreasing violent behavior could be completely reversed if new forms of

social control do not develop. But again: one has to be extremely careful in pushing such a bold hypothesis too far, especially as there are at least some cultural contexts that seem to contradict the European and American findings. Vital statistics in Japan, for example, show an extremely stable homicide rate between the 1950s and the end of the 1980s, which indicates that the impact of postindustrial structures is probably different in different cultural settings.

Thus far the focus has been on *individual* violence, whereas *collective* violence was not touched on at all. But of course, the question of whether modernization in some way led to a loss of social control and an increasing level of collective violence can be asked as well. As in the case of violent individual crime, however, there are strong arguments that disprove the theory of disorganization and anomie in the field of collective violence. As empirical research has shown, it is just not true that, in the 18th and 19th centuries especially, immigrants and poor inhabitants of the growing cities were the leaders or the most active population segment in collective uprisings and riots. These groups were not more prone to (violent) protest than were the more indigenous parts of the citizenry. The fast-growing and industrializing cities with their "uprooted" proletariat were—at least at the beginning of the industrial revolution—quite often less violent than the old towns where indigenous artisans used their resources to fight violently against social and economic changes. Charles Tilly especially argued that migration processes into big cities could decisively weaken the level of collective violence for at least two reasons: first, these processes withdrew potentially discontented people from their original communities where they had the means and resources for resistance and protest. In their new places migrants—at least temporarily—lost parts of their collective identity so that the potential for collective violence actually decreased. Second, migrants needed time to get used to city life so that they were not immediately able to join political and social struggles with their possibly violent outcomes.

But, as Tilly quickly adds, this does not mean that collective violence will gradually disappear in the process of modernization. It only means that forms of collective protest and violent conflict change their faces. Whereas before the industrial revolution people used rough music, food riots, machine breaking, and so on, to express their grievances, the social and political conditions of modern industrial society changed the repertoires of contention. Strikes, election rallies, demonstrations—in other words, more organized forms of protest—began to replace older and more spontaneous repertoires of collective action. Whether violence resulted from those actions was often a question of contingent circumstances.

In partial contrast to Tilly's view, it has been argued that in the process of modernization violent protest not only changes its *form* but decreases in *numbers*. This decline, so the argument goes, should be a realistic expectation as Western societies especially have become more and more democratic so that most of the people can express their social and political grievances by peaceful means. In addition, many of the often violent conflicts of the 19th century have been institutionalized and formalized so that, for example, conflicts at the workplace are no longer violent. However, one has to be careful regarding predictions, and one can even doubt whether the aforementioned view on our present does not neglect important phenomena that seem to contradict its optimism. Even in the democratic societies of the West, there are a number of citizens and groups that socially and politically are not integrated and whose exclusion from wider society produces quite a few tensions that result in violent behavior. Violent race riots in American cities in the 1960s and 1990s and violent ethnic conflicts nearly around the world are an indicator that collective violence might not disappear but will play a considerable role in the future.

One must keep in mind that those violent protests are usually not caused by a general state of anomie and a general loss of social control. On the contrary, those violent conflicts often have political aims. Collectively formulated political goals and collective actions are dependent on social relationships, and quite often are only possible within stable social structures. To speak of a general loss of social control in this context would falsely neglect the fact that political mobilization and political conflict (which might turn out violent) can only take place against the background of functioning social networks.

IV. INSTITUTIONS OF SOCIAL CONTROL AND THEIR EFFECT ON VIOLENT BEHAVIOR

After the arguments of the last section, which stressed among other things the secular decline of violent behavior in the process of modernization, it is not surprising to say that the genesis of modern police institutions and a modern criminal justice system was not a response to violent behavior of individuals—at least not in the United States and in Western Europe where research on the history of the police and similar institutions is an established subject of social history. When those institutions emerged in the first half of the 19th century they were either, as for example in the United States, a reaction of urban elites and politicians to political conflicts or an attempt by bureaucrats and "reformers" to concentrate the power of the central state by monopolizing the means of violence as it happened in England or—in a different setting—in Prussia (cf. Emsley/ Weinberger, 1991). If political elites aggressively responded to crime at all, it was property crimes and not violent crimes that seemed to be the most interesting objects of concern.

To be sure, English and American constables, German *Feldhüter*, *cavaliers* in the French *maréchaussée*, and so on, whose tasks were in some respect similar to those of modern policemen, did exist a long time before the 19th century. But modern police forces as established in the last century were remarkably different from their predecessors as they tried to establish some sort of a politically authorized, professionally organized, permanent control and surveillance of public spaces by using clearly defined violent and nonviolent means—tasks that were not even intended by premodern forces of order. Although control and surveillance were not primarily focused on violent acts—at least not in the last century—one might assume that those new forces of social control had some effect on the level of violence in society. It is reasonable to think that the new police contributed decisively to this aforementioned secular decline in the rate of violent behavior. But a couple of arguments obviously contradict such a hypothesis. First, as the cited research on the English county of Kent has demonstrated, the downward trend in violent behavior preceded the time when the first modern police institutions were created.

Second, it is doubtful that the existence of modern police forces really was some sort of a quantum leap in the degree of social control; especially in densely populated areas of the big cities policemen on the beat were not really able to control the behavior of all people. A relatively high policemen to population ratio of 2.5 : 1000, which was achieved in some European and American cities in the last century and which has not changed greatly to the present day, has never been high enough to prevent violent crime—especially as one has to keep in mind that not all policemen are on the beat all the time and that quite a high percentage of violent crime is not committed in public spaces but in privacy, for example, within the family. In that context it is important to mention that the existence of modern and supposedly effective police forces did not stop the dramatic rise in the rate of property crimes that have been observed since the beginning of industrialization. Even if one takes into account that (statistically) increasing property crime might be one of the most important effects of increasing police activity (the more policemen on the beat, the greater the possibility that cases of property crime will be dealt with by a judge), the existence of such a high level of property crime should be at least a reminder not to overestimate the power of police forces in general. Their capacity for surveillance is more limited than is usually assumed.

Third, as statistical data on the historical development of violent crime indicate, there is probably not a very high correlation between police density and violent crime. The temporarily high rate of violent crime, for example, in the period of the Great Depression or the rise of violent crimes since the 1960s in the United States was definitely not accompanied or even caused by a manifest reduction in the number of policemen. On the contrary: between 1965 and 1975 American society increased its police officers to population ratio from 1.9 to 2.5 policemen per thousand population. But at the same time there was a remarkable increase of violent crime as well. So it is reasonable to assume that the level of violence in a particular society is quite independent of the existence and the actions of police forces and other institutions of social control.

This claim can be affirmed by taking into account the research on totalitarian regimes. Although it is quite safe to say that in totalitarian regimes the institutions of social control (ordinary police forces, secret police, paramilitary organizations, etc.) were more powerful and present in everyday life than they were in democratic societies, and although it cannot be doubted that those totalitarian regimes—by the use of brutal force—achieved a level of surveillance that was unthinkable for democratic rulers, the "success" of those regimes in preventing violent crime was not impressive at all. Of course, court statistics in Nazi Germany indicate that between 1932 and 1938 the incidence of violent crime was reduced by about 40%. But it is not clear whether this was the effect of institutions of social control or only one of a different social and economic setting. In any case, this decreasing trend in violent crime in Germany was reversed as the war created conditions that led to a rise in (violent and nonviolent) crime again: the power of the state and its institutions of social control in reducing violent crime should not be overestimated.

This warning is even more valid when applied to punishment as one important element in the criminal justice system because it is clearly designed to prevent deviancy, to deter violent crimes, and thus to control the behavior of people. First of all, it seems necessary to point out that the decreasing secular trend in violent crime was accompanied by an equally observable trend that increasingly led to an abandonment of the death penalty in many European states and to a reduction of physical forms of punishment. The obvious brutality of traditional "correctional" measures gave way to more "humane" kinds of treatment without encouraging people to use more violent or "criminal" means to achieve their goals in everyday life. The effect of deterrence, which is often assumed in discussions about punishment, is difficult to prove. One of the reasons is simply that many forms of deviant behavior and especially many forms of violent action are not carefully planned so that "criminals" rationally evaluate the costs and risks of their particular behavior. Even among those who have felt the costs of committing a crime more than others—those "criminals" who, for example, have been imprisoned—the effect of deterrence by punishment is hardly visible as their chance of committing a crime after release from prison is quite high.

Thus, political strategies that are based on the assumption of the massively deterrent effects of punishment have usually not been successful as the well-researched case of the United States has clearly demonstrated in recent decades. Although American politicians have propagated and enforced tougher and tougher forms of punishment since the end of the 1960s—the death penalty was enforced again, the number of people under some form of correctional control increased to an extremely high level—the effect on violent crime was not very impressive as crime rates and especially those for violent crime tended to increase.

If the effects of institutions of social control were not that great regarding violent behavior of *individuals*, the question to ask is whether they were effective in the prevention of violent *collective* action? It is true that some forms of collective violence vanished when the modern state—at least in most countries of the West—successfully established its monopoly of violence. The danger of warlords violently contending for power, as often happened in the late Middle Ages, was largely over when states centralized the most important resources of power and deprived existing powerholders of their means of violence. Thus, the modern state sharply reduced the number of struggles for power that could result in a civil-war-like situation of bloodshed and collective violence. But this claim is probably only true in the Western world. In countries of the former communist bloc and in those of the Third and Fourth Worlds the legitimacy of powerholders is often questioned so that large-scale collective violence between contending groups is still a possibility that one has to reckon with.

However, it is doubtful whether agencies of social control were really able to repress other forms of collective violence, for example, violent demonstration, strikes, rallies, and so on, that usually are not intended to overturn existing structures of political power. Of course, it is true that communist and fascist regimes successfully destroyed existing structures of political participation and mobilization and thus made large-scale violent collective action nearly impossible. But it is rather unlikely that agencies of social control in democratic states are able to achieve the same effects without sacrificing democratic principles.

Modern police forces were created in the first half of the 19th century to repress new threats from the "masses" and to prevent collective actions that undermined the stability of regimes. In Britain, the United States, and Prussia, for example, modern police forces were established in periods of massive urban riots and political conflicts. But this does not mean that these measures by state elites always led to a real reduction of collective violence. Violent riots continued in the following decades and they exist today as, for example, race riots in the United States, violent demonstrations in Europe, and clashes between the police and protesters in other parts of the world indicate. Although one has to admit that the police have increasingly replaced the military in the containment of societal conflicts, it is still true that police forces can be overwhelmed by the power of protests so that even in Western democracies they sometimes have to be supported by armies or paramilitary organizations (e.g., national guards). Thus, the effect of institutions of social control on the level of collective violence in society is not that impressive, especially as one has to keep in mind that inappropriate interventions by forces of order quite often were and are the *cause* for violent demonstrations or strikes.

V. CONCLUSION

Although the concept of social control is still widely used in sociological discourse, its fruitfulness concerning the explanation of violent behavior is not always clear as the meaning of the concept quite often is too broad to instruct precise research questions. Nevertheless, by narrowing the meaning of the concept and by focusing on institutions (e.g., police forces) that explicitly try to "control" violent behavior by citizens, some fruitful questions can be asked: Did the process of modernization lead to a general loss of social control and as a result, to

an increase in violent behavior? Did institutions such as the police effectively prevent people from committing violent crimes or from protesting violently? Both questions could be answered in the negative.

Also See the Following Articles

CLASS CONFLICT • CRIME AND PUNISHMENT, CHANGING ATTITUDES TOWARD • CULTURAL STUDIES, OVERVIEW • DEATH PENALTY • LEGAL THEORIES AND REMEDIES • POLICING AND SOCIETY • SOCIAL EQUALITY AND INEQUALITY

Bibliography

Archer, D., & Gartner, R. (1984). *Violence and crime in cross-national perspective.* New Haven/London: Yale UP.

Bessel, R. (1993): Die 'Modernisierung' der Polizei im Nationalsozialismus. In F. Bajohr (Ed.), *Norddeutschland im Nationalsozialismus*, pp. 371–386. Hamburg: Ergebnisse Verlag.

Cockburn, J. S. (1991). Patterns of violence in English society: Homicide in Kent 1560–1985. *Past and Present, 130*, 70–106.

Cohen, S. (1985). *Visions of social control. Crime, punishment and classification.* Cambridge: Polity Press.

Emsley, C., & Weinberger, B. (Eds.). (1991). *Policing western Europe. Politics, professionalism, and public order, 1850–1940.* New York: Greenwood Press.

Gurr, T. R., Grabosky, P. N., & Hula, R. (1977). *The politics of crime and conflict. A comparative history of four cities.* Beverly Hills and London: Sage.

Johnson, E. A. (1992). Cities don't cause crime. Urban-rural differences in late nineteenth- and twentieth-century German criminality. *Soc. Sc. Hist., 16*, 129–176.

Lane, R. (1979). *Violent death in the city. Suicide, accident, and murder in nineteenth-century Philadelphia.* Cambridge, MA, and London: Harvard UP.

Liska, A. E. (1992). Introduction to the study of social control. In A. E. Liska (Ed.), *Social threat and social control.* pp. 1–29. Albany: SUNY Press.

Monkkonen, E. H. (1975). *The dangerous class. Crime and poverty in Columbus, Ohio, 1860–1885.* Cambridge and London: Harvard UP.

Ross, E. A. (1969). *Social control. A survey of the foundations of order.* With an introduction by Julius Weinberg, Gisela J. Hinkle, and Roscoe C. Hinkle. Cleveland and London: The Press of Case Western Reserve University. (Original work published 1901).

Scull, A. (1988). Deviance and social control. In N. J. Smelser (Ed.), *Handbook of sociology*, pp. 667–693. Newbury Park: Sage.

Shikita, M., & Tsuchiya, S. (1992). *Crime and criminal policy in Japan. Analysis and evaluation of the Showa era, 1926–1988.* New York: Springer Verlag.

Stone, L. (1983). Interpersonal violence in English society 1300–1980. *Past and Present, 104*, 22–33.

Tilly, C. (1979). Collective Violence in European Perspective. In H. Davis, T. Graham, & R. Gurr (Eds.), *Violence in America. Historical and Comparative Perspectives*, pp. 83–118. (Rev. Ed.). Beverly Hills and London: Sage.

von Hofer, H. (1990). Homicide in Swedish statistics, 1750–1988. In A. Snare (Ed.), *Criminal violence in Scandinavia: Selected topics. Scandinavian studies in criminology, Vol. 11*, pp. 29–45. Oslo: Norwegian UP.

Social Equality and Inequality

Jan Pakulski

University of Tasmania

GLOSSARY

Class Systems Stratification systems typical of industrial capitalism. They are contrasted with non- and precapitalist systems of inequality and stratification (e.g., caste, estate, political rank).

Inequality of Opportunities concerns the issue of barriers in social mobility.

Inequality of Position Concerns the distribution of resources and endowments.

Social Class Economically determined large grouping sharing similar occupational location, material rewards, and interests, and some form of consciousness (self-recognition) and identity.

Social Inequality Differential access to goods and services, rights and entitlements, power, and prestige.

Social Mobility Movements of incumbents (persons, groups, etc.) between social strata, classes or statuses, typically upward or downward.

Social Status Honor, prestige, social standing conventionally granted to individuals or social categories and reflected in social distances. It is often seen as attached to collectivities (status groups) and contrasted with class.

Social Stratification Enduring hierarchy; inequalities that form a stable pattern of positions and that are transmitted between generations.

Social Stratum A unit in a social hierarchy; persons or families sharing a similar position in a social hierarchy (stratification system).

Underclass Marginalized people, a "cultural stratum" locked in the vicious circles of marginalization, poverty and social deviance. In the United States the term has been applied to "ghettoized" racial minorities suffering from drugs, violence, crime, split families, and endemic unemployment.

UNDER THE LABEL OF SOCIAL INEQUALITY social scientists study differential access to goods and services, rights and entitlements, power, and prestige. Social stratification typically refers to such forms of social inequality that are structured, that is, that form discernible hierarchies of social strata. Inequality of position or outcome refers to the gap in assets (e.g., income, wealth, prestige, power) between different strata. Inequality of opportunity refers to barriers in social mobility, that is, movements up and down social hierarchies. Most of the historically important systems of social inequality were "harmonious" in the sense of wide social acceptance. This changed under the impact of the notion of "natural equality of men" popularized by the

French *philosophes* in the 18th-century Enlightenment movement. Since then, social equality has become the universal ideological aspiration in all modern societies, and social conflicts have been seen as attempts to redress social discriminations by the lower and/or aspiring social strata. Nineteenth-century theorists formulated what may be taken as classical insights into the relationship between social inequality and conflict. These were subsequently elaborated into more consistent theoretical packages, first by Karl Marx, and then by Max Weber, the elite theorists, and the functionalists. Contemporary social theories stress the complexity of social inequalities and revise the inequality-conflict nexus in light of the new postindustrial and postmodern developments.

I. SOCIAL INEQUALITY, STRATIFICATION, AND CLASS

While the terms "social inequality," "stratification," and "class" are often treated as synonyms in everyday language, they have different meanings in social analyses. Under the label "social inequality" social scientists study differential access to goods and services, rights and entitlements, power, and prestige. Social stratification typically refers to such forms of social inequality that are structured, that is, that form discernible hierarchies of social strata. Such strata, sometimes called "classes," persist between generations and are reflected in social distances, discriminations, and conflicts. Because of this persistence, they can be studied as systems of social positions and stratification systems. Movements between these positions up and down social hierarchies constitute social mobility. Stratification research aims at describing the relations between social strata (stratification systems), explaining their origins and persistence, and accounting for differences in stratification systems between different societies. Social mobility studies describe, compare, and explain mobility patterns and social barriers to mobility typically seen as symptoms of social class divisions. Thus the problem of social inequality has four aspects: the substantive aspect is related to the question about the nature of the key dimensions of inequality and the key "assets" and "resources" (e.g., economic, such as income, cultural, such as prestige, and political, such as authority); the distributional aspect focuses on the distribution of these assets and resources between individuals and groups; the relational aspect refers to the ways in which differently endowed individuals and groups relate to each

other and form social hierarchies; and the mobility aspect concerns movements up and down these social hierarchies.

While all societies are unequal and almost all are stratified, only some can be described as "class societies" (although many American scholars use the term "class" in a generic sense, as referring to all social strata). In the European tradition of research, "class" has a specific meaning, different from the term "stratum." It refers to large social groupings that form in the process of production around socioeconomic assets. Members of the same class share a position in relation to ownership of capital, marketable skills, and working conditions; they form working, middle, service, and ownership classes. In this specific sense, classes are parts of stratification systems that emerge together with industrial capitalism, and they are typically contrasted with status groups and strata in slave systems of stratification (e.g., in the Roman Empire), with castes in premodern India, and with medieval European "estates." In contrast with such preclass systems, the modern class system is open, dynamic and conflictual. Social mobility is typical and high, the number of classes and the patterns of relations between them change, and they oppose each other. Class theorists see classes as evolving from mere statistical aggregates ("classes in themselves" in Marxist terminology) to self-conscious, solidary groupings sharing interests and ideological commitments ("classes for themselves").

Distributional studies of social inequalities form the foundation for relational studies that "map" social strata or classes. Thus American researchers of stratification construct occupational socioeconomic status (SES) scales that typically combine income, education, and occupational prestige. They also chart gradational class/status hierarchies similar to those developed by neo-Weberian scholars. Neo-Marxists map the class structure along what they see as the key relations of exploitation and domination. Such maps, in turn, serve as bases of social mobility studies that focus on movements up and down social (stratum or class) hierarchies. They branch into studies of *patterns of mobility* and *causes of mobility*. The latter, studies of occupational attainment, identify and compare the main causes of occupational advance, in particular the ascribed factors, such as parental backgrounds, and "achievement factors," such as the level of education (e.g., Blau and Duncan 1967). Social closure, especially when based on ascriptive criteria, is seen as evidence of inequality of opportunity. By contrast, extensive mobility and attainment based on meritocratic achievement factors are symptomatic of egalitarian societies in the sense of equality of opportunity, or are seen as an indicator of weak class formation.

Thus the concept of social (in)equality has acquired two distinct meanings. Inequality of position refers to the gap in assets (e.g., income, wealth, prestige, power) between different strata. Inequality of opportunity, a concept favored by liberally minded scholars, refers to social barriers and unequal mobility chances. They may vary independently. For example, the gap between the wealthy and the poor in the United States is relatively wide (and growing), while social mobility is relatively high.

Both aspects of social inequality have been intensely researched and hotly debated by contemporary social scientists. Before these debates, especially those concerning the relationship between social inequality and conflict, are reviewed in section V, a brief excursus is made on the major historical systems of inequality, followed by a summary of the major classical and contemporary theories of social inequality (section (II), a brief assessment of the complex patterns of social inequality (section III), and a discussion of the major trends (section IV).

A. Premodern Inequalities and Modern Class Systems

Ancient societies, especially the Athenian and Roman Empires, had developed complex systems of stratification in which the freeman-slave division was pivotal. Economic inequalities could not override this principal inequality of social standing; a slave remained subordinate to a freeman, and could be killed almost with impunity by a freeman. Most free people were citizens, that is, they enjoyed certain rights protected by law and enforced by the state and private militias. Among the freemen in Rome the key status division was between the landowning patricians and landless plebeians. Access to both kinship links and patron-client connections were also important determinants of lifechances.

Feudal divisions in Europe from the 10th through the 12th centuries had laid the foundations of the European estate system, in which each estate—the clergy, the nobility and the "third estate" of peasants, merchants and artisans—had different traditional rights and a different lifestyle, and was subject to different laws. The Indian "classic" caste system was an extreme form of status stratification based on social conventions concerning the notion of purity and pollution. Caste inequalities, which have evolved into a broad variety of historical forms and mutations, have been legitimized by tradition and religiously sanctioned. Castes are hierarchical (although these hierarchies are seldom consistent and clear), socially segregated, and typically endogenous. In all premodern stratification systems social inequalities were wide and pervasive, mobility was rare, and inheritance was typical. However, such systems have been described as "harmonious" due to a strong traditional/religious legitimization and harsh sanctions for social dissent.

The modern class system (in diverse forms) evolved out of estate systems under the impact of three revolutions: national (formation of nation states), industrial-technological (machine production in factories), and political (popular sovereignty and civil liberties). Social positions in class societies are based principally on economic assets, mainly capital ownership and skills. Class systems were from the very start "insensitive" to traditions and religious status conventions, and they were relatively open. Class inequalities and divisions gradually replaced traditional status ("estate") divisions as the principal bases of social cleavages, although the latter survived in the form of nobilities, aristocracies, the "intelligentsia," and traditional peasants. Strong residues of traditional status inequalities and divisions have also survived in communist China, mainly in the form of traditional peasantry and the "officialdom." In the newly settled societies of North America, the class system emerged early and in the absence of feudal traditions. But the purity and sharpness of class divisions there was immediately blunted by the deep inequalities and divisions between White colonists, Black slaves, and displaced native peoples. While in Europe the formation of the class system was accompanied, first, by conflicts between the feudal strata and the ascendant bourgeoisie, and later by conflicts between working and ownership classes, the dominant social and political conflicts in post-revolutionary America evolved around the issue of slavery, civil liberties, and land rights.

Class inequalities, cleavages, and conflicts underlied revolutionary upheavals from the 19th into the early 20th century, especially in rapidly industrializing Europe. After the Bolshevik Revolution in 1917 and the formation of the Soviet Union in 1922, a new system of stratification emerged in Russia. In this system life chances depended primarily on the rank in the party-state command system and not on property and marketable skills, as in the class systems. Privileges were distributed according to the proximity to the political elite, and they were concentrated at the apex of the communist "nomenklatura"—a stratum of politically reliable and loyal people who could be approinted to strategic positions of command.

Both modern forms of stratification are changing. The capitalist class system is fragmenting (some argue decomposing) under the impact of occupational differentiation, technological change, expanding citizenship and globalization. In 1989–1991 "velvet revolutions" and postcommunist reforms have undermined the rank system in Eastern Europe and Russia.

B. Social Inequality and Conflict: The Modern Nexus

Ideological justifications of social hierarchies in premodern societies, often in the form of religious doctrines and creeds reinforced by ruthless sanctions, made such hierarchies "natural" and God-sanctioned in the eyes of all social strata. Slaves in ancient Rome, serfs in medieval Europe, untouchables in premodern India, or peasants in premodern China seldom contested the hierarchical social order. Occasional rebellions in such societies were typically triggered by violationis of traditional rights and obligations regarded as sacred.

The nexus between social inequality and conflict is therefore historically new—it shares its birth with the secular outlook and egalitarian ideology of the European Enlightenment. The notion of basic human uniformity and "natural equality of men," popularized by Jean-Jacques Rousseau and the French *philosphes*, became a powerful ideological current in the 18th-century Enlightenment movement. The principle of "natural equality" was enshrined in the revolutionary programs and democratic constitutions, but was also heavily qualified. It applied to civic status and not economic position, and it involved a notion of equality of opportunity and not equality of outcome. These "bourgeois" qualifications were criticized, in turn, by radical socialists, including Marx.

In the rapidly industrializing Europe and North America, passion for equality became a major ideological driving force of protest, revolution, and reform. Yet, until the mid-19th century, this passion did not turn against *all* inequalities, but mainly against feudal and aristocratic privilege; it did not radicalize the most downtrodden and dispossessed, but the middle strata and the "losers," the downwardly mobile craftsmen and artisans. August Saint-Simon, a French utopian socialist, and Alexis de Tocqueville, a conservatively inclined observer of postrevolutionary developments in France and America, together formulated what may be taken as key insights into the relationship between social inequality and conflict: it is not the most pervasive forms of inequality that provoke conflicts, but those which are most visible and ideologically questioned (de-legiti-

mized); conflicts erupt when "things get better"—when tyrannies start to reform; conflicts involve predominantly the middle strata: those resourced and aspiring, as well as those who risk sliding down the social hierarchy. Extreme poverty typically breeds apathy, while privilege breeds compliance. These insights were, in turn, elaborated into more consistent "classic" theoretical packages, first by Karl Marx, and then by his critics: Max Weber, the Italian elite theorists, and the French and American functionalists.

II. CLASSIC THEORIES OF SOCIAL INEQUALITY, STRATIFICATION, AND CONFLICT

Social inequality and conflict in advanced societies have been explained in the context of four theoretical models formulated by Karl Marx, elite theorists, Max Weber, and the early functionalists. They differ in the way they explain the sources of social inequalities, diagnose their major forms, and link these forms with social distances, conflicts, and social change. While the first two, the Marxist and the elite theories, describe inequalities and conflicts as polarized, the latter two see stratification as graded and potentially harmonious (see Table I).

Both Marx's and the elite models are *polar* in the sense of stressing the opposition between two basic social categories: the owners versus the labor-selling workers in the case of Marxism, and politically circumscribed elites versus the masses in the case of elitism. In classic Marxism, the main source of this polarity, and therefore of class conflict, is private ownership of the means of production that causes exploitation, conflict, and domination between the major classes. Other classes, such as the petite bourgeois and landowners, and class sections and strata are of lesser importance, and they are likely to wane in the process of class polarization. All important social inequalities and cleavages gradually coalesce with major class divisions. As the working class becomes more impoverished, it is also likely to gain class consciousness and political organization, thus becoming the major force of revolutionary change, inevitable in Marx's view. In this way, Marx also sees class conflict as the "engine of historical change."

The classical elite theories were formulated in opposition to Marxism by the "Machiavellians": Vilfredo Pareto, Gaetano Mosca, and Robert Michels. They stipulate that power comes from organization, rather than prop-

TABLE I

Classic Theories of Inequality and Stratification Compared

	Marxist	Elite	Weberian	Functional
Image of inequalities	polar-antagonistic	polar-domination	gradational-multidimensional	organismic-consensual
Sources of inequality	property relations, private ownership of the means of production	social organization, corporate hierarchy, political organization	property relations, cultural conventions, state & bureaucracy	functional imperative, dominant values, occupational differences.
Key dimensions of inequality	economic capital	political power	economic power, honor, command	occupational prestige, socioeconomic status
Key units of stratification	antagonistic classes & middle class(es)	elites vs masses	classes, status groups, power groups (parties)	social strata, hierarchical classes
Relations between units	exploitation, conflict and domination	domination & manipulation	domination, conflict & competition	competition & dependence
Trends & future developments	class polarization, conflict & revolution	elite circulation & replacement	emergence of new classes, status groups & parties	fragmentation & social mobility

erty ownership; that the most central division in society is between elites (the top power-holders) and masses, rather than the major socioeconomic classes; and that elites cannot be eliminated. Revolutions are just elite replacements, and classless society is a dream. Social organization and bureaucratization inevitably give rise to elites—a fact stressed by Gaetano Mosca and Robert Michels in his famous "iron law of oligarchy" (who says organization, says elites). These elites are conscious, cohesive, and conspiratorial, that is capable of defending their own interests. Due to their ability to control recruitment processes, they form self-perpetuating oligarchies. While the elite-mass gap is constant, the nature of elites changes with the processes of industrialization and bureaucratization. Elites replace each other in the eternal cycles of circulation and revolutionary takeovers or, as Pareto put it, "history is a graveyard of aristocracies" (for a review see Bottomore, 1993).

In contrast with these polar visions, the Weberian theory and the "mainstream" American theories of stratification reflect the *gradational* image of complex "social ladders" (upper, middle, lower, etc.). Social inequalities reflect historically variable patterns of property ownership, access to skills, social conventions regarding honor, and positions in political hierarchies, especially in the state. Although Weber refers to "common currencies" of social inequality as "power" and "life chances," he sees social hierarchies as multidimensional. Such hierarchies consist of classes, status groups, and parties either overlapping or cross-cutting each other. Different

combinations of economic power, social honor, and political command crystallize into distinct *social classes* that are separated by mobility barriers and social distances. The relative importance of inequalities generated by the market (class), cultural conventions (status groups), and the state structures of political command (parties) varies historically. Only modern Western societies can be described as "class societies"; premodern China and India were stratified predominantly along status lines, and they were described as "status societies." While Marx predicts inevitable growth of inequalities, class polarization, and intensification of conflict, Weber sees class conflicts as contingent on proximity and communication between class members, visibility of the "class enemy," ideological organization, and political leadership.

Finally, the functional theories see social inequalities as reflecting primarily popular evaluations of social standing. These evaluations, according to Emile Durkheim, accompany social classifications and reflect relationship to and distance from "the sacred," that is, special realm of objects, symbols, and formulas representing the collectivity. Social stratification inevitably follows social differentiation, and inequalities of social standing are anchored in social values. Conflicts are pathological symptoms of anomie, that is, normlessness or "moral vacuum." Such a view reflects an *organismic* image of society which has been elaborated by Kingsley Davis and Wilbert E. Moore (1945) and Talcott Parsons (1954). The fomer argued that social inequalities reflect "functional necessity" for optimal allocation of talent and motivation; the latter analyzed them as means for securing social integration.

III. CONTEMPORARY THEORIES AND RESEARCH

Contemporary social theorists supplement and extend the classic schemes. They stress the complexity of social inequalities, revise the class/strata schemes in the light of new developments, and suggest new forms of sub- and international divisions and conflicts.

A. Neo-Marxism: Class Maps and Dependency Theories

History proved unkind to Marx's expectation of class polarization, class conflict, and revolutionary overthrow of capitalism in the most industrialized countries, thus provoking a growing skepticism as to the validity and utility of his theory. This skepticism led to the reformulations of class theory that often went well beyond Marx's original statements and concerns. The first wave of such reformulations coincided with the failure of proletarian revolutionary movements in Europe at the beginning of this century and gave rise to "revisionist" theories of class fragmentation. The second wave followed the experience of Soviet communism and Nazism in the 1930s and 1940s, and the post-World War II political settlements in the West. The class scheme was adjusted to account for both the extremist movements, which were linked to the major "class bases," and "conventional" electoral politics seen as an expression of the "democratic class struggle." The third wave of class theorizing, triggered by class-partisan dealignment and "new politics" in the 1970s and 1980s, posed the most serious challenge to the very class interpretation of politics. In response to this challenge, Eric O. Wright revised the Marxist class scheme by redefining class inequality, playing down class polarity, and rejecting the centrality of class conflicts.

Wright (1985) sees class inequalities in terms of principal assets—capital, organizational assets, and skills—that are unequally distributed and that enable those who obtain them to exploit those who own nothing but their labor power. The principal assets determine the overall systems of inequality: under feudalism the key asset was the labor power; under "statism" (i.e., in communist societies) it was organizational assets; under capitalism it has been the means of production (capital); and under nonexistent socialism it will be

skills. In contemporary societies all these assets coexist, thus generating a complex class structure. Thus, according to Wright, there are *multiple* classes. Class cleavages and class conflicts in contemporary society are generated by unequal access and ownership of capital, organizational assets, and skills, respectively. Moreover, class cleavages are not necessarily the most important generators of social divisions and change; gender, racial, and ethnic conflicts may affect social dynamics to a similar or greater extent. In the most recent statements, Wright stresses that the relationship between class inequalities and social conflicts is mediated by the variety of political and ideological factors, and that class conflicts coincide with other types of social conflicts. While Wright continues his revisions of the Marxist theoretical schemes, others abandon them for the more mainstream functional and Weberian legacies (for an overview see Lee and Turner, 1996).

One of the most popular offshoots of Marxism, the so-called "dependency theories," analyze class inequalities, exploitation, and conflict on a global scale. They have been developed in the context of the theoretical confrontation between the "mainstream" modernization theorists (e.g., Talcott Parsons and Daniel Bell) and their neo-Marxist critics (e.g., Andre G. Frank and Immanuel Wallerstein). The latter chart the gap in wealth and power between the advanced "core" of the capitalist world system (the industralized "North") and the developing "periphery" (the industrializing "South"), separated by vaguely defined "semiperiphery" of advanced primary producers. Globalization of the world market (and, more recently, finance) has generated vicious cycles of developments and affluence in the "core" at the expense of dependency and impoverishment in the periphery. While popular in the 1970s, the dependency theories have been criticized more recently. Critics point to the closing affluence gap between societies, which is mainly due to the rapid economic growth of Asian societies. The defenders insist that while the East and South Asian region (as well as some South American economies) have been "upwardly mobile" in the world system, African countries remain in the periphery, and the Asian ex-Soviet societies show some symptoms of a downward slide. Both sides seem to agree that the world system today is quite open and mobile. The rapid reshuffles between the affluent "core" and impoverished "periphery," as pointed out by contemporary globalization theorists, make the notion of world polarization difficult to sustain, though more radical theorists suggest that international class divisions are, nevertheless, in the process of formation.

B. Contemporary Elite Theories: Power, Elites, and Democracy

While Marxist class theories seem to be losing popular appeal, the elite models of power inequalities have been experiencing a series of revivals. The first was prompted by the formation of fascist and communist dictatorships that restricted the power of property, subjected markets to political control, and generated a distinctive form of political stratification in which the overall life chances reflected a position in a command-political, rather than productive-economic, hierarchy. The second revival coincided with the corporatization of politics and the social structure in the industrialized West. The elite-mass model was embraced by many students of the power structure in the United States in the 1950s and 1960s. What was seen as a fusion of the executive-governmental, corporate, and military power during the Cold War era sparked the "power elite" visions, most notably by C. W. Mills (1956). Unlike in the orthodox class visions, in this elite account power inequalities were central, and power grew out of corporate hierarchies of the state-military-industrial complex. Although most of the elite theorists in the United States remained very sensitive to the power of property and to the class connection of the corporate elites, they refused to reduce the organizational-political power to the power of property and/or market relations. These "power elite" theorists clashed with the advocates of the "plural elite" model. The former saw power (especially in the United States) as concentrated in the hands of cohesive and conspiratorial "power elites." The latter saw political power as graded and dispersed between competing "strategic elites." Such plural strategic elites did not threaten democracy because they checked and balanced each other's power, and had to cultivate support of various nonelite categories.

The "power versus plural elite" debate generated some important methodological advances. Power was measured, and elites were identified, in three ways. The positional method relied on the assumption that power coincides with top positions in the largest organizations: governmental, private business, and voluntary associations. The reputational method relied on evaluation of power by well-informed panels of judges; those who were seen as the most powerful were included into the elite. Decisional studies identified power with decisional input. Those who shaped the key decisions (e.g., on declaring a war, introducing welfare programs, etc.) were selected as elites. American researchers extended the scope of power studies by identifying "nondecisions," that is, the capacity to shape the agendas,

to suppress or gloss over certain issues, as an important aspect of power. More synthetic measures of power and "snowballing" techniques of elite identification were applied in American and Australian studies.

The third revival of elite theory has been prompted by the development of what Giovanni Sartori (1965) called "a democratic theory of elites." It coincides with democratization in Eastern Europe and the ascent of the highly etatist and authoritarian "tiger" economies in Asia. Elites, as noted by contemporary analysts, have played the central role in both processes. However, unlike the second wave studies, these new studies emphasize the role of elites in democratic transition and in enhancing economic growth. When elite divisions trigger social and political conflicts, democracy cannot survive. On the other hand, elites, especially when they are open and unified, can contain social conflicts and craft stable and democratic "polyarchies" (for the overview see Etzioni-Halevi, 1996).

C. Neo-Weberian Theories: Complex Stratification, Mobility, and Conflict

Weber's critical appraisal of Marxism proved immensely fruitful in generating a powerful stream of heavily "weberianized" analyses of European neo-Marxist "Frankfurt School" theorists (e.g., Max Horkheimer, Theodore Adorno, Herbert Marcuse, and, more recently, Jurgen Habermas), inspiring the predominantly North American community studies (e.g., by Lloyd Warner and Paul Lunt), and in stimulating studies of social mobility, which was seen by Weber as the critical generator of "social classes." Above all, Weber's theories continue to provide an important springboard for contemporary theoretical and empirical studies of social inequalities.

Neo-Weberians chart social inequalities along the complex occupational hierarchies that combine market position with social prestige (status) and authoritative command. Ralph Dahrendorf and Anthony Giddens represent a more theoretically oriented European stream of neo-Weberian stratification research. Dahrendorf (1959) summarizes changes in the class structure of "industrial society" in six points: the decomposition of capitalist class into owners-shareholders and managers; the similar fragmentation of the previously unitary working class into skilled, semiskilled, and unskilled segments; the expansion of the "new middle class," itself divided into bureaucratic administrators and service staff; increased social mobility eroding class boundaries and dissolving class struggle into individualistic competition; the extension of citizenship rights;

and the institutionalization of class conflict through collective bargaining and arbitration procedures. These new developments cannot be directly attributed to the operation of traditional class mechanism, that is, productive/property and market relations. They are the outcomes of expanding organizational-authority relations, state interventionism, the growth of large corporations, and the technologically driven division of labor. Such relations reflect the primacy of control over (rather than mere ownership of) property, and they generate new forms of class inequality and conflict that differed from those envisaged by the Marxists.

Anthony Giddens (1973) suggests two principal processes of class structuration in advanced (that is, highly industralized) societies: through ownership of property, possession of skills and qualifications, and disposition of manual labor power, and through division of labor within enterprises, authority relations, and divisions due to consumption and lifestyles. Social stratification, in his view, involves classes, sublcass strata, and elites.

John Goldthorpe represents a more empirically informed stream of neo-Weberian research concerned mainly with the formation of "social classes" through mobility barriers. He has constructed an influential synthetic class scheme based on inequalities in employment status and conditions. This scheme served as a basis of a series of comparative studies of social mobility in 15 major industrial societies in the 1980s, known as the CASMIN Project (Comparative Analysis of Social Mobility in Industrial Nations). The study concludes that although there have been substantial increases in structural mobility rates (i.e., social mobility due to increasing differentiation in occupational positions), the relative gaps in mobility chances between the classes have remained stable over time or showed a "trendless fluctuation" (Erikson and Goldthorpe, 1992).

Daniel Bell's analyses of value change and postindustralism carry a clear Weberian imprint. Bell (1973) suggests a major overhaul in the vision of the "postindustrial" class structure. The shift from goods-producing to service economies has been associated with the growing preeminence of professional and technical strata, the increasing centrality of theoretical knowledge in all areas of social life, and the ascendancy of state-based knowledge classes and technocratic ruling elites. The historical shift in the base of social inequality and power has led from property to technical skills. Education and political mobilization replace inheritance and patronage as the principal mechanisms and routes of access in postindustrial society. The class system in such society is open and meritocratic. Although it does not dispose of the disparities of power and wealth, it nevertheless makes these disparities consistent with visions of equal opportunity, achievement, and merit.

The neo-Weberian stream of theorizing has also resulted in important reformulations of the links between social inequalities and communal conflict. Weber saw socioeconomic, sociopolitical, and sociocultural divisions as interacting in generating patterns of conflict—the point emphasized recently by Pierre Bourdieu (see section III.I). Social protest and reform movements led by charismatic leaders, according to Weber, challenge the social order and the established hierarchies of honor. Purely class (i.e., socioeconomic) conflicts are less frequent because classes, unlike status groups, seldom form conscious and organized communities, and because the idiom of class interests is less appealing that the value idiom of dignity and honor typical of status conflicts. Nevertheless, when interests are sharply polarized, class members are concentrated and communication among them is easy, and when they develop political and ideological leadership, conscious and solidary classes may emerge. Moreover, the Weberian emphasis on multidimentionality of inequalities allows for the analysis of "status discrepancy" or "crystallization" whereby different aspects of social position differ in their hierarchical status location. When widespread, this discrepancy, rather than inequality, may trigger social conflicts.

These Weberian points have been taken one step further by the proponents of "resource mobilization" and "political opportunity structure" theories of mass social movements, especially the civil rights movement in the United States. They see protest movements as collective responses to, on the one hand, structured social inequalities, especially of the discrepant type and, on the other, as symptomatic of access to resources by the discriminated social categories. Movement success depends on mobilization of resources, such as organization, moral commitment, solidarity, publicity, and so on, and on political opportunities. Movements mobilize when opportunities open up, and they subside when opportunities decline. Thus the civil rights campaigns in the United States coincided with urbanization of the Black population, the formation of a Black middle class, the growth of Black churches and unions, and the establishment of Black colleges. The antiracist and pro-democratic ideological commitments mobilized during the 1940s and 1950s, as well as the legal reforms banning discriminatory practices, were important parts of the new opportunities. So were the electoral dealignment and conflicts within the political elites.

D. Functional Theories: Inequalities, Values, and Expectations

The classic heritage of Durkheim was developed by the post-World War II structural-functionalists who stressed the multidimensional nature of inequalities, variability of stratification patterns, and intense social mobility. While Davis and Moore's (1945) version of "pre-requisite functionialism" was severely criticized, the more sophisticated version proposed by Talcott Parsons gained much broader currency. Parsons (1953) identified three bases of social ranking: *possessions* that people own such as capital or land; ascribed characteristics or *qualities,* such as abilities or lineage; and *performances* or achievements marking success in fulfilling role obligations. Value systems, and therefore the stratification systems, differ in the degree to which they stress possessions, qualities, and performances. For example, the dominant social hierarchies in feudal and caste-societies reflect ascribed qualities; capitalist hierarchies are built around possessions, and communist systems stress performance. Thus the system of inequalities performs not only the major function of strengthening value integration, but also motivation and value socialization. Conflicts erupt when values change and/or socialization fails.

Robert Merton added a less sanguine note. Value systems, according to him, could themselves become potential sources of conflicts when society promotes the ends (social goals) which cannot be achieved by socially approved means. Thus crime and rebellion may reflect not so much a failure of socialization, as an attempt to achieve goals by alternative (illegitimate) means, or as an attempt by the socially marginalized groups to legitimize the alternative set of achievable goals. This reformulation helped to shift attention to differentiation in group-specific value universes, and to the role of rising expectations and relative deprivations in social rebellions. It is not necessarily the level of deprivation or exploitation that triggers protest and dissent, but the level and dynamics of aspirations. This explains the rebellious and radical behavior of students and middle strata who experience economic and educational upgrading. Rising expectations, according to theorists of revolution, may lead to revolutionary upheavals if they are not accompanied by the opening up of opportunities. Social expectations are built, and accomplishments are assessed, in relation to some "benchmark" or "reference" social groups and categories. Conflicts erupt when the widely accepted relativities in social inequalities are violated.

Gerhard Lensky (1966) provides a most ambitious synthesis of the functionalist and Weberian theories of inequality and stratification. The process of stratification, that is, the distribution of privilege, prestige, and power (equivalents of Weber's class, status and party), is charted by Lensky in the context of a model of goal-pursuing individuals in historically evolving societies. Perhaps the most important claim concerns the reversal of the "age-old evolutionary trend towards ever-increasing inequality" in the most industrially advanced societies. Lensky credits this reversal to the growing complexity of knowledge and authority systems, increasing productivity, effective birth control, educational reforms, and the spread of the democratic ideology. Many of these themes have been further developed by the theorists of postindustrialism and human capital.

Perhaps the major contribution of functionalists to the study of social inequality was in the area of social mobility. This is because the core conclusion of functional theorists was that social closure, inheritance, and ascription are dysfunctional in the modern industrial order, and therefore should decline with industrialization. This optimistic proposition was tested, with various success, by studies of social mobility and attainment.

E. Social Mobility and Ascription

It can be argued that since the pioneering studies of Pitirim Sorokin, studies of social mobility have grown into an autonomous area of research and theorizing. There is a considerable convergence in this area between the major theoretical camps, especially the Marxist, Weberian, and functional. Comparative studies of mobility analyze movements between social classes, status groups, occupational categories, power groupings (e.g., elites and the masses), and the structural positions in the world system (e.g., core and periphery). Moreover, the conceptualizations of mobility and the techniques of measuring inequality of opportunity have been broadened and refined, especially thanks to the widespread use of multivariate analysis. Studies of class and occupational mobility, both intergenerational (father-to-son) and intragenerational (first-to-last job) have been supplemented by gender-specific analyses (e.g., mother-to-daughter), studies of elite recruitment and "underclass" formation, and the international analyses of movements of countries and regions within the world system.

The key debate in mobility studies is about the historical and current trends in equality of opportunity (that is, social openness as measured by mobility rates). One of the main points of contention in this debate is the importance of relative versus absolute mobility rates. Relative rates measure mobility net of marginal effects; the absolute rates are the raw flows between origins and destinations. The latter can be diagnosed by comparing the relative mobility chances of people from different strata or class locations. While the absolute mobility has been increasing, especially under the impact of the growing number of middle- and high-status occupational positions, the relative mobility rates remain relatively stable. This has provoked a question whether or not industrialization really promotes equalization of opportunities.

Studies of occupational and intersector mobility reveal that professionals are more likely to inherit their positions (i.e., show a high degree of closure) than other occupations, while the broad service, managerial, and clerical categories are relatively open in the sense of intergenerational mobility and frequent movements in and out of these occupations (career mobility). Similarly, skilled manual jobs are more open compared with unskilled ones. Thus, the results of social mobility and status attainment studies confirm that class divisions and boundaries are blurred and, by and large, permeable. While considerable inequalities of opportunity and pockets of inheritance still exist, the most industrially advanced societies, especially the bulk of the "middle mass" in these societies, show high level of openness combined with universalism. Social mobility, especially into and between "middle classes," is quite high. This is partly due to a structural shift—a rapid growth of white collar, technical, and professional positions and the corresponding decline in manual industrial and farm employment. First diagnosed as a universal trend associated with industrialization by Seymour Martin Lipset and Hans Zetterberg in the 1950s (the "Lipset-Zetterberg thesis"), this structural shift has eroded class and status group boundaries and increased the openness of industrial societies. Contemporary mobility studies confirm these regularities with some qualifications: while the absolute mobility rates vary between societies, the relative rates remain stable among the industrializing market societies (the "Lipset-Hauser-Jones thesis"). Another conclusion drawn from comparative studies has been that ascription declines. Education, which is an "achievement factor," grows in causal importance as propellant of occupational attainment (for a review see Heath 1981; Erikson and Goldthorpe, 1992).

In all industrialized societies a person's education, rather than parental occupational background, is the key causal factor in occupational attainment, thus confirming the strong connection between mobility and universalism. Social closure is high in less developed and industrializing societies, as well as in societies with long-lasting conservative regimes, such as Spain. The new attainment studies have also confirmed the expansion of universalism in the United States throughout 1970s and 1980s. Hout (1993), for example, observes that the effects of social origins on occupational destinations in the United States declined by more than one-fourth over the 1962–1973 decade, and by more than one-third over the 1972–1985 period. At the same time, however, the nexus between parental and children's education remained strong, thus pointing to the possibility of inheritance of "cultural capital" (see section III.E). Interestingly, a similar pattern of occupational mobility was identified in marketless and formally "classless" communist societies of Eastern Europe in the 1970s and 1980s, thus providing some support to the functionalists' view that the occupational differentiation and technological conditions, rather than property relations, are the key determinants of social inequalities.

The studies of marriage patterns do not alter this picture of relative openness. While they show a considerable degree of social homogeneity among marriage partners in advanced societies, this homogeneity (homogamy) varies among different social positions. Like social immobility, it tends to be highest on the two extremes of the social hiearachy and among farmers. Moreover, marriage partners in advanced societies are closest in educational and cultural (status) dimensions rather than in terms of socioeconomic class. However, there is also considerable evidence of strong and persisting racial, religious, and ethnic/national homogamy.

While these developments represent enormous advancements in comparison with the classic theories, they also triggered some criticisms. Contemporary researchers are accused of ignoring four aspects of contemporary social inequalities: political inequalities concerning citizenship status and democracy; inequalities associated with nationality, ethnicity, and race; inequalities of gender, especially in the familial/domestic realm; and inequalities in "cultural capital." I briefly review these four aspects.

F. The Impact of Citizenship

The original Weberian point about the role of the state and law in shaping social inequalities in modern societies was subsequently developed by T. H. Marshall in his seminal paper on "Citizenship and Social Class." Marshall (1949/1964) outlined what became a classical version of the theory of citizenship, which pointed to the global and profound impact of legislative-political interventions on social inequality and class divisions in Britain. Class and citizenship, according to Marshall, had always been at war. He distinguished three stages in this war and three respective aspects or components of citizenship, namely civil, political, and social. The civil component of citizenship—rights to personal liberties, freedom of speech, thought and faith, the right to property and justice—was instituted in the 18th century in the form of independent courts of justice. The political component, involving the right to vote and stand for political office, developed throughout the 19th century. Parliaments and councils of local governments were the key institutions securing political citizenship. Finally, the first half of the 20th century saw the extension of citizenship into the social sphere of welfare and social security rights. The formation of the welfare state corresponded to this final stage of citizenship extension. The most important and novel aspect of this stage was the collective mode of definition and implementation of rights. While the civil and political rights were attributed to individuals, and they were in many ways compatible with the operation of the "capitalist class principle," the welfare rights were defined in the collectivist idiom and extended under the pressure from working-class organizations. Their net effect was not the elimination of class inequalities, but the substantial abatement of their impact. Income inequalities were compressed, especially on both ends of the scale, the gap in culture and social experience narrowed, and citizenship extension cum inclusion became the major goals of the underprivileged.

Marshall's theory was subsequently extended and elaborated to fit other liberal democratic societies. Students of civil rights and minority rights movements highlighted the importance of inequalities in civic status as "triggers" and focus of social conflicts. The main actors in such conflicts have been status blocs, including African Americans, indigenous peoples, and women. For students of social inequalities this marks a clash between the formal, egalitarian, and rights-based status of citizenship, on the one hand, and informal, diverse, hierarchical statuses of honor, social standing, and "social worth," on the other. Citizenship is thus "at war" (to use Marshall's expression) not only with class inequalities, but also with much more deeply ingrained and "organic" social hierarchies of gender, racial, ethnic, and other statuses. This is one of the most important sources of tension and conflicts in contemporary societies, and the key area of struggle for egalitarian reforms in advanced Western societies.

G. Nationality, Ethnicity, and Race

National status is both egalitarian and hierarchical. It is egalitarian in the sense that within a nation, everyone is a brother/sister. It is hierarchical, often even polar, in the sense that national commitments presuppose ranking and/or polar divisions between friend and foe, us and them. The eruption of worldwide national conflicts in the opening decades of this century highlighted this point. Nationalism, especially in its most virulent ethnic/racial fascist and Nazi forms, represented an ideology of national, ethnic, and racial superiority and polarity. The notions of national-racial hierarchy permeated strong national identities. The Holocaust and the enslavement of "inferior Slavic races" reflected these hierarchies underlying the ideological principles of German National Socialism. Less virulent forms of racial and national discrimination and persecution survived in most multiracial and multiethnic societies, although only few countries, such as South Africa before 1994, institutionalized racial divisions.

The persistence of racial and ethnic inequalities and conflicts, especially in the United States provoked an open challenge to the class schemes. Salience and autonomy of race and ethnic factors suggested that ethnicity and race were a fundamental source of stratification. Not only did racial and ethnic inequalities prove remarkably salient and persistent, but they also permeated identities to a much larger extent than class. The civil rights movement, Black consciousness movements, and campaigns of ethnic revivalism became the central features of the North American social and political scene. Similar processes were diagnosed in the multiethnic and multiracial societies of Western Europe. However, racial and ethnic divisions there strongly correlated with socioeconomic divisions, thus provoking interpretations in terms of class-racial "internal colonization" (e.g., Hechter, 1975). The advocates of such interpretations in the West depicted the march of capitalism as involving the *divide et impera* tactic toward its working classes, combined with progressive expansion of exploitative relations. Racial and ethnic minorities were the intranational victims of this tactic.

More sophisticated explanations stress the cultural foundations of racial prejudice and discrimination. In almost all societies new generations are socialized to ethnocentric and stereotypical beliefs. More radical interpretations see prejudice and discrimination as expressions of the struggle for power. They converge with culturalist studies in a powerful stream of "underclass" research in the United States.

The increasing unemployment among socially segregated racial and ethnic minorities raises the prospects of new social divisions and conflicts. The typically racially distinct "new poor" populating "underclass"—an urban stratum of mostly colored "truly disadvantaged" (William J. Wilson) or "deviant poor" (Ken Auletta)—hardly resemble the industrial proletariat. Auletta (1982) distinguished four component types of the underclass: the hostile, the hustlers, the passive poor, and the traumatized. The first two of these types are not necessarily poor; they often draw considerable profits from illegal activities, such as drug trafficking. Moreover, most of them are outside the labor market. They either cannot find work, or are unable to work due to family circumstances or poor health.

Current studies of the underclass in the United States lean toward structural explanations. For example, Wilson (1987) sees the main causes of the formation of a Black underclass in urban deindustrialization, male joblessness, and middle class migration out of depressed areas. These processes start a vicious circle of social concentration, isolation, and "social denudation"—the flight of successful families from socially depressed areas. All of these are associated with the pathological sociocultural adaptation reflected in the formation of "ghetto subcultures of poverty and crime." More radical social analysts point to the legacy of racial discrimination and ethnic prejudice. "Ghettoized" racial minorities, they stress, suffer from long-term social discrimination. Legacies of this discrimination are visible in drug abuse, violence, crime, marital instability, teenage pregnancies, and endemic unemployment.

In spite of the signs of increasing unemployment and social segregation in Western Europe (35% of Turks were unemployed in Germany, and 42% of Moroccans were jobless in Holland, in 1994), there are few signs of an underclass forming there. The welfare system in Western Europe is more extensive than in the United States, the poor are less segregated, and their standard of living has risen in absolute terms, in spite of the widening income gap.

H. Patriarchy, Viriarchy, and the Gender Gap

Perhaps the most heated aspect of debate has erupted around the most common form of social inequality and division: the gender one. Criticisms of gender blindness directed against students of social inequalities has coincided with the increasing participation of women in the labor force, the second wave of feminism, and with political mobilization of multifaceted women's movements. The spotlight of these criticisms turns against mainstream stratification and class analyses that are accused of ignoring women, underscoring the significance of gender relations and domestic work, and distorting the class/strata maps by concentrating on the position of the male family head. Contemporary feminist thinkers argue that gender-based inequalities are an inherent feature of stratification, and that they have to be identified at its "source," that is, within the family and domestic sphere. They conceptualized gender inequality using the concept of *patriarchy*. While originally referring to the subordination of women and other household members to the male household head, *pater familias*, the concept of patriarchy has subsequently been stretched to cover all diverse forms of male domination both within and outside the domestic sphere. The domestic sphere, according to feminist theorists, cannot be reduced to a mere reproductive appendage to the occupational employment sphere. The domestic gender divisions are transmitted to, and reflected in, market fragmentation and unequal career structures ("viriarchy"). Separation and inequalities between genders are maintained in a broad variety of fields, resulting in the vast areas of "gendered" positions, which include manual outcontracted jobs, as well as "white blouse" jobs. This gender segmentation is to a significant extent a result of domestic arrangements and social conventions concerning decisional prerogatives (who makes the major decisions) and parental responsibilities (who is the principal child-carer). Similarly, careers are structured in a way that places heavy penalties for discontinuities experienced by child-bearing and child-rearing women. Since in contemporary society access to economic and symbolic rewards is heavily dependent on career developments, the viriarchal configuration produces a characteristic pattern of inequalities. This is also affected by the regulative role of the state, especially in the areas of taxation, labor regulation, and welfare provision (child care, family support, etc.). These two aspects—the projection of domestic relationships into the sphere of the market, and the progressive etatization of the formerly private sphere of biological and social reproduction—are difficult to incorporate into the mainstream theories of class and stratification (for an overview see Crompton and Mann, 1986).

Gender inequalities have been propelled to the top of the public agenda by the powerful "second wave" of the feminist movement. This successful mobilization of gender identities, issues and concerns seems to confirm the nature of the "modern nexus" between social inequality and conflict (see section I). Gender inequalities are highlighted not by the most discriminated, but by the least discriminated and most highly educated Western women. Feminism is weak or nonexistent in traditional societies where religious beliefs and practices, typically discriminatory of women, are strongly legitimized.

I. Education and Cultural Capital

Already in the 1960s and 1970s the American and European studies pointed to the growing importance of education as a major cause of status attainment and, more generally, social advancement. The importance of educational inequalities was confirmed by the studies of "human capital" (e.g., by Gary Becker) and postindustrial trends (e.g., by Daniel Bell). While Becker and Bell emphasize not only the centrality but also the legitimacy of educational inequalities, as representing the principle of achievement and merit, French neo-Marxists, such as Pierre Bourdieu, see the educational systems as perpetuating social class divisions. Conflicts in modern societies, according to Bourdieu, erupt around access to and prerogatives of both economic capital and social, symbolic and cultural "capitals," that is, around access to education, tastes, and cultural consumption.

Bourdieu represents the most radical break with the economism of the original Marxist version of class theory, which he accuses of ignoring "the positions occupied in the different fields and sub-fields, particularly in the relations of cultural production, as well as all those oppositions which structure the social field and which are not reducible to the opposition between the owners and non-owners of the means of economic production" (1994:244). The multidimensional social space he constructs engenders material and cultural inequalities, and it suggests multiple struggles for domination. The Weberian genealogy of this view is quite clear, though Bourdieu identifies his position with the Marxist theoretical legacy. However, unlike the Marxist schemes, his explanations of inequalities center on cultural differences. Relations of class domination—central in Bourdieu's scheme—involve neither exploitation nor even open antagonism and conflict. Economic capital is important, but it is not privileged over other forms of cultural, social, symbolic, and other capitals. Social agents can thus be located in the social space according to the type, composition, and volume of their multiple capitals. Classes, the categories of people who share similar location in social space, are likely to have similar interests and dispositions, although they seldom form social groups or act in a solidary manner.

The studies of education and cultural capital, as well as the analyses of gender gap, racial inequalities, and urban underclasses mentioned above, mark another important shift in inequality research. While earlier studies of social inequalities focused on their causes, aspects, and general patterns, the new generation of empirically informed studies emphasizes the complexity of consequences of social inequalities, including the impact of social inequalities on individual lifechances. The impact on physical and mental health, stress, confidence, sense of well-being, family relationships (including violence and stability), child legitimacy, social deviance, and crime became a standard part of the research agenda. Equally important became the questions of social policies aiming at tackling the problems of educational disadvantage, urban poverty, and underclass-related crime.

IV. CURRENT TRENDS: A NEW AGE OF INEQUALITY?

Are we entering a new "age of inequality" prompted by globalization and postindustrialism? The evidence of that, as indicated above, is patchy and mixed. Trends in socioeconomic inequalities are the easiest to discern, because these inequalities are widely assessed and measured. They show that income and wealth gaps are much wider in the developing than in the developed nations, and that these gaps are much larger in the ownership of assets (land, capital) than in income differentials (UNCTAD, 1997). The overall narrowing down of the affluence gap between nations in the 1960s–1980s was mainly due to the spectacular growth of the East Asian "tiger economies," China, and more recently India. The fact that high growth was occurring in the most populous societies (with interventionist governments in many of them) also led to a reduction of world poverty. In China alone the proportion of the population living in poverty decreased from 25 to 60% (depending on the measure used) in 1976 to 7 to 25% in 1994. The current economic decline in Asia may alter this picture.

While the *affluence gap* between nations may be narrowing down, the *income gaps* within nations have been increasing (UNCTAD, 1997; see Table II). The nearly century-long egalitarian trend stopped in the 1970s and early 1980s. The "third industrial revolution," combined with globalization and the contraction of the welfare state, have led to the widening of the gap between the wealthy and the poor. These effects are similar to those diagnosed in the first (1770–1840) and second (1880–1910) industrial revolutions and represented in the "Kuznets curve." Economic inequalities, according to this curve, increase in the initial stage of industrializa-

TABLE II

Income Inequality since 1970 by Region

Region	No. of countries	Gini Coefficient (%)*			Ratio of richest to the poorest 20%		
		1970s	1980s	1990–4	1970s	1980s	1990–4
Developed countries	12	32	32	33	5.6	5.6	6.0
Eastern Europe	4	22	23	28	3.1	3.1	4.1
Russia	1	n/a	26	31	n/a	n/a	5.1
China	1	n/a	32	36	n/a	4.7	6.1
Developing countries:							
Latin America	10	50	51	n/a	14.5	15.6	n/a
East Asia	7	41	41	n/a	8.3	8.2	n/a
South Asia	2	31	32	31	4.6	4.7	4.6
Sub-Saharan Africa	10	n/a	n/a	45	n/a	n/a	9.5
North Africa	4	n/a	n/a	38	n/a	n/a	6.6

* Gini coefficient ranges from 0 to 100. Zero = perfect equality, where everyone earns the same amount of income; 100 = perfect inequality, where one person earns everything and the others earn none.

Source: UNCTAD 1977:108.

tion and then level up or even decline. One may see the current widening of the income gap as a symptom of a new (post-) industrial revolution.

Wealth has always been distributed more unequally than income, but it had also been subject to egalitarian trends in the 20th century. More recently, these trends are also being reversed. Although with the spread of small ownership and the rapid growth of pension/super funds an increasing proportion of people in advanced societies become property owners, this ownership is highly uneven. Studies in the United States, for example, show a rapid growth in the number of superrich. A recent issue of *Forbes* magazine (October 13, 1997) lists 170 billionaires among the 400 richest people in the United States, up from 135 billionaires in 1996. Significantly, there is only one Black person among the top 400 wealthiest Americans (Oprah Winfrey, 349th on the list). The wealth gap seems to be increasing in all advanced societies regardless of the political regimes in power. Recent Australian studies, for example, show a growth in asset gap between wealthy and poor families between 1986 and 1993, a period of social democratic (Australian Labor Party) government.

Is this mirrored by widening status gaps, increasing social distances, growing political divisions and mobility barriers? The answer to this question is less clear. First, status inequalities are much more complex and difficult to assess, and studies of social distances are more fragmented than studies of income and wealth distribution. There is little doubt, however, that the

processes of modernization have flattened status hierarchies and undermined ascriptive statuses that had permeated "aristocratic" (Tocqueville's term) and "patriarchal" societies. But, as Durkheim and Weber warn us, modernization has also generated new bureaucratic hierarchies of authority and expertise. With a few dissenting notes (coming mainly from neo-Marxist scholars), contemporary students of social inequalities in advanced societies agree that occupational statuses are increasingly achieved. Ascription is rare and inheritance is restricted mainly to property-based (farming and small business) occupations. Studies of stratification point to fragmentation of inequalities—occupational differentiation, growth of middle strata, embourgeoisement of skilled workers, and increases in structural mobility—and to market clustering along gender, ethnic, and racial lines that result in the formation of "ethno-" and "gender-" strata. The large class-type clusters of positions with similar rewards, statuses, mobility chances, identities, and common political representation have been dissolving.

Perhaps the most widely studied and diagnosed of all status divisions is the gender gap. The resurgence of feminism coincides with (and prompts) the actual narrowing of this gap. The most recent studies of gender inequality in advanced societies point to:

• Persistence of unequal division of labor within the family and in the domestic sphere. Traditional stereotypes and practices persist particularly at the lower end of the status spectrum and among rural families. The "egalitarian shift" in domestic duties is most pronounced among the young, educated, white-collar working couples.

- The closing of gender gaps in education. Women undergo an "educational revolution" in advanced societies, and their proportion among university students has doubled in the last 10 years. However, women are still underrepresented among higher degree holders, and in education leading to high-status professional skills.
- A rapid increase in female participation in the labor force. Women's employment grows most rapidly in the service sector ("caring professions" and "white-blouse" jobs), in public sector, and in part-time positions.
- The persistence of gender gaps in authority. While women trickle into political elites, they are underrepresented in the top administrative layers of business and professions.
- A declining gender gap in politics and civic activism. The "second wave" feminism and other new social movements challenge patriarchal images and practices that disadvantage women.

These political mobilizations are strong in advanced Western societies. The proportion of women in political elites has been increasing rapidly, especially in Scandinavian societies.

Inequalities of power (general capacity to realize one's will and achieve one's goals) are as difficult to assess as inequalities of status. We can point to two contradictory developments. The trend toward power concentration identified by elite theorists at the beginning of this century seems to continue in advanced societies. Bureaucratic hierarchies and corporate pyramids seem to grow, if anything, steeper. Perhaps the most consequential aspect of change is the appearance of supranational power centers (UN, EC, World Bank, the IMF, etc.) and the declining willingness of governments to intervene in the economy, thus resulting in power vacuums in public spheres. On the other hand, power stratification has been affected by the extension of citizenship rights and democracy. As pointed out above, the extensions from civil, through political, to social rights have combined with widening scope of "subjects": from propertied adult males to all residents of the state. Some diagnose further extensions of citizenship rights into "human rights," which are independent of statehood, and "cultural rights" involving rights to dignified representation through the information systems and public arenas. Proliferation of these rights

raises the prospects of the continuation of egalitarian trends in the sociocultural and sociopolitical spheres.

Perhaps more controversially, one may argue that power gaps seem to be narrowing down due to the proliferation of democratic institutions and practices. Students of civil society point to the phenomena of "new politics," including the mobilization of "citizens' politics" and libertarian "new social movements." Internationally, Samuel Huntington (1991) has diagnosed the "third wave" of democratization, which involves the adoption of electoral mechanisms by more than thirty formerly authoritarian regimes. According to the Freedom House, for the first time in history the majority of regimes in the 1990s can be classified as democratic. Although the process of democratic consolidation is slow, and it may be reversed under the impact of elite divisions and backlash movements, democratic commitments and practices constitute a new orthodoxy both among elites and mass populations.

Thus the national and international patterns of inequality are affected not only by the economic trends, but also by increasing scope of egalitarian citizenship statuses (civil/legal rights) and new forms of civic activism. Whether or not it indicates restratification (formation of new strata) or destratification (further fragmentation) is a topic of intense debates. The former view, that of restratification, is taken by advocates of postindustrial trends. The latter position, that of progressive destratification, is represented by supporters of postmodern visions of social change.

A. Postindustrial and Postmodern Trends

The post-World War II studies of inequalities introduce new social strata: corporate elites, managerial classes, the rapidly expanding professional, service, and white collar classes, as well as the fluctuating underclasses of welfare dependents. The theoretical visions of "postindustrial society" (e.g., Bell 1973), and comparative studies inspired by the theorists of postindustrialism, present a more systematic map of these new strata and classes. For example, in a six-nation study of the United States, the United Kingdom, Germany, Canada, Sweden, and Norway, Gosta Esping-Anderson (1993) charts what he calls "the patterns of post-industrial class formation" in the following way:

- In all advanced societies proportions of qualified and high status positions—professional, managerial, technical, and semiprofessional—have grown rapidly. The lowest status jobs are either proportionally shrinking or growing slower than the higher status jobs. Even if the unskilled service jobs continue to grow, they are unlikely to form a large "proletariat-like" class. They are more diverse in nature (with less disadvantages in the welfare state sector and more in private sector), and more mobile. Such jobs typically form entry or stopover points rather than permanent positions.

- In all countries there is considerable social fluidity and mobility. However, this mobility is higher in the middle and at the bottom of the occupational strata, and lower at the top. In all countries (except Germany) there is considerable mobility to and from the lower status jobs, especially among the unskilled service workers.

- In the United States and Canada the lower status service positions serve as stop-gap jobs for youth who ultimately go to medium and high status positions. For example, 30% of these job holders in the United States in the 1980s moved to clerical/sale positions, and 17% experienced a long-distance rise into managerial, professional and technical jobs. There is no gender difference in this respect. By contrast, the low status service jobs in the United Kingdom and Germany seldom form springboards for upward mobility, especially for women.

- Lower status jobs are more confining for women than for men. This is partly the result of women's generally lower education, and partly reflects discontinuities in employment caused by childbearing. The occupants of the core low-status jobs are older, uneducated, and unskilled, often from racial and ethnic minorities. In the United States there is also another kind of "underclass core" consisting of predominantly Black single mothers and youth.

- Education proves to be the most important and universally effective means of status elevation and upward mobility. One may argue that this form of "human capital" becomes the key status determinant. Lifechances and occupational mobility are increasingly a function of education. This, paradoxically, means more openness at the lower status end due to widening access to basic education, and more closure at the top due to restricted access to tertiary education.

- While the middle and lower status sections of the social hierarchy look relatively open, there seems to be a relatively higher degree of closure within the upper echelons (Bell's "knowledge class"). Professions, in particular, show signs of closure, which reflects, to a large extent, restricted access to higher educational credentials. Managerial jobs, though, are more open.

Sociologists embracing the thesis of "postmodernization" see fragmentation of inequalities and class decomposition rather than the formation of new classes. They claim that as the old industrial classes decompose, and the old forms of class identity, solidarity and conflict are replaced by new forms of fragmented status identity and conflict. Advanced societies are unequal, but these inequalities do not give rise to socially distinct and politically active classes (e.g., Pakulski and Waters, 1996). The major trends can be summarized in six points:

- Education and skill-based inequalities in rewards are increasing. Over 50% of the GDP in the advanced (OECD) societies is estimated to be knowledge-generated and about 80% of newly created jobs in these societies are taken by educated knowledge workers. Unskilled and uneducated workers are increasingly marginalized, paid less, and threatened with unemployment.

- Deindustrialization (the shrinking of the manufacturing sector) in advanced societies produces structural unemployment and "jobless growth." Low-skill jobs are shifting to developing countries, and industrial companies, faced with deregulation and increased competition, are downsizing their staff. The unemployed in deindustrializing urban areas and "sunset regions" are often socially segregated. This gives rise to concentrations of the "new poor" and predominantly Black "underclass," especially in the United States.

- While profit levels increase, more people share them thus expanding the ranks of socially heterogeneous "middle mass." The "small owner" category grows rapidly and the boundary between owners and nonowners becomes blurred.

- Social mobility rates in the industrialized world are persistently high. While there are signs of inheritance on the top end of the social hierarchy, the large fortunes do not last long. There is no sign of the lower status service jobs forming distinct strata, let alone a class-type "new proletariat." The underclass seldom imprisons people for life and its members show little unity.

- While the income gap between rich and poor *within* the nations starts to grow, the rapid economic growth in the developing societies results in shrinking affluence gap *between* nations.

- Social inequalities detach themselves from social (especially socioeconomic class) positions. Contemporary inequalities seem to follow complex patterns of human capital more than structural positions in the economy. While material inequalities start to widen, there is no evidence of analogous increases in social status and power inequalities.

While "postindustrial class formation" involves *restratification*, that is, formation of new "knowledge classes," professional strata, and expert elites (all more open and meritocratic than their industrial predecessors), the advocates of "postmodernization" point to *destratification*. This destratification involves three shifts: from positional and economically determined "class systems" to increasingly complex patterns of "classless inequality" based on material *and* human (social, symbolic, and cultural) capitals; from relatively stable systems of politically organized classes to dynamic and fluid systems of changing identities and esoteric sociopolitical groupings; and from isomorphic national stratification systems to polimorphic inequality patterns.

B. Social Inequality and Conflict

Is the current wave of globalization and technological change likely to trigger new forms of social conflicts analogous to the conflicts accompanying the first (1770–1840) and second (1880–1910) industrial revolutions? As indicated above, answers to this question—whether in affirmative or negative—have to be heavily qualified.

For a start, there is little agreement as to whether or not social inequalities are, in general, increasing or decreasing, and whether or not social hierarchies in advanced societies are rearticulating (following restratification and formation of new classes) or getting blurred (following destratification and formation of "classless inequalities"). There are, however, some points of agreement in the current diagnoses. Material inequalities in the developing world are much wider, more entrenched, and increasing faster than in the industrialized West (see Table II). The unequal distribution of land, political and military conflicts, and corrupt administration are among the key factors responsible for the wide rich-poor gap. Status divisions, especially around gender, ethnicity, and race, are also much wider, mainly due to strong traditionalism. All of this increases the likelihood of violent social conflicts. However, there are also some mitigating factors. Status inequalities in the developing world tend to be more firmly legitimated than inequalities in the secularized and detraditionalized West. Moreover, while material inequalities are increasing, their impact may be cushioned by rapid economic growth. As long as the widening economic gap coincides with raising hopes of economic upgrading, reduction of proverty and, occasionally, with extensions of civil and democratic rights, it is unlikely to cause conflicts.

The rich-poor gap in advanced societies has been much narrower than in the developing world, and it is growing much slower (Table II). Nevertheless, after nearly a century of egalitarian trends, this increase, when combined with rapid detraditionalization, delegitimization of many social inequalities, and growing risk-awareness, is seen as socially destabilizing, marking a new era of social strife. Again, such scenarios should be treated with caution. For a start, the industrialized populations show a relatively high tolerance of inequalities, especially socioeconomic inequalities, which are legitimized in terms of merit (education, skills, productivity, etc.). Moreover, many see the current increases in wage/salary gap as temporary and conjectural: caused by declining state interventions, declining power of trade unions, dropping demand for unskilled workers (caused, in turn, by new technology and global competition from low-wage countries), and changes in the household structure (polarization between two-income households and households headed by a jobless single parent). This perception may reduce the conflict-inducing nature of inequalities. Finally, the advanced societies have well-developed infrastructure of conflict-defusing institutions, from democratic-political to welfare-administrative.

Indeed, the current increases in economic gap do not seem to trigger mass social conflicts and upheavals in advanced societies, similar to those which accompanied previous waves of change (e.g., the socialist movements in the 19th century, fascism and communism in the early 20th century). Industrial conflicts are at a historically low point, and there are few signs of social upheavals (though many signs of uncertainty and anxiety). International military conflicts seem to be abating, and democratic forms of government are widespread. The end of the Cold War has reduced the level of superpower conflict and tension, but also increased the prospects of social and political instability in Russia.

What are the reasons of these changing patterns of social inequality and conflict in advanced societies? There are a number of explanations suggested by the theories discussed above (section II). One may argue that the large-scale conflicts abate because of the declining popularity of socialism and the ascendancy of liberal ideologies help in legitimizing economic inequalities, and that the aspirations of the ascendant and strategically important social categories, especially the technical and professional workers, are largely satisfied; they are among the winners in a globalizing hi-tech world. One may also argue that class-type large scale conflicts are unlikely to grow when class structure is fragmented, and when the capacities of the most disadvantaged categories—the underclasses and the new poor—to form an organized "class for itself" or a challenging "counter-elite" are reduced by social isolation, denudation, and fragmentation. Contemporary neo-Marxists and neo-elitists seem to embrace this view. Finally, one may follow a neo-Weberian line of argument pointing to the multidimensional, cross-cutting, and compensatory patterns of inequalities, and the effectiveness of the modern state to control conflicts. In such a view, economic, cultural, and political aspects of inequalities do not go hand-in-hand, and they seldom cumulate in one social category. Moreover, as suggested by Weberian scholars, it is the combination of strong status divisions with the weakening state that trigger large-scale social conflicts. While circumscribing their activities, the state agencies (in advanced societies) show no signs of weakening, and ascriptive status divisions seem to be abating, thus reducing the likelihood of large-scale social conflicts. Small-scale conflicts continue to erupt around the issues of national, racial, and gender status divisions, as well as around the role of the state in securing and extending citizenship rights.

Also See the Following Articles

CLASS CONFLICT • COLONIALISM AND IMPERIALISM • CONFLICT THEORY • GENDER STUDIES • INDUSTRIAL VS. PREINDUSTRIAL FORMS OF VIOLENCE • POLITICAL ECONOMY OF VIOLENCE AND NONVIOLENCE • POWER, SOCIAL AND POLITICAL THEORIES OF • SOCIAL CONTROL AND VIOLENCE

Bibliography

Auletta, K. (1982). *The underclass.* New York: Random House.
Bell, D. (1973). *The coming of post-industrial society.* New York: Basic Books.
Blau, P., & Duncan, O. (1967). *The American occupational structure.* New York: Wiley.
Bottomore, T. (1993). *Elites and society* (2nd Ed.). London: Routledge.
Bourdieu, P. (1994). *Language and symbolic power.* Cambridge: Polity.
Crompton, R., & Mann, M. (Eds.). (1986). *Gender and stratification.* Cambridge: Polity.
Dahrendorf, R. (1959). *Class and Class Conflict in Industrial Society.* Stanford: Stanford UP.
Davis, K., & Moore, W. (1945). Some principles of stratification. *American Sociological Review, 10,* 242–249.
Erikson, R., & Goldthorpe, J. (1992). *The constant flux.* Oxford: Clarendon.
Esping-Anderson, G. (Ed.). (1993). *Changing classes: Stratification and mobility in post-industrial societies.* London: Sage.
Etzioni-Halevi, E. (Ed.). (1996). *Classes and elites in democracy and democratization.* Hamden, CT: Garland.
Giddens, A. (1973). *The class structure of advanced societies.* London: Hutchinson.
Goldthorpe, J. (1980). *Social mobility and class structure in modern Britain.* Oxford: Clarendon.
Heath, A. (1981). *Social mobility.* London: Fontana.
Hechter, M. (1975). *Internal colonialism.* London: Routledge.
Hout, M. (1988). More universalism, less structural mobility. *American Journal of Sociology, 93,* 1358–1400.
Huntington, S. (1991). *The Third Wave.* Norman OK: Oklahoma UP.
Lee, D., & Turner, B. (Eds.). (1996). *Conflicts about class.* London: Longman.
Lensky, G. (1966). *Power and privilege.* New York: McGraw-Hill.
Lipset, S. M. (1959/1981). *Political man* (1st/2nd Ed.). New York/Baltimore: Doubleday/Johns Hopkins UP.
Lipset, S. M., & Zetterberg, H. (1956). A theory of social mobility. *Transactions of the Fifth World Congress of Sociology,* 155–177.
Marshall, T. H. (1949/1964). *Citizenship and social class.* Cambridge: CUP.
Mills, C. W. (1956). *The power elite.* Oxford: OUP.
Ossowski, S. (1957/1963). *Class structure in the social consciousness.* London: Routledge.
Pakulski, J., & Waters, M. (1996). *The death of class.* London: Sage.
Parsons, T. (1953). A revised analytical approach to the theory of social stratification. In R. Bendix & S. M. Lipset (Eds.), *Class, status and power,* pp. 92–128. Glencoe: Free Press.
Putnam, R. (1976). *Comparative study of political elites.* Englewood Cliffs: Prentice-Hall.
Sartori, G. (1965). *Democratic theory.* New York and London: Praeger.
UNCTAD. (1997). *Trade and development report, 1997.* United Nations Conference on Trade and Development. New York and Geneva: UN Publications.
Walby, S. (1990). *Theorizing patriarchy.* Oxford: Blackwell.
Wallerstein, I. (1974). *The modern world-system.* New York: Academic Press.
Wilson, W. J. (1987). *The Truly Disadvantaged.* Chicago: Chicago University Press.
Wright, E. O. (1985). *Classes.* London: Verso.

Social Theorizing about War and Peace*

Hans Joas

Free University of Berlin

THE TOPIC OF SOCIAL THEORIZING about war and peace involves two questions. First, what do sociology and the social sciences tell us about the genesis and causes of war and about the effects of war on the development of humanity? Second, what light is shed on the major theoretical projects generated by our disciplines and on these disciplines themselves if they are viewed in light of the first question?

I. WAR AND PEACE IN THE SOCIAL SCIENCES TODAY

In this context, if one casts an initial glance over the social sciences at present the result is a highly contradictory impression. On the one hand, it looks as if pressing current global problems have had little impact on the dominating approaches in these disciplines. The major

theories that are the subject of general discussion today—for example, those of Habermas, Luhmann, or the Poststructuralists—contain hardly any mention of war and peace. On the other hand, approaches derived from the social sciences are of considerable importance both for the development of nuclear strategies and for peace movements. Game theories and conflict theories often constitute the core of lines of argumentation employed in strategic analyses, and as soon as the various trends in the peace movements quit the level of appeals to personal ethical convictions, they almost exclusively argue in terms of global analyses in the social sciences. The contradiction between these two observations resolves itself once it becomes clear that the social sciences have to a certain extent delegated the concern with war and peace to a separate area of its own. Peace research, military sociology, the study of international relations, the analysis of nuclear conflict scenarios in terms of game theory—none of these fields have had any noteworthy effect on the general development of the social sciences. The reasons for this segregation are by no means coincidental. Rather, they are closely linked to the definition of the concept of "society" that is constitutive for the social sciences. Alain Touraine and Anthony Giddens both criticized classic sociology for employing a concept of "society" that expressed only the reality of the 19th century European and perhaps also North American nation-state. All the asserted regular laws of development thus refer clandestinely to the reality of a state whose territories are clearly delineated and which is bound to a body of law, and administered

---

329

in a modern manner, whereas the dynamics of the relationships between these states is regarded as a purely historical contingency and otherwise hardly warrants interest. Consequently, such an approach cannot adequately thematize the particular internal characteristics of a nation-state as opposed to other historical structures; the dependence of intrasocietal processes on global economic, political, and military processes or on supranational cultural processes. The only exception, albeit not with regard to the fixation on the nation-state, but in the central treatment of war and peace, is a specifically German (and Austrian) tradition of historical humanities and political science. Yet, this tradition cannot simply be drawn on, given its strong connection to the glorification of power and chauvinism. If one criticizes classic sociology for neglecting to deal with international relations, one must at the same time ask whether the Enlightenment's optimism with respect to peace was a worthless illusion that had necessarily to be abandoned in favor of a realism based on power politics or whether it can be made the subject of a serious reconstruction.

II. THE AGE OF ENLIGHTENMENT

Thought on the conditions for peace began, of course, long before the Enlightenment. The late Middle Ages, at least, engendered a series of attempts to make the Christian religion, which linked the peoples of Europe, the core of a peaceful order patterned after the ancient Pax Romana. Such attempts, of course, hardly focused on the non-Christian world; and when they did, the conditions of a Christian peace would seem not to apply to it. It was the thinkers of the Renaissance as well as some from the radical sects of the Reformation who created a universalistic orientation toward peace. The historical impact of this was widespread and left its mark on many aspects of life in the North American colonies. The predominant line of development, however, lies in the subsequent period, namely in the consolidation of the territorial and/or nation-states of Europe and in the development of the ideology of the raison d'état and the balance of power. The discourse on peace can to a certain extent be regarded as a relatively quiet voice of the outsider being raised against the status quo; at this time it was the way of thinking for which standing armies and perpetual conflicts of interest between the states became ever more a matter of course. The reemergence of the issue of peace in France during the early Enlightenment was perceived

by contemporaries as abstruse rumination. Although the author of the early Enlightenment's most famous utopian vision of peace—the Abbé de St. Pierre—cannot complain that his proposals failed to attract any attention, the crude and polemic retorts were initially clearly the order of the day.

Nevertheless, it was the Enlightenment, which generated the first serious attempts to base the possibility of lasting peace on a change in the internal substance of the state, that continues to have an influence on the social sciences even today. A total of at least five such approaches can be discerned; they set their sights on guaranteeing peace respectively by means of the expansion of free trade, the founding of republics, the development of industrial society, the establishment of socialism, and, last, the existence of stable nuclear alliances. All of them have been, at least in the very basic form in which they were initially presented, sullied by historical events. This is not to say that they were falsified in some simplistic fashion. Their overall claims, however, were dashed by the emergence of wars which they had not foreseen and the causes of which apparently contradicted the expectations that had been nourished by theory.

The two oldest relevant models in the social sciences are associated with the names of Immanuel Kant and Adam Smith. Adopting motifs from Rousseau, Kant established a link between the capacity of the state for peace and its internal structure and spoke in terms of the peaceful nature of republics. His concept of the republic, however, was not at all aimed at deposing the monarch, but rather signified the constitutionalization and juridification of the power of the monarch. The well-understood interests of the citizens would have the effect of helping to avoid war and promote mutually beneficial relations between the states if these interests were only taken into account when making foreign policy decisions. On this point this "republican" model corresponds to the other great peace model that was represented in the emerging political economy. Adam Ferguson and Adam Smith sought to establish the pacifying impacts of free trade. It was, after all, possible to effect a peaceful exchange of needed goods instead of mutual threat, destruction, and pillage; the expansion of these exchange relations would serve the interests of both sides and render war superfluous.

However, both models soon ran into difficulty due to historical developments. This comes most blatantly to light in the case of Kant's position, which was totally in keeping with "republican" thinking in general, both in Germany and in France. Just after 1789, hopes in France were high that the revolution would also be a step toward eliminating the cabinet wars of the 18th century. Thus, a republican victory in the wars that were being waged against France by the monarchies of Europe would have been a contribution toward the emergence of a peaceful world. Instead, the increasingly offensive character of the French war campaign plunged the republican model of peace into a severe crisis. It was in particular the German intellectuals of the time who discussed the consequences of this state of affairs. Was it right for revolutionary France to use violent means to convert other states into republics and should the intellectuals who sympathized with the revolution support expansion of this revolution by armed force? After Napoleon's victory over Prussia in 1806, this issue necessarily became even more acute. It was now these same progressive intellectuals who began to regard the strengthening of a German national consciousness and, to an increasing degree, the armed struggle against the occupying forces as the only political conclusion. The justification of national consciousness still contained universalistic elements, yet the hope for a future peaceful world no longer played a role. As a result, in a peculiar about-turn, that philosophy gained the upper hand in the peace debate, which expected peace to come both from eliminating France as source of unrest through reinstating the legitimate monarchy and from a new balance of power coordinated in the spirit of a reinforced Christendom. The question as to how strong the break was between the justification of war and the philosophy of peace as based on natural rights and the universalistic ideals of the Enlightenment is an important issue for assessing the further development of German thought of the 19th century.

Smith's theory of replacing war with free trade was not at all as simple as it sounded. He was well aware that even communities engaged in trade still remained dependent on military protection indefinitely just as he was conscious of the question as to how trade between states that were totally different in terms of their military strength could be kept free of the influence of this strength. On the whole, however, his optimism in peace-making policy surely predominated. After all, free trade itself bolstered those social strata within society that opposed the traditionally bellicose nobility. The free-trade, liberalist model of peace, however, had a covert particularistic undertone. For the hopes for peace it nourished were usually not truly universalistic but, rather, limited to the circle of "civilized" people. Thomas More had already declared that such a war as was waged against a people that leaves land untilled while denying others use of that land was just. In many cases, "savages" were expressly excluded from the pro-

posals intended to foster peace. As an exception, Bentham had, as a consistent free trader, demanded as early as the end of the 18th century that the colonies be dispensed with; otherwise, it was to be feared that, even after curbing the power of war-mongering aristocrats, conflict over the colonies would give rise to ever more wars. In England, discussions that focused on peace and the appeal for free trade remained closely linked. For this very reason, those outside England felt that free trade in many cases merely served the interests of what was at that time the most economically and technologically advanced nation (England) and that it was therefore by no means simply an outgrowth of universalistic thinking.

III. MARXISM

In the 19th century the two models of peace discussed above were joined by two additional models, both of which were also closely linked to the ideals of the Enlightenment. Marxism took the stance against the non-constitutional state's lack of a capacity for peace and leveled it at capitalism: it was not the republic but socialism that provided the social conditions for peace. Capitalism is ascribed a violent and expansive character; the struggle to overthrow capitalism thus goes hand in hand with the struggle for peace. This is why the Marxist-inspired movements have always regarded pacifist policies that did not give priority to critiquing capitalism or efforts to reach a peaceful settlement of international conflicts at the level of international law with a fair degree of arrogance. The late Engels, however, showed a new receptivity to both a nonviolent upheaval within society and to the prospects for European disarmament. More recent Marxist attempts have been able to draw on this and have attested to the capacity for peace that capitalism, at least in principle, exhibits in the nuclear age. Mainstream Marxist thought, however, is shaped by the diverse attempts to draw up a theory of imperialism; this line of reasoning was developed immediately prior to the First World War and found its view that capitalism inexorably drifts into an imperialistic *stage*—in which conflict between the major "imperialist" powers is inevitable—confirmed by this war. This view of things determined the way people thought after the First World War and extended far into the social democratic camp, where admittedly older Enlightenment models of peace continued to have an effect. It was fueled by the impression that the foreign policy of the Soviet Union, being the only socialist state, was—

regardless of what one thought of the precise nature of this socialism—nonaggressive and aiming toward peace.

Outside the socialist and communist movements, the fear of a revolution within society of course allied itself early on with the fear that such a rebellion could be incited or supported by the Soviet Union or the Communist International. Within the working class movement, however, the Hitler–Stalin Pact of 1939 was the event that undeniably shook the foundations of those things that had hitherto been taken for granted. This was true not only for the members of the resistance who were fighting the Nazis within the Third Reich but was also exemplified by the abrupt cessation of all contacts made with a view to possible cooperation between the German Social Democratic and the German Communist Parties. It was true above all for the exponents of Marxist thought. The entire range of reactions can be understood if one takes a look at the controversy between Rudolf Hilferding, the Social Democrat and theoretician of "Finance Capital," and Walter Ulbricht, the later Communist leader of the East German State. At the end of 1939, convinced that Hitler's Germany and the Soviet Union of Stalin were hand in glove, Hilferding concluded that both had totalitarianism in common and that social democracy consequently had to take up the cause of supporting Great Britain and France in the fight against both of them. Ulbricht reacted to this with a polemical attack that attracted international attention; in it he characterized British imperialism as the principal enemy. Precisely because of its willingness to establish a pact with the Soviet Union, Nazi Germany, as Ulbricht saw it, had become the less aggressive form of imperialism. This, of course, demonstrated not only the bankruptcy of the Marxist theory of imperialism, which was completely functionalized to serve as a justification for Soviet foreign policy, but also its profound lack of consideration for the autonomous significance of democracy and constitutionality for an assessment of the capacity of states for peace. The German attack on the Soviet Union in 1941 albeit led to a renewed shift in emphasis, as now the principal opposition to fascism was again undisputed. Yet Soviet policy in Eastern and Central Europe after the Second World War, and especially in the cases of military intervention to repress internal reform movements in socialist states (Hungary, 1956, and Czechoslovakia, 1968), provoked large-scale discussions on both occasions about the capacity of socialism for peace; the simple thesis that eliminating the interests of the capitalist military–industrial complex would result in peace was, in any case, put to a hard test and gradually lost any credibility.

For the generation who rediscovered Marxism in the 1960s and 1970s and in so doing helped it to undergo a renaissance, with the exception of the suppression of the "Prague Spring" the events outlined above were already too far back in time to leave their mark on political perceptions. For this generation, the military conflicts between the socialist states (above all, between China and the Soviet Union) as well as the Soviet intervention in Afghanistan in 1979 played a decisive role. For many former Marxists this meant a simple switch, for they adopted a realism of power politics or even one of geopolitical power. This transformation is not all that plausible, since, despite all the evident gaps in the explanatory power of a peace model centered on capitalism or "imperialism," the basic question as to the internal economic, social, and political prerequisites for a capacity for peace in foreign policy cannot simply be abandoned.

IV. CLASSIC SOCIOLOGY

The theory of the peaceful nature of industrial society was constitutive for sociology. Auguste Comte and Herbert Spencer, the academic outsiders who propagated sociology as a new science without being able to give it institutionalized academic foundations, undoubtedly perpetuated the peace-oriented thinking of the Enlightenment by attempting to prove the peaceful character of the nascent industrial society. Spencer's distinction between two types of society, namely the "militant society" and the "industrial society," was particularly influential. According to Spencer, in the society of the militant type primacy was accorded to the collective capacity for violent action toward the outside. Such a society, he claimed, as a consequence completely subordinated the individual to a collective purpose; domination was structured around a unilinear hierarchy. By contrast, the industrial society tolerated relationships between individuals that were entered on a voluntary, contractual basis. In such a polity, individualism and the market flourish; the structure of domination is decentralized and multipolar. Such a polity aims externally at entering contractual relations with other polities for the purpose of mutual benefit. The evolutionist assumption that the "militant society" will inevitably die out may seem incredibly optimistic to us today; however, these assumptions were representative of the 19th century social sciences, especially in England and the United States. Even classic Marxism is more closely in tune with the optimism of these assumptions than may appear at first sight. It merely moves the dawning of the age of peace up one step in history, as it were: in this system, only the socialist industrial society is in itself peaceful in principle, not the capitalist society. The path leading to such a state leads via internal social changes, with an emphasis on violence. The success of these changes, however, as Engels puts it in *Anti-Dühring*, is evolutionistically guaranteed, for example, by the internal dissolution of capitalist militarism owing to the increasing inability to finance the arms burden and the arming of the class-conscious proletariat, which goes hand in hand with compulsory conscription. The period between 1815 and 1914, which was interrupted by only a few small wars, could serve as evidence supporting the assumption that industrial societies are peaceful. For this reason, the outbreak of the First World War was a severe shock in that it called the philosophy of history behind the social sciences into question. Even if the war as such did not contradict expectations, the course it took was the source of profound irritations.

The reaction of contemporary German sociologists to the First World War is extraordinarily interesting, particularly with regard to the various ways the cult of war and chauvinism deformed the glorious tradition of German historical thought in the humanities and political science; however, it is least revealing with regard to the intrinsic problems of the thesis that industrial society is peaceful. For this thesis was least widespread in Germany; generally speaking, the German founders of sociology took a contemptuous view of Comte and Spencer and were far removed from liberalism and positivism. Werner Sombart, Max Weber, and Georg Simmel can be treated here as three clearly distinguishable types. Whereas Sombart had put forward a substantial social scientific theory about the connection between war and capitalism prior to the outbreak of World War I, during the war he boiled this down to the fateful struggle between British utilitarian commercialism and German antiutilitarian heroism. Although Max Weber steered clear of such hyperbolizations of the War in terms of the philosophy of history, he, too, failed to develop any sociological analyses of the emergence and impact of war. Those of his publications that directly intended to have a political influence are pioneering achievements in the analysis of the link between the internal constitution of a state and the capacity for action in foreign policy. Georg Simmel, in turn, interprets the War only in terms of aesthetics and a philosophy of life and believes that the experience of war offers a possible escape from the tragedy of modern culture. Nor do the other authors of the period offer anything to overcome this failure of sociology; the only

exception is the work of Emil Lederer, who does not fall prey to unrestrained speculations about either the question of war guilt or the meaning of the war. Rather, he attempts a sociological interpretation of the surprising features of the war, namely the concept of total war and an increasingly autonomous war machinery.

The positions taken by the major sociologists of other countries at this time were just as favorable to their own respective national causes as they understood them. Yet, the relationship between such nationalistic positions and the universalistic Enlightenment ideals of a peaceful world order took a different form. In his political writings Emile Durkheim, the leading sociologist in France, did not believe that the War sounded the death knell for the pacifist ideal; rather, he regarded a victory for France as a contribution to the end of militarism and a step toward the ultimate triumph of peace. Theoretically, Durkheim differed from Spencer in predicting that the disappearance of war in industrial society would occur gradually and not in leaps and bounds. In a view that was nevertheless optimistic and evolutionist, Durkheim assumed a progressive adjustment from the continuous state of war in primitive communities to the permanent legislation of modern societies. But Durkheim failed to face up to the problem that a state structured by and through a legislative body could very well take a stand toward the outside world as a power-state bound by no law. Thus the events of the War proved too unwieldy for his categorizations. Durkheim could only attempt to prevent his normative ideals from being sucked into the vortex of nationalistic ideologies.

American sociological thought at the time was characterized less by a belief that followed Spencer in promulgating the pacifying effects of individualistic contractual freedom and more by taking a specific understanding of the republic and democracy and transposing them onto an international context. According to this view, the steadily progressing process of internationalization in economy and the sciences would no longer permit a mere coexistence of the states. The only alternative to solving conflicts without institutions, and this would always tend to be a violent solution, consisted in establishing a moral and legal level at which international disputes could be settled peacefully. For these sociologists, the outbreak of war was especially shocking since it contradicted their assumption of orderly progress and their strongly evolutionist belief in a decided trend toward the dissemination of democracy throughout the world. And indeed, the events of war in Europe were initially interpreted as being anachronistic, as the expression of European backwardness; it went without saying that America should stay out of such a war. During the course of the War, however, a line of argumentation became ever more prevalent which advocated America's entering the War on the side of the Allies, for which it perceived a universalistic justification. Joining the cause of democracy and abolishing war by setting up a League of Nations and guaranteeing the right to self-determination for the small nations—these were, however, entirely noble war objectives in the eyes of American reformist intellectuals.

The consequences of America's entrance into the War on domestic policy, however, dashed all hopes that the War would provide an opportunity for reform. The analysis of the War gave rise to a few fruitful approaches in the social sciences which were derived, above all, from the assumption that a relationship existed between "democracy" and "peace." For the most part, however, these approaches considered the socio-psychological level: here the possibility of social integration through loyalty-fostering participation in public and consequential processes of will formation was contrasted with integration via opposition to external or internal enemies. With a few exceptions—such as in Thorstein Veblen's 1917 book *The Nature of Peace and the Terms of Its Perpetuation*, for example—the relative weight of such sociopsychological factors, however, was only seldom considered in relation to economic, political, or military-technological factors in American social science at that time. It is interesting that Veblen quite clearly assumed that tension exists between democracy and capitalism. He views this as one of the reasons for modern nationalism to the extent that nationalism is promoted by the powers that be out of fear of demands for social equality. On the whole, however, he, too, considers nationalism obsolete and not modern enough or promising for the future. Here the sociopsychological considerations are not developed into an analysis of modern nationalism and the significance it had in the War.

V. THE SOCIAL SCIENCES AFTER WORLD WAR II

The four models of peace mentioned—free trade, the republican order, socialism, and the industrial society—continued to have a great deal of influence in modified form even after the end of the Second World War. However, all of them increasingly gave way to the realism of power politics. Just as the nuclear-armed superpowers and the alliances they set up confronted each other since the beginning of the Cold War, so,

too, did the "proletarian internationalism" of the one side and the democratic universalism of the other appear to be diametrically opposed, hostile, and mutually exclusive alternatives. In reality, both positions increasingly deteriorated into legitimatory ideologies that served the objectives of realists in the sphere of power politics. Although many social scientists made various declarations of their personal beliefs with regard to the problems of war and peace during the Cold War, or confessed that they could at best beat a retreat in the face of the intimidating horrors of nuclear strategies, they only rarely contributed more extensive analyses. The representative theorist of the time, Talcott Parsons, made little if any comment on the Cold War in the framework of his studies, and when he did, the statements did not go much beyond noting that international relations had become institutionalized to a slight degree. As leading representatives of Neo-Parsonianism themselves concede, Parsons not only had difficulty dealing with the present but also with the historical role of war when it came to fitting it into the framework of his evolutionary model based on the theory of differentiation. For in his theoretical framework, wars, like social movements, are only the agents of overarching processes of differentiation; at worst, they can divert or hinder the course of these processes in a minor way but cannot really have any decisive influence on them. For Parsons, there can be no question of such contingent processes of collective action constituting the direction or extent of differentiation.

The two most important voices in sociology during the 1950s and 1960s who consistently addressed the social meaning of war and the effects of the nuclear arms race were Raymond Aron and C. Wright Mills. Aron is being rediscovered in France and England with such enthusiasm because for decades he did not submit to the thematic repression of war-related problems and made an abundance of important contributions to the topic, both in his theoretical work and in his extensive political journalism. In his theories he always remained a neo-Clausewitzian strategic realist whose work can be helpful as an antidote to economic reductionists, but in my view it still cannot open up any approaches that take us further. Mills was the actual dissident in the "orthodox consensus" of an American-dominated sociology. His warning, which is still rousing today, on the "Causes of the Third World War" was based on his analysis of the power structures of American society in which he identified an elitist complex that controls military-strategic and general foreign policy decisions. This thesis of course proved to be too simple in empirical terms; his analysis of contemporary society focused too strongly on the opposition of the two superpowers and did not go into sufficient historical depth to warrant being adopted. Nevertheless, here was someone protesting against the carefree attitude with which the public and, implicitly, many social scientists believed in the stability of the system of deterrence. This belief was indeed very widespread. People called for at most the elimination of isolated elements that threatened the stability of this deterrence through arms control agreements; of course, the interest in the possibilities of conventional warfare below the nuclear threshold was kept alive in order to maintain the political scope for action.

VI. THE CONTEMPORARY THEORETICAL SITUATION

The situation changed fundamentally in the 1980s. For post-war theory—that is, the belief that peace is guaranteed through stable nuclear deterrence—this change plays the role of a "crisis experiment," which can, like the First World War, serve to make us aware of hidden assumptions. Innovations in weapons technology reduced the stability of deterrence or at least made us realize that radical destabilization is a possibility. This applies to the vision of a protective shield over the United States (Strategic Defense Initiative) as well as to new possibilities of a first-strike or limited nuclear war. The rapid escalation of international tensions in the early 1980s caused the populations of many European countries to become sensitive to the military nexus of conditions under which they lived. The extent of ecological problems that crossed all ideological bloc boundaries (Chernobyl) foreshadowed the need for global cooperation and to address the links between the economy, ecology, and armaments. All of these developments suggested that the world had moved beyond the deceptive security of this fifth model of peace, which in many ways is, of course, more similar to the old notion of a balance of power. From this viewpoint, the peace movements' most important contribution may have been that they once again rocked the foundations of power politics and generally reopened a public discourse about peace and war among citizens in an international context.

This debate was opened up, moreover, in a theoretical situation in which Marxism did not present itself as a convincing alternative. Major contributions by Marxists diverged greatly from the traditional ideas of Marxism; this is true of E. P. Thompson's thesis of an "exterminism," of an arms race that escalated primarily because of its own intrinsic dynamic and not because of economic or political interests, and it is equally true of Mary Kaldor's thesis of the "Baroque arsenal" with which she questioned the economic and military benefits of the new military technologies produced by the arms race. Most of the younger intellectuals in the social sciences, however, began, as already mentioned, to look more in the direction of Clausewitz and Aron or even to search for rejuvenated "geopolitical" views. The point is, however, that here all the elements of the peace models that are potentially worth preserving—even though they certainly cannot be upheld in their entirety—are lost in the process.

One way out of this situation is to undermine the too-easy identification of social order and nation-state. Indeed, in particular Alain Touraine and Anthony Giddens have called attention to the fact that tacit identification of the abstract concept "society" with the concrete reality of territorially delineated nation-states tends to obscure rather than shed light on the dependency of social processes on economic, political, military, and cultural complexes of an international nature. In classic sociology, the relationship between state and society as expressed is not reflected upon in terms of its historical and geographical particularity. Relativizing the concept of society implies that the widest variety of social processes can be analyzed using the category of action and thus suggests that the degree to which they exhibit a "systemic" character should not be prejudged in conceptual terms but rather be taken into account as being empirically variable. An approach that centers on the interweaving and intermeshing of actions and the consequences thereof yields a more differentiated picture than is afforded by the concept of system. The early transformation of Parsons' work in Etzioni's theory of the active society, Giddens's development of a theory of structuration via a critique of Marxism, Castoriadis's and Touraine's contributions to a theory of institutionalization as a creative process, and Michael Mann's historical sociology of power are cases in point.

What all of these authors have in common is that they renounce the granting of privileged status to one particular domain of society that then supposedly holds the key to understanding the totality of that society. Giddens, for example, attempted to analytically separate the dimensions of capitalism, "industrialism," the organization of military power as well as internal "surveillance" and control, and to retain them as possible variables to one another. Castoriadis stressed especially that democracy is not to be viewed as a superstructure of capitalism, but rather that it represents an autonomous dimension of the history of humankind. Etzioni wanted to show how additional strata of inter- or supranational regulations are established above the level of the nation-state; against this background he appealed for a dismantling of the military blocs by means of regulated forms for their cooperation as opposed to their renewed disintegration into rivaling nation-states. Michael Mann consistently distinguishes between four sources of social power (ideological, military, economic, and political) and analyzes societies as organized power networks. The program of such a family of theoretical approaches permits us to set our sights on integrating the assumptions of the models of peace in the social sciences and the social philosophy discussed above. Despite the fact that all of them were shaken by historical events, this is no reason to cast them aside. The theory of the peaceful character of industrial society, at least with respect to the process of internal pacification, which extends all the way to "civilizing" the military complex, has, after all, largely been proved correct in this narrower sense today. Kant's idea of republicanism still raises important questions with regard to the public control of foreign policy as a condition for its defensiveness. The Marxist assumptions regarding the interests of the capitalist defense industry are not mere figments of the imagination. Free trade and the prevention of both protectionism and export monopolies have essentially contributed to peaceful relations between the Western industrial societies. However, it is necessary to reflect in theoretical terms on the relative accuracy of every single explanation and to bring it to bear in the narrative totality of the analysis of the causes of war. Thus, it is surely too simple to explain the First World War in terms of the conflict of interests of various imperialist powers, the autocratic character of the German Reich, the existence of distinct export monopolies or Europe's backwardness in relation to the United States as various people did at the time. The combination of the rational core of the various approaches into one "integrated" concept of peace is the task of the day.

Also See the Following Articles

BALANCE OF POWER RELATIONSHIPS • COLONIALISM AND IMPERIALISM • ECONOMIC CAUSES OF WAR AND PEACE • EVOLUTIONARY THEORY • MILITARY CULTURE • NUCLEAR WARFARE • PEACE AND DEMOCRACY • POLITICAL ECONOMY OF VIOLENCE AND NONVIOLENCE • TRADE, CONFLICT, AND COOPERATION AMONG NATIONS • WORLD WAR

Bibliography

Doyle, M. W. (1997). *Ways of war and peace*. New York: W. W. Norton.

Giddens, A. (1985). *The nation-state and violence*. Cambridge, MA: Polity.

Joas, H., & Steiner, H. (1989). *Machtpolitischer Realismus und pazifistische Utopie: Krieg und Frieden in der Geschichte der Sozialwissenschaften*. Frankfurt/Main: Suhrkamp.

Johnson, J. T. (1987). *The quest for peace*. Princeton, NJ: Princeton University Press.

Mann, M. (1988). *States, war and capitalism*. Oxford, UK: Blackwell.

Senghaas, D. (1992). *Friedensprojekt Europa*. Frankfurt/Main: Suhrkamp.

Sociological Studies, Overview

Metta Spencer

University of Toronto

I. Peace and Conflict in Social Thought
II. Explaining or Managing Acts of Violence

GLOSSARY

Anomie A state of normlessness in society, most commonly occurring during periods of dramatic social change.

Dependency Theory The theory that under the capitalist system, economic development can take place in one country only if another country is kept underdeveloped, thus accounting for the widening economic gap between developed and underdeveloped nations.

Functionalism The belief that a social pattern is best understood in terms of the regular functions that it serves in a given society.

Noninstitutionalized Violence Violent actions that are carried out by individuals or groups acting independently without coordination or normative regulation.

Revolution Political conflicts aimed at changing the regime of a whole society.

THE TOPICS of this encyclopedia—violence, peace, conflict, and war—are all common objects of sociological research, though not equally so. Peace, for example, is infrequently the main theme of articles or books, whether one defines the term narrowly (as the mere absence of organized warfare) or broadly (as societywide harmony resulting from the prevalence of justice).

Violence, on the other hand, is a matter of widespread research and refers predominantly to the actual use or immediate threat of bodily injury as a form of intimidation. The sociologists who devote the most attention to the study of violence tend to be those who focus on its manifestations at the individual level or at the level of small groups, such as criminal gangs. Fewer analyze organized, institutionalized violence (warfare) and, among those few who do study war, there has been more interest in studying revolutions and other internal struggles than international wars. Finally, conflict is one of the main topics of sociology and therefore it will be our main topic in this article. Of the countless types of conflict, most do not involve warfare or even violence, but occur as everyday struggles between parents and children, say, or industrial firms and unions. Such battles often constitute the main objects of sociological research, though we shall devote less attention to these mundane conflicts here than to the more violent military activities. However, before addressing any empirical research along these lines, let us briefly review the major theories that inform sociological scholarship in matters of peace, conflict, and violence.

I. PEACE AND CONFLICT IN SOCIAL THOUGHT

Although rather few social theorists have sought to explain those conditions that are here termed peace, a great many have discussed a comparable condition that they call social order. For present purposes, we will not be amiss if we read the term social order as a synonym for peace in its broader definition: as societal harmony.

A. Peace as Social Order in Functionalist Theory

The most influential book on social order is Talcott Parsons's early masterpiece *The Structure of Social Action,* which outlined the framework for a generation of sociologists who called themselves "functionalists." Although not many sociologists today base their research on functionalism, most of them still do accept Parsons's account of how social order is maintained. He depicted this condition of societal integration (without calling it "peace") by contrasting it to the "war of all against all" that, according to Thomas Hobbes, is the natural condition of humankind in the absence of government. Parsons asserted that the primary theme of social theorists has been the effort to explain how social order is possible: In view of the infinite variety of goals toward which people may hypothetically aspire, how do they generally manage to curb their impulses; arrive at consensus; coordinate their joint activities, and produce orderly, stable, harmonious groups?

To Parsons, the key to social order was "normative regulation." In a well-ordered society individuals supposedly acquire their personal goals, as well as certain norms and values, by "internalizing" rules upheld within their social group, thereby minimizing conflicts—perceived incompatibilities between their wishes and the expectations of others. When functionalist theorists try to explain why a certain group emphasizes one particular value over other possible values, they usually argue that it contributes usefully to the maintenance of the group as a whole. And when functionalists have to explain violations of societal norms (such as criminal practices or individual unauthorized use of violence) they usually refer in the first instance to the inadequacy of the rule-breaker's upbringing or "socialization."

Socialization research is useful for explaining variations in degrees of personal, individual cooperativeness that we would recognize as peaceable behavior. To understand the maintenance of cooperative interaction as a system, however, social researchers must deal with social institutions and organizations. Each organization is structured by rules that are generally observed during peaceful interactions, and societies offer institutional mechanisms for handling infractions of those rules. At the societal level, the most conspicuous of these mechanisms is the legal system, which resolves disputes, judges who is responsible for blameworthy actions (crimes or "torts"—actions that inadvertently harm others or their interests), and imposes punishment or restitution for damages.

Preindustrial societies may not have formal laws and systems of law enforcement, but they do have other institutions of social control, such as the practice of convening village elders who are authorized to administer justice and restore peace to a community.

At the international level, legal institutions are not well developed. There are international laws, which are created through treaties between states, as well as recognized by custom. There are also a few law-making international bodies, such as the European Parliament, but these institutions are not as well-recognized as national legislative systems. The United Nations General Assembly, for example, cannot be regarded as a world parliament, for its decisions are not binding, and there are limited mechanisms of enforcement. There is a world court (the International Court of Justice), but countries are often able to ignore its decisions. An International Criminal Court is being created and will judge serious personal offenses such as war crimes. When all these international institutions become well-established, they will be the most important means of protecting peace, just as law-enforcement institutions at the local level are the most important ways of keeping peace in a neighborhood or province. You and I do not get into fist-fights about noisy parties or broken contracts; we complain to the police or go to court instead. In the same way, international law can become the main institution replacing warfare in the century ahead.

It was Parsons and the other functionalists who called sociological attention to the legal system and the other institutions that maintain social order. Today, even though functionalism has been almost abandoned, its account of social order still prevails, since no alternative sociological account of order been proposed that is markedly more satisfactory. However, its theoretical critics have long accused functionalists of portraying harmony and equilibrium as the usual state of human affairs and therefore focusing too little attention on conflicts. The main critics of functionalists tend to prefer one of the several versions of conflict theory, all of which pay particular attention to the great difficulty of fitting together the many contradictory objectives that may exist in any group.

B. Conflict Theory

Conflict theorists point out that we can find as much conflict as harmony or peace in society. In contrast to functionalists, they do not suppose that it is often easy to reconcile the opposing interests in situations of conflict. Here we shall discuss three influential variants of conflict theory: those initially elaborated by Karl Marx, Georg Simmel, and Max Weber. We shall also pay attention to a few more recent scholars who have continued to draw on their insights.

1. From Revolutionary Communism to World System Theory

Karl Marx's famous views contrast sharply with the functionalist views described above, for he viewed history as shaped by the process of class conflict. Social classes are groups of people who confront similar life circumstances because they have a similar relationship to the means of production. For example, some classes consist of people who own factories or land, while other classes consist of workers, who have nothing to sell except their own labor. Marx (1818–1883) did not endorse the functionalist notion that a common set of values guides all members of a single society in the direction of mutuality. On the contrary, when harmony seemed to prevail in a particular society, it meant to Marx that the workers probably were unaware of their own true interests, for a full grasp of reality would impel them to struggle against the social class that was exploiting them.

Marx not only recognized that conflict was a basic part of social life; he even joined the workers in their struggle against the owners, expecting it to culminate in a revolution that would usher in a new social order to supersede class conflicts. Though he certainly did not minimize the suffering that accompanied violent conflict, he regarded it as frequently necessary for human advancement and therefore as a struggle to be fought and won—not avoided, suppressed, or papered over with pacifist or religious rhetoric.

The 20th century has been the age of Marxism. Billions of human lives have been shaped (or ended) by policies carried out in his name. After the breakdown of communist regimes, intellectuals of the 21st century may be less receptive to Marxism than those of the 20th. Nevertheless, some elements of his theories have

so deeply penetrated the discourse of social science that his influence will continue for a long time, even among persons who do not consider themselves Marxist.

Marx recognized that social injustice kills more people than bullets or bombs. For that reason he regarded the mere absence of war as an inadequate objective. In fact, he preferred war (revolution) over an unjust peace—at least whenever, by revolting, the oppressed classes can improve their long-term prospects and create peace with justice. In this respect, Marxism probably offers a useful corrective to the facile imagery of the functionalists, whose thin concept of "social order" may mistakenly portray a situation as peaceable when in fact oppressed people are docile only because they have too little power to defend their own interests.

However, Marx the theorist has been dead for more than a century, and obviously history has not turned out as he had predicted. Other theorists have revised his ideas in a number of ways but even their revised predictions have rarely turned out as expected. Contrary to Marx's theory, for example, workers in capitalist countries have not become constantly more impoverished; their standards of living have actually improved. Moreover, communist revolutions have not taken place in advanced industrial societies, as he expected, but only in countries that were just beginning to industrialize. Had the Bolshevik revolutionaries acted in accordance with Marx's vision of the future, they would not have attempted to capture the Russian state and create the Soviet Union, which had only a small industrial working class. However, their leader, V. I. Lenin, adapted Marxism to suit his more urgent ambitions. Drawing upon a small point in Marx's Capital, he elaborated his own theory of imperialism.

In Marx's day each European capitalist country dominated overseas colonies as sources of raw materials for its industries and as markets for its finished products. Lenin took this observation as a basis for his theory of imperialism, arguing that any capitalist country always had to keep increasing its overseas holdings to maintain a constantly expanding market and opportunities for foreign investments. The capitalist countries, competing for imperialistic control of those colonies, would engage in warfare among themselves. By looting the colonies they might even be able to raise the living standards of workers in their own countries and postpone the day when profits would vanish and angry workers would carry out the communist revolution that Marx had predicted.

Lenin's theory of imperialism enabled Marxists to defend their doctrine for a long time, despite unexpected circumstances. This theoretical revision recast the class struggle as a struggle between nations that differed in terms of their class structure.

When most colonies gained formal independence after World War II, their people initially expected to become rich by developing industries of their own. As this hope dwindled, the theory that seemed best to explain their problem was "dependency theory"—a conflict theory that bore a strong resemblance to Lenin's theory of imperialism. Thus according to dependency theorist Andre Gunder Frank, many of the former colonies remained in much the same economic relationship to their European capitalist rulers as before gaining political independence and, indeed, were not "developing" economically but actually "underdeveloping"—going downhill. Their only prospect of improving their circumstances depended on their escaping from these exploitive economic relationships and regaining control of own systems of production and distribution.

Dependency theory became popular in the socialist countries, for it allowed the Soviets, for example, to claim that they were offering support to poor countries all over the world by providing them with the weapons and aid they needed to liberate themselves from the capitalist nations.

By the late 1970s, however, many of the "underdeveloping" countries had become disillusioned with their socialist allies, who for their part were clearly falling behind in the competition against capitalism. Moreover, some of the former colonies (such as Singapore and Hong Kong) that had retained close ties to capitalist societies had become extremely prosperous instead of "underdeveloping" as predicted. By the time the Soviet Union abandoned Marxism, dependency theory seemed largely discredited among those in the socialist bloc who had drawn on it as a rationale for the maintaining the defensive wariness and militarism that constituted the Cold War.

By then, however, dependency theory had changed somewhat in the West, where it still remains influential as a theory of international conflict. It has been absorbed into an approach called world system theory, which bears somewhat less resemblance to Marx's original writings. Where dependency theory began by portraying relationships between pairs of countries—one in the capitalist center, the other a former colony in the underdeveloped "periphery"—world system theory portrays all the nations of the planet as constituting a single interdependent system, all experiencing the effects of an increasingly globalized market. Moreover, world system theorists deny that the socialist bloc had remained unaffected by this global capitalist market. And finally, although world system theory predicts

nothing comparable to Marx's revolution of industrial workers, it does anticipate that international relations will continue to be marked by conflict and even violence. The world system approach is probably the most influential version of conflict theory today.

2. From Georg Simmel to Lewis Coser

Georg Simmel (1858–1918) was a German social theorist whose ideas were imported to the Chicago School of sociology by one of his former students, Robert E. Park. Later Simmel's ideas about conflict were systematized and promoted by Lewis A. Coser.

Simmel held that both conflict and cooperation are present in all human relationships. He analyzed what he called "the web of conflict"—the interdependence of cooperation and conflict. For example, whenever the conflict between two groups increases, one of the effects is usually to increase solidarity and cooperation within each of those groups. Modern society brings people into amazingly complex relationships because of the multiple groups to which we belong. We may be allies in one situation but opponents in another.

Though Simmel did not call it so, he introduced the concept of "cross-cutting cleavages"—a notion that other sociologists often use when trying to explain why conflict increases or decreases. For example, pluralist theorists claim that democracy is more stable in societies where people experience numerous cross-cutting cleavages. Democracy is unstable in polarized settings where a person's opponents on one issue tend to be her opponents on all other issues as well. Suppose you and I belong to different ethnic communities, each of which has its own language, religion, cuisine, and economic traditions. Our conflicts are likely to be intense because when we discuss almost any topic, you and I may disagree.

On the other hand, suppose you and I are on opposite sides of a dispute today in our committee meeting but we know that tomorrow we will be singing together in the same glee club or playing on the same soccer team. With this ambivalent relationship, we are likely to criticize each other only mildly, if at all. Whenever many people in a society are in such social structures that produce many ambivalent relationships, the prevailing spirit tends to be one of tolerance and moderation, making it easier to find a democratic compromise.

Simmel had only limited influence on political theorists, but quite a lot of influence on scholars studying ethnic conflict—a topic that was the special preoccupation of Robert E. Park and his fellow sociologists of the Chicago School during the first decades of the 20th century. The comparative weakness of Simmel's position among political theorists may have resulted from a weakness in his analysis: his tendency not to distinguish very clearly between conflict and violence. Though he was correct in noting the impossibility of eliminating conflict from social life, it is a mistake to conclude that the elimination of violence from society is also impossible. Societies differ considerably in the frequency with which their members resort to personal violence and their states resort to warfare. Some sophisticated modern societies have not experienced a war for several hundred years and, according to ethnographers, in some preindustrial societies (e.g., the Mbuti pygmies and the Semai) even personal acts of violence have been rare. Methods of managing conflict vary in countless nonviolent ways, ranging, say, from Amerindian ritual meetings in a sacred sweat lodge to billion-dollar lawsuits between huge corporations. Professional peace researchers all emphasize the distinction between conflict and violence. The whole objective of their discipline is to improve social institutions so as to enable people to wage their inevitable conflicts in noninjurious ways. The main shortcoming of Simmel's theory may have been its failure to hold that up as a realistic objective.

Lewis Coser's (b. 1913) work was so closely related to Simmel's that we need not try, for present purposes, to distinguish sharply between their approaches, except to note that Coser has distinguished more clearly between conflict and violence. Like Simmel, he has shown that frequently conflict has positive effects for a social group that undergoes it. For example, it can provide a safety valve in times of increasing tension, while at other times it stimulates innovations.

Unlike many other conflict theorists, however, Coser acknowledges that not all conflicts are based on genuinely contradictory interests. Often he judges that a particular conflict is "nonrealistic"—i.e., carried on as an end in itself. Even revolutionary violence can be based more on a group's sense of its own identity than on its material interests.

On the other hand, conflicts within a group sometimes reestablish unity and balance to that group. For example, Coser suggests that the main explanation for the absence of a bitter class struggle in North American society is that its workers participate in so many varied groups that have smaller-scale conflict among them. The workers do not store up their energy for use in one single, highly divisive struggle.

Both Simmel and Coser add subtle extra dimensions to our understanding of conflict. However, neither of these writers offers a systematic theory that has proved particularly useful in predicting the outcome of situations fraught with potential conflict. So far, we do not have any abstract sociological theory that predicts whether a conflict will destroy the internal relationships of a group or result in the positive outcomes that Coser, in particular, likes to envisage.

3. From Max Weber to Randall Collins

Max Weber (1864–1920) was a German scholar with whom Simmel was personally acquainted, but the two men approached their research in dissimilar ways. Whereas Simmel looked for universal, abstract generalizations about human relations, Weber grounded his observations on detailed studies of specific historical cases.

Weber also differed even more significantly from Marx, some of whose conclusions he specifically tried to disprove. However, many sociologists have mistakenly exaggerated the differences between Weber and Marx, whose views actually coincided in a number of ways. For example, Weber recognized conflict in all the societies that he studied and believed that people can generally be counted on to pursue their own interests. Unlike Marx, however, he saw groups as forming on the basis of a varied combination of interests, some of which were symbolic, not material—which meant that not all intergroup conflicts could be reduced to class struggle. People who occupy high statuses on the basis of their education, religion, ethnicity, or culture sometimes go to great lengths to maintain their prestige and to keep their social distance from other groups whom they regard as their inferiors. While Marx would have been unable to explain the upsurge of race riots and nationalistic wars of secession in the late 20th century, these events might not have surprised Weber at all.

Weber did not consider that the only important interests are material ones, for he attributed some major social conflicts to ideological differences instead. In distinction to Marx, Weber also believed that ideas often had independent causal impact on historical outcomes. For example, to a considerable extent he attributed the rise of capitalism in Europe to the unique system of values and religious doctrines held by Calvinists.

Weber did not minimize the phenomenon of power and social domination. However, when a social group was able to dominate a subordinate group, he believed that this was often because the subordinates believed that they should obey the dominant group. Power is the ability to coerce others to do what they may not want to do, but power does not always have to show its violent basis. Often the subordinate regards the power as legitimate and obeys it willingly, in which case power manifests itself as "authority" instead of naked coercion.

Authority relations are necessary aspects of many different kinds of groups, including business firms, families, and (especially) states. To Weber, the state was always at bottom a structure of domination, and its domination rested on its ability to coerce—by the use of weapons, if it came to that. Indeed, a defining trait of the state was that it possessed a monopoly on the legitimate use of violence within a particular area. However, Weber also emphasized the dependence of state officials on rituals and conventions (e.g., robes and wigs for judges, flags and marching bands for prime ministers) by which they overawe the public and pump up their own legitimacy. Indeed, when the state has to resort to overt violence, its legitimacy may be vanishing and a rebellion may be in the offing.

In the Germany of his day, Weber was a politically active centrist who never supported the Marxist revolutionary goal of ultimately abolishing the state. He seemed to suppose that every society needs a government for the maintenance of its social order (we might say "peace") and that, to keep the peace, every government needs to use violence, at least occasionally. Ironically, we can see this apparent contradiction—that peace requires violence, while it also opposes violence—as an illustration of Simmel's main point: conflict (or even violence) is a necessary and inevitable component of all social life, including harmonious social life.

Weber is perhaps second only to Marx as an influence on other sociologists. Perhaps the most influential exponent of Weber's views is Randall Collins (b. 1941). Collins's own research has been organized to match Weber's concerns. Like Weber, Collins became interested in the ups and downs of large societies over lengthy periods of history. Unlike Weber, however, he has tended to explain their growth and decline primarily in military or geopolitical terms. He has noted that there are inherent logistical difficulties in the maintenance of a huge empire with military threats on its borders. The degree of difficulty varies according to the geography of the terrain, such as mountain ranges and seacoasts, but ultimately the sheer distance makes it impossible to maintain an empire after it has come to cover too wide an expanse. Indeed, Collins (who is capable of thinking like a general) became one of the very few social analysts who correctly predicted the break-up of the Soviet Union, and his reasoning was based on the observation that as an empire it had become militarily overextended. Having read numerous historical studies of other empires, he predicts that Russia will continue to crumble into smaller states over the next century or more.

C. From Grand Theory to Middle-Range Theories

We have considered four "classic" sociological approaches: the Parsonian version of functionalism and the conflict approaches of Marx, Simmel, and Weber. Each of these grand theories has its followers among contemporary scholars. Indeed, every sociologist needs to know about these "grand theories" because they provide a framework within which various traditions of scholarship are located. Most sociologists identify with one of these traditions, and by publicly identifying themselves along these lines, they tell us something about the unexpressed presuppositions about conflict that inform their own work.

On the other hand, ideally theories ought to be "falsifiable"—specific enough to yield concrete hypotheses that empirical research can disprove or provisionally uphold. To some extent, Marxism fulfilled this ideal, for as we have seen, few of Marx's predictions have come true, and his followers either have had to abandon his theory or revise it so as to derive predictions different from his own. Even so, Marxism will continue to influence much scholarly research on conflict in the future. Unlike Marxism, however, the other theories that we have considered are not concrete enough to yield many falsifiable predictions, though that fact does not make them irrelevant to contemporary research. Like Marxism, the writings of Weber and Simmel constitute general frameworks within which to interpret various outcomes more or less plausibly.

On the other hand, empirical researchers do not necessarily depend on these grand classic theories, for many of them work instead with "middle-range" theories, addressing questions that are relatively specific to particular problems and issues. From this point on we shall focus on some of these middle-range accounts of violence.

II. EXPLAINING OR MANAGING ACTS OF VIOLENCE

It is sometimes useful to distinguish between noninstitutionalized and institutionalized manifestations of violence. The noninstitutionalized forms include such events as rapes, barroom brawls, homicides, riots, and terrorism. The institutionalized forms include a society's coercive system (e.g., the police and jails) and warfare. Under the heading "war" we may also include all the organized activities that are required for the preparation and waging of violent conflict—e.g., an arms trade, the routine maintenance of a military apparatus; and propaganda to whip up public support for military action. Since more sociological research has been devoted to the noninstitutionalized forms of violence, let us consider it first.

A. Noninstitutionalized Violence

Homicide, rape, and wife-battering are examples of non-institutionalized violence: ordinarily they are carried out by individuals acting independently. It is theoretically possible, for course, for these activities to be planned and organized and, when they are performed in that way, we might consider them institutionalized. For example, the mafia is a criminal organization that sometimes orders its "hit men" to murder a specific person. Rape, too, is occasionally carried out as an organized act of war, as happened in Bosnia during the early 1990s and during World War II, when numerous foreigners were imprisoned to serve as "comfort women" for the Japanese troops. Nevertheless, those who perpetrate the vast majority of homicides, rapes, and acts of domestic violence do so without any planning and certainly without being ordered by a superior officer to do so. For that reason, sociologists tend to consider such acts as "noninstitutionalized"—indeed, as forms of deviant behavior. The study of deviance has been a major subfield within sociology for many years.

1. Deviance

Scholars have proposed a variety of theories to account for deviance—actions that violate norms. Deviant behavior ranges from such minor infractions as slurping soup in public to serious ones (e.g., embezzling funds or even serial killing). Violence is only a small part of the wider spectrum of deviance, albeit probably the most serious part. Sociologists often explain noninstitutionalized violence in terms of the same theories by which they explain, say, narcotic use, prostitution, or car theft. Let us consider three theories in this connection: anomie, cultural transmission, and social learning theories.

a. Anomie Theory

Anomie refers to a state of "normlessness" in society—a condition that occurs most frequently during periods of dramatic social change. The great French sociologist Emile Durkheim explained that anomie occurs when old institutions are no longer functioning in a stable way and people no longer can count on receiving the expected rewards for conforming to expected standards. Robert K. Merton later formalized Durkheim's theory

and tried to show how it might explain various dissimilar responses, some of which would be considered deviant. During an economic crisis, for example, unemployment may reach high levels, while there may be insufficient public funds or political will to pay adequate unemployment or welfare benefits. In other words, the goals toward which people have been taught to aspire (e.g., to achieve prosperity by holding a well-paid job) do not correspond to the institutionalized means that are actually available and the norms by which people are supposed to compete.

When this frustrating situation arises, people may respond in a variety of ways. Ideally they continue to conform to society's standards, despite the difficulties, by trying harder to get ahead while following the rules. Analysts of violence are particularly interested in two of those deviant types, whom Merton called respectively innovators (those who adopt illegal or disapproved ways of reaching success, such as robbing banks or cheating in business) and rebels (who withdraw allegiance to the existing social system, which they consider unjust, and seek to rebuild society along different lines). Both of these types may (but do not necessarily) resort to violence. Rebels and innovators are mainly social outsiders rather than mainstream members of society. They are portrayed as marginalized people in periods of upheaval when large populations are having to migrate or adapt to a societal crisis after old relationships have broken down and before stable new ones have developed.

Anomie theory sometimes seems to fit empirical reality, but sometimes not. Take terrorism, for example. Often the terrorist is not a marginalized social isolate, but a leading member of some cult or political group whose members are collectively estranged from the wider society, whether or not they ever have been individually excluded from mainstream society. Indeed, a terrorist often comes from a rather privileged background and might have become a prominent person in mainstream society. This is true of many political assassins, who think of themselves as guerrilla warriors and revolutionaries. In their own way, terrorists of this sort are self-sacrificing idealists; it is just that the ideals they espouse are contrary to those shared throughout the wider society. Sociologists can explain little about them in terms anomie theory, but do better by applying an alternative theory of deviance, subculture theory, also known as "cultural transmission theory."

b. Cultural Transmission Theory

Cultural transmission theory occupies a place in sociology that is just as distinguished as the anomie framework, against which it stands in sharp contrast. Anomie theory portrays society as culturally rather uniform; its members uphold a common set of goals and institutionalized means, though these may be in some temporary disarray. Cultural transmission theory, on the other hand, sees most societies as comprising disparate groups that uphold their own distinctive cultures. When a person conforms to one of those "subcultures," he or she may automatically appear to be a deviant from the perspective of people in most of the other subcultures. To mention only one example, some years ago, hundreds of American followers of a religious fanatic, Jim Jones, committed suicide and murdered their own children at their compound in Guyana, all believing that they would gain immortality by doing so. None of these people were social isolates; all of them were avid conformists to a subculture that was deviant from the standpoint of most nonmembers. According to cultural transmission theory, the more one is integrated into such a deviant subculture, the more likely one is to live by its standards, even when those standards are antisocial vis à vis other groups. Thus the same processes of affiliation and conformity explain how one person may become a terrorist, while his brother or sister becomes a pool shark or stamp collector: by associating with a group of terrorists, billiard players, or stamp collectors, as the case may be.

c. Social Learning Theory

If cultural transmission theory is almost incompatible with anomie theory, it is entirely compatible with social learning theory. In fact, any attempt to explain the mechanism by which subcultural groups influence their members will probably point out that people tend to imitate the social behavior that they see around them. This is the core principle of social learning theory, an explanatory model that informs much of the research conducted by social psychologists. It is based on the principle that people do not usually invent their behavior independently, but try out for themselves actions that they have seen; when they selectively choose to copy the behavior of another person, that person is sometimes called a "role model." Social learning theory has been applied in ways that go beyond any envisaged by cultural transmission theorists.

Emile Durkheim specifically tried to base his research on social facts—objective conditions in the society—just to show the unimportance of imitation (social learning) as an explanation of social behavior. His book *Suicide* proceeds by ruling out a variety of possible explanations of suicide before positing his own alternative explanation. One of the theories that he attempted

to refute is the notion of "contagion"—the direct imitation of exemplified behavior. He acknowledged that there are many instances when a given suicide seems to have been influenced by familiarity with another preceding suicide, but he denied that the outcome can be explained by the simple process of suggestion. Instead, he promoted the assumption (which has been widely held ever since by sociologists) that the act must be attributed to some structural features of the person's social world. It was Durkheim, of course, who developed the notion of anomie as an element in his own theory of suicide.

This structural emphasis is the subject of a renewed debate, as some sociologists have come to deny that Durkheim had a sufficient basis for rejecting the theory of contagion. Statistical evidence shows that violent acts are often imitated. Abusive parents were almost always abused as children themselves. Moreover, a well-publicized suicide or homicide ends to be followed in the region exposed to the publicity by a rash of subsequent suicides or homicides a week or so later. Famous fictional events seemingly can have similar effects. Additional evidence along these lines comes from epidemiological research on the effects of television violence, which suggests that an increase of televised violence, witnessed by children, is followed by an upsurge in the frequency of violent crimes a few years later when the initial cohort of children exposed to these actions reach adolescence and young adulthood. The case of South Africa is taken as evidence to that effect, for that country adopted television several years later than most other societies. Its upsurge in violent crime shows on graphs as a curve similar to that of other countries, except several years off-schedule—a delay that has been attributed to the preceding delay in television exposure. This conclusion is not accepted by all sociologists, many of whom continue to emphasize the structural factors that they claim lie behind and actually explain all the apparent influences of simple suggestion or contagion that give rise to violent actions.

This debate mirrors another long-standing debate concerning the relative independence of culture, as distinct from social structure, in shaping social behavior. Structural analysts tend to look for objective facts and to regard as incomplete those explanations based on modeling, imitation, cultural habits, or tradition. Those who, on the other hand, argue that cultural explanations are in themselves sufficient or compelling usually defend their reasoning by appealing to Max Weber. It was Weber whose explanations (in contrast to those of Marx and Durkheim) sometimes referred to cultural factors, as when, for example, he attributed the rise of capitalism in part to the culture of Calvinism. (Of course, Weber also offered many structural accounts as well.)

2. Collective Behavior and Social Movements

Besides the unorganized acts of individuals we must also consider certain spontaneous activities carried out by larger groups, especially by a crowd, such as riots. These unplanned, unorganized acts of group violence tend to be studied, not by specialists in deviance, but by sociologists who specialize in collective behavior. As in the studies of deviant behavior, early theorists tended to portray violence as the irrational doings of isolated, "atomized" individuals. There is a substantial early literature, for example, attributing social strife mainly to "mass societies"—those societies in which numerous members live unsettled lives because the old institutions have been disrupted and populations uprooted from traditional rural settings. "Mass society" theory was used, for example, to explain totalitarianism in Nazi Germany and the Stalinist Soviet Union.

There are cases that seem to fit this model, but perhaps more cases that do not. Charles Tilly, for example, has focused on the many acts of unplanned, noninstitutionalized violence that are better seen as political acts than as irrational acts of deviant or frustrated individuals. He has shown that the people who carry out these political acts usually are not isolated "atoms" in a "mass society," but people with considerable influence in their own communities.

Social movements are emergent group phenomena that have a longer duration than the single events constituting collective behavior. Social movements vary in specificity; some aim only to change a particular law, for instance, while others seek to change a general value of the society. A social movement is usually a self-limiting phenomenon that surges for a few years, then subsides. However, if movement activists are unable to change public opinion or official policies in their direction, they may turn to violence. Terrorism, for example, is usually performed by the extremists within a social movement. A social movement may even become institutionalized and turn into a revolution. Let us consider next such institutionalized forms of violence.

B. Institutionalized Forms of Violence

Much of the violence that takes place in a modern industrial society is officially authorized, even normatively prescribed, by the wider community. Consider the police and prison guards, for example. Although law enforcement officers are supposed to use the minimum amount of violence required for restraining criminals, they are trained and equipped to use weapons, whereas private citizens are not legally entitled to engage in "self-help" by apprehending thieves or dangerous criminals. Justice is to be imposed by the state, not by individual vigilantes. Indeed, a police officer who needs to use violence on behalf of the public is, in fact, obligated to do so, rather than allow the criminal to escape.

A similar obligation may be imposed on other citizens as well in times of war. If the state goes to war, it may conscript citizens for military duty and require them to go into battle and shoot to kill, though generally those soldiers are personally very reluctant to do so. Those who actually kill are usually tormented psychologically for a long time thereafter. As Colonel Dave Grossman has shown in his book *On Killing,* in times past when warfare was conducted in face-to-face battles, most soldiers actually aimed over the head of their enemies so as to avoid killing them, even if this increased their own chance of being killed. In recent wars, however, soldiers have been more ready to kill, largely because their weapons land far away and the killer does not witness the effects of his own action.

Any civilian may refuse to obey the order to kill by declaring himself a "conscientious objector," but many states (including some that are otherwise democratic) do not legally permit anyone to refuse conscription and may imprison anyone who tries to avoid that "duty." Thus we see again that violence is normatively regulated—"institutionalized." Warfare is not the act of individual buccaneers with a penchant for violence. It is a social institution.

Researchers usually define a war as an armed conflict that has resulted in the death of 1000 or more people during a single phase. In the final decade of the 20th century, there have been 35–45 wars going on around the world during any given year. However, there is no reason to believe that war is a necessary institution in all possible societies. Slavery and dueling also have been widely practiced social institutions in times past but have been abolished, as war may also be abolished some day. Warfare is an extreme method of conflict resolution to which societies resort if they cannot resolve a seemingly intolerable conflict. When an enforceable system of international law becomes established, nations may go to court to seek justice instead of using war as a "self-help" measure. For the present, however, we must consider warfare at two different levels: as internal war (mostly "civil" war) and as international war.

1. Internal Wars

Sociologists have devoted a good deal of attention to accounting for revolutions, a form of warfare that takes place within a society, though it may be supported by an outside interest or nation. (We sometimes speak of "proxy wars" that are fought internally but virtually at the behest of a foreign state, which may even supply and train the guerrillas.)

Internal wars come in many variations, probably the most common being civil wars: conflicts between two or more different factions within a single society, all of which either seek to gain control of the state apparatus or to separate a portion of the country as an independent state. During the late 1990s, all the wars that were going on were civil wars; that is, not one war was being waged between the governments of two different countries. (This is a departure from past patterns; in general, during the past two centuries about 70% of all wars have been international in scope.) Some civil wars, especially those in which the combatants represent different ethnic groups, result in genocide—attempts to exterminate a whole ethnic group. (This can happen in international wars too, as in World War II when the Nazis tried to kill all Jews and Gypsies.) Alternatively, the objective may be to expel all members of a particular community, as happened during the war in the former Yugoslavia, when the perpetrators called their racist policy ethnic cleansing. Here we shall consider the two main types of internal war in the late 20th century: revolutions and wars of secession.

a. Revolution

The term revolution is often used in reference to any drastic social change affecting a whole society, including ones that are not violent, such as the industrial revolution. Although our attention here will focus on violent revolutions, it would indeed be a major mistake to suggest that all extreme changes of a political system result from the use of violence. Historians have greatly underestimated the number of successful nonviolent revolts using such tactics as boycotts, strikes, and other organized campaigns of civil disobedience that have overthrown a regime or made it unable to govern. The most famous example occurred when, by protesting for many years, Mohandas K. Gandhi and millions of his followers forced the British crown to grant political independence to India. However, Gandhi did not succeed entirely, for, against his wishes, the Muslim faction was allowed to secede and form Pakistan.

Sometimes an armed revolution succeeds or fails so quickly that very little blood is shed in the bid for power. Thus a handful of revolutionaries may capture the center of state power and eliminate the officials in a swift coup or putsch. At the other extreme, a revolution may begin as an unorganized popular rebellion at the grassroots of society—a circumstance that is more likely to result in large-scale violence. This was true, for example, in the case of the French Revolution, which overthrew the monarchy in 1791.

Still, spontaneous rebellions do not always become violent, and we see examples of peaceable revolutions in the astonishing changes that took place throughout eastern Europe as the year 1989 was drawing toward a close. In one country after another, crowds filled the streets, calling for the communist rulers of their countries to resign. Mikhail Gorbachev, President of the Soviet Union, refused to send troops to crush these rebellions, as some of his predecessors had done. Lacking Soviet support, the rulers of these regimes acquiesced and left office with very little blood being shed, except in the case of Romania.

Several sociological studies of revolution were partially confirmed by the revolutions of 1989. One was Theda Skocpol's book *States and Social Revolution*, which emphasizes this: Revolutionaries do not deliberately "make a revolution." Revolutions happen—often surprising the people who start them and whose original goals were far more limited than the outcome. Certainly all Eastern Europeans were astonished by the easy collapse of the communist regimes. However, some of Skocpol's generalizations do not fit the 1989 cases. She claimed that revolutions take place only in agrarian societies and are led by peasants, not city-dwellers. (This was not the case in 1989.) Further, revolution can come only when (a) the state breaks down and no longer can repress revolts and (b) peasants rebel against the landowners. An ordinary, reasonably effective state can repress rebellions and can undertake the necessary reforms in time to prevent peasant uprisings. However, in the three cases that she studied, the French, Chinese, and Russian Revolutions, the state was facing a variety of other threats simultaneously, which made it weak and ineffective. These events precipitated Skocpol's three cases of revolution, which led to the development of modernized states that (in her opinion) were too effective to be susceptible to revolution thereafter.

In 1989, effective repression was not even attempted, except in Romania. The eastern European rulers had not attempted any reforms and they did not try to use their armed forces to put down the protests. However, earlier that year the Chinese rulers had crushed a nonviolent, student-led protest in Beijing's Tiananmen Square. Neither the Soviet Union nor the eastern European communist regimes emulated that example. Had they even threatened to do so, perhaps the peaceable revolutionaries would have stayed indoors and their countries would still be socialist. Or perhaps not.

b. Wars of Secession

Wars of secession are internal wars in which the objective of at least one faction is to separate their country into two or more states. In the late 1990s, approximately half of all the wars going on around the world have been wars of secession, such as the wars in Sri Lanka, the former Yugoslavia, and Chechnya. In addition to these actual wars, dozens of separatist movements were going on (e.g., in Quebec) for which it was impossible to estimate the probability that war would result. Most separatist movements are easily repressed or simply never win enough support to matter. Eventually the remainder also usually fail, but only as a result of military defeat.

Robert Schaeffer has described the typical outcome of movements that successfully accomplished their goal: secession, which was based upon the presumed right of every "people" to "self-determination." Nationalists learned this notion from western politicians—especially Woodrow Wilson and V. I. Lenin, two men who otherwise agreed about almost nothing. Later, their respective successors, Franklin D. Roosevelt and Joseph Stalin, who shared a dislike for colonialism, encouraged independence movements to secede from colonial empires, though neither of them would countenance independence movements in most of the areas that their own countries dominated.

Schaeffer described two waves of partition: those in the British colonies, which were divided along ethnic lines, and those carried out by the victorious nations after World War II: Germany, Korea, China, and Vietnam. Since the downfall of communist regimes in 1990 there has been another wave of secessions such as those in Yugoslavia and Czechoslovakia. The timing enables us to establish the remarkable accuracy with which Schaeffer predicted the course of subsequent partitions.

An all-too-frequent outcome is that secession generates refugees and leads to bloodshed, the most dramatic case being that of India in 1947, where nearly one million were killed in the fighting. In all the cases that Schaeffer studied, partition separated families, disenfranchised minority populations, and deprived them of the right to vote. Often the new laws created second-class citizenship, curtailing minority language or religious rights. In his cases, and in others as well, the newly divided states have usually found themselves in worse financial circumstances after partition than be-fore, though occasionally one of them benefits while the other suffers.

Though partitions are carried out in order to resolve conflicts, the actual effect is usually to turn those internal conflicts into inter-state conflicts. Conflicts previously limited, thereafter continue indefinitely as full-scale wars. The conflicts in Northern Ireland, Israel, North and South Korea, and India–Pakistan illustrate the virtually interminable nature of these struggles. During the Cold War the newly divided states also found it necessary to ally either with the Soviet Union or the United States, and their conflicts became part of the global nuclear war plans. With this consideration, we arrive at last at the topic of international warfare.

2. International Wars

When we turn to the topic of international warfare, we encounter a peculiar paradox. World War II killed more than 50 million persons and, hypothetically, an unlimited World War III, using all the weapons that will still be available in the early 21st century, could destroy the entire human population and most other species. Yet sociologists have written almost nothing on the subject of global war.

In an unusual effort to explain the strange silence of his colleagues on this topic, the British scholar Anthony Giddens blames the 19th-century sociologists who are still inordinarily influential in the thinking of their successors. Giddens notes that for the circumstances in which we live now, traditional social theory (especially of the liberal or socialist type) has not prepared us, who live in a world of nations.

Both the socialist Marx and the liberal Durkheim anticipated a future in which, after the disappearance of social classes, there would be global unity. Of the 19th-century classical theorists, only the mildly nationalistic Weber came close to comprehending the growing power of the nation-state and its inherent reliance on territoriality and militarism. Moreover, according to Giddens, all of these social analysts conceived of industrialism as a pacific force that would unify the world through interdependent economic exchange. None of them anticipated the technological dangers of modern science, the horrific weapons, or the cultivated aptitude for cruelty that would be perfected during the 20th century. Their intellectual heirs therefore observe the key events of their own period with a detachment that comes of lacking a language by which to capture ongoing experience.

Michael Mann also has analyzed the indifference of sociologists toward issues of warfare with an argument similar to Giddens's, for he too believes that the nation-state has turned out to be more crucial than the "founding fathers" of the discipline expected. A nation-state, he argues, is not an ethnic state, but a citizen state. Regardless of nationalistic mythologies, the modern state is not an organization of people united by culture or a common genetic background. Instead, membership is defined on the basis of citizenship—a status that has been won only slowly by the middle classes, then the lower classes and women, who are still mostly preoccupied with domestic issues.

Mann does not promise that democratizing foreign and military policy would necessarily put an end to warfare, since he shows that public opinion is sometimes extremely militaristic. The middle class, for example, was remarkably enthusiastic about engaging in World War I. No social class is capable of supervising geopolitics, in his view. On the other hand, he does not suggest how geopolitics should be supervised.

Many other scholars are more confident than Mann that the spread of democracy is likely to usher in a far less violent period of history than can be found in the record of past centuries. There are two reasons for this conclusion. First, well-established democracies virtually never go to war against other democracies. They do go to war against nondemocratic states and, of course, nondemocratic states go to war against each other. Since there is a great upsurge in democratic governance around the world, we can reasonably expect that all states will eventually be democratic and that this will curtail or even eliminate warfare, especially if the internal democratization is matched by the strengthening and democratizing of international institutions.

A second reason for expecting democracy to reduce violence comes from research showing a U-curve in violence when we compare countries according to the strength of their states. Mark Cooney has shown that lethal conflict tends to be high where state authority is absent (mostly preindustrial states), low where states are present but where power is not centralized (in democratic states), and high again in very centralized states (which he describes as authoritarian or totalitarian in nature). In general, centralized states perpetrate violence against their own citizens by oppressing them for any act of political disobedience. Cooney cites research by R. J. Rummel, which estimates the number of people killed by the state per year per 100,000 population between 1900 and 1987. The communist states averaged 520 such deaths; the other totalitarian state (i.e., Nazi Germany) averaged 400; the authoritarian states averaged 210; and democratic states averaged only 10.

If we take a lesson from these impressive findings, it should be this: scholars who are committed to finding ways of reducing violence should dedicate themselves to the study of democracy and to discovering the most promising ways of establishing democracy in societies where it does not exist.

Much additional work needs to be done along these lines, but the present consensus of researchers points out one special prerequisite for the maintenance of democracy within a nation: the existence of a strong, independent civil society. By this term they mean the institutions of a society that exist independent from government—what are often called in western societies "nongovernmental organizations" or "NGOs." Totalitarian societies are notable for the way they have controlled all kinds of groups. Even private associations such as stamp collectors' clubs and prayer groups had to be registered and approved by the government, if not actually conducted under the auspices of the ruling party. This meant that individuals who shared some common interest or political value could not meet and discuss issues. Naturally, this limitation made it extremely difficult for dissenting groups to form that might offer a real challenge to the dominance of the political party or dictator in power.

The importance of nongovernmental organizations has long been recognized by political sociologists who have studied the prerequisites for democracy. What is somewhat new is the growing recognition by peace researchers that democracy is extremely important for the maintenance of peace and the protection of human rights. This recognition means that the encouragement of non-governmental organizations is therefore a vital aspect of peace-building.

Also See the Following Articles

INSTITUTIONALIZATION OF VIOLENCE • INSTITUTIONALIZATION OF NONVIOLENCE • SOCIAL THEORIZING ABOUT WAR AND PEACE • STRUCTURAL VIOLENCE

Bibliography

Black, D. (1993). *The social structure of right and wrong.* San Diego, CA: Academic Press.

Collins, R. (1986). The future decline of the Russian empire: An application of geopological theory. In R. Collins (Ed.), *Weberian sociological theory.* New York: Cambridge University Press.

Cooney, M. (1997). From warre to tyranny: Lethal conflict and the state." *American Sociological Review, 62,* 316–338.

Coser, L. (1959). *The functions of social conflict.* New York: The Free Press.

Durkheim, E. (1951). *Suicide.* New York: The Free Press.

Frank, A. G. (1970). The development of underdevelopment." In R. I. Rhodes (Ed.), *Imperialism and underdevelopment: A reader.* New York: Monthly Review Press.

Grossman, D. (1995). *On killing: The psychological cost of learning to kill in war and society*. Boston: Little, Brown.

Lipset, S. M. (1994). The social requisites of democracy revisited. *American Sociological Review, 59*(1), 1–22.

Mann, M. (1987). War and social theory: Into battle with classes, nations and states. In C. Creighton & M. Shaw (Ed.), *The sociology of war and peace*. London: Macmillan.

Merton, R. K. (1938). Social structure and anomie. *American Sociological Review, 4*, 672–682.

Mill, C. W. (1956). *The power elite*. New York: Oxford University Press.

Parsons, T. (1949). *The structure of social action*. New York: The Free Press.

Schaeffer, R. (1990). *Warpaths: The politics of partition*. New York: Hill and Wang.

Sharp, G. (1973). *The politics of nonviolent action*. Boston: Porter Sargent.

Simmel, G. (1955). *Conflict* (translated by K. H. Wolff). Glencoe, IL.: The Free Press.

Skocpol, T. (1979). *States and social revolution: A comparative analysis of France, Russia and China*. Cambridge: Cambridge University Press.

Sutherland, E., & Cressey, D. R. (1960). *Principles of criminology*, (6th ed.). Philadelphia: Lippincott.

Tilly, C., Tilly, L., & Tilly, R. (1984). *The Rebellious Century, 1830–1930*. Cambridge, MA: Harvard University Press.

Spirituality and Peacemaking

Graeme MacQueen

McMaster University

GLOSSARY

Altruism Positive regard for others and compassionate feelings toward them: delimited altruism is altruism restricted to traditional in-groups, while extended altruism is altruism that reaches groups traditionally considered as out-groups.

Historic Peace Churches Three religious communities within the Protestant Christian tradition (Mennonites, Quakers, and Brethren) that historically have regarded peace as one of their primary values and that have strong traditions of refusing military service.

Interior Life A turning away from external rewards, goals, and pressures, as well as from materialistic assumptions, in an inward movement of the mind in order to gain or renew (whether informally or through formal practices of contemplation, prayer, or meditation) a connection with ultimate realities and values.

Nonviolence A system of values, ideas, and practices that involves empathy with the potential object of violence, revulsion from violence, and a determination not to participate in it, and, in many cases, both theory and practice for achieving just ends without recourse to violence.

Peace Spirituality Any form of spirituality in which peace and peacemaking are accorded very high value.

Prophet As a religious type, one who obeys the urge to announce the truth because of a sense of duty or of having been commissioned, offering a criticism of existing affairs, and looking forward to a future situation.

Social Peace A condition within, or a relationship between, social groups that is characterized by high levels of harmony and accord and low levels of violent conflict.

Spirituality The interior life and the practices that sustain it.

Utopia An envisioned society, whether realistically achievable or not, that a community honors as the repository of its values, and that both allows the positive projection of these values and establishes a vantage point from which to criticize an existing social condition.

SPIRITUALITY, the interior life and the practices that sustain it, can be found throughout the world, often but not always in association with institutionalized religion. This article examines those forms of spirituality that take peace as a primary value—linking them under the term "peace spirituality"—and discusses their contributions to peacemaking under eight categories: moral grounding, vision, critique, resistance, nonviolence, conflict resolution, reconciliation, and building a tradition of peace spirituality. Historical examples are drawn largely from the recognized "world religions," the main exception being those taken from the religious life of the Five Nations (later called the Six Nations—also known as the Iroquois League), which are given in order to remind us of the existence of powerful peace spiritualities largely independent of the world religions.

I. INTRODUCTION

The 20th century has been a time of enormous violence but also of an unprecedented growth in movements and institutions for peacemaking. Among the most important sources of peacemaking have been the world's great spiritual traditions. The awarding of the Nobel Prize in Peace to Bishop Desmond Tutu in 1984, to Tenzin Gyatso, the 14th Dalai Lama, in 1989, and to Bishop Carlos Belo of East Timor in 1996, attests to the continuing importance of these traditions. More broadly, the influence of religion and spirituality on social movements against war, the initiation and development by religious groups of nongovernmental organizations working for peace, and the leading role of the historic peace churches in the development of peace and conflict studies in institutions of higher learning in the West all suggest the enduring importance of spirituality for peacemaking.

Criticism of war and violence developed in several distinct and sophisticated forms in the great urban centers of the Axial Period (Karl Jaspers' term, used to refer to 800–200 B.C.E.). In the Middle East, in India, in China, and in Greece powerful rejections of militarism and brutality were articulated. These rejections seldom achieved dominance in society—war was not ended, armies were not abolished, imperial projects were seldom abandoned—but they exercised, at times, a constraining influence, and they grew over the centuries both in their international legitimacy and their institutionalized power. Antiwar traditions have increasingly come into contact with each other in the past two centuries, while new antiwar spiritual traditions, such as Baha'i, have come into being. In the world today one can no longer find a Buddhist peace organization uninfluenced by the religions of the West any more than one can find a Christian peace organization of any size that is uninfluenced by spiritual practices and ideals from the non-Christian world. In short, as the 21st century begins one sees a cross-fertilization of peace spiritualities, even a global peace spirituality in the making.

II. CENTRAL CONCEPTS

A. Peace and Peacemaking

"Peace" refers in this article, when there is no indication to the contrary, to social peace, defined as a condition within, or a relationship between, social groups that is characterized by high levels of harmony and accord and low levels of violent conflict. Since genuine harmony and accord exist only when groups feel that social interaction is taking place according to accepted standards of justice and goodness, peace and justice are always in a close relationship. But, while there are some elements of the just society that are so common as to be almost universal, there are also significant variations from one culture to another. Hence, while this article assumes that peace implies justice it does not presuppose any particular form of just society.

"Peacemaking" refers here to the creating, maintaining, or deepening of social peace through nonviolent methods.

B. Spirituality

Spirituality is a complex concept with an evolving and culturally specific meaning. The word originated in the Christian tradition and continues to flourish there, but in the last century it has increasingly been used to refer to aspects of other religious traditions. In the last 40 years in North America there has been a proliferation of writings about spirituality, including feminist spirituality, native spirituality, and various forms of earth-centered spirituality.

This recent fascination with spirituality appears to result from unease with both the materialism and the institutionalized religion of the modern period. In the first case, spirituality protests the reduction of human beings and the world to material substance as well as the reduction of human life to the striving for material accumulation. In the second case, spirituality criticizes institutionalized religion for its parochialism, its sectarianism, its traditionalism, its accommodation with the secular world, and its emphasis on correctness (correct belief, correct ritual, and so on). Against all this "spirituality" has become a term for those elements of religion that are vital, unifying, grounded, and courageous.

Unfortunately, this understanding of spirituality is too subjective and value-laden to serve as a scholarly definition. In the present article, therefore, an old but somewhat more precise definition will be employed: spirituality is the interior life and the practices that sustain it. By "interior life" is meant a turning away from external rewards, goals, and pressures, as well as from materialistic assumptions, in an inward movement of the mind in order to gain or renew (whether informally or through formal practices of contemplation, prayer or meditation) a connection with ultimate realities and values. Although this understanding of spirituality is still to some extent culturally specific (this meaning of the term originated in Christianity), it is easy to show that spirituality of this kind is found in many different places, times and traditions and is not the property of any one culture or religion. The present discussion does not take Christian spirituality as normative, nor does it assume that spirituality is better than religion or represents the essence or highest aspect of religion.

Some contemporary writers assume that all spirituality has a positive relationship to peace and peacemaking. But on what basis does one exclude from the spiritual the various forms of holy war that religions have formulated and promoted? It is clear that such activities are sometimes undertaken with inward soul-searching, prayer, and the like. Or what is one to say about such religious practices as those of the *thugs* in India, worshipers of the goddess Kālī, who in the heyday of the sect assassinated wayfarers according to prescribed religious rites? Does one say that these rites did not involve spirituality? It is more helpful to allow the existence of numerous spiritualities or forms of spirituality. In many traditional religions it would readily be admitted that there are different forms of spirituality according to the nature of the "spirit" or power with whom one is communing. A person who worshiped the Roman god Mars, for example, may have been engaging in spiritual practice precisely in order to be able to prevail violently against an enemy. For these reasons it is important to establish within the category of spirituality the subcategory of *peace spirituality*, defined as any form of spirituality in which peace and peacemaking are accorded very high value. The remainder of this article deals exclusively with peace spirituality.

Since, in accordance with the above understanding of spirituality, this article is not concentrating on the institutional aspects of religion, it will not treat the social, cultural, and financial functions of church, temple, mosque, and the like; or the role of formal dogma, religious authority structures, church and state interactions; or the role of religious law. Important as each of these factors is for peacemaking, none falls within the category of spirituality as understood here.

III. EIGHT PRINCIPLES OF PEACE SPIRITUALITY

A. Moral Grounding

"Remember, O my soul," wrote the Quaker John Woolman, "that the Prince of Peace is thy Lord" (Steere, 1984: 217). Woolman, a key 18th-century figure in the movement for the abolition of slavery in the United States, regarded the divine as characterized above all by peace and justice. The divine communicated its nature to the human soul when the soul was able to listen in quietness and receptivity. Woolman's own spiritual practice, which was intense, was directed toward discovering through such discernment and receptivity what was required of him to manifest this nature, these values, in the world. One cannot understand the abolition of slavery without taking into account this form of spirituality.

In every major religious tradition, at one time or another, there have been people who have regarded peace as grounded in the very nature of ultimate reality and therefore as central to the spiritual life. They have likewise argued that peace is encouraged in scripture, is illustrated in the words and actions of the central religious figures in the tradition, and is for these reasons something people are called to bring into being in the world. In these ways they have attempted to put peacemaking at the center of their traditions.

According to the model of humanity implied in this form of spirituality a human being does not become moral merely through socialization and enculturation, nor through simple rational decisions of the self. Morality develops fully only when the human being is open to the distinctive "voices" of the transhuman as encountered in spiritual practice. Moral grounding, therefore, is simultaneously spiritual grounding.

From the point of view of such peace spirituality, there is great significance in the fact that the same word may be used—the English word "peace," for example—for profound inner tranquility and for absence of social violence: the reality encountered in the inner consciousness is seen as linked to the urge to create peace in the external world. Social peace and inner peace are regarded as part of the same reality. The practitioner does not regard peace as an abstract idea or moral ideal only but as an experienced reality known intimately.

Peacemaking in even its most mundane forms is, therefore, spiritual practice.

It follows that those committed to peace spirituality will regard peace as passing in value and significance all utilitarian and rational calculation, will be capable of great dedication and stubbornness in pursuing their ideal, and will regard as valuable all those things—symbols, narrative, ritual, and so on—that promote spiritual discernment and inspiration.

B. Vision

Spiritual traditions present powerful visions of society, and in the case of peace spiritualities these are visions of a peaceful society. These envisioned societies or "utopias"—the word is used here in a nonpejorative sense—may be pictured as belonging to the past, a golden age from which we have fallen but from which we can draw moral lessons (as in Confucianism); or as rooted in the past but recoverable in the future (as in Judeo-Christian religion); or as waiting in the future in genuine newness (also found in Judeo-Christian tradition and common in Western secular varieties of utopianism); or as recurring cyclically (as in several traditions from India); or as existing here and now, present but unseen (as in many mystical traditions).

In Buddhist utopias from the early Indian phase of the tradition, as pictured in texts such as the *Aggañña Sutta* and the *Cakkavattisīhanāda Sutta*, the cyclically recurring golden age is one characterized by peace and justice. Violence enters society through greed and in association with private property and the maldistribution of wealth. The degeneration of the world to its present condition of war and injustice has taken place both because of structural inequities and because of a downward spiral fueled by the self-perpetuating forces of violence and vengeance. Human beings can help reverse this degeneration by manifesting, in intentional communities, the values representative of the golden age: nonviolence, truthfulness, and so on. All those things that help human beings to remember who they really are and can be again are of value in this process of rescuing the world from holocaust. Mindfulness and meditation take a central place in removing greed, ill will and delusion from the mind and thereby aiding moral action.

Expectations of a perfected future state have generally played a role in promoting peace in the Buddhist community. Fervent and violent attempts to inaugurate this condition are, however, not entirely unknown—an example would be the White Lotus Rebellion in China at the end of the 18th century, which looked forward to the coming of Maitreya, the future Buddha, and which caused such military difficulties for the government that the Ch'ing dynasty never recovered.

Jewish and Christian scriptures have offered further utopian possibilities. The longing for the concrete re-establishment of God's sovereignty over the world through the reign of an ideal king is a major theme in the Hebrew Bible, and peace is a frequently mentioned characteristic of this kingdom. This longing finds expression in the New Testament as well, where Jesus is identified as the Christ—the Messiah, the ideal king, whose return is looked for. Historically, both Jewish and Christian traditions have at times hosted powerful messianic movements that have drawn on Biblical images, and these movements have sometimes involved their participants in direct political action (not always nonviolent) for the building of the ideal society. Other Biblical images have also been mobilized by utopian communities: the image of Eden, for example, where there is neither strife nor war and the man and woman do not even have to kill to eat; or, for Christians, the image of the sacred time when Christ formed, with his disciples, a spiritual community that offered a witness to the world through its material simplicity, faith and peacefulness.

The power of utopias lies both in the establishment of a positive vision toward which human beings can orient their strivings and in the creation of a position from which to criticize and judge the present visible, imperfect society. This utopian position can be transmitted from generation to generation via narrative, ritual, verbal formulas, doctrines, creeds and contemplative practice. All of these, however, make use of symbol, and all symbols are subject to interpretation, with the result that there is no straightforward and predictable connection between a given symbolic production and concrete action in the world. A utopian narrative may be handled by one society as an entertaining but rather unimportant story while another society uses it to create a revolution; or a narrative may inspire action in both groups, but with apparently contradictory results. The story of the exodus of the Hebrew people from Egypt and of their eventual entry into the promised land, for example, was read by Boers in southern Africa as legitimizing their violent subjugation of indigenous African peoples, while the same story has been read by many African American people as providing hope and inspiration in their struggle for liberation from racism and oppression. In the Jewish community the Hebrew prophets have provided inspiration to political Zionists, spiritual Zionists and anti-Zionists. *The Bhagavad Gītā*, the Hindu scripture that was so important to

Mohandas Gandhi in his pursuit of nonviolence that he referred to it as his mother, was drawn upon by the young Aurobindo Ghose to legitimate violent action against the British.

Finally, all symbolic formations are to some extent specific to a cultural or religious group, and symbols that are extremely meaningful and inspirational to one group may be completely opaque to another. This is one of the dangers of peace spirituality, since by its very nature peacemaking must be able to bring groups together.

In 1642 a Jesuit missionary to New France (in modern Quebec) was surprised to witness the arrival of a peace delegation from the Five Nations, dreaded enemy of the French and of their native allies. An old man in the delegation stood up and expressed in a loud voice his party's intention to make peace, so that "the land shall be beautiful, the river shall have no more waves, one may go everywhere without fear" (Wallace, 1946, 54). The Jesuit missionary and his associates did not understand that the delegation was drawing on its utopian vision as set forth in the Deganawidah Epic, a charter narrative of the Five Nations; they did not understand the positive value given to peace in this narrative; they were unaware of the Five Nations' sophisticated process of peacemaking, based on the narrative but concretized in specific practices that had been successfully used for many years to bring about peace; and they did not know what their own role in the peace initiative ought to be. They therefore behaved inappropriately and the opportunity for peace was lost.

C. Critique

Moral grounding and visions of a just and peaceful society make possible a criticism of existing states of affairs. Two styles of criticism within spiritual traditions may be distinguished, the prophetic and the renunciatory.

1. Prophecy

The prophet as a religious type is one who obeys the urge to announce the truth, not because he or she wishes to but because of a sense of duty or of having been commissioned. The prophet usually offers both criticism of existing affairs and a looking forward to a future situation. Prophets are by no means always agents of peacemaking. Often the criticism of existing social, political, or religious practices is fierce and the judgment—to be carried into effect either by human or transhuman agency—severe. Still, condemnations of violence, war, and brutality are common in many prophetic traditions.

Among the Five Nations, the prophet Deganawidah is represented (in narratives that precede contact with Europeans and their scripture) as saying that he has been sent to establish the Great Peace, which shall put an end to war among nations. Much later, the Seneca prophet Handsome Lake directed aspects of his message against violence.

Prophecy in the Hebrew Bible ("Old Testament" to Christians) has been extremely important historically in the West, not only because of the explicit moral content of the prophets' messages but because it helped establish a distinctive mode of speech or discourse: bold and even reckless truth-telling on behalf of the oppressed, from a position of political weakness but moral certitude. This mode of speech can be heard in 17th century English radicals such as Gerrard Winstanley as they declaim against the violent domination of the ruling classes; in 19th century feminists such as Julia Ward Howe as they denounce male warmaking or abolitionists such as William Lloyd Garrison as they attack slavery; and in Marxists such as Rosa Luxemburg as they condemn capitalism as the cause of world war. At the end of the 20th century prophetic speech remains strong in socialism and in Christian Liberation Theology.

In the Middle East, the Koran has joined Jewish and Christian sources to provide a powerful model of prophetic speech. It would be difficult to overestimate the historical importance of prophetic speech for this region of the world.

2. Renunciation

The distinction here between prophet and renunciant contrasts the fiery outrage of the prophet with the quietude and asceticism of the renunciant. It is not that a renunciant does not criticize the existing order—the criticism is often extreme—nor that the renunciant is necessarily disengaged from social activity—some renunciants have been deeply involved in social change—but that the renunciant tends to be focused on experimenting with alternative ways of living, trying to embody utopian values here and now, in private and social life. Typically, renunciants are less interested in denouncing than in relinquishing. Self-perfection through discipline and the letting go of wealth, power, and status must accompany social improvement.

One of the most important renunciatory movements in history began in the kingdom of Magadha in Northeast India sometime around the beginning of the 6th century B.C.E. This movement gave birth to both Jainism and Buddhism and helped in the formation of Hinduism. In Jainism and Buddhism (also in Hinduism, though in a more complex way) renunciation became part of a comprehensive system of human perfection, which included peace and nonviolence. This model of peacefulness was unique in the ancient world since it emphasized renunciation of violence against all living beings, human and nonhuman; integrated moral rules within a comprehensive system of training; and, in the case of Jainism and Buddhism, grounded these values in ultimacy but without theism.

Many modern Buddhist organizations committed to peace and justice, such as the Buddhist Peace Fellowship, retain the traditional flavor of Buddhist renunciatory teachings, stressing simplicity of lifestyle, meditation, and the development of compassion. At the same time, lay people of both sexes have taken a leading role in many such organizations and there exists a degree of criticism of traditional monasticism both for its tendencies to disengage itself from the world and for its tendencies to compromise with secular powers.

The influence of the ancient Indian stream of renunciatory spirituality and its critique of dominant society and the war system extends beyond Asia. Both of the central figures in the development of 20th-century nonviolence, Gandhi and Tolstoy, were deeply influenced by it, and it is, in part, through them that the renunciatory ideal has become entrenched in contemporary peace spirituality. Tolstoy was largely frustrated in his personal attempts to live a renunciatory existence, but Gandhi put his ideals into action. Gandhi became one of the most influential figures in the 20th century through his ability to merge an ancient Indian ascetical ideal, buttressed by a solid grounding in the Hindu religious tradition, with an activism, cosmopolitanism, and political sophistication that allowed him to be understood outside his own tradition.

In addition to the transmission from India, there have been other, largely independent renunciatory traditions, including Jewish, Muslim, and Christian traditions, and these too have developed a critique of the war system. In Judaism, the Essenes were an early renunciatory sect that apparently experimented with a doctrine of nonretaliation. In Islam, while the prophetic tradition has developed principles of just war, many powerful statements in favor of peace are found in the renunciatory tradition, in Sufism of both the early and late period. During much of Christian history, radical renunciatory spiritualities with a strong critique of war and violence developed as conscious alternatives to dominant forms of Christianity. Some of these groups were denounced and persecuted as heretical by the Church. Anabaptism and Quakerism, so influential in bringing pacifism and peacemaking into the modern world, were able to survive persecution, but pre-Reformation groups were often decimated. Few Waldensians and virtually no Cathars survived the medieval persecutions to carry forward their witness against violence. In the modern period, Roman Catholic renunciatory activism has been well represented by figures such as Dorothy Day, Thomas Merton, and Philip and Daniel Berrigan. Christian renunciatory traditions have been in direct contact with those originating in India and there has been an ongoing process of dialogue toward the formation of trans-sectarian peace spirituality.

D. Resistance

Critique develops into resistance when dissenters actively refuse to cooperate with systems they find unacceptable. An order to fire on a crowd of protesters is disobeyed by a soldier; a family refuses to hand over a hunted minority group; a community in a region occupied by a foreign power refuses to obey the orders of the foreign power's administrative authorities; an individual refuses to pay war taxes. Such actions can be found throughout the world and are not invariably linked to spirituality—in the modern period, especially, much resistance to violence has been based on humanitarian feelings or secular ideology—but the part spirituality has played historically in the development of resistance has been enormous.

Conscientious objection, the refusal on principle to serve in armed forces, illustrates the point. In Christianity the practice can be attested (though it was a minority practice) very early in the tradition. After the Protestant Reformation it became a characteristic of the "historic peace churches" (the Mennonites, Quakers and Brethren). At the end of the 19th and the beginning of the 20th centuries it was powerfully advocated by Leo Tolstoy, whose version of Christianity, as he set it forth in the later part of his life in such influential works as *The Kingdom of God is Within You*, had a great deal in common with earlier radical Christian sects. Tolstoy's Christianity entailed a rejection of much that was assumed good and just (including war) by dominant groups in society, and it was profoundly suspicious of institutionalized religion. In Tolstoy's view the key religious teaching, set out in Christ's Sermon on the Mount, was the distinction between the "law of love" and the "law of violence." Since one's loyalty to God and to Christ ought to be higher than one's loyalty to any human institution, one simply had to disobey human authority when it asked one to violate the law of love. If a young man was ordered to serve in the army he had to refuse. Tolstoy did not think one had to be a Christian to understand the law of love: he felt this law was also set forth in non-Christian religions and, moreover, that it was possible for human beings to grasp it without accepting any religion at all. Regardless of the source of one's knowledge of the principle, however, it gave one a sense of loyalty to something higher than earthly powers.

The commitment to a higher loyalty, of which Tolstoy is a modern spokesperson, not only sustains the resister in the face of persecution but changes the nature of the experience of persecution. Societies maintain order with the help of shame and ostracism as well as overt force. Incarceration, exile, denunciation, stigmatization, disfiguring, and public execution owe their force not only to their direct power to cause pain, but to their ability to cause people to feel rejected by society. The person whose resistance is grounded in spirituality may be able to surmount the fear of rejection. Of course, the existence of a like-minded supporting community helps greatly, but even alone some resisters have been able to withstand great pressure. The training of resisters will often include preparation for experiences of isolation and stigmatization. Both Gandhi and Martin Luther King, Jr., urged their followers in civil disobedience to look upon imprisonment as an honor and an opportunity. (Preparation for the 1963 Birmingham, Alabama, civil disobedience campaign exemplifies this.) Spiritual grounding of this kind may give a power to resisting individuals and groups that is difficult for secular politics either to account for or to duplicate.

In the extreme situation where the resister faces death, spiritual grounding may make death acceptable. Both Gandhi and King were assassinated, and both appear to have been prepared for it. All resistance movements have their martyrs, even cults of martyrdom; peace spirituality is unique only in that the martyrs give their lives nonviolently.

E. Nonviolence

The concept of nonviolence is complex, but at the root of the matter lies empathy with the potential object of violence, and a consequent revulsion from violence combined with a determination not to participate in it. It is in this very broad sense that the term is used here. Four aspects of nonviolence that merit separate treatment are altruism, nonretaliation, feminist nonviolence, and alternative technique.

1. Altruism

All societies recognize altruism—positive regard for others and compassionate feelings toward them. But the circle within which altruism is active varies a good deal from society to society, culture to culture. People may be encouraged to have strong altruistic feelings toward members of their in-group (community, clan, nation, or whatever) while being encouraged to regard those outside their in-group as subhumans to whom no respect or pity need be shown. It is, therefore, of great significance that there have arisen individuals and movements throughout history that have criticized delimited altruism and have tried to create forms of extended altruism, altruism that reaches those traditionally classed as members of out-groups. Extended altruism is not simply a matter of expressing pious sentiments about loving everyone. Where the attempt to champion it is made resolutely, traditional prejudices, loyalties, and boundaries must be criticized and transgressed. The price paid by the proponent of extended altruism can be very high.

One of the earliest and clearest attacks on delimited altruism as it relates to war was that made by the Chinese thinker Mo Tzu (flourished 5th century B.C.E.). Mo Tzu proclaimed that all rulers who ordered military expeditions for the enlargement of their power and territory—a common practice in his day—were criminals. Their criminality and their perversity arose, he said, from the habit of partial rather than universal love. They loved their in-group and had no regard for those outside it. Mo Tzu was not a pacifist—he even helped organize defensive brigades on behalf of states under attack—but his disgust with war was profound.

During the Axial Period, in China and elsewhere, other philosophical and religious thinkers also put forward notions of extended altruism. In India, ascetical groups such as the Jains and Buddhists experimented with extremely radical altruism, attempting to widen the circle of compassion to include all living beings and criticizing not only war but also animal sacrifice and the eating of flesh. While advocates of extended altruism were often ignored and sometimes harassed, their concepts and values laid the basis for later notions of universal human rights, as well as of the inherent value of nonhuman life forms.

Extended altruism is important to peacemaking, and in some forms of peacemaking it is an explicit dynamic. The Five Nations, for example, attempted to turn enemies ritually into kin so that the proscriptions against domestic and intracommunity violence could be used to prohibit warfare. The confederacy aimed to have an ever-increasing number of nations linked as kin under the Tree of Peace. The process, which was elaborated in sacred story and ritual, was both spiritual and practical.

2. Nonretaliation

Altruism and nonretaliation are by no means identical. There have been groups that have adopted a position of nonretaliation because of scriptural injunctions, doctrinal beliefs, or a desire for personal purity—all in the notable absence of altruistic feelings. Nonretaliation by itself does not, therefore, constitute nonviolence as the latter term is used here. It is, however, one essential aspect of nonviolence.

Retaliation for injury or insult to one's person or one's in-group has been one of the sustaining dynamics of war. The human psyche apparently offers fertile ground for doctrines of retaliation, which have been supplied and elaborated variously by culture. Retaliation may become the sacred duty of the good son, the brave warrior, or the loyal citizen. Attempts to break cycles of retaliation are therefore important to the history of peacemaking. In the West, New Testament ideas of nonretaliation have been of special significance, especially those teachings ascribed to Christ in Matthew 5–7 (the Sermon on the Mount) and Luke 6. Historically, these passages have been repeatedly rediscovered by new groups of Christians, who have sometimes encountered great opposition when attempting to put them into practice. Frequently marginalized within a Christendom deeply committed to warmaking, these dissidents laid the foundation for the historic peace churches, and their views have thus had growing legitimacy and influence from the 16th century onward. The development of peace groups in the modern sense, beginning in the United States and England in the early 19th century, was strongly influenced by Christian ideas of nonretaliation and nonviolence (or "nonresistance" as it was usually called in that century).

However important they have been historically, New Testament teachings on nonretaliation are not unique. In Judaism at the time of Christianity's origins and early history there existed a minority tradition of nonretaliation. Moreover, numerous other non-Christian traditions have acknowledged the principle. In the modern period nonretaliation has achieved a trans-sectarian status, as its proponents have drawn upon several spiritual traditions in their advocacy and development of it.

3. Feminist Nonviolence

Feminist spirituality has been of great importance for nonviolence, and for peacemaking generally, in the last two centuries, and has become a major area of discussion in the last decades of the twentieth century. Since there are numerous varieties of feminism, there are naturally numerous varieties of feminist spirituality; nonetheless, three major areas of feminist criticism relevant to the present discussion may be identified.

Feminist spirituality has tended to be highly critical of *dualistic* forms of spirituality that oppose the spirit to the body, the earth, or the material realm. Historically, such dualisms have often identified spirit with the male principle and have identified that to which spirit is opposed—all that which must be rejected and even despised in spiritual practice—with the female principle. The consequences of such spirituality, say feminists, have been devastating, both for women and for all those living beings, human and nonhuman, who have been symbolically allocated to the material realm. Such spirituality, they say, is an alienated spirituality that is not at home on the earth, has contempt for living systems and is prepared to destroy them as part of its quest for purity of spirit.

Feminist spirituality is likewise critical of ideologies, whether linked to religion or not, which legitimize *domination* as a central goal. The paradigm of domination in this criticism is the domination of women by men, but feminists have attempted to work out an emancipatory theory and practice that is critical of all systems of domination and that champions the liberation of all those who are oppressed.

Finally, feminist spirituality has, since at least as early as the 19th century, been critical of *war and violence*. Some forms of feminism have suggested that women are biologically less prone to violence than men. Some have held that women's position in society, which has often entailed primary responsibility for nurturing, care-giving and the affective side of human life, has made women more committed to life-sustaining activity. Others have held that feminism as a system of thought and practice, rather than women in themselves, is the carrier of values of life-affirmation and compassion. Whichever of these routes is taken, feminist spirituality is seen as taking women more deeply into the matter than mere theory, linking them with realities beyond abstract thought.

In response to these negative aspects of male-centered spiritual and intellectual tradition, feminists have formulated a spirituality that is embodied, emancipatory, and nonviolent. It is the third of these points that distinguishes feminist theory and practice from many other emancipatory systems. Of course, some varieties of feminism have been prepared to support armed struggle, but on the whole feminists have been less interested in the clash of arms than many opponents of oppression, and for this reason feminism has made serious contributions to nonviolence, both as an arena of value and as a repertoire of liberative technique.

Feminist spirituality represents a serious critique of traditional spirituality, but it can be accommodated within the definition of spirituality adopted in this article provided it is understood that the valuing of the material realm that feminist spirituality encourages is quite distinct from scientific reductionism and from ideologies of material accumulation, and provided our definition of the interior life is open to conceptions of community and social action.

4. Alternative Technique

Protests and hunger strikes, small- and large-scale noncooperation, symbolic delegitimation of tyrants, active unarmed confrontation, creation of alternative institutions, conversion of the enemy—all these techniques of struggle have existed since ancient times. It is not surprising that those whose spirituality inclines them to affirm justice but oppose violence should, over the years, progressively develop these methods of nonviolent social change, especially since they are often more ready than others to question secular authority and to deny its ultimate legitimacy. Nonviolent action is not always dependent on spirituality, but, historically, it often has been. Many of the great experimenters with nonviolent action, who have shaped the modern tradition, have operated from an explicitly spiritual base.

In the last four decades, feminist activists have been among the most creative experimenters with nonviolence, building sustained communities of resistance, inventing rituals for the collective expression of grief and rage, crossing boundaries and breaking taboos, and imbuing actions with a spirit both celebratory and indomitable. The women's encampment at Greenham Common in England, directed against the Cruise missile, exemplifies each of these elements.

In the Middle East both Jewish conscientious objectors and Muslim (sometimes Christian) Palestinians resisting the Israeli occupation of the Occupied Territories have experimented with varieties of nonviolent technique. The Israeli organization Yesh Gvul (literally, "there is a limit"), which decided to accept military service in principle but to refuse service in Lebanon and the Occupied Territories, provides an example of creative thinking in the area of conscientious objection; while the nonviolence, or in some cases limited violence, of the Palestinian *intifada* involved a broad range of methods of unarmed resistance. It would be wrong to characterize these movements as inspired chiefly by spirituality, but in the case of certain important individuals (for example, the Israeli Jew, Joseph Abileah) the connection to spirituality is clear.

Numerous spiritual traditions that have not histori-cally used the term "nonviolence" have begun to accept in the 20th century that the term expresses an important aspect of their self-understanding. The willingness of various unofficial representatives of these traditions to join the movement for the promotion of nonviolence was made clear in the Declaration of the Parliament of the World's Religions proclaimed in Chicago, 1993, which includes "commitment to a culture of non-violence and respect for life" (Kung, 1993: 24) as one of the four irrevocable directives for a global ethic supported by the world's religions.

F. Conflict Resolution

The desire for peace and harmony, the generation of utopian visions of a peaceful society, the rejection of violent actions and structures, the encouragement of altruism and of nonviolent ways of settling disputes—all these have combined in traditions of peace spirituality to produce innovation in conflict resolution.

Buddhist organizations, both in Asia and in the West, have in recent times been increasingly active in the study and promotion of conflict resolution, usually with an explicit link to nonviolence and to traditional Buddhist spiritual practice. In war-torn Cambodia, for example, each year since 1992 a Buddhist peace walk led by the venerable Maha Ghosananda (nominated several times for the Nobel Peace Prize) has taken place through regions of conflict, attempting to support the population of these regions in the hope for peace as well as to encourage leaders of the warring groups to negotiate. Although the 1994 walk was caught in a crossfire between government and Khmer Rouge forces—a monk and a nun were killed and five other walkers wounded—the walks have continued. The group sponsoring these walks has been inspired by scriptural accounts of the Buddha's own initiative in resolving conflicts, and has drawn upon the ancient practice of mindful walking—a form of meditation aimed at allowing the participant to attain clarity and calmness. Meditational practices aimed at cultivating the compassionate heart have also been important.

Another prominent Buddhist attempt at conflict resolution is the ongoing effort of the Tibetan community, led by the Dalai Lama, to reach an agreement with China on the status of Tibet. The Dalai Lama has not only refused to allow the militarization of Tibetan resistance to Chinese domination but has also put forward concrete proposals for the attainment of a political settlement. It is evident that he is respected by his people not merely as a wise and trusted leader but also as a man deeply devoted to the Buddhist spiritual tradition.

By his own testimony, his ability to persist in his difficult task is likewise a result of Buddhist spiritual practice.

In the West, Christians, especially from the historic peace churches, have played a pioneering role in the resolving of conflict. Beginning in the mid-19th century, Quakers began developing methods of private diplomacy, seeking out leaders or combatants in order to end existing conflicts. Mennonites have done likewise. Groups without sectarian affiliation but with a deep commitment to spirituality, such as the Fellowship of Reconciliation and Moral Rearmament, have carried out similar actions. Since World War II, the peace churches have played a key role in the development of peace and conflict studies in postsecondary institutions, with the result that there is now a considerable number of universities where students can study the theory and practice of conflict resolution.

In North America, Jews have been prominent in the development of theory and practice of conflict resolution. Implementing these methods in the conflict between Israel and its neighbors has, however, been difficult. Many Palestinians and members of Arab states have been suspicious of conflict resolution, seeing it as a method associated with power politics, superpower intervention and a legacy of imperialism. They have been, in general, more moved by appeals to justice within their own prophetic traditions. Meanwhile, the Jewish left, so active in the last two centuries in movements for social justice and peace, has been weakened in the last several decades both by the holocaust and by Zionism. Zionists have seen it as their duty to create a homeland where Jews can be secure and free from violence, and spiritual Zionists have, in addition, envisioned an Israel that will treat its neighbors justly and become a model of justice and peace for the world; nonetheless, it cannot be denied that the intense nationalism associated with the creation of a new nation state in a region where many of the inhabitants have not wanted it has narrowed the space available for Jews who have a different vision of a peaceful world.

These difficulties illustrate one of the dilemmas of conflict resolution in the modern world. Conflict resolution that becomes merely a way of reaching an agreement of some sort between the leadership of opposing parties, regardless of power imbalances and in the absence of a clear conception of justice, is unlikely to gain the enthusiastic support of oppressed peoples. If peace spiritualities have anything to contribute to this discussion it may lie in the insistence that all resolution of conflict take place within a framework of justice to which all participants subscribe.

G. Reconciliation

It has recently become increasingly recognized that conflict resolution, in regions where bitter war has been waged, is a dangerously incomplete process without attention to forgiveness, reconciliation and healing. Spiritual traditions have powerful resources for the accomplishment of these aims, especially in the form of scripture, sacred narrative, ritual, prayer, and meditation. Through these resources people are given access to levels of the self often closed to rational problem-solving.

In contemporary North America, first nations peoples have perceived the need for psychic and social healing of the wounds caused to their societies by the European conquest and by the continuing encroachment of dominant white society on their lands and cultures. For example, in all three major instances of armed conflict between indigenous peoples and the Canadian state in the 1990s, native healers were called upon during or after the conflict.

This need for healing as a component of peacemaking has been recognized for centuries by the Five Nations. According to the Deganawidah epic, Hiawatha was unable to join Deganawidah as a peacemaker until he was healed of the deep grief brought about by the deaths of his daughters. Deganawidah, with this end in mind, took him through a ritual of condolence. On the completion of his healing, Hiawatha was able to go with Deganawidah to cure the mind of the mad and violent Onondaga sorcerer Adadarhoh. When they had straightened out the seven crooks in his body, combed the snakes out of his hair, and made his mind healthy the Great Peace was finally inaugurated. This story was the basis of the Condolence Ceremony, a means by which the Five Nations attempted to put an end to revenge killing within the confederacy and thereby guard the Great Peace. It was clearly recognized that revenge, and subsequent chronic warfare, issued from unresolved grief. The Condolence Ceremony was practiced not only among existing members of the confederacy but as a way of attempting peace with groups (such as the French) outside the Confederacy.

A recent narrative that recognizes the profound connections between healing and peacemaking among indigenous peoples is Leslie Marmon Silko's remarkable novel, *Ceremony*.

Among modern Christian organizations, those in Africa have been especially active in reconciliation and healing. In Liberia the Christian Health Association has carried out reconciliation and trauma healing workshops, which have helped make clear the links between war trauma and violence and the need to address them simultaneously. In Mozambique the churches have addressed the problem of integrating the returning soldier in a scheme whereby the soldier hands over his or her gun to representatives of society, being given in return an instrument for promoting human dignity, such as a bicycle, cow, sewing machine, or typewriter. The process has included dismantling the gun and transforming it into a socially useful instrument. In such rituals the reintegration of the warrior into the community, the turning from death to life, the determination to set people's backs to war and to reconstruct society are powerfully enacted. In South Africa the Truth and Reconciliation Committee chaired by Bishop Desmond Tutu has attempted in an extremely difficult environment to find a way to avoid vengeance and recrimination by granting amnesty to those who have fully disclosed their acts associated with political objectives in the past conflict. Despite its shortcomings, and the inevitable difficulties of balancing the need for reconciliation with the need for justice, the commission has offered a powerful model for other societies emerging from violent conflict.

In Cambodia the Center for Peace and Reconciliation, established chiefly by Buddhists, has attempted, through nonviolence training, peace walks and other programs, to begin the process of healing and the restoration in Cambodia of a peace culture, while in Sri Lanka, a healing garden for children traumatized by the conflict has been established in the Batticaloa region. Although it has been designed to be nondenominational so as to transcend religious and ethnic divisions, the garden has drawn upon earth-centered symbols of peace and wholeness.

Religious organizations explicitly devoted to reconciliation have in the past few decades begun working together more closely than before and sharing strategies. The Fellowship of Reconciliation, for example, was formed in 1914 by Christians, but since that time it has become an interfaith organization, including as affiliates such groups as the Jewish Peace Fellowship and the Buddhist Peace Fellowship. This is but one case of the emergence of an transsectarian peace spirituality.

H. Building a Tradition of Peace Spirituality

However much spirituality may be a matter of the interior life, however much it may refuse to be institutionalized, the question inevitably arises as to what can be done to preserve, transmit and expand it. Can one build a tradition of peace spirituality?

A social group that emphasizes inwardness, contemplation, and the like must make available to its members, and to others it may wish to reach, the values, symbols, and practices that permit access to the spiritual realm. Where the dominant culture is inattentive to this realm, or even actively denies its existence, these values, symbols, and practices will necessarily be countercultural. It is not unusual for a serious tension to exist between dominant culture and the culture of peace spirituality. During the Cold War, it often happened that states spent considerable energy mobilizing populations against the official enemy through state rituals and myth, while those committed to a spirituality of peace tried to promote directly contrary perspectives. Creeds, prayers, and rituals directly parodying state versions were developed during the 1980s to keep alive an alternative vision.

Spiritual traditions grow through the selection of a corpus of texts, a set of practices and teachings, and organizational rules. The rules may be explicit and detailed and may deal openly both with spiritual practices and with issues of power and the interaction with the secular world. Monastic codes exemplify this combination of spiritual and wordily concern. Likewise, to take the Five Nations again as an example, the Great Law (also known as the Constitution of the Five Nations) completes the narrative of Deganawidah by bringing it into concrete realization: the use of consensus and discussion in decision making, the roles of women and men, the permissible uses of coercion, the procedures for the selection of leaders, are all laid down in detail with the explicit aim of preserving the Great Peace. The Religious Society of Friends has likewise given careful attention to the development of forms of organization, discourse, accountability and decision making that express the group's primary values and allow room for spiritual discernment.

Some spiritual traditions are so inward looking that they are content to preserve their vision without making any attempt to change the world. Quietism of this sort was common prior to the birth of the modern peace movement in the early part of the 19th century. In the past two centuries peace spirituality has undergone a transformation, becoming less content with witness to the world and more involved in struggle to change the world. Of course, not all varieties of peace spirituality are equally active. In the Asian Buddhist community, for example, there remains a good deal of controversy about the proper role of spiritual leaders and the extent to which it is acceptable for them to be involved in social and political matters. The International Network of Engaged Buddhists is an organization that attempts, with sister organizations, to work out what a socially engaged Buddhism in the modern world ought to look like. The organization sponsors numerous projects for peace and for social and environmental justice. Likewise, in the historic Christian peace churches one finds a range of views on the degree and sort of involvement with the world that is appropriate. Yet the formation of organizations such as Christian Peacemaker Teams (cosponsored by the three historic peace churches), which actively enter situations of violent conflict to help local efforts at peacemaking, witnesses to a powerful confluence of a traditional pacifism and a very modern concern for sophisticated political strategizing. More recent traditions of peace spirituality—those, for example, connected to feminism and environmentalism—are explicitly dedicated to engagement with the world and see this as essential to spiritual expression.

Many of the most active nongovernmental organizations dedicated to assisting people in war zones and other difficult situations came into being through one or another form of peace spirituality. Likewise, the lives and thinking of former Secretary Generals U Thant and Dag Hammarskjold, as well as numerous other officials in the United Nations, testify to the influence of traditions of peace spirituality on that organization.

On the other hand, judging from developments of the last 100 years, it can be expected that there will be increasing communication and cooperation between people belonging to different forms of peace spirituality. Many people who participate in the movement for a more comprehensive peace spirituality already find their identification with this movement stronger than their identification with the formal religion to which they belong. It can be expected that there will be increased borrowing of practices between religious traditions and a growth of interfaith spiritual practice relevant to peacemaking. Spirituality, which privileges direct experience and actual encounter with other human beings, may prove itself more adaptable and less dangerous than the relatively rigid religious dogmas and political ideologies that have often dominated human development in the past.

Also See the Following Articles

CONSCIENTIOUS OBJECTION, ETHICS OF • CRITIQUES OF VIOLENCE • ETHICAL AND RELIGIOUS TRADITIONS, EASTERN • ETHICAL AND RELIGIOUS TRADITIONS, WESTERN • INSTITUTIONALIZATION OF NONVIOLENCE • MORAL JUDGMENTS AND VALUES • NONVIOLENCE THEORY AND PRACTICE • PEACE CULTURE • PEACEMAKING AND PEACEBUILDING

IV. FUTURE PROSPECTS OF PEACE SPIRITUALITY

From the perspective of practical peacemaking, the weaknesses to which peace spirituality is prone are closely connected to the features that give it special strength. Utopian thought may be associated with serious naiveté and denial and can also, at times, lead to forms of millenarianism that are intolerant and even violent. The moral certitude of the prophet can make him or her ill-suited for the compromises sometimes necessary in peacemaking. The renunciant may be more interested in self-purification and perfection than in concrete change in the world. And while spirituality is often promoted as transcending the sectarianism of institutionalized religion, it can easily re-create the bases of division, demonizing its opponents, and expending its creative energies in exercises of self-legitimation. Finally, the need of spiritual traditions for highly specific symbols, narratives and practices is problematic in so far as these may be meaningless or repugnant to members of other groups with whom peace is sought.

Bibliography

Bainton, R. (1960). *Christian attitudes toward war and peace.* New York: Abingdon.
Blatt, M., Davis, U., & Kleinbaum, P. (Ed.). (1975). *Dissent & ideology in Israel: Resistance to the draft 1948–1973.* London: Ithaca Press.
Brock, P. (1991). *Freedom from violence: Sectarian nonresistance from the Middle Ages to the Great War.* Toronto: University of Toronto Press.
Brock, P. (1991). *Freedom from war: Nonsectarian pacifism 1814–1914.* Toronto: University of Toronto Press.
Crow, R., Grant, P., & Ibrahim, S. (Ed.). (1990). *Arab nonviolent political struggle in the Middle East.* Boulder: Lynne Rienner.
Dennis, M. (1993). *Cultivating a landscape of peace: Iroquois-European encounters in seventeenth-century America.* Ithaca: Cornell University Press.
Green, M. (1986). *The origins of nonviolence: Tolstoy and Gandhi in their historical settings.* University Park: Pennsylvania Univ. State Press.
Kotler, A. (Ed.). (1996). *Engaged Buddhist reader.* Berkeley: Parallax.
Kung, H., & Kuschel, K-J. (Ed.). (1993). *A global ethic: The declaration of the parliament of the world's religions.* New York: Continuum.
McAllister, P. (1988). *You can't kill the spirit: Stories of women and nonviolent action.* Philadelphia: New Society.
Paige, G., Satha-Anand, C., & Gilliatt, S. (Ed.). (1993). *Islam and nonviolence.* Honolulu: Matsunaga Institute for Peace, University of Hawaii.

Parker, A. (1968). *Parker on the Iroquois.* Edited by W. Fenton. Syracuse: Syracuse University Press.

Polner, M., & Goodman, N. (Ed.). (1994). *The challenge of Shalom: The Jewish tradition of peace and justice.* Philadelphia: New Society.

Queen, C., & King, S. (Ed.). (1996). *Engaged Buddhism: Buddhist liberation movements in Asia.* Albany: SUNY Press.

Schneiders, S. (1989). Spirituality in the academy. *Theological Studies, 50* (4), 676–697.

Silko, L. (1977). *Ceremony.* Viking, New York.

Smock, D. R. (1995). *Perspectives on pacifism: Christian, Jewish, and Muslim views on nonviolence and international conflict.* Washington: United States Institute of Peace Press.

Steere, D. (Ed.) (1984). *Quaker spirituality: Selected writings.* New York: Paulist Press.

Wallace, P. (1946). *The white roots of peace.* Philadelphia: Univ. of Pennsylvania.

Wink, W. (1992). *Engaging the powers: Discernment and resistance in a world of domination.* Minneapolis: Fortress Press.

Zerbe, G. (1993). *Non-retaliation in early Jewish and New Testament texts: Ethical themes in social contexts.* Sheffield: Sheffield Academic Press.

Sports

Gordon W. Russell

University of Lethbridge

GLOSSARY

Aggression Any form of behavior directed toward the goal of harming or injuring another living being who is motivated to avoid such treatment. However, the infliction of harm in interpersonal competition does not constitute aggression unless it is in violation of the agreed-upon rules of play.

Catharsis Aggression is thought to be reduced as a result of observing others behave aggressively or, by behaving aggressively oneself.

Competition The athlete(s) strives to perform well against some personal or external standard of excellence.

Correlation Refers to the strength of the relationship between two variables. The index ranges from -1.00 through zero to $+1.00$.

Rivalry The athletes' thoughts are directed toward defeating, hurting, or humiliating their opponents.

SPORTS and recreation play a significant part in the day to day lives of most people. The results of a U.S. national poll revealed that 71% of adults regarded themselves as sports fans while 73% reported participating in a sport or recreational activity. The potential benefits arising from their involvement are considerable both from the standpoint of the individual and society.

Sports can enrich the quality of our social interactions. As a topic for conversation, sports offer a refreshing alternative to sharing observations on the weather. Where a common interest is found people may be brought closer together as they exchange views on the reason for last Saturday's loss or share in their admiration of a team or sports figure. Of course, formal memberships, for example, supporters clubs, provide opportunities for even stronger bonds to be forged.

International competition is frequently touted as a means to foster liking among athletes and the nations they represent. The 1994 Goodwill Games and Richard Nixon's visit to China are often cited as examples of sport's capacity for bringing nations closer together. Nixon's invitation to visit China was linked to a tour by a U.S. Ping-Pong team in an act of what has been called "Ping-Pong diplomacy." Although Nixon's mission was successful, there is little to suggest that Ping-Pong provided anything more than a timely and convenient backdrop against which to stage his meetings with Chinese officials.

Individuals also stand to derive physical benefits from their active participation in sports and recreational activities. In recent years many people have turned to sports and/or exercise hoping to realize overall health benefits and thereby, an increase in life expectancy. Certainly, an active rather than a sedentary life style is beneficial but is longevity necessarily increased?

The answer is seen in the results of a Harvard study. Over 2000 men born between 1860 and 1889 were classified as either major athletes (lettered in major varsity sports, e.g., rowing, football, track), minor athletes (participated in minor sports programs, e.g., swimming, cricket, golf) or nonathletes. It was the category of minor athletes that clearly outlived both their extremely active and more sedentary classmates. Moderation then, would appear to be the best course.

In sum, sports offer us numerous benefits, whether as participants or spectators. Among the potential benefits are improved social relationships, personal satisfactions, physical well-being, and even an increase in life expectancy; all can be realized in the context of modern-day sports and recreational activities. However, there is a dark side to some sports, namely, gratuitous aggression. The study of aggression specifically in sports warrants brief mention, particularly as several of its features sets it apart from other research settings.

I. THE STUDY OF AGGRESSION IN SPORTS

Social scientists from a variety of disciplines and countries have in recent decades turned to sports as a setting in which to test aggression hypotheses. Foremost among several advantages to conducting research in sports is an always welcome gain in the triangulation of measurement. That is to say, the external validity of findings from the social science laboratory are greatly increased when confirmed in a naturalistic sports setting using entirely new measures. To this end, sports provide the means to develop behavioral measures of aggression either from the direct observation of athletes or from archival sources. Thus far a variety of innovative measures has been derived for the major sports of baseball, basketball, football, ice hockey, and soccer.

A. Quality of Data

The sports world has a passion for keeping extensive and detailed records. Sport statisticians meticulously record an exceedingly large—in some sports, excessive—number of individual and game events, for example, goals, assists, rule violations, attendance, temperature at game time, and so on. The event of immediate interest, aggressive rule violations, originates with highly trained and experienced experts, that is, game officials, who make on the spot judgments regarding the type and severity of acts of interpersonal aggression.

Researchers also benefit from the validity of behavioral measures derived from direct observation or official records. Few doubt that late hits, swearing at officials, and the ever-popular fistfight are anything other than unabashed acts of aggression. Such actions meet generally accepted definitions of aggression in reflecting the aggressive tactics of athletes intentionally attempting to do harm to others, actions that go beyond the agreed-upon rules of play.

B. Uninhibited Expression

Perhaps the most important advantage to studying aggression in sports lies with its freer and more natural expression. Wartime notwithstanding, sports is perhaps the only major sphere of human activity in which acts of aggression are not only tolerated by a large segment of society but enthusiastically applauded. Were the violence of the ring or gridiron to erupt on Main Street, court appearances would inevitably follow. The laws that normally ensure civilized conduct are temporarily suspended during play; athletes are instead governed by the official rules of their sport.

It can be argued that in this climate of approval athletes are relatively unconstrained by the usual concerns with social condemnation and the legal consequences of their actions. Coupled with puny and ineffectual punishments for transgressions, for example, being shown a yellow card, being sent to the showers, athletes are free to express their aggressive impulses in a natural, uninhibited and free-wheeling fashion. By contrast, aggression expressed in the laboratory is typically subject to distortion by a range of troublesome and potentially biasing artifacts such as social desirability, image management, anxiety, and guilt.

C. Trends

Aggression measures derived from sports records allow researchers to track trends. Official records and newspaper summaries, exist for most major sports and in some sports such as cricket, soccer, and rugby, date back to the 19th century. Historical records provide the means to see how rule changes, social norms, and so on have gradually transformed a sport into its present-day form. In some instances we find startling differences between current levels of violence and that which occurred during a sport's formative years. For example, a tally of deaths occurring in English rugby during the three years

1891 to 1893 shows that 71 players were killed in Yorkshire county alone.

Archival sources also provide the means for a continuous tracking of player violence over time. To illustrate, aggressive player infractions were tallied for all games played in the National Hockey League during the 1930–1931 season. Thereafter, the procedure was repeated at 5-year intervals to the present. On-ice aggression was found to have steadily declined from 1930 until approximately 1960 at which point the trend reversed. Since then player aggression has risen sharply and steadily reaching a level approximately four times that seen in the postwar years.

A few sports owe their very existence to violence, for example, professional wrestling, boxing. However, most others can and have been played with little or no violence. Regrettably, diverse forms of aggression have needlessly found their way into many of our major sports with accompanying personal and social costs. In addition to often life long debilitating injuries to participants, violent behaviors are often learned and put into practice by aspiring youngsters. Others watching player violence from the stands or on television may also be adversely affected. What follows then is an overview of sports aggression research highlighting selected findings. Coverage of the topic deals first with aggression at the individual and group levels with the focus then widening to include spectator violence, the role of media, and influences that reach far beyond the sports venue.

II. INDIVIDUAL AGGRESSION

A. Are Athletes More Aggressive than Others?

A perennial question asks if athletes as a group are more aggressive than others in society. One might speculate that a selection factor operates such that sports attract more aggressive people to their ranks or alternately, provide training or experiences that increase the aggressivity of athletes. Of course, those clinging to a belief in catharsis might see participation in combatant sports leading to levels of aggression lower than those in society. Evidence on the question is fairly clear. For example, the aggression of nonathletes, athletes in non-contact sports (e.g., tennis, swimming) and those in contact sports (e.g., football, wrestling) was compared in one phase of a controlled laboratory experiment. Using a behavioral measure, shock, the three groups of

subjects did not differ in the amount of aggression they directed toward a confederate.

Similar results were obtained in a second study that compared three groups of freshmen students, those who had never "lettered" in a sport, those who had discontinued playing football after high school, and members of the university football team. No differences were revealed on a measure of anger. Finally, a comparison of two university tennis squads and a noncompetitive student sample again failed to uncover differences in scores on a hostility inventory. However, in an exception to this pattern, high school football players were found to score higher on measures of hostility than were physical education students. On balance, the evidence for athletes being more aggressive than others in society is at best weak.

A companion question might ask if sports fans are more aggressive than others. Although the evidence is thin, the answer to our question is again, equivocal. In 1973, Stuart Miller administered his 20-item Football Fandom scale and several social-personality measures to a sample of college students. Men identified as fans scored higher than nonfans on measures of assaultiveness, hostility, and verbal aggression. More recently, however, a study comparing Dutch soccer fans with nonfans failed to reveal differences in physical assaultiveness.

B. Are Athletes More Likely to Rape?

Hardly a month goes by that we don't learn of a sexual assault by a member(s) of an athletic team. When allegations are made against celebrity athletes, the event is headline news for the weeks and months that follow. It is easy to understand why the massive publicity given to such stories would lead one to think that something is terribly wrong in the sports world. In recent years, speculation has raged in both the popular press and academic writings suggesting that all-male sports groups foster attitudes that cause their members to be disproportionately represented in rape statistics.

Is there good evidence to support these claims? First, only a handful of studies have addressed the question. The few existing studies have thus far been conducted on college campuses where reports of sexual assault have been tallied for the general student population and compared with those of student athletes and fraternity members. Taken together, the results of these studies contradict the view that athletes (and fraternity members) are any more likely than the rest of the male population to commit rape.

The persistent notion that all-male living arrangements, typical of athletic teams, tend to foster rape-supportive attitudes toward women and lead to a greater incidence of rape has also been tested. To the surprise of many, males living in mixed-sex housing rated the likelihood of their committing rape significantly higher than students in all-male housing.

At this juncture, a major recommendation to be drawn from these early studies is that educational programs and other means of reducing the incidence of rape should be directed at the general population of males. The tactic of specifically targeting athletes is likely misdirected.

C. Individual Differences in Aggressivity

A handful of studies has examined the relationships between athletic aggression and several models of personality, including the Type A, Macho, and Machiavellian personalities in addition to Locus of Control. For example, the Locus of Control model has proven useful in identifying the personality profiles of athletes occupying particular positions on sports teams as well as its overall relationship to aggression. The model makes a basic distinction between people with an external orientation who believe that events in their lives are largely under the control of external forces, such as luck or fate, and those with an internal orientation who believe that they can to a degree influence the course of events in their day-to-day lives. As predicted by the model, hockey players with an external orientation are involved in a greater number of on-ice fights than their teammates. They seemingly are less able than internals to utilize alternative, nonviolent responses, such as negotiation, in a developing confrontation and just let the "inevitable" happen.

A second personality model related to athletic aggression is the Machiavellian personality developed by Richard Christie and Florence Geis in the early 1970s. The profile of the Machiavellian includes a lack of concern with conventional morality, the absence of affect in interpersonal relations, and a lack of commitment to the goals of an organization. In addition to being aggressive, high Machs resort to guile, deceit, and deception in manipulating others in pursuit of their goals. In sports, hockey teams have a disproportionate number of high Machs playing on defence. Moreover, during the season these unscrupulous individuals are more heavily penalized for interpersonal aggression than are their teammates.

D. Social Influences on Individual Aggressivity

The sports world represents only a minor category from which youngsters choose their heroes. Rather, heroes appear to be drawn mainly from among friends and relatives and, to a lesser extent, the entertainment industry. By one tally, boys choose sports figures as heroes more often than girls (16% versus 6%), make a greater effort to emulate their choices and in turn, are influenced to a greater extent.

Concern is frequently expressed over the quality of exemplars, role models, heroes, and so on, who have achieved a measure of fame in their sport and serve as persons to be emulated by youngsters. Certainly, that concern is justified where sport celebrities are seen to be engaged in illegal, immoral, or unethical conduct and thereafter continue to be lavishly rewarded by society. That is, the pairing of a celebrity's antisocial behavior with public acclaim, prestige, and/or wealth creates a condition that maximizes their potential influence on admirers.

Athletes exhibit various attributes that make some worthy of selection as personal heroes, for example, exceptional skill, personal charm, and charitable deeds. Unfortunately, it is their aggressive behavior that sometimes forms the basis for their selection. Michael Smith has reported a positive relationship between young hockey players' estimates of how "aggressive" their favorite NHL player is and the level of aggression they themselves display in their own league play. Asked about their style of play, the youngsters admit learning dirty tactics from their heroes, tactics they put to use in their own games. Young football players similarly learn illegal tactics from older players in the college and professional ranks. Tactics ranging from spearing to late hits to stepping on downed opponents are observed and incorporated into their own play. Teams with a reputation for toughness are also singled out for emulation. That is, hockey teams rated as most popular by young players are overall those that have amassed the greatest number of penalty minutes for aggressive infractions.

In general, youngsters choosing heroes from high-contact sports are more aggressive in playing their own sport. More importantly, these same youngsters have been shown to be more aggressive than others in their day to day activities outside of sports, for example, in the home, at school, and on playgrounds. The influence of malevolent sports heroes then, can reach well beyond the playing field to adversely affect the social relationships of their admirers.

E. Environmental Influences

Environmental factors are often influential in determining the occurrence and intensity of aggressive behaviors exhibited by athletes, spectators, and others involved in sports. The list of factors thus far shown to affect people's aggression includes crowding, darkness, odors, ions, noise, colors, and temperature. Two studies will serve to demonstrate the influence of environmental factors specifically on athletic aggression.

1. Color

One of the first decisions for owners of a new sports franchise is the selection of the team's colors. The choice of color is recognized as a important consideration in creating a club's image for the public and of course, for their league opponents. In the case of black, everyone recognizes its long standing association with evil, death, and generally sinister forces. Throughout the tradition of cowboy movies, the villain trying to run the poor widow and her children off their homestead invariably wore black, whereas the Lone Ranger and other crime fighters principally wore white. Teams seeking to impress their opponents with their toughness or aggressive play typically have chosen black as the basic color for their uniforms.

An intriguing question is whether professional sports teams actually behave in ways that are consistent with the color of their uniforms. That is, are teams wearing black also "black-hearted"? The answer was found in the penalty records of the National Football League and the National Hockey League.

The uniforms from both leagues were first classified as being either predominantly black, for example, Los Angeles Raiders, or nonblack, for example, Miami Dolphins. An examination of league records showed that teams at or near the top of the standings in the penalty column typically wore black. Moreover, an increase in penalties occurred when teams switched from nonblack to black uniforms.

The results beg the question as to why the wearing of black results in teams being more heavily penalized. Is it perhaps because referees feel compelled to call a tighter game against teams wearing black? On the other hand, it is just as reasonable to suggest that players wearing black actually behave more aggressively.

It seems that neither referees nor players are colorblind. In a follow-up study using experienced referees, it was found that referees do indeed, call more penalties against teams attired in black. It also appears that when athletes don black uniforms they revert to a more aggressive style of play. The original finding of higher levels of aggression by teams that have adopted black uniforms then, has two explanations. It results from the combination of referees' calling a tighter game and, the players themselves giving freer reign to their aggressive urges when attired in black. As a footnote, black-uniformed teams in the NFL and NHL had the same percentage of wins as teams wearing nonblack uniforms.

2. Temperature

A second environmental question that has drawn considerable interest from researchers is the relationship between temperature and aggression. Research from archival investigations has established that as temperatures soar into the high 90s and above, people become increasingly aggressive. For example, police records in Texas show that when temperatures rise into the region of 100° Fahrenheit there is a corresponding linear increase in reports of homicides, assault, and rape.

Sports provided an alternative setting for testing the temperature-aggression hypothesis. The prediction that increases in interpersonal aggression accompany increases in temperature was tested using baseball records over three seasons of play in a Texas league. The researchers cleverly adopted the number of times batters were struck by an "errant" pitch as their measure of aggression. Consistent with a heat-aggression hypothesis, as the temperatures recorded at game time rose so too did the number of batters hit by pitches. There was no indication of a downturn at the highest temperatures as predicted by a rival, curvilinear model. Parenthetically, other explanations for their results such as sweaty palms or fatigue were ruled out in the analysis.

III. GROUP AGGRESSION

A. Group Perceptions

When people join a team or organization, they frequently undergo a fundamental change in their perceptions. More specifically, they develop strong "we" versus "they" views of their team vis a vis other teams striving for similar goals. These perceptions of one's team in relation to competing teams can lead to increased liking and cohesion among its members. However, at the same time these perceptions foster the development of rivalrous attitudes and behaviors toward members of the out-group(s). The phenomenon is seen in several studies involving young boys attending summer camp.

In an Oklahoma study, the campers were carefully

matched and assigned to separate cabins. Within each of the cabins, identified by the boys as the "Rattlers" and the "Eagles," strong bonds of friendship and loyalty quickly sprang up. However, hostility soon developed between the cabins with name calling and derogatory remarks highlighting their interactions.

The camp organizers arranged for the two cabins to compete against each other in a week-long series of competitive events. The result was that the initial antagonisms soon intensified. This phase of the study was abruptly halted when at week's end a full-scale food fight erupted in the camp dining hall. Seemingly, hostility between rival groups is fueled by "we" versus "they" perceptions that develop all too easily between newly formed groups.

Strong identificatory ties and in-group feelings of solidarity can also lead group members to see aggression where others might not. Leon Mann interviewed Melbourne fans at the conclusion of an Australian Rules football match. In what he describes as mild sore-loser reactions, fans of the losing team saw dirtier play, poor officiating, and felt the winning side benefited more from penalties. In recognition of the implications for fan violence, Mann has included these often bitter reactions to a loss as an important contributory factor in his taxonomy of sports riots.

B. Group Aggression

The aggression of groups (teams) in competitive play has received only limited attention from researchers. One of the more thoroughly researched questions is that of the course of aggression during a combatant contest. There is a virtual consensus on the question insofar as five studies in Canada and the United States point to increasing levels of player violence over the course of hockey games. Violence it seems, begets even more violence.

Does familiarity breed liking? In general, the answer is "yes." However, in the case of hockey teams meeting over the course of the season familiarity appears instead to breed hostility. Levels of on-ice violence have been shown to increase with the number of times any two teams meet. Much like the Rattlers and Eagles in Oklahoma, their initial hostility toward each other intensifies with repeated exposure to their rivals.

A feature of team aggression likely related to the above is the finding that intradivisional hockey games see more aggression than interdivisional matches. Games against opponents outside of one's division are fewer in number and hence, there is only limited exposure to rivals. Familiarity has fewer opportunities to breed hostility. Alternatively, traditional rivalries are generally fostered within a division. Such games are often touted as "battles" or "must wins" by local media. On those occasions players may well live up to media hyperbole and arrive at the arena more determined than ever to do battle.

A further question concerns differences in the aggression of teams playing at home versus on the road. As with the ubiquitous home field performance advantage, is there also a home field aggression "advantage"? Here the answer is one of no differences. A review of studies involving soccer, football, and hockey in four countries yielded nonsignificant results in five of nine cases. The remaining four studies were equally divided between greater aggression at home and greater aggression at away games.

The records of 297 Israeli soccer teams provided additional insights into the dynamics of group aggression. Teams at the top of their division and those at the bottom attempting to stave off relegation were more violent than teams occupying intermediate positions. Furthermore, the frequency of player fights was found to increase from the amateur to the top professional divisions. Finally, in the Israeli experience, teams playing for subordinate ethnic communities were more violent than those representing large urban centers.

Other studies of team aggression have been designed to test predictions from various theories of aggression. For example, hockey records provided one such test of the frustration-aggression hypothesis. Simply put, the closer people are to attaining a goal when they are impeded or otherwise thwarted, the greater the degree of frustration they will experience. Those experiencing the most frustration, being thwarted just short of their goal, will predictably exhibit the most aggression.

An index of aggression was developed for each team from the season records of a senior men's league. Interpersonal aggression was operationalized as the total penalty minutes awarded by game officials for aggressive rule infractions such as slashing, roughing, and fighting. The prediction then, was that teams falling just short of their goal—in this case, second place in the league standings—would be most severely thwarted and consequently exhibit the greatest amount of on-ice aggression.

As seen in Figure 1, this is precisely what occurred. As teams occupied first place at various times during the season they drew very few aggressive penalties whereas those most severely thwarted, occupying second place, incurred the greatest number of penalties. Thereafter, teams occupying third on down to sixth place during the season exhibited decreasing levels of interpersonal aggression.

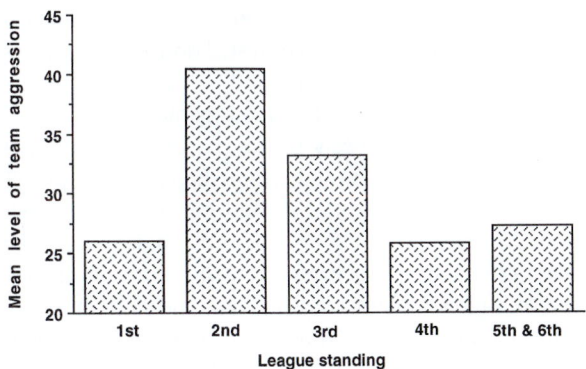

FIGURE 1 Team aggression and league standing. [From Russell, G. W., & Drewry, B. R. (1976). Crowd size and competitive aspects of aggression in ice hockey: An archival study. *Human Relations, 29*, 723–735.]

Commentary abounds to the effect that gratuitous interpersonal aggression in some combatant sports is to be expected, inevitable, or in the nature of the game. Quite the contrary. Athletes have it within their means to control their aggression. For example, in ice hockey there is a general recognition that drawing an aggressive penalty late in a close game can seriously jeopardize the final outcome. In such circumstances, when hockey teams are tied or within one goal of a tie, on-ice aggression is lower than when there is a larger differential. Thus, athletes can control their aggressive impulses and play within the rules when it is in their interests to do so.

IV. SPECTATOR VIOLENCE

A. Introduction

Riots have with some regularity occurred on a worldwide scale and have resulted in numerous deaths and a far greater number of injuries. Considering just the sport of football, Table 1 presents a sample of major tragedies that have been reported in this century.

Riots are an uncommon but nonetheless troubling feature of modern-day sports. They can erupt in any sport that attracts a large and passionate following. However, certain sports seem more prone than others to riotous behavior. One comparison simply tallied the number of sports riots that had occurred in the United States from 1960 to 1972. Football led the way (61) followed by baseball (58), basketball (46), hockey (29), and boxing (19). Of course, comparisons across sports are spurious without taking into account the frequencies with which they are played. However, it is noteworthy that with the possible exception of baseball, sports featuring interpersonal aggression and varying degrees of player contact dominate the list. The fans of equally competitive noncontact sports rarely if ever find cause to riot. Among the multiple causes of fan violence, just how important is the factor of player aggression?

B. The Effects of Observing Player Violence

Support for a connection between player violence and crowd violence is seen in an influential paper by Michael

TABLE I

Deaths and Injuries Associated with Football Disturbances

Date	Location	Deaths	Injury	Date	Location	Deaths	Injury
1902	Glasgow	25	350	1979	Lagos	24	27
1946	Bolton (UK)	33	500	1980	Calcutta	16	100
1957	Florence	—	120	1981	Athens	21	54
1959	Naples	—	65	1982	Moscow	60	—
1961	Chile	5	300	1982	Algiers	8	600
1964	Istanbul	—	84	1985	Peking	??	??
1964	Lima	350	500	1985	Bradford	57	200
1966	Cairo	—	300	1985	Mexico	10	30
1967	Kayseri	48	602	1985	Heysel	39	470
1968	Buenos Aires	72	113	1989	Hillsboro	95	400
1971	Glasgow	66	—	1991	Johannesburg	42	42
1974	Cairo	48	47	1996	Lusaka	9	78
1979	Hamburg	1	15	1996	Zaire	50	??

Smith of York University. He examined the events that precipitated hostile outbursts among sports spectators. His was an archival study that analyzed media accounts of crowd violence in a variety of sports from around the world. A major finding was that 74% of all hostile outbursts were immediately preceded by player violence. Parenthetically, controversial calls by game officials (15%) and spectators baiting players (11%) were identified as lesser causes.

The effects on spectators of witnessing player violence were formally investigated in an early field experiment. The study was conducted on the occasion of the Army-Navy football game held annually in Philadelphia. The design pitted three theoretical positions against each other, that is, a cathartic view, the frustration-aggression hypothesis, and Social Learning theory.

Men were intercepted on a random basis and asked to complete a hostility measure either as they entered or as they left the stadium after the game. The same procedure was followed at an equally competitive but nonviolent control event (gymnastics). Hostility was found to increase from before to after the football game whereas there were no changes at the gymnastics competition.

Neither the cathartic prediction of reduced hostility nor the frustration-aggression prediction that only fans of the losing team would show an increase found support in the results. In this instance, Social Learning theory was the sole beneficiary. It had predicted an overall increase in hostility resulting from a general weakening of inhibitions against the expression of aggression.

A replication subsequently examined sex differences and the effects of viewing fictional aggression. A number of writers have suggested that where aggression is seen as a spoof, for example, cartoons, roller derby, and professional wrestling, the audience members will experience a cathartic reduction in their aggressive urges.

In a test of the prediction, male and female Canadian university students were randomly assigned to either before or after conditions at a hockey game (realistic aggression), a professional wrestling card (fictional), or a major swimming competition (control event). Students overwhelmingly saw the wrestling violence as sham. Nevertheless, there was an overall increase in hostility. A similar increase also occurred for men and women attending the hockey game whereas there were no before–after differences at the swim meet.

The effects on spectator hostility of observing player violence have also been examined in a more detailed fashion. Before–after designs leave unanswered the question of the course of spectator hostility in relation to player violence during a contest. Additional measures administered during the first and second period intermissions of a fight-filled hockey game revealed that spectator hostility closely tracks player violence. That is, spectator hostility peaked immediately after a player brawl near the end of the second period. By contrast, levels of spectator hostility did not change over the entire course of a peaceable (control) game. From before to after a violent contest then, spectator hostility follows a curvilinear course the peak of which is centered over episodes of player violence.

The Israeli soccer study noted above adds an important footnote to the question of player aggression and its influence on spectators. Teams whose rosters include violent players are more likely to have violent spectators. However, the relationship was asymmetric. In the authors' words "Players ... exert a significant impact on spectators' violence, but spectators do not affect players' violence."

C. General Effects

Other aspects of our emotional state also undergo changes as a result of our attendance at combatant sports events. Physiological arousal is seen to increase and, as with hostility (above), has been shown to closely track the course of player violence. The importance of this lies in the fact that while arousal is neither a necessary nor sufficient condition for aggression, it acts to facilitate aggression. That is to say, spectators in a heightened state of arousal are more likely than unaroused individuals to respond aggressively to provocations.

Spectators also experience other affective mood changes. For example, over the course of witnessing a violent hockey game, there is a general deterioration in the quality of one's mood state. Social affection and surgency decrease while anxiety, fatigue, and hostility increase. Thus, although watching a violent contest may be an entertaining experience, there are nonetheless attendant emotional costs to the individual. Moreover singly or in combination, negative mood states may facilitate disruptive behaviors in the stands and the quality of spectators' postgame interactions with others in the community.

D. Football Hooliganism

Crowd disorders at sporting events have been a matter of concern to government and civil authorities, sport and entertainment officials, and the general public throughout recorded history. In recent times, public attention has been focused on violent excesses that have plagued football primarily in Europe and Latin America. Disturbances occurring before, during, and after matches have drawn media attention and have been a particularly worrisome matter for devotees of the sport.

Sociologists have taken the lead in their efforts toward identifying the biographical and societal factors associated with football violence. An extensive literature has consistently identified troublemakers as young, single males. They are further described as in some respects marginalized, often being unemployed, less well educated, and sharing a sense of being alienated from the mainstream of society. Interestingly, when questioned about their violence, they disavow responsibility for their actions and instead attribute their misconduct to external causes.

E. Who Riots?

Attempts to empirically investigate the dynamics of riots and the psychological makeup of those involved have been sporadic and infrequent. Studying riots in situ is of course, made difficult by the fact that they are unscheduled with respect to time and place. Moreover, given the illegality of riots, those involved generally are unable or unwilling to cooperate with researchers. Retrospective accounts by participants or observers are further subject to several biasing influences, for example, selective selection and selective recall of events.

The tack taken in a recent series of field studies has involved on-site interviews with Canadian, Dutch, and Finnish sports spectators, a small minority of whom (approximately 8%) indicate a strong likelihood that they would involve themselves in a riot were one to erupt in the stands. The format in which sports events are staged dictates a piecemeal approach if an investigator intends to pursue questions of individual differences using multiple inventories. In the case of ice hockey, spectators are available principally during the brief, 15-minute intermissions between periods of play.

The results of nine field studies are consistent with the European football literature insofar as those most likely to join a disturbance are typically young, single males. Several social factors have also been found to be predictive of men's self-reported likelihood of escalating a disturbance. Spectators who attend hockey games for the reason "I like to watch the fights" and those who have had numerous fights during the past year are also more likely to join a disturbance.

There has been a long-standing recognition that

groups rather than solitary individuals are more likely to initiate crowd violence. As Leon Mann and Philip Pearce have observed "exhibitionism and displays of bravado will be found virtually only among those who are part of a group and not among solitary spectators." The prediction found support in the series. Men attending hockey games in the company of other men foresaw a greater likelihood of joining a disturbance than those attending alone.

Cognitive variables may also play a part in disorderly behaviors. In addition to making external attributions for their misconduct, those who would involve themselves are subject to the false consensus effect. These people tend "... to see their own behavioral choices and judgments as relatively common and appropriate to existing circumstances while viewing alternate responses as uncommon, deviant, or inappropriate." Two studies in the series confirmed a prediction that those reporting a strong likelihood of joining in a developing riot believe that a disproportionately greater number of other spectators are inclined to take similar action.

The false consensus effect may contribute to the likelihood of crowd violence. One might speculate that those inclined to join a disturbance and who believe that a disproportionately large number of other spectators are similarly inclined may see such interventions as more normative. As a consequence, inhibitions that are normally engaged when one considers a deviant course of action may be weakened. Furthermore, individuals may act precipitously emboldened by the belief that others would approve of their intervention and are poised to follow their lead.

A battery of personality measures was administered piecemeal to spectators at various sports sites with a view to establishing the relationships between each measure and spectators' self-reported likelihood of escalating a disturbance. The battery included anger, physical aggression, public self-consciousness, psychopathy, impulsivity, and sensation seeking. Each measure was found to be related to the likelihood of spectators' involvement in crowd disorders when it was administered on one or more occasions in the series.

Many of the measures administered in the series are intercorrelated. For this reason, an overarching study involving the simultaneous administration of all previous measures was undertaken with a view to identifying a fewer number of measures predictive of joining in a disturbance. Male university students who regularly attend hockey games and who might be found in the stands on any given evening served as participants. As shown in Table II, all but one of the previous measures were again related to the likelihood of involvement.

TABLE II

Relationships Between Likelihood of Involvement, and
Social/Psychological Variables ($N = 78$)

	Likelihood of Involvement
Recency of fight	.67**
"I like to watch the fights"	.57**
Number of fights	.55**
Age	−.37**
Size of male group	.30**
False consensus effect	.20*
Physical aggression	.53**
Impulsivity	.46**
Anger	.31**
Psychopathy	.30**
Sensation-seeking	.21*
Public self-consciousness	−.06

* $p < .05$ (one-tailed).
** $p < .005$.
(Russell & Arms, 1998).

This, despite a much younger sample and different means of recruitment. Next, all measures were entered as predictors in a multiple regression analysis with the likelihood of involvement ratings serving as the criterion.

The analysis yielded a multiple correlation [$R = .807$, $F (12, 75) = 9.79$, $p < .0001$) that accounted for fully 65% of the variance. Just two measures emerged as significant predictors, namely, the amount of time that had elapsed since the participants' last serious fight and, their ratings of "I like to watch the fights" (the former measure was introduced for the first time). Seemingly, men who have recently been embroiled in fights and those who are drawn to an event by the prospect of witnessing player violence are especially likely to be found at the center of crowd disorders.

V. THE MEDIA AND SPORTS VIOLENCE

A. Introduction

Much of the public debate swirling around the question of media violence has centered on television and movie themes that feature violent excesses by agents of law enforcement, gangsters, and psychotic killers running amok in a community. Aggressive erotica too has drawn more than its share of public criticism. What has generally been ignored in the debate is the large amount of prime time viewing given over to combatant sports entertainment. The issue of televised sports violence is all but lost against the background of blood and mayhem so prominently featured in media programming and indeed, the evening news. Although deaths in sports are a rarity, viewers are nonetheless fed a steady and graphic diet of explicit violence. The effects on the viewing public are far from benign.

B. Competition with and without Aggression

Sports themselves clearly differ in their effects on observers, for example, boxing versus golf. In the case of combatant sports, the aggressive content has consistently been shown to elicit an aggressive response from observers. On the other hand, fast-paced, spirited, competitive play does not by itself appear to increase aggression in the viewer nor is it seen as any less entertaining.

The point is made clear by an experiment in which men were shown a short film clip of exciting, fast-paced hockey action that included several on-ice brawls. Other men watched the same clip with the acts of player violence edited out. Still others assigned to a control condition worked on a jigsaw puzzle for an equivalent length of time. Furthermore, within each condition half of the subjects were initially angered by a confederate or treated in a polite fashion. Those who viewed the aggressive version and who were initially provoked subsequently directed more aggression toward the confederate than angered subjects viewing either the edited version or those in the control condition. The fight scenes did not enhance the entertainment of the film, that is, subjects rated the two versions as equally entertaining.

While the study makes the point that media presentations of violent sports increase aggression in viewers, numerous other experiments also point to the same conclusion. Leonard Berkowitz and others used an especially brutal fight scene from the award-winning movie *Champion* in their early investigations of the role of aggressive cues in eliciting aggression from viewers. The film clip shows actor Kirk Douglas playing the part of an aging prize fighter who is savagely beaten by a young challenger. The subjects watched either the fight clip or a nonviolent but equally competitive control film. Again, half of the subjects in each condition were initially angered by another (confederate) subject with whom they watched the film. Among angered subjects, those exposed to the boxing film directed more aggression (shock) toward the confederate than angered subjects viewing the nonaggressive film.

C. Priming

The media sometimes contributes to sports violence in subtle and generally unrecognized ways. In a very real sense, we are often made ready to behave aggressively even before we take our seats at combatant sports events. The language and images contained in pregame publicity may increase the likelihood of altercations erupting among spectators and athletes alike.

Psychologists working in the area of cognitive processes are well aware of what are called "priming effects." Stored memories or schema can be activated by comments to which we attend and subsequently determine the kind of judgments we make in regard to our social situation. Thus, if friendly, cooperative schemas are activated, others in our social surroundings are likely to be seen in a positive light. On the other hand, if the content of pregame publicity activates antisocial or negative schemas, then others with whom we come in contact are apt to be judged unfavorably or be seen as personally threatening.

The clearest illustration of how mere words and aggressive associations can set the stage for open conflict is seen in the results of the following study. Students recited one of two lists of words. The first list contained the names of several nonaggressive sports such as golf, bowling, and billiards. The other list was identical except that the nonaggressive sports were replaced with sports having long-standing associations with aggression such as boxing, football, and hockey. Later, everyone was asked to describe an individual named Don. Those who had earlier recited the names of nonaggressive sports saw Don in a generally positive light. By contrast, students who recited aggressive sport names described Don as hostile and menacing.

It is important to recognize that we typically act on our perceptions of people quite apart from any objective facts that are known about that person. Don may be a very friendly and gentle person. Yet, if priming has led us to see him as hostile and threatening, then our responses to him will be framed in similar terms. When pregame hyperbole creates a hostile social climate in which competitors are described in aggressive language and imagery, the stage is set for conflict.

A Canadian study is especially persuasive in providing evidence of the effects of violent media content and violence-related cues, in this case, specifically on children. Second- and third-grade schoolboys served as subjects. High- and low-aggressive groups were initially formed on the basis of teacher ratings. Half of the boys in each group watched either an exciting "motocross-like racing team" in action or a violent film featuring a police SWAT team in a shootout with snipers. After watching their assigned film and with the study ostensibly over, the boys were taken to the gymnasium for a game of floor hockey. Just prior to the game, each boy was interviewed either with a microphone or a walkie-talkie similar to one seen in the violent SWAT team film.

During the games, trained observers recorded all instances of interpersonal aggression during the games, for example, tripping, name-calling, pushing, poking, pinching, or sitting on another boy. Those boys initially identified as aggressive showed increased aggression in response to the violent police film whereas nonaggressive boys failed to show comparable increases. Equally important, the group of aggressive boys who were exposed to violence-related cues, that is, a walkie-talkie, in addition to the violent film exhibited even higher levels of aggression during the game.

D. Other General Effects

The observation of combatant sports can produce effects in addition to an increase in viewer aggression. Finnish psychologist Kaj Björkquist has investigated the effects of repeated exposure to violent media fare on viewers' physiological responses. Young boys were shown videos of Kung Fu and karate action for varying lengths of time. Those exposed to the scenes for extended periods of time showed less of an emotional response than those youngsters seeing the scenes of violence for the first time. This process of desensitization is presumed to result in people becoming less anxious and more tolerant and accepting of societal violence. However, the extended notion that desensitized persons are more apt than others to behave aggressively has been challenged by Tedeschi and Felson. They cite the example of medical students who become desensitized in the course of their training with cadavers. Yet, physicians show no evidence of being more violent than other occupational groups.

E. Mitigating the Impact

Parents and others concerned about the harmful effects on children of watching violent programming are frequently counseled to have an adult watch with their children. The presence and/or explanations provided by the adult are presumed to be effective in neutralizing whatever harmful effects might arise from viewing violent content. While the literature on this important question is sparse, such evidence as we have does not offer encouragement for the success of the tactic.

The social context in which television is viewed can clearly determine the response of viewers. Belgium researcher Muriel Dunand and others arranged for subjects to watch either *Champion* or an equally exciting, nonaggressive track film. During the showings a confederate coviewer either watched passively or made enthusiastic remarks about each film ("hit him!" in the case of boxing). Predictably, subjects were more aggressive after seeing the boxing film. Equally important, the greatest amount of aggression was shown by those who viewed the boxing film in the company of the actively involved coviewer, that is, their aggression was significantly higher than that attributable to the event itself.

A test of the suggestion that coviewers actively disapproving of televised sports violence would also be beneficial in reducing viewer aggression was undertaken. Small groups of subjects watched a fight-filled clip of hockey action in the company of an attractive male or female confederate who interjected with comments that were either supportive, neutral, or critical of the violence being shown. Overall, the models were ineffective in their attempts to influence the degree of subjects' aggression toward a "hired" experimenter. However, a measure of social desirability had also been administered and provides a plausible reason for the models' apparent lack of success, that is, a remarks $\times$ social desirability interaction.

Subjects scoring high on social desirability are attuned to opportunities to be seen in a favorable light. Indeed, they faithfully tracked the indirect attempts of the confederate models to influence them, that is, when the model expressed support for the violence, they directed more aggression toward the experimenter; when the model deplored the violence, they were less aggressive. By contrast, those low on social desirability and relatively less concerned with being seen in a positive light responded totally opposite to the views expressed by the models. That is, when the model was heard to deplore the violence, they tended to be more aggressive and when the model was supportive of the violence, they tended to be less aggressive.

The behavior of subjects low on social desirability was explained by means of psychological reactance whereby people act contrary to even subtle attempts by others to limit their freedom of action. While a minority of individuals stand to be positively influenced by coviewers who openly deplore sports violence, any gains are likely offset by a roughly equal number of others who foil the models' efforts at influence and respond in an fashion opposite to that advocated.

F. The Attraction to Media Violence

Media coverage of violent sports events such as football, hockey, professional wrestling, and boxing attracts vast audiences. The popularity of combatant sports with the general public raises some interesting questions. For example, are the violent aspects of an event essential in order to ensure an audience for a sport or would a sport lose its appeal if violence were minimized? The answer seems obvious in the case of boxing; a boxing match without violence is not a boxing match. For other sports, one might ask if the public would still find them attractive with less-violent content.

Studies have shown that the popularity of television programming does not diminish when the violent themes are edited out. A similar result is seen with hockey audiences. Attendance at the next home game following each team's two most violent contests over an entire season were compared with attendance following each team's two least violent games. There was no indication that violent games subsequently influenced the number of fans passing through the turnstiles. However, more recently an association between hockey violence and attendance was found, but only in the case of U.S. expansion clubs where the sport is marketed with a strong appeal to its violent content.

People differ widely in their attraction to violent sports programming. From an individual differences perspective, those who are themselves aggressive have been shown to actively seek out opportunities to view violence. Additionally, it appears that aggressive individuals respond more strongly to depictions of violence. For example, macho males exposed to a boxing film exhibited a higher aggressive mood state than nonmacho men. The greater volatility of macho men viewing sports violence further suggests that coviewers and others nearby are at an increased risk of being targeted for aggression.

Advances in media technology have created vast audiences for many sports that previously were witnessed by thousands and are now seen by millions. Television coverage of combatant sports goes virtually unchallenged and presents something of a conundrum for those intent on reducing the amount of violent content in media programming. From most perspectives, to eliminate violence from coverage of some sports would be to emasculate these sports. Would millions still be content to watch shadow boxing, flag football, no-contact hockey, or amateur-style wrestling?

VI. THE LONG ARM OF SPORTS VIOLENCE

A. Campus Violence

With the arrival of autumn, the Saturday afternoon football game becomes a focal point for social activities on most U.S. college campuses. While college administrators welcome the revenues generated by a successful program, they are also painfully aware of the problems created for campus security personnel. The exuberance of fans is seldom confined to the stadium and frequently spills over into other areas of the campus community, sometimes with destructive consequences.

To assess the impact of football weekends on campus life, the records of unruly student behavior in the residence halls of a large southeastern university were examined for a 4-year period. An overall measure of disruptive behavior was developed and included acts such as disorderly conduct, destruction of property, assaults, and alcohol violations.

Football weekends were marked by a greater number of disciplinary cases than weekends when the team was idle. Disorderly behavior in and around the residence halls was also more frequent when the team played at home rather than away. Interestingly, whether or not the games were televised had no bearing on the number of reported incidents. Perhaps the most intriguing finding of all was that the disciplinary incidents were far more frequent during the celebrations following a *victory*.

B. Domestic Violence

With some regularity, health care workers and others have suggested that serious health risks are posed to people in the local community when violent sports events are staged in the region. Specifically, it is suggested that incidents of child abuse, spousal violence, and elder abuse increase when a family member(s) returns home from a violent event or after watching the event on television. A 1992 investigation by Garland White, Janet Katz, and Kathryn Scarborough offers support for these speculations.

The admission records of emergency wards in the District of Columbia-area hospitals were examined for the hours following the National Football League Washington Redskins home and away games. Redskins *victories* at home were followed shortly thereafter by increases in the number of women admitted for assaults, stabbings, "accidental" falls, and gunshot wounds. The number of admissions following losses remained unchanged.

The authors suggest that the greater incidence of interpersonal aggression following home town wins arises from an increase in power motivation. Football fans have been shown to derive an increased sense of personal power from observing their favorite team emerge victorious. That increase in power motivation then, is thought to find violent expression in interpersonal relationships in which disagreements that might otherwise be resolved by negotiation or compromise are instead settled by force.

C. Homicide

Other lines of investigation point to the lethal implications of major combatant sports events. One such study tested the hypothesis that important NFL games would be followed by increases in the local homicide rate. To this end, all playoff games from 1973 to 1979, including the Super Bowl, were examined as were the homicide rates for the metropolitan areas in which the franchise teams were located. An increase in homicides occurred consistently 6 days after the playoff games. However, the increase occurred only in those cities whose team had been eliminated from the playoffs a week earlier.

As the investigators point out, the 6th day following a playoff game falls on the eve of the next round of the playoffs. Whereas last week's winner is still in contention, fans of last week's losing team are forced to confront the realization that "their" season is over. For them there will be no game tomorrow, only an emotional void. Whether the lethal outcomes occur as a result of fans having their hopes so cruelly dashed or because of problems associated with gambling losses remains open to speculation.

Evidence that harmful effects arising from major combatant events reach far beyond the immediate area of the sports venue is also seen in the innovative program of sociologist, David Phillips. His measure of interpersonal aggression was derived from the registry of U.S. national death certificates which among several pieces of information, note the cause of death. One in a series of investigations tested the hypothesis that heavyweight championship boxing matches would trigger a rise in national homicide statistics.

All title fights for the period between 1973 and 1978 were examined in relation to homicide rates for a 10-day period following each televised bout. Homicides increased 12.5% on the 3rd day and 6.6% on the 4th day following the title fights. Furthermore, it was the most heavily televised fights that were followed by the steepest rise in homicides. As intriguing as the reason for the 3-day lag is the fact that the homicide victims resembled the losing fighter. Thus, if a Black fighter was defeated by his White opponent, there was an increase in the deaths of young, Black males. Conversely, a victory by a Black boxer was followed by a rise in homicides of young, White males.

The selective effects of witnessing title fights were foreshadowed by Berkowitz and others in a series of investigations designed to assess aspects of aggressive cue theory. In one condition, subjects were introduced to a confederate coviewer who had the same first name as the eventual loser in the film, *Champion*. Subjects subsequently directed more aggression at the confederate than when the initial introduction involved a neutral name. As with Phillips' homicide victims, those seen to have associations with a victim stand to be further targeted for aggression.

VII. POSTSCRIPT AND CONCLUSIONS

A. A Postscript

One conceptual thread in particular runs throughout this chapter. Most of the studies cited have provided formal or informal tests of catharsis hypotheses, namely, people become *less* aggressive as a result of behaving aggressively or observing others behave aggressively. Proponents have invoked a reservoir analogy wherein aggressive energy is constantly welling up within the individual and must be periodically discharged lest it spills over or breaks through to wreak havoc on those unfortunate enough to be in its path. It is a view that is widely shared by men and women alike with approximately two-thirds of North Americans subscribing to some form of cathartic belief. However, it must be said that there is very little support for the notion both in the sports and nonsports literature.

A glance back over the studies cited in this chapter provides no indication that behaving aggressively or observing aggression engages a cathartic mechanism. Athletes competing individually or on teams have not

been found to be less aggressive than others. At a group level, teams become increasingly aggressive over the course of a contest and with the number of times they have met an opponent. Fans too show no evidence of a cathartic discharge of their pent-up aggressive urges. As they watch player violence from the stands or on television, their aggression is likely to increase. Thus, as intuitively appealing as the concept is to most people, the body of scientific findings on the question cannot be taken to encourage them in that belief.

B. Conclusions

Sports and recreational activities offer us a wealth of potential benefits whether as a participant or spectator. Alongside these personal and social benefits, there is also a potential for physical and emotional harm to some among sports' vast following. These same risks may extend to others with little or no involvement in sports, often with traumatic if not lethal consequences.

Modern technology has enabled the media to bring a number of major violent sports to worldwide audiences. The challenge for sports officialdom is to minimize participant violence in a sport(s) while at the same time preserving what is socially beneficial. The equally daunting task for media researchers is to find means to mitigate or deflect the harmful effects of violent content. For both parties, the challenge is formidable.

Also See the Following Articles

AGGRESSION, PSYCHOLOGY OF • MASS MEDIA, GENERAL VIEW • NEUROPSYCHOLOGY OF MOTIVATION FOR GROUP AGGRESSION

Bibliography

Baron, R. A., & Richardson, D. R. (1994). *Human aggression* (2nd ed.). New York: Plenum Press.

Berkowitz, L. (1993). *Aggression: Its causes, consequences, and control.* Philadelphia: Temple University Press.

Giulianotti, R., Bonney, N., & Hepworth, M. (Eds.). (1994). *Football, violence and social identity.* London: Routledge.

Goldstein, J. H. (1983). *Sports violence.* New York: Springer-Verlag.

Guttmann, A. (1986). *Sports spectators.* New York: Columbia University Press.

Kerr, J. H. (1994). *Understanding football hooliganism.* Philadelphia: Open University Press.

Kerr, J. H. (1997). *Motivation and emotion in sport: Reversal theory.* Hove, England: Psychology Press.

Mann, L. (1989). Sports crowds and the collective behavior perspective. In J. H. Goldstein (Ed.), *Sports, games, and play* (2nd ed., pp. 299–331). Hillsdale, NJ: Erlbaum.

Mann, L., & Pearce, P. (1978). Social psychology of the sports spectator. In D. J. Glencross (Ed.), *Psychology and sport* (pp. 173–201). New York: McGraw-Hill.

Milgram, S., & Toch, H. (1969). Collective behavior: Crowds and social movements. In G. Lindzey & E. Aronson (Eds.), *The handbook of social psychology* (Vol. 4, pp. 507–610). Reading, MA: Addison-Wesley.

Phillips, D. P. (1986). Natural experiments on the effects of mass media violence on fatal aggression: Strength and weaknesses of a new approach. In L. Berkowitz (Ed.), *Advances in experimental social psychology* (Vol. 19, pp. 207–250). New York: Academic Press.

Russell, G. W. (1993). *The social psychology of sport*. New York: Springer-Verlag.

Russell, G. W., & Arms, R. L. (1998). Toward a social psychological profile of would-be rioters. *Aggressive Behavior, 24,* 219–226.

Smith, M. D. (1983). *Violence and sport*. Toronto: Butterworths.

Tedeschi, J. T., & Felson, R. B. (1994). *Violence, aggression, & coercive actions*. Washington, DC: American Psychological Association.

Structural Prevention and Conflict Management, Imperatives of

Christian P. Scherrer

Copenhagen Peace Research Institute and Institute of Ethnicity Research and Conflict Resolution

GLOSSARY

War A violent mass conflict involving two or more armed forces as combatants/actors in warfare. Regular state-armed forces are not involved in all cases. Nonstate actors are mainly so-called liberation movements having regular guerrilla or partisan armies, often recruiting along ethnic, national, or social class lines. Militias, gangs, and other irregular forces have different agendas; they have less or no centralized control or identifiable lines of command. Combat takes place with some degree of continuity.

Major War and Mass Violence Distinguished from other armed conflicts or massacres by various degrees of medium or high intensity, claiming usually more than an estimated average of 1000 victims per annum during the conflict period. In many cases the numbers of victims are contested or otherwise questionable.

Impure Types/Different Components Combining the basic types can adequately solve the inherent difficulty of all the "impure" types we find in the real world. That way we get closer to the "mixed types" encountered in the field.

Dynamics and Change To illustrate the dynamics and the changing composition of contemporary wars a second method was used: The diachronic development was cut in phases of warfare. Contemporary wars do not resemble football games anymore. For a given phase the register shows the primary or dominant type followed (if necessary) by a secondary or tertiary characterization of a particular conflict, hence describing the heterogeneous and dynamic nature of most modern non-Clausewitzean types of conflicts.

I. INTRODUCTION

Compared to the tremendous increase of intrastate warfare and nonwar types of mass violence such as genocide and mass murder, the Clausewitzean type of inter-state conflicts was in recent decades a rather exceptional phenomenon. In two-thirds of all contemporary conflicts the ethnic factor (e.g., ethnic nationalism) is a dominant or influential component.

The themes of intrastate conflict, its types, causes, and possible peace strategies, are highly topical. However, research deficits prevail regarding abundant issues and problems in this vast field. Research on the causes of wars was mainly concerned with classic types of conflicts between states but does not easily apply to intra-state conflicts. The lacunae of global surveys on mass violence can be identified. Present war registers overlook certain categories of violence. Most registers are constructing static entities instead of expressing the permanent mutation of conflicts in the real world. There are very few "pure types." Conflicts develop over time and may change in quality, with one component becoming dominant over the other(s).

The question "What to do in a particular situation?" is linked to the type of conflicts we are dealing with. The idea is that the results of systematic registers of mass violence point at priorities for action. The importance of timing in response to conflict will be stressed. Types of responses should be related to different types of conflicts and their underlying issues in order to be effective. The high frequency, and huge potential of ethnic types of conflict is decisive regarding the possibilities of structural prevention of violence, conflict management, and transformation as well as regarding the role of multilateralism in preventing violence. State failure and violent ethnic conflict are closely linked.

Ethnic and national groups' struggles for survival, rights, or recognition dominate contemporary warfare to an increasingly large extent and result in "anarchy" in the state system. In the so-called Third World a growing number of states cannot claim to have an effective monopoly of violence. Depending on criteria employed about half of those states are failed states and have potentially become dangerous states (repression, war, genocidal policy).

The second section expresses the view that ethnicity is not a "political pathology." It can be shown that militant ethnic nationalism can be avoided by recognizing "otherness" and accommodating just demands. Following a long phase of avoidance of the terms "ethnic group" and "ethnicity," these concepts have recently become much-used bywords. These concepts are in need of elucidation. The third section contains a presentation of the main concepts and definition of terms as well as a comprehensive typology of contemporary violent conflicts, a register of violent conflicts, and an analysis of current trends in international warfare and mass violence. The fourth section first looks at possibilities and conditions of conflict management in general by relating causes, triggers, threats, and issues with the type of conflict formation and the dynamics of destructive processes (escalation, violence, war, and/or genocide). The task is to look into conflict escalation and the parallel limitation of options for responses. The focus is on a variety of possible constructive responses according to the different stages of conflict. With regard to the nowadays most frequent conflict formation opposing states and nations/nationalities effective responses should prevent the process of escalation into violent confrontation at a very early stage. Some of the root causes and driving forces of violent conflicts can only be neutralized if the dynamics of destructive processes are not allowed to develop. The mandatory question of "lessons learned?"—asked on the basis of having proposed a typology and analyzed contemporary violent conflicts—shall culminate in the drafting of typologies of constructive responses to conflict. In Sections V to VIII the attempt of developing a theory of peaceful and structural prevention of violence will get major inputs: Sections V and VI discuss key elements of structural prevention of violent conflict such as autonomy arrangements, free association, and self-governance. Several examples of realized forms of structural prevention found in different world regions are described. In Section VII constructive structural elements for multiethnic states are discussed, starting with 18 guiding principles, which by linking forward and backward can produce the desired result—namely, the creation of balanced constitutional and social–political structures. Section VIII focuses on federation and decentralization as conflict prevention and resolution.

In the grand design the suggestion is to look at ethnopolitical conflict constellations as a structural feature of the new world order. Macrotrends have increasingly suggested since the 1980s that the world system is rapidly evolving into a complex multipolar order. Regional conflict scenarios make sense, even more so if they are determined not only by geographical but also by macrocultural (civilizational) and political criteria. To give an illustrative exemplification: The collapse of the USSR and the subsequent outburst of ethnic conflicts on the periphery of that former "empire" were closely linked. Some elements significantly differ from the situation in other world regions, particularly in the Southern hemishere. Ethnonationalism in the East grew almost institutionally. It is resulting from a form of administrative ethnicization, which was one of the main constitutive elements of the Soviet experience.

A sort of "Third World War" is in full swing. Warfare and mass violence are not going on between East and West, nor between North and South, but occurring in this very moment inside some 60 states on four continents. The regional distribution of contemporary wars shows a clear global trend: Warfare and mass violence is infrequent in the North and West but part of normality in the South and some areas of the East. Many wars in the South would not be fought without involvement of the North.

According to the Ethnic Conflicts Research Project (ECOR) register two-thirds of the violent conflicts from 1985 to 1996 had a dominant or influential ethnic component. Findings are based on first hand information and field experience. Case studies determined the approach of the ECOR, a research project on ethnicity and conflict resolution started in 1987.

There were some disturbing changes of the general trend in recent years. Foreign military intervention has not at all been an exception and has lately increased significantly. Complex emergency cases led to an alarming increase of conflict-induced mortality. Warfare and mass violence are becoming increasingly chaotic at a conceptual and practical level, with interethnic wars increasing at the cost of both inter-state and ethnonationalist wars, and gang wars nearly doubling in a 10 years' period. State failure, warfare, and mass violence are inextricably linked.

In view of the farily recent discovery of the ethnic phenomenon by the mass media and considering a general research deficit concerning these "forgotten wars" being fought in many third world countries, research deficits have prevailed. The attempt here would be ambitious: to propose an actor-oriented typology only indirectly related to root causes but directly linked with the main driving forces, the base of mobilization and manifestations of violent conflict worldwide.

One of the most dangerous sources of armed conflicts is the assertion of all powers by nation states in their relations to what they call minorities.

According to the ECOR's global survey nation-states are exceptions from the rule: Only a very small faction of the world's population lives in what could be called an ethnically homogenous state. Just 20 countries with a population average of 500,000 can be called nation-states. Very few states with considerably more than 10 million citizens are homogenous nation-states. Most states pretend to be nation-states but in reality have a multiethnic and pluricultural composition. This fiction is kept up at high costs. For instance in the USSR, the very coining of the term "titular nation" pointed at the fact that there is no single nation-state in the former Soviet space. In Africa, out of over 50 states only 5 are relatively homogenous regarding their ethnonational composition.

If we look underneath the structure of some 200 states there is an extraordinary multitude of perhaps 6,500 to 10,000 nations, nationalities, and peoples as ethnic entities of diverse size. Groups rank from 900 Rama Indians in Nicaragua to 25 or 30 million Oromo at the Horn of Africa and up to 1.1 billion Han Chinese. This diversity represents a tremendous richness of different cultures for most people, but a threat to others. Characteristics given to identify a ethnic group or a nationality are by no means an academic exercise but will gain more political relevance as relations between nationalities, nations, and states are increasingly seen as an important element of what is called international politics and international relations. The legacies of colonialism and other external conditions contributed to separate nations from nationalities. The invention of the nation-state, its official nationalism, and the high expectations raised by development ideologies in the former colonies are basic sources for past and future conflicts.

Since 1945 more than 250 major wars have taken place mostly in the third world, and recently in the Former Soviet Union (FSU) and Yugoslavia. Very few of these wars were inter-state conflicts. The last classic inter-state wars were fought for some weeks in 1995 between Ecuador and Peru, since March 1998 between Eritrea and Ethiopia, and between the NATO states and Yugoslavia in Spring 1999. Today, all wars are so-called internal conflicts, yet many are fought with outside assistance. Research to identify the root causes of the tremendous upsurge of ethnonationalism in the global framework leads to questions linked with the nature of ethnicity and the ethnic base of nations. Often these categories are not very adequately used.

II. THE QUEST OF UNDERSTANDING: ETHNICITY IS NOT A "POLITICAL PATHOLOGY"

Anyone posing the question of the ethnic basis of national identity often finds they have stirred up a hornet's nest. One largely unexamined presupposition underlying the idea of the nation-state in the European area was that a nation has a homogeneous basis—in other words, that ethnos and nation are one and the same. The terms "ethnos" and "ethnicity"—which have once again come into everyday use—are often devoid of content.

The state classes have sought to declare ethnicity a "political pathology." In political discourse, the term is mostly negatively charged, having connotations such as "primitive," "backward," or "irrational." Contrary to the prognoses of the political and social sciences in regard to the development of modern societies, ethnicity has lost none of its importance in recent decades. On the contrary, the importance of the ethnic dimension, and its politicization, have grown into issues of status and categorization in violent conflicts, civilian disputes, and instances of social demarcation and exclusion.

Different types of actors such as states, international corporations, liberation movements, migrants' organizations, political parties, pressure groups, strategic groups, military leaders, and populists all seek to make political capital out of "ethnic identity." Some actors deliberately try to influence and manipulate the ethnic identity set-up. In this study article, the term "ethnicity" is used to describe a variety of forms of mobilization, which ultimately relate to the autonomous existence of specifically ethnic forms of socialization and which politicize these. No clear-cut distinction can, however, be made between struggles by social classes and struggles by ethnic groups.

The formation of ethnic identity cannot be taken as a given; it is the result (not an inevitable one) of processes of interaction within an ethnos, between one ethnos and another, and between one ethnos or more and a state or states. Of these three areas of conflict, only the second, the interethnic, is generally taken into consideration—mostly in the form of supposedly tribal conflicts. In contrast, the conflictual relationship between ethnic groups and the state/states, which is of such significance when it comes precisely to ethnonationalism, is frequently neglected.

Ethnic identity can, for example, be interpreted as consciousness of cultural separateness or otherness. It is of utmost importance to understand that this collective consciousness is not an intrinsic reflection of objective cultural characteristics in a particular ethnic entity of whatever kind. Nor is it a matter of "free choice" resulting from subjective (individual or collective) identification with a specific ethnic group and its distinct character. It always exists within a conflictual context.

Following a long phase of avoidance and negativization of the term, or of the reality it represents, "ethnicity" has recently become a much-used byword. Reference to the supposedly ethnic character of a conflict often fulfills a purpose other than elucidation. Paradoxically, in those very conflicts that are described as "ethnic" in the media, there is nothing, or almost nothing, typically ethnic to be found. The intention, rather—as

in the coverage of the wars in Yugoslavia and the genocide in Rwanda—is to hamper the search for other causes. In extreme cases, the newly discovered byword "ethnicity" is intended to divert attention from the true causal process. The ethnic discourse and its appeal to a particular community has, in each case and from the very outset, a political significance that is linked to the particular case and to the respective interests.

The concepts of "minority" and "ethnic group," which are often used in connection with ethnonational conflicts, are in need of elucidation. Similarly, the almost customary confusion of the concepts of "nation," "state," and "nation-state" indicate a need for a complete definition of terms. Colonial expansion put an end to the autonomous existence of a variety of social formations and political systems. "Concepts" and reality were homogenized. The export of the nation-state model to the colonies ran into a host of difficulties because no appropriate foundation for this kind of construct existed in the extra-European world.

Characteristics that define an ethnos or indigenous people as a nationality or as a nation without its own state continue to be a subject of dispute for power-political (not analytical) reasons. Nowadays, however, stipulations are acquiring greater political relevance. The relationship between national minorities, nationalities, and nations, on the one hand, and recognized states on the other can no longer be declared to be solely an internal matter of states; it is increasingly being viewed as part of international relations.

Reference to ethnicity does not simplify the search for the causes of conflict. Ethnicity is not an "explanatory factor" in armed conflicts, nor should it be pressed into service as one because other explanations fail. Often—as in the case of Yugoslavia—one can talk of a hybrid ethnicization of religious groups. The violent conflict in Kosovo 1998/99 was the first war in the region showing a clear-cut ethnic component, with Serbian armed elements (army, police and paramilitary gangs) versus Albanian Kosovar civilians, from May 1999 UCK elements versus Serbian and Roma civilians.

To call for such "ethnic conflicts" to be labeled blanket-fashion as 'identity conflicts' because there is nothing very ethnic about them is simply playing with words. Amnesia about historical developments, and a lack of understanding for the justified fears of nondominant minorities, made comprehension of the wars in the Balkans impossible and encouraged the grotesquely distorted and more or less unquestioned coverage of them in the mass media.

A. Minority Conflicts? An Attempt at Definition

Where ethnonationalism is being discussed, there is often talk of minorities. This term seems in need of elucidation and should only be used with reservations. The ideologies bound up with it range, in ascending order, from racial segregation through unilateral assimilation and ideas about "melting pots" (racial amalgamation) to purely formally equal integration, then to the relativization of unitary-cum-homogenist ideas with the notion of "diversity in unity," and, ultimately, to respect, protection, and encouragement for otherness on an equal basis within the framework of a (con-)federal state. However, to place the content of ethnic conflicts on a par with that of minority conflicts or problems is, in many cases, mistaken. More far-reaching demands by many nations/nationalities point to structural differences between minority and nationality policy, explored in Sections IV–VI hereafter.

The concept of minority and the reality in which minorities are created and obliged to live points up a variety of facets that are often largely ignored in the debate about minority or ethnonational conflicts. The most important, however, seems to be that the concept of minority is essentially ascriptive in nature: as a rule, it is the state that decides what makes a minority and to which circle of people the term will apply. The state itself is dominated by, or in the ownership of, a particular ethnic group that defines itself as a majority but often is not one in demographic terms. National censuses and demographic statistics are just one more battlefield (for all the actors concerned). Statistics are usually presented according to predetermined political conditions. In extreme cases, the ethnic group apostrophized as a minority is only a political minority, measured in terms of power, while demographically it constitutes the majority. This is the case, for example, with the Oromo in Ethiopia or the Mayan peoples in Guatemala.

The concept of minority requires elucidation for a variety of "internal" reasons as well. Many nationalities that find their rights curtailed by the (new) states or are harassed, threatened, or persecuted by them, do not regard themselves as minorities. They do not share the sociopsychological characteristics of minorities. On the contrary, some cultivate a robust nationalism. National minorities, which are mostly regarded by the dominant ethnonational group as subordinate segments of a (more) complex state society, have special phenotypic and cultural "peculiarities" ascribed to them. These kinds of ascribed "markers" are often looked down on by those segments of the state society that are dominant (either in terms of power or numerically). But traditional societies derive their distinctiveness and reproduce themselves on the basis of their nonintegration into market economies; they have developed a whole series of autonomous, self-supporting modes of production.

The dual concept of the "national minority" has come into increasing use in recent years in the discourse about the minorities' question and in international politics. This is a consequence of the increased attention that has been paid to the contentious minorities issue in post-Cold War Europe.

B. The Concept of the Ethnos

The basic concept of the ethnos is not clearly defined. In ethnology and cultural anthropology it is delimited, but contentiously, within certain boundaries. The variety and number of categorizations offered by the different ethnological schools is very great. Combining the more accessible definitions is not really possible, given the differing approaches and standards. The most frequently mentioned factors are shared origin and similar culture, religion, class, and language. However, two of these (class and religion) are not apposite.

The ethnic form of socialization must be distinguished from socialization into social classes. The extent and boundaries of the two are often congruent, but they can also overlap, as in more complex societies, or exclude one another, as in egalitarian societies. Religion must be rejected totally as a criterion, since it is an ideological domain, which, within the framework of colonialism, was externally directed and fortuitously selected.

Imported religions and syncretist variants are more common and/or more dominant than indigenous religions among the 6,500 to 10,000 ethnic groups worldwide. The general supposition is that religions, like nationalisms, generate a transcendent identity-forming link, whereas ethnicity, though identity-forming, has a divisive effect. This supposition does not seem generalizable. Connections (or rather conflicts) between religion, nationalism, and ethnicity ought not to be denied.

One of several possible approaches to the subject focuses on attributes based on clusters of "special features" or on social specialization which are seen as constituting "ethnic markers." Such attributes are only relevant within the framework of interethnic relations. Often they only become a major focus of perception when situations of conflict arise. The attributes of an ethnic community include, as a minimum:

1. A historically generated or newly discovered community of people that largely reproduces itself.
2. A distinct name, which often simply signifies "person" or "people" in the ethnic community's language.
3. A specific, heterogeneous culture, including, particularly, a distinct language.
4. A collective (ethnic) memory or historical remembrance, including community myths (myths of foundation or emergence relating to shared ancestry).
5. Solidarity between members of the community, generating a feeling of belonging.

These attributes by no means constitute a definitive checklist; they are, rather, an attempt to get closer to the problem of ethnicity, the individual elements of which need to be examined more closely and be defined in detail for each concrete instance. Maintaining ethnic borders—and thus also being able to delimit different ethnic groups—has it's problems, for various reasons. Overemphasizing individual elements, such as participation in a shared culture or the social dimension (which sees ethnic groups as a particular form of social organization), would appear to be problematic.

From the point of view of those concerned (in the *emic* view), ethnic affinity is generally (emically speaking) not perceived in any way as ideologically generated. Neither is it a quasi-organic process, produced by specific socialization as a member of a distinct social group. In contrast to the hypothesis of ideological construction, some authors talk of affinity based on traditional ethnic solidarity, as related to groups with high coherence and cohesion, such as clans and other tribal entities, and which, say these authors, represents an almost naturally occurring form of "unconditional ethnic solidarity." The hypotheses on this subject are thus unusually far removed from one another.

First of all, it is indispensable to state a frame of reference and to designate theoretical axioms. Statements about group affinity and personal identity can turn out differently depending on the terms of reference used. In modern societies, very different conditions of group affinity obtain than in traditional societies. The ethnic and sociocultural identity of an individual varies according to the location or standpoint of the observer; identification of Other and Self can vary enormously;

conflict situations can bring about fundamental changes in frames of reference.

In a situation of threat, individual elements of personal and collective identity can become enhanced or diminish in influence. The political instrumentalization of mechanisms of demarcation (for the purposes of exclusion) plays a role here, as does recourse to (within the framework of peaceful coexistence) socially unconscious elements of group identity. Identity constitutes itself via processes of demarcation that do not occur within a nonauthoritarian space and whose modalities cannot be determined freely and independently. The abstract difference of others poses no problem; the experience of real threat from others, or a construed feeling of superiority vis-à-vis others, are, in contrast, results of processes of exclusion and polarization.

From an emic point of view, shared origin is crucial. The fact that this does not have to be real in origin, and is usually putative-cum-mythical or fictitious in nature, is often overlooked. Other central elements that determine affinity to an ethnically constituted group—the capacity to reproduce as a group, for example, or common cultural configurations, or a so-called "feeling of belonging" that implies group solidarity—may be regarded as too general to be able, ultimately, to provide precise empirical insights into the ethnic dimension of political processes in a conflict situation. Constant injury to central elements, either from within or from without, elicits specific forms of resistance in each particular case, ranging from withdrawal to rebellion.

C. The Concept of Nationality

Within the framework of sociopolitical or international legal categorization, an ethnic group or an indigenous people may be viewed as a nationality. This conceptual shift should essentially be seen as the result of a political process, which, in most cases, has followed a conflictual course. Factors relating to political power play a decisive role here. The conquest and dominance aspect is of central importance. This constitutive aspect has been acknowledged, notably in the definition of indigenous peoples and in particular in the elaboration of new instruments of international law designed to protect them.

In the concrete hostile conditions of internal or external colonization (with its unconditional claims of state sovereignty) an ethnos that does not reshape itself into a nation/nationality risks destruction as an independent unit. A cohesive nondominant ethnic group reshaped in this way will be recognized as a nationality if it possesses certain other characteristics to some degree (to be verified in each individual case).

The following five characteristics of nations/nationalities represent a maximum definition—that is to say, the more clearly the named characteristics fit a particular nation/nationality and the greater the number of them that apply, the nearer that nation/nationality comes to a hypothetical ideal type. An ethnos in the position of a nondominant social group can, accordingly, be regarded as a nationality if, despite the claims to dominance and sovereignty from outside:

1. It constitutes a distinct space of communication and interaction, i.e., it is able to form or maintain a public sphere of its own.
2. It has a particular mode of production and life identifiable with it and is able to reproduce it.
3. It has some form of political organization.
4. It has settled an identifiable area of land or demarcated territory.
5. It is distinctive, i.e., its members identify themselves or are identified by others as members of this particular community.

Ethnic characteristics are only relevant within the framework of interethnic relations and it is primarily in conflict situations that they become a major focus of perception. The same characteristics—particular sociocultural practices, for example—can (as with the example of cultural emblems) be totally unimportant in various interethnic situations, but in a different context they can suddenly acquire huge significance. For example, skin color and other phenotypical features are of secondary importance in many societies of the third world; but in Western societies, physical characteristics are one of the main distinguishing features at home (in relation to migrants and asylum-seekers) and abroad (e.g., in holiday resorts).

The attempted definition consists of about half (inter-)subjective and half objective features. The disputed point with some of the named features is precisely whether they can be described as "objective." Name-giving, certain cultural aspects (especially language), the association with a particular territory as a settlement area and site of economic activity (not with a mythical primeval homeland), the mode of production, and the degree of (present) political organization can, at least, be regarded as objective, empirically verifiable characteristics.

An ethnonational community that possesses some crucial attributes, or all these attributes, develops a distinct collective identity; it could, in political contention, invoke the international legal principle of self-determination. This in no way implies a right to secession—something never acknowledged by the community of states. The creation of new states occurs in accordance with political opportuneness. International law speaks of "nations" but actually means states; most states are multiethnic.

In actual political/legal practice, the right to self-determination is often not applied, even in the form of internal self-administration, because in these cases it is (allegedly) not linked to territoriality and because most peoples are generally not recognized as peoples but as minorities. The relevant legal basis is then human rights, which are generally individual rights. As a consequence, the rights of ethnonational communities are located in a precarious "gray area" between collective international law and individual human rights.

D. Politicization of the Ethnic

Whether affiliation to an ethnic community becomes politicized and whether the right to self-determination is demanded depend on a large number of factors. It may be said, however, that the fundamental right to self-determination is generally in antagonistic relation to the "inviolability of the borders" of existing state entities. In the third world, state territory only rarely corresponds to ethnic territory. State borders, often traced out with a ruler at some official's desk, cut across ethnic borders.

The politicization of the ethnic (thus ethnicity) is often seen as a precondition for conflictual processes between states and distinct ethnic groups. From the perspective of any ethnonational community, however, such politicization is, as a rule, not a precondition but a *result* of conflictual processes. Politicization of the ethnic is one of several possible lines that may be followed by macrosocial processes that develop as a reaction, but not an automatic one, to changes in social surroundings.

Ethnopoliticization is thus one possible (but not necessary) consequence of external interference. Such interference can either be destructive in its ultimate effects, as, for example, the preferential treatment of a particular ethnic group by colonial powers; or it can be destructively structured from the outset. The latter occurs in the form of external aggression, like the invasion of an ethnic territory for the purposes of exploiting resources or of expelling an ethnonational community from its ancestral lands.

III. TOWARD A COMPREHENSIVE TYPOLOGY OF MASS VIOLENCE

Practically all wars are nowadays intrastate wars. Since 1945 internal conflicts within the borderlines of a single state are by far more numerous than inter-state conflicts (international armed conflicts) between two or more states. Distinguishing internal and external conflicts— even thought politically as well as analytically relevant—tends to become invalid.

In two-thirds of all contemporary conflicts the ethnic factor (ethnicity) is a dominant or influential component. Ethnicity is mostly negatively charged in political discourse. Contrary to the prognoses of political and social sciences in regard to the development of modern societies, ethnicity has lost none of its importance in recent decades. On the contrary, the importance of the ethnic dimension has increased. Identification of the driving forces of ethnic nationalism in the global framework leads to questions linked with the nature of ethnicity and the ethnic base of nations. Underneath the structure of nearly 200 states there is an extraordinary multitude of distinct groups.

Whilst ethnic violence in the FSU was a nonintentional result of Lenin's policy of administrative ethnicization (the korenizatsiya), the legacies of colonialism and other external conditions contributed in the former third world to separate nations from nationalities. The legacies of colonialism and other external conditions contributed to the separation of nations from nationalities. The invention of the nation-state, its official nationalism, and the false expectations raised by development ideologies in the former colonies are some of the basic sources for past and future conflicts. The European nation-state project created large-scale disorder after being exported to the colonies. The official nationalism failed to satisfy its own aspirations of achieving an acceptable degree of development. State failure to safeguard internal peace and security created most extreme problems.

The sacrosanct principle of noninterference in the internal affairs of states has always been a shaky rule as the high number of foreign state interventions shows: States of the North were since 1945 actively involved in over 390 wars fought by state actors in the South. Compilations concerning the period of 1945 to 1991 go as high as 690 foreign overt military interventions. The principle of noninterference was respected or violated according to political or economic interests at stake. Interference traditionally takes place by supporting insurgents with arms and equipment and providing safe haven (hinterland) for rebels in neighboring states rather than through direct involvement of foreign states with combatant troops. In economy the principle of autarchy is long obsolete. Or let us take migration or ecological disruption. It does not stop at borders and could induce more conflict issues and threats in the near future. In the past noninterference was only honored according to political preferences—on a case-by-case basis.

The debate should best be linked with particular conflict issues and threats. The term internal conflict tends to become invalid regarding a number of is sues and threats that can no longer be considered as falling under the competence of the state. Thus the scope of what are "internal affairs" of states has to be redrawn.

A. Definitions of Mass Violence, Ethnicity, and Main Actors

Wars and nonwar types of mass violence (such as genocide or large-scale massacres) have to be clearly defined and distinguished.

• Major wars and mass violence are distinguished from other armed conflicts or massacres by various degrees of medium or high intensity, claiming usually more than an estimated 1000 victims per annum or as an average during the course of the conflict (see, for instance, CoW, SIPRI, and others). In many cases the numbers of victims are contested or otherwise questionable. Governments tend to reduce the number of victims while rebels usually inflate numbers. Additionally, in most wars the adversaries exaggerate enemy casualties. Verification of numbers of battle-related deaths and (even more so) of massacre-related deaths is an awesome task.

• War is defined as a violent mass conflict involving two or more armed forces as combatants/actors in warfare. Not in all cases are regular state-armed forces (such as military, police forces, militias, and other paramilitary troops) involved. Nonstate actors are mainly so-called liberation movements having regular guerrilla or partisan armies, often recruiting along ethnic, national, or social class lines. Tribal militias, gangs, and other irregular forces have different agendas; they have less or no centralized control nor identifiable lines of command. Referring to most types of contemporary warfare violent clashes and combat between the warring parties take place with some degree of continuity. Ethnonationalist wars especially tend to become protracted conflicts.

• Nonwar types of mass violence are characterized by a separation of perpetrators of mass murder and their victims. In most cases the victimization and aggression is organized, supported, or tolerated by state actors. Contrary to asymmetries in many types of wars (concerning quality of weaponry, use of resources, and level of training), in nonwar mass violence there is a clear difference to be made between armed perpetrators and the victimized nonarmed civilians, which are by definition defenseless. The worst type of mass violence is genocide.

• Genocide is defined as state-organized mass murder and crimes against humanity are characterized by the intention of the rulers to exterminate individuals because of belonging to a particular national, ethnic, "racial," or religious group. Mass murder committed against members of a particular political group (called *politicide* by Barbara Harff) or social group (called *democide* by Rudolph Rummel) are equally horrifying but do not legally fall under the Anti-Genocide Convention of 1948. The most deadly regimes in the 20th century have all committed total genocide against domestic groups, mainly in barbarian attempts to exterminate *their* minorities.

• Dominant groups got into positions of command over the so-called monopoly of violence. Their assertive relationship toward ethnically distinct nationalities (nations without their own state) became the most important dangerous source of violent conflict since 1945, increasingly so with each cycle of decolonization.

• Ethnic communities can be defined as historically generated or (in some cases) rediscovered communities of people that largely reproduce themselves. An ethnic or communal group has a distinct name, which often simply signifies "person" or "people" in the ethnic community's language. Such groups maintain a specific, heterogeneous culture, including, particularly, a distinct language, and a collective memory or historical remembrance, including community myths, producing a degree of solidarity between members and generating a feeling of belonging.

• Ethnicity as a term is used to describe a variety of forms of mobilization, which ultimately relate to the autonomous existence of specifically ethnic forms of socialization. No clear-cut distinction can be made between struggles by social classes and struggles by ethnic groups. To talk about the politicization of ethnicity seems tautological. Different types of actors such as states, transnational companies, liberation movements, migrants' organizations, political parties, pressure groups, strategic groups, military leaders, and populists all seek to make political capital out of "ethnic identity."

B. Typology of Contemporary Violent Conflicts

Typologies of conflicts are indispensable for any survey of conflicts. In order to register violent conflict comprehensively we need a sophisticated typology and an equally sophisticated methodology to codify conflicts and indicate change. The main lacunae of global surveys on mass violence can be identified:

1. Present war registers overlook or deliberately ignore certain categories and types of violence such as genocide, mass murder, communal violence and postmodern types of conflicts.
2. Some conflict types do not necessarily involve state actors.
3. Most registers are constructing static entities instead of expressing the permanent mutation of conflicts in the real world. Conflicts develop over time and may change in quality, with a new type becoming dominant over the other(s).
4. External factors cannot be ignored.

These shortcoming and gaps have serious implications: A critical limitation occurs if compilations exclude nonwar types of mass violence. This results in limited explanatory power since the latter account for a higher number of casualties than wars in recent years. For instance, the war that began in Rwanda in 1990 served only as a smokescreen for a much larger crime, the extermination of an entire population group, which killed more people than all wars in FSU and Europe since the end of the Cold War.

Based on over 10 years of fieldwork and conflict analysis ECOR developed the, at present, most advanced survey. Analysis illustrates that conflicts change over time and can have two or more different layers. Secondary and tertiary components have to be identified in order to understand changes and provide analytic insight for responses to conflict. This of course makes conflict analysis a complex task. In order to allow comparison with other compilations the ECOR register somewhat follows (in types A–D) standards set by AKUF, corrected by Nietschmann's early works.

The problem is that ethnicity was seen in much of the academia as a sort of taboo, and this has only changed recently. Regarding conflict actors the main criteria cannot be described adequately by the ownership of the state in all cases. The typology has been extended to include wars between nonstate actors (E and F). Not only wars but also organized mass murder such as genocide (G) have to be included.

The resulting typology allows an analysis of global trends in warfare and nonwar types of mass violence, which is otherwise not visible. The methods and techniques applied to read the database of traditional registers would not be able to detect the most disturbing trends and extreme problems the victims of conflict and the international community are facing today.

A. Anti-regime wars or political and ideological conflicts: State versus Insurrection (SvI). There are different forms: liberation movements vs colonial powers; popular movements and/or sociorevolutionary movements vs authoritarian state; destabilization or reestablishing a status ante. The aim is to replace the government of the day or to change the sociopolitical system. Destabilization conflicts started in the framework of the Cold War can be very violent and have long duration; exemplary cases are RENAMO in Mozambique or UNITA in Angola, Mujaheddin (until 1991) and Taliban in Afghanistan, and Contras in Nicaragua. Today some former destabilization conflicts have mutated to become dominantly ethnonationalist or ethnotribalist (e.g., in Afghanistan and Angola).

B. Ethnonationalist conflicts: In diverse forms, mostly as intrastate conflicts opposing states and national groups (State versus Nation, SvN); sometimes as inter-state conflicts (MSvN). Ethnonationalist SvN conflicts are the most frequent type of contemporary armed conflicts and wars; such conflicts are generally of long duration (decades)—even conflict resolution would only in a few cases afford to create new states. The aim is self-defense; in extreme cases as a struggle for survival against aggressive state policies and outright threats of extermination. Possibilities for conflict resolution range from concessions regarding cultural autonomy and diverse degrees of autonomy to (con-)federal solutions and sovereign statehood.

C. Interstate conflicts, State versus State (SvS): Earlier seen as the "classic type" of warfare. Cases: war at the Persian Gulf between Iraq and Iran (1980–1988), the 11 Days War between Mali and Burkina Faso (1985), or the invation of U.S. in Panamá (1989). The number is limited; according to the ECOR Register during the decade 1985–1994 there were only 12 cases (of 102 wars). Application of the Geneva Conventions is unproblematic. Coalitions or war alliances are seldom: multistate versus state (MSvS); several states vs several other states (MSvMS). This constellation was the classic World War; today it is rare, e.g., U.S., Great Britain, France, and others vs Iraq (1990–1991).

D. Decolonization wars of foreign-state occupations (FSO): There are still a few Afro-Asiatic cases: Western Sahara, East Timor, West Papua, and Palestine; Eritrea became a sovereign state in 1991–1992. Most examples of type D have a dominant ethnonational character. Because of its privileges in international law type D is different from type B (which is of decisive influence for a possible conflict resolution). Essentially former European colonial territories were occupied or annexed by non-European regional powers; the occupied peoples have a case in the UN.

E. Interethnic conflicts: Type E is, together with types B and D, part of the ethnic conflicts in a broad sense but is different concerning its actors and aims. They act according to particular collective (nonprivate) interests. The issues are manifold but usually sectarian and sectorial: particular interests, tribalism, clan conflicts, chauvism, and narrow nationalism. Economic aspects play a role but cultural and political aspects dominate. As in B the militants use their own group as a recruiting and support base; actors are not forced to develop a war economy above normal levels. Such conflicts are often fought without a state actor taking part

F. Gang wars: Nonstate actors (mixed with criminal elements), especially in situations of state collapse. They act according to particular or even private interests. Economic aspects seem to be dominant and a particular type of war economy is developed. Gang wars are fought over valuable resources (diamonds, gold, precious stones, drugs, etc.), land, or control of markets. Actors are village militias, demobilized soldiers, or mercenaries (*contras, re-contras, re-compas*), so-called "dead squads," the Mafia, (drug) syndicates (e.g., in Columbia or in the Golden Triangle of SE Asia), professional groups (e.g., Garimperos vs Indians in the Amazon), private armies of warlords (in Afghanistan, Liberia, Somalia, etc.), or big landowners (in Latin America vs landless *campesiños*), or settlers or migrants vs indigenous peoples (e.g., in mountain areas of Bangladesh, Tripura, and Assam; in the Kenyan Rift Valley, etc.).

G. Genocide: State-organized mass murder and crimes against humanity characterized by the intention of the rulers to exterminate individuals belonging to a particular national, ethnic, "racial," or religious group (genocide). Genocide is the worst type of mass violence and has to be clearly distinguished from warfare. Targets and victims are civilians (non-combatants) including old people, children, and even babies. Recent cases of large-scale genocide were the exterminations committed by states. The Khmer Rouge regime in Cambodia, during 1975–1979, exterminated Vietnamese, Cham, and Chinese minorities; mass murder was also committed against ethnic Khmer (autogenocide). Rwanda's Hutu power regime overkilled the entire Tutsi branch of the Banyarwanda in 100 days (April 7 to July 15, 1994); massacres were repeatedly committed against Tutsi since 1959 and against two other minorities (Gogwe and Hima). Since the early 1990s Sudan's NIF regime has committed genocide against the Nuba in Central Sudan and Dinka civilians in Southern Sudan; this continues to the present day.

On the basis of these seven core types of conflict diverse mixed forms can be identified. Their characteristics and main impulses can be analyzed, starting with their historical and regional backgrounds. The task of conflict research remains a Herculean one: to detect the roots, genesis, and dynamics of intrastate conflicts. The aim is to give a survey of conflict potentials, to identify belligerent actors and their goals, to analyze characteristics of rebel forces, and to research the course of a particular conflict and its means (resources, external support) as well as possible foreign involvement. Furthermore, the task for peace research is to think about ways of structural prevention, transformation, and resolution.

C. Registers of Contemporary Violent Conflicts 1985–1996

Registers of contemporary wars often blur the high proportion of ethnically determined or induced types of conflicts. Such conflicts appear in combination with other types and forms of intrastate conflicts; this blurs a clear assignment. Today the category of ethnic conflict has gained broad acceptance. A few years ago this category was generally avoided for different reasons: in many Third World countries it was because of the connotations with "backwardness," "primitive culture," and "premodernity"; in Europe (especially in Germany), because of political implications or historical reasons, somewhat "value-neutral" official and camouflage terms were used instead. Usually the findings/results of a register have to be analyzed and interpreted carefully, whereby the outcomes for the same period can show a high degree of divergence concerning the overall number of conflicts, the proportion of a particular type, e.g.,

ethnic conflicts or substitute categories. Some authors underestimate the potential of ethnic conflicts. Most experts agree that their number is increasing. One of six individuals belongs to an at-risk minority.

The number of conflicts remained high through 1995 and 1996. The absolute number of conflicts was not sharply decreasing as other sources suggest. Concerning the virulence of violent conflict in the Third World there is no reason to talk about a relaxation. Many endless civil wars are still being continued. In 1994 the worst genocide since the Holocaust claimed up to 1 million lives. In 1995 two new armed conflicts were started, in 1996 three were started, and in 1997 two. Some of the new wars are linked to older wars (Niger, Liberia, Eastern Zaire/Rwanda), others are truly new. The number of conflicts for the period of 1985–1994 (listed in Table I) is as follows (according to type): A, 69; B, 66; C, 18; D, 12; E, 39; F, 17, and G, 4, yielding a total of 225 conflicts. In the years 1995–1996 some 80 conflicts were fought (75 violent conflicts still continued and 5 new conflicts were started). See Table II; for this period the numbers of conflicts per type are given below Table II. Twenty-seven violent conflicts were settled within the 12-year period (1985–1994; a total of some 102 violent conflicts occurred); in some of these conflicts the end of the war or the cease-fire remained precarious.

D. Trends and Perspectives

The heterogeneous dynamic character of contemporary violent conflicts has to be expressed adequately. In ECOR's evaluation this has been solved as such: besides pointing at a dominant type secondary and tertiary components were also codified. In order to exclude multiple counting of particular components only the last phase of a war was considered relevant. In the register the composition of the seven types of wars (A–G) features a dominant component followed by a secondary or tertiary component. Table III shows results regarding the seven types of violent conflict.

Conflicts with a dominant ethnic-induced or ethnicized character (types B, D, E, and G) account for nearly two-thirds (64.7%) of all contemporary conflicts. According to the number of appearances ethnic components made up 53.7%. That means there is a significant trend: the ethnic factor bears a higher dominance than other conflict components such as the antiregime component; compared with ethnic-induced conflicts the antiregime conflicts are half as dominant.

The results show some clear trends: in the 12-year period (1985–1996) the ethnonationalist wars and

TABLE I

Register of Violent Conflicts from January 1, 1985 to December 31, 1994

World region	No.	Country	Nation(alitie)s/actors	Conflict types[a]	Period/phases[b]
Central America	1	Guatemala	Maya-Kiché, Ixil, EGP, others	B/GBA/BA	1954/1978–1985/1986–...
	2	Guatemala	URNG	AB	1960/1980–1992(?)
	3	Nicaragua	FDN-Contras/Re-Contras	A+/AF	April 1981–1990/...
	4	Nicaragua	Miskitu/Sumu, Rama	B+/B	Feb. 1981–1987/1990
	5	El Salvador	FMLN, Pipil	AB	1980/81–Feb. 1992(?)
	6	USA	Panama (LD-RP)	C	20–24 Dec. 1989
Caribbean	7	Haiti	Tonton Macoutes, FRAPH; US	FA/FA+	Sept. 91/Sept. 94–...
South America	8	Brazil	Gold searchers vs Yanomami	FE	1986(?)–...
	9	Columbia	FARC, EPL; ELN; M-19	AB; A; A	1964/65/1.74–3.90/...
	10	Columbia	Drug syndicates, death squads	AF	1970(?)–...
	11	Columbia	Guajiro	BA	1975(?)–...
	12	Suriname	Busi Nengee/Kalinja, Lokono	BA/B	21 June 1986–7 June 89
	13	Peru	Sendero Luminoso, militias	ABF	May 1980–...
	14	Peru	Aymara, Quichua, MRTA	BA	Nov. 1987–...
North Africa	15	Morocco	West Sahara: Sahrawi	DB	18 Nov. 1975–1992(?)
	16	Sudan	South Sudan: SPLA	BGA	Sept. 1983–...
	17	Sudan	SPLA-Dinka, SPLA-Nuer	BE+	Aug. 1991–...
	18	Algeria	GIA, AIS (Armée Isl. du Salut)	AF	1991–...
	19	Egypt	Moslem fundamentalists	A	1992–...
West Africa	20	Senegal	Diola, MFDC	BA	April 1990–...
	21	Liberia	NPFL, INPFL	EA/EA+	Dec. 1989/Aug. 90–...
	22	Sierra Leone	RUF, NPFL, ULIMO	AEC	Jan. 1991–...
	23	Mali	Burkina Faso	C	21–31, Dec. 1985
	24	Mali/Niger	Tuareg: MFUA, MPA, FIAA	BCE/BC	May 90–92/June 94–...
Central Africa	25	Chad	FAN, FAP, MPS	E/BAC+/BA+/B	June 1966/79/90/91–...
	26	Rwanda	Bahutu, Tutsi, FPR/RPA	BA+	Oct. 90/92–July 94
	27	Rwanda	Interahamwe/CDR/GP vs. Tutsi	GEF+	6 April 94–15 July 1994
	28	Burundi	Tutsi (army), Bahutu (militias)	G/EAC	1972–.../August 1993–...
	29	Zaire	Luba; Hunde, Nyanga, Hutu	EA/GEA	Aug. 1992/March 93–...
East Africa	30	Ethiopia	Eritrea: ELF, EPLF	DB/DAB	1962/1976–May 1991
	31	Ethiopia	Tigrai, TLF, TPLF, EPRDF	B/BA	1975–May 1991
	32	Ethiopia	Oromo: OLF, IFLO, UOPL	BAD/BDA	1976/May 1991–..,
	33	Ethiopia	Gojjam, Gondar: EPRP, EDU	A/AB/BA	Mar 74/Dec. 75/May 91–...
	34	Ethiopia	EPRDF: EPDM, OPDO, u.a.	AB	Jan 1989–May 1991
	35	Djibouti	Afar (FRUD, others.)	BEA/BAE	1981/Oct. 1991–...
	36	Eritrea	ELF-Idriss, Jihad, ELF-GC	EA+	1993(?)–...
	37	Somalia	Somaliland: Isaaq, SNM	BA+/BA	1980/1990–May 1991
	38	Somalia	Marehan, SSDF, SDM, USC	EA/E/E+	1988/Jan. 91/Dec. 92–...
	39	Uganda	NRM, Acholi, Langi, Bari	AB/EA	Feb. 1981/Feb. 86/–...
South Africa	40	Angola	MPLA; FLNA, UNITA	D/BAC+/BAE	1961–75/20 June 1991–...
	41	Namibia	SWAPO, Herero; !Khoi; TA	BD	1966–22 Dec. 1988
	42	Zimbabwe	ZANU, Ndebele-ZAPU	AB/EA	Jan. 1983/1987–May 1988
	43	Mozambique	FRELIMO; RENAMO	D/AC/AE+	1991/1975–Oct. 1992(?)
	44	South Africa	SNC, PAC/Inkatha, Boers	DA/DAE/EAD	1962/1976/1990–...
Western Europe	45	Spain	Euskadi, ETA, HB	BA	1937–...
	46	France	Corsica, FLNC	BA	1950–...
	47	N-Ireland	IRA, UVF, UFF	DB/DEA/EDA	1961–1969/1986–10/94(?)
Eastern Europe	48	Yugoslavia	Slovenia/Croatia	AB/CB	June 1991–July 91/Oct. 91
	49	Croatia	Serbs (Krajina, Slavonia)	G/BF+/EA	1940–44/mid-91–93/May 95
	50	Bosnia:	Tshetniki, Muslims, HOS, others	EFB+	March 1992–...
	51	Moldavia	Russians, Ukrainians, Kosaks	EF+	March–Aug. 1992
	52	Rumania	Securitate, Timisoara Magyar	AE	17–28 Dec. 1989

continues

continued

SE Europe	53	Georgia	Gamsachurdia rebels	A/AEF	Sept. 91/Jan. 92–Nov. 1993
	54	Georgia	S. Ossetia	B	Dec. 1990–July 1992
	55	Georgia	Abchasia; alliance, Russians	BC/BC+	Aug. 92/July 93–Dec. 1993
	56	Chechnia	Inguschi, North Ossetians	BE	Dec. 1991–March 1992
	57	Aserbaijan	Nagorny-Karabach	BE/CBE	88–90/1992–May 1994(?)
	58	Armenia	SW Aserbaijan	CBEF	March 1993–May 1994
	59	Chechnia	Russian Army vs Chechen	BEAF	11 Dec. 1994–...
West Asia	60	Libanon	Maronites/Druse, Shiites/Hesb	AE/CEA/EAC	April 75/78/82–1993(?)
	61	Israel	Palestine: PLO/Hamas; Druse	DB	1968–...
	62	S-Jemen	Tribes, clans, JSP	AEF	13–29 Jan. 1986
	63	N-Jemen	South Jemen	ABC/BAC	Dec. 91/March 94–July 94
	64	Turkey	Kurds, PKK, HRK	B/BADF	1970/1984–...
Persian Gulf	65	Iran	Aseri, Kurds, Turkmen	BA	July 1979–1988/...(?)
	66	Iraq	Kurds, PUK, KDP	BA/BAC/BA+	1976/Feb. 91/March 91–...
	67	Iraq	Iran (1st Gulf war), Kurds	CB	Sept. 1980–20 Aug. 1988
	68	Iraq	Kuwait	CD	2–4 Aug. 1990
	69	USA/GB a.	Iraq (2nd Gulf war)	C	17 Jan.–27 Feb. 1991/...
	70	Iraq	Shiites	AB/CAB	1990/2. March 1991–...
Central Asia	71	Tajikistan	CP, clans, Russian troops	EAF+	Aug. 1992–June 1993(?)
	72	Afghanistan	CP, Pathanen, Tajik, Usbek, a.	ABE/BAE+/EB	1973/Oct. 78/Apr. 92–...
	73	Pakistan	Sindhi, SNA, Muhajir, Paschtun	BEF	Nov. 1986–...
South Asia	74	India	Pakistan (Siachen glacier)	C	April 1984–1989(?)
	75	India	Kashmir: Muslim/Jamu/Ladakh	BE/BAE	1986/1990–...
	76	India	Punjab: Sikhs, KLF, KCF	BAE	July 1982–...
	77	India	Bihar: Naxaliten	A	1988–...(?)
	78	Sri Lanka	LTTE, EPRLF, Tamils, Muslims	B/BA+/BAE+	July 83/Sept 87/Mar 90–...
	79	Sri Lanka	JVP, Singhalese Youth	AE	July 87–Nov. 1989(?)
	80	Bangla Desh	CHT-Tribes, Chakma, SB, a.	BAF	1973–...
	81	NE-India	Tai-Asom, ULFA, Boro/Bodo	BEA	1990–...
	82	NE-India	West Begal/Himalaya: Gorkha	BA	1987–1988(?)
SE-Asia	83	NE-India	Naga: RGN, NNC, NSCN	BD/BEA/AB/BA	1954/1963/1972/Nov. 75–...
	84	NE-India	Manipur: KNA, NSCN, Meitei	BA/BEA/BAE	1960/75/84/May 92–...
	85	NE-India	Mizo: MNF, u.a.	BAE	1966–June 1986
	86	Burma	Karen: KNDO, KNU	BEA/B/BA	1947/1950/1988–...
	87	Burma	CPB (PVO, Red Flag), DPA	A/A+/AB	1948/1962/March 89–...
	88	Burma	KIO, Mon; NDF; Pa-O, KNPP	B/BAE/BA	1962/1976/Nov. 1988–...
	89	Burma	Shan, Da'an, ALF, Wa, a, a.	EA/EBA	1970(?)/1988–...
	90	Burma	DAB: NDF, ABSDF, PPP, a.	AB	Nov. 1988–...
	91	Burma	Opium guerrilla: KKY, MTA, Wa	EA+/EFA/FE	1950/1976/March 1989–...
	92	Thailand	Laos	C	Nov. 1987–Febr. 1988
	93	Laos	Hmong, LLA, drug wars	FEC+/FEA	1970/1975–...
	94	Cambodia	Khmer Rouge, ANS, Sihanouk	A/CA/G/AB+/A+	1968/70/1971–75/79/85–...
	95	Vietnam	Montagnards, KPNLA, FULRO	B/BA+/B	1964/1970/75–Oct. 1992(?)
East Asia	96	China	Vietnam	C	Feb./March 1979–1988
Island Asia	97	Philippines	NPA, Cordillera, CPA, Bontok	AB	1970–...
	98	Philippines	Mindanao: Moro, MNLF, MILF	BA+/BA	1970/1989–...
	99	Indonesia	Aceh, others	B	May 1990–...
	100	Indonesia	East Timor	DBA	Aug. 1975–...
	101	Indonesia	West Papua, OPM	DGB	1965–...
Asia Pacific	102	New Guinea	Bougainville	BAD	Feb. 1989–...

[a] Mixed types: AB, BA, BC, CB, AC, CA, AE, EA, ABC, BAC, etc. The first mentioned type is the dominant type for the given period (marked by a dash) in combination with a less influential secondary or tertiary type. Foreign actors: (+) direct interference/engagement of an outside power with combatants, not only presence of military 'advisors' or mercenaries.

[b] Phase/period: (/) slash between types or periods of time indicate different phases of war or paradigmatic changes in the course of warfare; periods of time: (...) indicates that war is continued after the register period end 1994 or end 1996 while (?) indicates that the date or the termination of warfare is questionable.

Sources: Scherrer (1988, 1997); ECOR (1991, 1992, 1994a., 1995, 1996, 1997); AKUF (1996, 1997); HIIK (1996); SIPRI; Gantzel/Schlichte (1994); Gantzel/AKUF (1992); Nietschmann (1987); SEF (1996, 1997); Wallensteen et al. (1993, 1997).

TABLE II

Register of Violent Conflicts from January 1st 1995 to December 31st 1996

World region	No.	Country	Nation(alitie)s/actors	Types of conflicts	Period/phases
Central America	1	Mexico	EZLN (Chiapas), Tzeltal, Tzotzil	BA/AB	Jan. 1994/2/1995–...
	2	Mexico	EPR/ELN (Guerrero, Oaxaca)	BA	June 1996–... (new)
	3	Guatemala	URNG	GAB/AB	1960/1980–12.96 (?)
	4	Nicaragua	(Re-) Contras, recompas, gangs	A+/AF	1981–1990/...
South America	5	Brazil	settler, gold rush vs indigenous	GE/FE	1986 (?)/1989–/...
	6	Columbia	FARC, EPL; CGSB	AB; A; A	1964/65/1.74–3.90/...
	7	Columbia	ELN vs S, TNC	AB; A; A	1965/74–...
	8	Columbia	Drug syndicates, death squads	F	1970 (?)–...
	9	Peru	Sendero Luminosa/Rojo; militias	ABF	1980–March 1995/...
	10	Peru	MRTA; Aymara, Quichua	AB	Nov. 1987–1992/...
	11	Ecuador	Peru	C	1/1995–2/1995
North Africa	12	Morocco	W. Sahara; Polisario; MINURSO	DB	Nov. 1975–1992/... (?)
	13	Sudan	South Sudan: SPLA	BA+	Sept. 1983–...
	14	Sudan	SPLA vs SSIA, Nuer u.a.	F/BE+	Aug. 1991–...
	15	Sudan	Arab militias vs SPLA	F/FE	1983/1991–...
	16	Sudan	Central Sudan: Nuba genocide	BGA/GBE	1989/91–...
	17	Sudan	NDA; Northern Sudanese+SPLM	AB+	Oct. 1989/1995–...
	18	Algeria	Muslim fundamentalists AIS, GIA	AF	1991–...
	19	Egypt	Muslim integrists/M. broderhood	AF	1992–...
West Africa	20	Senegal	Diola, MFDC	BAD/BA	1990–94/Jan. 1995–...
	21	Liberia	NPFL, ULIMO (K+J), LPC	EF/EA+/A	1989/95/April 96–...
	22	Sierra Leone	RUF, NPFL,ULIMO	EC/AE+	Jan. 1991–...
	23	Mali	Tuareg: MPA, FIAA; militias	BAE/BCE	1990–92/1994–... (?)
	24	Niger	Tuareg: FLAA	BAE/BCE/BC	May 90–91/Oct. 94–...
	25	Niger	Arabs, others; FDR	BE	1995–... (new)
	26	Ghana	Konkomba vs Nanumba, Gonja	EA	Feb. 1994–...
	27	Nigeria	Ogoni (MOSOP), others	BA	90er/
Central Africa	28	N. Chad	MDD, Frolinat, FNT	B/BAC+/BA+/E	June 1966/79/90/91–...
	29	S. Chad	CSNPD, FARF	BA/BEA	1985/91/Aug. 94–...
	30	Rwanda	Postgenocide/destabilization	EFC+/G/BA+	Oct. 90/Apr.–July 94/...
	31	Burundi	Tutsi/Hutu: Army vs FDD others	G/EAC	1972–.../August 1993–...
	32	Zaire-South	Luba; Katanga-Shaba; Lumumbist	EA/AE	Aug. 1992/March 93–...
	33	Zaire-East	Hutu, FAZ; Tutsi, Hunde	GEF	Summer 1994–...
	34	Zaire-East	Hutu+FAZ; AFDC, Banyamulenge	EA/A	Sept. 96/96–... (new)
East Africa	35	Ethiopia	Oromo: OLF, IFLO, UOPL	BAD/BDA	1976/May 1991–...
	36	Ethiopia	Somali, div.	BEA	1974/1992–...
	37	Ethiopia	Gojjam, Gondar: EPRP, EDU	A/AB/BA	Mar 74/Dec. 75/May 91–...
	38	Ethiopia	Somalia: ONLF, WSLM, others	CE	Aug. 1996–... (new)
	39	Djibouti	Afar (FRUD others.)	BEA/BAE	1981/Oct. 1991–...
	40	Eritrea	ELF-Idriss, Jihad, ELF-GC	EA+	1993 (?)–...
	41	Somalia	Clans; SNA, USC, UNOSOM	EF/EA/EF	1988/Jan. 91/Dec. 92–...
	42	Somaliland	Issa/other clans	EF	1992–...
	43	Uganda	LRA+HSM, WNBF; Acholi, Langi	AB/EA	Feb. 1981/Feb. 86/–...
	44	Uganda	MIR (Islamic), UDFM	EA+	1995–... (new)
	45	Uganda	Sudan; div. guerrilla groups	ECA	1991/1996–...
South Africa	46	Angola	FLEC-FAC, FLEC II	AE/AEF	1975/1993/1994–...
	47	South Africa	Kwa-Zulu: Inkatha IFP	EA	1990–...
West Europe	48	Spain	Euskadi, ETA, HB	BA	1937–...
	49	France	Corsica, FLNC	BA	1950–...
	50	N-Ireland	IRA; UVF, UFF	DB/DEA/EDA	1961–69/86–10/94/95–...
East Europe	51	Croatia	Serbs (Krajina, Slavonia)	G/BF+/EA	1940–44/mid-91–93/May 95
	52	Bosnia	Chetniks, Muslims, HOS, others	EFB+	March 1992–Oct. 1995 (?)
Southern Europe	53	Chechnia	Russian intervention vs Chechen	BEAF	11 Dec. 94–22 Aug. 1996

continues

continued

West Asia	54	Lebanon	SLA, Hisb-Allah, Amal, PFLP	EC/CE	1982–1993/1993–...
	55	Israel	Palästina: PLO/Hamas	DB	1968–...
	56	Turkey	Kurds, PKK	B/BADF	1970/1984–...
	57	Iran	Kurds, KDPI; Aseri	BA/BAD	July 1979–1988–...
	58	Iraq	Kurds, PUK, KDP	BA/BAC/BA+	1976/88/March 90–...
	59	Iraq	Shiits/Shia	AB/CAB/AB	1990/March 1991/1991–...
Central Asia	60	Tajikistan	CP, Clans, CIS/Russian troops	EAF+/EA+	Aug. 92–June 1993/93–...
	61	Afghanistan	CP, Pathans, Tajik, Usbek, a.	ABE/BAE+/EB	1973/Oct. 78/Apr. 92–...
	62	Pakistan	Sindhi, MQM, Muhajir, Pashtun	BEF/EF	Nov. 1986–1990/90–...
South Asia	63	India	Kashmir: Muslim/Jamu/Ladakh	BE/BAE	1986/1990–...
	64	India	Bihar: Naxalits	A	1988–...
	65	Sri Lanka	LTTE, Tamils	B/BA+/BAE+	July 83/Sept 87/Mar 90–...
	66	Bangla Desh	CHT: Chakma, Shanti Bahini	BAF	1973–...
	67	NE-India	Tai-Asom, ULFA, Bodo BSF	BEA	1989–...
SE Asia	68	NE-India	Naga: RGN, NNC, NSCN	BD/BEA/AB/BA	1954/1963/1972/Nov 75–...
	69	NE-India	Manipur: KNA, NSCN, Meitei	BA/BEA/BAE	1960/75/84/May 92–...
	70	Burma	Karen: KNDO, KNU	BEA/B/BA	1947/1950/1988–...
	71	Burma	Mon, NMSP	B/BAE/BA	11962/76/Nov. 88–June 95
	72	Burma	opium guerrilla: MTA, Wa	EA+/EFA/FE	1950/1976/Mar 1989–...
	73	Laos	Hmong, LLA, drug war lords	FEC+/FEA	1970/1975–... (?)
	74	Cambodia	Khmer Rouge/Ieng Sary; ANS	A/CA/G/AB/A+	1968/70/71–75/1979–...
Island Asia	75	Philippines	NPA, Cordillera, CPA, Bontok	AB	1970–...
	76	Philippines	Mindanao: Moro, MNLF, MILF	BA+/BA	1970/1989–Sept. 1996 (?)
	77	Indonesia	Aceh others.	B	May 1990–...
	78	Indonesia	East-Timor	DBA	Aug. 1975–...
	79	Indonesia	West-Papua, OPM	DGB/DB	1965–...
Asia-Pacific	80	New Guinea	Bougainville, BRA, BTG	BAD	Feb. 1989–Dec. 95/...

	Type							
	A	B	C	D	E	F	G	Total
No. of dominant type	18	31	3	4	17	5	2	80
Primary, secondary, tertiary 1995–1996	18-29-9 (56)	31-18-1 (50)	3-3-1 (7)	4-2-3 (9)	17-16-5 (38)	5-7-3 (15)	2-1-0 (3)	178

genocide became more dominant than antiregime wars or gang wars. Dominance and frequency are roughly balanced regarding inter-state wars, decolonization wars, and interethnic wars.

Particularly significant is the result concerning the two most frequent types of war (A and B): conflicts from 1995 and 1996 contain most frequently an anti-regime component (31.5%) and an ethno-nationalist component (28.1%) as a secondary or tertiary component (see Table IV). Most significantly is that the ethno-nationalist character of contemporary violent conflicts is almost twice as frequently in a dominant position then the character of anti-regime conflicts (38.75 to 22.5). This result is almost in line with the result from the decade 1985 to 1994 (44.1 to 19.6%); see Table III.

E. Reduction of Inter-State Wars and the Increase of Foreign Interventions

Shocking for mainstream security studies and conflict research is the fact that the Clausewitzean type of inter-

TABLE III

Violent Conflicts 1985–1994

	Conflict types (%)							
	A	B	C	D	E	F	G	B+D+E+G ethnic conflicts
Dominance	19.6	44.1	11.8	4.9	13.7	3.9	2.0	64.7
Mentioning	30.7	29.3	8.0	5.3	17.3	7.6	1.8	52.9

TABLE IV

Conflict Types over a 12-Year Period (January, 1985 to December, 1994 in %)

	A	B	C	D	E	F	G	B+D+E+G ethnic conflicts
Dominance								
1995–1996	22.5	38.75	3.75	5.0	21.25	6.25	2.5	67.5
1985–1994	19.6	44.1	11.8	4.9	13.7	3.9	2.0	64.7
Secondary components	31.5	28.1	3.9	5.1	21.3	8.4	1.1	55.6
Tertiary components	30.7	29.3	8.0	5.3	17.3	7.6	1.8	52.9

state conflict has practically disappeared. The most significant trend in recent years shows a progressive decline of the absolute number (and proportion) of inter-state conflicts. Today there are less than 1 in 20 conflicts of this type (3.75%, 1985–1996). Currently there are only three cases of a dominant inter-state conflict: the war between Pakistan and India in Kashmir 1998–1999, the war between Ethiopia and Eritrea, being fought with increasing intensity since March 1998, with spillover effects on Southern Somalia during 1999, and the 78-days air war of the NATO alliance against Yugoslavia 1999. The most costly of the three wars is the one at the Horn of Africa; the original issue was a territorial dispute about the Badme district. In half a dozen wars the inter-state conflict character became a secondary component of internal types of conflict, most prominently in Africa.

Even worse is that today inter-state conflicts increasingly mutate into a subcomponent or an extension of intrastate wars. In Africa this pattern can be demonstrated in several recent cases occurring in the years 1996 and 1997. Contrary to the classic types of inter-state conflicts and disputes, different types of ethnic conflicts/disputes could be compared to rhizome plants: growing for decades, nearly impossible to up-root, growing "everywhere," and always surfacing where and when you would least expect. In Africa, the new pattern can be shown to have emerged in the period 1996–1999. Inter-state conflicts are increasingly mutating into subcomponents or extensions of intrastate wars. The military involvement of eight African states and a dozen nonstate actors in the new war under way in the Democratic Republic Congo since August 1998 between the Kabila regime and the RCD rebels is the latest and most complex example.

From 1996 to 1998 the amount of foreign state participation increased to 17 cases (of 80 conflict cases). Compared to 1985–1994 there had been 27 cases of foreign state intervention; in 15 of those 27 cases the

intervention occurred in the last phase of the conflict, while in 12 cases the former state intervention took place in the 1980s. In the 2-year period of 1995 to 1996 the number of foreign state interventions was 23 cases, whereby in 6 cases the foreign intervention started before the mentioned period. Hence, recent foreign state intervention is, with 17 cases for 1995 and 1996, extraordinary high. Rarely do interventions occur of types B and E. The question of foreign state intervention is to be distinguished clearly from support by foreign states for one or more conflict actors (e.g., by providing hinterland or weapons).

F. Regional Distribution of Conflicts: Decrease in Asia versus Increase in Africa

The distribution of conflicts according to world regions shows the following picture. Today 45% of all violent conflicts are taking place in Africa, which is more than during the decade 1985–94 (Table V). The high share of Africa in the world's conflicts was further increasing since 1996 to about half of all conflicts.

During the period of 1985 to 1996 the regional distribution of violent conflicts was largely modified. While the proportion in Latin America remained constant, those in Asia and Europe were declining. On the other

TABLE V

Distribution of Conflicts by Region

World region	1985–1994	1995–1996
Asia	42.2%	33.7%
Africa	29.4%	45.0%
Europe	14.7%	7.5%
Americas	13.7%	13.7%

TABLE VI

Subregional Distribution and Change in Percentages

Region	No. of conflicts (1985–1994)	%	No. of conflicts (1995–1996)	%	Change
Latin America	14	13.7%	11	13.7%	0
Europe	15	14.7%	6	7.5%	−49%
Africa	30	29.4%	36	45.0%	+53%
Asia	43	42.2%	27	33.7%	−21%
World's conflicts	102	100%	80	100%	−/+

hand, the proportion of violent conflicts in Africa was increasing dramatically. In terms of number of cases and mortalities Africa has become the most war-torn continent in recent years, surging past West Asia and South Asia.

In Africa the civilian population suffered heavy losses through exterminatory mass violence, warfare, and war-induced famine. In 1996 five African countries were among the nine countries affected by major armed conflicts claiming more than 1000 lives: Algeria, Burundi, Congo-Zaire, Sudan, and Uganda (besides Afghanistan, Chechnia/Russian Federation, Sri Lanka, and Turkey/Kurdestan). In 1997 the number of African countries with major conflicts claiming more than 1000 violence-related deaths rose to eight (Angola, Rwanda, and Congo-Brazzaville) compared to three other cases in the rest of the world. In 1998 nine of the eleven major armed conflicts occurred in Africa: in Algeria, Angola, Burundi, Democratic Republic of Congo, Eritrea-Ethiopia, Guinea-Bissau, Rwanda, Sierra Leone, and Sudan; two more were fought in Asia (Afghanistan and Sri Lanka).

After 1990 Europe once again temporarily became one of the major theaters of war. The talk of "Europe as island of peace" was abruptly silenced in 1991. The most peaceful world regions were East Asia and North America (the latter without taking into account high rates of urban violence and criminality).

Six years later violent conflicts in Europe were reduced to half and conflicts in Asia decreased by one-fifth. Only conflict in Africa increased dramatically by more than 50% (Table VI).

The frequency of violent conflicts in the years 1995 and 1996 are categorized as follows. The most frequent dominant conflict type was ethnonationalist, with 38.75% of all cases (28.1% of mentioning). Next were antiregime wars (23.75%) and interethnic wars (20%), the latter with a strong increase, followed by gang wars (7.25%), decolonization wars (5%), and inter-state conflicts (3.75%). Genocide (2.5%) remains the most rare type of violent conflict but the one with the highest mortality.

The conflicts in 1995 and 1996 acquired a dominant ethnic character (types B, D, and E) and account for two-thirds (66.25%) of all contemporary violent conflicts. According to the number per type of conflict the ethnic conflict components appeared in over half of all cases (Table VII).

H. Most Dramatic Recent Trends: Increasing Complex Crisis and State Collapse

Genocide and mass murder of defenseless victims account for 2 and 2.5% of all conflicts in the respective

TABLE VII

Frequency of Violent Conflicts

Type of conflict	Dominance : frequency		Quota	
	1985–1994	1995–1996	1985–1994	1995–1996
Antiregime	19.2 : 30.7	23.7 : 31.8	0.63	0.75
Ethnonationalism	44.1 : 29.3	38.7 : 28.4	1.51	1.36
Interethnic conflicts	13.7 : 17.3	20.0 : 20.4	0.79	0.98

periods. This is an alarming sign and a matter of most serious concern. The number of victims of genocide and mass violence in the period of 1985–1996 is much higher than the frequency would suggest. The small numbers of genocide and mass violence show a higher mortality than those of all other conflicts combined.

In the 1990s a dramatic increase of extreme crisis situations and complex emergency cases led to an alarming increase of conflict-induced mortality. The state-organized genocide in Rwanda in 1994 alone took 1 million lives in a period of 100 days. This incredible number of victims is more than twice the number of victims caused by all violent conflicts taking place from 1988 to 1996 in the former Soviet Union and in the former Yugoslavia combined. Even more victims (an estimated 2.5–3 million people since 1954) were killed by genocide, war, and famine as consequences of successive Sudanese regime's onslaughts in southern Sudan. Sudan is the most deadly contemporary case of mass violence; at present this conflict is going on unabated.

Another matter of concern is the proportion of gang wars that was nearly doubling in a period of only 10 years (from 3.9% to 6.25%). Chaos and warlordism so far characterize only a small number of all conflicts (every 16th), but this could increase even further. This concern is based on the evidence that the higher proportion of mentioned cases compared to the proportion of dominance of this type of conflict indicate a trend toward further increases in dominance and frequency.

In the case of most ethnonationalist types of conflict the conspicuous silence of the Western mass media is even more suspicious; such conflicts account for 40% of all violent conflicts. The ethnonationalist character is increasingly becoming the dominant component of contemporary conflicts. One of the conflict impacts is the relatively low chance for peaceful conflict settlement. This is one of the main causal reasons for the steady increase (up to 1995) of such durable protracted conflicts. This again contributes significantly to the increase of the total number of contemporary wars.

The related conflict type of decolonization continuously accounts for 1 of 20 wars. Such conflicts also receive little attention by Western media.

Another matter of concern and cause for alert is the rising number of interethnic conflicts; those conflicts between ethnic groups without participation of state actors in most cases. This type of conflict increased by nearly one-third (30%; a 5% increase).

The trend points toward a further fragmentation within existing states. This results in a loss of hegemony of state actors in many countries in the South; state failure and warfare is inextricably linked.

IV. VIOLENT CONFLICTS, TIMING, AND TYPES OF RESPONSES

This section looks into peace strategies such as the possibility of structural prevention of violence and conflict management and transformation as well as the role of multilateralism in preventing violence. The question "What to do in a particular situation?" is linked with the type of conflicts we are dealing with as well as with the stage of escalation of the conflict at the particular time of intervention. In this section the importance of timing in response to conflict is stressed and the types of responses are related to different types of wars. Peaceful responses and peace strategies should learn from existing schemes and focus on long-term structural and interactive prevention of violent conflict rather than plunge into activism that only produces short-term bandages. Proven mechanisms range from minority protection (affirmative action to autonomy regulations), power-sharing, nationality policies, and federal schemes. Procedures and instruments include standard-setting for international laws and rules, such as those made to protect nondominant groups and regimes for secession.

A. The Crucial Question of the Right Timing for Peaceful Responses to War

Let us think about conflicts in a very general way. In daily social life conflicts make sense. Conflict is an essential form of social interaction. To argue with someone brings problems out. Problems should be expressed (not suppressed); only by this way can solutions be found. To have it out with a person makes arrangements possible with due respect for different interests and positions. Therefore the focus is not on preventing conflicts but on preventing destructive ways of dealing with differences. Interaction becomes destructive through the use of violence.

In processes confronting social groups or larger sections of society the option of violence should be prevented from the onset. Some may argue that pacifism in interethnic or international relations is a questionable position. For instance they might claim the right to self-defense. Here things already get difficult. Others think about revolutionary violence, which should be characterized as controlled violence against oppression. The ideal typical case would be a so-called natural right of resistance against tyranny. But we all know that there are no ideal typical cases in social life and in the real world. It may only be consequent and genuine common sense to say that violence bears violence and that prevention is better than cure.

B. Collective Memory and Dormant Conflict

Conflicts are a natural thing and mere differences as such are not conflictive and therefore do not usually carry or provoke violence. Cultural or ethnic differences can be interesting or attractive and make social life more colorful—as long as such differences are not politicized and exploited for particular interests, especially if states engage in such activity. Immanuel Kant's questions about sustainable peace by banning wars on a global scale "for all times," thus establishing eternal peace, seemed not from this world. Kant wrote his piece about eternal peace some 200 years ago—after the French Revolution and on the height of the era of enlightenment. Common sense maintains that wars have always been fought. Therefore, there is always a past full of memories of hostilities and despair. Past violence itself is a source for traumatizing memories.

A constitutive element for each and every society, community, or ethnic group is what has been called the collective memory. Other elements would be a common language, being part of a common culture, living in a particular place or territory as a space of communication and social interaction, and feeling some kind of solidarity of belonging to a particular group. It is the collective memory before all other elements that make up a community of people that is the most decisive element regarding conflict. The collective memory is a kind of living history book, giving a record of past traumatic experiences. Like official or written history it is full of myths. Common memories about the past reflect all kinds of events, including disputes, past injustices and traumas, violence and victimization, wars, and mass violence. In some cases the worst memory is about genocide. Psychologists talk about internalization such as "sleeping memories" that can suddenly be reactivated. Peace researchers should know very well that memories of past horrors are still virulent after generations of peace and stability.

C. Adequate Choice of Procedures and Use of Instruments at the Right Time

Like memories conflicts also can be pending in a subconscious or sleeping stage and can be suddenly reactivated. That is why this stage is the best time for prevention. Even weak preventive measures have an effect. Targeted measures against renewed violence should take into account the root causes of a dormant conflict (stage 1: sleeping conflict). The adequate choice of procedures and use of instruments is important. Galtung questioned the triangle of diagnosis, prognosis, and therapy. He correlated the time dimension with peace work (analysis and practice). Alternative options include either reliving the tragedy (Galtung) to stop traumatization or to neutralize the trauma through confidence building and empowerment (in order to prevent it from emerging again). Galtung asked, "Why should anyone relive a trauma?—To demystify the past. . . ." A typology of responses to conflict would have essentially to include all kind of procedures and instruments for prophylactic peace building and peace keeping at the stage of sleeping conflict. Thus a typology for crisis prevention and conflict management first characterizes institutions, procedures, and instruments for peaceful coexistence (see Table VIII). In a more specific typology for local and global peace-building (see Table IX) instruments for violence prevention and interethnic balance are listed.

D. Stages of Conflict Escalation and Possible Constructive Reponses

Let us now look into conflict stages and possible constructive responses in an abstract way. The Herculean task of peace-building is most effectively approached by various ways to structurally prevent violence on different levels. This includes different actors or institutions and can be achieved by using various means. In the enclosed general survey of types of crisis prevention and conflict management I tried to specify some aspects of my typology of peace in order to give a historic and structural view of existing institutions, procedures, and instruments for peaceful coexistence (compare Table IX). In much the same way the procedures and instruments for violence prevention and interethnic balance are given in a systematic overview (compare Table VIII).

E. Structural Prevention at the Stage of Dormant Conflict

Peaceful coexistence can be approached with a minimal level effort of enforced application of existing instruments: international law—not only on paper—but used to safeguard international security as well as internal peace. Concerning all forms of conflict characterized by ethnic factors structural prevention provides many options. It is best used to intervene at the stage of sleeping conflict. This is where and when the obstacles are few but the choices of possible approaches are fairly

TABLE VIII

Typology for Crisis Prevention and Conflict Management: Institutions, Procedures, and Instruments for Peaceful Coexistence

Peace-building/types	Scope, realm	Principle	Period	Models and processes/deficits/needs	Aims/objectives/expectations
Peaceful coexistence by structural prevention of destructive interaction	UN, regional regimes, states, societies, NGOs	Interactive, preventive, rule of law	Increasingly since 1945; still to be enforced	Application of existing instruments/laws (international pacts, conventions, declarations) as well as development of new instruments in international law; problem: how to break passive/active resistance of states?	New instruments to combat destructive interaction between states and nation(ality)s; rapid establishment of international criminal justice in high demand; lack of enforcement
Peaceful coexistence of granting comprehensive minority rights	States, multilateral regimes	Active, preventive, internal, rule of law	Since 1980s; increasingly since 1990	Protection of the rights of nondominant groups (OSCE HCNM); standard setting by UN-CHR toward Universal Declaration of the Rights of Indigenous Peoples	Internal peace and external security through interethnic balance and protection of new minorities; application of international law
Peaceful coexistence by power sharing	States/regimes/ civil actors	Active, preventive, innovative	Since many centuries; more cases still to be established	Lessons to be learned from experiences with different existing models of power sharing, representation, ethnically mixed elites, and their cooperation (CH, Lebanon, Malaysia, Benin); models of limited attractiveness	Comparison of existing models and their performance; development of new instruments to promote constructive interactiont and balance of different ethnic and national groups
Peaceful coexistence by granting internal right to self-determination and free association for all peoples	Cooperation of involved state(s) and peoples; facilitation by UN, regional regimes, INGOs/NGOs	Interactive, preventive, innovative	Increasingly since 1945; still to be established on larger scale	"Lessons learned?" from experiences with autonomy regulations and self-governance in all continents; models: *korenisazia* and autonomization in FSU and China; creation of new states in India, quotas for scheduled castes/tribes; autonomy regulations in Europe; lack of implementation	Comparison of existing models and their performance; development of new instruments to promote constructive interaction between states and nation(alitie)s; establishment of international regimes in high demand
Peaceful coexistence by establishing (con-) federal schemes	Cooperation of multiethnic state and people(s); facilitation by relevant actors	Interactive, preventive	Increasingly since 1945; still to be established	Lessons to be learned from experiences with federal schemes in all continents; models (also incomplete): FSU/RF, India, Nigeria, Tanzania, Ethiopia, new South Africa, Switzerland, Spain, etc.	Comparison of existing models and their performance; development of new models to promote (con-) federal and regional schemes
Peaceful coexistence by rules for the realization of the full right to self-determination	Cooperation of involved state(s) and international community	Interactive, preventive, innovative	Still to be established	Consequences to be drawn from experiences with destructive ethnonationalist civil wars in all continents; deficit of shared norms/standards for secession; global governance	Rules for the creation of new states; regimes for recognition of claims; new instruments to promote constructive transition

Preventing/transforming violent conflict by preventive diplomacy	State system primary; civil actors such as INGOs	Reactive/active; state-centered regime building	On the rise since 1990; medium-term	Multiethnic societies/states; actionistic activities/power mediation, conflict regulation/agreements between the parties to the conflict; little impact	Protection/minimal rights for nondominant groups; security through respect for others; recognition of multiplicity
Preventing violence by early warning linked to early action	UN, INGOs, regional regimes, states local civil actors	Active preventive	Still to be established	Increasing capabilities of early warning; full use of conflict prevention networks to be built-up jointly by multilateral regimes, research institutes and INGOs/NGOs	Top priority for bridging the gap between early warning and early action
Peace by peaceful intervention: mediation/facilitation	Civil society actors, NGOs/INGOs, some states	Reactive-activist interactive (mainly internal) preventive	On the rise since 1980s; short- to longer-term	Multiethnic societies/states; actionistic mediation/facilitation, conflict regulation/solutions through agreements between inside parties facilitated by outside parties	Empowerment for nondominant groups; security through respect for others, recognition of multiplicity/promotion of minorities' issues
Peace building by constructive dialogue	States external and local civil actors	Active/reactive processual preventive force innovative	On the rise since 1990s; medium term	Improvement of overall relationships in multiethnic societies/states; recognition and awareness about hidden perceptions/agendas of involved parties	Discovering shared needs; focusing on the future; translating common needs into "joint actions as stepping stones to agreements" (D. Weeks)
Peace building by constructive conflict resolution approaches	States external and local civil actors	Active/processual preventive innovative	Still to be established	Facilitation of conflict resolutions through negotiation about binding agreements as constructive medium- and long-term approaches	Shared needs and joint plans for the future; securing accountability of all parties and building sustainability
Peaceful interethnic coexistence by enforcing accountability and compliance of/by the states	UN/regimes under monitoring & watch by NGOs/INGOs	Interventive; rule of national and international law	Long-term approach; still at point zero	Enlightened civilized state leaders and civic organizations pushing for change; overall promotion of standard-setting in international law in order to force states to obey to the rules and comply with international law	Humanitarian minimum and respect of human and minority rights; no double standards; clear-cut sanctions to be introduced against deviation/crimes by repressive and intransigent state governments
Peace by peaceful means: education, culture of peace by lively cross-cultural communication	Civil society civilized states	Active, interactive preventive innovative	Medium periods	Enlightened libertarian sectors of societies/civilized states pushing for change; prevention of violence by getting to know each other (multikulti vs daily racism; travelling, cultural contacts, arts, etc.)	Conflict regulation through rights for nondominant groups (citizenship for 2nd-generation migrants); respect for other societies and different cultures/lifestyles

TABLE IX

Typology for Local and Global Peace-Building: Violence Prevention and Interethnic Balance

Peaceful coexistence	Scope, realm	Principle	Period	Characteristics/phenomena	Aims/objectives/results
Negative peace by threat of aggression pax americana/sovietica/etc.	Global state system globalize economy	Deterrence (external) and internal control	Short- and medium-term	Northern states or regional powers against weaker Southern states; exception: mutual deterrence of the super powers (Cold War)	Imposition of interest/containment/economic interest; result: hegemony
Negative peace by military intervention named "humanitarian"	State system (often against civil society); UN	External; state-centered; powered by legacy of Eurocolonialism/imperialism	Short-term since colonialism	Usually colonial powers, Northern states or regional powers against weaker states at the peripheries; expression of (post-) colonial dependency (dependencia); toppling of unfriendly governments, e.g., U.S. interventions in Latin America since Monroe	Often ultimate with no agreement proposed; control/imposition of "solutions"; result: conflict of interests; partial and nonsustainable effect, perpetuation of dependency
Coexistence/peace by arbitration and settlement of disputes	State system	External potentially also internal	Since 1899 First Hague Peace Conference	Establishment of the Permanent Court of Arbitration (PCA) 1899 and the Convention for the Peaceful Settlement of International Disputes (CPSID) provide for legal base	Peaceful settlement of disputes is a good old idea (reaffirmed by the UN Charter, 1945, Article 33c); result: PCA had little impact
Coexistence by agreements	State system (primary); TNCs	Internal/expansive state-centered; colonialism	Since the early 19th century	Settlers vs indigenous nations/weak settler states; conflict reduction by treaties, mostly broken after changes of the balance of power	First territorial invasion; control of lands and resources; population control
Coexistence through welfare state policies and agreements	State system (primary); economy civil society	Internal state-centered; expansive, internal colonialism	Longer periods since the early 20th century	Mainstream societies vs indigenous groups/strong settler states; attempted reduction of conflict, postcolonial trusteeship ideology; limited agreements with indigenous groups; reservation-type of system complemented by affirmative action (U.S., Australia, NZ)	Alien control of most indigenous lands and resources; population control
Internal peace and coexistence by means of modern treaties	State system economy civil society	Internal and state-centered; softened internal colonialism	Undefined periods since the 1980s	Mainstream societies, indigenous and other minorities/strong settler states; conflict prevention through treaties and agreements with indigenous peoples; partial to full self-governance (Canada, Denmark, Sweden)	Control and internal peace as aim; result: hopeful beginnings in Kalaallit Nunaat, Nunavut, Dené NWT, Saami Land

Coexistence by means of autonomy/conservation (in Southern neoliberal states)	State system (primary); civil society (only corporate)	Internal state-centered; internal colonialism by other means	Shorter and longer periods	*Mestizo* societies *vs* manifold indigenous communities/weak states (periphery); agreements with selected communities; type: *comarca* (Panama since 1920s), *resguardo*; nonintegration often broken by attempts of assimilation; self-rule in Eastern Nicaragua, flawed by neglect/paternalism	Traditional institutions (*caciques/congreso* system); control by concession of self-rule; aim to avoid structurally induced conflicts by territorial autonomy regulations (by law or constitutional, often ad hoc); real autonomy needs an economy
Peaceful coexistence by self-rule and free association (based on Northern welfare states)	State system and civil society	Associative non-expansive internal/external	Medium and longer periods after 1945	Enlightened/libertarian societies, indigenous minorities/social welfare states; structural conflict avoidance, conflict regulation or solution through rights and concessions, self-governance (Føroyar or Faroe Islands' home rule 1948)	Security through respect for others; high degree of organization; development and prosperity for many; few solid models for indigenous and minority self-governance realized (traditional institutions exc.)
Peaceful coexistence by neutrality and welfare	State (primary) civil society	External/internal	Austria, Malta a/o for 50 years	Liberal social-democrat societies, protection for minorities/welfare states; structural conflict avoidance (Austria: federal elements), prosperity for many in crisis	Conflict regulation through welfare state; proportional representation in parliamentary democracy; nonallied policy in crisis
Peaceful coexistence by neutrality and (con-)federation	State system and civil society	Stable self-centered	Swiss model 400 years (?)	Decentralization in multiethnic pluricultural Switzerland: confederation since 1848, linked with big-party concordiality in the central government; respect for other indigenous languages/cultures, but no inclusion of migrants; prosperity for many in crisis	Conflict regulation/solution by self-rule (canton system) and proportional/regional representation; elements of direct democracy overpowered by corporatist interests; serious abuse of federalism
Peace through involvement/peaceful intervention	State system/UN System OSCE, OAU, etc.	Reactive/active civil society actors only marginally inclusive	Since 1945, on the rise since 1990 short-term	Divided societies/states; UN operations; OSCE missions; in between intervention and mediation/facilitation	Conflict regulation/solution through agreements between parties to the conflict; security through interethnic balance and protection of national minorities

broad. The scope is large and open and a range of different actors and institutions can participate to take up their own initiatives.

Besides all forms of structural prevention there are other types of peace-building. For instance, there is the minority rights approach, which is best undertaken on different levels ranging from international standard-setting in the framework of the UN Human Rights Commission and at the conferences of the OSCE to the creation of national laws. Legislation is best done in an interactive process involving different actors and by consulting the groups that are to profit from it. An ideal case for that could have been the elaboration of the Declaration of Indigenous Peoples Rights at Geneva, which annually included hundreds of delegates from all over the world. This remarkable process was suddenly interrupted after 10 years of work.

A next type would be peaceful coexistence and inter-ethnic balance through a number of models for power-sharing. The cases to be mentioned as examples—as is easily seen in Table VIII—cannot be all that ideal. Other approaches for the realization of free association and internal self-determination of all peoples can be undertaken by way of autonomization—with a range of cases to be studied and compared. More systemic schemes for self-governance were realized by the nationality policies of large multiethnic states such as FSU, China, or India. These cases might be considered as incomplete models. Nevertheless lessons can be learned from these long-term experiences. A last type of preventive response is still somewhat utopian. It consists of regimes for secession and rules for the creation of new states or their international recognition.

F. Emerging Conflict Setting the Stage for Peace Workers and Nongovernmental Organizations

Most people in crisis areas never get involved in violent acts, and most do not support violence. They are potentially welcoming any initiative for peacekeeping and peace-building. Peace-loving people who are struggling for mutual understanding are found in every society and subgroup. The more intensively a conflict escalates the more such brave people are forced to be silent. In certain situations they will not be able to expose themselves without running high risks. A second group of people only gets involved if a conflict is already in an emerging stage (stage 2). They get involved by learning about past issues, threats, and horrors confronting their group, people, or party with another/other parties to the conflicts. Many people get involved only halfway. First, they do not want "to have something to do with

that savagery." In many cases they do not even know which party or group they should belong to.

In an emerging stage of conflict there are usually plenty of early warnings from the side of targeted groups as well as local NGOs, but often little or no action from the international community, at least no comprehensive action. The case of Rwanda showed this in the most shocking way. Rwanda of 1994 is the most striking example to show the gap between early warning and early action. In this case there was no early action at all, even in the wake of state-organized mass murder—announced in advance, incited by extremists by means of radio, and reported by several foreign TV stations.

In many cases nongovernmental local organizations such as popular associations, churches, and politicians try to mediate and facilitate dialogue. International NGOs might get involved. Preventive diplomacy would also include other states and multilateral organizations. The aim is to calm the waves and work for a peaceful settlement and constructive resolution approaches. In the nonviolent emerging stage of a conflict most options for reactive, active, and even interactive responses are still open. The structural prevention approach might already face more obstacles and difficulties to find broad-based political support in order to press for implementation and realization (often controlled by intransigent state actors). Adequate responses at this stage include early actions by manifold actors and constructive peace-building and peacekeeping measures such as dialogue, mediation, and facilitation of conflict transformation or sometimes resolution.

G. Escalation Sets Increasing Limits for Constructive Responses to Conflict

In the stage of escalation to violent conflict (stage 3) there is a serious limitation of options as well as of the types and number of actors involved. While at an emerging stage many actors are nongovernmental, at this stage governments take over and try to control possible responses to conflict. States increasingly try to monopolize the public sphere. Especially in ethnonationalist conflicts this could mean that collaborators of INGOs would be harassed or kicked out of the country. Local NGOs would be banned or restricted. The main conflict actors no longer hear appeals for constructive dialogue. Most parties to the conflict now find it impossible to compromise. The ideological battle is in full swing. In the omnipresent propaganda the enemy will be dehumanized, thus preparing the ground for full-scale violence.

The severe phase (stage 4) is characterized by a now fully violent and militarized conflict. Most doors are closed. Civil actors are out of the picture for the most part. Only combatant parties (governments and rebels), sometimes multilateral actors, have control. The vested interests of those intervening become clearer. The possibilities for responses other than military interventions are now totally restrained. All parties to the conflict find it impossible to do anything but fight it out.

In the phase of deescalation (stage 5) combatant parties sign cease-fire agreements. All conflict actors now look for repair and seek assistance and equipment in case of renewed violence. Some NGOs are welcome again, mostly those bringing in humanitarian aid and assistance. Here the classic peacekeeping efforts are started. The cases of headline conflicts as depicted by Western mass media (which often have the status of an involved actor since the media have great influence on local and international conflict actors) have their own externally induced dynamics. Sometimes peacekeeping includes the deployment of troops from major powers or the UN. In this case an eventual military intervention would be named "humanitarian." As many examples might show, the danger at this stage is that the cycle of violence turns backward and the conflict relapses to stage 3, only to escalate again. Power mediation, as a state-centered response to conflict, could also again be a possibility. International NGOs would try to push for peace-building. They would start confidence building measures and try to initiate dialogue between the parties to the conflict.

H. Peace-Building and Consolidation in the Postconflict Phase

Peace-building in the postconflict phase of rebuilding and reconciliation (stage 6) has short- to medium-term perspectives. War-torn societies need rehabilitation and reconstruction. The bulk of the NGOs come in at this time and they are allowed to bring in (often tax free) any amount of materials they may need for their work (including whatever luxury they need for their collaborators, e.g., expensive 4-wheel-drive cars).

Some of the critical skills of INGOs are in high demand by now, such as constructive conflict resolution approaches and cooperative planning. Arbitration by neutral outsiders or partial insiders is taken up in order to settle the conflict in a peaceful manner. Building a culture of peace at all levels also includes the grassroots level.

Of course conventional conflict management approaches only deal with the leadership of the former adversaries now searching for a longer-term solution. This would then best be accomplished in way of binding agreements or even spectacular peace treaties—with

donor countries promising a lot of aid and plenty of development projects to be set-up in order to consolidate the still-shaky negative peace.

I. Nongovernmental Organizations in Conflict Situations

Nongovernmental organizations have become a mass phenomenon only since the mid-1980s. There are three reasons why NGOs have become key players on an international level.

1. The first condition was set when neoliberalism became state policy in France, under Giscard d'Estaing, as well as in Britain, under the rule of Margaret Thatcher, and in the U.S. after Ronald Reagan was elected in 1980.
2. Governments created NGOs for intelligence purposes and used them as instruments for activities they could not carry out themselves, especially in situations of intrastate conflict and possible violations of noninterference.
3. Civil society-building in Western countries, as result of the 1968 rebellions, increasingly created a more and more complete network and a parallel infrastructure of civil society institutions which were assuming many functions of state institutions.

During the 1980s "conflict resolution" became an issue and developed into an industry in U.S. Before the mid-1980s assistance in conflict situations, especially in intrastate conflicts, was bound to strict rules. Assistance in war situations was only given after the adversaries agreed to a cease-fire. In the mid-1990s "conflict prevention" became more and more important. This is a result of large-scale failures of the international system. Effective prevention would make many NGOs jobless. Nongovernmental organizations were increasingly operating in conflict areas under ill-defined and self-appointed multitask mandates that included virtually everything from humanitarian assistance up to conflict resolution.

The crisis in Rwanda was among the most noticeable events to require mounting assistance of NGOs worldwide. The genocide in Rwanda resulted in an unprecedented loss of lives. More than 1 million Rwandans became the victims of the genocidal state machinery which is more than double the casualties recorded for all the violent conflicts in countries such as the former Soviet Union and Yugoslavia since 1990. The genocide in Rwanda sent shock waves throughout the international community. The very role of NGOs in conflict situations came under scrutiny. Some of these organizations were said to have been actively contradicting and precipitating the government's policy, especially the official policy concerning the internally displaced persons. The United Nations created UNREO, a specialized body to coordinate the NGOs in Rwanda.

Since the electronic media became more and more important for funding of nongovernmental organizations, the role of the media had to be reassessed. During the period of April and May of 1994 some NGOs such as Caritas or Care International received donations of up to 1.2 million U.S. dollars per day, from deeply concerned citizens, based on the images of refugees beamed into their living rooms by the international news media. The result of these developments is highly ambiguous: In some Third World countries humanitarian aid accounts for up to 50% of the value of the Overseas Development Assistance. The long-term perspective of development as an instrument for conflict prevention is increasingly challenged by short-term NGO activism.

J. Low Chances for Peaceful Settlement of Protracted Conflicts

In protracted conflicts negotiation or outside party (third-party) mediation are generally very difficult and rarely successful. In an analysis of the (potential) success of on-going mediation efforts (in 22% of 284 wars and crises from 1945 to 1990) Bercovich et al. concluded with a negative assessment: The longer the duration of a conflict the lower are the chances of reaching any settlement.

The principle of self-determination is a focal point of the programs of most insurgencies and ethnic resistance movements. The multiplication of states, a substantial growth of the number of independent states (currently nearly 200), has already started to become a real scenario. Secessionist movements have contributed to many deadly conflicts, but secession has also brought the resolution of a few protracted conflicts, as in the case of Bangla Desh and Eritrea (the latter only until warfare was resumed in March 1998).

Rules, procedures, and regimes for secession, federation, and interethnic power-sharing need to be developed. These issues may soon be ranking high on the agenda of the United Nations and regional organizations such as OSCE, OAU, OAS, and ASEAN. Resolving conflicts in Afghanistan, Somalia, Rwanda, or Bosnia required more-comprehensive UN interventions. Because of the events in Rwanda and the total failure of the international community to intervene, prevention of violent conflict has been put on the agenda of national, supranational, and multilateral

actors. The talk is mainly about acute prevention and crisis management.

However, to prevent or even "solve" conflicts is an awesome task since the targeted conflicts have, for the most part, already escalated and reached various stages of violence by the time they get the attention of the mass media and (with that) political clout in the West. This reactive approach is likely to overwhelm the capacities of conflict research and conflict management—and necessarily so. The acute-prevention approach is bound to become just another failure. More-constructive approaches have been discussed. Most of the latest conceptions are still in a somewhat embryonic stage. The danger is that integral approaches escape the short-term logic of policy-makers or do not usually deal with headline conflicts. Their success seems not measurable (in most cases a questionable perception).

Today there is much talk about response to crisis and other basically reactive responses and not much talk about structural and proactive prevention. Examples of different forms of national self-administration from all parts of the world should be scrutinized and analyzed. There is no link between conflict intensity and the degree of ethnic heterogeneity in a given territory. In many regions of the world distinctly different ethnic groups have for centuries coexisted peacefully. In traditional societies ethnic heterogeneity and cultural diversity were not per se sufficient reasons to cause intergroup conflicts. Only external intervention or asymmetric relationships—and as a reaction the politicization of ethnicity—brought disorder and violation of rules that often led to conflictive escalation. In the societal realm securing survival requires that the society produce its own mechanisms to effectively calm down, moderate, mitigate, regulate, and solve internal conflicts.

V. STRUCTURAL CONFLICT PREVENTION: AUTONOMY ARRANGEMENTS AND FREE ASSOCIATION

The different characteristics exhibited by different types of society have, correspondingly, different types of claims to autonomy or variant regulatory mechanisms, ranging from cultural autonomy, through regional self-governance, to *de facto* sovereignty. Protection of ethnic and national minorities by means of autonomy arrangements (of all kinds) did not begin until the 20th century. The problems with ethnonationalism, which had been sparked off by revolutions and by the regroupings that have occurred in the wake of the two World Wars, began to grow more acute. The progressive nationalities policy—including the right to secession—that had been adopted by the Socialist International in London in 1896 and taken over by Lenin in 1914 ("Right of Nations to Self-Determination") was applied only in a formalized way in the Soviet Union. At that time, the federal structure of the USSR, with what was initially four republics, contrasted with developments in Western Europe, which had led to ethnically more unified or homogenized states. Following the First World War the imperial multinational states (Ottoman and Austro-Hungarian empires) collapsed and fragmented into a host of smaller states.

From the 1960s, it was the new, recently independent Third World states that became the main locus of conflict and also, increasingly, the main theater of war in the struggle of nationalities for self-determination. In the 1970s, there were once again violent ethnonationalist conflicts in Europe—in the Basque country (Euskadi, northwest Spain, and southwest France), in Northern Ireland (part of the United Kingdom), and on Corsica (part of France). Toward the end of the 1980s mass violence broke out in the USSR, first in the Southern Caucasus and in Tajikistan, as well as in the fragmenting Yugoslavia (Serbian minorities in Slovenia and Krajina versus Croatia; multicultural Bosnia). In the Soviet Union, the so-called "imperial overstretch" manifested itself ever more clearly from 1985 and ever more dramatically from 1989–1990.

Because of the taboo attached to state integrity—that is to say, the inviolability of internationally recognized borders—and the acceptance of national sovereignty as a normative principle of international relations, the most realistic and promising regulatory mechanisms are those that do not aspire to independent statehood and sovereignty. For some categories of ethnic-cum-national conflicts, the remarks that follow here do not apply, since any realistic solution would entail the creation of a new state or (con-)federation of states. This is true for about 20% of those conflicts that may be interpreted as having an ethnic basis. Federalization, coupled with extensive autonomy rights, is often preferable to secession. To cite a current example: in Yugoslavia, a confederation would have been much more effective in protecting the rights of the individual nationalities than would secession by part-states, with the rise in group nationalism that would have resulted from this, even under controlled conditions. Violent follow-up conflicts that resulted from the break-up of Yugoslavia were foreseeable. The same would apply to any further instances of secession in the former Yugoslavia, and this is probably why they will not take place (e.g.,

Kosova). The latest round of violence is the result of ultranationalist policies from both sides and the exhaustion of peaceful political options.

The right of peoples to self-determination is laid down in the United Nations Charter and the major texts of international public law (such as the two international pacts, mainly the International Covenant on Civil and Political Rights). This basic right to self-determination is considered by some states as not necessarily calling into question the traditional state structure ("internal self-determination"). Emphasis is laid on requiring states (particularly Third World ones) to assume responsibility and jurisdiction ("accountability of states") and on creating procedures enabling national disputes and indigenous claims to self-determination to be brought before the International Court of Justice in The Hague.

The Vienna Declaration, issued by the World Conference on Human Rights in June, 1993, contains the first instrument of international law clearly proclaiming a (special) right to secession. Subjects are peoples "under colonial or other forms of alien domination or foreign occupation"—that is to say, a right of peoples "to take any legitimate action . . . to realize their inalienable right to self-determination" (article 2). Those states that violate the principle of equal rights and the right to self-determination and thus possess a government that does not "[represent] the whole people belonging to the territory without distinction of any kind" are explicitly excepted from the protection of territorial integrity that is a right of sovereign states.

The right of peoples to self-determination is increasingly being interpreted by some representatives of indigenous peoples in the sense of a free association between indigenous nations and former settler-colonies. This conflicts somewhat with the legal situation and with the unqualified adherence of most indigenous organizations to the right to self-determination, as repeatedly reaffirmed in recent times in representative documents:

- The Preamble and 109 articles of the Kari-Oca Declaration of May, 1992.
- The various drafts of the Preamble and 45 articles of the Declaration on the Rights of Indigenous Peoples drawn up between 1987 and 1993 by the UN Human Rights Commission Working Group on Indigenous Populations (UN-WGIP).

In the final draft of the latter declaration, the right to self-determination is clearly interpreted as the right to regulate one's own affairs. However, the form of a covenant or convention would be preferable to that of a declaration because this would afford better safeguards for the activation or enforcement of the rights that are called for. It would probably be difficult, in the near future, to return to anything below the legal norms and standards stipulated in Convention 169 of the International Labor Organization (ILO). Despite some awkward and disconcerting aspects, this convention represents to date the most detailed recognition in international law of the right of indigenous peoples to self-determination. Any binding codification of the interests of individual indigenous and nondominant nations would have to be sought chiefly via bilateral agreements between states and nations; but there has as yet been no clear precedent for such a course during this century.

The terms "autonomy" and "self-determination" are generally used more in relation to voluntary or enforced concessions on the part of states than to the realization of some legitimate legal claim granted binding international recognition. And there are other respects in which the concept of autonomy needs clarification.

A. The Right to Self-Determination in Relation to International Law

In the case of the Latin American states that emerged after 1840, it was 140 years before any mention was made in their constitutions about distinct, indigenous peoples living within their territory. Efforts have recently been made within the UN system—especially in the ILO and Human Rights Commission—to define the right to self-determination more precisely and to secure a revision of international law. Up to now, the situation of human rights and the rights of the peoples—which, illogically, are often mentioned in the same breath—has been shaped by the following five parameters:

1. As the modern system of states established itself, sovereignty shifted from peoples to states, which meant that indigenous and nondominant peoples lost their status as independent actors.

2. As a result, the self-declared "sovereign" state now constitutes the dominant form of political organization on the world scale and the "highest" in terms of status.

3. Yet only very few new states of the 20th century (in Africa and Asia) and the 19th century (in Latin America) are nation-states in the strict sense (they are, rather, multiethnic in structure).

4. This means that the nature of existing communities of states, general international law, the UN Charter, the human rights declarations to be ratified by states, international pacts on civil rights, conventions, other international agreements, and International Humanitarian Law (IHL) are an expression of the consensus of the states participating in them or are dependent on their good will.

5. There are contradictions between human rights and law of the nations; invoking international law, particularly the principles of nonintervention and unrestricted sovereignty, tends to promote dictatorships, which trample on the human rights and minority rights of "their" citizens.

International law talks of "nations" not of states. Worldwide there are thousands of nations but only 193 states. The number of nations is declining as a result of genocide and assimilation, whereas that of states is rising, chiefly as a result of the collapse of multinational states.

Yet aggressive claims by so-called nation-states vis-à-vis ethnically or nationally distinct groups (called "minorities," which are sometimes actually the majority) and/or indigenous peoples are a highly dangerous source of conflict. Peoples' right to self-determination is a central item on the agendas of almost all rebel ethnic movements, who call for "legitimate rights" and see international law as backing their case. In general, the demanding of rights proves problematic where reference is made to:

1. The right of divided peoples (nations or nationalities divided up into different states by arbitrary colonial borders) to be reunified.
2. The right of a nation or nationality to secede in order to form its own state.
3. The right of the population of an area that has been incorporated by a state through military annexation (FSO conflict) or contractual cession (colonial agreements, mandated territories) to reject this absorption either by means of a plebiscite or, where necessary, by armed combat.

In international law, it is the sovereign right of states to exist that has dominated in most interpretations of cases (1) and (2)—in other words, there was no recognition of the right to reunification or secession as a form of the right to self-determination. However, the increase in the number of states after 1990 ultimately found expression in the Vienna Declaration of the World Conference on Human Rights (June, 1993). The right to secession was recognized as legitimate in cases where the state against which the secession is directed treats minorities or indigenous peoples on its territory unfairly or discriminates against them in some other way. In case (3) the situation in regard to international law is disputed. In the end, what decides whether legitimate rights are realized is not an abstract claim to a right but the military strength of the respective liberation movements (like the Eritrean Peoples Liberation Front, EPLF) that have made it their aim to see that international law is enforced.

International law regulates rights, duties, and relations between states. During the 1960s, the United Nations also recognized anticolonial liberation movements as subjects of international law. In actual fact, it is states, not peoples that are sovereign and equal. In other words, it is states that claim power of definition when it comes to determining what is meant by the principle of self-determination in international law. It is they who decide what a "people" is and which communities may count as such. In practical political terms, the right to self-determination is not applied because in most cases it is (allegedly) not connected with territoriality and because as a rule most "peoples" are recognized not as peoples but as "minorities." The appropriate legal basis is then human rights and minority rights, which are generally individual rights. In practical political terms, international law nowadays constitutes a barrier to the extension of human rights and the rights of nondominant social groups.

The binding principles of state sovereignty and nonintervention remained resolutely in force *de jure* until the mid-1990s. *De facto,* there was a series of direct interventions by the major powers. It is true that equality and self-determination of peoples are recognized as rights in the UN Charter (article 1, 2, and 55) and have been embodied in numerous resolutions and pacts (notably the ICCPR, article 1), but they are regarded as general maxims, not as tenets of international law.

Many experts believe that the right to self-determination is the "opium for the people"; in the form of a right to secession, the community of states will always refuse to grant it, they say, purely out of a survival instinct. "No one," they claim, is prepared to bear the "anarchical consequences" of a systematic pursuit of it. Whether the use of the principle of *uti possidetis,* the transformation of administrative borders into state borders (as was done from 1840 in Latin America, from 1948 in the colonies, and from 1990 in the Eastern bloc), was a "prudent principle" that prevented endless conflicts or whether it merely postponed conflicts or actually caused their eruption (as in Croatia and Bosnia) is not easy to judge. Postulating a right to secession on a limited scale as "self-defense against extreme repression" (Fisch) is not sufficient and applies in more than just one case. Both the right to secession as a form of self-defense and the division into external and internal

self-determination are already progressive ideas in international terms.

International organizations consisting of government representatives and experts from recognized states often do not deny the right of peoples to self-determination directly but point to the difficulty of identifying legally binding, tangible criteria for deciding whether a particular nationality can be a subject of the right of self-determination as defined in international law. In order to mitigate these difficulties, the right to self-identification should be defined and embodied in international law. It must be said, however, that this suggestion has little chance of being accepted.

Ethnic nationalities defined as minorities by states are recognized as legal subjects with a partial status in international law. The so-called "minorities question" ought therefore to be resolved through mechanisms of minority protection, notably autonomy rights. These special rights should entail the replacement of state policies of assimilation, segregation, and integration of nondominant ethnic groups by a policy of guaranteed coexistence. The protection of ethnic minorities, based on the right of peoples to self-determination as proclaimed by the UN Charter, has not become accepted in international law and international politics. Up to now, the right to self-determination has been applied mainly in colonized areas and in federal substates.

However, the problem of internal colonization and the complex reality of primary ethnic affiliation and identity are being taken increasingly seriously. The explosive power of ethnicity in relation to foreign-dominated (centralized) states, as evinced in the Third World—and, after 1990, in the USSR—clearly demonstrates the need to refine and expand the right to self-determination.

B. The Concept of Autonomy and the Minorities Question in Europe

Autonomy rights have existed in different forms at different times and in very different societies. In Europe, such rights have been known since the Middle Ages (for the nobility, churches, cities, universities, etc; the two former categories have mostly been done away with, the latter have partly been preserved). The first agreements on minorities—in favor of religious minorities—were concluded within the framework of international law, at the Berlin Congress of 1878. The First World War was conducted (from the Western point of view) with the purpose—so the justification goes—of liberating oppressed minorities and ethnic groups in Europe and in the Ottoman Empire. In the Treaty of Versailles, the ethnic factor was strongly emphasized.

Revisionist claims made by Germany and Hungary from 1933 to the territories of "their" minorities in other countries (especially Poland and Czechoslovakia) contributed to the outbreak of the Second World War, which itself signaled the "final solution" of many minorities—in the form of genocide, flight, enforced resettlement, and expulsion.

At the start of this century, the highly explosive minorities question was seen as relating exclusively to Europe and the Ottoman Empire (or Turkey); in the Third World it remained "undiscovered" within the framework of international relations. The focal points of the minorities question in Europe were: European Jewry, Alsace-Lorraine, Schleswig-Holstein, Friesland (East, West, and North Frisians), Upper Silesia and the Sudeten Germans, the Ukrainians in interwar Poland, and the situation of numerous minorities in the context of Austro-Yugoslavian and Greco-Turkish relations. The "solution" to this latter situation came in the 1923 Peace of Lausanne in the form of a massive enforced exchange of religious and ethnic groups—a tragedy that continues even today to affect relations between the states concerned. After physical eradication (mass murder, democide, politicide, and genocide), this is the most brutal method of eliminating the problem of nondominant groups. It is a problem which, besides being a constant source of ethnic, linguistic, and religious discrimination and socioeconomic disadvantage, serves as a pretext for external intervention and is responsible for the outbreak of wars.

C. The Issues Surrounding Nondominant Ethnic Groups

The League of Nations system gave priority treatment to the "problem" of nondominant ethnic groups, particularly so-called "borderland minorities." The Geneva Convention of May, 1922 contained 100 or so articles on the protection of minorities. Article 147 provided for a direct right of petition by such minorities to the European Congress of Nationalities in Geneva; and, indeed, brisk use was made of this. The congress was officially viewed as an international forum for nondominant ethnic groups within the framework of the League of Nations—as the Working Group for Indigenous Populations is today within the UN system. For ethnic groups to be admitted, three criteria applied in 1920: the desire for an independent cultural identity (i.e., a distinct ethnocultural identity), political organization, and the assent or nonopposition of the majority.

The trend toward monolingualism or linguistic nationalization that emerged in most European countries

after 1880, and to an even more pronounced degree after 1918, necessitated the legal recognition of one or more other languages as official languages. More far-reaching forms of cultural autonomy, such as instruction in the mother tongue and the protection of cultural independence, were often regulated by law. The right to bilingualism (established in 1860) was in most cases far from entailing any kind of political participation or social integration (or nondiscrimination). In individual cases, decrees relating to language aggravated interethnic mistrust and encouraged the formation of negative stereotypes.

D. Creation of Territories with Limited Autonomy after 1919

The practice of declaring the settlement areas of ethnic minorities official territorial entities with limited (territorial) autonomy began only at the start of this century and was usually prompted by wars. Examples include:

- Lenin's policy of *korenizatsiya* in the Caucasus and the rest of the USSR, adopted as of the 1917 revolution and implemented from 1919
- The Ruthenians in Czechoslovakia in 1919
- The Swedish-populated Åland islands in Finland in 1921
- The establishment of South Tyrol as one of what is now a total of five autonomous regions in Italy from 1947
- Home rule for the Faeroese in the Kingdom of Denmark from 1948
- Regionalization and phase granting of autonomy to Basques, Catalonians, Andalusians, and Galicians in post-Franco Spain

In contrast, the safeguards for the Danes in the Federal Republic of Germany (in southern Schleswig, in the *land* of Schleswig-Holstein) and the Sorbs in the German Democratic Republic (incorporated into the regional constitutions of Saxony and Brandenburg after reunification) have no clear territorial components. Provisions contain, among other things, special regulations regarding voting rights as well as some degree of cultural autonomy. There are no such special conditions in force in the Federal Republic in regard to indigenous East Frisians, Cinti and Roma, Jews, or Poles (in the Ruhr), and especially not in regard to the new minorities. Observers await with interest the outcome of a constitutional appeal lodged by the Sorbs against the destruction of what would be the 129th Sorbian village to suffer this fate. The municipality of Horno/Rogow joined with 10 other municipalities under threat and, with the support of the Sorbian umbrella organization Domowina, lodged a complaint with the constitutional court of Brandenburg against the coal-mining activities that had been decreed. This action is apparently unprecedented in German legal history.

VI. STRUCTURAL CONFLICT PREVENTION THROUGH SELF-GOVERNANCE

In international law, autonomy is the contractually or legally established limited self-government of a territory that comes under the supreme territorial jurisdiction of a state (territorial autonomy). Autonomy was formerly regarded as being the prerogative of ethnic minorities. In individual cases, the introduction of a number of broad-based classic measures of minority protection have led or contributed to ethnonational conflicts being defused or, in some cases, resolved.

A. Nondiscrimination, Affirmative Action, and Self-Governance

The range of types of autonomy extends from minimum nondiscrimination against distinct nationalities (defined by states as minorities) through affirmative action (positive discrimination) to a gamut of solutions involving delimited and enhanced forms of self-governance. The home-rule arrangement created for the Faeroese as far back as 1948 has exemplary status here. Fully developed structures of self-governance constitute aspects such as might be found within the framework of more far-reaching policies on autonomy and nationalities. "Models" were implemented early on in the USSR, then in the Faeroe Islands, or are now in use in Euskadi and Catalonia. In principle, such solutions exceed the bounds of classic minority protection.

However, major elements of—what should ideally be—preemptive, preventive conflict avoidance in Europe (prophylaxis/prevention) are often actually concessions, made in what is already a crisis-laden situation in order to avert or contain conflict. Concessions to minorities have been made or demanded at various phases from 1878 to the present. Most notable concessions were made in the interwar period in regulations for borderland minorities; after 1945 in the post-war order; in the 1980s in autonomy regulations and protofederal decentralization in Spain; from 1991 in the Russian Federation in the expanded structures for au-

tonomous territories; and, after the end of the Cold War, within the framework of the C/OSCE process, with the appointment of a High Commissioner for National Minorities, agreed at Helsinki II in 1992.

The key elements of the various minority policies in Europe have been:

- Recognition of one or more other languages as official languages or languages of communication (radio, television, press)
- Instruction in the mother tongue and protection of cultural independence (cultural autonomy)
- Political representation and special regulations on voting rights (guaranteed seats, proportional representation, consensus-based decision-making or right of veto)
- Creation of a special territorial entity with full or partial autonomy (territorial autonomy)
- Limited, extended, or full-fledged self-governance

In Europe, the codification of minority rights has usually occurred via constitutional change or the law. In Anglo-Saxon colonies, the rights of ethnically distinct peoples were recognized contractually.

B. Transfer of Sovereignty Rights via Bilateral Agreements

A major extension of the ethnic problem per se has been reflected since the 1980s in demands made by indigenous and endangered peoples for full self-government. They want their own independent judicial administration and the power to decide economic activities (natural resources, ownership of land). Indigenous and endangered peoples refuse to be subjected to external rule. Such demands are reminiscent of days when the first treaties were concluded between European colonial powers and indigenous peoples, initially respected as sovereign nations.

There are a host of historical examples of relevant treaties dating from the 17th to the 19th centuries from North America and New Zealand/Aotearoa. The period from 1700 was characterized by a spread of the influence of the European powers abroad. This led, among other things, to the development of an extensive system of treaties, notably between the English and French crowns of their successors (mainly the United States) and large numbers of indigenous peoples. For the most part, these treaties were undermined or directly violated—usually after the military situation of the European settlers had improved.

Certain features of contractual law predetermine bilateral treaties as the form in which contemporary issues should be resolved between states and indigenous peoples:

• Such a contractual policy would currently fall somewhere between minority law and nationality policy. As in minority law, such treaties generally favor relatively small populations. And as in nationality law, the populations are granted a specific form of self-governance within the framework of a state organization.

• The contractual process is extremely bilateral, contains a strong internationalizing element, and offers a relatively flexible framework for protected agreements.

• There are no contemporary models for protected agreements so far, only approximations. The "modern treaties" between Canadian central government or the Quebec government with the Cree and Inuit should be viewed with caution in this regard. The debate in Australia about the relationship between (central) government and the aborigines, and the self-governance now in operation in certain areas, are a good beginning.

The treaties of recent times raise a number of legal and political-cum-moral problems. The "money for land" model of the James Bay Agreement is reminiscent of earlier 19th-century agreements. The package was the product of a bitter struggle waged by the Quebec Indians and Inuit against the building of the gigantic James Bay hydroelectric complex on their land, which had been begun without the consent of the landowners. It was only when these owners brought a legal complaint that a negotiating process began between the three parties, placing the government under a certain "pressure to act." The Inuit and Cree obtained only about 1.3% of the land they had demanded, but received quite high compensation (225 million Canadian dollars for 11,000 native inhabitants). In his global study of treaties and agreements between states and indigenous peoples, commissioned by the UN Human Rights Commission, Miguel Alfonso Martínez announced that he would be looking specifically at the validity of this agreement.

C. Elements and Evaluation Criteria

The following major instrumental elements are decisive in determining the quality of agreements on self-government for nondominant nations/nationalities:

• Self-governance, with requisite legislative, executive, and judicial bodies
• Existence of a mixed judicial–political body to act as arbitrator
• Control of the territory and natural resources by the nationality bound by the treaty
• Stipulation as to who has sovereignty over resources, how these are managed, and how profits from them are to be shared between regional and central government
• The autonomous government to have regional sovereignty over taxes: autonomous fiscal law, own revenue, own budget, own financial administration
• Central government development in autonomous regions to take place only in consultation with the autonomous regional/local authorities (possible right of veto)
• Protection and promotion of all forms of expression of own culture via own communications channels (especially radio and press)
• Fair representation in central government institutions (parliament, ministries, etc.)

Four of the eight items mentioned relate to the economic basis of self-governance, in line with the motto "No autonomy without economy." The areas that affect the life of a nation/nationality most decisively are the land issue and the management of natural resources.

Prime evaluation criteria and principles generally applicable to self-government would be:

• No paternalism in decision-making processes; acknowledgement of nation's responsibility for itself
• No imposition of foreign (Eurocentric) ways of thinking and concepts of state; respect for differently structured thinking, indigenous institutions, and traditional procedures
• Clear regulations, verifiability, and control mechanisms, in order to preclude nonactivity or obstruction by other parties to agreements

The above-mentioned instrumental elements and evaluation criteria are intended to prevent centralized states from continuing to ensure unilateral power of decision for themselves in certain key areas. States should be persuaded, or forced, to share power of decision on a partnership basis. The number of instruments and elements of self-governance, and the extent to which they have been realized, are indicative of the quality of agreements on self-government.

D. Examples of Self-Governance among Indigenous Peoples in America

Any claim that autonomy arrangements and nationality policies that have been put into practice (or are due to be) in all four corners of the world could serve as models must have a question mark after it. The degree to which individual models of autonomy are transferable is relatively limited and depends primarily on the particular region involved and the specific constellation of circumstances. "Model status" in a broader sense has more to do with use of the method of open dialogue between states and nations/nationalities and with the transfer of sovereignty rights in the form of bilateral agreements—one of the best-protected forms of agreement, legally speaking, and one which is viable internationally.

It remains to be seen whether the following examples can serve as models of self-governance for indigenous peoples elsewhere and whether they can stand up to detailed scrutiny and comparison. Representatives of indigenous movements and independent human rights organizations have at any rate, described them as capable of these things.

One scheme with model status is the system of home-rule created, as early as 1948, for the Faeroese. Almost no one has heard of the Faeroese system of self-governance and, although it has proved itself over a long period, it has so far been overlooked in the debate about self-government. The Faeroese model could be recommended for wider application in the (post-)colonial territories of France, Britain, the Netherlands, and the U.S. The better-known system of home rule in Greenland was first tried out in the Faeroes.

The Faeroe Islands, which are part of the Kingdom of Denmark, obtained an autonomy statute that covers everything except the legal, finance, and defense systems and foreign policy. The 47,000 Faeroe Islanders are culturally independent and speak Faeroes, which is related to Norwegian. They possess all the symbols of an independent state, such as their own flag, passport, stamps, bank notes, a parliament that serves as a forum for the wrangling of seven political parties, and their own separate "national" soccer team.

All five examples presented below involve legal provisions for populations that are relatively small (ranging from less than 50,000 up to 500,000), but which in some cases inhabit and husband large geographical areas. Many of these territories are, in addition, of great strategic importance to the economies of their respective states. The reason is the huge reserves of raws materials in them. This applies to the first three examples—Greenland, northwest Canada, and eastern Nicaragua—which have a further characteristic in common, namely the multiethnic composition of their naturally favored, mostly indigenous populations.

As may be demonstrated by the example of the Nicaraguan region of Mosquitia, the ethnic composition of a population has a decisive influence on the political model in operation in each case. Along with eastern Nicaragua, Greenland represents the only model of indigenous self-governance with a Western-style parliamentary system and a majority-party set-up (in Greenland there are three parties, in Mosquitia more than a dozen).

One crucial feature in regard to the overall economic and political context of the examples presented here is the fact that the indigenous peoples of Greenland and Canada unquestionably are part of the wealthy First World, whereas the Indians of Latin America occupy some of the poorest and most marginalized rural zones of the Third World.

Issues of collective ownership of land by indigenous peoples, and the related issue of who has power over natural resources, were the subject of political debates (internally) in Greenland and Nicaragua and also (externally) within the framework of the Inuit Circumpolar Conference and the international Indian movement. In the case of Mosquitia, the land issue was one of the factors that directly contributed to the outbreak of war. It has been agreed that revenues from natural resources will be distributed equally in Greenland and "in just proportion" in Nicaragua. In Greenland, a compromise was reached on the subject of underground mineral resources which elsewhere are generally excluded from consideration—in other words, are subject to the sole power of disposal of the central government (as is the case, for example, with the gold mines in eastern Nicaragua). In Greenland, the independent Inuit government and the Danish authorities decide this issue jointly, whereas in Mosquitia, the law merely provides for the conclusion of relevant agreements between central government and regional governments (without stipulating details). However, the Greenland model has existed 10 years longer, and the legal provisions have been implemented in their entirety, whereas unclear or missing provisions in the case of Mosquitia have provided central government with opportunities for inaction and obstruction.

E. Home-Rule in Kalaallit Nunaat (Greenland)

Kalaallit Nunaat (Inuit Greenland) is regarded both by North American Indian leaders and by the World

Council of Indigenous Peoples as a model for a constitutional-cum-legal solution (in the form of "home-rule") to the problem of autonomy for the indigenous peoples of America. Home-rule is interpreted as implying continued national (i.e., Danish) unity and excludes the option of a federation (of the Kingdom of Denmark). But Greenland can only serve to a limited extent as a model for the two Americas—more so for North America and the Polar Circle, especially the northern territories of Canada, Alaska, and northern Russia, which are inhabited almost exclusively by native peoples, Inuit, and Indians (and native Siberians). The common features comprise low population density (~55,000 Greenlanders, of whom 45,000 are Inuit and 10,000 Danish; 14% were born outside Greenland), welfare-state provision, mostly modern means of production, and a common culture among the native inhabitants. A complicating factor is the variety of restrictions stemming from the Cold War (such as being cut off from relatives in the USSR). The large numbers of military bases (Greenland itself has two U.S. air bases) are proof of the almost unparalleled extent to which Inuit settlement areas were militarized during the Cold War.

Greenland is part of the Kingdom of Denmark. Denmark pursued a liberal policy of modernization in its "provinces." The fishing industry and the concomitant urban development around the large fish factories caused profound upheavals in traditional society. But Danes and Inuit never waged war against one another. Home-rule in Greenland is not a concession made by a state that felt itself under pressure. The Inuit of Greenland were granted extensive home-rule between 1979 and 1987. This took place via the successive transfer of areas of administrative competence to the Inuit and the mixed Inuit–Scandinavian population. The transfer of a Scandinavian-style welfare state and of public enterprises in the fishing and fish- and shrimp-processing sector entailed much administrative work as well. Constitutional law, together with the legal system, the health service, the finance and currency system, and defense (the army) were excepted from the provisions. The educational system, in the author's opinion, is no more than a copy of the Danish one. Subsidies from the Danish state make up a large part of the government budget.

Self-determination also makes itself felt to some extent in foreign policy: following a referendum in 1982 (which took effect in 1985), Greenland withdrew from the EC, though it remains an associate. The Inuit Circumpolar Conference promotes cooperation between Inuit peoples in four states.

F. Canada: Indian Policy and the Nunavut Agreement

The new Canadian constitution brought with it undoubted advances, but the practical realization of these is still awaited. Since 1988–1989 the central government and some provincial administrations have hardened their positions (e.g., Quebec—see the harassment of Mohawks and their revolt at Oka in 1990). This has caused considerable detriment to the reputation of Canada as being a state with a liberal minorities policy.

Canada did not always pursue a "liberal minorities policy." In the 1960s its declared aim was the assimilation of indigenous peoples (as in the U.S.). At that time, parliament revoked all existing contractual rights. In 1969 the government declared the special rights for indigenous peoples to be a form of "discrimination" but was forced to agree to an investigation into indigenous land claims. In 1973 the Supreme Court (Calder vs Canada) passed what, for that time, was a sensational ruling to the effect that the claim of the Nishga Indians to their forefathers' land was still valid and had not been rendered null and void by their subjection. The Calder case forced the government to adopt a new policy toward Indians and to respect treaties already concluded. Like the Mabo case in Australia in 1992, it triggered a whole series of land claims by indigenous groups.

As of the late 1990s the focus is on control of the rich reserves of natural resources. Despite Canada's progressive policy toward Indians (compared with that of the U.S.), Indians are still divided into various categories, and the state still has a say on the important issue of control over resources. Since the late 1970s there has been a twofold division into (1) specific claims, i.e., special claims that have to do with the revision or interpretation of previous agreements, including those with individual Indian peoples; and (2) comprehensive claims, i.e., claims relating to the traditional use of land and estates belonging to Indians who have not yet signed any agreements and were not removed from their land. With the exception of the "modern treaties," the contractual process in Canada took place under the sovereignty of the British Crown. Up to now, the comprehensive claims have proved significantly more important for Indian policy as a whole. The first major case was that of the James Bay and Northern Quebec Agreement in 1975. The present-day agreements, concluded on a "money for land" basis, do, however, raise a whole series of legal and political problems, as mentioned previously.

An example of the inconsistencies in the recognition of indigenous territories is the case of the Dene nation, which reputedly became the largest landowner in America (so it was claimed by the Canadian delegate to the 1989 UN WGIP session), but which, again, has no control over the reserves of raw materials on its territory. One of the most recent agreements concerns the "land claim settlement" of the Gwich'in, who are part of the Dene Assembly of the Northwest Territory. The Gwich'in Denes obtained the land title to 20,000 square kilometers and the right of surface exploitation to a further 6,000 square kilometers; the amount of land involved is thus much less than in the Nunavut Agreement with the Inuit. But the Gwich'in agreement—like the Nunavut Agreement—provides for a share in the royalties resulting from the exploitation of resources and for representation in mixed management bodies that oversee the estates and waters and lay-down rules on hunting and nature conservation.

Clearly under the influence of the Greenland scheme of self-governance, the Canadian government concluded what is probably the most detailed and extensive exploitation agreement so far with the Inuit, covering their settlement areas in the Far North. This did not happen in the form of a bilateral treaty but as an agreement between the Tungavik (the Inuit of Nunavut) and the Ministry for Indian Affairs and Northern Development. This "Nunavut Agreement" is due to be fully implemented by 1999. It clearly represents the most detailed variant yet of self-governance for the thinly populated lands of the indigenous peoples of North America. However, given the low legal status of the affected areas in regard to future development, international experts are skeptical, though they see no immediate danger. Territoriality is inextricably bound up with self-determination and vice versa; according to Howard Berman, this is the basis on which every agreement must be assessed.

Within a huge area measuring 2.2 million square kilometers, the agreement transfers a few restricted settlement zones (~18% of the total area), and any resources located there, as collective property to the 17,500-resident Inuit on condition they renounce all claim to more extensive rights of use. It also regulates use of most of the remaining areas (excluding any resources located there). Inuit acceptance of the package was secured by means of, among other things, liberal helpings of cash. Over a hundred million dollars in cash are due to be paid out over the next few years, with an additional share of the profits from the exploitation of resources. The main weaknesses of the agreement are the low administrative-cum-legal status of the area and the lack of protection for it against possible mass migration (gold rush, oil finds), settlement, and the outnumbering of the Inuit on their own territory.

G. Nicaragua: Autonomy for the Caribbean Regions

Nicaragua's scheme of regional autonomy for its two Caribbean areas (Región Autónoma Atlántico Norte (RAAN) and Región Autónoma Atlántico Sur (RAAS) affects almost 50% of the national territory but only 9.5% of the population, which is multicultural in composition, comprising four indigenous communities, a somewhat large African diaspora (mainly in RAAS), and a number of Mestizos, who have immigrated to both regions. The system of autonomy in the two Caribbean regions is mentioned in the constitution and has existed on paper since September, 1987 (law no. 28: Estatuto de la Autonomía de las Regiones de la Costa Atlántica de Nicaragua) and concretely in a few pilot projects. The system of territorial autonomy does mention the indigenous peoples' settlement areas but affords them no further legal protection, as indigenous territories, against Mestizo immigrants. In practice, the agricultural border is being constantly shifted eastward as a result of immigration by impoverished campesinos; so far this has mostly occurred to the detriment of the Sumu Indians from Musawas and of the mining areas. Land is the Indians' major resource (along with fishing). Conflicts over it have been going on for decades.

Of positive value are the following rights and guarantees set out in law no. 28:

1. Confirmation of the multiethnic, pluricultural, and multilingual character of the costeños (coastal inhabitants) and stipulation of nondiscrimination against them (article 11.1). Particularly well developed are the cultural rights, such as bilingualism in education and administration, and the financial support, albeit modest, for indigenous and Afro-American cultures (articles 11.2 and 11.8).

2. Recognition of the communal property of the indigenous communities (225 Miskitu villages, 32 Sumu, and 4 Rama settlements), including the land, waters, and forests which they "traditionally work" (articles 9, 11.3, 11.6, and 36).

3. Establishment of two autonomous regions independently administered by elected regional parliaments and executives appointed by these; the parliaments have jurisdiction over the territory (articles 6,

7, 8). The division into two regions precludes dominance by one ethnic group (the Mestizos).

4. Institutionalization of a plural system of parliamentary democracy, but with elements of a presidential system, since not only a *junta executiva* but also a *coordinador* is elected, who, significantly, is called "governor" by the population, since he has wide-ranging powers. This executive oversees the work of the councils (articles 27 and 28) but without curtailing the coordinator's powers (article 30).

5. The system is based on a balancing and combination of demographic representation and the formal principle of equality vis-à-vis the six ethnic communities (termed *comunidades* in the law). The aim is to reduce interethnic tensions and protect the rights of the small ethnic groups (Sumu, Rama, Garifuna) against the disproportionate influence of the Hispanic Mestizos, the African-American Creoles (in the RAAS), and the Miskitu Indians (in the RAAN). The division into municipalities is made according to ethnic criteria; there is positive discrimination in favor of smaller ethnic groups in the electoral domain. Every ethnic community must be represented by at least one member in the regional government (junta executiva); there are six *comunidades* in the RAAS and four in the RAAN.

6. The right to self-identification was laid down in law (art. 12).

Of outstanding importance (though not stipulated in the law) is the fact that radio channels may broadcast in indigenous languages. The radio is either under the control of the Indian movement (Radio Miskut in Bilwi) or is made active use of by it (Radio Caribe). Broadcasters are flexible enough to make spontaneous changes to their fixed weekly schedule to accommodate debates, scandals, or political events—as happened in 1993 before the general congress of YATAMA (the Indian organization Yapti Tasbaya Masrika).

In the Spring of 1990 and in 1994 and 1998 secret, democratic, and plural elections took place in both autonomous regions (in addition to the general elections) for the purposes of appointing the regional councils (parliaments). Although YATAMA and the proautonomy Sandinistas (Frente Sandinista de Liberación Nacional) were approximately equally represented in northeast Nicaragua in 1990–1994 and represented the great majority of the electors, the implementation of the autonomy law was hampered by political conflicts and conflicts of interests from 1990 onward. This occurred despite the fact that the proautonomy forces still had four members in the central parliament in Managua who were vital to the survival of the centrist government

of former president Violetta Chamorro. The current president, Alemán, was elected with the support of the largest Indian faction, led by Steadman Fagoth Muller. The proautonomy forces are thus no longer in the position of holding the balance.

The political struggles between Sandinistas and the right in Managua are in a way continuing in eastern Nicaragua—and did so to an even more pronounced extent after the elections of 1994. But the autonomy arrangement is regarded by some conservatives in central government as going too far and by a small faction of Miskitu Indians as not going far enough. In 1990–1993 these two camps, curiously, came together, blocked the autonomy government in the northern region, and fueled the political trench warfare between the left-wing Sandinistas and right-wing former opposition (Unión Nacional Opositora) in the southern region. One serious setback for the Indian movement was the dissension and infighting before the 1994 regional elections: only a minority of Miskitu canvassed under the banner of YATAMA; others stood on the Sandinista or conservative lists. Despite this, the elections brought no fundamental changes.

The Nicaraguan autonomy law is undoubtedly imperfect, but qualitatively speaking it is the best so far produced in Latin America; how much influence it will have, however, depends on whether and to what extent it is ignored or dismantled by Managua. There are growing signs that this is indeed happening: clear regulations to preclude nonaction or obstruction on the part of the government are lacking. The weak point lies in the area of regional council control over territory and resources: neither the respective competencies nor the share of revenues between regional and central government is clearly stipulated.

But the process of rectifying the legal weak points and obscurities was dragged out. The same was true of the regional fiscal sovereignty of the autonomous governments, which have no tax powers and have only a limited income of their own. One cannot speak of an independent budget or financial administration. In sum: *No autonomía sin economía.*

H. Panama: The *Comarca* System

Panama is regarded as progressive when it comes to recognition of particular Indian rights and the granting of cultural autonomy (though not bilingual instruction in schools). Currently, territorial self-governance exists only for the Kuina and Emberá Choco, but not for the more numerous Ngobe (Guaymí) Indians, whose area—due to be designated a *comarca*—has been overrun by Mestizo settlers and banana companies.

The best-known area is Kuna Yala, the "land of the Kuna" (official name Comarca San Blas), with its reservation-style system of autonomy and self-governance. Forty-five thousand Kuna Indians inhabit a territory extending from El Porvenir up to the Colombian border—where there are also Kuna Indians living. Kuna Yala includes some 400 Caribbean coral islands. In Kuna Yala, too, penetration by Mestizo settlers, loggers, and drug-dealers (from Columbia) is difficult to halt. The Kuna largely manage their own affairs. However, the school system is currently run monolingually (in Spanish). Thanks to their being relatively sealed off from the world, their rigid sociocultural community has survived and their subsistence system is intact. However, the economy is partly dependent on the outside world, and unequal bartering goes on.

Native inhabitants have guaranteed representation in Panamanian parliament; this applies to the Kuna and Ngobe (Guaymí). However, the *cacique/congreso* system of internal Indian organization has its shortcomings. Where necessary, it can be manipulated more easily by the authorities than can an elected representative body (such as those in Mosquitia in Nicaragua); on the other hand, it keeps traditions alive.

In the case of the Emberá Indians' *comarca,* the official regulatory framework has built into it a provision instructing the state office for renewable resources (Dirección Nacional de Recursos Renovables) to ensure the conservation and rational use of such resources "jointly with" the Emberá community. Such a provision is an invitation for state bodies to intervene. Significantly, there is no mention of such an arrangement in the older statute of the Kuna *comarca.*

In the case of the Ngobe (Guaymí) Indians, the authorities have dragged their feet over autonomy negotiations in a series of protracted conflicts over land and wrangling over the division of political-cum-administrative competencies. Contributing factors have included, on the one hand, the size of the territory claimed, which extends over several provinces, and, on the other, the disunity, poor organization, and lack of militancy among the Ngobe. The indigenous peoples are now beginning to respond to the government's "divide and conquer" policy and in 1992 the various Indian congresses in Panama came together to form a union.

J. Colombia: The *Resguardo* System

The *resguardo* system in Colombia has its roots in the *encomienda* system of Spanish colonial times (which it began to replace from the 16th century). At the outset, it existed only in the Andean uplands (department of Cauca). An early form of self-governance was introduced in the form of the Indian *cabildos* as far back as 1537, and *cabildos* is still the name by which the bodies that run the *resguardos* are known. Some of these early *resguardos* survived the period of liberalism. A *resguardo* is a piece of land that may not be sold and forms part of the permanent property of an Indian community. In addition, there are *territorios tradicionales* (titleless), *reservas indígenas* (state-owned), and *comunidades indígenas civiles* on land belonging to large landowners. The *reservas indígenas* cannot be thought of as reservations in the "classic" (North American) sense—the history of these is, in any case, much more recent.

Until the 1960s, the upland Indians led a precarious existence. Encouraged by guerrilla activities in Indian areas and by the official land reforms, they began to demand their land back from the large landowners. From 1970, the Indian movement began to organize itself, first as a peasant movement, in the form of the Asociación Nacional de Usarios Campesinos (ANUC), and then as an Indian movement, in the form of the Consejo Regional Indígena del Cauca (CRIC, later renamed the Movimiento de Autoridades Indígenas de Colombia: MAIC). The peasant-based ANUC tried to take over the CRIC but was unsuccessful. Both organizations, together with the Organización Nacional Indígena de Colombia, founded in 1982, saw the struggle over land as part of the class war in Colombia. The Paez Indians, and later the Guanbianos Indians in the Andean Cauca region, proceeded to action as early as the mid-1970s, occupying land claimed by *hacienderos* (large estates of "Spanish" (i.e., White) landowners and smaller estates of Mestizo landowners). As justification for their action, they cited their historical rights of ownership—in other words, they acted as Indians, not as *campesinos*. In 1980, together with indigenous peoples from all over Colombia, they founded MAIC/AIC as a new organization representing the Indigenist Indian movement.

In 1945, the Colombian Institute for Land Reform (Instituto Colombiano de la Reforma Agraria) was forced to recognize the claims of the *cabildos*; since then, 258 new *resguardos* have been created in addition to the 67 existing colonial ones; 80% of them (covering a total area of 25 millin hectares) are located in the Amazonian rainforest region, where there were no *cabildos*. As in Panama, a measure of representation is reserved for the Indians in parliament; but this amounts to only 2 of 100 senator's posts or 2% of the seats—much less than their proportion in the population, which is at least 7%. The rights of the indigenous peoples are mentioned in the constitution in more than 20 articles. Only half a million Indians are identified as such by the state in Colombia. Officially, there are 81 ethnic groups speaking 64 languages from 14 families of languages. The MAIC, however, assumes a total of up to 5 million indigenous people. The Colombian Indian movement is one of the oldest in the two Americas; it has become an important political force that can no longer be ignored.

VII. CONSTRUCTIVE STRUCTURAL ELEMENTS FOR MULTIETHNIC STATES

The political sciences have made an exhaustive study of the question of how stability may be ensured in multiethnic states. The danger is that because of the preoccupation with stability, implications such as solidity, permanence, and, ultimately, immobility will be evoked, with the result that paths to conflict resolution will be distorted. Where the resolution of nationality issues is concerned, what is needed—in total contrast—is great flexibility on the part of all those involved and creativity on the part of the decision-makers. The search is for constitutional solutions, protective mechanisms, and cultural and economic policies that can balance the interests of the individual ethnic groups and thus ensure the proper functioning of the whole. These solutions have to be of a consensual nature, and all those affected must take part in working them out.

The formal, interdependent principles and conditions which must—in ideal terms—be observed when trying to create balanced constitutional and sociopolitical structures in multiethnic states can act as guides for innovative policies in the areas of legislation, internal political affairs, culture, and the economy. This presupposes that almost all states have a multiethnic and multicultural character and that—with one or two rare exceptions—it is not possible to talk of a state being ethnopolitically or culturally neutral. On the contrary, one has to assume inherent difficulties with such neutrality and also that there will be sectional interests on the part of the state classes.

A. Demands for Ethnocultural Neutrality on the Part of the State

For a state to be ethnically and culturally neutral runs counter to the whole European notion of the nation-state, as propagated all over the world through colonialism. Ethnicity was treated by the state classes as a "political pathology" (Mazrui). Integral to the nation-state model was both an attempt to standardize away ethnic identities and an overt cultural monopolism, often of a hybrid nature. The ideology of the nation-state, the arbitrary colonial drawing of borders, and the political constitutions of the new states hampered, or actually ran counter to, any harnessing of ethnic loyalties.

Given this situation, demands for ethnocultural neutrality on the part of the state, rather than the culturally monopolistic ideology of the nation-state system, and demands for decentralization and federalization rather than political–administrative centralization, require nothing less than an ideological conversion. There has to be a turning-away—if not a turning-around—from certain dubious doctrines of European nationalism and of its successor and imitator, the developmental nationalism in the colonies of the Third World. Only in this way will it be possible to avert the development of destructive forms of top-down ethnicization and the third phase of nationalism—namely, ethnonationalism.

The degree of "neutrality" sought, and the resolve to eliminate centralism, are crucial determinants of the state's ability to balance interests within society and to resolve ethnonational disputes. The further development of international norms and instruments that provide binding guarantees of equality of opportunity for ethnic groups will help reduce or eliminate the many diverse forms of disadvantage suffered by nondominant groups. Formal principles of a kind that will avert conflict thus presuppose a civilized state that makes serious efforts to ensure ethnopolitical or cultural neutrality, that derives part of its legitimization from this, and whose political options are not subject to external constraint.

The number and diversity of the following 18 principles for averting conflict reflect the obvious fact that there is no such thing as a simple cure-all.

1. Federalization
2. National self-government based on solid economic foundations
3. Internal self-determination
4. Protection of minorities, with right of veto
5. Equal access to central institutions
6. Balanced ethnic representation
7. Certainty of the law
8. Respect for human rights
9. Nonviolent resolution of conflicts
10. Use of consensus principle to limit the rights of the majority
11. Cultural autonomy and respect for tradition
12. Promotion of a democratic culture by means of participation
13. Right to equal development

14. Fair division of sovereignty over natural resources and land
15. Social security and economic equality of opportunity
16. Intersectoral linkage within civil society; multiple loyalties
17. Unity through diversity
18. Multiculturalism as an advantage

B. Democracy and Human Rights as Universal Values in Different Permutations

The different principles must interact and be brought into relation with one another. Participation, human rights, and civil society are parts of a democratic culture. When taken up by a mass movement, the ideals of democracy and human rights can shake authoritarian political structures to their foundations (USSR in 1985–1991, Burma in 1988, China in 1989, and Benin and Mali in 1990, etc.) and bring about their transformation. The demand for democratization, for example, cannot be equated with free elections between two or more parties. Even dictatorships occasionally conduct multiparty elections—only to ignore the results (as in Nigeria and Burma) or to resort to armed combat if they find them inconvenient (as in Angola). All the principles listed have to do with democracy and democratic culture. Only in combination with one another and only when linked with what goes before and what goes beyond do they produce the desired result.

Democracy and human rights are truly universal, behavior-relevant values which, in their different permutations, have their roots and history in societies and cultures on every continent. The question is: What concept is being assumed? Is there unvarying universalism? Are individual human rights more important than collective ones? Is voting more important than being involved? Is Western representative democracy the ideal form for all societies? Are paid—or indeed bought—parliamentary representatives superior to elders' councils? Is the multiparty system ideal for all societies? Why should a two-party system (such as that in the U.S.) be better? Why should the majority decide everything?

The sign of a genuine federation is, precisely, that majority decisions are not the measure of all things and that dictatorship by the 51% is prevented. The degree of decentralization and participation says more about the way a true democracy functions than does the number of ballots and parties. Democracy, so the UN Human Rights Conference stipulated in its Vienna Declaration

(June, 1993), is based "on the freely expressed will of the people to determine their own political, economic, social and cultural systems and their full participation in all aspects of their lives."

The arrogance of someone like Fukuyama makes him wax lyrical about Western liberal democracy's being "the ultimate form of human government" and even about "the end of history" rather than about an "end-product of Western social and intellectual history." The opposite point of view sees parliamentary democracy as "capital's extended board of directors" (Ziegler); it highlights what a fragile product of bourgeois society and globally oriented capitalism liberal democracy turns out to be in Third World conditions. At the periphery of the same global economic system, different rules apply. In certain circumstances, military dictatorships make better partners there for global players.

C. Guiding Principles for the Creation of Balanced Constitutional Structures

What is needed is an integrated and holistic viewpoint. In what follows here, the guiding principles, which, by linking forward and backward can produce the desired result—namely, the creation of balanced constitutional and sociopolitical structures in multinational states—are described in detail.

1. Federalization and regionalization on the basis of accepted or negotiable ethnic borders (otherwise federalist measures can foster the propensity to ethnonational conflict and encourage the collapse of the state).

2. National self-government for regions, and self-governed districts for nationalities/nations with small populations, with a satisfactory, negotiable degree of autonomy for each segment and a secured economic basis for self-regulation ("no autonomy without economy").

3. Abandonment of the option of secession and of (usually armed) transition to independent statehood in favor of internal self-determination in all ethnational or independent matters—as an exercise of the right of all peoples to independent development and self-determination but within the framework of existing states—assuming free association for individual nations/nationalities or peoples.

4. Constitutional protection for minorities, including affirmative action in favor of nationalities previously neglected or oppressed; right of veto for the affected ethnic groups when changes are made to laws on minorities.

5. Access to central institutions for all ethnic groups; power-sharing in mixed bodies and (proportionately) equal opportunities of participation in important decision-making processes.

6. The principle of balanced ethnic representation (e.g., in proportion to population) to be written into the electoral system. It has to be applied to the membership in central institutions such as parliament, central government, and also, preferably, to major ministries (controlled polyarchy); representation in the army and police and also in the secret services; smaller groups to be given guaranteed minimum representation in major institutions (parliament, the administration, the legal system) (preferably by the inclusion of relevant articles in the constitution).

7. Rule of law and certainty of the law to be ensured by strengthening democratic institutions; the executive's adherence to the law to be ensured by means of public control and institutional balance; control of state monopoly on force (penalties for arbitrary acts committed by the security forces); reliability and accountability help shape responsibility.

8. Respect for, and institutionalization of, human rights based on empirical values and norms corresponding to human needs; regard for the dialectic between rights and needs determines the degree of acceptance and respect accorded to human rights in a particular society; no monopoly in the shaping of binding human rights.

9. Nonviolent settlement of conflicts; reinforcement of all methods of peaceful dispute settlement, with involvement and supervision by civil society players; control of emotions; banning of ethnic and racist hate campaigns.

10. The rights of the majority (where these exist) to be limited by means of the principle of consensus and collective decision-making (negotiation and cooperation of ethnic elites in consociational democracies) within the framework of central institutions; or properly regulated, issue-specific rights of veto for minorities.

11. Cultural autonomy and respect for tradition through the preservation, promotion, and development of traditional institutions; cultural autonomy via bilingualism; subsidiarity principle and consensus based on traditional values.

12. Promotion of a democratic culture with broad-based participation; democratic behavior, including that on the part of the political elites and officials; civilization of relations through practice of mutual respect and cultural tolerance; development of a constructive conflict culture.

13. Right to equal development and to the satisfaction of basic human needs with particular attention being paid to the most disadvantaged sectors of the overall population and to all national groups; the right to development is integral to basic human rights and fundamental freedoms.

14. Fair division of sovereignty over natural resources and land; inalienable ownership of land by indigenous peoples and respect for the link between "Mother Earth" and spirituality.

15. Social security and economic equality of opportunity (fair division of public resources, nondiscrimination in the allocation of state posts and on the public employment market) as social rights and also as guarantees against destructive ethnopopulism and as a basis for interethnic and intercultural coexistence; investment in social rather than military security.

16. Promotion of intersectoral linkage of an integrating kind within civil society; each individual should have multiple loyalties and frames of reference—as a member of a national community, a religious group, a professional group, clubs, and associations.

17. Unity through diversity; ensuring the identity of the whole by promoting individual identity (respect for ethnic identity) while not neglecting joint identity; fostering shared features rather than highlighting differences.

18. Multiculturalism as an advantage, seen as a rich source of forms of thought and expression, not as a regretable lack of homogeneity.

D. Democracy Requires Favorable Sociocultural Preconditions

Democracy and human rights do not flourish when they are (bilaterally) imposed from outside. Some of the states that formerly propagated colonial oppression, inequality, and bondage must now face questions about their legitimacy and about their right to dictate to other states about democracy. For democracy to develop, favorable sociocultural and institutional preconditions are required. Grassroots democracy and peaceful dispute settlement are important sociocultural factors, which may very well be found in many societies of the Third World. What are missing, however, are the institutional preconditions at the state level and/or the political will on the part of the ruling class to share power and privileges. The resistance of regimes that block democratic reforms can often only be broken by a combination of internal and external forces. Democratic movements in repressive states should not be left to cope alone. Use should be made of the international community's existing sanctions options. Regional agreements and the further development of international standards can help to civilize authoritarian states.

Up to now, it is in the Nordic countries (Denmark, Sweden, Norway, and Finland) that the above catalog of ideal proposals for developing balanced structures in multiethnic states and societies has been implemented most consistently. These countries have elaborated exemplary anticipatory, conflict-averting schemes for their ethnonational minorities, indigenous peoples, and migrant communities. Progressive minorities policies (such as the Faeroan model) develop on a solid basis of political balance and social justice. The high level of political stability in these countries would not be conceivable without a highly developed welfare state. However, as members of the circle of wealthy industrial nations, they have far less pressing problems to cope with than most states in the third world, especially those in the African and Asian areas.

VIII. FEDERATION, DECENTRALIZATION, AND SELF-GOVERNANCE

Measures for greater decentralization have proved themselves all over the world as an appropriate framework for the coexistence of distinct peoples. In the context of the state system, this means, for example, federal structures based on specific sociocultural, linguistic, geographic, or ethnopolitical principles. Decentralization gives the part-states increased responsibility for their own affairs and it delegates administrative tasks to them.

Various large states such as the former USSR, China, and India have applied similar methods of decentralization of tasks and of regional or local self-governance with differing results. The state-based division of the Indian Union allows flexible, regionally adaptable responses to the aspirations of ethnic movements for autonomy and statehood within the framework of the union (the Punjab, Kashmir, and Naga are exceptions here). India can, despite one or two weaknesses, be described as a model that South and Southeast Asia, particularly Burma, would do well to imitate. The underlying principle is to create the greatest possible degree of ethnolinguistic homogeneity in the separate constituent states.

In Africa too, larger multiethnic states—such as Nigeria, Tanzania, and recently also Ethiopia and South Africa—have experimented with decentralizing, federalist, associative schemes. The new African states (like the Asian ones before them) had the disruptive factor of separatism to reckon with from the time of their creation by the colonial powers. The use of categories such as "native" versus "settler," and even the notion of minorities (where there are no majorities), has a very tenuous foundation in large parts of Africa. There is an extraordinary diversity of ethnic components and relations. With the exception of South Africa and the uplands of Zimbabwe and Namibia (and briefly also certain areas of Kenya, Uganda, and Tanzania), most areas of Africa were not attractive to prospective settlers from outside. Until recently, racial segregation in South Africa was one of the greatest strains to which the continent was subjected. The perverted form of federalization represented by the now-abolished Bantustans was the cause of many violent conflicts in the country. Nowadays, internal colonialism is the major cause of armed conflict, not only in Africa, but also in large parts of the world.

In the multinational construct that is Europe, there are also many more peoples than there are states. Some major nationalities—for example, the Basques and the Catalonians in Spain and the Tyroleans in Italy—nowadays enjoy a state-like autonomy. And indigenous and other minorities in the Nordic states and Switzerland enjoy extensive rights. Swiss federalism, with its self-governance by cantons, is an expression of a policy of internal balance between different confessions, cultures, and regions. However, most nationalities in Europe have not yet secured their right to self-governance. A "Europe of the Regions," as a counter-model to the authoritarian-cum-centralist Europe of the present-day Union, could, at some unspecified time in the future, help resolve acute minority and nationality problems in Western and Eastern Europe.

A. Federation and Association in Africa: Tanzania, Nigeria, and South Africa

In Africa, there has never been nationalism based on linguistic entities. However, as in Asia, the basic problem is the colonial state structure and the phenomenon of internal colonialism. In 1884 the Europeans divided Africa into 48 colonial possessions. Though the territorial jigsaw puzzle of the new states had been cobbled together in Europe, when decolonization of the first colonial possessions began, the new states and their regional organization (the Organization for African

Unity) declared the borders of these possessions to be "sacred" and nonnegotiable. Colonialism subsequently experienced a continuation in, as it were, an internal form. Only a handful of states managed to introduce elements and priorities of their own into this process of nation-building and, at least in part, to put their own stamp on it.

One arrangement regarded as exemplary by most African countries is the Tanzanian confederation uniting Tanganyika and the islands of Zanzibar and Pemba (and comprising 70–120 ethnic groups). However, representatives of some minorities and a number of groups in Zanzibar do not consider the state set-up such a good model. In Tanzania, no ethnic group has a majority or quasi-majority. In March, 1964, following the revolution in Zanzibar in the previous December, the islands entered a union with the mainland under which the individual administrations and political systems were preserved. The Chama Cha Mapinduzi party ("party of revolution") saw itself as avant-garde during the 1960s and 1970s, striving to create a democratic–socialist system (*ujamaa*). But it was unable to control the bureaucracy and brought about a weakening of existing organs of self-determination. As a result, participation was not very attractive to the population (especially the masses of the peasants and small-scale subsistent farmers).

Tanzania sought to follow an independent path and for certain periods was regarded as a model. The widespread adoption and promotion of Kiswahili as the national language of Tanzania and as a transethnic, cross-border *lingua franca* is an important binding link in the multiethnic state. Swahili also constitutes one of the politically important shared features of East Africa. However, the *ujamaa* ("community of interests") village cooperative movement was undermined by the bureaucracy and experienced a political and economic crisis during the 1980s. Although external factors (drop in prices of raw materials, war with Idi Amin, drought) played a part in the economic decline, it was ultimately home-grown errors of judgement (wrong investment policy, badly planned industrialization at the expense of agriculture) that was the determining factor. Last, the regions were granted few competencies within the framework of self-reliance. Given that the state structure was never to be brought into accord with the ethnic structure, there is also no basis for segmental autonomy.

A Zanzibari, Ali Hassan Mwinyi, succeeded the charismatic founding president Julius Nyerere in 1985. There continue to be forces in Zanzibar working toward separation (supported by A. M. Babu, who represents Zanzibar in the Unrepresented Nations and Peoples Organization). In 1992 it was decided to introduce a multiparty system.

The Tanzanian constitution safeguards traditional and indigenous rights of use and the right to a "decent" life; every individual has a right to land. However, pastoral peoples such as the Maasai are fighting for the return of their land-use rights and against encroachment by settlers.

Mention must also be made here—though with some reservations—of the Federal Republic of Nigeria, particularly the reconciliation achieved after the Biafra war and the administrative division into 30 constituent states. However, the annulment of the 1993 presidential elections (when Moshood Abiola, a Yoruba, was confirmed as the "wrong" winner) once again demonstrated the continued destructive role of the military. The dominance of the Muslim Hausa-Fulani groups of the north (24% of the total population) in the army and state apparatus became total. As in Tanzania and many other African states, there is no clear ethnic majority–minority situation in Nigeria. The second largest ethnic group after the Hausa-Fulani is that of the Yoruba (21%), followed by the Ibo (12%) in the east, who sought to break away to form Biafra. There are 430 minority language groups concentrated in the oil-rich southeastern coastal area and Niger delta (15%), in the northeast and southwest (7% each), and in the Benue area (21%).

Originally in order to break the power of the north, a federal structure was introduced. This was expanded to 12 states in 1966, 19 in 1975 under the reformist army officers Mohammed and Obasanjo, and finally to 30 states. Coming under these states are 589 local administrations. In 1983 (after the failure of a corrupt civilian government), the military, who had grown accustomed to enjoying the sinecures of power from 1966 to 1979, carried out another coup and have not relinquished power since (which means there has been a total of 25 years of military rule). Although Abiola's struggle against the military had multiethnic support, it was depicted in the international media as a purely Yoruba affair and as confined to western Nigeria. The strike staged in 1994 by the oil-workers in the south, and by other sectors, in support of the democratization in Nigeria—the first of its kind in postcolonial African history—was scarcely heeded in the West. Writers risk their lives if they speak up for democracy in their homeland: in October, 1995, Ken Saro-Wiwa and his fellow campaigners from the Ogoni people were executed. Africa's most famous writer and winner of the Nobel Prize, Wole Soyinka, lived in exile and was ambassador for the provisional government of the National Democratic Coalition (NADECO), the largest-ever opposition alliance in Nigeria.

In many Third World countries, the holding of elections involving more than one party is no sure sign of democracy—as is demonstrated by developments in Africa following the Cold War. Africa's most populous state, Nigeria, probably offered the clearest illustration of this. The local elections held there in March 1996 were merely a ploy by the weakened military regime. Moshood Abiola, the victor of the elections of June 1993, meanwhile, remained imprisoned until his death, and opponents were murdered or executed. At the end of 1998, under strong international pressure, a democratic opening-up occurred; but the ultimate test of this is yet to come—after the military had to relinquish power and the winner of the national elections, Olusegun Obasanjo, was sworn in May 1999 as Nigeria's new president.

Since the 1970s, the oil and gas economies and the fluctuation in prices on the world markets have largely determined the framework conditions for economic development and the state distribution of resources. If wrangling over distribution grow more acute, the dichotomy between north and south, and the opposition between central government and the federal states, may well grow worse. One dangerous scenario would be continued stagnation under military rule. A deepening of the existing antagonisms between the three ethnopolitical centers of gravity in the north (Hausa-Fulani), west (Yoruba), and east (Ibo)—within the framework of a badly balanced federal structure—could lead to new prosecession or antiregime conflicts. The appointment of a sovereign national conference of all the relevant ethnic, social, and political groups (as in Benin in 1991–1992) would be a good start. The stepping-down of the military (but their involvement in the national conference as one of the professional groups) and a genuine federalization of Nigeria would seem to be the only way out of the situation of permanent crisis in which Africa's most densely populated country finds itself.

In apartheid South Africa, a number of ethnically and racially based Bantustans were created as an instrument of White power retention. After centuries of disregard of ethnic languages, the new South Africa has recognized 11 official languages. The enforced schooling of millions of Black children in Afrikaans (a Dutch dialect) is over. Up to now, nationalism based on linguistically defined groups has not been very pronounced in Africa (unlike in India). But what South Africa did experience was various forms of so-called tribal nationalism fueled to the utmost by the apartheid regime. In most regions of Africa, tribalism was a colonial chimera and a useful construct for controlling rebellious colonies. In contrast to the situation in many cattle-breeding communities, tribal structures in most farming societies in Africa had long since disappeared. Violent Zulu nationalism, generated as a means of weakening the multiethnic African National Congress, is one of the burdens of the past that the new South Africa has to bear.

B. Ethiopia: Ethnicization and Decentralization

In the case of Ethiopia, it remains to be seen how far the newly initiated policy of balance between the "nations, nationalities, and peoples of Ethiopia" (as it says in the constitution of 1991) will succeed. Hopes that the proclaimed rights for "self-determination" would be implemented were raised by Ethiopia's swift recognition of Eritrea's de facto independence. Hopes among the Oromo majority group were shattered already after one year of relative freedom. Warfare resumed in the South, and, in Spring of 1998, also in the North, between Ethiopia and Eritrea. Subsequently, spillover effects threaten to affect the entire Horn of Africa region.

The new Ethiopia could become a model for other multiethnically structured states in Africa. Ethiopia (minus Eritrea) was seeking to institute national, regional, and local self-governance for its 100 or so nations and nationalities with elected bodies and fair representation in central government—in other words, a model somewhere between a federal state and a confederation. The country has been divided into 12 regions, 5 of which are mononational, the rest plurinational (for larger and smaller ethnic groups). The language of the titular peoples has been made the official language.

However, the weaknesses of the Ethiopian experiment have begun to show up in practice, at least since the regional elections of June, 1992. Elections were manipulated by the EPRDF coalition (Ethiopian Peoples Revolutionary Democratic Front) dominated by the small Tigrai or Tigrawai ethnic group, and they were boycotted by the opposition, notably the Oromo guerrilla movement, the Oromo Liberation Front. The EPRDF has declared its guerrilla force to be the country's regular army.

Since the summer of 1992 a despotic Abyssinian minority regime began once again to take shape. The second-largest minority after the 15% Amhara minority are the Tigrai, whose numbers following Eritrea's scission, now stand at only 6%. The Cushitic majority, comprising the Oromo, Somalis, and Afar, plus over 100 other ethnic groups (Cushitic, Lacustrine, Omotic, and Nilotic), continues to be excluded from power. The general election, postponed until 1995, did little to change this, since all autonomous political movements remained excluded from any kind of participation.

C. The "Special Case" of the Swiss Confederation and Its Abuse

The "special case" of multinational Switzerland, at the heart of Europe, officially declared to be a *Willensnation* ("nation founded on the will of the people"), is an example of almost mulish insistence on self-determination on the part of an ethnolinguistic majority, even at the price of economic disadvantage and political decoupling from the rest of the world. At the end of 1992, association with the rest of what was then the European Community (EC), within the framework of the European Economic Area (a prelude to the European Union), was rejected. During the past years, the Swiss electorate has also defeated a proposal to join in international peacekeeping operations (membership in the United Nations was rejected earlier), and scrapped a proposal for free transit for foreign trucks across the Alps. Switzerland's non-EU-compatible transport policy was accentuated even more with the acceptance of the "Alps initiative." The consequences of this aloofness are slowly being felt by the Swiss: for the first time since the economic crisis of the 1930s, joblessness in the land of social harmony and near-full employment has risen to alarming levels.

The national minorities in French-speaking Romandie and Italian-speaking Ticino had declared themselves clearly in favor of Europe but were silenced by a narrow majority among the German-speaking Swiss. The continuing economic crisis is having particularly serious effects in the French-speaking area, and the *Röstigraben* between Alemanics and Romanics has grown deeper (*Röstigraben* signifies the linguistic or ethnic borderline, jokingly defined in terms of the German liking for, and French dislike of, *Rösti*—thinly sliced fried potatoes.) Even trivial events send emotions rocketing. The prophecies of doom have been growing ever more dramatic since 1992. A German news magazine considered that the Alpine republic had failed as "a state based on harmony between the different language-groups, and therefore also as a model"; and it went on to ask "Is there not a danger that the Confederation itself will fall apart?"

The French-speakers have been outvoted half a dozen times since the EMR rejection at the end of 1992—but this had also happened previously. Anyone analyzing the results of the elections and ballots in Switzerland will conclude that the split between progressive electors, who are more open to the rest of the world and to new ideas, and the conservatives does not run precisely along the division of the two major language groups, but is prolonged into German-speaking Switzerland. Urban Switzerland very often votes in the same way—on both sides of the *Röstigraben*. The large cities of German-speaking Switzerland (Zurich, Basle, Bern, and a number of industrial cities in the central area) are to be found on the losing side in most ballots alongside the French-speaking area. It is simply the fact that Switzerland is not so much democratic as federalist—in other words, when there are ballots, the notorious no-voters from the rural regions always triumph despite a majority yes-vote.

Ballots fail because of the in-built cantonal majority: tiny cantons such as Appenzell, Uri, Schwyz, Unterwalden, or Zug, which have fewer than 10,000 voters, have as much voting power as large cantons (like Bern or Zurich) with a million or more inhabitants. A citizen of Appenzell has the voting power of 50 citizens of the state of Zurich. At the level of parliament, with its two-chamber system, the small "reactionary" *Ständerat* (upper chamber), which is composed of two representatives from each canton, regularly blocks the large *Nationalrat* (lower chamber), which is elected in proportion to the population. To ask whether this form of *Kantönligeist* ("cozy canton spirit") is still suited to the times is to assail the foundations of institutionalized conservatism. Another abuse of federalism occurs in the creation of cantonal tax havens for the superrich. The case of Marc Rich showed the depths to which this kind of policy can sink. The system continues at the local level (the local authorities have sovereignty over taxes). The result is "economic apartheid."

The full might of the Swiss financial marketplace, large-scale global enterprises, and provincialism—all exist side by side in a perverse combination. Tax fraud, economic crime, and money laundering have international implications. Every attempt to rectify the system of private wealth and public poverty—for example, by doing away with bank confidentiality or introducing a "wealth tax"—has failed. The Swiss oligarchy, the "invisible government," has (says Ziegler) "colonized" the indigenous political class and lulled the population into quietude. Because of the excessive influence exerted by the notorious "thumbs-downers," Switzerland has slowly developed into a model of political immobility.

The political crisis now risks developing into a national crisis for the Alpine realm. It is may be less easy to surmount than its economic counterpart. But now that cracks have developed in Switzerland's self-imposed isolation, the power elite at home could further aggravate the problem of acceptance for a policy of opening-up to the outside world. In their unthinking "stampede" to get things done, the elites are ready to sacrifice a "sacred value." One of the few things that bind the multiethnic federation together, apart from William Tell, the *Rütlischwur* (the mythical swearing of the oath at the formation of Switzerland, said to have taken place at Rütli), and the Red Cross, is Switzerland's allegedly now-meaningless neutrality.

The overwhelming majority of Swiss people believe that the policy of neutrality continues to be indispensable. In contrast to the imposed neutrality of Austria, that of Switzerland is not a product of the Cold War. Neutrality is an expression of the Swiss policy of internal balance (between Catholics and Protestants, between cantons and between the ethnocultural regions of the confederation) and of the 400-year-old 'special path' of successful self-assertion by the small Helvetian state. All the same, the country does lie wedged between some of the most bellicose nations that history has seen, the process of civilization of which many Swiss people consider is not yet complete. In principle, the question of whether neutrality is compatible with EU membership will not pose itself so long as there is no European system of collective defense, which would necessitate the abandonment of their now allegedly obsolete neutrality.

One possible role for Switzerland within the European framework would be, among other things, to work for the realization of a decentralized, federal structure as a way of satisfying "the vital interests of smaller communities" (Flavio Cotti). In a changed Europe, neutrality, "good offices," and direct democracy are political specializations for which the future European Union has a need. The search for appropriate, democratically legitimated European institutions and mechanisms could, for example, lead to the generalized application of direct democratic referendums (such as those that Switzerland practices). In 1995, despite the resistance of the ruling party, Bavarian voters endorsed a bill introducing direct democratic citizen participation at the local authority level.

D. A Europe of the Regions as a Countermodel to a European Union Superstate

A Europe of the Regions, which up to now has been regarded as a utopian countermodel to the authoritarian-cum-centralist Europe of the Eurocrats, could, at some point in the future, contribute to the solution of acute ethnonational problems in Western Europe (the Basque Country, Northern Ireland, Corsica, etc.) Since the Danish "No" to Maastricht I and the rejection of membership by the Norwegians, EC and later EU integration has ceased to be a self-propelling process. In Sweden, those apposed to the EU were victorious in the elections of September, 1995; they may call for Sweden to leave the Union. In other Western European countries too, stress is (increasingly) being laid on national self-will and regional particularities. Like a ritual, Euro-politicians keep repeating in vain—year after year—the need to create an effective Common Foreign and Security Policy (CFSP) of the Union.

There is a "fourth level"—in addition to Union leadership (Commission), member-state governments (Council of Ministers) and parliament (European Parliament)—that is not provided for in the treaty of Maastricht I, which came into force in November 1993. No form of democratically legitimated, institutionalized share in dceision-making was created for the regions. The only thing envisaged is a consultative committee for regional and other area authorities. The collective rights of official minorities and other ethnic groups will continue to be acknowledged only at the individual state level (if at all), not at the Union level. Furthermore, regions and minorities continue to have no right to bring actions before the European Court in cases when the Eurocrats—the Council of Ministers and the Commission—violate the principle of subsidiarity.

The second Maastricht conference, in 1996, was prepared by a so-called "reflection group" representing the 15 EU states. Maastricht I already envisaged the transfer of sovereignty "upward," the clearest example being the currency union, due to be implemented in the year 2000. Maastricht II is meant to introduce joint policy on issues of internal security, defense, and foreign relations. The first of these relates to the reinforcement of "fortress Europe" against waves of migrants and refugees and to the creation of a European police force (Europol) to fignt terrorism and organized crime. As a rule, states consider abandoning a foreign policy of their own more threatening to their national sovereignty than relinquishing economic self-determination, which in any case has long since been called into question by globalization and the world market.

However, a Common Foreign and Security Policy is still a long way off. Individual areas of operation—established by former colonial powers—are seriously disrupting the process of European union and the development toward the formation of a Western European great power. Within the framework of the EU, national identities are artificial hybrids and have much more to do with the political arrogance and the military or economic quest for power of the ruling classes than with the independent cultural and linguistic identity of the peoples.

Maastricht II was supposed to bring about a reform of the EU bodies and of the mechanisms of cooperation between them. The excessive influence of two democratically nonlegitimated bodies—the Commission and the Council of Ministers—is to be curtailed. The treaty aims to bring about increased transparency and foster citizens' acceptance of EU institutions, which are currently somewhat removed from reality. The strengthening of parliamentary aspects that has been called for is part of a comprehensive democratization of the justifiably disquieting European superstate. In order to increase democratic control, thought should be given to the creation of a second chamber of the regions alongside a European Parliament with enhanced status. Although the European Parliament is far from being a rubberstamp parliament, in the eyes of most Europeans it gained status only in 1999, with the dismissal of the entire European Commission (20 commissioners, including the president), following an outrageous corruption scandal involving several commissioners. In May the Parliament voted (392 to 72 with 41 abstentions) for Romano Prodi as President of a new Commission. Prodi's first task was to put together a new Commission. Unprecedentedly, proposed candidates will face parliamentary hearings (during summer and fall 1999). However, democracy deficits prevail. The Parliament and the Council have to settle outstanding differences over the statute; expectations of reaching an agreement before the year 2000 will almost certainly be frustrated.

By way of a feeble compromise, a Committee of the Regions, under the chairmanship of Jacques Blanc, was set up within the European Parliament, as a first step toward a form of representation for the regions. Demands for further institutional rights are to be pressed within the framework of the Maastricht II follow-up conference. The most important of these are: recognition as an independent body, reinforcement of legislative powers, more independence vis-à-vis the Economic and Social Committee, formal reaffirmation of the principle of subsidiarity, and clear demarcation of competencies within EU structures. Regional representatives could become direct "contacts" for people, if the regions were incorporated into the structure of the state-fixated EU. The call for stronger integration of the regions finds little favor with most of the governments of the 15 EU states. As is natural, it is primarily the states with strong regions, such as Germany, Spain, and possibly Italy, who are most supportive of the project; opposition to it comes from extremely centralist France and from Britain, which fears increased separatism on the part of Scotland.

TABLE X

Official Minorities and Other Ethnic Groups:
A European Overview

State	Historical nations, nationalities, minorities	Population (millions)	% of total population
Spain	Catalans (16%), Galicians (8%), Basques (2%), Gitanos/Roma (2%)	11–13	29
Britain	Welsh, Scots, Northern Irish, Cornish "gypsies," Manx. Migrants: Indians and Pakistani (2%), Caribs (1%)	10	17
Germany	Turks (2.2%), Kurds, Yugoslavs (1%), Italians (1%), Danes, Sorbs, Roma & Cinti, Frisians, others	8	10
France	Bretons (4%), Arabs (3%), Alsatians & Lorrainers (2%), Basques, Catalans, Corsicans, Flemings, others	4	7
Italy	Sardinians, Friulians, South Tyroleans, Ladins, Catalans, Provençals, Slovenians, Croatians, Albanians, Greeks, Roma	3–3.5	6

© Christian P. Scherrer, 1995. Sources: Internationaler Weltatlas (Hamburg: Xenos, 1993); pogrom, No. 174, Dec. 1993–Jan. 1994, 11; Minority Rights Groups reports.

A parliament of the regions, in which not only the geographic regions of Europe, but also its historic nations, nationalities, and minorities are represented on an equal footing, would create a "directness" that is currently lacking. The demand for representation as peoples could be satisfied in a more regular and more concrete way, which might generate a sense of belonging to Europe. This would also affect minority groups, whose affiliation and representation at national level is often not assured. The number of European minorities is considerable, and their populations range from a few thousand to several million.

In the multinational construct that is Europe, there are many more peoples than there are states. In some Western European states—notably in Spain and Britain—the populations of some minority nationalities or nondominant nations far exceed those of some small states (such as the Vatican State, Liechtenstein, and Luxembourg) and even the demographic size of other smaller states (Denmark, Switzerland, Belgium, and Austria). Table X gives an overview of official minorities and other ethnic groups in Europe.

In some potential EU member-states in eastern and southeastern Europe, the proportions of minority nationalities are even higher. In extreme cases (such as in the Baltic states and Turkey), they rise to one-third or one-half of the total population. Yet the participatory rights of these national minorities are rudimentary. In some cases, discrimination against them is institutionalized and systematic.

Only a few larger nations that do not have their own states (such as the Basques, the Catalans, and, to my mind, the Scots and the Welsh) currently enjoy a form of autonomy tantamount to statehood. Most endangered nations/nationalities have not yet managed to secure their right to self-governance (see Table XI). The most marginalized people in Europe are the 8 million Roma, who live scattered throughout almost every state on the continent. They were the second victims of the Holocaust and continue to this day to be victims of racial prejudice on an everyday basis. The largest communities of Roma live in Eastern Europe, mainly in Romania (2–2.5 million: 8–10% of the total population), the former Yugoslavia (1–1.5 million: 4–6%), Hungary (670,000: 5.2%), Turkey (650,000: 1%), the former USSR (640,000), and also in Spain (900,000). They have no political lobby. Only a strengthening of

their own organizations (e.g., the Romani World Congress, founded in 1971) could improve their situation.

"European Union semantics" has created yet another incomprehensible term with the coinage "external identity." This term, which means a special (Western) European identity vis-à-vis the outside, is devoid of content to many citizens. For the Eurocrats, "external identity" is something to be created. The guiding notion, they say, is not the U.S. ideology of the melting pot, whose alleged success they much admire, but the development of a "European facet" to existing multilayered identities—all the while preserving national, regional, cultural, and ethnic identities.

As we search for a new configuration for Europe—one that goes beyond the old nation-states—the issues of membership, citizenship, democratic representation, and demographic representativity pose themselves in an entirely different light. The new Europe must be, in equal measure, a Europe of the citizen and a Europe of the peoples.

Also See the Following Articles

COLONIALISM AND IMPERIALISM • CONFLICT TRANSFORMATION • ENEMY, CONCEPT AND IDENTITY OF • ETHNIC CONFLICTS AND COOPERATION • GENOCIDE AND DEMOCIDE • HUMAN RIGHTS • INSTITUTIONALIZATION OF VIOLENCE • NONGOVERNMENTAL ACTORS IN INTERNATIONAL POLITICS • WARFARE, TRENDS IN

TABLE XI

Minority Nationalities in Potential EU Member States in Eastern and Southeast Europe

State	Historical nations, nationalities, minorities	Popluation (millions)	Percentage of total population
Latvia	Russians (42%), Belorussians, Ukrainians, Poles, and others	1.2–1.4	48
Turkey	Kurds (15%), Arabs (2%), Roma (1%), Circassians, Armenians, Assyrians, Greeks, Turkomans, Jews, Bulgars, Georgians, Laz, and others	13–18	20–30
Croatia	Serbs (15%), Roma (3.7%), Slovaks, Italians, Germans, Chechens, Ukrainians, Ruthenians, and others	1–1.2	25
Romania	Roma (8–10%), Hungarians (7.5%), Ukrainians, Serbs, Bulgars, Banat Germans, Croatians, Slovaks, Russians, Chechens, Tatars, Turks, Greeks, Armenians, and others	3.5–4.5	15–25

Bibliography

African Rights (Omar, R., & de Waal, A.) (1995). *Rwanda: Death, despair and defiance.* London: African Rights.

Amnesty International. Annual Report. London: Amnesty International.

APC-EU (Africa-Caribbean-Pacific) (1996). Lomé Convention. *The Courier,* 155,

Asiwaju, A. I. (1985). *Partitioned Africans: Ethnic relations across Africa's boundaries 1884–1984.* Lagos: Lagos University Press.

Asmal, K. (1993). The democratic option, ethnicity and state power. Paper presented at Grahamstown (Rhodes University).

Assies, W. J., & Hoekema, A. J. (Eds.) (1994). Experiences with systems of self-government by indigenous peoples. IWGIA document no. 76, Copenhagen.

Barth, F. (Ed.) (1969). *Ethnic groups and boundaries.* Boston: Little, Brown.

Bercovitch, J., & Rubin, J. Z. (Eds.) (1992). *Mediation in international relations: Multiple approaches.* London: St Martin's Press.

Bertrand, M. (1995). *UNO: Geschichte und bilanz.* Frankfurt: Fischer.

Burger, J. (1987). *Report from the frontier: The state of the world's indigenous peoples.* London: Zed Books.

Burton, J. et al. (Eds.) (1990). *Conflict: Resolution and provention;* Houndsmills: Macmillan.

Cabral, A. (1974). *Die revolution der verdammten.* Berlin: Rotbuch.

Calließ, J., & Merkel, C. M. (Eds.) (1995). *Peaceful settlement of conflict I.* Loccum: EAL.

Calließ, J., & Merkel, C. M. (Eds.) (1994). *Peaceful settlement of conflict II: Third party intervention.* Loccum: EAL.

Calließ, J., & Merkel, C. M. (Eds.) (1995). *Peaceful settlement of conflict III: A task for civil society.* Loccum: EAL.

Foege, W. (Ed.) (1992). *Resolving intra-national conflicts: A strengthened role for non-governmental actors.* Atlanta: Carter Center.

Minugh, C. J., Morris, G. T., & Ryster, R. C. (1989). *Indian self-governance.* Kenmore: CWIS.

Churchill, W. (1989). Critical issues in native North America. IWGIA document no. 62; Copenhagen.

von Clausewitz, C. (1980). *Vom kriege: Hinterlassenes werk: Text der erstaufl, 1832–1834.* Frankfurt: Ullstein.

Conflict Management Group (Harvard University) (various years). *CMG Update* (quarterly newsletter).

Council of Europe (1994). Framework Convention for the Protection of National Minorities. Strassburg.

CSCE/OSCE (Conference/Oranization on Security and Co-operation in Europe) (various years since 1993). Documents/statements on or of the CSCE High Commissioner on National Minorities.

Deng, F. M., & Zartmann, W. (Eds.) (1991). *Conflict resolution in Africa.* Washington, DC: Brookings Institution.

ECOR (1998). *Struggle for survival in the decade of the world's indigenous peoples: Analysis and reports from the frontiers: Compilation of interviews.* Moers: IFEK.

ECOR (1997). *Ethnicity and State at the horn of Africa II (ECOR 14).* Moers: IFEK.

ECOR (1996). *Ethiopia versus Oromia: The empire strikes back (ECOR 13).* Moers: IFEK.

ECOR (1995). *The United Nations in the decade for the indigenous peoples of the world: New challenges after 50 years (ECOR 12).* Moers: IFEK.

ECOR (1995a). *Ethnicity and state in Rwanda 1994/95: Conflict prevention after the genocide: Assessment and documents (ECOR 11)* Moers: IFEK.

ECOR (1995b). *Ethnicity and state in Burma: Ethno-nationalist revolution and civil war 1949–1995 (ECOR 10).* Moers: IFEK.

ECOR (1993). *Ethnicity and state in Eastern Nicaragua: Autonomous governance in Yapti Tasba (ECOR 6).* Moers: IFEK.

Elwert, G. (1995). Kriegsökonomie und ethnische Mobilisierung. *Blätter iz3w, 209,* 19–21.

Elwert, G., & Waldmann, P. (Eds.) (1989). *Ethnizität im Wandel.* Saarbrücken: Breitenbach.

Ethnopolitical Studies Centre (1993). *Socio-political situation in the post-Soviet world* (E. Payne, Ed.). Moscow: Foreign Policy Association.

Evans-Pritchard, E. E., & Fortes, M. (Eds.) (1940). *African political systems.* London: Oxford University Press.

Freedom House. (various years). *Freedom in the world: The annual survey of political rights and civil liberties.* New York: Freedom House.

Galtung, J. (1994). Peace and Conflict Research in the Age of the Cholera. Malta: IPRA.

Galtung, J. (1994b). Conflict interventions. In Calließ/Merkel (Eds.).

Galtung, J. (1964). An editorial. *Journal for Peace Research, 1*(1), 1–4.

Gantzel, K. J. (1997). Kriegsursachen—Tendenzen und Perspektiven'; in: Ethik & Sozialwissenschaft, EuS 8: 3, 257–266.

Gantzel, K. J., & Schlichte, K. (various years). *Das Kriegsgeschehen: Daten und Tendenzen der Kriege und bewaffneten Konflikte.* Bonn: Interdependenz/SEF.

Gellner, E. (1983). *Nation and nationalism.* Oxford: Blackwell.

Goldstone, R. (1995). Exposing the truth: Interview with the UN prosecutor for the former Yugoslavia and Rwanda. *The Courier, 153,* 2–5.

Gurr, T. R. (1994). Peoples against states: Ethnopolitical conflict and the changing world system. *International Studies Quarterly, 38,* 348–377.

Gurr, T. R. (1993). *Minorities at risk: A global view of ethnopolitical conflict.* Washington, DC: U.S. Institute of Peace.

Gurr, T. R., & Harff, B. (1994). *Ethnic conflict in world politics.* Boulder, CO: Westview Press.

Héraud, G. (1963). *L'Europe des ethnies.* Paris: Presses d'Europe.

Holsti, K. J. (1991). War Issues, Attitudes, and Explanations. In *Peace and war: Armed conflicts and internatinoal order 1648–1989* (pp. 306–334). Cambridge: Cambridge University Press.

Horowitz, D. L. (1985). *Ethnic groups in conflict.* Berkeley: University of California Press.

Huber, K. J. (1994). The CSCE's new role in the east: Conflict prevention, RFE/RF-Research Report 3. Berlin: RFE.

International Alert (1994). *Self-determination: Report of the Martin Ennals symposium.* Saskatoon: International Alert.

International Alert (1994a). Towards a policy framework for advancing preventive diplomacy, paper. Amsterdam.

International Institute for Strategic Studies (1997). *The military balance 1996–1997.* London: Brassey's.

Instituto Indigenista Interamericano (1990). In R. Stavenhagen & D. Iturralde (Eds.), *Entre la ley y la costumbre: El derecho consuetudinario indígena en América Latina.* Mexico: Siglo XXI.

International Work Group for Indigenous Affairs (var. years). Documentation (on situation of indigenous peoples).

International Work Group for Indigenous Affairs (1989). *Indigenous self-government in the Americas.* IWGIA Document 63. Copenhagen: IWGIA.

Joint Evaluation of Emergency Assistance to Rwanda (1996). In D. Millwood (Ed.), *The international response to conflict and genocide: Lessons from the Rwanda experience.* Copenhagen: JEEAR.

Kidron, M., & Segal, R. (1992). *Der politische Weltatlas.* Bonn: Dietz.

Kiernan, B. (1998). *The Pol Pot regime: Race, power, and genocide in Cambodia under the Khmer Rouge, 1975–1979.* New Haven, CT: Yale University Press.

Lijphart, A. (1984). *Democracies: Patterns of majoritarian and consensus government.* New Haven, CT: Yale University Press.

Macrae, J. et al. (1994). *War and hunger: Rethinking international responses to complex emergencies.* London: Zed.

Mann, M. (Ed.) (1990). *The rise and decline of the nation state.* Oxford: Blackwell.

Martínez Cobo, J. R. (1986). *Study of the problem of discrimination against indigenous populations.* New York: UN.

Mazrui, A. (1994). Global Apartheid: Structural and Overt. *Alternatives, 19,* 195–293.

Moynihan, D. P. (1993). *Pandaemonium: Ethnicity in international politics.* Oxford: Oxford University Press.

Nietschmann, B. (1987). Militarization and indigenous peoples. *Cultural Survival Quarterly, 11*(3), 1–16.

Nohlen, D., & Nuscheler, F. (1992–1995). *Handbuch der Dritten Welt* (3rd ed.). Bonn: Dietz.

NUUK Papers/Johansen, L. E. et al. (1992). Report on Experience of Self-government for Indigenous Peoples. Geneva: UN (E/CN.4/1992/42/Add.1).

Pfetsch, F. R. (Ed.) (1991). *Konflikte seit 1945.* Freiburg: Ploetz.

PIOOM-COMT (1994). Contemporary Armed Conflicts. A Global Inventory. *PIOOM Newsletter, 6*(1), 17–21.

Phillips, A., & Rosas, A. (Eds.) (1993). The UN Minority Rights Declaration. Turku/Åbo: Åbo Academic Printing.

Plant, R. (1994). *Land Rights and Minorities*. MRG: London.

República de Nicaragua (1987). Estatuto de la autonomía de las regiones de la Costa Atlántica. La Gaceta, Diario Oficial 5/87. Managua: Imprenta Nacional.

Rothchild, D. (1991). An interactive model for state–ethnic relations. In Deng & Zartmann (Eds.),

Rummel, R. J. (1994). *Death by government: Genocide and mass murder*, New Brunswick, NJ: Transaction.

Rummel, R. (1994a). Power, genocide and mass murder. *Journal of Peace Research, 31*(1), 1–10.

Rupesinghe, K. (1992). *Early warning and conflict resolution*. Houndsmills, UK: Macmillan/St. Martin's.

Ryan, S. (1990). *Ethnic conflict and international relations*. Aldershot: Dartmouth.

Scherrer, C. P. (1997). *Ethno-Nationalismus im Zeitalter des Globalismus: Handbuch 2*. Münster: Agenda.

Scherrer, C. P. (1997a). *Ethnisierung und Völkermord in Zentralafrika*. Frankfurt/New York: Campus.

Scherrer, C. P. (1996). *Ethno-Nationalismus im Weltsystem: Handbuch 2*. Münster: Agenda.

Scherrer, C. P. (1994). *Ethno-Nationalismus als globales Phänomen*. Duisburg: INEF-Report 6.

Scherrer, C. P. (1994b). Regional autonomy in eastern Nicaragua (1990–94): Four years of self-government experience in Yapti Tasba. In Assies & Hoekema (Eds.).

Schlichte, K. (1994). Is ethnicity a cause of war? *Peace Review, 6*(1), 59–65.

Stiftung Entwicklung und Frieden (Development and Peace Foundation) (various years). *Eine Welt: Texte der Stiftung Entwicklung und Frieden*. Bonn

Stiftung Entwicklung und Frieden (Development and Peace Foundation) (various years). *Global trends*. Frankfurt: Fischer.

Singer, J. D., & Small, M. (1984). *The wages of war 1816–1980. A statistical handbook, with disputes and civil war data*. Ann Arbor, MI: University of Michigan Press.

Sivard, R., & Eckhardt, W. (1993). Wars and deaths 1945–1992. In R. Sivard (Ed.), *World military and social expenditures 93*. Washington, DC: World Priorities.

Smith, A. D. (1992). *Ethnicity and nationalism*. Leiden: Brill.

Smith, A. D. (1991). *National identity*. London: Penguin Books.

Stavenhagen, R. (1990). *The ethnic question: Conflicts, development and human rights*. Tokyo: UN University Press.

Tungavik (Inuit of Nunavut) and CANADIAN MINISTRY OF INDIAN AFFAIRS AND NORTHERN DEVELOPMENT (1993).

Agreement between the Inuit of the Nunavut Settlement Area and Her Majesty the Queen in Right of Canada, Ottawa.

UNCHR (United Nations Commission on Human Rights)/ECOSOC. (various years). Reports of the Working Group on Indigenous Populations. Annual sessions, July/Aug. in Geneva.

UNCHR/ECOSOC (1995). Considerations of a permanent forum for indigenous people (E/CN.4/Sub.2/AC.4/1995/7).

UNCHR/ECOSOC (Various years). Study on treaties, agreements and other constructive arrangements between states and indigenous peoples, Geneva: E/CN.4/Sub.2/A.4/.

UNCHR/ECOSOC (1993). Draft declaration on the rights of indigenous peoples (E/CN.4/Sub.2/1993/26).

UNDHA (United Nations Department of Humanitarian Affairs) (various years). DHA news.

UNDP (United Nations Development Programme) (various years). Human development report.

UNESCO (United Nations Educational, Scientific and Cultural Organization) (1994). First consultative meeting of the Culture of Peace programme (CPP-94/CONF.601/3.

UN General Assembly (1992). Declaration on the rights of persons belonging to national or ethnic, religious and linguistic minorities (General ssembly, 47th session, 1 Dec. 1992).

UNRISD (United Nations Research Institute for Social Development) (various years). UNRISD Discussion Papers (DP), Geneva.

UNRISD (various years). UNRISD Occasional Papers (OP).

UNRISD (1995). Ethnic violence, conflict resolution and cultural pluralism report.

UNRISD (WSP: War-torn Societies Project) (various years). The Challenge of Peace: An Interactive Newsletter, vol. 1.

Van Praag, W., & van Michael, C. (1994). UNPO was created and is run by the nations and people that are not represented in the UN and in international fora. *ECOR, 12*, 49–55.

Wallerstein, I. (1995). *Die Sozialwissenschaft 'kaputtdenken': Die Grenzen der paradigmen des 19, Jahrhunderts*. Weinheim: Beltz Athenäum.

Wearne, P./MRG (1994). *The Maya of Guatemala*. London: MRG.

Widerspruch (1995). Ethnische Politik, Krieg und Völkermord. Volume 30.

World Conference of Indigenous Peoples on Territory, Environment and Development (1992). Kari-Oca Declaration and Indigenous Peoples Earth Charter.

Yamskov, A. N. (1994). The "new minorities" in post-Soviet states. *Cultural Survival Quarterly, 18*(2–3), 58–61.

Zimmermann, K. (1992). *Sprachkontakt, ethnische Identität und Identitätsbeschädigung*. Frankfurt: Vervuert.

Structural Violence

Kathleen Maas Weigert

University of Notre Dame

GLOSSARY

Conflict As a noun, a relationship between actors in a system that is based on perceived or structurally embedded incompatible goals or values.

Nonviolence Between individuals, refraining from using violent means to achieve one's goals, either out of a religious or philosophical rejection of such means or because of a practical assessment that such means are the only ones available and/or are worth using in an effort to achieve one's goals while simultaneously reducing violence.

Power The capacity to effect change, differentiating power *over* others (to get others to do what you want) from power *with* others (to work together to achieve some common purpose).

Structure Patterned relationships among components of a social system that, although creations of human actors, constrain human behavior.

Violence Either the intentional use of force to harm others in order to achieve some goal or harm that results to some because of the unequal distribution of power and resources.

STRUCTURAL VIOLENCE (also called indirect violence and, sometimes, institutionalized violence) is differentiated from personal violence (also called direct or behavioral) and refers to preventable harm or damage to persons (and by extension to things) where there is no actor committing the violence or where it is not meaningful to search for the actor(s); such violence emerges from the unequal distribution of power and resources or, in other words, is said to be built into the structure(s). This article discusses the origins, dimensions, development, and use of the term as well as the relationships between the two types of violence and examines various advantages and disadvantages for the concept's use in peace research and peace action.

I. ORIGINS OF THE CONCEPT

While other social sciences (and, indeed, other fields) examine peace, conflict, violence, and nonviolence, it is in the field of peace and conflict studies where these terms take on central significance and, as a result, where sustained attention has been paid to them for an understanding of the preventing, waging, transforming, and/or ending of conflicts as well as, more generally, for the creation, maintenance, and transformation of structures and processes of peace from the personal to the global levels.

The definitions and dimensions of these central concepts are rich and subject to much discussion and debate. In this article the focus is on the relationships among the terms as they relate to the particular concept of structural violence. While the idea of structural violence, at least in an embryonic way, may be as old as the study of conflict and violence, the actual concept was introduced into the field and given salience by Johan Galtung in his 1969 seminal essay. Both he and other scholars have developed the concept in an attempt to provide a tool for peace research, education, and, at least for some, action. Several distinctions merit attention.

In his 1986 review essay on the concept of structural violence, Webb highlighted the debate in the field as represented by "subjectivists" and "objectivists." In addressing the issue of the ingredients needed to warrant labeling something a conflict, the distinction between these two groups focuses special attention on the role of actors and their perceptions in a conflict situation. The subjectivist model maintains that there must be at least some perception of incompatible values or goals by the actors involved to justify calling something a conflict. The objectivist model, on the other hand, argues that conflict can exist without the awareness of the social actors since conflict, in this view, has to do with "interests" and interests are not a matter of the subjective definition of the actors but are instead "determined" by the social structure. In short, conflict is incompatible interests embedded in the structure of the system where the conflict is found.

A second key distinction focuses on positive and negative peace. This distinction was apparently first presented by Wright in a discussion of pacifists and internationalists in his 1942 classic, *A Study of War*. He attributed to the former an "unsophisticated interpretation" of peace as negative (i.e., the absence of war) and contrasted this with the latter's more complex understanding of peace as something positive (i.e., international justice), which in turn implies "orderly procedures and a spirit of co-operation" in dealing with international problems which "can only be realized in a world-society." Wright concluded, "The positive aspect of peace—justice—cannot be separated from the negative aspect—elimination of violence."

It was Galtung who advanced the distinction. In his editorial in the very first issue (1964) of the *Journal of Peace Research*, Galtung referred to the two aspects of peace, calling negative peace "the absence of violence, absence of war" and positive peace "the integration of human society." In a 1968 essay, he defined negative peace as "the absence of organized violence between such major human groups as nations, but also between racial and ethnic groups because of the magnitude that can be reached by internal wars" and positive peace as "a pattern of cooperation and integration between major human groups."

This leads to a third distinction, that between violence and nonviolence, which helps pull together ideas from the previous two and brings us to the concept of structural violence. While the nonviolence–violence distinction raises such topics as definitions, tactics and strategies, and outcomes and evaluations, for this article the fundamental issue is conceptual. In defining violence, some choose to restrict the term to the intentional use of force (foremost, but not exclusively, physical) against one or more "others" (and in some definitions, to property) to inflict injury or death. Violence is seen as goal oriented; actors resort to violence in order to achieve some particular or general purpose(s). Thus, an actor, an action, and an "actee" (adapting a legal convention that avoids relying on the word "victim," a term which renders an individual, at least in ordinary usage, quite powerless) are necessary in this conceptualization of violence.

For others, violence is conceived in broader terms. In his 1969 essay, Galtung began with the idea that "*violence is present when human beings are being influenced so that their actual somatic and mental realizations are below their potential realizations*" (italics in original). Violence, then, was defined as "*the cause of the difference between the potential and the actual ...*" (italics in original). Note that here there is no need for an "actor" in the traditional sense of the term, while there is some kind of "action" and an "actee." This led Galtung to his formulation of structural violence:

> We shall refer to the type of violence where there is an actor that commits the violence as *personal* or *direct*, and to violence where there is no such actor as *structural* or *indirect*. In both cases individuals may be killed or mutilated, hit or hurt in both senses of these words, and manipulated by means of stick or carrot strategies. But whereas in the first case these consequences can be traced back to concrete persons as actors, in the second case this is no longer meaningful. There may not be any person who directly harms another person in the structure. The violence is built into the structure and shows up as unequal power and

consequently as unequal life chances (italics in original).

In a 1985 review of peace research, Galtung pinpointed the genesis of the term to his experience in what was then Southern Rhodesia, where he did statistical work on interracial violence. Acknowledging his debt to Gandhi (who apparently never used the term itself), Galtung commented that the concept of structural violence allowed him to get away from the actor-oriented perspective of much western social science. He elaborated by saying that structures are

> the settings within which individuals may do enormous amounts of harm to other human beings without ever intending to do so, just performing their regular duties as a job defined in the structure.... Structural violence was then seen as unintended harm done to human beings ... as a process, working slowly in the way misery in general, and hunger in particular, erode and finally kill human beings.

Galtung posited that the introduction of this concept offered a new thrust in peace research, namely a "critical analysis of structures and possibly to efforts to transform structures pregnant with violence into less violent ones."

His use of the term structure fits with a common approach found in the social sciences, namely, one that uses structure to refer to patterned relationships among components of a social system (although which patterns are discerned is related to one's perspective). A social structure can be considered a "social fact" (i.e., something external to individuals) with an independent reality that constrains their behavior and channels their actions. While that facticity suggests a determinism of some kind, many would hasten to add that structures are creations of human actors as well, a point to which we return in Section IV.

In his 1969 essay, Galtung offered several illustrations of structural violence. One focused on hunger: "if people are starving when this is objectively avoidable, then violence is committed, regardless of whether there is a clear subject–action–object relation, as during a siege yesterday or no such clear relationship, as in the way world economic relations are organized today." A second, perhaps more famous, example referred to husband–wife patterns: "Thus, when one husband beats his wife there is a clear case of personal violence, but when one million husbands keep one million wives in ignorance there is structural violence."

In the 1969 essay, Galtung proffered the word "social injustice" as a substitute to describe the condition of structural violence but rejected the term "exploitation," arguing that the latter belongs to a political vocabulary and, besides, it can all too readily change to the verb "exploit," which might draw attention away from structure ("and even lead to often unfounded accusations about intended structural violence"). Galtung linked structural violence with positive peace (i.e., the absence of structural violence was seen as positive peace) and equated positive peace with social justice, a positively defined condition of an egalitarian distribution of power and resources. While structural violence did not prevent social change, it did constrain it, making it difficult to accomplish. Lawler provides a helpful guide to and analysis of Galtung's developing framework.

II. DEVELOPMENT AND USE OF THE CONCEPT

A number of scholars took up Galtung's challenge to examine structural violence. Of those who did so in empirical research, the earliest operational definition of the concept took the form of life expectancy data (initially undertaken by Galtung and his colleague, Ted Hoivik) either within a country or between countries. Alcock and Kohler, for example, examined the global system for the relationship, both at a particular point in time and over time, between this manifestation of structural violence and wealth (measured by GNP per capita or energy consumption per capita). The conclusion from this line of research was straightforward: there were unnecessary (i.e., theoretically preventable or "premature") deaths, differentially distributed, and these deaths could be attributed to the structures of power and resource allocation in the particular arena (domestic or international)—in short, to structural violence.

For some scholars in the peace research field and in international relations more generally, these kinds of data were framed in different conceptual terms, such as development, where premature or unnecessary deaths were taken as indicators of uneven or maldevelopment. While not always directly referring to Galtung's work, researchers in other fields employed the term itself; for instance, in the areas of public health and preventive medicine. Gilligan, for example, following Gandhi, labels poverty as the "deadliest form of violence" and examines it as a form of structural violence, defined as "increased rates of death and disability suffered by those who occupy the bottom rungs of society, as contrasted with the relatively lower death rates experienced by those who are above them." Whether such researchers did not know of Galtung's work or simply found it not useful is an empirical question beyond the scope of this article. That in fact they employed the concept without reference to Galtung's work, however, suggests an issue raised by various critics of academic specialization, including deconstructionist scholars. They find fault with the dominant practice of a narrow specialization of knowledge, arguing that such an approach raises barriers to the inter-, multi-, or transdisciplinary research they contend would better advance our knowledge and understanding of social realities.

It appears that structural violence as a term has, nevertheless, entered the lexicon of peace studies and peace research and is widely used at least at a descriptive level, as indicated by an examination of introductory texts and anthologies in peace studies or by review articles of the field, such as Wiberg's. Certainly, some scholars have found the concept theoretically suggestive and have sought to employ and/or develop it. Recent empirical works, for example, essays by Kazak on the Middle East and Mathiot on India as well as more theoretical works, such as Eisler on human rights and especially Burton in his comprehensive examination of violence employ the term; the contributions of Eisler and Burton are discussed below.

It is perhaps Birgit Brock-Utne who has paid the most systematic attention to the term, which she does in her analysis of peace and peace education from a feminist perspective. She extended earlier works by including in the negative peace concept the absence of collective, personal violence against women. She employed the distinction between unorganized and organized violence and drew attention to structural violence that leads to a shorter life span and structural violence that leads to a less fulfilling life. She examined theoretical issues in peace education and looked at both out-of-school situations and more formal educational settings; her typology is examined in the next section.

III. RELATIONSHIPS BETWEEN DIRECT AND INDIRECT VIOLENCE

Granting for the moment the validity of the distinction between direct and indirect or structural violence, one of the important issues calling for attention is the relationship between the two types. In his 1969 essay, Galtung urged that the distinction between personal and structural violence be made the "basic one" in peace research and peace action. His justification was made in terms of the "unifying perspective" it offered to the study of violence, plus the advantage of not prejudging which caused more suffering. After a discussion of the means of personal and structural violence, he turned to the relationship between the two types, first arguing that there is a logical distinction between them. He then examined several possible hypothetical relationships between the two types (e.g., does one cause the other?; does the manifest form of one presuppose the latent existence of the other?; is one the price of the other?) and rejected reductionism in each case.

While originally eschewing the term "exploitation," as noted above, Galtung later included it as one of the "mechanisms" or "aspects" of structural violence (along with penetration, fragmentation, and marginalization). In a 1990 essay, he further pinpointed exploitation as a "center-piece" in his view of "the archetypal violent structure." He combined the distinction between direct and structural violence with four classes of "basic needs," yielding "a typology of violence" (see Table I). The distinction between Exploitation A and Exploitation B is that the former refers to the situation where the "underdogs may in fact be so disadvantaged that they die (starve, waste away from diseases) from it," while the latter refers to the situation in which the underdogs "may be left in a permanent, unwanted state of misery, usually including malnutrition and illness." Suggesting that it is possible to label this table "anthropo-centric," Galtung noted that a fifth column (for the rest of nature) could be added at the beginning. As he did in 1969, Galtung urged acceptance of the direct violence–structural violence distinction because to do otherwise (i.e., to restrict "peace" to the study of direct violence) is "narrow" and, furthermore, leaves out important interconnections among types of violence, "particularly the way in which one type of violence may be reduced or controlled at the expense of increase or maintenance of another."

In his 1990 article, Galtung expanded his work on direct and structural violence by introducing the concept of "cultural violence," which he defined as "those aspects of culture, the symbolic sphere of our existence—exemplified by religion and ideology, language and art, empirical science and formal science (logic, mathematics)—that can be used to justify or legitimize direct or structural violence." He conceived of three "super-types" or overarching categories to make a "(vicious) violence triangle" image, leading to a "violence strata" image, and suggested that, generally, the causal flow is from cultural via structural to direct violence (see Box).

TABLE I

A Typology of Violence[a]

	Survival needs	Well-being needs	Identity needs	Freedom needs
Direct violence	Killing	Maiming, siege, sanctions, misery	Desocialization, resocialization, secondary citizen	Repression, detention, expulsion
Structural violence	Exploitation A	Exploitation B	Penetration, segmentation	Marginalization, fragmentation

[a] *Source:* Galtung (1990, p 292). Reprinted by permission of Sage Publications Ltd.

Brock-Utne explored and expanded the relationship between direct and indirect violence as she applied it to the field of peace education in her 1989 work. Table II presents her updated summary frame. In her 1989 work, she argued that while the six cells are logically independent of one another, this does not mean there are no relationships between them; whether and what connections exist is to be decided empirically. She suggested research questions within each cell. For example, a focus on cell I (unorganized negative peace) could lead to an analysis of patriarchy and macho attitudes since they are relevant to both rapes and wife battery as well as to street killings. She also highlighted possible research questions for linking different cells. Is there, for example, more or less of cell I-type violence in periods of economic decline, which might lead to a type of structural violence, or in times of direct violence, i.e., war and revolution? Or what is the relationship between organized direct and organized indirect violence (for example, the relationship between the lives of women and children in developing countries and the money spent on weapons)?

While just briefly referring to one of Galtung's works, Riane Eisler is also concerned with the relationships between kinds of violence. She approaches the issue in her examination of human rights, calling for "a new integrated approach to both violence and human rights." As Table III shows, Eisler differentiates between two models of social organization. In the dominator model, differences are "automatically equated with inferiority or superiority" and the superior dominates the inferior. In the partnership model, difference is not

---

Box 1

Cultural, Direct, and Structural Violence: Militarization and Militarism as An Example

Let us reap an important harvest from this taxonomic exercise: we can use it to clarify the concept of militarization as a process and militarism as the ideology accompanying that process. Obviously, one aspect is a general inclination toward direct violence in the form of real or threatened military action, whether provoked or not, whether to settle conflict or initiate it. This inclination brings in its wake the production and deployment of the appropriate hardware and software. However, it would be superficial to study militarization only in terms of past military activity records and present production and deployment patterns; this would lead to facile conclusions in terms of personnel, budget and arms control only. Good weeding presupposes getting at the roots, in this case at the structural and cultural roots, as suggested by the three-strata paradigm. Concretely, this means identifying structural and cultural aspects that would tend to reproduce the readiness for military action, production, and deployment. This would include mobbing of young boys at school, primogeniture, unemployment, and exploitation in general. Further, the use of military production and deployment to stimulate economic growth and economic distribution; heavily nationalist, racist, and sexist ideologies; and so on. The combination of building military teaching and exercise components into high school and university curricula and structure, and disseminating militarism as culture, should merit particular attention. Yet structure and culture are usually not included in "arms control" studies, both being highly sensitive areas. Those taboos have to be broken.

Source: Galtung (1990, p. 296) Reprinted by permission of Sage Publications Ltd.

TABLE II

A Summary of the Concepts of Negative and Positive Peace[a]

	Negative peace	Positive peace	
	Absence of personal physical and direct violence	Absence of indirect violence shortening life span	Absence of indirect violence reducing quality of life
Unorganized	Absence of, e.g., wife battering, rape, child abuse, dowry deaths, street killings	Absence of inequalities in microstructures leading to unequal life chances	Absence of repression in microstructures leading to less freedom of choice and fulfillment
Organized	Absence of, e.g., war	Absence of economic structures in a country or between countries so that the life chances of some are reduced or effects of damage on nature by pollution, radiation, etc.	Absence of repression in a country of free speech, the right to organize, etc.

[a] *Source:* Brock-Utne (1997, p. 154). From *The Web of Violence: From Interpersonal to Global.* Copyright 1997 by the Board of Trustees of the University of Illinois. Used with the permission of the University of Illinois Press.

automatically equated with inferiority or superiority. She argues that the domination and violence that occur in the private sphere provide the basis for domination and violence in the public sphere; partnership and peace are juxtaposed with domination and violence.

Another scholar who addresses the links between kinds of violence, making direct reference to Galtung's work, is John Burton. Within a "human needs" framework, Burton offers his "problem-solving" approach to explaining violence and the means of "proventing" it (i.e., "taking steps to remove sources of conflict, and more positively to promote conditions in which collaborative and valued relationships control behaviors"). He attributes the origins of structural violence to "the pol-

TABLE III

The Dominator and Partnership Models[a]

Component	Basic configurations	
	Dominator model	Partnership model
Gender relations	The ranking of the male over the female as well as the higher valuing of the traits and social values stereotypically associated with "masculinity" rather than "feminity"[b]	Equal valuing of the sexes as well as of "femininity" and "masculinity" or a sexually egalitarian social and ideological structure where "feminine" values can gain operational primacy
Violence	A high degree of institutionalized social violence and abuse, ranging from wife- and child-beating, rape, warfare to psychological abuse by "superiors" in the family, the workplace, and society at large	A low degree of social violence, with violence and abuse not structural components of the system
Social structure	A predominantly hierarchic and authoritarian social organization, with the degree of authoritarianism and hierarchism roughly corresponding to the degree of male dominance[c]	A more generally equalitarian social structure, with difference (be it based on sex, race, religion, or belief system) not automatically associated with superior or inferior social and/or economic status

[a] *Source:* R. Eisler (1997, p. 174). From *The Web of Violence: From Interpersonal to Global.* Copyright 1997 by the Board of Trustees of the University of Illinois. Used with the permission of the University of Illinois Press.

[b] The terms "femininity" and "masculinity" as used here correspond to the gender stereotypes appropriate for a dominator society (where "masculinity" is equated with dominance and conquest) and *not* with any inherent female or male traits.

[c] As used here, the term "hierarchic" refers to what we may call a domination hierarchy or the type of hierarchy inherent in a dominator model of social organization based on fear and the threat of force. Such hierarchies should be distinguished from a second type of hierarchy, which may be called an actualization hierarchy (e.g., of molecules, cells, and organs in the body: a progression toward a higher and more complex level of function).

icy and administrative decisions that are made by some and which adversely affect others." He suggests that the structural violence concept is relevant to institutions throughout systems, beginning with the family, and in fact says "domestic violence, the sexual abuse of children and physical abuse even within the frame of learning and obedience, are all examples of structural violence."

The issue of decision-making is important for Burton in discussing direct and indirect violence. In his section on academe and public servants, he argues that "power elites" gain from the current structures (or at least do not experience structural violence in any significant way) and they assume that problems "can be taken care of within the social and legal compliance frame." In his discussion of the workplace, however, Burton does note that those in control of a system can also be "victims" of the system. If decision makers remain within what Burton labels the "power" frame and thus rely on enforced or induced compliance, then violence at all levels is likely to be considered appropriate by those in, as well as those out of, power positions. But if decision-makers could better estimate anticipation of responses to their decisions, they could better cost out the consequences of pursuing particular policies and, most likely, contribute to a lessening of violence. However, to do this—to better get at the roots of a problem—there must be collaboration with all those concerned; then, agreements can be reached without compromising human needs. Burton therefore argues for an alternative decision-making process that is based on "direct communication by decision-makers with peoples who suffer the structural violence that are the source of problems."

IV. STRUCTURAL VIOLENCE IN PEACE RESEARCH AND PEACE ACTION

As we consider the future of the concept of structural violence, at least two basic questions can be asked. First, how useful is the concept for those doing peace research? Second, how useful is it for those involved in action for peace?

As indicated in the above review, at least some scholars in peace research have found the term helpful. Perhaps an answer to this question depends, in turn, on how peace research is defined—another subject of differing perspectives. In his 1969 essay, Galtung argued for an enlarged version of peace research, "defined as research into the conditions—past, present and fu-

ture—of realizing peace," one that would of necessity be "equally intimately connected with conflict research and development research; the former often more relevant for negative peace and the latter more relevant for positive peace, but with highly important overlaps." In asking if research should emphasize negative or positive peace, Galtung cautioned that "too much research emphasis on one aspect of peace tends to rationalize extremism to the right or extremism to the left, depending on whether one-sided emphasis is put on "absence of personal violence" or on "social justice" and that the two types of extremism are related formally, socially, and "in a dialectic manner: one is often a reaction to the other." He urged attention and action to both types of peace and rejected the "pessimistic" view (i.e., that one could not meaningfully work for both negative and positive peace) by pointing to the many forms of social action (citing, for example, the field of nonviolent action); the theoretical work on symmetric, egalitarian organization; the theory of vertical development; and approaches to arms control and disarmament issues. Finally, he concluded that peace research could make "a real contribution" by recognizing the double goal (i.e., concern with the conditions for promoting both aspects of peace) and aiming for both: "there is no reason to believe that the future will not bring us richer concepts and more forms of social action that combine absence of personal violence with fight against social injustice once sufficient activity is put into research and practice."

In his 1996 comprehensive work, Galtung highlights the notion he used in earlier works that views peace studies as "an applied science similar to medical studies or health science, informed by an underlying D, P, T paradigm (diagnosis, prognosis, therapy)." In peace studies, diagnosis refers to states of violence, prognosis to processes of violence (increase, same, decrease), and therapy to processes of violence reduction (negative peace) and processes of life enhancement (positive peace). Table IV presents Galtung's detailed systematization of peace and conflict studies, and the place of "structural violence" in that system. As pointed out earlier, structural violence is seen as one of three violences that must be addressed if we are to better understand social reality and if we are committed to reducing violence at all levels.

Nevertheless, as noted above, not all scholars in the peace research movement have embraced the concept of structural violence. Four basic arguments can be cited. First, some argue that the term cannot be made adequately operational. Second, some contend that even if one could make it more operational, it would still

TABLE IV

Systematization II of Peace and Conflict Studies: Some Examples of Fields of Education, Research, and Action[a,b]

Direct violence (DV)	Direct (positive) peace (DP)
N: "survival of the fittest"	N: "mutual aid and cooperation"
P: violence to self, suicide	P: intra-, interpersonal growth
S: violence across fault lines	S: nonviolent liberation
W: war geography; genocide	W: peace movements; alternative defense
C: culturocide	C: cultural liberation
T: history and future of violence, war	T: history and future of peace
Structural violence (SV)	Structural (positive) peace (SP)
N: ecocide	N: non-homocentric eco-peace
P: psychopathologies	P: intra-, inter-personal peace
S: patriarchie, racism, class	S: development, parity, equity
W: imperialism, trade	W: peace regions; governance, UN
C: cultural imperialism	C: cultural coexistence
T: history and future of exploitation and repression	T: sustainability of the above
Cultural violence (CV)	Cultural (positive) peace (CP)
Religion: transcendent	Religion: immanent
Law: democracy, human rights	Law: democracy, human rights
Ideology: universalist, singularist	Ideology: particularist, pluralist
Language: sexist, racist	Language: humanist/non-speciesist
Art: patriotic, patriarchy	Art: humanist/non-speciesist
Science I: Western logic?	Science I: Daoist? Buddhist?
Science II: to destroy life	Science II: to enhance life
Cosmology: Occident I? Sinic? Nipponic?	Cosmology: Occident II? Indic? Buddhic?
School: militarization	School: peace education
University: militarization	University: peace study and research
Media: war/violence journalism	Media: peace journalism

[a] *Source:* J. Galtung (1996, p. 33). Reprinted by permission of Sage Publications Ltd.
[b] Key: N = nature; P = person; S = social; W = world; C = culture; T = time.

not be helpful to theory-building because it is rooted ultimately in "value." Here, two critiques are offered. On the one hand is the observation that not all researchers (or participants in a system) would agree on the importance of the implicit values which seem to undergird the term; for example, equality, basic needs, and so on. Some would go so far as to say that structural violence equals whatever the researcher does not like. On the other hand are those whose concern is that the use of such a term will undermine the "objectivity" of the science project (although this charge can be made as well against other concepts, such as development with its implicit values). Third, some lamented the use of the term because it side-tracked important work. In 1977, Kenneth Boulding, for example, claimed that the term is really a "metaphor" rather than a model and, in his opinion, a bad model at that: the metaphor of structural violence is "that poverty, deprivation, ill health, low expectations of life, a condition in which more than half the human race lives, is 'like' a thug beating up the victim and taking his money away from

him in the street, or it is 'like' a conqueror stealing the land of the people and reducing them to slavery." While Boulding thought there is "some truth" to that metaphor, very different processes create the two and by using the metaphor Galtung "diverted attention" from the very real problem of the structures that lead to violence. Fourth, for some the term does not seem to go beyond what basic stratification theory and research already have to offer, so there is no advantage to using a term like structural violence.

For those who employ the term, on the other hand, several arguments are put forth in its favor. Some contend that in enlarging the focus of violence from the behavioral to the structural, the concept provides a means for moving beyond psychologistic interpretations (which can seem to suggest "fitting" an actor into an existing system) and thus, quite importantly, allows for challenges to that system itself. Second, the enlarged view is an advantage to those who are interested in decentering the "state" as the only or main actor of any importance in global analyses, making room for an examination of other actors, issues, and social forces which, they argue, are necessary for an understanding of peace. In this vein, structural violence calls for attention to a particular historical situation as well as for studies of that concrete reality in comparative perspective. Which leads to a third advantage to the term, namely, that researchers from other disciplines not typically seen as part of the peace research movement (e.g., humanities and philosophy) may be interested in making contributions from their perspectives because of this more expansive view of peace. In the process, a richer understanding of the complexities of peace and violence can be advanced. Finally, for some, precisely because structural violence does imply value(s), as would-be critics contend, it is more appealing to them as researchers; they do not subscribe to the paradigm of "value-free" knowledge. Some extend this position by pointing out that such a value position is important because it allows for links between the academy and the peace movement, which leads to the second major question: How useful is the structural violence concept to those involved in peace action?

There are both disadvantages and advantages. On the negative side, there is for some a simple antitheory stance. Concepts at the level of abstraction that structural violence seems to be, are to be avoided because they obfuscate reality. For others, there is the possibility that the term may evoke a determinism. Structural violence seems, in effect, to reduce if not eliminate the notion of human agency. Worse yet, the concept may engender a fatalism which precludes action. If things "are as they should be," one can do nothing except become resigned—hardly the impetus to individual or collective action. Relatedly, it can imperil those who are less interested in more macro analysis to the extent it seems to overcomplexify the situation, enervating them in the process or adding to their sense of powerlessness. It can also discourage those who are simply less experienced in structural analysis because, as with any structural analysis, there are not always clear, obvious implications for action. The impulse is to retreat to the local scene, restricting one's vision and energies to what can be "done" in one's own backyard. The challenge then becomes to engage in more holistic thinking, to diagnose structures in such a way that individuals can see their positions in them but can also perceive the possibilities for change, which leads to a discussion of the advantages of the term for those involved in peace action.

To label something as "violent" often carries with it a general cultural valence of negativity which can elicit, at least theoretically and possibly in concrete actions

as well, the rejection of any such situation so defined; it is "wrong" and it should be "righted." Second, structural violence contributes to a focus on the larger system and helps deflect the commonly used, "blame-the-victim" approach for the cause of social problems. Third and relatedly, for some actionists an analysis that calls attention to structural issues, as long as it is done in conjunction with attention to the individual level, can encourage (if not in fact demand) work on both levels: actions to alter the violent structures and processes, and personal decisions to lead one's own life in a conscious way so as to lessen the suffering of others. Here the theoretical as well as experience-based redefinitions of power from "power over" and power as "zero-sum" to "power with" and "power to" become central to individual action as well as to community capacity-building in attacking roots of structural violence.

Fourth, with the concept of structural violence, the links between justice and peace become key and the question of nonviolent action essential. Here, such concepts as interdependence, solidarity, and conscience constituency and such metaphors as the "web" and "spaceship Earth" can help sustain and motivate those working for peace. Here, too, the importance of developing skills of imagination and of working to construct cultures of peace and new identities (e.g., "world citizen" as Wright called it or "global citizen" as is used more frequently today) take on more urgency.

Fifth, this leads as well to a discussion of social change, social movements and actions to reduce or eliminate structural violence. How one defines "democracy" and "democratic structures" becomes key. If, for example, democratic structures are conceived as those in which people have some voice in the decisions that most affect their well being, the call for changes in the current world system as well as systems at lower levels of analysis (down to and including the family) becomes imperative. And finally, peace action calls for an examination of education. Learning about structural violence is a beginning step in acting against it. Gleaning principles of action against both direct and indirect violence becomes essential if indeed the purpose of the study of peace and violence is not simply to advance theory but also to contribute to the decrease of violence and the increase of structures and processes of peace in the global community.

Also See the Following Articles

CONFLICT TRANSFORMATION • ENVIRONMENTAL ISSUES AND POLITICS • INSTITUTIONALIZATION OF VIOLENCE • NONVIOLENCE THEORY AND PRACTICE • PEACE CULTURE •

Bibliography

Alcock, N., & Kohler, G. (1979). Structural violence at the world level: Diachronic findings. *Journal of Peace Research, 16*(3), 255–262.

Boulding, K. E. (1977). Twelve friendly quarrels with Johan Galtung. *Journal of Peace Research, 14*(1), 75–86.

Brock-Utne, B. (1989). *Feminist perspectives on peace and peace education.* New York: Pergamon Press.

Brock-Utne, B. (1997). Linking the micro and macro in peace and development studies. In J. Turpin & L. R. Kurtz (Eds.), *The web of violence: From interpersonal to global.* (pp. 150–160). Chicago: University of Illinois Press.

Burton, J. W. (1997). *Violence explained: The sources of conflict, violence and crime and their provention.* Manchester, UK: Manchester University Press.

Eisler, R. (1997). Human rights and violence: Integrating the private and public spheres. In J. Turpin & L. R. Kurtz (Eds.), *The web of violence: From interpersonal to global.* (pp. 161–185). Chicago: University of Illinois Press.

Galtung, J. (1964). An editorial. *Journal of Peace Research, 1*(1), 1–4.

Galtung, J. (1968). Peace. In *International encyclopedia of the social sciences* (Vol. 11, pp. 487–496). New York: The Macmillan Company and The Free Press.

Galtung, J. (1969). Violence, peace, and peace research. *Journal of Peace Research, 6*(3), 167–191.

Galtung, J. (1985). Twenty-five years of peace research: Ten challenges and some responses. *Journal of Peace Research, 22*(2), 141–158.

Galtung, J. (1990). Cultural violence. *Journal of Peace Research, 27*(3), 291–305.

Galtung, J. (1996). *Peace by peaceful means: Peace and conflict, development and civilization.* Oslo, Norway: PRIO, International Peace Research Institute.

Gilligan, J. (1996). *Violence: Our deadly epidemic and its causes.* New York: Putnam's.

Kazak, A. M. (1994). Belief systems and justice without violence in the Middle East. In P. Wehr, H. Burgess, & G. Burgess (Eds.), *Justice without violence.* (pp. 217–232). Boulder, CO/London: Lynne Rienner.

Lawler, P. (1995). *A question of values: Johan Galtung's peace research.* Boulder, CO: Lynne Rienner.

Mathiot (Moen), E. (1994). Attaining justice through development organizations in India. In P. Wehr, H. Burgess, & G. Burgess (Eds.), *Justice without violence.* (pp. 233–256). Boulder, CO/London: Lynne Rienner.

Webb, K. (1986). Structural violence and the definition of conflict. In *World encyclopedia of peace* (Vol. 2, pp. 431–434). Oxford, UK: Pergamon.

Wiberg, H. (1981). JPR 1964–1980—What have we learnt about peace? *Journal of Peace Research, 18*(2), 111–148.

Wright, Q. (1942). *A study of war: Volume II.* Chicago: University of Chicago Press.

Suicide and Other Violence toward the Self

David Lester

Center for the Study of Suicide

GLOSSARY

Attempted Suicide/Parasuicide/Deliberate Self-Harm Suicidal actions that the person survives.
Completed Suicide Suicidal actions that result in the person's death.
Self-Mutilation Mild self-injurious behavior without suicidal intent.

SUICIDE is a behavior in which an individual acts in such a way as to intentionally cause his or her death. Typically, the actions must result in death in a short period of time and directly, such as hanging oneself by a rope, in contrast to a behavior such as smoking heavily with the intent to increasing the risk of death by lung cancer in the distant future. Suicide can be viewed as an act of aggression directed toward the self.

I. SUICIDE AND SELF-DESTRUCTIVE BEHAVIORS

Suicidal behavior that results in the individual's death is called completed suicide. Many more individuals, perhaps 10 times as many, attempt to commit suicide but survive the attempt. These individuals are called attempted suicides, but scholars have questioned whether the majority of the attempters really intended to commit suicide. As a result, it has been suggested that attempted suicide be called parasuicide but, in more recent years, the terms self-injury and deliberate self-harm have become common. The lack of suicidal intent in many attempted suicides has also suggested that those making "gestures" at suicide may share traits and psychodynamic forces with those who inflict minor damage on themselves, self-mutilators. Self-mutilators may cut their bodies, insert objects into bodily orifices, bang their heads, and so on, actions that seem to involve no suicidal intent at all.

In contrast to these trends, which remove the notion of suicidal intent from the terms describing those who fail to die as a result of their own actions, some scholars have suggested broadening the concept of suicide. For example, Karl Menninger viewed any self-destructive or self-limiting behavior as motivated in part, consciously or unconsciously, by suicidal impulses. Thus, Menninger saw behaviors such as alcoholism and drug addiction as methods of shortening an individual's life, and he called these behaviors chronic suicide. Behaviors in which individuals destroy part of their body, such as blinding or castrating themselves, were labeled by Menninger as focal suicide, since the suicidal impulse appears to be focused on one part of the body, leaving the remainder of the person to survive.

II. THE EPIDEMIOLOGY OF SUICIDE

Officially reported rates of completed suicide in nations of the world are very stable from year to year, ranging from less than 1.0 per 100,000 per year in 1990 in Egypt and Kuwait to 39.9 in Hungary and 33.2 in Sri Lanka (see Table 1). The most notable trends include an increase in suicide rates over the last century in most nations, and an increase in youth suicide rates in many nations in the last 20 years.

Suicide rates tend to increase with age, especially for men in developed nations. In less developed nations, suicide rates peak at earlier ages, sometimes in those aged between 15 and 24. Official suicide rates are higher in men than in women in all nations of the world, with the exception of China, which has recently begun to report suicide rates indicating a higher suicide rate for women.

In contrast to the sex difference in completed suicides, most nations report a higher rate of attempted suicide in women than in men. One explanation for this sex difference focuses on the fact that men and women choose different methods for suicide, with men choosing the more lethal methods for which survival of the suicidal act is less likely. However, within each method for suicide, men die more often and women survive the act more often. Hormones (in particular testosterone) and cultural expectations may also play a role in causing this sex difference in suicidal behavior.

Suicide rates are higher in the more developed nations with a higher quality of life. National suicide rates are also predicted by social variables such as divorce (nations with higher divorce rates have higher suicide rates) and religion (with Islamic nations having lower suicide rates).

III. EXPLAINING THE SOCIAL SUICIDE RATE

Explanations for associations such as those mentioned above include direct social causation theories and composition theories.

TABLE I

Suicide Rates Around the World in 1990
(collected by David Lester)

Hungary	39.9	Puerto Rico	10.5
Sri Lanka	33.2[d]	Scotland	10.5
Finland	30.3	Uruguay	10.3
China	28.7[g]	Northern Ireland	9.9
Slovenia	27.6	Netherlands	9.7
Estonia	27.1	Ireland	9.5
Russian Federation	26.5	Romania	9.0
Lithuania	26.1	Portugal	8.8
Latvia	26.0	United Kingdom	8.1
Germany, East	24.4	Korea, South	8.0[c]
Denmark	24.1	England & Wales	7.8
Austria	23.6	Italy	7.6
Switzerland	21.9	Spain	7.5
USSR	21.1	Zimbabwe	7.4
Ukraine	20.7	Uzbekistan	6.8[e]
Belarus	20.3	Liechtenstein	6.7
France	20.1	Argentina	6.7
Belgium	19.3[a]	Taiwan	6.7
Czech Republic	19.3	Israel	6.5
Kazakhstan	19.1	Chile	5.6[a]
Czechoslovakia	17.9	Costa Rica	5.2
Luxembourg	17.8	Venezuela	4.8[d]
Germany, West	17.5	Barbados	4.7[b]
Germany	17.5[f]	Ecuador	4.6[b]
Sweden	17.2	Macao	4.4[c]
Japan	16.4	Panama	3.8[c]
Iceland	15.7	Tadjikistan	3.8[f]
Norway	15.5	Greece	3.5
Yugoslavia	15.3	Bahrain	3.1[b]
Bulgaria	14.7	Columbia	3.1[c]
Mauritius	14.2	Armenia	2.8
Trinidad & Tobago	13.7	Malta	2.3
New Zealand	13.5	Mexico	2.3
Singapore	13.1	St. Lucia	2.3[c]
Poland	13.0	Albania	2.1[a]
Australia	12.9	Maldives	2.0[c]
Canada	12.7	Bahamas	1.2[c]
Krygyzstan	12.5	Kuwait	0.8[c]
USA	12.4	Egypt	0.04[c]
Hong Kong	11.7		

[a] 1990 rates not available—1989 data.
[b] 1990 rates not available—1988 data.
[c] 1990 rates not available—1987 data.
[d] 1990 rates not available—1986 data.
[e] 1990 data not available—1991 data.
[f] 1990 data not available—1992 data.
[g] 1990–1994.

A. Social Causation Theories

The classic direct social causation theory was proposed by Emile Durkheim in 1897. He suggested that the levels of social integration (the extent to which the members of a society are bound together in social networks) and social regulation (the extent to which the desires and aspirations of the members of the society are restrained by social norms, customs, and values) caused the societal suicide rate. Societies with extremely high or extremely low levels of these two social characteristics would have high suicide rates, and the type of suicide depends upon the level of the social characteristic (see Table II).

Modern revisions of this theory have noted that it is difficult to distinguish operationally between social integration and social regulation and, perhaps therefore, they should be combined into one broad social characteristic. Furthermore, suicide resulting from very high levels of social integration and social regulation (that is, altruistic and fatalistic suicide) are rare in modern societies. Thus, a modern version of Durkheim's theory states that societal suicide rates are negatively associated with the level of social integration/regulation.

This theory has had some success also in predicting regional variations in suicide rates within a nation. For example, for the states of the United States, the suicide rate is negatively associated with the level of social integration (based on a cluster of measures such as divorce rates, interstate migration rates, church nonattendance, and alcohol consumption rates).

B. Composition Theories

Composition theories propose that societies with a high proportion of those at high risk of suicide will have a high suicide rate as a result of large numbers of these individuals committing suicide. So, if men, the elderly, and the divorced have higher suicide rates, societies with higher proportions of men, the elderly, and the divorced will have higher suicide rates.

TABLE II

Durkheim's Four Types of Suicide

very low social integration	egoistic suicide
very high social integration	altruistic suicide
very low social regulation	anomic suicide
very high social regulation	fatalistic suicide

There is some evidence that composition theories are not sufficient to explain regional variations in suicide rates. For example, although the divorce rate of the states of America is positively associated with the suicide rate of the states, the divorce rate of the states is positively associated also with the suicide rate of the married, the widowed, and the single, as well as the divorced. Thus, for example, states with higher divorce rates also have higher suicide rates among married people. It appears, therefore, that the divorce rate may be a measure of a broader social characteristic of the regions, perhaps social integration as suggested by Durkheim's theory.

IV. EXPLAINING INDIVIDUAL SUICIDES

The strongest predictor of individual suicides is psychiatric disorder. Those with a psychiatric diagnosis of affective disorder (which includes depressive disorders and manic-depressive disorders), schizophrenia, or substance abuse have higher rates of suicide than those with other diagnoses or with no psychiatric disorder. In addition, the level of depressed mood is a strong predictor of suicide.

In assessing individuals for their potential for suicide in the future, the most useful predictors, in addition to psychiatric diagnosis, are a history of previous suicidal ideation and suicide attempts, current suicidal ideation and planning, experience of severe stress in recent months, and having few friends and family to use as resources (for support, comfort, and problem-solving efforts) or having resources who are hostile toward you.

Recent research has focused on neurophysiological factors, in particular the neurotransmitter serotonin. At first, serotonin was thought to be critical in causing depression and thence suicidal behavior, but later research has identified serotonin dysfunction in other disorders, including obsessive-compulsive disorder, eating disorders, and such behaviors as arson. Current speculation is that serotonin may be associated with impulse control, and the association between serotonin dysfunction and suicidal behavior may be a reflection of the suicidal person acting impulsively on their self-destructive impulses.

The prediction of potential suicides is made difficult, however, by the statistical rarity of suicide. The suicide rate in the United States is about 12 per 100,000 per year. If we have a population of, say, 100,000, and our prediction instrument is 75% correct, this means that we will predict 9 of the 12 suicides correctly, and we will classify three of the suicides as nonsuicides (false negatives). However, we will also predict 24,997 of the 99,988 nonsuicides as suicides (false positives). So we would have to monitor 25,006 individuals in order to save 9 suicides!

V. THE RELATIONSHIP BETWEEN MURDER AND SUICIDE

Sigmund Freud, in psychoanalytic theory, saw suicide as the opposite of outwardly directed aggression. When an individual is angry at someone, but for some reason this anger is forbidden (perhaps it is anger toward a beloved parent) or blocked, then the anger can sometimes be repressed (become unconscious) and can be directed inward onto the self. As Edwin Shneidman once said, suicide is murder in the 180th degree.

This view was applied by Andrew Henry and James Short to societal suicide rates. They argued that when people in a society are stressed and exist in misery, they look for external agents to blame for their misery. If they can find external agents to blame for their misery, then they will become angry and, in the extreme, assaultive and murderous. However, if they cannot find external agents to blame for their misery, then they are more likely to blame themselves and become depressed and, in the extreme, suicidal. Thus, suicide rates and homicide rates should respond in opposite ways to social variables.

There is some evidence for this. For example, nations with a higher quality of life have higher suicide rates and lower homicide rates. In nations where the quality of life for everyone is higher, there are fewer external agents on whom to place the blame for one's misery, and so people are more likely to blame themselves. Thus, suicide rates will be relatively high and homicide rates will be relatively low. The reverse is true when the quality of life is poor. However, not all associations between societal suicide and homicide rates and social variables show these contrasting associations.

In many nations, the oppressed have higher homicide rates whereas the oppressors have higher suicide rates, as for example, for African Americans and European Americans in the United States. Again, the oppressed have clear external agents to blame for their misery and so will more often be angry and, in the extreme, homicidal; the oppressors have fewer external agents to blame for their misery and so will more often be depressed and, in the extreme, suicidal. Other explanations have been proposed for such differences in suicide and homicide. For example, Herbert Hendin has noted that some suicidal African Americans are also

outwardly violent, and he sees both forms of violence as a reaction to the overt racism and hatred to which African Americans have been exposed (see Lester, 1998).

In general, at the individual level, there is a great deal of evidence that suicidal individuals are quite angry. Suicidal psychiatric patients are among the most violent and difficult to manage, and psychological tests often show levels of physical, verbal and indirect hostility in suicidal individuals. Thus, murder and suicide do not show such a clear contrast at the individual level of analysis.

A. Suicidal Murderers and Murderous Suicides

There are a number of phenomena that combine both suicidal and murderous impulses and behaviors. Marvin Wolfgang drew attention to the fact that some murder victims play a role in precipitating the interpersonal conflict that results in their death. They may have started the argument or provoked the attacker in some way. Wolfgang called this behavior victim-precipitated homicide, and some commentators see this behavior as motivated in part by suicidal impulses, especially in those for whom suicide is an unacceptable behavior (perhaps it is a sin in their moral system). Wolfgang felt that about a quarter of the murder victims in his study of murder in Philadelphia were victim-precipitated. "Suicide by cop," in which a criminal acts in such a way as to make it likely that he will be killed as the police try to arrest him, may be a similar phenomenon.

Some suicidal individuals are thought to destroy themselves in response to the conscious or unconscious murderous impulses of others. The psychological theory of transactional analysis, proposed by Eric Berne, argues that suicidal individuals are responding to injunctions made to them when they were infants by their parents that they ought not to have existed and that they have no right to exist. Such injunctions may operate at the unconscious level. Adolescents may also be especially susceptible to such wishes on the part of their parents. Joost Meerloo called this phenomenon psychic homicide, killing someone by getting them to commit suicide.

Alan Felthous and Anthony Hempel have proposed a classification of cases of murder-suicide based on the relationship between the people. In the consortial type—possessive subtype, the offender, typically a man, kills his wife or lover because she has rejected him. He then kills himself, sometimes after also killing the rival. In the consortial type—physically-ailing subtype, either one or both partners may be very sick, and the murder-suicide is to spare both partners the pain of a drawn-out dying process and the loss of the partner. In the adversarial type, a disgruntled employee returns to the place of employment and murders those whom he holds responsible for his frustration, after which he typically commits suicide.

In the filial type, depressed or psychotic parents kill their children prior to committing suicide. Here the murder of the children seems to be a response by a suicidal parent who wants to commit suicide and decides to kill the children too, perhaps to "spare the children further suffering" (misguided altruism) or because the parent sees the children as extensions of himself or herself. Research indicates that the rate with which infants are murdered (both across nations and across regions within a nation) is associated with the suicide rate of the regions, and not with the murder rate.

In the familial type, a person, usually the man of the family under severe stress often accompanied by psychiatric disturbance, annihilates his complete family. In the pseudo-commando type, a person, again usually a man, selects a public place and tries to kill as many people as possible. These mass murderers are usually resolved by the murderer committing suicide or being killed by the police. Here the suicide seems to be a way of escaping from the consequences of the murderous acts.

VI. SUICIDE AND WAR

Emile Durkheim noted that suicide rates decline during wars, both in men and women, as they sometimes do in other types of crises. More recent studies have confirmed this phenomenon. The decline has been noted, not only in the armed forces, but also in civilians. Furthermore, the decline has been observed in nations that were at war and those that stayed neutral, and in both the victorious and the defeated nations.

Since this decline is evident for people of all age groups, the decline is not due to suicides being concealed by the armed forces or by the potential suicides going off to fight and being killed in battle. (Those aged over 65, for example, would not have been in the armed forces). Similarly, the decline in suicide rates in neutral nations suggests that the decline is not due to suicides during battle being covered up by means of phoney causes of death on the death certificate or by being labeled as "war casualties."

There is sometimes a high rate of suicide in the military leaders of the defeated nations. This was ob-

served, for example, in both Germany and Japan after the Second World War. There are no data on whether other groups in nations (defeated, victorious, or neutral) have high rates of suicide after a war.

A. Suicide in Concentration Camps

Research on suicide in Jews held in concentration camps in Germany and German-occupied territories during the Second World War indicates a high rate of suicide in the late 1930s prior to placement in the camps, but mainly among the elderly, a low rate of suicide in the camps, and a high rate of suicide after liberation. It has been suggested, following Durkheim's theory, that the low suicide rate of Jews in the concentrations camps might have been due to the increased social integration forced upon them by conditions in the camps and, following Henry and Short's theory, to the existence of a clear external source to blame for their misery.

It might be thought that the intensive supervision in the concentration camps may have prevented suicide, but a high suicide rate on death row in American prisons has been documented despite the intense supervision.

B. Compassionate and Bellicose Nations

Nations of the world have been rated for their "compassion," a dimension that includes measures of civil violence, land and income inequality, health and education expenditures, international cooperation, support for world order, and international wars. Suicide rates are higher in the more compassionate nations while homicide rates are lower. However, nations more involved in warfare during the last 150 years have a lower recent homicide rate expressed as a proportion of the total lethal violence rate (the suicide rate plus the homicide rate).

C. Explanations

There are three explanations that have been proposed for the decline in suicide rates during wars. First, Durkheim argued that, at least for major wars, war increases the level of social integration as the citizens unite against a common enemy, and thereby lowers the suicide rate. Perhaps also, war diverts peoples' attention away from their personal problems toward the larger issues of the society, which reduces the risk of suicide.

Second, war may have an impact on other social conditions, such as the economy (for example, unemployment), and these changes may result in the causal relationship between war and suicide rates.

Third, following Freud's psychoanalytic theory in which suicide is viewed as partly a result of blocked aggressive impulses, since war is a time of externally directed aggression, war may legitimate other-oriented aggression. Consequently, war should be associated with a relative drop in the suicide rate. Commentators, however, have preferred Durkheim's explanation.

Bibliography

Durkheim, E. (1897). *Le suicide.* Paris: Felix Alcan. English version (1951). *Suicide.* New York: Free Press.

Felthous, A. R., & Hempel, A. (1995). Combined homicide-suicides. *Journal of Forensic Sciences, 40,* 846–857.

Henry, A. F., & Short, J. F. (1954). *Suicide and homicide.* New York: Free Press.

Lester, D. (1997). *Making sense of suicide.* Philadelphia: Charles Press.

Lester, D. (1998). *Suicide in African Americans.* Commack, NY: Nova Science.

Litman, R. E. (1967). Sigmund Freud on suicide. *Psychoanalytic Forum, 1,* 206–214.

Maris, R. W., Berman, A. L., Maltsberger, J. T., & Yufit, R. I. (1992). *Assessment and prediction of suicide.* New York: Guilford.

Meerloo, J. A. (1962). *Suicide and mass suicide.* New York: Grune & Stratton.

Menninger, K. (1938). *Man against himself.* New York: Harcourt, Brace & World.

Retterstol, N. (1993). *Suicide: A European perspective.* New York: Cambridge University Press.

Wolfgang, M. E. (1958). *Patterns in criminal homicide.* Philadelphia: University of Pennsylvania Press.

Technology, Violence, and Peace

Brian Martin

University of Wollongong

GLOSSARY

Artifact Individual piece of hardware.
Big Science Large-scale, bureaucratized scientific research.
Little Science Small-scale, low-cost scientific research by individuals or small groups.
Nonviolent Defense An alternative to military defense relying on nonviolent action by civilians.
R&D (Research and Development) Scientific research and technological design, modification, and testing.
Sabotage Violence against technology.
Technological System (or Technological Ensemble) Collection of technical and social systems built around a single focus.
Technological Vulnerability The risk that a technological system will break down due to a certain threat.
Technology Artifact and related social aspects.
Weapon A tool for inflicting violence.

TECHNOLOGIES have long been used as tools for violence, from clubs and swords to cluster bombs and precision-guided missiles. In a less obvious way, tech-nologies are vital to creating or maintaining peace in a society. For example, ample provision of food and shelter involves many technologies for agriculture, construction, and transport. Technologies can also be used to support nonviolent action, as in the case of communication systems designed to thwart aggression or surveillance.

I. TECHNOLOGY

Technologies are commonly thought of as individual pieces of hardware, such as pens, cars, and computers. These can be called artifacts. These artifacts are never created or used in isolation from people. Instead, they are aspects of relationships between people and relationships between humans and the environment. For example, most pens are manufactured in factories and are the product of a long process of design. The materials used to manufacture the pen, such as steel and plastic, come from a prior process of mining and manufacture. The plants used to manufacture pens involve workers whose work is possible due to their own skills and training and is influenced by employers, governments, and labor markets. When using the pen, a writer depends on social skills, including literacy, and also on other artifacts such as paper. In these and many other ways, the pen as an artifact is embedded in many social worlds. The word "technology" can be used to refer to both the artifact and its associated social aspects.

All technologies are social in this sense. They are

created by humans and used by humans in social contexts. Therefore, in order to understand technologies it is necessary to understand their social contexts, including violence, peace, and conflict.

Technologies can be used for many purposes. For example, electronic mail can be used by armies and peace groups. Even so, every technology is typically easier to use for some purposes than others. Electronic mail is easy to use for sending messages, but it doesn't even make sense to use it to hit someone over the head. Thus, although technologies are multifunctional, they are never neutral.

Weapons are tools for inflicting violence. A bare hand or foot can be used as a weapon, but today the most commonly used weapons are technologies such as knives, rifles, and bombers. It is true that weapons can be used for nonviolent purposes. For example, a grenade can be used as a paperweight and a fuel-air explosive can be used as a piece of art. It is even possible to caress someone with the barrel of a rifle. But it is far more common to use these technologies to inflict violence, since that is what they were designed for.

There are many different theories of technology; some are more useful for thinking about technology in relation to violence and peace than others. To treat technologies as inherently good or bad is not helpful, since technologies have multiple uses. A more common view is that technologies are neutral. It is true that many technologies can be used for both good and bad purposes, and for different purposes. But usually neutrality is taken to have a stronger meaning, such as that technologies are equally easy to use for different purposes, which is not helpful when comparing compact disks and cruise missiles. The approach taken here, a standard one in studies of technology, is that technologies are constructed for specific purposes and, as a result, are usually easier to use for those purposes. Users can choose and modify technologies for their own purposes but are constrained by the physical reality of artifacts and the inertia of associated social systems.

There is a lot of writing about the ways that society influences technologies. On the one side is the view that technologies are autonomous, following their own trajectories. On the other side is the view that technologies are largely determined by their origins and inevitably serve the purposes of their creators. A middle view is that technologies are "shaped" by the social conditions and groups that led to their creation but, once created, they can, within limits, be directly used or modified for other purposes.

It is conventional to think of humans and technologies as different categories: humans think, act, and design technologies, whereas technologies are not beings in the same sense. This conceptual division is breaking down somewhat as technologies take over more human functions ("thinking" by computers) and as technologies become part of humans (most dramatically as prostheses but more commonly as extensions of human senses and capabilities such as telephones for speaking and vehicles for moving). One perspective on technology is based on rejecting the conceptual distinction between humans and artifacts, referring to both as "actants" and analyzing the way different actants enroll support, resist change, and so forth. This perspective can provide a refreshing perspective on the dynamics of technological societies. Nevertheless, for the account here, a conventional picture is used distinguishing between artifacts and humans.

Technologies can be divided into two categories. First are those that are designed and most useful for violence and violent conflict. These are discussed in Section II. In the second category are all other technologies. The role of technologies in peace and nonviolent conflict is covered in Section III.

An overall conclusion is that each mode of dealing with conflict is associated with characteristic forms of technology. Some of the points raised in Sections II and III are summarized below.

Typical Technologies Associated with Methods of
Dealing with Conflict

Military forces: tanks, ships, bombers, radar, nuclear weapons
Defensive-only military forces: fighter aircraft and other weapons that cannot be used for offense
Guerrilla forces: small arms
Nonviolent defense: network communication systems, self-reliant energy systems
Negotiation: (technologies are not crucial)

II. TECHNOLOGY FOR VIOLENT STRUGGLE

A. Technology and the History of War

The human species is distinctive for its tremendous use of tools—another word for technologies. A few other species make limited use of tools, but for humans it has long been impossible to imagine society without tools; everything from sticks for knocking fruit from trees to clothing, roads, and electricity. Probably from the earliest use of tools, humans have used them for inflicting violence, including rocks and pointed sticks to kill animals and, sometimes, to attack other humans. Quite simple tools can be used to inflict horrific violence, and even today some mass killings are carried out largely by clubs and spears.

Weapons can be used to kill and subjugate other people. A society with a more powerful weapon can use it to help conquer others. In societies without agriculture, there is little to gain economically by conquering other people. Conflict between such societies often serves to maintain social cohesion, maintaining the in-group against the out-group. Battles are largely ritualistic, with few individuals hurt or killed. The technologies used in such conflicts are largely adapted from those used to hunt animals. There is little incentive for developing new technologies of violence.

With the development of agriculture some thousands of years ago, a new dynamic appeared. Agriculture depended on knowledge and artifacts for understanding and controlling natural cycles of plant life and required greater control of social life; for example, to ensure that adequate amounts of food and seed were preserved over the winter months. Agriculture was accompanied by the development of greater social differentiation, with individuals specializing in tasks such as producing agricultural implements and constructing major buildings. Agriculture made possible a greater surplus of food and goods, allowing some, such as priests, to live off the work of others. The gradual improvement of agricultural technology created greater surpluses, allowing more specialized roles and enabling innovation in other areas such as building.

With agriculture's greater surpluses came the possibility of attacking and subjugating another society in order to control that society and use its surpluses. This situation stimulated the production of weapons of attack and, in response, weapons of defense. The refining of new metals such as bronze and iron was used for producing more effective spears and arrows and, in defense, shields and armor.

For the past several thousand years, military priorities have played a significant role in technological development. For example, many early European cities were designed so that they could be defended against invaders, with a central area surrounded by city walls. Many inventors, such as Archimedes and Leonardo da Vinci, worked at developing more potent weapons.

On the other hand, technologies have repeatedly transformed the nature of warfare. The machine gun, for example, developed in the latter half of the 1800s, made it possible to overwhelm an opponent armed only with rifles. The British military used machine guns in defeating much larger forces in many of its colonial wars. In World War I, the machine gun gave a decisive advantage to the defense, and millions of men were killed in futile attempts to storm positions defended by machine guns. The development of the armored tank, in contrast, was a great advantage to the attacking side, used most decisively in early German victories in World War II. Since then, the development of nuclear weapons and long-distance delivery by bombers and missiles has created a mode of war preparation based on "deterrence," namely the threat to retaliate against attack with massive nuclear destruction.

These are only a few examples of the historical role of weapons. As technologies designed and mainly used for violence, weapons have played a key role in social evolution. Even those technologies that seem "peaceful," such as roads and factories, have been influenced by military priorities. More importantly, though, technologies have made possible ever-more-destructive forms of warfare.

B. Types of Technology Used for Violence

There are various ways to classify technologies used for violence. Military forces are commonly divided into the branches of army, navy, and air force. Each has its own characteristic types of technology. Army: jeeps, tanks, cannons, ground-launched missiles; navy: destroyers, battleships, submarines, sea-launched missiles; air force: fighters, bombers, air-launched missiles.

Only some technologies are really specific to these branches. Machine guns and explosives are used by all of them. Missiles are much the same whether launched from ground, sea, or air. In the former Soviet Union, a fourth branch of the military was the "missile forces."

Another way to classify weapons is by the primary means by which they cause destruction. Four categories are normally used.

1. Nuclear weapons, sometimes called atomic weapons, are explosives whose power comes from fission and/or fusion reactions involving atomic nuclei. Their effects include blast, heat, and radiation. Some radiation is short term, including neutrons, whose effect is enhanced in nuclear weapons called neutron bombs. Other radiation, especially fallout, is long term. It is also possible to have radiological weapons based on radiation from nuclear sources in the absence of an explosion.

2. Chemical weapons are chemicals, such as napalm and sarin, that wound or kill by direct contact with humans. They can be delivered in various ways such as by artillery shells or missiles.

3. Biological weapons are disease organisms, such as anthrax, that cause illness or death in humans.

Like chemical weapons, they can be delivered in various ways.

4. "Conventional" weapons are traditional weapons such as rifles and explosives. The explosive force behind these weapons is usually based on chemical reactions. But they are not called chemical weapons because they cause destruction primarily by physical processes, such as when a body is hit by a bullet or by shell fragments from a grenade, land mine, or artillery shell.

As well as nuclear, chemical, biological, and conventional weapons, there are also some other categories. So-called environmental weapons are based on triggering natural processes, such as earthquakes and tidal waves, by artificial means such as explosives.

Another important category is the "technology of repression," namely technologies used for torture, incarceration, area control, and surveillance. If military aggression is the use of force to attack, repression is the use of force to control. The technology of repression includes electroshock devices, leg shackles, trauma-inducing drugs, guillotines, plastic bullets, chemical irritants, night vision cameras, automatic vehicle tracking systems, telephone-tapping equipment, and human identity recognition systems. It also includes associated systems for production, skills, and training to use such equipment, including technical support and training in interrogation, torture, and assassination. Some of the technologies used for repression are just different uses of everyday technologies, such as cigarettes or electrical circuits used in torture or computer databases used to keep tabs on dissidents. Others are specially designed for the purpose, such as prefragmented exploding ammunition.

"Nonlethal weapons" are weapons designed not to kill or maim. They include electrical stunners, infrasound beams to cause disorientation, and chemical sprays. Many nonlethal weapons are used for repression.

Weapons are an important part of the technology of violence, but weapons can only exist if there are other technological support systems. Here are some of the components.

• Industrial systems are used to produce most weapons today. For example, artillery shells are produced in factories. This in turn requires designing and building the factory itself, training the workers, inspecting the products (quality control), and adapting to new specifications.

• Transport systems are needed to get weapons to battlefields, to move troops, and to serve the requirements of industrial systems.

• Communication systems are needed to plan and coordinate military operations, to gain information about enemy activities, and to coordinate industrial production.

• Various support systems are needed to sustain military operations. These include agriculture to produce food, energy to power transport and industry, and others including water, sewage, and medical services. In so-called "total war," such as World War II, nearly every sector of society is mobilized to support the war effort, including clothing workers, teachers, and artists. Technology plays a role in every sector in society and thus is implicated in the social mobilization for total war.

• "Weapons systems" are the full complexes of technologies that support a particular weapon. For example, a jet aircraft on its own is almost useless. It requires, among other things, fuel supply systems; regular and often intensive maintenance; spare parts; landing fields; weapons (such as missiles); training facilities for pilots; and research and development (R&D) efforts to design, build, and test the aircraft.

All weapons need to be understood in the context of associated technological and social systems. Even an apparently simple item such as a bullet exists only because of a complex of technological systems. So rather than referring to an artifact or a technology, sometimes it is useful to refer to a "technological ensemble," which is the full collection of technical and social systems built around a single focus. Rather than think of a submarine as an isolated piece of technology, it is helpful to think of it as a technological ensemble involving systems for design, manufacture, maintenance, communication, supply, training, and many other functions.

C. Characteristics of Technology Used for Violence

Since technologies have many potential uses, there is no definitive way to characterize technologies used for violence. Nevertheless, there are some criteria that provide insight.

1. Destructive Power

Weapons are typically oriented to destruction. Some bullets are designed to wobble in flight so that they destroy much larger amounts of human flesh. Fuel-air explosives are designed to maximize the destructive power of conventional chemical components; some of them have the explosive power of a small nuclear weapon.

However, destructive power alone does not distinguish a weapon from a nonweapon. For example, explosives used in mining can be extremely powerful.

2. Centralized Control

The ideal military weapon is one that can be totally controlled by the user but cannot be controlled—that is, resisted or evaded—by the enemy. Land mines, for example, are laid at the discretion of the user but are designed to be difficult to detect and defuse by others. A cruise missile, once launched, is extremely difficult to intercept and destroy before reaching its target.

Centralized control might be a military ideal, but it is never achieved. One problem is that other militaries often can obtain the same weapons. Both sides can use land mines and cruise missiles. Even nuclear weapons, subject to the tightest controls, cannot be monopolized. Many governments have developed them, and there remains the possibility of criminal or terrorist use.

Centralized control is not just a military goal. Many corporations, for example, seek to control production of goods, for example through secrecy and patents. As well, some types of weapons, such as guns, are widely available in at least some countries. Centralized control thus is a characteristic of some weapons systems but by itself does not distinguish weapons from nonweapons.

3. Offensive versus Defensive Weapons

It is common to distinguish between offense and defense in military operations, though often both sides claim to be defending rather than attacking. Technologies can be classified according to whether they are useful for offense. Technologies of offense include bombers and intercontinental ballistic missiles. Technologies that are not so useful for attack include fortifications, bomb shelters, antiaircraft artillery, and short-range fighter aircraft. A military system based around technologies that cannot easily be used for attack is called "nonoffensive defense" or "defensive defense."

Offensive weapons are often justified on the basis that they will deter attack. The classic case is nuclear deterrence, based on the threat to destroy enemy facilities or population centers if the enemy launches an attack.

4. Participation

When lots of people can use a technology it can be called "participatory." Some weapons are participatory, such as knives and rifles, whereas others are not, such as battleships and tanks. The most participatory weapons are those that can be used by individuals without much training and which can be cheaply produced in large numbers. For mass armies, from the French Revolution to the Iraq–Iran war in the 1980s, participatory weapons are commonly used. However, the trend in military R&D is to develop weapons that are less participatory, such as submarines and supersonic aircraft.

Two contrasting modes of warfare are (a) regular military forces led by and sometimes composed entirely of full-time professional soldiers and (b) guerrilla forces, which are "irregular" fighters typically operating by harassment and typically against regular forces that have standard large-scale equipment and control of major transport routes. Guerrillas are often drawn from the local population and have little formal military training. As a result, guerrillas typically use more participatory weapons such as rifles, traps, and explosives. This is partly due to the need to escape detection (a jet fighter is hard to conceal), partly due to lack of resources, and partly due to lack of skills and support personnel to maintain complex weapons systems. However, with the development of sophisticated small weapons that can be purchased more or less "ready to use," such as portable rocket-launchers, some guerrilla forces are upgrading their weapons. When guerrilla forces are successful militarily and begin to control substantial areas, typically they also acquire more large-scale military equipment.

It would be quite possible to produce vast numbers of deadly weapons that anyone could use, but few governments seek to arm their populations when it is not wartime. Those that do or have—most notably Switzerland, Sweden, and former Yugoslavia—usually restrict people to hand weapons such as rifles and do not routinely make available grenades, bazookas, land mines, nerve gases, or mobile missile launchers, though they may be trained in using some of these.

D. Gender and Technologies of Violence

Males carry out most of the physical violence in the world, both at an individual level and at an organized level, especially violence by militaries. Military and police forces are predominantly male, especially so in front-line positions. Since male domination is closely associated with violence and with the institutions—namely the police and the military—that are authorized by the state to use violence, it is to be expected that there might be some relation between gender and technologies of violence.

Some technologies for violence are designed for men, who tend to be larger and stronger than women. Many weapons, such as heavy swords and guns, are difficult to use for those who are small or relatively weak and thus are oriented to men. But this connection is not a tight one, since some women are larger and stronger than many men. It is better to say that such technologies are designed for certain types of people—those of a certain size and strength. These technologies are designed for young fit men, who are more likely to be selected for the military and police, and are hard to use by most women as well as by children, the elderly, people with disabilities, and men who don't fit the standard model.

It is quite possible to design many technologies so that size and strength do not affect one's ability to them. Pressing the buttons to launch nuclear weapons does not require any special size or strength. As soon as weapons become mechanically powered and automated, strength is largely irrelevant, and so in principle gender should become irrelevant. Yet gender divisions remain extremely strong even in the most technologically sophisticated military forces, especially in the production and use of weapons.

Gendered work roles are quite pronounced in factories, including weapons factories. Production work with certain technologies is conceived as a male domain, but the definition of what is a male task changes with time. For example, in the early days of the typewriter, typing was considered a male task. Later it became an overwhelmingly female area of employment. With the spread of word processors, it is more common for both sexes to use keyboards. A similar pattern is apparent in many areas involving weapons. Certain technologies are defined as male or female domains, even though in many cases there appears to be no objective reason for this assignment.

The patterns of gendered use of weapons suggest that male domination often shapes production and use of technologies of violence more than military efficiency. Militaries remain largely composed of young fit men even in highly technological forces where women and other poorly represented groups could be equally or more effective in the roles. In these situations, some technologies are gendered by design, but the most important factor is the imposition of gendered identities and uses on technologies.

E. Violence, Technology, and Social Organization

Through the ages, warfare has affected the way that societies are organized. One example is the rise of the modern state in Europe. Governments sought to maintain large standing armies in order to defend against enemies and needed new sources of money to pay the soldiers. New bureaucracies were established to collect taxes; the military was used to compel compliance. Warfare was thus integral to the development of the modern bureaucratized state.

In a few cases, the role of technology in such military-influenced social changes can be seen. For example, during the 1800s some railway lines in Europe were built so that they could transport troops to front lines. The pattern of railway development in turn influenced commercial transport.

With the rise of total warfare in the 1900s, the entire economic system is mobilized for war. This has led to the imposition of a command economy by governments, with centralized control over investments, distribution, and labor. During World War II, command economies were imposed in England and the United States as well as in the dictatorships of the Soviet Union and Nazi Germany where government control was already substantial. To run a command economy, it is helpful for military production to be organized in large factories, whose activities are easier to control centrally than production that is dispersed geographically and organizationally. Since the military itself runs on a command system, it might be said, then, that factory production fits into a military model. At a very general level, there are affinities between the military, as an organization of humans and technologies to exercise force, and factories, as command systems for industrial production.

Technologies of violence can also influence social relationships at a more intimate level. In societies where guns are routinely used for crime, people who are afraid are more likely to stay home and barricade themselves behind locked doors and windows. Although it is quite possible to attack someone with bare fists, various technologies, including shoes, brass knuckles, knives, and guns, increase the potential harm from assault. This in turn triggers technological development for protection or retaliation, ranging from alarms, bullet-proof vests, incapacitating sprays, and guns.

Technologies used for violence thus are implicated in the way people relate to each other at the face-to-face level as well as in the organization of factories, transport, and energy systems. But there has not been much study of these connections, so it is difficult to make definite conclusions about the connections between technologies and social organization.

F. Science, Engineering, and Technologies for Violence

Technologies are based on human manipulation, construction, and organization of materials. Engineering is a field whose primary activity is designing, developing, and maintaining technologies. Similarly, knowledge is based on human construction and organization of ideas. Science is a field whose primary activity is developing and testing knowledge about the natural world.

Before the 1900s, technological development, including weapons development, was primarily a matter of practical insight combined with trial and error. Early scientific theories seldom were used by inventors or manufacturers. Instead, often it was technological innovation that stimulated scientific theory. For example, science contributed little to the development of the steam engine, whereas the practical reality of the steam engine triggered the development of the laws of thermodynamics.

Beginning in the late 1800s, this situation began to change. In the German chemical industry, for example, scientific knowledge about synthesis of chemicals was used in developing systems for manufacturing them. In the years since, there has been an ever closer interaction between scientific knowledge and technological development, each being used to stimulate the other. For example, theoretical investigations into the field of numerical analysis (a branch of mathematics) sometimes have spin-offs in practical applications; at the same time, practical developments in computing sometimes stimulate new theoretical investigations. The interaction between knowledge and technology is so routine that it can be misleading to distinguish between them. Although terms such as "scitech" have not caught on, the word "technology" today often implies the involvement of science and the word "science" assumes a role for technology. This is true of weapons as much as anything else.

In the past century, weapons design, development, and production has become a carefully planned process involving scientific and engineering expertise. The single most important event in the mobilization of science and engineering for war and violence was World War II, during which time scientists and engineers in many countries—including Britain, Germany, the Soviet Union, and the United States—were put to work to aid the war effort. This led to rapid developments in many areas, including ballistics, explosives, manufacturing processes, cryptography (the study of codes), radar, and, most famously, nuclear weapons.

To be sure, scientists had applied their talents to war-making on many previous occasions. World War II was a turning point in that, for the first time, many governments systematically organized scientific talent for the purpose of making war. The most important case was the U.S. Manhattan Project, set up to produce nuclear weapons. This involved hundreds of top scientists and engineers, massive expenditure, and the establishment of organizational structures to harness intellectual and technical work for military purposes.

After the war, the military mobilization of science and engineering continued, often justified by the imperatives of the Cold War between the United States and the Soviet Union and their respective allies. Governments poured massive amounts of funding into science and engineering, much of it directly into military projects and much of the rest into areas with potential military spin-offs, such as microelectronics, meteorology, oceanography, and aeronautics. World War II thus symbolized a transition from "little science" to "big science." Little science was characterized by small projects run on a low budget by one or just a few scientists, often carried out by amateurs or university professors. Big science, by contrast, is characterized by large-scale projects with mammoth budgets and involving dozens or hundreds of scientists, typically funded by government or sometimes by industry.

One of the important features of big science is its bureaucratic nature. Whereas little science was—and still is to some extent—done at the initiative of individuals who relate to colleagues in their field as independent professionals, big science involves large teams organized bureaucratically, with direction from the top, both from funders and team leaders. The transition to big science was brought about largely by military projects, but now many civilian research enterprises are also run on the same lines.

In the United States, most military funding comes from the federal government but much of the R&D is carried out by industry, such as by automobile, aircraft, and chemical companies. The close link between military and industry is called the "military–industrial complex," a term that indicates the mobilization of industrial enterprises for military purposes and has also been referred to as "Pentagon capitalism." The application of science and technology for violence is central to the military–industrial complex, which is sometimes therefore called the scientific–military–industrial complex. Similar complexes are found in major arms-producing capitalist countries, such as Britain, France, Germany,

Italy, and Switzerland. In the former Soviet Union, on the other hand, industry was run directly by the government and the term is not so relevant.

In bureaucratized military R&D, individual scientist and engineers are cogs in a large enterprise. Often they work on specific tasks, such as some detailed aspect of developing a computer program or a propulsion system, which seems to have little immediate relevance to military purposes. Scientists are primarily problem-solvers and engineers are primarily makers, and they can carry out their tasks with little or no awareness of the end products and larger context of which their work is a part. This is similar to the factory worker on an assembly line whose narrow tasks are much the same whether the product is a car or an armored personnel carrier. Bureaucratic organization and large-scale projects thus help to insulate many scientists and engineers from the ultimate uses of the things they help produce.

G. Technological Vulnerability

Today's technological societies are remarkably vulnerable to breakdown or sabotage. Disabling a few key power stations and transmission lines could cripple electricity supplies; computer viruses can disable communication networks; deadly toxins in central water supplies could kill vast numbers of people. These technological vulnerabilities are especially acute in the case of military attack. A few bombs on key industrial facilities or communication nodes would be devastating. A single nuclear power plant, if targeted for attack, could release massive quantities of radiation into neighboring areas.

The only way to defend against attack on crucial facilities, it seems, is by military preparedness that will stop any aggressor at a country's borders or before. Since missiles can now penetrate many defenses, this becomes an argument for deterrence, namely developing the capacity and making the threat of counterattack in force. Technological vulnerabilities thus provide a justification for "forward defense," namely the capacity for military offense.

One way to reduce technological vulnerabilities is to create differently structured technological systems, often decentralized ones. An energy system based around energy efficiency and local renewable energy sources, for example, is far less vulnerable to a few bombs or saboteurs than centralized power sources. The Internet—which was originally designed by the military to survive a nuclear attack—is far less vulnerable to attack or military coup than a small number of large television and radio stations. Technological

systems based on networks, self-reliance, and low hazard are generally more resilient in the face of attack than centralized, expert-dependent, and potentially risky systems.

The issue of technological vulnerability illustrates how technological choice even in ostensibly nonmilitary areas can affect the need for military defense. Large-scale military weapons systems, including aircraft carriers, nuclear submarines, and ICBMs, are themselves prime vulnerabilities in the event of war and thus help justify their own existence.

III. TECHNOLOGY FOR PEACE AND NONVIOLENT STRUGGLE

Advocates of military defense sometimes argue that weapons—including weapons of mass destruction— are technologies for peace, since they operate to deter attack by enemies. Whatever one's assessment of this viewpoint, weapons are technologies for violence. In this section the focus is on technologies that are not designed for violence. Some of these are especially useful for preventing war; others are especially useful for dealing with conflict using nonviolent means or, in other words, waging nonviolent struggle.

A. Technology for Arms Control

When governments enter into treaties or agreements to control their armaments, there is often a suspicion that the other side might be cheating. One way to monitor treaties is by direct inspection of the other side's military facilities, but sometimes that is banned or restricted on the grounds that military secrets might be revealed. Another approach is to use technological means for monitoring compliance.

One example concerns the testing of nuclear weapons, which many militaries desire in order to ensure that their arsenals will work. In the 1940s and 1950s, atmospheric nuclear explosions could be detected by monitoring the levels of radiation in the atmosphere. Since the 1960s, earth-orbiting satellites have been used to look for tell-tale characteristics of nuclear explosions. When some governments agreed that all underground nuclear tests larger than a certain strength would be prohibited, compliance was checked by sensitive seismic equipment that can detect tremors in the earth at great distances.

Monitoring technologies are the most common ones used for arms control. Monitoring technologies are commonly used for military purposes, as in the case of surveillance satellites, but can be readily turned to the task of providing information to those aiming to limit the deployment or testing of weapons.

B. Economic Conversion

When technologies are changed from military production to civilian production, this is called "economic conversion" or "peace conversion." It has long been a routine occurrence in the aftermath of wars. Factories that produced jeeps are converted to produce cars, and facilities used to produce military electronics are converted to produce civilian electronics. Economic conversion is the opposite of military conversion, which routinely occurs before and during wars as economies are mobilized to support the military struggle.

Economic conversion is not just a matter of changing production from weapons to civilian goods. It involves a host of factors, including retooling of production facilities, designing products appropriate for civilian use, and retraining workers. One important change is in the market for goods produced. Much military-related production is made to order according to military specifications with a guaranteed purchaser: the military itself. For civilian production, sales are often less predictable. A different mindset is needed for competing in the market.

Up to and including the aftermath of World War II, economic conversion was not too difficult since factories that produced military goods relied on basic manufacturing processes such as metalworking. In recent decades, though, military technologies have become far more military specific. Today, many weapons are so highly specialized that it is far more difficult to convert facilities that civilian purposes. For example, facilities that produce missiles or nuclear submarines have few immediate civilian applications. This applies as much to the skills of scientists and engineers as it does to the actual buildings and equipment.

Even when military facilities can be converted, they lead down certain technological paths. For example, military aircraft engineers might turn their skills to high-speed mass transit; their skills and orientation are less likely to lead them to designing bicycles or cycleways. The result is that some civilian technologies and priorities are influenced by a past history of military investment. The most notable example is the push for nuclear power which drew heavily on personnel, skills, and commitments originally developed to produce nuclear weapons.

Many local communities and peace activists have devoted huge efforts at making economic conversion work. In many cases the task is enormous. The difficulties are in part a consequence of what can be called "technological momentum." The investments in military facilities create a continuing incentive—a momentum—to maintain themselves. This is partly due to the physical infrastructure of buildings and tools, partly due to the investment in training and development of skills, and partly due to workers and local communities developing ways of living that are tied to the facilities. Technologies by themselves do not perpetuate themselves, but humans can develop a strong adherence to behaviors that are linked to continuing the established technological framework. The more militarized the technological infrastructure, the greater the difficulty of economic conversion.

C. Technology for Nonviolent Action

Conflict can be waged by both violent and nonviolent means. The role of technology in violent struggle is well known, but technology can also play an important role in nonviolent action.

Some methods of resolving conflict, such as mediation and arbitration, are essentially human techniques. Technology such as pens, charts, or videoconferencing facilities can play a supportive role, but it is seldom vital to the success of such methods. Technology is more fundamental to what is called nonviolent action or nonviolent struggle.

Methods of nonviolent action include symbolic actions such as speeches, rallies, and marches; noncooperation such as boycotts and strikes; and interventions such as fasts and sit-ins. When thinking about methods such as speeches, strikes, or sit-ins, the main focus is on human bodies; technology seems incidental, such as the microphones used by a speaker. This is partly because activists have not paid much attention to the role of technology in waging nonviolent struggle.

1. Technology for Nonviolent Defense

To illustrate the role that technology can play in nonviolent action, it is useful to consider the case of defense against aggression or repression using nonviolent means. This is called nonviolent defense, social defense, civilian defense, or civilian-based defense. It is the application of the methods of nonviolent action for defending a community from military attack or authoritarian rule.

There are several factors that are important for the success of nonviolent defense. The most crucial are psychological and organizational factors, including the morale, unity, and will of the nonviolent resistance; the knowledge, understanding, and strategy of the resistance; and the coordination, decision-making, and leadership of the resistance. To improve the capacity of the resistance in these areas, psychological and sociological research and testing is valuable. Technology is not central to these areas.

Another set of factors, under the general heading of physical infrastructure, is also important. This includes communication systems; industrial production and distribution; and systems ensuring human survival, including food, water, clothing, shelter, energy, transport, and health. Technology is heavily involved in all these areas.

2. Communication Technology for Nonviolent Defense

Consider communication, probably the most important factor in nonviolent defense involving technology. An aggressor normally seeks to control means of communication. In a military coup, the first targets are television and radio stations. If a population is dependent on mass media—television, radio, and major newspapers—for information, it is vulnerable to political control by a small group. For effective communication in a nonviolent struggle, it is far better to use network media, including the mail service, telephone, fax, short-wave radio, and electronic mail. All of these use technology to enable one-to-one interaction. If there is a dense network of network media, then it becomes very difficult for a ruler to control the population.

After the Indonesian invasion of East Timor in 1975, the occupying forces tried to prevent any communication with the rest of the world. The Australian government aided this effort by shutting down a radio transmitter in the Northern Territory that was a link to the East Timorese resistance (which included both nonviolent and armed guerrilla components). In 1991, a journalist was able to film some of the brutal actions of the Indonesian military and smuggle a video out of the country. The subsequent worldwide publicity greatly helped the East Timorese cause.

After the Chinese government crushed the prodemocracy movement in Beijing in 1989, it publicized a phone line for citizens to inform on those who were involved in the movement. Prodemocracy supporters were able to communicate with supporters outside China using fax machines, which were not controlled centrally. Numerous callers around the world called the phone line in order to block its use by the Chinese government.

These are examples of how communication technology is crucial to nonviolent action. Just as R&D is vital in developing military technologies, so too is it vital in improving communication technology for nonviolent purposes. For example, telephone systems can now be monitored centrally, making it relatively easy for a repressive government to listen in or disrupt particular lines. In a nonviolent defense system, telephone systems would be designed so that central monitoring is either impossible or is able to be disabled in a crisis.

3. Survival Technology for Nonviolent Defense

Other technological systems vital to a nonviolent resistance are those that enable survival of the population. If the food supply, for example, is heavily dependent on fertilizers, pesticides, and transport systems, then it is possible to punish a population that refuses to acquiesce by disrupting food production and distribution. The food supply is less vulnerable to disruption if it relies more on local gardens. Rather than develop knowledge, skills, and technologies for monocultures and large-scale harvesting, the orientation would be toward knowledge, skills, and technologies to develop fruit-bearing trees, plants that are easy to cultivate in small local gardens, and convenient means of preserving food, among other possibilities. In the intifada, the unarmed Palestinian resistance to Israeli rule from 1987–1993, local food production was important, since the Israeli occupiers often punished the population by imposing long curfews, banning travel, and closing shops.

The basic strategy behind a physical infrastructure to support nonviolent action is to improve self-reliance of the population. This includes systems for energy, water, transport, and health.

In the case of industry, an aggressor may wish to run factories for its own purposes. It would be possible to design equipment so that it can be disabled by the workers in case of an emergency. For example, crucial software could be written that would irreversibly scramble the computer operating system if a suitable number of workers anonymously keyed in special individual codes. A back-up system could be stored safely, for example, in another country. With such a system, the workers could not be forced to get the system going, since they would lack the technical ability. In a sense, the resistance would be built into the technology.

4. R&D Priorities for Nonviolent Defense

The priorities for R&D for a system of nonviolent defense would be quite different from those for a military system. Military funding and priorities have helped shape the strong research emphasis on the natural sciences and engineering, which are especially relevant to weapons systems. In contrast, R&D for nonviolent defense would place much more emphasis on the social sciences, since factors such as morale, strategy, and coordination are central to organized nonviolent struggle.

A reorientation to nonviolent defense would also change the emphasis within numerous fields of study. Within materials engineering for example, the emphasis would shift from materials that can be used in weapons to materials that could be used by a people to build their own houses easily and simply. Within psychology, the emphasis would shift from ways to make soldiers more ready and able to kill during combat to ways to help nonviolent resisters sustain their commitment in the face of divide-and-conquer tactics. These are crude examples of how a shift of research priorities from military to nonviolent goals would change the problems studied, the knowledge gained, and the technologies developed.

5. Participation in R&D for Nonviolent Defense

The process of studying and developing technologies for nonviolent action provides a contrast to weapons R&D. Most military R&D is carried out by government or corporate laboratories, with scientists and engineers taking a leading role. Testing is done in labs and by the military itself, in exercises and on the battlefield. Thus, the whole process of military R&D is dominated by specialists, including scientists, engineers, and military personnel.

In contrast to this military model, nonviolent defense depends fundamentally on popular participation. Whereas most soldiers are young fit men, anyone can attend a rally or join a boycott, with few restrictions on the basis of age, sex, or ability. Furthermore, the success of nonviolent defense depends on widespread participation. As a general rule, technologies supportive of nonviolent action are those that allow or foster participation, such as telephones and faxes for communication or do-it-yourself building materials. This is because dependence on centralized facilities or on a small group of specialists makes a society vulnerable to takeover.

The implication is that development and testing of technologies for nonviolent defense also needs to involve as wide a cross section of the population as possible. For example, in designing a cheap and easy-to-use short-wave radio system, it makes sense to consider designs by many different users and to have lots of people try them out. When actually implementing a system of short-wave sets, it would help to run small-scale tests and full-scale simulations, analogous to military exercises. Whereas military training normally only involves military personnel, training for nonviolent de-

fense would need to involve the entire population. The same applies to the process of developing appropriate technologies.

In summary, reorienting technology from military priorities to the goal of supporting nonviolent action has major implications for several dimensions of R&D. The fields that receive the greatest attention and support would change: military-generated interest in engineering and the physical sciences would be replaced by nonviolence-generated interest in the social sciences. Within particular fields, the key problems would also change. Within architecture, for example, a key goal might be how to encourage the social solidarity that is vital to nonviolent action. Finally, the methods of R&D would change to become far more participatory. These implications show that the military influence on science and technology is deep and pervasive. It involves not just the technologies that are produced but also theories, intellectual priorities, technical training, skills, and research methods.

D. Sabotage

Sabotage can be considered violence against technology rather than against people. It includes actions such as putting sand in a tractor's fuel tank, programming a bug into a computer system, and putting spikes in trees that will wreck a sawmill blade. Sabotage is often covert, such as when a worker physically halts an assembly line.

Sabotage has been used to resist aggressors, such as by factory workers in Europe occupied by the Nazis. It is also commonly used by workers to resist their bosses, for example as a form of protest against production increases. Some environmental activists use sabotage to try to stop activities such as mining and forestry.

Sabotage occupies a position somewhere between violence and nonviolence. It can be used as part of a violent or a nonviolent resistance to aggression or repression. Some types of sabotage are visibly violent, such as blowing up buildings, whereas others are much less overtly damaging, such as deleting a computer file containing names of dissidents targeted for arrest. There have been many debates about the morality and pragmatic value of sabotage. In terms of the role of technology in conflict, the distinctive feature of sabotage is that it involves disabling a technology rather than using it for the purpose it was designed for. It is also possible to have sabotage of social and knowledge systems associated with technologies, such as the disruption of military training exercises. Propaganda and disinformation can be considered to be methods of sabotage in which the target is people's beliefs rather than technologies.

Although much sabotage is covert, some is open, such as when activists hammer nosecones of nuclear missiles or pour blood on military files and then wait to be arrested. In these principled sabotage actions, the symbolism of damaging technologies is of far greater significance than the actual physical damage. This sort of sabotage highlights the dual role of all sabotage, namely in actually damaging or hindering technologies and in symbolizing the existence of resistance to those using or running the technologies.

E. Strategies for Moving toward Technology Oriented to Nonviolent Action

The systems for designing, producing, and maintaining technologies are powerful. Societies have made enormous investments in current technologies, including everything from bricks and roads to pharmaceuticals and satellites. These "investments" include factories, physical infrastructure, systems of knowledge, training, bureaucratic routines, and regular ways of doing things. Therefore it is a mammoth task to transform these systems to reorient them in support of nonviolent action.

The easiest and most productive step is to find those technologies that already exist that can be used for nonviolent action and to encourage more people to use them for this purpose. Electronic mail, for example, is excellent for communicating in the face of repression. More people could learn how to do this and in particular learn tricks to reduce the vulnerability of e-mail being cut-off or monitored. Also, using e-mail to make contact with activists who oppose repressive regimes can be done immediately.

The next easiest step is to investigate options for using existing technologies. This could be done by searching publications or by talking to knowledgeable individuals. Through such an investigation, it might be found that there already exist procedures for protecting e-mail systems from takeover, such as using a duplicate password system.

Somewhat more difficult is to push for minor adaptations to existing technologies to make them more useful for nonviolent action. An example is the development of special software to run e-mail systems in a crisis, reducing the vulnerability of the system at central nodes of control.

Finally, there is the option of developing entirely new technologies, such as new ways of running e-mail. This is likely to require the most effort for the least return since, even after developing a good system, it would be necessary to convince people to adopt it.

Nevertheless, if technological systems are ever to be transformed from military to peaceful priorities, then R&D will have to be reoriented as well.

Fundamental to any of these changes is a greater awareness of the importance of designing and using technology for creating a society based on nonviolent rather than on violent modes of conflict. If existing technologies are just treated as a backdrop to action for peace, then a whole dimension of change is overlooked. A strategy for peace needs to include a policy for technology.

Also See the Following Articles

ARMS CONTROL • ECONOMIC CONVERSION • ECONOMICS OF WAR AND PEACE • MILITARY-INDUSTRIAL COMPLEX • NONVIOLENT ACTION • WARFARE, TRENDS IN • WEAPONRY, EVOLUTION OF

Bibliography

Dunnigan, J. F. (1983). *How to make war: A comprehensive guide to modern warfare.* New York: Quill.

Edwards, P. N. (1996). *The closed world: Computers and the politics of discourse in cold war America.* Cambridge, MA: MIT Press.

Ellis, J. (1975). *The social history of the machine gun.* London: Croom Helm.

Huxley, A. (1946). *Science, liberty and peace.* New York: Harper & Row.

Jasanoff, S., Markle, G. E., Petersen, J. C., & Pinch, T. (Eds.) (1995). *Handbook of science and technology studies.* Newbury Park, CA: Sage.

Kaldor, M. (1982). *The baroque arsenal.* London: Andre Deutsch.

Krause, K. (1992). *Arms and the state: Patterns of military production and trade.* Cambridge, UK: Cambridge University Press.

Lewer, N., Schofield, S. (1997). *Non-lethal weapons: A fatal attraction? Military strategies and technologies for 21st-century conflict.* London: Zed Books.

Martin, B. (1993). *Social defence, social change.* London: Freedom Press.

Martin, B. (1996). Communication technology and nonviolent action. *Media Development 43,* 3–9.

McNeill, W. H. (1983). *The pursuit of power: Technology, Armed force, and society since A.D. 1000.* Oxford, UK: Basil Blackwell.

Mendelsohn, E., Smith, M. R., & Weingart, P. (Eds.) (1988). *Science, technology and the military.* Dordrecht: Kluwer.

Noble, D. D. (1991). *The classroom arsenal: Military research, information technology, and public education.* London: Falmer Press.

Pearton, M. (1982). *The knowledgeable state: Diplomacy, war and technology since 1830.* London: Burnett Books.

Prokosch, E. (1995). *The technology of killing: A military and political history of antipersonnel weapons.* London: Zed Books.

Smit, W. A., Grin, J., & Voronkov, L. (Eds.) (1992). *Military technological innovation and stability in a changing world: Politically assessing and influencing weapon innovation and military research and development.* Amsterdam: VU University Press.

Southwood, P. (1991). *Disarming military industries: Turning an outbreak of peace into an enduring legacy*. Houndmills, Basingstoke: Macmillan.

van Creveld, M. (1989). *Technology and war: From 2000 B.C. to the present*. New York: Free Press.

Wilson, A. (1983). *The disarmer's handbook of military technology and organization*. Harmondsworth: Penguin.

Wright, S. (1991). The new technologies of political repression: A new case for arms control? *Philosophy and Social Action, 17* (3–4), 31–62.

Television Programming and Violence, International

Barrie Gunter

University of Sheffield

GLOSSARY

Arousal Physiological excitation within the nervous system caused by on-screen action and events, associated with the release of chemical substances in the body and brain, and experienced psychologically by the individual as an emotional reaction.

Content Analysis A research technique which involves objectively and systematically counting and cataloging predefined objects, incidents, or occurrences depicted on television.

Correlational Analysis A statistical technique for examining and quantifying the degree of association between two or more variables, whereby as the probability of occurrence of one increases, the probability of occurrence of another either increases (positive correlation) or decreases (negative correlation).

Cultivation Effects The tendency of media audiences to have their beliefs about the real world shaped by patterns of behavior and object or incident occurrences in the media.

Desensitisation Progressive reduction of psychological reactivity to an exciting media stimulus following repeated exposure to it.

Disinhibition The weakening of socially conditioned inhibitions against behaving violently as a function of exposure to violence in the media, especially when depicted as justified.

Imitation Behavioral copying by the media consumer of an action or incident portrayed in the media.

I. VIOLENCE ON TELEVISION: KEY ISSUES

A. Background

Concern about violence on television can be traced back to the earliest days of the medium. The roots of this concern can be found in the unease that has typically been expressed whenever a popular new entertainment medium emerges. Critical reactions occurred in response to the appearance of popular romantic and adventure novels in the 19th century and the growing popularity of motion pictures during the first half of the 20th century. The 1950s witnessed a redirection of public anxieties onto the rapidly spreading medium of television.

B. Key Concerns

There are several major issues on which debate about televised violence has centered. These typically relate to accusations leveled against television about its alleged enthusiasm for featuring violence in programs as an apparently essential ingredient of entertainment, and the impact that such material can have on viewers, especially upon children. A number of common assumptions are made in the recurrent debate about violence on television. First, it is frequently argued that television contains a great deal of violence. Second, there is a common belief that regular viewers are therefore exposed to large quantities of violence during the course of their everyday television viewing. Third, it is assumed that constant exposure to violent content in programs must have a deleterious effect upon viewers and contributes, as a causal factor, to the enactment of antisocial behavior in society. Fourth, evidence from public opinion polls is regularly cited to support the contention that viewers generally are concerned about the amount and nature of violence on television. Fifth, there is much dispute internationally about how effectively television violence is regulated or could be better controlled. This debate has been conducted all around the world and similar concerns have been expressed across Europe, Asia, and Australasia. While a great proportion of the empirical research studies on this subject have emanated from the United States, the current article reviews evidence from the rest of the world on each of the key issues of on-screen representation, audience impact, and public opinion concerning violence on television.

II. MEASURING VIOLENCE ON TELEVISION

A. Methodology

Traditionally, the most commonly used method for assessing how much violence television programs contain is known as *content analysis*. When measuring violence on television, researchers begin by setting up an "objective" statement of what they mean by violence. Violence is defined in broad terms. Accompanying this definition is a frame of reference which specifies how and where that definition should be applied in the assessment of programs. This instructional frame of reference is given to teams of trained coders who watch video-recorded samples of programs and count up incidents which match the *a priori* definition of violence. From this, a quantitative assessment of the "amount" of violence on television is produced in terms of the numbers of violent incidents or events cataloged by coders. Such analysis does not invariably involve counting every single punch

that is thrown, shot that is fired, or dead body in the battlefield. In some scenes, violence is cataloged at the level of continuous sequences where the flow of the action is uninterrupted.

This approach aims to yield an objective measure of the extent and location of particular classes of incident or event in television programs devoid of any element of subjective judgement about violent television portrayals. All violence tends to be treated in the same way by a content analysis, regardless of the type of program or dramatic context or setting in which it occurs. Thus, cartoon violence, for example, is treated no differently than violence occurring in a contemporary drama series. Violence in the news would be weighted no differently from violence in a situation comedy.

B. International Comparisons

The on-screen representation of violence has been studied in Canada, Europe, the Far East, and Australasia. This work has generally adopted a standard content analysis approach similar to that of George Gerbner and his co-workers in the United States.

1. Canada

With the rapid expansion of television worldwide during the 1980s and 1990s, the U.S. government has been pressured to bring violence on television under control not only from its own citizenry but also from those of foreign countries, especially where the latter are importers of substantial amounts of American productions. This point applies with particular acuity in the case of the United States' closest neighbor, Canada, where so many American programs are routinely broadcast.

Comparative analyses of violence in newspapers, radio, and television in Canada and the United States conducted for the 1977 Royal Commission on Violence in the Communication Industry analyzed 8000 news items and found that 45% related to conflict and violence. Of 2400 news items broadcast on 15 Canadian and American television stations, 48% were related to conflict and violence. The American stations were found to place greater emphasis on homicide and other physical violence than the Canadian stations, while the latter showed more of other types of conflict and property damage. Direct, physical violence (including natural and man-made disasters) was about 10% more common in television news than in newspapers. Television was more likely to personalize violence in terms of private gain or deviance.

Another major content analysis study conducted under the auspices of the Royal Commission on Violence in the Communication Industry cataloged an average of 18.5 acts of aggression per program hour on Canadian television. A total of 594 acts of physical aggression involving the body (assault or battery) or a weapon (typically a gun or object not intended for aggression) were observed in a sample of over 100 programs. These comprised mainly violence that involved the use of a body part (which occurred at a rate of 3.1 per program hour) or the use of a weapon (4.2 per program hour). In addition, there were acts involving physical threat (1.7 acts per program hour) and those involving the use of verbally threatening behaviour (3.4 per program hour).

2. Europe

A study of prime-time television programs was carried out during the late 1970s in The Netherlands and revealed less violence on Dutch television than on American television. Crime drama series, however, were found to be just as violent as American counterparts. These programs were mainly imported from Britain and Germany. In Germany, another analysis revealed almost 500 murder scenes during 1 week on the two major public and four most-watched private television channels. Research in Finland emphasized the need to take on board the nature and context of violence when analyzing televised violence. This is because viewers make perceptual distinctions between different forms of violence and react differently to violence displayed in different dramatic contexts. This study showed that television, in contrast to the real world, displayed more physical violence than verbal or psychological violence.

3. Israel

A small-scale study of violence on Israeli television was carried out as part of the U.S. Surgeon General's 1970 investigation of television and social behavior in cataloged 52 violent incidents in 1 week. Most of these incidents occurred in fictional drama programs.

Adults' programs were more likely to contain violence than were children's programs. Nearly half of all adult-oriented programs in Hebrew and nearly one in three in Arabic contained at least one violent incident. Just over one in five children's programs contained violence. Television series dealing with such themes as crime, detective stories, or espionage were the most violent programs, while long-running serials, especially historical dramas, were the least violent programs.

The majority of violent incidents were judged to have been presented in a fairly realistic style and were more likely to occur in serious than in humorous contexts. Over half the violence was physical and inten-

tional, while around one in five incidents comprised verbal violence. One in seven incidents comprised threatened physical violence. The majority of violent incidents resulted in no observable harm to victims or targets, and most of the remainder produced only minor pain or suffering. Just two incidents resulted in death and two further incidents caused significant pain and suffering. For the most part, violence produced no blood or wounds. Just two incidents produced a large amount of blood.

4. Japan and the Far East

Research into violence on television in Japan found that Japanese-made programs were as likely to contain violence as American-made programs, and the rate at which violent incidents occurred was identical. Japanese violence differed markedly from that in American-made programs with a much greater emphasis on suffering.

On Japanese television the "good guys" were as likely to be violent as were the "bad guys," which distinguished them from American programs in which villains tended to use violence more liberally than anyone else.

Research has been carried out in a number of Far Eastern countries comparing levels of violence on television in different national markets. In 1988, the Asian Mass Communication Research and Information Centre launched a study of violence on television in Asia which covered eight countries: Bangladesh, India, Indonesia, Japan, Malaysia, Pakistan, the Philippines, and Thailand. The monitoring work was carried out in 1989. The main objectives of the study were as follows:

- Determine the frequency and the level of violence on TV in Asia.
- Identify the types of violent programs.
- Determine the countries of origin of violent programs.
- Explore the sources of locally produced violent programs.
- Describe the dramatic contexts and the nature of violence.
- Analyze the trends in the depiction of violence in order to assess if levels of violence on television are increasing or decreasing.
- Examine the cross-cultural similarities and differences in the depiction of violence on television.

Four main categories of programming were selected for analysis: social dramas, action-adventures, cartoons, and comedies. Violence was defined as "the use of physical force or verbal abuse which is psychologically or physically injurious to a person or persons, including the destruction of property and animals." A total of 256 programs were analyzed ranging from 15 in Indonesia to 65 in Malaysia. The average number per country was 32. More than half the programs were local in origin. The biggest foreign supplier of programs was the United States, with Japan as the next most popular source of material. Nearly 6 in 10 of the programs monitored were classified as violent. The percentages ranged from around 18% in Bangladesh and 20% in Malaysia to 94% in Thailand and 100% in the Philippines. In India, which screened only locally produced programs, 72% of the programs were violent. In the Philippines, around one in four programs were local.

Foreign programs were reported to contain more violent incidents per hour than locally produced programs, reaching a high of 23 per hour in the Philippines and a low of 3.2 per hour in Indonesia. While foreign programs had more violent incidents, little or no blood was generally shown. In these programs the villains were drawn from upper and lower classes and violence usually related to social and institutional conflicts. Local productions featured fewer violent incidents, but these tended to be more bloody. Villains were mainly drawn from the upper classes and violence was chiefly due to personal vendettas and interfamilial conflicts.

5. Australasia

In Australia and New Zealand, much emphasis has been placed on comparing violence on domestic television channels with that occurring on television in other countries. One study found that just over half the programs (51%) and program hours (53%) monitored on major Australian channels contained any violence. The first measure was lower than other countries with which comparisons were made, which included the United States (80%), Japan (81%), New Zealand (66%), and the United Kingdom (56%).

Much of the violence contained in programs on mainstream Australian television occurred in fictional output, with very little being found in nonfiction programming. Crime drama shows were found to be almost uniformly violent (96.7%), and a clear majority of cartoons (85.7%) and action-adventure series (73.7%) also contained violence. Nonfiction programs represented 27.5% of the programs analyzed but only 2.4% of the programs with violence fell into this general category.

The intensity of violence was measured in terms of the rate at which violent episodes occurred in programs. There was an overall rate of four violent episodes per program and 5.4 per broadcast hour. When nonfiction programs were excluded, however, the average rate per hour increased to 7.4. Compared with other countries for which data were available at that time, this result placed Australian television within the mid-range. The rates per hour elsewhere were just over 4.0 in the UK, 5.7 in New Zealand, 7.0 in Japan, and 8.1 in the United States.

In the same corner of the world, several studies of televised violence in New Zealand over a period spanning almost 20 years from the mid-1970s have indicated that levels of televised violence have remained fairly stable. New Zealand compares favorably with other countries in respect to the amount of violence contained in home-produced programs. However, much of what is now shown consists of imported programs from overseas where program violence levels tend to be higher.

6. United Kingdom

The amount of violence on British television has been monitored in periodic studies since 1970. Much of this work has been funded by the broadcasting industry. Initial research was modeled on American work and was designed to enable comparisons to be drawn between the two countries.

Early findings showed that, although a common feature of programming, violence was not as prevalent on British television as on American television. In fictional drama, the only category of programming in which direct comparisons between American and British findings were possible, it emerged that around 6 in 10 programs contained violence—compared with a reported 8 in 10 fictional programs on American television.

There was somewhat less violence on British television in terms of the rate at which violent incidents occurred; average numbers of just under two violent incidents per program or just over two per hour were recorded. In the mid-1980s further research found that the overall rate for dramatic fiction had increased by more than one violent act per hour compared with that in 1971.

Over the same period, the two major channels, BBC1 and ITV, showed decreases from 49 to 28% and from 51 to 32%, respectively, while the minority channel, BBC2, showed a decline from 55 to 26%.

During the early 1990s, a series of monitoring studies was published by the Broadcasting Standards Council in Britain. These studies monitored not only how much violence there was on television, but also how much sex and bad language. These studies also incorporated an analysis of violence on the new satellite television channels. A little over half of the small samples of programs monitored on the four main public-service channels contained violence. Violence levels on these channels increased steadily between 1992 and 1994. Levels of violence on the satellite movie channels were generally much higher than those found on the public-service channels. Nearly three-quarters of movies on the satellite channels contained violence.

The latest research in Britain comprised a content analysis study covering 4 weeks of television broadcast output on eight channels (the four main terrestrial channels and four satellite broadcast channels) which covered more than 2000 programs and over 4700 hours of broadcast material. A complete week of output was taken during each of four waves of off-air recordings running from Monday to Sunday. All broadcast output was recorded around the clock.

Of the programs analyzed, 37% were found to contain violence. A total of 21,170 violent acts were coded over the 4 weeks' output, of which 71% occurred on the four satellite channels. Each violence-containing program contained around 10 violent acts and 5 violent sequences (scenes which contained one or perhaps more than one violent act in quick succession). This violence occupied over 51 hours or 1.07% of program running time. On the terrestrial channels (BBC1, BBC2, ITV, and Channel 4), just 0.61% of program output time was occupied by violence, representing a drop on the mid-1980s figure of 1.1%. The general level of violence on television was disproportionately inflated by a small number of programs that contained exceptionally large quantities of violence. Just 1% of programs across the eight channels were found to contain 19% of all violent acts coded. Further, just 2% of the programs monitored were found to contain 46% of all the program running time occupied by violence.

Most violent acts (70%) occurred in drama programs, with cinema films being the largest single drama genre contributor (containing 53% of all violent acts). The most commonly occurring form of violence involved the use of a body part (42%) or a hand-held weapon (31%). More than a third of violent acts (36%) depicted no injuries to victims, but few acts were found to be extremely graphic in terms of their portrayal of pain, blood, and horrific suffering.

III. PERCEPTIONS OF TELEVISION VIOLENCE

A. The Meaning of Violence

The quantitative measurement of violence on television via content analysis has been largely a process of defin-ing the concept of violence clearly and applying the definition in an accurate and consistent manner to television programs. What the commonly applied definitions overlook is that there are many forms of violence other than that which involves purely physical injury and harm. There is emotional and psychological violence, verbal violence, institutional violence, and symbolic violence. Of course, these can be as difficult to define and record as a general concept of "violence" as physical force. Research from several different countries has shown that audiences regard violence as a multifaceted concept which does not represent a unitary process or a single set of events. Violence can vary in its severity, justification, consequences, and in the intentions of the perpetrator. While physical violence may be the most commonly perceived form of violence on television, a more complete measuring procedure also might be to include other expressions of violence such as verbal violence and violent images.

Whether the use of force or infliction of harm or injury is perceived as violent clearly depends on a number of considerations associated with the particular circumstances surrounding the action. The total context in which the action takes place can exert a significant influence upon how the viewer will interpret the episode or image. Violence on television cannot be taken simply at face value. How violent actions are perceived is related to social norms, personal values, and the particular form and context of violence itself.

B. Insights from Viewers' Perceptions

International research has revealed that viewers can be highly discriminating when it comes to portrayals of violence. They do not invariably read into television content the same meanings as do researchers.

One method of analyzing viewers' perceptions is to obtain ratings and opinions from them about which programs are violent and how seriously so. In Britain, this has been done by asking individuals to indicate from a list of program titles which ones are violent and which are not. One problem with this kind of measure is that it cannot indicate how much violence there is in specific program episodes. Are respondents basing their opinions on one particular episode, several episodes, or the whole series?

Subjective ratings of television can also be made for actual program materials. Viewers can be invited to make personal judgements about the violence contained in program excerpts or in entire episodes. This technique allows the researcher to investigate the degree of variation in viewers' opinions about television violence and the specific ingredients of violent portrayals which affect those judgements.

Research by the BBC in Britain showed that when viewers were asked to fill out a questionnaire about specific programs shortly after they had been broadcast, in which reactions to violence and other aspects of the programs were probed, whether a particular program was perceived as violent did not depend on how many "violent" incidents it contained.

Research has indicated that adults and children alike are capable of highly refined judgements about television violence. Studies in Britain and in The Netherlands have shown that viewers have their own scales for deciding the seriousness of incidents and their opinions do not always concur with researchers' categorizations of violence. Researchers who have allowed viewers to decide for themselves about the seriousness of different portrayals of violence have found that viewers' perceptions can vary widely and are influenced by a number of attributes of the portrayals themselves. Purely quantitative counts of violence may be less valuable on their own than those qualified by knowledge of how particular portrayals are evaluated by or impact upon audiences.

Familiarity of surroundings, for example, is one of the most powerful factors influencing viewers' perceptions of television violence. The closer to home the violence is portrayed in terms of place and time, the more serious it is judged to be. Viewers in the United Kingdom generally rated violence in British crime series as more violent than similar portrayals on American-made series of the same type. Portrayals of "violent" behavior in cartoons or science fiction programs, however, were seen as essentially nonviolent.

Some audience perceptions, however, exhibit more complex patterns. One illustration of this was a set of paradoxical opinions about violence perpetrated by law enforcers and by criminals, or by men and by women, which varied with the origin of the program. With extracts from British crime series, for instance, viewers were most concerned about violence inflicted by men upon women; while in scenes from American series, they were concerned more by women being violent to men. In an American context, violence performed by criminals was perceived in more serious terms than that used by law enforcers (usually the police); while in British settings, it was law enforcer violence that viewers were more troubled by. Localized social, cultural, and moral values may influence the way audiences judge different styles of television violence.

Children, too, can make distinctions between different forms of violence on television. Dutch research has shown that while young viewers may not have the maturity of adults, they readily learn to distinguish broad program genres and the conventions to which they adhere in the kinds of portrayals they contain. Distinctions are made between violence depicted in cartoons and in action-adventure programs in terms of perceived realism, level of identification with characters, and degree and nature of emotional involvement with the action.

On the basis of the above findings with adults and children, it is clear that viewers classify program content differently from the descriptive analysis of research frameworks that employ narrow definitions of violence. Although objective cataloging of incidents in programs has the useful function of providing reliable counts of how often certain categories of items occur, the relevance or meaning of those items for the audience can be properly ascertained only through obtaining the perceptions of viewers themselves. There would be some merit in recommending a subjective approach rather than a purely objective one in the analysis of televised violence because this perspective enables one to identify the programs that viewers themselves take most seriously. A subjective audience input to a content analysis could therefore render a useful embellishment to an otherwise dry approach to analyzing the appearance of violence on television.

IV. EFFECTS OF TELEVISION VIOLENCE

A major bone of contention in the ongoing debate about television violence has focused on whether it causes aggressive behavior among viewers or could be considered to represent a significant contributor to crime and violence in society. In examining the effects of television violence, there are two principal questions that need to be considered. First, what kinds of effects are being referred to? Second, how are the effects measured and to what extent can the evidence deriving from these measures be unquestionably accepted? Research on television violence effects from around the world is reviewed in this section.

A. Types of Evidence

Television violence may have an impact on viewers at a number of psychological levels, allegedly being able to shape social attitudes and behavior and to color perceptions and feelings about the world. Behavioral effects have received the greatest attention, although sometimes these are operationalized simply as measures of attitudes toward particular forms of behavior as might be deployed in different situations. While concern about behavioral effects has tended to focus upon the influence of aggressors as role models on-screen, a further body of evidence has indicated that patterns of victimization on television can transmit important messages to the audience about risks and dangers from violence in the real world.

The extensive empirical research published about the effects of television violence, where the focus has been upon aggressor role portrayals, can be divided up according to the main research methodologies employed. Most of the work done so far can be broken down into six major categories: (1) laboratory experiments; (2) field experiments; (3) correlational surveys; (4) longitudinal panel surveys; (5) natural experiments; and (6) intervention studies. Victim-focused research is considered under the single heading of cultivation effects.

1. Laboratory Studies

These have been designed to demonstrate a causal relationship between watching a violent event on television and increased viewer aggressiveness. The findings to emerge from this form of investigation have often been taken as evidence of a causal connection between watching television violence and increased viewer aggressiveness. Typically, however, these studies have tested only small, unrepresentative groups of people under highly contrived or unnatural viewing conditions. Their measures of television viewing and aggressive behavior tend to be far removed from normal everyday behavior. Thus, whether laboratory findings provide any meaningful indications of how people behave in the outside world has been strongly debated.

Using laboratory research during the 1960s and 1970s, behavioral psychologists in the United States investigated the propensity of children to model their behavior on examples seen on-screen and through the aggression-eliciting properties of violent film portrayals among young males. Outside the United States, a handful of studies investigated similar media violence effects during the early 1970s. Some evidence emerged from Britain that children would imitate a film model when placed in a similar play situation after viewing. However, this effect did not occur for all children and also appeared to be weakened for some children by prior experience in the play setting, especially among middle-class children. If children played beforehand with the same toys as a film model they subsequently watched, their own play patterns submerged any new behaviors being modeled on film.

Just as American research had shown differences in the degree of aggression simulation as a function of the realism of filmed violence, so too did evidence emerge from Britain that children exhibit different degrees of sensitivity to real and fantasy violence. Children were found to play significantly more with war toys after watching a war film as compared with a puppet film and tended to play less constructively following exposure to the war film. This last effect was much more pronounced among working-class than middle-class children.

American research has indicated that a key factor in whether children are likely to copy behaviors they see on screen is the extent to which they identify with the central characters. British research has shown, however, that such identification is not always forthcoming and that even when it is, young viewers do not automatically endorse a character's conduct. No indication emerged, for instance, that delinquent boys, who demonstrated a propensity toward violent conduct anyway, identified any more than did nondelinquent boys with television action heroes. More recent research revealed little difference between 1990s delinquent adolescents with a criminal record and nondelinquent teenagers in Britain in their media usage habits or movie or television program preferences. Even when a character is liked and identified with, children will not necessarily accept violent behavior from that character. However, aggressive children may display more sympathy for the antisocial behavior of a lesser known character when his behaviour matches the way they would tend to behave.

The aggression-eliciting effects of aggressive images found to occur in the United States were also found among Belgian French-speaking military recruits mostly in their late teens and early twenties. Exposure to images displayed on slides that depicted weapons was associated with a greater subsequent propensity to display aggression in a contrived laboratory setting. The effect was weakened, however, if viewers were instructed beforehand to focus on and evaluate the aesthetic qualities of the images they were shown. These results illustrated the significance of paying attention to the mediating effects of social contexts of viewing and the different ways in which media violence could be interpreted by viewers.

2. Field Experiments

To avoid some of the problems associated with laboratory research, while retaining a few of its advantages, some researchers have conducted field experiments. In these studies, children or adolescents are generally the object of investigation and are randomly assigned to view either violent or nonviolent television material for a period of a few days to a few weeks. Measures of aggressive behavior, fantasies, or attitudes are taken before, during, and after the period of controlled viewing. In order to ensure control over actual viewing, young people have usually been studied in group or institutional settings. The two most common settings have been nursery schools and residential schools or institutions or summer camps for adolescents boys. In most cases, these studies have indicated a link between viewing a diet of mainly violent programs and increased levels of aggressiveness among those individuals observed.

One comparison between adolescent boys in the U.S. and a similar group in Belgium found an increase in aggression on some measures for boys in both countries who watched mainly violent films over a several-week period, particularly among those boys initially high in aggression anyway. Exposure to a diet of mainly nonviolent material, much of which contained comedy material, was associated with a drop in violence levels among boys who had initially scored quite high in terms of their inherent aggressiveness.

Another international study that took place in the United States, Canada, Britain, and Italy reported relationships between the type of movie seen and the punitiveness of moviegoers who were interviewed either as they entered or came out of the movie theater. Respondents were asked to state what they felt the maximum penalties should be for persons convicted of assault and battery, rape, robbery, and murder in terms of years of imprisonment. In all four countries, those who had just seen a violent movie exhibited greater punitiveness for the perpetrators of violent crimes.

3. Correlational Surveys

The basic approach in correlational research is to obtain a measure of viewing violent programs and to relate this to a measure or battery of measures of aggressiveness. The ultimate goal is to demonstrate a causal relation, with the first step being to find out whether the possibility of a relation exists in the first place between two variables which happen to be correlated. Viewers often have to identify or recall from lists of program titles which ones they like best or watch most often. Occasionally, more-effective diary measures are used, but even then assumptions are made about the probable violent content of programs viewers say they have seen, which are not backed up by any better evidence. If some doubt exists about amounts of violence watched on television, there must also be doubts about the evi-

dence offered on the supposed effects of this conduct. In any case, correlational surveys are unable to demonstrate causal relations. They can simply show where degrees of statistical association exist between certain reported sets of behaviors and attitudes. Even then the small size of most of the correlations reported to date indicates only very weak associations.

Early work in Britain following the introduction of television for the first time in certain parts of the country used fairly superficial measures of aggression based on teachers' reports about pupils' behavior and found no evidence of a link with television. Later studies have shown how correlational analyses can yield spurious links between television and antisocial conduct. One study of the relationship between television viewing and delinquency among adolescents in Britain indicated that the differences between a group of delinquents and nondelinquents in antisocial behavior levels was more to do with their social class and family upbringing than their television watching.

Research among children ages 11 to 16 in Northern Ireland examined relationships between children's aggression, television viewing, and enjoyment of televised violence, while also obtaining detailed information about family background and personality characteristics. The sample comprised 386 sibling pairs who therefore shared genetic stock and the same early development environment. No evidence emerged that general television viewing was associated with manifest aggressive tendencies. However, children who scored high on a measure of psychoticism were both more aggressive and enjoyed watching television violence. Reported levels of enjoyment of television violence within sibling pairs were unrelated, even though they did exhibit similar television viewing patterns. The more aggressive sibling did not tend to watch more television violence, but did enjoy it more if they had a high-scoring psychoticism personality profile. The results were interpreted as showing that family background and largely inherited personality characteristics underpin aggressiveness and enjoyment of watching violence on television.

4. Longitudinal Panel Studies

These studies can test causal hypotheses and they usually employ sound sampling methods. The aim of this type of investigation is to discover relationships which may exist or develop over time between television viewing and social attitudes and behavior. In this respect, such research addresses the notions of the cumulative influence of television violence. This view posits that links between watching television and personal levels of aggressiveness should increase with age and repeated exposure to televised violence.

In the United Kingdom, a major investigation of the impact of television violence on the behavior of adolescent boys used a simulated panel survey in which the respondents were not actually studied across separate points in time, but were questioned retrospectively at a single point about their habits over previous years. Detailed and lengthy interviews with these teenage boys revealed a relationship between certain aspects of their claimed viewing behavior and self-reported attitudes and dispositions toward the use of violence in their lives. In particular, the more the boys claimed to watch particular types of dramatic television content—preclassified as containing violence—the more likely they were to report having used aggression themselves under different circumstances.

Critics have challenged these results, focusing in particular on the validity of the biographical information obtained from the young respondents about not only their current viewing habits and behavior, but also those they tried to recall from 10 years earlier. Some of the programs listed had been taken off the air when the respondents were just 3 years old. Further analysis revealed that the correlations between reported exposure to television violence and personal aggressiveness were not as clear-cut as originally reported.

A major American longitudinal study of the impact of televised violence on people during their early years of development reported that exposure to televised violence at age 8 was correlated with reported aggressiveness at age 18 among a cohort of young people interviewed on two separate occasions 10 years apart. A further follow-up with the same respondents at age 30 continued to find a role for television in the development of aggressive tendencies, but acknowledged the impact of other genetic and environmental factors. This study was extended internationally, with further surveys being launched in Finland, Poland, The Netherlands, Israel, and Australia. Fewer data emerged from either Australia or from among children studied in Israel who lived in a rural location to support a link between television viewing and aggression. Weak links were suggested by the studies among children who lived in an urban location in Israel and among children in Poland. The Finnish work corroborated the American findings. The Dutch study moved off in a different direction when its researchers decided to develop their own measures of television viewing and aggression rather than adopt what were seen as inferior measures from the original American study. The Dutch results failed to support the view that television violence is a likely long-term

factor of any significance in the development of personal aggressiveness.

5. Natural Experiments

Some researchers have attempted to assess relationships between the presence of television and shifts in social conduct over time in natural environments. These studies fall largely into two categories. The first involves a longitudinal assessment of occurrences of certain forms of conduct, often as documented by authorities, before and after television was available. A different version of this type of study has attempted to find out if media depictions of certain kinds of behavior can spark subsequent similar behaviors in the real world. The first type of study has taken place in communities in which television had been introduced for the first time. Thus, the effects of television on previously unexposed populations can be examined.

In measuring the impact of the introduction of television to a society for the first time, some researchers have simply examined degrees of association between the growth in numbers of television set owning households in the population over time and official crime trend statistics. One such investigation, which compared statistics for the United States, Canada, and South Africa reported that White homicide rates doubled in North American societies after the introduction of television, but the same result did not appear in South Africa, where television was introduced only in 1976. Although controlling for a variety of other factors known to affect crime rates such as urbanization, economic conditions, alcohol consumption, firearms availability, and so on, the weakness of this study was that it did not measure actual levels of exposure to television programs among members of the public. Television can only influence viewers if they watch it, and statistics showing extent of television set ownership say nothing about how much people actually use their sets or about what kinds of things they watch.

The study of the impact of television on previously unexposed communities has been a fairly rare occurrence partly because of the resources needed to mount such a study and partly because it is increasingly difficult to find populations in the world with no prior experience of television. In one investigation with small communities in Canada, many measures were taken of children's behavior. The research occurred in three towns which at the outset either had no television reception (NOTEL), only one channel available (UNITEL), or several channels available (MULTITEL). By the end of the research, NOTEL had one channel, UNITEL had two channels, and MULTITEL still had four channels.

The three towns were compared at the outset and then again 2 years later in order to find out what impact television had had on other activities.

The major finding of the study was that the aggressive behavior observed in the school playground of children ages 6–11 years increased in NOTEL over the 2-year period, while similar behavior in the other two towns exhibited no such increase. This pattern of increased aggression was true for both physical and verbal aggression; among boys and girls, for younger (6–7 years) and older children (8–9 years), for children who were initially high or low in aggressiveness, and among light and heavy television viewers.

Another similar Canadian study compared a Cree Indian community into which television was introduced with a control Indian community and a control Euro-Canadian community. No before- and after television differences in levels of aggression occurred between the experimental and control communities, taken as a whole. When children were classified by the amount of daily exposure to television, however, significant differences in aggressive attitudes emerged. The introduction of television into the community increased the aggressiveness of those children who watched a lot of television.

Other real-world phenomena have been explained in terms of television effects. There have been cases noted in different parts of the world where extremely violent events depicted or reported on television, such as airplane hijacks, civil disturbances, and acts of murder and suicide have apparently led to simlar copycat incidents. One such case was investigated in Britain. A central character in a major UK soap opera was depicted attempting to commit suicide through taking a drug overdose. The program was followed by an alleged increase in overdose-related suicide attempts among members of the public. A study of individual cases and general patterns of suicide rates yielded insufficient evidence to prove a link between the television portrayal and real-life incidents.

B. Intervention Studies

In the sphere of violent portrayals, the worst is usually assumed of television. Exposure to televised violence is generally hypothesized to exert potential harms on unsuspecting viewers, especially upon vulnerable young children. A number of studies have started from the assumption that harmful impact is contingent upon watching television violence, but have then asked if this is so, what, if anything, can be done to alleviate this undesirable effect? Intervention projects have explored ways of inoculating viewers against television's influences. Such exercises have normally been conducted among children with the aim of improving young viewers' television literacy, that is, their critical appraisal and understanding of television content. Intervention studies in Europe have yielded some evidence that increased awareness of television techniques can reduce harmful reactions to television violence.

One UK study was designed to modify 8- to 9-year-old children's comprehension and awareness of violence on television. The intervention included television show visits, witnessing two male actors demonstrate a fight sequence which was seen on video as well as live, watching educational films about the making of action movies, and discussions of violent television excerpts. Results showed that even a short-duration intervention program can bring about substantial changes in children's comprehension and awareness of violence on television and in their daily lives.

In The Netherlands, Dutch researchers have reported educational effects of a six-part school television series designed to encourage children ages 10 to 12 to become more discriminating consumers of violent television crime series. Children were taught to deconstruct television dramas, recognize their fictional nature, and critically appraise their use of violence as a storytelling device. Interviews were filmed with real police officers talking about their work and offering their opinions about the veracity of fictional police depicted on television. In particular, contrasts were drawn between the extent to which the police on television and in real life use violence to subdue criminals. This course produced a significant lowering in children's perceptions of the realism of violent crime dramas and increased recognition of the risks and harms associated with real violence.

C. Cultivation Effects

Cultivation effects of television are those which are envisaged to influence and shape individuals' beliefs and opinions about the world around them. In this context, television is envisaged to represent one among a number of sources of information about the world which people take into account when developing their opinions and impressions of social reality. While direct experience and conversations with other people remain important, increasingly information about conditions and events near and far are conveyed by the mass media.

In the more specific context of discussions about public perceptions of crime and violence, the role of the media has achieved prominence. There has been an assumption that television, in particular, with its apparently regular portrayal of crime and violence, can have a major impact on public beliefs and concerns about crime. American research has indicated that people who are heavier viewers of television exhibit greater perception of personal risk from crime and greater fear of victimization. Research outside the United States has not universally supported this relationship.

A Canadian study among residents of Toronto found that when the actual incidence of crime in the respondent's neighborhood was controlled, no overall relationship emerged between television viewing and fear of being a victim of crime. Enhanced fear was most closely associated with overall amount of viewing only among people who lived within high crime neighborhoods.

British researchers have also failed to replicate American findings on the relationship between total television viewing and public fear of crime. Perceptions about crime and violence were related more to viewing particular categories of programs than to total amount of viewing. Furthermore, public perceptions of dangers from real-life violence were influenced by television programs only insofar as these programs represented a main source of information about the locations being asked about. Thus British viewers' perceptions of the potential risk from violent crime in American cities was related to how often they watched U.S.-produced crime dramas, while their viewing of UK-produced crime programs appeared to exert little impact upon their perceptions of the potential risks of attack in British locations.

V. PUBLIC OPINION AND TELEVISION VIOLENCE

In addition to the significance of viewers' perceptions of television violence to identify the salience of violence on-screen and to supplement content analysis in providing audience-based distinctions between violent portrayals in terms of their inherent seriousness, in many countries wider public attitudes about television content are regarded as an important area of feedback in establishing the status of public tastes and values in relation to television output. Public opinion about violence on television, however, can easily be misrepresented. Viewers' opinions about televised violence can give rise to apparent contradictions and may depend crucially on how questions about televised violence are asked.

A. Violence in Drama

When asked about violence on television in the context of things that have caused them offence, only a minority of viewers (30% or fewer) claim to have been offended at all by television violence. When the question is re-framed by asking viewers to indicate the kinds of things which should never be shown on television, an even smaller number (16%) reject violence, brutality, and cruelty as wholly inappropriate for television. Concerns about violence on television can vary with the nature of the violence. Thus, more than half of British viewers (55%) said they would not want to see a scene depicting a woman being raped, while far fewer (14%) said they would not wish to see television depict a scene of the killing of a criminal.

The context of violence can make a significant difference to viewers' opinions about it. In Britain, clear majorities of viewers agreed that: "people are justified in being concerned about the impact of TV violence on children today"; "there are too many programs on television that contain violence" (60%), and that "we would be better off without violence on television." When the same viewers were asked for their opinions about the violence in a number of popular American- and British-made crime drama series, more than 8 or 9 of 10 took a tolerant view about the violence in these programs, and fewer than 1 in 10 generally regarded the violence in these shows as too extreme.

B. Violence in Factual Programs

Much of the news featured on television revolves around issues of conflict. Frequently this takes the form of political conflicts, industrial disputes, or arguments about the economy. From time to time, the news may be dominated by crime, violent civil disturbances, terrorism, or war. Viewers in Britain have been found to state a preference for less news about violent incidents, but this is often associated with long-running conflicts for which no clear resolution can be envisaged. Even with short-term conflicts, such as the Falklands dispute and the Gulf War, in both of which British forces were involved, an initial public appetite for information from television about these events quickly waned, especially when nothing really new or dramatic was happening.

As with public opinion about violence in fictional drama, opinions about violence in factual programs are mediated by contextual and stylistic factors relating to the way violent incidents are treated. Public anxieties about violence in the news are especially likely to be aroused in connection with stories which involve ordinary people and in relation to the depiction of certain graphic images of real life violence which may be distressing to people in general or more especially to the victims or their families.

Violent events involving private individuals, such as the victims of murder, rape, or other crimes, or the cases of individuals involved in violent disasters, can cause deep concern among many people in Britain. Although the public may show a degree of sympathy for news editors and reporters who wish to include violent incidents among their reports, sympathy for the needs of victims and their families tends to be greater. Reporting of violence involving ordinary citizens may be regarded as acceptable if it can be justified in terms, for example, of being for the greater good of people in general. Where such a justification does not exist, most people express a natural sympathy for the victims and a concern about the trauma which further reminders of critical incidents might cause to them. Women may be especially sensitive to certain kinds of violence, such as rape, particularly where it is covered on regional news, thus bringing it closer to home. Such stories may, of course, perform a constructive function in informing women that there is a rapist at large and may also, on some occasions, play a part in aiding the apprehension of the assailant.

Tolerance for potentially distressing images involving private citizens can vary with the purpose of showing them in the news as well as by the time when they are included in bulletins. An overwhelming proportion of viewers (78%) surveyed across Britain felt that it was unacceptable for television news broadcasts to include scenes from a major incident which showed the dead or seriously injured in such a way that they were recognizable. However, pictures from the same scene after the bodies had been removed or where the camera was placed at such a distance that the bodies or injured were not recognizable were both generally regarded as acceptable (by 87 and 76% respectively).

Respondents to a large national British survey generally felt that reconstructions of violent crimes in the news were either completely (59%) or fairly (29%) acceptable. People who had themselves been victims of violent crime were even more emphatic with two out of three (66%) finding such reconstructions "completely" acceptable. By comparison, nearly two out of three viewers in general (64%) felt that dramatic reconstructions of natural disasters were either completely or fairly unacceptable, while nearly one in five (18%) felt they were not acceptable at all. The lower level of endorsement of the latter scenes stemmed from a concern that they served no useful purpose. Reconstructions of vio-

lent crimes, to which there may have been witnesses, could at least function to solicit the help of those witnesses in coming forward and sharing whatever they know with the police.

News editors often face difficult choices when deciding whether to use televised reconstructions of potentially distressing events. They not only have to consider the range of possible reactions of the general audience to such scenes but also the degree of distress they might cause to the survivors of such events or their families. Among the latter group, reactions can in turn vary with oppositional points of view taken up by different individuals. British research again found that some rape victims endorsed the use of reconstruction techniques, while others could not tolerate them. There was general recognition of the rights of the individual to decide whether such techniques should be used. For some the need to obtain help in apprehending their assailant outweighed the pain of living through the event again, while for others that pain was just to great to experience once more.

C. Conflict in the News

Research carried out in Britain during the Gulf War in 1991 found that viewers were prepared to tolerate certain images of war and not others. When viewers nationwide were asked to get their views about four specific events from the war which were shown on the television news coverage—(1) the bombing of a bunker/shelter in Baghdad that resulted in heavy civilian casualties; (2) coalition pilots captured by Iraq and displayed on Iraqi television broadcasts; (3) the filming of Iraqi troops surrendering; and (4) the aftermath of coalition air attacks on Iraqi forces as they were withdrawing from Kuwait in the final days of the conflict—most thought it had been right to show pictures of these incidents on television. The exception was the transmission of Iraqi film showing captured coalition pilots including two Britons. Here, viewers questioned the decision to show this because of the potential upset such images might have caused to viewers in general and most especially to the families of war victims.

Despite a certain degree of tolerance among many members of the public for scenes showing the outcomes of war, few people were willing to accept close-up shots of the dead or dying, whether featuring British or Iraqi casualties.

Apart from wars and military conflicts, civil disturbances and attacks on private citizens provide other sources of real-life violent injury and death which may be covered in the news. The 1980s, for example, witnessed a number of urban riots in Britain's inner city areas which were vividly reported by television news bulletins. Through this reporting, fire and fighting became familiar sights leading some commentators to allege that this coverage may have led sections of the disaffected population to be more ready to take part in such incidents. A debate thus was fueled about television's role on such occasions. One body of opinion held that television had a duty to report the facts and to do so by showing what really happened. This responsibility needed, however, to be weighed against the possibility that reports of civil disturbances could produce imitation elsewhere or alternatively might serve to limit any further spreading of such events by causing an informed public to prompt its politicians to take remedial action.

There are clearly many different considerations which must be borne in mind by news editors when deciding how to cover violent events in the news. Many similar considerations are relevant also to the producers of other types of factual programming. Television audiences comprise a variety of types of people whose personalities, values, and opinions vary widely. In turn, these psychological aspects of their make-up play an important part in determining what kinds of factual violence they will find acceptable or unacceptable and how strongly they will react to different types of violence in the news or other factual programs. Audience research has begun to provide some insights into these matters. It is important, however, to establish just what appears on screen. The analysis which follows attempts to provide further evidence on this issue.

D. Liking of Violence on Television

Some commentators have argued that violence on television is an internationally marketable commodity. Violence is a key ingredient underpinning a program's popularity and helps to sell programs to audiences worldwide. Program-makers are therefore under pressure to inject a dose of violence into their productions in the belief that this is what audiences both want and enjoy. This intuition is not supported by audience research.

In Britain, where much research has been conducted into the antecedents of program appreciation, repeated studies with nationally representative viewing panels have found little evidence to support the contention that violence enhances program popularity. Instead, there are some sections of the audience, most notably women, for whom violence reduces their enjoyment of programs. There is some suggestive evidence, however, that not all violence should be regarded in the same

way in this context. Retributive violence in which the ends justify the means and villains are severely punished for their wrongdoing may enhance program appreciation.

VI. RESEARCH, REGULATION, AND CONTROL

The debate about television violence has given rise to many conflicting points of view. These stem not simply from contradictory research findings in which one study fails to corroborate the findings of another, but from a deep-seated academic divide between social scientific and media researchers who exhibit allegiances to fundamentally different theoretical and methodological approaches to the subject. The United States was the home of Behaviorism and its perspective on measuring and explaining human behavior influenced approaches to media research. In Europe, a different approach has placed greater emphasis on cognitive factors and their central role in mediating the way audiences interpret and respond to media messages.

The ideological biases of these two schools of thought have shaped the dominant methodological perspectives. American researchers have tended to place greater emphasis upon experimental methodologies in which externally observable behavior is assessed and effects are precisely quantified in numerical terms. The aim is to find consistencies across viewers in patterns of response to television portrayals. Outside the United States, the more cognitive approach of European critical media studies places more emphasis upon the analysis of meanings conveyed by media "texts," the mental "scripts" which audiences develop as "readers" to anticipate plot developments and contextualize events on-screen, and different kinds of judgements which may be placed on the same text by different viewers. This approach tends to use qualitative research methods to measures audience reactions to television content and eschews the methodological straitjacket of quantitative methods which attempt to measure viewers' involvement with television in purely numerical terms. The general view is that quantitative approaches fail to represent the rich and varied nature of audiences' understanding of television programs.

Even social science researchers outside the U.S. have criticized the validity of many of the conclusions that have been drawn from American media effects research. Among the major problems identified are: a failure to report nonsignificant results in correlational surveys which contradict a television violence effects conclusion; a failure to represent the true nature of television viewing in laboratory based experiments accompanied by measuring aggressive behavior in a fairly narrow, unrealistic fashion; and a failure to represent sufficiently the various psychological processes that can mediate viewers' responses to television. This kind of effects research has so far given insufficient attention to the concept of identification with characters on-screen, which qualitative research has revealed to be a prominent factor that cannot be properly represented through simplistic experimental manipulations in the laboratory.

There have been calls for a rethink of the most appropriate paradigm to adopt to achieve any real progress in establishing the significance of television violence in the lives of viewers and the nature and extent of its impact upon them. While the possibility that television can influence audiences on a number of psychological levels is not doubted, a big question mark is drawn over the contribution that has so far been made by behaviorism-oriented research to the general understanding of this relationship.

Outside the United States, therefore, while caution is generally exhibited over the depiction of violent portrayals where there is some suspicion that adverse audience effects may follow, more immediate weight is attached to adverse public opinion about programs. Thus, broadcast regulations often stress that television broadcasts should not offend common standards of public taste and decency in addition to ensuring that material is not transmitted which would be likely to incite people to commit violence themselves. While being mindful of not wishing to incite viewers to commit crimes or take part in civil disturbances through things shown on television, broadcasters and their regulators in many parts of the world beyond the United States are more immediately responsive to breaches of public codes of good taste and social and moral values than they are to accusations of causing increased social violence or individual acts of interpersonal aggression.

Also See the Following Articles

AGGRESSION, PSYCHOLOGY OF • BEHAVIORAL PSYCHOLOGY • CHILDREN, IMPACT OF TELEVISION ON • JUVENILE CRIME • MASS MEDIA, GENERAL VIEW • POPULAR MUSIC • PORNOGRAPHY • TELEVISION PROGRAMMING AND VIOLENCE, U.S.

Bibliography

Belson, W. (1978). *Television violence and the adolescent boy.* Aldershot, UK: Saxon House.

Berkowitz, L. & LePage, A. (1967). Weapons as aggression-eliciting stimuli. *Journal of Personality and Social Psychology, 7,* 202–207.

Berkowitz, L., Parke, R. D., Leyens, J. P., & West, S. G. (1974). The effects of justified and unjustified movie violence on aggression in juvenile delinquents. *Journal of Research in Crime and Delinquency, 11,* 16–24.

Bouwman, H., & Stappers, J. (1984). The Dutch violence profile: A replication of Gerbner's message system analysis. In G. Melischek, K. E. Rosengren, & J. Stappers (Eds.), *Cultural indicators: An international symposium.* Vienna, Austria: Austrian Academy of Sciences.

Broadcasting Standards Council (1994). *Monitoring report II.* London: Broadcasting Standards Council.

Broadcasting Standards Council (1995). *Monitoring report III.* London: Broadcasting Standards Council.

Centerwall, B. S. (1989). Exposure to television as a cause of violence. *Public Communication and Behavior, 2,* 1–58.

Cumberbatch, G., & Howitt, D. (1989). *A measure of uncertainty: The effects of the mass media.* London: John Libbey.

Cumberbatch, G., Jones, I., & Lee, M. (1988) Measuring violence on television. *Current Psychology: Research and Reviews, 7*(1), 10–25.

Doob, A. N., & Macdonald, C. E. (1979). Television viewing and fear of victimization: Is the relationship causal? *Journal of Personality and Social Psychology, 37,* 170–179.

Freedman, J. L. (1984). Effect of television violence on aggressiveness. *Psychological Bulletin, 96*(2), 227–246.

Gauntlett, D. (1995). *Moving experiences: Understanding television's influences and effects.* London: John Libbey.

Ginpil, S. (1976). Violent and dangerous acts on New Zealand television. *New Zealand Journal of Educational Studies, 11* 152–157.

Gordon, D. R., & Ibson, T. L. (1977). Content analysis of the news media: Radio. In *Report of the royal commission on violence in the communications industry: Violence in television, films and news (Vol. 3, pp. 677–703). Toronto, Canada: The Royal Commission.*

Gordon, D. R., & Singer, P. D. (1977). Content analysis of the news media: Newspapers and television. In *Report of the royal commission on violence in the communications industry: Violence in television, films and news. (Vol. 3).* Toronto, Canada: The Royal Commission.

Granzberg, G., & Steinbring, J. (1980). *Television and the Canadian Indian.* Technical report, University of Winnipeg, Department of Anthropology.

Gunter, B. (1985). *Dimensions of television violence.* Aldershot, UK: Gower.

Gunter, B. (1987). *Television and the fear of crime.* London: John Libbey.

Gunter, B., & Harrison, J. (1997). *Violence on television: A content analysis of British programs.* London, UK: Routledge.

Gunter, B., & Wober, M. (1988). *Violence on television: What the viewers think.* London: John Libbey.

Gunter, B., & Wober, M. (1993). The Gulf crisis and television: The public's response in Britain. In B. Greenberg & W. Gantz. (Eds.), *Desert Storm and the mass media.* pp. 281–298. Cresskill, NJ: Hampton Press.

Gurevitch. M. (1972). The structure and content of television broadcasting in four countries: An overview. In G. A. Comstock & E. A. Rubinstein (Eds.), *Television and social behaviour: Media content and control* (Vol. 1, pp. 374–385). Washington, DC: U.S. Government Printing Office.

Haines, H. (1983). *Violence on television: A report on the mental health foundation's media watch survey.* Mental Health Foundation of New Zealand, Auckland.

Halloran, J. D., & Croll, P. (1972). Television programmes in Great Britain: Content and control. In G. A. Comstock & E. A. Rubinstein (Eds.), *Television and social behaviour: Media content and control.* (Vol. 1, pp. 415–492). Washington, DC: U.S. Government Printing Office.

Himmelweit, H. T., Oppenheim, A. N., & Vince, P. (1958). *Television and the child: An empirical study of the effect of television on the young.* London: Oxford University Press.

Hodge, B., & Tripp, D. (1985). *Children and television.* Cambridge, UK: Polity Press.

Huesmann, L. R., & Eron, L. D. (Eds.) (1986). *Television and the aggressive child: A cross national comparison.* Hillsdale, NJ: Erlbaum.

Iwao, S., de Sola Pool, I., & Hagiwara, S. (1981). Japanese and US media: Some cross-cultural insights into TV violence. *Journal of Communication, 31*(2), 28–36.

Kniveton, B. H., & Stephenson, G. M. (1970). The effect of pre-experience on imitation of an aggressive film model. *British Journal of Social and Clinical Psychology, 9,* 31–36.

Leyens, J. P., & Parke, R. D. (1975) Aggressive slides can induce a weapons effect. *European Journal of Social Psychology, 5,* 229–236.

Linton, J. M., & Jowitt, G. S. (1977). A content analysis of feature films. *Report to the royal commission on violence in the communications industry: Violence in television, films and news.* (Vol. 3, pp. 574–580). Toronto, Canada, The Royal Commission.

Lynn, R., Hampson, S., & Agahi, E. (1989). Television violence and aggression: A genotype-environment, correlation and interaction theory. *Social Behavior and Personality, 17*(2), 143–164.

McCann, T. E., & Sheehan, P. W. (1985). Violence content in Australian television. *Australian Psychologist, 20*(1), 33–42.

Menon, V. (1993). Violence on television: Asian data for an Asian standard. *Intermedia, 21*(6), 40–41.

Morrisson, D. (1992). *Television and the Gulf War.* London: John Libbey.

Morrison, D. (1993b). *The viewers' view of violence: Attitudes to violence in relation to television guidelines.* Leeds: Leeds University Institute of Communication Studies, Report to the British Broadcasting Corporation.

Murdock, G. (1973). Political deviance: the press presentation of a militant mass demonstration. In S. Cohen & J. Young (Eds.), *The manufacture of news.* London: Constable.

Mustonen, A., & Pulkkinen, L. (1993). Aggression in television programmes in Finland. *Aggressive Behaviour, 19,* 175–183.

Mustonen, A., & Pulkkinen, L. (1997). Television violence: A development of a coding scheme. *Journal of Broadcasting and Electronic Media, 41,* 168–189.

Noble, G. (1975). *Children in front of the small screen.* London: Constable.

Platt, S. (1987). The aftermath of Angie's overdose: Is soap (opera) damaging to your health? *British Medical Journal, 294,* 954–957.

Shaw, I., & Newell, D. (1972). *Violence on television: Programme content and viewer perception.* London, UK: British Broadcasting Corporation.

Shearer, A. (1991). *Survivors and the media.* Broadcasting Standards Council Research Monograph Series: 2. London: John Libbey.

Sheppard, A., Sheehy, N. P., & Young, B. (1989). *Violence on television: An intervention.* Report to the independent Broadcasting Authority. Leeds, UK: University of Leeds, Department of Psychology.

Shinar, D., Parnes, P., & Caspi, D. (1972). Structure and content of television broadcasting in Israel. In G. A. Comstock & E. A. Rubinstein (Eds.), *Television and social behaviour: Media content and control* (Vol. 1). Rockwell, MD: National Institute of Mental Health.

Stewart, D. E. (1983). *The television family—A content analysis of the portrayal of family life in prime time television.* Melbourne: Institute of Family Studies.

Van der Voort, T. H. A. (1986). *Television violence: A child's eye view.* Amsterdam, Holland: Elsevier.

Vooijs, M. W., & van der Voort, T. H. A. (1993). Teaching children to evaluate television violence critically: The impact of a Dutch schools television project. *Journal of Educational Television, 19*(3), 139–152.

Watson, C., Bassett, G., Lambourne, R., & Shuker, R. (1991). *Television violence: An analysis of the portrayal of "violent acts" on the three New Zealand broadcast television channels during the week of 11th–17th February 1991.* Research project for the Broadcasting Standards Authority by the Educational Research and Development Centre, Massey University.

Wiegman, O., Kuttschreuter, M., & Baarda, B. (1992). A longitudinal study of the effects of television viewing on aggressive and pro-social behaviors, *British Journal of Social Psychology, 31,* 147–164.

Williams, T. M. (Ed.) (1986). *The impact of television: A natural experiment in three communities.* London: Academic Press.

Williams, T. M., Zabrack, M. L., & Joy, L. A. (1982). The portrayal of aggression on North American television. *Journal of Applied Social Psychology, 12*(5), 360–380.

Wober, J. M. (1992). Violence and appreciation: The broken chain. *Medien Psychologie, 4*(1), 15–24.

Wober, J. M. (1997). Violence or other routes to appreciation: TV program-makers' options. *Journal of Broadcasting and Electronic Media, 41,* 190–202.

Wober, M., & Gunter, B. (1988). *Television and social control.* Aldershot, UK: Avebury.

Television Programming and Violence, U.S.

Leonard D. Eron and L. Rowell Huesmann

University of Michigan

I. Introduction
II. Research Evidence
III. Manifestations of the Television Effect
IV. Psychological Processes
V. Counteracting Media Effects

Television Violence Graphic display of aggressive/violent acts on the television screen.

GLOSSARY

Aggression/Violence An act intended to inflict physical harm on another person.
Cuing/Priming When observation of something in the environment activates associated thoughts, beliefs, or scripts making their retrieval more likely (priming) or signals that a particular belief or script is appropriate (cuing).
Desensitization Reduced physiological and psychological responses to observation of violence after repeated exposure.
Moderator A factor, e.g., age of viewer, that exacerbates or mitigates the effects of TV violence.
Normative Beliefs Beliefs about the appropriateness of aggressive and violent behavior.
Observational Learning Imitation by an observer of behavior displayed by a model or adoption of attitudes and beliefs displayed by a model.
Scripts Sequences of stimuli, behaviors and outcomes that are learned by observation and encoded in memory and which guide an individual's behavior.

I. INTRODUCTION

Television is the most obvious, ubiquitous, and potent source of information available to children growing up in the U.S. Children are not only being entertained but also educated by television. The information they receive from the endless number of cartoons, sitcoms, and prime time programs that pervade the airwaves cannot but affect the way they interact with and view society. Since violent content is a staple of American television programming, it should not be surprising that extensive exposure to this medium in early childhood promotes cognitions (i.e., beliefs, attitudes, and justifications) that support the use of aggressive and violent behavior in solving interpersonal problems, relieving frustration, and acquiring material possessions as well as power and influence over others. The cognitions learned through this early exposure affect behavior not only concurrently but also over time and their influence can be detected in the aggressive, antisocial, and criminal behaviors of young adults. There also is abundant evidence that witnessing television violence can influence the behavior of adult viewers, at least in the short term by cuing aggressive ideas and scripts. In order to counteract the influence of what is learned via the media and to counteract such cuing effects, children and ado-

Encyclopedia of Violence, Peace, and Conflict, Volume 3   477   Copyright © 1999 by Academic Press.
All rights of reproduction in any form reserved.

lescents must develop attitudes and normative beliefs about the appropriateness and frequency of aggressive behavior which do not support the use of violence to solve the problems noted here. This article documents the above conclusions.

A. Definitions

In this article, we are concerned primarily with aggression and violence as acts that are intended to injure or irritate another person. This does not refer to assertive behavior. Thus, a so-called "aggressive" salesperson would not be considered aggressive according to this definition unless, of course, he or she committed acts intended to injure another person. Television violence, in this article, refers specifically to graphic visual portrayals of acts of physical violence by one or more persons against another person or persons. However, this does not include references to off-screen violence that are not actually portrayed on the program but merely mentioned or later described in some detail.

B. Pervasiveness of Television

Television was introduced to the U.S. at the New York World's Fair in 1939, and on July 1, 1941 the Federal Communications Commission (FCC) licensed and approved the first commercial television stations. However, World War II interrupted development in this country and full-scale broadcasting was suspended until 1946. Currently, at least 98% of households in the U.S. have a television set, more households than have indoor plumbing. During the 1970s, a new dimension was added with the introduction of cable television. In 1992, 60.2% of the households with television sets had cable. Video cassette recorders (VCRs) became very popular in the 1980s, and in the early 1990s it was estimated that at least 75% of households with televisions also had VCR equipment. The availability of VCRs in most homes provides children with the opportunity to view violent films and interferes with efforts to control what children watch. These are fairly stable patterns that have been revealed over many years of research. It has been found that television occupies more time than any other nonschool activity and takes up more than half of children's leisure activity time. By the time children graduate from high school, they will have spent 54% more time in front of a television set than in front of a teacher. Also, there is more viewing among African-American and Latino children, independent of socioeconomic status. Many of the poorest and potentially most vulnerable groups in society are the heaviest viewers because of the lack of alternative activities for them (Comstock, G. & Paik, H. Television and the American Child. 1991, Academic Press).

C. Extent of Violence in Programming

The content of television programming is heavily devoted to depictions of violence. A number of studies have estimated that every hour of prime time television programming contains 5 violent acts, whereas 1 hour of Saturday morning children's programming contains an average of 20–25 violent acts. An average child watching an average amount of TV will see about 20,000 murders and 80,000 assaults by the onset of adolescence. A 1992 study of 1-day's programming (from 2:00 A.M. to midnight) on broadcast and cable channels in Washington DC notes 1980 violent scenes including murder, assault with and without guns, athletic violence, and property destruction. Highly violent acts occur in 15% of all programs shown in the U.S. Children's cartoons contain an average of 23 acts of violence per hour. Children's programs are 9% above the overall average for percentage of programs with violence, as indicated in the study described in the following paragraph.

More pertinent, perhaps, to the relation between viewing violence on TV and subsequent behavior than the total amount of violence watched is the context in which the violence is presented. In a report released in 1996, a team of researchers from the University of California in Santa Barbara, the University of North Carolina, the University of Texas, and the University of Wisconsin presented data based on 2500 hours of entertainment, movies, and reality programs (but excluding sports and nightly newscasts) on 23 cable and broadcast channels, including PBS, during the 1994–1995 season. The study monitored programs between the hours of 6:00 A.M. and 11:00 P.M. over a 20-week period. It was found that the majority of programs on television contained violence, that one out of four violent interactions involved use of handguns, that the perpetrators largely went unpunished, and the most violent portrayals did not show the negative consequences of the act. Indeed, 47% of all violent conflicts on TV showed no harm to victims and 58% showed no pain. Only 16% of all programs showed the long-term negative effects of violence including psychological, emotional, or financial harm. The perpetrators went unpunished in 73% of the incidents. It is the contention of the authors of this study that the context and explicitness of the portrayed violence is at least as important as the total quantity of violence. Another important finding of this study was that antiviolence messages are scarce on television despite their demonstrated effectiveness. Finally, in their executive summary of the research report, the investigators stated "The sheer frequency with which violence is encountered throughout the television landscape and the number of violent incidents that are observed by most viewers can contribute to desensitization and fear as well as providing ample opportunities to learn violent attitudes and behavior." These effects, among others, are discussed below.

II. RESEARCH EVIDENCE

Since 1960, a body of evidence coming from both laboratory research and survey studies based on real-life experience has confirmed that there is a causative relation between the observation of aggression and violence on television and subsequent aggressive and violent behavior on the part of the observer. This is especially true for young children, and for these observers, the effect is not just temporary, but is sustained over the years. For example, one study has shown that the amount of violence youngsters watch on television at age 8 is related to their aggressiveness 10 years later and to the seriousness of criminal acts 22 years later at age 30. These relations hold up even when initial aggressiveness, IQ, and social class are statistically controlled.

Over 35 years of research by many behavioral scientists has validated the causal connection between the observation of television violence and the subsequent violent behavior of young viewers, with a significant carryover into adulthood. A number of national commissions composed of eminent scholars who have reviewed all of the available studies have all come to the same conclusion—there is a causal relation between viewing violent television and subsequent behavior. The National Commission on the Causes and Prevention of Violence, which issued its report in 1969, was the first of this series. In 1972, the Surgeon General's Scientific Advisory Committee on Television and Social Behavior came to the same conclusion, as did the National Institute of Mental Health in 1982 and the American Psychological Association, in reports issued by two panels in 1989 and 1993. The Centers for Disease Control and the American Pediatric Association have issued similar reports.

Of course it is not contended that television violence is the only cause of aggression and violence in society today. Aggression is a multiply determined behavior. It is the product of a number of interacting factors—genetic, perinatal, physiological, neurological, and environmental. It is only when there is a convergence of factors that violent behavior occurs. No one factor is necessary or sufficient to produce long-term antisocial behavior. Thus, media violence alone cannot account for the development of serious antiviolent behavior. It is, however, a potential contributor to the learning environment of children who eventually go on to develop aggressive behavior. Furthermore, research supports the view that the effect of violence viewing on aggression is relatively independent of other likely influences and is of a magnitude great enough to account for socially important differences. The current level of interpersonal violence has certainly been boosted by the long-term effects of many persons' exposure to a steady diet of TV violence when they were children.

A. Field Studies

The many correlational field studies demonstrating a relation between violence viewing and aggressive behavior at one point in time have been correctly criticized by some writers as not being proof of cause and effect. However, these studies do not stand alone. Longitudinal studies, when both the predictor (violence viewing) and the criterion (violent behavior) are measured at two or three different points in time, have provided compelling evidence of a causal effect over time for TV violence. For example, in the 22-year longitudinal study mentioned above, it was demonstrated that those boys who at age 8 were highly aggressive but were not watching violent television were significantly less aggressive at age 19 than those boys who were similarly highly aggressive at age 8 but were indeed watching violent television. By age 30, these same subjects who had been viewing violent television had more serious and more frequent criminal records.

The longitudinal findings of this study have been corroborated by research in a different area of the U.S. and in other countries, e.g., Finland, Poland, and Israel, supporting the position that the viewing of televised violence leads to increases in subsequent aggression and such acts can become part of a lasting behavioral pattern. These later studies have also demonstrated that the effect is present now for girls as well as boys in at least three of the countries. Other longitudinal studies conducted by different researchers have reported similar results.

B. Laboratory Studies

The final piece of evidence proving causation has been provided with classroom experiments where conditions are experimentally controlled and there is random assignment of subjects to conditions. Cause and effect are unambiguously demonstrated in these experiments. The typical paradigm is that randomly selected children who are shown either a violent or a nonviolent short film are observed immediately afterward as they play with each other or with objects. Consistently, it has been found that children who see the violent film clips behave more aggressively than those who view the non-aggressive clips. Just as children learn cognitive and social skills from watching people act out such skills, they learn violent behaviors from watching other people behave violently. It is also true that in the laboratory children can be taught to be less aggressive by showing them films with prosocial models. The findings of these laboratory studies complement those of the field studies in affirming the causal relation between viewing violence and subsequent violent behavior on the part of its observer. These destructive effects are not limited to children. Laboratory experiments have demonstrated that adults can be affected by observed violence as well as children, at least for short periods subsequent to the viewing. In adults the observation of violence seems to trigger aggressive ideas and scripts that have been learned earlier in life more than it teaches new aggressive habits.

C. Meta-Analysis

Meta-analysis refers to a quantitative aggregation of research results permitting conclusions about the size of the causal effect from an objective and comprehensive survey of the literature. To date, there have been at least four meta-analyses of the extant literature, all of which come to the same conclusion; there is a causal relation to varying degrees between observation of television violence and subsequent violent behavior. The most recently published meta-analysis summarized and aggregated 217 of the best studies done between 1957 and 1990, and the authors concluded that research findings obtained during that period strengthen the evidence that viewing television violence increases aggressive and antisocial behaviors. The results from study to study are robust. All types of aggressive behavior, including illegal behaviors and criminal violence, had highly significant effect sizes associated with exposure to television violence. The studies using criminal violence and other illegal activities as criteria of aggressive behavior yielded comparable findings to studies in which less-violent aggressive behavior was the criterion.

III. MANIFESTATIONS OF THE TELEVISION EFFECT

Viewing television violence affects individuals differently. While it is scientifically undisputed that viewing violence on TV leads to an overall increase in violence behavior, the effects show up in a number of ways.

A. Copying Aggression

The most obvious effect, of course, is the actual copying of the behavior—when the actors who carry out the mayhem on screen serve as models for behavior. This is especially effective when the observers are young children. Young children very often imitate what they see other persons do—particularly if the other person is a desirable hero. Observational learning is one of the most powerful mechanisms through which children acquire social skills and learn how to behave in society. There are a number of factors which, it has been shown, affect the learning of behavior observed on the TV screen. Whether the child identifies with the actor and whether the actor is perceived as possessing valued characteristics affects the likelihood of observational learning. If the actor is rewarded for the aggressive behavior, the observer is more likely to model the behavior. On the other hand, if the observed aggressive behavior is punished, the child is less likely to imitate the behavior. If a child is constantly exposed to television and film heroes solving problems aggressively without any subsequent punishment for the aggressor, the child will mimic these behaviors. In the study of television program content and context noted previously, the researchers assessed the rewards and punishments associated with violence and found that in the majority of violent scenes aggression is neither rewarded nor punished. However, it is explicitly rewarded (15%) almost as often as it is punished (19%) at the time it occurs. When punishment does occur, it is usually toward bad characters and only rarely toward good characters. Thus, the characters that children are most likely to identify with are rarely discouraged from acting aggressively by punishment for their acts.

B. Desensitization

A second effect of continued watching of violence is desensitization. The continuous habitual exposure to media violence desensitizes children, and adults as well, to the negative emotional reactions that aggression and violence normally produce. After enough exposures, the physiological signs of unpleasant emotions disappear, and the viewer becomes relatively unaroused by violence. This makes the viewer less affected by his or her own violent acts as well as insensitive to violence perpetrated by others and leads to the decreased likelihood of taking any action to help a victim of violence (the so called "bystander effect"). Contributing to desensitization is the humor that often accompanies aggressive interchanges (39% of violent scenes). This is especially apparent in children's cartoons so that children come to believe that acting aggressively is funny.

C. Attitude Change

A third effect is attitude change. Viewers of violence become more accepting of violence and adopt attitudes condoning violence. Viewers of violence also display increased fearfulness about becoming a victim of violence and mistrust of others. The child comes to believe the world is a dangerous place, the so called "mean world syndrome," and modifies his or her behavior with either a heightened alertness and precautions (including arming oneself) or withdrawal to supposed safe havens. Important in the development of these fear responses is the fact that a higher percentage (73%) of violent scenes do not show the perpetrator being punished. Viewers shown violence that is unpunished are significantly more likely to become anxious and fearful especially if the violence is undeserved or targeted against innocent victims. Such persons come to believe that the world about them is full of potential dangers of which they are likely to be victims unless they take extreme precautions.

IV. PSYCHOLOGICAL PROCESSES

What are the psychological processes that bring about these effects and/or account for the relation between viewing violence and subsequent violent behaviors? These intervening variables have been termed mediators. Also important are moderators, which function to diminish or increase the relation, and correlated factors, which, in themselves, have no apparent effect on the relation but often help to recognize it. The most impor- tant psychological process accounting for the appearance of aggressive behaviors is learning. Over 50 years of research on human aggression indicates that habitual aggressive behavior is largely learned in the child's early interactions with the environment. While genetic and physiological factors may predispose some children more than others toward aggression, for most children it is their early learning experiences, both observational and actual, that mold them into youths who behave more or less aggressively. In this regard, television, as indicated above, is a powerful teacher and also, as indicated above, provides many opportunities for the learning of such behaviors by impressionable young children.

A. Observational Learning of Cognitions and Behaviors

Previously it was thought that observational learning of behaviors, as described above, by itself accounted for the relation between viewing of violence on TV and its subsequent enactment by the viewer. More recently, it has been demonstrated that by frequent observation of violence children also learn cognitions that support the use of violence in interpersonal actions; it is these cognitions that often mediate or provide the link between observation and later behavior. Not only do young viewers adopt specific behaviors modeled by others but they also tend to adopt evaluative standards used by those models. By observing violence in the media, children learn scripts for complex aggressive behaviors and at the same time adopt attitudes about the appropriateness of aggressive and violent behavior. The latter have been termed normative beliefs. Scripts are programs for behavior that lay out a sequence of events that the individual believes is likely to happen and how one is to respond given what is appropriate and possible for a particular situation. Normative beliefs act as internal self-regulatory standards serving to filter out behaviors that are not acceptable. Cognitive rehearsal of these scripts and normative beliefs occur whenever the child is exposed to a violent sequence on TV or fantasizes about a sequence previously observed. These reexposures and fantasy experiences serve as rehearsals of the violent sequences which are then more readily called up from memory and serve as guides to action. An individual who has previously learned mostly violent scripts and very few prosocial scripts, for example, will likely resort to the violent ones when faced with an ambiguous social interaction since they are better learned than the prosocial scripts and thus will be retrieved from memory more readily.

There are also at least five variables that are important in affecting the magnitude of the television viewing–aggression relation mediated by cognitions. These are the child's intellectual achievement, social popularity, identification with TV characters, belief in the realism of violence shown on television, and the amount of fantasizing about aggression in which the child engages. These variables are considered moderators of the relation. These and other moderators are discussed below.

B. Cognitive Cuing and Priming

Television violence not only teaches aggressive scripts and beliefs, it can also stimulate the use of aggressive scripts or beliefs learned in other ways. According to this perspective, observation of an aggressive sequence can prime or "trigger" other related thoughts that increase the probability that the observation of a specific aggressive act will induce other aggressive ideas, e.g., aggressive ideas brought on by viewing violence on TV can prime other semantically related thoughts, increasing the probability that they will come to mind. In this way, when an individual views an aggressive act on television it activates other thoughts that are cognitively associated with aggression. Once these additional thoughts have come to mind, they can influence aggressive responding in a variety of ways. This explains why observation of aggression in the media is often followed by acts of aggression that might differ from the actual aggressive sequence which has been observed. For example, it has been demonstrated that merely the sight of a gun can stimulate other aggressive ideas and emotions which can then affect the viewer's subsequent attitudes and behaviors. In one study it was found that college students who viewed slides of weapons were immediately willing to punish a target more severely than were those who had viewed neutral slides. Presumably, viewing the weapons stimulated other aggressive ideas and emotions which then affected the viewers' attitudes and behavior.

C. Cognitive Justification

The justification hypothesis posits that people who are aggressive like to watch violent television because they can then justify their own behavior as being normal. It involves the observational learning of attitudes, but it operates in the opposite direction from the process described above. According to this theory, television violence viewing not only stimulates the child's aggressiveness; it results from it. A child's own aggressive behaviors normally should elicit guilt in the child, but this guilt is relieved if the child who has behaved aggressively watches violent television. Thus, the child who has behaved aggressively very often watches violent television shows to justify his or her own aggressiveness.

D. Physiological Desensitization and Excitation Transfer

Along with these cognitive explanations of the connection between observing violence in the media and subsequent violent behavior of the individual, there have been physiological explanations which by themselves account for violent behavior or are presumed to be antecedents and/or accompaniments of the various cognitive processes we have described. Observation of violence heightens physiological arousal and this arousal heightens the propensity of the person to behave aggressively (excitation transfer). For example, it has been demonstrated that violent videotapes elicit both aggressive cognitions and higher systolic blood pressure in college students. However, the evidence for physiological explanations is not as clear cut as the data which indicate the importance of cognitions as mediators in the relation between TV violence and behavior. Generally, research on affective reactions to violent displays has been concerned with the probability that continued exposure to violence on TV will lessen negative emotional reactions to violence as well as feelings of concern, empathy, or sympathy that viewers might have toward victims of active violence (desensitization). It should not be surprising that emotional and physiological responses to violent scenes habituate as do responses to other stimuli. The difference from other stimuli is that the arousal that is naturally stimulated by observing violent behaviors is usually unpleasant and therefore inhibits aggressive action. Once this arousal habituates, however, aggression is no longer inhibited.

E. Moderators

There are a number of factors, both societal and individual, which, while not causes of the relation, serve to exacerbate or mitigate the influence of television violence on aggressive behavior. Studies have shown that in societies or segments of societies where there are powerful norms against expression of aggression, television has much less influence on its expression, e.g., in the Israeli kibbutz for both boys and girls and generally for girls in many Western countries. Family characteristics have also been shown to moderate the relation between TV violence and behavior. In families where parents have more interactions and discussions with children and where television viewing is controlled by the parents there is less evidence for the TV violence–aggressive behavior connection.

Individual characteristics that influence the size and direction of the relation include age of the observer. The younger children are, the more likely they are to be influenced by viewing violence in the media and the more likely is the effect to be cumulative and long lasting. This is because young children are more impressionable and have less-mature cognitive standards which makes it more difficult for them to distinguish what they observe on the screen from "real life." However, no age is immune from influence. Similarly, while there is some evidence that low IQ is important in the relation, with less-intelligent children being more affected, it has been demonstrated that individuals at all levels of intelligence can be affected by the observation of violence on TV. Also, it is not true that only individuals who are already prone to being aggressive are affected. Children at all levels of initial aggression have been shown to be influenced in their behavior by observation of television violence.

Other related moderating variables are the child's academic achievement and social popularity. Children who behave aggressively are less popular and, perhaps because their relations with their peers tend to be unsatisfying, less popular children watch more television and view more violence. The violence they see on television may reassure them that their own behavior is appropriate or teach them new coercive techniques which they can attempt to use in their interactions with others. Thus, they behave more aggressively which in turn makes them even less popular and drives them back to the television. The evidence supports a similar role for academic failure. Those children who fail in school watch more television, perhaps because they find it more satisfying than schoolwork. Thus, they are exposed to more violence and have more opportunities to learn aggressive acts. Since their intellectual capacities are more limited, the easy aggressive solutions they observe may be incorporated more readily into their behavioral repertoires. In any case, the heavy violence viewing isolates them from their peers and gives them less time to work toward academic success. And, of course, any resulting increase in aggression itself diminishes the child's popularity. Thus, the cycle continues with aggression, academic failure, social failure, and violence viewing reinforcing each other.

Ethnicity and social class have also been invoked as correlates or moderators of the relation between media violence and behavior. However, although it is true that certain social and economic populations may be more influenced by TV violence because they watch more violence, there has been no research demonstrating that these populations are differentially affected by the same amount of exposure, both from each other and from the majority White population.

Another variable presumed to be a moderator has been gender. Since up until very recently most studies have indicated that girls are less aggressive than boys, girls were presumed to be less affected by TV. In a large-scale study done in 1960, this was indeed the case. However, more recent longitudinal studies done from the late 1970s to the 1990s indicate that girls too are now affected by television violence. This change may be a function of an increased number of aggressive female models on television and a gradual change in our cultural mores making it more acceptable for females in our society to be physically aggressive.

V. COUNTERACTING MEDIA EFFECTS

As might be expected in light of the overwhelming evidence linking television violence to violent behavior, especially in children, training programs have been introduced which, it is hoped, will ameliorate this effect. Most of these are school based and are conducted by the regular teacher during school hours. There have also been efforts to educate parents and other caretakers about these harmful effects and what they can do to prevent and/or ameliorate them.

A. An Experimental Study

An early, now-classic study was conducted over 2 years in the late 1970s with more than 700 children in the 1st and 3rd grades in a suburban Chicago school district and two inner-city schools of the Chicago archdiocese. Training procedures were aimed at changing attitudes about the acceptability of aggression in interactions with others and about the realism of television portrayals. The intervention also emphasized the undesirability of acting like aggressive television characters. Procedures were based on those used successfully in attitude change experiments—crediting the children for possessing attitudes it is hoped they would adopt, encouraging perception of personal responsibility, inducing the belief that one is participating out of free choice, and promoting the perception that the consequences of one's behaviors are important. This was accomplished by asking children in the experimental group to make videotapes to be shown to other children in Chicago who had been "fooled" by television and "got into trouble by imitating TV although they (the experimental subjects) knew better." They then composed essays explaining how TV is not like real life and why it would be harmful to watch too much TV and to imitate the violent characters. The children were videotaped reading their essays, and the tapes were then played before the entire group. This gave the children an opportunity to see themselves advocate an antiviolent position and it also made their position public so that other children knew their feelings and attitudes about both television and aggressive behavior. Four months after the intervention was completed, those children in the experimental group were significantly less aggressive than children in the control group who had similar aggression and television violence scores at the start but had a different, yet equivalent treatment over the 2 intervention years. Further, the more the youngsters' attitudes and normative beliefs changed over the 2-year period, the more their peer-nominated aggression score decreased.

B. Media Literacy Interventions

"Media literacy" and "critical viewing skills" are terms used to describe interventions that are aimed at teaching children—and occasionally parents—how to watch television without being affected by the violent and other antisocial messages that television seems to be delivering. For example, students are taught how unrealistic sequences can be put together spuriously with visual and sound effects to be made to look realistic. Thus, by developing critical viewing skills, it is hoped that the effect of observation will be ameliorated. Curricula are also designed to recognize certain types of negative portrayals of social behavior and to point out alternative ways of interpreting those portrayals. Further, these curricula also are designed to give the viewer the ability to devalue the source of information, assess the motivation for presenting the information, and to judge the reality of the presentation. Unfortunately, there have not yet been any rigorous evaluations showing that these program have long-lasting effect.

C. Role of Parents

Training for parents includes informing them of the negative effects that viewing of violence on TV can have for their children and, at the same time, teaching them how to control and shape their children's television habits. The first thing parents can do is limit the number of hours the child is permitted to watch TV. Since violence is so pervasive in both adult's and children's programming, merely limiting the number of hours will reduce the amount of violence to which the child is exposed. Some researchers suggest that preschoolers should watch no more than 2 hours daily. The American Psychological Association has issued a number of recommendations to parents on how to reduce the effect of television on children as follows.

To reduce the amount of TV viewing: (1) Parent and child can work together to keep a time chart of the child's activities, including TV viewing, homework, and play with friends. Then, the parents can discuss what they believe to be a balanced set of activities. (2) Parents should set a weekly viewing limit. At the beginning of the week, children should select programs approved by the parents from television schedules. (3) TV should be ruled out at certain times, such as before breakfast, during meals, or on school nights. (4) Together, the parent and child should make a list of alternative activities—riding a bicycle, reading a book, or working on a hobby. Before watching TV, the child must choose and do something from the list. (5) Planned viewing should be encouraged. The parent should have program choices in mind before turning on the TV set in the child's room. (6) It should be remembered that children learn from their parents. If parents watch a lot of TV, chances are their children will also watch a lot. As for controlling the amount of violence observed by the child, parents should try to watch at least one episode of the programs the child is watching so as to get first-hand knowledge of the violent content. And they should consult the ratings in the TV sections of the newspapers and/or *TV Guide*. Rankings of the most and least violent shows are also published by such organizations as the National PTA TV Action Center. When violence does appear during programs, the parent should discuss with the child what it is that motivates the characters to act in this way, what a better response could have been, how the character might have solved the problem differently, and what the painful consequences of violence really are. Parents should explain to the child how the violence has been faked, that it really hasn't happened, and explain how sound and visual effects can make the sequence appear realistic and how most persons never react in this way. Also, the child should be encouraged to watch other programs with characters and situations that demonstrate helping, caring, and cooperation of which there are a number.

D. Role of the Media

But just because there are these things parents can do, however, does not absolve the film and television industries from their responsibility for reducing the level of violence portrayed on the screen. There are too many instances in which parents cannot comply with such suggestions. In families with single parents or two working parents TV often acts as a baby-sitter. Or in more fortunate families with more than one TV in the home, it becomes difficult for parents to monitor their children's TV behavior. Similarly, monitoring children is difficult when they can go to friends' houses to watch programs forbidden at home. And unfortunately there are too many families in which the parents do not care or do not know about TV's effects. Therefore, the TV and film industries should accept their responsibilities to protect children from this mayhem and reduce the amount of violence on the TV screen. Of late there has been some indication that the industry is responding to pressure from viewers—and governmental agencies (see below)—to do something about the problems.

Earlier we discussed the large-scale study sponsored by the cable stations and conducted by faculty members at four universities in which the amount and context of violent displays are being monitored over a 3-year period. Results for the first year have been published and, as pointed out above, the amount of violence in TV programming is indeed at a very high level and is especially harmful to young viewers as a result of important contextual factors. Perhaps this has been a watershed year and the following years will show a marked decline in such programming on the cable stations. A similar study is being conducted by an independent group of scholars for the TV broadcast networks. As of the date of this writing, no final report by this group has been issued other than a brief one indicating there has been a reduction over the past year in the extent of violence depicted on four networks.

Is it too much to expect that the TV industry will voluntarily curtail to any appreciable degree the amount of violence portrayed on the screen? Probably so. After all, violence supposedly sells and many of the most popular programs for both adults and children have contained violence, at least over the past 3 decades. Even a 1% increase in viewers can increase profits by millions of dollars, so the ability of violence to attract viewers is an important measure of financial success. Also, violence is generally less expensive to produce because one can get by with scripts that are trite, poorly written, and poorly acted, while successful dramas that contain little or no violence are more expensive to produce and require greater writing and acting talent. Thus it is probably too much to expect the TV industry to do much to reduce violence in its presentations without some prodding from the government.

E. Role of Government

Indeed the government has recently weighed in on the side of concerned parents and other citizens. Both candidates for the presidency in the recent campaign inveighed against violence in television programming and the general lack of support for "family values" seen in such programming, indicating there would be some official actions if the extent of violence in the media did not subside. Already, however, government has had some influence. In response to prodding by Senator Paul Simon of Illinois and other Congressional figures, the networks have instituted warning labels which are flashed on the screen before the showing of violent sequences. Also, legislation has been passed and signed by the President to require all new TV sets to be outfitted with an electronic device, the V-chip, by which parents or other supervisors can block out programs deemed not appropriate for child viewing. Further, the FCC has issued requirements for licensing of TV stations that include a minimum number of hours per week devoted to children's educational programs. Presumably, if children are watching educational programs they will not be watching violence. Also, the educational programs could offer alternative solutions to solving problems and discourage the use of aggression and violence. The effectiveness of any of these measures will depend to a great extent on their implementation. Currently, it appears that the government is ready to allow the purveyors of violence to develop a single rating code for each program that is supposed to capture all objectionable aspects, e.g., violence, sex, and language. This effort is proceeding despite the fact that polls show that the public wants a system with separate ratings for violence that can be read by the V-chip. Furthermore, the rating effort is controlled by an advocate for the film industry who has in the past vigorously denied that media violence has any effect on behavior. Given the well-known penchant for youths to be attracted to R-rated films, a single rating system may well be ineffective. On the other hand, the possibility of affecting even small segments of audience may well motivate ratings-conscious sponsors and producers to reduce violence despite such an imperfect system.

The prospect of censorship by government agencies

does not appear likely at this time because of objections on the basis of First Amendment rights. However, the Centers for Disease Control has termed youth violence an epidemic, threatening the health of young persons throughout the nation. Soon serious consideration may have to be given to whether this proven threat to the nation's public health is outweighed by threats to free speech.

Also See the Following Articles

CHILDREN, IMPACT OF TELEVISION ON • JUVENILE CRIME • MASS MEDIA, GENERAL VIEW • POPULAR MUSIC • TELEVISION PROGRAMMING AND VIOLENCE, INTERNATIONAL

Bibliography

Bandura, A. (1973). *Aggression: A social learning analysis.* Englewood Cliffs, NJ: Prentice–Hall.

Bandura, A. (1986). *Social foundations of thought and action: A social cognitive theory.* Englewood Cliffs, NJ: Prentice-Hall.

Bandura, A., Ross, D., & Ross, S. A. (1961). Transmission of aggression through imitation of aggressive models. *Journal of Abnormal and Social Psychology, 63,* 575–582.

Berkowitz, L. (1974). Some determinants of impulsive aggression: The role of mediated associations with reinforcements for aggression. *Psychological Review, 81,* 165–176.

Berkowitz, L. (1984). Some effects of thoughts on anti- and prosocial influences of media events: A cognitive-neoassociation analysis. *Psychological Bulletin, 95*(3), 410–427.

Berkowitz, L. (1993). *Aggression: Its causes, consequences and control.* New York: McGraw-Hill.

Bushman, B. J., & Geen, R. (1990). Role of cognitive-emotional mediators and individual differences in the effects of media violence on aggression. *Journal of Personality and Social Psychology, 58,* 156–163.

Comstock, G. A., & Paik, H. (1991). *Television and the American child.* San Diego, CA: Academic Press.

Comstock, G., & Paik, A. (1994). The effects of television violence on antisocial behavior: A meta-analysis. *Communication Research, 21,* 516–546.

Eron, L. D. (1987). The development of aggressive behavior from the perspective of a developing behaviorism. *American Psychologist, 42,* 435–442.

Eron, L. D., Huesmann, L. R., Lefkowitz, M. M. & Walder, L. O. (1972). Does television violence cause aggression? *American Psychologist, 27,* 253–263.

Eron, L. D., Walder, L. O., & Lefkowitz, M. M. (1971). *The learning of aggression in children.* Boston: Little, Brown.

Gerbner, G., & Gross, L. P. (1980). The violent face of television and its lessons. In E. L. Palmer & A. D. Orr (Eds.), *Children and the faces of television: Teaching, violence, selling,* pp. 149–162. New York: Academic Press.

Huesmann, L. R. (1988). An information processing model for the development of aggression. *Aggressive Behavior, 14,* 13–24.

Huesmann, L. R., & Eron, L. D. (1984). Cognitive processes and the persistence of aggressive behavior. *Aggressive Behavior, 10,* 243–251.

Huesmann, L. R., Eron, L. D., Brice, P., Klein, R., & Fisher, P. (1983). Mitigating the imitation of aggressive behaviors by changing children's attitudes about media violence. *Journal of Personality and Social Psychology, 44,* 899–910.

Huesmann, L. R., Eron, L. D., Lefkowitz, M. M., & Walder, L. O. (1973). Television violence and aggression: The causal effect remains. *American Psychologist, 28,* 617–620.

Huesmann, L. R., Moise, J. F., & Podolski, C. (1997). The effects of media violence on the development of anti social behaviors. In D. Stoff, J. Breiling, & J. Maser (Eds.), *Handbook of antisocial behavior.* New York: Wiley.

Kunkel, D., Wilson, B. J., Linz, D., Potter, J., Donnerstein, E., Smith, S. Z., Blumenthal, E., & Gray, T. (1996). Violence in television programming overall: University of California, Santa Barbara Study. In J. Federman (Ed.), *National television violence study: Scientific papers.* Studio City, CA: Mediascope.

Singer, J. L., & Singer, D. G. (1981). *Television, imagination, and aggression.* Hillsdale, NJ: Erlbaum.

Territorial Disputes

Paul F. Diehl

University of Illinois at Urbana–Champaign

GLOSSARY

Border Dispute Disagreement between two or more states over the delimitation or demarcation of an international boundary.

Contiguity The sharing of a common land or sea border between two or more states.

Intrinsic Importance Inherent value that a piece of territory has for the sovereign, including the availability of resources (water, minerals, etc.), space for development and living and the like.

Opportunity Effect The result of sharing a border that makes interactions, including conflict, between neighbors more likely than between other pairs of states.

Proximity Effect The result of states being geographically close such that conflict is more likely because states are able to project military power more easily against their neighbors than against other states.

Relational Importance The specific and sometimes unique value that a given territory might have for a particular state; what may be regarded as important territory for one state because of location or historical

associations may not be as important to the other disputant.

Territorial Change The voluntary or involuntary transfer of control over a given territory from one political entity to another.

TERRITORIAL DISPUTES, reflecting disagreements between states over the same pieces of territory, are critical phenomena in understanding the conditions for war and peace in international relations. This article surveys the different conceptual and operational definitions of territorial disputes and summarizes the research findings on when territorial disputes and changes are likely to escalate to war or be resolved peacefully. Final consideration is given to promising questions for a future research agenda.

I. INTRODUCTION

Geographic concerns have often been at the center of studies of international war, violence, and peace. Early studies of geography and war launched prescriptive notions that control over certain areas of the European continent was a necessary and sufficient condition for preeminence in world affairs. Thus, studies of territory and conflict focused on strategy and conflict over the "Rimland" (proposed by Nicholas Spykman) or "Heartland" (proposed by Halford Mackinder) areas of Europe. More recently, scholars have considered the role that territory plays in conceptions of national interest and the development of grand strategy. Attention has also focused on how territorial disputes are resolved (or not), with a special emphasis on when states will use military force against one another in their attempts to resolve those disputes.

One significant segment of the scholarly literature on geography and war is concerned with territory as a *facilitating* condition for conflict. In this conception, war or violent conflict is partly a function of "opportunity," and geography affects substantially the opportunities that states have for conflict. Factors such as physical proximity or a large number of borders influence a state's ability to fight, and most states do not have the capacity to project military force far from their national borders (thus, most wars are fought between neighbors). Geography also conditions the number of interactions between states and therefore the opportunities for war (as neighbors tend to have more interactions, both friendly and hostile, than more distant pairs of states). Finally, geographic proximity facilitates the spread of conflict from one area to another, and a broad series of studies analyzes how geography can be the agent of conflict diffusion. Although all these studies link geography to violent behavior, they are not centrally concerned with disputes over territory.

The focus of this article is on territory as a *source* of conflict, that is, when states contest the control or the sovereignty of a given piece of land or a waterway (an understudied subject). Here, territory is not merely an agent that facilitates the conflict interactions of states but rather is the basis or central issue over which they are fighting. There are two sets of questions about territorial disputes that have dominated their study in the field of international peace and security studies. The first concerns the role that territorial disputes play in national decisions for war. Among the key questions are: Are territorial disputes more or less likely than other disputes to lead to war? Under what conditions do territorial disputes escalate to the use of military force and war? What characteristics of territory make such disputes particularly susceptible to violent conflict? Studies addressing these questions have placed territorial disputes among a series of other concerns such as alliances, power distributions, and regime types in seeking to build general knowledge about the conditions for military conflict and war.

A second set of concerns revolves around the resolution of territorial disputes and the promotion of peaceful relations between states. The key questions here are: Can territorial disputes be peacefully resolved? When a territorial change or transfer occurs, how and when

can it be achieved peacefully? Do territorial changes resolve territorial disputes or do they merely fuel a cycle of territorial conflict? Although to some degree the concern with territorial disputes and conflict resolution is the inverse of the question set concerned with war, those studies that focus on peace have had greater concern with policy implications that traditional theoretical studies on the causes of war.

In this article, empirical evidence on these and related questions are summarized and integrated. As a first step, there is a discussion of the definition of territorial disputes, given that most inter-state conflict might be said to have at least a latent territorial component to it. Then, we move to a discussion of the different varieties of territorial disputes. We then present a review and synthesis of the conditions under which territorial disputes lead to violence, and especially war, between states. Following this is a discussion of the conditions under which territorial disputes actually lead to alterations in international borders. The discussion also includes an analysis of when territorial changes are achieved through military force and when they are achieved peacefully. Finally, an analysis of how territorial changes affect the future conflict relationships of the parties is given. This article concludes with a synthesis of what we know about territorial disputes and, more importantly, identifies the research gaps or questions that may form the basis for a future research agenda.

II. DEFINITION OF TERRITORIAL DISPUTE

A key research problem in the study of territorial conflict is the conceptual and operational definition of what constitutes a territorial dispute. This is not simply a semantical or esoteric matter. Distinguishing territorial-based conflict from other kinds of confrontations is essential for understanding the unique features (if indeed any exist) of territorial disputes and aids in making a more precise theoretical framework for explaining international conflict.

The distinction between territorial and other disputes is not a straightforward matter and at least four problems are encountered. First, at one level, one might regard almost all disputes between states as having a territorial component to them. Most obvious are conflicts over the delineation of an international border or a given piece of territory, as occurred between Argentina and Chile over the Beagle Channel. More problematic are cases involving disputes over resources (e.g., Iraq's complaints against Kuwait), when control over those resources is tied to control over the territory where they are located. Even more difficult to distinguish are ethnic or religious conflicts when such differences are intimately tied to specific territories (e.g., Jerusalem, Kashmir). Definitions must distinguish between those disputes that are primarily over territory versus those that merely have a territorial component.

A second difficulty is deciding what constitutes an active territorial dispute. Does the mere existence of competing territorial claims constitute a territorial dispute? There are various instances of competing claims (e.g., many states claim Antarctica), but it is often the case that such claims are not being actively pursued by the state claimants. Erich Weede refers to such claims as "latent territorial conflict." One might suggest that some type of severity standard be applied to territorial disputes before they might receive consideration. One possibility is that territorial disputes must be actively pursued and for those interested in violence, one might add the requirement that there be some realistic chance that states would use military coercion in pursuit of their territorial claims. The problem with this solution is that territorial disputes can quickly cycle through active and latent stages. From a scholarly perspective, one runs the risk of either including what may be irrelevant and fundamentally different situations (e.g., latent claims) *or* excluding some such cases that may suddenly become active; such a trade-off is only avoided if the research question focuses on the transition points between the active and latent stages (yet this has not been a prominent scholarly concern). Also, adding a militarized dimension to the territorial dispute definition may lead one to miss disputes that are managed peacefully. A corollary problem is determining when a territorial dispute is over. John Allcock and his colleagues include in their compilation of territorial disputes those cases in which there has been some or total resolution of competing claims. Their argument is that such conflict resolution could (and has in some cases) quickly disappear and that even those cases that have been allegedly resolved must be considered in any listing or analysis of territorial disputes. As noted below in the discussion of recurring conflict, there may be some empirical merit to this argument, although it begs the question of understanding when territorial conflict is over.

A third definitional problem is the focus of some scholars exclusively on territorial changes. There is little question that such transfers are an important component for issues of peace and violence. Yet an exclusive focus on territorial changes leads scholars to ignore a whole set of territorial disputes that do not result in

territorial adjustments. A similar problem is encountered in the scholarly literature on deterrence, where there is a tendency to focus on deterrence failures to the exclusion of successful deterrence cases in which the visible manifestations are less apparent. This is not to say that theory-building is not possible in focusing on territorial changes but rather that territorial disputes cannot be treated as synonymous with cases of territorial transfer. Indeed, some might also argue that territorial transfers may not involve any real dispute between the parties at all, as some territorial changes are merely business transactions in the sale of property (e.g., Louisiana Purchase) and may not have been preceded by any competing territorial claims.

Wrestling with these problems, several studies have developed some convergence around conceptual and operational definitions (conceptual and operational are frequently indistinct in presentation) for territorial disputes. Allcock et al. are a bit vague on inclusionary rules for what constitutes a territorial dispute, but they specifically do not include "boundary demarcation problems when these do not involve contentious territorial claims by one state against another…" (1992, p. xi). They also exclude maritime boundary disputes unless such disputes are made in conjunction with landward claims as well. Finally, they retain on their listing "certain historically significant disputes which appeared settled or dormant…" (1992; p. xi). The basis for distinguishing those included and those excluded on this last point is not apparent. It evident that not all of the definitional problems cited above have been addressed or resolved by that source.

Stephen Kocs uses a strictly legal definition of territorial disputes: "when two or more states formally claim legitimate jurisdiction over the same piece of territory" (1995, p. 161). He makes a number of modifications to this basic definition, with the net effect of narrowing dramatically the scope of cases for his empirical analyses. He only includes cases in which the territorial demands are reasonably specific, excludes cases in which an international boundary lacks adequate definition, excludes cases in which a territorial dispute is manufactured by a state to justify aggressive action, and, finally, excludes claims on territory that are not contiguous to both parties in the dispute (this is largely done because the author was interested in conditions for war and geographic contiguity is almost a necessary conditions for war initiation—a concern that is relevant for studies of war, but not necessarily for identifying territorial disputes).

Paul Huth adopts the broadest and yet the most precise definition: "a territorial dispute involves either a disagreement between states over where their common homeland or colonial borders should be fixed, or, more fundamentally, the dispute entails one country contesting the right of another country even to exercise sovereignty over some or all of its homeland or colonial territory" (1996, p. 19). More precisely, he identifies a series of situations that qualify as territorial disputes: (1) disagreement over a boundary line of a border, (2) opposing definitions of a boundary line and no legal or historical documents establishing that line, (3) occupation of another state's territory without consent, (4) claims by one state against the occupation by another state of a portion of territory located within the latter, and (5) when one state does not recognize the sovereignty or independence of another entity and seeks to control all or part of that entity's territory. Unlike others, Huth is more explicitly concerned with conditions for the end of a territorial dispute, defined as any of the following: (1) a territorial change in which the challenger state gains territory and this is legitimated by the losing state, (2) the challenger state formally relinquishes future claims, or (3) the challenger state agrees to accept the ruling on the dispute given by an international adjudicatory panel.

Conceptually, these most prominent approaches attempt to exclude from consideration disputes that only have a secondary territorial component. Thus, there is a tendency for territorial disputes to be primarily conflicts over boundaries or border delineations rather than a broader conception of territorial conflict. The conceptual definitions also tend to ignore maritime disputes and focus almost exclusively on conflicts over land. A comparison of the operational outputs of these definitions reveals some broad tendencies in identifying territorial disputes.

The scholarly literature does not generally include compilations of territorial disputes prior to World War II; generally then, there are only single case studies of disputes or territorial concerns are embedded in a broader listing of conflict events. Huth lists 129 territorial disputes (including 116 disputed borders). First, the most common kind of territorial dispute according to Huth is a disagreement over boundary delineation, constituting almost 40% of his cases. Many of Huth's cases are of long duration, and almost 45% were still ongoing at the cut-off point for the data.

It is possible to compare the results of Kocs' more restrictive listing of territorial disputes with that of Huth, given the strong temporal overlap of the two, with Kocs covering the 1945–1987 period. Kocs identifies only 41 territorial disputes, but 36 of these also appear on Huth's list, indicating some strong, albeit

imperfect, convergence among the two leading data sets in the field. The listing of Allcock et al. is less easy to evaluate given that it mixes contemporary territorial disputes with a smattering of resolved but historically significant ones. That list has 84 different territorial disputes, some of them multilateral, but it is much less clear whether such a list could be used for systematic quantitative analysis rather than merely as an information resource.

Although there are few systematic listings of territorial disputes, a number of data sets dealing with international conflict provide information that might be suitable for analysis of territorial-based conflict. Of course, such data sets include only conflict events meeting a certain threshold of severity, and therefore one may miss territorial disputes without the use or threat of military force. These type of data sets are most suitable for assessing when an already-militarized territorial conflict escalates to war. The most prominent collection is the Correlates of War Project Militarized Interstate Dispute data set. For each of the 2042 disputes over the 1816–1992 period, there is a code for the type of revisionist demand made in the dispute and 28.7% of those disputes are coded as having territory as a primary issue for at least one of the participants. The International Crisis Behavior (ICB) data set is more restrictive, focusing only on crises (rather than disputes in general) and extends from 1919 to 1994. Nevertheless, within that data set, it is difficult to disentangle territorial disputes from other types. The data set has a coding for issues, but these are largely defined by their military–security content, and territorial disputes may or may not be coterminous with security issues. Slightly more promising is the "gravity of threat" variable, which includes a "threat to territorial integrity" category. Yet territorial disputes involving a "threat to the existence of another state" fall outside this category and it is unclear whether it is possible to use the ICB data to learn anything about territorial conflict.

Overall, there remain some vagaries in defining what constitutes a territorial dispute, and extant approaches have not solved all the definitional problems. There are few efforts to identify a full population of territorial disputes and these are limited to the post-1945 time period, severely restricting comparative longitudinal analyses. International conflict data are a potentially richer source of identifying territorial conflict, but current data compilations necessarily ignore nonviolent territorial disputes and are not well designed to separate territorial from other kinds of disputes.

III. KINDS OF TERRITORIAL DISPUTES

Much of how one determines different kinds of territorial disputes is affected by the breadth of one's definition of the phenomena. Broad definitions of territorial disputes, such as that by Huth, naturally lead to identifying multiple types; as noted above, Huth defines several different types of competing territorial claims as territorial disputes. Others focus exclusively on one type of territorial dispute, that being conflict over the delimitation of an international border. Indeed, an obvious distinction among territorial disputes is the difference between border/boundary and other disputes. The former category includes serious and minor differences alike over the exact location of a dividing line between states; this is what Friedrich Kratochwil and his colleagues refer to as a "positional" dispute. The latter includes disputes over dependent or colonial properties, competing claims to large tracts of territory, or politically/economically strategic areas (e.g., Walvis Bay) that are not necessarily centered on national border areas. Although such distinctions may be useful in classification, differentiating disputes on these kinds of dimensions have primarily served a descriptive rather than a theoretical function. More relevant are distinguishing different kinds of territorial disputes according to the precise dimensions or characteristics that assist us in understanding which can be peacefully resolved or which are likely to escalate to war.

One obvious approach is uncovering the aspects of territorial disputes that lead states to consider the territory important enough to potentially fight over; this is consistent with the idea that issue salience is an important factor in assessing conflict escalation to war and some territories are regarded as more important than others. One obvious distinction is between territorial disputes that are ethnically based versus those that are not. Ethnically based disputes are those in which the territorial claims are based on some ethnic (and sometimes religious affinity) with the population of the disputed territory. Another dimension may be the relative economic value of the territory, mostly its resource utility, although this may be difficult to estimate in practice. For scholars who seek a longitudinal analysis, it may be impossible to ascertain what the prevailing perception of the actors at the time was vis-à-vis a given disputed territory (e.g., oil-rich Alaska was considered a worthless, frozen piece of land when it was purchased by the United States in the 1860s.)

A third territorial dimension thought relevant is the strategic value of the territory. This is most often determined by how control over the disputed territory affects the opportunity for offensive attacks and defensive actions by the disputing states. A different approach to defining kinds of territorial disputes is by reference to territorial importance, which may cut across underlying issues. Gary Goertz and Paul Diehl look at the "intrinsic" and "relational" importance of territory when states dispute territorial control. Intrinsic importance refers to the inherent value that a piece of territory has for the sovereign; this includes the availability of resources (water, minerals, etc.), space for development and living, and the like. In contrast, relational importance signifies the specific and sometimes unique value that a given territory might have for a particular state; this often involves some religious, ethnic, or historical attachment between the people of one state and the territory in dispute. Significantly, relational importance recognizes that what may be regarded as important territory for some states because of location or historical associations may not be as important to the other disputant; unfortunately, most work on territorial disputes wrongly assumes a symmetry of importance for all protagonists. Equally relevant, this approach allows a territory to have both relational and intrinsic importance simultaneously and to varying degrees on each respective continuum. Other approaches tend to classify only one element of a territory and then the determination is made dichotomously.

A dramatically different approach shifts the focus from the underlying importance to the territory to the status of the dispute itself. Kocs makes the distinction between *previously resolved* and *never-resolved* disputes. Previously resolved disputes are a bit of a misnomer in that the disputes may be still ongoing, but there is some legal basis (treaty, other agreement) that has at one time established a boundary location or territorial ownership. Implicitly, Allcock et al. note the distinction between resolved and unresolved disputes, although they also explicitly indicate that the empirically there may be little difference with respect to state behavior in some cases.

IV. TERRITORIAL DISPUTES AND MILITARIZED CONFLICT

The central concern of scholarly research has been with more than with identifying competing territorial claims, but rather also with understanding when those claims involve the threat or actual use of military force. Specifically, the key research questions focus on how violent territorial disputes begin, what characterizes their dynamics, and when they escalate to war. Most of the research is framed so as to compare the initiation, dynamics, and escalation of territorial disputes vis-à-vis other kinds of inter-state disagreements. That is, most international conflict scholars strive for a general explanation of inter-state conflict, of which territorial disputes are a part, rather than seeking only to understand that particular phenomenon and its conflict correlates.

A weakness of the international conflict literature in general is a propensity to take violent conflict as a given and therefore ignore the origins of what made the dispute militarized. There seems to be some expectation that territorial disputes arise inherently because of poorly drawn boundary lines. Yet this does not explain why some of the disputes become militarized and further ignores the origins of other disputes that occur over clearly defined demarcations. Furthermore, if poor mapping were the sole source of territorial disputes, then one might expect a decline in the number of such disputes over time as more borders are carefully defined; exploration of the globe is complete, and mapping has become a scientific exercise. From extant compilations, however, there is no indication that such a trend toward fewer territorial disputes exists.

Territorial disputes with a violent component do not simply appear, they are the product of a political choices, and states choose to press territorial claims on some occasions and refrain from doing so on others. Many of the suggested processes parallel those in the general international conflict literature. For example, some scholars have argued that territorial disputes occur following a change in the relative strength of the states involved, with the stronger state in position to press its territorial claims. Yet what empirical evidence we have on these matters suggests this is not necessarily the case.

Robert Mandel finds that border disputes occur more frequently among states that are roughly equal in power, belying the expectation that only stronger revisionist states start territorial disputes. He also reports that border disputes are more common among low-technology rather than advanced industrial states (consistent with other findings that such states are more likely to intervene over territorial concerns); he argues that the greater functional role and prestige given to weaker states by territorial possession may account for their propensity to fight over territory. Of course, he also acknowledges that more advanced states may have already resolved their boundary demarcation problems and therefore the association with technology is spurious.

In contrast, Huth offers another view on power distributions and the initiation of territorial conflict. He uses a modified realist model, which includes both domestic and international political factors, to explain how states become involved in territorial disputes and in enduring militarized rivalries over territory. Because of their salience, territorial disputes, as opposed to other kinds of conflicts, have a greater propensity to involve military force and recur, thereby producing long-term rivalries, even if not all territorial disputes evolve into long-term conflicts. Importantly, he notes that the relative strength of the challenger does not have much of an effect on the initiation of territorial disputes, and that states also do not frequently challenge allies or extant treaty commitments by resort to militarized action. Rather, domestic concerns, especially ethnic and linguistic ties between one's own population and those living in the disputed territory, are significantly associated with the recurrence of militarized conflict. Bikash Roy finds that similar domestic political considerations are critical in generating territorial disputes.

Significantly more scholarly attention has been devoted to understanding the escalation of territorial conflict; that is, most studies take violent conflict as a given and then seek to explain variations in severity, with special attention to the conditions for war. Yet few studies explore variations across territorial disputes. One exception is Mandel, who finds that territorial disputes are more "severe" when they occur in low-technology states, are fought over ethnic rather than resource issues, occur in dyadic rather than triadic state configurations, and occur between members of different ideological blocs. Huth again cites domestic considerations as critical in the escalation of territorial disputes; yet he also finds that other factors are also key elements in the escalation process, especially relative military strength, common security interests, the involvement of the challenger in other disputes, and the value of the territory. The vast majority of studies, however, look for variations across all types of disputes, looking at territorial conflict to help uncover which disputes are more prone to escalation.

Two general studies of international conflict highlight the centrality of geographic concerns, but neither is able to discern what conclusions about territorial disputes might be drawn from the strong relationships reported. Paul Diehl studied major power war over the 1816–1976 period and discovered that 12 of the 13 wars that occurred did so when one side was contiguous to the site of the dispute; contiguity was a virtual necessary, although far from sufficient, condition for conflict escalation to war. Similarly, Stuart Bremer found geographic contiguity to be one of the strongest dyadic conditions in assessing the probability that two states will go to war.

Although the findings on geographic contiguity are stark and significant, it is not entirely clear what they signify. Is the strong association between contiguity and war a reflection that territorial disputes are more dangerous than other conflicts? Or does contiguity indicate merely that there is greater opportunity for interactions between states who border each other, and therefore one might expect more hostile (and peaceful ones as well) interactions between neighbors? Might it also be that contiguity represents a proximity effect, whereby most states are only able to project military power to neighboring areas and therefore are incapable of warfare with other than contiguous states? Note that the "loss of strength gradient" is dramatic from most states outside of their region. In a series of studies, John Vasquez has attempted to sort out which of these contiguity effects is really present: opportunity, proximity, or territoriality. Vasquez initially argued that the contiguity–war relationship was a reflection of territorial disputes and not incidental to opportunity or proximity effects. His steps-to-war model includes unresolved territorial claims as an essential component; that is, states that have settled all outstanding border and other territorial disputes are unlikely to go to war, except in a contagion process in which existing war "spreads" to them. In a follow-up study, he more systematically looks at the logical structure and corollaries of the three competing explanations. Using scientific standards and extant empirical findings, he argues that the territorial explanation is compelling, and therefore territorial disputes are much more dangerous than other kinds of inter-state confrontations.

Vasquez's initial analyses were not based on new empirical studies and there was some doubt as to whether the three explanations could be sorted out empirically. Nevertheless, a series of new empirical studies are strongly consistent with Vasquez's assertions. Kocs controlled for contiguity and discovered that war was about 40 times more likely if neighbors were involved in a never-resolved territorial dispute versus when they were not. Never-resolved territorial disputes did not account for all wars, but they were a significant component. Vasquez himself demonstrated with empirical data over the 1816–1992 period that territorial disputes have a higher probability of going to war than other kinds of disputes, and such disputes account for a majority of war outbreaks. The results he presents generally hold across different time periods,

lengths of rivalry, and different power levels (e.g., major, minor) of states.

Consistent with the notion that territorial disputes are more likely to escalate to war are findings that the bargaining behavior of states in territorial disputes is more severe or coercive. Paul Hensel looks at over 2000 militarized disputes since 1816 and assesses the relative behavior of states when territorial issues are involved versus when they are not. He notes that territory-based disputes are generally more severe and more likely to prompt violent responses from the target of the initial militarized action (whereas many other disputes end quickly when the target states do not respond with military actions and/or launch diplomatic initiatives). Although Hensel notes that territorial conflict is less likely to end in a stalemate, this should not imply that territorial conflicts are easily resolved. Indeed, Hensel finds that territorial conflict is more likely to recur and to do so in a shorter period of time than disputes over nonterritorial issues. Paul Senese looks at the same militarized disputes as Hensel, but there are several unique elements to his analysis. Senese confirms Hensel's findings that territorial disputes are more severe overall than other conflicts, and he also notes that geographic contiguity contributes to greater severity (as it may be easier to project military force close to home). Yet, he finds no strong evidence that geographic concerns lead to the escalation of disputes. That is, geography is important in influencing the probability of militarized conflict arising and may even affect the severity of the initial actions in the conflict, but other processes (involving, for example, democratic regimes) determine whether states will choose a progressively more hostile series of actions during a dispute.

A final set of research concerns related to territorial disputes are the roles that territory can play in the termination or resolution of militarized conflict. This consideration is rarely given much attention in the international conflict literature. Yet one of the keys to understanding the recurrence of conflict, and therefore enduring rivalries, is to determine how that cycle of conflict can be broken. In his survey of alliances, Douglas Gibler has discovered that a significant portion of peaceful alliances contained territorial settlement agreements; that is, the agreements resolved long-standing territorial claims between states. Critically, he reports that alliances of this variety are not followed by war. In effect, the territorial settlement treaties removed one of the contentious issues between states and ushered in a era of peaceful relations (this is similar to the argument made by Vasquez). Thus, territorial settlement treaties may be one mechanism for ending war and rivalries between states, and indeed Huth reports that borders that are well defined by a legal settlement and fully demarcated are unlikely to be disputed.

Of course, there are multiple ways besides alliances to get a settlement of territorial disputes. Yet a formal agreement may not be a guarantee that conflict will not reoccur. What is necessary is that the settlement must be acceptable to all parties; it must be regarded as "fair." The concept of "fairness" is difficult to define operationally and it may vary substantially depending on whose perspective is adopted. Nevertheless, Steven Brams and Jeffrey Togman employ a model called "Adjusted Winner" (AW) that looks at the resolution of conflict from the perspective of the multiple issues that often characterize conflict and the differing values often attributed to those issues by the disputants. From the AW perspective, they explore whether the Camp David Accords, perhaps one of the most significant peace agreements since 1945, could be judged as "fair," especially when it is not necessarily regarded as such by many observers. This examination is of particular interest here in that many of the key issues surrounding the Arab–Israeli peace process have a central territorial component; these include disputes over the Sinai, Jerusalem, and a Palestinian state among others. Perhaps surprisingly, the Camp David agreement meets the standard of fairness, with both Israel and Egypt getting at least two-thirds of their main interests satisfied. Indeed, this fairness may help explain why the signatories have had relatively peaceful relations in the past 20 years after several previous decades of war. The AW method suggested by Brams and Togman may be the mechanism to resolve territorial conflicts and promote long-term conflict resolution, especially when territorial concerns are arrayed and interwoven in a complex pattern with other issues.

Part of the equation in settling territorial disputes is the willingness of the challenger state to seek compromise, as a final resolution is rarely a complete victory for the state that wants a revision to the status quo. Huth's findings indicate that a challenger is more likely to seek a settlement if it suffered one or more military defeats at the hands of the status quo state, if it shared some common security interests with that state, or if it was involved in other disputes. These incentives prompt the challenger to settle in the hope of gaining the best deal it can and/or so the extant territorial dispute does not impede the pursuit of other national interests.

There are several conclusions about territorial disputes and militarized conflict that can be drawn from these research findings. First, it is clear that territorial disputes are more prone to coercive bargaining behavior and escalation than other kinds of inter-state disputes. Such an effect is also not merely the result of proximity or opportunity effects, but rather stems from the significance that states attach to territorial versus other conflicts. It is also evident that territorial conflict can be solved and that different treaty or settlement approaches might be the vehicles to achieve this.

V. TERRITORIAL CHANGES

One key segment of international conflict research has been concerned with conditions surrounding territorial changes. Territorial changes may play a central role in understanding territorial dispute and how they might be resolved. Erich Weede argued that "the history of war and peace is largely identical with the history of territorial changes as results of war and causes of the next war" (1973, p. 87). Thus, we might look at territorial changes as outcomes of territorial disputes and potentially such transfers may either resolve the dispute or further intensify the hostility associated with still competing territorial claims.

Despite their importance, there are some limitations to focusing on territorial changes as we noted above; territorial changes will not cover dispute over territories that do not result in geographic alterations and some territorial changes are completed amicably from start to finish, much like a mutually beneficial business transaction. Nevertheless, by looking at territorial changes it is important to understand when they can be achieved peacefully and when they lead to lasting peace between the parties.

Over the period 1816–1996, there have been approximately 800 territorial changes involving at least one state. The typical (median) territorial change involves over 20 thousand square kilometers of territory and directly affects 400 thousand people living in the territory transferred. Although there are an average of more than 4 territorial changes per year, such transfers tend to be concentrated around major wars.

Territorial changes are spread across the different continents with perhaps only the Western hemisphere experiencing disproportionately fewer, perhaps because most boundaries were settled there by the end of the 19th century. Major power states occupy 9 of the first 10 slots on a list of states most involved in territorial changes in the past 2 centuries.

Descriptive data indicates that territorial changes are frequent phenomena. Further study reveals, however, that they are not as associated with violence as has been implied and that their study may reveal the conditions under which change can be managed peacefully. Only 27% of territorial changes occur with military conflict between the parties within 1 year of the transfer; put another way, almost three-fourths of territorial transfers take place peacefully according to Gary Goertz and Paul Diehl. Furthermore, the percentage of violent transfers has declined over time with changes only half as likely to involve violence since World War II as compared to the period before. Although we must be careful about drawing too many inferences from territorial change data, there is a suggestion that much territorial conflict can be handled without military force.

These general patterns suggest that certain kinds of territorial changes are most dangerous and therefore others are more benign. Two extended studies provide insights into the relevant conditions; one framing the question to understand the conditions for conflict and the other to account for the conditions for peace. Goertz and Diehl looked at territorial changes from 1816 to 1980 and focused on three concerns of violence surrounding cases of national independence, inter-state territorial transfers, and the aftermath of territorial changes. The first falls largely outside the scope of our focus on inter-state territorial disputes. Yet their findings on inter-state territorial transfers (specifically transfers of homeland as opposed to dependent territory) indicated that states were more likely to fight over territory that was regarded as valuable. Expansionist pressures (economic, military, population) on the states involved also encouraged violence although there were significant differences over time. Expansionist pressures on the gaining side were related to violence after 1914; the stronger, gaining side seemed to prey on the decline of the losing state and seized new territory through the use of military force. Nevertheless, decline on the part of the losing side in the exchange was associated in military conflict prior to that. These results are consistent with earlier findings on territorial disputes that relative capabilities, and changes in those affected whether territorial disputes would escalate.

Goertz and Diehl also looked at whether military conflict between the same two states followed a territorial change, specifically in the 30 years following that exchange. Although they cannot be sure that any subsequent conflict was over the same territory, such an analyses helps us understand whether peace and stability are promoted by the transfer of territory. They report that almost 40% of territorial changes are followed by a militarized dispute between the same parties. Future conflict was more likely when material capabilities were in favor of the losing side, and the territory involved held great intrinsic and relational importance (espe-

cially for the losing side). Counterintuitively, Goertz and Diehl report that the presence of a formal treaty transferring the territory (which was thought to indicate the legitimacy of the exchange) was *positively* associated with future conflict; the authors do not have a compelling explanation and their results are contrary to earlier findings on territorial disputes that indicated that legally recognized boundary lines helped promote peaceful resolution of disputes.

Arie Kacowicz was concerned with what conditions promote peaceful territorial change and he looked at a smaller subset of cases over the same time period as Goertz and Diehl. He finds that an asymmetrical power distribution was actually associated with the success (i.e., achieved peacefully) of a territorial transfer; particularly important is when the distribution of power is favorable to the status quo power. Of course, this may only indicate that when a strong state gives up territory, it is bound to do so voluntarily (when conflict does occur, one might expect that no transfer will occur as the strong state will be able to resist change). Consistent with the democratic peace idea, both Kacowicz and Huth find that peaceful territorial settlement is also more likely when there is a compatibility of the regimes of the two states. Kacowicz also notes that various international norms (e.g., decolonization, sovereignty) may help promote peace, and this comports with Goertz and Diehl's strong finding that international norms help assured peaceful transfers of sovereignty in colonial cases. Finally, Kacowicz identifies the importance of domestic political incentives for states to willingly (or not) relinquish territory. Goertz and Diehl argue that territorial importance is a key factor in determining when states will fight. Kacowicz suggests that the question of "important to whom?" must be answered by reference to the domestic actors in each state.

An analysis of territorial changes reveals that most exchanges of territory occur peacefully. Yet violence is likely when the territory is regarded as especially important by disputants, international norms do not provide restraints on state behavior, and various distributions of power facilitate the pressing of territorial claims through military force. The occurrence of a territorial change is not necessarily an indicator that territorial or other conflict between the same states will be avoided in the future.

VI. FUTURE RESEARCH DIRECTIONS

Research on territorial disputes has been hampered by the lack of systematic data on the subject and the tendency to focus on geography as a facilitating condition rather than as a source of conflict. Although there has been significant progress in documenting territorial disputes and understanding the conditions under which they may lead to war or be resolved peacefully, there are several questions or concerns that seem to form the centerpiece of a future research agenda.

Most studies of territorial disputes seem to take them as a given without consideration to how they arise. It is evident that there are many different kinds of territorial disputes, but we have little basis for understanding how such disputes move between latent and active stages and then back. As the territory itself remains constant over this time (except perhaps for some estimations of strategic and economic value), scholars must look to the international political conditions that lead states to press claims; domestic political concerns would also seem to be paramount, but these are thus far underemphasized by the literature.

A second item for the research agenda would be the need to understand why territorial disputes are more violent than other kinds of conflicts. The typical study uses a territorial issue variable as a surrogate for an unspecified set of factors that make states more willing to fight. But what is it about territory that makes it so important? And why are some territorial disputes more benign than others? Scholars may look to identify and measure issue salience more precisely, rather than to use issue types as imperfect indicators. When we know what makes a dispute important to states, we will be able to understand why territorial disputes in general are more dangerous and why within territorial disputes some types of conflicts are easier to manage than others.

Finally, research on territorial disputes, much like international conflict in general, needs to pay greater attention to concerns of peace and conflict resolution. Beyond generally studying conditions for peaceful resolution, scholars must focus on long-term stability and conflict resolution and not merely on whether a single dispute or territorial change is resolved. Effective schemes at conflict resolution are those that do not prompt renewed cycles of territorial conflict. Understanding conflict resolution will be essential for accurately modeling the dispute initiation process noted above, as the beginning of a territorial dispute is often the renewal of territorial conflict captured in a broader time frame.

Also See the Following Articles

CONFLICT MANAGEMENT AND RESOLUTION • ETHNIC CONFLICTS AND COOPERATION • INTERNATIONAL RELATIONS, OVERVIEW • PEACE AND DEMOCRACY • POWER, SOCIAL AND POLITICAL THEORIES OF

Bibliography

Allcock, J., Arnold, G., Day, A., Lewis, D. S., Poultney, L., Rance, R., & Sagar, D. J. (1992). *Border and territorial disputes.* (rev. 3rd ed.). London: Longman.

Brams, S., & Togman, J. (1996). Camp David: Was the agreement fair? *Conflict Management and Peace Science, 15,* 99–112.

Bremer, S. (1992). Dangerous dyads: Conditions affecting the likelihood of interstate war, 1816–1965. *Journal of Conflict Resolution, 36,* 309–341.

Diehl, P. F. (Ed.) (1996). *Territorial dimensions of international conflict. Conflict Management and Peace Science, 15,* 1–112. [Special Issue].

Diehl, P. F. (1991). Geography and war: A review and assessment of the empirical literature. *International Interactions, 17,* 121–137.

Diehl, P. F. (1985). Contiguity and military escalation in major power rivalries, 1816–1980. *Journal of Politics, 47,* 1203–1211.

Gibler, D. (1996). Alliances that never balance: The territorial settlement treaty. *Conflict Management and Peace Science, 15,* 75–97.

Goertz, G., & Diehl, P. F. (1992). *Territorial changes and international conflict.* London: Routledge.

Hensel, P. (1996). Charting a course to conflict: Territorial issues and interstate conflict, 1816–1992. *Conflict Management and Peace Science, 15,* 43–73.

Huth, P. (1996a). *Standing your ground: Territorial disputes and international conflict.* Ann Arbor: University of Michigan Press.

Huth, P. (1996b). Enduring rivalries and territorial disputes, 1950–1990. *Conflict Management and Peace Science, 15,* 7–41.

Kacowicz, A. (1994). *Peaceful territorial change.* Columbia: University of South Carolina Press.

Kocs, S. (1995). Territorial disputes and interstate war, 1945–1987. *Journal of politics, 57,* 159–175.

Kratochwil, F., Rohrlich, P., & Mahajan, H. (1985). *Peace and disputed sovereignty: Reflections on conflict over territory.* Lanham, MD: University Press of America.

Mandel, R. (1980). Roots of modern interstate border disputes. *Journal of Conflict Resolution, 24,* 427–454.

Roy, A.B. (1999). *Blood and soil.* Columbia: University of South Carolina Press.

Senese, P. (1996). Geographical proximity and issue salience: Their effects on the escalation of militarized interstate conflict. *Conflict Management and Peace Science, 15,* 133–161.

Vasquez, J. (1995). Why do neighbors fight?: Proximity, interaction, or territoriality. *Journal of Peace Research, 32,* 277–293.

Ward, M. (Ed.) (1992). *The new geopolitics.* Philadelphia, PA: Gordon and Breach.

Weede, E. (1973). Nation–environment relations as determinants of hostilities among nations. *Peace Science Society (International) Papers, 20,* 67–90.

Terrorism

David C. Rapoport

University of California, Los Angeles

I. History, the Concept, and the Problem of
   Definition
II. Contemporary Terrorism
III. The Future

GLOSSARY

Assassins (*Ismaili-Nizari, Fedayeen*, 1090–1275) Early
Islamic (Shia) millenarian terrorist group. It maintained a state as the launching pad and sanctuary for
international assaults and was crushed when Tam-
erlane destroyed that state. Victims were high-ranking officials and assailants were long time "loyal"
retainers who always used daggers, weapons which
precluded escape and facilitated martrydom. The
term "assassin" came from the word "hashish," which
the assailants were suspected of using.

Aum Shinrikyo ("Supreme Truth," 1984–1995) A
Fourth Wave Japanese religious group which
breached the barrier of using weapons of mass destruction by employing nerve gas (sarin) in a Tokyo
subway in 1995, killing 12 and injuring some 5000.
The group was crushed after this attack. The move
toward violence came after Aum was unsuccessful in
elections (1990). It combined Hindu, Buddhist, and
Christian millenarian themes which visualized the
end of the world. Like the Thugs, who worshipped a
similar deity, Aum preferred to kill without shedding
blood. A transnational religious community, Aum

had over 40,000 members with assets of more than
a billion dollars.

Front de Liberation National (FLN, 1954–1962, An
effective Second Wave Algerian separatist group that
initiated a long savage struggle against France and
those Algerians opposed to FLN purposes. It created
a secular socialist one-party state (1962), which provided sanctuaries to various foreign left-wing terrorist groups. Since 1992, the FLN government has been
the target of the Armed Islamic Movement's ferocious uprising.

Irish Republican Army (IRA, 1916) A Second Wave
separatist group. It is the most durable modern terrorist organization, originating in the Easter Uprising
(1916). The peace treaty establishing the Irish Free
State (1922) split the IRA occasioning a civil war in
the face of the refusal by some to accept the status
of a mainly Protestant Northern Ireland as British.
Subsequent campaigns to gain the North occurred
in 1939–1941, 1955–1962, and 1967–present. After
1969, IRA splits over tactics and Marxist influences
created the Provisional IRA (Provos,the main body),
Officials, and the INLA (Irish National Liberation
Army).

Irgun (**Irgun Zvai Leumi,** National Military Organization, 1937–1948) A Second Wave Zionist Revisionist
group initially formed to cope with Arab terrorist
attacks. Menachem Begin became leader in 1941 and
beginning in 1944 led strikes at British targets, tying
down some 100,000 troops after World War II. Irgun
members joined the Israeli army in 1948; and after

independence was achieved, established a right-wing political party, Herut. Menachem Begin became the Israeli Prime Minister in 1970s and later received a Nobel Peace Prize.

Masada Ancient Jewish mountaintop fortress occupied by the Sicarri (Daggermen). The Romans captured it, ending the massive revolt (67–73 A.D.). It is sometimes identified as the earliest terrorist campaign in history. Some 1000 Jews killed themselves in the fortress, presumably to avoid capture. Masada today is a major contemporary shrine which has different conflicting meanings to various Jewish groups.

Millenarian A term given to religious groups that live in imminent anticipation that the world as we know it will end. They believe that justice will be administered which will lead to the destruction of the wicked and will give the righteous an earthly paradise. Millenarian groups often turn to terrorism, partly because terror is part of the end-time vision.

M-19 (April 19th Movement, Moviemento 19 de Abril, (1970–1990) Third Wave Columbian revolutionary group founded when presidential candidate Rojas Pinilla's election was lost. The M-19 saw Columbia as being in the grip of the U.S. Supported by foreign Marxist terrorist groups and states, particularly Cuba, it had temporary alliances with drug cartels. Their tactics were characterized by spectacular hostage-taking. They reentered Columbian politics in 1990 but drug traffickers killed the party's presidential candidate.

Narodnaya Volya ("The Will of the People," Russia, 1879–1892) The first modern rebel organization to call itself "terrorist." Their influence was great and they argued that terrorism reduced the massive bloodshed normally associated with revolution and that understanding the mechanics of terrorism was a scientific achievement. The populist group developed a systematic assassination campaign of high officials culminating in the assassination of Tsar Alexander II (1881).

Oslo Peace Accords (September 13, 1993) Agreement between Israel and the Palestinian Liberation Organization (PLO) to initiate a process to establish a peace treaty and to relinquish territories conquered in the Six Day War (1967).

Palestine Liberation Organization (PLO, 1964–present) A Third Wave confederation of major Palestinian groups aiming to create a Palestinian state. Yasir Arafat, head of Fatah, the largest group in the PLO, became PLO leader in 1969 and was successsful in getting all Arab states to recognize the PLO as "the sole, legitimate representative of the Palestinian

people (1974). In the 1970s, it became virtually synonymous with international terrorism, training many foreign groups in Lebanon and operating with other foreign terrorist groups in many foreign states especially in Europe.

Revolutionary Catechism (1869) Written by Sergei Nechaev. The first "mini-manual" on the "science of destruction" or terrorism. The influential Russian document was extraordinary, waiving all moral limits to the struggle and suggesting that terrorists had to understand themselves wholly as "instruments" of a cause. The work visualized a variety of ways to provoke government repression in order to generate uprisings.

Thugs (Phansigars, "Stranglers") A Hindu group, worshippers of Kali, goddess of creation and destruction. Existed from the 13th (possibly the 7th) to the 19th century C.E. Thugs killed without shedding blood, the goddess' food. Their victims were travelers whose goods they confiscated. The most durable terrorist body known which killed several million, many more people than any other group.

Tupamaros Movimiento de Liberacion National, MLN, 1963–1972) A Third Wave revolutionary group lionized by the New Left because of its daring "Robin Hood-like" tactics and their hostility toward the U.S. The name "Tupamaro" comes from the 18th-century Inca "pretender." The prominent role of the armed forces in destroying the Tupamaros gave the military leverage to dismantle the Uruguayan democracy.

Zealots (qa'nana) and **Sicarri**, ("Daggermen") The two principal groups leading the Jewish millenarian revolt against Rome in the 1st century (C.E.). The Zealots were more numerous, but both drew their inspiration from Mattathias, leader of the Maccabees, and most of all from his Biblical predecessor Phineas, the High Priest, who averted a plague by killing an Israelite tribal leader and his Midian consort who were defiling a holy place. The Sicarri concentrated on attacking Jews, while the Zealots struck Romans.

I. HISTORY, THE CONCEPT, AND THE PROBLEM OF DEFINITION

Terrorism has an ancient lineage. It is evident sometimes in preliterate or primitive societies and has a long significant history in various religious traditions. But the concept of terrorism, as distinguished from the phenomenon, is a recent development, produced by the secular French Revolution. Terrorism was seen as an indispensable tool to establish a democratic order, and the term "terrorism" initially referred to government acts. Thus, the *Oxford English Dictionary* says the term originated in 1795, meaning either "government by intimidation" or "a (government) policy intended to strike with terror those against whom it is adopted." "Terrorists" carried out those policies.

The architects of the French Reign of Terror believed that they possessed a new *purpose* and *method*, and when Robespierre proclaimed "either virtue or the terror," he meant that only terror would produce true democratic dispositions. The practices of the "Revolutionary Tribunal" ("People's Court") exemplified the new purpose and method best. An ordinary court assessed the *behavior* of potential defendants; but the People's Court treated "enemies" or those with "impure" hearts. Motive not behavior was its chief concern, and the ordinary rules of evidence (those developed to assess behavior) were scrapped as being impediments to accomplishing the new task. Conventional notions of guilt or innocence thus became irrelevant. The issue for the Revolutionary Tribunals was not justice, but how to manipulate a prisoner's fate so that it would serve as a didactic lesson, i.e., the identification of appropriate and inappropriate civic dispositions for a democratic ethos.

Nearly a century later, Narodnaya Volya ("The People's Will," 1879) emerged, the first rebel movement to characterize *itself* as terrorist, one whose successors haunted Russia for nearly 4 decades. Like the French before them, the Russians sought popular rule, understood terrorism to be a temporary necessity to "raise the consciousness of the masses," and they chose victims for "symbolic" reasons or for political effects. The Russians never achieved their immediate political objectives, but their influences endured as they generated a "culture of terror" for successors to inherit and improve.

Russian writers (i.e, Nechaev, Bakunin, Mozorov, Stepniak, and Kropotkin) addressed the double despair of revolutionaries; the sense that spontaneous mass uprisings had become impossible and the gnawing anxiety that revolutionaries had become "idle wordspillers." In their view, the solution was a new way of acting, calculated to bring recognized but latent diffused social tensions to the surface and then direct them toward their proper objects.

The doctrine was developed partly from studying the Tsars' own Balkan intrigues. The latter organized assassinations of Turkish officials knowing that the Turks would then massacre Christian subjects, who in turn would revolt, provoking critical international responses. *Publicity* and *provocation* not pure terrorism;

these were the objectives of Tsarist atrocities, a lesson Russian revolutionary terrorists absorbed.

The revolutionary atrocities would transform society through publicizing a cause and provoking the opposition to violate its own norms in efforts to root the terrorists out, responses which invariably created serious international concern. Beyond their several political purposes, atrocities had therapeutic value, promoting self-confidence in revolutionaries freeing their souls from the paralyzing weight of moral conventions. Successful terrorism entailed learning both how to kill and how to *die*, a death best culminated in a public trial where, in circumstances maximizing publicity and empathy, one simultaneously accepted responsibility and indicted the regime. "The terrorist," Stepniak wrote, "is noble, terrible, irresistibly fascinating (uniting) the two sublimities of human grandeur, the martyr and the hero."

The Russians had so many successors, and such articulate ones, that most people came to associate terrorist activity exclusively with rebels. After the rise of the totalitarian state in the 1930s, state terrorism eclipsed that of the rebel briefly; but since the 1960s, rebels have preoccupied the public and they are the focus here.

In the 1960s, the problems of definition for the first time became acute, a matter which many find unresolved still. Schmid and Jongman discovered more than 100 definitions, and Laqueur's widely read text finds the issues so vexing that it oddly refuses to provide a definition.

Subsequent political developments help explain this confusion. The term "terrorist" suggested so many abusive connotations and created such enormous political liabilities that terrorists stopped calling themselves terrorists. Lehi (the "Stern Gang"), a Revisionist Zionist group that split off from the Irgun in the fight for Israel's independence, was the last group to describe *itself* as terrorist. Afterward, only one's enemies were terrorists. Rebels characterized every government that opposed them as terrorist no matter what tactics it employed; governments returned the compliment, deeming every rebel who used violence a terrorist.

Simultaneously, the link between terror and democracy became more complicated. So often were democratic states plagued by terror that the conventional wisdom reckoned all terrorists to be hostile to the democratic ideal. Many "freedom fighters" who fought against colonial rule after World War II used terrorist methods, but few were willing to call participants terrorists. Simultaneously, the media, Rapoport noted, corrupted or confused language even further, deliberately refusing to use terms consistently, apparently to avoid being seen as blatantly partisan. The American media developed an extraordinary policy of describing identical persons in the same account alternatively as "terrorists," "guerrillas," and "soldiers." Similar, less blatant, inconsistencies plague academic accounts too.

Uncertainties concerning the term were effected by historical events. Over time some terrorists became something else; and these changes were often so dramatic that one could hardly remember earlier characterizations. When Britain recognized the Irish Free State (1922), Michael Collins became the first terrorist to be acknowledged as the political leader of a legitimate government. After World War II similar, though not identical, developments occurred when Kenya, Algeria, and others achieved independence. By 1996 four persons once known as terrorists had even received Nobel Peace Prizes. Menachem Begin and Anwar Sadat shared one (1978) for leading Israel and Egypt to a peace treaty. Nelson Mandela (1994) was indispensable in leading South Africa to reconciliation. Yasir Arafat (1996) was still in charge of an active terrorist organization, the Palestine Liberation Organization (PLO), when he signed the Oslo Peace Accords (1993). In these four instances the terrorists did something to change their status. But occasionally the reputations of terrorists were transformed without a change in behavior. A most striking historical instance was the reputation of those who fell at Masada. Jewish rabbis for nearly 2 millennia rejected them as unsavory criminals, but modern secular Israelis hail them as heroes, and Masada has become an important site for military ceremonies.

Finally, the recourse to terror has become "cheapened." Initially, only the idea of a perfect society could be powerful enough to justify extranormal violence, i.e., attacks on the unarmed or innocent. But today a vast array of groups whose only common feature is a strong feeling that some alleged injustice requires attention use terror. Even groups organized around a "single issue," such as abortion, environmentalism, animal rights, and exclusion of immigrants have engaged in acts of terror; inevitably private persons with personal concerns have followed suit. In the 1980s Action Directe, (AD), a left wing French group, moved from issue to issue vainly seeking one which would give them a popular constituency.

The events described above worked to alter definitions. Most observers today agree that terrorism is a means to achieve a public end, but two major differences divide them still. Some emphasize that terrorism is distinguishable from other forms of violence, while others minimize that distinction. For those who emphasize differences, Walters' study of Zulu government terrorism provided the most useful and influential account. Here terrorism is described as extra-*normal* violence and as such goes beyond the rules (informal and formal) governing coercion, a violence which ignores conventional distinctions between guilt and innocence and/or between combatants and noncombatants. The "target" is not persons directly assaulted, but the public as a whole. Similar views are expressed by a variety of scholars, including Thornton, Rapoport, and Schmid. The definition conforms to the conceptions the original terrorists had of themselves, provides a good way to link rebel and state terrorism, and allows one to anticipate direction, i.e., the pronounced tendencies of terrorist campaigns to escalate atrocities.

A second less satisfactory view makes terrorism synonymous with all forms of illegal rebel violence. Although most legal definitions, or definitions by states, incorporate this view, i.e., the UK (1974) and the West Germany (1985), the difficulties are conspicuous. To use the term consistently and retrospectively, soldiers like George Washington and Robert E. Lee would become terrorists, indistinguishable from their contemporaries who really were terrorists, i.e., the Sons of Liberty and the Ku Klux Klan (KKK). This definition also obscures relationships between state and rebel terrorism, hiding a crucial and often-forgotten fact, namely that the public does distinguish the different means rebels use. Governments oblivious to that fact create sympathy for the rebels and much more trouble for themselves. The classic instance was the British decision to shoot leaders of the Easter Rising (1916), who fought in uniform and only against soldiers, making those executed into martyrs for a hitherto indifferent public.

II. CONTEMPORARY TERRORISM

A. Culture

French and Russian speculations and actions produced a "culture of terror." Sergei Nechaev's *Revolutionary Catechism* (1868) proclaims a "science of destruction," one in which individuals took lessons from anyone. The result may be seen in the history of modern terrorism. Successive generations participate in fresh efforts to alter the range and character of terrorist activity. In contrast, earlier groups, such as the Sons of Liberty and the KKK, did not explain their success, partly because they did not visualize successors. Thus, their efforts remained isolated episodes, not lessons to be studied and emulated.

Nor did the classic religious expressions produce such a culture. Divine precedents always determined the religious forms, precedents peculiar to specific religious traditions. Classic Islam illustrates this point. Believers were forbidden to use the sword against Muslims, and terrorists interpreted this prohibition to mean that only other weapons were permissible. Thus various groups chose different tools. The Assassins, (Fedayeen, 11th to 13th centuries) were the most effective, selecting the dagger while other groups used ropes or clubs. In each case, the weapon precluded the assailant's escape, making martyrdom likely, and the martyr is the critical agent for message-giving religions. Weapons that would make escape possible, i.e., missiles and poisons, were never chosen. Moreover, only important officials were struck down, an extraordinary limitation made explicable by the religious injunction to avoid *fitna* (civil strife). When ritual is so important, these can be no warrant to "improve" the practices. Justifications to go outside the tradition, to "borrow" something that worked elsewhere, were "unthinkable."

Nechaev's "science of destruction" could only develop in a larger society, which characteristically attempts to make all activities conform to standards of efficiency and utility. Ironically, the classic ancient terrorist groups (i.e., the Assassins (Islam), the Zealots (1st century Judaism), and the Thugs (Hinduism, 13th to the 19th centuries)) were the most durable, and despite or perhaps because of primitive technologies they were probably the most destructive (measured by casualty estimates and political turmoil generated). Their strength derived from extraordinary commitment, organizational ingenuity, and favorable public responses, including international support.

B. The Four Waves

Since the 1880s, four major waves of terror have washed over the international world, each with its own special character, dominating purposes, and peculiar tactics. The first three lasted from 35 to 40 years each, and the fourth, which began in 1979, is still in process. The waves overlapped, and each left organizations which survived (i.e., the Irish Republican Army, IRA) as it receded. Each surge was closely connected to major unexpected political turning points, exposing government vulnerabilities, and making it possible to define new issues or give older ones greater salience. Hope, thus, was excited; and hope is always the main lubricant of rebel movements.

The First Wave began in Russia during the 1880s and was precipitated by the massive reform efforts the

Tsars introduced to bring Russia up to Western standards. The hopes aroused could not be fulfilled quickly enough; and in the wake of inevitable disappointment, systematic assassination campaigns against prominent officials began. The best known groups aimed to reconstruct society radically; but others, such as the Poles and Armenians, sought more modest goals of national independence.

Within a decade, the Russian pattern of systematic assassination of high officials for revolution and/or separatism spread. Assassins struck in the Ottoman Empire (i.e., The Federation of Armenian Revolutionaries in 1890). Then the Balkans exploded during the 1890s when many found the boundaries of the states recently torn out of the Ottoman Empire too constricting and formed a variety of terrorist groups, i.e., Internal Macedonian Revolutionary Organization, Young Bosnia, and the Serbian Black Hand. International support materialized occasionally, as foreign states provided sanctuaries for terrorists on the run, and foreign constituencies largely organized by refugees gave moral aid and funds. Meanwhile, in the West revolutionary Anarchists mounted assassination campaigns to frustrate drives toward universal suffrage, a provision they thought could make existing political systems invulnerable.

The Second Wave began after World War I and continued for 2 decades after World War II. The principal stimulus was national self-determination, the war aim of the Allies. Articulated to undermine enemy empires, the principle ultimately destroyed the legitimacy of retaining colonial possessions also by the victors themselves, at least in the West. By the 1960s, as Western colonial empires gave way to many new states (i.e., Ireland, Israel, Cyprus, Yemen, Algeria, etc.), the Second Wave receded. The new terrorists "improved" the tactics of their predecessors. Their assassination campaigns were waged against police forces, the "eyes" and "ears" of government. The terrorists had larger forces, more significant social support, and their major energies went into guerrillalike (hit and run) actions against troops. But as the operations were conducted with concealed weapons and without identifying insignia, they were beyond the rules of war. Imperial territories were normally populated by different ethnic groups with conflicting concerns, and the terrorists commonly made indiscriminate attacks against those civilians opposed to independence, i.e., Cypriot Turks, Algerian Berbers, and European residents everywhere.

The international world was a much more active element, too, and crucial for the limited successes achieved in the Second Wave. The new rebel purpose induced the more favorable international climate. Nationalism was less threatening than the revolutionary ethos of the first wave especially since the colonial empires were overseas empires and not contiguous, as were those of the First Wave. Nationalism also provided a better unifying purpose for diaspora communities. United Nations resolutions encouraging national liberation movements were simultaneously symptoms, causes, and consequences of this international support.

The Third Wave began in the late 1960s and embraced a revolutionary ethos again, making the West, especially the U.S., its principal target. The political turning point was the Vietnam War. The effectiveness of Vietcong terror against the American Goliath armed with modern technology kindled hopes that the heartland of the Western world was vulnerable. The U.S Weather Underground, the German Red Army Fraction, the Italian Red Brigades, and French AD saw themselves as vanguards for the revolutionary masses of the Third World and looked to the Tupamaros (Uruguay) as a model for effective activity in urban contexts. The Soviets encouraged these movements covertly.

Sometimes the new revolutionary ethos was linked to separatist purposes, i.e., the Basque Nation and Liberty (ETA); the Armenian Secret Army for the Liberation of Armenia; Peasant Front for Liberation of Corsica; the PLO; and the IRA. But over time in each case, separatism proved more important than revolution.

When the Vietnam War ended, the PLO replaced the Vietcong as the heroic model for revolutionary terrorists. The PLO turned to terrorism in the aftermath of the Six Day War (1967) when the extraordinary collapse of three major Arab armies gave credibility to those arguing that the established structures simply could not muster the commitment needed. Although the PLO, with so many different and mutually hostile revolutionary and nationalist elements, seemed like an odd model for revolutionaries, the PLO's principal antagonist, Israel, had become an integral element of the West, and Soviet ties strengthened PLO revolutionary elements.

Observers of the Third Wave coined the term "international terrorism" to describe the "new" terrorists. A widespread revolutionary ethos created bonds between separate groups which transcended national lines, and a terrorist organization (the PLO in Lebanon) provided facilities to train other terrorists in different groups from many countries. The targets of the actual assaults also reflected an international dimension; some groups conducted more assaults abroad than in indigenous territories. The PLO was more active in Europe than on the West Bank, and sometimes more active in Europe than the European groups! On their own national soil,

groups sought targets with international significance especially Americans and American installations abroad. There were striking instances of different national groups and teams composed of separate nationals cooperating on attacks in third countries (i.e., the massacre at the Munich Olympics, 1972; the kidnapping of OPEC Ministers, Vienna, 1975; and hijackings to Entebbe, Uganda, 1976, and Mogadishu, Somalia, 1977). States (i.e., Libya, Iraq, and Syria) used foreign terrorists as instruments of their international policies, a practice called "state-sponsored terror."

Airline hijacking was the period's novel tactic, numbering over 100 every year in the 1970s. The assaults symbolized the era's unique international character because foreign landing fields normally were required. Hijacking also reflected the impulse for spectacular acts, a theme expressed in the assassination proclivities of the First Wave but abandoned largely in the Second to organize more effective militarylike strikes. Planes were hijacked to secure hostages, and a variety of different sorts of hostage-taking incidents dominated the period, the most memorable being the kidnapping of the Italian Prime Minister Aldo Moro, who was then murdered when his government refused to negotiate for his release (1979). The Sandinistas took Nicaragua's Congress hostage (1978), an act so audacious that it sparked an insurrection, bringing the Somoza regime down 1 year later. The Columbian M-19 tried to duplicate the act, taking the Dominican Republic's embassy in the Columbian capital (1980) but to no avail. Subsequently, when the M-19 took the Supreme Court, the government killed over 100 members, including 11 justices, rather than yield. The most recent failure, perhaps the last spectacular gasp of Third Wave revolutionaries, occurred when a Peruvian Marxist group, Tupac Amaru, held 72 hostages in the Japanese embassy for more than 4 months (1996–1997). A rescue operation killed all the terrorists.

Many right-wing terrorist groups, frustrated with what they understood as unjustifiably slow, compromising government responses, also emerged. (Parallel expressions in the First and Second Waves were the Russian pogroms of Jewish villages and the Secret Army Organization (OAS) of French colonists in Algeria). Neo-Fascist Italian groups (i.e., the New Order, the National Vanguard) caused more casualties, and more indiscriminate ones, than did their better-known revolutionary counterparts, a pattern exhibited in the first two waves also. In Latin America "death squads" operated secretly, assassinating purported revolutionaries and those "too critical" of government. Only a few such groups identified themselves, i.e., the Argentine Anti-

Communist Alliance, the Communist Hunting Command (Brazil), and the Secret Anti-Communist Army (Guatemala). The Grey Wolves and the Apostolic Anti-Communist Alliance plagued Turkey and Spain, respectively. Northern Ireland has the Protestant Ulster Defence Association (UDA). Right-wing terrorist groups shun publicity partly because police and military personnel contribute direct support. (Experience shows that only revolutionary governments can be open in their use of terrorism and only during their initial phase when the claim of weakness is most credible and an enthusiasm for the vision most compelling.)

The Third Wave began ebbing in the 1980s. Revolutionaries were defeated in one country after another. The Israeli invasion of Lebanon (1982) eliminated PLO facilities to train other terrorist groups, and international cooperation against terrorism became more effective. The dramatic unexpected political turning points, the necessary condition for a new wave, were two related events, the revolution in Iran and the Soviet defeat in Afghanistan. Both "demonstrated" that religion provided more hope than did the prevailing revolutionary ethos. When the Soviet bloc disintegrated (1991), partly because of the Afghanistan disaster, new separatist rebel movements, often with a religious base, appeared.

Religious elements were common in earlier waves because religious and ethnic identities overlapped. But the earlier objectives were establishing independent states, and the tactics were understood as human or secular creations (i.e., Ottoman Turkey, Macedonia, Cyprus, Israel, Algeria, Northern Ireland). The Fourth Wave produced a new sacred terrorism form, one in which religious justifications and precedents shaped both the aims and the tactics. No wave, moreover, produced more brutal and deadly attacks.

Islam generated the earliest examples. Inspired by the Iranian Revolution and aided by Iranian governments, Shia terrorists (i.e., *Hezbollah*) operated both in Middle Eastern and European states to support objectives in the Islamic world. A striking new tactic was suicide bombing (self martyrdom) which proved effective against Western targets in Lebanon and reasserted in a new way the crucial martyrdom theme of the First Wave, which was neglected in the two successive waves.

Sunni Islam also produced some extraordinary events, i.e., the storming of the Grand Mosque in Mecca (1979) and the assassination of Egypt's President Sadat (1981). Sunni terrorism appeared in many states with large Islamic populations, i.e., Syria, Tunisia, Morocco, Algeria, the Philippines, and Indonesia, and it rivaled the PLO in strikes against Israeli targets. Muslims from all parts of the Islamic world fought in Afghanistan, developing an international *esprit* which enabled them to return home with the will, confidence, and training to begin terrorist operations. Ironically, American support had been crucial in getting most outsiders to Afghanistan, including some involved in the World Trade Center bombing (1993).

During the 1980s, other religious communities spawned their own forms of terrorism. Sikhs sought a separate religious state in the Punjab. A persistent and extraordinarily bloody struggle was waged between Sri Lankan Buddhists and Hindus, one in which suicide bombings became common and whose most prominent victim was Indian Prime Minister Rajiv Gandhi. Jewish terrorists attempted to blow up Islam's most sacred site in Jerusalem, the Dome of the Rock, waged a campaign against Palestinian mayors, murdered 29 worshippers in Hebron (1994), and assassinated Israeli Prime Minister Yitzak Rabin (1995). In 1995 *Aum Shinrikyo*, a Japanese religious movement which combined Hindu and Buddhist elements with millenarian Christian themes, released nerve gas on the Tokyo subway killing 12 and injuring some 5000, creating an enormous world-wide trauma that a new threshold in the terrorist experience had been crossed.

Christian expressions materialized in the U.S., largely the product of elements in the amorphous decentralized Christian Identity movement, which proclaims a racist doctrine including a Bible-based justification for exterminating all Jews. In typical millenarian fashion, members, sometimes with their families, often withdrew to armed rural communes to wait for the Second Coming and expecting racial war. Counterfeiting and false lien campaigns were mounted to indicate the rejection of state authority and generate funds. Secessionists seized small territories inevitably provoking sieges. So far, the level of violence has been minimal, although the Oklahoma City Bombing (1995), the most deadly terrorist act ever on American soil (168 killed), seems connected with the movement.

C. Organizations

Terrorist groups are generally very small. Few contain more than 50 members; but for each member, four to six persons outside are required to provide essential logistic support. At their peaks, extraordinarily effective groups like the Irgun, the National Organization of Cypriot Struggle for Union with Greece (EOKA), the IRA, and ETA had between 200 and 400 members. But there have been larger organizations. The *Montoneros*, operating openly in the Argentine chaos, had over 1,500 members in 1974. The PLO in Lebanon before the Israeli invasion numbered 25,000, but no other terrorist organization has ever been allowed to operate so freely, and their numbers reflected an effort to establish a regular army.

Urban terrorist groups are normally divided into 4- or 5-person cells, which are virtually sealed off from each other to limit police penetration. This need for cell autonomy often creates serious obstacles to effective control from above. Outside the city, units are significantly larger because natural terrain provides better opportunities than the city can for concealment.

Modern terrorist organizations, compared to their ancient counterparts, have short lives. The overwhelming majority, perhaps as many as 90%, do not last a year. Nearly half of the surviving groups collapse before their 10th anniversary. On the other hand, short-lived groups frequently have successors because their more durable constituencies survive and furnish new recruits for the next generation. Often there are secure foreign sanctuaries which are useful too in generating successor organizations. A few organizations are very durable; the IRA has operated intermittently for 80 years, making it by far the most long-lasting modern group. Its "competitors" are the Basque group ETA, active for 38 years, and the PLO, which survived for 29 years as a terrorist organization. It is no coincidence that these groups are principally ethnic ones. The durability of the new forms of sacred terrorism is still unclear.

Normally, terrorists fight a "poor person's war"; but larger, more durable organizations need capital. They get money in several ways; one is "expropriation" in the forms of in bank robberies, forced donations, ransoms, protection rackets, drugs, and services. Private parties, especially those in diaspora communities, and foreign states voluntarily provide aid. In the case of the PLO, legitimate investments and taxes from the Palestinian diaspora have been crucial.

The only demonstrable common characteristic of active terrorists is their youth; very few reach the age of 30. The reasons are obvious. The activity attracts persons at the peak of their physical strength, individuals with enormous enthusiasm, little patience, and the willingness to take great risks. Beyond that, attrition rates are very high. Males predominate, but left-wing revolutionary groups attract many females; Vera Figner was the second commander of Narodnaya Volya; women dominated the Weather Underground, the RAF, and constituted 40% of the *Tupamaros* in its final stage. Conversely, in right-wing groups and in separatist organizations lacking a revolutionary component, women and children invariably provide logistic services but, compared to their left-wing counterparts, bear arms infrequently.

Social compositions change over time. The Russians were originally middle-class university students, and some minorities, especially Jews and Poles, always had a disproportionate influence. But over time the Russian groups diversified and approximated society as a whole more. A similar pattern appears in later revolutionary terrorist groups but insufficient data prevent conclusive pictures. Weinberg and Eubank note that the social profiles of leaders and followers in the Italian revolutionary and right-wing terrorist groups resemble those of left- and right-wing parliamentary parties.

Information on contemporary sacred terrorist groups is sparse, but social profiles vary greatly even within the same religions. In Egypt, middle-class university students with technological interests are highly represented; in Lebanon and Iran, the poor led by religious clerics predominate. Women generally have smaller roles in sacred groups. In Islam women are generally excluded, but they do participate in Christian groups and are especially important in Sri Lanka among the Hindu Tamils.

D. Outcomes: Domestic and International

The overall impact is difficult to gauge without distinguishing between immediate victims, political reactions, intended and unintended consequences. Sometimes terror is the principal tactic, (Narodnaya Volya); other times, it is part of a larger political and military effort, as in Vietnam, or is a tactic of one group for an objective that others are vying for in different ways, (i.e., the Irgun in the struggle to establish Israel). In every case, alternatives must be considered too. But no systematic discussion of effects using these distinctions exist. The most one can do here is provide some general observations.

Some effects can be measured rather precisely, like the cost of airport surveillance, an omnipresent feature of our lives. Other important features are prominent, but scarcely known and not easily measured. For example, most ununiformed or undercover police forces (such as the Russian Okhrana, the FBI, Scotland Yard, etc.) were created initially to cope with terrorist threats, but they became permanent institutions with many tasks significant to the community even when no terrorist threat existed.

Victims have received some attention. But the statistics are inadequate, and cumulative figures are available only for international incidents since 1968. Even here, the data sources employ different definitions which make the gross numbers for international terror vary widely. Domestic terror statistics are much larger but even more unevenly collected. Often countries with the most victims (i.e., Peru and Sri Lanka) keep the least reliable statistics. Most countries, however, experience far more deaths from highway accidents than from terrorism. Israel, for example, through 1993, experienced 20 times as much.

Data on international incidents reveals that the overwhelming number of assaults involve bombings, and are performed for the same reasons as in the 19th century. Most (over 40%) are strikes against property, 20% involve attempts to kill persons, and 10% are kidnapping and hostage-taking efforts. Most international victims are government officials, usually diplomats, and one-third represent business interests. Approximately one-third are Americans with the Israelis, French, and British far behind, in that order. Despite the high profile of international terrorism, casualties have averaged some 350 annually since early 1970s, and an American is as likely to die in an international incident as from an animal bite, and in 1998 was more likely to be hurt taking a bath!

Domestic terror figures, terror within particular states, however, are often 20 to 30 times the international statistics. But the domestic totals vary considerably depending on the length of the campaign and the "moral" limits accepted in the struggles. The campaign of the Irgun and Lehi in Palestine (1944–1948) consumed 371 lives while that of the Algerian Front de Liberation National (FLN) (1954–1962) took over 95,000. There have been more than 60,000 deaths in the recent on-going struggle that Algerian Islamic militants have waged (1992–present) against the FLN government.

Terrorist groups rarely succeed. Revolutionary groups without a distinct ethnic base have the greatest failure rate, as both Latin American and European experiences during the Third Wave demonstrate. But groups that fail sometimes alter the political landscapes in ways they did not intend. The Tzarist efforts to reform Russia, and perhaps to create a parliamentary government, were abandoned, a fact which may have had immense consequences for Russia and for the world. In the wake of the Tupamaro attacks, a Uruguayan military junta (1974) took over a country known then as the "Switzerland of Latin America." Similarly, terrorists induced Argentinian (1976) and Turkish armies (1980) to abort fresh attempts at democratic government.

Separatist groups have, however, produced some striking successes. When rebels and governments have distinctly different ethnic bases and everyone understands the situation as colonial, usually empires with overseas territories, terrorist activity has sometimes helped establish a new state. But when dominant communities do not perceive themselves as colonial powers, the outcome is different. A special autonomy might be the most achieved, i.e., the German-speaking Trento-Alto-Adige region in northern Italy. To defuse ETA, Spain has given the Basques greater regional autonomy, a concession which has led some to lay down their arms and may ultimately bring peace. The Oslo Accords (1993) may produce a separate Palestinian state at some future time, but if that occurs it will be noted that Israel had never incorporated the West Bank and that few issues have generated more international concern.

Terrorist activity normally creates even greater gaps between neighboring ethnic groups, often making it impossible either to achieve their larger objective or to live with the more limited alternative achieved. The EOKA eliminated British rule in order to gain a union with Greece. Instead, the state of Cyprus (1952) was established, the only entity that the frightened Turkish Cypriots would tolerate. But the hatreds and fears EOKA atrocities exacerbated have made achievement of a single state for that island impossible so far, especially as Turkey refused to accept Turkish Cypriot refugees, and thus alter the ethnic character of the island. In Algeria the European population's fear was so great that flight was the only solution because, unlike Turkey, France accepted the refugee burden. The PLO's terrorist tactics achieved something, but the distrust evoked is a major, perhaps insuperable, obstacle for gaining more and may ultimately be a crucial factor in dooming the Oslo Accords. Has 2 decades of IRA terror made the Protestant majority in Northern Ireland more or less implacable?

Separate spaces may be the best solution for separated peoples. But where that is not possible, as in South Africa, President Mandela's extraordinary experiment, a "Truth and Reconciliation Commission" (1995) to enable the perpetrators of atrocities (*both* the government and rebels) the opportunities to gain legal immunity by confessing, may produce a bridge between populations. The effort could have significant consequences for other terrorist struggles.

In the international world, terrorist activity generally creates and exacerbates tensions between states. The most dramatic example is the assassination of the Austrian Archduke, which precipitated the First World War, transforming the political map of the world. The truly explosive question was the extent of foreign involvement, an issue always raised when borders are crossed. In the wake of President Kennedy's assassination, the American government's most pressing problem was to convince its people that no foreign power was implicated. The Israeli–Egyptian War (1956) and the Six Day War (1967) were occasioned partly by terrorist raids, and the Israeli invasion of Lebanon (1982) was precipitated by an attempted assassination of an Israeli diplomat in Britain. Iraq cited Shia terrorist attacks against Iraqi officials to justify the initiation of a war against Iran in 1980. The American raid on Libya (1986) was a direct response to a series of terrorist attacks implicating that country. In the same decade, Britain severed diplomatic relations with Syria and Libya for sponsoring terrorism on British soil, France broke with Iran when Iran refused to let its embassy members be interrogated, the United States broke with Iran when many American embassy staff members were taken hostage in 1979, and Iran's encouragement of Shia groups in Lebanon to hold Europeans and Americans hostage intensified tensions between Iran and the West. During the 1991 Gulf War, Iran thought that a more desirable relationship with the U.S. required Iran to facilitate the release of hostages held by Lebanese groups sympathetic to Iran.

Even friendly states find that terrorism creates frictions between them. France has refused to extradite some PLO, Red Brigade and ETA suspects to West Germany, Italy, and Spain respectively. Italy spurned American requests to extradite the person alleged to have organized Palestinian terrorists to seize the vessel, *Achille Lauro* in 1985. The U.S. often refused British requests to extradite IRA suspects. In 1998 Italy spurned Turkish efforts to extradite a Kurdish terrorist leader, because Turkey would probably execute him and Italian law forbids capital punishment. Such events will recur until the laws and interests of separate states are identical, a virtually unimagineable condition.

State-sponsored terrorism, i.e., using foreign rebels or domestic surrogates, in the international sphere is rarely productive. Only Iran and Syria acting jointly have been successful in a strategic sense, and then only in one country, Lebanon (1984), where after dramatic self-martyrdom attacks, the multinational forces withdrew. In that unusual case, the sponsors hid their involvement well, local elements were deeply committed, and the confused objectives of the multinational forces had little support. Normally surrogates have their own agenda and eventually may expose the sponsoring state to retaliation itself. The limited power of the state-sponsored international terror is indicated also by the striking Iraqi unwillingness to use it during the Gulf War, despite widespread predictions that Iraq would. Had it done so, bringing Saddam Hussein to trial for war crimes would have become a war objective, and avoiding that certainty is the most plausible explanation for the uncharacteristic restraint.

State-encouraged terrorism, however, can create enormous domestic problems for other states. Embassy hostages held by Iranians after the Shah escaped to the United States humiliated President Carter and caused excessive and harmful obsessions with the issue, as spectacular terrorist acts always do. Carter's poor crisis management probably wrecked his bid for reelection in 1980. In the complicated Iran–Contra Affair, precipitated by efforts to get hostages in Lebanon released, the Reagan administration nearly unraveled, but these events did not benefit the hostage holders.

E. Explanations and Conditions

The explosion of rebel terrorism in the 1960s surprised almost everyone. No scholarly consensus emerged to explain the Third Wave which most believed was an unprecedented phenomenon. The favored explanations are offered singly or in combination. A "technological explanation" sees terrorism as a by-product of innovations in transportation, weapons, and communication technologies, which made it easier to travel, destroy targets, and transmit messages quickly to large numbers. Psychological explanations describe terrorists as abnormal personalities with identifiable character traits. A widespread conspiratorial theory explained terrorism as a Cold War product, a Soviet-inspired and organized "surrogate war." All these explanations have some element of truth, but they are seriously deficient even when employed collectively. Conspiratorial theory grossly underestimated the strength of local concerns, psychological theories became increasingly inadequate as the data accumulated, and while modern technology influences terrorist practices, a technological theory of the sort described is implausible because terrorism had a significant history long before the 1960s.

The most significant dimension of terrorism, its political roots, received little attention. Terrorism is an aspect of the French revolutionary tradition and has been a constituent feature of our life for 2 centuries. In specific periods, different methods (mass uprisings, terrorism, *coups d'etat*, and guerrilla wars) have supplanted each other as the magic tool for successful revolution.

One legacy of the French Revolution was a set of unusual concepts, pertinent to understanding the terrorist phenomena. A new idea of the sovereign, i.e., the "People," distinct from the institutions designed to embody it, made rebel claims to represent the "People" always conceivable and sometimes credible. The problem became particularly vexing when a "national self-determination" claim was made because existing states contained several "Peoples." The "promise" of the Revolution was that a perfect world would emerge once social institutions were refashioned, a promise which could generate "guilt" when injustice was pointed out. At the minimum, these themes could create serious public ambivalences, leading often to indecision, always an advantage to potential terrorists.

Terrorist activity occurs most often in states that are democratic, in states that are moving toward democracy, and in states in which a significant move toward democracy has been arrested. The most oppressive states may contain the most injustices, but they also destroy the hope that terrorists require. In Tsarist Russia, rebel terror began only after dramatic reforms. It ceased after an attempt on Lenin provoked savage repression, but when Gorbachev introduced the policy of *perestroika* (relaxation) in the Soviet Union, hope was rekindled and rebel terror began again.

Terrorism is always associated with attacks on "innocent" victims. The Reign of Terror tried to redefine the meaning of innocence and constructed a doctrine of "total war" to be invoked when the life of the community was at stake. Total war obliterates crucial but fragile (and in a sense quite arbitrary) distinctions between combatants and noncombatants, permissible and impermissible military methods. Because democratic states increasingly depended upon conscription, there were pressures to justify every war as one of self-defense and total war became more congenial. After 1945, the doctrine's implications became visible for the first time in peace, embodied in terrifying weapons of mass destruction. In these circumstances, rules of combat which might have inhibited rebels earlier no longer did so.

The "right" to use terror, moreover, is claimed as an entitlement of the "weak," a startling perversion of democratic egalitarianism. Rebels portray themselves as weak and normally "claim responsibility" for their assaults, while states normally conceal responsibility because the public understands that states have alternatives. Only states in the initial phase of a revolution, when their weakness is known and their desperation plausible, will state terror accepted.

When it is not at war, the concern for the sanctity of life is another feature of the democratic state, one which seems wholly opposed to its propensity to make wars total. In placing a high premium on the lives of hostages, for example, democratic states become vulnerable in ways in which other contemporary states are not. For example, when Iraq found that Iran would not negotiate for hostages, Iraq stopped taking them. The same reason convinced Lebanese Maronites in 1986 to stop taking Shia hostages. Tactical success of terrorists thus depends upon their abilities to turn an antagonists' moral strength into a political weakness.

Ever since **Narodnaya Volya** recognized the importance of the press, terrorists have struggled to make the communications network give them attention. Opportunities are maximized in democratic states because the public finds terrorist activity interesting. For 16 days in July, 1985, some 65% of national TV coverage in the United States was concerned with the hijacking of TWA Flight 847, and between 1981 and 1986 terrorism received more national TV attention than poverty, unemployment, and crime combined.

The unhealthy tendencies of democratic governments to become preoccupied with terrorist incidents and to make unrealistic promises about quick results partly reflects media-generated pressures. Restrictions on the media consequently have been imposed often, even in genuinely liberal states like Britain where Prime Minister Margaret Thatcher complained the media provided "the oxygen" terrorists need.

Yet as terrorists themselves stress, the media affect terrorist groups adversely, too, by painting grotesque portraits. A less obvious important point is that the desire of terrorists to exploit media opportunities sometimes distracts them from more important questions concerning organization and strategy. Thus, the irony may be that while the media encourages more terrorist groups to emerge, it simultaneously shortens their life expectancies.

F. Counterterrorist Policies

There may be no "solutions" to terrorism in a democratic state. But specific conditions and particular public responses do help explain the ebb and flow of terrorist activity. Terrorism normally combines criminal and political (or religious) activity with a mode of violence so peculiar that it eludes ordinary conceptual categories. Terrorists will always claim a prisoner-of-war status, even though they reject the associated traditional military norms; and their dependency upon secrecy makes it necessary for governments to waive their claim to have military immunities from interrogation. Yet a policy of regarding all terrorists as criminals simply is unwise, because sometimes it strengthens those with significant political constituencies.

In coping with terrorist campaigns, as distinguished from terrorist episodes, there are three major concerns: pertinent domestic political grievances, police action, and international issues. Each concern has significant costs and limits, and in particular cases, one or another is more significant. When a group has viable durable political support, the aim is to divorce that connection, which may necessitate timely concessions. Yet demands cannot always be met without generating terror from those who oppose them (i.e., Northern Ireland and Israel). Other times there may simply be no ability to meet stated demands, i.e., the South Moluccan demand that the Dutch compel Indonesia to establish a South Moluccan state.

The most effective police power against secret organizations is intelligence activity which normally requires undercover agents. But this device can have a high cost; gaining information may require participation in the group's activities and the agent's commitments may become confused. A police agent, Azeff, led the Terrorist Brigade of the Russian Social Revolutionaries (1905), and nearly 40% of its members were on the Tsar's payroll. Similarly, though less profound, abuses plagued the FBI's efforts to deal with American terrorism during the Third Wave. In countries with serious terrorist problems the necessity to interrogate prisoners quickly frequently produces torture. In democratic states, the enlargement of surveillance powers always occurs at the expense of traditional civil liberties; and powers taken are not always restored. Yet sometimes when democratic governments did not use the powers needed, the military, determined to "get on with the job," have overthrown them.

Special immunities for repenters sometimes can have enormous significance by demoralizing organizations, as the Italian experiences with the BR and the neo-Fascist groups illustrate. In this respect, revolutionary groups seem more vulnerable than separatists, especially separatists with important international resources.

Groups normally go to the international sphere to compensate for serious domestic weaknesses; a decision which often compounds their weakness, by making them dependent on forces with different, often conflicting, interests. Some groups will never get much support no matter how just their claims, i.e., a state for the Kurds will mean territorial concessions from four states. But many groups will find that the separate interests of sovereign states with different traditions of political dissent provide leverage.

There are several ways for governments to alter the international scene to their advantage. The first is by changing International law. Some political offenses once immune to extradition, like the assassination of heads of state, no longer are. The League of Nations (1937) drafted two conventions for an international court with jurisdiction over all cases involving international terrorism cases; but war broke out before the conventions went into effect, and the UN did not reestablish them. Since 1970 many bilateral, regional, and UN agreements affecting aircraft, diplomats, hostages, and the transportation of nuclear materials have been concluded. Those regulating hijacking have been the most effective, reducing the number of incidents enormously since the high point in the late 1960s and early 1970s. Increased hijacking difficulties ironically may have promoted a tendency to destroy aircraft in flight (Air India over the mid-Atlantic, 1985 and Pan Am over Lockerbie, Scotland, 1988).

A second way to deal with the international dimension is to improve cooperative mechanisms. In the 19th century, police forces of different states intermittently and informally cooperated. After the dramatic upsurge in Middle Eastern terrorism in Europe during the 1980s, a formal mechanism to transmit information regularly, Interpol (which now has 142 member states), was established. In 1986, TREVI (*terrorisme, radicalisme, extremisme et la violence internationale*) was created by the European Community to enable regular consultations on extradition matters.

A third method to deal with international terrorism is reprisals by individual or allied states. As early as the 1st century, terrorist groups gained foreign sanctuaries, training facilities, and logistical support, and aggrieved states responded. In most cases, a neighbor acts alone, sometimes with overwhelming force. When everything else failed to stop the Thugs, the British incorporated hitherto independent Hindu states into British India and, significantly, no international reaction materialized. A century later, states found such options limited considerably. Rescue operations like Entebbe (1976) and Mogadishu (1977) are generally acceptable, but punitive reprisal raids are less so. During the Algerian uprising against France, the French attacked FLN bases in Tunisia and Morocco, generating so much adverse international reaction that the raids became counter-productive. Israeli raids in Egypt, Jordan, and Syria deprived the PLO of its bases. The tactic was much less successful in Lebanon because the bases were deliberately placed in refugee camps, and the attacks incurred a difficult-to-estimate cost in world opinion. The Israeli invasion (1982) of Lebanon eliminated the bases at enormous political and military costs.

Multinational sanctions have been rare, but the U.S. air raid against Libya (1986) received British aid and was supplemented by a European Community arms embargo. Subsequently, Libya seemed to reduce involvements with terrorist clients or, perhaps more precisely, Libya reduced the more overt signs of that connection. European governments also expelled Libyan diplomats and students, and Libya became increasingly isolated in the Arab world. Evidence that Libyan officials were involved in the Pan-Am Lockerbie crash (1988) led a unanimous UN Security Council to demand that Libya extradite the suspects (1992), a wholly unprecedented UN step. Many thought that this might signify a new era of international cooperation against terrorism, but Libya has not yet complied. A new opportunity for multinational sanctions occurred when a Berlin court (1997) found that Iran's "highest political leadership" ordered the murder of Kurdish refugees on German soil, but it is likely that the results will be as barren as they were in similar instances when the French Revolutionary, Nazi, and Fascist regimes organized assassinations on foreign soil.

Various states have imposed measures against individual state sponsors, but no consistent policy of serious sanctions against *all* identified sponsors exists. Mindful that American citizens have been the principal targets Secretary of State Alexander Haig described terrorism as *the* most important international problem (1980), but the U.S. has only fitfully dealt with the issue because other concerns and interests are more important.

III. THE FUTURE

Terrorism will remain part of the landscape indefinitely, and we cannot forecast its ebb and flow, because terrorism is likely to remain linked, as it has in the past, to unexpected major political transformations. There is no way of determining when the current religious element runs its course, but it seems likely that separatism, a persistent dimension in every wave, will remain significant afterward.

The anxiety that terrorists will exploit each new technological development has been part of the intellectual landscape ever since 19th-century police reports argued that no defense against the bomb would ever materialize. The most prominent fear today is that future terrorists will use weapons of mass destruction (chemical, biological, and nuclear) which can also produce mass panic. The "culture of terror" expressed in Nechaev's writings suggests that the day may come, and many think that Aum Shinrikyo's Tokyo attack indicates that it has.

Yet significant differences between doctrine and practice exist, and the issue should be put in appropriate historical perspective. Opportunities to employ chemical weapons had been available for some 80 years and ignored, before Aum struck, the barriers, against biological and nuclear weapons were intact. Since the 1880s explosives and firearms have been the principal weapons for all groups. The changes characterizing each wave have been largely differences in targets, strategic priorities, and different methods of delivery, but the weapons remained the same.

Three reasons explain this restraint. A desire to win public support is generally understood as the major inhibition, although ironically states with political agendas have used such weapons. A second reason is that terrorists themselves often have moral reservations. And finally there are considerable operational difficulties. Terrorist groups must assemble and reassemble weapons while in constant flight and, consequently, they have always been very prone to accidents, and accidents account for perhaps as many terrorist casualties as those inflicted by security forces. More complicated or more volatile weapons, especially weapons of mass destruction, will produce many more accidents and more lethal ones. Larger less-mobile units will be needed, and secrecy, the rebel terrorist's indispensable condition, will be compromised.

Aum's unusual circumstances illustrate these issues. No underground group could have Aum's facilities; a worldwide organization of perhaps 50,000 members, assets over a billion dollars, and many professionally trained scientists. As a religious group it had special immunities under Japanese law which prevented investigations of complaints. It made 12 efforts; 10 were aborted by accidents, and only 2 injured those outside the group. To make the gas less dangerous to members delivering it, the dose was diluted which was why so few (12 including 1 Aum member) were killed in the major subway attack. Only persons who came in contact with the liquid were injured and the group destroyed itself in the gamble.

Many argue that the sacred terrorist groups of the Fourth Wave lack the restraints which characterized those in earlier waves. Their political agendas are less compelling, and religious commitments make them less vulnerable to moral issues and cost. Certainly, sacred groups have inflicted and taken more casualties than their secular counterparts in the 20th century. But neither statistics nor doctrine suggest wholesale indifference to such concerns. The past will never be a conclusive guide to future, but it is one always worth consulting.

Also See the Following Articles

ASSASSINATIONS, POLITICAL • ETHNICITY AND IDENTITY POLITICS

Bibliography

Anderson, S., & Sloan, S. (1995). *Historical dictionary of terrorism*. Metcuchen, NJ: Scarecrow Press.

Barkun, M. (1994). *Religion and the racist right: The origins of the christian identity movement*. Chapel Hill, University of North Carolina Press.

Billington, J. (1980). *Fire in the minds of men: Origins of the revolutionary faith*. New York: Basic Books.

Crenshaw, M. (1981). The causes of terrorism. *Comparative Politics, 13*(4), 379–397.

Hewitt, C. (1984). *The effectiveness of anti-terrorist policies*. New York: University Press of America.

Laqueur, W. (1987). *The age of terrorism*. Boston: Little, Brown.

Marx, G. (1975). Thoughts on a neglected category of social science movements participants: The *agent provocateur* and the informant. *American Journal of Sociology, 80*(1), 401–442.

Nechaev, S. (1971). *The revolutionary catechism*, reprinted in David C. Rapoport, *Assassination and terrorism*, Toronto: Canadian Broadcasting Corporation.

Rapoport, D. C. (1971). *Assassination and Terrorism*, Toronto: Canadian Broadcasting Corporation.

Rapoport, D. C. (1977). The politics of atrocity. In Y. Alexander & S. M. Finger (Eds.), *Terrorism: Interdisciplinary perspectives*, pp. 46–59). New York: John Jay Press.

Rapoport, D. C. (1982). State terror. In D. C. Rapoport & Y. Alexander (Eds.), *The morality of terrorism*, (Part 2, pp. 127–216). New York: Pergamon.

Rapoport, D. C. (1984). Fear and trembling: Terror in three religious traditions. *American Political Science Review, 3*, 658–677.

Rapoport, D. C. (1988a). *Inside terrorist organizations*. New York: Columbia University Press.

Rapoport, D. C. (1988b). Messianic sanctions for terror. *Comparative Politics, 20*(2), 195–213.

Schmid, A. P., & Jongman, A. J. et al. (1988), *Political Terrorism: A new guide to actors, authors, concepts, data bases and literature*, 2nd ed. New Brunswick: Transaction.

Simon, J. (1989). *Terrorists and the potential use of biological weapons*, R-3771–AFMIC. Santa Monica, CA: Rand Corporation.

Simon, J (1994). *The terrorist trap: America's experience with terrorism*. Bloomington: University of Indiana Press.

Thornton, T. P. (1964). Terror as a weapon of political agitation. In Harry Eckstein (Ed.), *Internal war*. New York: Free Press.

Walter, E. V. (1969). *Terror & Resistance* New York: Oxford Univ. Press.

Theories of Conflict

Ho-Won Jeong
George Mason University

THIS ARTICLE focuses on the diverse social environments that generate conflict. Research on conflict, political violence, and revolution has been popular among those who are anxious to do research on both social stability and the process of structural transformation. Several different theoretical traditions can be identified in understanding social conflict. Some focus on human nature and biological conditions. Others, on the other hand, emphasize a social structure and relations within groups. The analysis of sources and the nature of conflict helps us explore the conditions needed for its resolution.

GLOSSARY

Conflict Groups Organized either to defend or challenge the legitimacy of existing authority relations.
Nonrealistic Conflict Not directed toward achieving specific goals; merely releasing tensions.
Rational and Legal Authority Based on the principles of the universal and impartial applications of rules.
Realistic Conflict Serves as a means for obtaining specific outcomes.
Relative Deprivation A perceived gap between the expected conditions of life and the actual conditions of life.

I. PARADIGMS ON SOCIAL CONFLICT

Conflict can be examined in terms of the dynamics of group interactions. The causes of conflict have been investigated by the sociopsychological and structural analyses of social relations. The existence of conflict can be ascribed to relative deprivation, dissatisfaction of basic needs, failure of organizational functions, asymmetric power relations, and dominant social structure. The roots of the modern theories of conflict can be traced back to Max Weber, Karl Marx, and Sigmund Freud.

Social psychologists find the sources of violent human behavior in the inner psychological environment. War and violence are inherent in human nature. Some believe that aggressive behavior is genetically fixed and biologically functional. Others explain conflict in terms of feelings of deprivation and frustration brought about by rapid social change. The collapse of social norms often allows the expression of frustration in violent forms.

Social relations among and within groups have also been an important aspect of analysis in looking at conflict. The patterns of conflict can be analyzed in terms of collective action. Social stability is maintained by the legitimation of authority relations between superior and subordinate groups. Problems are seen in terms of how a society evolves in response to challenges to its survival. Functionalism emphasizes that social disintegration results from the failure of basic functions of a social system. Conflict is equated with social instability. Exchange theories explain the sources of power in terms of the ability to supply goods and services desired by others. Cultural norms are affected by the structural conditions of exchange relationships. The existence of social consensus reduces unreasonable expectations.

In contrast with a consensus model of social relations, the nature and types of conflict can be studied in terms of how a hierarchical structure produces antagonistic relations among opposing classes or interest groups. Social and economic inequity generates struggle in a modern political economy. In the Marxist paradigm, power relations between different classes are determined by an exploitative economic structure. Coercion is used to maintain unequal relations between the rich and the poor. While disagreeing with the Marxist emphasis on the sources of class antagonism, sociologists Lewis Coser and Ralph Dahrendorf challenged the assumption of functionalist approaches that conflict is pathological and dysfunctional. Under certain circumstances conflict can contribute to social cohesion. The struggle between dominant and subordinate groups in a modern society has been stabilized through institutionalized mechanisms of dealing with social conflict.

II. SOURCES OF AGGRESSION

Aggressive behavior injures someone psychologically or physically. Some researchers argue that aggression stems from an instinct linked to an inherently violent human nature. Violence is explained by an inner cause. Particular psychological propensities were pointed out as the origin of aggression by several well-known social psychologists. For Freud, a desire for destruction results from a death instinct. According to others, most people have within them an autonomous source of aggressive impulses. Pathological psychological impulses largely

account for outbreaks of war and mass killings. Competitive sports may also be considered as one of the means by which to express aggressive human nature.

In psychological approaches to conflict, the theory states that most humans have a natural build-up of blocked energy that searches for release. Aggression stems from a genetically based innate drive that has to be satisfied. Aggressive behavior is triggered by the excessive frustration of goals. Frustration is further accumulated by the outside interference with the achievement of certain objects. The perception of threats and uncontrolled emotion strengthen aggressive postures. The failure of adaptation to frustration thus leads to violence.

If aggression is believed to be a response to certain biological and psychological stimuli, the origin of conflict is exclusively attributed to aggressive impulses that invite violent expression no matter what the object might be. Given that aggressive energies have to be worked out by themselves, natural limitations are not likely to be imposed on the intensity of behavior. Since humans are assumed to be, by instinct, aggressive, conflict cannot be resolved peacefully. This innate propensity to aggression, therefore, is responsible for individual and group violence. The suppression of violent propensities within a group results in the pursuit of their outlets in relations with other groups.

Violent conflict does not need to involve a contentious issue if we assume that violence is the result of the desire for the release of tension. The attainment of specific outcomes does not necessarily mean the termination of conflict. Only external order would be able to control a tendency toward destructive behavior. If we believe that the motivational propensities for aggression are ascribed to the struggle for survival in a resource stricken world, then aggressive behavior can be reduced by creating a more caring world.

III. RELATIVE DEPRIVATION AND BASIC NEEDS

Mass violence can be caused by feelings of relative deprivation and dissatisfaction with basic human needs. A prolonged period of economic and social development generates heightened expectations. There is a certain level of expectations for social and economic conditions to which people believe they are rightfully entitled. However, these expectations are not always met even though people have the ability to achieve them. Relative deprivation exists when people feel that their expectations of conditions for life have not been satisfied.

The perception of deprivation is subjective. If people's hopes and desires far exceed what they can realize, they may have more dissatisfaction with their current situation. The expectation to improve unsatisfied material and social conditions tends to go up with time. However, the economic and social capacity to meet these expectations does not increase simultaneously. Thus expectations are likely to rise disproportionately to what society can actually provide. Frustration deepens when manifest reality does not match anticipated reality.

An intolerable gap between expected social conditions and actual achievement of these conditions can be a precondition for widespread unrest and political violence. Poor economic performance, along with rapid social change, strengthens the belief that unfair economic and political conditions have been imposed on those who suffer loss. A lack of opportunities as well as unequal distribution of benefits generates contention. A sharp reversal of gains, compared with others, in particular, leads to the increased perception of discrepancy between what people have and what they feel they are entitled to enjoy.

Regardless of subjective perception, there are basic requirements for the survival and development of human beings in both physical and psychological terms. Some sets of fundamental universal human needs cannot be denied. The maintenance of decent human life requires self-fulfillment as well as physical survival. Food, shelter, and other basic material necessities are needed for physical survival. Love, affection, security, and self-esteem satisfy psychological needs. Human emotions are constructed within the framework of social life. No meaning in life is found if people's self-esteem is destroyed. The denial of collective identity is a source of ethnic conflict. Needs can provide factual and objective criteria for analyzing a social situation that contains the potential for the emergence of conflict.

IV. RATIONALITY AND SOCIAL ORDER

Social relationships are based on mutual consent between groups of people. However, society is not monolithic, and a specific interaction may have a different meaning to those who are engaged in it. People fight for control over advantages and opportunities. Actions may be taken intentionally to repress the resistance of others. Conflict is considered as a type of social relationship in which one party undertakes action against the other. Nonviolent and regulated conflict may be called competition.

In the Weberian tradition, a legitimate social order is maintained by a set of rules and norms. Social action is affected by accepted norms and, in many societies, laws are used as a major means to contain conflict. Social tensions are regulated by agreed values and mechanisms. Thus the acceptance and rationalization of conflict are made in terms of established sets of institutional procedures. While this approach legitimizes certain types of conflict, it gives power to a particular group of people who are in a position to make and enforce rules.

The ideas of conflict management are based on rational approaches to all aspects of social problems. Legal authority is the foundation for order. Authority, justified in the light of rational and legal political order, is impersonal compared with charismatic authority, which depends on personal appeals and qualities. The principles of the universal and impartial applications of rules are the basis of a modern political system. The rational management of conflict legitimizes the status quo and represents efforts to contain conflict within an existing political structure. In order to engage in conflict, parties have to agree on certain formal rules of the game that provide the framework of their relations.

V. SOCIAL EXCHANGE

Humans pursue diverse social and material objectives. Exchange is inevitable since individuals have limited resources. In general, an exchange relationship is based on voluntary actions of individuals who are motivated by the returns they want to get from others. Goods and services can be tangible or intangible. Social associations are formed by the process of exchange activities between at least two people. Exchanging goods and services serves not only to create the bonds of friendship but also to produce power relations.

Establishing and maintaining relations emanates from the calculation of benefits and costs. Depending on the level of satisfaction, some exchange relationships are more rewarding than others. Benefits ought to be reciprocated in order to continue to receive them. Though obligations may not be specific, commitments to the other party are entailed in the relationship.

The fulfillment of exchange obligations generates trust. Social exchange is not likely to happen without a promise from others to reciprocate favors. Thus, trust is essential for maintaining stable social relations. Bonds and indebtness are perpetuated by obligations. Conflict may originate in the failure to reciprocate benefits. Disagreement on norms of fair exchange can also produce tension.

A group structure emerges from social interaction. Exchange processes may lend themself to the differentiation of status and power. The unilateral supply of goods and services can be contingent on the acceptance of unequal power relations. The ability to provide resources, essential for the survival of the community, fortifies distinctions between superiors and inferiors. Those who hold higher power ranks in a group tend to feel the greater pressure to share their wealth with others. In many tribal societies, superiority is established by distributing gifts or offering religious services.

A differentiated status structure necessitates legitimation and organization. Norms of reciprocity are developed to maintain social associations. Collective approval gives legitimacy to the power of the leadership. The failure to distribute social and material rewards can generate opposition and the call for new leadership.

In the absence of mutual consent, exchange relationships may be forced on the other side. Threats and violence are used in the case of robbery. Explicit and implicit forms of coercion are employed to guarantee the continued supply of goods and services. One example would be the exploitative economic and political structure set up by colonialism.

VI. FUNCTIONALISM AND SOCIAL SYSTEMS

Functionalist theories view society as an entity that can be reduced to its constituent parts. A social system has a specific structure that is composed of relationships among the constituent parts, including polity, economy, and culture. These parts carry out basic functions for maintaining the whole society. Functions of a social system are defined in terms of processes that are essential for the survival of the system. The solidarity of a society relies on the integration of its components.

Actors in a social system fulfill their required role assignments. Institutionalized patterns of interaction among actors are regulated by cultural patterns. The educational component of the social structure has the function of transmitting the existing culture to future generations. Socialization helps keep a kinship structure, which in turn has the function of sustaining family ties.

Social structure is based on the consensus of values among its members. The overall pattern of interrelationship is geared toward order and harmony. An inefficient response to disturbances from an environment causes malfunction of the system. For instance, social instability can arise from the incompatibility between modernization and traditional value systems. The domination of a new religion or ideology follows changes in power distribution in various subsystems.

According to functionalism, progress means increased specializations and complexities in the functions of society. The economic structure of any given society should be compatible with the political structure and normative values. More specifically, an increased capacity to mobilize economic resources is based on the development of modern political institutions, which support market operations. In addition, the penetration of a free market economy is accompanied by the replacement of traditional cultural norms by universalistic values and generalized rules. The dissatisfaction with the existing system demands the adjustment of relationships among components. Deviant behavior is treated like a disease that should be cured.

Coerced change does not necessarily engender either the political solidarity or cultural legitimation that sustains commitment from members of a society. Coercive order is not stable unless it brings changes in cultural norms to subjugated people. The subjugated groups should be willing to accept the dominant group's cultural orientations as well as institutional models.

Society can fail to respond to the challenges coming from the disequilibrium between the demand and the supply of resources. The failure of normal functions leads to pathological states. Abnormal states are considered harmful to the survival of the system. Systemic crisis or stress disrupts normal patterns of interactions among components within a system. The failure of critical social functions creates conditions for radical social change such as revolution. Since conflict is associated with disunity, it is seen as dysfunctional.

VII. CLASS CONFLICT

In the Marxist paradigm conflict between classes arises out of differing material interests. The political economy of social relations is important in understanding the causes of conflict. A basic assumption of Marxism is that a social and political structure is determined by the mode of production. The economic structure determines forms of social consciousness as well as types of legal and political institutions.

Conflict is rooted in class antagonism, which results from the historical conditions of production. In a capitalist society, two main classes can be identified. The means of production such as land and factories are monopolized by a few people, the bourgeois class owns the capital and material resources needed for mass production. The workers provide labor in exchange for the wages that are essential for the subsistence of their physical survival. The power of the bourgeois derives from the ownership of the means of production. The business class dominates the working class until the latter organizes to protest exploitation. The exploitation of one class by another is the main source of conflict.

Workers are alienated since their work is not related to the realization of their needs. The work does not reflect a worker's desire or nature. It only serves the interests of the owner of the means of production. The ultimate cause of all crises in a capitalist system is poverty and restricted consumption of the masses. The emancipation of the working class results from the elimination of private properties. Class struggle is a vehicle for structural change. Conflict can be eventually eliminated in a classless society.

Class conflict is characterized by the absence of mobility and the concentration of power and property among a few elites as well as the superimposition of economic and political interests on the masses. A clear correlation exists between the distribution of power and social stratification. The intensity of conflict in a capitalist society is linked to the concentration of political and economic power in one class. Post industrialized societies have reduced the degree of class antagonism, in part, by introducing effective conflict regulation mechanisms such as mediation and arbitration and, in part, by allowing workers' participation in electoral processes.

VIII. DISCOURSE AND DOMINATION

In postmodernism, the social world is divided into a multitude of communities, cultural traditions, and knowledge. The primary forces of domination are not economic exploitation. The sources of conflict can be related to the subjugation of differing identities and understandings of reality that belong to particular groups of people. The process of discourse plays an important role in shaping subjectivity, social institutions, and politics. Language mediates between individuals and the conditions of their existence.

A discourse can be characterized as a set of rules for speech. Rules of discourse dictate who is accorded the right and the status to make authoritative statements. Such mechanisms as newspapers and television ensure the survival of a dominant structure under the mask of knowledge. There are close connections between knowledge and power. All knowledge claims are moves in power games. Methods of social control serve as instruments of those who have power.

Subjecting each individual to a specific identity contributes to the regulation of differences in a modern society. In a rationalized world, human beings are transformed into manipulative subjects. Modern industrial society allots each person to a specific role or an operation that characterizes the person. The individual is carefully fabricated in the social order. Hegemony is maintained by a complex web of conceptual and material arrangements producing the very fabric of everyday life. Hegemony at the workplace, for instance, is enforced by economic arrangements such as contracts and reward systems that are supported by laws. Discipline is based on more than physical coercion.

The goal of postmodernism is emancipation from the dominant discourse by creating a social space that tolerates differences and favors autonomy. Emancipation can be achieved by privileging local narrative over metanarratives. The dominant paradigm and its language need to be deconstructed by the analysis of the existing patterns of culture. In empowering the local narrative, postmodernism acknowledges that one's reality is shaped by cultural and social circumstances. Gender, race, and class relations are located in specific situations. Identity is fluid as one's reality also fluctuates. Postmodern theory challenges the dominant discourse, which represses the voice of marginalized groups.

IX. STRUCTURE OF AUTHORITY

Status differences are entailed in most social relations. Power imbalance characterizes asymmetric relations. The unequal distribution of decision-making power is a source of latent conflict. The structural origins of group conflicts can be related to the arrangement of social roles attached to domination and subjection. The two distinctive sets of groups are produced by authority relations. One group has a position of domination with the other in a position of subjection. Opposing interests derive from power differences.

Identical authority positions develop common group interests. Conflict groups are organized either to defend or to challenge the legitimacy of the existing structure. The creation of conflicting parties can be prevented by the lack of freedom of speech and associations. Communication among those who share the same interest is also essential in the formation of groups. Thus the conditions for the formation of conflict groups do not exist in a repressive political system.

The dominant group wants stability while the dominated group pursues change. The dominant group is interested in the preservation of a social structure that legitimizes their authority. Change is resisted by the party benefiting from the structure. Those on top interpret conflict in terms of law and order. For the subjugated group, the existing situation is perceived as unjust and exploitative. Those in a disprivileged position look for opportunities to establish a new set of relations.

Conflict involves struggle between the forces of status quo and challenge. Opposing groups mobilize resources. The problems of maintaining or changing a given structure are interpreted in terms of the legitimacy of existing authority relations. Since conflict arises out of tensions between subordinate and dominant groups, solutions on individual issues do not eliminate the possibility of recurrent conflicts. Conflict regulation mechanisms may prevent violence but do not deal with sources of conflict. As far as asymmetric patterns of interaction exist, conflict cannot be avoided. Conflict resolution needs to be based on structural changes that lead to egalitarian relations.

X. FUNCTIONS OF CONFLICT

While conflict may bring about radical social change, it can also enhance the function of a social system. Pressure for innovation and creativity prohibits the ossification of a social system. Social life is not entirely harmonious, and conflict does not need to be considered disruptive. A certain degree of conflict is, in fact, essential in promoting unity. Since conflict is natural in every society, productive relations may emerge from well-managed conflict. Group solidarity is more easily maintained by allowing conflicts. However, consensus on basic values is critical if the conflict is to be functional. The existence of established rules of competition can help the regulation of conflict within the system.

If conflicts are superimposed on each other, they endanger social stability. In superimposed conflicts, the same groups face each other in various types of conflicts. The emergence of overriding interests increases the intensity of conflict with the concentration of emotional energies. On the other hand, the criss-crossing of conflicts cancel each other out. They prevent disintegration of a whole society along one primary line of cleavage such as class, religion, or ethnicity. Threats to consensus on core values would be reduced by the existence of multiple conflict groups engaged in many different issues.

A conflict, which serves as a means for obtaining a specific outcome, can be called a realistic conflict. Particular demands are directed at the presumed objects. The antagonistic actions of labor unions against management are said to be realistic if these actions are organized to achieve such results as an increase in wages or benefits. The sources of realistic conflict exist in every social system as long as people raise opposing claims to power positions and economic resources as well as argue about different values. If conflict is a means to an end, it can be resolved by achieving specific goals. Different forms of contention are assessed in terms of their effectiveness in promoting interests.

In nonrealistic conflict, conflict is an end in itself. Finding a solution for the unsatisfactory situation is no longer a major concern. The aim of conflict is simply releasing tensions. Hostilities may be diverted toward substitute objects. Safety valve mechanisms function as channels for cathartic release. The weaker party in conflict especially uses displaced means to express feelings of frustration. However, the displacement of goals does not change the terms of the relationship.

This distinction between realistic and nonrealistic conflicts has important implications for conflict management and resolution. A realistic conflict can be resolved if the desired outcome is obtained. Conflict is channeled into productive social activity. However, the hostility expressed in nonrealistic conflict is destructive and needs to be controlled. A safety valve function may be employed to avoid tensions between primary parties in conflict but does not solve the root causes of problems. Mediation is supposed to help adversaries direct their energies from engagement in the emotional aspects of nonrealistic conflict to discussion about substantive issues.

XI. IMPLICATIONS FOR CONFLICT RESOLUTION

Depending on the assumptions of social order, different approaches to resolving conflict can be suggested. The emphasis on coherence and order may justify the use of force and other means of restricting behavior. If it is assumed that social order results from a general consensus on the core values of society that outweighs actual differences of opinions and interests, main concerns remain with conflict reduction and regulation. Since conflict appears to be avoidable, major efforts are made to strengthen the mechanisms of social control that minimize conflict. Social tension and strains may be ascribed to psychological maladjustment. Psychiatric approaches need to be used if problems are rooted in individuals. Stress is placed on the adjustment of individuals to given structures.

The efforts to preserve existing institutional arrangements lead to the ignorance of pressures for change. An unstable social order is explained in terms of the breakdown of control mechanisms. The regulation of social conflict is more concerned with the way conflicts are expressed than understanding their causes. The functions of conflict regulation have been performed by conciliation, mediation, and arbitration. The ideas of alternative dispute resolution represent the philosophy of regulation by adopting a less costly method to handle the symptoms of conflict. Regulation methods have been designed to reduce physical violence. In this approach, the routinization of problems prevents the explosion of a superimposed conflict.

In contrast with a consensus model of social order, society can be viewed as held together by force and constraint. Changes are inevitable given that coercive relations cannot be maintained forever. Social conflict could be eliminated only through structural change. Conflict resolution should address the causes rather than the symptoms of social conflict. If progress is made possible by a struggle, the task would be to overcome the resistance of those who benefit from the current system against changes. Since conflict is inherent in the social structure, the complete elimination of conflict is not possible and desirable. The suppression of conflict is not an effective means of dealing with its sources. Most importantly, efforts to ignore conflict are, in the long run, counterproductive.

Conflict can be transformed and resolved by adopting nonviolence principles established by Tolstoy and Gandhi. Nonviolence has often been used as a strategy to break intolerable situations. The ideas of nonviolence suggest resolving conflict through persuading oppressors in a nonthreatening manner. At the same time, nonviolence can also be used to promote a culture of self-sacrificing love. Reconciliation is built in a nonviolent approach to conflict resolution which transcends dichotomization. Its aim is to resolve sources of problems rather than annihilate adversaries. All parties are encouraged to participate in the process to explore a just solution to the conflict.

XII. CONCLUSION

The struggle against dominant social relations and oppressive cultural norms has existed throughout human history. The large question for research on conflict analysis and resolution is, then, how we can identify the sources of dominant relations that generate conflict. Examining the impact of conflict on human well-being has to be one of the most important tasks in analyzing the causes and nature of environmental conflict, labor disputes, problems in urban communities, and a violent culture.

Also See the Following Articles

CLASS CONFLICTS • NONVIOLENCE THEORY AND PRACTICE • POWER, SOCIAL AND POLITICAL THEORIES OF

Bibliography

Blau, P. M. (1964). *Exchange and power in social life*. New York: Wiley.

Bottomore, T. B. (1964). *Karl Marx: Selected writings in sociology & social philosophy*. New York: McGraw–Hill.

Colomy, P. (Ed.) (1992). *The dynamics of social systems*. London: Sage.

Coser, L. (1964). *The functions of social conflict*. New York: The Free Press.

Dahrendorf, R. (1959). *Class and class conflict in industrial society*. Stanford, CA: Stanford University Press.

Davies, J. C. (1971). Toward a theory of revolution. In J. C. Davies, (Ed.), *When men revolt and why* (pp. 134–148). New York: The Free Press.

Foucault, M. (1994). Genealogy and social criticism. In S. Seidman, (Ed.), *The postmodern turn* (pp. 39–45). Cambridge, UK: Cambridge University Press.

Jeong, H. W. (1998). *Peace and conflict studies: An introduction*. Dartmouth: Aldershot.

Lorenz, K. (1966). *On aggression*. New York: Harcourt, Brace & World.

Weber, M. (1964). In T. Parsons (Ed.), *The theory of social and economic organization*. New York: The Free Press.

Torture (State)

Raymond R. Corrado and Irwin M. Cohen

Simon Fraser University

GLOSSARY

Crimes of Obedience Acts that are perpetrated under the explicit or implicit orders of the authorities that would not occur without official authorization.

Process of Authorization The belief in victimizers that they are serving a higher purpose which serves to allow them to neutralize any negative feelings they may have about participating in torture.

Process of Dehumanization The process of objectifying an individual in the eyes of the victimizer.

Process of Routinization The professionalization and normalization of the practice of torture.

State Torture Acts of torture that are carried out by a government or its agents.

I. INTRODUCTION

The use and practice of state torture is not a modern phenomenon. Since the earliest conflicts between people, political torture has been justified, legitimized, and institutionalized by the state. From our oldest accounts, state torture was seemingly a regular occurrence. Instances of widespread systematic torture of large numbers of people were sanctioned by governments. The fact that the ruling authority demanded or created a climate in which torture was either tolerated, accepted, or required indicates the very nature of state torture and reflects where responsibility for acts of torture to a large degree lie. In modern times, the use of state torture is a growing worldwide phenomenon in that the number of states that practice torture continues to grow.

This article deals exclusively with the use of torture perpetrated by the state in an attempt to achieve some political, social, and/or economic objective. While it must be kept in mind that not all instances of torture are committed by governments or their representatives, this article focuses on state torture. Certain acts by nongovernmental agents, such as death squads, revolutionaries, or terrorists, and certain cultural norms that may be sanctioned but not carried out be the state, such as foot-binding or genital mutilation, clearly constitute torture; however, our focus is on the actions of governments and their agents.

Moreover, human rights literature distinguishes between ill-treatment and state torture. For instance, under human rights law, rape committed by a soldier against a prisoner may be regarded as ill-treatment and not torture due to the personal or individual motivation for the act. While a recognition of this distinction is important in debates on what constitutes torture and the relationship between gender and torture, this article makes no such distinction. Acts that might be defined as ill-treatment are, for the purposes of this article, recognized as instances of state torture.

As mentioned above, state torture is simply a method used by governments to effect compliance and obedience or to achieve some ideological goal. For instance, in ancient Rome, torture was used in the judicial system to maintain conformity to the dictates of the Empire and, to a lesser degree, to force people to renounce their faith. During the Inquisition, the Church systematically used torture to combat heresy. In Europe, with the revival of natural law in the 12th century, torture became a legitimate form of punishment for a variety of criminal code offenses in addition to its judicial role of helping the prosecution secure a confession. Finally, during the contemporary period, torture has been used, among a myriad of other reasons, as a form of punishment, not only for common criminals, but also most frequently for political prisoners. Torture, therefore is a state activity used against specific individuals or groups that the state defines as a threat to the achievement of certain goals, be they ideological, political, economic, militaristic, religious, or social.

II. CONCEPTUALIZATIONS AND DEFINITIONS OF STATE TORTURE

Definitions of torture generally include the notion that it involves the deliberate infliction of pain or suffering, but frequently these definitions also include the motivations for torture, its specific goals, and the identity of its agents. Acts of systemic torture are overwhelmingly "political" in the sense that it is inflicted directly or indirectly by agents of the government against people who are targeted for any number of reasons and that is explicitly authorized either by law or as part of a standing internal policy. The centrality of torture as a state activity was made explicit in 1984 in the United Nations Convention Against Torture:

> . . . any act by which severe pain or suffering, whether physical or mental, is intentionally inflicted on a person for such purposes as obtaining from him or a third person information or a con-

fession, punishing him for an act he or a third person has committed or is suspected of having committed, or intimidating or coercing him or a third person, or for any reason based on discrimination of any kind, when such pain or suffering is inflicted by or at the instigation of or with the consent or acquiescence of a public official or other person acting in an official capacity.

This definition makes several characteristics of torture quite clear: first, it involves either physical or mental pain; second, it is either to obtain information, to extract a confession, or to simply inflict punishment; third, torture includes acts performed against an individual or to intimidate a third party; and, fourth, it is an activity carried out under the authority of the state.

In the Convention's subsequent documents, the United Nations has rejected some of the more common defenses and justifications for the systematic use of torture. Most importantly, the Convention denies government agents the right to torture under the pretext of following orders. The United Nations also wants public officials and other persons involved in the custody, interrogation, and treatment of prisoners to be instructed on the prohibition against torture (1984, Article 10). In effect, the UN is directly addressing the most commonly employed explanation and justification used by torturers that they were following legitimate or legal orders.

At the level of nation-states, this issue has been addressed, for example, in the United Kingdom, where legislation defines torture not only in terms of public officials or people engaging in violence in an official capacity, but also of giving the orders to torture. The defence of simply following orders also is not legally acceptable (1988, Section 134). These international and national laws identify the essential elements of torture. Torture involves at least two people with one individual, namely the torturer, having all the power while the victim is virtually powerless. This power primarily manifests itself in terms of the application of pain, both mental and physical. According to Amnesty International, the aim of torture is a systematic activity rationally designed to break the will of an individual in order to achieve "lesser" goals such as obtaining a confession or information.

Several theorists have defined torture as a crime of obedience unlike ordinary crime. Torture would constitute an ordinary crime if it was carried out by officials at their own behest and in disregard of the policies and orders under which they function. However, for an act to be defined as torture it must be carried out under the explicit or implicit orders of the authorities. As such, torture is defined as a crime of obedience because of the presumption that the act would not take place without official authorization.

III. SPECIFIC OBJECTIVES OF STATE TORTURE

Peter Suedfeld (1990) provides a useful taxonomy for the main goals of state torture.

1. Information: Torture has always been associated with obtaining confessions. During the Middle Ages, the practice of torture attained prominence as the most efficient method of procuring a confession in legal proceedings. Yet, torture has always been used to force victims to provide information concerning criminal, political, or military knowledge to which the victim is presumed to have access. Although this motivation remains the most readily cited basis of implementing a strategy of state torture, the resulting information is not necessarily reliable. A recurrent theme in the literature is that torture is a rather inefficient method of acquiring reliable information.

2. Incrimination: A related purpose of torture is to force individuals to divulge information that can be used to either incriminate themselves or others. However, this objective is often secondary to the primary motivation of intimidating all political opponents. This is evident since the victim normally will confess or admit to anything to stop the torture. In effect, incrimination and information gathering can be secondary to the goals of isolation, indoctrination, or intimidation of the direct victim in a manner that will terrorize others.

3. Isolation: Isolation refers to severing the prisoner from all contact. Isolation conditions victims that they are helpless and that the torturer is omnipotent. This experience can create a new identity, defined by the state, for the victim. If torture cannot produce this new identity, or the state strategy does not require the victim to rejoin society, the prisoner is frequently killed.

4. Indoctrination: The goal of torture in indoctrination is to force the victim to abandon their previously held beliefs and to adopt those of the regime.

5. Intimidation: Intimidating others beyond the immediate victim can be an important goal of torture. In effect, a specific act of torture is seen as a general deterrent to intimidate others from behaviors that the authorities considered unacceptable. Torture is a particularly effective general intimidation tactic beyond the immediate victim when the victim or the media disseminates the gruesome details of certain methods of torture or by allowing people to see the frightening results of victims. All of these reasons for torture must be understood as being part of the process of establishing complete domination over a victim's physical and mental world and imposing the will of the state on the immediate victim as well as on others. Torture may also be employed to intimidate people into denouncing other groups or their own groups.

IV. MODERN TORTURE TECHNIQUES AND THE ROLES OF TORTURERS

Over time, torturers have developed an exhaustive number of techniques and instruments to torment their victims. In order to differentiate the many different methods of torture that are at a torturer's disposal, Suedfeld (1990) has created six general categories that attempt to distinguish the essential elements of torture techniques.

1. Active Physical Pain: The most common techniques are the use of active physical pain. At least 90% of all Amnesty International reports of torture indicate its use. This form of torture includes beating a victim with fists, boots, clubs, whips, barbed wire, and other blunt instruments. Electric shocks to sensitive body parts and vicious sexual assaults are often part of the sequence of escalating physical pain. The next stage can include mutilating body parts through a myriad of methods. Any form of torture that involves the physical application of pain on a victim would be defined as active physical pain torture.

2. Passive Physical Pain: Physical pain can also be applied in a passive form, for instance, by tying an individual up, making prisoners stand in a stationary position for long periods of time, or forcing them to remain in an uncomfortable position for an extended period of time. All of these techniques produce severe physical pain without the torturer having to touch the victim. Passive physical pain techniques are also effective because they inflict intense physical pain without leaving scars on the body.

3. Exhaustion: Other techniques that leave little or no evidence on the victim's body are those that produce extreme exhaustion. These methods involve forcing a prisoner to engage in strenuous physical ac-

tivity until total and complete exhaustion sets. For instance, torturers might force victims to carry heavy weights or have them perform vigorous exercises. Exhaustion is generally accompanied with other specific torture techniques, such as sleep deprivation, beatings, or humiliation.

4. Fear-Inducing Techniques: These techniques, such as near-drowning or near-suffocation, generally do not leave any evidence on the body and do not have many long-term physical effects on their victims. Instead, these techniques are generally associated with severe psychological side-effects. These torture tactics are frequently implemented by torturers because they again require very little direct contact between torturer and victim and these methods heighten the victim's sense of dread.

5. Combined Mental and Physical Pain: These forms of torture techniques include placing a victim in complete darkness or in intensely lit cells, sleep deprivation, constant questioning, or sexual assaults on them and/or on family members. These practices have both tremendous physical and mental effects on the victim.

6. Mental Pain: Finally, torture techniques can focus entirely on the mental stability of the victim. Perhaps the most common forms of mental torture are the constant use of death threats, threats of bodily mutilation, or being forced to watch others being tortured. Other techniques, such as being forced to eat excrement or drink urine, being forced to engage in grotesque acts, or being forced to participate in other humiliating behaviors concentrate exclusively on the victim's mental state. In general, the choice of torture techniques is directly related to the nature of the torture complex in terms of its level of sophistication and the goals that the state is using torture to achieve. For those who wish to indoctrinate their victims, mental forms of torture seem to be most efficient, while those interested in either information, intimidation, and murder tend to employ physical and passive physical torture techniques. The effectiveness of these techniques is evident in the long term and often tragic mental disorders that occur, including suicide.

Predominately soldiers or members of the secret police directly engage in torture. However, abuses of psychiatry or medicalized torture are more often the domain of physicians. Soldiers do engage in these forms of torture, but efficiency often requires a trained medical practitioner. Doctors play a myriad of important roles that are necessary for a torture complex to exist and to function. A primary duty of doctors is to examine a victim to ensure that they are fit to undergo a session of torture or are fit to be tortured again. Doctors ensure that prisoners do not die during questioning. Doctors are required to recommend how much torture a specific victim can endure and to make recommendations on how to use a prisoner's particular psychological state or physiology to torture them more effectively.

Other important roles for doctors in torture are to give legitimacy and credence to false autopsy reports on torture victims, to agree to falsify postmortem records, to provide false medical certificates for persons who are tortured to death, and to disguise the cause of a torture victim's death, often without ever having examined the body. Doctors resuscitate victims or advise when torture should be discontinued or resumed. Perhaps most prevalent, doctors treat those who have been tortured with the full knowledge that once the victim is well enough they will be tortured again. Doctors are also encouraged to develop more effective torture techniques.

In some cases, the participation of doctors in torture is clear by the forms of torture that are practiced. For instance, the use of psychoactive drugs or brainwashing techniques suggest the assistance of a physician. Doctors administer involuntary and painful medications, place patients in debilitating restraints, and participate in the process of humiliating and degrading patients. Finally, doctors are relied upon to preserve the sanity of the torturers so that they may go on torturing without any undue psychological or behavioral problems.

V. HISTORICAL THEORETICAL BASIS OF CONTEMPORARY THEORIES OF STATE TORTURE

There are a myriad of theoretical approaches to understanding why states resort to the use of torture. However, space limitations do not allow us to deal with all of them effectively or to evaluate those mentioned below critically. Yet, most contemporary theories incorporate central themes from the utilitarian–expediency perspective, which was among the earliest systematic attempts to explain torture.

A. Utilitarian–Expediency Perspective

This perspective evolved from the more general theoretical debate about a government's legitimate use of various types of coercion and violence to enforce controversial and even revolutionary forms of criminal justice.

Enlightenment-influenced theorists, such as the Italian Caesare Becarria, argued that medieval forms of torture were barbaric and ineffective in stopping crime. Whether torture should and/or could serve as a rational policy tool became an important issue.

During the 18th century, Jeremy Bentham asserted that given the right set of circumstances, torture should be sanctioned. He argued that there are two main points concerning the expediency of torture. First, torture is less penal than many of the other forms of punishment that society regularly uses, such as the death penalty. Second, torture is more efficient than other punishments. Bentham claims that society's most basic response to those who violate the law is imprisonment. The utilitarian–expediency argument is that one has to be kept in prison for a long time to achieve the desired punitive and deterrent goals of the state. However, if torture can effect such state goals in a shorter period of time, torture can be justified regardless of the mental pain and the long-term effects associated with being subjected to torture.

According to this perspective, there is a clear distinction between punishment and torture. Punishment is directed at past actions, while torture is directed at future actions. As such, depending on the goals of the state, there are times when torture would be easier to justify than punishment. Bentham contends that torture may be better than punishment for the simple reason that once the goal has been achieved, the torture can stop. The utilitarian argument has no contemporary theoretical policy proponents as no government has publicly institutionalized torture as a legal method of governance, although the argument for its use has been made in the case of counterinsurgency warfare. Still, the crucial theme of the efficiency of torture as a method to implement or obtain political goals is central to most contemporary theories of torture.

B. Duvall and Stohl's Cost–Benefit Analysis Model

Duvall and Stohl demonstrate in a mathematical model that torture as part of a general policy of state terrorism can be an efficient method to achieve political goals. In effect, certain governments can expend fewer resources to gain a political objective using torture than by using nonviolent tactics.

Duvall and Stohl provide a rational choice model for understanding the utility of torture. They argue that the decision to engage in torture is based on the belief that the benefits of torture would outweigh its costs and that the desired outcome, however that is defined,

will be achieved through torture. Duvall and Stohl argue that these conditions are most likely to be met at the two extremes of the power continuum, when a state feels an overwhelming sense of powerlessness or is supremely confident in their strength. They suggest that a sense of governmental powerlessness is conducive to a policy of state torture in two situations. First, a politically fragile state may resort to torture as a way of combating a perceived challenge or threat from a large portion of the society it is attempting to rule. Second, torture may be employed in a conflict with a "strongly committed, elusive adversary group." Still, torture can also be used from a position of relative strength.

As mentioned above, a decision to torture is based in part on an estimation of the relative effectiveness of the policy. An estimation of effectiveness depends on the ability to command relevant resources and the vulnerability of the target group. Duvall and Stohl argue that three considerations are most important in making this assessment. The first is the process of learning, where torture is considered a viable policy option based on its past success. Second, if a government believes that it has the ability to engage in torture and control the process, they are more likely to engage in it. Finally, the degree to which the target group resides outside the dominant social fabric also impacts on the decision to engage in torture. The state must be convinced that either the dominant segment of society will not strongly object to their actions or that their tactics will not disrupt, to a significant degree, the everyday functioning of the state. Given these considerations, and a situation in which the government finds itself in actual or potential conflict with some socially marginal segment of society, a state is more likely to engage in sustained torture.

Another factor in making an evaluation of the utility of torture is its relative cost. The costs may be measured in terms of the financial commitment required to established and maintain a large, complex, and active torture infrastructure. As many authors have pointed out, the military, judicial, and administrative components of state torture operate on budgets large enough to threaten the economic stability of the state. Moreover, the costs of this repressive apparatus continue to rise even during periods of economic decline. Therefore, the financial cost of adopting a policy of torture is an important aspect of the decision-making process.

A state must also consider the response costs of their actions. In other words, a state must assess the reactions of others to their actions and include this in a decision to engage in torture. Concern over response costs is much greater in advanced industrial societies than in Third World nations. The more reclusive the state, the less concern rulers need to be about external response costs. Interestingly, Duvall and Stohl contend that a regime's vulnerability to domestic retribution or to international pressure is generally less in the contemporary Third World than in the First World. This is due to the practice of the international community not considering a government's human rights record when establishing trade agreements and the ability of Third World nations to achieve a degree of domestic conformity through the use of sustained torture. The other main cost concern of states is production costs. These are the costs, other than financial, associated with creating and maintaining torturers and a torture complex.

Therefore, Duvall and Stohl provide a model predicated on the objective assessment of evidence. Their model focuses on a cost–benefit analysis for engaging in torture. Policy-makers estimate their opponents' capability to either undermine their authority or to jeopardize their vision of the social and political order and weight this assessment against the financial, response, and production costs of sustained torture. In effect, instead of persuading and/or affecting expensive, and often unavailable, lifestyle incentives to follow demanding revolutionary objectives, governments terrorize the general population into obeying by torturing a small portion of citizens. The time and material cost of torture, relative to the same costs of other persuasive methods is usually very low. For Nazi Germany and Stalin's Soviet Union and in Saddam Hussein's Iraq, torture was and is an efficient policy instrument.

C. Kelman's Threat Assessment Perspective

Edward Peters claims that torture arises out of a combination of the state's vast power and its vulnerability to enemies from within and without. To combat these real and supposed threats, the state adopts a policy of torture. This argument closely resembles the approach taken by Herman that only the state has the resources and mechanisms to adopt a policy to torture people systematically and efficiently. A torture complex is created with standard operating procedures and multiple detention centers that practice torture routinely.

According to this policy approach, the primary goals of torture are to maintain the authority of those in power by systematically destroying those who are a threat to them and to intimidate all others into conformity. Kelman argues that in order to legitimize the use of torture, the authorities frequently point to a history of violence against the state, real or imagined. This

violence generally takes the form of insurgency, guerrilla operations, or terrorist acts. Often people can be subjected to torture not because of criminal acts that they have performed or are planning to perpetrate but because they hold political or religious beliefs that are deemed dangerous to the authority of the ruling elites. Therefore, torture becomes a highly efficient and relatively inexpensive tactic in fulfilling the state's policy of repression against a defined target group.

This perspective suggests three points at which the perceived threat to the state provides the basis for a policy of torture. First, any possible threat to the state enables the authority to create a purpose and a justification for the implementation of a torture policy, i.e., usually to maintain law and order. Second, the state sanitizes torture in the eyes of the public. Torture is seen as an honorable profession, with highly trained experts, who serve to protect society from internal and external threats. Third, the state determines the legitimate targets of torture by successfully applying negative labels to specific groups or individuals. As the research of Lauderdale and Corrado demonstrate, if required by a state's political ideology, the "enemy" is defined in such strong terms as to gain popular support for the implementation of a policy of torture.

D. Lopez's Scheme for the Government as Terrorist

George Lopez argues that specific political climates make torture more viable and defensible. He contends that new regimes feel extreme pressure to consolidate power, especially after a coup d'etat, widespread revolt, or long-term rule by force. In these situations, governments may resort to purges, exterminations, and torture as well as other tactics like detention, press censorship, travel restrictions, and economic coercion of certain groups. Lopez points to the state-sponsored ethnic violence in Uganda and the executions during the first years of the Khomeni regime in Iran as examples of this kind of political climate. Another type of political climate that leads to torture is characterized by the severe pressure placed on the ruling elites for social, economic, and political reform. Lopez suggests that the inevitable result of this situation, regardless of the dominant ideology of the government, is torture. This style of governing is most pervasive in developing nations.

Lopez also examines the effects of civil war on political climate. Frequently, the torture of groups or individuals that are hostile to the perspective of the victors is viewed as the final and logical conclusion to the war.

In addition, sustained torture is an effective method of achieving postrevolutionary goals such as changes in the distribution of wealth.

Lopez examines the role of ideology in state torture. The importance of ideology is that it holds together all the other variables that are associated with being the root causes of torture. Lopez focuses on the ideologies of authoritarianism, militarism, national security consciousness, and patriarchy as being mostly responsible for human rights violations in the contemporary period. Lopez contends that this is due to the fact that these ideologies place as the highest value the maintenance of the state and the dominance of the ruling elites.

National security consciousness is "a set of ideas about the tasks of geopolitical security and economic development in the post World War II world and the crucial role that governing elites play in these distinct but highly related processes." Lopez contends that concerns about internal security, the military capabilities of unfriendly neighbors, and local and international attempts to destabilize programs of national development combine to entrench an ideology that demands repressive means to control and restrict dissent. In addition, the use of force in small states is sometimes used to demonstrate their resolve and power to other states. Lopez argues that the actions of the Afghani armed forces against their own people was an attempt to demonstrate this aspect of national security consciousness to the Soviet Union.

In terms of the ideology of patriarchy, Lopez posits that the dynamic of patriarchy emphasizes characteristics of masculinity in governing. These "male" attributes express themselves as violence, an aura of the male as a fighter, and through a rejection of all "feminine" characteristics like sensitivity, pity, and emotionality. According to Lopez, as a result of a cultural and historical acceptance of these values, rulers are socialized to use violence and even torture to avoid appearing weak in achieving their ideological goals.

Another crucial variable that Lopez considers is the support mechanisms for torture. Lopez contends that sustained torture could only exist with either internal or external support. Most of the literature focuses on the development of external support through international trade. Lopez suggests that there are internal forces that sustain and legitimize torture. Beyond those in the ruling regime who directly benefit from policies of torture, a history of violence in a state forces its citizens to self-censure themselves. Members of the general population who are not subjected to torture benefit from a policy of sustained torture because it provides a deterrent to

social unrest and upheaval which, in turn, may promote social and economic development.

The final factor that Lopez suggests must be considered as a root cause of torture is the results that torture achieves. He argues that torture is sustained and legitimized based on its past successes. History demonstrates that governments are frequently successful in accomplishing their political and social objectives through the use of torture. Luigi Bonante suggests that the successful use of repressive measures prevents alternative approaches from being attempted, thus institutionalizing torture tactics. Once torture has been used against a target group successfully, it is unlikely that other approaches will be tried. Jeane Kirkpatrick contends that once revolutionary autocrats see the utility of torture, it is unlikely that they will abandon these tactics on their own. Therefore, Lopez suggests that the root causes of torture may be found in a state's political climate, ideology, support mechanisms, and the perceived outcomes of past repressive measures.

E. Corrado and Tompkins' Economic Dependency Model

Corrado and Tompkin's model concentrates on those variables that resist the rise of severe methods of political repression. Corrado and Tompkins begin by examining the economic structures of the state. They contend that advanced industrial societies are characterized by a large, relatively affluent middle class that acts as a stabilizing force removing the need for sustained political repression. They contend that while there does exist conflict over social, political, and economic policies, the legitimacy of the state itself is rarely challenged. Unlike in developing countries, the lack of a fundamental challenge to the right of the state to exist removes a principal need for brutal repressive measures such as torture. Moreover, Corrado and Tompkins argue that stable economic growth allows for a degree of political stability and political stability removes many of the motivations for torture.

There is also a clear relationship between economic dependency and political repression. Corrado and Tompkins contend that the greater the level of international economic dependency in a state, the less likely torture can be sustained. Due in part to the attention directed against governments by the media and the international community, states that engage in torture are likely to either find little international economic support or the imposition of severe economic sanctions, at least in theory. The recent example of the release of many political prisoners in China to maintain their favorite-nation status with the United States demonstrates the influence of economic dependency. However, not all foreign investors or governments base their economic decisions with other countries on human rights concerns. For the most part, states are more interested in economic gain than ensuring that their trading partners adhere to international standards for human rights. For instance, Canada refuses to join the United States in linking trade policy to improvements in Cuba's human rights record.

In addition to the role of economics, Corrado and Tompkins examine the impact of a state's structure of government on the use of state terrorism and torture. They argue that a well-established tradition of liberal democratic institutions reduces the likelihood of torture. The relative political stability that is associated with liberal democracies reduces the need for leaders to engage in repressive methods of governance. In more authoritarian political systems, such as those found in many developing countries, leaders are freer to use torture tactics due to their nation's institutionalized styles of governing, such as a declared state of siege or the lack of an independent press, judiciary, and legislature.

Corrado and Tompkins also argue that military takeovers are often followed by an escalation in state torture as military regimes commonly abolish many of the fundamental principles of democracy, such as due process guarantees, free press, and freedom of assembly. Furthermore, overt military interference in civilian governments is another important variable in state torture. Perhaps the one clear exception to this rule in First World nations is the strong role in policy decisions of the military and security forces in Israel. Not surprisingly, Israel is likely to become the first advanced industrial, liberal democracy to legalize the use of torture in interrogations of political prisoners.

Other variables associated with the structure of government that Corrado and Tompkins point to as crucial in developing a policy of torture are the strategies of the ruling elites, the degree of civic participation in politics, and the existence of diverse political parties. Corrado and Tompkins contend that the more the ruling regime resorts to illegal or unethical political strategies to ensure their positions of authority, the more likely the state will engage in torture to eliminate dissent. Moreover, they argue that a significant segment of the population can become alienated from the political process if there are not efficacious political parties with which they can identify. This alienation may lead to the formation of widespread political unrest which may then be used by the government to implement repressive measures such as torture to maintain authority.

The other significant variables that Corrado and Tompkins identify as correlates of torture are ethnicity, ideology, and specific events and conflicts. They argue that torture is more common in countries with a high degree of ethnic differentiation and where different political communities have a strong ethnic identification. Violence involving groups that define themselves by their differences of ethnicity is today's paramount human rights problem. Therefore, strong ethnic differentiation combined with failing economic and social development programs and the manipulation of conflict issues by political and cultural leaders is a persistent root cause of torture in contemporary Third World nations.

Corrado and Tompkins' model contends that the higher the ideological commitment of individuals who control or represent the government, the more likely state terrorism. Secular ideologies of militarism, authoritarianism, fascism, and Marxism in developing countries frequently do result in policies of sustained torture. The national security doctrine of Brazil, which has been adopted by numerous Third World countries, provides a good example. This doctrine was devised by Golbery de Couto e Silva between 1949 and 1964 and focused on the elements of total war, which involves the whole economic, political, cultural, and military capacity of the nation against perceived enemies of the state, i.e., anti-government terrorists, their supporters, and even sympathizers. Torture becomes a key tactic in the ensuing "dirty wars" along with thousands of extrajudicial executions.

In addition, Corrado and Tompkins argue that religious ideologies can also provide the justification for sustained torture. Iran under the leadership of the Ayatollah Khomeini (1982–1989) provides a clear example of the relationship between religion, power, and state torture. In addition, there is a substantial rise in religious fundamentalism in Third World countries that contravenes the principles of toleration and equal rights and often manifests itself as a policy of torture against all dissenters. What this discussion makes evident is that a strong ideological commitment by the ruling elites, alone or combined with the elements of a fragile political system and a high level of ethnic or class differentiation, is a leading root cause of sustained torture.

Finally, Corrado and Tompkins argue that specific events and conflicts can provide the root cause for torture. They contend that a dramatic event, such as a direct challenge to state authority, an assassination of a general or of a key political figure, increases the likelihood of torture. Moreover, the more widespread the incidence of civil conflict, the higher the likelihood of torture.

F. Michel Foucault

Although Foucault examines torture in 18th-century France, his approach to the use of torture as ideologically based punishment is still relevant today. Foucault stresses the instrumental and utilitarian nature of modern punishment. The use of punishment serves the ideological goals of the state, at least in the state's theoretical assumptions about how the use of a particular form of discipline will impact on society. Foucault's analysis concentrates on the transformation of punishment from disciplining the physical body of the offender to focusing on an offender's soul. Foucault suggested that the purpose of torture was not to demonstrate why the law was enforced but to demonstrate who were its enemies. Torture, therefore, must be seen as a process; torture is an expression of state power and a method of constituting and expressing the domination of the state over its subjects. Accordingly, it establishes and maintains conformity to state goals.

Foucault contends that the institutionalization of state torture to obtain information or confessions is just one of the state's strategies. The torture situation itself is focused on creating "truth." For the ruling regime, objective truth is always in danger of being forgotten but is produced through the use of torture. More than this, the use of torture serves to transform an individual into the enemy. The use of torture fabricates the enemy for all to see and thus validates the state's use of torture. This transformation is perhaps the most important aspect of torture for Foucault.

VI. THE MAKING OF THE MODERN STATE TORTURER

Crelinsten suggests that there are four main routes that a person can take to becoming a torturer.

A. Career Advancement Route

The individual is promoted from within a military or civilian organization into a special unit that engages in political torture. The individual is not seeking out the role of a state torturer, but by demonstrating the necessary qualities and skills for being a successful torturer, such as a willingness to follow orders or having an extreme loyalty to the organization, that individual is deemed suited for this duty.

B. Direct Conscription

Some individuals are simply drafted into specialized units of the armed forces. The traditional profile of these individuals is that they are from the lower-income groups, poorly educated, and come from families that share the same ideological orientation as the regime in power.

C. Serendipity

An individual chooses to join a specific unit not because of its duties but because of some other instrumental reason, such as its location or its prestige.

D. Counterinsurgency and Antiterrorist Campaigns

Captured insurgents, guerrillas, or terrorists can be made to torture their own people in exchange for the promise of good treatment.

Once a successful recruitment occurs, however, the more difficult part begins—the transition process of an individual into a state torturer. There are two main goals in the conversion process. The first objective is to impart in the new recruit an obedience to authority that allows them to follow exceptional and disturbing orders. The second aim is to create a level of desensitization regarding torture. This objective is aimed at providing torturers with the necessary psychological defenses to perform their duties. There are several processes used by the state to transform ordinary people into torturers.

E. The Process of Authorization

For torturers to carry out their duties they need to believe that they are serving a higher purpose or a greater good. The significance of this higher purpose justifies the use of torture. Authorization is aimed at providing recruits with the justifications that enables them to neutralize their negative feelings about committing brutal acts. The process of authorization also allows recruits to view themselves as playing a vital and necessary role in the protection of the state. Authorization not only trains recruits for their future duties, but also introduces them to the hierarchical structure of the torture complex. Understanding that they must obey orders, torturers are able to justify their actions as simply following orders and doing what a good soldier's duty requires.

F. The Process of Routinization

As Kelman suggests, the "professionalization of the practice of torture clearly contributes to normalizing their work." Routinization is aimed at enabling recruits to view their participation in torture as a profession, like any other profession. The basic training of torturers is carried out in groups where individual's learn the necessary skills of torture from their superiors. The reasons for torturing people are constantly reinforced as are the attitudes that recruits should have for the enemy. The routinization process involves building an individual's tolerance and confidence levels to the point where they can function without hesitation. Recruits learn the skills of torturing, they learn these skills from other torturers, they learn the techniques to neutralize their aversion to torture, and they learn the justifications for why some people must be tortured. The process of routinization involves training, socialization, and indoctrination in addition to normalizing and professionalizing torture.

The training process involves recruits enduring large amounts of pain and suffering that is aimed at breaking the wills of the recruits and removing their disdain for inflicting pain and suffering on others. Creating a torturer involves having recruits take many of the small steps that culminate in the torturing of another individual. For instance, training might include having to feed victims or watch intensely graphic films of physical abuse. Doctors might be called on to examine people before they were tortured or to falsify coroner reports. The process of routinization includes attending special classes where torturers learn what torture looks like and what is involved in torturing another person. The ultimate goal of routinization is to normalize the torturer's work. The aim is to desensitize and resocialize the torturer to such an degree that being a torturer is viewed as a vocation, a necessary task, and a duty that one should be proud of. Torture is transformed into what is being done, namely performing one's duty and demonstrating one's loyalty.

G. The Process of Dehumanization

The aim of dehumanization is to turn the victim into an object, to strip victims of all their human status in an attempt to legitimize and rationalize the appalling treatment of that individual. The main source for the dehumanization of victims evolves from their designation as enemies of the state. Prisoners are defined as terrorists, insurgents, or dissidents who do not have to be accorded the same treatment as those who support the ruling regime.

The process of torture helps to dehumanize the individual and this dehumanization helps the torturer to continue applying torture. Staub alludes to the substantial amount of research that indicates that when people witness the suffering of others, they tend to devalue the victims. There are numerous techniques that are used to dehumanize victims. Placing a bag or a hood over a victim's face allows the torturer to ignore the fact that they are torturing a person. Denying prisoners the ability to wash themselves allows the torturer to conceive of the victim as an animal or a nonperson. Tactics such as making victims eat their own excrement, drink their own urine, or sexually assault each other clearly devalue the individual. It has even been suggested that the screams of those being tortured sound so much like the howls of animals that this factor is a strong element in the devaluing of victims. What this analysis has made clear is that torturers must build up internal defenses for them to be able to carry out their work. As they routinize and legitimize their actions, torturers also need to dehumanize their victims.

H. Doubling

Doubling refers to "an active psychological process, a means of adaptation to extremity … The adaptation requires the dissolving of 'psychic glue' as an alternative to a radical breakdown of the self." Doubling is a defense mechanism where the self is divided into two distinct beings, one that participates in torture, and one that is understood as being the "true" moral nature of that person. However, when the individual must function within the torture complex, it is the self that engages in torture that acts as the entire self. There needs to be a dialectic between the two selves so that the torturer can function psychologically in an environment that violates their ethical and moral standards and still view his- or herself as a decent human being.

Doubling must be subjectively understood as a life or death choice. It is necessary for the individual to understand that the creation of a personality that can function within a torture complex is necessary survival. Finally, doubling must occur, to a certain degree, on an unconscious level and must be accompanied by a significant change in one's moral consciousness.

I. The Use of Euphemisms

The language of torture is one that replaces the words that describe cruelty with euphemisms. The use of jargon helps to create a shared culture and lessens the torturer's confrontation with the meaning of his or her actions. Things and persons are not called by their real names, while the techniques of torture frequently refer to the worlds of cooking or medicine. For instance, in Zaire, the torture session begins with *le petit dejeuner,* where victims are forced to drink their own urine, followed by *le dejeuner*, or "the lunch," where victims are beaten on their shoulders, and concludes with a *diete noire*, where victims are not allowed to have any food or water. It is far easier to say that one has placed a prisoner on a diet than it is to admit that you are personally responsible for starving another human being to death.

In terms of medical euphemisms, the interrogation itself is referred to as "treatment." Other examples include the "Operating Table," which allows torturers to beat victims while forcing them to support their upper torso by lying on a table that only supports the lower torso, and by torturers referring to each other as "doctor." The conclusion that can be drawn from these examples is that the language that torturers use helps to bond them together and form a cohesive group with their own distinct subculture. The jargon is a mechanism that allows torturers to ignore the reality of what they are doing to other people.

VII. TYPOLOGY OF STATE TORTURERS

Crelinsten (1993) has devised a typology of different kinds of state torturers.

1. Zealots: Zealots are individuals who are generally emotionally detached from what they are doing. They are unflinching, cruel, and in complete control of their emotions. The frightening aspect of these kind of torturers is that they are ordinary people who simply believe fanatically in what they are doing and in the ideological goals of the ruling regime. People who generally fit into the zealot category are those who are not well educated, but have a strong positive orientation to authority, an enjoyment of military activities, and a strong "us" versus "them" differentiation.

2. Careerists: These torturers are interested in career development and see torture as a job that needs to be done efficiently in order to earn a promotion. They are often intelligent, educated, and disapprove of the excesses of the torture process. These torturers may be distinguished from other types of torturers because they are not particularly interested in torture, but see it as a means to an end. In many cases, careerist torturers have the fact that they have chosen this kind of lifestyle in common.

3. Sadists: Sadists are very rare despite popular conceptions of torturers; nonetheless, there is evidence that some derive pleasure from inflicting pain.

VIII. INTERNATIONAL RESPONSE TO THE USE OF STATE TORTURE

In the contemporary period, the prohibition against the use of torture can be seen as a universal value, much in the same way as the prohibition against slavery. Amnesty International has played a crucial role in promoting this idea through its publications that focus on incidents of torture wherever they occur and by trying to identify those responsible for ordering, sanctioning, or participating in any aspect of torture. Amnesty International and other human rights organizations link their policies to several key pieces of UN legislation that attempt to deal with the increased use of torture by governments. Regional political organizations, such as the European Union and the Organization of American States, which include most North American and Latin American countries, have adopted laws and a declaration against torture. However, it appears that the United Nations is the most important international organization that provides the best hope in effecting a long-term policy to reduce the practice of torture.

A. Charter of the United Nations

In 1945, the United Nations attempted to ensure that governments would be concerned with universal human rights. Article 5 of the United Nations Universal Declaration of Human Rights (1948) states that: "No one shall be subjected to torture or to cruel, inhuman, or degrading treatment or punishment." Like previous attempts to codify into international law respect for human rights, this declaration was criticized because it was viewed by the international community as a recommendation without any binding force within individual states. This declaration depended upon the goodwill of states for its implementation and was unnecessarily vague as to intent and meaning. In an attempt to address some of these concerns, the United Nations adopted Resolution 3452, or the Declaration for the Protection of All Persons from being Subjected to Torture and Other Cruel, Inhuman or Degrading Treatment or Punishment (1975). The main points of this resolution would be repeated in the United Nations Convention against Torture and Other Cruel, Inhuman or Degrading Treatment or Punishment (1984).

Article two of the Convention states that there are no legitimate justifications for torture, be they war, a state of emergency, or, in the case of the individual torturer, an order from a superior officer. Article four states that all countries must make torture an offense under the criminal law, while Article 11 requires that a state's procedures of interrogation and their treatment of prisoners must be kept under systematic review. The United Nations Convention Against Torture also declared that governments must educate "all law enforcement personnel, civil or military, medical personnel, public officials, and other persons that may be involved in the custody, interrogation, or treatment of any individual subjected to any form of arrest, detention, or imprisonment." Finally, Article 13 of the Convention states that all witnesses and complainants, with respect to torture, must be "protected from ill-treatment or intimidation as a consequence of his complaint or any evidence given." Nonetheless, reports of torture continue to emerge from states that were signatories to the declaration.

B. The World Medical Association

Due to the increase in reports citing the participation of medical professionals in torture, several medical organizations and associations have attempted to implement policies and directives to combat the use of physicians in torture. The World Assembly of the World Medical Association adopted the International Code of Medical Ethics (1949), which states that under no circumstances was a doctor permitted to do anything that might weaken the physical or mental resistance of a patient unless it was in the patient's best interest. The World Medical Association adopted the Declaration of Tokyo (1975), which states that doctors should not condone or participate in the practice of torture regardless of the offence that the patient is suspected of, accused of, or guilty of in all situations including civil strife and war. The Declaration of Tokyo stated that doctors could not attend torture sessions, that they had to insist on complete independence with respect to their patients, and that they could not participate in force-feeding prisoners who were competent to make the decision to continue a hunger strike.

The United Nations General Assembly adopted the Principles of Medical Ethics (1982), which states that doctors had to give the same degree of medical care to prisoners as they gave to free citizens and that they must not participate in torture. Specifically, this proclamation states that it is a contravention of medical ethics for health personnel "to apply their knowledge and skills in order to assist in the interrogation of prisoners and detainees in a manner that may adversely affect the physical or mental health or condition of such prisoners or detainees."

C. World Psychiatric Association

For psychiatrists, the World Psychiatric Association adopted the Declaration of Hawaii (1977), which states in part that doctors must never use their professional abilities to violate a patient's human rights and that they must refuse to cooperate with anyone who demands that they "treat" patients once the absence of a mental illness has been established. The British Medical Association's policy is very clear. Medical ethics prohibit *any participation* by doctors in torture. Doctors have an obligation to assist other physicians who attempt to resist their government's policies of torture and human rights violations.

D. Amnesty International

The focus of Amnesty International is to assist political prisoners or "prisoners of conscience" wherever they are found, regardless of ideology, religion, cultural background, or race. In 1972, Amnesty International officially begun its campaign for the abolition of torture. In terms of its mandate, Amnesty International is a worldwide movement that is independent of any government, political grouping, ideology, economic interest, or religious creed. It opposes the death penalty and torture or other cruel and inhuman treatments or punishments.

Amnesty International acts on the basis of the United Nations Universal Declaration of Human Rights and has formal relations with the United Nations, the Council of Europe, the Organization of American States, and Organization of Africa Unity. While it has thus far failed in its goal of achieving the abolition of torture worldwide, Amnesty International has been very successful at focusing international attention on cases of state torture. Amnesty International calls on all governments to condemn torture officially, to allow independent investigations of reports of torture, to exclude all statements extracted under torture, to prohibit the use of torture in law, to prosecute all alleged torturers, to train all officials in the prohibition against torture, and to compensate and rehabilitate all victims of torture.

IX. CONCLUSION

The existence of international standards for the prevention of torture is not enough in the attempt to impose a fundamental respect for basic human rights. States still practice or use techniques of torture. In 1995 alone, over 10,000 detainees were reportedly tortured in 114 countries. Torture and other human rights violations are overwhelmingly perpetrated by governments in an attempt to achieve their political, social, or economic objectives. Like any other governmental policy, torture becomes simply another tool used by the state to assist in the achievement of these goals.

Three broad conclusions can be drawn about torture. First, torture is the result of historical or situational dynamics as well as political processes created by the authority structure or governments. Second, it is not too difficult in the right circumstances to convince an individual to torture. Third, torture should be considered a complex construct encompassing a variety of violent acts. What acts are defined as torture can be the subject of considerable controversy. It is possible to argue that even liberal democracies such as Canada condone certain forms of "torture" in terms of legitimate forms of punishment, such as long-term imprisonment, solitary confinement, and the death penalty. Prisoners' rights activists maintain that incarceration produces the same physical and psychological effects as torture, yet such effects are considered acceptable and legitimate to most citizens. Perhaps, like terrorism, torture is an elastic concept, or a value judgment, based on our definitions of torture or our personal biases or is a moral decision based on the acceptable level of pain one can inflict on an individual to force that individual to conform to the requirements of the state. While attention to victims of torture is very important, perhaps a more effective means of combating torture is to understand fully the processes that create torturers, including the complex combination of social, situational, and political factors discussed in this article and then to utilize the global media and international political and economic organizations to mitigate these factors.

Nonetheless, for all the public protests, resolutions passed, and amendments to codes, torture and psychiatric abuses continue to be two of the most common features of political repression. Clearly, prevention strategies must be aimed at those in positions of power within the state. As Stover and Nightingale suggest, those who have the power to prevent such abuses are generally those who benefit most from it, while those who are most interested in abolishing torture are not in a political position to do so.

Also See the Following Articles

ENEMY, CONCEPT AND IDENTITY OF • ETHNICITY AND IDENTITY POLITICS • HUMAN RIGHTS • MILITARISM • TERRORISM

Bibliography

Amnesty International (1984). "Torture in the eighties: An Amnesty International report." London: Amnesty International.

Amnesty International (1996). "Amnesty International report: 1996." London: Amnesty International.

Bentham, J. (1973). "Bentham manuscripts: Of torture." *Northern Ireland Legal Quarterly*, 24(3), 305–320.

British Medical Association (1992). *Medicine betrayed: The participation of doctors in human rights abuses.* London: Zed Books.

Corrado, R. (1991). *Contemporary political crime: National and international terrorism.* Toronto: Harcourt, Brace & Jonanovich.

Corrado, R., & Tompkins, E. (1992). *Terrorism.* Burnaby, BC: Simon Fraser University Press.

Crelinsten, R., & Schmid, A. (Eds.) (1993). *The politics of pain: Torturers and their masters.* Leiden: COMT.

Duvall, R., & Stohl, M. (1983). *Governance by terror.* New York: Marcel Dekker.

Foucault, M. (1979). *Discipline and punish: The birth of the prison.* New York: Vintage Books.

Lauderdale, P. (Ed.) (1980). *A political analysis of deviance.* Minneapolis: University of Minnesota Press.

Lifton, R (1986). *The Nazi doctors: Medical killing and the psychology of genocide.* New York: Basic Books.

Lopez, G. (1984). *A scheme for the analysis of government as terrorist.* Westport, CT: Greenwood Press.

Peters, E. (1985). *Torture.* London: Basil Blackwell.

Rejali, D. (1994). *Torture and modernity: Self, society, and the state in modern Iran.* Oxford, UK: Westview Press.

Schmid, A. (1992). *Research on gross human rights violations.* Leiden: COMT.

Stohl, M., & Lopez, G. (Eds.) (1984). *The state as terrorist: The dynamics of governmental violence and repression.* Westport, CT: Greenwood Press.

Stover, E., & Nightingale, E. (Eds.) (1985). *The breaking of bodies and minds: Torture, psychiatric abuse, and the health professions.* W.H. Freeman, New York: W. H. Freeman.

Suedfeld, P. (Ed.) (1990). *Psychology and torture.* New York: Hemisphere.

Total War, Social Impact of

Sheldon Ungar

University of Toronto at Scarborough

GLOSSARY

Civil Religion Fundamental or sacred beliefs about a nation that set it apart and render it special.

Home Front Impacts The creation of a distinct mode in society during war that is unimaginable in peacetime. A key question is to the extent to which these changes are reversible.

Identification Problem The difficulties in determining whether the outcomes following a war can be directly ascribed to it or are the result of trends that are independent of the war.

Moral Panics The perception of extraordinary threats to societal values and interests that are presented in a stereotypical fashion and can result in accelerated demands for extreme political responses.

Resource Mobilization Theory A sociological approach to social movements that focuses on the capacity of contending groups to assemble adequate means to attain their ends.

Social Exchange Perspective The view that social order depends on ongoing transactions between different segments of society.

Watershed Hypothesis The postulate that war is a crucial dividing line that affords segments of society that participate in the war the opportunity to gain new benefits subsequent to the end of hostilities.

DESPITE THE MASSIVE CHANGES that occur during the course of total war, it is very difficult to identify the specific, long-term consequences that follow. After reviewing some of the home front impacts of the world wars, this article finds limited and mixed evidence to support the "war-as-watershed" hypothesis. In contrast, the nuclear arms race, which involved prolonged preparations for the ultimate total war, had several clear social consequences. First, it unleashed moral panics that resulted in the institutionalization of the military–industrial complex. Second, it created levels of secrecy and deception that helped spawn distrust of governments. This article concludes by pointing out new questions pertaining to the civil wars that have followed the ending of the Cold War.

I. INTRODUCTION

WAR. What is it good for? Absolutely NOTHING!

From the song, War,
by Baron Strong and Norman Whitfield

This rock anthem, which was popular in the 1980s, suggests that war no longer commands patriotism among the richest nations but is mostly regarded with abhorrence. To understand war, it is sufficient, according to the popular culture, to know that it maims and kills. If this sentiment is sincere but superficial, it does reflect some real changes in warfare during the Twentieth Century. For one, the link between war and national aggrandizement has attenuated as seizures of territory have proved to be transitory and reversible. As well, the threat of escalation in a nuclear world undermines the idea of national security and cautions that peace ought to take precedence over war.

At the same time, scholars have defaulted to some extent on the issue. While they have produced a rich literature on the nature and causes of warfare, the effects of the preparation for war and the conduct of wars on the social order have secured relatively little research attention. Beyond some informative case studies, there is a paucity of theorizing and systematic comparative data on the social consequences of war.

Clearly, this article cannot redress this neglect. Rather, it pursues more modest ends. It first asks how the total wars fought this century affect social inequalities among different groups in society. It then looks at how preparations for the most extreme total war—the nuclear arms race—redounded on society. The importance of the latter is underscored by its duration and the continued possibility of nuclear proliferation as well as terrorist use of weapons of mass destruction.

II. PROBLEMS IN IDENTIFYING THE SOCIAL IMPACTS OF WAR

A major problem in grasping the effects of total wars is that it seems obvious, at least initially, that they impact on all relations and alter the entire social fabric. Certainly contemporary observers of these wars held such a view. Subsequent commentators, insulated by the passage of time and perhaps looking for a new interpretive angle, began to challenge the theme that war is an engine of social transformation. Above all, despite the massive changes that occur during war, it is difficult to identify the specific, long-term consequences that follow.

To begin, we can ask whether it is possible to formulate *any* empirical generalizations that establish a strong link between war and specific social changes? If we are looking for invariant relationships, the research is apt to disappoint. At a very broad level, we might postulate that war is essentially destructive. However, this gener-

alization befits the total wars of the 20th century more than the dynastic struggles of Renaissance Europe, to take one example. Overall, if we take an anthropological and historical perspective, the sheer weight of variation over time is probably too complex to lend itself to any coherent relationship.

Even in the total wars that we focus on here, the differences in degrees of destruction are so great as to thwart generalization. Thus the physical impingement of war on Russia utterly overwhelms the impacts felt in Canada, even though the latter was a combatant in both World Wars. The distinction between frontline and more distant states—encompassing parameters such as physical destruction, death rates, involuntary population movements, scarcities, and starvation—is further complicated by differences in political systems, social structures, and levels of economic development. A collapse of state functioning in Russia merged with prior trends to lead to revolution in 1917. Such an outcome was unimaginable in Canada, where the First World War forged, for the first time, a strong sense of national identity and nationhood.

Wars, one might argue, are always unexpected and arrive at the wrong time. In terms of a model of social change, wars are exogenous or external factors, erratic interludes that interrupt prevailing social trends and tendencies. Presumably, they can retard some changes, accelerate others that were already taking place, and introduce novel developments as well. Since total wars operate on such a massive, all-encompassing scale and are superimposed on trends and tendencies that predate hostilities, it is exceedingly difficult to identify their specific consequences. If we observe that "A" follows the war, we are still left with the counterfactual question of whether "A" would have happened anyway? There is also a problem of timing. That is, we need to ask how soon after the war must "A" happen for it to be counted as a war consequence? More concretely, are changes that take a decade or two to manifest themselves attributable to war effects, or are they independent of it?

III. THE MILITANCY WATERSHED HYPOTHESIS

Of all the impacts ascribed to total wars, the watershed hypothesis has probably received the most attention. In its strongest "militancy" form, it suggests, to take one example, that the African-American civil rights movement in the United States truly began during the Second World War. These were the watershed years, when new techniques, leaders, organizations, race consciousness, and militancy came into being. For the first time, African-Americans fought independently and effectively for their rights. Proponents of this thesis point to the outspokenness of the African-American press, mass involvement in political activities, as well as race riots and the March on Washington. Critics raise questions about both the uniqueness and the magnitude of African-American militancy during the war. Thus one key question is whether the level of African-American militancy during the war was actually greater than the level of militancy during the 1930s

While varying in detail, the essentials of the watershed hypothesis have been applied to other groups. Thus it has long been a truism that total wars are critical for promoting the demands and the respectability of organized labor. In Europe, at least, wars are also associated with a shift to the left of the political spectrum and the undermining of mass support for the dominant social system. Political crises ensue and, as exemplified by Greece at the end of World War II, civil war almost led to communist victories.

The watershed hypothesis also applies to the liberation of women and the accelerated emergence of multicultural societies. But, as in the case of African-American militancy, revisionist scholars have challenged this hypothesis, especially for women workers. Before we consider in more detail the identification problems associated with the watershed hypothesis, it is essential to delineate the home front impacts of war that led observers to conclude that the social fabric was undergoing revolutionary and irreversible changes.

IV. SOME EFFECTS OF TOTAL WAR ON THE HOME FRONT

The immediate effects of total war on a society are typically so immense and immeasurable that they are best grasped by metaphor. In this regard, James Lowell aptly compared war to a "great seething cauldron." The idea of a cauldron implies an intermingling and shaking up, a series of collisions that disturb and unsettle relationships and patterns. Total war entails concatenating mobilizations—of troops; industrial workers, and other population segments; supplies; productive capacity; administrative expertise; propaganda. Customary social relations and social exchanges are abruptly terminated. The outbreak of hostilities ushers in a distinct mode in society that is unimaginable in peacetime.

Above all else, total war calls for far-reaching domestic sacrifices. As resources are diverted to the military effort, people face shortages, substitutions, and ra-

tioning. Much of this is carried out through the bureaucratization of the life world: the national registration of people, the issuing of food stamps, scrap collecting, neighborhood block captains (who, among other things, are to guard against the black market and hoarding), and civilian defense efforts. War reaches the kitchen, as official propaganda urges homemakers to attend special classes and to act as "home engineers" who give "ration parties," develop good eating habits with less, and learn to curb all waste.

The churning up of society propels people out of their customary orbit. In the United States, demand for labor in war industries pulled previously ostracized African-American and displaced or marginal workers into factories. More than 700,000 southern African-American tenant farmers and field workers migrated north and west, transforming what was still thought of as a southern problem into a national one. An unprecedented number of women also joined the work force, although the recruitment of women for work was not universal. In both Germany and Japan, war production proceeded with hardly any change in female labor-force participation. In Japan, women workers increased by less than 10% between 1940 and 1944.

Overall, the accumulated changes were dislocating—and in multiple ways. To maintain a common front against the enemy, states also had to prevent segments of society from uniting against each other. Industry often opposed women workers, especially in the early stages of war. Hence women were mostly forced into poorly paid jobs. To maintain the idea of women's work as temporary, strong opposition was mounted against day-care programs in the U.S. This gave rise, in turn, to concerns about latch-key kids and increases in juvenile delinquency. Effectively, the image of "Rosie the Riveter" bore a heavy weight of mythology. For the most part, women factory workers were segregated from men and were paid less.

The movement of workers into industrial areas created shortages of housing, schooling, and recreational facilities, and this served to especially intensify racial hostilities. Whereas the movement of people in war seems to imply a forced intermingling of groups with perhaps some leveling of differences, the American South opposed any threat to segregation. To maintain continuity with prewar practices, African-Americans were largely trained for menial positions and segregated at work and in the military. Secretary of War Stimson argued that the army should not be used as a "sociological laboratory." The mixture of state impositions, rising expectations, and challenges to customary social relations and practices rendered race riots and wildcat strikes relatively commonplace during World War II. There were, in other words, sufficient organization and protest activities by different groups to suggest that war-related changes could have enduring effects.

V. IDENTIFYING POSTWAR EFFECTS

The key question here is to what extent various alterations of the social fabric during wartime prove to be transient or, in contrast, persistent. Judging the consequences of war is partially a matter of expectation. Should we count on a linear pattern of change or should we anticipate hiatuses or uneven development? Given the challenges in the immediate aftermath of war—shortages of food and fuel plagued Europeans, while U.S. consumers faced a steak shortage—followed by the need to reconvert the economy, build new housing, and so on, it is reasonable to expect a period where many issues remain in limbo. In effect, those desiring recognition and compensation for their contributions generally have to wait for more opportune times.

At the same time, segments of society attempt to turn the clock back and restore "normal" relations. While the war drew women into the workforce, signs of its ending pushed them out. From June to September, 1945, one of every four women in U.S. factories lost her job. Male-dominated unions, undoubtedly fearing a new depression, pushed their own bread-and-butter issues. One of these was to make sure that women did not compete with men for well-paid factory jobs. In virtually all countries where women were mobilized on a large-scale, the ending of overt hostilities saw efforts to return them to either the household or to their traditional, low-paid service occupations. While the numbers of women workers generally remained above prewar levels and subsequently rose again, it is unclear how much of the ensuing rise was due to the war or to secular economic developments.

In Western nations, the most common changes following World War II occured in labor relations and in the social responsibilities accorded the state. Many of the elements of the welfare state were institutionalized after the war. But again, the identification problem arises. Were these welfare reforms, as some scholars claim, a result of the war? Or were they the crowning of processes that began during the Depression and would have happened anyway? The issue has not been resolved.

In the case of labor relations, however, it is probably safer to see the war as a harbinger of change. In this case, there are both theoretical and empirical reasons for upholding its transforming potential. Examining the factors underlying the success of labor serves to clarify the findings for women and African-Americans.

A. Social Exchange and Resource Mobilization

According to the social exchange perspective, social order depends on ongoing transactions between different segments of society. For example, a basic exchange takes place in work, where the outcomes that people receive (such as income, benefits, job security, social status) depend largely on the level of their inputs (the education, skills, dedication and so on that they bring to the task). Social order is best served by the negotiation of fair or equitable relationships between a group's inputs and its outcomes. However, the links between inputs and outcomes are often based on "tacit equations" that, to put it plainly, need to be enforced. Thus it is not uncommon for the state or employers to attempt to reduce workers' outcomes or to impose new demands on them. Resistance may or may not follow, depending on such factors as timing and the capacity of the affected group to mobilize resources in response to challenges.

The impositions states impose during wars would be utterly unacceptable were it not for a sense of necessity created by the common enemy. As well, groups may tolerate *temporary* inequities in exchange relations because they expect future compensation. In order to assure productivity during the war, U.S. unions agreed to a no-strike pledge as well as to limits on income. In return, labor representatives were appointed to government boards, and the War Labor Board aided unions by policies that made, for example, the check-off for union dues almost universal.

It is widely held that members of the three groups under discussion anticipated that they would make gains as a result of their war contributions. But implicit "understandings" about future compensation are not sufficient. Just as critical is the organizational capacity and power to consolidate wartime gains. For example, while Britain promised political freedoms to colonies that participated in the fight against Nazi Germany, it did not grant these outcomes automatically but had to have its hand forced following the war.

Compared to African-Americans and women, industrial workers were in a better position in peacetime to convert their war contributions into enduring gains. From a resource mobilization perspective, a key issue is the capacity of groups to assemble sufficient resources to attain their outcomes. With their new respectability, a steady flow of income from union dues, and a stranglehold on some industries, organized labor was in the best position to exact new outcomes from employers and the state. Subsequent to the war, labor protests were more marked than those found with the other groups and they made the biggest gains in income and welfare benefits.

B. The Hiatus Problem

Gains made from participation in wartime do not automatically translate into peacetime gains. This is apparent from the experiences of African-Americans and women. Despite wartime activism, the U.S. civil rights movement did not surge until the early 1960s; the women's rights movement did not take off until the end of that decade. Clearly, these groups lacked the resources and political opportunities to exact concessions after the war. Because of these extenuated hiatuses, proponents of the watershed position tend to fall back on psychology. Thus it is claimed that, as a result of wartime experience, women and African-Americans gained a new self-confidence and a new willingness to assert themselves. But just why this new independence took so long to manifest, and why it did so in the 1960s remain largely unaddressed.

Sociological speaking, the link between contributions to total war and subsequent gains is contingent. Wars appear to create the potential for altering social relations and inequalities, but seemingly promising changes can be reversed. If they are to be consolidated, they must be actively pursued and converted into successes. This requires more than shifts in the psychology of contending groups. The latter must be able to mobilize adequate resources and to do so at politically opportune times.

Given these hiatuses, a key question that emerges for future research is what role did those affected by the wartime experience play in the ensuing struggles for civil and gender rights? To give credence to the psychological aspects of the watershed hypothesis, the evidence should indicate that those caught up in the cauldron of war, rather than a new generation, provided the leadership in the emergent social movements.

V. MORAL PANICS AND THE ARMS RACE

The idea of total war reaches its apogee in the threat of nuclear war. While arms races do not cause the social cauldron to boil as intensely as world wars, they are often more enduring. Hence the nuclear arms race, which lasted about 35 years, had a number of unforeseen and somewhat insidious effects on the social order. War preparations often result in the redistribution of

income, especially to the benefit of large industries. To take one example, Britain and Germany began a naval arms race in the 1880s that greatly accelerated after the turn of the century. This arms race transformed social exchanges between government and industry. Governments required the existence of large industries whose weapons-producing capacities were far in excess of peacetime requirements. To secure a sufficient supply of arms should war transpire, nations were forced to guarantee the existence of national armament industries. Hence they were obliged to pay most of the cost for technical innovations and to shelter arms industries from the vagaries of the marketplace.

Studies of the economic effects of World War II reveal that, despite labor's gains, the greatest benefits accrued to the 100 largest corporations in the U.S. Before the war, a combination of the fear of taxes, isolationism, and the relative safety of "fortress America" impaired the formation of a military–industrial complex (MIC) in the U.S. The MIC that emerged during the war was sharply curtailed at its end. In the postwar period the U.S. rapidly demobilized its armed forces, rejected universal military service, and so restricted military budgets that even the Manhattan Project and the production of atomic bombs and delivery systems suffered. Fiscal restraint in military matters was due, in good part, to the erroneous belief in an enduring atomic secret that would enable the U.S. to be the greatest military power on Earth for minimal cost.

Resistance to taxes, however, was soon overtaken by the fear of communism. The emergence of the Cold War in 1947 was followed by several moral panics over startling Soviet nuclear developments. Moral panics involve the perception of extraordinary threats to societal values and interests that are presented in a stereotypical fashion by elites with high credibility. At their worst, moral panics occasion accelerated demands for extreme responses in the political arena.

Nuclear moral panics had cascading effects because they created the perception that both national security *and* the sanctity of the American way of life were imperiled. That is, the panics challenged the fundamental beliefs embodied in the nation's civil religion. According to sociologists, practically every nation has a set of sacred beliefs that set it apart and render it special. The U.S. civil religion holds that democratic America is God's primary agent in history and that the nation has a distinct destiny or mission. One manifestation of this was the claim, by President Truman, that the atomic bomb was a "sacred trust" given to America to preserve freedom.

Not surprisingly, then, the first panic was precipitated by the announcement of a Soviet atomic explosion in 1949. This unexpected event, which overlapped with the communist victory in China, led to National Security Memorandum 68 (which called for the global "containment" of communism), a massive increase in the American nuclear stockpile, the decision to build a hydrogen bomb, and a near-quadrupling of the military budget. It also lent support to the unexpected American-led intervention in Korea. Finally, it helped underwrite the McCarthyist witch hunts and the trial and execution of the Rosenbergs. While most of the attention to McCarthyism focused on national political figures and Hollywood celebrities, the hysteria reached into state legislatures and affected local politics as well. An unprecedented level of peacetime government secrecy now became the norm.

A. Sputnik and the Consolidation of the Military–Industrial Complex

With the loss of its nuclear monopoly, America's faith was transferred, as if by sleight of hand, to nuclear superiority. Technological competition in the arms race became the focal point of the Cold War rivalry, especially as the Soviets sought to demonstrate "socialist superiority" by making an all out effort to prevail in that competition. Thus the two camps vied, in front of the whole world, for triumphs that involved not only prestige but a sense of which system would predominate historically. By implication, the Soviet launch of the *Sputnik* satellite on October 4, 1957, launched a moral panic that touched on practically every American institution and seemingly discredited the most sacred beliefs about the nation.

With the new Soviet credibility gained by beating the U.S. in the missile race, not only science and technology, but education, race relations, and economic development became points of comparison between communism and democracy. The initial foreboding and recriminations in the U.S. gave rise to a sense of sacrifice and rebirth. *Sputnik* "woke up the country" and led to four major initiatives: the doubling of research and development funds by 1961, federal aid to education, defense reorganization, and the space program. The satellite had a tremendous impact on the U.S. nuclear arsenal. By 1956, 150 well-targeted missiles were thought to be enough, and at no time before 1958 did the ballistic missile group recommend more than 200 missiles. But *Sputnik* cut loose the purse strings and President Eisenhower approved almost 1100 missiles by the end of his term.

Before the panic, American resistance to federal control of education and research, unconstrained military spending, and social engineering remained intact. After the start of the panic, Eisenhower still fought a rearguard action against government control and the technocratic threat to traditional American values. But the "emergency means" that he was compelled to put in place became permanent. A U.S. technocracy was forged at the end of the Eisenhower years and embraced and institutionalized by the Kennedy administration. Where state-funded and state-managed research and development seemed to contradict the tenets of a liberal economy, so great was the perceived threat to America's special destiny that the restoration of technological superiority was undertaken at the expense of these other values.

There was also a felt need to reinvigorate American life and prove the superiority of its institutions. The Rockefeller Panel, for example, was one of many committees of leading citizens brought together to established new goals for Americans. The National Defense Education Act made available $250,000,000 for public school facilities. Sputnik was taken as evidence that the Soviets had managed to get ahead here as well as in science, technology, and engineering.

Sacrifice was a commanding theme of the Kennedy administration. When the Soviets, in what amounted to a second *Sputnik,* sent the first person into space, there were calls to mobilize the country on a wartime basis. The ensuing decision to go to the moon was the culmination of the new American technocracy. What had started as a military challenge was transformed into a civilian competition. In an ironic twist of Eisenhower's faith in traditional American values of free enterprise and government non-intervention, the Apollo program was dubbed a peculiarly "American" enterprise. In the new America of command technology and command innovation, the Apollo project, like the earlier Manhattan Project, became the model for further projects, particular President Johnson's Great Society program to fight poverty. As a result of Soviet challenges to sacred beliefs about the future of the nation, the U.S. sought to develop superior skills in every field of human endeavor, and government-led and government-sponsored programs became the primary means of doing so.

B. The Enduring Consequences of the Nuclear Arms Race

As illustrated above, the moral panics that attended the arms races had strong economic effects. In the U.S. and the Soviet Union, and to a lesser extent Britain, the spiraling arms competition created what C. Wright Mills called a permanent war economy. Overall, the evidence suggests that massive military spending has negative effects on the economy. With the Soviet Union, the diversion of resources from civilian to military production was clearly a factor in the collapse of the nation. Despite the promised technological innovation, the U.S. fell behind Japan and West Germany in civilian-oriented technological competition. Where the ending of the Cold War engendered visions of a "peace dividend" in the U.S., most independent military analysts concede that cutbacks to the military budget have been too slow and too modest. In entrenching a permanent war economy, the MIC spread its production tentacles into the vast majority of congressional districts, resulting in widespread local opposition to cutbacks.

If the idea of free enterprise was bent out of shape in the institutionalization of the MIC, the very existence of nuclear weapons (allied with plans to use them and a staggering amount of media coverage) has had a variety of other subtle and not-so-subtle psychological, political, and social effects. In this context, Victor Sidel, past president of the American Public Health Association, speaks of "destruction without detonation." Even without being used in war since Hiroshima and Nagasaki, the accumulation of these weapons has left a dark cloud over society.

The psychological effects of the nuclear threat are cleverly understated in a once-common bumper sticker: "Just one nuclear bomb can spoil your whole day." Studies done during the 1980s reveal that many children believed that a nuclear war was likely during their lifetimes. Not surprisingly, results also indicate that children viewed the future with uncertainty and unease. Public recognition of the corrosive influence of the arms race probably peaked with the televised broadcast of the film "The Day After." Coming during the period when President Reagan spoke loosely about winning a nuclear war, parents were advised not to let children watch the film alone and to let them discuss their fears afterward. For all that, the psychological effects probably did not approach the sheer terror felt by many of those who experienced the Cuban Missile Crisis during their childhood.

Moral panics require the creation of folk devils, and the vilification of the Soviet Union—an amoral communist state bent on world domination—reached unprecedented levels. The projection and mirror-imaging that ensued as each side exaggerated the inherent evil of its opponent poisoned the international political atmosphere and undermined chances for cooperation. Projection also afforded what amounted to paranoid justifications for spiraling weapons programs. President Reagan, for example, tried to justify the MX missile by

claiming that the Soviets could launch a first-strike that would destroy about 90% of America's land-based intercontinental missiles. Not only was the 90% figure greatly exaggerated, but even if it were true, the remaining 10% of these missiles would provide a sufficient second-strike to deter the Soviets. Omitted from these calculations were the other two elements of the American nuclear triad—the missiles on aircraft and those on submarines.

The creation of a demonic enemy to whom was ascribed many of the powers of Satan inevitably redounded on the domestic political scene as well. Starting with the clandestine Manhattan Project, secrecy became a mainstay of the American political system. Not only did the military evolve a huge bureaucracy to withhold information, but both the surveillance of civilians and the creation of misinformation became commonplace activities. At the same time, the need for constant readiness to protect against a Soviet preemptive strike gave rise to what has been termed an "imperial presidency." The delegation of powers to the executive branch coupled with secrecy allowed the MIC to thrive without many of the congressional and public checks that are critical to an informed democracy.

Documents declassified subsequent to the end of the Cold War substantiate prior claims that the MIC and the government frequently deceived the American public. In particular, there were systematic cover-ups of the amounts of radiation troops and the general public were exposed to as a result of atmospheric nuclear tests in the 1950s and early 1960s. In some instances, high levels of exposure were purposively employed to test their effects. Taken in tandem, Cold War secrecy and revelations, coupled with official duplicity in Vietnam and the Watergate scandal, have created a pervasive sense of distrust in national institutions. The civilian militia movement is an extreme response by those whose regard the expansion of government powers as a communist-inspired conspiracy. With the end of the Cold War, the military has engaged in a hunt for new threats and has managed to create fear (but not quite panic) over the possibility that rogue states or terrorists could come to possess nuclear weapons. It remains to be seen whether these nuclear wild cards will be sufficient to justify major new weapons programs as well as extreme levels of government secrecy.

VII. FUTURE RESEARCH DIRECTIONS

Advances in conventional arms allied with nuclear realities have probably rendered future total wars too costly, especially for the richer industrial nations. Since the end of the Cold War, the most prominent conflicts have involved civil wars and wars of succession. Several of these have been exceptionally brutal, involving the systematic gang raping of women, ethnic genocide and cleansing, and forced population movements. Whereas extant evidence on the long-term impacts of war is largely based on the European and American experiences, there is a pressing need to gather comparative data on the effects of civil wars. Here we can suggest several critical questions. What happens to rape victims and their offspring—and to what extent does their experience vary in different cultures? How do population displacements, starvation, and related aspects of civil wars affect the young and especially their opportunities as they come of age? And finally, what are the long-term political, social, and economic consequences for nations set asunder by domestic conflicts?

Despite the transparent horrors, the United Nations and Western nations in general have been slow in responding to these conflicts. Yet interventions need not be limited to the ending of active hostilities. The Truth and Reconciliation Commission in South Africa offers one potential model for the restoration of relations in postwar periods. In other words, the social impacts of war are not simply preordained. Rather, under the auspices of proactive peace movements, there is the possibility of creating some degrees of freedom for consciously managing them.

Also See the Following Articles

CIVIL WARS • COLD WAR • MILITARY-INDUSTRIAL COMPLEX, ORGANIZATION AND HISTORY • NUCLEAR WARFARE • WORLD WAR II

References

Ausenda, G. (1992). *Effects of war on society.* San Marino: CA Center for Interdisciplinary Research on Social Stress.

Creighton, C., & Shaw, M. (1987). *The sociology of war and peace.* London: Macmillan Press. Duis, P. & LaFrance, S. (1992). *We've got a job to do: Chicagoans and World War II.* Chicago: Chicago Historical Society.

Kolko, G., (1994) *Century of war: Politics, conflict and society since 1914.* New York: The New Press.

Kurtz, L. (1988). *The nuclear cage: A sociology of the arms race.* Englewood Cliffs, NJ: Prentice–Hall.

Miller, M. S. (1988). *The irony of victory: World War II and Lovell, Massachusetts.* Chicago: University of Illinois Press.

Titus, J. (1984). *The home front and war in the twentieth century.* Washington, DC: U.S. Government Printing Office.

Ungar, S. (1991). Civil religion and the arms Race. *Canadian Review of Sociology and Anthropology, 28,* 503–525.

Ungar, S. (1990). Moral panics, the military industrial complex and the arms race. *Sociological Quarterly, 31,* 165–186.

Ward, B. (1994). *Produce and conserve, share and play square: The grocer and the consumer on the home-front battlefield during World War II.* Hanover: NH University Press of New England.

Totalitarianism and Authoritarianism

Martin Palouš

Ministry of Foreign Affairs of the Czech Republic

I. INTRODUCTION

Totalitarianism and authoritarianism are relatively new political terms that have appeared only in the 20th century. In short, it can be said that they denote contemporary autocratic political regimes; i.e., the form of government where the ruler is endowed with and exerts absolute power. Such political regimes, however, have existed from the very beginning of human history. Therefore, the first question a student of totalitarianism and authoritarianism may like to have answered touches upon these terms themselves. How are they related to other, older concepts that were used previously and actually are still being used as a name or "label" for autocracies, such as tyranny, dictatorship, despotism, or absolutism? The answer to this question can be obtained when we look at the history of political discourse in the 20th century. Before we do that, however, let us try to clarify the generic problem underlying our theme: what are autocratic and nonautocratic forms of government?

II. AUTOCRATIC AND NONAUTOCRATIC POLITICAL REGIMES

The distinction between autocratic and nonautocratic governments seems to be as old as the very concept of Western politics, which emerged with the birth of the city-state (poleis) in ancient Greece (8th–6th centuries B.C.) Until then existing states—empires often stretching over huge masses of land—might have reached quite an impressive level of technical development and sophistication. Nevertheless as far as their form of government was concerned, they were administered like great households. The imperical rulers assumed the role of guarantor of order, imposing their rule from above, and acted as mediators between immortal gods and mortal men. They exercised complete administrative, managerial, judicial, military, and fiscal authority and were free to accept or to repudiate any laws and norms governing the society of their subjects in any time. No matter how different the style and results of their administration of human affairs might have been, they all were "despots." There was no "politics" under their domination. The "hydraulic" societies of the Old World, "political systems dependent on the maintenance of large-scale irrigation systems for their survival," to use the terminology of Karl Wittfogel, could be poor or rich, underdeveloped, or, on the contrary, have a highly sophisticated and differentiated structure. They nevertheless lacked that dimension of human life for which the necessary condition is the existence of public space and which cannot materialize in the company of slaves but only among one's peers: freedom.

The Aegean region inhabited by the Hellenic tribes was located on the outskirts of the world and organized from the capitals of mighty ancient empires. The state power was weak and decentralized and the region was highly unstable, finding itself in permanent flux and reconfiguration. Whereas the traditional "imperialistic" approach to the problem of instability and disorder would have been conquest followed by centralization of power, the Greek solution was radically different. It was achieved gradually in a process that extended over centuries and which is known as "synoeicismos." Those who administered their affairs at home, i.e., within their own "private" households (oikiai), as autocratic despots, established polis—a common space to deal with common matters. The rule (arche), instead of being in possession of one, was put, as Herodotus reports several occasions, into the midst of the people (es meson toi demoi). As opposed to "barbarian" autocratic rule, there was no human ruler in the Greek polis endowed with the supreme authority. Not the divine will of Emperor or Pharaoh, but the law, nomos, was accepted as the genuine source of order in the human world.

This change had a revolutionary implication: Whereas prepolitical societies are structured hierarchically—Egyptian pyramids were, indeed, the materialization of this social form—the constitution of a political community ruled by law presupposes a principally horizontal organization. Isonomia, the equality of citizens before the law, required the radical limitation of ruling power and introduced an entirely new concept of governance. Citizens should have felt free of the risk of being killed, imprisoned, enslaved, or otherwise harmed in their daily lives by the actual ruler. The elementary intention of the "rule of law" was to give them freedom and to protect them against wilfull tyrants and usurpers, inclined to overstep their human

lot and to seek illegitimately their own personal aggrandizement. Conflicts and disputes in polis could not be resolved by intervention of absolute power from above, but strictly within the margins of political justice. Binding decisions in all disputed matters could be taken only by the proper judiciary organ of polis in a "due process of law." Freedom and equality of citizens in the sphere of justice meant that they had the right to submit accusations against each other and when sued they were entitled to a fair and public trial. Elected jurors who sat in judgement of their fellow citizens, swore to listen impartially to both sides and vote strictly on the issue at hand.

There is no doubt that the ancient and modern rules of law can be compared only with great caution. The ancient society and state differ substantively from their modern equivalents. Not including the fundamental difference between the Greek "pagan" understanding of human identity and the Christian idea of humanity, it is true, for instance, that in protecting "common good" polis enforced "public interests" by means which modern Europeans would certainly label as evident violations of individual rights. This fact, however (the historical records establish the evidence that the restrictions of the personal freedoms of citizens did not happen often nor in many matters in the ancient Athenian democracy), is simply irrelevant for our current analysis. The point is that the political use of power, when the ruler acts as a "guardian of law," and the seizure of power, when he promotes his self-interests and uses his tyrannical will, were perceived by the Greeks—as they are by us—as two entirely different things. Despite the realistic observations of historians that these rulers did not always live up to their own promises and often disregarded moderation and self-control, the love of freedom and the contempt for tyrants represented undoubtedly the fundamental values underlying the Greek mentality. As we know from Herodotus, it was this distinction between the autocratic and nonautocratic forms of government, between sheer life and "good" life, in the words of Aristotle, between the slavish life of a society pursuing the goal of its self-preservation, sheltered by the superhuman activities of its divine ruler and organized as a kind of household and the life that can be led only in the plurality of free human agents assembled in public space, acting and thinking in its light that brought the Greeks into revolt against the Persian king. And it is the same distinction, representing the core political idea of Western civilization, we want to comprehend and study when examining the contemporary phenomena of totalitarianism and authoritarianism.

III. TOTALITARIAN SEARCH FOR A NEW CONCEPT OF STATE

As we said, totalitarianism and authoritarianism represent specific forms of autocracy that came into existence only in the 20th century. However, when these terms appeared in the European political discourse for the first time in the 1920s, they were not used by opponents of totalitarian or authoritarian political regimes, but by their own propagators and protagonists. They appeared in the language of those who were looking for some solutions to escape the evils of modern liberalism.

It was Benito Mussolini and the theoreticians of Italian fascism (Giovanni Gentile) who coined the term *totalitario* in the early 1920s to describe a new type of state whose task it was to lead Italy out of the postwar crisis. Also, Antonio Gramsci, the most prominent Italian Marxist, presented the Communist Party as the vanguard of a "totalitarian movement." In Germany, the word *totale* was introduced into the political vocabulary by the 19th-century Prussian military strategist Carl von Clausewitz, who dealt with the concept of "total war." *Der Totale Krieg* by Erich Ludendorff and *Die Totale Mobilmachung* by Ernst Junger, published in the 1930s, departed from the German interpretation of World War I and yet reflected an attitude that was deeply rooted in the German mind, one that viewed war not only as the use of force in the relations between the states competing in the international arena, but as an eminent act of culure, *eine innere Notwendigkeit* ("a spiritual necessity") (Eksteins, 1989). The "turn to the total state" was seen by Karl Schmitt, the most prominent legal scholar at the time and briefly the "crown jurist of the Third Reich," as a necessary step in strengthening the feeble governance in the Weimar Republic, which came into existence after the loss of the War. Schmitt's critique of liberalism is especially important. Schmitt was definitely not a political radical; on the contrary, he was a conservative. What he was afraid of was European nihilism and the decline of European spirit. Schmitt's remedy for the political crisis of the Weimar Republic was to revive the use of strong authority through an authoritarian rather than Nazi (national socialist) state.

The slogan of Mussolini, "All within the state, none outside the state, none against the state," demonstrates clearly what totalitarians disliked in liberalism. It was "too little state" and too much privatization of life in liberal "bourgeois" society and its essentially negative concept of freedom as freedom *from* politics. It was its conformism, mediocrity and easiness. It was its alien-ation from the public sphere which, they believed, ought to be again animated by the ancient Roman or traditional Germanic spirit, and its contempt for, or at least indifference to, the "classic" virtues. It was the fact that under the conditions of "mass society," emerging as a final result of the process of modernization, the form of government that was almost automatically associated with the general idea of progress—liberal democracy—was sinking into a deep crisis.

The totalitarian search for a new concept of state, both in its Italian and German versions, did not come out of the blue but was catalyzed by the catalysmic, epoch-making event of the Great War (1914–1918). The first pan-European all-out military conflict after 99 years of peace entirely changed the social and spiritual climate on the continent. The "Golden Age of Europe" had ended. First, the unprecedented mass mobilization of whole national societies and then the horrors of the front severely undermined the self-confidence of the European middle class and subverted the central dogma of modern Europe: the belief in progress. The old certainties and the prudent, cultivated optimism of the past disappeared. Practically all European national societies, with the middle class decimated in the carnage that lasted for more than 4 years, suffered great instability as a result of the War. The new European political architecture and the harsh reparations imposed on the defeated Central Powers by the Paris Peace Conference provoked in Germany the "Versailles syndrome," making the revision of the Versailles Treaty a major German political objective in the interwar period. The inability of the European nation-states to implement even the most basic objectives of the postwar plans for European unity paved the way for Hitler's constitutional coup d'etat and for laying the foundations of a totalitarian state through the Nazis' Enabling Act of March, 1933.

IV. THE INTELLECTUAL RESISTANCE OF THE 1930S AND 1940S

Artists such as Arthur Koestler, George Orwell, Ignazio Silone, and Albert Camus, to name only the most prominent ones, were among the first to criticize the autocratic new states emerging in Italy, Germany, and the Soviet Union. The open-minded, critical intellectuals became suspect in the eyes of the new political leaders and were quickly turned into state enemies. The stream of emigrants, especially from Germany, appeared first in many European cities and then later in the United States. Prominent philosophers, scientists, writers, and journalists opened a kind of intellectual front against

Nazism, Fascism, and Bolshevism and began their struggle for freedom by theorizing about totalitarianism and authoritarianism, mostly from either a liberal or Marxist point of view. Karl Manheim, Ludwig von Mieses, Friedrich Hayek, Herbert Marcuse, Mark Horkheimer, Franz Neumann, Sigmund Neumann, Victor Serge, Emil Lederer, Raymond Aron, Franz Borkenau, Ernst Fraenkel, Herman Rauschning, Rudolf Hilferding, Eric Voegelin, Karl Popper, and many others, including Leon Trotsky, tried to cope with totalitarian phenomena in their writings and to formulate the principles of intellectual resistance. Marcuse's *The Struggle Against Liberalism in the Totalitarian View of the State* (1934), Horkheimer's *The Authoritarian State* (1940), and Sigmund Neumann's *Permanent Revolution: Totalitarianism in the Age of International Civil War* (1942) are definitely classics.

Totalitarianism and authoritarianism, through the Nazi, Fascist, or Bolshevik states, made a significant number of European public intellectuals refugees and stateless cosmopolitans and forced them to test their ideas against harsh reality. As Jeffrey Isaac pointed out, a new literary form was, in fact, invented, or at least reinvented, on this occasion: the political book combining history and political criticism. It is important to realize that totalitarianism was not only condemned by its enemies, but was also a new and shocking but still fascinating source of inspiration, something that was closer to their state of mind than they wished and were ready to admit. The totalitarian world was phantasmagoric, it was a living nightmare, but still it "could not be written off as unrealizable" (Isaac, 1992). It "seemed literally to defy comprehension; it was confusing not only to its protagonists but to its victims and potential victims as well" (Isaac, 1992). A puzzling question come back again and again: What is the nature of this monstrosity? How can anything like this come into existence in the human world? What part of the human condition can come up with the idea of the "Final Solution" and then bring into existence a bureaucratically organized and technologically advanced system of death factories?

V. THEORIZING TOTALITARIANISM AND AUTHORITARIANISM DURING THE COLD WAR

The "classic" period in the history of these concepts started with a conference on totalitarianism held by the American Academy of Arts and Sciences in Boston, March 6–8, 1953. Organized by Carl J. Friedrich, who

later published a seminal work in the research of totalitarian phenomenon with Zbigniew Brzezinski *Totalitarian Dictatorships and Autocracy* (1956), and opened by a lecture of George Kennan, the conference made the first step to a comprehensive definition of totalitarianism based on the presupposition that "totalitarian regimes constitute a relatively novel species in the long history of autocratic government" (Friedrich et al., 1969).

Since the times when European public intellectuals began launching their antitotalitarian campaign, the political situation in the world changed. World War II ended in Europe by the unconditional surrender of Nazi Germany on May 8, 1945. Only a few years later, however, the victorious coalition of the United States, The United Kingdom, and the Soviet Union (which was joined by France) broke up and Europe was again torn apart by a new "ideological" conflict between the liberal West and the communist (i.e., totalitarian) East. The "old" continent definitely lost its supremacy in the world' affairs and was divided into two "antagonistic" camps lead by the United States and the Soviet Union, which emerged from the war as the new superpowers. The Western perspective was clear enough: one form of totalitarianism was defeated, but the second one became much stronger than ever before. The European civilization and its liberal principles were again endangered and forced to struggle for survival. The Fulton speech of Churchill in March, 1946 and the Long Telegram of George Kennan from Moscow to the State Department in the same year, followed by the famous "X" article on "Containment" which appeared in *Foreign Affairs* in Summer 1947, represent unmistakable signs that times were, indeed, changing. Within a few years, the Cold War was in full swing and this has to be borne in mind when looking at all attempts, especially those in the 1950s, at a new conceptualization of the 20th century autocracy.

First of all it was argued by Friedrich and Brzezinski that "totalitarian dictatorship is historically unique and sui generis ... that fascist and communist totalitarian dictatorships are basically alike, or at any rate more nearly like each other than like any other system of government, including earlier forms of autocracy" (Friedrich & Brzezinski, 1967). This argument brought about the next step: to attempt to define it.

The result of these endeavors was the following proposition: the totalitarian dictatorship can be characterized by six basic features or traits (Friedrich & Brzezinski):

1. an official ideology, consisting of an official body of doctrine covering all vital aspects of man's

existence, to which everyone living in that society is supposed to adhere, at least passively; this ideology is characteristically focused and projected toward a perfect final state of mankind, that is to say it contains a chiliastic claim, based upon a radical rejection of the existing society and conquest of the world for the new one;

2. a single mass party led typically by one man, the "dictator," and consisting of a relatively small percentage of the total population (up to 10 per cent) of men and women, a hard core of them passionately and unquestioningly dedicated to the ideology and prepared to assist in every way in promoting its general acceptance, such a party being hierarchically, oligarchically organized, and typically either superior to, or completely intertwined with the bureaucratic government organization;

3. a system of terroristic police control, supporting but also supervising the party for its leaders, and characteristically directed not only against demonstrable "enemies" of the regime, but against arbitrarily selected classes of the population; the terror of the secret police systematically exploiting modern science, and more especially scientific psychology;

4. a technically conditioned near-complete monopoly of control, in the hands of the party and its subservient cadres, of all means of effective mass communication, such as the press, radio, motion pictures;

5. a similarly technologically conditioned near-complete monopoly of control (in the same hands) of all means of effective armed combat;

6. a central control and direction of the entire economy through the bureaucratic co-ordination of its formerly independent corporate entities, typically including most other associations and group activities.

This definition can still serve undoubtedly as a good point of departure for any research of totalitarian phenomena. Nevertheless, it must be noted that the expectations of those who needed such terms to use in various fields of value-free scientific research remained unfulfilled. The problem was methodological: As the proceedings of the mentioned Boston conference demonstrate, what characterized this gathering of prominent personalities was an atmosphere of mobilization. The Cold War context set the tone of the totalitarianism debate and created around it, "the mood of political crisis and ideological urgency" (Friedrich et al., 1969).

It was generally believed that the Western civilization, with all its values and principles, was again exposed to an imminent and very serious threat. Totalitarianism, which took now the shape of Soviet communism, represented not so much a scientific problem, but a serious challenge to Western freedom and its clarification became, in Friedrich's words, "the central problem of our time" (Friedrich & Brzezinski, 1956). Or as George Kennan put it in the first sentences of his opening lecture: "We have come together to discuss a phenomenon of our time that has brought the deepest possible misery to untold millions of our contemporaries … (which) has demeaned humanity in its own sight, attacked man's confidence in himself, made him realize that he can be his own most terrible and dangerous enemy, more bestial that the beasts, more cruel than nature" (Friedrich & Brzezinski, 1956).

The question that must be raised immediately, when we read Kennan's arguments 45 years later, runs as follows: Did George Kennan speak here as a public intellectual regardless of his actual position in the American political system or as an official herald of American postwar realism in international affairs? What was more important for him, the shock, supported by the well-proven empirical evidence, that totalitarian dictatorships are materialized evil, transforming the human world into hell? Or the fact that such regimes, because of their devilish nature, had to be regarded by the State Department as hostile or at least unfriendly to the United States?

As I do not think that the principal intention of those who tried to "define" totalitarianism was to find its place in value-free social and/or political science, I am also not convinced that the main framework of the debate of totalitarianism was the postwar American policy of containment. The idea that the Soviet Empire should be at least "contained," if it could not be defeated and its population "liberated," offered without doubt a clear direction to the U.S., as its foreign policy (driven by American national interests), perceived one of its main tasks to protect the "free world" in the age of the atomic bomb. It should not be overlooked, however, that as far as the nature of totalitarianism itself is concerned, this perspective rather blurred important distinctions and can be easily seen as the root cause of many serious confusions. The largest among them concerns the distinction between totalitarian and authoritarian autocratic governments that started to gain currency in the political vocabulary of the Cold War period, especially in the United States, misleading not only those who studied contemporary autocratic forms of government, but also those who had to use these concepts in practice.

It was undoubtedly true that there were very remarkable differences between the military dictatorships in Latin America or Southeast Asia (which were labeled as authoritarian) and the Stalinistic form of government that spread to eastern Europe and embodied, according to the experts from the Pentagon and the State Department, pure totalitarianism. Nevertheless, the fact that the former were friends and the latter foes of the United States could be accepted as sufficient reason only by those who relied on the use of force in international relations, who most probably rightly argued that the United States should not hesitate to protect freedom by intervening militarily in the American "zone of influence" and to head-off the communist world revolution by all available means. However, as far as the debate on totalitarianism is concerned, it was only a matter of time before it became apparent that this type of reasoning was too narrow and too much determined by the spirit of the "imperialistic republic," to use the phrase of Raymond Aron (1974).

VI. RETREAT FROM TOTALITARIANISM AND ITS SURVIVAL: THE ATTEMPTS TO DECONSTRUCT THE CONCEPT IN THE 1960S AND 1970S

The process of gradual change in the Soviet Union and in the other socialist countries in eastern Europe, which started in the middle of the 1950s and culminated at the end of the 1960s, still bears a name that explains how strongly the communist variety of totalitarianism was connected with the chief dictator: de-Stalinization. Joseph Stalin died in 1953. Nikita Khrushchev delivered his famous secret speech, denouncing the "cult of personality" of the previous adored leader and disclosing the horrible crimes of Stalin's regime, in 1956 to the 20th CPSU Congress. No matter whether Khrushchev's proclaimed goal to return from Stalinism to true Leninism was meant sincerely and regardless of the principle question whether any reform of communism was only a vain effort and an attempt to "square the circle," the political situation in Europe at the end of the 1960s was remarkably different from the previous decade.

Thanks to Khrushchev and other reformers, communism lost its cruel, numb, but at the same time unfathomable face and acquired at least some human qualities. The whole world was observing with a kind of relief and with hope that what was going on in the socialist camp under the label of de-Stalinization was showing unmistakable signs of being capable of at least some positive developments. For sure, there were crises within the system (the Hungarian Revolution of 1956) or crises between superpowers (the Cuban missile crisis of 1962, which brought the world closer to nuclear conflict than ever before). Nevertheless, all these problems were overcome in the end, free from the pure totalitarianism known in the Stalin era. In spite of various setbacks, the reformist spirit seemed to be prevailing, even gaining, step by step, new ground. The ideological confrontation between East and West was being reformulated. If at the outset of the Cold War the East–West relations were characterized by an uncompromising Manichean struggle between life-and-death enemies, the relaxed 1960s gave birth to a much more benign concept of "peaceful coexistence of the countries with different social systems."

The "thaw" in the Eastern bloc contributed positively to the stabilization of the international situation. The Cold War was not over, but no one could doubt that it entered a new, qualitatively different phase. The tension declined and in retrospect, the 1950s could be easily perceived as a "nightmare." The scene cleared up and in daylight, everything that had come into existence in the darkness began to reveal its ghostly nature. This shift was also found in political terminology and it is not at all surprising that under the new circumstances, the classic definition of totalitarianism came under fire.

Two trains of argument were used, due to the essential ambiguity of political terms noted previously. On the one hand all political terms describe political phenomena and serve as instruments for historical analysis. On the other hand, they design political ideas that have the power to "act" in the human world and to change eventually the course of human matters; political ideas as used by politicians whose discourse is not descriptive but prescriptive.

Subsequently, one type of criticism was coming from those who intended to clarify the content and validity of the term "totalitarianism" from the point of view of the behavioral social and political sciences. What behaviorists disliked, when they tried to find its place in the context of their research, was that they heard in it—as Michael Curtis put it—too much of "emotive overtones" (Friedrich et al., 1969). According to these critics, the term "totalitarianism" should be tested as an analytical tool to be used in the process of causal explanations and for that purpose it had to be, above all, depoliticized. The "counter-ideological uses of totalitarianism" could not guarantee that this term was justified from the point of view of value-free, neutral, and objective science; that there is at all such a social and political reality (Friedrich et al., 1969).

A scientific term, it was argued, can be useful only if it is sufficiently general to be applied to a number of cases. As a matter of fact, all available definitions of totalitarianism—sometimes reflecting the reality of Hitler's regime in Germany, sometimes corresponding to the Stalinist period of Soviet communism—were strangely at odds with this requirement. Even if we could omit all the differences between Nazism and communism and focus on what they had in common, "there is hardly much to be gained by having the term so highly specified that it merely replaces one or two proper names," argued Stanislav Andreski (Mason, 1967). Those who suggested that societies formed by these regimes should be studied as examples of a new social "species," of a new type of society characterized by a number of distinctive traits, simply did not respect well-established scientific methodology. Such an approach to social phenomena involved too much of categorization, too much essentialism, and an excessive concern with the uniqueness of extremist criminal regimes which in their pure form existed only for a very limited period of time (the Nazi regime in Germany became truly totalitarian only after 1939 and Stalin's regime in the Soviet Union corresponded to the above suggested definition in the period of the "great purges" in the second half of the 1930s and again after World War II until Stalin's death in 1953). The conclusion, which was supported by Benjamin Barber, Michael Curtis, and Herbert Spiro, among others, was clear: the concept of totalitarianism was of very limited analytical or heuristic value. The best thing would be to "retreat from it," to not use it at all and let it disappear from the political lexicon.

The second type of criticism was opposite to this ambiguous definition. Those who belonged to this "school" fully agreed with the first group that the phantoms and shadows of the 1950s should be disposed of and thrown away. Nevertheless, they were convinced that what was at stake in the on-going totalitarianism debate concerned above all the realm of prescriptive political ideas. In other words, their argument against totalitarianism was not scientific, but, on the contrary, political.

It belongs to the very essence of politics, however, that it is decisively country specific. In order to understand the political dynamism behind the totalitarianismus debate in the 1960s, let us examine it not from the American but rather from the German perspective. For in Germany, for obvious reasons, it was more difficult than anywhere else, or rather impossible, to separate social and political sciences from politics and to keep the scientific discourse neutral and value-free in the Weberian sense. Throughout the postwar period, the German debate concerning the nature of contemporary autocratic regimes took place in a very specific context that can be characterized by one word: denazification.

Germans, burdened with their own totalitarian past, simply could not identify themselves with the American slogan "save the Western civilization from a deadly enemy." No doubt that American policy, which began with the Marshall Plan of postwar reconstruction of Europe, helped to overcome the gap which the war opened between Germany and all other Europeans. No doubt that it was the pro-American foreign policy of the first chancellor of the post-Nazi German state, Konrad Adenauer, that helped build a bridge from the past toward a "better" future and enabled Germany to raise from the ashes and to overcome the postwar marasmus and disorder. Nevertheless, as the heated polemics that burst out at the beginning of the 1960s concerning the scandalous discoveries of the Nazi pasts of many then-prominent German politicians clearly demonstrated, neither American money invested in future European stability nor Adenauer's awareness of the importance of close transatlantic cooperation could solve the central problem of the newly democratic and newly liberal German political community: how to achieve a real reconciliation; how to restore the shattered spiritual balance; how to heal the German mind, which seemed to be still disturbed by what had happened during the war despite all undisputable signs of economic growth and political recovery.

While the dominant feature of the American perception of totalitarianism was that it was communism that had to be contained and kept out of the free world, the German focus was clearly on the homefront. The arguments that appeared first in the 1960s, however, indicate that real soul searching was extremely difficult in the existing climate of ideas. The thaw in the East did not provoke so much questions concerning the future of the divided European continent, but inspired left-wing western European intelligencia to take up sometimes very militant anti-American attitudes and to condemn, as had happened many times before, the antihuman traits of world capitalism.

The renaissance of the left in the 1960s brought another resolute attack against those who used the term "totalitarianism." It was criticized as an instrument of the Cold War, serving above all the interests of American hegemonic policy. Especially in Germany, it could be unmasked as part and parcel of a self-righteous strategy of those who wanted to divert attention away from their own disgraceful Nazi past and make a new career in the democratic regime. If the principal argument of Friedrich and Brzezinski was that "totalitarian regimes constitute a relatively novel species," the left-wing opponents of the term—who openly professed their own political bias—were suggesting its deconstruction, i.e., the return to the traditional, ideological antagonism and to the terms "fascism" and "communism." Whereas the reforms in the East demonstrated dynamism and the still-unexploited potential of the socialist movement, the right-wing extremism (i.e., an aberration of "capitalist" social order and the unmistakable sign of the "decline of the West") had to be condemned by all "progressive" people in the world—not only on moral grounds but for pragmatic reasons because history itself was following the path of progress.

With this move, the debate on contemporary autocracies came, as Karl Bracher, who opposed the left-wing criticism of totalitarianism, pointed out, full circle. The arguments that were based on the differences between fascist and communist political ideas and socioeconomic concepts—rather then on similarities between the "forms of government" and social realities produced by the communist and fascist political praxis—were unpleasantly reminiscent of the critique of Western liberalism in the 1920s and 1930s.

The Marxist or neo-Marxist projects of a rational social order, based not on exploitation so common in the old, corrupted world, but on equality and justice, and the intellectual appeals promoting a new politics and a new governance of human matters might easily be labeled as potentially dangerous products of utopian, constructivist thinking. On the other hand, however, the problem was that this criticism did not do away with the fundamental problem of contemporary politics concerning both constitutional guarantees of freedom of individuals and the governance among nations which "after Auschwitz" was even more real and more pressing than in the 1920s and 1930s. The global agendas superseded the European hegemony, taken for granted in the world of yesterday and setting hitherto the tone of the totalitarianism debate. The independence of India in 1947, the emergence of the Third World, the discussions around the "limits of growth," new disturbing questions concerning the environment, and other explosive issues that suddenly emerged, clearly indicated that in spite of the victory over fascism in World War II and the successful containment of communism during the Cold War, despite all attacks on "totalitarianism" and suggestions to get rid of it, this debate was not at all over.

Bracher's criticism of the left-wing deconstruction of the term "totalitarianism" is worth mentioning. According to Bracher (and we can add Hans Mommsen and Ernst Nolte, to introduce just two names from the long list of German historians and other public intellectuals), to dump this term "is historically wrong, because this move simply fails to consider the long history of the totalitarianism debate started in 1922 and 1933." The criticism of the Cold War uses of the term—which had its champions still in the 1970s and 1980s—might be justified and at least debatable. What was not acceptable for Bracher—and what makes this strategy to "solve" the problem more than dubious from any reasonable point of view—was the unreflected ideological bias of those who presented it. What seemed to be completely forgotten by the left-wing critics was the original meaning of the term: that what is at stake here is the struggle of European civilization in the 20th century for its freedom; that it is vital in this struggle to be able to distinguish, under the conditions of the contemporary world, between dictatorship and democracy.

Bracher agreed with Friedrich and Brzezinski and other supporters of the classic definition that the structural similarities are more important than the ideological differences between left-wing and right-wing totalitarian governments. On the other hand, he was neither on the side of those who were actively engaged in Cold War international politics and were striving to "contain" the archenemy nor did he subscribe to any value-free, neutral scientific methodology. As a German, he was quite aware of the political dimension of the totalitarian problem. On the other hand—and again as a German, we may add—he was also aware that to understand totalitarianism requires a different type of knowledge. What must be looked for in the totalitarian debate is a knowledge that "knows" how to cope with the generic problem of autocratic versus nonautocratic forms of government in our times and that is able to see the general dilemma our civilization was confronted with from the very beginning in the concrete social and political, i.e., historical context we are part of. However, it is this context that has to be properly reflected in the first place. The totalitarianism debate itself represented a serious problem for Bracher, a problem that by its nature, as we will see in the final section of this article, opens the door not only to the core problem of European politics, but also of European philosophy. What matters, is not only the term itself, but—to repeat once more Bracher's argument—how it was used under the given concrete circumstances, what set in motion its own history.

VII. TOTALITARIANISM LIVED AND REVISITED

The political developments of the "golden sixties" reached their peak in 1968. The student protest movements sweeping throughout western Europe and the United States, and the Prague Spring—an unprecedented attempt in the east European socialist camp to open the closed communist system and to endow it with a "human face"—were a monument of the spirit of the times and marked the end of an era. The prevailing climate of ideas in the 1970s and 1980s was very different. Contrary to the idealistic optimism and sometimes exorbitant expectations of the previous decade, the social and political atmosphere was much more sober and realistic. The students of the French, German, or American universities returned to their classrooms with the sense of urgency and mobilization among western public intellectuals withered away; also, East–West relationships were characterized by a return to more "realistic" policies possible within the existing bipolar political architecture. The reformist spirit of the 1950s was replaced by a more traditional version of international politics—conceived as an interplay of security and "national" interests of the principal actors of the international system; defined and hammered out under the conditions of the Cold War, predominantly by the two leading superpowers, whose competition for influence and control over world affairs was moderated by their shared concern for avoiding nuclear conflict and for keeping global balance and stability.

However, what on the western side of the Iron Curtain—which ran across the European continent and was generally recognized as an undisputable aspect of political reality—could be registered as a change of political atmosphere, the coming of a new generation or a shift of paradigm, was rightfully perceived by the open-minded and liberal inhabitants of the "socialist" camp of the East as a catastrophe. Hundreds of thousand people fled from Czechoslovakia after the invasion of the Warsaw Pact troops on August, 21, 1968, convinced that there was no future for them or for their children in this part of the world. The icy blow of "Realpolitik," which replaced the "thaw" of the Prague Spring, the fact that the Soviet step was in fact approved by Washington as an operation within the confines of the Soviet "zone of influence," gave to the new emigrants a lesson that was later best articulated by Milan Kundera, a Czech writer, living in exile in France, as a central European "tragedy." The tragic fate of central Europeans consisted, according to Kundera, in their unfortunate

geostrategic location. They found themselves sandwiched between and crashed by the great historical powers. Central Europe, wrote Kundera,

is a family of small nations (which) has its own vision of the world, a vision based on a deep distrust of history. History, that goddess of Hegel and Marx, that incarnation of reason that judges and arbitrates our fate—that is the history of conquerors. They cannot be separated from European history; they cannot exist outside of it; but they represent the wrong side of history; there are its victims and outsiders. (Kundera, 1984)

With due respect to Kundera and all others who solved this central European problem in their individual lives by escaping to the West, it was not in the circles of emigres, but among those who stayed at home—and this is definitely different from the situation in the 1930s and 1940s—where important arguments emerged that significantly enriched the on-going totalitarian debate. The Orwellian vision of *1984* did not materialize in the practices of eastern European governments, whose ideologues coined the term "Real Socialism" after 1968, and new voices could be heard in the 1970s and 1980s coming from central Europe that did a kind of live reporting—as if following the theme of the one of Orwell's (1970) essay—from the "inside the whale."

There are many names, many outstanding figures in all countries behind the Iron Curtain that should be mentioned in this context. Certainly not only central Europeans but also Russians contributed in a substantive manner to the uneasy task of disclosing the real nature of the socialist regimes that had tried to hide beneath more fashionable clothes in the changing world of the 1970s and 1980s to secure favorable conditions for their survival. For the purpose of this article, however, only one of them will be referred to in this section, a Czech dissident and playwright and later the president of the newly liberated, postcommunist state, Václav Havel.

Václav Havel belongs to the same generation of Czech intellectuals as Milan Kundera, also appearing on the public scene of his country in the 1960s. The Prague Spring of 1968 also represented a significant crossroads in his life. Nevertheless, not only was he never a member of the Communist Party—which is why he did not need to "sober up" after having been temporarily intoxicated by the Marxist ideology—but his choice in the aftermath of the Soviet-lead invasion that crushed the experiment with the "socialism with human face" was different from Kundera's. Having decided not to leave his country under any circumstances, he has become undoubtedly one of the most sensitive and most penetrating observers of the post-1968 transformation of the central European communist variety of totalitarianism.

His reflections on the nature of contemporary autocratic governments noted the remarkable difference between the "revolutionary ethos and terror" of the Stalinist 1950s and the depressive, deadening atmosphere—"dull inertia, pretext-ridden caution, bureaucratic anonymity, and mindless, stereotypical behaviour"—so typical of the era of "normalization" that spread throughout Czechoslovakian society after the defeat of the "counter-revolution" in 1968 (Havel, 1992).

In its original version, the defining feature of a totalitarian regime was the combination of idealistic hopes for a better world with the use of brute force and physical violence:

In the fifties there were enormous concentration camps in Czechoslovakia filled with tens of thousands of innocent people. At the same time, building sites were swarming with tens of thousands of young enthusiasts of the new faith singing songs of socialist construction. There were tortures and executions, dramatic flights across borders, conspiracies, and at the same time, panegyrics were being written to the chief dictator. (Havel, 1992)

The society that was essentially liberal and "open" in the past (and already the Nazi occupation and the horrors of World War II (1939–1945) had strongly undermined this capacity) was being forcibly "closed" after the communist constitutional coup d'etat in February, 1948. The building of a socialist "radiant future," foreseen in Marxist–Leninist ideology, was accompanied by the ruthless and oppressive policies of the Communist Party, which seized the monopoly of power and quickly formed a totalitarian political regime. It must be noted, however, that it was not only the immoderate lust for power of the new rulers combined with the blind conviction and commitment of the "enthusiasts of the new faith" that sent the Czechoslovakian democracy into the abyss. The Czechoslovakian communists certainly had their share in it, but the real "historical force" behind their success was the Soviet Union, whose territorial and political gains had to be recognized in postwar Europe and whose emerging global influence was also reflected in the American policy of "containment."

In spite of the fact that the 1950s could indeed be perceived in retrospect as a "nightmare," there was something in this period that surprisingly Havel could label as "positive." Even though the closing of society—the systematic destruction of all social institutions, structures, and intermediary bodies (in the sense of Tocqueville) whose nature and mission was simply not compatible with the idea of total control by the state, led by the "vanguard" political party—was carried by all sorts of brutal and ruthless means, this "revolutionary transformation" took place in an environment that was still nontotalitarian. As is evidenced by all sorts of historical records, the customs and habits of society, including the lifestyles and self-presentations of the communist leaders themselves, still bore some traces of the old, prerevolutionary world. It was this "ancestral" aspect that gave the beginning phase of Czechoslovakian totalitarianism its specific "local color" and, if we are allowed to use this word with regard to the enormous suffering and tragedy experienced by thousands of innocent people, its flavor.

The song of idealists and fanatics, political criminals on the rampage, the suffering of heroes—these have always been part of history. The fifties were a bad time in Czechoslovakia, but there have been many such times in human history. It still shared something, or at least bore comparison with those other periods; it still resembled history. No one could have said that nothing was happening, or that the age did not have its stories.

What was not entirely missing in the 1950s and what immediately took on more visible, more touchable, and socially more significant forms after the "nightmare" was gone, was the hope for the future. When people began first to feel and then later to perceive the signs of a dawning new day, appeared the dimension of the human condition that is able, despite all terrors, tragedies and deaths, to impart meaning to human life: the fundamental sense of historical continuity of time and the faith that the painful experiences of the past and the irreversible losses could be healed and saved from oblivion through recording and telling the story. It was this attitude that was helping people to see the light at the end of the tunnel, even when there was no real reason to believe that the communist regime had to collapse quickly and when it turned out that the broadly spread speculations concerning the American or western interventions against communism were from the very beginning a sheer illusion. And it was this same state of mind that nourished the gradual change in the social and political atmosphere of the 1960s; what made the vast majority of Czechs and Slovaks believe, during the Prague Spring of 1968 and even still when they saw Soviet tanks in the streets of Prague and other cities in August of that year, that socialism—whatever this word meant—was after all reformable, that central Europeans were not doomed to remain forever—as Kundera said in 1984—the "victims and outsiders" of European history.

The 1970s and 1980s meant, first of all, the end of this hope, the unpleasant discovery that there was no saving bridge over the gap between the past and the future and that central Europe was indeed finding herself at a kind of dead-end. The bipolar political architecture of the Cold War turned out to be a much stronger element in shaping her destiny than the desire of the central Europeans to actively participate in its creation. The period of "normalization" in Czechoslovakia started not at the moment of Soviet occupation, but when the huge majority of Czechs and Slovaks simply gave up and conformed to their historical lot—by either willingly cooperating with a "rehashed" ruling power or retreating to the private spheres of their lives and succumbing to passivity. The spirit of resistance of 1968 was taken over in 1969 by the "captive mind," named and analyzed by another outstanding central European, the Polish poet Czeslav Milosz. The regime that emerged under the domination of this "captive mind" could serve, as Václav Havel pointed out in 1986, "as a textbook illustration of how an advanced or late totalitarian system works":

> (It) depends on manipulatory devices so refined, complex, and powerful that it no longer needs murderers and victims. Even less does it need fiery Utopia builders spreading discontent with dreams of a better future. The epithet "Real Socialism", which this era has coined to describe itself, points a finger at those for whom it has no room: the dreamers. (Havel, 1992)

In other words: being exposed to the influence of an external totalitarian power and in a desperate effort to adopt itself to the geopolitical conditions in the changing world (this was, after all, also the principal reason for the Soviet intervention in Czechoslovakia), totalitarianism dramatically changed its style and external manifestations. The main force of Havel's writings on totalitarianism consists in his unique ability to offer an authentic, exact, and thoughtful analysis of this— sometimes horrifying, sometimes only ridiculously absurd—metamorphosis.

First, what got lost entirely was the revolutionary character of totalitarian government. Although politi- cally it uncompromisingly adhered to the dogma of the "leading role of the Communist Party," at the same time it dropped its original intention to transform the existing social and political order according to the ideo- logical Marxist–Leninist blueprint. It "set itself a single aim: self-preservation." Instead of using the straightfor- ward Draconian policies of its early days, instead of perpetrating acts of open violence against the defeated social classes (which were to be physically destroyed), the "normalization" regime was created by unprincipled opportunists who simply desired to keep themselves in power by any means. With the exception of a relatively small group of "counterrevolutionaries," who deserved exemplary punishment, all others were to be offered a possibility to preserve their own well-being and their relatively safe and undisturbed existence. The ticket one had to buy to be admitted was quite cheap and the vast majority were easily persuaded. No class origin, no conviction, no commitment, not even difficult moral choices were required to get on board, just the formal agreement with the Soviet occupation and at least tacit consent with the basic goals of "normalization"; the readiness to give up all ideals and noble visions and to just play the game and be flexible enough to adapt oneself to the requirements of a new situation. All ideal- istic motivations and aspirations had to be rejected at this stage of the history of communism, and what re- mained was a strange variety of petty and down-to- earth political realism.

The ruling power simply offered to the ruled a kind of bizarre "social contract"; a contract comparable to the similar acts that have been described by political philosophers as being behind the making of modern states in European history: offering a relatively undis- turbed private life and even some personal benefits in exchange for loyalty to the regime, the willingness to accept its concept of politics, and understanding what the nature and role of public space is in "socialist" so- ciety.

Here the history of totalitarianism made another full circle. It began by critiquing the "bourgeois" ideal of private liberties and the liberal claim for freedom from politics. The Italian Fascists and the German Nazis em- phasized the necessity of building a strong state and strived to impose a new concept of politics on the "deca- dent" western societies and to solve the crisis of Euro- pean civilization by reviving the ancient virtues and values. The communist revolutionaries, departing from the progressive teachings of Marx, Engels, and Lenin, wanted to see the bourgeois oppressive state "wither away" and their ambition was also to replace it with a political order of a new type, with a new form of administration of human matters, based in this case not on the mythologized past, but on a future-oriented, so-far unknown and that is why the utopian project (*utopia, a-topos,* in Greek means "out of place," i.e., what cannot be found in the space of the real world). However, what the disciples and heirs of the totalitarian "founding fathers" got and what they found themselves actively supporting, after the power of their ideological premises and political enthusiasm "burned out," was quite opposite to their original intentions: a kind of facade—and a thousand times worse, we can add—an imitation of the "rotten" and supposedly outdated "bourgeois" political regime.

The politics that pursued the idea of the total state ended in the "lessons of the years of crisis" (1968/1969) which used the language of the old revolutionary slogans, but whose message had an entirely different meaning:

1. Any effort to open up the "socialist" system and to reform its form of government was considered dangerous and leading to destabilization, intolerable to the ruling forces of this world.

2. Only fools and martyrs could be so foolish as to act against this fundamental and invincible "law" of human history.

3. In the era of Real Socialism, politics should be understood not as a sphere of human responsibility and agency, but as a kind of ritual. Its aim was not to change the course of human matters but to keep them in the state in which they already were.

4. It was perfectly acceptable that, under the given circumstances, not everybody had the ambition, or the stomach, to become a politician. In that case he was only advised to mind his own business and to stay away from politics.

There is no doubt that the "liberalization" of the traditional elements of totalitarianism (i.e., their reinterpretation in connection with the above-mentioned "social contract") made life much easier and more bearable for the enslaved peoples. At the same time, however, it obviously did not include any increase of their freedom, but on the contrary their further enslavement. A society where an advanced or late totalitarian system came into being was not any more decimated by the revolutionary "reigns of terror and virtue," and some socialist governments even managed to offer to their population quite a high standard of living. But it did not mean, on the other hand—and that is the principal

message of Václav Havel—that the inhabitants of the world of "Real Socialism" were safe from the destructive effects of totalitarian radiation.

There was no unmanipulated public space available for them, no ideologically undistorted language to address the relevant social issues and to formulate and discuss new political ideas. There was no communication as regards the public good and common matters, there were no citizens committed to rediscovering the original meaning of politics in their concrete situations. There were no events besides various anniversaries to make the news and to form stories; no social movements to be seen; no experiences to be transformed into political knowledge; no hope, at least for the living generations, that the political situation could be ever changed. What remained was a society, relatively well fed, surviving under a kind of socialist welfare condition, but suffering a strange disease that Havel compared to asthma: one is still alive but struggling for air to oxidize the blood, having permanent difficulties in breathing:

It is not true that Czechoslovakia is free of warfare and murder. The war and killing assume a different form: they have been shifted from the daylight of observable public events, to the twilight of unobservable inner destruction. It would seem that the absolute, "classical" death of which one reads in stories (and which for all terrors it holds is still mysteriously able to impart meaning to human life) has been replaced here by another kind of death: the slow, secretive, bloodless, never-quite-absolute, yet horrifyingly ever-present death of non-action, non-story, non-life and non-time; the collectively deadening, or more precisely, anaesthetizing, process of social and historical nihilization. This nihilization annuls death as such, and thus annuls life as such: the life of an individual becomes the dull and uniform functioning of a component in a large machine, and his death is merely something that puts him out of commission. (Havel, 1992)

Havel's description of the destruction of "stories" in a world controlled by totalitarian forces, his story about a deep crisis that points to the very core of our humanity—to the primordial need of every human being to impart meaning to his or her life—reveals undoubtedly a new truth concerning the essence of totalitarian government. It illustrates on the one hand the closed totalitarian mind in action, endless conformism and hopeless thoughtlessness—the "stupidity beyond remedy"—of its protagonists. On the other hand, however, it also articulates the reasoning behind the dissident revolt against this system that spread all around central Europe in the late 1970s and 1980s. It testifies to the dissidents' "heroic" struggle with "nothingness" and social amnesia, but also to the essential uncertainty, vulnerability, and a kind of nakedness that accompanied this enterprise:

> I am attempting to say that the struggle of the story and of history to resist nihilization is in itself a story, and belongs to history.
>
> It is our special metastory.
>
> We do not know how to talk about it because the traditional forms of storytellling fail us here. We do not yet know the laws that govern our metastory. We do not even know yet exactly who or what is the main villain of the story (it is definitely not a few individuals in the power center: they too are victims of something larger, just as we are).
>
> It is clear: we must tell the story of our asthma, not despite the fact that people are dying from it, but because they are not.
>
> One small detail remains: we have to learn how to do it. (Havel, 1992)

The history of dissident movements and their role in the miraculous liberation of central Europe still needs to be properly explored. The collapse of communism in the fall of 1989 and all subsequent events opened many fundamental questions that simply cannot be answered right now. Was it the policy of American President Ronald Reagan, who launched his campaign against the "evil empire" at the right moment and sent it down to its knees, that contributed more than anything else to the western victory in the Cold War? Or was it rather the programs of "perestrojka" and "glasnost" of the new Soviet leader Michail Gorbachev, who came to power in 1985? Or the combination of both? Or was it all a logical and predictable outcome of the Helsinki process, which had already in 1975 started to erode the postwar European division and the European political architecture? What place in this unexpected outcome of the East–West confrontation can we give to people like Polish electrician Lech Walesa or Czech playwright Václav Havel?

After the fall of the Berlin Wall, totalitarianism lost not only its power and ability to keep the people closed in and in slavery, but also its prestige as a strong, respected, and somewhat mysterious player in the realm of international relations. In fact, it might be another aspect of its strange nature that this theme has been so far only rarely studied by social or political scientists. A British conservative, Roger Scruton, who focused on the total absence of the rule of law in a totalitarian political system, and a British liberal thinker (John Gray), who analyzed totalitarianism as social and/or political system that succeeded in destroying entirely all intermediary bodies of civil society, undoubtedly belong to the most distinguished and the most attentive scholars. Their arguments, which will not be commented on here, also corroborate the importance of the central European dissidents' perspective for the study of totalitarianism. The thing is, with due respect to the robust effects of heavy-handed American international policy or the perhaps unintentional outcomes of the Gorbachev strategy of modernization of the Soviet empire, it was Walesa and Havel rather than the armies of learned western Sovietologists and Kremlinologists who taught us by far the most important lesson concerning the totalitarianism's last—at least for the time being—metamorphosis.

VIII. HANNAH ARENDT'S DIFFICULTIES OF UNDERSTANDING AND THE FUTURE OF TOTALITARIANISM IN THE ERA OF GLOBALIZATION

The last word is usually given to someone who is capable of summing up the previous discussions and to bring contradictory positions into proper perspective. Hannah Arendt was definitely not a harmonizer. She developed her own way of writing about the political crisis of European civilization in the 20th century and—especially the way she approached the Jewish tragedy of the World War II when she agreed to go to Israel in 1962 as a journalist to cover the trial of Nazi war criminal Adolf Eichmann and publish her report on "Eichmann in Jerusalem"—the Banality of Evil (Arend 1994)—openly went against the mainstream understanding of the totalitarian phenomenon and was controversial, at the very least. It seems to me, however, wholly compatible with and commensurate to the nature of the subject under investigation to conclude with the most challenging, the most provocative author in the field.

Hannah Arendt (1906–1975) was a German Jew. Her first exposure to "totalitarian radiation" took place when Hitler seized power of the Weimar Republic in 1933. She fled from Germany in the same year, but before she left—first to work in France in an organization that facilitated Jewish emigration to Palestine and later to start a new life and a distinguished academic career in America—she had a chance to observe the emerging totalitarian regime in the first months of its existence, i.e., literally *in statu nascendi*. She related her experiences of 1933 more than 30 years later in an interview she gave on German public television in 1964. What was shocking for her at the moment when the new regime emerged was not the radicalism of its political program and, above all, its openly anti-Semitic policies, but the strange social change that occurred almost instantly. Anti-Semitism as such was definitely not anything new. As were all Jews in Germany, Arendt was used to its occasional manifestations. The radicalism of the Nazis in this respect was indeed a gloomy, ominous sign for the future of Jews in Germany. Nevertheless, it was not at all surprising: "We didn't need Hitler's assumption of power to know that the Nazis were our enemies!" (Arendt, 1994b)

Much more depressing than the political changes resulting from the nature of the Hitler's Nazi regime, was when Arendt characterized as a "personal problem"—to see "not what our enemies did but what our friends did," how quickly they "'co-ordinated' or got in line."

> In the wave of Gleichschaltung (co-ordination), which was relatively voluntary—in any case, not yet under the pressure of terror—it was as if an empty space formed around one. I lived in an intellectual milieu, but I also knew other people. And among intellectuals Gleichschaltung was the rule, so to speak. But not among the others. And I never forgot that. (Arendt, 1994b)

Isn't it exactly this "unforgettable" trait characterizing the majority of German intelligentsia in the 1930s that should actually be identified and factored in as an important, but too often forgotten, element in the history of German totalitarianism? Isn't it here that the research of the nature of totalitarian regimes should start from? Isn't it true that—despite the "others" being absolved by Hannah Arendt from the sin of "co-ordination" with totalitarian evil—the capacity for coordination was definitely not limited only to the German intellectuals and occurred in many other forms and in many other situations in Europe in the 20th century? Hannah Arendt's answer to these disturbing questions, based first on her own personal experiences and then tested

against the shocking realities and brutal facts of the European politics of her times, was unequivocal. The position she departed from in her inquiries into the nature of totalitarianism could be then formulated as follows:

• The emergence of autocratic political regimes in the 20th century that can be labeled totalitarian was not the result of an attack against Europe led by barbarous villains who came from the outside and struck like a bolt from the blue.
• It was enabled or at least facilitated by the striking inability of modern European societies to find individually or collectively, in the framework of the international system they created, an adequate response in the moment when the barbarians appeared.
• The rise and hitherto only temporary success of totalitarian movements is a historical turning point. Both Hitler's and Stalin's regimes were in the end defeated, but something irreversible and epoch-making happened through their attempts at global domination. After Auschwitz the world simply cannot be the same as before: "The subterranean stream of Western history has finally come to surface and usurped the dignity of our tradition." (Arendt, 1973)

Totalitarianism represents the most radical denial of human freedom, unknown and unprecedented in human history, and that is why the politics whose aim is to ward off this danger needs to start from a new beginning. The crimes again humanity, committed against millions of innocent people, genocides such as the Holocaust, which took place in the heart of "civilized" Europe, in the milieu of modern, enlightened, and progressive European society, whose most common reaction to all these horrors was neglect of the victims and the attitude of "coordination," have revealed the depth of the crisis of European civilization.

What comes under fire in the moment of confrontation with the totalitarian threat are not only the institutions of the modern nation-state but also the basic ideas and fundamental values underlying the modern European concept of politics. Neither social sciences, describing and analyzing social reality from the neutral, value-free point of view (equating totalitarianism "with some well-known evil of the past, such an aggression, tyranny, conspiracy"), nor the perspective of traditional liberal politics (committed to the protection of the free western world and fighting against its external totalitarian enemies) can help us find an adequate response to the most fundamental political problem we have faced in the 20th century. According to Hannah Arendt, the main difficulty with totalitarianism lies in out inability to understand it; "to reconcile ourselves to a world in which such things are possible at all; (Arendt, 1994a) to regain the capacity to act in the moment when totalitarian tendencies emerge in the midst of turmoil and political crises; to keep public space open even if the plurality of existing options are fading away under the given social and political circumstances and the seemingly invincible Laws of Nature or Laws of History are requiring our unconditional surrender and "coordination."

According to its own anamnesis, modernity liberated man from the shackles by which his Promethean human nature had been bound to the earth. It was the era of reason and science; the era of technological advances, industrialization, and urbanization; the era of fast development in all spheres of human life and the visible improvement of people's living conditions; the era that introduced the concept of religious tolerance; the era of social and political emancipation reaching all layers of the European population; the era when democracy, the rule by the many, which had appeared for the first time in ancient city-states, was rediscovered and adapted to the new conditions as a political form corresponding better than any other form of government to the progressive trends within European society; the era of constitutionalism, the rule of law and liberal politics, based on common sense and enlightened self-interest, subscribing to the concept of limited government and declaring respect for the unalienable, i.e., natural, rights of man; the era when equal sovereign states replaced the medieval Christian Empire in Europe and gradually invented all new forms and procedures of international law and politics; the era when the world—literally discovered by Europeans—was really "Eurocentric," i.e., Europe undisputedly played a leading role in world affairs.

The actual political experience of the 20th century, however, puts the whole modern period into a radically new perspective. Totalitarian governments have been created by political movements that have come into existence in the nontotalitarian world (Surely "they have not been imported from the moon," remarks Arendt ironically.) If we want to understand this event—according to Arendt the central event of our times and the main symptom of the crisis of European civilization—it is Europe's modernization project that has to be questioned and thoroughly reconsidered in the first place. Totalitarianism must be studied in the proper historical perspective and its "crystallizing elements" traced back to their origins in previous centuries.

Besides the rise of totalitarian movements themselves in the 1920s, whose sharp criticism of Western "decadent" liberalism was accompanied on the one side by their "avowed cynical 'realism'" and by "their conspicuous disdain of the whole texture of reality" on the other, there are two other 19th-century elements of totalitarianism that Arendt suggests we must take into account: anti-Semitism, which became a kind of secular ideology, widespread in the emancipated European national societies; and imperialism, the element of "expansion for expansion's sake," the limitless pursuit of power," which grew out of colonialism and was caused by the incongruity of the nation-state system with the economic and industrial developments in the last third of the nineteenth century." (Arendt, 1973)

> In this sense, it must be possible to face and understand the outrageous fact that so small (and in world politics, so unimportant) a phenomenon as the Jewish question and antisemitism could become the catalytic agent for first, the Nazi movement, than a world war, and finally the establishment of death factories. Or, the grotesque disparity between cause and effect which introduced the era of imperialism, when economic difficulties led, in a few decades, to a profound transformation of political conditions all over the world. (Arendt, 1973)

However, going back before the final crystallizing catastrophe took place in the 1930s, when Hitler seized power in Germany, does not mean for Arendt to get involved in anything like a scientific historiography: "I did not write a history of totalitarianism but an analysis in terms of history," she replied to Eric Voegelin's critical review of her seminal book. The aim of her study was not to offer a causal explanation of historical phenomena, but to let the event of the emergence of totalitarianism "illuminate its own past"; by enfolding the "story" in historical time to obtain better comprehension and it

> does not mean denying the outrageous, deducing the unprecedented from precedents, or explaining phenomena by such analogies and generalities, that the impact of reality and the shock of experience are no longer felt. It means, rather, examining and bearing consciously the burden which our century has placed on us—neither denying its existence nor submitting meekly to its weight. Comprehension, in short, means the unpremedi-

tated, attentive facing up to, and resisting of, reality—whatever it may be. (Arendt, 1973)

"The process of understanding is clearly and perhaps primarily, also a process of self-understanding," says Arendt, connecting her studies on anti-Semitism, imperialism, and totalitarianism with the debate concerning contemporary European politics. As we already said, the totalitarian movements emerged in Europe after the Great War (1914–1918). This first pan-European military conflagration after the long period of relative peace and prosperity (which began in 1815 when the Vienna Congress of leading European states ended the decades of turmoil and disorder triggered by the French Revolution) was indeed an epochal event. What changed after its termination was not only the political map of Europe, but also the general climate of ideas on the continent. European politics after the Paris Peace Conference (1919–1920) took place in an environment that was radically different from the prewar period, from the "world of yesterday" as we can learn about, for instance, from the autobiography of Stephan Zweig. As distinct from the wonderful and in many ways delirious and seductive "Belle époque" that European society was living through immediately before the First World War, the postwar era made Europeans to wake up to very different realities. What disappeared in the first place was the relaxed, self-confident "Eurooptimism" that accompanied the European politics throughout the whole 19th century. Four million members of European middle-class societies killed on the fronts were not the only victims of the first all-out conflict after 90 years of stability in Europe; there was also the central political idea of European modernity: the idea of progress.

The 20th century "has become indeed, as Lenin predicted," Arendt stated in the opening sentence of her study *On Violence,* "a century of wars and revolutions, hence a century of that violence which is currently believed to be their common denominator." (Arendt, 1970) It has become a century when European civilization, instead of leading the world to its better future, has found itself in mortal danger, threatened by the totalitarian attempt at global conquest and total domination. It has become a century that has undermined and radically problematized the very foundations of European modernity.

Never has our future been more unpredictable, never have we depended so much on political forces that cannot be trusted to follow the rules of common sense and self-interest—forces that

look like sheer insanity, if judged by the standards of other centuries. It is as though mankind had divided itself between those who believe in human omnipotence (who think that everything is possible if one knows how to organize masses for it) and those for whom powerlessness has become the major experience of their lives. (Arendt, 1973)

To understand the nature of totalitarianism presupposes the realization above all that in spite or their opposite attitudes as far as the necessary outcome of historical processes is concerned, "Progress and Doom are two sides of the same medal" that the task is not to stick to the one or the other and to become either a reckless optimist or a reckless prophet of despair, but to emancipate our thought from the superstition that all events in the human world are in the end dictated by "historical necessity." What Arendt tried to open up when studying totalitarian phenomena is an entirely new, paradigm of modernity that transcends the way we think about human history. What she had been looking for with her writing was a comprehension of the human situation that would help people regain insight into what they—and not the blind forces of Nature or History—are doing; a comprehension that aims at restoring the original "free," spontaneous character of human political activity, at recovering the dignity and the full power of human agency. To comprehend the totalitarian attempt at global conquest and total domination does not mean only to study certain sets of empirical observable facts—political and social systems, the methods of enforcement of state power, spontaneously grown worldviews and popular beliefs, the official state ideologies, and so on—but above all to be ready to receive from God the greatest gift a man could desire: the open or "understanding" heart King Solomon was praying for: "the divine gift of action, of being a beginning and therefore being able to make a beginning.

What can save us from the spell or curse our century of totalitarianism imposed on us is not an intervention from outside or from above, but our own capacity of what Arendt calls the faculty of imagination.

which alone enables to see things in their proper perspective, to be strong enough to put that which is too close at a certain distance so that we can see and understand it without bias and prejudice, to be generous enough to bridge abysses of remoteness until we can see and understand everything that is too far away from us as thought it were our own affair....

Without this kind of imagination, which actually is understanding, we would never be able to take our bearings in the world. We are contemporaries only so far our understanding reaches. If we want to be at home on this earth, even at the price of being at home in this century; we must try to take part in the interminable dialogue with the essence of totalitarianism. (Arendt, 1994a)

… human dignity needs a new guarantee which can be found in a new political principle, in a new law on the earth, whose validity this time must comprehend the whole of humanity while its power must remain strictly limited, rooted in and controlled by newly defined territorial entities.

IX. CONCLUSION

Hannah Arendt's reflections on the nature of totalitarianism bring us not only to the present stage of the totalitarian debate, but also back to the beginning of our article. What is at stake today is actually the original dilemma, the generic problem accompanying Western politics from the very beginning. The question is whether mankind will be able, under the conditions of global communications, complex inter-dependence and multiculturalism, to protect the fundamental human "value," that, according to Aristotle, makes the difference between the life whose aim is survival and self-protection and the "good" life. The question is whether the global commons, which are more and more on the agenda of world politicians, will enhance the need for global administration of human matters or will increase the chance for genuine global politics. Totalitarianism of the past should make us alert and cautious. Any future totalitarianism, using the lessons from the defeat of its predecessors and technically much more advanced, would undoubtedly be even more destructive and more dangerous to the human species.

Our global situation is rapidly changing and the New World Order is being designed and crafted. The collapse of communism put the end to the twentieth century, which was characterized by the emergence of totalitarian governments and by the domination of political ideologies. The case for freedom now seems to be pretty strong. So far, so good. But I am convinced that the idea of total domination is not going to disappear easily from our world and that the following appeal or maybe advice of Hannah Arendt, reacting to the totalitarian

horrors of World War II, should still be seriously considered and thought out by our politicians:

… human dignity needs a new guarantee which can be found only in a new political principle, in a new law on the earth, whose validity this time must comprehend the whole of humanity while its power must remain strictly limited rooted in and controlled by newly defined territorial entities. (Arendt, 1973)

Totalitarianism, in short, remains with us as the greatest threat for our civilization and the greatest temptation for those who are endowed in the current world with power. The future is open and if its openness is not to be lost, mankind must be aware what is going to be at stake after the great anniversary 2000: to maintain in emerging world politics the element of freedom which is still the essence and very nature of our humanity.

Also See the Following Articles

COLD WAR • GENOCIDE AND DEMOCIDE • PEACE AND DEMOCRACY • POLITICAL THEORIES

Bibliography

Arendt, Hannah (1970). *On Violence,* (Harcourt, Brace and World, Inc., New York, 1970).

Arendt, Hannah (1973). *The Origins of Totalitarianism,* (Harcourt, Brace, Jovanovich, New York and London, 1973).

Arendt, Hannah (1994a). Understanding and politics, in *Essays in Understanding 1930/1954,* (Jerome Kohn (ed.), Harcourt, Brace and Company, 1994).

Arendt, Hannah (1994b). What remains? The language remains: A conversation with Guntehr Gauss, in *Essays in Understanding 1930/1954,* (op. cit.)

Arendt, Hannah (1994c). A replay to Eric Voegelin, in *Essays in Understanding 1930/1954* (op. cit.)

Arendt, Hannah (1994d). *Eichmann in Jerusalem, The Report on the Banality of Evil,* Penguin Books, 1994.

Aron, Raymond (1974). *The Imperial Republic (The United States and the World, 1945–1973),* trans. by Frank Jellinek, (Prentice Hall Inc., Englewood Cliffs, New Jersey, 1974)

Bracher, Karl D. (1980). *Totalitarismus and Faschismus. Eine wissenschaftliche und politische Begriffskontroverse* (Kolloquium im Institut fuer Zeitgeschichte, am 24. November 1978, Muenchen-Wien-Oldenbourg, 1980)

Ecksteins, Modris (1989). *Rites of Spring. The Great War and the Birth of the Modern Age* (Lester and Orpen Dennys, 1989)

Friedrich, Carl J. (ed. and intro.) (1954). *Totalitarianism* (Proceedings of a conference held at the American Academy of Sciences, March 1953, (Harvard University Press, 1954)

Friedrich, Carl J. (ed.) (1967). *Totalitarian Dictatorship and Autocracy,* Frederick A. Praeger, New York, 1967)

Friedrich, Carl J. and Brzezinski Zbigniew (1956). *Totalitarian Dictatorships and Autocracy,*

Friedrich, Carl J. and Brzezinski Zbigniew (1967). Totalitarian dictatorship and autocracy, in Paul T. Mason (ed.), *Totalitarianism, Temporary Madness or Permanent Danger,* (D.C. Heath and Comp., 1967)

Friedrich Carl J., Curtis Michael, Barber Benjamin (1969). *Totalitarianism in Perspective. Three views,* (Praeger Publishers, New York, 1969)

Havel, Václav (1992). Stories and totalitarianism, in *Open Letters* (ed. by Paul Wilson, Vintage Books, 1992)

Isaac, Jeffrey C. (1992). *Arendt, Camus and Modern Rebellion* (Yale University Press, New Haven and London, 1992)

Kirkpatrick, Jean (1980). *Dictatorships and Double Standards,* (Harper, New York, 1980)

Kundera, Milar (1984). The Tragedy of Central Europe, *The New York Review of Books,* April 26, 1984

Mason, Paul T. (ed.) (1967). *Totalitarianism, Temporary Madness or Permanent Danger* (D.C. Heath and Comp., 1967)

Milosz, Czeslaw (1981). *The Captive Mind* (Vintage Books, New York, 1981)

Orwell, George (1970) Inside the Whale, in *A Collection of Essays,* (Harcourt, Brace, Jovanovich, 1970)

Patočka, Jan (1996). *Heretical Essays in the Philosophy of History* (transl. by Erazim Kohák and ed. by James Dodd, Open Court, Chicago and La Salle, 1996)

Paul, Ellen Frankel, (ed.) (1990). *Totalitarianism at the Crossroads,* (Transaction Books, New Brunswick, USA, and London, UK, 1990)

Spiro, Herbert J. (1970). Counter-Ideological Uses of Totalitarianism, *Politics and Society,* No. 1, (November 1970)

Vernant, Jean Paul (1982). *The Origins of Greek Thought,* transl. from the French, (Cornell University Press, Ithaca, N.Y., 1982)

Voegelin, Eric (1978). What is right by nature, in Gerhart Niemeyer (trans. and ed.) *Anamnesis,* (University of Missouri Press, 1978)

Wallace, Robert W. (1996). Athenian Law, Freedom, Rights, in (eds.) Josiah Ober and Charles Hedrick, *Demokratia: A Conversation on Democracies, Ancient and Modern* (Princeton University Press, 1996)

Wilson, Kevin and Dusen van der Jan (eds.) (1995). *The History of the Idea of Europe* (Routledge, London and New York, 1995)

Zweig, Stephan (1943). *The World of Yesterday: An Autobiography,* (Cassel, London, 1943)

Trade, Conflict, and Cooperation among Nations

Solomon W. Polachek and John Robst

State University of New York at Binghamton

Peace is the natural effect of trade. Two nations who traffic with each other become reciprocally dependent: for if one has the interest in buying, the other has the interest in selling; and thus their union is founded on the mutual necessities (Baron de Montesquieu, 1748).

GLOSSARY

Conflict Includes wars and other military acts as well as verbal expressions that display hostility.
Cooperation Includes voluntary unifications, formation of alliances, cultural or scientific agreements, and verbal expressions of support.
Trade The buying, selling, or exchange of commodities.

TRADE is hypothesized to reduce conflict and increase cooperation between countries. This article discusses the various approaches used to test these hypotheses and their results including the relationship between trade levels, trade gains and conflict–cooperation, methods for addressing causation issues, and the role of trade in determining whether democracies fight each other.

I. INTRODUCTION

Eradicating hostility and promoting cooperation is an important step leading to peace. Attempts to diminish hostility and bring about cooperation (between two countries) are often initiated by third-party nations. The problem is that "peace" imposed by others may be innately unstable, especially if the underlying differences originally separating the countries remain. For this reason, it seems that a more viable peace is one that exists naturally, without the need for outside intervention. This article concentrates on such types of coexistence in the hope that the peace science field has more valuable insights to gain from such a perspective.

Not all countries are in conflict. In fact, data indicate that, on average, more cooperation exists than conflict. Yet, during the Cold War some country pairs (dyads) such as the United States and the USSR exhibited great amounts of hostility even though the U.S. as well as the USSR relations with many other countries were extremely cooperative. If differences in dyadic conflict can be explained, these insights could help us understand how natural dyadic cooperation can evolve.

Specifically, a natural peace is one based in part on mutual dependencies. As will be explained, mutual dependence makes conflict more costly, thereby increasing the incentives toward cooperation and, hence, toward peace. Probably many kinds of mutual dependencies affect dyadic conflict–cooperation levels. By concentrating solely on mutual dependencies of an economic nature, this article provides only a partial illustration of the assertion.

In this article, international trade is taken as a measure of international economic dependence. How trade can enhance cooperation between countries is modeled. While perhaps an old idea, the article presents a cogent theoretical model with rigorous empirical tests. The logic is simple. If conflict leads to a cessation or at least a diminution of trade (perhaps through tariffs or quotas), then countries with the greatest gains from trade face the highest costs of conflict and hence engage in the least conflict and the most cooperation. In addition, the more essential and strategic the trade (i.e., the stronger the dependence), the greater the deterrent effect of trade on conflict.

II. INTERNATIONAL TRADE

Individuals do not produce everything they need. They find it advantageous to specialize. Division of labor comes about because persons work at what they do best and trade for what they produce inefficiently. International trade occurs for the same reason. One country is not able to produce all it needs as efficiently as another. A country is said to have a comparative advantage over another when it is relatively more efficient in the production of a particular commodity. The existence of comparative advantages enables both countries to increase their own welfare through trade. Loss of existing trade because of conflict, for example, would imply potential welfare losses. It is these potential welfare losses that deter conflict.

The inverse relationship between trade and conflict is not merely asserted. Instead, a logical justification using economic theory is given. The basic model assumes what is standard economic theory, namely that countries maximize their own social welfare by obtaining the highest levels of material well-being possible. Given cross-country differences in technology and factor (resource) endowments, any one country can raise its social welfare by specializing in domestic production of commodities for which it has a comparative advantage and trading for commodities produced relatively less efficiently. Thus, given different technologies and factor endowments across countries, trade patterns emerge.

A world system encompasses numerous countries, many trading with each other because the virtues of trade make each country better off economically. What results is a system of intercountry interdependencies, which, if based on free market principles including free trade and the full mobility of resources, would result in maximal global output. As discussed above, any country breaking off such a trade relation would decrease its own long-term economic well-being, as well as perhaps the well-being of its trading partners and other countries. As such, reneging on a trade relationship is costly from a private as well as a global perspective.

Dyads with the most trade are expected to exhibit the least conflict (and most cooperation). This hypothesis has a history emanating from the intellectual and commercial exchanges that brought long eras of peace throughout the 19th and early 20th centuries. Blainey (1988, p. 18) states: "The long peace that followed the Battle of Waterloo was increasingly explained as a result of the international flow of commodities and ideas." Read (1967, p. 146) says: "Cobden (the renowned 19th-century British statesman) hoped that he had begun genuinely to persuade the peoples and Government of Europe that free trade could be 'not only a law of wealth and prosperity but a law of friendship … a web of concord woven between peoples and people.'" Others, such as John Bright, Henry Thomas Buckle, Sir Robert Peel, William Gladstone, John Stuart Mill, and Albert the Good proposed "variations of the same idea" (Blainey, 1988, p. 19). Unfortunately World War I—the most bitter, long-lasting, all-encompassing war among trading partners—seems to have been sufficient to dispel much faith in this theory of peace. The abandonment of this theory based on one data point (albeit one carrying a strong weight) may have been premature.

Hirschman (1945) emphasizes "the politics of foreign trade" by which he means "the possibility of using trade as a means of political pressure … in the pursuit of power" (pp. v and xvi). Decreasing trade lowers the gains from trade though the losses can be mitigated if the country finds other trading partners. Nevertheless, the cost of conflict is the resulting lost gains from trade associated with lower trade levels as well as the higher costs of trade associated with finding new trade avenues. As such, conflictual behavior is more costly the greater

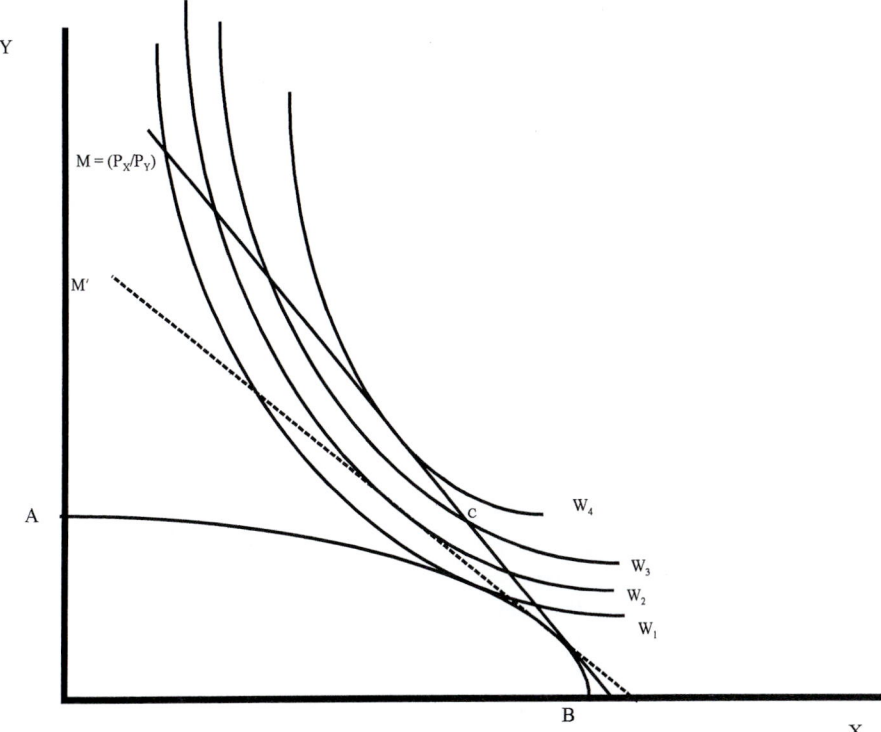

FIGURE 1 The gains from trade (X and Y are representative commodities).

these gains-from-trade losses. As indicated, the mechanism by which a country decreases trade is tricky. Obviously embargoes and quotas are possibilities. This leads to a predicted inverse relationship between trade and conflict.

Conflict is assumed to affect the terms of trade. Specifically, greater levels of conflict make trade more difficult. Reasons include retaliatory tariffs, quotas, embargoes, and other trade prohibitions. Conflict raises the costs of trade, thereby making at least one of the countries worse off (in a welfare sense). The implicit price of being hostile is the diminution of welfare associated with potential trade losses.

This can easily be illustrated geometrically (Fig. 1). Define curve AB to reflect a country's production possibility frontier. This curve defines the maximum combinations of commodities x and y that can be produced in a given country. Curves w_1, w_2, w_3, and w_4 represent, in ascending order, potential domestic welfare levels. Welfare level w_1 would be the maximum attainable if no trade were permitted. However, if trade is permitted at the price ratio given by the line segment with slope m, this welfare level can be raised to w_4. Restrictions of trade such as embargoes that do not affect the terms

of trade lower potential welfare perhaps to w_3 (point C). Restrictions of trade that affect prices may result in less desirable terms of trade m' and a new equilibrium and welfare level, w_2. Thus the price of being belligerent is an implicit price that increases with the level of trade. *Ceteris paribus*, the greater the amount of trade, the higher the price of conflict and the less the amount of conflict that is demanded.

III. MEASURING POLITICAL INTERACTION

There are many philosophical problems in measuring political interactions. Questions exist concerning what constitutes hostility and cooperation as well as how and to whom such activities occur. Presumably, measures of interaction should entail answers to these questions. Unfortunately, as we shall see, this is often not the case.

Many deficiencies are embedded in various measures. Common measures include defense expenditures, data on wars, and casualty estimates. However, there are problems with these measures. In a sense, defense expenditures indicate general levels of a country's hostility. Yet defense expenditures need not reflect aggressiveness at all. In fact, such expenditures could be viewed as a warning to other nations, serving the purpose of deterring the outbreak of armed conflict. Alternatively, they can even be a measure of domestic repression. Yet, even if defense expenditures did constitute a measure of conflict, such expenditures do not yield information about to whom hostilities are vented. Nor can one infer the type of conflict. War data, such as Correlates of War (COW), yield information on a particular kind of conflict and on the particular participants. However, war (defined in COW as 1000 or more battle-related deaths) is a particularly intensive form of interaction, and the number of dead or wounded varies with technology as well as country size. The Militarized Interstate Dispute (MID) data includes a broader range of conflict than COW, but still excludes relatively minor forms of conflict. None of these data deal with cooperation between countries. Similarly, United Nations General Assembly voting behavior need not reflect actual conflict between countries and often deals with a subset of possible country interactions.

Because of these deficiencies, a different measure of dyadic interaction is frequently used, entailing the use of events data. The problem with events data is that they comprise interactions reported in newspapers. Many secret treaties and negotiations as well as subtle international dealings not reported in newspapers are obviously omitted. However, the benefit of events data is that they measure cooperation as well as hostility. In addition, actor and target countries can easily be identified. Precise measures of the amounts of different kinds of hostility can be ascertained as well.

Studies discussed in this article typically use the Conflict and Peace Data Bank (COPDAB), an extensive, longitudinal collection of more than 350,000 daily and yearly events reported by dyad from 47 newspaper sources. The COPDAB data span 1948–1979, starting with a 35 country sample and eventually increasing to 135 countries. Events are coded on a 15-point scale representing different kinds of conflict and cooperation. The annual frequency of events in each category represents the amount of each type of dyadic interaction from an actor to a target country. The overall amount of conflict between two countries is often denoted as net conflict (NETF) and computed as the frequency of conflictual events (those in categories 9 to 15) minus the frequency of cooperative events (1 to 7). A negative value of NETF implies that more events fall into categories 1–7 than 9–15; hence, that a cooperative interaction exists. A positive value implies that the preponderance of events fall into categories 9–15 so that on balance a conflict relationship exists. It is interesting to note that this summary conflict statistic is comparable to that suggested by Richardson (1960, p. 30), who states:

> Usually both threats and co-operation are going on simultaneously; so that as we have restricted ourselves to a single variable for one group, that variable must represent the net result, the excess of threats over co-operation.

The NETF differs from Richardson, as the research discussed here use frequencies of events data.

IV. CONFLICT AND TRADE

Polachek was among the first to examine the relationship between trade and dyadic interactions. He claimed that dyads with the most trade have the most to lose from conflict and hence have lesser amounts of conflict. This section analyzes the validity of such a supposition.

Bivariate regression analysis treating conflict as a function of trade is used initially. Its form is given in Eqs. (1) and (2) below:

$$NETF_{ij} = \alpha_0 + \alpha_1 x_{ij} + \varepsilon \qquad (1)$$
$$NETF_{ij} = \beta_0 + \beta_1 m_{ij} + \varepsilon, \qquad (2)$$

where NETF = net conflict of country i toward country j, x_{ij} = exports of country i to country j in U.S. dollars, m_{ij} = imports to country i from country j in U.S. dollars, and ε = a random error term assumed normally distributed with mean zero. The problem with bivariate regression is that other factors such as country attributes can influence this relationship. In general, country size would affect conflict and trade. So might population density (crowding hypothesis), defense expenditures (a general measure of country hosility), as well as other considerations. To net out these latter factors, multiple regression analysis is considered in addition to the bivariate regressions models. The equations take the forms:

$$NETF_{ij} = \alpha_0 + \alpha_1 x_{ij} + \alpha_2 A_i + \alpha_3 A_j + \varepsilon \qquad (3)$$
$$NETF_{ij} = \beta_0 + \beta_1 m_{ij} + \beta_2 A_i + \beta_3 A_j + \varepsilon, \qquad (4)$$

where A is a vector of country attributes for each actor and target country and other variables are as defined above. Negative coefficients for α_1 and β_1 would imply that countries with greater trade dependencies engage in less net conflict. For these coefficients a consistent pattern appears. Whether bivariate or multivariate forms are used, negative and statistically significant signs pervade for a sample of 30 countries from 1958 to 1967 (see Table I). This means that dyads engaged in the most trade have the least conflict even when adjusting for country attributes. A 1% increase in trade would decrease conflict (increase cooperation) by between .15 and .19%. Thus doubling trade between two countries would lead to about a 15 to 19% decline in the net frequency of dyadic hostility.

We argue that trade is generally a beneficial form of interdependence; however, Gasiorowski suggests interdependence can be both beneficial and costly. Trade is considered to be a beneficial aspect of interdependence due to the existence of "gains from trade." Countries with few (or one) trading partners, may find such interdependence costly as adjustments to trade disruptions may be difficult (see the section on trade gains for a more detailed discussion of this issue). Gasiorowski makes several extensions to Polachek's work, expanding the COPDAB sample to 130 countries covering 1948–1977. Polachek aggregates events without regard to the intensity of the events, with wars and other serious events given the same weight as mild conflict. Gasiorowski uses weights to adjust for the intensity of the event. Further support is provided for an inverse relationship between conflict and trade.

Arad and Hirsch concentrate on the potential gains from peace in the Middle East. As tensions between

Egypt and Israel fell with the signing of the Egyptian–Israeli Peace Treaty in 1979, Arad and Hirsch argue that trade should increase, making both countries better off economically. While trade has increased, tensions in the Middle East continue to be high, limiting increases in trade.

Domke (1988) examines the relationship between exports (as a share of GNP) and the outbreak of war. Instead of using data on dyadic relationships, Domke uses monadic data, treating each country as an observation. Separate regressions are estimated for 31 of the 98 years between 1877 and 1974. An inverse relationship exists in 10 of the 14 years considered before World War I and 9 of the 10 years looked at after World War II. The conflict–trade relationship is weakest between the wars, but an inverse relationship is found in 4 of the 7 years during this time frame.

Sayrs also examines the trade–conflict relationship using COPDAB data but considers conflict and cooperation separately instead of using net conflict. She finds support for the proposition that trade reduces conflict but does not find evidence trade increases cooperation.

Studies also focus on more severe forms of conflict in war data. Mansfield (1994) focuses on several different types of wars to examine the trade–war relationship. All inter-state wars, wars including major powers, and those that do not involve a major power are considered. Instead of looking at dyads or monads, Mansfield examines global trade and conflict. In each case, global trade reduces the likelihood of war.

An alternative vantage is to examine whether conflict influences trade. For example, Pollins and Gowa each consider trade to be the endogenous variable and conflict to be the exogenous variable. Each find a significant negative relationship between trade and conflict, with these results suggesting that the direction of causation (whether trade reduces conflict or conflict reduces trade) is an important issue. We address this issue below.

Yet, another group of researchers argues that trade increases conflict. World resources are scarce and countries compete for such resources. Trade often leads to friction between countries as scarce resources become depleted. Others suggest that countries attempt to acquire the resources of other countries through military force instead of trade. Thus countries may view conflict and trade as substitutes to acquire resources. While not focusing on these theories Barbieri finds economic interdependence increases the likelihood of militarized inter-state disputes but has little impact on the likelihood of war.

TABLE I

Impact of Trade on Net Conflict[a]

Equation	Adjustment for country attributes	Independent variable	Intercept	Coefficient
(1)	No	Exports	−1.3241 (13.7)	−.0028 (13.3)
(2)	No	Imports	−1.3341 (13.8)	−.0027 (12.8)
(3)	Yes	Exports	−.0984 (0.1)	−.0023 (9.8)
(4)	Yes	Imports	−.1119 (0.1)	−.0023 (9.9)

[a] Absolute value of t statistics in parentheses.
Source: Polachek (1980).

V. SIMULTANEITY

The results linking trade and conflict discussed above do not indicate the direction of causality. They cannot ascertain whether trade diminishes conflict or whether, in fact, the reverse is true, and it is really conflict that reduces trade. This distinction is crucial for policy purposes. Trade is postulated as an instrument to reduce conflict. If trade is only a response to preexisting conflict levels, then no viable policy implications for the reduction of conflict would be obtained.

One approach entails the use of dyadic time-series data. If changes in trade levels are associated with corresponding changes in political behavior, then causality can be established on the basis of leads and lags in the time series data. To illustrate, Gasiorowski and Polachek take advantage of COPDAB's long time span to examine the U.S. and Soviet Union between 1967 and 1979. These countries are important because of the volatility in U.S.–Soviet relations during these years. Recall the easing of U.S.–Soviet hostilities in the détente period of the late 1960s and early 1970s and the abrupt shift that began to take place in the mid-1970s.

Figure 2 plots the trade–conflict relationship. Warsaw pact conflict directed at the United States is given on the vertical axis and U.S.–Warsaw Pact trade is on the horizontal axis. The trade measures, consisting of the sum of imports and exports, are given in real quar-

terly dollars. The conflict measures are intensity-weighted sums of conflictual events, aggregated quarterly from the COPDAB data. The solid lines are linear and hyperbolic fits of the 1967–1976 data. The inverse relationship between conflict and trade is clear in this figure. In addition, it is evident that the relationship is hyperbolic rather than linear. The data from the 1976–1978 period appear to have a flat but slightly negative slope, indicating that the level of conflict varied little in this period with changes in the level of trade.

Time-series data enable one to compute Granger-type causality tests. With time-series data, one can ascertain whether trade levels in one period affect future conflict levels and vice versa. Put simply, increases in explanatory power induced by lagged trade values in a regression expressing conflict as a function of trade would be indicative of causality running from trade to conflict. Table II contains probability values for Granger F tests of the null hypothesis that trade does not cause conflict (column 1) and that conflict does not cause trade (column 2). Low probability values (e.g., less than .05) indicate rejection of the hypothesis while high values indicate no causality. The null hypothesis that lagged values of trade do not significantly affect present conflict is rejected for the first six lag periods. The hypothesis that lagged conflict does not affect present trade is rejected only in lag periods 4 through 6. These results are consistent with trade affecting political inter-

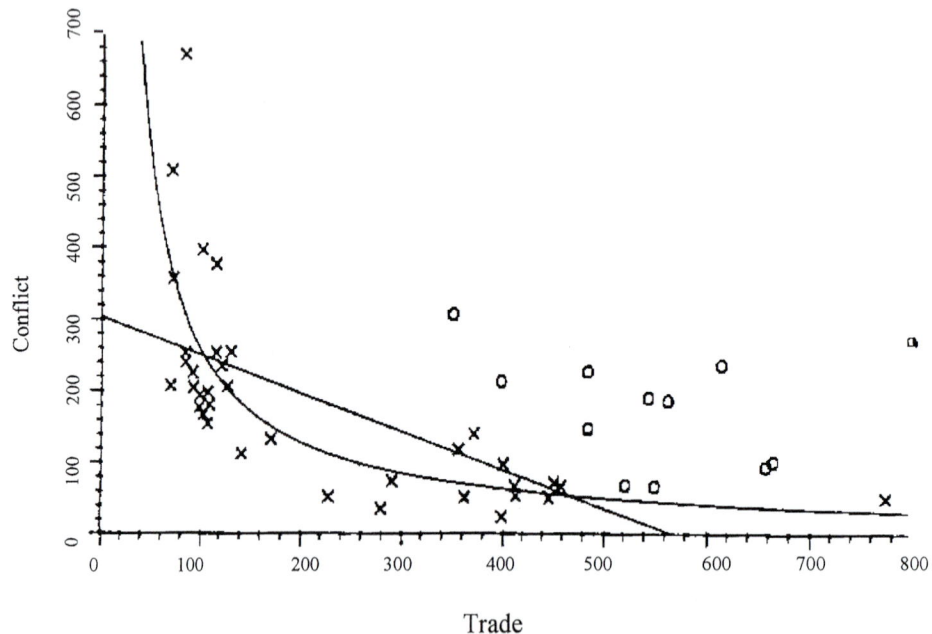

FIGURE 2   Conflict versus trade (1967–1975 values: X; 1976–1978 values: O).

TABLE II

Probability Values for the Granger Causality Test, 1967–1978[a]

Lag periods	(1) Trade causes net conflict	(2) Net conflict causes trade
1	.0009	.1046
2	.0018	.3165
3	.0004	.1394
4	.0054	.0110
5	.0071	.0201
6	.0126	.0240
7	.0874	.0661
8	.0515	.0604
9	.1917	.1486
10	.2739	.2300

[a] Column (1) gives the probability values for tests of the hypothesis that trade does not cause conflict. Column (2) tests the converse hypothesis that conflict does not cause trade. Low probability values (e.g., less than .05) indicate that the hypothesis is rejected; high values indicate acceptance. Lag periods indicate the number of quarters over which Granger causality is tested.

Source: Gasiorowski and Polachek (1982).

actions. These results were viewed as strengthening the findings that trade affects conflict.

Reuveny and Kang extend Gasiorowski and Polachek's research. Instead of looking only at U.S.–Warsaw pact or U.S.–Soviet.Union relations, they consider 18 different dyads that include developing and developed countries; major powers such as the U.S. and USSR; and countries from Africa, Europe, Asia, and South and North America. They also use Granger causality tests and find trade reduces conflict *and* conflict reduces trade. Interestingly, they also show the number of significant lags on net conflict is only one to four quarters. Thus the use of annual data may not reveal a conflict reduces trade result.

In subsequent work, Reuveny and Kang take this issue a step further by disaggregating trade based on commodity groups. Trade data from the United Nations are used to divide total trade into 10 commodity groups. Conflict tends to Granger cause trade in metals, petroleum, manufactures, and high technology. Trade causes conflict when measuring trade in food, live animals, beverages, and consumer goods. These results suggest a model is needed that simultaneously determines trade and conflict.

Polachek uses such a model. In effect, trade is an endogenous predetermined variable in the equations. As such, two-stage least-squares (TSLS) is an appro-

priate econometric technique for estimation in the presence of endogeneity. In fact, not using TSLS would imply potentially biased estimates because trade would be correlated with the residual (ε). Results indicate that causality is as predicted. An even stronger, more negative coefficient is obtained. Thus even when accounting for simultaneity, causality still runs from trade to conflict. Increases in trade diminish conflict. In elasticity terms, the coefficients imply that a doubling of trade could reduce conflict by over 30%.

An alternative approach entails appropriately lagging the trade data. If trade is measured before the conflict occurs, clearly trade must be the causal variable. Oneal et al. use such an approach with MIDs data from 1950 through 1985 and find lagged trade reduces conflict.

VI. TRADE GAINS

Thus far, theory has shown that trading countries experience a welfare gain. Conflict was assumed to hamper trade by implicitly raising costs through tariffs, quotas, and other means. Trading countries with significant trade relations would thus engage in less conflict because they are most threatened by welfare losses associated with lost trade. It seems at least intuitively clear that a corollary exists. Conflict would be most sensitive to trade of commodities particularly strategic to an economy. The reason is obvious. Even small amounts of trade of essential commodities yield high welfare gains. However, Dumas argues that exploitative trade may increase conflict. Thus, the country owning the strategic commodity has an incentive not to exploit its market power. Both countries must have welfare gains in order for trade to have a mitigating effect on conflict.

To test these hypotheses, one would need data not only on gross commodity trade flows, but also on some measure of the welfare gain (a synonym for how strategic the commodity is to the country's welfare). Initial studies did not have such data and thus only perform cursory tests.

It is well known that certain countries have unique attributes that give some indication of their trade. For example, Saudi Arabia exports mostly oil—a strategic commodity to many countries. (Saudi Arabia's exports outweighed its imports 4 : 1 for the 1958–1967 time frame.) A priori because of the strategic value of oil, one would expect countries trading with Saudi Arabia to experience large welfare losses if trading were to cease. Thus, these countries should be sensitive to Saudi Arabian trade. Since Saudi Arabia is such a large exporter of strategic material, it need not be as sensitive to other countries.

This hypothesis concerning the sensitivity of the trade–conflict relationship to the strategic nature of trade is tested. Regressions of the same nature as above (Eqs. (1) and (2)) run on a country-by-country basis yield insight concerning this relationship. For example, to use the Saudi Arabian illustration, regressions should yield a low export elasticity (i.e., a small impact of trade on conflict) when Saudi Arabia is an actor trading with the rest of the world and a high elasticity when Saudi Arabia is treated as a target by the rest of the countries.

Regressions limiting the actor or target to particular countries yield these kinds of expected results. The trade–conflict elasticity with Saudi Arabia as actor is −.15. The negative sign implies that trade actually increases hostility. A country exporting an exceedingly strategic commodity can use its monopoly power without worry about being hostile. When Saudi Arabia is viewed as a target, the elasticity is well above average at 0.65. Apparently oil importers minimize hostility to Saudi Arabia.

These kinds of patterns emerge during the 1958–1967 time frame for other countries as well. Libya, also an oil exporter, has the same pattern of coefficients. Similar results are obtained for East Germany, which appears to be a net exporter. The same logic should apply to large self-sufficient countries. Thus the United States, with large amounts of trade, should have a large trade–conflict elasticity when viewed as a target country. Small countries with a balance of payments problem should be highly sensitive to trade. This is the case for Israel and Lebanon.

Subsequent studies take steps to more directly incorporate welfare gains, though data limitations still force certain simplifications. One must obtain welfare gains implicitly as consumer and producer surpluses computed as the area under import–demand and over export–supply curves. The more inelastic the import–demand and export–supply curves the greater the levels of consumer and producer surplus. The greater these surpluses, the smaller the incidence of conflict, holding trade levels constant. For this reason inelastic import–demand curves and export–supply curves should serve to decrease conflict just as does greater trade. Aggregate import demand curves are used rather than commodity specific demand elasticities. An actor's demand from the rest of the world is used rather than dealing with dyadic bilateral demand though this simplification is eliminated below.

Regressions are run looking at the relationship between import demand elasticities, levels of trade, coun-

try attributes, and a measure of conflict. Countries are used as the unit of observation since elasticities are computed at the country level. Despite drastic aggregation, a statistically strong positive association between conflict and the import–demand elasticities emerge. The more inelastic the import–demand curve, the less the conflict. Further, the inverse trade–conflict relationship's statistical significance strengthens considerably.

The International Monetary Fund Directions of Trade data has been used to compute dyadic import elasticities, including income (both long-term and short-term), price, and cross-price elasticities. Eight country groups to match the Federal Reserve Board Multicountry model were considered: Canada, Germany, Japan, United Kingdom, United States, Other Industrial countries, OPEC, non-OPEC developing countries, and the rest of the world. The disaggregation yielded 178 dyads. The regression results are reported in Table III. As before, trade is inversely related to conflict for these dyads, but the relationship is far stronger than before. Import elasticities also remain a strong deterrent to conflict.

This analysis is extended by incorporating bilateral demand elasticities disaggregated by commodities. Three merchandise trade categories (manufactures, agricultural goods, and raw materials) for 14 of the largest OECD industrial countries are considered. Again, the results are consistent with expectations, as a positive

TABLE III
Impact of Trade on Net Conflict Enhanced by Dyadic Trade Elasticities[a]

Variable	Coefficient
Constant	−50.49
	(3.12)
Dyadic trade elasticity	37.62
	(2.63)
Exports (billions U.S.$)	−4.49
	(4.47)
Imports (billions U.S.$)	−8.21
	(6.86)
GNP (actor)	.0178
	(0.46)
GNP (actor) − GNP (target)	−.056
	(2.20)
R^2	.35
Number of observations	178

[a] Absolute value of t statistics in parentheses.

Source: Polachek (1992).

relationship emerges for commodity import elasticities and conflict.

VII. DEMOCRACY, TRADE, AND CONFLICT

Ever since 1979, when Rudolph Rummel cited Babst's 1972 war data research that wars are not fought between democracies, a plethora of empirical work evolved attempting to test the proposition that democracies rarely fight each other. This proposition is noteworthy because earlier work considered democracies to be no less war prone than other states.

Steve Chan rectified these differences regarding whether democracies deter conflict. His solution to the problem is mostly methodological: Monadic studies using single countries as the units of observation fail to support the contention that democracies rarely fight. On the other hand, strong support emerges that democracies rarely fight each other using dyads as units of observations. Indeed, using the Correlates of War data, Chan finds overwhelming support that "the more libertarian *two* states [are] the less the *mutual* [our emphasis] violence" (Chan, 1984, p. 620) while he finds little support that "the more libertarian a state, the less its foreign violence" (Chan, 1984, p. 620). Chan's study thus served as an impetus for a number of dyadic-based tests of the hypothesis. These, in turn, have led to a number of further studies seeking reasons why the relationship holds.

Polachek also analyzes the question of why democracies fight less. The innovation is to show that democracies are richer and have more trade. To protect this wealth democracies conflict somewhat less and cooperate considerably more. Nondemocracies have less to protect and as a consequence conflict more and cooperate less. In fact, when controlling for trade, democratic dyads have net conflict similar to nondemocracies. These results are provided in Table IV. Oneal et al. consider a similar question using MIDs data and find that both trade and democracy reduced conflict between 1950 and 1986.

VIII. EXTENDING THE BASIC MODEL

Whereas liberal theory stops with the basic trade–conflict relationship, the model can be extended to derive additional results. Polachek et al. extend the expected utility approach to derive propositions relating how other political and economic factors affect conflict.

TABLE IV
The Impact of Democracy and Trade on Net Conflict[a]

Variable[b]	(1)	(2)	(3)	(4)	(5)
Intercept	−1.92	−1.01	−1.91	−1.71	−3.00
	(8.42)	(8.11)	(8.42)	(9.20)	(10.0)
DD	−1.51		−0.48		0.37
	(4.18)		(1.26)		(0.9)
DN	0.85		0.94		2.1
	(2.60)		(2.91)		(5.50)
ND	2.58		2.66		2.4
	(7.78)		(8.91)		(6.10)
Exports		−0.003	−0.003	−.003	−.003
		(10.39)	(8.23)	(8.50)	(6.80)
GNP-actor				−1.3 E-8	−1.4 E-8
				(11.7)	(12.5)
GNP-target				7.6 E-9	6.5 E-9
				(6.60)	(2.50)
Pop-actor				2.0 E-5	2.0 E-5
				(12.4)	(12.0)
Pop-target				4.7 E-6	4.3 E-6
				(2.80)	(5.0)
R^2	0.025	0.021	0.038	0.08	0.09

[a] Absolute values of t statistics in parentheses.

[b] DD is a dummy variable equaling 1 if the actor and target are democracies; ND equals 1 if only the target is a democracy; DN equals 1 if only the target is a democracy.

Source: Polachek (1994).

A. Tariffs

Tariffs imposed by a target decrease the price the actor country receives for imports. Thus, tariffs can be viewed as directly reducing trade. As such, tariffs have the same impact as a trade reduction; hence, tariffs increase conflict. An actor increases conflict with trading partners that impose tariffs.

B. Foreign Aid

Political scientists often look at the impact of foreign aid on international relations. One can view foreign aid simply as a transfer payment from one country to another. Take the case when an actor has political relations with two target countries and examine the effect of one target country offering aid to the actor. To the extent such aid must be used to purchase the target's exports, foreign aid enables the actor to purchase additional imports from the actor. The increased trade increases the actor's cost of conflict with the target. Foreign aid reduces the actor's conflict vented toward the foreign aid provider.

C. Contiguity

Many argue that contiguous countries are more conflict prone, thus implying that distance deters conflict. Others provide evidence of a link between distance and trade. Many of the same arguments are used to support an inverse relationship between distance and trade and distance and conflict. It has been suggested that contiguous countries have greater conflict since they have more contact, while common interests lead to greater trade between contiguous countries. Contiguous countries may be more conflictual; however, an indirect effect of distance on conflict exists through trade. Although transportation costs are a relatively small component of trade, distance nevertheless makes trade more expensive. As a result contiguity enhances trade thereby indirectly decreasing conflict or at least increasing cooperation.

D. Economic Size of Country

Economic theory distinguishes between small and large countries. A small country by virtue of its economy's size has no real influence on international prices. On the other hand, a large country can affect the international price through its volume of trade. This means that the effect of trade on conflict might differ depending on whether one trades with a small or large country.

Two vantages are considered. First, from the actor country's vantage and, second, from the target country's vantage. Viewing interaction from the actor's viewpoint (see Fig. 3), there are two possibilities: (1) the actor can trade with a small country or (2) the actor can trade with a large country. Trade with a large country decreases conflict more than trade with a small country. The logic is as follows: Conflict with a large country is

more costly since large countries more dramatically influence trading prices. These effects have a greater impact on the cost of conflict the higher the level of trade.

Similarly, changes in actor size are important. But since relatively small targets have less of an influence on price, trade results in a greater reduction in conflict for a small actor trading with a large target than a large actor trading with a small target.

IX. CONCLUSION

This article has provided an overview of the conflict–trade literature. The majority of the literature supports a link between conflict and trade, with trade reducing dyadic conflict and increasing cooperation. There are exceptions to this general conclusion and future work should attempt to reconcile the findings. There are many areas that still need to be addressed in this literature. While trade tends to reduce conflict for most dyads, there are cases where trade increases conflict. It would be useful to study possible reasons for the differing relationships between dyads.

Also See the Following Articles

CONFLICT MANAGEMENT AND RESOLUTION • ECONOMIC CAUSES OF WAR AND PEACE • PEACE AND DEMOCRACY • SOCIAL THEORIZING ABOUT WAR AND PEACE • TERRITORIAL DISPUTES

Bibliography

Arad, R. W., & Hirsch, S. (1981). Peacemaking and vested interests: International economic transactions. *International Studies Quarterly, 25,* 439–468.

Azar, E. (1980). The conflict and peace data bank (COPDAB) project. *Journal of Conflict Resolution, 24,* 143–152.

Babst, D. V. (1972). A force for peace. *Industrial Research, 14,* 55–58.

Barbieri, K. (1996a). Economic interdependence: A path to peace or a source of interstate conflict? *Journal of Peace Research, 33,* 29–50.

Barbieri, K. (1996b). Risky business: The impact of trade linkages on interstate conflict, 1870–1985. In G. Schneider & P. A. Weitsman (Eds.), *Enforcing cooperation: "Risky" states and the intergovernmental management of conflict.* London: St. Martin's Press.

Blainey, G. (1988). *The causes of war.* Basingstoke: Macmillan.

Chan, S. (1984). Mirror, mirror on the wall . . . are the freer countries more pacific? *Journal of Conflict Resolution, 28,* 617–648.

de Montesquieu, B. (1748 1900). *The spirit of laws* (translated by T. Nugent) New York: Collier.

Domke, W. K. (1988). *War and the changing global system.* New Haven: Yale University Press.

Dumas, L. (1990). Economics and alternative security: Toward a peacekeeping international economy. In B. Weston (Ed.), *Alter-*

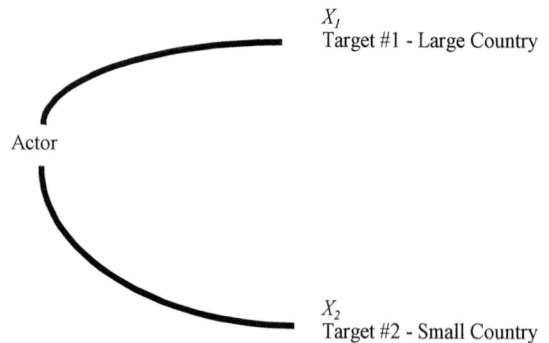

FIGURE 3 Interactions by size of country. X_1 = actor's exports to target 1 (target 1's imports from actor); X_2 = actor's exports to target 2 (target 2's imports from actor).

native security: Living without nuclear deterrence. Boulder, CO: Westview.

Gasiorowski, M. (1986). Economic interdependence and international conflict: Some cross-national evidence. *International Studies Quarterly, 30,* 23–28.

Gasiorowski, M., & Polachek, S. W. (1982). Conflict and interdependence. *Journal of Conflict Resolution, 26,* 709–729.

Gowa, J. (1994). *Allies, adversaries, and international trade.* Princeton, NJ: Princeton University Press.

Hirschman, A. O. (1945 1980). *National power and the struggle of foreign trade.* Berkeley: University of California Press.

Mansfield, E. D. (1994). *Power, trade and war.* Princeton, NJ: Princeton University Press.

Oneal, J. R., Oneal, F. H., Maoz, Z., & Russett, B. (1996). The liberal peace: Interdependence, democracy, and international conflict, 1950–86. *Journal of Peace Research, 33,* 11–28.

Polachek, S. W. (1978). Dyadic dispute: An economic perspective. *Papers of the Peace Science Society, 28,* 67–80.

Polachek, S. W. (1980). Conflict and trade. *Journal of Conflict Resolution, 24,* 55–78.

Polachek, S. W. (1992). Conflict and trade: An economics approach to political international interactions. In (Eds.) W. Isard & C. Anderton (Eds.) *Economics of armies reduction and the peace process,* New York: Elsevier.

Polachek S. W. (1994). Cooperation and conflict among democracies: Why do democracies cooperate more and fight less?" Paper presented at the Peace Science Society (International) Meeting, Urbana–Champaign, November. Forthcoming in M. Wolfson (Ed.) *The political economy of war and peace.* Norwell, MA: Kluwer.

Polachek, S. W. (1997). Why democracies cooperate more and fight less: The relationship between international trade and cooperation. *Review of International Economics, 5,* 295–309.

Polachek, S. W., & McDonald, J. (1992). Strategic trade and incentives for cooperation. In M. Chatterji & L. Forcey (Ed.), *Disarmament, economic conversion and the management of peace.* New York: Praeger.

Polachek, S. W., Chang, Y. C., & Robst, J. (1997). Extending the role of trade to better understand international interactions. Working paper, SUNY–Binghamton.

Pollins, B. (1989a). Does trade still follow the flag? *American Political Science Review, 83,* 465–480.

Pollins, B. (1989b). Conflict cooperation and commerce: The effect of international political interactions. *American Journal of Political Science, 33,* 737–761.

Read, D. (1967). *Cobden and Bright: A Victorian political partnership.* London: Edward Arnold.

Reuveny, R., & Kang, H. (1996). International trade, political conflict/cooperation, and Granger causality. *American Journal of Political Science, 40,* 943–970.

Reuveny, R., & Kang, H. (1997). Bilateral Trade and Political Conflict/Cooperation: Do Goods Matter? *Journal of Peace Research, 35,* 581–602.

Richardson, N. R. (1960). *Arms and insecurity.* Chicago: Quadrangle.

Rummel, R. J. (1979). War, power, peace: Understanding conflict and war (Vol. 4). Beverly Hills/London: Sage.

Sayrs, L. W. (1989). Trade and conflict revisited: Do politics matter? *International Interactions, 14,* 155–175.

Trade and the Environment

Janet Welsh Brown

World Resources Institute

I. INTRODUCTION

The 1990s have been marked by sharp disagreements between environmentalists and promoters of trade. Many environmentalists think that the environmental effects of increasing trade flows must be tackled within the trading system itself and regulated through trade agreements, while most of the trade enthusiasts think of the liberalization and expansion of trade as a goal in itself and of environmental effects as externalities that should be controlled in the production process or use of products, but not within the trading system. This on-going controversy is further complicated and intensified by competition for markets among the largest trading powers—the United States, the European Union (EU), and Japan—and between states (divided roughly North and South) that operate at very different levels of development, international economic power, and effectiveness of domestic environmental protection. Even within states, both North and South, the trade and environment issue reflects an on-going tension between the generally more powerful, established trade ministries and the more recently estab-lished, less powerful environmental ministries. For both developing and highly industrialized states, some international realities complicate the politics further: the largest trading states with big markets and lots of leverage in negotiations can get away with lots more—either in protecting the environment or upholding traditional trading rules—to the detriment of smaller, weaker trading partners.

A. The Impact of Trade on the Environment

All products that enter into international trade (and all services, too, though less directly) have an impact on the environment through their production, transport, use, and disposal. This is true of both manufactures and natural resources that are traded. As the volume of trade swells in an era of trade liberalization and globalization, the environmental impact grows, too, of course. The demand for products and the need of all governments (especially of developing-country governments) to attract capital, create jobs, build foreign exchange, and pay off foreign debts makes selling products on the international market a high priority—so high that it shapes policies that govern important national choices on investments, taxes, subsidies, and other incentives. In countries heavily dependent on trade and investment from abroad or those dependent on exporting a single valuable commodity, trade imperatives may be the single most important determinant of development policy, creating a pressure that is often disrespectful of environment concerns in both exporting and importing countries.

Pressure to increase exports may be felt acutely by developing countries in search of foreign exchange to finance importation of goods and services required by their development goals. The drive to export minerals, forest products, fiber and food crops is also fueled by demand from the highly industrialized nations of the North that have experienced exponential economic growth since World War II. Structural adjustment reforms imposed by the International Monetary Fund (IMF) and the World Bank to rescue countries from the 1980s' debt crisis also have had the effect of increasing pressure on exports to finance further growth and to meet annual interest payments that in many countries required more that half the value of their exports.

Export pressure has thus contributed heavily to unsustainable exploitation of minerals, forests, fisheries, and farm lands and to uncontrolled pollution from processing and manufacturing. To compete against other developing countries in the same fix, governments often underpriced their goods. In the late 1980s, stumpage fees charged to the logging companies (often foreign-owned) by the Philippines and Indonesia ($3 and $4 per cubic meter, respectively) were one-fifth to one-tenth the real value of logs as calculated by the Asian Development Bank. The use of irrigation and the application of chemical fertilizers and pesticides, usually for high-valued export crops, has been heavily subsidized in many developing countries. Studies in the 1980s revealed subsidies of over 80% of the actual cost of the pesticides, use of which was encouraged and often paid for by international assistance and loans. This led to excessive use of the chemicals, thousands of poisoning cases, and water supplies contaminated from the runoff. Because the prices of the resulting exports do not reflect environmental costs to the resource base or health costs in the communities of origin, the environment and health of poor countries may be seen as subsidizing the consumption of the wealthier nations.

Damage to the environment from goods produced for export occurs in the highly industrialized countries as well, though they are better protected than developing countries by stronger environmental laws and enforcement. A host of European and U.S. subsidies support their agricultural exports, leaving behind serious soil and water problems and distorting world prices. For instance, protection of U.S. and European beet sugar producers (through a series of quantitative barriers, or import quotas) not only inflates the cost of sugar to the domestic consumer and distorts the world price of the commodity, but its production also uses large

quantities of herbicides that damage soils and contaminate runoff. Similarly, intensive cattle production in the Netherlands, now curtailed for environmental reasons, caused water contamination in that low-lying country.

B. The Role of the Trade Community

Following World War II, as part of a much larger effort to coordinate world economic recovery and growth (institutionalized in the IMF and the multilateral development banks), the major trading nations met to negotiate ground rules for trade. In 1948, they concluded the General Agreement on Tariffs and Trade (GATT) and intended to establish an international trade organization, which did not materialize until 1995. The negotiators' main purpose, indeed their philosophy, was to achieve trade liberalization (as a means of increasing prosperity), especially by reducing tariffs and other barriers to trade, and to avoid protectionism and the trade wars that had so severely damaged the world economy, contributing to the depression of the 1930s. Trade has grown about twice as fast as the world economy has grown since World War II. The GATT has been quite successful in reducing tariffs, though the reductions were sometimes replaced by "voluntary" restrictions on exports such as sugar and automobiles.

The GATT rules have developed slowly through a series of difficult negotiations, the most recent of which, the Uruguay Round, was also the longest, ending in 1994 with the formal establishment of the World Trade Organization (WTO) in 1995. What was a small organization in 1948 (23 signatories), dominated by the major trading nations, has become a near universal agreement (128 in 1995 with another 25 expected early in the 21st century), but it is still dominated by the major trading states. In both large and small states, it is producers rather than consumers whose interests are represented by their governments' delegations in the negotiations, as governments everywhere promote international sales rather than imports. Thus, the United States has clung to its textile tariffs and sugar quotas even though dropping such barriers to cheaper imports would result in lower prices for consumers.

The GATT Secretariat in Geneva is run by a cadre of professionals devoted to the concept of liberalization and chary about all trade barriers, including nontariff barriers, a category in which they include measures to protect the environment. Not until 1992 did the annual GATT report even acknowledge the environmental issue, and then only to dismiss the environmental effects of trade by asserting that trade and the resulting economic growth would enable developing countries to better protect their environment. Trade negotiations are conducted by government trade representatives, and all others, except for invited industry experts, are excluded. GATT dispute-settlement procedures (conducted behind closed doors and decided by consensus) have been the source of complaints for years by representatives of smaller, especially developing countries.

C. Development of the Issue

Environmental and trade objectives were pitted against each other as early as the 1972 UN Stockholm conference on the environment, where prominent developing-country fears included concerns that environmental protection would be used to limit their economic development and further obstruct entry of their products into the industrialized countries. Several international environmental conventions—the Whaling convention (1946), the Convention on International Trade in Endangered Species (1973), the Montreal Protocol protecting the ozone layer (1987), and the Basel convention (1989) seeking to control trade in hazardous wastes, among others—sought to limit trade in shrinking resources or dangerous substances or to use trade measures (as a penalty) to protect the world's natural resources. Only in 1987 did the World Commission on the Environment and Development (the so-called Brundtland Commission) point out the broader implications of expanded trade for the environment and the ways in which the poor countries, through pressure to export, were being caused to subsidize unsustainable practices in their own countries, especially with respect to commodity exports.

It was not until the 1990s, however, that the outspoken opposition of environmentalists and free-trade enthusiasts created the trade and environment "issue" in international politics. Several major international efforts contributed to the effort. In the European Community, as nations integrated their economies, the pressure also grew to "harmonize" their environmental requirements—that is, to bring their environmental standards into line with one another. Under the 1988 U.S.–Canadian Free Trade Agreement, most of the disputes in the early years were over environmental issues. The issue was put on the agenda of the 1992 UN Conference on Environment and Development (UNCED), which came to be known as the Earth Summit. Making trade and environment mutually supportive was the first substantive recommendation of *Agenda 21*, the Conference's detailed blueprint for achieving sustainable development. Environmental concerns were raised in the on-going GATT Uruguay Round of negotiations and in

negotiating the North American Free Trade Agreement (NAFTA) at an earlier stage, early enough to negotiate a side agreement on environmental cooperation.

United States environmental organizations were slow getting into the trade issue, urged on by Canadian and agriculture colleagues. Indeed, few can be said even now to have really mastered the issue, considering how important trade is to achievement of their international goals. Nor can the promoters of trade liberalization be said to have internalized the environmental values that might temper their unrestricted enthusiasm for free trade. The first significant publication by a nongovernmental organization (NGO) came out of the World Wildlife Fund's Geneva office only in 1991, not much before some nontrade intergovernmental organizations of considerable prestige—such as the Organization for Economic Cooperation and Development (OECD), the World Bank, and the Organization of American States (OAS)—undertook their own efforts to reconcile what founding chairman of the OAS Committee on the Environment, Heraldo Muñoz, called the "goal of prosperity through free trade and the imperative of protecting the environment."

II. TRADE–ENVIRONMENT DISPUTES

Each environmental case brought before the GATT (and those brought before the World Trade Organization when it superceded GATT in 1995) has been surrounded by controversy. It is in these challenges that the trade and environment protagonists' interests and basic assumptions have crystallized for the public. The word *environment* is not mentioned in the GATT, though there are provisions (Article XX) allowing nations to protect human, animal, and plant life and health and to protect exhaustible natural resources. Under GATT, the general rule governing nations' treatment of imports is that governments can require anything of importers that they do of their own products; for example, U.S. rules setting maximum pesticide residue requirements on fruits and vegetables must be the same for both imported and domestically grown products. But, according to GATT's approach, only the environmental effects of the imported products can be considered, not the effects of the processes that produced them. Thus, a nation could require that its own forests be regulated to prevent unsustainable harvests, but it could not prohibit importation of, nor could it tax wood products from, a country with no regulations or conservation measures for its forests. This kind of situation (and similar ones in the manufacturing sectors where trading partners may require vastly different degrees of pollution control) leads to protests by both environmentalists and producers in the receiving country of "unfair advantage" for exporting countries avoiding environmental costs. The GATT/WTO environmental disputes have involved this kind of conflict, and in several cases it was an action of the United States, mandated by national law to protect the environment, that was challenged.

The first case was a 1991 complaint by Mexico (and supported by Venezuela) that the United States was blocking importation of Mexican tuna because Mexican fishing vessels killed twice as many dolphins as U.S. ships. Though the U.S. Marine Mammal Protection Act required the ban, the GATT dispute panel ruled for Mexico, because the U.S. ban was concerned with process not product. The panel ruled further that GATT Article XX provisions protecting health and conservation of animal and plant life did not apply in activities beyond a nation's territory, that is, in international waters.

In a follow-up case in 1994, the European Union complained because the United States rejected EU tuna exports that came from intermediary countries that did not certify that they did not buy from nations embargoed by the United States. In what may have been the first breach in the dike, the GATT dispute panel rejected the EU arguments that dolphins were not an exhaustible resource but it ruled nevertheless that Article XX applied only within the territory of the country imposing the ban and that such measures could only be used directly and not to change the policy of another state—a puzzling distinction at best.

Two other cases challenged U.S. laws meant to increase fuel efficiency in automobiles sold in the United States. One required a manufacturer's fleet to achieve an average minimum mileage per gallon of fuel. The GATT panel found that the 1978 American "gas guzzler" tax on automobiles that fall below the required average was a legitimate nondiscriminatory conservation measure, even if not as effective as a fuel tax. In the second instance, however, on the charge that 1975 U.S. Corporate Average Fuel Economy standards put an unfair burden on European companies that exported primarily top-of-the-line models, the panel ruled that because the U.S. requirement was based on ownership and control relationships, it put the imports at a competitive disadvantage and was not aimed at conserving fuel, and the panel requested a change in the U.S. law. These rulings, which seemed to weaken U.S. environmental laws that had been hard won, incensed American environmentalists and sharpened their opposition to NAFTA, the Uruguay Round, and the new World Trade Organization.

Two other challenges to national environmental laws were brought under GATT rules, but the laws were nullified before the disputes were settled. Hoping to curtail tropical forest loss, Austria passed a law in 1990 that required various degrees of labeling of tropical timber products and imposed hefty duties on imported products made from lumber harvested in unsustainable fashion. The income from the duties was to be used to fund sustainable tropical forest management projects in the exporting countries. Malaysia and Indonesia, whose exports would be affected and who, more importantly, feared the Austrian example would be a precedent that would force tropical countries toward sustainable forestry management practices, got the ASEAN (Association of Southeast Asian Nations) countries to agree to boycott Austrian exports if Austria implemented the law, and Austria withdrew the plan before it ever went into effect. Tiny Netherlands, in 1993, adopted similar legislation that would ban importation of tropical timber that was not harvested in a sustainable way, but it was not implemented either. It is possible that if a larger trading country with bigger markets, such as the United States or Germany, were to enact such a law, the outcome might be different, even in the face of GATT rules.

Four more complaints over environmental trade measures have been brought under WTO dispute settlement rules operating since 1995. In each case the complainant state challenged national or EU environmental-protection measures. In each case, the WTO ruled against those measures. In the Venezuela Reformulated Gasoline Case, Venezuela and Brazil claimed to be discriminated against by a U.S. Environmental Protection Agency (EPA) rule, promulgated under the Clean Air Act, that required all refineries to make cleaner gasoline, using the 1990 U.S. industry standard as a baseline. Since fuel from the foreign refineries was not as "clean" in 1990 as that from U.S. refineries, the importing countries were starting their clean-up efforts from a different starting point. The WTO panel ruled in 1997 for Venezuela and Brazil, and EPA set about revising its rules to bring them into compliance with the WTO.

A second WTO ruling found against the European Union, which imported 7 percent of its bananas from some small Caribbean states under a special duty-free preference. Grown primarily on very small farms, these bananas used smaller amounts of pesticides than those grown and exported by big corporate growers. Under charges brought by larger banana-exporting countries, Ecuador, Guatemala, Honduras, and Mexico, plus the United States (on behalf of two large U.S. banana-growing companies that operate in those Latin American countries), the WTO panel in 1997 approved the duty-free preferences (a concession to poor states allowable under GATT), but found that the EU was deliberately favoring the Caribbean countries in its allocation of quotas. Subsequent changes in EU have not satisfied the United States or WTO. In 1999, as the United States prepared to impose retaliatory sanctions against selected European exports, the U.S. press again began to write about "trade wars."

In yet another EU–U.S. case, the United States charged the European Union with discrimination against exports of U.S. beef treated with growth hormones, the use of which had been banned in European cattle. In 1997 the WTO, citing international scientific findings on the safety of the specific hormones in question, ruled against the European Union, ignoring overwhelming democratically determined consumer preferences for hormone-free beef.

In a fourth case, four developing countries (India, Malaysia, Pakistan, and Thailand) have charged that a U.S. ban on the importation of shrimp caught by vessels that kill endangered migrating sea turtles violates WTO rules that no nation can use trade restrictions to influence (fishing) rules of other countries. The United States argues that there are relatively simple and inexpensive "turtle-extruder-devices" that shrimp fishers could use to save the turtles and that their failure to do so will negate all other conservation efforts to protect these acknowledged endangered species of turtles. The case is a near replica of the earlier tuna–dolphin cases. In 1998, the WTO found against the United States in a sweeping ruling that appeared to label all national laws protecting species in international waters unacceptable violations of the World Trade Agreement. The United States then changed its application of the law, accepting importation of shrimp caught by fleets using protective gear, regardless of the policy of the country of origin, and thereby achieved a much narrower ruling on appeal before the WTO later that year. That decision in turn has been challenged, and the dispute continues.

One case brought thus far under NAFTA has similar possibilities of trade agreements overriding national environmental measures. In this case, Canada has legislated to ban the importation and interprovincial transport of a gasoline additive called MMT because it is a toxic substance, already banned in the United States. The Ethyl Corporation, the U.S. company that makes and distributes MMT in Canada, is suing the Canadian Government, as NAFTA allows it to do independent of U.S. government backing, for $251 million to cover its loss of earnings and reputation. Canada lost some early

procedural battles in the case, and, realizing that a ruling favorable to Ethyl could attach an immense price tag to national environmental-protection laws, settled out of court, basically conceding Ethyl's claims.

In venues other than WTO and NAFTA, the settlement of trade–environment disputes has come out differently. The European Court, for instance, which has jurisdiction in disputes among member states of the European Union, has generally upheld the right of individual countries to protect their environment.

A. The Dilemma of the Developing Countries

Most of these trade and environment cases brought before the GATT have been battles among the industrialized states, but the pro- and anti-environmental arguments continue to be articulated most forcefully by northern nongovernmental organizations (NGOs) on the one hand and developing country governments on the other. By the 1990s the developing countries had been struggling for years to lower the tariff and other barriers to their products in the big industrial markets. Even though many of them had reduced their own import restrictions in the 1980s in response to structural-adjustment imperatives, they still faced a number of high hurdles for some of their exports. Their weaker position compelled them to accept "voluntary" agreements to limit the number of automobile parts or the amount of sugar shipped to certain countries. Japan and Taiwan's preference for raw logs over processed lumber prevailed over Southeast Asian nations' hope to export the higher-valued processed wood. In the United States, escalating tariffs (tariffs that increase with each step of processing) effectively limit textile and footwear exports to the United States.

The developing countries also had bad experience with the U.S. anti-dumping measures—meant to keep subsidized goods from U.S. consumers, but used also to protect U.S. producers. And they were well aware of the leverage the vast U.S. market could bring to bear when it came to imposing demanding standards on food imports. (When the United States promulgated maximum thresholds for pesticide residues on fruits and vegetables, those rapidly became in effect the standard for countries such as Mexico and Chile, which export large quantities of fresh produce to U.S. consumers.) The developing countries were, therefore, sensitive to the possibility that the environmentalists' demands would be used to give advantage to competing U.S. producers and manufacturers. Their suspicion was deepened when U.S. labor organizations and Congressional supporters, often sounding quite protectionist, joined the environmentalists in opposition to NAFTA and the Uruguay agreements. Developing countries therefore maintain their opposition to integrating environmental concerns into trade negotiations. Nevertheless, in a concession to environmentalists' pressures, NAFTA set a precedent by adding a side agreement to deal with environmental issues among the signatories, and that compromise is likely to set the minimum standard for subsequent U.S. trade agreements within the region. For more than a generation the developing countries have been audible critics of the powerful trading nations' leverage within GATT, especially with regard to dispute settlements and the exclusionary character and secrecy of the proceedings in Geneva. Now their opposition to introducing environmental considerations into trade negotiations has put them in the uncomfortable position of clinging to established GATT traditions to protect access for their products.

B. Environmentalists' Concerns

Environmentalists in the United States and other industrialized countries fear that trade agreements will overrule their environmental-protection laws, as in the tuna–dolphin and fuel-conservation measures in the GATT cases. They are aware that the officials of the WTO, which has much stronger dispute enforcement powers than its predecessor GATT dispute panels, still have not internalized the sustainable development goals embraced at the 1992 Earth Summit. Along with labor organizations and businesses that sought to maintain the predominance of their own services and goods, the environmentalists picked up on the arguments about competitiveness, that is, their concern that developing countries with less stringent and poorly enforced environmental regulations and low-paid, unenfranchised workers without benefits or security would enjoy a competitive advantage—at the price of continuing environmental degradation and pollution. Their environmental concerns fed the fear, alive in the United States from the 1990 presidential elections onward, that U.S. industry (and jobs) will escape to the less exacting and more profitable climate of the developing countries. These arguments were raised, unsuccessfully, in the Congressional NAFTA ratification debate and successfully in President Clinton's 1997 effort to get "fast-track" legislation he wanted for subsequent trade negotiations. Although there is no documentation that U.S. companies move to developing countries to avoid environmental costs (around 2% of total cost of production), the argument nevertheless carries weight as workers

see downsizing, plant closures, and moves to the South for whatever reasons, while corporate earnings and executive compensation remain at an all-time high.

Environmentalists demand, so far unsuccessfully, that trade agreements like NAFTA and the Uruguay Round include environmental considerations as legitimate factors in trade agreements. For the first time, an environmental addendum was attached to a treaty in creating NAFTA's Commission for Environmental Cooperation, which is to investigate environmental complaints, and a modest fund to assist Mexico in achieving higher levels of environmental protection. And the Uruguay Round agreed to creation of a Trade and Environment Committee, but its functions and authority are still under debate. Essential to making either of these bodies effective in defending the environment is adoption of rules guaranteeing useful levels of transparency and access (for NGOs, the press, and the public) to WTO and NAFTA meetings and documents. GATT's closed processes, rejection of most NGO input/participation, and lack of transparency are resisting a trend common in all the multilateral development banks, UN, and other international bodies such as the OECD and the ASEAN. Without access and transparency there can be little expectancy that the trade community will feel any real pressure to take up environmental or social considerations.

C. The U.S. Role

Recent U.S. Administrations of both parties have sought to free themselves from Congressional interference on the details of trade negotiations. Relying on the expansion of trade to help "grow the economy," create jobs, and correct the balance of trade, Administration officials have to bargain hard with their international competitors and, at the point of ratification, do not want to face a barrage of demands from the many interest groups represented in Congress. At the end of the century, remaining Japanese barriers to U.S. products, competition for the growing Chinese market, and concern over the increasing leverage of a consolidated European trading bloc far outweigh any environmental worries that U.S. trade negotiators may experience.

On the other hand, the United States has strongly defended unilateral measures to protect an international resource (as in the tuna–dolphin case) and other national conservation laws in other GATT and WTO cases. Starting with the Bush Administration, the United States has championed NGO participation in environmental negotiations and subsequently in other UN meetings, and, more recently, in trade negotiations. U.S. representatives have also pursued greater transparency, first in the multilateral development banks, and now in trade processes, albeit with less vigor than in other forums.

However, on issues where specific U.S. interests are directly involved, as in some of the disputes between Canada and the United States under the Free Trade Agreement (FTA), U.S. environmental leadership is less clear. The United States, for instance, has challenged the British Columbia government's financial assistance to Canadian companies for reforestation, charging that it constitutes unfair competition on the international market for U.S. lumber exports. And in the various disagreements between the United States and Canada over salmon fishing in the northwest waters, the U.S. position seems motivated as much by defense of the U.S. fleet as by conservation concerns. Nor has the Clinton Administration followed up vigorously on its NAFTA environmental obligations, even though it employs environmental rhetoric. It is often difficult, as the GATT, WTO, and FTA cases illustrate, to sort out the mixed motivation of protection of the environment versus protection of a domestic industry and promotion of U.S. growth exports.

III. EFFORTS TO RECONCILE TRADE AND ENVIRONMENT GOALS

Numerous bodies, both governmental and nongovernmental have produced intellectual arguments for reconciling trade and environment goals. The OECD's Committee of Experts on Trade and Environment called for coordination of policies on trade and environmental protection so as better to serve the overall goal of sustainable development. In an attempt to calm developing-country fears that trade would be used as a weapon to force nontrade policies, the Clinton Administration, in 1994, attempted to clarify the limited circumstances under which trade measures might be used for environmental ends. The International Institute for Sustainable Development, a publicly funded Canadian NGO think tank, with an international group of authors, has developed a set of principles to guide all players in the trade–environment negotiations— principles that could expand trade and create new wealth and jobs that would address poverty without degrading either global or local ecosystems. Based on assumptions of the need for poverty alleviation as well as the importance of both environmental protection and reduction of trade barriers, the principles include efficiency and full internalization of environmental costs, respect for the regenerative capacity of ecosys-

tems, decision-making as close as possible to the affected population, and adherence to science and the precautionary principle. A 1992 western hemisphere conference convened in Chile under OAS auspices sought to harness the "world's largest market" to reconcile trade and environment goals. Academics have written on the "Greening of GATT." Economic policy analysts have pointed out that both trade liberalization and environmental protection seek to use available resources more efficiently, and that environmental damage in the absence of environmental protection carries higher costs for the economy of a country than the cost of environmental controls.

There are many changes in trade policy that would benefit the environment—for example, faster reduction of agricultural subsidies that dictate anti-environmental technology choices, or the use of trade and investment concessions, as in the NAFTA, to stimulate international environmental cooperation. And there are environmental policy changes that would benefit international trade, such as universal adherence to the "polluter pays" principle, internalizing the environmental costs of all products, and eliminating under-pricing of natural resources. There is much unfinished environmental business before the WTO, the EU, and NAFTA. Whether there is the collective political will and leadership among the largest trading nations to reconcile environmental and trade interests and to overcome the fears of developing countries is another question.

Though GATT/WTO officials seem begrudgingly to have accepted the legitimacy of the environment/trade connection, they have made no substantive concessions to change. The Trade and Environment Committee of the WTO continues to debate the agenda, and the NAFTA Commission for Environmental Cooperation's operations fall far short of environmentalists' expectations. But the trade–environment issue is joined, and it will not go away. Environmental concerns will be part of every trade negotiation going into the 21st century.

IV. CONTINUING ISSUES

At the end of the Uruguay Round, weary delegates agreed to creation of a WTO Committee on Trade and Environment and essentially dumped on it all the unresolved environment-related issues. The Committee was instructed to "examine" all relevant issues: existing trade measures employed by international environmental treaties; charges and taxes for environmental purposes; harmonization of environmental standards, regulations, labeling, packaging, and recycling requirements; mechanisms for settlement of disputes; the effect of environmental requirements on market access; the export of goods that are prohibited from sale in domestic markets (e.g., DDT); transparency; NGO participation; intellectual property rights; and possible environment/trade conflicts in the service sectors. Of these, the NGOs consider the questions of access to deliberations and transparency the most important, within a larger debate on the definition of the authority and agenda of the Committee itself. With all these persistent controversial issues still before the negotiators, it is no wonder that the debate over the specific role of the Committee is itself intense.

Even before the completion of the Uruguay Round, there was talk of subsequent "Green Round" negotiations on the GATT. Environmental critics of the trading system, clearly dissatisfied with the Uruguay Round's inability to deal with environmental issues, think the whole unfinished agenda needs attention. But they are not agreed among themselves on the approach to GATT reform. Some argue that Article XX of GATT, which makes possible exceptions for the health and protection of plants and animals, is sufficient to meet environmental concerns, that the article requires only a more expansive interpretation than it has been given over the years. These critics argue that conservative, single-minded officials have gone way beyond the intent of the original signatories and need to be corrected, and that the WTO staff of trade officials needs to be augmented by addition of environmental expertise.

Other critics, more despairing of changing the mindset of WTO staff, call for a new forum for the discussion of trade and environment issues. Some want to create an intergovernmental panel (modeled after the respected International Panel on Climate Change) of experts in economics, international law, and the natural sciences to do research and make recommendations on technical strategies such as the reduction of trade distortions and the internalization of environmental costs. Still others hope for a new overarching world environment agency that would counterbalance the WTO through its responsibilities for monitoring compliance with treaties and advocacy of increasing environmental protection.

While no new institutions are likely to be created in the near future, it is likely that steps will be taken to open WTO processes to greater public scrutiny and NGO participation, and to craft transparency rules that make trade documents available to the public before irrevocable decisions are made. Such steps would make the facts and the politics of the trade system much more visible to the news media and to nontrade interests and would move toward equalization of the parties in the trade–environment debate—which is precisely why they are so stubbornly resisted by the trading community. If the WTO cannot make minimum reforms in these key areas, however, it will find itself increasingly sidelined as the action around trade and environmental issues moves to a different playing field.

Also See the Following Articles

ECOETHICS • ENVIRONMENTAL ISSUES AND POLITICS • NONGOVERNMENTAL ACTORS IN INTERNATIONAL POLITICS • TRADE, CONFLICT, AND COOPERATION AMONG NATIONS • TRADE WARS (DISPUTES)

Bibliography

Arden-Clarke, C. (1991). *The General Agreement on Tariffs and Trade: Environmental protection and sustainable development.* World Wildlife Fund International, Gland, Switzerland.

Esty, D. C. (1994). *Greening the GATT: Trade, environment, and the future.* Institute for International Economics, Washington, DC.

French, H. (1993). *Costly tradeoffs: Reconciling trade and the environment.* Worldwatch Institute, Washington, DC.

French, H. (1998). *Investing in the future: Harnessing private capital flows for environmentally sustainable development.* Worldwatch Institute, Washington, DC.

International Institute for Sustainable Development (1994). *Trade and sustainable development principles.* Winnipeg, Canada.

Low, P. (Ed.) (1992). International trade and the environment. Discussion Paper 159, World Bank, Washington, DC.

Munoz, H., & Rosenberg, R. (Eds.) (1993). *Difficult liaison: Trade and the environment in the Americas.* Transaction Publishers, New Brunswick, NJ.

Repetto, R. (1995). *Jobs, competitiveness, and environmental regulation: What are the real issues?* World Resources Institute, Washington, DC.

Trade and Environment Committee, National Advisory Council for Environmental Policy and Technology (1993). *The greening of world trade.* Environmental Protection Agency, Washington, DC.

Zaelke, D., Orbach, P., & Housman, R. (Eds.) (1993). *Trade and the environment: Law, economics, and policy.* Center for International Environmental Law. Island Press, Washington, DC.

Trade Wars (Disputes)

Gabriella Cagliesi

Rutgers University

GLOSSARY

Trade War The use of trade restrictions to achieve purely economic objectives related to trading activities.
Trade War Duration Rounds of interactive retaliations.
Trade War Intensity Degree of government involvement and institutionalization of the trade conflict.

THE PURPOSE of this article is to reexamine the evolution of trade disputes using new international trade theories to explain causes, dynamics, and effects of a variety of trade conflicts around the world in the modern and contemporary era. The process of reading the past through a richer theoretical and analytical apparatus should enhance our ability to identify the risks faced by the current international trading community and should provide us with some solutions to avoid repetitions of old mistakes.

I. INTRODUCTION

Since the first prehistoric act of barter individuals have realized the mutual advantages of trading. In any epoch commercial relations have been regulated by tacit or explicit trading rules. Any unilateral act intended to extract additional benefits over the trading partner by reneging on the rules has always been perceived as a challenge and has usually called for a reaction. Confrontations over trade have evolved or —perhaps we should say—have degenerated into situations that range from embittered relations to trade conflicts. Sometimes, conflicts have even escalated into pernicious trade wars.

The practice of trade warfare has modified over time in terms of duration of conflicts, intensity, number, and identity of conflicting countries and the "trade weapon" used in the bargaining process. Equally dramatic have been the developments of economic theory in analyzing positive and normative aspects of trading activities and policies. All these facts are considered in analyzing trade wars.

II. THE LANGUAGE OF ECONOMIC CONFLICT

Trade disputes can vary in intensity and duration. In this light, trade disputes can be conceived as a continuum ranging from virtually zero to a very high level of conflict. The highest level is constituted by a trade war and is characterized by high intensity and by the escalation of interactive retaliation. This definition of trade conflicts, that is, the use of economic instruments to achieve economic objectives, does not suggest that trade wars are apolitical or that they preclude the use of military force. It confines the implications of the analysis to the economic level.

In reviewing historical cases of trade conflicts that conform to the above definition of a trade war, I make use of some game theory concepts. Each trading country is viewed as a player who can choose either to use or not to use trade restrictions in maximizing his or her own welfare. Games can be bilateral or multilateral depending on the numbers of players, and they can be zero-sum (the gains of one player must be the loss or the cumulative losses of all other players) or variable-sum games (all players may gain from some solutions of the game); thus, unlike zero-sum games, mutually beneficial cooperative strategies are possible. Games can be iterative or static depending on the possibility of retaliation.

The most famous game used to model international conflicts is a particular variable-sum game known as "prisoners' dilemma" (PD). Although in this type of game both countries prefer mutual cooperation to mutual defection, cooperation is not guaranteed. A bilateral static PD trade game always induces very conservative, noncooperative strategies because of the fears of facing a noncooperative trading partner. An iterative bilateral PD game induces cooperative strategies, as the threat of retaliation deters free-riding temptations. A multilateral PD game implies a nondiscriminatory principle in the strategies of multiple actors (if this were not the case, then the game could break into a set of bilateral games). In trading practices the nondiscriminatory rule in a multilateral trade arrangement is better known as the Most Favored Nation (MFN) norm. The MFN rule requires that any trade concession is to be extended to all participants in the MFN system, even those who refuse to grant similar concessions. Thus, it creates an incentive to free-ride on the cooperativeness of others. Cooperation is discouraged even in iterative games.

When there is a substantial asymmetry in size between actors in terms of economic power, neither bilateral nor multiple games will evolve into cooperation, as the hegemonic actor will try to maximize his income by imposing optimal tariffs on smaller actors rather than by engaging in free trade. Notice that if all countries are small, the individual player's decision has no effect on the final outcome. Trade relations are competitive rather than strategic and the natural result of the game is cooperation.

III. THE EVOLUTION OF THE INTERNATIONAL ECONOMIC THEORY OF TRADE

The mere existence of trade weapons, such as tariffs, and the record of their long tradition corroborate the view that the international arena is populated by interdependent actors in situations of competitive or conflicting interests. Different trade theories have emphasized different aspects of this view.

A. Mercantilism

Until the end of the 18th century, economic trade theory was predominantly mercantilistic theory. This theory stressed the relevance of exports over imports for the welfare of a nation in a world where volume of trade was perceived to be static and fixed. In the mercantilistic view relations between actors were perceived to be extremely conflicting, as their interests were mutually exclusive (technically a static zero-sum game), so that cooperative solutions were not achievable. Because the static nature of the trade game, where retaliation was not contemplated, mercantilism advocated aggressive government interventions, such as import tariffs and export subsidies, to win a trade war.

B. The Comparative Advantage Theory

The theory of comparative advantage (CA) developed as a reaction to the mercantilistic system. Actors' interactions are perceived to by dynamic rather than static and competitive rather than strategic. The interrelations among actors are mainly thought of in a general equilibrium sense such that the sum of all actions influences the final equilibrium. However, no actor can individually influence the moves and the payoffs of other actors in the game. Thus trade barriers erected by an individual country become self-defeating. Its choice is therefore between freely trading or not trading at all.

Since the trade game is perceived as a variable-sum game, trading is the Pareto efficient solution, as it enables countries to take advantage of their differences in tastes, technologies, or endowments. Policy guidance is straightforward: restraining trade does not help in obtaining new gains, as free trade cannot be improved upon. If free trade is the optimal rule, then trade wars are suboptimal and, thus, they are the result of irrational behaviors. This position has been a creed for 2 centuries until the development of new theories of trade challenged it.

C. New Theories of Trade

As world trade has boomed, it has become more and more evident that the predictions of the comparative advantage paradigm have failed to explain the observed pattern of trade and that the assumptions underlying the CA analysis did not suit the kind of firms and industries participating in international trade. The main point of the new theories of trade is that commerce increases market size and lowers average costs. Economies of scale, imperfect competition, and externalities are independent causes of trade not present in the traditional theory of CA.

The trading environment is not competitive, as firms have a mutually recognized strategic interdependence that makes each firm vulnerable to the moves of its adversary. Among all noncompetitive market structures, oligopoly offers more interesting implications, as it gives insight into the basic game theoretic structure of strategic trade policy: governments have the power to make strategic moves that affect the conditions of oligopolistic firms and impart strategic advantages to domestic firms over foreign firms. In their influential 1983 theoretical contribution Brander and Spencer proved that, under some circumstances, trade aggressiveness has the potential to increase national welfare. Although policy implications are similar to the old mercantilistic policy prescriptions, there are two main differences with the old mercantilistic view: first, the trade game is an iterative game that could require more rounds of retaliations and, second, the variable-sum nature of the game implies that cooperation is possible and is possibly Pareto superior. Thus, in only some circumstances may free trade fail to be the optimal rule. However, when political economy considerations enter into the analysis, free trade is nevertheless the more reasonable, and safe, policy.

The normative conclusion that free trade is the best rule and that trade wars are to be avoided since they produce adverse results for everyone, have been challenged in some studies. However, these analyses of trade bargaining and trade wars have been either purely theoretical, with very special hypotheses and heroic assumptions, or have empirically focused on a very narrow subset of the subject. Because they represent an attempt to develop a theory of trade war, some interesting studies that have undertaken such an endeavor are briefly described.

D. Conditions for Winning a Trade War

In his 1993 contribution MacMillan tackles the issue of if and when it is possible for a country to gain from a trade conflict. He argues that if the initial situation is free trade, the conjecture that a trade war is detrimental for all countries involved is still valid. If the initial status quo is reciprocal trade tariffs and each country is not using its optimal tariff—intended here as the best-response tariff given the trading partner's tariff—then it is possible for a country to be better off by increasing its protection than by engaging in a bargaining process for trade concessions, even if the other country retaliates.

This outcome occurs because when a country is using a tariff below the optimal level, any tariff reduction involves a cost. In reciprocal trade concessions, tariffs are bargaining chips used to gain access to the foreign country. If the cost of reducing its own tariff is greater than the benefit of lower foreign tariffs, the status quo is preferable to reciprocal trade concessions.

A country may even prefer a higher level of tariffs, by engaging in a trade war, if it is able to achieve improvements of its terms of trade and at the same time to retain its volume of exports to the foreign country. Thus, a country is likely to gain from a trade war when the following occurs: its existing tariff if well below its optimal tariff, the world price is more responsive to domestic tariffs than to foreign tariffs (as this situation enhances the country's chance of terms of trade improvements), and foreign consumption and production are not very responsive to foreign tariffs (so that the domestic country is able to retain its volume of exports to the foreign country).

Harrison and Rutstrom in their 1991 study investigate the value of trade negotiations and the conditions for a country to gain from participating in retaliatory trade war. To this purpose they used a calibrated general equilibrium model to simulate trade wars and alternative strategies. Although results of calibrated models require a cautious interpretation, as they are very sensitive to the choice of the calibrated values of trade elasticities, their exercises show some interesting features.

They assume that the United States (U.S.), Japan, and the European Economic Community (EEC) increase their existing protection structures and they simulate a trade war between these three trading partners, while assuming the rest of the world is passive. They find that by improving their terms of trade sufficiently, the U.S. and the EEC are able to gain from this trade war, whereas Japan and, more heavily, the developing countries (LDC), lose from the war. From a global perspective the world in general would lose, whereas it would gain from global free trade. They also claim that a country can gain from trade wars if it is large relative to its trading partner since the world price is more responsive to the domestic tariff than to the foreign tariff.

In the alternative scenario of trade negotiation, they find that the cooperative solution implies a level of protection higher than the status quo, but lower than that under a trade war. They find that negotiations carried under retaliation threats induce a higher cooperative level of tariffs than negotiations conducted under no threat of conflict escalation.

These findings add force to the argument that the cooperative activity stimulated by the presence of the General Agreement on Tariffs and Trade (GATT) reduces protection under the level that would prevail otherwise. The changes that take place from one negotiation to the other may be relatively small, but at least they preserve what cooperation has already been obtained.

Similar results have been found by Kennan and Riezman in their 1988 work. They claim that if one country is substantially larger than its trading partner it can expect to win tariff wars despite retaliation. By using a different analytical apparatus (Edgeworth's box) they were able to state this result not in terms of elasticities, as in the case of Harrison and Rutstrom, but in terms of endowments. If both countries have the same endowment distribution (i.e., the same dimension), both will lose from a trade war; but if a country is larger than its trading partner, it may expect to win a trade war.

So far the issue of winning a trade war has been analyzed under the assumption that the status quo is tariff protection. Johnson, in his famous 1953 study, reasserts the proposition that a country may gain from a trade war as compared to free trade. He also offers the conditions under which, in a particular case, the country will indeed improve its welfare. Johnson's study may be taken as representative of a monopolistically competitive situation with two countries, where retaliation takes the form of imposing the optimal tariff after the first country has imposed its optimal tariff and on the assumption that the other country's optimal tariff will remain unchanged.

Starting from a point of free trade, if a country provokes trade tension by imposing its own optimal tariff, the adjustment process may lead to one of two possible outcomes: either it may evolve into a policy equilibrium with both countries imposing consistent optimal tariffs at either higher or lower levels than at the beginning of the retaliation process or the adjustment mechanism

may stall into a tariff cycle where countries keep changing tariffs and keep retaliating. If and when a policy equilibrium is attained, one country at least must be worse off as compared to free trade. Both countries may lose, but it is not necessarily true that both will lose.

Johnson shows the conditions under which a country will gain by imposing an optimum tariff, even if the other country retaliates by following the same policy. He claims that under the special case of constant elasticity offer curve for each country—a condition that makes each country's optimal tariff independent of the other's—trade wars are beneficial for the home country if the following conditions are met: the price elasticity of demand for imports is higher in the home country than in the foreign country and the foreign country's consumption responds little to the foreign country's tariff increase. Both these conditions are analogous to those claimed by Harrison and Rutstrom.

This evolution of the theoretical analysis of trade has been to some extent prompted by the historical evolution of trading activities and strategies. The steadily progressive increase of trade volumes has created deeper interdependence among the actors and more sources of tension. The next section presents an overview of how trade wars have changed.

IV. THE HISTORICAL EVOLUTION OF TRADE WARS

Trade wars that fit the definition adopted here began with the establishment of a reasonably sophisticated international trading system. In the ancient and feudal period trade consisted of highly complementary exchanges of essential commodities, such as food and raw material, that made any potential trade conflict very costly. This situation discouraged engaging in trade wars. The level of trade conflicts was kept at the low end of the continuum.

Until the decline of Britain as the hegemonic power and the rise of the U.S. and Japan, trade wars mainly involved large European states. Trade wars were essentially bilateral conflicts of the PD type: large actors capable of manipulating their terms of trade for the purpose of deriving income gains, as suggested by the mercantilistic practice. The big actors engaged often in aggressive protectionism through governmental interventions that provoked high-intensity and long-lasting trade conflicts, as shown by the period of mercantilistic practices.

The much-analyzed free trade movement began in the 19th century. The hegemonic country of that moment, Britain, engaged in unilateral reductions of tariff barriers. The disputes of this period were mainly between large powers and small countries and were paradoxically initiated by small countries to react to the vicious commercial behavior of the hegemonic states. In fact, as the big countries (namely Germany, Britain, and France—the U.S. at that time was only supplying raw material to Europe and was not a major trading nation) realized that they were capable of inflicting damage to each other, they pursued tranquil bilateral relations toward freer trade by granting mutual MFN status. However, the extending MFN status to small countries was not necessarily in their best interest because of the asymmetry in economic power. In fact, the MFN clause incited countries to adopt the practice of having a high general level of protection as a bargaining chip so as to negotiate specific concessions on the general rate to be extended to other countries by the MFN clause. Thus, the MFN clause made it important to raise tariffs before engaging in any important negotiations.

The asymmetry of economic power gave larger countries the incentive to keep their tariffs high while lowering the tariffs of smaller trading partners. Some small countries did not react while others reacted by increasing their tariffs and initiating trade wars and were severely punished for not being acquiescent to the larger countries' trading behavior. In general, trade negotiations in the prewar system had benefited from a climate of prosperity, the presence of a major actor committed to free trade (Britain), by a small number of actors (particularly big actors), and by the practice of stipulating long-term treaties to enhance free trade. All these circumstances reduced the incentive toward free-riding on the MFN and kept trade tension to a low-intensity level and duration.

World War I changed the pattern of trade: many additional small countries entered the scene and some other countries that had been peripheral became significantly more important. The U.S. and Japan emerged as potential major actors. United States' trade became more concentrated in manufacturing than in primary goods, making the country more vulnerable to geographic discrimination. Because of the large number of trading nations, the MFN rule was more and more frequently used.

However, as already pointed out, the MFN norm has an intrinsic problem of creating free-riding incentives. The presence of a large number of *asymmetric* countries intensifies this problem: in fact, because small countries individually lack the power of effective retaliation, they cannot prevent the larger countries from defecting.

Thus, the history of trading disputes in the postwar period, until the 1930s, is governed by the U.S.' attempt to further exploit its rising hegemonic power by free-riding on the MFN norms. Moreover, by misperceiving other countries' economic power and the possibility of coordinated retaliation, the U.S. went even further with its hegemonic predation behavior by increasing its tariffs with the 1930 Smoot–Hawley tariff, thus benefiting even more from the lowering of foreign tariffs.

With the Smoot–Hawley tariff, protection was extended to 12,000 products and the U.S. average tariff level rose to 60% of dutiable products. The tariff provoked a near-universal retaliation that escalated into a trade war that brought world trade virtually to a halt. The dramatic general increase in tariff protection to the U.S. hurt all participants and showed the necessity to correct the free-riding problem in the MFN system. Some countries resorted to nontariff types of protection such as quotas, some to exchange rate controls. As a result of this unfolding of events, the attempt to reduce tariffs multilaterally was abandoned, to be pursued instead on a strictly bilateral basis.

The U.S. changed its negotiation tactic in the 1934, although not its hegemonic predation strategy, in the form of the Reciprocal Trade Amendment (RTAA), which authorized the President to undertake bilateral tariff negotiations on an MFN basis with foreign countries. The RTAA allowed the U.S. to obtain large concessions from small primary producers for small counterconcessions while negotiating more equitable concessions on the effective rate of protection only with larger partners. Both the break-down of the MFN system into bilateral interaction and the U.S.'s new bargaining tactic fostered a reduction of protectionism, even though the larger powers' tariffs remained high.

The collective learning experience of the 1930s, that large-scale trade wars are harmful for everyone, and, later, from the potential dynamic gains from expanding trade in the aftermath of the Second World War oriented countries toward favoring better trade relations. Several new organizations were instituted for this purpose. The most important was the GATT. The GATT served two main purposes in the international community. First, it set rules and principles of reciprocity and nondiscrimination—the MFN rule—for conducting international commerce and, eventually for resolving international commerce disputes with justifiable retaliation. The second main purpose of the GATT was to provide a forum for a series of multilateral talks aimed at lowering the general level of protection. Relative to its second role, it launched and completed between 1947 and 1993 eight rounds of talks which, cumulatively, have reduced the general level of protection by a significant amount: overall tariffs have been reduced by 90%.

Since the post-World War II period the international community has significantly changed its attitude toward trade protection: countries have embraced the cause of freer and less-turbulent trade relations and have negotiated reciprocal barrier reductions under the GATT's rules. The slow-paced but progressive process of trade liberalization has been fostered even further by the formation of the EEC, which has increased the effectiveness of the bargaining power of all its members, and by the growing economic strength of Japan.

Beginning at the end of the 1950s, trade has expanded at dramatic rates: by the end of the 1980s world exports were 1000% higher than in 1950, while world output had risen more than 400%. Trade liberalization has created more trade. Of course other factors have also contributed to this incredible performance of trading activity: in particular, technological improvements in transportation and communications.

With the expansion of trade, commercial disputes have arisen. They are typically centered on trade in specific commodities, and so far they have not repeated the pattern of the trade wars experienced before the GATT's establishment. Trade games have generally become multilateral asymmetric conflicts and involve two levels: at one level, there are trade disputes and negotiations between three major trading actors (that is, the U.S., Japan, and the European Union (EU)) and at another level, simultaneously, there are conflicts between the economically developed countries versus the Less Developed Countries (LDCs) and the Newly Industrialized Countries (NICs).

The success of the extended decline in multilateral tariff levels has been accompanied by the rising importance of various kinds of exceptions that, if not properly monitored, could lead to a vicious reversion to high protectionism. Among the potentially harmful exceptions are: "special" protection associated with safeguard actions, exceptions for "unfair" foreign trade associated with antidumping and countervailing duty, exceptions for "justified" disobedience associated with Section 301 of the U.S. trade act of 1974, and exceptions from the MFN rule associated with the formation of regional trading blocks. These four cases are briefly outlined below.

The rise in "special" protection is demonstrated by the growing use of quantitative controls of imports or exports, such as, for instance, Voluntary Exports Restraints (VERs), Voluntary Import Expansions (VIEs), Orderly Market Arrangements (OMAs), and by tariffs that are created to suit the need of particular industries. The use of this "special" protection allows countries to "manage" trade so as to dampen the underlying changes in trade flows and trade balances. The increasing use of antidumping and countervailing duties raises questions concerning the abuse of "unfair trade laws" such as when firms value the competition-dampening effect of an on-going investigation for its own sake and not because it represents a real case of unfair foreign practice.

Strong reactions of resentment and condemnation of the U.S.'s practice of aggressive unilateralism have been triggered by Section 301. This section identifies a list of "priority" countries that may be pressured, with ultimatum tactics and even retaliation, to remove those trading practices that the U.S. has perceived and designated as unacceptable. This assertiveness is the result of the inability of the GATT dispute settlement procedure to enforce the rights of the U.S. With Section 301, however, the U.S. President is allowed the authority to unilaterally enforce the perceived rights of the U.S. under GATT and to respond to unfair foreign practices where international agreements do not exist. Finally, the formation of regional trading blocks, such as the EU and the North American Trade Agreement (NAFTA), raises a number of questions about their role in broader efforts to liberalize trade on a multilateral basis.

The last and most ambitious of the GATT multilateral talks to liberalize trade was the Uruguay Round (UR). Since the beginning of negotiations, it has been clear that the UR would represent a serious attempt to limit the risks of aggressive unilateralism and managed trade as well as the problem of regional protection. This round of negotiations started in 1986, had a long impasse during which the bargaining process seemed irrevocably destined to fail, and finally was completed in 1993 after some laborious compromises were reached by the U.S. and the EU in the agricultural sector, which was one of the major stumbling blocks to successful resolution. The UR also achieved some success in liberalizing international trade in services and in strengthening dispute settlement mechanisms through the establishment of the World Trade Organization (WTO), which replaces the old GATT.

To summarize: the historical overview of trade wars and trade accords has shown that, using game theory, trading practices have evolved from static or dynamic Prisoner's Dilemma types, where actors are balanced, to those that are asymmetric, with large numbers of actors and with significant inequalities in size and vulnerability. Trade conflicts have over time become higher in intensity but shorter in duration.

Trade wars now may be solved more easily thanks to more rapid diplomacy and communication, the presence of international institutions, and the fact that deeply integrated economies have to reduce the likelihood of spillover into other sectors. It also appears that trade disputes have become less "brutal," as the multilateral character of negotiations has reduced the actors' aggressiveness and has made it thus less likely for an economic conflict to degenerate into a large full-scale military war that has long-term, debilitating consequences for the protagonists. To paraphrase, a duel (i.e., a bilateral trade war) is harsher than a saloon brawl.

The next section uses strategic trade theory concepts and simple game theory models to review some specific episodes of past trade conflicts to understand how those of the past have influenced the current international pattern of specialization and trade. This kind of historical/strategic analysis should alert us to and explain the reasons for trade conflicts, how they escalate, and the kinds of outcomes to expect.

V. THE GAME THEORY ANALYSIS OF FOUR HISTORICAL TRADE DISPUTES

Four cases of trade rivalries and wars that exemplify the different type of trade conflicts in the continuum of trade relations are presented: the Anglo–Dutch Rivalry, the Chicken War, the Steel Turmoil, and the Textile Dispute.

A. The Anglo–Dutch Rivalry

The analogy between mercantilism and the modern theory of strategic trade policy is based on the fact that imperfect competition, with strategic interaction between firms, was a feature of 17th-century trade. In fact, the exploration of Asia, Africa, and America in the 16th century opened up many profitable opportunities for trade in the 17th century. Long-distance trade from Europe was undertaken by state-chartered monopoly trading companies in a few advanced countries. Thus, a small number of firms were competing for the same lucrative trade routes. Recognition that the government could be strategically used to alter the international distribution of profits in such trade gave monarchs and statesmen a clear incentive to intervene in order to promote domestic firms.

Notice that in the mercantilistic view, increasing one country's trade share can only be achieved by displacing existing merchants. A classic example of this type of trade disputes during this period is the Anglo–Dutch rivalry for East Indian trade. The situation conforms well to a Cournot duopoly for conquering a third market. A static bilateral PD zero-sum game, like this one, predicts unconditional noncooperation, with the elimination of one player and dominance of the third market by the winner.

In East Indian trade two companies, the English East India Company and the Dutch United East India Company, were given by their respective governments exclusive trading privileges in India and southeast Asia. Like the English, the Dutch company mainly imported and reexported spices to European markets. Neither company had an initial inherent advantage in East Indian trade. The Dutch proved very tenacious in their efforts to eliminate foreign competitors and dominate the scene. A particular type of strategic policy endorsed by the government—through a managerial incentive scheme—facilitated their success in dominating the trade in the region.

To understand the indirect influence of the Dutch government in this success, it is important to look at the institutional structure of the two competing firms and at the particular managerial incentives that motivated manager's choices. The English East India Company was a private firm run solely by merchants without any government involvement beyond the granting of the monopoly charter. The objective of the Company was to choose the quantity of pepper to ship each year to Europe to maximize the returns of its investors.

The objectives of the Dutch company differed significantly from the English objectives. The Dutch government had institutionalized in the monopoly charter a managerial incentive that promoted aggressive behaviors and exclusionary tactics against the English rivals. According to this scheme, Dutch managers were compensated on the basis of both the firm revenues and the firm profits, thus giving them an incentive to increase the trading volume and the turnover of the company. As a result, the company adopted hostile trade behavior.

The optimal profit-maximizing response of the English was to reduce their output. This strategic trade game is interesting, as it alerts us to the significant effects of implementing government policies that cannot be clearly recognizable as interventionist. In fact, without resorting to exports subsidies, the Dutch government was able to create strategic advantages for the domestic firm.

B. The Chicken War

This contemporary conflict over the poultry trade involved the U.S. and the EEC in the late 1950s. It represents the case of a bilateral iterative PD trade conflict. The prediction of a dynamic PD game that a tariff war between two large countries should evolve from mutual defection to mutual cooperation did not occur. Three main factors contributed to this outcome: the EEC's need for unity, the misperception of payoffs to the other actor, and, ironically, the GATT.

The formation of the EEC and its highly protective agricultural policy (i.e., the Common Agricultural Policy (CAP)), considered a foundation stone of the EEC itself, are at the core of the chicken war conflict in 1962. Like the U.S., the strong European agricultural lobby was interested in favoring greater protection of the poultry industry. This was incorporated into the CAP and deeply damaged U.S. farm exports of frozen chickens. The U.S., under GATT's article, requested a compensation for the losses caused by the chicken policy, but they could not reach an agreement on the amount of the compensation.

The obstinate European behavior induced a more belligerent U.S. policy. The U.S. glass, carpet, and rug industry received escape clause protection from EEC exports, allegedly causing serious injury. Thus, a tactic of cross-retaliation was adopted by the U.S. in an attempt to induce the EEC to abandon or revise the agricultural protection. The possibility of granting concessions to the U.S. created many divisions among the EEC members. The "unfair" U.S. cross-retaliation reinforced the EEC's position to refuse all modifications of the CAP, as the CAP became a symbol of the need for EEC unity in the face of a common adversary. In game theoretical terms, this European unconditional preference for defection changed the structure of the simple PD game into a prisoner's dilemma deadlock. This game is characterized by the fact that one player prefers mutual defection to mutual cooperation. This variation of the simple iterative PD structure prevented U.S.–EEC cooperative solutions.

Finally, in September, 1963, the issue was submitted to a special GATT tribunal that found the U.S. claim justified, but almost halved the U.S. damage claim to a level much closer to the EEC's own estimates. The GATT's finding was accepted by all parties. The U.S. showed its dissatisfaction over the chicken battle by imposing some penalty tariffs on particular countries—those who had showed a strong interest in not modifying the chicken protection. The GATT's intervention prevented the conflict from spilling over into other issues but, at the same time, by setting a final compensation, removed the need to cooperate on the issue of the Chicken War itself.

C. The Steel Turmoil

The steel conflict involved the U.S., Japan, the EEC, and many other smaller countries for the partition of the U.S. steel market. This case presents several important peculiarities. First, the conflict remained confined to a low-intensity level. Second, although there was interactive bargaining in steel, no formal retaliations typically associated with trade wars occurred (with only one exception). Third, it started the practice of managed trade with heavy use of antidumping, countervailing duties, subsidy charges, and bargaining over quantity restraints and quotas.

The structure of this game is a dynamic multilateral asymmetric game with many players of substantially different size. The larger countries involved were the U.S., Japan, and the EEC; all the others were small players. According to game theory predictions, the presence of many actors, under the MFN rule, creates the incentive to free-ride. The outcome of the game is therefore mutual defection and noncooperative strategies. This prediction actually occurred. In the chronology of events the larger countries initiated trade barriers.

To understand how the conflict started and developed, we need to look at the beginning of the century. By 1900 the U.S. was the major steel-exporting country, and it was dumping in foreign markets. The steel industry was a symbol of national economic power, as it was found in only the most advanced countries and was a component of other advanced economies. The higher productivity of the new Japanese plants, the much lower employment costs, and the low cost of capital due to the government interventions (through low interest rates, tax breaks, and direct subsidies) increased Japanese competitiveness and contributed to its emergence as a main exporter in the steel market.

This rapid and large-scale success in penetrating the U.S. market induced the U.S. firms to seek protection by invoking countervailing duties, antidumping, and escape clause actions. These relatively unsuccessful actions induced the U.S. government to negotiate a temporary Voluntary Restraint Agreement (VRA) with Japan and the EEC. The EEC and Japan were given 41% of a fixed import tonnage. After the last expiration of the VRA, the U.S. filed the largest dumping suit on record against six Japanese steel firms. As a result of a long negotiation process, a Trigger Price Mechanism was adopted in 1978, which set the import price based on Japanese production costs. Any import from Japan below that price would automatically trigger a dumping investigation.

Overall, the trading relations between the U.S. and Japan and the U.S. and the EEC in the steel market have not shown any signs of significant antagonism. The system of voluntary restraints, instead of tariffs, was tolerated by Japan and the EEC mainly because these quotas were freely given without any cost to the exporter country for its allowed amount of trade in the U.S. The quota system also made it easier to squeeze out more efficient third-country competitors in the target market.

Moreover, in Japan the quota system, as opposed to the tariff system, was particularly favored because it promoted the formation of a steel-exporting cartel that could raise its prices and reap monopoly profits. Actually Japan's rapid emergence as a massive exporter of steel and the decline of the U.S. is the most widely cited example of a successful industrial policy combined with acquiescent U.S. behavior producing a nonsignificant response to trade policies.

Among others, one interesting aspect of the multilateral steel trade rivalries involves the LDCs and the new rising competitors. At first the larger economies did not pay much attention to the impressive rates of export growth of some of the LDCs and the NICs. Since these countries were not perceived as a major threat, they could gradually penetrate the markets of the three cyclopes (U.S., Japan, and the EEC) almost unnoticed and could take advantage of the restrictions negotiated by the three larger economies. The first suits filed against individual developing countries were recorded in 1979 with dumping actions filed against South Korea, Taiwan, and Brazil.

It was not until 1984, with the Reagan plan, that the threat of their rising role in world trade was fully perceived. They were targeted as a whole through forced quantitative limits on their exports to the U.S. with no concurrent reduction of U.S. imports from either Japan or the EEC. In fact, the Reagan plan restricted steel imports from the LDCs to 18.5% without significantly changing either the EEC or the Japanese shares of the U.S. market. The LDCs had effectively become the target of a U.S./Japan/EEC coalition to reduce and hold the LDCs share of the U.S. market at a minimal level. This dubious tactic to shut down smaller economies because of their limited or ineffective ability to retaliate was even more dramatically implemented in the textile trade with the Multi-Fiber Arrangement (MFA) and has become a concern and a complaint of the LDCs ever since.

D. The Textile Dispute

This case of trade conflict is also characterized by the presence of influential players (i.e., Japan and the U.S.) and by a large number of smaller countries. Although the structure of the game is very similar to the one presented in the steel case, the outcome has a unique feature of "collusive" noncooperation, as the large countries colluded in noncooperating strategies directed against developing countries. Thus, to some extent, under the MFA all countries actively or passively agreed to not cooperate.

The textile industry has a long historical tradition of trade conflicts, in part because textiles is one of the first sectors that developing countries have traditionally entered. After the War World II and until the end of the 1970s, Japanese firms attempted to conquer the U.S. market. The U.S. resolutely responded to the Japanese invasion by resorting to quantity restraints, which induced Japanese reactions and embittered U.S.–Japan relations.

By the time these two countries reached an agreement, other developing countries, especially those in Asia, managed to break into the sector and to produce even more cheaply than Japan. Moreover, these emerging economies benefited from the trade restrictions imposed on Japanese exports and expanded their textile exports to the U.S. The American industry requested the government to enlarge the scope of bilateral restraints and to establish a multilateral control system over textiles. As a result of a U.S. proposal, importing and exporting countries spent more than 6 months in tough negotiations under the auspices of GATT and concluded the MFA on December, 1973. The basic objective of the MFA here was to achieve expansion of trade and progressive liberalization of world trade in textile products, ensuring the equitable and orderly development of this trade.

The Arrangement is a *de facto* derogation of the free trade principle of GATT. It allows the developed countries to deviate from the basic GATT rules of nondiscriminatory acts and eliminations of quantitative restraints and permits them to impose quotas on products from developing countries. Although the MFA also provides some provisions for importing countries to secure access to textiles and garments from developing countries, it was primarily meant to protect the interests of the developed countries by providing "breathing space" to make adjustments.

During the second of the three extensions of the MFA, the LDCs realized that their negotiating position could be strengthened only if they were united. Thus, they established a formal institution to improve coordination among themselves and to provide technical assistance in textile negotiations. Their coalition has proved to be successful. In fact, among the important provisions of the UR there is the condition to replace the quotas under the MFA with less-restrictive tariffs over a 10-year period.

VI. CONCLUSIONS: WHAT ARE THE FUTURE TRADE CHALLENGES?

The analysis of the past should alert us to the risks of the future. Since the late 1940s it has become evident that the use of economic "weapons" to achieve national security objectives is preferable to more violent options. The experience of two world wars, the threat of nuclear weapons, and the demise of the Cold War have deeply influenced the ways in which single nations, as well as the entire international community, deal with conflicting interests. However, if the use of military threat both for aggressive or defensive purposes has, fortunately, become more parsimonious, the use, and sometimes the abuse, of economic weapons has, regrettably, escalated. The risk is that military rivalries and arms races will be replaced by economic rivalries and forms of commercial warfare. In this light, we can consider the success of the Uruguay Round as a big step forward in the direction of the international trade disarmament.

The implementation of the Uruguay Round is expected to increase world trade by some $270 billion per year by the end of the year 2002 and increase the standards of living throughout the world. The success of the UR goes well beyond these figures. Its early collapse would have been disastrous psychologically and could have led to an unrestrained proliferation of trade restrictions and destructive trade wars. Despite the success of the Uruguay Round, many serious trade problems remain. Among the new challenges are the following: renewed interest in protectionism to assure "special" protection of high-technology industries and to satisfy a future demand from the developed countries against manufactured exports of the NICs; increases in regionalistic tendencies; and escalation and proliferation of aggressive unilateralism. Although free trade must be viewed as the ultimate goal and although countries are heading slowly but consistently in that direction, it would be advisable in the immediate future to set a less ambitious and more modest goal in regulating trade relations, namely to skew the system toward freer trade by defining the terms and the rules for fair and mutually beneficial trading activities. These tasks will require countries to abandon any "special" excuses for protectivist measures and heartily justified retaliation and to banish aggressive unilateralism.

The December, 1988 Uruguay Round of the GATT specifically addressed the above trade disarmament issues. A member of the U.S. delegation for the UR wrote that there is a growing consensus that if we can defuse the trade weapons that encourage trade conflicts, this in itself will create a better environment for peace and prosperity based on growth. The UR is a good start in the direction of commercial disarmament.

The issue of preferential trade agreements is more controversial. One can argue that these free-trade areas represent a progression toward freer trade and more peaceful trade relations and that they complement, rather than undermine, the WTO. However, protection toward nonmembers just may create interbloc trade conflicts and trade wars between alliances. After all, these regional agreements embody the logic of discrimination, and this principle has proved to create more adverse than beneficial effects. The economic consequences of regionalistic tendencies are not so clear cut, as they are intertwined with political, social, and cultural factors. It may be possible that free trade starts from "befriending thy neighbor," but in order for free trade to progress countries must understand, or simply remember, that the earth is round.

Also See the Following Articles

DECISION THEORY AND GAME THEORY • ECONOMICS OF WAR AND PEACE, OVERVIEW • TRADE, CONFLICT, AND COOPERATION AMONG NATIONS

References

Bhagwati, J., & Patrick, H. T. (1990). *Aggressive unilateralism.* Ann Arbor: The University of Michigan Press.

Brander, J., & Spencer, B. J. (1983). International R&D rivalry and industrial strategy. *Journal of International Economics, 18,* 83–100.

Conybeare, J. A. C. (1987). *Trade wars: The theory of international commercial rivalry.* New York: Columbia University Press.

Harrison, G. W., & Rutstrom, E. E. (1991). Trade wars, trade negotiations and applied game theory. *The Economic Journal, 101,* 420–435.

Irwin, D. A. (1991). Mercantilism as strategic trade policy: The Anglo-Dutch rivalry for the East India trade. *Journal of Political Economy, 99*(61), 1296–1314.

Johnson, H. G. (1953). Optimum tariffs and retaliation. *Review of Economic Studies, 21,* 142–153.

Kennan, J., & Riezman, R. (1988). Do big countries win tariff wars? *International Economic Review, 29*(1) 81–85.

Krugman, P. R. (1986). *Strategic trade policy and the new international economics.* Cambridge, MA: The MIT Press.

MacMillan, J. (1993). Trade accords and trade wars. In L. H. Horst & N. Van (Eds.), *Trade welfare and economic policies* (pp. 167–176). Ann Arbor: University of Michigan Press.

Nivola, P. S. (1993). *Regulating unfair trade.* Washington, DC: The Brooking Institution.

Staiger, R. W. (1995). International rules and institutions for trade policy. In G. Grossman & K. Rogoff (Eds.), *Handbook of international economics* (Vol. III, pp. 1495–1551). New York: Elsevier.

Woronoff, J. (1984). *World trade war.* New York: Praeger.

Transnational Organizations

Jackie Smith

State University of New York at Stony Brook

GLOSSARY

Global Civil Society "That domain of associational life that exists above the individual and below the state yet across state boundaries through which people experience the virtues of sociality and represent themselves in a social context" (Wapner, 1996, p. 7). Global civil society interfaces with international political institutions, often pressing these institutions toward more humane purposes.

International Nongovernmental Organization (INGO) A formal organization composed of a membership base that comes from more than two countries. International nongovernmental organizations pursue purposes independent of national governments and intergovernmental agencies, although some INGOs also receive government funding and include government employees among their members.

Social Movement A more or less cohesive collection of individual and organizational actors excluded from routine decision-making processes that engages in various collective attempts to promote social and/or political change.

Transnational Social Movement Organization An international nongovernmental organization engaged in explicit attempts to "[change] some elements of the social structure and/or reward distribution of society" (McCarthy & Zald, 1977, p. 1217).

TRANSNATIONAL ORGANIZATIONS are nongovernmental entities with some degree of formalization that involve members from more than one state. These organizations, often referred to as international nongovernmental organizations (or INGOs), represent efforts of individuals and organizations to address common problems by working across national boundaries. Transnational organizations vary considerably in the nature and extent of transnational cooperation they actually generate, but they are all shaped by similar global processes and trends. Particularly in the latter half of the 20th century, the numbers and geographic scope of transnational organizations have expanded dramatically. Large numbers of transnational organizations now promote economic interests, cultural and religious values, recreation, public service, and social and political change.

Transnational organizations are key indicators of an emerging "global civil society." As efforts of those acting beyond state boundaries to address collective goals, transnational organizations can provide essential tools for global political and social change. They provide foundations for transnational social movements by aggregating interests beyond state boundaries and articulating these interests in transnational policy-making arenas. To the extent that these organizations facilitate communication and cooperation among people from different national backgrounds, they generate definitions of global problems and their solutions that transcend those formed by a single national perspective.

I. FORCES SHAPING TRANSNATIONAL ORGANIZATION

Kriesberg describes four global trends that have affected the emergence of transnational nongovernmental organizations, including: growing democratization, increasing global integration, converging and diffusing values, and proliferating transnational institutions. Over the past several decades, there has been a growing acceptance of democratic values, and greater numbers of people around the world now enjoy the right to participate in political decisions affecting their lives. Democratization within nations helps provide the skills and resources necessary for transnational organization. And increasing recognition by governments of democratic principles and rights has allowed greater international efforts to secure such rights for individuals, even when this has compromised national sovereignty.

Second, increasing global integration has advanced both the opportunities and the demands for transnational organization. The increased mobility and ease of transnational communications that have enabled the growth of a global economy have also facilitated transnational communication and cooperation for noneconomic purposes. At the same time, as the global economy extends its reach and increases its influence on national and even local market dynamics, the world's citizens are increasingly dependent upon transnational ties in order to protect their interests. Indeed, in order to check the negative impacts of global economic forces, transnational citizens' organizations may need to enhance their abilities to operate efficient and responsive transnational organizational structures similar to those that advance transnational economic operations.

Third, globally converging and diffusing values help shape the emergence and form of transnational organization. The expansion of transnational economic exchange has created common experiences such as urbanization and industrialization, which are shared by individuals in many countries. Transnational communication facilitates business transactions, but it also helps convey other ideas and cultural artifacts beyond national boundaries. Shared values and symbols can facilitate transnational communication and cooperation by providing common points of reference and even shared targets for action.

Finally, the proliferation of transnational institutions helps to generate opportunities and incentives for transnational organization. The development of inter-state organizations such as the United Nations or the European Union has heightened the need for similarly organized nongovernmental efforts. In order to attempt to influence these intergovernmental organizations, citizens are formally required to adopt transnational organizational forms. To obtain consultative status at the United Nations, an organization must be international in scope. For this and other reasons, transnational organization improves citizens' organizations' abilities to monitor relevant international developments and to influence decisions taken in multilateral political forums.

II. FORMS OF TRANSNATIONAL ORGANIZATION

A. Types of Organization

Transnational organizations are formed to promote economic interests as well as to further noneconomic goals, and thus they take on many forms. The principal focus of this article is on transnational organizations that pursue noneconomic goals. But clearly many transnational organizations exist to expand international economic activities and to perform functions of governments. Thus, we can consider three main "sectors" of transnational organization: the intergovernmental, economic, and voluntary sectors. Each of these sectors is introduced and defined, but the voluntary sector and its relations with transnational organizations in other sectors is explored in much greater detail. Table I provides examples of organizations in each of these sectors.

While most transnational organizations in the economic and voluntary sectors are not founded specifically for political purposes, whenever these actors consciously employ their resources to constrain the choices or influence the behaviors of states or other transnational actors, they are involved in transnational politics. Transnational organizations are relevant to global peace, violence, and conflict to the extent that they are involved in such political processes. The purposes and functions of transnational organizations influence the extent and the nature of their contributions to global politics.

TABLE I

Types of Transnational Organizations

Type of Transnational Organization	Characteristics	Examples
Intergovernmental	Formed by agreement among states	United Nations World Trade Organization
Economic	Seeks economic benefits/profits	IBM Corporation
	Includes transnational criminal organizations using illicit means to pursue profit	Transnational drug cartels
Voluntary	Formed by citizens to further what is seen as a public good or to advance the rights or interests of a particular group	International Olympic Committee International Peace Research Association
	Most pursue nonpolitical goals of recreation, service, professional association, etc.	Amnesty International

1. Intergovernmental Sector

The main actors in the intergovernmental sector are intergovernmental bureaucracies, which are created by formal agreements among states. These bureaucracies or agencies are designed to implement international agreements and are instructed by intergovernmental decision-making bodies and allotted resources to carry out their tasks. Once in place, however, these agencies take on their own internal dynamics, which can lead to widely divergent perspectives between the states that established the agency and the bureaucrats who carry out their formal missions. The interests of these actors, combined with their formal authority and access to governments, create important strategic possibilities for transnational social movements.

As is the case with national and subnational bureaucracies, it is not uncommon for officials within intergovernmental agencies to find it in their interest to cooperate with other nonstate actors who share their goals. This is particularly true for actors who enjoy widespread support and little organized opposition within the broader population (e.g., "consensus movements"). McCarthy and Wolfson describe the relationships between government officials and movement agents within countries:

In contrast to the criticism from partisan and grass-roots sources that is likely to follow from governmental facilitation of conflict movements, similar attempts to aid the mobilization of consensus movements are almost certain to generate legitimacy [for the agency], and perhaps even resources, for the beneficent unit of the state. The managers of state agencies, then, can be expected

to see major advantages in aiding the activists of a consensus movement (1992, p. 288).

Similarly, international bureaucrats who are constantly plagued with resource deficits that frequently prevent their agencies from effectively fulfilling their missions are likely to be open to collaborative relationships with certain other nonstate actors. In their analysis of transnational relations, Keohane and Nye concluded that there is much room for transnational actors and intergovernmental organizations' secretariats to be "potential allies" (1972, pp. 395–398). For example, agencies such as the UN High Commissioner for Refugees and the UN Commission for Human Rights currently rely quite heavily on information and services provided by transnational citizens' human rights, development, and aid organizations. As intergovernmental organizations become increasingly strapped for resources and inundated with global problem-solving tasks, their agents may be even more open to collaborative relationships with nonstate actors capable of furthering organizational goals.

2. Economic Sector

The most visible and influential actor in the transnational economic sector is the transnational corporation (TNC), which is a profit-oriented business operating in more than one country. Transnational corporations are perhaps most clearly interested in and able to influence major (economic-related) policy decisions of state actors. They command vast amounts of resources and can therefore use considerable incentives and threats against states that challenge their interests. For instance, according to a study by the Institute for Policy

Studies, of the 100 largest economic units in the world, only 49 were countries while the remaining 51 were TNCs. And the gross revenues of a number of the largest corporations exceed the gross domestic products of states like New Zealand, the Philippines, and Indonesia.

Industry associations, which may technically be nonprofit organizations, are also part of the economic sector, as their purpose is to maximize the profits of members. Examples of these include regional or global associations of subnational, national, and transnational producers in a particular industry such as the International Association of Refrigerated Warehouses, the Nordic Hotel and Restaurant Association, or the Textile Industry Federation of Africa and Madagascar. Occasionally, the names of these organizations belie their true purpose; for instance, the Global Climate Coalition was set up to protect the interests of fossil fuel industries against threats of new environmental regulations. These organizations provide services for members such as information and assistance with establishing new national operations and with meeting international industry standards. Occasionally they engage in advocacy on behalf of their members by lobbying for industry interests in intergovernmental organizations.

Another nonstate actor in the economic sector is organized labor. While less influential than TNCs and far from a globally coordinated movement of the world's working people, transnational labor organizations maintain a presence in transnational politics. Their presence, moreover, is likely to expand as regional integration agreements such as the European Union and the North American Free Trade Agreement develop. The International Labor Organization has provided an intergovernmental forum where transnational labor organizations such as the World Federation of Trade Unions have regular access to business and government officials where they can work to protect workers' rights and interests.

In addition to these entities, transnational organizations also exist to pursue illicit economic and political goals. Such organizations are, for obvious reasons, more difficult to identify. Occasionally, such organizations will operate out of apparently legitimate front organizations. For instance, the Third World Relief Agency worked to channel humanitarian relief aid but also weapons to Bosnian Muslims during the international embargo on such transfers. Phil Williams details the forms of transnational organization used to promote drug trafficking, smuggling of goods and people, nuclear materials trafficking, and other illegal activities. Transnational corporations dealing in international transfers of hazardous wastes will frequently establish temporary shell organizations to complicate efforts to track illegal shipments. While difficult to track and monitor, these transnational organizations can pose new threats to the international system, and they can complicate efforts to resolve violent conflicts. Their work, however, is facilitated by the increasing steps to liberalize international trade.

3. The Transnational Nonprofit or Voluntary Sector

Until fairly recently the transnational nonprofit or voluntary sector has been the most neglected by scholars of international relations. Young defines a nonprofit organization as a "body of individuals who associate for any of three purposes: (1) to perform public tasks that have been delegated to them by the state; (2) to perform public tasks for which there is a demand that neither the state nor for-profit organizations are willing to fulfill; or (3) to influence the direction of policy in the state, the for-profit sector, or other nonprofit organizations" (1991, p. 923). The categories of cultural, religious, and service organizations generally perform public tasks for which there is a demand (although at times some of these groups might engage in attempts to influence policy). Advocacy organizations, on the other hand, include TSMOs and other organizations whose primary mission it is to influence the policies of public and private institutions, or to otherwise promote social change.

Most scholars of international relations—if they mention them at all—refer to all the actors in this category as nongovernmental organizations or NGOs. Failing to distinguish among organizations in the nonprofit sector, however, has meant that many scholars have ignored the various roles these organizations can play in transnational politics. It is clear that the main activities of the European Sleep Research Society have quite different political implications from those of, say, the International Association for Non-Violent Sport or the Union of European Federalists. Specifically, we would expect that, of these three, the Union of European Federalists would be most engaged in transnational political processes. And yet, most scholars persist in considering all of these organizations "NGOs."[1] A

---

[1] Some researchers have attempted to refine the concept of NGOs. Boulding, for instance, uses the term "global social change organizations" (GSCOs) to refer to transnational advocacy groups, while Willetts calls them "global pressure groups."

major exception is the work of Peter Willetts, who adapts the work on domestic interest groups to transnational interest groups. Willetts distinguishes "global pressure groups" from other NGOs, classifying these into categories of sectional groups and promotional groups. Sectional groups are those that "seek to protect the interests of a particular section of society" and include economic, professional, and recreational associations, while promotional groups "seek to promote causes arising from a given set of attitudes" and consist of welfare agencies, religious groups, communal groups (e.g., women, ethnic groups), political parties, and issue-specific promotional groups (1993, p. 6).

Nongovernmental organizations in the voluntary or nonprofit sector play important roles in transnational politics. They press for the establishment of international norms such as the recognition of human rights, promote and monitor states' compliance with these norms, and challenge states that violate international standards. When they carry out these tasks, nongovernmental organizations play an essential part in promoting the development and effectiveness of intergovernmental institutions.

The transnational nonprofit sector, while quite large, is very diverse. Moreover, only a small proportion of these organizations ever becomes actively involved in transnational politics (although few can prevent their work from being affected by transnational politics). Transnational politics was defined above as "relationships in which at least one actor consciously employs resources, both material and symbolic, including the threat or exercise of punishment, to induce other actors to behave differently than they would otherwise behave" (Keohane & Nye, 1972, p. xxiv). Thus, our primary concern here is to define the major categories of transnational nonprofit organizations and their potential for political activity. Modifying Willetts's categories somewhat, four major categories of NGOs are identified below as cultural, religious, service, and advocacy organizations.

a. Transnational Cultural NGOs

A considerable proportion of transnational activity is organized into recreational associations. Perhaps the most prominent transnational recreational organization is the International Olympic Committee. Other organizations in this category are the World Organization for the Scout Movement, the European Camping Federation, and the World Bridge Federation. Also included in this category are transnational research institutes. Transnational research institutes typically aim to facilitate international scholarly cooperation and informa-

tion exchange, thus fostering scientific or scholarly advancement.

Recreational and cultural organizations are not generally involved in transnational politics. There are, however, occasions when they may be forced to make decisions that have broader political relevance. One example of this is when the U.S. branch of the International Olympic Committee was forced to decide whether to boycott the 1980 Olympics in Moscow to protest the Soviet invasion of Afghanistan. Research institutes, while not generally designed for political purposes, can become involved in transnational politics either as part of what Haas calls "epistemic communities" or more directly by lending their expertise to broader political movements, such as the environmental movement.

b. Transnational Religious NGOs

Perhaps the oldest category of transnational nongovernmental actor is the religious NGO. The Catholic Church is one example of such an actor as is the World Council of Churches (WCC), the World Muslim Congress, and the World Fellowship of Buddhists. Besides formal church institutions, there are also numerous associations outside formal church structures that are based on religious identity. Examples of these are the Baptist Press Service, Youth for Christ International, and the Muslim Women's Organization as well as transnational religious orders.

While most of the activities of religious organizations remain outside of transnational politics, it is not uncommon for transnational religious organizations to act as transnational political actors. For example, the WCC has several standing committees devoted to global social justice work. Catholic, Protestant, and Jewish religious organizations have been heavily involved in promoting the cause of international human rights and thus have gained considerable experience as transnational political actors. Analyzing the role of transnational religious solidarity structures in challenging authoritarian regimes in Latin America, Pagnucco and McCarthy concluded that the strategic advantages of transnational mobilization of religious identity

> may be summarized as the [ready] creation of solidarity across national boundaries ... the development of mechanisms of mutual support, the creation of international legitimacy for local claims and action, and international mobilization in support of local activists. The leaders of core states where religious freedom is a norm tend to be diffusely supportive of such freedom for

members of such communities in non-core states. Second, the many other advantages of transnational SMO structures . . . allowed a cadre organization with few resources made up of a very small number of activists to exert telling pressure on parochial and repressive regimes (1992, p. 145).

In short, transnational religious institutions and networks can serve as important mobilizing infrastructures for political movements. Churches and religious organizations can bring solidarity, concrete resources, and political legitimacy to a movement and help raise the political salience of the issues it seeks to address. This may be particularly true in cases of transnational efforts to protect the civil and political rights of individuals. Religious organizations often claim the loyalties of individuals from numerous states and can therefore more readily sensitize members to the experiences of those in other countries.

Transnational religious organizations may also become involved in politics less directly by providing resources and protection for fledgling movements. After the demise of the Soviet empire, churches mobilized globally to provide aid to their East European counterparts. Churches and religious orders may contribute personnel and other resources to transnational political groups such as Pax Christi International, Service for Peace and Justice in Latin America, or Amnesty International. Finally, churches and religious orders are also important sources of funding for international aid and relief efforts. Indeed, Catholic Relief Services is one of the largest funders of international development projects. Increasingly, church (and other) institutions established to promote development work find it difficult to avoid engaging in policy advocacy as they pursue their development or aid missions.

Some religious institutions also have an indirect impact on transnational politics, since they are often responsible for cultivating global awareness on the part of their members. Whether this awareness grows from a religious group's ethnopolitical liberation activities, missionary work, or international giving and service activities, churches are routinely encouraging members to take some kind of action in response to injustice, suffering, or oppression in the world. Even when religious organizations are not involved in transnational political activities, it is not uncommon to find that many individuals involved are motivated by religious beliefs. As Zald and McCarthy observed, "while religious groups may serve as infrastructures for broader social movement action, minority dissident factions within local religious groups may be important cells in broader movements even if they cannot convince the majority of their congregation to support them" (1987, p. 88). The apparent prominence of religiously motivated individuals in transnational movements suggests that prior participation in religious institutions may somehow encourage or predispose individuals to take part in transnational service and advocacy.

c. Transnational Service NGOs

Transnational service organizations are those that aim to provide relief aid to needy populations. Among these groups are the Save the Children Federation and World Vision. While most transnational service organizations struggle to keep their work clearly within the realm of service, many find it difficult to avoid engaging in efforts at institutional development and policy reform as they carry out their service missions. Transnational service NGOs have proven a fairly efficient means of disseminating international aid from governments and from intergovernmental agencies. Indeed, according to a study by Anheier and Cunningham, since the 1970s, when the U.S. Congress promoted a "new directions" approach to international development, the amount of U.S. aid channeled through service NGOs nearly doubled to over a billion dollars. United Nations agencies such as the World Health Organization also depend quite heavily on the assistance of nongovernmental service organizations in promoting their work in remote regions. For instance, a study by Kathryn Sikkink illustrates the work of such groups in promoting new practices in the marketing of baby food.

We can see that by serving as conduits of governmental aid and by facilitating the work of intergovernmental agencies, transnational service NGOs often work quite close to the transnational political arena. Indeed, supporting intergovernmental agencies' work may serve to enhance the effectiveness of intergovernmental institutions—and that would have direct implications for transnational politics. However, these political impacts are incidental to the main goals of these organizations, which are decidedly nonpartisan or impartial in their aims to provide some form of aid or service to needy populations.

d. Transnational Advocacy NGOs

The category of transnational advocacy NGOs includes Willetts's categories of professional associations, communal associations, political parties, and a fourth category, transnational social movement organizations. These groups share the characteristic that their organizational aims involve influencing policy and therefore bring them into *routine* involvement in transnational politics.

Transnational professional associations such as the International Federation of Accountants or the International Association for Cross-Cultural Psychology seek to protect the interests of their members in transnational politics. They also perform nonpolitical tasks such as harmonizing professional standards and providing professional advice and research on international dimensions of the particular field. In addition to advocating professional interests in global political forums, transnational professional associations may also become involved in broader campaigns for political change. For example, in the 1980s, many professional groups formed special committees to address issues of nuclear arms control. Professional organizations may also join international human rights campaigns aimed at protecting individual members of their organization or profession from human rights abuse by their own government(s).

Transnational communal groups also seek to protect and promote the interests of a specific category of people (e.g., Jews, women, francophones). These groups primarily engage in activities aimed at serving members directly, and occasionally they enter transnational politics to promote or defend group interests. For instance, in recent years indigenous peoples' groups have organized transnationally to defend common interests and to resist new forms of control by national governments. Often such groups resist change and promote a return to status quo arrangements. Those communal groups, whose goals demand some form of social or political change, are considered as part of the subset of transnational social movement organizations discussed below.

Transnational political parties are usually federations of national parties organized to coordinate national party platforms and particularly national positions with regard to regional integration policies. While important structural differences limit the abilities of such groups to coordinate electoral strategies across national boundaries, such groups often seek to help members develop more coherent and complementary national policies on key transnational issues.

Finally, transnational social movement organizations (TSMOs) are those voluntary sector transnational organizations that are generally of greatest interest to peace and conflict researchers. Transnational social movement organizations differ from other transnational advocacy organizations in that they are explicitly designed to further social change goals. They are part of broader social movements, which result when networks of actors excluded from routine decision-making processes engage in collective attempts to "[change] some elements of the social structure and/or reward distribution of society" (1977, p. 1217). Transnational social movements involve *conscious* attempts to develop transnational cooperation around shared social change goals. They do this by developing ongoing communication among organizations and activists that allows them to share technical and strategic information, coordinate parallel activities, or even to cooperate in truly transnational collective action.

Transnational social movement organizations are critical in generating the transnational linkages necessary for effective global change action. They actively attempt to mobilize new human and material resources for social change and to activate and coordinate strategic collective action throughout the ebbs and flows of a movement. Thus, they are principal carriers of social movements, even when they are not the sole organizations active in social movements. Some TSMOs serve as important nodes that help link the different elements of transnational social movements, although the extent to which they can successfully coordinate movement activities varies. Like national movements, transnational social movements incorporate a range of individual and organizational actors, including individuals, church groups, professional associations, and other social groups. Thus, TSMOs often work closely with the other types of transnational organizations described above.

B. Growth and Change

The transnational voluntary sector has expanded considerably since the early 1950s. Over 4 decades, transnational nongovernmental organizations of all different kinds developed to foster cultural exchanges, facilitate international recreational activities, and to organize individuals around common religious identities, among other functions. The numbers of such organizations rose from just around 1100 groups in 1953 to over 9000 by 1993 (see Fig. 1). At the same time, the number of TSMOs grew nearly sixfold from just around 100 organizations in 1953 to over 600 in 1993.

As a percentage of all INGOs, the population of TSMOs has grown more slowly than the general population of INGOs. In 1953, TSMOs represented 9.7% of all INGOs, but by 1993, they were just 6.8% of the population. The most extensive growth in the number of transnational organizations came after the early 1970s, when the total number of INGOs more than quadrupled. Not coincidentally, this period also marked the origins of UN global conferences, which aimed to

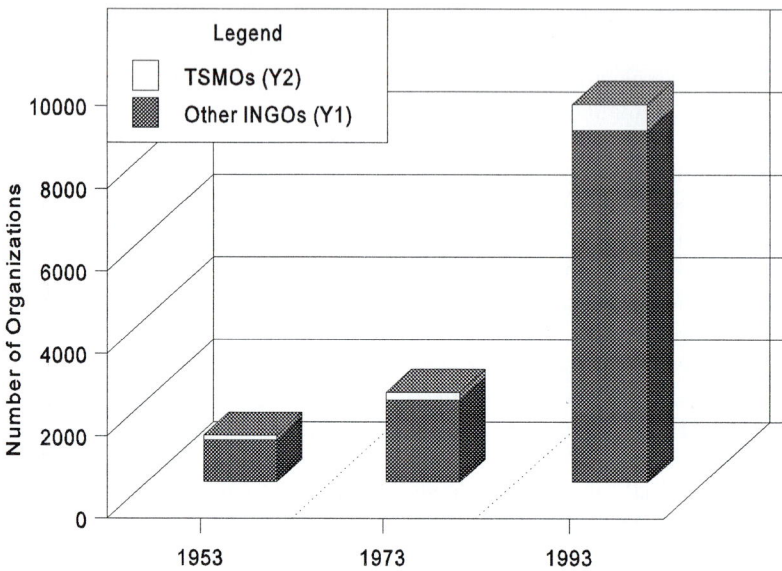

FIGURE 1   Expansion of INGOs, 1953–1993. The years surveyed begin in 1953 because that was the first edition of the *Yearbook*. Source: Yearbook of International Organizations.

expand public and government awareness of increasingly evident global problems such as food scarcity, environmental degradation, and population pressures. During the same period, the numbers of intergovernmental organizations has risen from only a few dozen in the years following World War II to over 2500 organizations today.

Global conferences occur outside routine meetings of the United Nations, and the agencies responsible for organizing these meetings have often sought to maximize the participation of INGOs, including TSMOs, at these meetings. Transnational organizations have proved valuable from the perspective of United Nations planners because they provide channels of communication from these global meetings to the local and national constituencies represented by these organizations. Not only do transnational organizations help convey information from international conferences to their constituents, but they also aggregate the interests of their members and articulate these interests in global conference settings. The existence of transnational organizations has been crucial to bringing previously unheard voices into the global political arena.

Global conferences signaled growing recognition that a series of problems required the attention and coordinated responses of numerous governments. On a growing number of issues, states found that they could no longer manage their external affairs without deliberate efforts to coordinate their policies with those of other governments. Thus, the United Nations and other intergovernmental organizations (IGOs) were created by formal agreements among states in order to manage problems that transcended state boundaries. The expansion of IGOs and the range of issues they address have generated a sphere of multilateral politics that has necessitated a parallel rise in a politically engaged global civil society. This global civil society is manifest in transnational organizations which serve to help individuals develop understandings of how trends in the intergovernmental sphere impact their interests and values. Transnational social movement organizations and other transnational organizations also allow for communication that turns diverse perspectives of constituents from varying political contexts into more or less coherent statements of collective goals and interests. This interest aggregation function plays an important role to manage conflict in a world experiencing increasing political and economic integration.

1. Transnational Issue Advocacy

By working to shape individuals' perceptions of global problems and by seeking to influence individual and government behaviors, transnational organizations have generated what Wapner calls "world civic politics." World civic politics involves attempts to shape the underlying institutions, beliefs, and practices that condition national, subnational, and individual actions and thereby to influence elite, inter-state negotiations and policies. Transnational organizations have also been pivotal players in government-level negotiations, pressing states to expand international cooperation around emerging problems and at times providing proposals about how to structure international cooperation. As governments organized—often in response to pressure from nongovernmental organizations—to address a growing number of common problems, they created institutions that provided various openings for transnational organizations of individuals and organizations to attempt to influence inter-state politics. These openings, in turn, have affected patterns of transnational organization.

Table II summarizes the numbers of TSMOs organized around issues that have motivated the largest numbers of transnational organizations. Human rights has remained the predominant area of transnational social movement activity throughout the entire post-WWII era, representing the oldest transnational issue area. Among the human rights TSMOs are some of the oldest transnational organizations, including the Anti-Slavery Society for the Protection of Human Rights, which was founded in 1823. Some of the newest transnational social movement organizations have emerged to work on environmental issues. Although very few environmental TSMOs existed prior to 1973, that issue represents the main focus of the largest proportion of contemporary TSMOs. Transnational social movements around the issues of peace, women's rights, world order, and the international language Esperanto have also consistently attracted some of the largest numbers of TSMOs.[2]

2. Geography of Transnational Organization

Transnational social movement organizations are most frequently based in the Northern hemisphere, largely centering around cities that serve as bases of political and economic power. But even as they represent disproportionately individuals and groups from the more industrialized regions of the globe, these organizations are incorporating increasingly global memberships. Figure 2 illustrates the shifts in geographic distribution of TSMO memberships. While West Europeans and North Americans retain the largest share of memberships in TSMOs, individuals and organizations from Southern, less-industrialized regions have become increasingly incorporated into these global networks.

In addition to expanding their memberships in developing regions, TSMOs are increasingly headquartered in the global South. In 1983 only 17% of all TSMOs based their international offices in the Southern hemisphere. By 1993 this figure rose to 24%. Thus, although the integration of Southern memberships has been slow, the trend is that TSMO memberships are becoming more balanced in terms of geographic representation.

III. GLOBAL CIVIL SOCIETY, SOCIAL MOVEMENTS, AND TRANSNATIONAL ORGANIZATIONS

Global civil society is "that domain of associational life that exists above the individual and below the state yet across state boundaries through which people experience the virtues of sociality and represent themselves in a social context" (Wapner, 1996, p. 7). The proliferation and expansion of international NGOs and of transnational alliances among national and local NGOs signal the presence of a global civil society with deepening roots. But as the broader global society has expanded, so too has its politically engaged sector. Thus, we can now speak of a global public sphere, where critical discourse about collective interests and values and their

TABLE II

Transnational Social Movement Issues

	1953	1973	1993
Total No. organizations	110	183	631
Issue area[a]			
Human Rights	30.0	22.4	26.6
International Law	12.7	13.7	4.1
Peace	10.0	7.7	9.4
Esperanto	10.0	15.3	8.6
Women's Rights	9.1	8.7	9.7
EthnicUnity/Group rts.	9.1	9.8	4.6
World Order	7.3	6.6	7.6
Development	2.7	3.8	5.4
Environment	1.8	5.5	14.3

[a] These are given in percentages.

Source: Kathryn Sikkink and her research assistants gathered information from the 1953 and 1973 Yearbook of International Organizations.

[2] These conclusions are based on data on transnational organizations available in the *Yearbook of International Organizations*, the most comprehensive source of such information. This source is useful for understanding broad patterns, but it undoubtedly underestimates some types of transnational association, especially those engaged in violence or in other illicit activities and those with less formal organizational structures.

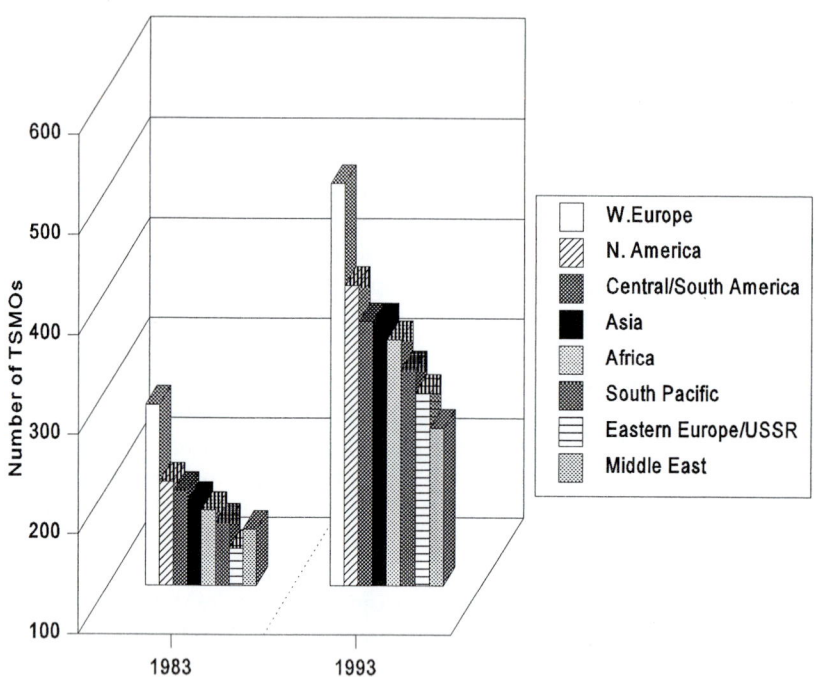

FIGURE 2   Geography of TSMO memberships: the number of TSMOs with members in each region. Source: Yearbook of International Organizations.

relation to national and international policy can take place. Transnational social movement organizations constitute a subset of INGOs that is routinely engaged in this emerging global public sphere. Transnational social movement organizations are organized across national boundaries to advocate some form of social and/ or political change. Their routine involvement in politically motivated social change advocacy distinguishes them from recreational, professional, and other INGOs that may enter into political debates at times, but whose organizational missions prevent them from doing regular social change activity.

A. Organizations, Social Movements, and Networks

As nodes in much broader networks of individuals and social organizations seeking a particular social change goal (social movements), TSMOs help frame global issues, mobilize broader publics around their social change frames, and promote activities in national, subnational, and transnational contexts to advance movement goals. They help identify, frame, and disseminate important technical and scientific information that is relevant to policy debates, and their political orientation helps channel such information into and through policy processes. Effective transnational movements attract

different clusters of organizational and individual actors that offer varying degrees of material, logistic, and solidary support for the movements' goals.[3] Often transnational organizations as well as national NGOs (e.g., church organizations or professional associations) participate in social movements, working alongside TSMOs, and bringing the movement both an expanded legitimacy and broader constituencies.[4] Differences in the numbers of people and groups a movement mobilizes around a movement's goals produces "cycles" or "surges" of movement activity. The surges in movement activity can produce government responses (both positive and negative) that have wide impacts for social change.

Social movements incorporate a broad range of actors, including both organizations and individuals. Occasionally, they will be supported by individuals or agencies employed by governments or by the economic sector. For instance, Greenpeace and the WorldWatch

---

[3] At the same time, these movements often generate organized opposition to such goals, and this opposition takes the form of a movement, earning it the label "countermovement."

[4] Because many churches are already transnational in character, these may be more likely sites of transnational movement-building than are other social infrastructures that lack transnational organizational structures.

Institute have sought the support of the global insurance industry for international action to curb global warming and its associated risks. Thus, as they seek to advance their collective goals, movements can serve as bridges between elements of civil society and political and economic realms of society. In this sense, they play a role that contributes to the management of global conflict by anticipating imminent crises and disseminating analyses on how to resolve these crises.

Transnational social movements vary dramatically in the number and strength of the organizations they incorporate and in the extent to which they are coordinated by a single organization or cluster of organizations. Some movements are represented by strong national (or transnational) umbrella organizations that help to coordinate action and provide a unified image of the movement. But the influence of a single transnational organization on a movement varies over time, and it is rare that any organization will retain undisputed leadership. Other movements are less able to unite under a common organizational banner, remaining more diffuse in structure than are movements with strong centralizing organizations.

Another crucial variable for the impact of transnational organizations is the amount and combination of human, material and political resources they bring to their social change efforts. Money and members alone will not usually translate into political influence. Neither will the presence of political allies without the financial resources and activists to generate sustained political pressure. In addition, social movements often challenge the interests of other social groups, and they can generate opposition from countermovements. The strength and organization of the opposition to a social movement influences that movement's potential for political impact. All of these variables will be important for explaining the varying impacts movements have on the global political process.

1. Issue Networks

The set of actors involved in collective attempts to bring about social or political change may be more or less tightly integrated through social networks and routines. Social networks are informal collections of individuals and/ or organizations that—because of social or work routines—have either incidental or deliberate contact on a regular basis. Social networks formed around the pursuit of particular social change goals are social movements, and movements frequently incorporate clusters of social networks sharing a common issue of concern. Technologies that facilitate international communication and transportation have contributed to the development of what Margaret Keck and Kathryn Sikkink have called transnational "issue networks." In Sikkink's definition, issue networks form from clusters of activists and movement organizations, policy-makers, intergovernmental officials, media, and foundations pursuing a common, principled goal. Linked by a common interest in advancing a particular value, these networks aid communication and strategic coordination and learning, thereby facilitating movement activity.

Sometimes networks of actors choose to create formal organizations, or coalitions, that serve on an ad hoc, temporary, or on a permanent basis to facilitate routine communication and to coordinate members' (usually organizations) activities. Coalitions, for instance, may be formed to better focus the actions of a diverse range of organizations and to enhance the movement's efficient use of resources. Coalitions typically form around campaigns, which are deliberate efforts to coordinate movement actions around a particular policy or event and to thereby extend the movement's message beyond its elite and informed publics to a more general audience. Chatfield describes such coalitional efforts in his analysis of U.S. pacifist organizations in the interwar period. By creating structured communication links between movements and other societal organizations, coalitions help to disseminate movement frames, or definitions of problems and proposed solutions, into more general public debate, thereby shaping evolving public opinion on a particular issue.

2. Organizational Integration

Most transnational organizations take on a networklike structure where an international office helps facilitate communications with different members (individuals and organizations). Frequently transnational organizations are loose federations of nationally organized sections. They can vary dramatically in the quantity and quality of transnational communication. Thus, comparing such organizations or generalizing about their significance for global politics remains problematic. Nevertheless, to the extent that the existence of a formal transnational structure indicate at least some minimal level of communication and coordination among individuals and/or groups from more than two countries, we can say that these organizations represent tools for nongovernmental, global problem-solving.

Dennis Young analyzes the challenges transnational organizations face when attempting to mobilize individuals across national boundaries to affect global change. A fundamental task of transnational organizations is to achieve the *integration* of their memberships. This entails cultivating common interpretations of collective goals and the means of achieving these. These common frames can only develop through extensive, two-way communication, and they are facilitated only through strong leadership that provides a unifying focus for members of highly diverse political and cultural backgrounds. Transnational organizational integration is therefore costly. It requires money for long-distance telephone lines, international postage, translation, transportation, and other costs associated with communicating across national boundaries. It also demands greater amounts of time and patience from members, as common positions and organizational decisions must be generated from a body of members or delegates whose backgrounds and perspectives are likely to differ much more dramatically than will those of leaders in local or national groups. Often financial subsidies must be made by sometimes cash-starved Northern affiliates to enable greater participation from members in less-industrialized countries. These and other obstacles to organizational integration continue to favor local and national forms of organization over transnational ones.

B. Transnational Organizations and Global Change

Transnational organizations typically bring together members or delegates from a number of different countries to consult on the organization's policy goals and to respond to changing political environments. These gatherings, whether in the form of actual meetings or telephone conferences, serve as opportunities for individuals from varying cultures and polities to learn about each others' experiences, observations, and interpretations of global problems. They often present participants' with views from other countries that contradict official government policies. Frequently, participants in transnational organizational meetings must work to overcome intense differences among their numbers regarding definitions of priorities and courses of action.

To the extent that they bring together delegates and members from different countries to discuss global problems, transnational organizations contribute to global conflict resolution efforts. As they grow in numbers and in experience, we can expect at least some of these transnational organizations to become more effective at influencing transnational political processes, both within and outside of formal inter-state institutional arenas.

Also See the Following Articles

CIVIL SOCIETY • ENVIRONMENTAL ISSUES, POLITICAL

Bibliography

Archer, A. (1983). Methods of multilateral management: Tie Interrelationship of intergovernmental organizations and NGOs. In T. T. Gati. (Ed.), *The United States, the UN and the management of global change* (pp. 303–325). New York University Press.

Boulding, E. (1991). The old and new transnationalism: An evolutionary perspective. *Human Relations, 44,* 763–786.

Feld, W. (1972). *Nongovernmental forces and world politics: A study of business, labor, and political groups.* New York: Praeger.

Feraru, A. T. (1974). Transnational political interest and the global environment. *International Organization, 28,* 31–60.

Gilpin, R. (1975). *U.S. power and the multinational corporation.* New York: Basic Books.

Goldman, R. M., (Ed.) (1983). *Transnational parties: Organizing the world's precincts.* Lanham, MD: University Press of America.

Haas, P. (1992). Introduction: Epistemic communities and international policy coordination. *International Organization, 46,* 1–35.

Keck, M., & Sikkink K. (1998). *Activists beyond borders: Transnational advocacy networks in international politics.* Ithaca: Cornell University Press.

Keohane, R., & Nye, J. (1972). Transnational relations and world politics: An introduction. In R. Keohane and J. Nye. (Eds.) *Transnational relations and world politics* (pp. ix–xxvii). Cambridge, MA: Harvard University Press.

Kriesberg, L. (1997). Social movements and global transformation. In J. Smith, C. Chatfield, and R. Pagnucco (Eds.) *Transnational Social Movements and Global Politics: Solidarity Beyond the State* (pp. 3–18). Syracuse: Syracuse University Press.

Livezey, L. W. (1989). U.S. religious organizations and the international human rights movement. *Human Rights Quarterly, 11,* 14–81.

McCarthy, J. D., & Wolfson, M. (1992). Consensus movements, conflict movements, and the cooptation of civic and state infrastructures. In A. Morris & C. McClurg Mueller (Eds.), *Frontiers in social movement theory,* (pp. 273–300). New Haven, CT: Yale University Press.

Meyer, D. & Staggenborg, S. (1996). Movements, countermovements, and the structure of political opportunity. *American Journal of Sociology, 101,* 1628–1660.

Pagnucco, R., & McCarthy, J. D. (1992). Advocating nonviolent direct action in Latin America: The antecedents and emergence of SERPAJ. In B. Misztal & A. Shupe (Eds.), *Religion and politics in comparative perspective* (pp. 125–147). New York: Praeger.

Sikkink, K. (1986). Codes of conduct for transnational corporations: The case of the WHO/UNICEF code. *International Organization, 40,* 815–840.

Smith, J., Chatfield, C., & Pagnucco, R. (Eds.) (1997). *Transnational social movements and world politics: Solidarity beyond the state.* Syracuse, NY: Syracuse University Press.

Wapner, P. (1995). Politics beyond the state: Environmental activism and world civic politics. *World Politics, 47,* 311–340.

Willetts, P. (Ed.) (1982). *Pressure groups in the international system,* (pp. 1–25). New York: St. Martin's.

Williams, P. (1994). Transnational criminal organisations and international security. *Survival, 36,* 96–113.

Young, D. R. (1991). The structural imperatives of international advocacy associations. *Human Relations, 44,* 921–941.

Zald, M., & McCarthy, J. D. (1987). Religious groups as crucibles of social movements. In M. Zald & J. D. McCarthy (Eds.), *Social movements in an organizational society,* (pp. 67–95). New Brunswick, NJ: Transaction.

Urban and Community Studies

D. B. Tindall, Fiona M. Kay, and Kerri Lynn Bates

University of British Columbia

GLOSSARY

Alternative Dispute Resolution A variety of nonjudicial processes for resolving conflict (e.g., negotiations, mediation, arbitration).

City A relatively large, dense, continuous settlement in which the majority of inhabitants do not produce their own food.

Civil Disobedience A nonviolent action where one refuses to obey a law for moral or philosophical reasons; also, a tactic employed by social movement adherents as a catalyst for change.

Civil Disobedience Movements Social movements that use civil disobedience as one of their tactics or as the main tactic (e.g., Satyagraha in India; the antiabortion movement, the civil rights movement in North America).

Collective Action A sustained and coordinated group action oriented toward achieving a collective goal. When a collective action is directed toward achieving social change it is referred to as a social movement.

Collective Behavior Forms of social behavior where dominant norms for social behavior are ignored or bypassed and new or emergent behavior norms arise that subvert conventional standards. Collective behavior is relatively spontaneous and is collective in that it involves groups of individuals acting and interacting in a common time and place. Generally, this term refers to behavior that is not formally organized (by authorities, formal organizations, etc.). Some examples of collective behavior involve reactions to natural disasters, crowd behavior, and fads.

Community A social grouping whose members have (1) a common geographic location (e.g., reside in the same neighborhood); (2) shared social identification and sentiments of collective solidarity; and (3) a significant degree of social interaction with one another—and hence form a network of social relations. These three dimensions comprise the classic definition of community. The relative importance of each of these dimensions of community can vary, and contemporary communities are sometimes defined by making reference to only one or two of these criteria. Urban scholars have been particularly interested in how the characteristics of communities have changed as a result of urbanization.

Community Policing The expansion of policing beyond the traditional reactive style. A more traditional model of policing has crime control as the guiding organizational mandate.

Environmental Criminology The study of crime and the physical, situational, and geographic context of its occurrence.

Human Ecology A perspective that involves the application of ideas from plant and animal ecology to the study of the relationship between humans and their physical habitat.

Nonviolence The ethic underlying civil disobedience which advocates action in the presence of openness and love and the absence of any form of violence (physical, verbal, property, or intimidation).

Racial and Ethnic Segregation The separation or marginalization of particular racial or ethnic groups. Ethnic segregation usually involves one or more visible minority group(s) living in disadvantaged economic conditions.

Social Network A pattern of relationships among a set of social entities (e.g., individuals or groups).

Strong Tie A emotionally close social relationship between two individuals (e.g., the kind of relationship characteristic of ties among immediate kin or among close friends).

Urban A collection of specialized, nonagrarian activities (e.g., administration, commerce, manufacturing) that are distinctive of (but not exclusive to) city residents.

Urban Area The definition of what constitutes an "urban area" varies by country, but definitions usually make reference to the number of persons living in a continuously built-up area with a given total population (relatively large) and population density (relatively high). The most characteristic urban form is the city. Rural areas, by contrast, have lower total populations and population densities.

Urbanization In the context of urban studies, urbanization has two related meanings. (1) An increase in the proportion of the population inhabiting urban areas such as cities and their surrounding areas (e.g., suburbs) and (2) The social and economic changes associated with population increases in urban areas.

Virtual Community A new type of community that has been made possible through the development of new technologies such as the Internet. Virtual communities are computer mediated social networks where there is no requirement for members to reside in common geographical locations, or to interact face to face. The absence of both face to face interaction and space as a barrier to interaction has opened up a variety of new possibilities for community life.

Weak Tie A social relationship of low emotional intensity between two individuals (e.g., the kind of relationship characteristic of ties among acquaintances).

THIS ARTICLE REVIEWS and discusses scholarly literature on violence, peace, and conflict in the context of urban and community studies. Specifically, the following topics in the community and urban studies literatures are covered: (1) social change and communities, (2) social psychology and life in cities, (3) models of urban development, (4) urban dimensions of crime, (5) collective behavior and collective action, and (6) resolution of community-based conflicts. Conflict refers to the struggle between individuals or groups within a society and often arises from competition over access to, or control over, limited resources. Both group and individual violence are more likely to occur in cities than rural settings, and thus this article focuses on the urban context. While urban studies is a multidisciplinary enterprise, urban sociology constitutes one of the core disciplines within this area of inquiry and as such it merits a brief description. *Urban sociology* can be defined as the study of social relationships and structures in the city. Cities are places where large concentrations of people work in a variety of specialized and interdependent occupations that for the most part do not involve the primary production of food. In studying cities and urban places, sociologists and other urban scholars frequently contrast cities with rural areas. In particular, such social scientists are interested in how people in rural and urban areas differ in the organization of their work, their social lives, and their personalities.

Group conflict often takes the form of struggle between communities. The problematic concept of community is central to this literature and thus deserves some explanation at the outset of this review. Three standard conceptual dimensions of community exist; these include (1) shared geography, (2) collective identity, and (3) structural integration. While these three dimensions of community are interrelated, they can be analytically separated and treated as semiautonomous indicators of "community." Shared residential location is probably the most frequently used "geographical" definition of community. This definition is used by geographers, sociologists, and planners alike. Collective identity is a cognitive aspect of community that refers to the way in which people identify themselves with some larger social group. Identification can be made both about who belongs to the group and who are outsiders. A related cognitive aspect of community is "sentiments of solidarity." While identification refers to the cognitive content of group affiliation, solidarity refer to its emotional intensity. In other words, sentiments of solidarity refer to the existence of strong emotional ties to the group. Although analytically part of the cognitive domain, this concept is sometimes conceptualized as part of structural integration. Structural integration, the final concept to be considered here, refers to patterned interactions among community members. These patterned interactions can take a number of forms. Many social scientists utilize social networks to depict the structural dimension of communities. Analysts who focus on community as shared geography or neighborhood frequently overlook, or assume the "identity" and "social structure" parts of this definition—and, hence, neglect obtaining empirical data on these aspects of community. In recent years, a number of authors have emphasized the structural dimension of communities and have conceived of communities as "networks"; this is an approach we favor. This approach better enables one to examine how communities change in response to industrialization, urbanization, and technological change.

I. SOCIAL CHANGE AND COMMUNITIES

A. Urbanization and Communities: The Community Question

Drawing upon the work of a number of urban scholars (e.g., Wirth, 1938; Whyte, 1955; Kornhauser, 1959; Gans, 1962; Fischer, 1976), sociologist Barry Wellman has posed what he calls "the community question": How have large-scale divisions of labor associated with urbanization and industrialization affected the organization and content of interpersonal ties? This is an issue of ongoing interest to urban and community scholars and one that has helped to structure much empirical investigation. As suggested by the "community question," social scientists of various stripes have been especially concerned with the impact of urbanization on various types of primary social ties: including those in the home, the neighborhood, the workplace, with kin and friends, and among interest groups. Of central concern is "whether such ties have diminished or have continued to flourish in contemporary societies?" Wellman uses the variable of social networks as an analytic tool to examine this question.

Three lines of argument have been made about social change in the developed world. (1) The community-lost argument asserts that the things that define community are missing in contemporary society, especially in urban neighborhoods. It is argued that in contemporary society there is little social solidarity, people are poorly integrated, and they have few informal social resources (e.g., neighborhood friends) to draw upon for support.

(2) The community-saved argument maintains that just the opposite is true; there are considerable social solidarity, integration, and supportive social resources to be found in the urban neighborhoods of contemporary societies. (3) The community-liberated argument, while agreeing with parts of the first two arguments, breaks new ground in asserting that a variety of structural (e.g., division of labor) and technological developments (e.g., the automobile and telephone) have liberated communities from the confines of geographical neighborhoods. Personal networks in urban communities are geographically dispersed and involve greater specialization. (People get different things from different network members; e.g., advice, emotional support, financial support, time spent together relaxing).

The community lost argument is based on theoretical speculation by Durkheim, Töennies, and others. This perspective maintains that the transformation of Western societies to centralized industrial bureaucratic structures has seriously weakened primary ties (e.g., family, close friends) and communities—thus making the individual more dependent on formal organizations (e.g., employment agencies, welfare bureaus). According to this view, as urbanization has taken place, face-to-face interactions with primary relations have been replaced with indirect secondary relations. Scholars within this tradition see modern urbanites as alienated isolates who bear the brunt of the transformed society on their own.

A rather dark portrait of the human condition has been painted by scholars working in this tradition. Where communal structures have been destroyed by social change, these theories argue that a variety of maladies from robbery and riots to revolution are posited as being likely to occur. Scholars working within this tradition have been pessimistic about the effectiveness of, and hence the need for, social reform and social welfare programs. While the community lost argument has persisted as an explanatory account of the consequences of urbanization, it has received relatively little empirical support.

The community saved argument is based on findings of field researchers in the 1940s, 1950s, and 1960s (such as Herbert Gans and William F. Whyte) who studied urban neighborhoods (primarily in the United States). The community saved argument asserts that neighborhood communities have persisted in industrial bureaucratic societies and that these communities are very important sources of social and economic support and stability for individuals. Scholars within this tradition argue that—paradoxically—the formal, centralizing tendencies of bureaucratic institutions have encouraged the maintenance of primary ties as more flexible sources of social support. It is argued that people who live in cities continue to organize personal communities on the basis of neighborhood, kinship, and work. These communities help individuals to cope with bureaucratic institutions as well as to give them support and a feeling of solidarity.

The community saved perspective paints a much sunnier portrait of people's ability to adaptively cope with challenging social conditions. Even under dire economic and physical conditions, people have the potential to organize into mutually supportive social structures. This perspective sees the community neighborhood as an ideal and asserts that many supportive neighborhoods exist in urban environs. One policy implication of this perspective is recognition of the functions that neighborhood social structures play in the provision of social support and the corollary that urban renewal projects must recognize and encourage such social structures. In fact, supporters of this tradition point to the rise of movements to protect urban neighborhoods from "urban renewal" as a logical development of these insights.

The Pruitt–Igoe housing project in St. Louis provides a good illustration of different aspects of the community-lost/community-saved debate. The Pruitt–Igoe project was built in the inner city of St. Louis in 1954. This project involved relocating 12,000 people from poor neighborhoods in the city into 43 buildings, 11 stories high, containing 2,762 apartments, and covering 57 acres. The buildings were designed so that there were no public gathering spaces for people to congregate in—a design that was praised by architects of the day because no space was "wasted." The project was very costly. The "industrial design" of the complex included details such as institutional wall tile (which facilitated the removal of graffiti), indestructible (and inelegant) lighting fixtures, vandal-proof radiators, and elevators. The Pruitt–Igoe project was seen as a model social program for the modern welfare state city.

Shortly after its construction, however, observers were stunned to learn that residents quickly turned the housing project to shambles. There were broken glass, tin cans, and abandoned cars in the playgrounds and parking lots. Many windows were broken and/or covered up with plywood. Inside the buildings there was a smell of urine and garbage. Elevators were in a state of disrepair. Plumbing and electrical fixtures had been ripped from the walls. There were gangs in the complex, and reports of rape, vandalism, and robbery were frequent. Upper floors of the buildings were abandoned—as crime often occurred in stairwells and eleva-

tors. By 1970 over half of the buildings were vacant and now all have been demolished. The question raised by social scientists is Why did this "state of the art" housing project fail so miserably?

On the surface, the history of this project appears to confirm the community-lost view. However, community saved advocates argue that certain physical conditions of neighborhood development can encourage or prevent the emergence of adaptive social structures. In the case of the Pruitt–Igoe project it is argued that there were so few physical spaces or facilities that promoted the formation of informal social networks that such supportive networks failed to develop. As noted above, field researchers have found that informal personal networks are very important in lower-class neighborhoods and that such networks often develop from encounters in informal spaces outside people's homes. Network formation is facilitated in "slums" by low-rise tenements, narrow streets, and multiple doorways in which to do business and stop and talk. In sum, the physical design of many urban renewal projects such as Pruitt–Igoe do not enhance the types of social interaction that are critical for the development of "community"—and in the absence of integrative and supportive social structures, the negative social outcomes predicted by the "community lost theorists" have been observed.

The third perspective, the community liberated argument, agrees with aspects of the first two. Scholars who developed this argument, agree with the community-lost argument's assertion that the nature of industrialized/urbanized society has weakened neighborhood communities. They also agree with the community-saved argument's contention that primary ties have remained important. Finally, there is agreement with the community-saved argument's assertion that communities still thrive in the city. So how are these seemingly contradictory assertions reconciled? Scholars working within the community liberated tradition disagree that contemporary societies are primarily organized on the basis of geographical neighborhoods. The community-liberated argument asserts that a variety of structural and technological developments have "liberated" communities from the confines of local neighborhoods. These developments include: (1) cheap, effective transportation and communication facilities; (2) the separation of workplace and kinship ties into nonlocal, nonsolidary networks; and (3) high rates of social and residential mobility. As a result, personal networks have taken a new form in contemporary cities. Supportive social networks still exist but they are dispersed spatially. Rather than dense clusters of "multiplex" ties (relationships based on multiple, overlapping ties), social ties tend to be more sparsely interconnected and pairs of ties tend to be based on fewer relationships or to be uniplex (based on single relationships).

Scholars working in the community liberated tradition have the most optimistic view of people's adaptability. According to this view, people are not restricted to the neighborhood for community, nor do they rely exclusively on formal institutions for support. Contemporary urban spaces vary in the degree to which they match any one of these three "ideal types" of communities described in the literature. Variation can occur between communities within single cities or between cities. (See Michelson, 1985, for research on gender issues related to community, paid-work, domestic-work, and transportation.) Cities in North America appear to more closely resemble the characteristics of the community liberated.

While patterns of urbanization in developing countries have varied from the North American model in many instances, some of the same debates have arisen about the consequences of urbanization and the nature of urban life. For example, during the 1970s there was a great deal of scholarly interest in slum and squatter settlements in India. This interest was spawned by government policies of the day, which—mirroring "urban renewal" in North America ghettos—involved removal and clearance of slums and squatter settlements. These types of housing settlements were inhabited by a substantial proportion of Indian urban residents; people living in such settlements comprised between 15 and 25% of the total urban population during this time. Mathur notes that during the 1970s many policy makers and scholars made no distinction between slums and poverty: "it was assumed that poverty and slums were synonymous." Further, slums were assumed to be a haphazard collection of huts and shelters. However, Singh drew conclusions that parallelled research observations of North American community-saved scholars by arguing that the development of such settlements was not the result of a random process; rather, such developments involved some degree of strategic planning—which had important consequences for social interaction.

> The settlement of bastis is not a haphazard process but involves a good deal of social manipulation of physical space. This manipulation may strengthen or limit social interaction in many important ways (Singh, 1978, p. 66, as cited in Mathur, 1994).

It should be noted that in India, caste membership plays an important role in how such settlements are physically structured. Members of dominant castes cluster their residences together so as to exclude or minimize social interaction with members of minority castes.

The basic lines of argument contained in the community-lost/saved/liberated debate have also surfaced in other areas of urban and communities studies. In particular, these arguments have been used in both theoretical and empirical contexts to explain the social psychology of urban life, differences in crime rates between urban and rural areas, and the occurrence of collective behavior and collective action—areas that are examined in following sections.

B. Virtual Community

When computer networks link people as well as machines they become social networks. A formal term for computer mediated social networks has been developed: computer-supported social networks (CSSNs). Another term for such networks is virtual communities (see Howard Rheingold's *The Virtual Community*). The nature of CSSNs can either liberate or facilitate social control. Computer-supported social networks have spawned their own culture (cyberspace) and, as part of this, norms and structures specific to life on the Internet. To date, many of the sociological arguments made about virtual communities are consonant with the community liberated thesis.

As with other communication technologies (e.g., the telephone), the Internet often supports rather than supplants other forms of social interaction. Some scholars have suggested that "teleworking" through the Internet and other computer mediated forms of communication may liberate workers who are faced with constraints associated with parenting, location of residence, or physical disabilities. Critics have noted that such liberation often comes at a price. Companies often implement teleworking to cut costs and in many cases actually increase control over employees. The consequences of teleworking have not been distributed equally. It is argued that while professionals have gained more autonomy, managers have increased monitoring and control over those who telework.

One author has suggested that CSSNs may counter the trend within contemporary western societies toward the privatization of community. Through virtual communities people seek companionship, information, and social support. Computer-supported social networks have the potential to both increase global connectivity and to deemphasize the importance of social solidarity at the neighborhood level. For example, as this volume was going to press, news media accounts were heralding the cyberspace victory of grassroots social movement organizations who mobilized over the Internet against the proposed Multilateral Agreement on Investment. Ironically, for the time being at least, corporate and business leaders who support a form of globalization (freer trade and investment) were outfoxed by groups (e.g., worker and environmental groups) who opposed economic globalization—but who took advantage of another form of globalization (a global communications network) to further their cause.

With regard to issues of inequality, some scholars have argued that the Internet has a leveling quality. For example, the lack of social and physical cues online mask the social characteristics of participants. Members of minority groups can participate in community life with a certain degree of anonymity and hence participate in "community life" with less risk of being subjected to prejudice and discrimination. Furthermore, the relatively anonymous and egalitarian nature of the Internet can facilitate a focus on the message rather than the characteristics of the messengers. Counter to this view, access to the Internet tends to be correlated with socioeconomic status, gender, and race.

As has been said of technology in general, the Internet is not inherently good or bad. Neither is it neutral. Web sites have been constructed by both progressive social movement organizations and by hate groups. Other negative aspects of virtual community life include: the ability of those who control the network to eavesdrop upon the communication of others (e.g., employers monitoring the communications of employees); new possibilities for malfeasance—con artists bilking "customers" in economic transactions (e.g., obtaining and using credit card numbers for illicit purposes); people misrepresenting themselves in personal relationships (e.g., to obtain "real life" sex). (For a review of research on computer supported social networks and virtual community see Wellman et al., 1996.)

II. SOCIAL PSYCHOLOGY AND LIFE IN CITIES

We now turn from the level of the community to the experience of individuals in urban environments. A great deal of work in social and environmental psychology has been done examining the effects of physical and social environments upon human behavior. Up until the mid-1970s much of this research took place in

laboratories and under experimental conditions. Since then, a growing number of field studies examining the causes and effects of environmental stress have been undertaken. One development of this line of inquiry is the development of "environmental load theory." The environmental load perspective focuses primarily on the individual as a unit of analysis but is complementary to the community lost thesis.

Stanley Milgram and others have suggested that because people have a limited ability to process information, they tend to experience negative effects to environmental stressors (e.g., noise, crowds, etc.). When the amount of exposure to environmental stressors exceeds the individual's capacity to process all that is relevant, "information overload" occurs. Individuals, in responding to this overload, attempt to cope by ignoring some of the stimulus inputs. In general, stimuli most important to the task at hand are allocated as much attention as needed, and less important stimuli are ignored. Even after exposure to a stressor has ceased, behavioral after-effects, such as decreased tolerance for frustration, errors in mental functioning, and less frequent altruistic behavior, may result.

Environmental load theory has been used to explain the deterioration of social life that occurs in some urban areas. It is argued that many negative phenomena, such as bystanders ignoring others in distress, may be due in part to an environmental overload in which the hustle and bustle of everyday life in the city requires so much attention that few cognitive resources remain for attending to "peripheral" social concerns. It is argued that city dwellers develop an "aloof attitude" toward others in order to allocate enough time and energy to everyday functioning.

This general line of argument can be traced back to earlier in the century to the works of George Simmel and Louis Worth. Simmel argues that since urban dwellers come into contact with vast numbers of people each day, they conserve psychic energy by becoming acquainted with a smaller proportion of people and maintaining more superficial relationships with these fewer acquaintances than do residents of rural areas. Wirth also describes this phenomenon in referring to the "superficiality, anonymity, and the transitory character of urban social relations." Milgram states that the ultimate adaptation to an overloaded social environment is to totally disregard the needs, interests, and demands of those with whom one is not directly connected and develop a highly efficient system of making such evaluations.

Research on "bystander effects" and "helping behavior" constitutes an avenue of inquiry that has developed from the environmental load perspective. Latné and Darley have conducted a number of experiments studying the bystander effect. Their research established the following principle: the larger the number of bystanders, the less likelihood that any one of them will intervene in an emergency. Other researchers have focused on "screening strategies." Some authors suggest that ethnic allegiance may be one strategy that people use to cope with overload. By screening out excessive demands and responding only along ethnic lines, overload is decreased. Milgram calls this making overload more manageable by limiting "the span of sympathy." This, of course, is a social process that reinforces discrimination and racism in urban spaces.

While various authors describe social life in cities as "often hectic" and "lacking in the common courtesies" that are said to exist in small communities, critics argue that this generalization oversimplifies reality. It is not merely that traditional courtesies are violated in the city but rather that new norms of noninvolvement have evolved in cities. It is argued that these are so well defined and so deeply a part of city life that they actually constitute the norms that people are reluctant to violate. In discussing the contrast between city and rural dwellers regarding such behavior, social psychologists have generally argued that observed differences reflect the responses of similar people to different situations rather than intrinsic differences in the personalities of rural and city dwellers.

Crowding is a favorite topic of scholars interested in environmental stressors. It has been argued that there is no simple linear relationship between density and the cognitive experience of crowding. Rather, expectations and cultural norms are important variables that mediate the relationship between density and crowding. For example, an individual sitting in a sports stadium with 60,000 others generally does not feel crowded—but if this same individual finds them self suddenly thrust into a similarly sized group of people in the middle of a downtown riot, they are likely to make markedly different evaluations in their perceptions of crowding. (For research on the relationship between human density and perceptions of crowding, see Gillis, 1974).

Similarly, the hypothesized negative relationship between urbanization and the provision of help has been criticized on both empirical and conceptual grounds. For example, in one experiment on helping behavior it was found that subjects with an urban background were more helpful than those with a rural background in their response to a laboratory accident. Other criticisms include limitations associated with conceptualizing urbanization. In particular, criticisms have been aimed at conceptualizations that ignore important variations and complexities related to urban form such as differences within a single urban environment and between urban environments in different cultures as well as the failure to identify the particular factors that influence the level of helpfulness and mutual aid. However, in recent years, support for the generalizability of urban–rural differences in helping behavior has been bolstered. In fact, it has been argued that the urban unhelpfulness effect is one of the most generalizable findings in social psychology. Yousif and Korte (1995, p. 474) state: "There have now been more than 60 comparisons of the level of helpfulness observed in urban and nonurban settings, and recent reviews have been unanimous in confirming this behavioral characteristic of urban environments." It should be noted, though, that this effect occurs primarily when social interactions involve neighbors or strangers and does not apply to strong ties (e.g., family and close friends). Steblay conducted a meta-analysis of research on urban–nonurban differences that included the following countries: the United States, Canada, Australia, Israel, Holland, and Turkey. The urban–nonurban difference in helping behavior was replicated in all of these countries except Holland (where only one study had been conducted). Yousif and Korte (1985) examined the possibility of the modifying effects of culture on this relationship. They conducted a comparative study of urban–nonurban differences in helping behavior between England and the Sudan. Similar urban–nonurban differences were found in both countries. Based on their findings they conclude "… the urban unhelpfulness effect is very robust across quite diverse cultural variations and … is not reducible simply to an attitudinal or normative explanation" (p. 488).

While much of this research has focused on understanding negative behavioral outcomes stemming from environmental overload and the relative anonymity of city dwellers, it should be noted that anonymity and related variables can serve to enhance or enable certain types of behavior or lifestyles. For example, stigmatized social groups and those living "deviant lifestyles" are generally found in higher proportions in urban settings—at least openly—because the individual anonymity typical of city life implies a reduction in the level of social control typical of small, close-knit communities. From the perspective of members of such subgroups, life in the city has a liberatory aspect. Thus, for people wishing to avoid the conformity pressures of the larger society, life in the city can be described as "community liberated."

III. MODELS OF URBAN DEVELOPMENT

We now turn from considering the experience of life in cities to explanations for the ways that cities and urban spaces develop. There are two broad approaches to theorizing about urbanization and urban communities. These can be referred to as (1) ecological approaches (including human ecology) and (2) structural approaches (including Marxist and other political economy approaches). (John Hannigan, 1995, offers an extensive review and assessment of a recently developed perspective on urbanization—namely, postmodernism.).

A. Ecological Approaches

1. Human Ecology

"Human ecology" is one of the most influential theories explaining the growth of cities. This perspective involves the application of ideas from plant and animal ecology to the study of the relationship between humans and their physical habitat. An early model of human ecology was developed by Burgess and is called the "Concentric Zone Model." This model uses terms such as "segregation, competition, invasion, succession, and natural areas" to explain patterns of behavior in urban spaces. Segregation refers to the tendency for particular types of groups or enterprises (e.g., different ethnic or income groups, commercial or residential activities) to cluster and segregate themselves by excluding other activities from their territory. When such entities are successful in creating a relatively exclusive area or homogeneous neighborhood they are said to have formed a natural area.

Competition involves conflict over territory. If one group invades another's space then succession is said to have occurred. Burgess based his concentric zone model on the city of Chicago. The concentric zone model describes different patterns of urban activities and their tendency to concentrate, segregate, and create natural areas. Competition for scarce resources is seen as being more intense at the center than at the periphery.

In Burgess's model, the zones radiate from the center of the city in the following order: (1) the central business district or CBD (the commercial and geographic center of the city), (2) the zone of transition (the main area of competition between residential and commercial activities), (3) the zone of working-class houses, (4) the middle-class residential zone, and (5) the commuter

zone. In addition, two other zones are sometimes included as part of the model: (6) peripheral agricultural areas and (7) the hinterland.

In this model the boundaries of zones are blurred, and people and activities in one zone often invade or migrate to another and are replaced by people or activities from an adjacent zone. For example, with different waves of immigration—especially among poorer immigrants—one ethnic group may occupy the zone of transition and then migrate to the working-class residential zone. In later years, this ethnic group may migrate to more distant zones (e.g., the middle-class residential zone) as it achieves material success and is replaced by a migrating "less advantaged group."

For a proper understanding, the model needs to be viewed as a "dynamic" system rather than as a "static" description of a city, as the concentric zones themselves are not very useful for describing the form of actual cities. It has been argued that the concentric zone model provides some important general insights into the processes and forms of urban growth. For example, it is maintained that in North American cities, activities and groups do tend to concentrate in particular areas. In fact, in recent decades there is evidence that socioeconomic and residential segregation has increased within larger cities. Also, there has tended to be a positive correlation between the socioeconomic status of urbanites and the distance of their residence from the core of the city. While this latter observation is generally accurate for North American cities, it should be noted that in countries where the development of cities preceded industrialization, this pattern does not hold. Further, cultural and physical constraints can affect the development of cities in ways that allow them to take very different forms. For example, in reviewing the application of the human ecology model to Brazilian cities, Valladares and Coelho (1994) state "... in contrast to the Spanish colonial city, Brazilian cities do not have a common physical layout ... [Brazilian] cities adapted to physical conditions, with spatial organization according to function and principle activities."

In recent decades gentrification has been a factor in the changing character of a number of North American cities. In these cities, deteriorated sections of both commercial and transitional areas have been reclaimed, renovated, and inhabited by those with higher socioeconomic status. (For a review of research on gentrification see Zukin, 1987.)

2. Other Ecological Models

A number of other models have been developed within the human ecology tradition in an attempt to improve upon the concentric zone model. Some of these include: the sector, the multiple-nuclei, and edge city models. The sector model emphasizes transportation arteries. Like the concentric zone model, the sector model conceives of activities and social groups as being concentrated. But in contrast to the concentric zone model, the sector model argues that commercial and residential areas expand from the center of cities in wedge-shaped sections that are molded by natural boundaries and transportation arteries.

The multiple-nuclei model contrasts with earlier models by arguing that cities develop as a series of centers, or nuclei, that attract similar activity patterns or social groups. Nuclei emerge around mutually supportive commercial activities, industrial activities, and residences (for example, an urban university campus with residences, bookstores, diners and cafés, photocopy shops, sports complexes, etc.). It has been argued that this model is most appropriate for cities that have been designed since the development and widespread use of the automobile.

A recent variation of the multiple-nuclei model has been developed that refers to the phenomenon of edge cities. This model describes residential areas in suburbs where people live during their nonworking hours. Over time, shopping centers are developed to serve suburbanites living in these residential areas. As these suburbs grow, an ample supply of labor becomes available. In response to the increased supply of workers, industry develops in these areas. Thus, the area becomes transformed from a residential suburb or "bedroom community" into "an edge city"—a place where people work as well as live.

All of these models highlight different aspects of urban growth and to different degrees describe the expansion of cities in North America. The ecological tradition has been criticized for being more descriptive than theoretical. It is argued that the ecological approach has described the growth of particular cities, but not provided an adequate explanation of patterns of growth. Of particular concern, the approach has given inadequate attention to intergroup conflict. While it has described intergroup competition over space (e.g., conflict between successive waves of immigration of different ethnic minorities) it has failed to adequately conceptualize and account for the role of power in such conflicts.

B. Structural Approaches

Structural approaches can be roughly organized under the rubric of "political economy." In the context of urban studies this perspective focuses upon the distribution of power and the allocation of resources in cities. The political economy of cities involves examining cities as parts of social systems, in particular, as spaces where capital accumulation is produced as part of global capitalism. Walton, in reviewing the contribution of political economy to urban sociology, argues that political economy has been the dominant paradigm for the past 25 years. In sociology, in recent years, this perspective has also become known as the *new urban sociology*. An important early contributor to this tradition was Charles Tilly, who explained urbanization in 19th-century France by referring to the interrelated processes of capitalist development and state formation. Processes such as migration, proletarianization, and collective action are all arise out of these two processes.

Scholars working within the structural tradition have focused on two problems: (1) a concern with collective consumption and (2) a theoretical concern with the function of space in the process of capital accumulation. For example, David Harvey argues that under capitalism, both capital accumulation and class struggle are important to the development of urban spaces. Cities serve to facilitate production, circulation, and consumption. Urban areas change as a results of periodic crises inherent within capitalism.

1. The Growth Machine: The Logic of Urban Growth

One of the most influential recent contributions in this tradition is the work of Logan and Molotch, who developed a structural model of urban development they call "the growth machine." Logan and Molotch conceptualize markets as social constructions that arise in the conflict between urban residents interested in the use value of property and entrepreneurs seeking to realize exchange value in the "urban growth machine." Logan and Molotch argue that by showing "how social factors shape prices of places and humans' responses to those prices, we can understand the physical and social shape of cities."

As suggested above, Logan and Molotch make the Marxist concepts of use value and exchange value central in their analysis of contemporary conflict over urban spaces. In particular, these concepts are applied to place. Hence, exchange values refer to the utilization of property to generate profit, and use values refer to values that individuals bestow upon property that are not part of commodified exchange. Place, they argue, is unlike any other good; the unique qualities of any given place mean that there are no substitutions with identical characteristics. Ownership of property is a type of monopoly.

There can be no additional entrepreneurs or any new product. The individual owner also has a monopoly over a subsection of the marketplace. Every parcel of land is unique in the idiosyncratic access it provides to other parcels and uses, and this quality underscores the specialness of property as a commodity (Logan & Molotch, 1987, p. 23).

According to this analysis, there is an inherent tension between those who see urban places as a source of exchange values (various types of property landlords and real estate speculators) and those who conceive of urban places in terms of their use values (e.g., homeowners and renters). Logan and Molotch outline how those who rely on urban spaces as sources of exchange value inevitably manage to form coalitions to promote their ongoing interest in furthering development and thus increasing exchange values. The need to increase exchange values is what drives the system of urban growth, often to the detriment of those who rely on the city for use value.

2. Other Contributions of Structural Approaches

The development of structural or political economy approaches to urban studies has facilitated a substantial amount of comparative research. Also, current trends and recent historical events have provided a number of "natural laboratories" to various urban scholars. Developing countries have provided a focus for those studying urban migration and modernization. The end of the Cold War during the 1980s has produced new research opportunities for comparative research between eastern and western Europe.

Another recent development is a focus upon "global cities." Global cities are international nodes in an international flow of capital and information. Such centers are often more strongly linked to other global cities than to cities within their own nation state or region. One argument suggests that in a relatively few global cities, the functions of finance and control of the economy become more concentrated while production increasingly becomes more decentralized. A variety of structural patterns accompany this process, including the transfer of manufacturing to various nonmetropolitan areas, low-wage enclaves, and off-shore enterprises. Within such global cities, there is increasing proletarianization of the urban population and a growing gap between well-paid upper-middle class professionals and those who support this class through various low-paid activities in the service sector (e.g., cooking, cleaning, work in the new "electronic sweatshops," etc.).

Within the "developing world," there has been a recent focus on "urban primacy" as a relatively unique form of urbanization that contrasts with patterns in North America and Europe. Urban primacy refers to a situation where one city (or a very few cities) dominate other cities within a country. Primacy is used to describe social systems where there is a lack of economic, political, and social integration among a given set of cities (within a region or country). Unequal patterns of urbanization are seen as being indicative of "underdevelopment." Primacy is also seen as a structural barrier to future development, as there are few incentives to invest in rural areas. As a result, patterns of fertility, mortality, and political integration are adversely affected.

A distinct but related concept is "overurbanization." Overurbanization refers to the idea that urbanization in developing countries is too great for one or more of the following reasons: the level of existing industry (or mix of industries) is too low, national reserves of capital are too low, there is an inability to provide social services to the urban population, or pollution and congestion are too great. Critics of the "overurbanization" thesis have questioned whether the historical experience of Western nation-states should be used as a norm by which to evaluate urbanization in developing countries. For example, while there has been ongoing debate among some Indian urban scholars as to whether India is "overurbanized" or "underurbanized," others have argued that the phenomenon of Indian urbanization is qualitatively different from patterns of urbanization in the developed world and have referred to the Indian pattern as "subsistence urbanization," "pseudo urbanization," "dysfunctional urbanization," or "urban atrophy" (Mathur, 1994). (For a review of theory and research on urbanization in developing countries, see Karsarda & Crenshaw, 1991; Stren, 1994).

Another important contribution of this tradition is documentation of the "informal economy." The informal economy refers to a variety of economic activities that are undertaken outside of the auspices of official state regulation. Such activities are run though households, social networks, and clandestine businesses. Most notably, research focusing on urbanites in developing countries documents a gap between the number of people who are employed or economically active compared with official statistics. Another line of inquiry is research on "flexible specialization" in manufacturing. Flexible specialization is one response to the loss of traditional manufacturing jobs and working class institutions in "post-Fordist" cities.

Finally, in contrasting some of the concerns of urban scholars in the developed and developing world, it should be noted that urban poverty and deprivation—while a concern in the developed world—is a central concern of scholars in developing countries. For example, Mathur (1994, pp. 54–55) cites the National Commission on Urbanisation, which in 1988 stated that the Indian urban poor live under "... the most brutal and inhuman living conditions, with large sections of the citizens (almost half in Bombay and Delhi) living in squatter settlements." Mathur notes that "[a] little over 41 million persons, or 20.1% of the total urban population, live under conditions of absolute poverty in that they do not have the necessary incomes to secure 2,100 calories per day, this being the official statistical cut-off point between the poor and the non-poor."

Scholarly work within the structural tradition has been criticized for being overly formulaic and deterministic. Critics have pointed to the need for theories that facilitate the possibility of discovering new problems, and uncovering new empirical phenomena. Scholars working within this tradition have responded to these criticisms over the past decade by describing a variety of new processes and phenomena—such as those described in the preceding paragraphs.

IV. URBAN DIMENSIONS OF CRIME

A. Dimensions of Social Inequality and Urban–Rural Differences in Crime Rates

We now turn from examining models of urbanization to a review of research on crime in urban spaces. Research examining social inequality and urban/community conflicts highlights several distinctive patterns, including racial and economic segregation within North American cities. Racial and ethnic segregation across cities is well entrenched and appears resistant to change. Contemporary social research investigating the rise of an urban underclass and the ghettoization of inner-city areas suggests that the geographic isolation of low-income urban blacks from predominantly white and more prosperous neighborhoods presents significant obstacles to many urban blacks. Edward Shishadeh and Nicole Flynn argue that ethnic isolation leads to weakened labor force attachment. In extreme cases, it can create an environment that fosters a self-image based on violence and reinforce a variety of behaviors that increase the social disadvantage of African Americans. Racial and ethnic

isolation can also divest communities of pluralist politics and render them vulnerable during periods of economic decline and government cutbacks.

In the U.S., research has consistently shown that crime rates are higher in urban than in rural areas. In addition, it is known that African Americans and other visible minorities tend to locate in larger cities. The question that arises is whether there is a confounding effect between urbanism and race in accounting for variation in urban–rural crime differences. The urban–rural crime difference holds for several different societies and across several different historical periods. Cross-national research and studies of cities in the third world offer considerable evidence of resilient urban-rural differences in crime rates (see, for example, Archer & Gartner, 1984). Contemporary research reveals that this difference remains strong after controlling for race, age, and sex population compositions. The urban–rural crime relationship is stronger and more consistent in the case of crimes against property and so-called "victimless crimes" than in the case of interpersonal violence.

Attempts to explain the relationship between crime and urban vs rural residence find their origins in the work of Louis Wirth and the community-lost thesis. Wirth contended that size, density, and heterogeneity of urban places undermine patterns of personal and social control. In turn, these factors increase the risk of crime and other social ills. Wirth argued that "urbanism as a way of life" promotes social estrangement and alienation, which allows urban residents to escape the influence of informal social controls that operate more effectively in less urbanized places. Reduced controls over deviant motivations encourage predatory behaviors.

Other researchers suggest that the deterministic model provided by Wirth fails to consider the ways in which the composition of urban and rural populations differ and thus the differences in the types of people who generally live in urban and rural locations. For example, Herbert Gans maintained in his 1962 book *The Urban Villagers* that Wirth's depiction of the city as alienating and anomic was inconsistent with a large body of ethnographic literature demonstrating that urban settings are diverse in their characteristics, many of which are characterized by thriving communities (reflective of the community-saved thesis). From this point of view, sometimes termed the population composition theory, higher crime rates in urban places do not result from structural factors such as size, density, and heterogeneity (which lead to diminished social and personal control). Rather, higher crime rates are an outcome of the fact that cities are more likely to be home to people (such as the young or socially disadvantaged) whose individual characteristics are associated with higher rates of crime.

B. Urban Gangs

Youth gangs have made up part of the urban "social" landscape of North America for over 200 years. The United States gang problem remains concentrated in larger cities. Curry, Ball, and Decker report in their analysis of the National Institute of Justice 1994 survey that the United States has more than 16,000 gangs with more than a half million members who commit nearly 600,000 crimes per year. They report a national estimate of 735 jurisdictions with a population of at least 25,000 having gang crime problems. Malcolm Klein documents the rapid spread of street gangs to as many as 1,100 cities in the United States compared with the relatively few large cities in which gangs presented a problem a few years ago. These staggering figures underscore the growing concern with gang violence.

Several themes from recent studies of gangs are noteworthy. The number of gangs in the United States has increased rapidly in recent years. Gang membership is becoming more diverse in terms of age, sex, and ethnicity. Most gangs are neither stable in membership nor cohesive. The age range of gang members has increased. Longer gang "careers" are one of the important changes in gangs since the late 1980s. As young adults remain in gangs longer, their own crime rates and their influence on those of younger members is likely to increase. Although there is little evidence that gangs evolve into adult criminal organizations, gang membership may be salient to organized crime opportunities.

Gang violence has also become more widespread and lethal. There are several factors driving this trend. The presence and availability of high-caliber automatic weapons changes strategic thinking about violence, and this technology makes lethal violence easier. Gang members report they steal guns from homes or other gun carriers, they buy guns from drug sellers who are trading up in firepower, or they buy them from the vast informal economy of guns. Some gang researchers have also noted a spread of urban street gangs to suburban and rural communities.

Criminological research demonstrates that gang members are more likely than nongang members to commit offenses, especially serious and violent offenses, and to do so with high frequency. Drug use and selling by gang members has increased. However, gangs also exhibit considerable diversity. Ronald Huff's anthology

of gangs, *Gangs in America*, demonstrates that there are different types of gangs, with different organizational structures, possessing different levels of violence, and directed toward different purposes (fighting, drug dealing, protection).

Classification of gangs is a daunting task. In addition to diversity and change, gangs come in many forms, which sometimes merge or change in other ways. Research to date has documented drug gangs, or "crews"; "wilding" groups; milling crowds; mods; rockers; football hooligans; skinheads; and bikers; "tagged crews"; prison gangs; and many other forms of gangs.

Explanations of gang violence center upon community disorganization and social control. Frederic Thrasher's early work was the most important study of gangs at the time. Thrasher was the first to treat the gang as an organizational phenomenon focusing on adolescent gangs and the conditions under which they emerged and the stages of development. Thrasher asserted that: (1) gangs emerge in poor and socially disorganized neighborhoods, (2) boys join gangs because there are a lack of opportunities to engage in legitimate work, (3) boys who join gangs lack skills and the drive to compete with others for legitimate jobs, (4) gangs are differentiated by age, and (5) gangs facilitate crime and delinquency.

Extending Thrasher's work, Cloward and Ohlin theorized that limited opportunity structures influence gang involvement and delinquency. Albert Cohen argued that lower-class youths blocked from status within the larger society turn to gangs to create their own subculture in which to achieve status. However, Shaw and McKay's social disorganization approach is the most widely used to account for the social ecology of crime across geographical units. According to this theory, low economic status, heterogeneity, and residential mobility are social factors that impede the ability of communities to produce an effective system of institutional control. Differences in the level of this control explain intra- and inter-city variation in crime rates. Yet, each of these theories share an emphasis upon the gang's role in lower-class youth delinquency.

More recent studies seek to explain gang behavior and crime as an outgrowth of the persistent and pervasive poverty that has afflicted many Black and Latino communities in the United States. William Julius Wilson, for example, demonstrates the rapidity with which poverty has become urbanized in the United States. Wilson documents the decline of manufacturing jobs in large metropolitan inner cities. This decline has occurred at the same time as increasing labor market segmentation, characterized by Whites having improved access to better-paying jobs and minorities being consigned to low-wage work, welfare, and the illegal economy. The result has been the emergence of a permanent underclass in several U.S. cities. Included in this underclass are gang members who have been unable to move out of gangs into conventional jobs. During the 1970s, when the decline in manufacturing jobs in large U.S. cities was steepest, gang formation occurred in communities that experienced the most extreme forms of economic disinvestment, labor market contraction, and social dislocation. The location of gangs in low-income neighborhoods reflects the political disadvantage of the residents of these neighborhoods compared with people in communities of greater wealth. In response, both William Wilson and John Hagedorn have called for the introduction of massive federal job programs. Wilson's policy agenda includes provision of child care services and subsidies to working-poor parents. He argues that government must address the larger problems in a more comprehensive way, thus improving the conditions of the ghetto underclass and significantly reducing youth gangs, whose membership is comprised largely of the inner city underclass. In a similar vein, John Hagedorn contends that public policy ought to stress jobs and investment in underclass neighborhoods, program evaluation, family preservation, and community control of social institutions.

However, Jankowski observes in his book *Islands in the Street; Gangs and American Urban Society* that public policy-makers are unable or unwilling to take actions to ameliorate urban poverty and instead focus on tougher law enforcement and longer prison sentences. (This is a common response of community-lost advocates, whose policy prescriptions result from an underlying pessimism about urban life.) Jankowski argues that this strategy fails to reduce gang activity for two reasons. First, improved law enforcement becomes compromised by the development of relationships between gang members and government and law enforcement agents. Second, longer jail terms fail to diminish gang persistence because gang members reproduce their gangs in prison.

C. The Physical Environment and Crime

Environmental criminology represents a field that explicitly attempts to merge the social and spatial analysis of events into a broader understanding of crime and victimization. The field developed largely out of the work of two scholars. C. R. Jeffrey, in his book *Crime Prevention Through Environmental Design* (1971), argued that the modification of specific features of urban design would serve to reduce crime. Oscar Newman, in his book *Defensible Space: Crime Prevention Through Urban Design* (1972), called for architectural features, such as public space dividers, greater visibility, and low-rise designs in multiunit buildings, to encourage residents to exercise territorial control. Many of the principles of defensible space are explicitly designed to encourage greater social contact and communication among neighbors and a proprietary sense of community.

Environmental criminology shifts the focus of study to locations of crime, the characteristics of those locations, the paths that bring offenders and victims together in space and time, and people's perceptions of crime locations. This approach suggests that careful predictive crime analysis will make it possible for government to reduce urban crime rates through improved justice resource allocation and informed urban planning decisions. For instance, the development of geographic information systems in police departments and the use of small-area crime profiling techniques have been demonstrated to be effective research tools in the study of the patterning of crime and victimization.

V. COLLECTIVE BEHAVIOR AND COLLECTIVE ACTION

A. Theories of Collective Behavior and Collective Action

In this section we explore explanations for a set of phenomena that are frequently associated with cities and urbanization, or that frequently have an urban or community basis, namely: riots, demonstration protests, and social movements. Why do people participate in riots and other forms of collective protest? This fundamental question has been considered by social scientists, philosophers, and political pundits for at least the past 2 centuries. Most early accounts focused upon collective behavior—such as riots and rebellions—in urban settings. Classic formulations (such as those of Le Bon & Tarde) conceived of collective behavior as irrational and as based upon "social contagion." Oberschall (1973, p. 12) depicts LeBon's view as follows:

> In a crowd, the rational faculties of the individual, his [sic] moral judgment and conscious personality come under the sway of contagion and suggestion frequently originating with a leader. These produce a "mental unity" or uniformity. The char-

acteristic mark of crowds is credulity, mobility, exaggeration of both noble and base sentiments, and suggestibility. The law of the mental unity of crowds applies not only to the "criminal" crowd, e.g., the type of crowd that stormed the Bastille, but to crowds that possess a sense of responsibility, e.g., juries, the electorate, and parliamentary assemblies. . . . Revolutionary crowds are drawn from the rootless, disorganized, mentally disturbed, criminal classes of big cities. . . .

1. Collective Behavior

Early North American theorizing about collective action (a particular focus was behavior in crowds but also included social movements) referred to this set of phenomena as collective behavior. Explanations for collective behavior that were developed during this period drew heavily upon the imagery of the community-lost thesis. Collective behavior was said to occur when a large number of people failed to accept some of the dominant values, norms, and/or leaders in a society. One of the earliest North American sociologists to give this problem serious attention was Herbert Blumer. Blumer's work followed in the footsteps of earlier European theorists (such as Le Bon and Tardé) in that he concurred that "social contagion" was the main process underlying collective behavior. However, Blumer contrasted circular reaction with "interpretive" behavior. Interpretive behavior refers to actions that are guided by thoughtfully interpreting the behavior of others.

Also working within the interpretive tradition (e.g., the symbolic interaction perspective), and hence, building upon Blumer's work, Turner and Killian developed "emergent norm theory" to account for collective behavior. In contrast to Blumer, Turner and Killian argued that there is substantial diversity among the participants in collective behavior. The "emergent norm" concept is used to explain the empirical fact that crowds are not unanimous in their feelings and expressions; individuals are quite diverse in terms of their sentiments as well as their motives and actions. An illusion of unanimity arises or is constructed because the behavior of part of the crowd becomes salient and is perceived both by observers and by crowd members as being the sentiment of the whole crowd. Variant views and divergent behavior are overlooked. Shared definitions about crowd behavior becomes an emergent norm. This norm inhibits behavior contrary to it and leads participants to implement sanctions against norm violators. (For research on a wave of rioting of widespread contemporary interest—the 1992 Los Angeles Riots—see Baldassare, 1994.)

2. Mass Society Theory

Another theory intimately connected with the community-lost thesis is "mass society theory", developed by Kornhauser. Mass society theory argues that with industrialization and subsequent social changes, people have become isolated and alienated. Mass society, as depicted by Kornhauser, refers to a social system in which elites are readily open to influence by nonelites. Simultaneously, nonelites (in particular, those occupying marginal positions in society) are also highly available for mobilization because they lack attachments to independent groups, the local community, voluntary associations, and occupational groups. Social conditions resemble a "mass society" when populations and elites can emotionally incite one another to extreme actions. Under such circumstances unconstrained social and political movements can develop (even totalitarian ones such as in Nazi Germany). This type of theorizing about collective behavior and social movements is also sometimes referred to as "breakdown theory," for obvious reasons.

In sum, in mass society (or the breakdown perspective), there is a lack of local primary groups and secondary associations to integrate individuals into the normative constraints of the larger society. According to this argument, people who join mass movements are those with relatively weak social ties. Research, however, has found that the participants in collective actions—and organizers in particular—generally tend to disproportionately be of higher socioeconomic status and to be more integrated and better connected to societal institutions than nonparticipants. This empirical insight has led to new lines of theorizing of which the most notable is resource mobilization theory, to be discussed shortly.

3. Relative Deprivation

A social psychological approach was developed during the 1960s that attempted to explain collective behavior by referring to psychological states. *Relative deprivation* refers to a difference or gap between what people believe they have a right to receive (their expectations) and what they actually receive (their achievements). Expectations and achievements may diverge for a number of reasons. First, both achievements and expectations may rise, but expectations may rise faster than achievements. Second, expectations may remain constant while achievements decline. A third possible scenario is when there is a period of rising expectations and rising achievements which is followed by a decline in achievements while expectations continue to rise. This latter pattern is know as a J-curve (because it can be graphically represented as an upside down and sloping "J"). Relative deprivation arguments have been used to explain protests associated with the civil rights movement in the United States during the 1960s.

Many studies of urban social movements that occurred during the 1970s adopted the relative deprivation approach. For example, urban social movements played an important role in the Brazilian social landscape during this period. Mobilization began in factories but soon spread beyond the labor movement. Residents of both poor and middle class neighborhoods mobilized to demand the right to basic services such as water supply, sewerage, school facilities, health facilities, and roads. There were protests against ecological dangers, development plans, housing evictions, and so on. The first studies of these protests described them as a reaction to the barriers that existed during previous periods of authoritarianism that prevented citizen participation in normal channels of dissent—such as political parties and trade unions. Researchers argued that the growth of movements during this period was facilitated by the increasing impoverishment of the urban population and the state's failure to provide collective goods and services.

Some critics have argued that relative deprivation focuses primarily on the conditions that immediately precede a social movement or a revolt. They state there is an assumption that if we can identify and understand discontent just prior to an uprising then we have explained it. The question is raised, What if people had been just as dissatisfied at earlier points in time and yet did not rebel? For many revolts, this has in fact been shown to be the case. In many instances equally intense discontent surfaces years before a revolt occurs but without the same consequences. If this observation is true in general then relative deprivation theory merely identifies the factors that precipitate revolts. Much empirical research has been done on these questions and has failed to provide strong support for relative deprivation as the primary cause of revolts.

4. Resource Mobilization and Collective Action

Another approach to explaining the rise of social movements and collective action is resource mobilization. The insights of the resource mobilization approach have constituted the conventional wisdom of the social movement literature over the past 2 decades. This view sees individual participation in social movements as being largely rational on the part of the individual and

emphasizes decision-making processes (and subsequent participation) as taking place in the context of group life. The assumptions contrast resource mobilization theory with classic formulations (such as those of Le Bon), which saw collective behavior as irrational and based upon "social contagion," and with mass society theory (as formulated by Kornhauser), which painted social movement participants as being alienated, atomized individuals and highly susceptible to the influence of extremist leaders (and ideologies).

The resource mobilization perspective conceives of collective action in terms of the mobilizing, converting, and transferring of resources from one group and one arena of action to other groups and actions. Mobilization refers to the process by which a discontented group assembles and invests resources for the pursuit of shared goals. While not explicitly linked to the community-liberated thesis, resource mobilization theory shares some of its characteristics. For example, people are seen as being largely rational and practical as opposed to being irrational and subject to contagion. Behavior is seen as being goal oriented. Other than the assumption that organization is a necessary condition for collective action to be successful, there are no assumptions about the nature of social structure—for instance, that it is locally based.

Collective action, thought of in these terms, covers a wide range of social phenomena. An aggrieved ethnic group organizing an economic boycott of a company, a team of community members attempting to clean up a neighborhood, and the members of a trade union seeking to raise their wages are all examples of collective action. Collective action goes on continually. Every day, people participate in collective efforts of some sort in such diverse settings as the home, the workplace, the meeting hall of a voluntary association, or a sports arena decorated for a political rally.

Not all collective action is the same; its character varies widely. Scholars working within the resource mobilization perspective argue that it is this variation that we should study. In addition to describing changes in the character of collective action, scholars also try to explain why such changes occur. In undertaking this challenge, they focus on the underlying social bonds and divisions in the society and seek to understand how these structural conditions change over time. For each historical period, one needs to determine the particular combinations of people that are likely to engage in collective action. Two important factors are focused upon: (1) cleavage factors, which tend to separate people from one another or set them at odds, and (2) integrating factors, which pull people together in social groups (whether or not collective action usually occurs).

A basic argument of the resource mobilization perspective is that both cleavage and integrating factors are necessary conditions for social movements to occur. The resource mobilization approach is critical of relative deprivation theory. In particular, it questions the emphasis that has been placed on discontent as a condition for social unrest. It is asserted that discontent, though perhaps a necessary condition, is not a sufficient condition for social unrest. Discontent must become mobilized. People who are dissatisfied have to come together and organize to act collectively. Their goals must be defined, they must be persuaded to join forces, and their activities must be coordinated.

5. New Social Movements

One theme that has emerged in the social movement literature in recent years, of particular relevance to urban and community studies, is that new social movements have arisen in reaction to certain modernization processes in late capitalist societies. The birth of these new social movements has been facilitated by the rise of new values. New social movement theorists argue that there has been a qualitative shift in the nature of sociopolitical action in the western hemisphere. In particular, these new social movements are thought to be "postmaterialist." The new middle class is said to be discontented with the nature of postmodern society. New values are seen as providing the ideological and motivational background for the emergence of the new social movements. The values important to these new social movements include a desire for *community*, self-actualization, and personal as opposed to occupational satisfaction.

A number of urban-based movements can be seen to fall into this category. (For research on urban-based movements see Castells, 1983.) For example, recent explanations for the rise of Brazilian urban social movements have drawn, in part, upon ideas from new social movement theory. For instance, Valladares and Coelho argue that such social movements have shifted from "the questioning of meeting 'needs' to the demand for citizen rights, and thus have become expressions of a new identity." South Africa provides another example of this transition. In South Africa, the Soweto Riots during the 1970s were a precursor to the rise of urban social movements in the 1980s, which in turn were an important force in the struggle against apartheid. Current urban movements are concerned about the nature of "civil society" in the transformed South Africa.

B. Social Networks and Community Organizing

Granovetter, in discussing the role that informal social networks play in community organization, raises the question: "Why do some communities organize for common goals easily and effectively whereas others seem unable to mobilize resources, even against dire threats." In discussing this question, he reviews Gans's study of the Italian community in the West End of Boston. This community—an archetype of the community saved thesis—was unable to organize to fight against the "urban renewal" that ultimately destroyed it. This outcome seems particularly surprising in view of Gans's description of West End social structure as cohesive. Granovetter explains this result as due to the nature of the interpersonal ties that existed in the community. Granovetter speculates that all ties were either strong or nonexistent; the consequences of this were that the community broke down into isolated cliques.

Granovetter suggests that for a community to have many weak ties that *bridge* different subgroups (or cliques), there must be several distinct ways or contexts in which people may form them. In developing these insights Granovetter constructs a rough principle that might be used for future investigation: the more local bridges (weak ties that link otherwise sociometrically distant cliques) in a community and the greater their degree, the more cohesive the community and the more capable it is of acting in concert. In recent years a number of authors have focused on the role that social networks play as a form of *social capital*. Social capital is seen as a resource that facilitates collective action. For example, communities who have greater social capital—in the form of integrating social networks—are better able to mobilize against opponents and to organize to positively adapt to change.

C. NonViolent Civil Disobedience

1. NonViolent Civil Disobedience (NVCD): A Definition

Civil disobedience is both a political tactic and the basis of movements that advocate social change. Civil disobedience is a nonviolent action engaged in by an individual who refuses to obey a law for moral or philosophical reasons. The participants in civil disobedience willfully and openly refuse to comply with a law in order to dramatize the issue that they, or the group, find unjust. An example of civil disobedience would be an environmentalist blocking a logging road by laying upon it—

and thus preventing the passage of logging trucks loaded with timber—when the logging company has obtained a court injunction prohibiting blocking the road.

Civil disobedience differs from other illegal acts because it is engaged in by people who commit the action knowing and accepting the penalties and consequences of breaking the law. Breaking the law is a means toward changing the law, the justice system, government policy, or the culture. Civil disobedience is also often called nonviolent action. The word *action* is significant—as the objective of civil disobedience is to actively seek change through protest or disruption, not through passively waiting for change.

It is an important distinction that civil disobedience campaigns are based on a philosophy of nonviolence. There is a history of collective protest being violent or involving damage to property (e.g., riots). Nonviolent action is not simply the absence of physical violence but includes the absence of verbal violence, intimidation, and property damage. Many nonviolent movements advocate the presence of openness and love used as a means through which to *convert* their opponent to the ideology of the civil disobedience campaign. Those who are participants and leaders in civil disobedience campaigns seek to change the worldview of those involved in the conflict so that the conditions that led to the conflict do not recur. Civil disobedience campaigns and movements accordingly often have a religious, spiritual, or philosophical foundation.

2. Community and Urban Aspects of Civil Disobedience

Nonviolent civil disobedience is related to both specific communities and national and international campaigns. In some instances civil disobedience is tied to specific geographic communities as they deal with local issues such as nuclear power plants near a city, defense of particular wilderness areas, or the protest against a particular abortion clinic. In the above cases, the movements are directly related to geographic communities. In other cases, the use of civil disobedience is tied to the freedom of a people, nation, or biological ecosystem and is therefore not bound to a specific geographical location. This, however, is not to say that these nongeographical cases do not have ties to a community. In order for any social movement to mobilize enough support to engage in a civil disobedience campaign there needs to be a community of people who identify themselves ideologically with the goals and strategy of the social movement. Therefore, in the case of national or international campaigns there is a sense of community, but a nongeographically specific community formed through collective identification.

Additionally, both the civil disobedience movements that share a geographic element and those that do not have an aspect of community referred to as social interaction. The members of both geographic and nongeographic civil disobedience movements meet together to plan campaigns and sometimes live or camp communally or travel together to actions and thus develop a community through social interaction and shared identity.

As with other forms of collective action, civil disobedience campaigns and movements tend to be disproportionately based in urban centers. They tend to have a leadership who originate from urban centers, recruit their membership from urban centers, and seek media attention to bring the issues to the attention of members of urban centers. Civil disobedience campaigns need to engage in actions that educate the public (including their opponents) in order to be successful. Therefore, actions tend to be geared toward urban centers with media outlets where the news stories get dispersed to a primarily urban audience (e.g., such tactics as protests at the urban head office of a company clear cutting a wilderness area).

3. Purpose of Civil Disobedience

The purpose of civil disobedience from the point of view of those who engage in it, as Martin Luther King Jr. (1963, p.2) stated, is "to create such a crisis and foster such a tension that a community which has constantly refused to negotiate is forced to confront the issue." The act is used to morally and politically expose an issue that the individual or group sees as unjust. Those who argue for civil disobedience assert that citizens need to be able to look at the law as a question: Should I obey this law or not?

Proponents of civil disobedience argue that breaking the law is legitimate because they are following a higher moral code. They argue that there are just and unjust laws. It is one's moral and legal obligation to follow just laws and to *not* follow unjust laws. Their peaceful *acceptance* of the consequence of breaking the law, they argue, shows their respect for the law. In addition, proponents argue that civil disobedience is not a problem to society if their campaign is ultimately seen by the public as wrong or misguided, it is only when civil disobedience movements gain widespread public support that they present a problem for society—namely, the need to change laws and other aspects of culture in accordance with the philosophy of the movement.

Those who oppose the use of civil disobedience—at

least those critics residing in democratic societies—argue that laws are the duty of citizens to obey because they are created by the people. Opponents to civil disobedience argue that it undermines the justice system and promotes anarchy because people are taking the law into their own hands and exposing their contempt for the justice system. Another argument against civil disobedience is that the participants are putting their selfish interests ahead of the interests of the community or the society. Further, opponents to civil disobedience argue that the practice of civil disobedience is self-defeating because it fosters anger and resentment from the opponents and thereby undermines potential negotiation efforts.

4. Consequences of Nonviolent Civil Disobedience for Communities

Civil disobedience campaigns can have a variety of potential effects on geographically based communities. These include, an increase in outsiders in the area, a disruption in the local economy, or even a boost to the economy. There are effects associated with policing, including the number of officers needed to arrest and process the protesters. There are effects on the courts, jails, and the legal aid system, as these institutions are forced to deal with larger case loads. There are also effects on individuals who have been civilly disobedient such as public condemnation, disruption in home and work lives, costs related to legal defense, time spent in jail, and permanent criminal records. Opponents of civil disobedience campaigns are affected emotionally by being made the target of public outcry and economically by incurring financial costs in terms of lost profits, costs related to legal representation, and costs associated with mounting public relations campaigns. In states where authoritarian regimes hold power, proponents of civil disobedience campaigns can face more dramatic consequences: prison, torture, and execution.

VI. RESOLUTION OF COMMUNITY-BASED CONFLICTS

In this final section we consider various efforts to resolve conflict and violence in a community context.

A. Alternative Dispute Resolution

1. A Definition of Alternative Dispute Resolution

Alternative dispute resolution (ADR) refers to a variety of nonjudicial processes for resolving conflict. These include: negotiation, mediation, arbitration, conciliation, private judging, neutral expert fact-finding, mini-trial, summary jury trial, and moderated settlement conferences.

2. Brief History of the Development of ADR in Canada and the U.S.

Alternative dispute resolution, in the U.S., emerged out of the legal reform and civil rights movements in the late 1960s. Excessive delays in the legal process from court overload and rising legal costs also encouraged more widespread support of ADR methods. In the U.S., ADR grew primarily as an alternative to the court system.

Alternative dispute resolution in Canada has come about, partially, from observing the success of early ADR processes in the U.S. as well as from a desire to find alternative ways to solve conflict in society. Advocates of ADR are motivated by the wish to seek nonadversarial approaches to conflict resolution. Some values that people express in seeking an alternative to the adversarial approach to conflict (through the court system) are: support for consensus-based decision-making, a desire for accessible and community-oriented resolution processes, a desire for economically accessible processes, and a desire for more efficient processes.

Alternative dispute resolution in Canada is constituted by a group of related processes that can be used with, or in place of, the legal system. Additional pressure to develop ADR in Canada has come from international companies wanting to use the process because of the costs and delays in the court system that exist in some provinces.

3. Some Pros and Cons of ADR

a. Pros

First, there are *economic savings* from not needing to hire lawyers, from time saved, and from having an arbitrator with expertise in the specific area (thus relieving the cost of retaining expert evidence). Alternative dispute resolution can, however, increase costs in some situations, such as in family negotiations and in large public disputes. Second, ADR allows a person or company to retain their *privacy*. By contrast, courts keep records of transcripts and judgements that are published and become a part of the permanent public record. Third, ADR often *saves time* because one does not have to deal with the overloaded courts and the delays inherent in the court system. Fourth, in ADR, parties have *more control* over the process including the solution (especially if they engage in mediation). People may feel more bound by their agreements if they have had more say in the process and if they feel their side of the story has been heard, and if they have played a role in designing the solution. Finally, since in ADR much time is spent listening to the other party and negotiating, there is more of a capacity to *preserve relationships* than in traditional conflict resolution methods.

b. Cons

Stobo identifies five possible draw backs to ADR: (1) there is no public scrutiny of the "case," (2) There is no opportunity for precedent setting, (3) certain disputes are unsuitable to ADR (e.g., where there has been abuse between the parties who might otherwise wish to negotiate), (4) sometimes there is a lack of commitment from participants that makes ADR difficult, and (5) there are limitations in fact-finding within ADR. Also, there is often a reluctance by lawyers to recommend ADR to clients, even if it is the best option, because they are not familiar with the benefits and processes of ADR.

4. Definition/Explanation of Some ADR Processes

There are many ADR processes (for example, arbitration, adjudication, conciliation, mediation, minitrials, moderated settlement conferences, multidoor courthouse programs, negotiation, private judging, summary jury trials and community mediation centers). Some of the processes work completely outside the court system, and some work in cooperation with the court system. It is outside the scope of this article to describe every ADR process. We describe briefly the most common ADR processes:

Adjudication: a process in which those in conflict present evidence and arguments to a neutral third party. The adjudicator, commonly a judge, has the power to provide a binding decision. Such decisions are often guided by a set of preexisting standards.

Arbitration: a process where a neutral third party conducts an informal hearing and makes a decision based on the information provided at the hearing. The arbitrator is a knowledgeable and mutually acceptable person. Arbitration may be administered privately or publicly, it may be voluntary or compulsory, and it may be binding or nonbinding.

Mediation: in a mediation process, a mutually acceptable third party helps the conflicting parties develop their own resolution. The mediator structures negotiations, facilitates communication, and makes suggestions or recommendations aimed at bringing the parties

to an agreement. However, the mediator leaves it to the disputants to decide the outcome. In mediation, the process is voluntary.

Negotiation: negotiation refers to communications or discussions between contending groups that are aimed at resolving the issues in dispute or coming to an agreement.

Community Mediation Centers (or Neighborhood Justice Centers): private or not-for-profit centers for conflict resolution that provide a number of different processes for the community such as mediation of community, neighbor, or family conflict. As well, these centers may provide training in conflict resolution and mediation skills and give educational seminars.

5. Three Examples of How ADR Processes, Initiatives, and Education Can Be Implemented in Communities

Alternative dispute resolution is highly applicable to communities. Community mediation centers and private mediators can provide an alternative to the court system that has many benefits for individuals such as saved time, cost, and privacy. Issues that are most likely best dealt with outside the court (such as landlord–tenant disagreements, family issues, and victim–offender reconciliation) may be most effectively dealt with from within the community. Citizens now have several types of community-based ADR processes to chose from in dealing with conflicts.

Alternative dispute resolution is also beginning to be used in school settings (mostly in the U.S.); one example is peer mediation in schools. Children are trained in mediation and conflict resolution skills and then serve as "conflict managers" in helping to solve the playground conflicts of their peers. An exciting development in some schools systems is the development of programs that provide mediation opportunities between students and school authorities on discipline and other matters. One potential outcome—and hope of ADR advocates—of teaching ADR skills to youth is that it can lead to the emergence of an entire generation of people who have skills in managing private conflicts.

A further application of ADR in community settings is the use of mediation to settle disputes between contending parties and governmental agencies. For instance, an organizational structure can be created that is comprised of representatives from different groups who have specific stakes in the outcome of an issue (called stakeholders), who would then work toward a reaching a consensus-based decision with the help of a mediator. One illustration this type of "round-table" approach is provided by a recent attempt to resolve land use disputes in British Columbia, Canada. In this case, different parties have been involved in making decisions about how land and natural resources will be used; the parties include diverse stakeholders such as representatives from different levels of government, aboriginal peoples, representatives of the mining and logging industries, environmentalists, local business people, and community members. If these types of public processes are well structured and facilitated, citizens have an unparalleled opportunity to be directly involved as partners in government and policy decisions.

B. Community Policing

The final approach to reducing conflict that we discuss is community policing. It has been argued that traditional methods of policing, which emphasize motorized police patrols, rapid response to citizens' reports, and crime investigation have done little to assuage public fears of crime. Some criminologists argue that innovative styles of community policing may prove more effective in addressing the public's fear of crime. For example, several research studies show that where foot patrols are used, residents report less worry and concern about crime. Horse patrols in urban parks and bicycle patrols in downtown neighborhoods are also becoming increasingly popular.

Several factors contributed to the advent of community policing, including the isolation of police officers in patrol cars, the narrowing of the police mission to crime fighting, increased reliance upon technology to manage efficiency over human interaction, insulation of police administration from community input, and a long-standing concern about police violation of human rights. Community policing (sometimes termed "community-based policing" or "community-oriented policing") developed out of a critique of the conventional model of urban policing. The philosophy of community policing challenges the view that the primary activities of police should be making arrests, law enforcement, and crime investigation. Rather, this approach emphasizes peacekeeping, order maintenance, and public service operations as central functions of policing. The community policing literature asserts that the most effective basis of social control and order in society is community based. Modern police have removed themselves organizationally and operationally from the community. Policing has been rendered less effective and communities have become increasingly disorderly as a result of this separation of police from the community. The literature suggests that in order for modern police to become effective and efficient agents of social control

in urban settings, police must reintegrate their operations to respond to the community's concerns and priorities.

Four major features of community-based policing include: (1) community-based crime prevention, (2) proactive service as opposed to emergency response, (3) public participation in planning and supervision of police operations, and (4) shifting command responsibility to lower-level ranks. Furthermore, community policing requires that police be encouraged to seek out alternatives other than law enforcement. This philosophy requires that urban policing be organized and operated at the community or neighborhood level. Police also need to address social issues and public order problems in addition to breaches of law. Finally, this approach claims community residents want more police presence, more visible and accessible police, and more personal contact with police.

Community policing is intended to improve relations between police and minorities through increased daily face-to-face contact with communities, with the same officers working in the same neighborhoods to develop long term rapport and mutual trust. The philosophy of community policing is designed to encourage community input into the police agenda and an emphasis on experimentation with creative solutions to problems as opposed to isolated incidents. This philosophy also encourages the recruitment of minorities and members of local communities into policing. In the Canadian context, community-based policing models have included recruitment of First Nations (or aboriginal) officers, as well as the development of Native police programs that emphasize cross-cultural policing and an understanding of traditional native policing and alternative dispute resolution strategies. (For a review of community policing and aboriginal peoples in Canada, see Depew, 1992.)

VII. CONCLUSION

This article has reviewed the scholarly literature on violence, peace, and conflict in the context of urban and community studies. Six key areas, drawn from the community and urban studies literatures, were examined: (1) social change and communities, (2) social psychology and life in cities, (3) models of urban development, (4) urban dimensions of crime, (5) collective behavior and collective action, and (6) the resolution of community-based conflicts.

We began with a critical discussion of the concept of community. Next we reviewed explanations of the relationship between social change and the nature of communities. In particular, we explored how large scale urbanization and industrialization have impacted on the formation and stability of communities within cities. The debate over whether communities have been lost, saved, or liberated within urban settings was discussed as a backdrop to the social psychology of urban life, differences in crime rates between urban and rural locations, and the occurrence of collective behavior and collective action. Concerns about the changing nature of communities, the degeneration of social life as a result of urbanization, and the persistence of supportive community structures in urban contexts are three (apparently contradictory) themes that recur throughout the urban and community studies literature. Support for these different arguments (community-lost, -saved, or -liberated) depends partly on what features of urban communities are emphasized. The community-lost and community-saved arguments use "neighborhoods" to define communities, while the community-liberated argument conceptualizes communities as social networks. The final topic we explored in examining social change and communities was the implications for communities posed by the Internet. Here we considered the relevance of computer-supported social networks to our understanding of "virtual" communities.

In the following section, we focused on the individual unit of analysis to consider the experience of life within urban environments and examined the contribution of environmental load theory to our understanding urban–rural differences in helping behavior and related phenomena. Perceptions of, and responses to, crowding are topics of interest to scholars in this area. With regard to helping behavior, social psychological studies have consistently found that help is more frequently provided in nonurban communities. However, urban–rural differences apply primarily to interactions with strangers, not to interactions with "strong ties."

Next we turned to the macro level of analysis in reviewing different models of urban development. Here, we emphasized the importance of human ecology to our understanding of the growth of cities and considered the contribution of structural approaches to our understanding of the role that cities play within larger processes of capital accumulation. Within the human ecology tradition, a number of related models were reviewed. These models described somewhat different trajectories of urban development that have occurred in different North American cities. In reviewing structural (or political economy) approaches to urban development, we describe how this tradition focuses upon the distribution of power and the allocation of resources

in cities. One model of urban development, entitled the "growth machine," emphasizes the role of "place" entrepreneurs in promoting development. This model argues that in contemporary cities exchange values of urban spaces are favored over their use values. This process has negative consequences for urban residents. We also examined the recent development of "global cities" as international nodes in the international flow of capital and information and described some differences that have been observed in urbanization processes between the developed and developing worlds.

In discussing urban dimensions of crime, we considered patterns of social inequality and the persistence of urban–rural differences in crime rates. Three themes are relevant to the study of crime in cities: racial/ethnic segregation and poverty within cities, the increase in gang-related crimes and lethal violence, and the physical environment of cities in relation to criminal behavior.

Next we turned to a consideration of phenomena frequently associated with urban locations: riots, demonstration protests, and social movements. We examined explanations of collective behavior and collective action, highlighting aspects of mass society, relative deprivation, resource mobilization, and new social movement theories. The role played by social networks in community organization was described. Our discussion of collective action then turned to consider the nature and purpose of nonviolent civil disobedience campaigns, which tend to be disproportionately based in urban centers.

Finally, this chapter concluded with a discussion of various efforts to resolve community conflict and violence in a community context. We offered a brief history of the development of alternative dispute resolution procedures, the strengths and limits of different ADR models, and provided definitions of various ADR processes such as: adjudication, arbitration, mediation, negotiation, and community mediation centers. We also examined a final approach to reducing conflict within communities, that of community-based policing, which poses a sharp contrast to traditional procedures and philosophies of policing urban centers.

Also See the Following Articles

GANGS • URBAN VIOLENCE, YOUTH

Bibliography

Archer, D. & Gartner, R. (1984). *Violence and crime in cross-national perspective.* New Haven, CT: Yale University Press.

Baldassare, M. (1994). *The Los Angeles riots: Lessons for the urban future.* Boulder: Westview Press.

Burgess, E. W. (1925). The growth of the city: An introduction to a research project." In R. E. Park, E. W. Burgess, & R. D. McKenzie (Eds.), *The city.* (pp. 47–62). Chicago: University of Chicago Press.

Castells, M. (1983). *The city and the grassroots: A cross-cultural theory of urban sociology.* Berkeley: University of California Press.

Depew, R. (1992). Policing native communities. In R. A. Silverman & M. O. Nielsen (Eds.), *Aboriginal peoples and Canadian criminal justice.* (pp. 97–109). Markham: Butterworths.

Fischer, C. S. (1976). *The urban experience.* New York: Harcourt, Brace, Jovanovich.

Gans, H. (1962). *The urban villagers.* New York: Free Press.

Gillis, A. R. (1974). Population density and social pathology: The case of building type, social allowance, and juvenile delinquency." *Social Forces, 53,* 306–314.

Granovetter, M. (1973). The strength of weak ties. *American Journal of Sociology, 78,* 1360–1380.

Hagedorn, J. M. (1991). Gangs, neighborhoods, and public policy. *Social Problems, 38,* 529–542.

Hannigan, J. (1995). The postmodern city: A new urbanization? *Current Sociology, 41,* 152–217.

Harvey, D. (1985). *The urbanization of capital.* Baltimore, MD: Johns Hopkins University Press.

Karsarda, J. D., & Crenshaw, E. M. (1991). Third world urbanization: Dimensions, theories, and determinants. *Annual Review of Sociology, 17,* 467–501.

King, Martin Luther, Jr. (1963). Letter from Birmingham Jail. In *Why We Can't Wait.* New York: Harper & Row.

Kornhauser, W. (1959). *The politics of mass society.* Glencoe, IL: Free Press.

Logan, J. R., & Molotch, H. L. (1987). *Urban fortunes.* Berkeley: University of California Press.

Mathur, O. P. (1994). Responding to the urban challenge: A research agenda for India and Nepal. In R. Stren (Ed.), *Urban research in the developing world:* Asia (Vol. 1, pp. 47–100). Toronto: Centre for Urban and Community Studies.

Milgram, S. (Ed.) (1970). The experience of living in cities. In *The individual in a social world: Essays and experiments.* Reading, MA: Addison-Wesley.

Oberschall, A. (1973). *Social conflict and social movements.* Englewood Cliffs, NJ: Prentice-Hall.

Standing Committee on Administration of Justice (1990). Alternative dispute resolution. Presented to the 2nd Session, 34th Parliament of Canada, Ottawa, Ontario.

Stobo, C. (1995). An alternative dispute resolution primer and survey of current government initiatives in Ontario: Current issue paper 165, (pp. 1–27). September, Ontario Legislative Library.

Stren, R. (Ed.) (1994). *Urban research in the developing world* (Vol. 1–4). Toronto: Centre for Urban and Community Studies.

Tilly, C. (1978). *From mobilization to revolution.* Reading, MA: Addison-Wesley.

Turner, R. H., & Killian, L. M. (1972). *Collective behavior.* Englewood Cliffs, NJ: Prentice–Hall.

Wellman, B. (1979). The community question. *American Journal of Sociology, 84* 1201–1231.

Wellman, B., Salaff, J., Dimitrova, D., Garton, L., Gulia, M., & Haythornthwaite, C. (1996). Computer networks as social networks: Collaborative work, telework, and virtual community. *Annual Review of Sociology, 22,* 213–238.

Whyte, W. F. (1955). *Street corner society.* Chicago: University of Chicago Press.

Wilson, W. J. (1987). *The truly disadvantaged: The inner city, the underclass, and public policy.* Chicago: University of Chicago Press.

Wirth, L. (1938). Urbanism as a way of life. *American Journal of Sociology, 44,* 3–24.

Wondolleck, J. M., Manring, N. J., & Crowfoot, J. E. (1996). Teetering at the top of the ladder: The experience of citizen group participants in alternative dispute resolution processes. *Sociological Perspectives, Pacific Sociological Association, 39*(2), 249–262.

Yousif, Y. Korte, C. (1995). Urbanization, culture, and helpfulness. *Journal of Cross-Cultural Psychology, 26*(5), 474–489.

Zukin, S. (1987). Gentrification: Culture and capital in the urban core." *Annual Review of Sociology, 13,* 129–147.

Urban Violence, Youth

Amy Leventhal, Deborah Gorman-Smith, and Patrick Tolan

University of Illinois at Chicago

I. THE ECOLOGY OF THE INNER-CITY NEIGHBORHOOD

Inner-city violence has become an issue of national concern and much of this public concern is targeted toward youth. Rates of serious and lethal crimes among juveniles have shown a steady increase since the late 1980s. These rates are highest in inner cities and have shown the greatest increases in urban areas with a population of more than one-quarter million people; violence is one of the leading causes of death for youth living in the inner city. Violent victimization rates indicate that the percentage of youths ages 10–16 ever victimized is highest in large cities, among African-Americans and Latinos, and among youths whose family income is under $20,000 per year. Adolescence and early adulthood are also when individuals are at greatest risk for becoming victims of violent crime. In addition to victimization, children living in inner-city communities also witness high rates of violence. Repeated exposure to violence can have negative consequences for families and psychological and emotional ramifications for youth.

Children growing up in disadvantaged inner-city neighborhoods routinely face harmful and potentially life-threatening circumstances. The risks and obstacles to healthy development and safety are extensive within the inner city. Disadvantaged neighborhoods are characterized by high rates of social problems such as adolescent pregnancy, drug problems, crime, gang activity, and racism. Children living in disadvantaged communities are more likely to have poor achievement, not complete high school, and exhibit high rates of aggression and other forms of psychopathology. As a part of their regular experience, inner-city youths must navigate their environment to avoid being victimized by violence, cope with observed violence, and manage possibilities for participating in violence.

An inner-city youth's survival may depend on everyday decisions that require sophisticated problem-solving. Youth constantly exposed to potentially dangerous situations must learn to anticipate and negotiate their environment to avoid harm. For example, the consequences of simply deciding which way to walk to school could be life-threatening because youths must be aware of and avoid dangerous situations such as crossing gang territories or going into a common drug-dealing area. Not only must youth understand societal rules governing behavior, they must also understand the rules governing behaviors that are specific to their community in the midst of gangs, drugs, and violence. Developing awareness and skill in managing the risks inherent in inner-city environments can be beneficial for their safety, but these skills may develop at the cost of aspects of cognitive, social, and emotional development.

Risks for violence faced by inner-city youth cannot be adequately explained by differences in income across neighborhoods. The correlates of poverty rather than poverty itself may best predict community violence. Inner-city youth grow up in communities where joblessness is high, poor housing is the rule, neighbors face similar economic plight, and few positive social opportunities for recreation or other positive engagement exist. More often than not, fathers live outside the family home; gang activity is common; and drugs, crime, and violence are pervasive. The convergence of these characteristics creates and sustains an ecology of violence within these communities.

Hopelessness among youth growing up among these obstacles is not surprising. Conventional means of success become perceived as increasingly more remote and unattainable to those living in the inner city. Two changes in the job market have led to fewer job opportunities and higher unemployment for those living in the inner city. Job opportunities have moved out of the city center and thus out of reach of the poor living in the city. The loss of jobs has resulted in those in disadvantaged neighborhoods becoming increasingly and homogeneously economically disadvantaged. Middle-income residents leave neighborhoods that are hit by these economic changes. This, in turn, compounds the deterioration of the community as businesses and community institutions and organizations receive less economic support when community members are homogeneously disadvantaged. Furthermore, inner-city youths have few models in their community of economic accomplishment through conventional channels. In these situations neighborhoods become physically run down. The physical decay of the neighborhood becomes a marker of few opportunities and poor resources in a community which, in turn, invites unconventional sources of opportunity such as drugs and prostitution.

In addition to having few economic resources, there tends to be significant discrepancies in other types of resources available within these disadvantaged inner-city communities as compared to neighboring communities. In large public housing complexes, which are common in poor inner-city neighborhoods, high residential instability and anonymity weaken informal social controls. In addition, inner-city neighborhoods have higher rates of single-parent families, which has been suggested to be related to weaker social networks and poorer monitoring of youth. Educational institutions in poor urban neighborhoods are affected by the

same problems that plague the communities in which they inhabit. Schools in poor inner-city communities have too few economic and social resources and must function in the face of competing and disruptive problems such as adolescent pregnancy, drug use, violence, and gang activity.

Together, these economic and social problems lead to the isolation and alienation of these neighborhoods from mainstream society. As many opportunities for gaining social status become more remote to inner-city residents, material acquisition takes on increasing importance as one of the few ways to gain social status. The attraction and plausibility of conventional accomplishments diminishes and standard markers of success become equated with acting "White" and abandoning one's ethnic identity. Furthermore, the inaccessibility of conventional success strengthens the unconventional systems of advancement that have taken hold in the inner city, such as prostitution and drug sales. To youths growing up in these urban areas, the choices are limited and seeing beyond the opportunities of the neighborhood poses a difficult challenge. The strengthening of these unconventional systems continues the cycle of disadvantage, supporting an ecology of violence.

Gang activity is one primary source of inner-city violence. According to Fagan and Wilkinson, a variety of factors typically present among gang members increase the risk for violence in these groups. Specifically, the probability of violence may be high within and among gangs as a result of repeated interaction among individuals, the presence of third-party observers, a high value placed on status, low social control, and a high value on masculinity expressed through toughness. Gang violence takes on a variety of forms and is driven by multiple motivations and functions. Gang violence serves as an expression of grievance, a mechanism for material gain, to maintain social order or gain a social position, a method of self-defense, and a reinforcement of a collective identity. Gang violence and youth violence are overlapping phenomena of which neither subsumes nor can fully explain the other.

II. EXPOSURE TO VIOLENCE

Exposure to violence is an unfortunate reality for inner-city youths, who are likely to be confronted by violence in a variety of forms. Rates of violence exposure are particularly high among children and youth living in poor, urban communities. Surveys indicate that more than half of inner-city youths have witnessed a violent attack in the previous year and even more children report staying inside their home out of fear of violence. Across studies, 14 to 46% of inner-city youth report having witnessed a shooting.

Exposure to violence can have emotional and psychological ramifications for children. For example, Gorman-Smith and Tolan found relations between exposure to community violence in the past year and current level of aggression and depression after controlling for previous symptom level. Fagan and Wilkinson suggest that violence is perpetuated, in part, by children internalizing experiences and beliefs about violence to which they are exposed. As a consequence children can develop conflict resolution skills that are aggressive and violent. Violent events in this context are, by nature, unpredictable. Garbarino, Kostelny, and Dubrow suggest that the combined commonality and unpredictability of violence can lead to posttraumatic stress symptoms such as emotional numbness and preoccupying vigilance.

III. PROTECTIVE FACTORS OF YOUTH VIOLENCE

Clearly, there are a multitude of risks facing youth that can relate to involvement in violence. However, not all children living in inner-city neighborhoods participate in violence. The question becomes, what factors might serve to protect them from becoming involved in violence? Are there characteristics of youth's lives and the contexts in which they live that may serve to protect or enhance risk for involvement in violence? The protective factors against involvement in violence have not been entirely specified to date. However, a number of factors may relate to decreased risk for youth. These include family functioning, coping, methods and style, social control, economic aid, and gun control.

A. Family Functioning

The influence of family on youth violence is well established. Families are the most proximal influence on children's aggressive and delinquent behavior. Family predictors of delinquency have been divided into two domains representing related, yet distinct, aspects of family functioning: (1) parenting practices and (2) family relationship characteristics. Parenting practices such as discipline and parental monitoring have been associated with involvement in violent and delinquent behavior. In addition, family relationship characteristics such as emotional cohesion (warmth), structure, organiza-

tion, and beliefs have been related to violent behavior among youth.

However, few studies examine the role of community influences on the relation between family functioning and youth violence. The influence of family on risk for violence appears to differ across community context. While family factors may protect against youth violence in other than the most devastated communities, in the most economically and socially disadvantaged inner-city neighborhoods where violence is a part of daily life, the risks posed to children may override good parenting practices or healthy family functioning. Consequently, the role of family functioning as a protective factor against youth violence appears to be community specific and may not be the same in the poorest urban neighborhoods.

B. Coping

Youth and families living in poor urban neighborhoods must cope with multiple stressors that arise from poverty, living in a disadvantaged neighborhood, having few resources, and exposure to violence and social problems. Children and families living in inner-city neighborhoods have a higher likelihood of experiencing stress than others. Also, chronic environmental stress is a constant presence among inner-city residents and is largely uncontrollable.

In addition to experiencing more stress than others, inner-city youth may be more vulnerable to the impact of stressful events. Studies have shown that those in lower socioeconomic-status groups are more vulnerable to negative effects of job loss than those in the middle class. Moreover, African-American males, when compared to White males, report more physical and psychological problems and more family problems after job loss. As yet, it is unclear whether poor ethnic minority children will show increased vulnerability to stress. Tolan et al. speculate that children with limited social and economic resources who experience chronic environmental stress and increased stressful life events may have greater difficulty managing day-to-day hassles. It seems likely that inner-city children not only experience high amounts of stress but also may be more adversely affected by this stress.

Stressors may have an indirect effect on children's adjustment through their effects on family functioning. Stressful events have been associated with psychological distress among adults. Psychological distress experienced by parents as a result of stressful events can negatively effect parenting and family relationship characteristics. In turn, poor family functioning may then increase the risk for behavior problems among youth.

A preliminary test of a stress and coping model suggests that inner-city children's coping can play a role in moderating the influence of stress on psychological functioning, but only for particular types of stress. Tolan et al. make an important distinction between the objectives of adaptive coping and effective coping. Adaptive coping minimizes stressors or their long-term impact and effective coping provides relief from distress but does not minimize the stressor in the long run. Effective coping may be more likely to facilitate involvement in violence. For example, a youth may join a gang for protection and, as a consequence, be involved in or exposed to violence. When youths are commonly confronted with potentially dangerous situations requiring sophisticated decision-making skills while their problem-solving skills are still developing, effective coping may be utilized more often than adaptive forms of coping. Further examination of coping that distinguishes between adaptive and effective coping may serve to clarify the relations between children's coping and negative outcomes within a family context.

C. Social Change

Given the amount and pervasiveness of disadvantage facing poor, urban, ethnic minority youth, it is unlikely that shoring up resources at the individual and family levels will be sufficient for broad, long-term change in overall rates of urban youth violence. Without decreasing community level and social structural risk factors inner-city communities will continue to be havens for violence.

Change can be effected at the societal level by providing economic assistance to urban communities in need. Facilitating employment opportunities and increasing resource allocation to schools and community organizations are ways through which communities can protect against youth violence. As noted earlier, the lack of employment opportunities in poor inner-city communities produces a gap that is filled by unconventional means of economic gain. Pervasive unemployment further marginalizes poor urban residents from mainstream society. Increasing viable employment opportunities may disrupt the cycle of hopelessness and strengthen connections to conventional sources of success. Increasing employment opportunities within poor inner-city communities would also indirectly minimize youth violence risk by facilitating greater economic diversity within communities, which supports the growth of business development. Furthermore, financially and structurally strengthening the educational system as a whole and increasing job training opportunities appear to be necessary components in preparing youth to engage in socially sanctioned means of economic gain.

D. Neighborhood Control

Characteristics of community social organization have been considered important deterrents of community violence. Social organization refers to aspects of communities that regulate the behavior of those in the community. Formal and informal social controls are aspects of social organization that play a role in deterring urban violence.

Formal social control is expedited by institutional bodies created on behalf of the society at large to facilitate the adoption of behavioral guidelines among citizens. Two separate initiatives in two large cities are strong examples of the positive impact of formal social control on rates of violence. These two initiatives, in Boston and New York City, made institutional changes in police-monitoring patterns and formal recreational opportunities for youths through community organizations and improved informal agency–resident relations. Following the implementation of these programs there was a significant decrease in overall violent crime rates in these cities. These programs lowered violent crime by instituting changes such as increasing the number of police in high-crime areas (increasing beat/neighborhood patrols), developing structured activities for youths, strengthening relationships between residents and police, and involving residents in monitoring and deterring crime. The success of these programs suggest that changes at this level can be important in deterring youth violent crime.

Collective efficacy is a form of social organization that has been related to lower community violence rates. Collective efficacy refers to the social cohesion among neighbors as well as their willingness to exert informal social control such as monitoring the activities of those in the neighborhood or intervening on behalf of the common good. High collective efficacy with youth translates into intervening and monitoring youth activities such as skipping school or hanging out on the corner. Collective efficacy appears to exert influence on violence by increasing residents' awareness and response to problematic activities in the neighborhood. Strengthening collective efficacy among neighborhood residents may be a way to decrease risk for youth violence by addressing informal social controls.

In addition to the role of social networks in facilitating informal social control, social support and social isolation appear to have important implications for youth violence indirectly by influencing parenting behavior. Social isolation and social support have been linked to parenting behavior and child maltreatment rates. A positive social relationship or involvement in social networks appear to influence parents' general psychological well-being and positive parenting behaviors. However, not all studies in this area have found positive relations between social support and positive parenting. For example, Weinraub and Wolf found high levels of social network contact associated with low levels of maternal nurturance among single mothers. While research suggests that poor social networks in disadvantaged communities relate to violence, the association between social support and youth violence among those in disadvantaged communities has not been examined at an individual level and remains unclear.

Sampson suggests that public housing policies contribute to poor informal social control. Urban public housing projects are typically large and residential instability is quite common among those who receive federal aid through public housing. The size of public housing projects and the anonymity that results from residential instability and safety concerns serve to undermine social control. Effecting policy changes in public housing to increase residential stability and strengthen ties between neighbors may indirectly decrease youth violence. For example, changes in the size and location of public housing residences may aid in deterring crime.

E. Gun Control

The use and availability of firearms has become an increasingly worrisome concern effecting youth in the inner city. In 1989 Sullivan reported that there were more guns on the streets and that they were more frequently in the hands of younger offenders. The number of homicides from firearms has continued to rise alarmingly since 1980. Firearm involvement in deaths among adolescents are particularly worrisome.

From a historical perspective, only recently have firearms played more than a limited role in delinquency. For much of the 19th century, homicides were declining and use of firearms by inner-city youths was not an issue in discussions of delinquency. The presence of guns in the inner city contributes significantly to the current trends in inner-city violence. Differences across countries in gun control laws demonstrate a clear relation between firearm accessibility and homicide rates. Guns are so common in the inner city that they have become notoriously easy to obtain at low cost. Guns appear to be increasingly more acceptable as a way of resolving disputes. According to Fagan and Wilkinson, the increased availability of guns in the inner city has increased the stakes of the code of the streets where social identity and respect are priorities. With such alarming statistics on the use of guns, particularly among youth, it is clear that this issue needs attention.

IV. DETERRING VIOLENCE

Explanations of violence have advanced beyond understanding and explaining violence in relation to poverty and toward an understanding of the array of social and organizational characteristics of poor communities that coalesce to create contexts ripe for violence. Poor, urban, ethnic minority youth are at great risk for involvement in youth violence. The numerous risks they face include limited social and economic opportunities, poverty, lack of resources, and rampant social problems. Prevention of youth involvement in violence begins by identifying protective factors against involvement in violence and strengthening those factors within high-risk groups. Research to date suggests that the factors with the most potential for prevention are family functioning, stress and coping, social control, economic aid, and gun control. These factors suggest intervention opportunities at the individual, proximal, and distal levels.

The relationships between family and community factors associated with urban youth violence are more complex than the literature suggests. Strengthening family functioning may be one way through which youths can be protected from involvement in violence. However, the neighborhood context seems to also play a role in determining whether family functioning can protect youths against involvement in violence. In particular, while family functioning acts as a buffer for the effects of stress on youth involvement in violence within urban poor neighborhoods, among those living in the most poverty-stricken neighborhoods of the inner city, this same relation may not occur.

Stress and coping appear to play a role in youth involvement in violence. The particular relations between stress and youth violence are unclear, but there is evidence that inner-city youth experience higher amounts of multiple types of stress than others. These stressors can impinge on children's adjustment directly and indirectly by negatively affecting family functioning. The amount and type of stress experienced by families and youth may differentiate those at high and low risk for involvement in violence.

Coping styles mediate the effects of stress on youth involvement in violence. An important distinction exists between adaptive coping strategies, focused on long-term resolutions, as opposed to the immediate reduction of stress through effective coping. Understanding the type of coping in which children and families engage will further clarify how stress and coping are associated with youth involvement in violence.

Clearly research indicates the importance of considering contextual factors specific to inner-city neighborhoods when developing preventive intervention toward deterring youth involvement in violence. In translating this knowledge to intervention, the particular focus of intervention with families may shift based on context. It appears even within urban contexts preventive interventions around violence would be most effective if tailored to the community. For example, in one community preventive intervention may most effectively lower youth violence by addressing stress management and, in another, it may be parenting practices or strengthening social networks. Intervening at the individual level or the proximal level with families may facilitate change within only certain community contexts or only to a certain degree. It remains unclear how coping and stress at an individual level are related to youth violence. These relations are likely complex and need further study to inform preventive intervention.

At a broad level, community factors can play an important role in effecting changes in youth violence. There are aspects of informal and formal social control that appear to mediate rates of violence among youth in urban contexts. For example, strengthening collective efficacy to increase monitoring and resident cohesion would be expected to have a broad impact on youth violence. Two initiatives in large cities that made organizational changes in policing patterns and structured community social opportunities for youths and subsequently lowered rates of violent crime citywide suggest that these are useful tools to lower violent crime in general. Providing economic and social resources to needy communities and addressing gun prevalence are also expected to have an indirect positive effect on youth violence. These broad-based changes appear to be an important level at which change is often neglected.

Exposure to violence as bystanders rather than as participants or victims put youth at risk for negative psychological and behavioral consequences. Decreasing risk of the negative ramifications of exposure to violence can be accomplished by preventing exposure to violence by youths. One intervention to lower exposure to violence would be to intervene at the community level to decrease the overall incidence of violence. Many of the strategies discussed earlier will indirectly result in less exposure to violence when levels of community violence decrease.

Also See the Following Articles

CLASS CONFLICTS • DRUG CONTROL POLICIES • GANGS • MINORITIES AS PERPETRATORS AND VICTIMS OF CRIME • URBAN AND COMMUNITY STUDIES

Bibliography

Belsky, J., & Vondra, J. (1989). Lessons from child abuse: The determinants of parenting. In D. Cicchetti & V. Carlson (Eds.), *Child maltreatment: Theory and research on the causes and consequences of child abuse and neglect.* (pp. 153–202). New York: Cambridge University Press.

Dobrin, A., Wiersema, B., Loftin, C., & McDowall, D. (1996). *Statistical handbook on violence in America.* Phoenix, AZ: Oryx.

Elliott, D. S., Wilson, W. J., Huizinga, D., Elliott, A., & Rankin, B. (1996). The effects of neighborhood disadvantage development. *Journal of Research in Crime and Delinquency, 33,* 389–426.

Fagan, J., & Wilkinson, D. L. (1998). Social contexts and functions of adolescent violence. In D. S. Elliott & B. Hamburg (Eds.), *Violence in American schools: A new perspective* (pp. 55–93). New York, NY: Cambridge University Press.

Federal Bureau of Investigation (1992). *Uniform Crime Reports.* Washington, DC: FBI.

Gorman-Smith, D., & Tolan, P. H. (1998). The role of exposure to community violence and developmental problems among inner-city youth. *Development and Psychopathology* Vol 10(1), Win 1998, 101–116.

Gorman-Smith, D., Tolan, P. H., & Henry, D. (1999). The relation of community and family to risk among urban poor adolescents. In P. Cohen, L. Robins, & C. Slomkowski (Eds.), *Where and when: Influence of historical time and place on aspects of psychopathology* (pp. 349–368). Hillsdale, NJ: Earlbaum.

Loeber, R., & Dishion, T. (1983). Early predictors of male delinquency: A review. *Psychological Bulletin, 94,* 68–99.

McLoyd, V. C. (1990). The impact of economic hardship on black families and children: Psychological distress, parenting, and socioemotional development. *Child Development, 61,* 311–346.

Office of Juvenile Justice and Delinquency Planning. (1995). *Report on trends in youth crime.* Washington, DC: U.S. Government Printing Office.

Richters, J. E., & Martinez, P. E. (1993a). The NIMH Community Violence Project. I. Children as victims of and witnesses to violence. *Psychiatry, 56,* 7–21.

Sampson, R. J. (1990). The impact of housing policies on community social disorganization and crime. *Bulletin of the New York Academy of Medicine, 66,* 526–533.

Sampson, R. J., Raudenbush, S. W., & Earls, F. (1997). Neighborhoods and violent crime: A multilevel study of collective efficacy. *Science, 277,* 918–924.

Tolan, P. H., & Gorman-Smith, D. (1997). Families and the development of urban children. In H. J. Walberg, O. Reyes, & R. P.

Weissberg (Eds.), *Interdisciplinary perspectives on children and youth*. Newberry Park: Sage.

Tolan, P. H., Guerra, N. G., & Montaini-Klovdahl, L. R. (1997). In S. A. Wolchik & I. N. Sandler (Eds.), *Handbook of children's coping: Linking theory and intervention* (pp. 453–479). New York: Plenum.

Wilson, W. J. (1991). Studying inner-city social dislocation. *American Sociological Review 56,* 1–14.

Wilson, W. J. (1987). *The truly disadvantaged: the inner-city, the underclass, and public policy.* Chicago, IL: The University of Chicago Press.

Veterans in the Political Culture

F. Lincoln Grahlfs

National Association of Radiation Survivors

GLOSSARY

Agent Orange Defoliant agent used in Vietnam. Veterans of that war blame their exposure to it for illnesses affecting both them and their children.

Boot Camp Term used to designate military basic training. For a period which usually lasts approximately 12 weeks, recruits are virtually isolated from outside contacts and experience rigid discipline and intensive training in military behavior and practices.

Esprit de corps A sense of union and common interest that develops among a group of persons who are associated with one another.

Patriotism Loyal and devoted support and defense of one's country.

Primary Group Group in which there is an intimate, personal quality to the social relationships which bind every member to every other member.

Resocialization The process of restructuring a person's view of the world around him or her, whereby the individual assumes a new and different role and begins conforming to a different set of norms.

Total Institution As conceived by Erving Goffman, a total institution is a human group in which one is completely immersed. The individual goes through his or her entire daily routine in the company of the same individuals.

VETERANS, like any other segment of the population, vary in many ways. They do, however, have one thing in common; they have borne arms for their country. And that common experience carries a number of implications for their relationship to the political culture.

I. THE MILITARY EXPERIENCE

A military organization is, in a very real sense, what Erving Goffman called a *total institution*. It is a social group in which one participates 24 hours a day. He works, eats, sleeps, and, to a large extent, engages in recreational activities with those same people. Its impact upon his or her lifestyle, attitudes, and behavior is therefore both profound and persistent. There are features of the military in particular that strongly reinforce this effect. Of particular note are the timing of the experience, the thoroughness of the socialization process, and the intensity of the social bonds one forms in the process of military service.

A. Timing

The timing of events in the life of an individual has a great relationship to the relevancy they will have in his life. It is, of course, a truism that we interpret today's experiences in the light of what has preceded them and, therefore, that what happens to one today will have some influence on his or her behavior tomorrow. But the context within which an experience occurs is also very important. The nature and extent of the impact of a given experience on an individual is related both to what else is happening in that individual's life at the time and to what is happening in the world around him or her.

1. Age at Induction

The overwhelming majority of persons who serve in the military enter service somewhere between 16 and 25 years of age. This time in a person's life, variously referred to as late adolescence or early adulthood, is a crucial one. It is precisely at this point when one is severing childhood ties and establishing the basis of an adult identity. Because of this timing, and because they are part of many individuals' first occupational experience, the guidelines acquired at this juncture are second in importance only to those learned from one's family.

2. World and National Contexts at Time of Service

Nothing happens in a social vacuum; it is inevitable that world and national events at the time of one's military service will color the experience and will be linked with it in one's feelings. Studies indicate, for instance, that Allied veterans of World War II are more accepting of nuclear weapons than are other veterans. When asked why, they cite their belief that the atomic bombing of Japanese cities saved them from participation in an invasion that could have cost them their lives.

Another example of the effect of social context invokes the concept of relative deprivation. Veterans who joined the service during the Depression, for instance, tended to have a much more positive feeling about the military because it compared favorably with what they perceived civilian life to hold for them at the time.

It is also worth noting that in spite of the long protracted entente between the United States and the Soviet Union there is a reservoir of positive feelings between veterans of those countries who had fought together against the Nazis.

B. Socialization

Of primary consideration is the fact that military service involves a very effective resocialization process that begins in boot camp and is continually reinforced as long as one is in the service. While it can be argued that the process by which one is converted from a civilian to a member of the military will vary from one country to another, there are probably more similarities than differences. At any rate, in the 1990s the United States has emerged as a world leader both in military power and in the production of military hardware. Thus, many other nations tend to model their military training programs on that of the Americans. Training of various kinds is, in fact, provided by the United States to military personnel from a number of other countries, most notably those in Central and South America. A description of the American model of military socialization, therefore, affords some insight into a process which affects more than just Americans.

Typically, a collection of recruits are sworn in early in the morning at some central assembly point in their region. They then board a public conveyance for the journey, which takes at least a full day, to a basic training facility. Upon arrival they have their hair cut as short as possible and are instructed to remove their clothes and take a shower. After moving naked from one medical officer to another for a series of examinations, they are issued uniforms. By the completion of these procedures it is very late, perhaps past midnight, and they are physically and psychologically exhausted. They are shown to their barracks and permitted to sleep.

The recruits are awakened the next morning at an hour much earlier than most of them have been used to. At this point they have been stripped as completely as is reasonable of their former identities; they have relinquished their hair, their clothes, and even their first names, for on those occasions when names are used, it will always be last names. For at least 4 weeks they will be quarantined and will not have contact with anyone from outside the base. They are now dressed alike and they begin the process of learning a new vocabulary, a new set of rules and relationships, and the dimensions of an authority structure in which they are starting at the very bottom. These dimensions will be paramount in their lives for at least as long as they are in military service.

This resocialization process is so effective and is so effectively reinforced throughout one's military career, that aspects of it linger long after most veterans have left the service. Among the most important things that it inculcates are patriotism, obedience, loyalty to the group, and a willingness to employ violence in the resolution of disputes.

1. Patriotism

Obviously patriotism is important to a military organization. It is a motivating factor for most who enter military service; for the remainder it must be instilled. If one is to be counted on to risk his life for something, his or her belief in it must be firm. So military training dwells upon the history and traditions of one's nation. It instills pride in those traditions and emphasizes the necessity for upholding them.

2. Obedience

There is probably nothing more important to a military organization than absolute obedience. In the life-and-death situations that military personnel are often called upon to face there is no room for questioning or thinking about an order. At the very beginning, therefore, the new recruit pledges his obedience to all those in authority over him. He is required from that time on to show respect for his superiors and to obey their orders without question. This is constantly reinforced by ceremonial honors accorded to persons of rank, ranging from the simple hand salute of a superior officer to the 21-gun salute for a head of state. Insubordination in any form is considered to be a very serious fault in the military and is dealt with severely. This process is so effective that is not unusual for a person recently released from military service to continue addressing any man he or she does not know well as "sir."

3. Loyalty to the Group

Success in any group endeavor depends upon cooperation. In fact, in the military staying alive frequently requires cooperation. Military leaders recognize this and emphasize it. No matter what the military organization or unit, its members are encouraged to think of themselves as members of the unit and not as individuals. They are told that this is the best organization of its kind and that they are special precisely because they belong to it. This is the phenomenon known as *esprit de corps*. The highest honors in a military organization, moreover, are most often awarded to those who have subordinated their own interests to those of the group.

4. Willingness to Employ Violence

Underlying everything else, the basic purpose of a military force is combat. In the military one must therefore be prepared for combat. Even those technicians who are somewhat removed from the front lines might, for one reason or another, someday find themselves face to face with an enemy. Military training thus includes learning about weapons and how to use them as well as instruction in techniques of hand to hand combat. Military personnel also have impressed upon them the idea that if they ever come face to face with an enemy it is a situation of "kill or be killed." And for those

who actually do participate in front-line combat, seeing enough death and destruction can result in many of them becoming hardened to it.

This effect of conditioning to violence is exemplified not only by American veterans who look back in amazement at the ease with which the service turned them into killers, but also by such examples as the young man in pilot training in the Royal Australian Air Force, who claimed never to have even considered picking up a gun before but now is quite comfortable using an automatic rifle. Discussion of the role of former soldiers in the establishment of communist regimes in both Russia and China, moreover, alludes to their training in the skills of violence as an implicit threat to bolster political persuasion. And it has been pointed out that young recruits in the Russian Army are still the victims of cruel hazing that conditions them to violence.

C. Identification with Other Veterans

Military service is a unique experience and that uniqueness is constantly reinforced. It is reinforced by all the symbols that identify military personnel; it is reinforced by the isolation imposed upon military personnel much of the time; and it is reinforced by the intensity of the experience. The sense of that uniqueness becomes a kind of shared identity among veterans.

Throughout history some veterans have articulated this feeling of uniqueness and common identity by forming organizations. In ancient Rome there was an organization of veterans of the wars against the barbarians. Numerous veterans organizations exist in the principal nations of the world today. In fact, a coordinating organization, the World Veterans Federation, exists with affiliates in more than 50 countries. Although only a small proportion belong to any of these organizations, the larger and more active ones seem to articulate the attitudes and sentiments held by the majority of veterans, who tend to accept their positions. The influence of these organizations on politicians is therefore considerable.

1. Shared Exposure to Danger Creates a Bond

For military personnel, the bond of shared experience and exposure to danger results in identification with a formidable reference group, first one's comrades-in-arms and later one's fellow veterans. The armed forces thus engender two important bonds or loyalties; one is to the formal entity, the military establishment, and the nation, the other is to one's comrades-in-arms. This is not really unique. The presence of both "formal" and "informal" structures has been identified in many contexts. But primary relationships in a military organization are more intense and more pervasive for a variety of reasons. And, while it is vital to the discipline and efficiency of a military unit that the norms of the primary group be generally compatible with the institutional goals, one should not tacitly assume that they always are.

2. Lifelong Identification and Esprit of a Unit

A military unit is a tightly knit and self-sufficient entity, and it is virtually impossible to belong to such a unit for any length of time without incorporating it, in a sense, into one's own being. Veterans, therefore, tend to identify themselves for the rest of their lives as members of the units of which they were a part. Evidence of that identification is to be found in the many pages listing military unit reunions that appear in periodicals and newsletters addressed to veterans. Moreover, it generally does not matter whether two people have ever met each other before or whether they were even attached to a given unit at the same time. Upon discovery that they both served in that unit there is immediate recognition of a bond. Nowhere, probably, is this phenomenon better articulated than in the following statement that appears on the first page of a 1990 roster of former crew members of the USS Mount McKinley, a ship that had been out of commission for more than 20 years. "She is physically gone now, but this valiant ship lives forever in the minds and hearts of the many Americans who called her 'my ship.'"

II. ULTIMATE CONSEQUENCES

As a consequence of their military experience, veterans possess a strong but highly ambiguous potential to influence the political life of a country. Having fought in the name of certain key values, they are thought of not only as being owed a debt of gratitude, but also as exemplifying those values. Their experience, moreover, has given them both organizational skill and a strong sense of group identity. It should not be surprising, then, for veterans to show above-average participation in the political process. They are most usually, but not always, advocates of patriotism, nationalism, and the status quo. In addition, however, they insist that their service should be recognized and attention given to any disabilities suffered by them or their fellows. At the same time, when a significant number of them feel strongly that the leadership of their country is in some way compromising the principles that they hold to be

important they can and do employ the same qualities in opposition to that leadership.

A. Desire for Recognition, Treatment, and Compensation for Their Problems

Veterans, virtually by definition, are persons who have served their country when it needed them, sometimes at great risk and sacrifice. They would like to feel appreciated. In premodern times it was frequently the case that members of a victorious army would share in the spoils of victory. This is no longer the case; today men and women are asked to fight for a cause, a principle, to defend a way of life. Many of them, when questioned, indicate that what they really want is recognition for the importance of the part they have played.

Modern governments generally commit themselves to care for any injuries or disabilities incurred in the course of military service as well as to provide compensation both for widows and families of those killed in the line of duty and for potential loss of earning power as a consequence of service injuries. This is almost universally considered to be a moral obligation of government. But, when the war is won and there are bills to be paid, care and compensation for veterans are frequently cut. So when veterans gather and when they organize, these concerns are high on their agendas.

B. Support of Fellow Veterans

Veterans are not particularly joiners (only a little over a quarter of American veterans say they belong to a veterans organization). Nevertheless, they do tend to perceive themselves as special and to feel connected to one another. Moreover, throughout their lives they identify with other veterans in general and in particular with those who participated in the same war or campaign. They are also supportive of other veterans, particularly those who are suffering or in need. And a veteran running for elective office can usually count on many fellow veterans' votes.

C. Respect for Constituted Authority

The man who has been taught strict obedience and respect for "the chain of command" will, in most cases, have come to be comfortable with the order and predictability those things engender. Veterans organizations, in particular, both support and participate in national observances. They also sponsor various youth programs that focus on understanding and respect for government and are in the forefront of efforts to assure proper respect for the national flag.

D. Support of "Military Preparedness"

Almost all veterans profess a desire for peace. Having participated in warfare, they are aware of its negative aspects and would like to avoid their recurrence. They differ greatly, however, with regard to how to assure that peace. While some feel that the maximum effort should be exerted to promote universal disarmament, far more support the idea of "peace through strength" and favor a strong military deterrent.

E. Participation in the Political Process

Military force is an instrument of government. Military personnel are therefore directly affected by government policy. In addition, as at least one psychologist has pointed out, there is the need to feel that one's risks and sacrifices were taken in the interest of something that is meaningful and worthwhile. Thus, upon return to civilian life, many of these men and women have a heightened awareness of the political process and an interest in seeing that it follows what they perceive as their country's and their best interests. When such men and women decide to run for public office they have the advantage of being perceived as articulating important patriotic values because they have served their country. In addition, they are quite likely to have the support of many other veterans. Veterans thus have much input into the political life of their country.

III. SITUATIONAL DIFFERENCES

As has been indicated, veterans, like any element of the population, are not all alike in their thinking, in their attitudes, or in their behavior. These things are affected by the background and experiences of each group of veterans and of each individual veteran. Among the important influences on them are such factors as the type of government in their country, the size of the veteran cohort both in absolute terms and relative to the rest of the population, and, inevitably, how much public support there was for the struggle in which they participated and the extent of their success or failure.

A. Type of Government

In an autocracy, of course, the regime tends to be supported by a loyal military establishment. Civil and military power, in effect, are coterminous, and much of the bureaucracy tends to consist of inactive military personnel. Where there is a hereditary aristocracy, moreover, the officer corps tends to be drawn from that stratum and enlisted personnel from commoners.

In new nations, or nations recently emerged from colonialism, those who fought for freedom (veterans of the revolution) will probably have a high degree of motivation to be involved in the political process. Their countrymen, moreover, will have become accustomed to looking to them for leadership. The dynamic of the revolution can, under such circumstances, continue into the emerging regime. By the same token, veterans of a defeated regime may continue for some time to engage in protest and disruptive activity.

In a participatory democracy, of course, there is a strong tendency for veterans to be highly regarded because they are perceived as having been willing to risk their lives in support of their country. For this reason, and because of their own feeling of commitment, there is great potential for the veterans' voice in the political life of the country. However, both attitudes toward veterans and the sentiments of the veterans themselves are affected by a number of factors.

B. Relative Size of Veteran Cohort and Nature of the Conflict

Such factors include the relative size of a particular veteran cohort and the extent of both popular and press support of the military actions in which they participated, as well as their possible exposure to any unusual negative circumstances or experiences. Wartime perceptions, memories, and associations have a tendency to persist for a lifetime. This is adequately demonstrated by the hundreds of reunions of military units that are held annually in all the major countries as well as by the strong efforts of veterans groups in support of memorials to their successes and in opposition to any acknowledgments that they might have done wrong. All these factors are discernible in one or another of the experiences of various nations.

IV. SPECIFIC CASES

A. The United States

The United States began with a breakaway revolution by a group of colonies and veterans of that revolution were active in establishing the new government. But in 1787, some Revolutionary War veterans, disgruntled because they had not received all the pay they felt they had been promised, and because their property was being confiscated for nonpayment of taxes, organized in protest. When about 1200 of these men, under the leadership of Daniel Shays, marched toward a federal installation, they were confronted and fired upon by government troops and three of them lost their lives. Occurring at roughly the same time as the constitutional convention, this perhaps underscored the need for a strong central authority with fiscal responsibility.

The pattern, unfortunately, was to be repeated all too frequently. Through the wars of the 19th century: The War of 1812, the Mexican War, the Civil War, the Spanish–American War; just as after the revolution, the government made promises to the veterans, but always told them to wait. The veterans tended to feel that they were eagerly sought when the country needed them to fight, but soon forgotten when the battle was over. And, as a rule, they did not get adequate recognition for their demands until they mounted a show of strength. In the resulting skirmishes with police or federal troops people were sometimes injured.

The conclusion of World War I, in 1918, was followed by high rates of both inflation and unemployment, which made adjustment to civilian life particularly difficult for the returning veterans. To be sure, the 1920s were a boom time for the American economy. But they were also a time of great discrepancy between rich and poor. Conscious of having risked their lives for less than a dollar a day while bonuses were being paid to those on the home front who met production quotas, large numbers of returned veterans now encountered considerable difficulty in finding employment.

There was much popular support for paying these veterans a bonus, but Congress debated the issue for a long time. When they finally passed a bonus bill, it was vetoed by two successive presidents, Harding and Coolidge. In 1924 Congress finally overrode the President's veto, but the bonus they legislated was not to be paid until 1945. The delay was justified by the argument that in 21 years most of the veterans would be at an age when the assistance would be more useful to them. What nobody said, of course, was that the Congress which passed this bill, by deferring it for such a long time, was leaving it for a future Congress actually to appropriate the funds to cover it.

In 1932, at the height of the Great Depression, a number of unemployed veterans, numbering more than 30,000, converged on Washington demanding an early lump-sum payment of the bonus they had been promised. The chief of the Washington police department,

who was a veteran himself, was sympathetic to their cause and made every effort to see that they were treated reasonably. The "bonus marchers" camped out in a public area and staged protests rallies to further their cause. Someone in the administration of President Hoover ordered the intervention of federal troops with fixed bayonets and tear gas to disperse them.

Although the World War I veterans did not get their bonus, they did gain a lot of public sympathy for their cause and the administration's clumsy handling of the affair was one factor in the loss of the election several months later. After the election a second bonus march developed and President Roosevelt, although he did not favor a bonus for the veterans, handled the matter more astutely, seeing to it that a camp was established for them. Soon afterward Congress did pass a cash bonus over President Roosevelt's veto.

More importantly, with increased awareness of the plight suffered by many veterans of the First World War there was finally a recognition of the need to coordinate services for veterans. In 1921 the various government programs assigned to take care of veterans needs were consolidated into the Veterans Bureau. This agency was, however, underfunded, inefficient, and crippled by graft. By 1930 the inadequacy of this system was recognized and Congress passed legislation authorizing establishment of the Veterans Administration as an independent federal agency. Eventually, in 1988, a bill was passed to convert this agency to a cabinet department, the Department of Veterans Affairs.

In spite of their negative experiences with government officialdom, America's veterans as a category have generally been patriotic and loyal citizens and have figured prominently in the political life of the nation. Through the years many veterans have served in Congress and of the 41 men who have been President of this country, 22 were veterans. Significantly, 9 of the 10 presidents between 1945 and 1997 have been veterans; 8 were veterans of World War II. An analysis by the veterans newspaper *Stars and Stripes* revealed that in the 104th Congress (1995–1996) 49 of 100 senators and 127 of 435 members of the House of Representatives were veterans.

To note that veterans are significantly numbered among officeholders, however, is to look only at part of the picture. In a democracy elected officials are accountable to an electorate. There are, in the mid-1990s, more than 26 million veterans in the United States, over 20 million of whom are identified as "war veterans." Surveys show, moreover, that veterans tend to vote in greater proportion than nonveterans. Among respondents to the General Social Survey, for instance, 69%

of nonveterans and 79% of veterans said that they had voted in the 1992 election.

Of just over 20 million persons in the United States today who are identified as war veterans, almost 8 million are veterans of World War II. This number is second only to the Vietnam veterans, who number just over 8 million. But this country's active participation in World War II lasted less than 4 full years, compared with a decade in the case of Vietnam, and normal mortality has had more years to take its toll on WW II veterans. In fact, over 12 million men and women (a figure which approximated 10% of the population) served in the United States armed forces in World War II. There was thus hardly an American without relatives or friends who were veterans of that war. In fact, in 1946 World War II veterans comprised such a large proportion of the young adult male population in this country that their thinking would be influential in shaping events of the next several decades. Moreover, to a large extent, the experience of the World War II veteran was far better than that of virtually any other in history. To understand fully the implications of this one must to take a brief look at the circumstances that produced the WW II veteran.

World War II was a popular cause whose veterans were welcomed home and rewarded by the United States government to a greater extent than any other veterans in our history. Add to that the fact that the men and women who served in that war grew up during the Great Depression of the 1930s, when high school students spent much time wondering and worrying over whether they would be able to find a job when they graduated. Not only did military service relieve them of that worry, but overnight they were treated as heroes. All the major cities and many smaller ones established recreation centers for them; some municipal transit systems let them ride free; people bought them meals and drinks.

And when they got out, there was the *Servicemen's Readjustment Act*, more familiarly known as the GI Bill of Rights. This legislation provided a bonus at separation, a weekly check until the veteran found a job, options for up to 4 years of education at government expense, and government-guaranteed loans to buy a house or start a business. To borrow a phrase, they never had it so good. So, for all these reasons, veterans of World War II, for the most part, have fond recollections of their military experience, they tend to be somewhat chauvinistic, and they are in favor of a strong military posture. They also appear to have a somewhat more positive attitude than many others regarding nuclear weapons.

This last point, the somewhat more positive attitude regarding nuclear weapons, reflects some of the "traditional wisdom" concerning World War II. Right or wrong, most veterans of World War II believe that the atomic bombing of Japan shortened the war, sparing them from the prospect of a costly invasion.

From the late 1940s to the break-up of the Soviet Union in 1991, United States foreign policy was driven by an extreme antipathy toward communism which led, directly or indirectly, to a number of military actions, none of which had the popular support enjoyed by World War II. Veterans of the Korean War and, more particularly, of the Vietnam War were keenly aware that many of the people "back home" were not fully supportive of the government's position, and many of them questioned what they were doing. Some returning Vietnam War veterans became outspoken opponents of the war, while others resented the less-than-cordial reception they received and fought hard to get positive recognition for their service.

At the same time, advances in emergency medical practice coupled with the ability to evacuate wounded personnel by helicopter in both Korea and Vietnam produced a larger number of wounded survivors than ever before. At the same time, the use of poison gas in World War I, the development of nuclear weapons at the end of World War II, and the use of *Agent Orange* in the Vietnam war all created health hazards for large numbers of military personnel. Most recently, large numbers of veterans returning from Operation Desert Storm have experienced unexplained illnesses.

Meanwhile, tight budgets have combined with a reluctance to acknowledge fully the human costs of the country's military campaigns. And, since these new kinds of disability frequently do not manifest themselves until somewhat later, their connection to military service is frequently denied. It is this kind of situation, no doubt, that prompted Severo and Milford to assert in *The Wages of War* that ". . . even after 'popular' wars, veterans have had to struggle against a government that has mostly sought to limit its financial liability, more like a slippery insurance company than a polity rooted in the idea of justice and fair reward."

Thus, a newer cohort of veterans has been emerging, veterans who are much more prone to question government policy and to demand that the country for which they risked their lives "do the right thing." At the same time, 5 decades of political and economic cooperation between the United States and Japan notwithstanding, it is not unusual for the conversation with World War II veterans to reflect a hatred for everything Japanese with which they were so thoroughly indoctrinated. And, if one is alert to them, there are frequent reminders of the extent to which the memories and attitudes of the World War II veteran still have an effect on American thinking and American policy.

One example is the 1995 program on American Public Radio, recognizing the 50th anniversary of the Battle of Iwo Jima. A Washington reporter had gone out to the memorial that commemorates that event, the bronze statue of the marines raising the flag on Mt. Suribachi, and was interviewing people who were at the memorial. Almost all the people interviewed were too young to remember the events of 1945, but virtually without exception they told of having a father or grandfather, or at least an uncle, who had been in the war and who had imparted to them a sense of the importance of those events.

Another reminder of the influence of the World War II veteran occurred when the Smithsonian Institution, 50 years after the atomic bombing of Hiroshima, was planning an exhibit featuring the plane that had dropped that bomb. It was originally planned to show the destruction caused by the bomb, but veterans groups, particularly Army Air Corps veterans, mounted a protest. They said that to focus on the destruction caused by the bomb without giving attention to the atrocities perpetrated by the Japanese would put the United States in a bad light. As a result the plans were modified and the plane was exhibited by itself. These older veterans still have a great deal of influence on American society, but as they die off and are supplanted by the newer generation, there are liable to be some significant changes.

B. Japan

Japan, prior to the mid-19th century, was essentially a collection of feudal fiefdoms. Each feudal lord, or *daimyo,* had a band of loyal retainers, or *samurai,* who paid fealty to him in return for a rice stipend. In the beginning, *samurai* had followed their lord in war and tilled the soil in times of peace. However, with the advent of the use of firearms and the need for strong defenses, the *samurai* left the fields and were aggregated into castle towns as full-time warriors. Beginning as early as the 12th century, the country was controlled by what amounted to a succession of military dictatorships, with the most powerful of the *daimyo* assuming control and adopting the title of *shogun* (roughly translated as generalissimo). There was an emperor with succession tracing back to earliest times, but the royal family was comparatively weak. The royal court continued to exist, but the real power lay with the *shogun.*

The Tokugawa Shogunate, which assumed power early in the 17th century, maintained stability for $2\frac{1}{2}$ centuries by the use of some extreme measures. Fearing the colonial expansionism of the western powers, they established an almost complete isolationist policy. Also, as a means of solidifying control, they required all other *daimyo* to spend half their time in Edo (today's Tokyo), which was the Tokugawa capitol. An important consequence of this latter policy was that certain *samurai* who were left in charge back home acquired key administrative skills.

But peace and stability had been achieved at a price. When the more modern western powers came knocking at the door in the 1850s, Japan was hardly in a position to resist. And, when the Shogunate, unable to resist, acceded to trading treaties with these powers, large numbers of extremely nationalistic *samurai* allied themselves in a countermovement. In 1868 the existing feudal arrangement was essentially replaced by a unified central government under the Emperor Meiji, to whom imperial power was restored.

For the central government to be capable of coping with external relations, as well as to foster a strong sense of nationhood, it would be necessary to have a national army. Upon relinquishing their fiefdoms the *daimyo* had, of course, pensioned off the *samurai* and one solution might be to aggregate them into an army. This option was rejected in favor of universal military conscription which, it was felt, would be more representative of the entire nation. The officer corps, however, was to be made up of former *samurai.*

The government was established on a cabinet model with a number of interesting features. Active military officers could serve in the cabinet, and the army and navy ministers were coequal with the prime minister and had direct access to the throne. In addition, a number of those *samurai* with administrative skills found a place in the new bureaucracy. Thus, veteran members of what had been essentially a warrior caste, imbued with a strong sense of nationalism, were well situated to have a major impact. Some were a part of the day-to-day government operations; others were in a position where they could have a great influence on the young men of the country; and some had special access to the emperor.

For the next three quarters of a century the Japanese pursued a course of aggressive expansionism. By the time of World War I they had occupied the Korean peninsula and many of the nearby islands, including Formosa (Taiwan). In the process they waged successful wars against China in 1895 and Russia in 1905. In 1914 they joined the allies in declaring war against

Germany, and at the conclusion of the war they were awarded administrative control of the former German colonial islands in Micronesia.

All these successful campaigns produced new cohorts of veterans and greatly reinforced the national fervor, and after World War I there was an increasing build-up of nationalist fervor. By the 1930s the militarists were virtually in control and in 1938 the prime minister called for the political and economic integration of East Asia, under Japanese leadership, as a bulwark against domination by the western powers. Ultimately this concept led to competition with the United States over control of the Pacific Ocean and finally precipitated World War II with disastrous results.

After Japan's defeat the allied powers created *The International War Crimes Tribunal for the Far East,* which tried the key political and military leaders of that country for "crimes against peace." The United States also insisted on the adoption of a new constitution that included an article asserting that "... the Japanese people forever renounce war as a sovereign right of the nation and the threat or use of force as a means of settling international disputes."

The scope of the war had been so great that the entire population had been directly or indirectly involved. But, at least to all outward appearances, the Japanese people accepted the military defeat and went about the business of rebuilding their country, and the veterans maintained a generally low profile. At least as long as the American occupation forces were there (1945–1951) it was not sensible to do otherwise.

A half-century later, though, that part of the constitution which precludes the building up of an army has been reinterpreted to allow the establishment of a home defense force, and there has been some suggestion that there should be further modification to accommodate their sending peacekeeping forces to troubled areas. Also, as a new generation has been assuming leadership, some deep differences have been surfacing.

In a way that is remarkably similar to events in the United States, controversy was generated by activities initiated to commemorate the 50th anniversary of the end of World War II. One of these activities was the drafting of a 50-year postwar resolution in the Diet. Many of the legislators favored an apology that acknowledged Japan's responsibility for invading foreign territory and precipitating the War. This was opposed by a large body, including former military men, who asserted that the war was fought for justice to release Asia from western imperialism. A reconciliation was achieved by passing a compromise resolution which asserted that "Europe and the U.S. conducted invasions and colonial rules mercilessly, but Japan did the same thing."

The flames of controversy were then fanned by the decision to build a history museum to mark the 50th anniversary of the conclusion of World War II. Historians on the advisory commission for the museum started by suggesting a forthright discussion of the road to the Pacific war that would be a lesson to young people and hopefully a deterrence to going down the same path again. This drew quick responses from ultranationalists, who wanted a display suggesting that economic forces in the 1930s compelled Japan to start the war. The same veterans groups who had opposed the parliamentary apology for World War II took up this battle, asserting that the museum was originally meant to be a memorial to the war dead but people were trying to use it to depict Japanese war atrocities. In the end, plans for the museum have focused excessively on less-controversial artifacts such as uniforms and boots worn by Japanese soldiers.

An added dimension of controversy derives from the fact that the museum is located adjacent to the Yasukuni Shrine. The Yasukuni Shrine is a national shrine of the prewar period, symbolic of Japanese militarism, and soldiers who died while engaged in war are worshipped there as "military gods." A campaign conducted largely by former military men resulted in 14 convicted war criminals being enshrined there.

C. Germany

The German people were effectively unified into a single nation in the 1860s, with Wilhelm I as Kaiser and Otto von Bismarck as chancellor. Under the conservative leadership of Bismarck the nation experienced a period of rapid industrialization, colonial expansion, and cultural development. By 1890 the political coalition that had supported Bismarck fell apart and he was forced to resign from the chancellorship. Wilhelm II, the grandson of Wilhelm I, who had by then succeeded to the throne, attempted to dominate German politics himself. However, a number of serious blunders by him and his advisors resulted in a serious constitutional crisis as well as defeat in World War I.

In 1918, when it became necessary for the Germans to surrender, the military were prominently among those who forced the Kaiser's resignation and established a republic. But the new government encountered difficulty from the beginning. Not only was the nation fragmented politically to the extent that it was difficult to forge a ruling coalition, but it was subjected to the extreme vindictive conditions imposed by the victorious allies in the Versailles peace treaty.

Germany's slow recovery was cut short by the world Depression of the 1930s, and severe social disorganization followed. Amid conditions that sometimes approached anarchy, militarists were able to organize the discontented, very many of whom were unhappy veterans of the recent war, into a coherent force. One of those veterans, a former corporal named Adolf Hitler, became leader of the National Socialist, or Nazi Party, which offered a combination of extreme patriotism and radical solutions to the nation's economic problems.

In 1933 Adolf Hitler, the former corporal, was appointed chancellor and proceeded forthwith to establish a totalitarian state and to take the nation down the road to World War II. At the end of that war the nation was once again economically devastated and at the mercy of its victorious foes. This time, in fact, its cities lay in ruins and it was divided into two separate nations, each occupied by different foreign powers.

In Germany, as in Japan, many of the officials of the wartime regime were tried by the allied powers as war criminals. The German people, in general, said they were glad to be free of the Nazi regime, and set about to rebuild their economy.

Great effort was made to convey the idea that the ordinary soldier was a reluctant accomplice of the Nazis. The German government, in fact, continues to pay veterans pensions to former members of the military, as well as "victim pensions" to those who were injured and to families of veterans who were killed in the war. At the same time, the law permits cessation of pensions to those who may be "war criminals." It has been alleged that the German government has been concealing the fact that such pensions are being paid to a number of former members of Hitler's elite units.

Again, the really divisive issue has arisen over a memorial exhibit. In 1995 a Hamburg research foundation mounted an exhibit that graphically contradicted the popular conception that the *Wehrmacht* was an army properly fulfilling its duty of fighting enemy soldiers and that it was only the elite SS unit who engaged in extermination of Jews, Gypsies, and others whom the high command designated as "undesirable." The exhibit, which had visited some 16 cities in Germany and Austria over a 2-year period, featured photographs of civilians being shot and hanged as well as letters and diaries written by ordinary soldiers recounting their participation in mass killings, leaving little doubt about the zeal with which German army units carried out a policy of systematic extermination.

The exhibit encountered mild opposition in a number of locations but announcement of its planned February, 1997 opening in Munich, capital of the conservative state of Bavaria, was greeted with organized protest by large numbers of people including both veterans and neo-Nazi groups.

D. USSR

The bivalent potential of veterans in the political arena is nowhere better demonstrated than by the early years of the Soviet Union. Russia's communist revolution occurred in the midst of World War I and former peasants who were serving in the army at the time were readily transformed into supporters of the new ideology. Some were recruited into the new bureaucracy; others returned to their villages as partisans and grassroots representatives of the Soviet regime. On the other hand, ex-soldiers also figured prominently in the short-lived anti-Bolshevik rebellions of 1920–1921. Following that, for the next 7 decades Soviet power was effectively in the hands of a powerful oligarchy.

The Soviet Union was one of the victors in World War II, but they had well over 6 million killed in battle as well as an even higher civilian mortality. This was a higher casualty rate than was sustained by any other nation in that war. Nevertheless, by 1985 the Soviet leadership had achieved control over most of eastern Europe and had deployed troops in Afghanistan, Syria, Vietnam, Cuba, and, to a lesser extent in more than a half dozen other countries. In addition they were engaged in a massive nuclear arms race with the United States. Eventually, these attempts to maintain superiority in troop strength and in nuclear arms precipitated both economic collapse and social unrest, which brought about the dissolution of the Soviet Union into its constituent independent republics.

The Soviet occupation of Afghanistan in 1979 had been a costly mistake which many have compared to the experience of the United States in Vietnam. Their forces encountered strenuous native resistance and sustained considerable casualties. Eventually they withdrew, but only after having incurred considerable resistance to the campaign by a large number of Soviet citizens, both civilians and military personnel. As a consequence, present-day Russia has two quite different cohorts of veterans. There are those who fought in World War II and are revered as heroes; then there are those who participated in the Afghan campaign, who are not particularly revered as heroes and feel resentful. The younger generation harbors some resentment toward the United States as the Cold War foe who supported their opponents in Afghanistan, whereas many of the older men remember the Americans as allies in the fight against Hitler.

E. China

In a sense, 20th-century Chinese history involves a succession of two revolutions that produced two rather different sets of veterans. In 1911 the traditional dynastic system was replaced by a republican form of government. The central authority, however, was quite weak and prone to corruption. It was, nevertheless, the recognized ruling entity in China and received considerable support from the Western powers in its resistance to Japanese invasion. The republican government was located in the southern part of the country, while the communist faction gained considerable strength in the north, and a bitter civil war between these two factions went on for several decades.

With the defeat of Japan in World War II, Taiwan was turned over to the Chinese Nationalist Government. In 1949 the nationalist forces were defeated and the communists established the People's Republic of China as the ruling authority on the Chinese mainland. At that time nationalist troops, government officials, and many other refugees moved to Taiwan and established themselves. Since that time the Chinese government on Taiwan has operated as a separate entity although the mainland government (the People's Republic of China) consider them to be a renegade province.

In the years immediately following the communist takeover, demobilized members of the People's Liberation Army, having been thoroughly indoctrinated with the ideology of the new regime, were accorded honorific status and returned to their home villages as important spokesmen for the new order. Soon after that, moreover, the government established a system of military conscription, thus assuring an ongoing flow of ex-service personnel into the countryside.

Because the People's Republic of China is an autocratic state it is able to exert somewhat more control over the destinies of its citizens than is the case in some other countries. Thus, it not only ascribes higher status to its military veterans, (and employs many of them in the government apparatus) it is also able to impress them back into service in case of any civil disturbance. Furthermore, official government policy has stressed ideological education of servicemen about to be demobilized so they may become leading cadres in productive construction and the building of the militia.

In this instance, then, veterans were consciously utilized by the state as an instrument of its own policies.

There were, however, some negative consequences. It has been noted that the special status accorded to former service personnel caused some of them to become arrogant and overbearing, creating some degree of tension between them and the civilian operatives with whom they had to work. Additionally, because of the special status accorded them, ex-soldiers have on a number of occasions been able to operate rather effectively as a pressure group and to obtain concessions, particularly from local authorities.

The government on Taiwan, which was for a long time after 1949 referred to as the "Chinese Nationalist Government," under the leadership of Generalissimo Chiang Kai-shek, was dominated by veterans of the war against Japan and of the unsuccessful struggle against the communist forces. There was, understandably, a bitter division between these Chinese mainlanders and the native Taiwan Islanders who regarded them as an occupation force.

For the Chinese Nationalists, withdrawal to Taiwan constituted a bitter defeat, and they long harbored a dream of returning to the mainland, defeating the communists, and reestablishing their former ruling status; some, in fact, still do. Both because of this long range dream and as insurance against any insurgency by the native Taiwanese, they continued to maintain a large military force and ready reserve. As long as the original migrants from the mainland retained a large degree of control, these conditions persisted. But by the 1970s many of them had died (Chiang Kai-shek died in 1975) and the new generation, as it assumed control, was somewhat less authoritarian and began recruiting a greater number of Taiwanese into the government and the military.

F. Israel

The modern state of Israel had its origins in the Zionist movement of the late 19th century. This was, in turn, the latest in a succession of attempts, over the centuries, to encourage resettlement by Jews in that part of the Middle East that they regarded as their ancestral homeland. But this area, generally referred to as Palestine, had by that time come to be populated largely by Arab people.

Having occupied Palestine during World War I, the British were awarded the right to administer the area under a League of Nations mandate that committed them to prepare the population for future self-rule. In accordance with the 1917 *Balfour Declaration,* the British were to assist Jewish immigration to Palestine with a view to the Jews becoming a majority and thereby achieving self-rule. Predictably, frequent clashes broke out between Arabs and Jews over diverse religious practices in places that were regarded as sacred by both Moslems and Jews. But with the rise of Nazism in the 1930s, migration of Jews to the area increased greatly.

In 1939 the British, courting cooperation of the Arabs on the eve of World War II, reversed their policy and declared that Jewish immigration and land purchases in the area would be seriously curtailed for 5 years, after which they would be banned. Because of the importance to both of them of defeating their common enemy, Nazi Germany, the Zionists cooperated with the British in World War II. But beginning in 1945 there was armed conflict between the British, who imposed very strict quotas on migration to Palestine, and the Zionists, who insisted that there should be a policy of open immigration for all European Jewish refugees who had survived the Holocaust.

In 1947 the British turned the entire problem of Palestine over to the United Nations, who approved a plan to partition the area into separate Jewish and Arab states. In May, 1948, when the state of Israel was proclaimed, the guerrilla forces who had fought against the British now found themselves defending their new nation against invasion by neighboring Arabs.

Many of the veterans of those bitter struggles against the British and the Arabs became key political leaders in the nation of Israel and they have been extremely effective in assuring that their country has maintained a hard line both in their relationships with surrounding countries and in the treatment of the large Arab population within their borders.

V. IN SUMMARY

The cited examples demonstrate how attitudes of veterans are affected by several dimensions of timing and circumstance. They also underscore the extent to which the collective memory and nostalgia of veterans foster in them a desire to have their contributions viewed in a positive light. Finally, they suggest a tendency for them to lean toward the philosophy of "might makes right." Most importantly, veterans can exert an influence on the political culture that the smart politician does not ignore.

Also See the Following Articles

COMBAT • CONFORMITY AND OBEDIENCE • MASS CONFLICT AND THE PARTICIPANTS, ATTITUDES TOWARD • MILITARY CULTURE • MILITARISM • PROFESSIONAL VERSUS CITIZEN SOLDIERY • PSYCHOLOGICAL EFFECTS OF COMBAT • WARRIORS, ANTHROPOLOGY OF

BIBLIOGRAPHY

Cancian, F. M., & Gibson, J. W. (Eds.) (1990). *Making war making peace: The social foundations of violent conflict.* Belmont, CA: Wadsworth.

Elder, G. H., Jr., & Clipp, E. C. (1988). Wartime losses and social bonding: Influences across 40 years in men's lives. *Psychiatry, 51,* 177–198.

Fussell, P. (1989) *Wartime: Understanding and behavior in the second world war.* New York: Oxford University Press.

Grahlfs, F. L. (1996). *Voices from ground zero: Recollections and feelings of nuclear test veterans.* Lanham, MD: University Press of America.

Ivie, R. L., Gimbel, C., & Elder, G. H., Jr. (1991). Military experience and attitudes in later life: contextual influences across forty years. *Journal of Political and Military Sociology, XIX,* 101–117.

Moore, B. L. (1996). *To serve my country, to serve my race: The story of the only African American WACS stationed overseas during World War II.* New York University Press.

Murphy, B. C. et al. (1990). Atomic veterans and their families: Responses to radiation exposure. *American Journal of Orthopsychiatry, LX* (3), 418–427.

O'Connell, R. L. (1989). *Of arms and men.* New York: Oxford University Press.

Severo, R., & Milford, L. (1989). *The wages of war.* New York: Simon and Schuster.

Victimology

Jukka-Pekka Takala and Kauko Aromaa

National Research Institute of Legal Policy, Finland

GLOSSARY

Dark Figure Hidden criminality, those criminal offenses that remain undetected or unrecorded.

Indirect Victimization Fear of crime, and also such safety precautions that deteriorate the quality of life, that is caused by the fear of crime.

Record Check (also reverse record check) Presenting a victimization survey to known crime victims and comparing their responses with the original data (such as police records).

Secondary Victimization Various uses: (1) the upsetting and humiliating experience within the criminal justice system that a crime victim encounters when seeking justice and redress for the original victimization; (2) pain and suffering by relatives and friends of the primary victim and other concerned people, same as *derivative victim*; (3) cases in which the victim is not an individual person but an impersonal, commercial, or collective entity; in this usage, *tertiary* victimization refers to cases in which the victim is the community at large.

Telescoping Remembering incidents as occurring more recently (forward telescoping) or in the more distant past (backward telescoping) than they actually occurred. Incidents that took place before a survey's reference period are often forward telescoped into that period (external telescoping).

Victim Facilitation, Precipitation, and Provocation Ways the victims contribute to their own victimization. The terms have various and sometimes inconsistent uses. Victim facilitation applies to a victim who unknowingly, carelessly or negligently brings about circumstances that make it easier for the offender to commit a crime. Precipitation and provocation usually imply a more determinate activity on the victim's part.

VICTIMOLOGY is usually defined as a field of criminology devoted to the study of victims. While traditional criminology has focused on the offender, victimology focuses on the victim of crime. Several traditions and lines of inquiry have developed within victimology. One of the best established general traditions is the victimization survey, in which a sample of the general population, or of a special target population, are asked about their experience as victims of crimes and related matters. National crime victimization surveys are used, for instance, as indicators of the extent of criminality, including unrecorded crime, that supplement the picture available from police statistics and other official records. Victimologists use police records, survey data, and other sources to analyze regularities in the patterns of victimization, e.g., how the risks of victimization vary by different demographic, social, psychological, situational, and other categories; or what sort of regularities interactional offenses exhibit. These findings have relevance for crime prevention and control policy. Victimology also studies the consequences of victimization to victims and other people. In addition to studying how offenses cause injuries, losses, and psychological trauma, victimologists have been interested in finding out how victims experience the way in which society and authorities handle their grievances. For instance, victims often feel that the way they are treated by the police, the courts, and other authorities adds to their victimization rather than helps alleviate it. Evaluation of different procedures, regulations, and organizations that are meant to help and assist victims of crime is an important part of victimology. Different mediation and restoration schemes that are meant to heal relationships that offenses have broken in the community are also studied by victimology. While the bulk of victimological research has dealt with victimization to crime, some researchers favor taking into account also victims of other types of behavior or sometimes even of events other than human actions. Just as criminology itself, victimology is a multidisciplinary field, and its practitioners may often define their work rather as a part of sociology, social policy, social work, law, psychology, psychiatry, and the like than as victimology or criminology.

> [Victimology] does not seek to explain why some people become criminals but why some people become victims and others do not.
>
> *Ezzat Fattah*

I. THE EMERGENCE OF VICTIMOLOGY

A. The Pioneers

The term "victimology" was apparently first introduced in print by Frederick Wertham, an American psychiatrist, in his 1949 book *The Show of Violence*. He wrote: "One cannot understand the psychology of the murderer if one does not understand the sociology of the victim. What we need is a science of victimology." However, as early as 1947, Beniamin Mendelsohn, one of

the recognized pioneers of victimology, had presented a paper titled "New Bio-Psycho-Social Horizons: Victimology" at a meeting of the Rumanian Society of Psychiatry and circulated the paper among Rumanian psychiatrists and lawyers.

Hans von Hentig's book *The Criminal and His Victim* (1948) is often cited as the first systematic treatment of victims of crime. von Hentig criticized criminologists' exclusive attention to the offender and suggested instead an approach that would pay equal attention to the victim. One of the chapters of the book was titled "The Victim's Contribution to the Genesis of the Crime." It was an early treatment of an issue that has generated one of the enduring controversies concerning victimology and victim policy: to what extent does the analysis of the causal or precipitating role of the victims in the origin of offenses imply attributing them moral or legal responsibility for the events. von Hentig and other early victimologists argued that many crime victims contribute to their own victimization by their conscious or unconscious choices. "Looking into the genesis of the situation, in a considerable number of cases, we meet a victim who consents tacitly, co-operates, conspires or provokes," von Hentig wrote. He suggested that certain individuals were "victim-prone" and they could be classified on psychological and social variables. Mendelsohn, whose work was published in English in 1956, drew on an analogy with accident causation and attempted to quantify the extent of the victim's "guilty contribution to the crime"; he was proposing a model on which programs aimed as preventing victimization might be based, but his categories of victims ranging from the "completely innocent" to the "most guilty victim" could easily be seen as "victim blaming."

Ten years after von Hentig's book, Marvin Wolfgang's study suggested that victim precipitation indeed played a crucial role in a considerable number of homicides. By Wolfgang's calculation, 26% of 588 homicides in Philadelphia resulted from victim-initiated resorting to violence. As Wolfgang's study exemplifies, this early victimology was interested mainly in crimes against individual persons, in identifying those characteristics of individuals that increased their susceptibility to victimization, and in studying the victim's participation in the bringing about of criminal events.

B. The "Dark Number" of Crime and Victimization Surveys

A different line of inquiry leads to today's victimization surveys. Over 100 years ago the Belgian social statistician Adolphe Quetelet (1796–1874) noted that reported crimes are only a part of the unknown total number of crimes. By the early 1960s, several small scale studies had confirmed this notion but also seemingly promised means to tap that great part of criminality that was not reported to the authorities. Large-scale victimization surveys were then designed to uncover the unrecorded "dark number" of crime. (Another line of inquiry probing the dark number is self-report studies asking subjects to report on their own commission of offenses—and some surveys include questions of both types.) There had been earlier scattered instances of questions regarding victimization to crime in different opinion polls in different countries. For instance, a Gallup poll conducted in Finland in November, 1945 contained such a question. The tradition of crime victimization surveys began in earnest in the U.S. during the 1960s. The early systematic studies were conducted on behalf of the U.S. President's Crime Commission and published in 1967. However, Finland may have been the first country to conduct a national victimization survey, namely a 1970 survey on violence. In the US, National Crime Surveys—now called National Crime Victimization Surveys—have been conducted since 1973. The finding that many, and in several crime categories most, offenses are not recorded in official statistics has since been borne out in many victimization surveys in many jurisdictions.

C. Victim Movements and Victim Assistance

Apart from improving upon the analysis of victimization processes and the counting of victimization, victimology has been interested in deeper analyses of the victims' experiences and positions. This cognitive concern is parallel to the political and advocatory movements that have attempted to bring the crime victims' problems and needs to the forefront. The victim movements comprise different types of organizations and interests. They range from attempts to influence penal codes, punishment latitudes, and parole rules in the name of victims' needs to programs that offer to help victims to cope with their experience; from voluntary organizations to statutory victim compensation programs and rules that guarantee the victims certain rights and privileges in the criminal justice system; from telephone hot-lines to victim–offender mediation. The growth, since the 1960s and 1970s, of victim movements has been attributed to various factors, including increasing awareness of the consequences of victimization and greater recognition of the shortcomings of the criminal justice system in responding to the needs of

victims. Also the emerging philosophies of justice that emphasize the informal and emotional aspects of dealing with crime and its consequences and see many crimes in terms of conflicts rather than as clear-cut breaches of categorical rules have contributed to the growth of mediation and restitution programs.

1. Victim Aid and Assistance

Different organizations have emerged to address crime victims' needs. Their activities range from offering assistance to victims with their emotional and practical problems to advocating legislation to better meet their needs. Some organizations deal with particular crimes and others focus on certain victims, such as those of violent crime or sexual assaults. In the U.S., victim movements include such organizations as the National Organization for Victim Assistance (NOVA), which was founded in 1975, the National Victim Center, Mothers Against Drunk Drivers, and Parents of Murdered Children. In Britain, a national organization called Victim Support listed 7,000 volunteers who made contact with almost 600,000 victims in a year (1990).

Shelters or refuges for women and children who are victims of domestic abuse are an important development. In 1974, the first battered women's shelter in the United States was opened in St. Paul, Minnesota, and there are hundreds, if not several thousands of shelters for battered women in the United States. In Britain, the first refuge for battered women was established in 1972. During one year (1977–1978), 150 British refuges admitted 11,400 women and 20,850 children. In Finland, exant shelters for unwed indigent mothers and their newborns also started to offer shelters for battered women in 1979.

Although many feminist-linked rape crisis services criticize the term *victim* as too submissive and so prefer the term rape *survivors*, these rape crisis centers and support lines can be considered part of a broadly defined victim movement. The women's movement in general has been very influential in bringing about greater awareness of the victimization of women and children.

An important part of the work of victim movements is the aid and assistance they offer victims in their dealings with the criminal justice system.

2. Victims in the Criminal Justice System

The victims experiences with the police and the officers of the court and its proceedings may amount to "secondary victimization"—humiliation and unreasonable challenges and demands on the victims' resources, time, and honor. Police officers may be insensitive during questioning, the victims may be blamed for contributing to their own victimization; testifying in open court may be upsetting; they may find defense attorneys hostile and the defendant's family or friends threatening; court schedules may be inconvenient; information about the court proceedings and correctional treatment may be difficult or impossible to get; and trial outcomes may seem grossly unjust or incomprehensible.

Such experiences, in turn, may lead to disillusionment with the system and distrust in law and order—and not only by the immediate victims but also by other people close to them. This rising concern has led to the development of state compensation schemes for victims of violent crime almost everywhere in the Western world. The victim's rights to be informed about and to participate in the judicial proceedings have also been enhanced in several jurisdictions. For instance, 49 states in the U.S. have a Victims' Bill of Rights (1996), most of them enacted during the past 20 years. Twenty-two states have passed constitutional amendments requiring the provision of certain services to crime victims.

3. Victim–Offender Restitution

One important development associated with the victim movement, maybe paradoxically, involves attempts to bring the victims into closer contact with their offenders. Often these pursuits are pictured as attempts to regain the victims' "stolen" rights back from the state and the criminal justice system. This aspect is aptly titled, "Conflicts as Property," in an article by the Norwegian criminologist Nils Christie (1977), who argues for face-to-face encounters of victims and offenders and the use of the victims' moral resources when dealing with crime.

The victim–offender reparation, mediation, and reconciliation programs stress the affective and emotional sides of dealing with victimization. These programs are expected to help the victims express their anger and indignation at the offender in a constructive way. Simultaneously they are designed to allow the offenders a forum for expressing their remorse in an environment of trust. They are also supposed to produce settlements that directly compensate the victims instead of just providing symbolic compensation through being able to witness the handing down of a state-imposed punishment.

II. VICTIMOLOGY AS A DISCIPLINE

There is no broadly agreed-upon theory of victimology, a fact which, combined with the amorphous nature of many victimological endeavors, makes a number of researchers deny victimology the status of a scientific discipline. Nevertheless, victimology satisfies at least some important requirements of a minor scientific discipline. There is a body of empirical knowledge about victimization that is shared and largely agreed upon by the practitioners of victimology. Crime victimization surveys are regularly conducted in several countries and constitute an important tradition of inquiry. There are scientific societies, journals, conferences, university courses, and textbooks devoted to victimology. There are also various advocacy groups for victims' rights, some activities of which border on, or can be included within, the scope of victimology. Working within victim assistance programs—be that salaried or volunteer work—can be considered one of the practical societal tasks that victimology as a discipline supports.

A. Questions of Theory and Demarcation

Victimology is a field with a less-generally agreed-upon theoretical framework or research paradigm than many longer established disciplines. There have been discussions on whether victimology is only a nontheoretical field of inquiry or whether a theory of victimization has been or can be developed. Similarly, the relationship between victimology and criminology has been questioned. Is victimology an independent discipline or is it a subdiscipline of criminology?

Other debates concern the limits of the subject matter of victimology. Should victimization to behaviors other than crime be included? Or how should one go about crimes that have no well-defined individual victim? Or when the victim is a corporate entity? How about "indirect" victimization, such as the debilitating or annoying fear of crime, or being ill-treated by the police and the courts when searching for justice?

B. A Nontheoretical Problem-Centered Field of Inquiry?

The main defining feature of victimology has to do with a portion of the empirical world: the phenomenon of being victimized. Victimologists are researchers who are interested in that phenomenon and obviously would agree that it is worthwhile to know that phenomenon better. There may be little else that is universally agreed upon by victimologists. There are few or no universally accepted theories or paradigms that would define the discipline. The methods and theories are mostly borrowed from the neighboring more established disciplines of sociology and different schools of psychology or psychiatry, and they are often fragmentary.

However, there have been attempts to define victimology more rigorously and to develop it into a proper discipline. One of the propagators of this idea is Professor Ezzat A. Fattah of Simon Frazer University, British Columbia, who suggests that the study of victims and victimization has the potential of offering "the long awaited paradigm shift that criminology desperately needs." Even if that is too hopeful, it is conceivable that victimology as an empirically driven discipline will develop a stable body of knowledge whose main characteristics will be broadly agreed upon even when their "ultimate" theoretical explanations and interpretations remain controversial.

C. Victims of Crimes and Other Behaviors and Events

The definition of victimology as a study of victims of *crimes* obviously makes the scope of the discipline dependent on how crimes are defined. (It also has repercussions on the question of whether or to what extent victimology should be considered a part of criminology or as an independent discipline.) And, as is well known, the definitions of crimes vary to a greater or lesser extent between jurisdictions and historical periods. Nevertheless, one could claim that these are only peripheral issues since some important acts are defined as crimes in virtually all societies and criminal victimology has very much concentrated on those kinds of offenses.

However, more profound issues remain. Victimology may also be helpful in shedding light on other kinds of victimizing behaviors that could be prevented. It could even be helpful for defining what types of behaviors ought to be criminalized, decriminalized, or controlled in some other ways. Victimological studies may inform the public and politicians about the consequences of different behaviors that endanger the life, health, or property of other individuals—drunk driving, speeding, and safety at the workplace are obvious cases in point. It is possible that taking the victim's view would reveal regularities that underlie victimization to noncriminal untoward events.

It is often instructive to compare the injury, damage, pain, and suffering experienced by victims of direct personal crimes with those endured by victims of other types of events; for instance, victims of accidents that are not intentional crimes but do sometimes involve criminal negligence. For instance, Finnish national victimization surveys include data on injuries caused by accidents in addition to those caused by deliberate vio-

lence. They show that, measured by either hospital days, days of convalescence in bed, or total days of restricted activity, deliberate violence caused considerably fewer injuries to Finns than did accidents in any one of the five categories that included: traffic accidents, work-related accidents, accidents at home, sports-related accidents, and other accidents.

Certainly there are victims of many other behaviors and conditions that would be important to study in order to gain a more comprehensive picture of human victimization. For instance, much pain and suffering can be caused by political acts that are not necessarily defined as crimes, or are not effectively prosecuted, because the criminal justice system is in disarray or ineffective in times of war or other international or national conflicts. A number of victimologists have focused on issues such as genocide, "politicide," or less dramatic but ubiquitous instances of abuse of power.

The list of conceivable sources of victimization is, of course, endless. One could think of studying the victims of cigarettes, food poisoning, industrial waste, sports injuries, divorce, tort, gossip, mental cruelty, bad publicity, noncriminal intrusion of privacy, or the withholding of love. In many fields it is also quite likely that taking into account both the perspective and the role of the victim it is possible to discover worthwhile information. Also, from the point of view of offering help to victims, there may be many more similarities than dissimilarities in helping victims of crimes and victims of disasters.

D. World Society of Victimology

There is an international scientific and professional victimological organization called the World Society of Victimology (WSV). The WSV's purposes include the following: to promote research on victims and victim assistance; advocacy of their interests throughout the world; to encourage interdisciplinary and comparative research in victimology; and to advance the cooperation of international, regional, and local agencies, groups, and individuals concerned with the problems of victims. Its members include victim assistance practitioners, scientists, social workers, physicians, lawyers, university professors, and students. The WSV traces its origins to the First International Symposium on Victimology organized by Israel Drapkin in Israel in 1973. The WSV is a nonprofit, nongovernmental organization with consultive status category II with the ECOSOC of the United Nations and the Council of Europe. The 9th International Symposium on Victimology took place in the Netherlands in 1997. While most victimological research is published in general criminological and other professional journals, there are journals focusing on victimology, such as *International Review of Victimology*, published by A B Academic Publishers (UK) in association with the World Society of Victimology, and *Violence and Victims*, published by Springer (New York, NY).

III. THE VICTIMIZATION SURVEY

The victimization survey was developed to illuminate the "dark number" of crime that the police and other official records do not contain. The typical victimization survey asks a sample representative of the general population (with some restrictions) about their victimization to a number of crimes, including incidents not reported to the police, during a certain period. In addition to obtaining information about concrete crime victimization events and what the respondents did about the incidents, surveys usually also ask questions about victims' reactions to crime overall and their views of the functioning of crime control authorities.

The victimization survey is best suited for measuring crimes against the person and property of private citizens. Crimes against corporate entities are more difficult to measure, although commercial victimization surveys have been conducted in many counties. Local crime surveys give a more detailed picture of local circumstances. Surveys can also target specific groups, such as women, teachers, police officers, prison inmates, and so on.

A. National Victimization Surveys

The most influential model for victimization surveys worldwide is the U.S. National Crime Victimization Survey (NCVS). Before a major redesign in 1992 it was called the National Crime Survey. The NCVS uses a continuous, nationally representative sample of households in the United States. Approximately 50,000 households and 100,000 individuals ages 12 or older are interviewed for the survey annually. In Britain, comparable national crime surveys have been conducted since 1983, but more rarely and using smaller samples than in the U.S. Because crimes are relatively rare and some serious crimes very rare, large samples are needed to ascertain any meaningful information of them. This means that crime surveys are quite expensive.

In general, the news from the large victimization surveys is not very dramatic. Most events recalled are not serious and, for most people, criminal victimization is still not very frequent. For instance, for an average household in the industrialized countries, a household burglary is to be expected once in 20 to a 100 years, a car theft even less often. However, the surveys also bring out that there is a large amount of repeat victimization, and they give indications that the risk of victimization varies greatly depending on the person's sex, age, way of life, place of residence, and so on.

As was originally expected, the general population victimization surveys reveal a considerably higher frequency of crimes than do police statistics. For instance, the first British Crime Survey (1983) found that only 25% of property crimes and 20% of violent offenses were recorded in the official statistics. Repeated surveys have also put finally to rest Adolphe Quetelet's 19th century axiom that the proportion of the number of known crimes to the unknown total number of crimes remains constant from year to year. Later British surveys have found a greater proportion of the offenses reported to the police. The Finnish national victimization surveys present roughly similar proportions of crimes reported to the police and also a similar trend toward more frequent reporting from the first survey of 1980 to the later ones.

B. International Comparisons

International comparisons of crime rates based on police and court statistics are fraught with difficulties because crime definitions differ, as do police and court practices, statistical conventions, and citizens' reporting of crime to the police.

Victimization surveys using a similar questionnaire in different countries allow a direct way of making offense definitions similar. However, even comparisons of victimization surveys must be done cautiously because of differences in sampling, methodology, and content. Even when questions about victimization are worded similarly, differences in sampling, fielding, and survey methodology, e.g., how different known sources of errors are taken into account, may produce great differences.

An illustration of the differences between police statistics and surveys in international comparisons is provided by the International Crime Survey (ICS), designed to overcome a number of basic comparability problems. The study found that the police recorded crime statistics and the survey rank ordered the jurisdictions more or less identically in the case of car thefts. Auto theft is a relatively well-defined offense that is reported to the police much more frequently than the average offense. With respect to some other crimes, however, there were great differences. For instance, for domestic burglaries the ICS put Norway 60% higher than Finland, while Interpol statistics had seven times higher rates for Finland than Norway. However, a closer analysis of national police statistics reveals that once incomparable categories are sorted out, this incongruity disappears.

C. Rates of Victimization for Common Crimes

As an example of rates of victimization for common crimes, Table I gives the figures for a number of crimes from the 19 industrialized countries that have participated in at least once in the International Crime Survey, which has been conducted three times (1989, 1992, and 1996). The ICS uses computer assisted telephone interviewing. The sample size is usually 2000, which is small by national victim survey standards. Nevertheless, this study is so far the only one using reasonably sized samples, identical questions, and a similar methodology across countries. Thus, while there is a fairly wide sampling error in the estimates, it is a unique source for international comparisons.

The ICS asked respondents about their experiences concerning 11 crimes during the previous year (crimes not included in Table I are: motorcycle theft, bicycle theft, attempted burglary, and sexual incidents). In two of the jurisdictions, The Netherlands and England and Wales, a little more than 30% had been the victim of at least one crime. Ten countries fall between 24 and 30%, while six European countries have overall victimization scores of under 22%. Japan is unique with 8.5%, about half that of the lowest European countries.

IV. ASSESSING VICTIMIZATION SURVEYS

The victimization surveys depend on reaching people who are both able and willing to tell about their victimization. While it might seem that crimes are salient and easily recallable events in the lives of individuals and

TABLE I

Percentage of Those Victimized at Least Once over the Previous Year (1996 or Latest Available)

	11 crimes[a]	Car theft	Theft from car	Car vandalism	Burglary	Robbery	Personal theft	Assault & threats
England & Wales	30.9	2.5	8.1	10.4	3.0	1.7	5.0	5.9
Scotland	25.6	1.7	6.6	9.8	1.5	0.8	4.5	4.2
Northern Ireland	16.8	1.7	3.1	6.7	1.5	0.5	2.5	1.7
Netherlands	31.5	0.4	5.4	10.0	2.6	0.6	6.8	4.0
Germany (1989)	21.9	0.4	4.7	8.7	1.3	0.8	4.0	3.1
Switzerland	26.7	0.1	3.0	7.1	1.3	0.9	5.7	3.1
Belgium (1992)	19.3	1.1	3.9	6.2	2.1	1.0	3.1	1.8
France	25.3	1.6	7.2	8.3	2.4	1.0	4.0	3.9
Finland	18.9	0.4	2.9	4.3	0.6	0.5	3.2	4.1
Spain (1989)	24.8	1.4	9.6	6.6	1.7	3.1	5.2	3.1
Norway (1989)	16.4	1.1	2.8	4.6	0.8	0.5	3.2	3.0
Sweden	24.0	1.2	4.9	4.6	1.3	0.5	4.6	4.5
Italy (1992)	24.7	2.7	7.0	7.6	2.4	1.3	3.6	0.8
Austria	18.9	0.2	1.6	6.7	0.9	0.2	5.1	2.1
U.S.	24.2	1.9	7.5	6.7	2.6	1.3	3.9	5.7
Canada	25.2	1.5	6.2	6.2	3.4	1.2	5.7	4.0
Australia (1992)	28.6	3.1	6.6	9.5	3.7	1.3	6.5	4.7
New Zealand (1992)	29.4	2.7	6.9	8.0	4.3	0.7	5.3	5.7
Japan (1989)	8.5	0.3	0.7	2.7	0.7	0.0	1.3	0.5

[a]Victimization to any of the following: car theft, theft from car, car vandalism, motorcycle theft, bicycle theft, burglary, attempted burglary, robbery, personal theft, assault or threat, and sexual incidents.
Source: Mayhew & van Dijk (1997).

families, this is not always the case. There are many potential problems that threaten to compromise the accuracy of victim surveys as a measurement instrument. There are biases in who is reached and how different types of offenses are recalled. In addition to the obvious case of murder victims, many other crime victims are also difficult to reach, respond reluctantly to victim surveys, or give inaccurate answers. Some measurement problems seem surprising from a common sense point of view.

The validity and reliability of surveys can be tested in various ways, including analyses of the internal structure of survey data and its relationship to the instruments used, methodological experiments using more than one method to gather data from parallel samples, and the use of external benchmarks, such as police records. In a police record check—also called "reverse record check" and the "test of known crime victims"—crime victims are sampled from police records and they are contacted and asked to respond to a victimization survey questionnaire. The individuals are approached as survey respondent from a probability sample without being told of their known victim status. The responses are then compared with the data from the police records.

A. Measurement Issues

1. Conceptualization of Offenses

A prominent issue concerns the way people perceive and remember crimes. Most of the time they quite easily conceptualize an event as a crime and recall the event later when it is a question of a theft of or damage to a very valuable piece or property or of a violent offense by a stranger that causes distinct injury. They are more reluctant to classify as a crime the removal of an object of lesser value, particularly if it is removed by a family member, a friend, a colleague, or an acquaintance or cases of physical encounters with a family member, even if the episode leaves them with bruises. Many people apparently tend to think that incidents such as these are "none of the government's business." This makes the measurement of domestic violence a difficult matter. Other types of incidents whose character as an offense is greatly dependent on changeable norms and ways of perception are threats of violence and indecent sexual acts.

2. Type of Crime

The reliability of surveys varies greatly by type of crime. Crimes that cause immediate tangible damage to an individual or to a household are in principle easier to

account for by victimization surveys than are crimes of endangerment or slowly accumulating damage to third parties or society at large.

Some types of crimes are difficult to measure by the victim survey because the victim does not know the pertinent facts in the first place. Shopkeepers may be able to assess the number or the value of the merchandise items they have lost, but they usually have little idea of how many events of shoplifting or employee theft this may have involved. Some cases of embezzlement are never noticed. The same goes for many cases of tax fraud and the like. Obviously, victimization surveys are not very good in measuring offenses such as speeding or traffic ticket evasion, either. In the last cases there is no identifiable individual victim, but the "victim" is rather the state, society at large, "law and order," or some other more abstract entity.

Even when there is a clearly identified victim who should know about the offense there are great differences in the recall rates of different types of crime. Record check studies show that, for instance, few cases of domestic violence are recalled. In a Finnish study, only one-fifth of cases of domestic violence known to the police were retrieved by the survey; most of this drop was due to the refusal of victims to respond to the survey in the first place. The highest recovery rates were for sexual assaults and property offenses. In a San Jose (CA) record check, only 22% of the known victims of assaults by a family member or a relative recalled the event in the victimization survey interview (while the general recall rate for assaults was 48%, and that for events involving strangers was 76%). In a Canadian record check study, only 29% of assaults committed by someone related to the victim were recalled to survey interviewers, but as many as 71% of assaults by strangers were recalled.

3. Comparing Records: Not Telling

In a Finnish police record check, less than one-half of those offenses the police already knew of were reported in the survey. The gap accumulated in three stages. One-tenth of the subjects could not be reached. As many as four-tenths of those who were contacted refused to be questioned. Finally, one-fourth of those who did respond failed to mention the offense that they had reported to the police. The results are comparable to those from similar method checks in the U.S. and elsewhere.

It seems probable that in addition to some trivial offenses that people simply do not recall they can fail to mention some serious offenses that they have been victims of, particularly if they involve persons of their own household (domestic violence) or offenses in which victim-precipitation is frequent (such as some assaults).

Police records and victimization surveys, then, ascertain different, only partly ovelapping, sets of offenses, and it would be a strange coincidence if between them they would give a comprehensive picture even of those types of offenses that the surveys measure—it is far more probable that a considerable number of individual victimizations that could reasonably be classified as offenses are not measured by either method.

4. Who Is Reached?

Many considerations suggest that those who are the most vulnerable to victimization also tend to be the most difficult to reach by means of large victimization surveys. Data supporting this assumption derive, for instance, from checks of police records. When crime victims from police records are included in victimization survey samples, a great proportion of them cannot be found or refuse to be interviewed. In one U.S. study that had addresses of victims from police records embedded in a general population sample, 97% of the interviews of the general population sample were completed while only 63.5% of the known victims sample were. Tests of known victims in other countries have yielded comparable results.

Also, other considerations support the assumption that many crime victims may be difficult to reach by regular surveys. Victimization is often high among homeless persons, prison inmates, the mentally ill, and misusers of alcohol and other drugs, people who are not usually adequately covered by normal population samples. Furthermore, even outside these categories, women who are violently victimized by their husbands or boyfriends may present an especially difficult case. In many cases, the abuser's objective is to control the woman's social contacts to the outside world. Thus consenting to a lengthy interview with a stranger—be it face-to-face or by telephone—or responding to a mail questionnaire may be deemed a type of behavior that is best avoided in order not to prompt further violence from the partner. Also many victims of violent crime by strangers change their address and withdraw from activities they enjoy and become difficult to reach.

Victimization surveys of the very young and very old are difficult or impossible. Family members can be asked about victimization of the children of the family, but this is unlikely to reveal many cases in which the offender is a family member. One can try to devise ways in which medical and social workers can gather data on this sort of victimization.

Another group not easily interviewed in a standard victimization survey is the elderly and others who live in elder care facilities and are heavily dependent on their nurses and other staff.

5. Sampling and Fielding

Sampling methods are dependent on the available population registers and available methods for contacting respondents. In the Scandinavian countries, the registers often make it feasible to draw a probability sample representing virtually all the *individuals* of a given age or other category while in some other countries the relevant unit would be the *household*.

An early assumption was that one adult member of a household would be able to give information of the victimizations of all the household members. However, surveys asking either one household representative or all household members show that asking everyone produces considerably more victimization events. In one U.S. study, the difference was 1.7- to 2.2-fold, depending on the type of offense. In a German study, personal interviews brought about almost 50% more victimization events than interviews with only heads of household.

In some cases, the problems of sampling compound with those of determining the proper victimized unit. For instance, when asking a sample of individuals questions about household-level victimization, it may be difficult to determine whether a reported property offense (for instance, one involving a car) really concerned individual property or that of the whole household; the choice obviously affects the crime rate estimate.

Also, mail questionnaires, telephone interviews, and face-to-face interviews are known to differ in how they reach the desired individuals and how they elicit responses.

6. Questionnaire Effects

As simple a fact as the order of questions in the interview instrument has shown to have considerable impact on the amount of victimization events collected. If each "yes" answer to a screening question, such as "Did you experience an offense x during the past y months," is immediately followed by queries of the details of the incident, the respondents may learn to answer "no" to the subsequent screening questions just in order to avoid further tedious detail questions. Questionnaires that first ask all the screening questions produce more victimization reports, as they do not allow the respondents to become testwise during the interview.

7. Forgetting and Telescoping

Checks with police records have shown that the respondents' recall rate is heavily dependent on the length of time that has lapsed between the offense and the interview. In the San Jose record check, the respondents recalled 69% of those incidents that had taken place 1–3 months before the interview, but only 30% of those that had taken place 10–12 months earlier. This by itself would imply that the period of time that the respondents are asked to consider should be kept short. However, very short reference periods also mean that fewer offenses are captured in the survey unless the sample—and the cost—is amplified as well. The problem is further complicated by the respondents' tendency not to stick to the given reference period. Record checks have shown that respondents often "telescope" into the reference period events that actually happened before it (forward external telescoping), while the opposite type of telescoping, moving events from the reference period outside it, is much rarer. This phenomenon may have to do with the respondents' need to give the interviewer "satisfying" answers. One way to prevent respondents from telescoping earlier events into the reference period is to interview them two or more times and to use the previous interview as a boundary point. Such *bounding* by repeat interviews is now the routine in the U.S. National Crime Victimization Surveys.

B. Improving the Surveys

1. More-Sensitive Instruments

Large general victimization surveys tell us very little about the social and personal settings in which crime takes place. They also seldom probe "the psycho- and sociodynamics of criminal behavior, the process of selecting the victim, victim–offender interactions and the victim's contribution to the genesis of the crime" (Fattah, 1992).

To alleviate these problems, specialized surveys have been conducted, such as those designed to uncover the types of violence that women experience. Specialized surveys targeted to domestic violence are one way to get a more comprehensive coverage of these types of crimes. Another is to redesign general surveys.

In Canada, a survey was conducted to measure violence against women. This Violence Against Women Survey (VAWS) addressed only women and only violent offenses; unlike standard victimization surveys, it included questions of adult lifetime victimization. Only women acted as interviewers. If it transpired that the respondent was abused in a current relationship, she

was asked if she was able to continue the conversation freely, and interviews were rescheduled if needed. The productivity of this approach is illustrated by comparing different estimates of wife assaults. In 1993, the police recorded 46,800 wife assaults in Canada; the General Social Survey estimated 107,500 incidents of such assaults, while the VAWS uncovered 210,000 women (1-year prevalence) who had been assaulted by their spouses that year. Similarly, a Finnish national survey of violence against women (1998) unveiled a clearly higher prevalence of victimization as compared with standard victim surveys.

In the U.S. crime survey redesign, introduced in 1992, questions were added that broadened the type of attack or threat that the respondent could choose and encouraged respondents to include events they were not certain would be considered crimes. Furthermore, subjects were told that "incidents involving forced or unwanted sexual acts are often difficult to talk about," and were specifically asked about such incidents involving strangers, acquaintances, and known offenders. Thus, within the categories of violent crime measured by the survey, the redesign produces fuller reporting of those incidents that involved intimates or other family members. The redesigned NCVS also broadens the scope of covered sexual incidents beyond the categories of rape and attempted rape (sexual assault other than rape, verbal threats of rape or sexual assault, or unwanted sexual contact without force but involving threats or other harm to the victim). Explicit cuing for rape and other sexual assaults was included in the new screening instrument. The redesigned survey elicits information on about three to four times as many sexual crime victimizations as the earlier instrument.

2. Redesign Effects

As an example of results from the U.S. Victimization Survey, some rates are presented in Table II. This table also shows how the different versions of the same survey produce different results. The redesign of the victimization survey was an effort to improve its ability to measure victimization, particularly crimes like rape and sexual assault.

V. OTHER APPROACHES TO THE STUDY OF VICTIMS

The number of methods that may have victimological applications is potentially unlimited. Of course, the main method that predated victimization surveys, the use of police and court or hospital/medical records, is

TABLE II

A Comparison of U.S. Victimization Rates for 1992 from Two Versions of the National Crime Victimization Survey

	Rate per 1000 persons or households		
	After redesign (NCVS)	Before redesign (NCS)	NCVS/NCS ratio
Personal crimes			
Violent crime	47.8	32.1	1.49
Rape	1.8	.7	2.57
Robbery	6.1	5.9	1.03
Aggravated assault	11.1	9.0	1.23
Simple assault	28.9	16.5	1.75
Personal theft	1.8	2.4	.75
Property crime	325.3	264.5	1.23
Household burglary	58.6	48.9	1.20
Household theft	248.2	195.5	1.27
Motor vehicle theft	18.5	20.1	.92

Source: National Crime Victimization Survey, Criminal Victimization, 1973–1995, April, 1997, NCJ-163069. By Michael R. Rand, BJS Statistician; James P. Lynch, Ph.D., American University, David Cantor, Ph.D., Westat.

still one of the most important methods of the study of victims. For some crimes, such as homicides, it is often the most important method. Apart from their normal routines, the police and other authorities can also devise specific methods to measure victimization in a more reliable way. The police and court records can also be linked, e.g., to mortality and morbidity data that the medical authorities keep.

Other methods include in-depth interviews with victims in order to find out long-term effects of victimization or about the interactions leading to a violent crime. For instance, employees can be interviewed to find out typical situations that lead to angry encounters with people they meet at work. Police documents describing offenses are also used to tease out other aspects of the interaction in victimization processes. Hospital records may be used to supplement other data on victimization or as an independent source for estimating assaults and batteries.

Over a period of 3 years, Shapland et al. (1985) interviewed 276 victims of violent crimes (assaults leading to injury, robberies, and sexual assaults) at four different stages of the criminal justice process in England. They found, for instance, that while most victims were quite satisfied with their first encounters with the police, they were usually less satisfied with the scarcity of information of the further processing of the case by the police and the courts, and many felt that they had not been treated with adequate consideration.

The clients of victim assistance institutions is another population that has been studied. For instance, Dean Kilpatrick and his coworkers gathered data on patients who sought treatment at a crime victims center in Charleston, South Carolina, and found that many of them could be diagnosed as suffering from posttraumatic stress disorder. This is consistent with the everyday experience of many people who work with them that crime victims often tend to be severely upset by their experience. Also, many studies have shown that victims of violent crimes or their attempts, such as rape, robbery, and assault, tend to have considerably more traumatic psychological symptoms than nonvictims. However, when evaluating cross-sectional studies showing this connection one must bear in mind that part of the association is probably due to the fact that individuals suffering from such traumas are more likely to be victimized than other people.

VI. REGULARITIES OF VICTIMIZATION

The victimization survey data and other sources allow probing into how the risk of victimization varies by different respondent characteristics, such as gender, age, lifestyle, and occupation.

A. The Similarity of Victims and Offenders

Contrary to popular impressions, the victims and the offenders of interactive crimes are not clearly distinct populations but share a number of common characteristics—particularly where the gravest crimes of violence are concerned. As Anttila (1974) said, "the same individuals may alternatingly or even simultaneously turn up as offenders and victims, while the majority of society's ordinary citizens are outside." According to a Canadian survey, the profile of the victim of crime has these characteristics: young unmarried male, living alone, probably looking for work, or a student, and with an active life outside the home. The profile of the offender would not be very different.

The similarity of the offender and victim is greatest in those crimes that involve personal interaction, such as assaults and robberies. It does not apply to crimes such as burglary or car theft in which there is no personal interaction between the victim and the offender.

B. Repeat Victimization

Most of the offenses recalled in victimization surveys are reported by a small proportion of the respondents. In the British Crime Survey, 70% of all incidents were reported by 14% of the respondents. In a Finnish survey, 1% of the respondents recalled one-fourth of all violent victimizations, and 5% more than one-half. Another British study concluded that once a house had been burgled, its risk of further victimization was four times the rate of houses that had not been burgled. Analysis of multiple victimization data suggests that some individuals and households have characteristics that increase their risks for victimizations. Some authors have suggested that crime prevention efforts should focus on those that run the highest risk of repeat and multiple victimization, and some projects show promising results in this regard.

C. Gender and Violent Victimization

Victimization survey data and other sources allow the establishment of many virtually universal regularities in the distribution of victimization events across different variables, such as demographic categories, situations, lifestyles, and occupations. Risks vary depending on the crime category. For instance, the ownership of potential targets of property crimes are not equally distributed among social strata. Young males run an overwhelmingly higher risk of personal violent victimization than do females or males who have reached middle age.

One stable finding from victimization studies is the qualitative difference of the distribution of violent victimizations between males and females. Women are much more often assaulted and battered by their spouses or other intimates than are men. In the U.S. National Crime Victimization Survey two-thirds of female victims of violence were related to or knew their attacker. Almost 30% were intimates such as husbands or boyfriends and 35% were acquaintances. In contrast, men are significantly more likely to be victimized by strangers or acquaintances. In the same study, 50% of attackers against men were acquaintances and 44% were strangers. Victimizations by intimates and other relatives accounted for only 5% of all violent acts against men.

Victim surveys from other countries give a broadly similar picture. For instance, in a 1988 Finnish victimization survey, only 30% of violent victimizations

against women were by strangers; in 1993 the proportion was 40%. Between 1988 and 1993, according to the Finnish National Victimization Survey, victimization of women by spouse or boyfriend or another member of the nuclear family decreased while violence experienced at the workplace became the most common type of violent victimization of women, counting all occurrences; however, when looking at violence that caused injury, domestic violence was still the leading category; it accounted for nearly one-half of the violent victimizations causing injury experienced by women; it was also a unique category in that it was the only category in which events causing injury comprised a major share (over 50% as compared to 10–20% in other types of violence.) When this is viewed in light of the fact that domestic violence is particularly difficult to detect by means of regular surveys, one can say that domestic violence is probably severely underestimated by general victimization surveys.

D. Safe and Risky Lifestyles, Situations, and Places

Using data from victimization surveys, researchers have found some regularities in the selection of victims.

Using U.S. National Crime Survey data, Cohen et al. found that among young (16–29), unemployed, low-income Blacks who lived alone the risk of being a victim of robbery was almost 10 times higher than the national average. Among older (50+), home centered, high-income whites who did not live alone, it was only one-eighth of the national average. The risk for burglary varied differently from that of robbery. One important variable explaining the variation was the amount of time that the household was unoccupied during the week. Interestingly, the risk of burglary was highest in the lower-income households, next highest in the high-income households, and lowest in the middle-income households. While high-income households are likely to contain more attractive targets, low-income households are more likely to be unguarded and conveniently located for potential offenders.

In a Canadian (Vancouver, British Columbia) victimization survey, Corrado et al. found that people who went out during the evening more frequently than the median had more than threefold more violent victimizations than those whose frequency of going out was less than the median. Similarly, data from the British Crime Surveys indicate that violent victimization is positively associated with the frequency of going out in the evening and the amount of drinking. This survey also related the risk of victimization to the subjects' own behavior: individuals who admitted they had, during the past year, carried a weapon, started a fight, or intentionally injured someone were three to five times more likely to have been victims of violent offenses than those who reported no such offenses.

E. Occupations

Some occupations carry higher risks of violent victimization than others. Particularly risky are occupations having to do with the control of crime and disorderly behavior, such as those of policemen, watch guards, and prison guards. Taxi drivers are vulnerable as their work requires them to pick up strangers and drive them to wherever they desire and because they are expected to have money on hand. Those transporting people to public entertainment have an elevated risk, as well as those working in restaurants and other places of entertainment.

"People in lines of work involving face-to-face contact with large numbers of persons on a routine basis involve a higher risk of criminal victimization than those with less accessibility to the public" (Fattah, 1991). The more the occupation involves public accessibility (face-to-face dealings with strangers), mobility (in- and out-of-town), and of handling money, the higher the risk of victimization.

Some illegal occupations, such as fencing, drug trafficking, illegal gambling, prostitution and procuring, black marketing, and so on carry a greater risk of victimization. This elevated risk is largely due to the fact that there are few legal means of dealing with business conflicts arising in such occupations. In other words, the victimizations are often acts or attempts of "social control" by the victims' customers or associates in these illegal activities.

F. Fear of Crime and Protective Measures

Apart from questions about direct victimization, crime surveys often ask questions about fear of crime and behaviors undertaken in order to avoid victimization. Besides the practical connection, debilitating fear of crime can be considered a problem in itself.

One of the stable findings is that women and elderly people tend to be more worried about crime, particularly violent crime and robbery, than are men and young persons. These people are also more likely to avoid going out at night. More recently, it has also been found that middle-aged men are often worried about property crime, and it seems that they are often the people who own property attractive to thieves. In a Danish study

in 1987 it was found that—when elderly women were excluded—there was a positive correlation between fear of crime and having been a victim of theft.

G. The Victim's Contribution and the Problem of Blaming the Victim

Wolfgang's Philadelphia homicide study brought forward the notion of victim precipitation. Wolfgang estimated that it is often only chance that results in one becoming a victim and the other an offender. In many of the cases, the victim shared most of the characteristics of the offender. In several cases, for instance, a male had started using physical force against his female partner, who retaliated with a knife, resulting in fatal consequences. Wolfgang's study challenged the black-and-white stereotypes of victims and offenders that many of us have.

Later, Menachem Amir applied the notion of victim precipitation in an analysis of 646 forcible rapes recorded by the Philadelphia police. He identified 19% of the crimes as precipitated by the victim. The study has been much criticized, however. Amir's definition of precipitation has been seen as too broad. It included instances in which the offender had interpreted the victim as having first consented to sex but then retracted and even instances in which the victim entered sexually charged vulnerable situations. The study was severely criticized, particularly by the emerging feminist movement, for confounding the allocation of blame, on one hand, with an analysis of the chain of events, the victim–offender interaction, and the motivation of the offender, on the other.

Several U.S. studies in the 1960s estimated the relative frequency of victim precipitation in different personal contact crimes. Studies found that about 11% of armed robberies and 6% of unarmed robberies were "victim-precipitated" in the sense that in a temptation–opportunity situation, the victim's behavior clearly had not been reasonably self-protective when handling money, jewelry, or other valuables. While Amir found that 19% of rape cases were victim-precipitated, the rate given by the National Commission on the Causes and Prevention of Violence was 4%. Forcible rape was considered victim-precipitated when a female first agreed to sexual relations, or clearly invited them verbally and through gestures, but then retracted before the act.

Karmen proposed a typology of auto theft victims that assigned different degrees of innocence and responsibility to the victim. A "totally innocent" victim takes special precautions to minimize the risk of theft. A partly innocent one facilitates theft through negligence. A "substantially responsible" victim wants the car to be stolen and precipitates theft by leaving the car exposed and vulnerable, while a "largely responsible" one goes even further and arranges with criminals for the car to be stolen. Finally, a "fully responsible" "simulator" fabricates the theft of a nonexistent car. The latter individuals are hoping to gain money from insurance, and they are actually committing insurance fraud. At the time of Karmen's study, it was estimated that carelessness—usually meaning that car keys were available—accounted for 20% of all car thefts in the U.S., and that at most 25% of thefts were due to the action of motorists who wanted their car to be stolen.

The new victimology added hues of gray to the black-and-white stereotypes of the innocent victim and the guilty offender. "In some instances the balance may even have swung too far in the other direction," wrote the Finnish criminologist Inkeri Anttila in 1974. It would suggest that "victims of assault have no one except themselves to blame if they deliberately walk in dark alleys after dark; that young girls actually wanted to be raped if they did not heed the warnings of their mothers; and that the stores deliberately provoke thefts by exhibiting goods in as tempting a way as possible."

The very notion of victim precipitation has been criticized as victim-blaming. Even victimology itself has been branded an academic institution of victim-blaming and, particularly in the context of women-battering, as an attempt by male victimologists to persuade the public that by changing the female's behavior, the problem of domestic abuse can be controlled.

However, as Fattah maintains, the notion of victim precipitation is basically sound. The problems have to do with the way it has been operationalized in some studies. Much of the criticism is based on a confusion of causal explanation with the issue of assigning moral and legal responsibility. From the finding that some courses of action that potential victims choose reliably increase their chances of being victimized it does not follow that the victimizers would be any more justified or excused when they do commit the offenses. Neither does the fact *per se* that certain behaviors do increase the risk of victimization in any way change the potential victims' *right* to engage in those behaviors. However, these findings may be taken into account by prudent persons when making choices, by society when it seeks to decrease unnecessary temptations of crime, and, after separate discussion that involves moral and legal values, by legislators and courts of law when deciding what sort of circumstances may be deemed valid justification, excuse, or mitigation. (The treatment of intoxication is a familiar case in point. There is little doubt that intoxication, overall, increases the probability of being both a victim and a victimizer. Nevertheless, intoxication is virtually universally considered an *invalid* excuse or mitigation.)

Also See the Following Articles

CRIMINOLOGY, OVERVIEW • HOMICIDE • PUNISHMENT OF CRIMINALS • WOMEN, VIOLENCE AGAINST

Bibliography

Doerner, W. G., & Lab, S. P. (1995). *Victimology*. Cincinnati, OH: Anderson.

Fattah, E. A. (1992). Victims and victimology: the facts and the rhetoric. In E. A. Fattah (Ed.), *Towards a critical victimology* (p. 32). New York: St. Martin's Press.

Fattah, E. (1991). *Understanding criminal victimization: An introduction to theoretical victimology*. Scarborough, Ontario: Prentice–Hall.

Fattah, E. A. (Ed.) (1986). *From crime policy to victim policy: reorienting the justice system*. Houndmills, England: MacMillan.

Karmen, A. (1984). *Crime victims: An introduction to victimology*. Monterey, CA: Brooks/Cole.

Lurigio, A. J., Skogan, W. G., & Davis, R. C. (Eds.) (1990). *Victims of crime: Problems, policies, and programs*. Newbury Park, CA: Sage.

O'Brien, R. M. (1985). *Law and criminal justice series: Crime and victimization data* (Vol. 4). Beverly Hills: Sage.

Rock, P. (Ed.) (1994). *Victimology*. Aldershot, England: Dartmouth.

Violence as Solution, Culture of

Robert Elias

University of San Francisco

GLOSSARY

Favorable Business Climate Circumstances for enhancing multinational corporate profits, often imposed by repressive policies such as banning labor unions, committing violence against community activists, and imposing structural adjustment programs.

Feminization of Poverty The tendency, beginning in the early 1980s, for the increasing U.S. poverty to disproportionately afflict women and children.

Hate Crimes Violence committed, with increasing frequency in the U.S., against groups such as women; homosexuals; and racial, ethnic, and religious minorities for no other motives than the victims' characteristics.

Hostile Takeover Merger of two corporations where one corporation aggressively buys up controlling stock of another corporation against its will.

Legitimate Violence Violence used by the state (or other elites) that it justifies as appropriate to pursue its policies and that it distinguishes from other, and therefore illegitimate, violence.

Low-Intensity Warfare Violence sponsored by U.S. foreign policy abroad that avoids the commitment of U.S. military forces yet that pursues military objectives such as containing dissident groups, ensuring a favorable business climate, and imposing compliant leaders.

New World Order Term used since the 1989 fall of the Berlin Wall, and especially since the 1991 Gulf War, to describe a new, post-Cold War environment, often associated with the triumph of capitalism and the rejuvenated role of the U.S. as the world's policeforce.

Official Narratives Packaging of domestic and international events by U.S. officials and other elites into stories that help sway public opinion toward supporting conventional political and economic policies.

Social Control Use of official force, and often violence, to shape the behavior or control the lives of people within certain groups in society that U.S. officials regard as a problem or threat and have targeted because of their characteristics rather than their antisocial or violent behavior; often the real motive behind conventional crime control policies.

Social Darwinism In this context, a rejuvenated perspective, pursued in the U.S. since the 1980s, of promoting "survival of the fittest" policies toward the ill, the poor, and the unemployed.

Structural Adjustment Program promoted by U.S. foreign policy and by international financial institutions such as the International Monetary Fund that exchanges foreign aid, usually in form of loans that increase a country's national debt, for state policies within the recipient nation that impose austerity measures on much of the population, especially the poor; often cited as an example of structural violence imposed for the benefit of local elites and foreign multinational corporations.

Structural Violence The violence imposed on people not by the behaviors of violent individuals but rather by organized, usually official, policies and institutions, such as structural adjustment programs abroad and labor, health, education, and poverty policies in the U.S.

Symbolic Violence Representational violence displayed in popular discourse, social intercourse, and the mass media, such as violent metaphors in language and music and violent images in films or television, and advocated in official policies, such as declared wars on crime, drugs, and poverty.

Wilding Committing acts of violence in increasingly random and brutal ways with little remorse toward victims; an "anything goes" mentality of behavior, often with violent means or outcomes that has been used to describe contemporary U.S. life and policies, whereby personal gain or automony is pursued at almost any cost.

I. INTRODUCTION

While we in the United States deplore violence, we nevertheless live in a very violent society. However, our society is not merely plagued by "illegitimate" violence. Arguably, even more violence is generated by "legitimate" behavior, engaged in by individuals, and by institutions, ranging from corporations to governments. Violence, on various levels, is standard behavior in U.S. society. It is justified by rationales ranging from "buyer beware" to "the need for domestic order" to "protecting U.S. interests" to "promoting national security."

Thus, much American violence is tolerated, perhaps even encouraged. Even more important, violence is viewed as a legitimate means of solving problems, even if the problem is violence itself. To seriously address a problem, we must "declare war" on it. Arguably, we are a culture of violent solutions. Using violence to solve social and other problems comprises a large portion of the violence we commit in U.S. society.

But, who are "we"? As we will see, "we" are sometimes all, or most, of us in this society. The public widely endorses "legitimate" violence and sometimes even "illegitimate" violence, although we should recognize the powerful forces of socialization and propaganda that often underlie that public support. But at other times "we" constitutes the society characterized less by its members and more by its leaders—that is, those who wield power. Of course, in a purportedly democratic society, our leaders claim to exercise power in our name, but, as political scientist Michael Parenti has argued, the reality may be quite different.

Thus, while we should be concerned with the "we" of the general public, we should be even more interested in the "we" of the powerful few people and institutions who really run our society, arguably more for their own interests than for ours. So let us consider the American people but also the American state—those elites both in and out of government who really rule our nation.

With this in mind, we can survey the way we, as a society, use wars and other violence to solve various American problems ranging from the government of Saddam Hussein to escalating crime. Doing so allows us to examine the role our own "legitimate" violence plays in creating new violence, which we then come to regard as a social problem. We then see how we routinely react to that violent social problem by committing more "legitimate" violence to try to solve the problem—thus producing a cycle of violence.

What are the characteristics and results of using violence as a policy for solving problems? Who benefits and who loses? What are the alternatives?

II. OUR VIOLENT SOCIETY

We are an undeniably violent society, where violence has become not merely a characteristic but rather a way of life, proliferating throughout the U.S. system. First, the U.S. arguably has the highest crime rate in the world. Beyond the tremendous violence to property, ranging from theft to wanton destruction, there is an even greater violence against people, ranging from muggings to beatings to sexual assaults to murders. This violence is becoming more organized and more systematic, with an increase in serial or mass murders, in gang violence, and in hate crimes against women and other groups in society.

Second, for all the violence of crime, even more violence results from harmful behavior which we thus far have refused to define as crime. As Jeffrey Reiman demonstrates, even more than from crime, people suffer from the violence (measured in terms of losses, illnesses, disabilities, and deaths) of extensive but preventable workplace injuries and diseases; of environmental degradation; of unsafe food, pharmaceuticals, and other products; of unnecessary surgery and incompetent emergency care; and of corporate and government wrongdoing that devastates individuals, groups, and communities alike.

Third, violence permeates U.S. culture. It characterizes our sporting life, for example. Some of our sports, such as ice hockey and football, exist specifically to measure which team can administer the most effective violence against the other. Increasingly the violence spills beyond the "game," such as in bench-clearing brawls. But our less violent sports have become more violent as well and being a sports spectator is now more likely to involve us in violence, either as a victim or as a perpetrator. Consider the "kneecapping" of an Olympic-bound ice skater in Detroit and the beer bottles thrown at professional baseball players. Likewise, we have an overwhelming amount of violence in our news, and we daily ingest hundreds of images of the violence of crimes or wars and so forth.

Our visual entertainment is also dominated by violence, from our television programs to our films. With the advent of videos, even more of that violence now comes into our homes. Violence has increasingly become part of our children's play: it is in the cartoons and other television they watch, in the movies they see, and in the computer games that now overwhelm so many of our households. But arguably, this violence is not play: is it not appropriate as play in the first place and it is not play when it makes us and our children more violent in our daily lives.

Fourth, our system routinely represses various groups and communities in our society. The powers that be have used social institutions to administer violence against politically unpopular groups such as the American Indian Movement, the Black Panthers, and Earth First. They use violence as social control (rather than as crime control) when they warehouse people of color in the nation's burgeoning prisons, when they promote forced sterilization campaigns against minority women, when they conduct drug and radiation experiments on unsuspecting subjects, when they discriminately administer the death penalty, when they conduct police raids to terrorize communities, and when they tolerate the institutionalization of police brutality.

Fifth, our society suffers from the violence of neglect and irresponsibility. Tens of millions of Americans are unnecessarily victimized in the richest nation in the world by the structural violence of hunger and malnutrition, homelessness, unemployment, illiteracy, untreated illness, and other symptoms of poverty, racism, and sexism.

Arguably, this violence is escalating, both tangibly and symbolically. There is more actual violence, the new scares concerning juvenile violence and workplace violence being only two of the latest symptoms. And there is more symbolic violence, in our language and in our various representations of violence, especially in the media.

While as a people we claim we deplore this violence, alarming numbers of us practice it in our daily lives. We also celebrate it in our heroes and, increasingly, in our heroines. As Jack Levin has suggested, "violence is hip right now." But as David Gelman argues, it is "better than hip: it's commercial."

In 1989, a young woman was brutally assaulted by six youths in New York's Central Park. The violence was bad enough, but the attitude displayed by the perpetrators was even more shocking. They had committed a savage crime but showed no remorse and no surprise that they had committed such an act. Raping and beating someone to near death seemed almost appropriate or at least acceptable—"it happens all the time." From this apparent smugness and insensitivity was born the term "wilding."

Wilding became the new violence of U.S. society: the indiscriminate violence of "mindless marauders seeking a thrill." As Charles Derber suggested, it was violence committed by people who, according to media characterizations, "seemed stripped of the emotional veneer of civilized humans, creatures of a wilderness where anything goes." But "wilding" is hardly reserved to marginal groups in our society. As Derber shows, "wilding" permeates our culture, from Main Street to Wall Street. The hyperindividualism and anything-goes environment of the 1980s "Age of Greed" has turned many of us into actual or potential wilders. No means to "get mine" (and everyone else be damned) is too extreme, not even murder.

Just as alarming is the fact that we increasingly use violence to solve our problems—both legitimate and suspect. It is remarkable, when we examine it, how many problems we now believe, or say we believe, can be solved by using violence.

III. DOING VIOLENCE TO OUR PROBLEMS

The problems to which we now routinely apply violence are both domestic and global and sometimes a combination of the two. Indeed, we can see the interrelationship between our domestic problems (from the interpersonal to the national) and our global problems, and the interrelationship of the techniques of violence we use against them.

But what elites view as "problems" might not be viewed as such by the masses. Violence, drugs, poverty, and even enemies (depending on who is targeted) might be legitimate problems to address. But what about when children, women, or minority races or religions are treated as problems, as we so often see in our society? And what about when enhancing profits for the few and maintaining U.S.-dominated international capitalism are treated as problems to solve? Whether legitimate or suspicious, the following "problems" (some at home, some abroad) have nevertheless been addressed, most often by seeking solutions through violence (see Table I).

A. Violence

As just illustrated, violence itself is a major problem. In the U.S. for example, there is a concern about controlling the high level of violent crime. Yet we routinely respond by escalating the violence. We declare "wars" on crime. We adopt more sophisticated weapons and military models. Our punishments increasingly promote deprivation, physical abuse, longer sentences, capital punishment, and even sterilization. When physically abused children grow up and commit their own violence, we call for greater violence against them to "teach them a lesson."

We unleash the police, tolerating increasing levels of brutality, making incidents like the Rodney King beating commonplace rather than exceptional. When communities like South Central Los Angeles erupt as a response to state violence and injustice, we send military troops to violently quell the riots. As Lillian Rubin has shown, when state violence fails, and citizens like Bernhard Goetz—the so-called "subway vigilante"—use their own violence against the threat of criminal violence, we applaud.

Abroad, we claim we are concerned about the problem posed by two other forms of violence: state repression and group terrorism. Yet most often, we respond with new violence. We send military aid to "professionalize" the Salvadoran army and its allied death squads. We bomb Libya to curb its terrorism campaign in Europe. We declare war on Iraq to reverse its invasion of Kuwait. When officials are too slow in responding with their own violence, they are chastised, such as with President Clinton's being criticized for his reluctance to "get tough" in Bosnia.

B. Drugs

Another major problem is the proliferation of drugs in our society. Yet predictably, we respond first and foremost by declaring a "war" on drugs. No need to spend much time on better health, education, or rehabilitation; only a violent response will seriously address drug users and dealers. No matter that these wars have turned many parts of our cities into armed battlefields, as Clarence Lusane has demonstrated.

Abroad, we follow the same policy. One response has been to sponsor the police and militaries in drug-producing or drug-processing nations so that they can conduct their own campaigns of violence. When that is not good enough, we send our own police (such as the Drug Enforcement Agency) and military, as Jonathan Marshall documents, to raid suppliers, poison crops, kill drug lords, and commit other violence to solve the problem.

C. Poverty

The U.S. also has a serious problem of poverty. Yet even in the 1960s, when we were willing to consider

TABLE I

Real Legitimacy?

Legitimate	Illegitimate
Problems	
Safety	Power
Crime control for everyone	Social control for the few
All crimes	Some crimes
All drugs	Some drugs
All repression	Some repression
All aggressors	Some aggressors
Poverty	Welfare
Underdevelopment	Foreign autonomy
Childraising	Controlling children
Authoritarianism	Too much democracy
Race relations	Other races
Intl. relations	Other nations
Eliminating arms	Maintaining arms
Female/male relat's	Controlling women
Decent work	Controlling workers
Wars	Conduct/win wars
Solutions	
Real attempts	Feeble attempts
Reasonable means	Unreasonable means
Good motives	Ulterior motives
Substance	Rhetoric
Solve	Manage
Attention for the many	Neglect for the few

"softer options" for dealing with poverty, our response was still a war: the War on Poverty. As we moved into the 1980s and early 1990s, our solutions for poverty became ever more abusive and violent. According to Frances Fox Piven and Richard Cloward, instead of fighting poverty, we have been fighting the poor: cutting assistance, pushing people off welfare, blaming them for their poverty, brutalizing and jailing the homeless, and swelling—rather than reducing—the ranks of the destitute.

Abroad, we purport to solve the problem of underdevelopment. Yet, in practice, we intensify underdevelopment with policies that can only be viewed as escalating the structural violence that already plagues most people in the world. According to Frances Moore Lappe, our development model, based on austerity programs and "structural adjustment," undermines local economies, ravages the environment, robs natural resources, exploits workers, represses communities, and generally enhances the misery of the world's poor. When confronted with millions of starving people, we ignore the institutional causes of hunger, such as the incentives we give other nations to squander their resources on militarism rather than nourishment. When we intervene, we commit our military troops to "take the problem seriously," even when—as in Somalia—the military solution only makes the problem worse.

D. Enemies

We in the United States have been preoccupied, perhaps uniquely, with the problem of our "enemies." Yet we may not agree on who or what constitutes the enemy. For example, at home, we might be united in thinking that criminals are our enemies, but the more we examine the double standard we use to define crime and criminals, the more we might begin to disagree.

After criminals, our "real" enemies might be even more obscure. Are dissidents, for example, our enemies or, rather, as some would argue, those most responsible historically for promoting rights and social progress? In practice, we have treated most dissidents as enemies. And we have routinely used violence to fight those enemies, whether in the assassination of Black Panthers, the "turkey shoot" attack on Attica prisoners, the armed raids on American Indian Movement members at Wounded Knee, the crippling or killing of antiwar activists in Oakland, or the bombings of the MOVE group in Philadelphia and the Branch Davidians in Waco.

Dissidents are not alone among our domestic enemies. We often perceive other threats, especially to our economic well-being, such as from other races, ethnicities, religions, classes, or genders, as being dangerous. The state might respond directly to these threats (such as through its racist immigration policies or its racist attacks by police officers on African Americans such as Rodney King) or indirectly by abetting (through divisive policies that, for example, pit races against each other in a competition for artificially scarce public resources) individual (usually white male) responses to these threats. In either case, the response is violence more often than not, emerging as state repression or, increasingly, as hate crimes. Mexican nationals are terrorized by border patrols or attacked by U.S. citizens for robbing "American" jobs. Asian Americans are bashed for ruining the U.S. auto industry. Arab Americans are victimized for threatening "our" oil supply in the Middle East.

Abroad, we face the problem of enemies or aggressors who we believe want to attack us or otherwise undermine our way of life. Again, violence dominates our choice of responses. In its 200 years, the U.S. has launched 200 military interventions, varying in scale but all making the same statement: "we will beat you into submission." If Mohammar Khaddafi insists on promoting international terrorism, then we can only stop him by bombing Libya and killing 100 innocent civilians. If Manuel Noriega continues to run drugs and to refuse to toe the U.S. line, then we can only stop him by invading Panama, killing several thousand people, and leaving tens of thousands homeless.

For the decade of the 1980s, solving the problem of Central American unrest relied on promoting the unrelenting violence of U.S.-sponsored murder, assassination, torture, terrorism, repression, invasion, starvation, military coups, crop poisoning, economic destabilization, psychological warfare, environmental destruction, and low-intensity warfare. As former Assistant Secretary of State Elliot Abrams said, the purpose of the contras in Nicaragua was "to permit people on our side to use more violence." According to Noam Chomsky, the contras never had, and never claimed they could gain, the support of the Nicaraguan people: "nothing counted except for the increase in violence." United States policy-makers had similar concerns about whether the violence was sufficient when we were in Vietnam.

The "new world order" promises no respite from this pattern, and the U.S. continues to prepare itself for new interventions against other nations, revolutionaries, and terrorists. The U.S. still promotes weapons sales to nations around the world, further buttressing the profitable war system. Yet, we threaten violence against nations whose growing conventional and nuclear weapon capability begin to concern us, even if we were instrumental—as in the case of Iraq—in creating it. The U.S. delivers "spankings" to "teach lessons," such as with President Bush's outgoing attacks on Iraq and President Clinton's bombing strikes on Baghdad—to prove he was not a foreign policy "wimp." When we attack Iraq during the Gulf War and kill 200,000 people, we have not attacked Iraqis but rather its leader, Saddam Hussein, whom we demonize as Hitler and invest with mythical powers that must be thwarted.

Nonviolent alternatives to violence and to military intervention against our "enemies" are options only at the risk of "backing down," or "appearing weak." A CBS News poll of U.S. popular support for the Gulf War best reflects the lack of alternatives to violence: When asking Americans what we should do in the Gulf, it offered only the following options: attack now, attack later, attack by air, attack by ground, and no opinion. So much for the possibility of not attacking at all.

E. Children

Yet another problem is how to successfully raise our children. Somehow childrearing often gets reduced to the problem of disciplining children, at home and in school. Curiously, we seem more preoccupied with the "negative" problem of keeping our children in line instead of the more "positive" problem of providing our children with a stimulating and fulfilling environment. Children seem more like an impediment than a national resource. In any case, again, our solution seems to emphasize violence.

Certain ideologies, such as fundamental Protestantism, encourage this violence in particular: "sacralizing" violence has been linked to the values of salvation, divine will, and obedience to authority. Accordingly, people are born with sin, and it is their human nature to rebel and to be selfish and evil. From this perspective, corporal punishment is not only acceptable, it is crucial to good child development. These views, once treated as old-fashioned, have made a comeback not merely among fundamentalists but throughout society, despite the overwhelming evidence that such violence is actually harmful and counterproductive.

Abroad, our problem is not our children but rather people who we routinely treat as if they are children. Foreigners are viewed as unruly, immature, disobedient, ignorant, incapable, and underdeveloped, precisely the traits we attribute to our children. Thus, they require the same kind of discipline, and violence seems to be the "only language they understand." As with our children, we are not beating them down for our own sake but rather so that we can, paternalistically, do what is in their best interest.

F. Women

As are children, women are often treated as problems. Rather than being valued for what they contribute to society, they are often viewed as threats to that society not only by the few in power but also by the masses. Gains in equality for women have been welcomed by some, especially those who have directly benefited. Yet for many more, gains against sexism and the movement (feminism) that has produced them are regarded as threats, even by many women.

Thus the challenge of maintaining a patriarchal society constitutes another problem. Violence is routinely the means used to help preserve male control in U.S. society. Men's power relies on the control of authority, resources, reproduction, and decision-making. Much of this is established in contemporary U.S. households, most of which can still be described as being organized on an authoritarian model. Family violence, which has grown to epidemic proportions, not only results from patriarchy, but it also provides a major means of enforcing patriarchy.

Likewise, women are often systematically victimized by other kinds of violence in U.S. society. They are sexually and physically assaulted. They are subjected to dangerous and unnecessary surgery. Women are the major victims of increasing serial and mass murder in the U.S. Women are economically deprived, confronting—along with children—the growing "feminization of poverty." And they are the increasing victims of hate crimes: violence committed against women specifically because they are women and because they therefore constitute some threat to men.

Abroad, we can see further, sometimes more severe, instances of global sexism. Yet despite human rights rhetoric to the contrary, preventing the victimization of women abroad has been a very low priority. In fact, we are more likely, with our policies, to promote this victimization. Equality for women abroad provides the same threat as it does at home. Thus the real problem is maintaining, not eliminating, global patriarchy. And again, the means are primarily violent. For example, according to Kathleen Barry, our foreign and development policies help promote or condone prostitution, the sex trade and "sex vacations" for men, female labor exploitation, female circumcision, sexual assault, and life-threatening female poverty.

G. Profits (for the Few)

In U.S. society, we must also be concerned with business profits. Driven by capitalism, we worry about how to maximize profits to produce the direct and indirect rewards they promise all Americans. Yet even (and some would say, especially) here, violence is routinely used to solve this problem.

Business-as-usual entails a stream of violence that if effectively checked would challenge the viability of the American economic system. Unchecked, it primarily victimizes workers and consumers; in other words, most of us. It is justified as the means of making profits, even if they are profits for the few, rather than the many. Business success, usually measured by the bottom line—how much profit—seems to hinge on violent policies.

The doctrine of "the buyer beware," for example, generally means that to maximize profit, a seller can swindle the consumer or even injure or kill the consumer with the product. To enhance profits, the Ford Motor Co. can decide not to replace tens of thousands of Pintos that contain gas tanks which it knows may explode on impact, causing injuries and deaths. To increase the bottom line, U.S. companies can underpay their workers compared to the value and profit their labor has created. They can also lay off workers in profitable enterprises, such as General Motors in Flint and U.S. Steel in Youngstown, and move elsewhere where profits (and usually labor exploitation) are even higher. In both cases, workers must endure the structural violence of low or nonexistent wages, and the devastated communities—which helped build those companies—must endure their own deterioration.

Other kinds of violence are also used to maximize profits: Large U.S. companies can use predatory policies to fuel "hostile" takeovers or drive smaller competitors out of business. Savings and loan banks can squander the life savings of thousands of elderly people who will then spend their waning years in hardship. Business enterprises can maintain the dangerous or lethal environments of their workplaces, thus sacrificing the lives of tens of thousands of Americans annually to workplace "accidents" and diseases. United States firms can, with minimal restrictions, pollute the natural environment, promoting illness and premature death. And, as suggested, this kind of violence intensified during the "Age of Greed" of the 1980s, as "wilding" in U.S. society moved from the back alleys to Washington and Wall Street.

Abroad, the problem is promoting capitalism and maximizing profits for U.S. multinational firms. Many of the same strategies used at home are used abroad. Thus, violence figures prominently in promoting business success; indeed, there are even fewer restrictions on the use of violence. Violent business practices are perpetrated not merely by U.S. multinationals but also by governments: local governments such as those in El Salvador or in white South Africa have promoted foreign business on their soil through state repression. At the same time, the U.S. government promotes its multinationals through aggressive, often military, strategies which help develop a "favorable business climate" abroad.

Such a climate is produced by blocking, often violently, progressive change and by combating challenges to the capitalist system generally, such as the "threat of a good example" provided by the economic reforms of the Sandinista government in Nicaragua. According to Noam Chomsky, it means accepting "austerity programs" that prime the economy by further impoverishing and violating local populations abroad. It means the violent repression of workers, especially if they try to organize for better conditions, wages, and so forth.

IV. ANATOMY OF OUR VIOLENT SOLUTIONS

A. Defining Problems

How can we explain the violent solutions we so routinely apply to our problems? First, how we define our social and other problems determines whether there is a problem, which problems will be recognized, and perhaps even which solutions will be adopted. Who helps us define our problems? Which language helps identify problems and their solutions? What process do we use to work problems through? And how do we choose among possible solutions to those problems?

1. Intellectuals

As suggested, violence is the solution-of-choice for many of our most important social problems. We have an intellectual culture which is so committed to the rule of force that it never ceases to be baffled when this violence routinely fails (e.g., in "convincing" the Vietnamese, in stopping crime, and so forth). Domestic and foreign policy-makers tell us that violence is the answer. As this author has shown, experts such as criminologists are largely responsive to officials and their war-based approaches to problem solving. Arguably, criminology perpetuates violence by accepting official (often violent) models and ideologies and by producing criminal justice technocrats who continue the violence process.

2. Media

After the policy-makers and experts, the media then dutifully set the context and report the solution to our problems: The Committee in Solidarity With the People of El Salvador (CIESPES) is violent, former President Duarte is a democrat; antiwar activists are violent, military planners are peaceful. Violence in response to these threats is regrettable but it is a necessary evil. As this author has argued, the media routinely "forget" our violence's past failures (such as our failed crime and drug wars) or its so-called "successes" (such as the Gulf War and our nuclear build-up). Or, as Edward Herman shows, the media only selectively report violence, such as "their" human rights abuses but not "ours."

3. Narratives

Language can make all the difference in defining our problems and in making violence the inevitable solution. Officials have learned this lesson, and have co-opted peaceful language to disguise violent activities: police officers are now referred to as peace officers, offensive weapons are peacekeepers, the War Department has become the Defense Department, and—according to military billboards—"peace is our [the military's] profession." Nevertheless, the media is filled with the language of war and violence when it describes our responses to problems such as crime.

Beyond words, our view of the world, and of our problems and their solution, is shaped substantially by public narratives. While there are competing, alternative narratives, the state has the resources to ensure that the dominant narratives describing our public problems are convenient for elite purposes, often demonizing the enemy to help justify a violent response.

Accordingly, most official narratives insist on violence to solve (or supposedly solve) our problems. Those narratives describe our violence as necessary, heroic, or altruistic. We are using violence only as a last resort (it is a shame how often it comes to that), pursuing innocent motives against Satanic forces. Or, we are only defending ourselves, or rescuing others—and we have been asked to help. Or, it is a struggle between good and evil, for our legitimate interests and, besides, violence is an inevitable part of human nature.

For example, in the international realm, the dominant narrative of the Gulf War demonized Saddam Hussein as the enemy, painted Kuwait as the innocent victim raped by Iraq, and portrayed the U.S. as the heroic avenger coming to the rescue. Similar narratives have been played out in Panama, Libya, Vietnam, and so forth. In the domestic realm, we saw Bernhard Goetz vindicated for his violence by narratives that justified his individual aggression because the state had failed (using its own violence) to stop crime. Thus, Goetz was portrayed as acting in self-defense: he was the romantic hero while his victims were unfairly demonized. Even though this narrative eventually weakened, it helped Goetz from being dealt with seriously for his violence.

As John Galliher has suggested, so strong are these narratives of violence that they can cause us to begin with the solution—violence—even before we have sufficiently understood or defined the problem. For example, we often seem to begin with a violent solution, such as capital punishment, and then look for theories or definitions of the problem that warrant this violence. After this kind of analysis, resolving crime through social and economic change, such as through conciliation, mediation, education, and other more peaceful means becomes impossible by definition, and the war-making solution moves forward.

Narratives of violence make violence legitimate; that is, some violence is legitimized if put into acceptable narrative form. Almost all state violence is thus legitimized and excused. Legitimacy is determined not just by raw power or position, but by public beliefs, which are substantially shaped by successive state narratives about good and evil. Thus, public opinion supports most state violence.

4. Assumptions

There are several apparent assumptions behind the U.S. use of violence to solve problems, both at home and abroad: First, violence is considered to be natural and inevitable, despite the evidence to the contrary, such as the findings of the 1986 Seville Statement on Violence. Second, the U.S. and the men who run it are entitled to control. Third, violence is viewed as permissible because it helps achieve appropriate ends such as instilling obedience, stimulating development, promoting democracy, protecting national security, and teaching lessons. Fourth, U.S. male aggressors are acting morally. Fifth, violence will be effective. Sixth, suffering is pre-destined, not created. Seventh, violence will not produce threats or harms for ruling U.S. males since there will be insufficient legal enforcement or counterforce against them.

B. Legitimizing Violence

Elites do not always need legitimacy to rule, but having it makes their exercise of power far easier. They want to first portray themselves as addressing legitimate problems. Then they want to legitimize their choice of violence as the solution. But official versions of legitimacy may differ dramatically from more objective assessments.

1. Which Problems?

For example, what are the legitimate social problems that should be addressed? In line with some of the examples we have used here, we, the public, might say that safety is a problem, yet while officials may pay lip service to that objective, they might privately be worried far more about the problem of their own power. We might want crime control but officials might prefer the social control of disgruntled groups such as poor African-Americans—and might be using the criminal law to pursue it, quite apart from any real questions of public safety.

We might view all crimes and drugs as the problem while officials might care only about certain crimes and drugs. We might want to stop all repressors and aggressors while officials might want to stop them selectively, according to old Cold War divisions, for example. We might view the problem as poverty while officials might view it as welfare. We might see productive international relations as a challenge while officials see other nations (i.e., enemies) as the problem. We might see the problem as one of eliminating weapons while officials might want to maintain them. We might want to prevent wars while officials might want to conduct and win them (see Table II).

Admitting these motives would usually put officials in a bad light. These definitions of the problems are considered illegitimate. Thus, instead officials rhetorically commit themselves to a higher duty and more acceptable definitions of public problems, even if they abandon them in actual practice. Indeed, taking the "high road" of addressing "legitimate" problems gives them greater freedom to choose the solutions.

2. Which Solutions?

To be legitimate, the state must approach the solutions to our public problems as follows: The solutions must be real, not feeble attempts, using reasonable, not unreasonable, means. They require attention, not neglect, and must be substantive, not merely rhetorical. They must proceed from good, not ulterior, motives, attempt to solve, not merely manage, the problem, and be designed to help the many, not merely the few. When officials choose violence as a solution, it must generally be done and justified within this framework.

TABLE II
Violence

Officially legitimate (what the State does or finds acceptable)[a]	Officially illegitimate (what the State finds unacceptable)
By government	Against government
By corporations	Against corporations
By the rich	Against the rich
Against women	By women
Against children	By children
Against foreigners	By foreigners
Against immigrants	By immigrants
Against people of color	By people of color
Against workers	By workers
Against homosexuals	By homosexuals
Against environmentalists	By environmentalists
Against the poor	By the poor
Against the powerless	By the powerless
Against activists	By activists
By the workplace	At or vs the workplace
By the police	Against the police
Against prisoners	By prisoners
Murder by rich	Murder by poor
Cap. Punish. vs poor people	Cap. Punish. vs rich Whites
Against terrorists	By terrorists
Against revolution	For revolution
By medical profession	Against medical profession
Against environment	By environment
By sports athletes	By sports spectators
In media	Against the media

[a] The state is defined as ruling elites and institutions, both inside and outside government.

For example, it would be scandalous for the public to learn that our violent crime policy does more to maintain than to reduce crime and is serving instead both ideological and social control functions for the powerful, as Jeffrey Reiman demonstrates. Nor would it be wise for the public to know that our violent drug policy has often done more to promote the drug trade than to stop it, especially when it has helped to promote other objectives such as our anticommunist crusades abroad or our ghetto-control crusades at home.

Taking the correct rhetorical approach to addressing social problems provides the building blocks for creating narratives that justify the use of violence. Typically they will be filled with distortions to achieve the desired effect but will be convincing enough to bestow legitimacy on the violent policy.

3. Using Violence

Despite all the efforts to justify their own violence, elites draw a sharp line between what they regard as legitimate state violence, or violence the state finds acceptable, and illegitimate violence directed at the state or which the state finds otherwise threatening or unacceptable. Certainly the state would not admit to most of the violence it views as legitimate; rather, it acknowledges only the violence it commits or endorses in response to the high-sounding, legitimate problems that we just examined.

For example, despite the democratic rhetoric, in practice officials accept violence committed against women but not by women and against immigrants, workers, activists, prisoners, foreigners, the poor, and people of color but not the violence committed by them. Officials accept violence by the police but not against them, by the rich but not against them, and by the medical profession but not against it. The state accepts violence caused by the workplace but not violence that invades the workplace. It accepts capital punishment against poor people but not against rich Whites. Officials accept government and corporate violence but not violence committed against these institutions.

C. War Model

As a matter of routine, we use violence to address our social problems. When that fails, we typically choose between two alternatives. On the one hand, we might give up, assuming the problem cannot be solved. As George Santayana once suggested: "Americans never solve any of their problems; they just amiably bid them good-bye." On the other hand, we might just as easily conclude that we were not using enough violence to address the problem. Sally Gearhart suggests how we trap ourselves into assuming that our only responses are either to be a victim or to strike back with more violence:

> ... objectification is the necessary, if not sufficient component of any violent act. Thinking of myself as separate from another entity makes it possible for me to "do to" that entity things I would not "do to" myself. But if I see all things as myself, or empathize with all other things, then to hurt them is to do damage to me ...
>
> ... Our world belongs to those who can objectify ... and if I want to protect myself from them I learn to objectify and fight back in self-defense. I seem bound to choose between being violent and being victimized. Or I live in a schizophrenic

existence in which my values are at war with my actions because I must keep a constant shield of protectiveness (objectification) intact over my real self, over my empathy or my identification with others; the longer I keep up the shield the thicker it gets and the less empathetic I am with those around me. So every second of protecting myself from violence makes me objectify more and ensures that I am more and more capable of doing violence myself. I am caught always in the violence–victim trap (Gearhart, 1982).

When we choose violence, as we usually do, we often declare war, both symbolically and tangibly. As former prosecutor Alice Vachss argues:

> A rapist is a single-minded, totally self-absorbed, sociopathic beast—a beast that cannot be tamed with 'understanding.' We need to stop shifting the responsibilities, to stop demanding that victims show "earnest resistance," to stop whining and start winning. And one of our strongest weapons must be fervent intoleration for collaboration in any form. We need to go to war (Vachss, 1993).

Apparently, only going to war will show how serious we are about the problem.

The linkages between our crime wars and our international wars are also revealing. We are a nation at war with ourselves: a civil war involving the forces of law enforcement against the forces of crime. We imagine this, however cynically, as a conflict between good and evil where only superior firepower will ensure our security and win the day. We imagine the same things when we attack Panama, Grenada, or Iraq. Thus, as Kay Harris suggests:

> ... the civil war in which we are engaged—the war on crime—is the domestic equivalent of the international war system. One has only to attend any budget hearing at which increased appropriations are being sought for war efforts—whether labeled as in defense against criminals, communists or other enemies—to realize that the rationales and the rhetoric are the same. The ideologies of deterrence and retaliation; the hierarchical, militaristic structures and institutions; the incessant demand for more and greater weaponry, technology, and fighting forces; the sense of urgency and willingness to sacrifice other important interests to the cause; the tendency to dehumanize and objectify those defined as foes; and the belief

in coercive force as the most effective means of obtaining security ...

People concerned with international peace need to recognize that supporting the "war on crime" is supporting the very establishment, ideology, structures, and morality against which they have been struggling ... (Harris, 1991).

To perpetuate the war model of solving problems, officials coopt the vehicles of peace for violent purposes. We noted earlier the cooptation of language, brought to its full absurdity and Orwellian dimensions in George Bush's claim—when describing his foreign policy—that "I want to win the peace war" and Norman Schwartzkopf's comment, when responding to the Bosnian fighting, that "I am violently opposed to the atrocities." But it is also a matter of coopting institutions. During the 1980s the U.S. used the Arms Control and Disarmament Agency as a forum for promoting weapons. In the early 1990s, the U.S. has coopted the United Nations—purportedly born to promote world peace—to instead allow the U.S. to assume its unchallenged role as the world's policeforce, and to justify its continuing military conquests.

Guns and other weapons figure prominently in the war model. Just as we resist any real gun control at home, we also shun any real arms control abroad. Arms, we are told, are allowed, even encouraged, to protect us from our enemies, yet actually they expose us to more not less danger. Weapons escalate the violence we claim we are trying to protect ourselves from internationally. And in the U.S., public health studies have shown that our guns are more likely to be used against us, or result in violent "accidents." Nevertheless, we persist, figuring we can use more violence than the "enemy," and thus win out.

Even when we "win" (usually superficially) any particular war, we know little about how to win the peace. If we were ever to really win a war on crime, wouldn't the prisoners of that war soon be the enemies in future wars? And although we "won" the Gulf War, with an awesome display of violence, what have we really won in peacetime?

V. The Impact of Violent Solutions

Having described how problems are defined and how violent solutions are legitimized, how well has violence worked to solve our problems? The answer is mixed. Violence has failed to solve our legitimate problems: those that affect the broader society. But violence has succeeded in solving some of our illegitimate problems; that is, violence has helped elites fend off challenges to their power and resources. Arguably that, and not any serious concern about solving legitimate problems, is primarily why violence is used in the first place.

A. Failures

Violence has failed to solve our legitimate social problems. There are many apparent reasons for this: Emma Goldman once claimed that "it is organized violence on top which creates individual violence on the bottom." Rather than inhibit violence by others, official violence instead provides a model that legitimizes such behavior. Violence hardly seems appropriate to address the problem of the violence that results when we willingly provide the instruments for such behavior to others, such as when we arm foreign dictators like Saddam Hussein. Violence provides a poor solution to problems, such as terrorism, which were generated by violence in the first place.

We should avoid violence for moral reasons. But violence is also inefficient, ineffective, even counterproductive. It not only fails to solve problems such as crime and foreign threats, it intensifies them. It promotes resentments if not hatreds, stimulates new problems, and invites retaliation in kind. Even though violence itself is becoming increasingly more highly organized, its use reflects a dysfunctional and disorganized society. Violence is a substitute for the kind of honest policy, resolve, organization, and social change required to solve most social problems.

Arguably, violence purposely avoids solving problems, perhaps because those practicing violence have other, ulterior motives. Some may want to use violence to deal with crime even though they know it will not work: this may be because they are more interested in punishing certain groups than in really reducing crime. As Carol Nagy Jacklin puts it, "On the one hand, we seem to deplore [the problem of] violence but, on the other, we are not stopping it in the ways we know it needs to be stopped."

More specifically, violence has been counterproductive in solving the problem of crime. The violence of imprisonment has only increased the violence prisoners commit in our overcrowded prisons, whose population has at least doubled since the mid-1980s, and then in society when they are released, sometimes prematurely, because of that very overcrowding. According to this author, imprisonment helps officials, not victims, who may not be so intent (as we assume they are) on revenge anyway. The war model of crime control applies military concepts (such as viewing criminals as the enemy) and solutions (such as violent punishment) to social, political, and economic problems. It contradicts the offender's need not for violence but rather for restoration and resocialization.

Our crime policy, like our foreign policy, was founded on violence. Coercive force has been legitimized to protect what we assume to be a just and humane system when actually it is violence being used to protect violence. It is force being used against people, like Rodney King, who are demonized as being inhuman. Conventional crime programs such as Crime Stoppers, Neighborhood Watches, McGruff and even the Guardian Angels adopt a violent worldview based on paramilitarization and a fortress mentality. Crime control policy adopts the language, ideology, and methods of war and then coopts the public as the foot soldiers in battle. Preventing crime becomes a holy crusade, like the Christian Crusades, and just as violent. The violence of crime control is a substitute for social progress that could more effectively solve crime and other social problems.

Even as a response to crimes against women, where some believe we impose our weakest punishments, greater violence is not the answer. The biggest detriment to enforcement against crimes such as sexual assault comes not from the weakness of our laws against rape and not from judicial lenience but rather from the discouragement victims receive from police and prosecutors. Actually the conviction and punishment rate is as high for sexual assaults as for other violent crimes. Most feminist criminologists agree that, even with more convictions, the violence of imprisonment would be ineffective. As Macmillan and Klein have argued:

If all men who had ever raped were incarcerated tomorrow, rape would continue outside as well as inside prisons. Incarceration does not change the societal attitudes that promote rape. In a society that deals with symptoms rather than causes of problems, prisons make perfect sense. Confronting the causes of rape would threaten the basic structure of society ... Prison is vindictive—it is not concerned with change but with punishment. And its real social function is similar to that of rape—it acts as a buffer, as an oppressive institution where a few scapegoats pay for the ills of society (Macmillan and Klein, 1974).

Just as we lose our repeated wars on crime, so too do our wars on drugs routinely fail. For all the violence they entail, the results have been feeble, if not counterproductive. Drugs continue flowing into the country, drug abuse remains extensive, and civil liberties have all but disappeared. Double standards of enforcement have promoted injustice and racism. Criminalizing drugs has manufactured criminals and promoted the social violence that is the price of taking risks in the high-stakes drug world. Unnecessary new crimes of violence are committed for resources to buy drugs at state-generated, artificially high prices. We are worse off each time we launch these wars.

Likewise, using violence against our "enemies" has been counterproductive. Many of our so-called enemies are not our enemies at all. Shouldn't African Americans and Native Americans be embraced rather than scorned after all the victimization they have endured through the centuries? Shouldn't peace activists, who oppose our society's illegitimate violence, be applauded rather than persecuted? Shouldn't we recognize that rather than our enemies, those who come from different races and ethnicities and genders have far more in common with us than not: we would all benefit by reforming our classist, racist, and sexist society.

Rather than blaming impoverished immigrants, why not examine the violent U.S. domestic and foreign policies that have forced their flood into the country. As for foreign enemies, isn't our national security threatened far more by not having enough educated people than by not having enough weapons and far more by threats to our natural environment than to the international political environment?

As for dealing with our real enemies, violence has been ineffective and inappropriate. According to Myriam Miedzian, we pursue violent national security policies that tend to make us *less* rather than more secure. Violence employed to suppress those who want to pursue their own political and economic systems returns against us many times multiplied in the form of revolutionary insurrections. Pushing weapons to maintain the war system inevitably generates new enemies that must be violently crushed, giving the defeated even more reason to violently retaliate some time down the road: our violence has generated widespread hatred of the U.S. in places such as Asia, Latin America, and the Middle East.

If we took a cost–benefit analysis of our violence in Central America, we would see the blood and misery of causing hundreds of thousands of deaths; millions of refugees; and unknown numbers of people tortured, raped, and starved. In exchange we have created resentment among millions of our Southern neighbors and a mockery of real democracy among the Central American governments. The U.S. is militarily strong but politically weak. We can kill but not persuade: our violence will never win the hearts and minds of others.

As for the problem of domestic poverty, our violent crackdowns on the "irresponsibility" of the poor has not reduced poverty. Instead, it has helped increase and institutionalize poverty. Rather than social policy addressing poverty's causes, punishment is our policy: a rejuvenated social Darwinism in which pain and further sacrifice are the cures. But the pain is administered unequally, with children, women, the powerless, and people of color the disproportionate victims.

The workplace has become an ad hoc battlefield for a "war of haves and have-nots." But rather than promoting the social change and full employment that would prevent disgruntled workers from returning to their workplace to do violence, instead only better protective strategies are proposed. No need to address the sources of this violence, when we can line up new violence to try to repel it.

Similarly, we ignore the causes of poverty abroad. The violence of "austerity" or military intervention is easier than promoting real development. Yet with that violence, the rich keep getting richer and the poor keep getting poorer. The violence of "structural adjustment" produces a net drain of resources from the "have-nots" of the developing world to the "haves" of the developed world and from the destitute to the already rich in the poor nations.

We may be more successful using violence to solve some of our other problems, such as controlling women and children and maintaining high profits for the few. But here we are using violence to solve illegitimate problems whose solution does not help the masses; indeed, they make most people's lives worse.

B. Successes

With these kinds of failures, why would we continue to use violence to try to solve our problems? First, although the quick fix of violence will not solve legitimate social problems, people are reluctant to accept the real social change our problems require. Thus, instead of challenging the use of violence, they often support it. Second, the few in power have little incentive to solve our legitimate problems: not solving those problems allows them to justify the continued use of violence, although for quite different ends. Violence also lets the elite few solve illegitimate problems that threaten their position and resources. Most violence in the U.S. is used to keep power, not to solve problems, no matter how high-sounding the rhetoric.

For example, violence does nothing to reduce crime; in fact, it helps maintain crime, targeting "common" criminals, diverting people's attention from much greater social harms, and enforcing the laws against the have-nots, who most threaten mainstream social relations. In other words, as Jeffrey Reiman shows, violence promotes the real goal of social control, not the secondary objective of crime control. Likewise, violent drug policies do nothing to curb illicit drug use; rather they help promote it. But those same policies have provided elites a cover for worldwide anticommunist crusades, for raising illegal foreign aid, for justifying military interventions, and for rationalizing the domestic social control of the nation's ghettoes, as Jonathan Marshall demonstrates.

The violence of antipoverty programs does not reduce poverty. But it does help control the unruly masses, it does fuel economic gains for the few, it does generate a "reserve army of unemployed" to help suppress wages and labor agitation, and it does promote—abroad—a model of development that helps the U.S. more than poor nations. Violence does not eliminate our enemies; arguably it creates more enemies. But it does provide at least short-term benefits for the few. It checks dissidents, blocks real democracy, assassinates unruly domestic and foreign leaders, controls foreign enemies, and rationalizes the profits and armaments of the military–industrial complex. And violence generated between races, ethnicities, and genders over artificially scarce resources diverts people's attention toward scapegoats rather than toward their real enemies: those few who monopolize the nation's power and resources.

Besides these legitimate problems, which have been slighted to pursue other motives, violence is also used—often successfully—to solve several illegitimate problems. Violence does keep children in line, training many of them to be pliant cogs in the domestic and world economic systems, even though that violence sometimes resurfaces when some of those children become adults and commit their own violence. Violence does maintain patriarchy, controlling and degrading women, keeping them subordinate and subservient to preserve male power and resources. And violence does maintain a favorable business climate at home and abroad, ensuring profits for the few at the expense of the many. It also maintains the war system as a source of those profits.

C. Micro–Macro Linkages

Whether a failure or a success, violence predominates. In an environment so saturated by violence, a relationship between the violence occurring in different realms no doubt exists. Among the linkages, it is difficult to distinguish cause and effect. Does our violence abroad, for example, help promote violence at home, is it vice versa, or both? Yet despite that cloud, increasingly we see that the linkages exist: violence on the micro and macro levels is connected.

We know that intrafamilial violence against women and children results, in part, from the broader society's *laissez faire* attitude toward the household. We know that family violence is, in part, responsible for subsequent violence committed by children who were previously abused. We know that the tolerated victimization of women in the home has undermined women's full protection under the norms of international human rights law and enforcement. We know that the violence of wife-beating escalates simultaneously with the structural violence of increasing unemployment. We know there are linkages between the violence of poverty and teenage violence in the U.S.

We know that "war" is the model we use universally to address our problems, whether at home or abroad. We can increasingly see the connections between the battering of children (and others) in the U.S. and the battering of foreigners (such as Central Americans) abroad. The two kinds of violence have similar natures, sources, processes, justifications, and vocabularies. When we typically treat foreigners as people who must be disciplined like our unruly children, we can understand the connection between militarism and corporal punishment.

Even governments acknowledge the micro–macro linkages. Some U.S. cities, for example, now offer tickets to professional football games to people who surrender their guns. One (admittedly more lethal) form of violence is being exchanged for another: state governments obviously know there is a connection. Internationally, another government—the United Nations—has acknowledged the linkage between criminal violence and state violence in passing its Declaration on the Victims of Crime and Abuses of Power. Not surprisingly, the U.S. opposed it.

D. Social Disintegration

Surely other linkages will keep emerging. As they do, we will see them comprising a seamless web of violence. But aside from these concrete results, what does our use of violence say about our society? This violence questions our social values. It suggests our growing powerlessness and lack of control. As Harold Pepinsky argues, it forebodes decline, even disintegration.

Former U.S. Supreme Court Justice Felix Frankfurter once warned:

Loose talk about war against crime easily infuses the administration of justice with the psychology and morals of war ... The process of waging war, no matter how it is rationalized, is a process of moral disintegration.

Similarly, Walter Schafer has argued that: "The quality of a nation's civilization can be largely measured by the methods it uses in the enforcement of the criminal law." If so, then ours is a civilization in decline.

Our repertoire of options for addressing social problems has narrowed, leaving us with little more than a menu of violence to apply. Accordingly, our use of violence has grown since the late 1970s: as official violence has grown, so too has public violence. We have more prisons and more corporal and capital punishment. We hit and punish our children more. We have more gang violence and hate violence. Violence permeates our homes. Crime has invaded new communities.

Our violence is increasingly gross, insensitive, and desperate. In response, society encourages violence (even when it breaks the law) as a means of resolving conflict and fighting back. Ironically, as Lillian Rubin shows, Bernhard Goetz's vigilante violence was applauded because the criminal process was viewed as too lenient. In fact, the process had failed because it was too harsh, too violent.

When societies are fragmented, alienated, and disintegrating, they use more violence—even if they have other means—to maintain order and solve problems. Societies impose social control by using either ideology, the law, or violence. According to Alan Wolfe, sophisticated or developed societies like the U.S. rely more on the former than the latter. When a once sophisticated society begins to decline, however, violence increasingly supplants ideology and the law. While in the 1970s the U.S. had been moving away from the "iron fist" toward the "velvet glove" for controlling society, that process has reversed. Even worse, we seem increasingly addicted to violence, gripped in a downward spiral, capped by a politics of denial about our desperate situation.

Internationally, the U.S. has lost considerable moral power (given its support of repression), political power (given its unpopular views in the United Nations), and economic power (given the competition of Europe and Japan). But the U.S. maintains its dominance and has regained its leadership of the United Nations through its undisputed military power. Yet despite appearances, militarism is often the last gasp of power for dying empires. Our obsessive rallying around the flag belies fundamental weaknesses and insecurities. Militarism blocks the search for ways to rejuvenate our society, such as the military-to-civilian conversion we need so desperately to rescue our economy.

Despite the warning signs, the U.S. system will no doubt continue its violence for some time to come. Under the "new world order," we will continue careening around the world like a rogue elephant in a china shop. Thanks to our military aggressiveness in the 1980s, capped by the Gulf War, the U.S. has now overcome the Vietnam syndrome of the 1970s and stands ready to unleash more lethal violence around the world. The absence of the Cold War has led only to a search for new military targets: drug lords in Latin America, communist holdouts in Cuba and Korea, regional conflicts in the Middle East and Eastern Europe, and even hunger in Africa.

Our relentless use of violence betrays our national purpose and our moral and intellectual culture. No crime, no matter how grotesque, is too great to fit into our system of intellectual self-defense which labels all our violence as simply a reflection of our good intentions.

VI. More Peaceful Solutions

We are a "culture of violent solutions." But violence will not solve our problems; violence is itself a problem and the root of most of our other social problems. There are alternatives to violence for addressing public problems. We should consider them not merely in principle (for moral reasons) but also for pragmatic reasons: unlike violent solutions, peaceful and nonviolent alternatives actually work.

But we should have no illusions about adopting more peaceful solutions to social problems. Pursuing them requires significant social change and a forceful political challenge to those who now benefit from our culture of violence. We have too long acquiesced to our leaders' justification of violence. We must decide whether we want the "new world order" of escalating U.S. violence or an "alternative world order" of peace and progress.

Also See the Following Articles

INSTITUTIONALIZATION OF VIOLENCE • STRUCTURAL VIOLENCE

Bibliography

Barak, G. (Ed.) (1991). *Crimes by the capitalist state.* Albany, NY: State University of New York Press.

Barry, K. (1984). *Female sexual slavery.* New York: New York University Press.

Chomsky, N. (1988). *The culture of terrorism.* Boston: South End Press.

Derber, C. (1992). *Money, murder and the American dream: Wilding from wall street to main street.* Boston: Faber and Faber.

Elias, R. (1986). *The politics of victimization.* New York: Oxford University Press.

Elias, R. (1993). *Victims still.* Newbury Park, CA: Sage.

Elias, R., & Turpin, J. (Eds.) (1994). *Rethinking peace.* Boulder, CO: Lynne Rienner.

Galliher, J. F. (1991). The Willie Horton fact, faith and commonsense theory of crime. In H. Pepinsky & R. Quinney (Eds.), *Criminology as peacemaking.* Bloomington, IN: Indiana University Press.

Gearhart, S. M. (1982). The future—If there is one—is female. In P. McAllister (Ed.), *Reweaving the web of life: Feminism and nonviolence.* Philadelphia: New Society Publishers.

Harris, M. K. (1991). Moving into the new milennium: Toward a feminist vision of justice. In H. Pepinsky & R. Quinney (Eds.), *Criminology as peacemaking.* Bloomington, IN: Indiana University Press.

Herman, E. (1982). *The real terror network.* Boston: South End Press.

Lappe, F. M. (1986). *Aid as obstacle.* San Francisco: Institute for Food & Development Policy.

Lusane, C. (1991). *Pipe dream blues.* Boston: South End Press.

Macmillan, J., & Klein, F. (1974). *Feminist alliance against rape newsletter* (September–October).

Marshall, J. (1991). *Drug wars.* Forestville, CA: Cohan and Cohen.

Miedzian, M. (1992). *Boys will be boys.* New York: Doubleday.

Parenti, M. (1991). *Democracy for the few.* New York: St. Martin's Press.

Pepinsky, H., & Quinney, R. (Eds.) (1991). *Criminology as peacemaking.* Bloomington, IN: Indiana University Press.

Piven, F. F., & Cloward, R. (1982). *The new class war.* New York: Pantheon.

Quinney, R., & Wildeman, J. (1991). *The problem of crime: A peace & social justice perspective.* Mountain View, CA: Mayfield.

Reiman, J. (1988). *The rich get richer and the poor get prison.* New York: Wiley.

Rubin, L. (1986). *Quiet rage.* New York: Farrar Straus & Giroux.

Turpin, J., & Kurtz, L. (Eds.) (1996). *The web of violence.* Urbana, IL: University of Illinois Press.

Vachss, A. (1993). *Sex crimes.* New York: Random House.

Wolfe, A. (1978). *The seamy side of democracy.* New York: Longman.

Violence Prediction

Ira Heilveil

UCLA School of Medicine

GLOSSARY

Low Base Rate The infrequent occurrence of a behavior. When a behavior occurs infrequently, it is generally difficult to predict accurately.

Outcome Studies Research into the extent to which a particular methodology or treatment has been effective.

Prediction The likelihood of someone committing a specific act in the future.

Predictor Variables Those variables that common sense, prior research, or experience would indicate might account for or predict future behavior.

Simulation Studies Research that substitutes descriptions or simulations for the actual events being studied.

Statistical vs. Clinical Prediction Statistical (or actuarial) prediction uses data that are converted into formulas in order to make predictions, while clinical prediction relies on subjective, individual judgement based on experience.

I. Introduction

The prediction of violent or dangerous behavior is one of the most important and controversial topics in the fields of psychology, sociology, criminology, and the law. In each of these arenas, people are called upon to advise and make decisions about the likelihood of a particular person or group of people to commit violent acts in the future. The consequences of these decisions can be grave and often involve striking a careful balance between the needs and rights of those whose future violent behavior is in question and the need and rights of a society to be protected from egregious violent behavior.

The actual prediction of violent behavior existed long before academicians began studying it. The human need to predict future events is tied to survival itself; knowing what plants might be toxic to consume, what animals threaten our existence, and what environmental conditions might ensue keeps human and other species from extinction. The ability to predict the next monsoon will determine the time spent on creating adequate shelter, while the ability to predict landslides might determine where that shelter is placed. In a seminal review of the history of prediction in the legal arena, noted American attorney Alan Dershowitz wrote that "the preventive confinement of dangerous persons who cannot be convicted of past criminality but who are thought likely to cause serious injury in the future has always been practiced, to some degree, by every society in history regardless of the jurisprudential rhetoric employed ... it is likely that some forms of preventive confinement will continue to be practiced by every society" (1974, p. 57).

According to Foucault, the search for predictors of violent behavior had its roots in the latter part of the 19th century, when it became apparent that the penal system could not achieve its ideal of reforming the criminal. The criminal justice system shifted from a focus on legal responsibility and rehabilitation to the protection of society. As this shift occurred, the demand on mental health professions in the judicial system increased. In the past, professionals were called upon primarily to explain criminal behavior and recommend treatment; they were now being asked for predictions as well. By the early 20th century, the concept of a "dangerous being" had become established. Clinicians in the criminal justice system answered to the demands of judicial priorities instead of responding to a more realistic or scientific appraisal of just what they could reasonably offer. As scientific evidence mounted that accurate predictions of violence were difficult if not impossible to make with much greater probability than chance, clinicians became stuck between the "rock," of growing judicial demands to help identify and predict dangerous behavior, and the "hard place" of their own knowledge of their limitations in doing so.

The prediction of dangerous or violent behavior can be viewed as a public health issue. While public health and general socioeconomic advances are reducing the prevalence of communicable diseases, the relative importance of accidents and violence is increasing. Certain types of violent behavior seem to be increasing on a worldwide scale. The importance of violent events in causing morbidity and mortality is growing.

Similarly, the links between health systems and criminal justice systems are expanding in many countries. This might be due to attempts to reduce the number of people in mental hospitals who are there because of their violent behavior or to attempts to improve treatment modalities for dangerous offenders incarcerated in the criminal justice system. There are also human rights concerns because the conclusions of predictions of violence often lead to decisions concerning the liberty of those whose future behavior is in question. The balance between the public's interests in being protected and the individual's liberty is a central issue in public health policy.

Shah (1978) has enumerated 15 points in the legal system in which the prediction of violent behavior are often made. They include:

1. Decisions concerning bail or release on personal recognizance for people accused of crimes, including a determination of the level of bail.
2. Decisions concerning the waiver to adult courts of juveniles charged with serious crimes.
3. Sentencing decisions following criminal convictions, including decisions about release on conditions of probation.
4. Decisions pertaining to work-release and furlough programs for incarcerated offenders.
5. Parole and other conditional release decisions for offenders.
6. Decisions pertaining to the commitment and release of "sexual psychopaths," "sexually dangerous persons," "defective delinquents," and the like.
7. Determinations of dangerousness for all indicted felony defendants found incompetent to stand trial (in some American states).
8. Decisions pertaining to the special handling of and transfer to special prisons of offenders who are disruptive in regular prisons.
9. Commitment of drug addicts (because of fears that they will commit violent crimes to support their drug habit).
10. Decisions concerning the emergency and long-term involuntary commitment of mentally ill people who may be considered a "danger to self or others."
11. Decisions concerning the "conditional" and "unconditional" release of involuntarily confined mental patients.
12. Decisions concerning the hospitalization (on grounds of continuing mental disorder and dangerousness) of persons acquitted by reason of insanity.
13. Decisions regarding the transfer to security hospitals of mental patients found to be too difficult or dangerous to be handled in regular civil mental hospitals.
14. Decisions concerning the invocations of special legal proceedings or sentencing provision for "habitual" and "dangerous" offenders.
15. Decisions concerning the likelihood of continued dangerousness of persons convicted of capital crimes as a basis for determining the use of the death sentence.

The predicting of violent behavior stretches well beyond the confines of the legal system itself into nearly every niche of society. Parents of schoolchildren must be able to predict whether their or someone else's child may become violent at any particular moment and pose a threat to their own child or someone else's at home or in the schoolyard.

Lovers, engaged in the ordinary conflicts of life, must be able to predict when an argument or disagreement might spiral into physical violence.

Shopkeepers must be able to predict when a particular character entering their shop might engage in violent or threatening crime.

Airlines must work hard to predict when a passenger might be inclined to exhibit or engage in potentially violent or disruptive behavior.

Barkeepers must predict when intoxicated customers have reached a point where they may become dangerous to themselves or to others.

Mental health practitioners must predict when their own clients or patients might put themselves or others at harm and act in a way to protect their patients and society.

Family members and individuals must seek to predict when a troubled teenager, who might have just broken off a relationship, or a parent or grandparent, who might have lost a job or suffered a debilitating illness or loss of a loved one, might take his or her own life.

The prediction of violent behavior in groups, such as the prediction of riots, mob behavior, and war, is beyond the scope of this article.

II. CURRENT CONTROVERSIES

The most central controversy in the area of violence prediction has remained whether it is even possible to predict violent behavior with any meaningful or practical accuracy. Monahan mentions two other controversies; these include the controversy over whether violence prediction, even if possible, should be undertaken at all in that doing so would violate the civil liberties of those whose violent behavior is being predicted. And finally, there are those who believe that even if accurate prediction were possible without violating the liberties of those accused, psychologists and psychiatrists who are often engaged in making these predictions should refuse to do so because it is a form of social control that is at variance with their role as helping professionals.

A. Is Accurate Prediction
Empirically Possible?

The question of whether it is possible to predict violent behavior has consumed researchers and theoreticians now since the 1950s. Initially excited over their ability to use sophisticated tools and their clinical acumen, psychologists and psychiatrists were often eager to offer their expertise to the legal system. Likewise, excited over the possibility of bringing scientific respectability to what was often perceived as an overly subjective assessment, judges and magistrates were eager to entertain the advice of these mental health professionals. In fact, for a period of time, the legal system became so enamored with such "expert witnesses" that it became commonplace for many judicial decisions to be made primarily on the weight of such testimony.

As actual predictions were put to empirical tests, however, it became clear that prediction of violent behavior based on empirical analyses left much to be desired. Methodological and statistical problems have plagued the research into violence prediction.

B. Methodological Concerns

The ideal form of research into violence prediction would be an experimental design in which subjects are randomly assigned to different conditions, something is done to manipulate a situation, and a violent outcome would be measured. Immediately it becomes clear that such an experiment would likely be unethical. It also is impractical in that the population of interest is often incarcerated to begin with, and such designs often call for decisions about when and how to release prisoners, decisions that are essentially out of the hands of those conducting research. The decision-making process concerning who is released and under what conditions is replete with multiple considerations and unrepresentative samples, making empirical research in a traditional sense difficult at best.

An alternative to a true experimental design is to begin with a set of "predictor variables"—those variables that common sense, prior research, or clinical experience would indicate might accurately account for or predict violent behavior. Subjects would be followed over a length of time, and these predictor variables would then be measured against specific outcome or "criterion variables"—measures of whether violent behavior actually occurred. This is the model that has often been used, but it too has limitations. It is often difficult, for example, to track enough people to measure their behavior at some specified time in the future. Similarly, the decision about what criterion measures to include is often a problem; if you use subsequent arrests as a criterion for whether someone is violent, how do you account for those who might have been violent who have managed to avoid being arrested? If you use the self-report of your subjects, how do you know they are telling you the truth, especially given a lack of trust of authority figures who might report them? If you use probation or parole officers' reports, you frequently come up against an overloaded caseload in which accurate reporting is unlikely for a variety of reasons.

C. Statistical Concerns

The primary statistical obstacle to predicting violent behavior is the problem of low base rates. The term "low base rate" is used to describe any event that occurs infrequently in the general population. Statistically, any event that occurs infrequently is difficult to predict. If you knew, for example, that the chances of something happening were 1 in 100, you could accurately predict that it was not going to occur. All you would have to do is predict each time that it was not going to happen, and you would be right about 99% of the time. But if you predicted that the event was going to happen, you would be wrong almost all the time. In the United States, violent behavior is estimated to occur at the rate of roughly 200 incidents per 100,000 persons per year. That is equivalent to a .2% base rate per year. If you were to observe any individual for a year and predict that that person would not be violent, you would be right about 99.8% of the time. On the other hand, if you were to attempt to predict which individual would actually engage in violence, and when, the odds would be stacked against you.

In practical terms, this means that any time anyone is engaged in attempting to predict a low-frequency behavior such as violence, especially if they are attempting to predict violent behavior in the general population, they are likely going to be incorrect more often than they are going to be correct. In order to increase the probability of predicting violence accurately, researchers must limit the scope of their investigations; yet the more limitations that are placed on the prediction process, the less generalizable the results are to the larger population.

D. Does Prediction Violate Civil Liberties?

In the early 1960s, the iconoclastic psychiatrist Thomas Szasz took the position that preventive or therapeutic measures based on a prediction of future violence violates a fundamental right in a democratic society, the right that one should only be punished for past acts and not detained for some act that has yet to occur.

Further, the label that an individual is "dangerous" becomes a stigma leading certain segments of society, particularly the so-called mentally ill, to be treated unjustly. Szasz eloquently points out that

> Drunken drivers are dangerous both to themselves and to others. They injure and kill more people than, for example, persons with paranoid delusions of persecution. Yet, people labeled 'paranoid' are readily committable, while drunken drivers are not. Some types of dangerous behavior are even rewarded. Race car drivers, trapeze artists, and astronauts receive admiration and applause. In contrast, the poly-surgical addict and the would-be suicide receive nothing but contempt and aggression. Indeed, the latter type of dangerousness is considered a good cause for commitment. Thus, it is not dangerousness in general that is at issue here, but rather the manner in which one is dangerous (Szasz, 1963, p. 46).

The issue of confinement based on the prediction of future violent behavior begs a fundamental question. Supposing, for example, that one is able to predict with great accuracy whether someone is likely to commit a crime in the future. Is it justifiable, in a democratic society, to incarcerate or continue to confine someone based on a prediction of violent behavior, no matter how accurate, if the person has yet to commit the crime?

There is also a basic contention over legal strategies that do not rely on statistical measures of prediction or even on the advice of a mental health professional on the likelihood of an individual to hurt others in the future. For example, there exists in many legal jurisdictions the "just desserts" model of imprisonment in which predictive considerations are replaced with explicitly normative and moral judgements of relative harm and the culpability of the offender for having committed a crime in the first place.

E. Should Mental Health Professionals Engage in Prediction?

Following the realization that empirically based approaches to prediction often turn out to be a fruitless endeavor, many psychologists and psychiatrists have turned the tables on their critics by not only agreeing with them, but by taking their criticism one step further. Not only is it impossible to predict future behavior accurately, many mental health practitioners argue, but it is also an activity that mental health practitioners should not engage in to begin with. To engage in the predictive enterprise is to become an agent of social control rather than an advocate for the emotional health of your patient. The controversy played itself out in the classic case of Tarasoff vs. the Board of Regents in which a psychotherapist, bound by law and ethics to protect the confidentiality of his clients, did not notify the intended victim that she might be the target of his client's violent behavior. The courts ruled against the psychotherapist, stating in essence that confidentiality ends "where the public peril begins." Psychologists and other mental health professionals are now by law in most states required to inform any potential victim of danger, even if it entails breaking the confidentiality of their patients. Interestingly, no similar law currently exists requiring attorneys to break the confidence of their clients if their clients' violent inclinations are revealed in the confines of their offices.

Many mental health professionals continue to reject the role of social control agent, instead claiming that their historical role and training has always been to improve the mental health of their patient and not of society. Others, by embracing the legal mandates that place them in the role of protecting society, define their roles more broadly. These professionals often argue that mental health practitioners are, whether they admit it or not, engaged in a process that is inextricable from societal norms and expectations.

III. FACTORS RELATING TO VIOLENT BEHAVIOR

The classic formula of the sociologist Kurt Lewin is often referred to whenever the prediction of future behavior is at stake. According to Lewin, an individual's behavior cannot be fully understood in isolation, and at any particular moment a person's behavior is a function of the interaction between individual personality factors and the environment in which the person is functioning. Reduced to a formula in which b = behavior, p = person, and e = environment, it can be stated that $b = f(p,e)$, or behavior is a function of the person and the environment. If one is to predict future behavior, it is necessary therefore to look both at personality or individual factors and situational factors and, ultimately, the combination of both.

A. Personality Factors

The psychologist Hans Toch developed a typology of the "violence-prone" person based on extensive research. His classification scheme consists of 10 catego-

ries, each one describing an approach to interpersonal situations that is likely to result in violent behavior. The 10 categories can be classified into two larger groups, one group that encompasses *self-preserving strategies*, in which violence is used to bolster one's ego, and the second group which includes *approaches that dehumanize others*. In this latter category, other people are viewed only as a means to end. The self-preserving strategies include:

Rep-defending: people are allocated by public acclaim a role that encompasses the exercise of aggressive violence.

Norm-enforcing: people are on a self-assigned mission involving the use of violence on behalf of norms that the violent person sees as universal rules of conduct.

Self-image compensating: various types of compensatory relationships between low self-esteem and violence which comprise the subcategories of *self-image defending* (a tendency to use aggression as a form of retribution against people who the violent person feels have cast aspersions on his self-image) and *self-image promotion*, in which violence is used as a demonstration of worth by people whose self-definition places emphasis on toughness and status.

Self-defending: A tendency to perceive others as sources of physical danger which requires neutralization.

Pressure-removing: A propensity to explode in situations with which one is unable to deal.

In the general category of approaches that dehumanize others, Toch lists:

Bullying: an orientation in which pleasure is obtained from the exercise of violence and terror against people uniquely susceptible to it.

Exploitation: a persistent effort to manipulate others into becoming unwilling tools for one's pleasure and convenience with violence used when other people react against this effort.

Catharting: a tendency to use violence to discharge accumulated internal pressure or in response to recurrent feelings or moods.

A similar typology was proposed by Megargee, who developed a framework in which personality factors thought to predict violence could be divided into three groups. These included *motivation, inhibition,* and *habit. Motivation* included the categories of "angry aggression," in which someone wishes to hurt another and is reinforced by the victim's suffering, and "instrumental aggression," in which aggressive behavior is a means to some other end and is reinforced or driven by other motives, such as murdering a taxi cab driver in order to steal his money. Megargee points out that these two motives can easily be mixed, such as when a husband strikes a spouse in order to stop being taunted by her while simultaneously seeking a means to express his anger and punish her.

Inhibition includes the notion that there are certain internal restraints or taboos against violence. Violence occurs when motivation exceeds inhibition. Inhibitions can be lowered by drugs and can vary depending on the target of violence and the method used. For example, someone may be less likely to be violent toward their boss than their child and more inhibited in using a gun than throwing a punch. In some cases, people who resort to violence exhibit a mix of high levels of inhibition and high levels of violence; this usually occurs as a result of suppressed aggressive feelings mounted over time to override even high levels of inhibition.

Megargee uses the concept of *habit strength* to describe those individuals who are consistently reinforced for committing violent acts in the past. If, for example, someone consistently is successful at obtaining drugs as a result of violent burglaries or at obtaining sex through violent means, their "habit strength" for committing violent acts will increase.

Recently, Bowlby's attachment theory has been utilized in an effort to understand the origins of violent behavior. Bowlby's theory stressed the propensity of people to make strong emotional bonds to others and the fact that disturbances in early forms of attachment should predict later emotional difficulties. Greenberg et al. found that a high percentage of preschool boys who presented at a clinic exhibiting disruptive behavior disorders showed an insecure-controlling pattern of attachment relative to a comparison sample of boys who did not demonstrate aggressive behavior patterns. Reporting on the results of two studies, Holtzworth-Munroe et al. found that relative to nonviolent husbands, violent men were more insecure, preoccupied, and disorganized in their attachment; they were anxious about being abandoned and uncomfortable with closeness. They were typically more dependent on and preoccupied with their wives and exhibited more jealousy and less trust in their marriages than men who were nonviolent.

Similar results were reported by Dutton et al., who found that men who were entering marital violence treatment programs scored significantly higher levels of fearfulness and preoccupation with attachment, as well as higher levels of jealousy. Nonviolent men by comparison scored significantly higher than violent men on a scale measuring secure attachment. Similarly, Murphy et al. reported that violent men scored considerably higher than comparison groups on measures of dependency, while Barnett et al. did not find differences between violent and nonviolent men on measures of desperate love or jealousy.

B. Mental Illness and Violence

Mental illness, which is often popularly thought to contribute to violent behavior, does not seem to be related to violence unless the mentally ill person also has had a previous history of violent behavior. Interestingly, when demographic variables are controlled for, prisoners do not have a higher incidence of mental illness than the general population, and, in fact, mental patients who do not have a record of violent arrest are apparently less violent than the general population. While there has been considerable research on the area of whether or what kind of mental illness might be predictive of violence, results are often contradictory. Klassen and O'Connor identified a group of mental patients, 60% of whom were arrested or committed violent acts within 6 months after release. Other studies have shown that demographic factors usually associated with violence in "normal" offender populations were not associated with violence among mentally disordered groups, while still other studies have reported a relationship between rates of violent offending and specific clinical diagnoses. Monahan, in summarizing these studies, noted that the most striking characteristic of these studies is that the research is so inconsistent. He states:

> For every study that reports increases in predictive accuracy, there is another that finds clinical risk assessments no better than chance. Studies concluding that the relationship between demographic factors and violence among the mentally disordered is weak can be placed side by side with equal numbers of investigations finding strong correlations (p. 251).

C. Environmental or Situational Factors

Violent behavior, whether toward oneself or others, cannot occur in a vacuum. Even an act of violence toward oneself usually requires access to the means to do harm: pills, weapons, or a bridge high enough from which to leap. Further, a suicide is often sparked by an external situation, such as a breakup with a boyfriend or girlfriend, the loss of a job, or the loss of one's health.

Concerning violence toward others, Megargee lists immediate situational factors, such as the availability of weapons, the presence of witnesses, and the behavior of the victim, as well as more pervasive situational factors. These include the level of frustration in the environment or the social approval of violence in a particular subculture. It is more likely, for example, that a violent act will be committed in a drinking establishment in which the usual clientele are violence prone and the standard method for resolving conflicts is through fighting.

Although not necessarily considered either "situational" or "personality" variables, other variables studied when attempting to predict violence include demographic ones, such as socioeconomic class, age, history of violent behavior, gender, race, the use of alcohol and other drugs, employment history, and criminal history.

D. Interactions

Ultimately, violent behavior is best understood, explained, and predicted when considering the interaction between individual variables and environmental variables. A linear equation, in which the degree or presence of a certain number of personality indicators is simply added to the degree and nature of certain environmental variables, will not necessarily predict violent behavior successfully. There are certain people, for example, who may have certain violence-prone characteristics who will be violent only in a specific setting, while others with similar violence-prone characteristics will be violent only in a different setting. Predictions of violence are most likely to succeed when knowledge of a specific individual is matched with knowledge of the specific environmental factors that contribute to violence uniquely for that individual.

Similarly, individual variables and situational variables are not truly independent. People do not usually find themselves in situations randomly, but instead seek out or are drawn into them. One can easily say, for example, that as long as a violent drug addict is paroled into a part of town where drugs are unavailable, that person is not likely to commit a violent act. Clearly, however, that drug addict is likely to return to the part of town where drugs are available. A prior gang member may move to a town where no gang exists, but create one out of an individual need.

There is also an overlap among all predictor variables of violence, including an overlap between personality and situational variables. As Monahan (1981) points out,

One cannot simply add together all the predictor variables to arrive at a total 'score' for violence potential, since the items are not independent.... Assume being poor is related to committing violence and being unemployed is also related to committing violence. If one were asked to predict violence in a person who is both poor and unemployed, one could not add the 'plus' for being poor with the 'plus' for being unemployed, since being poor and being unemployed are *themselves correlated*. More unemployed than employed people are poor, and vice versa. One would want to know how much *new* (i.e., independent) information is conveyed by knowing one factor when we already know the other (p. 53).

E. Childhood and Family Factors

Much has been written about the influence of childhood factors on the future development of violent behavior. These writings are often speculative, and the research that has been conducted is by necessity often ex post facto, an examination of adults who have been violent and extrapolating chronologically backward. Recently, along with the quality of early attachment mentioned above, issues such as the nature and quality of parental supervision, parental criminality, and alcoholism have been examined as contributing factors. Justice et al. undertook a comprehensive survey of 750 professionals, 1000 clinical case histories, and over 1500 references to violence in the psychological and psychiatric literature in order to assess the most frequently cited childhood predictors of adult dangerous behavior. The results were distilled into four "early warning signs" of future violence: fighting, temper tantrums, school problems, and an inability to get along with others. Although little sound research support exists to support the notion, the triad of enuresis, pyromania, and cruelty to animals is often cited as a key predictor of future violence. After concluding discussions with a large number of clinicians, Goldstein found that the following factors were used by the bulk of them in predicting adult violence: a childhood history of maternal deprivation, poor identification with fathers, or both, along with enuresis, fire-setting, violence toward animals, and brutalization by one or both parents.

Taking a more rigorous approach, Lefkowitz et al. followed over 400 boys and girls in Columbia County, New York from ages 8 to 19. Using a variety of measures, such as peer ratings, self-report, a personality test, and parent ratings, they found that the best predictor of aggression at age 19 was aggressive behavior exhibited at age 8. Other statistically significant variables for predicting later aggression included father's upward social mobility, low identification of the child with his or her parents, and a preference among boys for watching television programs with more violent content.

In 1979, McCord reported on a 30-year follow-up of over 200 Massachusetts boys who were first evaluated between 1939 and 1945. She found that the boys who experienced a lack of supervision, had mothers who lacked self-confidence, and were exposed to parental aggression at early ages were more likely to be convicted for personal crimes.

One of the most comprehensive studies on childhood predictors of adult violence was conducted by Wolfgang et al. They followed nearly 10,000 boys who lived in Philadelphia in 1945 from the age of 10 through the age of 18. They found that the variables of race and socioeconomic status were most strongly correlated with reported delinquent behavior. Those children who became chronic offenders, with five or more violations of the law, had lower IQ scores, more residential moves, and lower levels of education than other offenders, even when accounting for race and socioeconomic status. In 1977, Wolfgang updated his study, reporting on the same children, now adults, up to age 30. He found that the likelihood of multiple arrests increased in direct proportion to the number of prior arrests.

The extensive use of illicit drugs and alcohol is correlated with violent behavior among adolescents and adults. Chaiken and Chaiken observed that those violent offenders among prison and jail inmates often had a history of very heavy drug use both as adolescents and adults.

Another factor consistently related to violent behavior among youth is involvement with delinquent peers, often including gang involvement. There are some who believe, however, that peer delinquency may be less important for violent youths and that aggressive youth are frequently rejected by peers.

As is the case with adults, one pattern that emerges from the literature on childhood predictors of later violence is that the best predictor of violent behavior is a history of previous violence. In a large study of youthful parolees, serious offenders were often rearrested for the same type of crime—such as robbery, fraud, or assault, for which they were originally incarcerated. Those youths with a prior arrest for a violent offense were rearrested more often for a violent offense than were those without prior violent histories. If you were arrested for a violent crime, but had no prior arrests, you were least likely to be rearrested. Similarly, a large scale study conducted by Lattimore et al. of nearly 2000 people paroled by the California Youth Authority in 1981 and 1982 indicated that prior criminal history and socioeconomic variables are powerful predictors of both the timing and the charge of first arrest following parole. In their study, rearrest for violent behavior was significantly influenced by prior arrests for violence and evidence of family violence and parental criminality. Prior gang involvement and use of alcohol and other illicit drugs had little predictive ability for violent recidivism in their sample.

Weiner's analysis of the Philadelphia sample mentioned above, who were studied in 1945 and 1958, revealed that a prior arrest record for a violent crime was only slightly predictive of future arrests for a violent crime. Weiner also failed to identify any particular risk variables that were consistently associated with risks for rearrests for violent crimes.

Other factors show some promise in predicting the future violent behavior of youthful offenders. Age of onset of offending is one variable that has been shown to correlate with serious delinquency. The onset of violent offending usually occurs in late adolescence or early adulthood, usually following the onset of nonviolent offending. Likewise, juvenile careers that include violent offenses usually begin earlier than nonviolent careers. Therefore, if a young person has an established career of offending, an earlier age of onset would most likely predict rearrest for violence.

Monahan points out that the main conclusion to be drawn from research into childhood predictors of adult violence is that the distinction between childhood and adulthood is not a meaningful distinction when it comes to predicting violence. It appears in examining this research that the same factors influence the occurrence of future violent acts regardless of age. Age is an important factor primarily because the earlier someone begins a career of violence, the longer and more extensive that history may be.

F. Child and Spousal Abuse

A substantial body of literature exists that examines characteristics that contribute to or maintain physical violence within the family, either against children or against spouses. Factors that lead to the abuse of children often include parental psychological characteristics, the quality of the marital relationship, parent–child interactional factors, and family stress factors. The risk of child abuse increases when the following factors are present: a history of violence within the family, socioeconomic problems, the presence of someone else in the home, whether the parent in the home is single or separated, whether the mother is under 21 years of age, and a history of drug abuse.

While controversial, certain characteristics of abused children themselves appear to contribute to violence perpetrated against them. These include temperamental factors, significant and unrelenting behavior problems, and perinatal events. Typically, when these factors are present, stress within the family is augmented, and the increased stress level might contribute to an outbreak of violence.

The area of violence toward spouses is extremely complex and inextricable from its cultural context. A thorough examination of spousal violence in its cultural context is beyond the scope of this article, although it is clear that spousal violence in all cultures must be examined at many different levels in order to be understood. Explanations which might eventually lead to the prediction of violent behavior toward a spouse range from the social legitimation of such behavior, to individual factors such as personality and biology, and nearly everything in between. Clearly, the individual factors mentioned above, an examination of cultural and political factors, and situational variables are important in assessing and understanding the likelihood of future spousal violence. Situational events, such as the discovery of infidelity, or the actual or perceived threat of one spouse leaving a relationship, clearly contribute to the likelihood of violent behavior, especially when violence in the relationship has occurred repeatedly in the past.

IV. OUTCOME STUDIES

Once the factors that are deemed relevant to the prediction of violence are isolated, the question arises as to whether professionals are able to successfully predict violent behavior based on clinical observations or tests. These outcome studies apply a series of criteria in order to classify people into "dangerous" or "not dangerous" categories and then follow these people in order to see the percentage of those classifications that are correct.

Monahan summarized and evaluated five major studies reported in the United States during the 1970s. They included studies by Kozol et al., who conducted a 10-year study of nearly 600 men convicted primarily of violent sex crimes; studies by Steadman and Cocozza in which nearly 1000 people designated as "some of the most dangerous mental patients in the state (of New York)" were released from hospitals for the criminally insane to considerably less restrictive civil mental hospitals; a study by Cocozza and Steadman of over 250 felony defendants in New York State; a study by Stead-

man of over 400 patients at an institution in Maryland; and a study by Thornberry and Jacoby of over 400 patients released in Pennsylvania.

With the use of rigorous psychological testing, extensive case histories, and interview data, many of these researchers were able to successfully classify people into categories based on whether they are likely to be dangerous in the future. Unfortunately, when attempting to predict future violent acts, there was a consistent tendency to overpredict. Monahan concluded that

psychiatrists and psychologists are accurate in no more than one out of three predictions of violent behavior over a several-year period among institutionalized populations that had both committed violence in the past (and thus had high base rates for it) and who were diagnosed as mentally ill (p. 77).

Menzies, Jackson and Glasberg evaluated nearly 700 cases at an assessment center in Toronto between 1978 and 1979 and found that those individuals with a history of violence, previous incarcerations, and facing a charge of violence at the time of assessment were more likely than others to receive high ratings of dangerousness. Yet beyond these considerations, Menzies et al. concluded that decisions made about these patients appeared not to have depended on their individual or personality characteristics, but instead on the general belief systems of the clinicians doing the rating. Pfafflin reached a similar conclusion based on a study he conducted in Hamburg, Germany. There, he examined over 900 files of sexual offenders and found that biases and error entered into the selection process by which people became subject to court-ordered opinion. Pfafflin believed that the majority of cases were judged unfairly due to manifest prejudices, insinuation, circular reasoning, or moralizing.

In California, Konecni, Mulcahy, and Ebbeson coded information on mentally disordered sex offenders (MDSOs) and non-MDSOs from reports by psychiatrists and probation officers as well as psychiatric diagnosis and judges' decision. Results of their study indicated that once a negative impression is created based on prior offenses, it continues through the system with its own momentum. Negative probation officers' reports led to a greater classification of people as MDSOs by psychiatrists, and the psychiatrist's negative reports clearly influenced judges' decisions.

Pfohl studied decision-making processes of interdisciplinary teams assigned to the task of reclassifying 700 criminally insane patients in Ohio in 1974. Pfohl found that the professional members of the team often reconstructed reality by selectively choosing "facts" from file data in order to provide "valid" grounds for confirming an a priori decision. The team appeared to form their impressions primarily by reading the patient's record prior to their interview. Once they conducted their interview, they focused on evidence to support their previously determined hypotheses.

Cooper and Werner examined the ability of experienced psychologists and case managers within the Federal Bureau of Prisons to predict violence during the first 6 months of incarceration of 33 male inmates. They found that the professionals were individually unable to accurately predict which inmates would subsequently become violent, but that they achieved greater accuracy when their decisions were pooled to form a composite score. Even then, predictive accuracy was low. The authors believe that this was likely due to the professionals' failure to accurately weight the information available to them at intake.

Janofsky, Spears, and Neubauer assessed the ability of two psychiatrists to predict whether 47 newly admitted inpatients to a psychiatric treatment unit would commit battery or demonstrate threatening or suicidal behavior within 7 days. The psychiatrists were not able to accurately predict battery or suicidal behavior, but were somewhat effective in predicting threatening behavior. These authors also found that the presence of assaultive or threatening behavior at the time of admission, hallucinations, and a discharge diagnosis of mania were useful in predicting battery, while a discharge diagnosis of mania was useful for predicting threatening behavior.

Several "simulation studies," in which differing information is given to raters in order to understand how they make their judgments, provide some interesting clues to other factors that enter into clinician's judgements of dangerousness. Jackson gave psychiatrists, judges, and lay people different amounts and types of information about a hypothetical defendant; i.e., a positive or negative social history, a positive or negative psychiatric assessment, and a description of a serious or minor offense. The three groups of raters were asked to decide on a number of relevant issues, including a prediction of potential dangerousness. Jackson found that the less attractive, intelligent, and less likely to be chosen as a friend, the more dangerous the person was judged. Another study by Jackson attempted to adjust for the fact that case summaries or scenarios were poor representations of how people are actually asked to make decisions. Instead, he utilized videotaped interviews and had psychiatrists, attorneys, social workers, and lay people decide on key issues such as dangerousness. The raters were trained extensively to determine fitness to stand trial from the tapes but were given only short definitions to consider when asked about other issues, including dangerousness.

Jackson found that with structured training, interrater reliabilities were high, indicating that when given specific criteria, people from different perspectives do agree. But when given only short descriptions, as was the case for dangerousness, differences among groups emerged. In particular, judges found individuals more criminally responsible than did psychiatrists or lay people, while psychiatrists predicted a greater likelihood of future offense than did judges or lay people. These findings suggest that with specific criteria and training, the predictive enterprise could be made more reliable (but not necessarily more valid.)

A. Psychological Tests

In a prison, McGuire combined a variety of psychological test data, including the MMPI and the Q-sort, into a computer-analyzed formula in order to predict dangerous behavior. In so doing, she was able to accurately predict violence approximately one-third of the time. She states that while this approach is simpler than the labor-intensive approach of conducting interviews and reviewing case histories, the success rate does not warrant its use in making decisions about individuals. It's also questionable whether her results would generalize to a nonprison setting.

Sloore attempted to use the MMPI to predict dangerous behavior and found that no single scale was able to reliably predict violence, although several scales in combination can be helpful when combined with other information about an individual in making predictions.

Megargee reviewed the use of psychological tests to predict violence in the decades prior and concluded that no single test could accurately predict violent behavior. While many clinicians utilize a variety of tests and combine their results with other factors in order to make as accurate a prediction as possible, no single combination of test results has resulted in a highly successful approach to accurate prediction.

B. Neurological Tests

Attempts to account for violent behavior have at times focused on neurophysiological causes. These have included hypotheses about brain dysfunction resulting from a disease (such as cancer), head injury, or toxic substances. While some researchers noted high levels of lead, cadmium, and copper in some violent prisoners, Gottschalk et al. were unable to replicate these findings. They did, however, find high levels of manganese in prison versus control groups, which they were unable to account for in the prison environment. In one study by Tancredi and Volkow, positron emission tomography (PET) studies revealed that defects in brain functioning are related to particular behavior and that specific defects may be at the basis of an individual's dyscontrolled violent behavior. Jarvie, although he investigated only six cases, found frontal lobe region lesions acting as disinhibitors of social controls, while Grafman, Vance and Weingartner reported personality changes following frontal lobe damage. Results of these and other studies are inconclusive in that no one has successfully used this information to accurately predict acts of future violence. Most of this research is ex post facto in nature and merely correlates certain neurophysiological characteristics with people who have already been violent. In any case, it is likely that whatever neurophysiological correlates of violent behavior may emerge as predictive, whether they will manifest in a violent episode will no doubt be determined by the interaction of these factors with environmental and personality factors.

V. STATISTICAL APPROACHES TO PREDICTION

Statistical approaches to the prediction of violent behavior differ from clinical approaches in two aspects: different kinds of data are used, and the methods used to predict differ as well. Data are often more basic, consisting of facts that can be easily converted to numbers or either–or situations. Statistical prediction use data such as demographics, ethnicity, or scores on test results, whereas clinical prediction utilizes more abstract data, often requiring an element of subjective judgement. In statistical approaches, data are converted into predictions about future violence by means of automatic, mechanical rules and are applied equally to all cases; in clinical prediction, rules are often bent or ignored if in the judgement of one of the raters the complexities of the particular individual case warrants doing so. Essentially, clinical prediction requires a certain amount of intuitive judgement, whereas statistical prediction relies on rigid, hard-and-fast rules that apply to all cases across the board.

Generally speaking, statistical prediction— sometimes referred to as actuarial prediction, yields better results than the more subjective methods. For

that reason, many researchers in violence prediction hold out continuing hope for the refinement of statistical or actuarial methods in improving the success of the predictive enterprise.

In Monahan's review of statistical methods conducted prior to 1980, he concluded that actuarial research yielded a wide variety of results, ranging from "substantially less accurate to substantially more accurate than the studies of clinical prediction, depending upon what criterion of violence was used" (p. 127). These included important studies by Wenk, Robison, and Smith, Murphy, Wolfgang, Petersilia et al., Hindelang, Pritchard, Cook, Hamparian et al., Guze, and Diamond. Monahan found that the most significant predictive factors emerging from statistical-based approaches include past violence, age, sex, race, socioeconomic status, and opiate or alcohol abuse. Less predictive, although still correlated with violent behavior, is estimated IQ, residential mobility, and marital status.

These studies share many methodological problems that must be overcome if the state of knowledge in this area is to advance significantly. In general, these include impoverished predictor variables (violence is multifaceted, so research must consider a wide array of predictors), weak criterion variables (often violent behavior goes undetected by virtue of the methodologies of these studies), constricted validation samples (validation samples vary considerably, and validation of results must consider the wide array of conditions under which patients are released in order to accurately assess the accuracy of prediction efforts), and, finally, unsynchronized research efforts (lack of communication among researchers leading to idiosyncratic and fragmented results).

Even though statistical approaches hold out many advantages over clinical methods, especially in the ease in which prediction can be carried out, there are disadvantages to this method as well. Statistical approaches cannot take into consideration rare events, for example. If a statistical procedure predicts someone is likely to commit a violent act and that person then becomes crippled as a result of a car accident, the likelihood of the person committing a violent act is decreased significantly. Statistical approaches are also more suited to long-term predictions in that statistical procedures have yet to be developed to deal with emergency situations. In other words, no statistical procedure has yet to be developed that addresses a situation in which an individual is brought to an emergency room after being injured in a violent altercation and the person has no history of previous incarceration, arrests, or violent behavior and is not charged for a crime.

VI. HOW VIOLENCE IS PREDICTED IN ACTUAL PRACTICE

This article has so far concerned itself with whether violence can be predicted, controversies surrounding the prediction of violence, and research attempts to predict violence. Regardless of these issues, the fact remains that people *do* predict violence. One line of inquiry has been into how violence actually is predicted by those who do it on a regular basis.

An international collaborative study conducted under the aegis of the World Health Organization sought to clarify how dangerousness is assessed in Brazil, Denmark, Egypt, Swaziland, Switzerland, and Thailand. The authors concluded that although the criterion of dangerousness was widespread in both the arenas of mental health and law in these countries, the criterion for dangerousness is nearly always ill defined. In all the countries participating in the study, dangerousness was assiduously assessed, but with little scientific or actuarial bases for the assessments. They also concluded that the level of agreement reached on assessment of dangerousness was generally poor and that the level of agreement among psychiatrists was no better than among nonpsychiatrists.

Mental health professionals engaged in examining patients and predicting their violent behavior at Lima State Hospital for the Criminally Insane in Ohio were observed by Pfohl. Past violent behavior was the primary factor in judging patients to be violent in the future. The professionals assigned greater weight to more recent violent behavior as well as to those patients who had entrenched paranoid or "dangerous delusions" even when those patients did not have a violent history.

Monahan summarizes the observations of Dix in which Dix observed the staff meetings at a California state hospital where decisions were made about which mental patients should be released to the community because of their predicted level of dangerousness. Dix isolated eight factors that contributed to the staff's predictions:

1. Acceptance of guilt and personal responsibility for the offense.
2. Development of the ability to articulate resolution of stress-producing situations.
3. Presence of fantasies about dangerous acts.
4. Degree of violent behavior during hospitalization.
5. Duration of hospitalization.
6. Achievement of maximum benefit from hospitalization.
7. Change in community circumstances.
8. Seriousness of the anticipated conduct.

In one study, Yesavage et al. found that psychiatrists used patients' level of hostility as a predictor of future violence, along with suspiciousness, tension, excitement, and prior assaultive acts.

One important issue in understanding how people predict violence is the extent to which those who predict violence actually do what they say they do. In other words, one person might state that she considers history of violent behavior as a paramount consideration but in actuality might use other criteria, such as the race or gender of the subject. In one study, Konecni, Mulcahy, and Ebbeson found that psychiatrists gave multiple reasons for determining whether someone was a mentally disordered sex offender (a label that requires an attribution of future dangerousness), while in fact only one factor alone predicted both the psychiatrist's and the court's determination. That factor was whether the subject had previously been convicted for sexual offenses.

Similarly, Cocozza and Steadman found that of all the reasons psychiatrists gave for predicting violence, only 11% of those reasons correlated with the one factor they actually did use to primarily determine future violence—the type of crime with which the person was charged.

The prediction of violence calls for a careful balance between individual rights and the protection of society at large. Clearly, the rise in violent crime makes such efforts even more important, yet the tools for predicting violence remain unsatisfying. While there are ongoing efforts underway to resolve the methodological difficulties inherent in such an endeavor, the factors that contribute to predicting whether someone will be violent in a specific situation are complex. The current state of knowledge indicates that the best predictor of violent behavior remains whether someone has been violent in the past. This fact alone, however, can never predict when someone will be violent for the first time, nor does it say much about the situations or events that will spark a violent episode for a particular person. Other factors, such as the use of alcohol and other drugs, certain personality characteristics, age, gender, and socioeconomic status, have been shown to relate to dangerous behavior, but these factors do little to enhance the ability to predict violence in a clear and consistent way. Essentially, the prediction of violence is best accomplished when the particular personality characteristics of an individual are combined with knowledge of what environmental factors typically incite that individual to a violent episode. The more thoroughly an evaluator investigates the multiple determinants of violence for a particular individual, along with considering the specific circumstances under which that person is likely to become violent, the more likely the evaluator is to be successful in predicting violent behavior.

Also See the Following Articles

AGGRESSION, PSYCHOLOGY OF • BIOCHEMICAL FACTORS • CRIMINAL BEHAVIOR, THEORIES OF • MENTAL ILLNESS • PUNISHMENT OF CRIMINALS

Bibliography

Barnett, O. W., Martinez, T. E., & Bluestein, B. W. (1995). Jealousy and romantic attachment in maritally violent and nonviolent men. *Journal of Interpersonal Violence, 10,* 473–486.

Cooper, R., & Werner, P. (1990). Predicting violence in newly admitted inmates: A Lens model analysis of staff decision making. *Criminal Justice and Behavior, 17,* 431–447.

Davis, S. (1991). An overview: Are mentally ill people really more dangerous? *Social Work, 36,* 174–180.

Dershowitz, A. (1974). The origins of preventive confinement in Anglo-American law. Part I. The English experience. *University of Cincinnati Law Review, 43,* 1–60.

Dutton, D. G., Saunders, K., Starzomski, A., & Bartholomew, K. (1994). Intimacy-anger and insecure attachment as precursors of abuse in intimate relationships. *Journal of Applied Social Psychology, 24,* 1367–1386.

Fagan, J. (1990). Intoxication and aggression. In M. Tonry & J. Q. Wilson (Eds.), *Crime and justice: A review of research: Drugs and crime* (Vol. 13, pp. 241–320). Chicago: University of Chicago Press.

Farrington, D. P., Loeber, D. S., Elliott, J. D., Hawkins, J. D., Kandel, D. B., Klein, M. W., McCord, J., Rowe, D. C., & Tremblay, R. E. (1990). Advancing knowledge about the onset of violent crime. In B. B. Lahey & A. E. Kazdin (Eds.), *Advances in clinical child psychology* (Vol. 13, pp. 283–342). New York: Plenum.

Greenberg, M. T., Speltz, M. L., DeKlyen, M., & Endriga, M. C. (1992). Attachment security in preschoolers with and without externalizing behavior problems: A replication. *Development and Psychopathology, 3,* 413–430.

Gottschalk, L. A., Rebello, T., Buschbaum, M. S., Tucker, H. G., & Hodges, E. L. (1991). Abnormalities in hair trace elements as indicators of aberrant behavior. *Comprehensive Psychiatry, 32,* 229–237.

Harding, T., & Adserballe, H. (1983). Assessments of dangerousness: Observations in six countries. *International Journal of Law and Psychiatry, 6,* 391–398.

Holtzworth-Munroe, A., Stuart, G. L., & Hutchinson, G. (1997). Violent versus nonviolent husbands: Differences in attachment patterns, dependency, and jealousy. *Journal of Family Psychology, 11,* 314–331.

Janovsky, J. S., Spears, S., & Neubauer, D. N. (1988). Psychiatrists' accuracy in predicting violent behavior on an inpatient unit. *Hospital and Community Psychiatry, 39,* 1090–1094.

Klassen, D., & O'Connor, W. (1990). Assessing the risk of violence in released mental patients: A cross-validation study. *Psychological Assessment: A Journal of Consulting and Clinical Psychology, 1,* 75–81.

Monahan, J. (1988). Risk assessment of violence among the mentally disordered: Generating useful knowledge. *International Journal of Law and Psychiatry, 11,* 249–257.

Monahan, J. (1992). Mental disorder and violent behavior: Perceptions and evidence. *American Psychologist, 47,* 511–521.

Monahan, J., & Steadman, H. (Eds.) (1994). *Violence and mental disorder: Developments in risk assessment.* Chicago: University of Chicago Press.

Mulvey, E. P., & Lidz, C. W. (1993). Measuring patient violence in dangerousness research. *Law and Human Behavior, 17,* 277–288.

Murphy, C. M., Meyer, S., & O'Leary, K. D. (1994). Dependency characteristics of partner assaultive men. *Journal of Abnormal Psychology, 103,* 729–733.

Otto, R. (1992). Prediction of dangerous behavior: A review and analysis of "second-generation" research. *Forensic Reports, 5.* 103–134.

Palermo, G., Liska, J., Palermo, M., & Dal Forno, G. (1991). On the predictability of violent behavior: Considerations and guidelines. *Journal of Forensic Sciences, 36,* 1435–1444.

Pollock, N. (1990). Accounting for predictions of dangerousness. *International Journal of Law and Psychiatry, 13,* 207–215.

Shah, S. (1978). Dangerousness: A paradigm for exploring some issues in law and psychology. *American Psychologist, 33,* 224–238.

Sloore, H. (1988). Use of the MMPI in the prediction of dangerous behavior. *Acta Psychiatrica Belgica, 88,* 42–51.

Toch, H. (1992). *Violent men: An inquiry into the psychology of violence.* Washington, DC: American Psychological Association.

Violence to Children, Definition and Prevention of

John Kydd

Child VIP—Child Violence Identification and Prevention Project

GLOSSARY

Abuse Any specific proscribed trauma to children as defined by a legal authority.

Caregiver(s), primary Anyone who is responsible for providing for the daily care, nurturing, food, and housing for a child.

Child An individual who has not reached the age of 18.

Household A group of individuals who function as a unit socially and economically and who share cooking facilities.

Maltreatment An action or failure to act which results in physical or emotional trauma or the threat of such trauma (see also Trauma).

Neighborhood A geographical area which recognizes itself as a community.

Primary Prevention Programs addressed to the general population that have been designed to reduce the occurrence of the particular form of violence.

Secondary Prevention Programs designed to deter violence from specific groups at-risk for same.

Tertiary prevention Programs designed to address those children and families who have already been harmed by a form of violence and to reduce the consequences and prevent recurrence of same through treatment and rehabilitation (see also Treatment).

Short-Term Trauma Complete recovery within 6 months from an incident of violence.

Long-Term Trauma Impairment or delay with developmental, physical, or psychological sequelae resulting from any form of violence.

Treatment Techniques to prevent the recurrence of violence to a child and to reduce the harm resulting from the violence (see also Tertiary Prevention).

Violence Preventable trauma of human origin. This includes nonaccidental trauma that can be physically documented, trauma without physical signs, or threat of trauma including violation of one's legal rights.

Developmental Violence Failure to provide the child the necessary nutrition, love, care, education, culture, and play to realize its developmental capacity.

Economic Violence Poverty, homelessness, nonaffordable healthcare/daycare, and absence of work paying sufficently to adequately provide for self and family.

Environmental Violence Short- or long-term trauma

resulting from exposure to pollutants, teratogens, or other biohazards.

Structural Violence Trauma due to economic or governmental policy.

I. DEFINING VIOLENCE

Violence is like history; a concept immediate and millennial, local and universal, individual and societal. As a term it is as easy to misuse as it is difficult to define. Violence is at once *natural* and *innocent* (a *violent* storm, a *violent* volcanic eruption) and *unnatural* and *guilty* (a *violent* attack, a *violent* murder).

Violence is an exercise of power of which we do not approve. This exercise of power can be active (i.e., injury), passive (i.e., neglect or deprivation), intentional, or negligent. It is a creature of culture and time. Many acts considered violent today were not considered violent in the past (e.g., child abuse, exploitative child labor). The reverse is also true (e.g., heresy and apostasy).

Violence is also contextual. *Peace* could be considered a reciprocal of *violence*; each being defined as the absence of the other. In this sense, peace-*making* and violence-*unmaking* (*prevention*) are synonymous. They are synonymous both in their goals and in their dependence upon what we define to be violent. Peace-*making* and violence *prevention* depend upon violence *definition*.

What we consider to be violent has changed with *who* we consider to be responsible. In many less-individualistic cultures, the responsibility for misdeeds is shared by the entire extended family. In the more individualistic Western European cultures, the responsibility for violence is more focused upon a "perpetrator." The United States takes this notion the furthest, in trying 13- and 14-year-olds as adults for capital offenses and other serious crimes. No Northern European countries do this, preferring to focus more upon prevention than upon "getting tough on crime." In this sense the responsibility of the individual alone for violence may increase in proportion to the degree of individualism supported by their culture.

This decline of communal or societal responsibility for violence is sometimes paralleled by the decline of church, temple, mosque, and God. Many diseases (e.g., Bubonic plague) and depravities that were considered acts (or influences) of God are now considered only the actions of microbes and humans.

Where responsibility for violence migrates away from the extended family, community, and the state, there is greater tolerance for economic violence (e.g., child poverty, homelessness, and absence of affordable health care or day care), community violence (e.g., unsafe physical and mass media environments), and developmental violence (i.e., failure to provide each child the necessary nutrition, love, care, education, culture, and play to realize their developmental capacity). Most squarely put, *denying childhood for any child is developmental violence.*

A. Metaphoric Definition

Since violence has so many dimensions and its domain changes with culture and context, any concise denotative definition is inadequate. A metaphoric or symbolic definition could capture more of it. For example, if violence were a single substance, it would be a hard substance capable of harming any surface. It would have to be durable, as the impact of violence creates scars that can endure for generations. It would have to be multifaceted, both to reflect the many dimensions of violence and to afford each culture its own unique combination of facets. If it were a gem it would be the "diamond of our disapproval." History reminds us that revenge, like diamonds, can be forever.

While viewing violence as a gem may be unsettling, an unsettling image can sometimes teach more than an acceptable one. For example, as a diamond is highly valued so too has been a society's capacity to inflict violence. Astonishing sums are spent on both diamonds and military defense. A nation's power is traditionally defined by military capacity (e.g., the power to inflict violence for defense or other military purposes) and we define as "superpowers" those few countries that are able to eradicate much of humanity.

To inflict violence demands the hardest of hard feelings; to endure violence creates the hardest of hard feelings. Some historians argue that one effort of civilized humanity for the past millennia has been building the capacity to inflict violence (e.g., smelting ever rarer metals for ever harder swords and shields and isolating ever more dangerous elements (or microbes) for ever more intimidating armaments.

B. Theologic Definition

"The diamond of our disapproval" is a symbolic secular definition that needs a theological counterpart. Christianity, unlike many Eastern religions, lacks a god that embodies violence (e.g., Kali, the creator/destroyer, in Hinduism). Where there is no god with the capacity of violence, violence can be perceived as being godless and, thereby, inhuman (or inherently evil). When violence is defined as being a godless evil, it is more difficult to admit and more likely to be denied. The shame and stigma of admitting godless behavior can be greater than the shame of denying it. To cope with this shame, violence will be practiced in a manner that is not defined as violence. The Crusades were quite violent (and the Christians more violent than the Islamists) and involved the slaughter of thousands of innocent people who happened to reside in the "Holy Land." The death and destruction wreaked upon them was recognized not as violence but as an attempt to rescue the "Holy Land" from the "infidel." The conquest (and near genocide) practiced against native peoples in the Americas and Australia was not recognized as violence, but as the exercise of "dominion" and "assimilation."

C. Defining the Shadow of Violence

The shadow of violence is, in the Jungian sense, those forms of violence we do not wish to define as violence. Young children compelled, for economic reasons, to live in grossly polluted and dangerous environments can suffer greater developmental harm than children of affluent families who were physically abused. Homeless children, with the added elements of undernutrition and lack of reasonable medical care, can suffer far greater harm. Just as the Church did not recognize the Crusades as sinful, our society creates (or allows) a large shadow where violence is practiced but not admitted. Children experience poverty as violence, yet we do not define as violent an economy that pays such low wages that two parents can work full-time and still not be above the poverty level. Parental unemployment or underemployment can be very traumatic to children, yet many economists argue that an unemployment rate of 6% and a low minimum wage are healthy for the economy. However, placing children in poverty due to parental unemployment or underemployment for a year creates a loss of the child's future economic productivity that is greater than paying his/her family sufficient benefits to be out of poverty for the same year.

A society that is able to provide day care, health care, and comprehensive education to children and yet fails to do so is practicing structural or developmental vio-

lence. Blaming parents for their poverty, unemployment, or underemployment does not remedy the developmental violence to their children.

Another facet of the shadow of violence is the deprivation of culture or sacredness. What a land developer sees as the "harvesting" a stand of older trees, the child (and their extended family) may experience as the destruction of a sacred grove that has been a sacred site of worship, ceremony, fasting, and initiation for centuries. When the child's identity includes access to ancestors, ancestral sites, and the spirits that reside with ancient trees, the loss of the same is not unlike the murder or abduction of significant family members. Maurice Eisenbruch (1994) notes from studies of Cambodian children that the forced relocation of children from their ancestral sites was more traumatic than being physically injured or wounded.

Thus, any definition of violence is necessarily multidimensional, involving traumas that are difficult to recognize as violent. The dimensions offered here are (1) the personal–communal and (2) the perceptual. The personal–communal continuum allows us to map "who" was traumatized.

Regarding the personal-communal continuum, a single act of violence may harm the body, leaving bruises, cuts, and scars (Fig. 1). The act can also create psychological harm. More damaging still are acts that violate the soul or spirit (in cultures where these are recognized to exist). On the other end of the continuum is communal harm. Violence to a child creates trauma to that child's family and community just as violence to the family can create trauma due to the fear of violence on the part of the child. It is important to note that many Western cultures assume that other cultures share (or should share) their commitment to individualism. Where well-being is defined individually, less attention is paid to the well-being of the family and community of a child. Likewise, individualistic cultures tend to define violence individually, failing to detect the subtle and perhaps more damaging traumas to the extended family and community (Fig. 1).

The perceptual continuum maps the epistemology of the trauma or "how" we know or perceive it (Fig. 2). Empirical perception is that which is physically verifiable in the present scientific sense. Rational per-

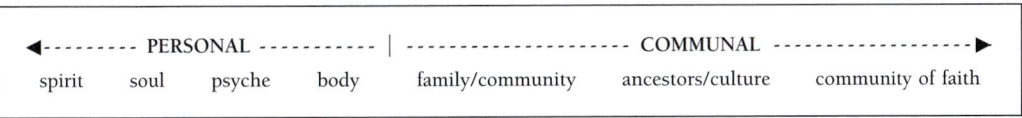

FIGURE 1   The personal-continuum.

MODE OF PERCEPTION

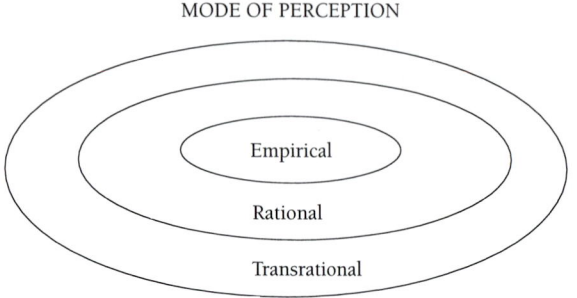

FIGURE 2 Map of perception.

ception includes but extends beyond the empirical to include moral and legal reasoning. Transrational perception includes and extends upon the others including intuitive and mystical perceptions of what is termed in the West to be "metaphysical." (Fig. 2) In a broader sense each of these is a type of evidence and a type of experience. The empirical is physical evidence physically experienced. The rational includes the physical and extends to psychological/emotional evidence which is so experienced. The transrational includes the former two and further includes metaphysical evidence that is intuitively, spiritually, or mystically experienced.

In application, the empirical covers all those traumas where we can find clear medical evidence. This covers all medically defined injuries. The *rational/sensate* includes a variety of categories where the harm or the cause is less physically clear. It includes those acts we consider wrong but for which we cannot prove medical harm. For example, we would find it unlawful for a distraught parent to hold an infant out the window threatening to drop it onto the street below or to hold a gun to the head of an infant threatening to kill it. The infant may not experience this as physical harm and will, due to its infancy, likely have no recall of the incident. Nevertheless, we uniformly define this as unlawful. In a different vein, a parent may be accused of sexual abuse for genital fondling of the child, who may not experience the fondling as anything other than neutral due to the child's young age. While the child would not find the experience harmful, with some uniformity we would find such touching to be unlawful.

D. Acceptable Violence

On the other hand, there are acts the child finds to be quite painful or harmful that are not defined as being violent. Different cultures find a number of actual harms to be "acceptable." Male genital circumcision is undeniably traumatic to the child but, for reasons of faith and culture, is tolerated. Female circumcision still occurs but is less tolerated. Spanking a child is traumatic but, for parent's "right to discipline," it is deemed acceptable. While there is clear evidence that poverty and homelessness can and do stunt the child's development, a number of affluent countries prefer to hold the parents responsible for the economic well-being of their children even though these countries could provide adequate housing, health care, and education at the governmental level.

Whereas faith-based cultures may choose to ignore certain acts of violence on religious grounds, many secular-based cultures choose to ignore state responsibility for violence on economic grounds. A double standard emerges: if the parents fail to feed the child, it may be deemed neglect but if the economy fails to provide employment at a wage sufficient to allow the parent to secure reasonable day care, health care, and lodging, there is no remedy to the trauma despite the fact that it can be quantified medically as being more detrimental to the child's long-term well-being than individual acts of physical violence by the parents. Poverty and homelessness are part of the larger category of "deprivation" traumas.

E. Deprivation as Violence

A child deprived of emotional nurturance, although well fed and cared for, can suffer long-term emotional impairment. Environmental deprivation concerns children compelled to live in highly dangerous environments and/or highly polluted environments. Aspirational deprivation includes children who may be quite well cared for, but who are set on a course of athletic stardom whereby they are forced to sacrifice their childhood to a sport (i.e., tennis) or to their parents' desire for a career (i.e., child actor/actress). The United Nations Convention on the Rights of the Child recognizes the above deprivations. It finds that each child has a right to the highest attainable standard of health; to a comprehensive education; to be spared violence, maltreatment, and other forms of trauma; and recognizes that each child has a right to some degree of leisure or "play" as a necessary part of his or her development. Perhaps most importantly, it recognizes within the child a right to "development" and thus any force, whether it be pollution, poverty, politics, or parental actions, that impair the child's physical, emotional, psychological, intellectual, cultural, or spiritual development is subject to sanction. In the broadest sense, violence to children may be defined as: failure by the parents and the state to provide a child's developmental needs.

Violence to a child's soul or spirit is more difficult to define, since the concepts of the same vary significantly by culture. However, in a general sense "soul" refers to the animating force or being of each individual. A violence toward one's soul can create soul sickness or even death. Children are often deemed to be more vulnerable to soul sickness than adults, just as they are more vulnerable to viruses and bacteria. As they mature they build stronger immune systems on both a physical and a metaphysical level. In this context, maintaining the health of a child's soul is a task both for parents and for ancestors of the child who have passed away. Traditional healers serve, in part, as go-betweens from the physical and metaphysical relatives and supporters to a child. In this context, the failure to support traditional forms of healing and the failure to honor worship and communion with ancestors undercuts that culture's capacity to provide for the metaphysical well-being of its children.

Soul may be defined as that metaphysical entity which resides within the body of the individual. Spirit is that which resides within the body of many individuals and is collectively experienced (i.e., the Holy Spirit, the Buddha, Allah, or the Creator). More often than not, spirit includes a community of faith. Violence to a community of faith (whether to the individual's access to spirit or to the community's access to worship) can have devastating effects on the participants, particularly to the children. Understanding these phenomena in Western cultures is largely being pioneered by parapsychology, whereas for indigenous cultures, excellent work is being done by medical anthropologists who are endeavoring to translate indigenous concepts of soul and spirit health and well-being into Western psychiatric terms.

F. Toward a Map of Violence

Just as a metaphor for violence (the diamond of our disapproval) can be helpful in aiding perception, so too can a visual map. This map should integrate the personal–communal continuum with the continuum of perception (Fig. 3).

The above image should be perceived as a series of concentric spheres. The inner sphere of bodily violence is subject to empirical perception. The next sphere includes violence to the psyche on the personal level and violence to family/community on the communal level. It may be perceived or proven by rational (including empirical) means. The next sphere includes the soul (on the personal level) and ancestor/culture (on the communal level). Here trauma can be perceived by empirical, rational, and transrational means. The last sphere consists of trauma to the spirit and trauma to the community of faith. Again, the mode of perception is transrational. This map of violence is also a map of peace-making. The absence of peace in one sphere can disturb the peace in others. Much of peace-making depends upon finding the underlying traumas, be they personal or communal.

G. Understanding Our Limited Knowledge of Violence

If violence were likened to pollution, then we may be at the early stages of the environmental movement. In the 1950s, it was scientifically absurd to suggest that DDT or other common insecticides could affect seabird eggs thousands of miles away. The focus then was on pollutants that were local and undeniable. Now, decades later, there is clear scientific evidence that many

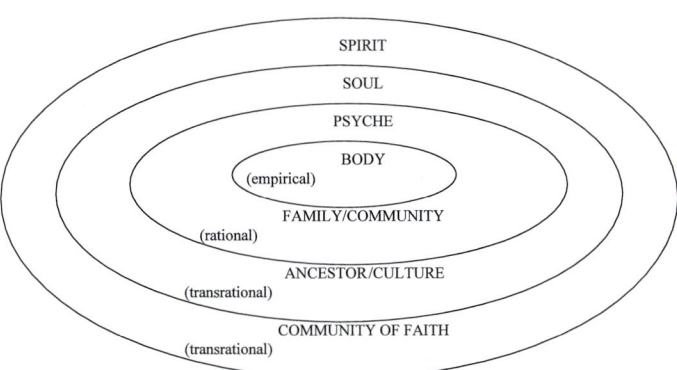

FIGURE 3. Map of perception including the mind–body continuum.

pollutants have global impact. Likewise, there is clear scientific evidence that local pollution can have long-term impact of a far greater severity than ever imagined. It is suggested that most violence against children, except for that which is local and obvious, goes largely undetected. We are just at the beginning of our capacity to detect the long-term effects of different types of violence. Certain acts of violence in one community can significantly raise the perception of fear and lack of safety in communities thousands of miles away. In this sense, violence can be seen as a psychic pollutant of considerable toxicity. We are just beginning to develop the technology to measure the toxicity, developmental impact, and recovery needed from exposure to violence. Just as, during the 1950s, commonly accepted methods of manufacturing seriously polluted part of the earth, today commonly accepted methods of entertainment (graphic mass media violence) may be seriously harming the psyches of those children watching it.

H. Standards of Definition for Violence to Adults and Children.

Much of what follows is an edited version of the Child Violence Identification and Prevention Protocols that were prepared for the United Nations Committee on the Rights of the Child and were endorsed by the Second World Congress on Children. These initial standards attempt, in the language of public health, to describe a taxonomy of trauma (maltreatment). They are, understandably, constantly changing. Those desiring further information (and updated information) should view the Protocols currently appearing at the Website: www.childvip.org.

These protocols also allow for a definition of violence toward adults by removing the standards that relate to the developmental stages of children. Focus upon children is necessary because they have less capacity to prevent violence to themselves and their communities and have a much greater potential of suffering harm long into the future than do their mature adult counterparts.

II. VIOLENCE TOWARD CHILDREN

A. Importance of Defining Violence toward Children

1. History of Harm

For a variety of reasons, children are the last major group in our society to be given access to their full civil rights. Though children are protected by criminal law from assault by strangers, they are not well protected from harm from family members and other forms of violence. Children are far more likely to be maimed, harmed, or killed by family members than by strangers. The child killed by a stranger is often considered a homicide, whereas if the child is killed by a parent, it is often considered a lesser crime than murder (i.e., infanticide). Infanticide, although almost universally illegal, is tolerated in many countries. Infanticide of illegitimate children was not uncommon in Western countries, such as the United Kingdom, through the 18th century (de Mause, 1991, as cited in *Innocenti,* 1997, page 5). An analysis of homicides in the United Kingdom from 1989 to 1991 involving victims under 18 years of age found that 60% of the children were killed by parents (*Innocenti,* 1997, page 5).

In a similar vein, many countries allow children to be physically beaten by a parent provided that the punishment is "reasonable." In stark contrast, no amount of beating is tolerated between parents in most Western developed countries. Children thus have less protection from acts of violence than adults. Family members, who have a special duty to protect them, are less likely to be punished for harming them. The first successful child abuse case in the United States was brought in the 1800s. Since there was no law preventing parental harm to a child, the case was brought under a prevention of cruelty to animals statute. Most of the legal protections of children prior to the 1900s were to prevent harm by strangers. These laws were often based upon protecting the productivity of that child as property of the father.

In ancient Rome, the act of "raising" a child was conditioned upon the father's acceptance of the child as being his. The mother would place the newborn at his feet and if the father accepted the child as his, he would raise (*tollere,* Latin "to raise") the child by lifting it up to his chest and embracing it. If the father refused to do so, this child's right to remain within the family was terminated. If another family could not be found to raise the child then the child would be left out in a public place. The practice was so common in ancient Greece and Rome that the term "alumni" was given to such children abandoned by their family and raised as foster children by others.

2. Family Violence Research

While there has been significant research on family violence, the degree of knowledge is quite disparate. An international literature review on violence in the family, consisting of over 1500 articles from 1985 to 1992 compiled by the UN, found that 79% of the articles about violence during their childhood often have recollections that are significantly influenced by the passage of time. The small amount of research that has been done with children indicates that violence is significantly underreported in official statistics. A 1994 survey of 16-year-olds in the United States found that the rate of rape was 500% greater than official figures, that 5% of the children reported being physically victimized (excluding physical punishment) in the prior year. Over 33% reported an attempted or actual physical victimization. Slightly under a third of those victimized in the previous year reported having suffered physical injuries as a result of the assault. (Finkelhor & Dziuba-Leatherman, 1994) The authors of the above study deplore the fragmented approach to researching violence upon children. They note: "in recent years there has been a great deal of public and media attention to victimized children, the concern has been largely fragmented. Professionals have focused on specific forms of victimization, such as child abuse, sexual abuse, hand gun violence, and kidnapping, mostly as separate problems. *But the fragmentation has inhibited a comprehensive perspective on the overall victimization of children.* Such comprehensive perspective would emphasize better the true toll of violent victimization. For example, one reality, not widely appreciated, because of the fragmentation, *is that children are far more prone to victimization than adults*" (UNICEF, 1997, p. 413, emphasis added).

Violence to children has only recently become an issue of public health. The "battered child syndrome" was first proposed in the 1960s. More recently there have been successful efforts to stop sex tourism (child prostitution), sexual abuse, and child pornography and to limit exploitative child labor. Good work is being done for children living in war zones such as Guatemala, Somalia, Uganda, South Africa, and the Balkans, particularly in comparing their struggle to children in high crime areas of inner cities in the United States.

A part of the comprehensive study of violence toward children should include child exposure to armed conflict, preventable poverty, environmental trauma, exploitation, homelessness, and other deprivation.

3. United Nations Recognition of Violence toward Children

The single greatest authority available for both understanding and preventing violence against children is the UN Convention of the Rights of the Child. This convention functions as a binding treaty upon countries that have ratified it. It was adopted by the United Nations General Assembly in 1989 and, as of November, 1997, had been ratified by 200 countries. It was ratified more rapidly than any other UN convention. Two countries have not ratified this convention; they are the United Arab Emirates and the United States of America. Any country ratifying the convention is considered to be a Participating State.

The Preamble of the convention declares that the child, by reason of his or her physical or mental immaturity, needs "special safeguards and care." Violence is most specifically raised in Article 19 and binds each Participating State to:

Take all appropriate legislative, administrative, social and educational measures to protect the child from all forms of physical or mental violence, injury or abuse, neglect or negligent treatment, maltreatment or exploitation including sexual abuse while in the care of parents(s) legal guardian(s), or any other person who has the care of the child.

In American terms, the convention functions essentially as a bill of rights and responsibilities regarding children. Decisions concerning the welfare of the child must be the primary consideration (Article 3). Article 6 states a child does not simply have the right to life, liberty, and pursuit of happiness but also has the right to "development to the maximum extent possible." Article 24.3 notes that Participating States should take measures to abolish traditional practices that harm the health of children. Articles 28.2 indicates that school discipline should be administered "in a manner consistent with the child's human dignity and in conformity with the convention." Articles 34, 35, and 36 protect children from abduction, sale, trafficking, sexual exploitation, and all other harmful forms of exploitation. Article 38 directs states to use all feasible methods to protect children affected by armed conflict and Article 37 specifically protects children from "torture or other cruel, inhumane or degrading treatment or punishment." In addition, Participating States have a duty to provide rehabilitative care for victims of violence under Article 39 and have a further duty to assist families that lack the resources to provide adequate care for their children. In stark contrast to punitive trends in the United States, such as trying 13-year-olds as adults, the UN Convention focuses on rehabilitation and public safety rather than retribution. Article 37 bans capital punishment and life in prison for offenses committed by children under 18 years old. Per the same Article, "*Enforcing the Convention,*" incarceration should be "a last resort" and "only for the shortest appropriate time."

Unlike many other United Nations Conventions, the Convention on the Rights of the Child is not simply a declaration of rights that is unmonitored and unenforced. The convention has its own process of implementation. The Convention is enforced by the Committee on the Rights of the Child, which is composed of approximately 15 State representatives who are elected by the representatives of all Participating States. The Committee is based in Geneva, Switzerland. It reviews, in writing, the efforts of each state to comply with the convention. Upon ratifying in a public dialogue, each Participating State must make a comprehensive report within 2 years. The report is reviewed by the Committee and by interested advocacy groups. Then the Committee meets with State representatives, exploring various issues. Later, based upon the commitments made by the State, the Committee makes specific written findings and recommendations in writing which are published globally. Thereafter each State reports on a 5-year cycle. This periodic assessment encourages each country to think more comprehensively about how it provides for its children, and the process often culminates in each State making specific commitments on what steps will be taken to further protect and defend the rights of its children. The mandate of the Committee could be furthered by creating an effective and comprehensive definition of violence toward children.

III. DEFINITION AND PREVENTION

If we wish to stop violence in society, we must prevent it from occurring to our children. The Australian National Committee on Violence noted:

> "The greatest chance to prevent violence in society is to raise children who reject violence as a method of problem solving, and who believe in the right of the individual to grow in a safe environment" (Australian Institute of Criminology, 1990).

As Peter Newell, an internationally prominent British child advocate, notes:

> "Violence to children is inextricably linked to violence by children, and to manifestations of adult violence. No country can be complacent about any level of violence involving children. Insensitive and violent treatment of children, like insensitive and violent treatment of the environment, threatens not just the quality of human lives to-

day, but the very survival of the human society in the future (UNICEF, 1997).

A. Violence Definition as Violence Prevention

Violence can be defined in many ways (e.g., medically, psychologically, theologically, anthropologically, historically, and legally). Legal definitions of violence are commonly found under criminal law. However criminal law is usually based upon adult standards and frequently fails to address many common forms of violence against children. Criminal law tends to punish the offender publicly with little attention given to the rehabilitative needs of the child victim.

In contrast, defining violence preventively demands that violence be defined not in terms of public retribution toward the actor but rather (1) in terms of the harm it creates to the child and (2) by incorporating the best methods of preventing the harm and reducing the likelihood of its reoccurrence. Since most violence toward children occurs within the family, punishing the family member may create further harm to the child due to the loss of the parent, the removal of the child from the family home, or the child's placement in inadequate foster care.

In public health terms, violence to children may be likened to a disease that maims and kills. The first stage in attempting to map an epidemic disease is to determine whom it has struck and to ascertain the common factors shared by those afflicted. Since violence is a complex process composed of myriad factors and causalities, the state of our understanding of violence is rather like the maps of the Portuguese navigators in the 1400s. For them, the world outside of Europe and North Africa was flat, unknown, and malevolent. In the 1500s, various voyagers improved on the map so that at least the edges of many continents were outlined with some accuracy, but the territory within remained *terra incognita*. In this light, the task at hand is to begin to explore the world of potential violence to children and begin to map the continents of violence that we can prevent.

B. Primary, Secondary, and Tertiary Prevention

Just as defining a disease should, at every stage, be linked to its cure, defining violence to children should be linked to its prevention. In epidemiological terms prevention has three stages.

Primary prevention concerns programs or actions for the general public that serve to prevent the violence described. For example, a series on TV exploring the traumas resulting from physical punishment could have a primary preventive effect in that the general population will learn more about the harm to children from corporal punishment.

Secondary prevention concerns programs or actions aimed at specific populations that are at risk. In the case of corporal punishment, it is children who are at risk. School programs concerning "good touch/bad touch," and explorations of the children's rights not to be physically punished, can have the effect of limiting harm.

Tertiary prevention concerns those who have already been harmed and seeks to prevent repetition of the harm and to reduce the extent of harm. Tertiary programs for parents might include anger management and education about local, national, and international laws that forbid physical punishment of children.

In addition, a punishment prevention program might also deal with religious authorities to challenge a traditional Christian explanation for physical punishment as "spare the rod and spoil the child." First, this is not a direct quotation from the Bible but is based on Proverbs 13:24 (King James version), which states, "He that spareth his rod hateth his son: but he that loveth him chasteneth him betimes." Those seeking to excuse physical punishment being a Christian duty could be referred to Psalm 23, Verse 4 which reads, "your rod and your staff they comfort me." Thus, one could argue that the word for rod has a meaning that does not reconcile with corporal punishment. The Hebrew term for rod, used both in Psalms and Proverbs, is *shabat*. A *shabat* was a wooden rod used by a shepherd in caring for sheep. It had many practical uses. First, it was a symbol of a shepherd's guardianship of the sheep. Second, it was easily thrown just ahead of a fleeing sheep to send the animal back to the flock. It could also be used to ward off an intruder and protect the sheep from dangerous animals that might attack. It was used to count the sheep as they passed under it, and it was likewise used to part the wool in order to examine for disease, wounds, or other problems that would require treatment. There is no evidence in the Bible that the rod was ever used to strike sheep.

Considering classic uses of *shabat* and applying it symbolically to parenthood, the *shabat* should first provide security, letting the child know that he or she is safe and accepted; second, prevent the child from going astray; third, protect the child, not allowing outsiders to hurt the child; fourth, aid in evaluating the child, ensuring the child's growth and development is monitored and supported; and fifth, aid in diagnosis, looking for signs of maldevelopment or trauma in the child that require treatment. In other words, the rod should be a comfort to the sheep and likewise a comfort for the child. Loving and firm discipline can be a comfort to the child.

The second half of Proverbs 13:24 uses the word "chasteneth," which comes from the Hebrew term *yasar*, which could be translated as "discipline." *Yasar* has both positive and negative connotations indicating "to chase and correct and punish" balanced by "a duty to admonish, build up, and instruct." Parents eager to follow the Bible could be directed to Colossians 3:21, which states "do not provoke your children to anger lest they be discouraged." The Greek word for discourage is *athymeo*. To "dis-courage" is to diminish the spirit of the child. Thus, the parents should be informed that discipline should not be extend to discouragement and that discipline must always contain a clear element of encouragement for a child.

IV. DIFFICULTY OF CREATING DEFINITIONS

Definitions are necessarily reductionistic. Wherever we define, we exclude something. Today's broad comprehensive and preventive definition could be tomorrow's constrictive albatross that prevents further understanding. Thus, our definition of violence must be plastic: able to accommodate new information and incorporate new ideas. Legal (statutory) definitions of violence toward children are not plastic. They are fixed in specific form until the legislature revises them. Legislatures also have to answer to the public's perception as to what forms of violence deserve to be sanctioned and which should be ignored. Public perception is often at odds with modern medical understanding of what circumstances creates the most harm to a child. Legislators are reluctant, historically speaking, to enact laws that could invade the privacy of the home.

This reluctance to legislate in the home is a fundamental principle of English common law. It is not shared by many countries outside the United States and the UK. For example, in 1979, Sweden became the first country to ban physical punishment of children. Their legislation was preventive, not punitive. In the next 16 years following that passage, there was only one prosecution in Sweden for what might be regarded in other countries as "ordinary physical punishment." In that case a father was given a small fine for spanking his 11-year-old son. The impact of this law was striking. A 1994 research study by the Swedish Department of country to ban physical punishment of children. Their legislation was preventive, not punitive. In the next 16 years following that passage, there was only one prosecution in Sweden for what might be regarded in other countries as "ordinary physical punishment." In that case a father was given a small fine for spanking his 11-year-old son. The impact of this law was striking. A 1994 research study by the Swedish Department of Health and Social Affairs found that approval of physical punishment had dropped from 65% in 1979 to just 11% in 1994. Only 1% of a sample of Swedish 15-year-olds reported ever having been struck with an implement, as contrasted with 25% of children in the United Kingdom and other developed countries.

Finland, Denmark, Norway, Austria, and Cyprus have also prohibited all violent and humiliating punishment of children (Statistics Sweden, 1996). In contrast to this are dozens of countries that have no statutory definitions of child abuse or child neglect and dozens more that have general definitions that are not subject to either enforcement or oversight.

Those countries that do have comprehensive definitions of violence to children often have significant definitional differences. A World Health Organization report notes that "conflicting definitions of child abuse and neglect, difficulties in identifying cases of child abuse and neglect, and variations in recording requirements make cross-national comparison virtually impossible" (Belsey, 1993). Common terms such as "child" or "best interests of the child" or "violence" translate poorly in many languages. The "childhood" commonly assumed in affluent developed countries is not a reality in many other countries.

This increases the difficulty of legal definitions, which, being legal, are usually universal. A child's right to culture and familial integrity can conflict with their right to health and right to be free of violence. A definition of violence demands a reconciliation of cultural rights, and human rights. Philip Alston, a renown authority on the Convention on the Rights of the Child, notes that any attempt at definition must avoid "Approaches which involve the embrace of an artificial and sterile universalism through the acceptance of an ultimately self-defeating, cultural relativism" (Alston, 1994).

A further challenge can be found in defining institutional or structural violence, such as poverty, homelessness, famine, and environmental degradation, that may result from the actions or inactions of the countries themselves or from neighboring countries. Laws of one country are rarely written to compensate for environmental or economic harm to children in a neighboring country.

A. Challenges of Medical Definitions of Violence

The first challenge of defining violence in medical terms may be that medical definitions do not recognize the concept of violence *per se*. Medicine recognizes harm, trauma, or illness, but a diagnosis of violence is rare.

If we choose to define violence as "preventable trauma of human origin" then we have to establish "harm" before we can diagnose "violence." If, in an example cited by James Garbarino, an infant child is tossed out a third-story window and lands on the convertible top of an automobile and yet suffers no detectable trauma, then how can this obviously violent act be deemed medically violent in the absence of detectable harm?

Like law, medicine faces the dilemma of universalism versus relativism. The concepts of "violence" and "health" varies markedly by culture. Measurements of child wellbeing, depression, and child function commonly used in Western "developed" countries assume a universal psychological reality that does not exist in many countries and indigenous communities. The penchant for individualism in some developed countries leads to an individual-based diagnosis relying on a very substantial investment in development of, within each child, an independent ego.

Likewise harm to the child is based on individual ego state assessment, individual self-esteem and individual losses of control leading to individual psychological intervention and treatment. Such methods of treatment have been quite ineffectual in cultures where the greater trauma has been defined in terms of harm to family and community (Lykes, 1994).

V. OVERVIEW OF CHILDRENS' SPECIAL NEEDS

No one questions an adult's right to be free from physical trauma by another. Children have vulnerabilities that adults do not and deserve no less protection from violence. Violence interferes with the positive growth and development of children. Even witnessing violence, such as violence between the child's parents, can harm that child's future development, parenting skills, and ability to contribute to a civil society.

signs, (such as psychological abuse, some effects of armed conflict; and threats of trauma, such as leaving a small child unattended next to a body of water. Violence should include harm to one's legal rights.

The Convention on the Rights of the Child by the United Nations in 1989 and its ratification by 200 countries creates a clear global responsibility to address the rights of children and are listed in Table I.

Denial of such rights is a form of violence to the child, just as the denial of basic legal rights is to an adult.

Violence cannot be defined adequately by law alone or by medicine alone. Medical definitions capture types of violence where there is detectable physical or psychological harm, yet there are many acts which are considered violent where physical trauma cannot be demonstrated, such as sex with or improper touching of a child. There are also many acts where traumas can be demonstrated that are not considered violent, e.g., sports such as rugby or football. Legal definitions of violence do not include all acts that harm children, e.g., chronic verbal abuse of a child Battery of a child is unlawful, yet all but a few countries allow it in the context of parental discipline. Thus the proposed definition of violence includes acts that are demonstrably harmful to children and acts that are considered violent where the harm is not yet demonstrated. Violence that cannot be defined cannot be prevented.

A comprehensive and effective definition demands the following:

1. Describing, in medical terms, all traumas to the body and psyche of the child that are likely to be nonaccidental.
2. Determining how each trauma can be most accu-

rately diagnosed and the short and long term harms assessed.
3. Describing which programs in what cultures and contexts that are most effective in preventing the identified traumas to children.
4. Posting the existing legislation and suggesting model legislation for every country that addresses protection of children from violence.
5. Surveying and posting research and research-in-progress on violence to children and its prevention.
6. Based on the above identifying the best methods for comprehensive, confidential diagnosis and reporting by those who are in frequent contact with children such as health care workers and teachers. This includes programs to educate personnel on how to better detect such traumas.
7. Maintaining a child violence identification and prevention Website with proposed definitions, model legislation, research, links to relevant organizations, and an Internet conference for discussing future research and policy development.

A. Toward a Taxonomy of Trauma

Any review of legislation to protect children reveals the use of labels of child trauma that frequently overlap, contradict, or simply fail to describe known harms to children. If all children of the world are vested (per Article 19) with the right to protection from violence, then prevention demands that we attempt to define all forms of violence possible to a hypothetical global child. Since the description and treatment of traumas differ by language and culture, great care must be taken that the definition does not exclude viable concepts in the child's culture and community. Otherwise the definition itself could function to harm the child's well-being by not recognizing a value or activity central to that child's culture. Before examining proposed categories of trauma, we must consider how the categories will be distinguished.

B. The Problem of Exclusivity

Using categories in English (or any other single language) creates problems of both translation and understanding in other languages. Northern European languages have many terms recognizing particular harms to an individual but a dearth of terms describing harm to the child's relationships to others and their community. Any single language, like the any single definition, excludes some form of violence.

TABLE I

Articles of the Convention on the Rights of the Child

Article	Rights of child
19	Protection from all forms of violence
24	Access to the highest attainable standard of healthcare
28	Access to the highest attainable standard of education
30	Protection of cultural integrity
38 and 1	Assurance of a safe and nurturing environment
27 and 31	Leisure time (play and commonly accepted medical procedures often involve risk of trauma that is not considered violence.)
32	Reasonable limits to work

C. The Problem of Data Retrievability

A Spanish-speaking researcher searching the category of "child abuse" would find that the term translates poorly into other languages. First there are significant differences in the term "child"; Vietnamese has, for example, eight different terms for what English lumps into the word "child." Next, there are problems with the term "abuse," not the least of which is that it is not a term of law or medicine in Britain and other European countries. They prefer the term "child maltreatment." In addition the term "child abuse" in the U.S. includes many acts that are not considered abusive in some Middle Eastern, African, or Asian countries. Likewise, English fails to capture categories of trauma in non-English cultures such as damage to a child's heart-mind (e.g., *khooc cet* in Cambodian). Thus any person trying to retrieve global data on a *verbal* category of data will be frustrated.

The only remedy to the above is to use *numeric* categories that allow each language and culture to define child trauma in their own terms. Numeric categories likewise allow for easier searching of subcategorizes.

D. A Taxonomy of Trauma

Most violence to children is multi-causal. Children are mistreated by parents, siblings, families, communities, corporations, states, and nations. While parents are primarily responsible for the welfare of their children, they cannot fairly be held responsible for inadequate child health care programs; underfunded, overcrowded or nonexistent daycare programs; decrepit school buildings with underpaid and undersupported teachers; dangerous housing; easily available handguns; violent gangs; drugs and other pollutants which foul the child's internal (addiction and fetal alcohol syndrome) and external environments. When parents work full time and, due to a low minimum wage, still find themselves below the poverty line, it is nonsensical to hold them responsible for the many harms resulting from child poverty. Laws that find only parents responsible for neglect and abuse cannot prevent many forms of maltreatment.

An effective taxonomy of maltreatment cannot simply be descriptive, like the careful Latinate classification of butterflies. It must also be preventive. To be preventive it must also identify all causal agents, their roles and the "best practices" for identifying, diagnosing, and treating the harm and preventing future harm. The categories below divide causal agents between (a) *parental–familial,* and (b) *communal–societal.* For example, a child beaten in a hate crime would fall in (b) *communal–societal.*

Within each causal category violence resulting from a failure to act, protect, or provide for the child is divided between *neglect* and *deprivation. Neglect* occurs where the agent has the capacity to prevent the trauma (e.g., failing to nourish where nourishment is available). *Deprivation* occurs when the agent lacks the capacity to prevent the harm (e.g., failing to nourish in a famine). Preventing *neglect* usually requires different actions by different entities than preventing *deprivation.* Only by detecting all dimensions of harm and determining all the agents of causation can we hope to effectively prevent violence to children.

Because many signs and symptoms of maltreatment vary, conflict, or overlap depending on the medical coding system used, an agreed taxonomy must be developed. If research in one country is to have any value in other countries we must have consistent terminology. The proposed numerical categories limit the ambiguity of translation and aid in research.

A. PARENTAL–FAMILIAL CAUSATION
1. Physical
2. Sexual
3. Psychological
   - Threats
   - Insults (includes humiliation, degradation, attacks on self-esteem)
   - Witnessing trauma to others, particularly to loved ones
4. Neglect or Deprivation (Parental neglect is the failure to provide or act when capable of doing so. Parental deprivation is the failure to provide or act when not capable of doing so—e.g., child malnutrition due to famine, war or refugee status. Most deprivation occurs on the communal–societal level.)
   - Food
   - Housing
   - Emotional nurture and affection
   - Sensory (Includes all forms of restraint and imprisonment)
   - Care and supervision
   - Medical attention
   - Developmental opportunity, including education
   - Play
   - Environmental (includes noxious pollutants, poverty, civil conflicts, high crime areas, access to drug paraphernalia, guns, etc.)

- Play
- Environmental (includes noxious pollutants, poverty, civil conflicts, high crime areas, access to drug paraphernalia, guns, etc.)

B. COMMUNAL–SOCIETAL CAUSATION

1. **Physical**
2. **Sexual**
3. **Psychological**
   - Threats
   - Insults (includes humiliation, degradation, attacks on self-esteem)
   - Witnessing trauma to others, particularly to loved ones
   - Denial of child rights
4. **Deprivation/Neglect** (Societal neglect is the failure to provide or act when capable of doing so. Societal deprivation is the failure to provide or act when not capable of doing so—e.g., child malnutrition due to famine, war or refugee status).
   - Food
   - Housing
   - Emotional nurture and affection
   - Sensory (Includes all forms of restraint and imprisonment)
   - Care and supervision
   - Medical attention
   - Developmental opportunity, including education
   - Play
   - Environmental (includes noxious pollutants, poverty, civil conflicts, high crime areas, access to drug paraphernalia, guns, etc.)
5. **Exploitative child labor**
6. **Effects of armed conflict**

E. A Few Methodological Issue Challenges

It is hoped that recognizing challenges such as the following will lead to improved identification and prevention measures.

- The need for balance between medical, social science, legal, public health, and cultural perspectives.
- Remedying the lack of uniformity in research on child trauma such as lack of agreement on definitions, sampling differences, bias of reporter, and representativeness.

- Implementing uniform national and international tracking systems, that can also reflect culture and context.
- Determining an objective method for assessment of each country's awareness and recognition of the issues, support for surveillance, and legislative and administrative commitment to addressing the problem.

VI. CATEGORIES FOR VIOLENCE DEFINITION, IDENTIFICATION, AND PREVENTION

Section 1.0 defines the general type of trauma.

Section 2.0 defines the clinical signs and symptoms evidencing the trauma.

Section 3.0 addresses the best present method of diagnosis of the specific trauma.

Section 4.0 describes the known short-term traumas to children by developmental stage. These traumas occur within 6 months of the time of injury and do not continue for an extended period of time.

Section 5.0 describes the known long-term traumas from the particular type of violence. Long-term trauma are those where impairment or delay with developmental, physical, or psychological sequelae are present and result from the identified form of violence.

Section 6.0 describes factors in the child, family, and the community known to mitigate the effects of the particular form of violence on the child.

Section 7.0 describes factors in the child, family, and the community known to exacerbate the effects of the particular form of violence on the child.

Sections 8.0, 9.0, and 10.0 describe the known primary, secondary, and tertiary prevention methods in standard epidemiological terms.

   Primary prevention (Section 8.0) programs addressed to the general population that have been designed to reduce the occurrence of the particular form of violence.

   Secondary prevention (Section 9.0) programs designed to deter violence from specific groups at-risk for such trauma.

   Tertiary prevention (Section 10.0) programs designed to address those children and families who

A. Expanded Categories

1.0 Definition. Violence is defined as preventable trauma of human origin. Trauma can be physical, psychological, or emotional. It includes all nonaccidental traumas that can be physically documented as well as the more subtle traumas of sexual abuse, forms of violence that may leave no physical signs, such as psychological abuse or effects of armed conflict, and threats of trauma, such as leaving a small child unattended next to a body of water. Violence includes trauma to one's legal rights. "Preventable trauma" is preferred to "violence" because it translates better into other languages, is more commonly understood among health care professionals, and because it decreases the perceived risk of reporting since the individuals involved are not labeled initially as being "violent." This definition is designed to maximize the early reporting of traumatic behaviors and thereby to maximize their prevention. Labeling such behaviors as "violent" at the outset would, in many cultures, reduce the rate of reporting.

1.1–1.10: Types of Trauma

1.0.0 Existing Definitions of Each Type of Trauma
    1.0.1 Legal definitions globally.
        Catalog of legal statutes by country.
    1.0.2 Medical/ definitions globally.
    1.0.3 Cultural/definitions globally.
    1.0.4 Other definition references globally.
2.0 Clinical assessment of the trauma (as defined in section 1.0 above).
    2.0.1 Patient history.
        2.0.1.1 Presenting problem.
        2.0.1.2 Present history.
         • Location(s) of trauma(s).
         • Description of trauma(s).
         • Pattern(s) of trauma(s).
         • Age.
         • Developmental history.
        2.0.1.3 Past medical history.
        2.0.1.4 Family history.
        2.0.1.5 Social history (i.e., religious, socio-economic, cultural).
        2.0.1.6 Drug/alcohol history.
        2.0.1.7 Third-party/collateral reports (i.e.: public health nurse, physician, or social worker).
    2.0.2 Physical and mental status examination.
        2.0.2.1 Description of trauma(s).
        2.0.2.2 Location(s) of trauma(s).
        2.0.2.3 Description of mental status.
        2.0.2.4 Pattern(s) of trauma(s).

    2.0.3 Clinical test data.
        2.0.3.1 Laboratory.
        2.0.3.2 X-ray and imaging.
        2.0.3.3 Psychometric.
    2.0.4 Other data.
    2.0.5 Differential diagnosis.
3.0 Diagnosis by level of certainty.
4.0 Short-term effects of the trauma.
5.0 Long-term effects of the trauma.
6.0 Factors exacerbating the trauma.
7.0 Factors mitigating the trauma.
8.0 Primary prevention.
9.0 Secondary prevention.
10.0 Tertiary prevention.

1. Subcategory Explanation

Level one (before the first decimal point): Designates overall framework for the definition, assessment, diagnosis, and prevention of the designated form of violence.
    1.*.* Definition
    2.*.* Clinical assessment
    3.*.* Diagnosis
    4.*.* Short-term trauma
    5.*.* Long-term trauma
    6.*.* Factors exacerbating the trauma
    7.*.* Factors mitigating the trauma
    8.*.* Primary prevention
    9.*.* Secondary prevention
    10.*.* Tertiary prevention

Level two (before the second decimal point): Designates form of trauma and is consistent throughout document.
    .1. Physical trauma
    .2. Threat of physical trauma
    .3. Sexual trauma
    .4. Threat of sexual trauma
    .5. Verbal insult (includes humiliation, degradation, attacks on self-esteem, etc.)
    .6. Witnessing trauma to others (particularly loved ones)
    .7. Inappropriate child labor
    .8. Threat to Human Rights of Child
    .9. Effects of armed conflict and children
    .10. Deprivation

Example: 2.1.* signifies: clinical assessment * physical trauma

Level three (before the third decimal point): Designates subtext related to respective form of trauma and is an expansion of level two topics.

Level three (before the third decimal point): Designates subtext related to respective form of trauma and is an expansion of level two topics.

Example: 1.1.3 represents the cultural/religious definitions of physical trauma: definition * physical trauma * cultural/religious definitions

Level four: Designates subtext to level three.

Example: 1.1.2.1 represents: definition * physical trauma * medical/psychological definitions globally * commentary on medical/psychological definitions globally

VII. DRAFT DEFINITION FOR PHYSICAL TRAUMA TO CHILDREN

The following is an example of the format that will be developed for other forms of preventable trauma to children, such as sexual trauma, emotional/psychological trauma, neglect, effects of armed conflict, and inappropriate child labor. The medical knowledge upon which they are based is constantly expanding and thus requiring ongoing revision to insure they are current. The revised version can be found on the CVCP website.

1.1 *Physical trauma definitions globally.*
Physical traumas are all nonaccidental cases of violence of human origin that can be physically documented. This may result from another person "punching, beating, kicking, biting, burning, throwing, [poisoning,] or otherwise harming a child... The injury may be the result of a single event or of repeated episodes and can range in severity from minor bruising to death" (Depanfilis & Salus, 1992). Play often involves injury which is not considered violence. Further details can be found at <www.child.vip.org>.

1.1.1 Legal definitions globally.

Any extreme and repeated cruelty; or physical injury which is nonaccidental or negligent and without justifiable cause, including: death, permanent or temporary disfigurement, illness, impairment of any bodily organ; or causing any nonaccidental physical injury, or an injury which is at variance with the history given. (Arkansas statute)

1.1.2 Medical/psychological definitions globally.

Physical trauma includes injury of a child (including while *in utero*) by nonaccidental actions or inactions, causing:
• death
• disfigurement
• visible or internal injury
• impairment of physical health and development or
• loss or impairment of any bodily function.

2.1 *Clinical assessment of specific trauma.*
(As defined in section 1.1 above)

2.1.1 Patient history.

2.1.1.1 Presenting problem.

2.1.1.2 Present history.
• Length of exposure to trauma(s)
• Intensity of trauma(s)
• Relationship of perpetrator(s) to victim
• Presence of existing trauma(s) to siblings

Note: Be aware of consistency in the patient's and parent's(s')/caretaker's(s') description of present history.

• **Location(s) of trauma(s)**
• **Description of trauma(s)**
• **Pattern(s) of trauma(s)**
  • Multiple injuries
  • Type and severity of injuries
  • Time of infliction
  • Cited reason for trauma (e.g., bedwetting, poor school performance, etc.)
• **Age of child**
• **Developmental history of child.**

Assessment of trauma cases must consider the child's developmental stage. For many types of trauma, each developmental stage requires different methods of evaluation and diagnosis. This raises the problem of defining developmental stages in an agreed manner. The proposed categories below are derived mainly from medical sources. Noting the developmental stage allows for more accurate diagnosis and a more accurate assessment of harm to the child's future development. Dimensions of development to consider are: physical, sexual, behavioral, intrapersonal, interpersonal, developmental, psychopathological.

TABLE II

Developmental Stages of Children

Developmental stage	Age
Intrauterine	Prebirth
Neonate	First 28 days of life
Infant	28 days–1 year
Toddler	1–3 years
Preschool	3–5 years
School-age	5–8 years
Preadolescent	8–12 years
Adolescent	12–18 years

Categories of development
Intrapersonal development
Interpersonal development
Physical development
Sexual development
Behavioral conduct
Developmental psychopathology

the child's development than traumas we prosecute as abusive (Table II).

Age commentary.
The age of the victim plays an important role in learning about the source of the trauma. "For children under three, practitioners are primarily reliant on physical evidence and its congruence with the explanation of the adult caregiver[s]. For older children, the children themselves can potentially be the most credible source of information if they are given the opportunity to give that information in a confidential setting with appropriate questioning" (R.E. Behrman, personal communication, February 18, 1997).

Infants and toddlers.
Particularly for children under two years of age, there is a higher risk of fatality of abuse.

Adolescents.
Approximately 25% of adolescent abuse cases in the United States begin during the adolescent years.

2.1.1.3 Past medical history.
- Health problem(s)
- Developmental disability
- Low birth weight or prematurity
- Severe emotional disturbance

- Child's previous exposure to any form(s) of trauma(s)
- Response to any previous trauma(s)
- Length of exposure to trauma(s)
- Intensity of trauma(s)
- Relationship of perpetrator(s) to victim
- Presence of previous or existing trauma(s) to sibling(s)

2.1.1.4 Family history.
- Composition and size of household (i.e., a group of individuals who function as a unit socially and economically and who share cooking facilities)
- Marital status of primary caregiver(s)
- Birth order and sex of child(ren) in household
- Illness or death in family
- Depression
- Hopelessness
- Availability of an extended family network
- Inadequate access to and use of medical services
- No or limited enjoyment in caring for child(ren)
- Inadequate child care arrangements
- Domestic violence in household
- History of the parent/caregiver abused as a child

2.1.1.5 Social history.
- Socioeconomic status of primary caregiver(s)
- Family's housing situation
- Educational attainment of primary caregiver(s)
- Employment status of primary caregiver(s)
- Cultural background
- Religious background
- Mobility
- Degree of involvement with social groups (i.e.: clubs, church, community, extended family, or other organizations)
- Perception by parent(s)/caretaker(s) of social norms with respect to trauma to child

2.1.1.6 Drug/alcohol history.
- Abuse of alcohol and/or other sub-

stance(s) by primary caregiver(s) (Briere, 1992)
- The treatment efforts and outcomes of primary caregiver(s) who abuse alcohol and/or other substance(s)

2.1.1.7 Third-party/collateral reports (i.e.: public health nurse, physician, or social worker).

It is appropriate to include a note here regarding international use of coding and medical databases. Any effort to propose new ways to define violence to children must be mindful of prior efforts to do so and existing medical databases. The Child VIP Project does not seek to "remake the wheel" of medical databases. Instead it seeks to strengthen the "spokes" within the wheel in a manner that allows more effective identification and, thereby, prevention of violence. What follows is a cursory summary of relevant medical databases.

ICD-9
The most popular coding for diagnoses and some procedures is the International Classification of Diseases (ICD).

United States and Canada
In the United States ICD-9-CM, a clinical modification of ICD-9 (Ninth Revision), is used by all nonmilitary hospitals for discharge coding purposes and must be reported on the bills submitted to most insurance companies. The Current Procedural Terminology (CPT), developed by the American Medical Association, is widely used in producing bills for patients.

This pattern is consistent with the use of medical databases in other countries. In Canada, for example, hospitals report on discharges to the Canadian Institute of Health Information using ICD-9-CM and will begin converting to ICD-10 in 1999. Physicians use ICD-9 or ICD-9-CM to code diagnosis for billing the provincial medical insurance schemes but usually use other coding schemes for services. Canadian hospitals often use software called a "grouper" to derive Case Mix Groups (CMGs) from the ICD-9 codes and other data such as age and gender. Case Mix Groups are quite similar to the Diagnostic Related Groups (DRGs) used in the U.S.

In Canada and the U.S., the International Classification of Health Problems in Primary Care (ICHPPC) is also used to code symptoms and diagnoses in primary care. About 85 to 90% of these translate to ICD-9, but some detail can be lost in the translation.

ICD-10
ICD-10 has been available for implementation from the World Health Organization since 1993. Over 30 national-language versions of ICD-10 have been developed or are in development.

Europe
In European countries, the International Classification of Primary Care (ICPC) is often used to code the symptoms and diagnosis in primary care, while ICD codes are used in acute care and for statistical purposes.

United Kingdom and Australia
In the United Kingdom, ICD codes, Ninth or Tenth Revision, are usually used by hospitals and physicians to code for statistical analysis while the Read Codes are used for recording details of clinical care. Read Codes were developed in the early 1980s so that electronic patient records could hold clinical concepts in a concise, compact, and unambiguous manner. They became the United Kingdom primary care standard in 1988 and are also in use in Australia.

2.1.2 Physical and mental status examination.

2.1.2.1 Description of physical trauma(s).
The International Classification of Diseases, Ninth Edition (ICD-9) has been chosen to classify the physical status of the patient because it is the most popular global coding system for diagnoses and some procedures. ICD-10 will be used once it is fully implemented.

The following list of injuries is partial. A complete list can be found at <www.child-via/org>. The injuries above are generally not dispositive for diagnosis of physical abuse, maltreatment or neglect.

Bruising. ICD-9: 372.72; 459.89; 772.6; 920–924

Bruising commentary.
Accidental bruises are usually found to be circular and over bony prominences on parts of the child's body with which they lead in activity.

Possible nonaccidental bruises are often located in protected areas such as the buttocks, thighs, genitalia, trunk, neck, cheek, and ear. Additional signs of nonaccidental bruises include old and new bruises in combination, bruises on several areas of the face, or bruising on an infant. It is important to observe the pace at which the bruise is resolved. The deeper the bruise, the longer it takes to heal.

- *Age-appropriate bruising.* Toddlers often have bruises on the forehead. Preschoolers and school-aged children often present with knee and shin bruises.
  Note: Any bruise on a child younger than nine months is an indicator that abuse may be present.
- *Patterned bruising.* Non-accidental bruises often reveal the object with which the child was struck. The skin surface may also be lacerated if the impact of the striking object was with enough force.

Typical patterns are:
- *whipping marks*, such as looped cords, belts, switches, and rulers
- *slap marks* reveal a faint hand print;
- *pinch marks*
- *ligature marks* when the child is restrained
- *bite marks* showing the assailant's tooth prints
  Note: The size of marks from other children will be small. Two to 4-year-olds sometimes bite other children, but the marks will be small
- *twin bruises* on either side of mouth, cheeks, or ears caused by pinching or grabbing
- *grip marks* on infants
- *black eyes*

Burns. ICD-9: 906; 910–917; 919; 940–949; E860–864; E896–899; E968; E988; E990

Burns commentary.
Nonaccidental burns. The two most common types of burns often associated with abuse are contact burns.

- *Contact burns* are often scarring, but not life-threatening. They usually involve hot metals or smoldering objects. If the injury is accidental, the contact with the injuring device is normally single and brief, resulting in a blurred pattern of injury. Burns are generally shallow due to

quick and evasive movement of the child upon contact.

Cigarettes are frequently used in cases of abuse and result in multiple burn marks applied to palms of the hand, soles of the feet, and clothed or protected body parts.

Hot metal objects are common weapons of abuse, sometimes leaving a recognizable print of the object due to the force with which it was applied to the child's body part.

- *Hot liquid or caustic substances burns.* Temperature and length of exposure are directly related to the severity of the burn. The placement and distribution of the burn on the child's body can help to identify possible abuse.

Accidental spilling injuries often show splash marks on the underside of the chin and the armpit on the side of the body which the child used to reach up and pull the container.

In *hot liquid immersion injuries*, there is a distinct boundary between the affected and unaffected areas of the child's skin, along with unburned crease marks with the affected area due to the restraint of the child. The most common nonaccidental immersion burn occurs with toddlers after toileting accidents with burns on the buttocks or sock-like or glove-like burns from placing the child's feet or hands in hot water.

Burns from caustic substances may occur when the liquids are thrown at or placed on children.

Note: In the United States, accidental tap water burns are becoming increasingly less common due to the lowering of water temperatures in hot water heaters.

Fetal alcohol syndrome. ICD-9: 760.71

Fetal alcohol syndrome (FAS) "is the primary *preventable* cause of mental retardation in the United States and Canada" and it results in lifelong impairments due to alcohol exposure *in utero* (Kydd, 1992). Fetal alcohol syndrome infants are at risk for central nervous system dysfunction, weak suck, feeding and sleeping difficulties, and failure to thrive. Children with FAS have compromised intellectual capacities, a high need for attention, multiple impairments and behavioral problems, and are frequently smaller. "By adolescence, FAS children often engage in inappropriate behaviors leading to expulsion from school for males and premature sexual activity for highly suggestible females" (Kydd, 1992).

Fractures. ICD-9: 767.2–4; 800–829; 850–854; 905; E887

Fractures Commentary.
The pattern of a fracture is often an important determinant in the etiology of the injury.

The *epiphyseal/metaphyseal chip fracture* is the "classic fracture of abuse" and occurs near the end of long bones due to jerking or shaking of a child's limbs (Feldman, 1993).

Mid-shaft humerus or femur fractures in infants are strongly associated with abuse unless a clear explanation is given.

Rib fractures need to be investigated in children three years of age or younger. Such fractures are present in nearly one-quarter of abused infants, usually due to squeezing or shaking. These fractures are often difficult to detect. Irritability is a common sign in infants.

Spiral fractures are strongly associated with cases of abuse and may be caused by twisting a child's limb (Bannister, 1987).

Munchausen syndrome by proxy. ICD-9: 301.51

An adult inflicts injury on a child to attract medical attention and support. (*Understanding Child Abuse and Neglect*, 1993). Symptoms are contrived usually by the mother and can include the following: seizures, hematemesis, hematuria, false temperatures, poisonings, diarrhea, and respiratory arrest.

This results in extensive medical attention, undue screenings, and invasive tests. In many cases, the mother is very familiar with medical terminology and the father may not be aware of the mother's actions. Many mothers are considered *normal* and free from psychiatric illness. While this is a rare form of physical abuse, nine percent of cases in the United States result in mortality (Fontana & Besharov, 1996).

Open wound of lower limb. ICD-9: 890–897

Open wound of upper limb. ICD-9: 880–887

Prenatal exposure to cocaine. ICD-9: 760.75

Cocaine can cause serious harm to a fetus including limiting or cutting off the normal oxygen and blood flow. Cocaine may also cause premature birth, kidney dysfunction, strokes, and malformations of the central nervous system, the heart, and the gastrointestinal tract (Kydd, 1992). *Note*: Children who are prenatally exposed to drugs may be at a higher risk for subsequent maltreatment if there are noticeable effects from the exposure.

Poisonings by drugs, medicinals, and biological substances. ICD-9: 960–979

Prenatal noxious influences. ICD-9: 760.7

Shaken Baby Syndrome.

A child is violently shaken, subjecting the child's head "to a repetitive, acceleration–deceleration, whiplash-type motion which causes severe intracranial injury, often without signs of trauma" (Fontana & Besharov, 1996). The child may present respiratory distress, retinal tears, and little external evidence of physical trauma. Shaken Baby Syndrome occurs in children less than 2 years, and usually in infants younger than 6 months.

Classic signs:
• Apnea
• Bradycardia

- Bruising, especially of the upper arms or shoulders
- Tense or bulging anterior fontanelle
- Coma, altered consciousness
- Fixed or dilated pupils
- Retinal hemorrhage (occur in over 50% of cases)
- Subdural hematoma (may cause vomiting, irritability, and low temperature)
- Head circumference greater than the 90th percentile for age

Other signs:
- Hyperthermia
- Leukocytosis
- Nuchal rigidity
- Posturing
- Respiratory distress unaccompanied by lower airway sounds or stridor
- Seizures
- Associated fractures of ribs or long bones
- Skull fractures
- Vomiting in small infants in the absence of diarrhea
- May be no external signs of physical trauma

Shaken Baby Syndrome commentary. Pale retinal hemorrhages are commonly found in cases of Shaken Baby Syndrome.

Sprains and strains of joints and adjacent muscles. ICD-9: 840–848

Superficial injury. ICD-9: 910–919

Toxic effects of substances chiefly nonmedicinal as to source. ICD-9: 980–989

2.1.2.2 Location(s) of physical trauma(s).

Head.
Bruising. ICD-9: 772.6, 920–924
Burns. ICD-9: 910.0–910.1, 919.0, 919.1, 940–941, 946, 948, E890–899, E924, E968, E988
Contusions. ICD-9: 800.1, 800.6, 801.1, 801.6, 803.1, 803.6, 804.1, 804.6, 851, 906.3, 920
Crushing injury. ICD-9: 906.4, 925, 929
Dislocations. ICD-9: 830 (jaw)

Effects of foreign object entering through orifice. ICD-9: 935.0 (mouth)
Fractures. ICD-9: 800–804, 905, E887
Hematoma. ICD-9: 432.1, 852.4, 853.0
Hemorrhage. ICD-9: 430–432; 852; 853
Injury to blood vessels. ICD-9: 900
Injury to nerves and spinal cord. ICD-9: 950–951, 957
Intracranial injury (excluding skull injury). ICD-9: 850–854
Late effects of injuries. ICD-9: 905.0, 906.0, 907.0, 908.2, 908.3, 908.5, 908.6, 909
Open wound. ICD-9: 873
Poisonings by drugs, medicinals, and biological substances, prenatal noxious influences. ICD-9: 960–969

Head injury commentary. Children with head injuries often show signs of altered consciousness, coma, seizures, vomiting, and/or irritability. This injury is the most frequent cause of death in victims of physical trauma.

- *Nonaccidental head injuries.* The forceful impact of blunt objects is often the cause of severe head injuries caused by abuse. Upon initial exam of an infant, it is important to closely scrutinize the scalp for bruising from the base of avulsed hairs. More complex skull fractures which involve more than one bone, cross sutures, or involve intracranial injury with wide fractures are often associated with abuse. Such fractures are uncommon from a simple fall.

Subdural bleeding and subarachnoid bleeding are caused by forceful impact and tend to be associated with abuse. Symptoms of subdural bleeding in infants include fever, irritability, bulging fontanelle, and convulsive seizures (Kempe, 1962; study by Merritt, as cited in: Iverson & Segal, 1990).

- *Accidental head injuries.* Accidental skull fractures are usually simple.

Trunk.
Bruising. ICD-9: 860–869, 922.0–922.3, 922.8, 922.9

Burns. ICD-9: 911.0, 911.1, 912.0, 912.1, 919.0, 919.1, 942, 946, E924, E968

Contusions with intact skin surface. ICD-9: 906.3, 922.0–922.3, 922.8, 922.9

Crushing injury. ICD-9: 926.1, 926.8, 926.9

Dislocations. ICD-9: 832 (shoulder), 835 (hip)

Effects of foreign object entering through orifice. ICD-9: 934 (trachea, bronchus, lung), 935.2 (stomach), 936 (intestine/colon), 937 (anus/rectum)

Exposure to elements (heat, cold, wind). ICD-9: 991.8

Fractures. ICD-9: 805–809

Hematoma. ICD-9: 864–866; 922

Hemorrhage. ICD-9: 578

Injury to blood vessels. ICD-9: 901–903

Injury to nerves and spinal cord. ICD-9: 952–957

Internal injury of chest, abdomen, and pelvis. ICD-9: 860–869

Late effects of injuries, poisonings, or toxic effects, and other external causes. ICD-9: 905–909

Open wound of head, neck, and trunk. ICD-9: 875–877; 879

Poisonings by drugs, medicinals, and biological substances. ICD-9: 960–979

Sprains and strains of joints and adjacent muscles. ICD-9: 846–848

Superficial injury. ICD-9: 911

Trunk injury commentary. The majority of rib fractures in infants less than 2 years of age are found to be abuse-related (Spivack, 1992).

Abdominal trauma commentary. Abdominal injuries which are abusive are normally inflicted by a fist or a foot. Frequently, there are no external bruises present in the abdominal area; however, other injuries are usually present in other parts of the child's body. Vomiting, abdominal pain, and signs of shock may be present. Anemia and/or bloody urine suggest that there has been internal bleeding, while a higher white blood cell count suggests that infection may be present. Accidental abdominal injuries often involve the spleen, while abusive injuries rarely involve the spleen.

Common accidents to children where there is damage to the abdominal region are motor vehicle passenger injuries, auto–pedestrian accidents, bicycle handlebar penetrations, and falls from significant heights.

Note: Abuse victims are normally infants or toddlers, in contrast to accident victims of abdominal trauma who are normally grade school age.

2.1.2.3 **Description of mental status (using DSM-IV terms per the American Psychiatric Association).**

- Disorders usually first diagnosed in infancy, childhood, or adolescence:
  - Learning disorder
  - Communication disorder
  - Attention deficit disorder (ADD)/Attention Deficit Hyperactivity Disorder (ADHD)
  - Elimination disorders
  - Disruptive behavior disorders
  - Other disorders of infancy, childhood, or adolescence
    - Separation anxiety disorder, selective mutism, reactive
    - Attachment disorder, or stereotypic movement disorder, etc.
  - Pervasive developmental disorders
  - Schizophrenia with childhood onset
- Mental disorder due to a general medical condition
- Mood or other affective disorders
- Anxiety disorders
- Eating disorders
- Sleep disorders
- Adjustment disorders
- Relational problems
- Problems related to abuse or neglect
- Substance-related disorders

2.1.2.4 **Pattern(s) of trauma(s).**

- Multiple injuries
- Type and severity of injuries
- Time of infliction
- Direct "cause" of physical trauma (e.g., bedwetting, poor school performance, etc.)

2.1.3 Clinical test data.

- Laboratory
- X-ray and imaging
- Psychometric

2.1.4 Other data.

- The same injury on children may have different outcomes, influenced by the "child's prior health, the immediate medical care received or not received, and subsequent care and rehabilitative interventions" (Dubowitz, 1991).
- Most injuries are not unique to preventable physical trauma, making it particularly important to consider the broader issues such as family interaction, cultural traditions, and psychosocial health.

2.1.5 Differential diagnosis.

Differential diagnosis identifies the basis for false positives. This is a key area for defining cultural differences in diagnosis and treatment. What western medicine may define as an injury may be an accepted result of healing methods in another culture. *Moxibustion* (discussed below) is an example of this. Modern western medicine is available only to a small percentage of the world's children. We must, therefore, honor the healing methods available to the children and note that, in some cases, traditional methods of healing have been shown to be more accepted and more effective (Eisenbruch, 1994).

Some examples of differential diagnoses are as follows:

Skin

- *Scars of acne, insect bites, and similar skin lesions* which have become infected often occur on the back and face and may cause puckered circular scars in random distribution (Medical Foundation for the Care of Victims of Torture).
- *Mongolian spots* is a harmless, bluish-black spot, occurring over the sacrum between the hipbones or the buttocks of some newborns and is common among blacks, Native Americans, Southern Europeans, and Asians (Fontana & Besharov, 1996; Glanze, Anderson, & Anderson, 1987).

- *Henoch–Schönlein Purpura* is a short-term allergic disorder of blood vessels. Symptoms include bruiselike areas on the lower abdomen, buttocks, and legs, pain in the knees, ankles, or other joints, and bleeding in the stomach and intestines as well as blood in the urine. The disease lasts up to 6 weeks and often does not have long-term effects (Glanze, Anderson, & Anderson, 1987).
- *Erythema multiforme* is an allergic condition with a rash on the skin and mucous membranes. Various sizes and shapes appear and include nodules, pimples, blisters, and bull's-eye shaped areas (Glanze, Anderson, & Anderson, 1987).
- *Platelet aggregation disorders*
- *Autoimmune diseases*
- *Blood dyscrasia* is a condition in which any of the blood elements are abnormal, as in leukemia or hemophilia (Glanze, Anderson, & Anderson, 1987).
- *Traditional healing* with knives or razor blades may leave scars in a circumscribed area. For example, in West Africa, skin is pinched up and then cut across with a razor blade to produce three or four short clean, parallel scars, usually in groups. This is used for counterirritation of painful areas.
- *Girpma* is a traditional remedy used by Kurds to "purify the blood" in infants and leaves a series of vertical parallel linear scars on the back close to the spine.
- *Moxibustion* is used to relieve pain. A slow-burning substance is lit and held close to the skin without causing burning (Glanze, Anderson, & Anderson, 1987).
- *Coining* is a southeast Asian treatment for symptoms such as fever or headache. Hot oil is rubbed on the skin and massaged in a downward motion with the edge of a hot coin. Parallel scars may result. (Research by Yeatman, Shaw, Barlow, & Bartlett, 1976 as cited in Iverson & Segal, 1990).

Fractures
Medical conditions which may predispose soft bones to minor injury (i.e., prolonged and difficult labor in infancy) (Fontana & Besharov, 1996):
- *Scurvy*, though it rarely occurs before five months of life.
- *Syphilis* causes lesions which are usually sym-

metrical. Its presence can be confirmed by serological testing

- *Infantile cortical hyperostosis* can result in swelling deep in soft tissues associated with cortical thickening in the skeleton; usually occurs within the first three months of life
- *Hyperostosis* usually involves the mandible, clavicles, scapulae, ribs, and tubular bones of the extremities
- *Osteogenesis imperfecta* is usually present in bones throughout the body and often occurs in the shafts. "The presence of multiple fractures associated with blue sclera, skeletal deformities, and of a family history of similar abnormalities usually confirms the diagnosis" (Fontana & Besharov, 1996)
- *Infectious osteitis*
- *Rickets*

3.1 *Diagnosis by level of certainty.*
- Reason to suspect
- Reasonable degree of clinical probability
- Reasonable degree of clinical certainty

4.1 *Short-term harm to child from physical trauma.*
Short-term trauma is characterized by complete recovery within 6 months from an incident of violence. The harm to the child varies significantly by the child's developmental stage. for example, a toddler who loses an older sibling would experience far less trauma than an adolescent losing a sibling. Likewise a toddler losing a mother is likely to experience far more trauma than an adolescent facing such a loss.

Trauma must also be categorized according to its symptoms within each developmental stage. The symptom categories are derived from standard medical diagnostics. The symptom categories are Physical, Behavioral, and Emotional.

4.1.1 *Intrauterine* (prebirth).

Physical
- Death
- Injury
- Permanent disability

4.1.2 *Neonate* (first 28 days of life).

Physical
- Death (Denham, 1995)
- Injury

- Permanent disability
- Mal- or undernutrition
- Eating disorders
- Sleep disturbances

Behavioral
- Impaired attachment relations (Culbertson & Schellenbach, 1992; Garbarino, 1987).

4.1.3 *Infant* (between 28 days and one year of age).

Physical (Denham, 1995)
- Death
- Injury
- Permanent disability
- Mal- or undernutrition
- Eating disorders
- Sleep disturbances

Behavioral (Denham, 1995).
- Withdrawn
- Impaired attachment relations (Culbertson & Schellenbach, 1992; Garbarino, 1987)
- Clingy

Emotional (Denham, 1995)
- Psychiatric illness (Brown & Anderson, 1991; Mullen, Martin, Anderson, Romans, & Herbison 1996)

4.1.4 *Toddler* (between 1 and 3 years of age).

Physical (Denham, 1995)
- Death
- Injury
- Permanent disability
- Mal- or undernutrition
- Eating disorders
- Sleep disturbances

Behavioral (Denham, 1995).
- Withdrawn
- Impaired attachment relations (Culbertson & Schellenbach, 1992; Garbarino, 1987)
- Clingy
- Communicates poorly
- Low impulse control (Veltkamp & Miller, 1994)
- Aggressive and violent behavior to self and others

Emotional (Denham, 1995)
- Post-traumatic stress disorder (Famularo, Fenton, & Kinscherff's study (a) as cited in Jenny, Taylor, & Cooper, 1996; Briere, 1992)
- Uncontrollable emotions
- Depression
- Blame, guilt
- Conflictual beliefs
- Anxiety
- Other psychiatric illness (Brown & Anderson, 1991; Mullen, Martin, Anderson, Romans, & Herbison 1996)

4.1.5 *Preschool* (between 3 and 5 years of age).

Physical (Denham, 1995)
- Death
- Injury
- Permanent disability
- Mal- or undernutrition
- Eating disorders
- Sleep disturbances

Behavioral (Denham, 1995)
- Withdrawn
- Impaired attachment relations (Culbertson & Schellenbach, 1992; Garbarino, 1987)
- Clingy
- Communicates poorly
- Overly adaptive behavior such as acting inappropriately adult or infantile
- Low impulse control (Veltkamp & Miller, 1994)
- Aggressive and violent behavior to self and others

Emotional (Denham, 1995)
- Posttraumatic stress disorder (Famularo, Fenton, & Kinscherff's study (a) as cited in Jenny, Taylor, & Cooper, 1996; Briere, 1992)
- Uncontrollable emotions
- Depression
- Blame, guilt
- Conflictual beliefs
- Hopelessness
- Anxiety
- Other psychiatric illness (Brown & Anderson, 1991; Mullen, Martin, Anderson, Romans, & Herbison 1996)

4.1.6 *School-age* (between 5 and 7 years of age).

Physical (Denham, 1995)
- Death
- Injury
- Permanent disability
- Mal- or undernutrition
- Eating disorders
- Sleep disturbances

Behavioral (Denham, 1995)
- Withdrawn
- Impaired attachment relations (Culbertson & Schellenbach, 1992; Garbarino, 1987)
- Clingy
- Communicates poorly
- Overly adaptive behavior such as acting inappropriately adult or infantile
- Rigid sex-role expectations
- Precocious sexual behavior
- Low impulse control (Veltkamp & Miller, 1994)
- Aggressive and violent behavior to self and others
- Compromised school performance (Howing, Wodarski, Kurtz, & Gaudin, 1993)

Emotional (Denham, 1995)
- Posttraumatic stress disorder (Famularo, Fenton, & Kinscherff's study (a) as cited in Jenny, Taylor, & Cooper, 1996; Briere, 1992)
- Uncontrollable emotions
- Depression
- Blame, guilt
- Conflictual beliefs
- Hopelessness
- Anxiety
- Codependency
- Other psychiatric illness (Brown & Anderson, 1991; Mullen, Martin, Anderson, Romans, & Herbison 1996)

4.1.7 *Preadolescent* (between eight and 12 years of age).

Physical (Denham, 1995)
- Death
- Injury
- Permanent disability
- Mal- or undernutrition

- Eating disorders
- Alcohol or other substance abuse
- Sleep disturbances

Behavioral (Denham, 1995)
- Withdrawn
- Impaired attachment relations (Culbertson & Schellenbach, 1992; Garbarino, 1987)
- Clingy
- Communicates poorly
- Overly adaptive behavior such as acting inappropriately adult or infantile
- Rigid sex-role expectations
- Precocious sexual behavior
- Low impulse control (Veltkamp & Miller, 1994)
- Aggressive and violent behavior to self and others
- Compromised school performance (Howing, Wodarski, Kurtz, & Gaudin, 1993)

Emotional (Denham, 1995)
- Posttraumatic stress disorder (Famularo, Fenton, & Kinscherff's study (a) as cited in Jenny, Taylor, & Cooper, 1996; Briere, 1992)
- Uncontrollable emotions
- Depression
- Blame, guilt
- Conflictual beliefs
- Hopelessness
- Anxiety
- Poor self-esteem
- Codependency
- Other psychiatric illness (Brown & Anderson, 1991; Mullen, Martin, Anderson, Romans, & Herbison 1996)

4.1.8 *Adolescent* (between 12 and 18 years of age).

Physical (Denham, 1995)
- Death
- Injury
- Permanent disability
- Mal- or undernutrition
- Eating disorders
- Alcohol or other substance abuse
- Sleep disturbances

Behavioral (Denham, 1995)
- Withdrawn
- Impaired attachment relations (Culbertson & Schellenbach, 1992; Garbarino, 1987)

- Clingy
- Communicates poorly
- Overly adaptive behavior such as acting inappropriately adult or infantile
- Rigid sex-role expectations
- Precocious sexual behavior
- Low impulse control (Veltkamp & Miller, 1994)
- Aggressive and violent behavior to self and others
- Compromised school performance (Howing, Wodarski, Kurtz, & Gaudin, 1993)

Emotional (Denham, 1995)
- Posttraumatic stress disorder (Famularo, Fenton, & Kinscherff's study (a) as cited in Jenny, Taylor, & Cooper, 1996; Briere, 1992)
- Uncontrollable emotions
- Depression
- Blame, guilt
- Conflictual beliefs
- Hopelessness
- Anxiety
- Poor self-esteem
- Other psychiatric illness (Brown & Anderson, 1991; Mullen, Martin, Anderson, Romans, & Herbison 1996)

5.1 *Long-term harm to child from physical trauma.*
Long-term trauma effects a delay or impairment of development with resulting physical, behavioral or emotional or psychological sequelae. Traumas that lead to long term impairment are potentially the most damaging to the child. They can often be comparatively subtle. Dr. Judith Wallerstein, in her 25 year follow-up study of children of divorce, reports that young children who witnessed domestic violence between their parents (but did not experience any violence from their parents) suffered from life-long difficulties with relationships, in parenting their children, and with heightened vulnerability to substance abuse (personal communication, 1997)

5.1.1 *Infant* (between 28 days and 1 year of age).

Physical
- Permanent disability
- Physical developmental delays

Behavioral
- Impaired attachment relations (Culbertson & Schellenbach, 1992; Garbarino, 1987)
- Avoidance (Briere, 1992)

Emotional

- Posttraumatic stress disorder (Famularo, Fenton, & Kinscherff's study (a) as cited in Jenny, Taylor, & Cooper, 1996; Briere, 1992)
- Altered emotionality (Briere, 1992)
- Disturbed relatedness (Briere, 1992)
- Anxiety
- Psychological developmental delays
- Speech and learning problems (Garbarino, 1987)
- Attention deficit disorder (ADD)
- Other psychiatric illness (Brown & Anderson, 1991; Mullen, Martin, Anderson, Romans, & Herbison 1996)

5.1.2 *Toddler* (between 1 and 3 years of age).

Physical

- Permanent disability
- Physical developmental delays

Behavioral

- Impaired attachment relations (Culbertson & Schellenbach, 1992; Garbarino, 1987)
- Avoidance (Briere, 1992)

Emotional

- Posttraumatic stress disorder (Famularo, Fenton, & Kinscherff's study (a) as cited in Jenny, Taylor, & Cooper, 1996; Briere, 1992)
- Cognitive distortions (Briere, 1992)
- Altered emotionality (Briere, 1992)
- Disturbed relatedness (Briere, 1992)
- Depression
- Anxiety
- Psychological developmental delays
- Speech and learning problems (Garbarino, 1987)
- Attention deficit disorder (ADD)
- Aggression to others and self (Briere & Runtz, 1990)
- Other psychiatric illness (Brown & Anderson, 1991; Mullen, Martin, Anderson, Romans, & Herbison 1996)
- Eating disorders (Rorty, et al., 1994)

5.1.3 *Pre-school* (between 3 and 5 years of age).

Physical

- Permanent disability
- Physical developmental delays

Behavioral

- Impaired attachment relations (Culbertson & Schellenbach, 1992; Garbarino, 1987)
- Avoidance (Briere, 1992)

Emotional

- Posttraumatic stress disorder (Famularo, Fenton, & Kinscherff's study (a) as cited in Jenny, Taylor, & Cooper, 1996; Briere, 1992)
- Cognitive distortions (Briere, 1992)
- Altered emotionality (Briere, 1992)
- Impaired self-reference (Briere, 1992)
- Dissociation (Briere, 1992)
- Disturbed relatedness (Briere, 1992)
- Depression
- Anxiety
- Psychological developmental delays
- Speech and learning problems (Garbarino, 1987)
- Attention deficit disorder (ADD)
- Aggression to others and self (Briere & Runtz, 1990)
- Other psychiatric illness (Brown & Anderson, 1991; Mullen, Martin, Anderson, Romans, & Herbison 1996)
- Eating disorders (Rorty, et al., 1994)

5.1.4 *School-age* (between 5 and 7 years of age).

Physical

- Permanent disability
- Physical developmental delays

Behavioral

- Impaired attachment relations (Culbertson & Schellenbach, 1992; Garbarino, 1987)
- Avoidance (Briere, 1992)

Emotional

- Posttraumatic stress disorder (Famularo, Fenton, & Kinscherff's study (a) as cited in Jenny, Taylor, & Cooper, 1996; Briere, 1992)
- Borderline personality disorder (Herman, Perry, & van der Kolk, 1989)
- Cognitive distortions (Briere, 1992)
- Altered emotionality (Briere, 1992)
- Impaired self-reference (Briere, 1992)
- Codependency
- Dissociation (Briere, 1992)
- Disturbed relatedness (Briere, 1992)
- Depression
- Anxiety

- Psychological developmental delays
- Speech and learning problems (Garbarino, 1987)
- Attention deficit disorder (ADD)
- Aggression to others and self (Briere & Runtz, 1990)
- Suicidal ideation (Council on Scientific Affairs, 1993)
- Compromised school performance (Howing, Wodarski, Kurtz, & Gaudin, 1993)
- Alcohol or other substance abuse (Cavaiola & Schiff, 1988)
- Eating disorders (Rorty, et al., 1994)
- Other psychiatric illness (Brown & Anderson, 1991; Mullen, Martin, Anderson, Romans, & Herbison 1996)

5.1.5 *Pre-adolescent* (between 8 and 12 years of age).

Physical
- Permanent disability
- Physical developmental delays

Behavioral
- Impaired attachment relations (Culbertson & Schellenbach, 1992; Garbarino, 1987)
- Avoidance (Briere, 1992)
- Criminal behavior

Emotional
- Posttraumatic stress disorder (Famularo, Fenton, & Kinscherff's study (a) as cited in Jenny, Taylor, & Cooper, 1996; Briere, 1992)
- Borderline personality disorder (Herman, Perry, & van der Kolk, 1989)
- Cognitive distortions (Briere, 1992)
- Altered emotionality (Briere, 1992)
- Impaired self-reference (Briere, 1992)
- Codependency
- Dissociation (Briere, 1992)
- Disturbed relatedness (Briere, 1992)
- Depression
- Anxiety
- Psychological developmental delays
- Speech and learning problems (Garbarino, 1987)
- Attention deficit disorder (ADD)
- Aggression to others and self (Briere & Runtz, 1990)
- Suicidal ideation (Council on Scientific Affairs, 1993)

- Compromised school performance (Howing, Wodarski, Kurtz, & Gaudin, 1993)
- Alcohol or other substance abuse (Cavaiola & Schiff, 1988)
- Eating disorders (Rorty, et al., 1994)
- Other psychiatric illness (Brown & Anderson, 1991; Mullen, Martin, Anderson, Romans, & Herbison 1996)

5.1.6 *Adolescent* (between 12 and 18 years of age).

Physical
- Permanent disability
- Physical developmental delays

Behavioral
- Impaired attachment relations (Culbertson & Schellenbach, 1992; Garbarino, 1987)
- Avoidance (Briere, 1992)
- Criminal behavior
- Juvenile delinquency (Garbarino, 1987)
- Teen pregnancy (Washington Alliance Concerned with School Age Parents as cited in: *Colorado 1*, 1995)
- Domestic violence
- Homelessness
- Later unemployment (*Colorado 1*, 1995)

Emotional
- Posttraumatic stress disorder (Famularo, Fenton, & Kinscherff's study (a) as cited in Jenny, Taylor, & Cooper, 1996; Briere, 1992)
- Borderline personality disorder (Herman, Perry, & van der Kolk, 1989)
- Cognitive distortions (Briere, 1992)
- Altered emotionality (Briere, 1992)
- Impaired self-reference (Briere, 1992)
- Codependency
- Dissociation (Briere, 1992)
- Disturbed relatedness (Briere, 1992)
- Depression
- Anxiety
- Psychological developmental delays
- Speech and learning problems (Garbarino, 1987)
- Attention deficit disorder (ADD)
- Aggression to others and self (Briere & Runtz, 1990)
- Suicidal ideation (Council on Scientific Affairs, 1993)
- Adolescent suicide (Garnefski, Diekstra, & de

Heus's study (b) as cited in Jenny, Taylor, & Cooper, 1996)
- Compromised school performance (Howing, Wodarski, Kurtz, & Gaudin, 1993)
- Alcohol or other substance abuse (Cavaiola & Schiff, 1988)
- Eating disorders (Rorty, et al., 1994)
- Other psychiatric illness (Brown & Anderson, 1991; Mullen, Martin, Anderson, Romans, & Herbison 1996)

6.1 *Factors exacerbating the trauma.*

Any effort to prevent violence, like any effort to prevent disease, must recognize the particular strengths and weaknesses intrinsic to the child, the child's family, the child's community and the child's society. By noting factors that exacerbate trauma we can begin to identify and protect those children most vulnerable to particular traumas. By reducing or eliminating exacerbating factors in the family, community and society we can reduce both the frequency and severity of harm to the child. The destabilized communities and unraveling of societal "safety nets" now common in many major cities increase both the risk and the impact of violence to children.

6.1.1 *Child.*

- Child exposed prenatally to teratogens such as alcohol. (Fontana & Besharov, 1996)
- Birth difficulty (Korbin, 1987)
- Low birth weight (Browne & Saqi, 1988)
- Failure to thrive
- Disability of the child or deformity
- Infant separated from mother for greater than 24 hours postdelivery (Browne & Saqi, 1988)
- Infant never breast-fed (Browne & Saqi, 1988)
- Undernutrition/malnutrition
- Intellectual deficits (Iverson & Segal, 1990)
- Earlier developmental stage at time of maltreatment
- Born unwanted (Roberts, 1988)
- Difficult child temperament (Brayden, Altemeier, Tucker, Dietrich, & Vietze, 1992)
- Dysfunctional parent–child relationships (Wiehe, 1992)
- Social isolation (Wiehe, 1992; Garbarino et al., 1980)
- Inappropriate child labor
- Adolescent pregnancy

- Other significant life stress (Kotch, et al., 1995)

6.1.2 *Child's associates*: family, friends, caregivers, teachers, etc.

Family Composition
- Unsustainably large family size (Belsky, 1993)
- Child spacing is less than two years (Altemeier, O'Conner, Sherrod, Tucker, & Vietze, 1986; Browne & Saqi, 1988; Wallace, 1995)
- Single-parent household (Browne & Saqi, 1988)
- Absence of father (Wiehe, 1992)
- Presence of unrelated live-in companion

Family Characteristics
- Young parents (under the age of 21) (Browne & Saqi, 1988; Roberts, 1988)
- Limited education
- Unemployment (Cantrell, Carrico, Franklin, & Grubb, 1990; Browne & Saqi, 1988)
- Frequent job changes (Tzeng & Hanner, 1988)
- Poverty
- Illness or death in family (Roberts, 1988)
- Lack provision of basic needs
- Move place of residence frequently
- Social isolation (Wiehe, 1992; Garbarino et al., 1980)
- Faith-based beliefs toward medical care (AAP, 1988)
- Alcohol or other substance abuse by primary caregiver (Roberts, 1988)
- Domestic violence (Browne & Saqi, 1988)
- Parent(s) abused as children
- Parent(s) incarcerated
- Psychopathology in primary caregiver (Veltkamp & Miller, 1994)
- Other extreme life stress (Kotch et al., 1995)

Parental Skill and Performance
- Poor parenting skills
- Inappropriate expectations of child
- Indifferent or intolerant toward child (Browne & Saqi, 1988)
- Overanxious
- Dysfunctional parent–child relationships (Wiehe, 1992)
- View child as a possession or chattel
- Rejection of unwanted child

Characteristics of Other Associates of Child
- Poverty
- Change place of residence frequently
- Presence of other significant life stress

6.1.3 *Child's community*: the social, religious, and cultural influences in the life of the child and his/her family.

- Poverty
- Healthcare facilities are inaccessible, inadequate, or of poor quality (Kaufman & Zigler, 1992)
- Social services are inaccessible, inadequate, or of poor quality
- Presence of unsafe neighborhoods (Garbarino, et al., 1980)
- Support for unsustainably large family size (Belsky, 1993)
- Values child spacing which is less than 2 years (Kaufman & Zigler, 1992)
- Support for viewing child as a possession or chattel
- Tolerance of inappropriate expectations of child
- Presence of other significant life stress (Kotch et al., 1995)

6.1.4 *Child's society*: those who share the history, social, economic, and political background with the child.

- Poverty
- Lack of provision of basic needs
- Lack of adequate adult supervision
- Presence of other significant life stress (Kotch, et al., 1995)
- Maintain high rate of unemployment (Cantrell, Carrico, Franklin, & Grubb, 1990; Browne & Saqi, 1988)
- Healthcare facilities are inaccessible, inadequate, or of poor quality (Kaufman & Zigler, 1992)
- Social services are inaccessible, inadequate, or of poor quality
- Tolerance of domestic violence (Browne & Saqi, 1988)
- Cultural influence and response to children with low birth weight
- Stigma against children with deformities or impairments

- Support for unsustainably large family size (Belsky, 1993)
- Support for child spacing which is less than 2 years (Kaufman & Zigler, 1992)
- Support for viewing children as possessions or chattel (Korbin, 1981)
- Tolerance of inappropriate child labor
- Differential views of male and female children

7.1 *Factors mitigating physical trauma.*
By noting personal, familial, communal and societal factors that mitigate trauma we can begin to reduce the risk of trauma and increase the child's resilience to it. Supporting the creation of mitigating factors to violence is like fluoridating the water to prevent future tooth decay. Minor measures can have immense effects.

7.1.1 *Child.*

- Healthy
- Reached appropriate developmental level
- Supportive helping network (Korbin, 1981; Gelles, 1983 as cited in Gelles, 1987; Kotch, et al., 1995)
- Presence and involvement of extended family and/or a mentor
- Secure attachment (Cicchetti, Carlson, Braunwald, & Aber, 1987)
- Coping skills (Werner & Smith, 1982; Rosenberg & Sonkin, 1992)
- Likable attributes (Kaufman, Johnson, Cohn, & McCleery, 1992)
- Good interpersonal skills (Kaufman & Zigler, 1992)
- High IQ
- Child believes in a purpose for life
- Seen as a separate individual
- Resilient personality (Werner & Smith, 1982)
- Interpretation of maltreatment

7.1.2 *Child's associates*: family, friends, caregivers, teachers, etc.

Family Characteristics
- Healthy
- Parental maturity
- Mother is present and supportive
- Father is present and supportive
- Nurturing family relations
- Parents exhibit coping abilities to meet child's needs

- Interdependent social structure (Korbin, 1981)
- Parents share in child-related responsibilities (Kaufman, Johnson, Cohn, & McCleery, 1992)
- Educational attainment
- Stable marriage
- Stable employment
- Parents have stable living conditions
- Parents enjoy personal interests
- Parents had supportive role models during childhood and adolescence
- Child was planned for
- Parents practiced family planning

Characteristics of Other Associates of Child
- Supportive helping network (Korbin, 1981; Gelles, 1983 as cited in Gelles, 1987; Kotch et al., 1995)
- Secure attachment (Cicchetti, Carlson, Braunwald, & Aber, 1987)
- Coping skills (Werner & Smith's study as cited in *Colorado 2*, 1995; Rosenberg & Sonkin, 1992)
- Overall economic and employment stability
- Provision of basic necessities: food, clothing, shelter, etc.
- Presence and involvement of extended family and/or additional caretakers
- Good interpersonal skills (Kaufman & Zigler, 1992)
- Had supportive role models during childhood and adolescence

7.1.3 *Child's community*: the social, religious, and cultural influences in the life of the child and his/her associates.

- Presence of stable living conditions
- Presence of social and economic supports for at-risk families "at the neighborhood level, where neighborhood is defined by geographic boundaries" (U.S. Advisory Board on Child Abuse and Neglect,1993)
- Supportive helping network (Korbin, 1981; Gelles, 1983 as cited in Gelles, 1987; Kotch et al., 1995)
- Support for effective coping skills (Werner & Smith's study as cited in *Colorado 2*, 1995; Rosenberg & Sonkin, 1992)
- Presence and involvement of extended family and/or additional caretakers

- Presence of affordable, accessible, quality child care
- Opposed to violence
- Availability of an interdependent social network (Korbin, 1981)
- Support for family planning

7.1.4 *Child's society*: those who share the history, social, economic, and political background with the child.

- Socio-economic stability
- Provision of basic necessities: food, shelter, health care
- Culture opposed to violence

8.1 *Primary prevention*.
Programs addressed to the general population that are designed to reduce the occurrence of a particular form of violence.

8.1.1 *Child* (including school-age, preadolescent, and adolescent age groups).

Activities
- Participation in constructive extracurricular activities

Education
- Participation in life skills education which includes topics such as self-esteem, empathy, conflict resolution, communication skills, and stress management (*Colorado 2,* 1995; Garbarino, 1992)
- Participation in violence prevention education
- Participation in alcohol or other substance abuse awareness and prevention program
- Participation in preparenting education by adolescents

8.1.2 *Child's associates*: family, friends, caregivers, teachers, etc.

Education
- Participation in preparent and/or parent education in the community, health/social service agencies, and/or at the worksite including topics such as child development (i.e., ages and stages), nutrition, nonphysical discipline, anger management, and communication (Depanfilis & Salus, 1992)

Health Services

- Utilize prenatal and childhood health care services
- The participation of high-risk pregnant women in prenatal screening (Fontana & Besharov, 1996)
- Home visits for new parents by a health worker (Olds & Kitzman, 1993)

Provision of Basic Needs

- Provide basic necessities, i.e., food, clothing, shelter, nurturing, etc.
- Assure provision of affordable, accessible, quality child care

Promotion

- Promote and practice family planning
- Promote alcohol and other substance abuse awareness and prevention
- Promote the value of healthy family functioning

8.1.3 *Child's community*: the social, religious, and cultural influences in the life of the child and his/her associates.

Activities

- Provide constructive after-school activities for students
- Provide high quality out-of-home child care settings

Education

- Provide education in the community, health/social service agencies, and at the worksite to parents on topics including nutrition, child development (i.e., ages and stages), nonphysical discipline, self-esteem, empathy, conflict resolution, stress management, and communication (Depanfilis & Salus, 1992; Garbarino, 1992; *Colorado* 2, 1995)
- Provide comprehensive, integrated prevention curricula to children and parents which include self-protection training and family life education (Depanfilis & Salus, 1992)
- Educate professionals in healthcare, social service, education, child care, and legal services to identify and report physical abuse
- Provide violence prevention education to children and parents
- Provide alcohol and other substance abuse awareness and prevention programs to children and parents
- Provide preparenting education to adolescents and adults
- Train all citizens to recognize and report child maltreatment

Health and Social Services

- Provide prenatal and childhood health care
- Provide screening to children, adolescents, and parents for maltreatment (Council on Scientific Affairs, 1993)
Health workers offer home visits to new parents (Olds & Kitzman, 1993)
- Provide accessible, affordable, quality mental health care
- Provide crisis helpline with information, referrals, and counseling services
- Assure accessible, affordable, quality childcare programs are available
- Provide basic needs: i.e., food, clothing, shelter, nurturing, etc.
- Develop link between health care and community agencies (Drotar, 1992)
- Facilitate collaborations between informal and formal community support and resource systems (*Colorado* 2, 1995)
- Provide social and health services which are accessible by any family, including "decent housing, job training, employment, and money" (Dubowitz, 1988; Thyen, Thiessen, & Heinsohn-Krug, 1995)

Promotion

- Provide child maltreatment awareness and education through mass media
- Promote the value of healthy family functioning
- Promote family planning
- Promote and implement workplace support for family needs
- Promote constructive extra-curricular activities for children

8.1.4 *Child's society*: those who share the history, social, economic, and political background with the child.

Activities

- Develop and monitor worksite parental leave policies
- Facilitate collaboration between informal and

formal community support and resource structures (*Colorado 2*, 1995)
- Link health care and community agencies (Drotar, 1992)

Education
- Provide support for child abuse education and awareness through mass media and the education system

Health and Social Services
- Provide prenatal and early childhood health care
- Assure affordable, accessible, quality mental health care is available
- Assure affordable, accessible, quality child care programs are available

Promotion
- Promote the value of healthy family functioning
- Promote family planning
- Promote workplace support for family needs

9.1 *Secondary prevention of physical trauma to children*
Programs designed to prevent violence to specific groups of children at-risk for such trauma.

9.1.1 *Child* (including school-age, preadolescent, and adolescent age groups).

Activities
- Participation in counseling (group/individual)
- Participation in constructive extracurricular activities

Education
- Participation in human development education, i.e., classes addressing: coping mechanisms, communication skills, conflict resolution, etc.
- Participation in alcohol and other substance abuse awareness and prevention education

9.1.2 *Child's associates*: family, friends, caregivers, teachers, etc.

Education
- Participate in parent education in the community, health/social service agencies, and/or at the worksite including topics such as nutri-

tion, child development (i.e., ages and stages), nonphysical discipline, anger management, and effective communication (Depanfilis & Salus, 1992)

Health and Social Services
- Provide protection to children living in high-risk environments (Thyen, Thiessen, & Heinsohn-Krug, 1995)
- Provide counseling to at-risk children and/or parents
- Provide alcohol and other substance abuse treatment
- Develop system of identifying at-risk families (*Colorado 2,* 1995)
- Provide social and health services to at-risk families
- Develop and provide community social and health information resources
- Provide home visits for at-risk families by a health worker (Olds & Kitzman, 1993)

Promotion
- Provide child maltreatment awareness and education through mass media
- Promote alcohol and other substance abuse awareness and prevention
- Promote and implement workplace support for family needs
- Promote parent support groups, particularly for parents of special needs children

9.1.3 *Child's community*: the social, religious, and cultural influences in the life of the child and his/her associates.

Education
- Provide parent education in the community, health/social service agencies, and/or at the worksite on topics including nutrition, child development (i.e. ages and stages), non-physical forms of discipline, anger management, and effective communication (Depanfilis & Salus, 1992)
- Provide violence prevention education
- Provide human development education

Health and Social Services
- Provide counseling to at-risk children and/or families
- Provide alcohol and other substance abuse treatment to adolescents and adults

- Provide screening for high-risk mothers during prenatal period (Fontana & Besharov, 1996)
- Provide screening to at-risk children, adolescents, and adults for maltreatment (Council on Scientific Affairs, 1993)
- Develop and monitor a system of identifying at-risk families (*Colorado 2*, 1995)
- Provide social and health services to at-risk families, including "decent housing, job training, employment, and money" (Dubowitz, 1988; Thyen, Thiessen, & Heinsohn-Krug, 1995)
- Develop and provide community information resources
- Provide services for families of children with special needs (*Colorado 2*, 1995; Kaufman, Johnson, Cohn, & McCleery, 1992)
- Provide parent aide programs: supportive, one-on-one relationships for parents at-risk of maltreating their children (Depanfilis & Salus, 1992)
- Provide foster care for children who cannot safely live with their parents
- Provide adoption for children without parents and where the parents cannot or will not parent the child

Promotion
- Provide child maltreatment awareness and education through mass media
- Promote affordable, accessible, quality child care
- Promote alcohol and other substance abuse awareness and prevention
- Promote workplace support for families
- Promote parent support groups, particularly for parents of special needs children
- Promote constructive extra-curricular activities for children

9.1.4 *Child's society*: those who share the history, social, economic, and political background with the child.

Education
- Provide support for education on healthy family functioning
- Provide awareness and prevention education on abuse of alcohol and other substances

Health and Social Services
- Provide foster care for children who cannot safely live with their parents
- Provide adoption for children without parents and where the parents cannot or will not parent the child
- Develop and monitor a system of identifying at-risk families (*Colorado 2*, 1995)
- Develop linkage between health care and community agencies (Drotar, 1992)
- Assure affordable, accessible, quality child care
- Assure affordable, accessible, quality mental health services

Promotion
- Promote healthy family functioning and prevention of child maltreatment through mass media and the education system
- Promote socioeconomic development
- Promote workplace support for families
- Promote family planning

10.1 *Tertiary prevention of trauma to child*
Treatment or rehabilitative programs for those children already harmed by violence which reduce the consequences of and/or prevent recurrence of the trauma.

10.1.1 *Child* (including school-age, preadolescent, and adolescent age groups).

Activities
- Participate in counseling (group/individual)
- Participate in peer support group
- Hospitalization
Involvement in a day or residential treatment center
- Participate in alcohol and other substance abuse treatment
- Utilize respite and crisis care
- Provide crisis helpline with information, referrals, and counseling services
- Participate in constructive extracurricular activities

Education
- Participate in job skills training for late adolescents
- Participate in life skills training for adolescents

10.1.2 *Child's associates*: family, friends, caregivers, teachers, etc.

Activities
- Participate in counseling (group/individual)
- Utilize parent aide programs: supportive, one-on-one relationships (Depanfilis & Salus, 1992)

Education
- Provide parent education in the community, health/social service agencies, and/or at the worksite on topics including nutrition, child development (i.e., ages and stages), nonphysical discipline, anger management, and effective communication (Depanfilis & Salus, 1992)

Promotion
- Promote use of shelters for maltreated children
- Promote alcohol and other substance abuse treatment for parents and adolescents
- Promote and provide parent and child/adolescent support groups
- Promote crisis helpline with information, referrals, and counseling services

10.1.3 *Child's community*: the social, religious, and cultural influences in the life of the child and his/her associates.

Education
- Provide parent education which includes topics such as nonphysical discipline and child development (i.e., ages and stages), and offered in the community, health/social service agencies, or at the worksite (Depanfilis & Salus, 1992)

Health and Social Services
- Provide respite and crisis care
- Provide crisis helpline with information, referrals, and counseling services
- Provide careful follow-up with abusive families (Rivara, 1985)
- Develop and implement system to identify victims of child maltreatment
- Provide parent support groups
- Provide parent aide programs: supportive, one-on-one relationships for parents (Depanfilis & Salus, 1992)

- Develop linkage between health care and community agencies (Drotar, 1992)
- Provide advocates for individual mistreated children to reduce the chance of additional injury
- Provide foster care for children who cannot safely live with their parents
- Provide adoption for children without parents and where the parents cannot or will not parent the child

Promotion
- Provide child maltreatment awareness and education through mass media
- Promote socioeconomic development
- Promote constructive extracurricular activities for children

10.1.4 *Child's society*: those who share the history, social, economic, and political background with the child.

Promotion
- Promote healthy family functioning and prevention of child maltreatment through mass media and the education system
- Promote socioeconomic development

Health and Social Services
- Develop linkage between health care and community social service agencies (Drotar, 1992)
- Develop and monitor a system to identify victims of child maltreatment
- Provide advocates for individual mistreated children to reduce the chance of additional injury
- Provide foster care for children who cannot safely live with their parents
- Provide adoption for children without parents and where the parents cannot or will not parent the child

Model Prevention Programs
The following is a brief sample of prevention programs which have been shown to reduce some of the risk factors associated with physical abuse of children. There are a multitude of others as well. Please list additional programs you would recommend that have demonstrated success.
- Center for Child Protection, San Diego, CA

- KEEPSAFE therapeutic preschool (Oates, Gray, Schweitzer, Kempe, & Harmon, 1995)
- Home visitation programs (Olds & Kitzman, 1993)
- Children's Institute International (http://www.childrensinstitute.org)
- Child Protection Center Lubeck (Thyen, Thiessen, & Heinsohn-Krug, 1995)
- Project TRUST (Hays & Megel, 1996)
- Hawaii Healthy Start, Honolulu
- Commentary on Prevention

VIII. DEFINING VIOLENCE TOWARD ADULTS

Much of the definition of violence to adults can be derived from the definition of violence to children. The chief difference is absence of developmental trauma since adults have, by definition, reached their full physical maturity. However, there remains substantial trauma due to developmental deficits, whether congenital or environmental. Also of note is the needs of the elderly who can suffer substantial loss of capacity and function as they age. The dynamics of abuse of dependent children and dependent elders are not dissimilar.

Parents increasingly face responsibility for both dependent children and dependent elders. Meeting the needs of one diverts attention from the other. To begin to address this issue there must be a method of reasonably assisting parents to meet the needs of their dependents. It is not sufficient to vest children with rights to food, shelter, and nurture that they, due to their age, are unable to exercise. Rights must be extended to the parent to be able to provide for and protect their children. In other words, each Nation should owe a duty of support to each parent to insure that the developmental needs of each child are met. The UN recognizes such a right in its Convention on the Rights of the Child. Recognizing this right would be another important step in reducing violence to children and thereby reclaiming the full potential of each child and reducing that child's potential for becoming violent.

Acknowledgments

This endeavor would not have been possible without the significant and essential contribution of Diane Riter M.P.H., Fredrick Rivara M.D., & David Hall M.D. Ms. Riter was the primary researcher and drafter of section VII. Any shortcomings elsewhere are the responsibility of the author.

Also See the Following Articles

CHILD ABUSE • CHILDREARING, VIOLENT AND NONVIOLENT • FAMILY STRUCTURES, VIOLENCE AND NONVIOLENCE • PUBLIC HEALTH MODELS OF VIOLENCE AND VIOLENCE PREVENTION • STRUCTURAL VIOLENCE • TELEVISION PROGRAMMING AND VIOLENCE

Bibliography

Alston, P. (1994). *Best interest of a child: Reconciling culture and human rights.* New York: UNICEF and Oxford Clarendon Press.

Australian National Committee on Violence (1990). *Violence: Directions for Australia.* Canberra: National Committee on Violence, Australian Institute of Criminology.

Belsey, M. (1993). Child abuse: Measuring a global problem. *World Health Statistical Quarterly, 46,* 69–77.

Belsky, J. (1993). Etiology of child maltreatment. A developmental-ecological analysis. *Psychological Bulletin, 114,* 413–434.

Briere, J. (1992). *Child abuse trauma.* Newbury Park, CA: Sage.

Cicchetti, D., Carlson, V., Braunwald, K., & Aber, J. (1987). The sequelae of child maltreatment. In R. Gelles & J. Lancaster (Eds.), *Child abuse and neglect: Biosocial dimensions* (pp. 277–298). New York: Aldine de Gruyter.

Depanfilis, D., & Salus, M. (1992). *A coordinated response to child abuse and neglect: A basic manual* (DHHS Publication No. ACF 92-30362). Washington, DC: U.S. Government Printing Office.

Eisenbruch, M. (1992). Towards a culturally sensitive DSM: Cultural Bereavement in Cambodian Refugees and the traditional healer as taxonomist. *Journal of Nervous and Mental Disease 18*(1), 8–10.

Eisenbruch, M. (1994). Resources and limitations in meeting the health needs of the Cambodian Population. Paper presented at Conference on Mental Health Education for Medical Doctors in Cambodia" Phnom Penh, 19–21, April.

Finkelhor, D., & Dziuba-Leatherman, J. (1994). Children as victims of violence: A national survey. *Pediatrics, 94*(4), 413–420.

Fontana, V., & Besharov, D. (1996). *The Maltreated Child* (5th ed.). Springfield, IL: Charles S. Thomas.

Garbarino, J. (1986). Can we measure success in preventing child abuse? Issues in policy, programming, and research. *Child Abuse and Neglect, 10,* 143–156.

Haj-Yahia, M., & Shor, R. (1995). Child maltreatment as perceived by Arab students of social science in the West Bank. *Child Abuse and Neglect, 19*(10), 1209–1219.

Hays, B., & Megel, M. (1996). Evaluation of the effectiveness of Project TRUST: An elementary school-based victimization prevention strategy. *Child Abuse and Neglect, 20*(9), 821–832.

Johnson, O. (1981). The socioeconomic context of child abuse and neglect in native South America. (pp. 56–70). Langness, L., Child abuse and cultural values: the case of New Guinea. (pp. 13–34). Le Vine, S. & Le Vine, R., Child abuse and neglect in Sub-Saharan Africa. (pp. 35–55). In J. Korbin (Ed.), Child abuse and neglect: Cross cultural perspectives. Los Angeles, CA: University of California Press.

Kempe, C. (1982). Cross-cultural perspectives in child abuse. *Pediatrics, 69*(4), 497–498.

Korbin, J. (1987). Child maltreatment in cross-cultural perspective: Vulnerable children and circumstances. In R. Gelles & J. Lancaster (Eds.), *Child abuse and neglect: Biosocial dimensions* (pp. 31–56). New York: Aldine de Gruyter.

Kotch, J., Browne, D., Ringwalt, C., Stewart, P., Ruina, E., Holt, K., Lowman, B., & Jung, J. (1995). Risk of child abuse or neglect in a cohort of low-income children. *Child Abuse and Neglect, 19*(9), 1115–1130.

Kydd, J. (1992). Abandoning our children: Mothers, alcohol and drugs. *Denver University Law Review, 69*(3), 360–479.

Leach, P. (1994). *Children first.* New York: Alfred A. Knopf.

Ludwig, S., & Kornberg, A. (Eds.) (1992). *Child abuse: A medical reference.* New York: Churchill–Livingstone.

Lykes, B. (1994). *Terror, silencing, and children: International multidisciplinary collaboration with Guatemalan, Mayan communities. Social Science Medicine, 38*(4), 543–552.

Mullen, P., Martin, J., Anderson, J., Romans, S., & Herbison, G. (1996). The long-term impact of the physical, emotional, and sexual abuse of children: A community study. *Child Abuse & Neglect, 20*(1), 7–21.

National Center for Health Statistics (1995). International Classifications for Diseases, Ninth Revision-Clinical Modification (ICD-9) [CD-ROM].

National Research Council (1993). *Understanding child abuse and neglect.* Washington, DC: National Academy Press.

Oates, R., Gray, J., Schweitzer, L., Kempe, R., & Harmon, R. (1995). A therapeutic preschool for abused children: The KEEPSAFE Project. Kempe Early Education Project Serving Abused Families. *Child Abuse & Neglect, 19*(11), 1379–1386.

Rivara, F. (1985). Physical abuse in children under two: A study of therapeutic outcomes. *Child Abuse & Neglect, 9*(1), 81–87.

Sedlak, A., & Broadhurt, D. (1996). *Executive summary of the third national incidence study of child abuse and neglect.* U.S. Department of Health and Human Services, National Center on Child Abuse and Neglect. Available: http://www.calib.com/nccanch/data/nis3.txt

Trickett, P. K., and Schellenbach, C. J. (Eds.) (1998). *Violence against children in the family and the community.* Washington, DC: American Psychological Association.

UNICEF (1997). *Innocenti digest no. 2: Children & violence.* Florence, Italy: International Child Development Center.

U.S. Advisory Board on Child Abuse and Neglect (1993). *Neighbors helping neighbors: A new national strategy for the protection of children.* Washington, DC: U.S. Government Printing Office.

Veltkamp, L., & Miller, T. (1994). *Clinical handbook of child abuse and neglect.* Madison, CT: International Universities Press.

World Health Organization (1994). Protocol for the study of interpersonal physical abuse of children (WHO Publication WHO/FHE/CHD/94.1). Geneva, Switzerland.

For additional references see the Child VIP protocols at <www.childvip.org> or write to the author at <jkydd@helsell.com>.

War Crimes

Howard S. Levie
United States Naval War College

GLOSSARY

Concentration Camps The establishments to which the Nazis sent Jews, Gypsies, Soviet prisoners of war, and other "undesirables" to be executed. At the Auschwitz concentration camp alone, established by the Nazis in Poland, more than 4,000,000 individuals were put to death in gas chambers and by other methods.

Crimes against Humanity This term, as defined in the 1945 London Charter of the International Military Tribunal, includes many customary war crimes; however, it is also the basis for the crime now known as "genocide."

Flyer Lynching When the Allies had secured control of the skies over Germany in World War II, the Nazi Government ordered that the police and the military were not to interfere if angry civilians attacked Allied air crews who had parachuted from downed aircraft. As a result many Allied aviators died at the hands of crowds of German civilians.

Grave Breaches The breaches of the four 1949 Geneva Conventions for the Protection of War Victims specified in Articles 50/51/130/147.

International Military Tribunal The title of the war crimes court established by France, Great Britain, the Soviet Union, and the United States by the 1945 London Charter for the trial of the major Nazi war criminals in Nuremberg.

International Military Tribunal for the Far East The title of the war crimes tribunal established by General MacArthur as Supreme Commander for the Allied Powers for the trial of the major Japanese war criminals in Tokyo.

Military Commissions Military courts established by orders of local military commanders for the trials of individuals charged with having committed war crimes.

I. INTRODUCTION

The trials of war crimes were very much in the forefront of the news during the years immediately after the end of World War II. They then ceased to be of news value except on rare occasions such as the My Lai Massacre, and even then much of the media did not really view that as a war crime. With the events in Bosnia-Herzegovina and in Rwanda, war crimes and war crimes trials have once again become front-page material. This article reviews the history of the international treatment of war crimes and the conduct of war crimes trials so as to ensure a better understanding of what is now transpiring in the two International Tribunals established by the Security Council of the United Nations and of what actions in this respect may be expected from the international community in the future.

II. HISTORICAL

While certain rules of warfare developed early in present-day civilization, the humanitarian law of war was late in coming into being. There are innumerable instances of extreme cruelty in war to be found in the Bible. Thus, for example, in 1 *Samuel* 15:3, the following appears:

> Go now and fall upon the Amalekites and destroy them, and, and put their property under ban. Spare no one; put them all to death, men and women, children and babes in arms, herds and flocks, camels and asses.

This was an early instance of what we would now consider an act of genocide, but which at that time was a customary procedure.

The fate of a prisoner of war under Persian, Greek, Roman, and Muslim custom, and during the Crusades, was little better. While there were some instances of prisoners of war being enslaved or ransomed, rather than killed, it was not until the Middle Ages that ransom became a practice, and even then it applied only to knights and not to foot soldiers. The latter would still either be killed or enslaved, although some peace treaties did provide for the release of prisoners of war.

During the late 18th and early 19th centuries the practice of exchanging prisoners of war arose and while it is sometimes claimed that Napoleon I destroyed this humane system, as late as the American Civil War (1861–1865), the two sides entered into such an agreement. However, it failed to function as intended, and after the war the United States tried a number of former members of the Confederate Army for the war crime of maltreatment of Union prisoners of war. The most famous of these cases was *United States v. Henry Wirz*. Wirz was the commander of the notorious Confederate prisoner-of-war camp located at Andersonville, Georgia. He was found guilty of gross violations of the law of war in his treatment of the prisoners of war in his custody and he was sentenced to be executed.

On April 24, 1863 the United States War Department issued its General Order No. 100, a code of the law of war drafted by Francis Lieber, an emigre from Prussia, a veteran of several European wars, and then a Professor of Political Science at Columbia University in New York City. This order, known generally as the "Lieber Code," was the first attempt to codify the law of war and it served as a major source for subsequent international codification efforts. Two relevant provisions of that Code stated:

> 59. A prisoner of war remains answerable for his crimes committed against the captor's army or people, committed before he was captured, and for which he has not been punished by his own authorities.

All prisoners are liable to the infliction of retaliatory measures.

> 71. Whoever intentionally inflicts additional wounds on an enemy already wholly disabled, or kills such an enemy, or who orders or encourages soldiers to do so, shall suffer death, if duly convicted, whether he belongs to the Army of the United States, or is an enemy captured after having committed his misdeed.

In 1874 a Diplomatic Conference which met in Brussels drafted an "International Declaration Concerning the Laws and Customs of War." Unfortunately, this Declaration never became effective. Then in 1899, and again in 1907, so-called "Peace Conferences" were conducted at The Hague. The First (1899) Hague Conference drafted a "Convention with Respect the Laws and Customs of War on Land," to which were attached "Regulations Respecting the Laws and Customs of War on Land." The Second (1907) Hague Conference drafted a total of 14 conventions of which Convention No. IV and its Regulations were largely the same as the 1899 Convention and its Regulations.

III. WORLD WAR I

World War I began just 7 years later and numerous violations of the laws adopted at The Hague occurred during that war and both sides conducted war crimes trials during the course of that conflict. One of the most famous of those trials was that of Captain Fryatt of the merchant ship *Brussels*. At the outbreak of the war the British Admiralty instructed merchant ship captains that if their ship was approached by a German submarine, they were to attempt to ram it. Captain Fryatt's ship was hailed by a German submarine and he attempted to ram it, driving it away and saving his ship. He was praised in Parliament and was given an inscribed gold watch by the Admiralty. Sometime later he had the misfortune of having his ship captured by the Germans, who tried him as having acted as an illegal combatant, the gold watch being received in evidence. His defense was that he had merely obeyed the orders of his Government. The German court found that this was not an excuse, convicted him, and sentenced him to be executed. This was done a few hours later. The British were incensed and called it "judicial murder." However, it now being firmly established that governmental orders are no defense, if Captain Fryatt were to be tried today, the result would very probably be the same as that reached by the German court.

The Treaty of Versailles, which ended that war, provided that Germany would turn over to the Allies for trial for war crimes those individuals who were charged with violations of the law of war and who were requested by the Allies for trial. The treaties with each of Germany's former allies also contained such a provision—but very little use was made of those provisions. Inasmuch as it was recognized that compliance by the weak Weimar government with the lengthy Allied demand, which included many of the major figures of Germany, would have resulted in the fall of that government and chaos in Germany, the Allies ultimately accepted a German proposal that individuals named by the Allies would be tried in Germany by the Supreme Court of Leipzig. This proved a fiasco, as guilty men were acquitted and convicted men received completely inadequate sentences. After 12 trials the Allies discontinued submitting names of proposed defendants to the Germans. (The Treaty also provided that ex-German Kaiser Wilhelm was to be arraigned before an *ad hoc* international tribunal "for a supreme offence against international morality and the sanctity of treaties." However, he had sought and obtained refuge in The Netherlands, which refused to extradite him for trial.) The French tried hundreds of cases *in absentia* but the British took no further action. This experience indicated that permitting a defeated nation to try its own personnel for war crimes committed against the enemy was not a viable solution to the problem of punishing individuals for violations of the law of war. The members of the German court, although an appellate court consisting of experienced judges, allowed their personal feelings as Germans to influence their decisions. Unfortunately, when such trials are conducted by the victor or victors, there is the danger that they will be a mockery of justice and, even if they are fairly conducted, they

are labeled "victor's justice," the implication being that trials by the victors of members of the defeated nation could not possibly be fair.

One case tried by the Supreme Court of Leipzig is worthy of mention. In the *Llandovery Castle Case* two officers of a German submarine were charged with joining their captain in machine gunning the lifeboats of a ship that the submarine had sunk. Their defense was that they were obeying the order of their commanding officer. The Leipzig Court held that there was no duty to comply with obviously illegal orders, such as those present in this case, and found the two officers guilty. That precedent remains a valid rule of the law of war.

In 1929 a Diplomatic Conference which met in Geneva drafted a Convention Relative to the Treatment of Prisoners of War. With the exception of Japan and the Soviet Union, almost all of the participants in World War II were parties to this Convention. It was, therefore, the provisions of this Convention that governed the treatment of prisoners of war by most of the belligerents during World War II, and a great number of the war crimes trials conducted after World War II involved violations of the provisions of the Geneva Convention.

IV. WORLD WAR II

A. Europe

War crimes trials, like all penal trials, have two functions: (1) to make it clear to other individuals that they will be punished if they violate the law of war and (2) to inflict punishment on those who do violate the law of war. Unfortunately, when war crimes trials are not conducted until after the conclusion of hostilities, the first function mentioned above is completely lost.

On a number of occasions early in World War II the Allied powers (then known as, and hereinafter referred to as, the "United Nations" although that organization was not yet in existence) announced that at the conclusion of hostilities they intended to try those individuals who had committed violations of the law of war. (According to one author, in September, 1939, only a few days after Germany's invasion of Poland, the German Army had created its own "War Crimes Bureau.") On January 13, 1942 the Declaration of St. James was issued by the nations then at war with Nazi Germany. It stated that at the conclusion of hostilities they would try and punish those persons who had been found guilty of having violated the laws and customs of war—war crimes. This proposition was repeated in a number of statements thereafter issued by the Chiefs of State of the Soviet Union, the United Kingdom, and the United States. (After the beginning of the general war in the Far East, the Republic of China joined in similar statements with respect to violations of the law of war committed in that area.) On October 20, 1943 the United Nations (with the exception of the Soviet Union) established the United Nations Commission for the Investigation of War Crimes, subsequently renamed the United Nations War Crimes Commission.

Upon the termination of the war with Germany in May, 1945, representatives of the four major powers (the Provisional French Government, the Soviet Union, the United Kingdom, and the United States) met in London and on August 8, 1945 agreement was reached on the Charter of an International Military Tribunal, a court established for the purpose of the trial for war crimes committed by the major Nazi war criminals. Nineteen other nations subsequently adhered to the Agreement to which the Tribunal's Charter was attached. While it was unique in many ways, special attention must be given to the novel provisions which (1) made Crimes Against Peace a war crime, (2) made persons who participated in a conspiracy to commit a war crime subject to punishment, and (3) made membership in an organization found by the Tribunal to be criminal in nature a war crime. Because of the limitations on the trial of Germans for war crimes committed against other Germans and because of the vast number of persons who were members of organizations found by the Tribunal to be criminal in nature, the task of trying these individuals was subsequently turned over to the courts of the Federal Republic of Germany, which tried many thousands of such cases. To be guilty, the accused had to be found to have known that the organization was criminal when he or she joined it or to have him-/herself participated in criminal acts. In view of the enormousness of this task it still engaged the attention of the German courts in the 1960s when the German statute of limitations for crimes was about to put an end to such prosecutions. In order to prevent such an occurrence the General Assembly of the United Nations caused to be drafted, and recommended that States ratify, a Convention on the Non-Applicability of Statutory Limitations to War Crimes and Crimes Against Humanity. In the end this proved unnecessary, as the Federal Republic's legislature enacted a law extending that nation's statute of limitations for war crimes.

The International Military Tribunal consisted of one judge and one alternate from each of the four original signatories. The indictment contained charges against 24 defendants but one of them committed suicide and another was found to be mentally incompetent, so 22

were actually tried. The arraignment took place in Berlin on October 18, 1945 and the trial itself began in Nuremberg, in the American Zone of Occupation, on November 30, 1945 and continued until August 31, 1946. The judgment, rendered on October 1, 1946, found 19 of the accused guilty of war crimes and acquitted 3. (All three of the men acquitted by the International Military Tribunal were subsequently found guilty of various offenses by German courts and were sentenced to terms of imprisonment by those courts.) The decision of the Tribunal was unanimous except that the Soviet Judge, General I. T. Nikitchenko, while concurring generally, dissented from the three acquittals and from the decisions that certain of the organizations charged were found not to be criminal in nature. Of those found guilty, 12 were sentenced to death, 3 to life imprisonment, and 4 to terms of imprisonment. Only 10 were actually executed, as Martin Bormann, Hitler's deputy, was tried *in absentia* and was never captured and Hermann Goering committed suicide by taking poison just before he was to be hanged. (All of their bodies were cremated and their ashes were scattered at random.) Rudolf Hess was the only accused tried by the International Military Tribunal at Nuremberg who was still in prison when he died (or committed suicide) in 1987. The judgment of the Tribunal was final, there being no provision for review or appeals.

Subsequent to the delivery of the judgment by the International Military Tribunal, the General Assembly of the United Nations adopted a Resolution affirming "the principles of international law recognized by the Charter of the Nuremberg Tribunal and the judgment of the Tribunal" and directed the Committee on the codification of international law (now the International Law Commission) to formulate those principles (UNGA RES 95(I), December 11, 1946). The International Law Commission complied with that directive, formulating seven principles which may be regarded as mandatory rules of international law ([1950] YB ILC, II, at 374). And on December 9, 1948 the General Assembly of the United Nations adopted a Convention on the Prevention and Punishment of the Crime of Genocide and proposed its ratification by the individual nations.

In order to have some uniformity in the actions taken in the four occupation zones of Germany, on December 20, 1945, the unified governing body, the Allied Control Council, adopted Law No. 10, entitled Punishment of Persons Guilty of War Crimes, Crimes Against Peace and Against Humanity. The United States implemented that law by establishing a series of courts, each consisting of three American civilian judges, which sat at Nuremberg. They tried 12 cases involving a total of 177 high civilian and military officials and leaders of Nazi Germany. They acquitted 35 and sentenced 24 to be executed. (These 12 trials are known generally as the Subsequent Proceedings.) As reasoned opinions were required and rendered, these 12 cases represent a large part of the judicially stated law of war crimes. It is, therefore, appropriate to review a few of them.

The *Medical Case* (*United States v. Karl Brandt*) concerned doctors who had been involved in using prisoners of war, Jews, Gypsies, and other "asocial" persons for medical experiments, usually with dire results for the persons who were the subjects of the experiments. (The Japanese followed a similar procedure in what is known as the *Kyushu University Case*.) During the course of its opinion the Tribunal enunciated 10 principles that must be met before medical experiments can be made on live human beings, the first of which was that: "The voluntary consent of the human subject is absolutely essential." Of course, there had been no such consent by any of the subjects of the German experiments. The *Justice Case* (*United States v. Josef Alstoetter*) named as accused judges, prosecutors, and officials of the Nazi Ministry of Justice. They were charged with and found guilty of enforcing laws that did not exist or that violated international law and with conducting grossly unfair trials. The *Pohl Case* (*United States v. Oswald Pohl*) named as defendants members of the Nazi SS, the organization that, among its many activities, operated the concentration camps. In addition to other offenses, they were found guilty of the use of slave labor. The *Hostage Case* (*United States v. Wilhelm List*) involved the trial of high-ranking officers of the German army who were charged with ordering their troops to commit so-called "reprisal killings," the killing of large numbers of innocent members of the civilian population of occupied countries as reprisal for actions by local resistance forces, the usual order being for the execution of 100 civilians for each German soldier killed by the resistance. The *Flick Case* (*United States v. Friedrich Flick*), the *I. G. Farben Case* (*United States v. Carl Krauch*), and the *Krupp Case* (*United States v. Alfried Krupp*) all involved leading industrialists, many of whom had been responsible for Hitler's rise to power and who had then taken advantage of the available opportunities to gain possession of factories in occupied territory, to take possession of and to move to Germany machinery from such factories, to use slave labor, and so on. The *Einsatzgruppen Case* (*United States v. Otto Ohlendorf*) was concerned with the units consisting of members of the SS (so-called "Extermination Units") who accompanied the German armies as they moved forward into the Soviet Union and who were found

to have murdered over a million Communists, Jews, Gypsies, and so on. (This trial was labeled "the biggest murder trial in history." In truth, as we discussed below, that prize should actually go to the Polish trial of Rudolf Hoess.) Finally, in the *Ministries Case* (*United States v. Ernst von Weizaecker*) the accused were all high officials of the Nazi government or of the SS. (For some reason one banker, not directly connected with the government, was included as a defendant.) This case is notable for the fact that it is the only European trial, apart from that of the International Military Tribunal at Nuremberg, in which an accused was found guilty of crimes against peace.

However, these trials accounted for only a very small percentage of the persons alleged to have committed conventional war crimes and crimes against humanity during the course of World War II in Europe. The chore of trying these cases for the United States was assigned to military commissions sitting in Dachau. (It was probably no coincidence that these trials were held at Dachau, which had been one of the more notorious Nazi concentration camps.) While there were a great many different offenses tried by these military commissions, the majority of the cases they tried fell into three categories: (1) concentration camp personnel, the trials of persons who had maltreated and murdered anti-Nazis, Jews, Gypsies, prisoners of war, and so on while acting in some capacity in a concentration camp; and (2) flyer lynching cases, the trials of persons involved in the killing by German civilians of United Nations airmen who had parachuted to the ground after their planes had been shot down. The murder of these downed airmen was official policy as the Nazi government had issued the "Terror Flyer Order," which prohibited the military and the police from interfering to protect these prisoners of war from the actions of the civilians (it must be borne in mind that anyone, including civilians, may commit a war crime); and (3) euthanasia, the trials of persons involved in the execution of the habitually criminal, the aged, the insane, the tubercular, and so on, the persons whom Hitler called the "useless eaters" or the "idle eaters" because while they consumed food, they were nonproductive. Inasmuch as the great majority of the victims of this policy were Germans, the German courts tried most of the cases of this category. And it must be borne in mind that similar and other types of war crimes were being tried not only in the other zones of occupied Germany but also in Poland and in a number of the nations that had been allies of Nazi Germany but now had new democratic governments. The British tried most of their cases before regular military courts, while the French tried most of their cases before their Permanent Military Tribunals. All of the members of the United Nations War Crimes Commission submitted copies of the records of their war crimes trials to that organization. As the Soviet Union was not a member, it did not submit any information to the Commission, which did, however, include in its files data with respect to some of the trials conducted by the Soviet Union obtained through the medium of the interception of radio broadcasts. The Commission published a 15-volume set of books entitled *Law Reports of Trials of War Criminals* in which there are lengthy discussions of many of the cases tried and of the law that they represent.

The first concentration camp case was tried by the British. It involved the Belsen concentration camp. The trial began on September 17, 1945 and ended 2 months later. Of the 44 accused, 14 were acquitted, 11 were sentenced to be executed, and 19 received prison sentences. (A well-known British professor of law, representing the accused, contended that to be a war crime the act charged had to have had a direct connection with the operations of war and that this could not be said of the concentration camps. Neither the court in the *Belsen Case* nor any other court or commission trying a concentration camp case accepted this theory.) Subsequently, the British tried another famous concentration camp case, that of Ravensbruck. An unusual aspect of this latter case was that five women were sentenced to death. Military commissions of the United States tried personnel of the concentration camps at Buchenwald, Dachau, Flossenburg, Mauthausen, and Nordhausen. The French tried 50 accused connected with the Natzweiler concentration camp. Of the accused, one was acquitted and 21 were sentenced to death. As discussed below, Poland tried two cases involving the concentration camp (better known as an extermination camp) at Auschwitz and one involving the concentration camp at Majdanek. Czeckoslovakia tried one case involving a high-ranking Nazi official who had been in charge of the supervision of a number of concentration camps.

One of the accused tried by the International Military Tribunal at Nuremberg was Ernst Kaltenbrunner, who oversaw all the concentration camps maintained by the Nazis. At that trial Rudolf Hoess, who had been the commandant of the concentration camp at Auschwitz in Poland for about $3\frac{1}{2}$ years, testified that during that period $2\frac{1}{2}$ million people had been executed and another half-million had died of starvation. Subsequently, he and his successor, with a number of the other Nazi personnel who had functioned at that concentration camp, were the subjects of separate trials by Polish

courts and a large number of them were convicted and sentenced to be executed. (These are the trials that are undoubtedly entitled to the title of "the biggest murder trials in history.")

Probably the most important flyer lynching case tried by the United States was the *Borkum Island Case*. An American bomber made a forced landing on Borkum Island, occupied by German military and civilians. Seven members of the crew surrendered to the German military. The latter were subsequently ordered to take their prisoners to the airport by what was the most dangerous of several available routes and the police were reminded of the "Terror Flyer Order" issued by the Hitler Government, which prohibited the police and the military from interfering to protect flyers who had been shot down and who were taken prisoner from civilians. The flyers were beaten by the civilians (at the urging of the mayor) and were shot to death. A number of the persons involved were tried and the mayor was sentenced to death.

A well-known British case involving the lynching of downed airmen was the *Essen Lynching Case*. There the German air officer commander, Heyer, ordered a military escort to take three captured British airmen to the Luftwaffe interrogation center, reminding the members of the escort that they were not to interfere to protect the British airmen from the German civilians. The crowd of civilians attacked the airmen and beat them to death, with no action being taken by the escort to protect them. Heyer and one civilian were sentenced to death. The escort and several civilians were sentenced to prison terms.

The most important euthanasia case is the so-called *Hadamar Trial* in which seven persons connected with the Hadamar Institute were charged with killing more than 400 Russian and Polish men, women, and children, who allegedly suffered from incurable tuberculosis. It is estimated that a total in excess of 10 thousand mentally ill Germans were killed under this program. As late as 1966, the Federal Republic of Germany, which tried most of these cases because the victims were German, requested and obtained the extradition from Ghana of one of the doctors who had participated in this program.

The *Stalag Luft III Case* (*Trial of Max Wielen*) demonstrated once again Hitler's (and the Nazis') lack of respect for the specific provisions of the law of war. Article 92 of the 1929 Geneva Prisoner-of-War Convention provided that the penalty for a prisoner of war's unsuccessful attempt to escape was disciplinary punishment only. Articles 89 and 90 provided that disciplinary punishment was limited to confinement for 30 days and certain additional minor punishments such as fines, discontinuance of extra privileges, and so on. When some 80 British prisoners of war escaped from the prisoner-of-war camp called Stalag Luft III, Hitler ordered that "more than half of the escaped officers will be shot." Actually, 50 of them were captured and shot by the Gestapo. The war crimes trial was conducted in Hamburg and in September, 1947 each of the accused who was found to have killed a recaptured prisoner of war was sentenced to death.

The *Ardeatine Caves Massacre (Trial of Albert Kesselring)* was tried by the British in Venice early in 1947. Twenty-eight German policemen who were marching in Rome were killed by a bomb. (Four more died later.) Hitler immediately ordered the execution within 24 hours of 10 Italians for each German policeman killed. Kesselring, the Commander of German forces in Italy and von Mackensen and Maelzer, his subordinates, claimed that Kappler, the head of the SD in Rome, told them that there was an adequate number of prisoners under death sentence. (Kappler denied this.) Three hundred and thirty-five prisoners, including a man of 70 and a boy of 14, one individual who had been tried and acquitted, and a number of Jews, some of whom were not even Italian, were taken to the Ardeatine Caves where they were shot and then the cave was blown up.

Kesselring was found guilty. Von Mackensen and Maelzer had earlier been tried in Rome and had been found guilty. All three received the death penalty but in all three cases this was commuted to life imprisonment. Kappler was turned over to the Italians by the British. He was tried and convicted by an Italian court. One Caruso, who had been the Chief of Police of Rome at the time and who had collaborated with Kappler, was also tried by an Italian court and was convicted and sentenced to death, much to the satisfaction of the Romans. (Maelzer was also tried and convicted by a United States Military Commission in Florence, charged with parading British and American prisoners of war through the streets of Rome in violation of the provision of the 1929 Geneva Prisoner-of-War Convention, which prohibited subjecting prisoners of war to public curiosity.)

The *Abbaye Ardenne Case (Trial of S.S. Brigadefuhrer Kurt Meyer)* was a famous war crimes case tried by a Canadian military court, the accused being charged with ordering his troops to deny the granting of quarter and to shoot prisoners of war. He was found guilty of giving the order for no quarter and of permitting the shooting of prisoners of war on two occasions. The military court adjudged the death sentence but this was reduced to life imprisonment by higher authority.

Numerous war crimes trials were also conducted in Denmark, France, Greece, Italy, the Netherlands, Norway, and the Soviet Union, as well as in former enemy countries such as Austria, Germany, Hungary, and so on.

B. The Far East

After the Japanese surrender in September, 1945, somewhat similar judicial events occurred in the Pacific. On January 19, 1946 General Douglas MacArthur, acting as the Supreme Commander for the Allied Powers occupying Japan, issued a proclamation establishing an International Tribunal for the Far East with a charter very similar to that of the Nuremberg Tribunal. However, here there were 11 judges, one from each of the nine countries that had signed the instrument of surrender on the U.S.S. Missouri, as well as India and the Philippines; and General MacArthur retained the right to review any case involving a death sentence. One of the major preliminary difficulties encountered was in reaching a decision as to whether Japanese Emperor Hirohito should be named in the indictment as an accused. When it was pointed out that the Emperor was regarded as a god by the Japanese and that the unrest in Japan caused by his indictment would necessitate a number of additional army divisions to maintain order throughout the occupation, the decision was reached by the Far East Commission, the international political governing body for occupied Japan, that he would not be included in the indictment. It was a wise decision because the extent of the Emperor's involvement in Japan's decision to go to war was debatable and, perhaps as a result, the occupation was one of the most orderly of recent times. (Individual occupation personnel could go anywhere in Japan without any danger of being interfered with by the Japanese people.)

Twenty-eight accused were arraigned before the International Tribunal for the Far East in Tokyo on May 3 and 4, 1946 and the trial proper began a month later on June 3, 1946. (Two of the accused died during the course of the trial and the trial of one other was severed because of his mental condition.) It ended almost two years later, on April 16, 1948, and the reading of the opinions occurred during the period between November 4 and 12, 1948. Unlike the results reached in the decision of the International Military Tribunal at Nuremberg, where there was only one majority opinion and the only dissent was that of the Soviet Judge with respect to the findings of not guilty, in the International Military Tribunal for the Far East, in addition to the majority opinion, there was one separate opinion as well as three concurring opinions and three dissenting opinions. The judges from France, India, and the Netherlands dissented. Judge Pal, the Indian judge, had announced his intention to vote to acquit all of the accused immediately upon his arrival in Tokyo, before the trial had even started, and his dissenting opinion contains numerous errors of fact and of law. Parts of the latter challenged the very jurisdiction of the Tribunal. Once again there was no provision for appeal but, as noted above, death sentences required General MacArthur's approval. The majority of the Tribunal adjudged seven death sentences. However, unlike the procedure followed in Europe, here the cremated ashes of the executed war criminals were preserved. Years later they were buried with honors by the Japanese and their graves are now a shrine.

In the Far East there were also trials for conventional war crimes and crimes against humanity conducted by Australia, China, the Netherlands, the Philippines, the United Kingdom, and the United States. Such trials were conducted not only within some of those countries but also on many Pacific Islands and elsewhere. (The United States Navy tried cases on Guam and Kwajalein. While the United States Army tried cases in the Philippines and in China, the majority of its war crimes trials took place before military commissions sitting in Yokohama.) The United Kingdom tried a number of cases in China as well as in Hong Kong, Singapore, and India. Once again, little is known as to the procedures followed by the Soviet Union in this regard. Of course, the Soviet Union only became a belligerent in the war in the Far East on August 9, 1945, a week before the surrender by the Japanese. However, several thousand Japanese were still being held in Siberia as convicted war criminals as late as 1956.

The very first case tried in the Far East was that involving Japanese General Tomoyuki Yamashita, who had commanded the Japanese forces during the battle to retake the Philippines conducted by the United States beginning late in 1944. On September 25, 1945 he was served with charges that he had

> unlawfully disregarded and failed to discharge his duty as commander to control the operations of members of his command, permitting them to commit brutal atrocities and other high crimes against people of the United States and of its allies and dependencies.

Yamashita's defence was based primarily on the ground that he was unaware of the war crimes that were being conducted by his troops. He was found to be guilty of the offense charged. Defense counsel (a group of American military lawyers) appealed to the Supreme Court of the Philippines and then to the United States Supreme Court. The latter Court denied Yamashita's petition by a vote of 6 to 2. (Unfortunately, the dissenting opinions of Justices Murphy and Rutledge have received far more publicity than the majority opinion of Chief Justice Stone despite the fact that they are based on numerous errors of fact.) This case applied the rule that a superior is responsible for the violations of the law of war committed, or about to be committed, by his subordinates if he knew, or should have known, that they were committing war crimes, or were about to commit war crimes, and he takes no action to prevent the commission of such acts or to punish those who have committed them. It also established the rule that the provision in the 1929 Geneva Prisoner-of-War Convention to the effect that prisoners of war were to be tried by the same courts as would try members of the armed forces of the Detaining Power applied only to offenses committed while in the status of prisoner of war and did not apply to trials for crimes committed prior to capture or to trials for war crimes. This latter rule was followed by all the countries trying war crimes cases. (A French court decided otherwise, but its decision was not rendered until most of the European war crimes programs, including those of France, were all but at an end. A provision of the 1949 Prisoner-of-War Convention attempts to change this rule, but its effect is subject to debate.)

Japanese General Masaharu Homma was also tried for having taken no action when the troops under his command had committed war crimes. He had commanded the Japanese troops in the Philippines at the outset of the war and his headquarters had been located close to the line of march used for the Bataan Death March. He was found guilty and sentenced to death. His petition to the United States Supreme Court was also denied by a vote of 6 to 2.

A rather unusual case tried by the United States at Nanking (with the permission of the Chinese Government) was *United States v. Lothar Eisentrager*. The accused were German intelligence agents or Embassy personnel stationed in China who had continued to assist the Japanese after the German surrender. This was a violation of the German capitulation, which was binding on all German citizens, wherever located, and, as such, was a war crime. They were found guilty of violations of the law of war. Six of the accused were acquitted. Twenty-one were convicted. Eisentrager was sentenced to life imprisonment. The other twenty were sentenced to varying terms of imprisonment. The decision was affirmed by the United States Supreme Court. (The *Trial of Gerhard Grumpelt* and the *Trial of Stever Ehrenrich* were two cases involving the scuttling of German U-boats after the German capitulation. Both accused were also found guilty of violating the terms of the surrender.)

The *Trial of Masao Baba* was conducted by an Australian military court sitting in Rabaul. It involved forced marches of Australian and British (and, perhaps, American) prisoners of war from Sandakan, Borneo, to Ranau, a distance of 165 miles over mountainous terrain with no well-traveled road and grossly inadequate arrangements for feeding them while en route. Few of the prisoners of war survived the lengthy march and many of those who did died soon thereafter or were shot by their Japanese guards. Japanese Lieutenant General Baba was found to be responsible for these death marches and for the executions and was sentenced to death.

In 1949 the Soviet Union conducted a war crimes trial in Khabarovsk in the Soviet Union in which the accused were members of a Japanese unit that had maintained laboratories in China in which it was alleged that experiments in bacteriological warfare had been conducted with prisoners of war, mostly Chinese, but some Russians, as the guinea pigs. All of the accused pleaded guilty and were sentenced to prison terms. The fact that they adopted the unheard-of procedure of implicating the Japanese Emperor in their actions and that they did not receive the death sentences customary in Soviet war crimes trials is some indication of the nature of the trial. Uncharacteristically, in 1950 the Soviet Union took the unusual step of publishing a book containing much of the record of this war crimes trial. In 1982 the Government of Japan admitted that the unit had existed but denied the use of prisoners of war for test purposes.

There is one other case involving the Soviet Union which is of interest. In 1956 the Soviet Union advised the Japanese government of the death in the Soviet Union of Japanese Prince Konoye. The Japanese asked how it happened that he had still been in Siberia, the Soviet Union having previously advised the Japanese government that all Japanese prisoners of war had been repatriated. The Soviet Union stated that Prince Konoye had not been a prisoner of war, but a convicted war criminal. When queried as to the nature of his war crime, the Soviet Union replied: "Supporting capitalism." Of course, if this is a war crime, then every soldier fighting against a communist country would be guilty of it. It would be difficult, indeed, to find any provision of international law, customary or conventional, that

would justify the designation of "supporting capitalism" as a war crime. (The North Vietnamese followed a somewhat similar procedure during the hostilities in that country (1965–1975) by taking the position that every American prisoner of war was a war criminal captured *in flagrante delicto*.)

V. POST-WORLD WAR II

In 1949 a Diplomatic Convention sitting in Geneva drafted four Conventions for the Protection of Victims of War. Each of these Conventions contains an article specifying the acts considered to be "grave breaches" of that Convention as well as provisions requiring a Contracting Party to

> enact legislation necessary to provide effective penal sanctions for persons committing, or ordering to be committed any of the grave breaches of the present Convention defined in the following Article.
>
> Each High Contracting Party shall be under the obligation to search for persons alleged to have committed, or to have ordered to be committed, such grave breaches, and shall bring such persons, regardless of their nationality, before its own courts.

Identical language is found in Articles 49/50/129/146 of the four Conventions. Articles 50/51/130/147 of the Conventions specify the "grave breaches" of each Convention. Grave breaches of the Conventions are, of course, war crimes. (There are, of course, war crimes other than the grave breaches of these Conventions.)

On August 21, 1996 the Congress of the United States enacted the War Crimes Act of 1996, adding a new provision to Title 18 of the United States Code. It states:

> Sec. 2401. War crimes
>
> a. Offense.—Whoever, whether inside or outside the United States, commits a grave breach of the Geneva Conventions, in any of the circumstances described in subsection (b), shall be fined under this title or imprisoned for life or any term of years, or both, and if death results to the victim, shall also be subject to the penalty of death.
>
> b. Circumstances.—The circumstances referred to in subsection (a) are that the person committing such breach or the victim of such

breach is a member of the Armed Forces of the United States or a national of the United States (as defined in section 101 of the Immigration and Nationality Act).

c. Definitions.—As used in this section, the term "grave breach of the Geneva Conventions" means conduct defined as a grave breach in any of the international conventions relating to the laws of warfare signed at Geneva on 12 August 1949 or any protocol to any such convention, to which the United States is a party.

While this is certainly belated legislation inasmuch as the United States ratified these 1949 Geneva Conventions in 1955 (it has not yet ratified the 1977 Additional Protocol I) and thus at that time took on the obligation of punishing violations of the grave breaches listed in each of the four Conventions, it is believed that existing law could have been found to punish most, if not all, of the violations of the grave breaches provisions to which reference is made. However, it is obviously preferable to enact specific legislation implementing the grave breaches provisions, as the United States was committed to do by the article quoted earlier, which precedes the grave breaches provision in each Convention.

During the period from 1950 to 1990 there were more than 100 international conflicts in many, or all, of which war crimes were committed, but not a single war crimes trial was conducted. During the hostilities in Korea (1950–1953) the United Nations Command had identified as persons who had committed war crimes, and had confined in a single prisoner-of-war compound, about 200 communist prisoners of war who were to be tried for their illegal actions upon the conclusion of hostilities. There were no trials because the Armistice Agreement required the repatriation of all prisoners of war who desired to be repatriated. During these hostilities, tuberculosis was found to be prevalent among the North Korean prisoners of war held by the United Nations Command. Although their medical treatment in a prisoner-of-war hospital received the approval of the Delegate of the International Committee of the Red Cross, who frequently inspected it, after the hostilities had terminated and the prisoners of war had been repatriated, the Chinese Red Cross Society leveled charges of maltreatment of these prisoners of war by the United Nations Command. (This was just one of innumerable offenses alleged by the Chinese Red Cross Society to have been committed by the United Nations Command—perhaps on the theory that the best defense against the fact of maltreatment of prisoners of war

by the Chinese Communists was to charge that these offenses had been committed by the United Nations Command.)

As noted above, during the hostilities in Vietnam (1965–1975) the North Vietnamese announced their intention to try captured Americans as war criminals captured *in flagrante delicto*. However, they apparently changed their minds as, when queried, Ho Chi Minh announced that no war crimes trials were contemplated. (For some unknown reason, when a nation tries one of its own citizens for a violation of the law of war, it is not considered to be conducting a war crimes trial. Thus, when the United States tried Lieutenant William Calley for his actions at My Lai during the hostilities in Vietnam, it was not considered to be a war crimes trial, although it most certainly was. This now appears to have been changed insofar as the United States is concerned by Section 2401(b) of 18 U.S. Code, quoted above. Had the North Vietnamese tried Calley for the same actions, it would have been considered to be a war crimes trial.) In 1966 one of the groups fighting for the sovereignty of Angola announced that it considered mercenaries to be illegal combatants and, some years later, after that group had acquired sovereign power in Angola, it tried, convicted, and executed a number of captured mercenaries. At that time being a mercenary was not a violation of the law of war and the trial was not a valid war crimes trial. (Article 47 of the 1977 Additional Protocol I now provides that "a mercenary shall not have the right to be a combatant or a prisoner of war." This was the first international legislation with respect to mercenaries and there had been no prior customary rule on the subject.) After the 1972 war between India and Pakistan when India released Pakistani prisoners of war in 1974, it withheld 195 of them for Bangladesh to try for the war crime of genocide. However, India eventually released all of these prisoners of war without any trials having taken place. (Trials such as that of Adolf Eichmann by Israel and of Klaus Barbie by France arose out of World War II events.)

In 1993 the United Nations Security Council adopted Resolution 827, which established an International Tribunal for the Prosecution of Persons Responsible for Serious Violations of International Humanitarian Law Committed in the Territory of the Former Yugoslavia since 1991. This was the first tribunal for the trial of war crimes not established by the victor or victors. It has 11 judges elected by the United Nations and is composed of two trial chambers of three judges each and an appeal chamber of five judges. Thus, it is also the first war crimes court in which there is a right of appeal. In the *Tadic Case* the Appeals Chamber of the

Tribunal held that it was properly established and that it did have jurisdiction to try cases involving violations of the law of war that had occurred in the former Yugoslavia. At this writing the *Erdemovic Case* is the only case that has been tried and in that case there was a guilty plea. (The defendant has filed an appeal based on the grounds that his 10-year sentence is too severe.) In 1994 the United Nations Security Council adopted Resolution 955, establishing a similar Tribunal to try war crimes committed in Rwanda or in neighboring states by Rwandan citizens. The statute for this Tribunal is identical, *mutatis mutandis*, to that of the Tribunal for the former Yugoslavia. Then in 1994, the International Law Commission released a draft of a statute for an International Criminal Court, of which the largest part of its jurisdiction would be violations of the humanitarian law of war. That proposal is still under discussion but the General Assembly of the United Nations has adopted Resolution 51/207, calling for the continued activities of a Preparatory Commission and for the convening of a Diplomatic Conference in 1998 to consider the matter.

VI. SOME LEGAL PROBLEMS

A. Rules of Evidence

There are a number of problems of law that arise with respect to war crimes trials that do not arise or arise only infrequently in ordinary criminal trials. One that caused the most dissension among American lawyers was the rule followed by all war crimes tribunals after World War II relating to the receipt of evidence. The civil law rules of evidence are far less rigid than those of the common law and the rule with respect to evidence which appeared in the 1945 London Charter, and which was generally followed by most of the post-World War II war crimes tribunals, courts, and military commissions stated:

> Article 19. The Tribunal shall not be bound by technical rules of evidence. It shall adopt and apply to the greatest possible extent expeditious and nontechnical procedure, and shall admit any evidence which it deems to have probative value.

Under this provision affidavits could be used instead of live witnesses. However, the opposing side could challenge the affidavit and demand the production of the affiant. Strange to relate, the defendants in the Subsequent Proceedings introduced 10 times as many affidavits as the prosecution and, apart from one case, the prosecution challenged more affidavits than did the defendants. (The Rules of Procedure and Evidence adopted by the International Tribunal for the Former Yugoslavia are equally liberal in the receipt of evidence.)

B. Acts of State

Prior to the attempt to try German Kaiser Wilhelm after World War I it had been an accepted rule that acts of state, no matter how reprehensible, could not be considered to be war crimes for which the responsible representative of the state could be tried. The 1945 London Charter made it clear that such a rule no longer existed. It provided:

> Article 7. The official position of defendants, whether as Heads of State or responsible officials in Government Departments, shall not be considered as freeing them from responsibility or mitigating punishment.

A provision to the same effect will be found in Article 7(2) of the Statute of the International Tribunal for the former Yugoslavia. There is little doubt that this now represents the general rule of international law.

C. Command Responsibility

We have seen the problems raised in the *Yamashita* and *Homma* cases with respect to the responsibility of the commander for the war crimes committed by his subordinates. The rule regarding "command responsibility" is now codified in the following manner:

> 2. The fact that a breach of the Conventions or of this present Protocol was committed by a subordinate does not absolve his superiors from penal or disciplinary responsibility, as the case may be, *if they knew or had information which should have enabled them to conclude in the circumstances at the time*, that he was committing or was going to commit such a breach and if they did not take all feasible measures within their power to prevent or repress the breach. (Emphasis added)

This rule is set forth in Article 86(2) of the 1977 Protocol Additional to the Geneva Conventions of August 12, 1949, and Relating to the Protection of Victims of International Armed Conflicts (Protocol I). The comparable provision in Article 7(3) of the 1993 Statute of the International Tribunal for the Former Yugoslavia more closely resembles the language of the rule expressed in the Yamashita case. It uses the expression: "if he knew or had reason to know."

Another rule with respect to the responsibility of commanders adopted at the same time, and set forth in Article 87 of the 1977 Additional Protocol I, provides:

> 3. The High Contracting Parties and Parties to the conflict shall require any commander who is aware that subordinates or other persons under his control are going to commit or have committed a breach of the Convention or of this Protocol, to initiate such steps as are necessary to prevent such violations of the Conventions or this Protocol, and, where appropriate, to initiate disciplinary or penal action against violators thereof.

D. Superior Orders

In the war crimes trials after World War II it was to be anticipated that most, if not all, of the defendants would plead that they had committed the war crime or crimes for which they were being tried because they had been ordered to perform the illegal act by a superior and that to have refused or to have failed to comply with the order would have resulted in serious consequences, even death, for the subordinate. With respect to such a defense the 1945 London Charter stated:

> Article 8. The fact that the Defendant acted pursuant to order of his Government or of a superior shall not free him from responsibility, but may be considered in mitigation of punishment if the Tribunal determines that justice so requires.

Despite the foregoing (or perhaps because of the provision with respect to mitigation of punishment), it was a rare case in the war crimes trials conducted after World War II in which the defense of "superior orders" was not interposed. It was uniformly rejected as a defense but without question it frequently had an effect on the sentence adjudged.

Beginning with the drafting of the four 1949 Geneva Conventions for the Protection of Victims of War and continuing with every convention on the humanitarian law of war that has been drafted since then, proposals have been made to include a similar provision with respect to "superior orders"—and in every case such a proposal has been rejected. Diplomatic conferences are apparently afraid, with good reason, that such a provi-

sion will adversely affect discipline in their armed forces. Such a provision will be found in the statute creating the Tribunal for the former Yugoslavia—but there no one involved in the drafting or adoption of the statute was concerned about adversely affecting discipline in the Serbian army.

E. Civil Wars

War crimes trials in civil wars have been rare for a number of reasons. If they are conducted during hostilities, there will be retaliation, frequently against innocent persons; and they are not conducted after one side has triumphed because, unfortunately, the successful side usually settles the matter without the formality of trials. (The American Civil War was an exception to that statement.) The "grave breaches" provisions of the 1949 Geneva Conventions do not apply to civil wars, which are covered by Article 3 thereof, entitled Conflicts Not of an International Character.

VII. CONCLUSION

There appears to be little doubt that the members of military forces should be thoroughly educated with respect to the provisions of the humanitarian law of war. They should be made aware of the fact that they will be tried by their own organization for violations of those laws and that, if they are captured, they will be tried by the other side for having committed war crimes, with the possibility of being subjected to severe punishment, including death, if convicted of a violation of the law of war or of a war crime. If this is done there will be a far greater tendency for compliance with the law of war on the part of the participants. Despite one much delayed claim of a violation of the humanitarian law of war, the Falklands War (1982) demonstrated that a war can be fought in accordance with law.

Also See the Following Articles

GENOCIDE AND DEMOCIDE • JUST-WAR CRITERIA • WARFARE, MODERN

Bibliography

Appleman, J. A. (1971). *Military Tribunals and International Crimes.* Greenwood.
Bosch, W. J. (1970). *Judgment on Nuremberg.* Chapel Hill: University of North Carolina Press.
Brackman, A. C. (1987). *The other Nuremberg.* New York: William Morrow.

Davidson, E. (1966). *The trial of the Germans: An account of the twenty-two defendants before the international military tribunal at Nuremberg.* New York: Macmillan.

Dinstein, Y. (Ed.) (1996). *War crimes and international law.* New York: Martinus Nijhoff.

Friedman, L. (Ed.) (1972). *The law of war: A documentary history.* New York: Random House.

Hosoya, C. (Ed.) (1986). *The Tokyo war crimes trial: An international symposium.* Tokyo: Kodansha.

Levie, H. S. (1993). *Terrorism in war: The law of war crimes.* Oceana.

GPO, Washington (1947). *Nazi conspiracy and aggression: Opinion and judgment.*

Roling, B. V. A., & Ruter, C. F. (Eds.) (1977). *The Tokyo judgment.* Amsterdam: University Press of Amsterdam.

United Nations War Crimes Commission (1947–1949). *Law reports of trials of war criminals.* London: HMSO.

de Zayas, A. M. (1989). *The Wehrmacht war crimes bureau, 1939–1945.* Lincoln: University of Nebraska Press.

Warfare and Military Studies, Overview

Juanita M. Firestone

University of Texas, San Antonio

GLOSSARY

Institutional Military Military organization designed around obligations of citizenship; members are recruited through a draft that obligates citizens of specified age to serve.

Occupational Military Military organization designed around market incentives; members are recruited through an open labor market in competition with civilian firms.

Group Cohesion Commitment to military unit (horizontal cohesion), the larger military structure (vertical cohesion), and military organization in general; associated with reduced combat stress and increased levels of performance.

Professional Soldier Value to military lies in professional expertise rather than loyalty; associated with the occupational model of the military.

Military Pipeline The rigid hierarchical structure in which individuals must enter at low ranks and move up to higher ranks.

Civilian Control The military institution is ultimately under the control of civilians rather than military professionals; for example, the U.S. where the civilian president is also the commander-in-chief of the military.

Convergence The ideology and structure of the military as an institution becomes more similar to civilian institutions; associated with the occupational model of the military.

Draft A system of insuring that citizens serve in the military for specified periods of time rather than allowing individuals to serve at their own discretion.

Don't Ask, Don't Tell Policy which allows homosexuals to serve in the military as long as they do not openly admit their sexual preference; others are not allowed to ask a soldier about his or her sexual preference.

Two-Person Career Outdated belief that higher-ranking soldiers needed a wife as a "silent partner" in order to meet the demands of a military career.

24-Hour Duty Day Military members are on call 24

hours a day, unlike civilian jobs, which generally have a limited time commitment.

Civil–Military Relations The type and extent of linkages between the military institution and various civilian institutions.

Deterrence The concept that a country must maintain a strong military organization in order to prevent other countries from attacking.

Constabulary Force Military used primarily for peacekeeping missions or to provide assistance during national disasters.

I. INTRODUCTION

A brief overview of warfare and military studies is a monumental task given the extensive history and rich material available. Not only is there a wealth of research, but it is interdisciplinary and cross-national in focus. This article presents a brief and selective overview of the ideas reflected in this history. It focuses on the changes that have occurred since the early 1970s and that seem to capture the changing nature of the research. For the most part these changes have been framed around the following questions: should the military be an autonomous organization or one subjected to civilian control, should military service be an obligation of citizenship or one of many voluntary choices available to potential members, and should the primary mission of a military be winning wars or maintaining peace? A centerpoint for attempts to answer these questions has been the debate about the merits of an institutional military based on obligations of citizenship versus an occupational military based on market driven incentives (see Table I). Regardless of ones' position in this debate, most agree that there is a change toward "civilianization" of modern militaries, producing a more occupational than institutional structure. Whether viewed as a potentially dangerous trend or an inevitable benign trend, this debate has emerged at the forefront of U.S. and international military studies. The information in Table I summarizes material from Moskos and Janowitz on the trend toward civilianization.

The study of warfare and the military is rooted in such classic works as Sun-Tzu's *The Art of War*, Thucydides' *The Peloponnesian War*, Julius Caesar's *Commentaries on the Gallic Wars*, Clausewitz' *On War*, and Mao Tse-tung's, *On Protracted War*. While the major thrust of these works was on specific strategies for winning wars, they also provided interesting insights with respect to the soldiers and officers who participated in those battles. From these classic strategic histories, military studies have evolved into a focus on the interrelationships among various political, economic, social, and military institutions within specific countries, nations, and nation-states. Most recently, the relationship between war and peace using a global perspective has enriched work in military studies.

TABLE I
Some Characteristics of Institutional and Occupational Militaries

	Military as institution	Military as occupation
Motivation to join	Duty, honor, country	Pay, benefits, bonuses
Work roles	Based on rank	Based on task/situation
Recruitment process	Draft	Compete in labor market
Ethics	Loyalty	Job performance
Authority	Chain of command	Professionalism
Influence	Leadership	Managerial
Structure	Bureaucratic	Functional
Family roles	Distinct from job	Interrelated
Civilian labor	Unnecessary, use soldiers	Contract labor needed
Civil–Military linkages	Autonomous military	Few differences
Laws/policies	Institutional needs	Individual rights
Minority relations	Insensitive	Tolerance
Personnel mix	Homogeneous	Heterogeneous
Culture	Masculine warrior	Professionalism
Status in system	Member of primary group	Expert in field

II. EARLY MILITARY STUDIES: WINNING WARS TO INSURE PEACE

Most studies of warfare and of military issues begin with the basic assumption that war is inevitable; thus, an important issue has always been devising a strategy to win. An important component in this process is the attempt to take advantage of the strengths of "your side," while exploiting the weakness of the "other side." Basic military strategy focusing on the ability to win a war has been viewed as an important part of deterrence. Thus the ability to maintain peace has been directly linked to the ability to totally destroy an enemy in war. Almost 3000 years ago Sun Tzu wrote "In peace prepare for war, in war prepare for peace. The art of war is of vital importance to the state. . . . Hence under no circumstances can it be neglected. . . ." In modern times the names of weapons and weapons systems reflect the same idea of a strong link between war and peace: the "Peacekeeper" and the "Strategic Defense System." Furthermore, in the American historical tradition, war is waged to save "good" people from the control of "bad" governments. This provides an interesting social backdrop for understanding why America can destroy countries like Germany and Japan and then turn around and help them rebuild their infrastructure.

One element of modern military strategy concentrates on weapons and logistics. President Dwight D. Eisenhower warned U.S. citizens about the possibility of "unwarranted influence" by the "military–industrial complex" in 1961. The ascendance of the military–industrial complex began with industrialization and continues with the allocation of billions of dollars to sustain permanent war capability. And, as recent events in Iraq, Africa, and Bosnia have shown, permanent war footing is a worldwide phenomenon.

III. TECHNOLOGY AND INDUSTRIALIZATION

Various new tactics designed to overcome the enemy were made possible by the industrialization of weaponry and the creation of nation-states. Civilians could be drafted, trained to fight, and armed with modern weapons at a relatively cheap cost. Industrialization also allowed mass-produced, low-cost uniforms and food so that large armies could be maintained during times of peace as well as during times of war. In a like manner, communication and transportation systems were modernized, solving logistic problems and making long dis-

tance wars more viable. Progress in all of these areas has continued so that in today's world, war is considered a normal part of society, the economy, and foreign policy. The lexicon of today includes varieties of war such as global war, limited warfare, guerrilla war, nuclear war, strategic war, and low-intensity conflict, as well as alternatives to the more typical war strategies such as creating a constabulary, or civilian-based, defensive military system. All of these focus on whether a military organization (either offensive or defensive) is needed in order to maintain peace and insure that countries remain intact. Early research was primarily concerned with threats from outside a nation, as exemplified by the so-called Cold War strategies and policies. Since the collapse of the Soviet empire, attention has shifted to internal threats, whether regional, nationalist, ethnic, racial, or religious in nature. In the case of either external or internal threats, a standing military is considered an important part of the efforts at managing conflict.

With the prevalence of standing armies, soldiers themselves became a factor in military strategy. Early studies focused on individual satisfactions among soldiers and between soldiers and their leaders and the combined impacts on horizontal and vertical unit cohesion. Researchers were primarily attempting to ascertain what kept soldiers fighting even when the odds seemed against them. Reported benefits of cohesion include reduced combat stress casualties, increased primary group solidarity, and increased performance, all of which translate into stronger commitment to the unit, the larger organization, and the military in general. Stronger commitment presumably would translate into battlefield accomplishments and expedite winning wars. These early works suggest that the primary group bonding that defines horizontal cohesion is the key to combat success. Vertical cohesion means that soldiers are willing to obey the orders given by superiors, and horizontal cohesion leads to liking, trust, and understanding among peers. Savage and Gabriel pointed out that while soldiers fighting in Vietnam exhibited strong horizontal cohesion, the goals of the primary groups they formed (e.g., use of drugs, "fragging" leaders thought of as incompetent) were quite often opposed to the goals at higher levels. These problems were exacerbated by the continuous rotation of individuals within combat units, which further disrupted vertical cohesion. At any given point in time there were always a few new "isolates" willing to go along in order to become accepted into the primary group or to enhance their chances of survival. Johns et al. suggested that cohesive groups alone do not necessarily produce increased combat effectiveness; but group members must also feel an attachment/commitment to higher levels of the military chain of command. Most typically officers were viewed as providing those linkages.

IV. PROFESSIONALS AND MILITARY SERVICE

Huntington and Janowitz highlight a shift from thinking of soldiers as "warrior heros" to viewing them as professionals and the importance of this shift for maintaining both civilian control of the military and creating an ethos of "duty, honor, country," which provides the basis for going into battle when necessary (see Feaver, 1996, for a critque of both their postions on civilian control). While all military members are socialized into loyalty, obedience, integrity, and courage, officers are supposed to both exemplify these characteristics and help inculcate them in subordinates. Additionally, officers are supposed to be role models through demonstrating their willingness to subordinate themselves to the good of their unit, the military, and the nation. The socialization processes that produce such loyalty and integrity necessitate an institutional structure in which military service is legitimated by values and norms that transcend individual self-interest in favor of the higher

good of the needs of the country. Thus, the motivation for joining the military comes from a sense of duty and service to one's country, not from the need for a decent-paying job. Moskos noted a shift in the U.S. military away from the institutional form toward an occupational model that creates commitment through market-based reward structures. He attributed this shift to the creation of the all volunteer force (AVF) as opposed to the draft-based military. Both the institutional and occupational models have implications for military operations and for civil–military relations.

Figure 1 provides a conceptual model of the institutional/occupational continuum. The model displays the interrelationships among some of the factors important for understanding changes and provides the organizing framework for this essay.

V. INSTITUTION AND OCCUPATION: OPPOSITE ENDS OF A CONTINUUM

The institutional and occupational models are often presented as polar opposites, each with its own benefits and drawbacks. The professional duty and obligation that were considered vital for military victories may be eroded by occupational values that suggest that responsibilities are not moral but contractual in nature. Thus

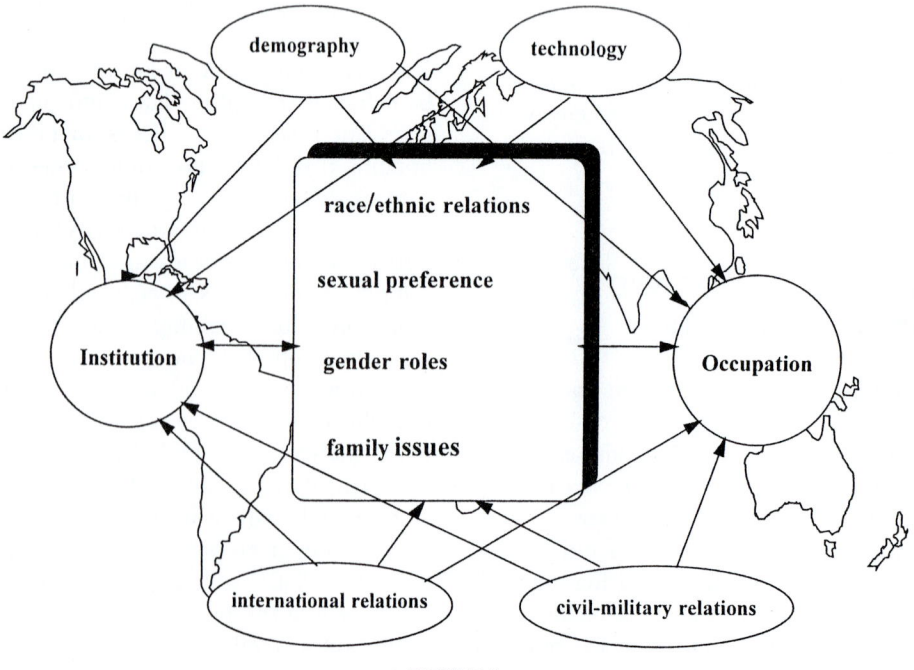

FIGURE 1

if the terms of the contract are not met, members may feel no obligation to continue fighting during seemingly hopeless battles such as many of those fought during Vietnam. Alternatively, the institutional structure may create values among members that are different from the civilian society. Among those who see the military as "a very different organization" may be leaders who believe they are unable to operate effectively under civilian control. In such a case military systems that diverge considerably from the remainder of society hold the power of internal dissolution because their leaders control the mode of destruction. Coup d'etat resulting in military rule can be one result. In reality institutional and occupational formats may be at opposite ends of the same continuum and the success of modern military organizations may rest in finding the spot where the tension between the two has reached equilibrium. It seems likely that this point of equilibrium is impacted by the immediate mission of the military: to win a war or to maintain the peace.

Recent changes in the international order have already produced a shift in strategy from an all-out war among superpowers to use of a constabulary military in limited or well-defined circumstances. This process is reinforcing the change from an institutional military designed to win wars to an occupational model where professional expertise is more valued than loyalty. While nations still perceived as "major powers" are likely to maintain larger militaries, at least in the short term, their mission is changing to reflect the need for smaller, more highly skilled mobile units. Additionally, the fit between organizational needs and the skills and abilities of personnel has become more important than such ascriptive characteristics as race, ethnicity, and gender, which were used in the past as predictors of institutional loyalty.

The changes in mission and structure coincide with demographic and economic changes, which further reinforce the occupational process. Economic changes have meant shifts in allegiance to and the need for alliances with superpowers for protection. Clearly, even relatively wealthy countries like the U.S. cannot afford to provide "free" military protection to other countries. Thus global "peacekeeping" forces comprised of troops from several countries, such as the forces deployed in the Gulf War and to Bosnia, may become the norm. As forces become more global in nature it seems likely that the old institutional structures highlighting duty, honor, and country above professional expertise will become obsolete. Technology further pushes this trend. As military equipment becomes more technical, sophisticated, and expensive, the need for highly skilled personnel with professional and technical expertise increases. As is the case in many profit-oriented businesses, fewer expert soldiers will be able to provide more military capabilities than the large soldier-intensive forces of the past.

VI. DEMOGRAPHIC CHANGE AND MILITARY PERSONNEL

Demographic changes add another dimension to transformations in the study of warfare and the military. Low birth rates and shifting age structures in highly industrialized countries mean fewer individuals available for military service. As a result, many groups of individuals seen as "unfit" for military service in past times are becoming an integral part of modern militaries. Expanding utilization of minority groups has been viewed as a means of acculturation into mainstream values of new immigrants in Israel and ethnic minorities in Greece, Turkey, India, and Ethiopia. Even in the absence of a major war, population pressures—decreasing birthrates, smaller cohorts of males between 18 and 25 eligible for military service—have increased the need to utilize qualified minority group members, such as Blacks, women, conscientious objectors, and homosexuals in the U.S., Australia, Canada, Israel, and the Netherlands. Additionally, both sexes and all races and ethnicities can also be conscientious objectors and homosexuals. All of these have challenged the status quo of the male-defined military culture and the outdated focus on the warrior-hero rather than the competent military professional. In fact an important focus of recent military studies has been the impact of such change on military structure and readiness. The U.S., with its large racially and ethnically diverse society and military, has been a major focus of such research.

One interesting aspect tied to the exclusion of various groups from military service in the past relates to issues of leadership. Because the military is a very structured hierarchical system, individuals must come in at a low rank and move up through the organizational pipeline to attain a higher rank. Thus, members of the highest ranks are most likely part of the old guard and may not be in touch with changing attitudes or with the types of problems encountered by new members. This may be amplified when the recruit is a member of a minority group who may perceive his or her superior as out of touch and unsympathetic. This could be particularly problematic if it leads to lower promotion rates, which ultimately create higher attrition among minority members. The important point is that minority group members must remain in the pipeline and become part of the leadership before many of the negative attitudes about their competence as soldiers change.

VII. RACE RELATIONS

While Blacks served in an integrated American militia both prior to and during the American Revolution, after that time segregated units became the norm. In the wake of World War II, when Black leaders began asking how Black soldiers could be asked to die for a country and an organization that treated them as inferior and kept them in segregated units, the military again changed its policy to one of fully integrated units. As noted by Janowitz (1976, p. 192) "from World War I onward, citizen military service has been seen as a device by which excluded segments of society could achieve political legitimacy and rights." Initial opposition suggested that widespread integration, even if it was a desirable social goal, would noticeably reduce combat efficiency by intruding on the unit bonding necessary for battle. According to official documents such as the "Gillem Report," issued in 1945, the full integration of African Americans would disrupt troop cohesion, undermine morale, incite greater violence against African Americans, decrease discipline, and seriously compromise combat readiness—thus creating a national security risk. Not only did none of these dire predictions prove true, the military has since been lauded as an exemplar of progressive social change. The armed forces, perhaps the most conservative of all institutions, indeed were able to move toward the goal of racial integration far more rapidly and completely than the civilian sector. Which is not to say that the process has been without criticism. As the quota on the proportion of Blacks allowed in the military was lifted, the percentage has steadily increased, bringing with it a different set of issues.

With the advent of the all-volunteer force in the U.S., the percentage of Blacks increased relative to Whites, and questions have been raised as to the impact of this structural shift on the military organization. Butler suggests that convergence with the civilian employment sector predicts racially segregated occupations becoming the norm within the military. Furthermore, as personnel return to their segregated communities after work the contact between the different groups characteristic of the institutional military will erode. Additionally, as the percentage of Blacks increases, they are more likely to end up in less technical and more directly combat related positions because of differences in education. This process has led some Black leaders like Jesse Jackson to suggest that young Black men are being used as "cannon-fodder" during armed conflict. If the military is perceived as just another job, rather than a commitment of citizenship, such pronouncements by political leaders may carry more weight, creating strained race relations. Butler and Holmes found that Blacks in the Marines perceived less racial discrimination than those in other service branches after controlling for rank, occupation, and education. This is interesting because the Marines maintains the most traditional (i.e., institutional) structure of the military service branches. This suggests that the "civilianization" of the military may make it less isolated from society but at the same time more vulnerable to the pressures and social problems that occur in the rest of society.

Military leaders might argue that having to pay attention to racial dynamics above military mission could negatively impact their ability to effectively and efficiently make personnel decisions. Interestingly, using a survey of former Soviet citizens, Ball determined that while the structure of the military itself neither exacerbated or alleviated ethnic conflict in the former Soviet Union, ethnically homogeneous units outperformed ethnically mixed units. Thus, using the military as a means of integrating society resulted in poor overall military performance. Data from the U.S. military, however, suggest that desegregation of military units had a positive rather than a negative impact on performance both prior to and after the creation of the all volunteer force.

VIII. ISSUES OF SEXUAL PREFERENCE

Recent attempts to establish that the ban of homosexuals from the military serves the public interest are reminiscent of the arguments used to exclude African-Americans from integration in the military prior to 1948. The debate has focused on whether open acceptance of homosexuals will disrupt the horizontal cohesion necessary for wartime successes. Homosexuals obviously participate in the military now, and there is absolutely no evidence that this has decreased morale, disrupted cohesion, increased promiscuity, diminished combat readiness, or threatened national security. To the contrary, the recent success of Operation Desert Storm suggests the effectiveness of the military in meeting the goal of victory does not depend on the sex or the sexual orientation of its soldiers. To illustrate more clearly that sexual orientation is not related to performance in the military organization, let us apply the same arguments to a scenario where the ban under consideration is against heterosexuals.

Admitted heterosexuals cannot be allowed in the military because the fact of having to hide their heterosexuality makes them vulnerable to blackmail, which in turn puts military secrets at risk. Furthermore, many books and movies have documented how men have given military secrets to their female lovers.

It is obvious that the inclusion of admitted heterosexuals to the military will greatly reduce combat readiness and endanger national security. Perhaps heterosexuals will argue that what they do in the privacy of their own bedroom, and with whom they do it, has no impact on their ability to function as soldiers. After all, they have participated effectively in the past, it is just that they never had to admit their heterosexuality before. While this may seem sensible, military and political leaders claim to know better.

Heterosexuals are indisputably interested in publicly displaying their sexuality; thus promiscuity will rise if the ban is lifted. After all, heterosexual couples wear wedding bands, have children, and constantly make sexual innuendoes and jokes, thus openly proclaiming their sexual identities. Of course, it would be unfair to allow such openly sexual individuals to join the military because they would have to take a vow of celibacy in order to serve effectively. Undoubtedly serving in the military would be a strain on heterosexual men, especially in situations where they would have to interact with women, and would have to control their insurmountable sexual desires (Adam, 1994, p. 111).

Clearly these statements do not make sense to most people, in part because heterosexuality is implicit in most elements of U.S. society. We do not recognize the integration of heterosexual identity into all aspects of our lives. The discussion of banning homosexuals from the military focuses solely on sexual orientation to explain behaviors. *One* aspect of our identity cannot explain the complexity of all our thoughts and actions as human beings. Yet, the ban on homosexuals in the military attempts to do just that, reducing human beings to one trait—their sexual orientation—and proposing that job performance and concern for national defense are based only on their sexual activities. An important aspect of this reductionism is the implication that ho-

mosexuals are too "feminine" to make good soldiers. If homosexuals (and women) are successful, it challenges the stereotype of the "macho" male soldier while reinforcing the stereotype that homosexuals are not "real" men. Finally, the current ban denies the rights of individuals to voluntarily serve their country through military service based solely on activities considered "private" by most people.

In such countries as Canada, the Netherlands, Norway, France, and Israel sexual orientation is not a criterion used to assess acceptance into the military. Other countries such as the United Kingdom and Germany have adopted an informal "don't ask, don't tell" policy similar to the U.S. As reported by the National Defense Research Institute report (1993, p. 103) ". . .in none of these countries were there significant disciplinary problems caused by homosexuals within the ranks. . . [m]oreover, in all countries, openly homosexual service members were appropriately circumspect in their behavior while in military situations. . ." In fact in the face of social change, the open inclusion of homosexuals in the military could be viewed as another example of extending citizenship rights to a group formerly perceived as unworthy and inferior.

IX. WOMEN AND MILITARY SERVICE

As pointed out by Jeanne Holm (1982), women have served effectively either officially or unofficially in the U.S. military since its incipiency. Furthermore, women have proven effective soldiers in such countries as Israel, Africa, and Russia. Women's roles in various militaries have been steadily increasing and by most accounts women have performed their responsibilities on a par with men. Within that context it is interesting to observe the renewed debate on the utilization of women occurring in the U.S.

Recent scandals such as the rape of women enlistees at the Aberdeen Army training facility; the prosecution of Second Lieutenant Kelly Flinn, the first woman to fly a B-52, on charges of adultery and sexual misconduct; the exposure of the secret club of Air Force pilots whose members boasted of excessive drinking and womanizing (Barstoolers Association); and the Tailhook scandal in which Navy Lieutenant Paula Coughlin blew the whistle about the good-old-boy pilots who think sexually assaulting women is fun have led many high-ranking military members to suggest that the military needs to reevaluate the utilization of women in the Armed Forces. Individuals at high levels of command have expressed surprise and chagrin over the public revelations of the sexist treatment of many women in today's military. Survey data collected by the Department of Defense in 1988 (and again in 1995) belie their expressions of surprise. Detailed information has been readily available for nearly a decade.

In fact the 1988 survey showed that about 52% of the males who responded and about 75% of the females who responded said that they knew someone who was the target of sexual harassment of some for. Proportions of women reporting that they had received *uninvited and unwanted sexual attention* during the previous 12 months from someone where they worked in the active-duty military ranged from 5%, who said they had experienced actual or attempted rape, to 58%, who said they were the targets of sexual teasing and jokes. Similar results were found for each of the four service branches and for the Coast Guard. And while women officers were *slightly* less likely to report being harassed (about 64% said they were), it is clear that rank did not provide much protection from reported harassment. Among enlisted personnel who have served less than 2 years, about 75% of the women reported they were targets of harassment within the previous 12 months. A report on these findings was published by the Defense Manpower Data Center and briefings were held at the highest command levels prior to the official release of the report in 1990.

In response, sexual harassment policies were updated and the content of human relations training courses included training specifically focused on sexual harassment. Part of the problem with these training sessions is that often they are not taken seriously. Indeed, sometimes the group facilitator does not seem to understand the seriousness of the issue or even identifies with the perpetrator and downplays its importance. While many workshop facilitators take their roles seriously, those that do not reinforce an environment that suggests sexual harassment is just fun and should not be viewed as an important problem. In spite of these efforts, the replication of the 1988 survey in 1995 produced similar results. Small declines in the percentages reporting sexual harassment are offset by its continued prevalence. Nearly 12% of men and over 59% of women reported some form of harassment within the previous 12 months of service.

The incidents at the Aberdeen training facility further complicate issues related to gender relations of women by refocusing the problems as racial in nature. Some have suggested that in the past White women would make sexual advances toward Black males and then exonerate their interest by claiming rape. As an idea this scenario seems to titillate a portion of the

military as well as the general public. Ultimately, whether the women "came on" to the drill sergeants is less important than the fact that these drill sergeants have been in the Army for a long time and they know the rules. Just because a woman makes a sexual advance (regardless of her race) does *not* mean the person in a position of power has to respond in kind. Clearly the person with more organizational power must control the situation and "just say no."

Once again, data from the 1988 survey are enlightening. About 47% of the Black women and about 54% of the White women who responded to the 1988 survey said that they were harassed by members of the *same* race. In addition, 20% of Black women and 18% of White women said they were harassed by members of their own as well as members of other races. The reports of harassment by someone of a different race do not constitute the majority of the incidents and do not seem to reflect a tendency for White women to be more likely to perceive or label the actions of men of a different race or ethnicity as harassment.

The military leaders who blame women for problems such as fraternization, adultery, sexual misconduct, and single parenting, none of which are solely or primarily related to women may reflect the disjuncture between leader and soldier attitudes produced by the pipeline effect discussed earlier. The fact that the military is still viewed as a masculine arena is not seen as problematic, nor is the fact that women in the military are still few in number and thus isolated within a principally male hierarchy. Both points are related and importantly produce a structure where women are expected to report any difficulties to a unit commander who may be part of the problem.

Further examples include the fact that issues such as pregnancy are presented as if they are the sole responsibility of women and are never described as "male problems." Accounts of men leaving their progeny in foreign countries after a war abound, but they are never used as a reason to exclude men from military service. The enormous number of calls which resulted from opening a sexual harassment hotline is also illustrative. As Dr. Charles Moskos recently suggested, perhaps a "chain of complaint" as well as a "chain of command" is needed to sort through the treatment of women. Such a system would reflect a more occupationally oriented system than the rigidly hierarchical institutional military.

Without an evidence-based assessment of these situations, the "old saw" about women not being suited for military service could easily resurface. Recent attempts to "blame" women for their own sexual assaults and/

or harassment seem based on antiquated beliefs about men's inability to control their sexual urges. This reinforces the documentedly outdated belief that women do not really belong in the military because they stir these male sexual urges and disrupt the male bonding necessary for maintaining military order and discipline.

Women are a readily available resource for enabling the military to accomplish its mission. However, before their utilization can be optimized, women must be accepted as fully integrated members of the military organization. In 1973 Goldman wrote: "with an increase in the proportion of women in the armed forces, the problem of protocol between the sexes will also have to be faced together with that of integrating the women personnel into the social life of the military" (p. 114). Current scandals emphasize the fact that this has not yet happened.

Using cross-national data, Segal argued that the utilization of women in armed forces is correlated with the extent of gender role egalitarianism in societies. Thus, as laws prohibiting discrimination based on gender are passed, women's roles in previously male-dominated arenas such as the military also expand. While this may indeed be the case, the U.S. experience suggests that increasing utilization does not necessarily have to be associated with equal treatment.

X. MILITARY AND FAMILY LINKAGES

Another interesting aspect associated with the change away from a more traditional military has been a focus on issues related to the service members' family. Until recently the military ignored issues related to family and forced the compartmentalization of military members sense of commitment to each. Most typically, family obligations were sublimated to those of the military because of historical context and occupational demands. Historically, soldiers (in particular enlisted soldiers) were discouraged from creating family obligations. This occurred explicitly with pay scales so low that family maintenance was difficult and often very precarious and implicitly through such adages as "if the military had wanted you to have a wife, you would have been issued one." One justification for this discouragement was also stated as a primary difference between the military and civilian organizations: the military duty day is 24 hours.

Moreover, the sense of duty related to the military has until recently been defined as an obligation of citizenship based on "duty, honor, and country" rather than economic rewards. In 1973, the conscription of

military members was discontinued and a voluntary format established. The military became more directly competitive with civilian organizations for members and began to adopt some civilian orientations. For example, Coser argues that the family as an institution in American society remains viable in part because modern institutions tend to make "limited" demands on individuals. For example, work hours are established by law thus allowing time for family and other activities. Segal relates Coser's discussion to the military, describing the competition between the two "greedy institutions (military and family)" as having greater conflicts than in the past.

Thus, changes in the military from a strongly institutional format based on conscription to an all-voluntary force, where obligation based on economic rewards is emphasized, along with changing roles of men and women in society have brought family issues to the attention of military planners. The focus seems to be on "helping" families adjust to the demands of the military, with little research attempting to identify and sources of strain between the two. This section attempts to identify potential sources of strain, presenting a framework for future research.

Most families demand emotional commitment, including displays of affection and a sense of belonging, as well as more practical obligations such as physical survival, child care, and homemaking activities. While these demands may fall differentially on individual members, they are continuous and critical for family survival. Demographic changes, such as greater numbers of divorced couples, single-parent families, and mothers with young children who work outside the home, reinforce the strain attached to meeting the needs for family survival.

Overall, however, family obligations are considered more inclusive and time-consuming than those related to one's job. For example, time commitments to the job are established by law, while those to the family are not. Because in the past, family members have been willing and able to accept different orientations to those obligations, the two institutions, family and work, have maintained a tenuous balance.

In other words, typically in the past, wives were more likely to be full-time homemakers, to be the "silent partner" in two-person careers, and/or to adopt intermittent (or part-time) work patterns than husbands in order to devote much of their time and emotional commitment to the family. Thus, husbands could spend much of their time and emotional involvement in job activities. In an institution such as the military, where the duty day is defined as 24 hours, this separation of family and work obligations seems critical. However, many of the changes suggested above have interfered with family members' abilities and willingness to maintain such differential patterns of obligation.

Family patterns in the military are becoming more similar to those in the civilian world; thus, the military is experiencing more dual-earner/career couples, more divorced couples, and more single-parent families. All these patterns can create strains and conflicts within the family system. But because many of the demands of the military are unusual compared to the demands of civilian organizations, these strains may be exacerbated. We have already mentioned an important one—the 24 hour duty day. Because today's military wives are more likely to be employed, their ability to perform as the "silent partner" in a two-person career has diminished. Moreover, similar to changes in the larger society, military wives' sense of identity and role obligations are becoming more and more independent from their husbands'. These changes must introduce strain into both institutions—the family and the military—and create a need for research rather than anecdotal accounts of successes and failures.

Dual military couples intensify the problems associated with dual career couples. The 24-hour duty day obligation, along with institutional requirements for unaccompanied (without family) tours of duty and frequent moves and job changes in order to progress in rank, magnify problems associated with individual career management. Military personnel are presented orders based on organizational needs, regardless of impact on family arrangements. If couples wish to reside together, often one must forgo optimal career choices for him- or herself. This could create either a sense of sacrifice or of resentment, both of which can create and/or amplify strains. Furthermore, a dual-earner couple, with one civilian and one military member, has all of the above problems with the added difficulty that the civilian spouse may be less understanding of military demands.

Whether true or not, military members' perceptions that the military is a "high risk" occupation, especially during times of war, seem to be an important difference. That is, members can be transported with little notice to areas of armed conflict. While all occupations may offer risk of accidental death and injury, the military is a case where individuals are asked to knowingly put themselves at risk without the ability to exercise personal choice. In and of itself, little research has focused on this particular source of family strain.

Furthermore, changes in today's military mean that not only men but women may find themselves at risk for injury related to conflict. The idea that the mother, rather than the father, is the parent at risk is very new to American definitions of a soldier as well as to ideas of appropriate roles for men and women. In a related vein, most family research related to parental absence focus on the impact of the father's absence, particularly with respect to the impact on boys. While women comprise only about 14% of the total U.S. military force, media portrayals of the Gulf War directed attention to mothers (but not fathers) who were absent from their families.

In spite of the issues raised, the proportion of married military personnel continues to increase. Furthermore, some research has pointed to the impact of family on military recruitment, morale, and retention. Thus, the successful completion of the military mission could be enhanced by research addressing changing family patterns and the interaction of these changes with military demands. A solid research agenda could provide the necessary information for insuring that individuals can create a balance between the demands of the military and those of the family.

XI. CIVIL–MILITARY RELATIONS AND ORGANIZATIONAL CONTEXT

The demographic/personnel trends highlight the structural changes that occur when the military is organized around voluntary membership as opposed to conscription. Assuring enough qualified volunteers means that the military must compete for personnel in the civilian marketplace in which workers have more control over work contexts and individual rights take precedence over institutional needs. Initially questions were raised concerning whether a more occupationally oriented military will have concomitant negative impacts on troop morale and performance, particularly in the event of a war. When cross-cultural data are examined, little evidence supports any negative impacts.

Coinciding with these demographic changes have been a diminishing base of military service in the U.S. from an all-time high during World War II to a current all-time low. This becomes very important when we remember that civilians (the majority of whom now have no prior military service) control the military's budget and approve the promotions and assignments of senior military ranks and the firing of high-ranking leaders. For example, much media attention has centered on the lack of military experience of President Clinton, current commander-in-chief. This may be compounded by budgetary constraints that have forced the closing of military bases diminishing the military presence in some regions of the country. Base closures have weakened the social and the economic linkages between these civilian communities and the military. All of these have greatly decreased the importance of the military–industrial complex in defining civil–military relations and military studies. A diminishing emphasis on the military–industrial complex will impact relations with other nations as well as internal military affairs. Certainly changes in international security have been precipitated by "civilian" terrorism. In addition, protection of space, the ecology, public health, and communications networks must be defined in international terms. These concerns highlight both the international focus of contemporary military studies as well as the emphasis on the relationship between war and peace studies.

XII. INTERNATIONAL RELATIONS AND THE MILITARY MISSION: WAR OR PEACE?

In 1988, Lester Kurtz documented how the new peace consciousness was global in form, which helped undermine the idea of international enemies and the need for nuclear war as a mechanism of deterrence. Without a need for military deterrence, the value of maintaining a large expensive standing army became questionable. This view was exacerbated with the reorganization of the Soviet Union. Recent U.S. concerns focus on uncertainty about the effectiveness of using force and on whether society will continue to value a military focused on keeping peace rather than on waging war. In other words, if the military must compete in the civilian labor market, will military service become just another low-waged, low-esteem service sector job? Additionally, concerns have been expressed that the organizational changes associated with a peacekeeping military might produce soldiers with "civilian" attitudes who might refuse to fight or who might desert their units during battle. Survey data suggest that these concerns are not supported by evidence.

Moskos tested the hypothesis that soldiers who served in United Nations peacekeeping forces would be more likely to develop what he labeled a "constabulary ethic." Such an ideology would focus on attaining political compromises with limited, if any, use of force. Indeed his findings indicated that "adaptation and adherence to constabulary standards derives from commonly shared peacekeeping experiences in the field following assignment to a United Nations force, rather than from prior peacekeeping training and orientation" (Moskos, 1976, p. 134). Thus, experience rather than prior civilian training or attitudes were more important in producing a constabulary ethic among the United Nations soldiers surveyed.

More recently, Segal and Tiggle surveyed volunteer reserve soldiers who served a 6-month rotation as part of a multinational composite reserve and active duty peacekeeping force in the Sinai Desert in support of the Camp David Accords. Results indicated that a majority of those responding supported the basic peacekeeping norms of minimal use of force and conflict resolution tactics, although the size of the majority decreased over time during the mission experience. Nor did participants express stronger pacific or internationalist world views then they held previously to the mission. Miller found similar results from soldiers serving a peacekeeping mission in Macedonia if they approved of the initial mission, although support for use of soldiers to keep the peace dropped among those who did not support the mission. Seemingly then, participation in a successful mission is the most important factor in forming attitudes with respect to the legitimate use of the military, whether the mission was one of war or peace. Note the positive attitudes toward the use of limited warfare after the Gulf War victory. Of course, since that victory frustrations with the ability to find consensual solutions to problems in Bosnia and Somalia may undermine the use of military for future peacekeeping missions.

XIII. THE FUTURE

Future research into warfare and military studies will undoubtedly be framed by the same debates as the past, because no clear or universally accepted answers have been found. Thus research continues to search for answers to the same questions: should the military be an autonomous organization or one subjected to civilian control, should military service be an obligation of citizenship or one of many voluntary choices available to potential members; and should the primary mission of a military be winning wars or maintaining peace? The difference in prospective studies will be the emphasis on global rather than national, regional, or international concerns. This will necessitate the use of multinational forces and raises questions about where the command of such forces will emanate. Furthermore, the inclusion of individuals from different cultures and socioeconomic backgrounds will mean that the legitimacy of any military operation must be established from an inclusionary rather than an isolationist perspective. All of these derive from a principal that peace and security cannot be attained by individual nations but must be global in orientation. Unilateral military actions will not make a nation or its citizens secure from war or from other terrorist acts.

For the moment we are still able to confine our thinking about civil–military relations and warfare and military studies to Earth as we know it. Given rapid technological and communication advances, that may last for only a short duration. In a recent editorial General Howell M. Estes III (1997) commented that:

> The U.S. military is already heavily dependent on space for support in five areas: navigation, communication, weather, warning and intelligence. In my opinion, the military's dependence on space will only grow in the years ahead.

Very soon, in order to remain an important arena for research, rather than a world perspective, peace and military studies will have to incorporate the important aspects of the past as well as the lessons we learn as we begin explorations into the universe.

Also See the Following Articles

COMBAT • MILITARISM • MILITARY CULTURE • MILITARY-INDUSTRIAL COMPLEX • PROFESSIONAL VERSUS CITIZEN SOLDIERY • PSYCHOLOGICAL EFFECTS OF COMBAT • WARFARE, STRATEGIES AND TACTICS OF • WARFARE, TRENDS IN • WOMEN AND WAR

Bibliography

Butler, J. S. (1976). Inequality in the military: An examiniation of promotion rates for black and white enlisted men, *American Sociological Review, 41*(5): 807–818.

Caesar, J. (1851). *Caesar's Commentaries on the Gallic and Civil Wars.* W. A. McDevitte, & W. S. Bohn (Trs). London: H. G. Bohn.

Crocker, C. A., Hampson, F. O., & Aall, P. (1996). *Managing global chaos: Sources of and Responses to international conflict* Washington DC: U.S. Institute of Peace.

Feaver, P. D. (1996). The civil-military problematique: Huntington, Janowitz, and the questions of civilian control. *Armed Forces & Society, 23*(2), 149–178.

Firestone, J. M., & Harris, R. J. (1994). Sexual Harassment in the U.S. Military: Individual and environmental contexts. *Armed Forces & Society, 21*(1), 176–185.

Holm, J. (1982). *Women in the military; An unfinished revolution.* Navato CA: Presidio Press.

Huntington, S. P. (1957). *The soldier and the state; The theory and politics of civil–military relations.* New York: Vintage Books.

Janowitz, M. (1960). *The professional soldier: A social and political portrait,* Glencoe, IL: The Free Press.

Kurtz, L. R. (1988). *The nuclear cage: A sociology of the arms race.* Englewood Cliffs, NJ: Prentice-Hall.

Marshall, S. L. A. (1947). *Men against fire.* New York: Harper and Row.

Moskos, C. C. (1977). From institution to occupation: Trends in military organization. *Armed Forces & Society, 4*(1), 41–50.

National Defense Research Institute. (1993). *Sexual Orientation and U.S. Military Personnel Policy: Options and Assessment.* Santa Monica, CA: Rand.

Savage, P. L., & Gabriel, R. A. (1976). Cohesion and disintegration in the American army: An alternative perspective, *Armed Forces & Society, 2,* 340–479.

Scott, W. J., & Stanley, S. C. (Eds.) (1994). *Gays and lesbians in the military: Issues, concerns, and contrasts,* New York: Aldine de Gruyter.

Shils, E. A., & Janowitz, M. (1948). Cohesion and disintegration in the Wehrmacht in World War II, *Public Opinion Quarterly,* 12, 29–42.

Stouffer, S. A., Lumsdaine, A. A., Lumsdaine, M. H., Williams, R. M., Smith, M., Brewster, J. L., Star, S. A., & Cottrell, L. S. (1949). *The American Soldier: Combat and its Aftermath.* 4 volumes, Princeton, NJ: Princeton University Press.

Sun Tzu (1983). *The art of war.* J. Clavell (Ed.), L. Giles (Tr.). New York: Delacorte Press.

Thucydides (1910). *History of the Peloponnesian war.* R. Crawley (Tr). New York: E. P. Dutton.

Tse-tung, Mao (1965). *On protracted war.* Peking: Foreign Languages Press.

von Clausewitz, C. (1984). *On war.* M. Howard and Peter Paret (Eds. and Trans). Princeton, NJ: Princeton University

Warfare, Modern

Antulio J. Echevarria II
United States Army Training and Doctrine Command

I. The Technological Revolution and Modern Warfare
II. The Future of Modern Warfare
III. Conclusions

GLOSSARY

Center of Gravity Defined by Prussian philosopher of war Carl von Clausewitz as the focus or "hub around which all else revolves."

Élan A military unit's fighting spirit and sense of cohesion.

Lethality An expression of the deadliness of a combat environment.

Offensive à outrance The offensive spirit; sometimes taken to an extreme—attacking everywhere and anywhere.

Tempo The pace of military activity.

THE NATURE OF WAR, defined by Carl von Clausewitz as the interplay of violence, chance, and political forces, has remained remarkably consistent throughout history. Warfare, or the process of waging war, on the other hand, has varied greatly over time and among cultures. Historians disagree over whether modern warfare began with the military revolution launched by Gustavus Adolphus in the 17th century or with the

operational-level innovations implemented by Napoleon Bonaparte in the 19th. In fact, each of these changes, while significant, pales in comparison to the transformation of warfare caused by the Technological or Second Industrial Revolution that took Western society by storm between 1890 and 1918. During this quarter-century, a rapid flood of technological innovations changed the conduct of war in ways that would remain relevant for another 100 years.

I. THE TECHNOLOGICAL REVOLUTION AND MODERN WARFARE

Among new military technologies that appeared at the *fin-de-siécle*, or the turn of the 19th and 20th centuries, were submarines and airships, which made operations practicable under water and in the air, thereby adding two new dimensions to military strategy. Steam ships, airplanes, motorized vehicles, the telephone, and the wireless continued the process of compressing time and space already begun by the railroad and telegraph. Smokeless powder, magazine-fed rifles, quick-firing artillery, and the machine gun raised battlefield lethality to unprecedented levels, creating a continuously unfolding crisis in the tactical procedures of land forces. The appearance of dreadnought-class battleships, high-speed battle cruisers, destroyers, torpedo-boats, self-propelled torpedoes, improved submarines, and underwater mines increased both the deadliness and complexity of war at sea. In addition, airships and airplanes promised to affect the conduct of war on land and sea in manifold, if still uncertain, ways. In little more than a quarter of a century, therefore, the Technological Revolution had irreversibly expanded both the conceptual and material requirements for waging war.

A. The Land-Power Crisis

By the end of the 1880s, the increased accuracy, range, and rate of fire of direct- and indirect-fire weapons had produced a nearly impenetrable fire-swept zone that threatened to eliminate the possibility of driving home an attack and, consequently, of achieving decisive victory on the battlefield. Over the next 25 years, the fire-swept zone expanded with the growth of weapon effectiveness. By 1900, it exceeded 800 meters; and the secondary or danger zone, which prohibited the movement of close formations, had reached 2000 meters. In 1909, Count Alfred von Schlieffen, one-time Chief of Staff of the German Great General Staff, wrote that "weapon technologies now celebrate their greatest triumph" without, however, having brought about "the long-sought-after advantage over an opponent." Schlieffen concluded, as did a number of other military writers, that the technological situation required a complete revolution in tactics in order to overcome the possibility of deadlock on the battlefield. The threat of tactical stalemate, in turn, meant that strategy—traditionally considered an art open to the inspirations of genius—would devolve to little more than a crude calculus of attrition, as in the American Civil War. In addition, the era's leading social scientists, philosophers, historians, and military thinkers believed that modern societies were incapable of producing a warrior willing and able to endure the hardships likely to attend a protracted conflict. In short, the Technological Revolution had created a multidimensional crisis for the conduct of war on land, a crisis that centered on the problem of how to execute the infantry attack.

Initially, military theorists sought to solve the problem through the use of skirmish tactics—infantry advancing in open order and using the terrain for cover and concealment—which had proven effective in the Franco-German War (1870–1871). While the Boer War (1898–1902) later confirmed that such tactics were still an effective means for reducing an attacker's casualties, it also showed that they required considerable time to execute properly, time that a defender could use to reinforce his defense. War plans and mobilization schedules placed a further premium on time. Tacticians therefore settled upon extended-order tactics—infantry advancing in lines with broad intervals between individuals—as a compromise between the efficient movement of troops in formed order and the near-chaotic nature of skirmish tactics. Strategic and operational requirements had thus begun to dictate tactics, a complete reversal of Helmuth von Moltke's principle that tactical successes should direct strategy. A third solution developed in the wake of the Russo–Japanese War (1904–1905). Military observers noted that artillery inflicted very few casualties upon an entrenched enemy unless it used large-caliber projectiles fired in a steep trajectory. However, they also noted that, regardless of caliber, artillery functioned extremely well as a weapon of suppression. In other words, when timed properly, artillery could protect an attacking force by keeping the defender's head down until the final assault was driven home. Such tactics would deprive the defender of sufficient time to engage the attacker while he crossed the deadly zone. Accordingly, military theorists began to advocate synchronizing the advance of the infantry with a protective "curtain" of fire, a sort of "symphony" of fire and maneuver.

The priority that political and military leaders gave to the *offensive à outrance* or to the spirit of the offensive was less an attempt to cross the deadly zone through mere *élan* than an overreaction to the perceived decline of the warrior spirit in modern cultures. Such emphasis acted as a counterweight to the exuberant enthusiasm, typified by the rapid growth of cults of speed and movement within *fin-de-siécle* Europe and the United States, that the era exhibited toward technology. The Russo–Japanese War, perhaps more than any other conflict prior to 1914, proved that technology alone—massive doses of firepower—would not suffice to bring about an opponent's defeat. Time and again, an attacking force had to use a bayonet assault to dislodge the defender from his position, particularly if he was ensconced in well-developed fortifications or trench-works. The ideas contained in French Colonel Ardant du Picq's *Études sur le Combat* (*Battle Studies*) did not address the reinforcing influence that such structures might have on a unit's cohesion and morale. Formations occupying entrenchments did not break and run in quite the same way as those that fought on open battlefields. Soldiers were less inclined to leave the relative safety of their trench for an open-ground environment that was many times more lethal to them. Ironically, the era of unparalleled technological change required that armies possess an even greater will to win.

Military thinkers had thus responded to the land

power crisis with a combination of tactical, technological, and socio-psychological solutions. They did not ignore Ivan S. Bloch's question *Is War Now Impossible?*, a question derived largely from the extensive military literature on the deadly zone, as much as they sought to avoid capitulating to its tendentious argumentation, which rested firmly and irreversibly upon his faith in pacifism. Bloch's most important contributions, in any case, stemmed not from his discussions of modern weaponry, which were already outdated by the time his multivolume work appeared in 1898, but from his analyses of the political and economic costs of waging war in the modern age. By 1913, both General Helmuth von Moltke the younger, then-chief of the German General Staff, and Marshal Joseph Joffre, chief of the French General Staff, had already expressed serious doubts about the possibility of achieving a quick, decisive victory in the next general conflict.

B. The Transformation of Sea Power

The land power crisis had barely unfolded when naval theorists detected a similar emergency for sea power. Real and anticipated improvements in underwater mines and in the range and accuracy of self-propelled torpedoes threatened to restrict the movement and therefore the influence of capital ships—the classic foundation of sea power. Underwater mines, which were relatively inexpensive and easy to produce, could deny passage through important straights or channels as well as prevent access to harbors vital for resupply. Armed with the new self-propelled torpedoes, highly maneuverable torpedo-boats posed a serious threat to the more expensive but slower moving capital ships, which did not possess a targeting system capable of tracking the smaller, more maneuverable vessels. The earliest warnings of this crisis came from the *Jeune École* (*Young School*) of the French navy, whose response was to advocate a defensive naval strategy, a solution that also satisfied the preferences of France's influential socialist party. Modest investment in underwater mines, torpedo-boats, and submarines, it was argued, would obviate the need to maintain a large navy to protect lines of communication and commerce at sea. However, other naval theorists, particularly those in Britain, responded by advocating the development of balanced fleets capable of meeting a variety of threats.

Along this line, the British Admiralty conducted a series of studies in the mid- to late 1880s, that ultimately provided the basis for the Naval Defense Act of 1889. Although its most immediate contribution was to renew Britain's commitment to the "Two-Power Standard" by which she agreed to maintain a navy more powerful than that of the next two greatest navies combined, the act also established several policies of nautical reform that other naval powers soon would follow. It set forth, first of all, that steam would serve as the basic means of propulsion for future battleships, thereby increasing their speed and reliability. It also directed that battleships should possess a complement of small-caliber guns for close-in defense against torpedo-boats. Further, it authorized the construction of "torpedo-boat destroyers" to protect capital ships. In addition, it outlined the requirement for a new class of armored cruisers capable of bridging the gap between the greater firepower but slower speed of battleships and the less-well-armed but faster destroyers. Finally, it directed the development of a class of mine-sweeping ships to counter the underwater mine threat. These measures preempted an emerging crisis in naval warfare by transforming the battle fleet from a relatively homogeneous assemblage of capital ships to an aggregate of heterogeneous vessels all functioning as parts of an integrated system.

Between 1895 and 1905, a series of technological innovations both reinforced the principles laid down in Britain's Naval Defense Act and further improved the offensive capabilities of battle fleets. New types of gunpowder and innovations in fire-control systems increased the range and accuracy of naval gunfire by a factor of 4. The development of the wireless allowed better command and control at sea. Quick-firing artillery, mounted on ships, virtually negated the threat from torpedo boats. Lighter steel and more efficient steam engines increased the range and speed of ships at sea. Thus, by 1905, long-range naval operations, once in jeopardy, had become a reality. However, in 1906, Admiral Sir John Fisher helped launch yet another revolution, this time in battleship design. Over the next 8 years, battleships, cruisers, and destroyers virtually doubled in size, speed, and firepower capabilities. In 1905 a typical battleship displaced some 13,000 tons and was armed with 4 12-inch guns (along with several smaller quick-firing guns for close-in defense) with a range of 6,000 yards. In 1906, on the other hand, the newly launched H.M.S. *Dreadnought* displaced nearly 18,000 tons and was armed with 10 12-inch guns, each capable of ranging to 13,000 yards. A new type of steam-turbine engine allowed her to reach speeds of 21 knots, 2 to 6 knots faster than existing battleships. By comparison, at the turn of the century, destroyers displaced less than 500 tons and were only armed with a few 3-inch quick-firing guns and, of course, a few small-diameter torpedoes. By 1914, they displaced nearly

1,000 tons, could reach speeds of 35 knots, and were armed with 4 4-inch guns and several 21-inch torpedoes.

In the meantime, the development of other supporting and enabling technologies, namely the gyro compass, periscope, and the diesel engine, had refuted H.G. Wells' *Anticipations* in which he declared that the submarine would do little more than "suffocate its crew and founder at sea." By 1914, the submarine had become not just a "thinking mine" fit only for coastal defense, but a weapon suited for commerce raiding and blockading. Ironically, it was the Germans who would make submarine raiding infamous in the First World War. Yet, in 1914 they possessed only 45 of the vessels, half of which were obsolete, while the British, who also maintained the largest surface navy, owned 97. While it added a new dimension to warfare, the submarine complemented rather than disproved the fundamental principles of Alfred Thayer Mahan and Julian Corbett concerning the nature of naval warfare and the importance of command of the sea. In other words, throughout 1914–1918, the struggle at sea centered upon the control of sea lanes of communication and commerce. And battle at sea remained a battle between fleets, though fleets now consisted of a variety of integrated systems coordinated by wireless and operating perhaps hundreds of miles apart either below, on, or above the water's surface.

C. The Ascent of Air Power

Although lighter-than-air balloons had been used for reconnaissance and observation as early as the late 18th century, they were not very successful because steering and communication difficulties imposed significant limitations upon their use. Nonetheless, by 1879, France had developed permanent balloon units for the purpose of aerial reconnaissance. Five years later, Germany followed suit. In the early 1880s, the introduction of electrically driven propellers gave balloons better navigation capabilities. This and similar aeronautical innovations inspired a flurry of interest in professional military journals and popular magazines. The literature of the day teemed with speculations and prognostications about the ways that aviation would revolutionize modern warfare. However, enthusiasm waned in the mid-1890s when the anticipated "conquest" of the air failed to take place as rapidly as expected. In 1900, Count Ferdinand von Zeppelin rekindled that interest when he successfully flew a gas-powered, hydrogen-filled aluminum airship across Lake Constance. Zeppelin's airship design would become the forerunner of the famous dirigible. In 1903, the Wright brothers piqued public enthusiasm further when they conducted the first successful flight of a heavier-than-air aircraft. Indeed, the conquest of the air now seemed imminent.

The French and German general staffs displayed keen interest in powered air vehicles almost from the beginning. Aircraft appeared to provide a means by which to bypass the deadly zone vertically, to acquire intelligence about the enemy's defensive preparations, and possibly to strike at his capital, then considered the heart of his will to resist. However, parliaments and war ministries, concerned with minimizing development costs and responsible for prioritizing competing financial requirements, proceeded slowly. Ironically, while one aeronautical record after another was broken between 1905 and 1913, particularly by the French, who led aviation development in nearly every category, both airships and fixed-wing aircraft had difficulty meeting design specifications laid down by military procurers in Europe and in the United States. Initially, Zeppelin's airships appeared to have greater speed, stability, and range than the rather flimsy fixed-wing aircraft. However, in 1910, German tests showed that airships were very vulnerable to fire from howitzers and antiballoon guns and, as a result, interest in the expensive Zeppelins began to decline.

Airplanes, on the other hand, seemed to have more military potential. By way of illustration, German investment in fixed-wing aircraft increased from 36,000 to 25,920,000 Reichsmarks between 1909 and 1914. During the invasion of Libya in 1911–1912, the Italians used a few airplanes to conduct aerial bombardments with hand grenades. The maneuver caused a panic at first, but it was soon discovered that alert sentries and timely, well-directed "anti-aircraft" fire could keep small numbers of aircraft at a safe distance. The Balkan Wars of 1912–1913 saw similar aerial assaults, but these, too, were easily countered by ground fire because they were not conducted in massed formations. Each of these conflicts, however, did demonstrate that aircraft would have a combat as well as a reconnaissance role in the next war. Consequently, airplanes required appropriate armament for air-to-air and air-to-ground fighting. As one German report concluded, "It will not be possible to operate in the air without weapons." In the autumn of 1913, the Germans conducted the first large-scale army air maneuvers to include night air operations. These maneuvers further clarified the roles of military aviation: strategic, operational (i.e., in support of cavalry divisions), and tactical reconnaissance; artillery observation; air-to-air combat; combat against ground troops; destruction of enemy installations; liaison; and troop transport.

By 1914, Germany and France possessed the most advanced air arms. The former had over 230 airplanes operating with her armies and another 39 with her navy, while the latter had about 100 fewer in total. In the opening phases of the World War I, each nation's air arm served its country well. German reconnaissance aircraft played an indispensable role during the Battle of Tannenberg in which the Russian Second Army was encircled and destroyed. As the German commander, General von Hindenburg later testified, "Without the airplane, there is no Tannenberg." Likewise, intelligence delivered by the French air arm literally made possible the "Miracle of the Marne" that saved the British and French armies on the western front. For a time, the air services of Germany and Britain aggressively pursued the idea of long-range strategic bombing. However, this idea proved less effective than originally hoped, as antiaircraft systems improved and civilian populations learned to adjust to the bombardments. Also, intermediate and long-range interdiction operations were attempted against key rail yards and naval ports. These strikes did cause some immediate disruption, but the effectiveness of new antiaircraft weapons made such operations costly; and the destructive power of air-delivered ordnance was not sufficient to produce long-term damage. The German use of radio-equipped aircraft in mass for close-air support proved highly effective during the campaigns of 1917 and 1918, both in defensive and in offensive roles. Navies also came to appreciate the value of air power at sea. The allies lost a number of merchant and warships, submarines, and patrol boats to German aircraft armed with bombs and torpedoes. By the end of the war, naval-air services had developed the capability to launch aircraft from sea vessels, forerunners of aircraft carriers.

From the standpoint of mechanical maturity, the First World War came about a decade too soon. Communication, aviation, and maneuver technologies, still in their infancy, were too limited and too prone to mechanical failure to enable an effective synchronization of fire and movement. As a consequence, the land-power crisis remain unresolved, the great symphony unfinished. After 8 weeks of fast-paced maneuver warfare, the Great War became the bloody, attrition-based struggle that Europe's war planners had for decades sought to avoid. Whereas railroads, telegraphs, and steam ships had increased the speed of strategic-level transportation and communication, they did little for operational-level maneuver. In fact, such technologies tended to shackle armies to rail terminals and sea ports.

Even the subsequent development of poison gas, flame-throwers, light-weight machine guns, and storm-troop or infiltration tactics—a return to the skirmish tactics of the 19th century but with an emphasis on operational penetration rather than tactical assault—failed to break the deadlock. Also, optimism regarding the efficacy of the infantry–artillery tandem precluded the full development of alternative operational-level maneuver technologies such as the tank, capable of rapidly penetrating a defense in depth to reach operational objectives. Even those armored fighting vehicles that appeared in the last 2 years of the war actually possessed neither the range, speed, nor communications capabilities necessary to make them operationally decisive.

D. Blitzkrieg: Theory and Practice

During the post-war period, communication, aviation, and maneuver technologies finally matured to the point that a practicable synchronization of fire and movement became possible. A doctrine for employing these more mature systems in a coherent and decisive manner emerged from the fertile soil of so-called *Blitzkrieg* theories generally associated with the military writings of B. H. Liddell Hart, J. F. C. Fuller, and Heinz Guderian. The *Blitzkrieg*, or lightning war, centered on the idea of using of air bombardments, artillery fires, and ground attacks to break through an opponent's defensive lines and penetrate to operational distances to disrupt his command and control and sever his lines of supply. At best, the psychological shock of an attack of such concentrated tempo and lethality would cause the defender's resistance to collapse suddenly (see Fig. 1). At worst, it would force him to fight in encircled pockets,

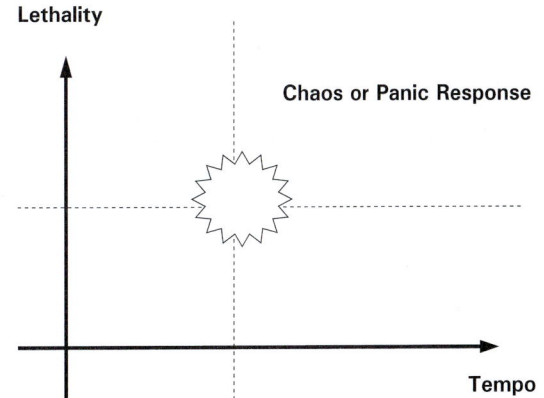

FIGURE 1 Lethality and tempo combine to produce a panic response.

against overwhelming odds, and with rapidly diminishing supplies. Germany's attacks against Poland, Denmark, Norway, France, and the low countries are illustrative of the former, while campaigns fought after 1941 generally conformed to the latter.

As the Second World War progressed, however, adversaries grew less susceptible to the psychological shock of a *Blitzkrieg*-style attack. Armies, navies, and air forces learned to cope both intellectually and emotionally with the war's tempo and lethality. Thus, more often than not, victory had to be won through the deliberate annihilation of the enemy's armed forces. On the Russo–German front, where the fighting was particularly bitter, encircled forces tended to hold out for extended periods of time, depriving the *Blitzkrieg* of its most appealing characteristic, its potential for delivering swift, lightning-like decisions. Even Japan's early victories in the South Pacific and the subsequent Allied counter-offensives demonstrated that, with some modifications, *Blitzkrieg* would work in theaters where naval and amphibious operations were more useful than armored pincer movements. The essential ingredient was not the armored fighting vehicle but the pinpoint location and timing of an all-arms attack, followed by a rapid operational-level exploitation before the enemy could recover. The years following World War II saw *Blitzkrieg* or the idea of a decisive all-arms attack change more in form than in substance. The object remained to integrate of air, ground, and naval power into a single decisive stroke or series of strikes designed to break an opponent's will to fight or, failing that, to destroy his armed forces, thereby removing his capacity to resist.

E. Strategic Bombing and Nuclear Warfare

The concept of strategic bombing emerged concurrent with but independent of *Blitzkrieg* theories. The so-called "true believers"—Giulio Douhet in Italy, Hugh Trenchard in Britain, and Billy Mitchell in the United States—believed that air power truly had revolutionized warfare. Although poorly understood and ultimately of dubious influence, these theorists argued that air power was the best arm for striking at the enemy's psychological center of gravity. Via strategic bombing, air power could circumvent the tactical and operational stages required of surface attacks and strike directly, and if necessary incessantly, at an opponent's heart and nervous center. The underlying principles of strategic bombing and *Blitzkrieg* thus shared a common theme—the use of selective destruction to trigger chaos or a panic response. Each theory thus saw technology as

little more than a tool, albeit a vital one, for attacking the all-important human dimension of warfare.

However, the concept of strategic bombing fell short of expectations during the Second World War. Strikes against major cities and industrial centers proved to be a necessary but not a sufficient cause for victory. Opponents reacted to the bombing with better defensive measures; and civilian populations became inured to the massive devastation, of which strategic bombing was merely a part, that the war produced. Here again, concept was ahead of technology. While the bombing of London by the Germans in World War I had created a panic response among the British population, the state of aviation and munitions technologies could neither sustain the tempo nor produce the lethality necessary to generate a decisive, war-winning effect. A certain technological optimism during the interwar years led theorists to believe that air power alone could achieve these effects in a future conflict. In fact, all evidence indicated that this relatively new arm did possess enormous potential. However, even in World War II, the state of long-range bombing technologies did not permit the preemption of an adversary's intellectual and emotional learning curves. On the other hand, while neither world war proved the case for strategic bombing, neither actually disproved it either. The right combination of tempo and lethality seemed literally just over the horizon. Indeed, with the dropping of atomic bombs on Hiroshima and Nagasaki—President Truman's "rain of ruin from the air"—strategic bombing technology at last matched the concept. Now the means existed to combine lethality and tempo in a strategically decisive manner.

By the mid-1980s, precision guided munitions had extended the tactical deadly zone to 4000 meters. Operational-level weapons such as the Tomahawk cruise missile could strike targets at ranges hitherto associated with the strategic level of warfare. Intercontinental ballistic missiles, armed with nuclear, biological, or chemical warheads, not only expanded traditional strategic distances to global proportions, but gave the principles of Douhet renewed relevance. For a time, the ability to send long-range weapons of mass destruction, whether dropped from B-52's or launched from submarines or underground missile silos, against major cities and industrial centers appeared to render conventional forces obsolete. Strategic attack became synonymous with nuclear attack; and strategic theory centered more on discussions of nuclear deterrence, flexible response, and mutual assured destruction. Nonetheless, while the means for delivering weapons of mass destruction evolved considerably, it remains to be seen (fortunately) whether they will prove effective against opponents who, despite egregious casualties, defy the rational actor model and simply refuse to submit.

F. Asymmetric Warfare

While the rapid victories associated with the Arab–Israeli Wars (1948, 1956, 1967, and 1973), the Falklands (1982), Panama (1989), and the Persian Gulf (1990–1991) suggest that limited, all-arms operations will remain viable, conflicts in Korea (1950–1953), Vietnam (1946–1954, 1960–1975), and Afghanistan (1979–1989) warn that such an approach has limits. Revolutionary wars, such as the civil wars in Spain (1936–1939) and Cambodia (1970–1975), have more often than not tended toward the extremes of political genocide rather than the limited goal of collapsing an opponent's will to resist. Most conflicts fought since 1945, in fact, have not involved limited aims or sophisticated technology but have centered on insurgency and counterinsurgency operations and acts of terrorism. These types of conflicts remain the Achilles' heels of both *Blitzkrieg*-style warfare and strategic bombing.

The essential ingredient for waging this sort of "protratcted" war, as Mao Tse Tung pointed out, is not overwhelming might but patience. The key element is time rather than speed. With time, an adversary's intellectual and emotional learning curves eventually level off and, if the war does not proceed as expected, begin to slope downward (Fig. 2). Understanding thus gives way to confusion and finally exhaustion. Such was the case with the analytical approach and strategic theories of U.S. Secretary of Defense Robert McNamara during the Vietnam conflict. As the war dragged on, U.S. citizens lost faith in the military's ability to win it

on favorable terms and at an acceptable cost. Although they endured tremendous losses, particularly during the Tet Offensive (1968), the Viet Cong and North Vietnamese regulars could avoid a general panic response or quickly recover from one by melting into the jungle. Mounting friendly and noncombatant casualties, on the other hand, eventually eroded support for the war at home; and U.S. military forces were withdrawn. A steady and seemingly pointless attrition had produced psychological exhaustion. An adversary not equipped to wage a high-tech, *Blitzkrieg*-style war can therefore still defeat one who is.

II. THE FUTURE OF MODERN WARFARE

Modern societies are currently undergoing a period of rapid technological change that may prove as revolutionary as the one that transformed Western society over 100 years ago. This revolution, which originated with the development of microchip technology in the latter half of the 20th century, portends a second transformation in modern warfare. This military–technological revolution (MTR), or a revolution in military affairs (RMA), presents armed forces with a number of opportunities as well as challenges. In the way of opportunities, the MTR or RMA may lead to important advances in precision targeting, information, propulsion, and biogenetic technologies. Precision weapon systems will continue to evolve toward greater range and accuracy, with the tactical deadly zone likely to extend to 200 kilometers within the next quarter-century. At the same time, information systems have begun to revolutionize command and control via the potential for real-time situation awareness. The near-instantaneous flow of critical information will enable decentralized operations to take place at a much faster tempo. Linear conceptions of the battlefield are already evolving toward a multidimensional, volume-centered representation. Such a reconceptualization makes it possible to conceive of an all-arms strike delivered across the tactical, operational, and strategic levels of war simultaneously. Successful execution of these operations will require an exquisite level of precise, yet flexible, synchronization between land, air, sea, and space systems. Protection for such a composite assault force will assume many forms, not the least of which will be synchronization with an "electronic curtain of fire." Research centers across the globe are currently studying alternative fuel and propulsion systems in the hope of radically reducing the cumbersome logistical tail of

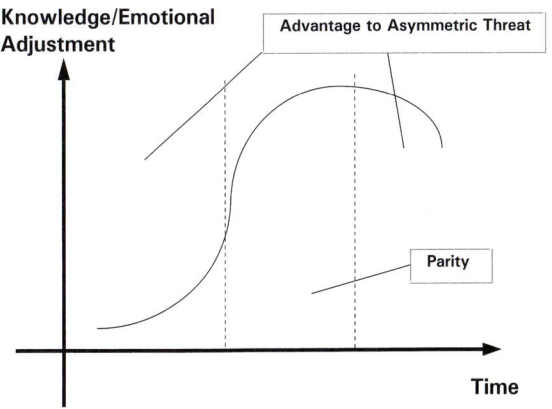

FIGURE 2 Learning and emotional adjustment curves.

modern armies. If successful, future armed forces will no longer have to execute linear, sequential campaigns defined by logistical consumption. Finally, various endeavors in biogenetic engineering might reveal ways to increase the endurance and cognitive capacities of individuals. Related research may lead to better methods for matching individual attributes with specific specialties.

However, these developments pose challenges for land, sea, air, and space power that may culminate in a new crisis for modern warfare. Within the next quarter century, even the most obscure of anational or metanational forces will be able to wage some form of electromagnetic warfare. The future deadly zone will include not only precision and area-fire weapons linked together via urban centers and complex terrain but also space-based lasers, satellites, unmanned aerial vehicles, and a variety of electronic weaponry. The greater speed of future operations will generate higher levels of physical and emotional stress for military leaders. Even sophisticated information aids may have difficulty keeping pace with the demand for decisions. Military personnel will probably fight under conditions that are far more psychologically demanding than those of past wars. Real-time information may influence political leaders to delay or change their decisions based upon the continuous flow of data received from the combat zone. Hence, future political objectives may become as fluid as tactical situations.

III. CONCLUSIONS

Many of the principles and concepts for the conduct of modern war through land, sea, and air power thus were developed or revised during the period of 1890–1918. Much of modern weapons technology, too, albeit in rudimentary form, originally emerged during this period. The marriage between concept and technological capability has been a difficult one at best. And, contrary to conventional wisdom, military thinking has not always lagged behind military technology. Undoubtedly, the further evolution of technology will bring new capabilities and new challenges. For this reason, the conduct of future war probably will remain more an art than a science. Yet, as Clausewitz pointed out, warfare deals with an opposing force, the opponent's will, which makes it neither an art nor a science in the truest sense of these terms. If history offers any lessons, therefore, one of the most important may be that the successful conduct of war requires knowing how, *or whether*, an opponent's will to resist is linked to his capacity to do so.

Also See the Following Articles
COMBAT • WARFARE, STRATEGIES AND TACTICS OF • WARFARE, TRENDS IN • WEAPONRY, EVOLUTION OF

Bibliography

Bellamy, C. (1987). *The future of land warfare*. New York: St. Martin's.

Bond, B. (1984). *War and society in Europe, 1870–1970*. New York: Free Press.

Brodie, B. (1969). *Sea power in the machine age*. Westport, CT: Greenwood.

Crane, C. (1993). *Bombs, cities, and civilians: Airpower strategy in World War II*. Lawrence: University of Kansas Press.

van Creveld, M. (1985). *Technology and war*. New York: Free Press.

Dupuy, R. E., Dupuy, T. N. (1970). *The encyclopedia of military history*. New York: Harper & Row.

Dupuy, T. N. (1980). *The evolution of weapons and warfare*. New York: Bobbs–Merrill.

Frankland, N. (Ed.) (1989). *The encyclopedia of twentieth-century warfare*. New York: Crown.

Forschungsamt, Militärgeschichtliches (Ed.). *Die Militärluftfahrt bis zum Beginn des Weltkrieges 1914*. Frankfurt am Main: E.S. Mittler.

Howard, M. (1976). *War in European history*. Oxford.

Jones, A. (1987). *The art of war in the western world*. Oxford.

Kennett, L. (1991). *The first air war, 1914–1918*. New York: Free Press.

Morrow, J. H., Jr. (1993). *The great war in the air: Military aviation from 1909 to 1921*. Washington, DC: Smithsonian.

Paret, P. (Ed.) (1986). *Makers of modern strategy: From Machiavelli to the modern age*. Princeton, NJ:

Strachan, H. (1983). *European armies and the conduct of war*. New York:

Taylor, J. R. (1974). *A history of aerial warfare*. London:

U.S. Army War College (1998). *Landpower in the 21st century: Preparing for conflict*. Carlisle, PA:

Wohl, Robert. (1994). *A Passion for Wings: Aviation and the Western Imagination, 1908–1918*. New Haven, CT: Yale University Press.

Warfare, Strategies and Tactics of

Hubert C. Johnson

University of Saskatchewan

GLOSSARY

Grand Strategy Planning at the highest level of the state for future campaigns.
Large-Scale Tactics Determination of the means and resources to be used to achieve a battle objective.
Military Strategy Implementation of Grand Strategy by the military services.
Small-Scale Tactics Determination of small unit operations on the battlefield.
Warfare A state of war and the waging of war.

WARFARE, found throughout human history, was depicted in the cave drawings of southern France and North Africa. These anonymous artists portrayed groups of warriors shooting arrows at other groups in struggles for game or territory. Since then war has played almost a determinate role in the rise and fall of civilizations. By the end of the 20th century we realize that the scale and destructiveness of warfare was much greater in that century then in any previous one. Truly we are molded by war.

I. WARFARE: A CONTINUATION OF STATE POLITICS

One of the greatest of military theorists, Carl von Clausewitz, indicated in his *On War* that war was the means the rulers of states attempted to protect and enhance their national interests when the regular mode of diplomacy failed. Many political theorists, if not Plato, have argued that the state has one fundamental duty: to protect and better itself. This concept is embodied in the term *Realpolitik*, which was popularized in Germany during the 19th century. Perhaps the best exponent of this doctrine was Machiavelli. In effect, the state, as an embodiment of citizens in a commonwealth, has no conscience, no morality, and serves only to pursue ruthlessly the realistic and materialistic goals that supposedly would benefit the populace. Early economic theorists, called mercantilists, argued the state should set policies that would result in a favorable balance of trade. If this goal could not be obtained peacefully, the state had the right to go to war and to destroy the enemy's trade by sinking its ships or invading its borders. Colbert, the great minister of Louis XIV, argued that a trade war might become a shooting war if the state could not get its way.

Therefore, the rulers of the state employ force and controlled violence in order to serve the interests of the commonwealth. Warfare is permissible and controlled violence.

II. GRAND STRATEGY

Once the decision is made to go to war the government has to establish a plan of action or to prepare what is called a "grand strategy." In Japan in 1941 when a cabinet crisis put Hidelki Tojo in as prime minister, he had to work out a new direction for the conduct of war. Prior to that time Japan had conducted an inconclusive war with China and lost a border skirmish with the Soviet Union, but since 1939 had had increasing trouble in its relations with the United States. Tojo had to determine either a northward (and Russia-based) and China-based plan of warfare or a southbound one. The Japanese Navy favored the latter because, if successful, it would result in the conquest of the rich petroleum reserves of Dutch Java. Only after much argument was a grand strategy adopted which gave primacy to the navy and enabled planning to commence for the Pearl Harbor attack of December 7, 1941. A grand strategy is an overall plan for the conduct of war that determines the aims, objectives, and limits and allocates the resources for a campaign. Only the civilian leadership of the state can determine such a policy because it transcends the capabilities of the military and naval leadership.

At the highest levels of statecraft, in the cabinet rooms, a grand strategy is determined that will mobilize the civilian resources of the state as well as those of the military in order to achieve a desired result. Fundamental in the establishment of a grade strategy is the decision to employ as much force as necessary to bring a satisfactory conclusion.

Famous examples of grand strategies include Julius Caesar's plans to conquer Gaul and to cross the channel, the preparations of William of Normandy for his invasion of England in 1066, and the plan of William Pitt the Elder in 1757 to fight the French in North America, Germany, India, and on the high seas. In more recent days, the collaboration of Churchill and Roosevelt in planning the defeat of the Axis powers in World War II provides a famous case.

Without a grand strategy a government cannot go to war with any hope of success, but the objectives of such a policy may not be immediately apparent. When Saddam Hussein determined to invade Kuwait in 1990 did he hope just to seize oil fields, or to unite his own people under his rule, or to claim

leadership of an international coalition of Islamic states as the leader of a new jihad? A grand strategy may be vaguely formulated or only partially revealed. It can be contradictory.

III. MILITARY STRATEGY

Once the government of a state has approved a grand strategy it is up to the military (including air forces) and naval forces to prepare a plan that will utilize trained personnel and weaponry to achieve the permitted objectives of warfare. Roosevelt and Churchill did not dictate to the armed forces of the Allies the format of the Normandy landings of 1944 but entrusted this plan to General Eisenhower and his subordinates. A large international and interservice group within the British forces, including representatives of the commonwealth as well as the Royal Navy and officers of the U.S. Army, Navy, and Air Force, had to prepare the intricate plans for collecting hundreds of thousands of troops at debarkation ports, hundreds of tanks, motorized vehicles and aircraft, and scores of ships under the condition of absolute secrecy. The planning for the Normandy invasion, entrusted by Eisenhower to General Bernard Montgomery, was the most detailed overall military strategy ever produced.

Other military strategies may or may not be well constructed. When the United States found itself embroiled in the Vietnam War, the Joint Chiefs of Staff prepared a military strategy that was limited by instructions from the president and the cabinet. President Lyndon Johnson sought advice from the joint chiefs as well as from his cabinet and determined to escalate American troop strength but to limit the operations of such troops. At no time could the U.S. armed forces use tactical nuclear weapons and most of the time they were given restrictions on what they could bomb and where they could send troops. A fundamental problem in Vietnam also was guerilla warfare, which provided a number of problems that the strategic planners could not solve very well. In Clausewitz's terms the U.S. armed forces had to fight a "limited war" as opposed to the "total war" waged in World War II. Limited wars are determined by political decisions as much as, or more than, strictly military and operational decisions. As the inconclusive war dragged on, opposition to it mounted within the United States and eventually forced the government to begin the process of troop withdrawal. A war that started out as a strategy designed to support the South Vietnamese government and escalated to become a major conflict between the United States and its South Vietnamese allies and the forces of North Vietnam and the guerilla movement, the Viet Cong, ended ignominiously in 1975.

IV. LARGE-SCALE TACTICS

If one plans warfare one is making strategic planning decisions. When the armed forces are given their lead to implement strategy they have to made plans for engaging in actual battle. Tactics consist of the planning for the use of troops and weapons to achieve victory in battle. Naturally there is a blurring between strategic planning and large-scale tactical planning. Napoleon was given the job of planning a campaign in Italy in 1796. When he marched into the Po Valley he arranged that the military units under his command would interact just prior to anticipated contact with the enemy as well as when battle was joined. The last arrangements were tactical and flowed out of strategic planning. In other words, Napoleon planned the strategy that resulted in the invasion of Italy and made the tactical decisions that that strategy called for in order to do battle. In 1942 Admiral Nimitz wanted to begin offensive operations against the Japanese in the Pacific but could not develop a large-scale strategy because of limited resources. He chose to send the First Marine Division to Guadacanal and to support it with the few aircraft carriers and other warships he had at hand. Because his strategy was limited his tactical possibilites were also limited.

Large-scale tactics, then, consist of the allocation of troops, weapons, and other resources to a battlefield commander who is entrusted with coordinating these assets in order to win battles. Australian General Monash described the role of such a commander succinctly; a general is like the conductor of an orchestra because he has to see that all the diverse types of units under his command function together in combat. The conductor has to make sure that the violins, oboes, and other instruments come in as the score dictates; the general has to make sure that the infantry, armored forces, air forces and other units play their assigned roles as the battle plan dictates. Unlike the conductor, however, the battlefield commander has to add other forced changes to the scenario because combat never follows prearrangements. Everything is subject to what J. F. C. Fuller called the "fog of war" when, in combat, things go wrong, the enemy does something unanticipated or one loses touch with some of one's own forces.

V. SMALL-SCALE TACTICS

Minor tactics consist of the training schemes all armed forces develop for inculcation in the minds of the troops and others who do the actual fighting on the spot. The U.S. Marine Corps developed amphibious warfare between 1920 and 1941 and trained frequently during that period. This training supplemented the ordinary "school of the soldier," which consisted of the tactical training of a Marine to work as a member of a squad, to acquire proficiency in marksmanship, to achieve a good physical standard, and to obey orders. Age-old, similar goals were set for the recruits to the Roman legions. Field training of recruits stresses advancing under fire, seeking cover when doing so, and converging on enemy points of resistance. For this reason the minor tactics of the infantry call for the most courage and result in the most casualties in warfare, both ancient and modern. Tactics require the infantrymen to get in "harm's way" to an extent unknown in artillery, armored, and logistical units. Others certainly find themselves in danger: the crews of submarines, air crews, tank crews, but all of these have impressive support structures. Behind front lines are large numbers of noncombat troops, mechanics, technicians, and so on. The infantryman must rely on his squad mates and is at the very source of extreme danger, even in modern combat situations. For this reason the infantry is known as the "queen of battle." The most coveted decoration in the United States Army, aside from the Medal of Honor, is the Combat Infantryman's Badge because its award is proof that the holder stood in harm's way.

When the squad advances under orders of the platoon commander, each soldier has an assigned role, either to carry a heavy weapon or to support those who do and to work, not as an individual seeker after glory, but as a member of a combat team. Success in battle often results from the coordination of firepower, which can only be achieved by constant field training and astute leadership. The arrangements for the combat of troops are minor tactics.

VI. CONCLUSIONS

To summarize, the government determines whether a state of war exists and also determines the order of priority the military services must use in the subsequent fighting. President Roosevelt had to give the bulk of troops available in 1942 to the European theater because of his Europe-first strategy determined with

Churchill. He permitted the bulk of the U.S. Navy to be deployed in the Pacific theater nevertheless. The government also determines whether limited or total war will be waged. To what extent will the civilian economy, for example, be harnessed to the war effort? These arrangements are examples of grand strategical thinking.

Strategical planning by the professional military, air, and naval commanders and their staffs then flow from the grand strategy. The Joints Chiefs of Staff had to prepare plans for the utilization of their units in a campaign as part of a war.

Battlefield commanders such as General Patton then had to arrange to have their units engage in combat. Patton and his staff of the Third Army determined the overall battlefield objectives with lower-unit commanders. This overall tactical work produced, at the final stage, the firing of artillery batteries, the advance of infantry, the movement of tanks, the use of tactical air support, and all the other elements of combat. Major tactics produced minor tactics.

Modern war, highly technological in nature, still relies on the use of force and violence to achieve political goals that could not be achieved by ordinary diplomatic means. One can recoil in horror from the killing and the destruction that inevitably result, but Mars continues his course, indifferent to the protests. The 20th century has seen continual violence. In fact, it would be hard to find a single day, anywhere in the world, absolutely free of civil or international war. A century since the Hague Tribunal and the international peace movement has not seen the triumph of peace and the outlawing of war.

Also See the Following Articles

WARFARE AND MILITARY STUDIES, OVERVIEW • WARFARE, MODERN • WARFARE, TRENDS IN • WEAPONRY, EVOLUTION OF

Bibliography

von Clausewitz, Carl (1976). *On war* (translated by M. Howard & P. Paret). Princeton, NJ: Princeton University Press.

Frank, R. B. (1990). *Guadalcanal: The definitive account of the landmark battle.* New York: Random House.

Johnson, H. C. (1994). *Breakthrough! tactics, technology, and the search for victory on the western front in World War I.* Novato, CA: Presidio.

Millett, A. R. (1991). *Semper fidelis: The history of the United States Marine Corps.* New York: Free Press.

Summers, H. G., Jr. (1982). *On strategy: A critical analysis of the Vietnam war.* Novato, CA: Presidio.

Wallach, J. L. (1986). *The dogma of the battle of annihilation.* London: Greenwood.

Warfare, Trends in

Nick Fotion

Emory University

GLOSSARY

Cooperative Engagement Capability The ability of a disparate military force to gather and process information instantly, communicate that information to all the units of the force, and respond as if the force is one close-knit unit.

Defensive Function of Weapons The ability of weapons to defeat the enemy's attempt to reach, locate, and disable targets.

Disabling Function of Weapons The ability of weapons to actually harm targets.

Locating Function of Weapons The ability of weapons to find targets. The dimensions of this function are distance, speed, time, and weather. Possessing ideal locating abilities, a weapon can find a target halfway around the world, do so in a few minutes, assess the features of the target in great detail, do so day or night, and in all weather conditions.

Reaching Function of Weapons The ability of weapons to take themselves to the target. The dimensions of

reach are distance, speed, and accuracy. Possessing ideal reach, a weapon can take itself to a target halfway around the world, do so in a few minutes, and be guided directly onto the target.

Real-Time Information Information about the enemy, one's own forces, weather, and so on that is provided and processed instantly.

I. RECENT TECHNOLOGICAL TRENDS

Trends in war, that is, changes in how often and how wars are fought, are largely a function of technology. This has always been so. New equipment and weapons in the past such as the stirrup, the long bow, the crossbow, and, most of all, guns, permanently changed the nature of war. But even as late as the 18th century, technology seemed to move at the pace of a slow walk. In the 19th century the pace became a brisk walk. During that century breech-loaded rifles came into use, giving soldiers greater firepower. Instead of firing two or four shots each minute with a musket, soldiers could now fire seven or more. Artillery gained power and range. In addition, weapons were put into the hands of the military in greater numbers. Technology made it possible to manufacture rifles by the millions and thus made armies in the millions possible. Technology even helped move these millions and their equipment to the battle lines so they could be deployed in the killing fields more quickly. Trains, as early as the American Civil War, moved troops quickly from one battlefield to another. Communication in the form of the telegraph made it possible for a central commander to coordinate the movement of his armies, even though they were hundreds of miles apart. At sea, steam power replaced sail, steel replaced wood, and the exploding shell replaced the cannonball.

The 20th century has seen the pace of technological development move from a walk to a jog to a run. Spurred by the two world wars, a variety of technologies were introduced in the first half of the century, including the airplane, the machine gun (although it was anticipated in the previous century), motorized equipment, the tank, radar, the submarine, and the atomic bomb. Spurred by the Cold War, the pace of weapons did not slow as one might expect after a major war. Instead, it accelerated. In terms of their function, here is an account of some of the significant weapons developed since World War II.

1. Reaching function: This is really three subfunctions. The first is distance. Post-World War II weapons, as represented by the intercontinental ballistic missile (ICBMs), the cruise missile, and the long-range bomber, can reach any point on the planet. Helicopters can drop troops deep behind the enemy lines, thus extending the field of battle well beyond the front lines, and artillery, firing improved conventional munitions, has a range twice what was achievable during World War II. The second subfunction is speed. Intercontinental ballistic missiles can reach their targets within 30 minutes; fast jet fighter planes can travel well over twice the speed of sound (vs much less than the speed of sound during World War II) and the mobility of troops on the ground has been enhanced since whole armies are now motorized (in contrast to World War II where at most 10% might be). The third subfunction is accuracy. As they reach out, delivery systems can be placed right on rather than somewhere near the target.

2. Locating function: This has four subfunctions. The first is distance once again. With the use of satellites, potential targets can be located no matter where they are. During World War II the Japanese built two superbattleships that were, more or less, a surprise to the Americans. Today such ships would be located even during the early stages of construction. The second subfunction is accuracy. Satellite information, various active and passive radars, and other sensor equipment can give details of enemy activity and position. Today not only the numbers but types of ships,

missiles, airplanes, tanks, and other equipment can be identified in detail even though they are deep behind enemy lines. The third subfunction is time. Battles need no longer take place mainly in daytime. Various radars and light-enhancing instruments make it possible for the battle to be fought 24 hours a day. Time is made irrelevant in another way. Unmanned air vehicles can locate enemy targets and accurately report where they are as of the moment (i.e., in "real" time). As a result, the artillery knows that its targets are where they are supposed to be. The fourth subfunction is weather. All-weather radars, infrared sensors, and other electronic capabilities enable the enemy to be found in foul as well as good weather conditions.

3. Disabling function: This function focuses on the actual damage done by a weapon. Even here there has been spectacular progress. Not only are explosives more powerful, but submunitions have made it possible for one shell or one bomb to do the damage that only many could do before. Submunitions are smaller warheads carried by a larger one. At the right time, the larger weapon disgorges the "baby" weapons. These offspring disperse over a wide area and either explode or lie dormant like a mine until a suitable target is found. They have become so widely available today that people rightly speak of the "submunitions revolution."

Of course, beginning at the end of World War II and developing rapidly thereafter, the nuclear revolution also took place. Since that war, nuclear weapons grew both in number and size. The number of nuclear warheads went from 6 in 1945 to close to 70,000 in 1986 (today the number is close to 36,000). In terms of size, one has only to compare the power of the World War II bombs (equivalent to 20,000 tons of TNT) with those of modern hydrogen bombs (equivalent to millions of tons of TNT) to realize how extensive the nuclear revolution has been.

4. Defensive function: Again progress in weapons development has been extensive enough to be revolutionary. The defensive function can best be understood as an effort to frustrate the other three functions. Here are some examples. The reach of airplanes and helicopters is frustrated by surface-to-air missiles (SAMs) that themselves possess more-than-adequate range, much speed, and great accuracy. One side's attempts to locate weapons, equipment, and personnel on the other side is frustrated by stealth technology as exemplified in the U.S.'s F-117 fighter bombers and by U.S. and Russian quiet

submarines. These attempts can also be frustrated by electronic countermeasures. Radar signals bouncing off airplanes can be distorted. Also, attempts to disable high-value tanks can be frustrated by so-called reactive armor. Such armor consists of explosive packets placed on the surface of tanks. As antitank warheads strike the tank, the reactive armor sets off small explosions that encourages the enemy warhead to dissipate its power outside the tank.

5. Supporting functions: Perhaps the most important revolution of all has and is taking place in the electronics field, especially with computers. Computers have entered all aspects of the weapons field. They allow information to be processed quickly enough to make the locating, reaching, and even the disabling functions of weapons more successful. In addition, computers help process information about supplies, equipment, personnel, weather, enemy positions, and everything else commanders want to know about. The electronics revolution via satellites has also expanded the military's ability to communicate. Even distant and isolated units can communicate instantly with headquarters and other units when there is a need to do so.

II. THE FUTURE

Although it is dangerous to project from past and present to the future, certain trends in the future are obvious. For one thing the electronics revolution shows no signs of abating. Computers promise to become much faster and contain much more memory. The military can harness the fruits of these promises, since war is an information-hungry activity. A naval operation centered upon an aircraft carrier is a case in point. The carrier and its accompanying escorts of cruisers, destroyers, and submarines need information about incoming ballistic missiles, cruise missiles, and airplanes. They also need to know where, nearby, enemy submarines and surface ships are lurking. Information gathered from various types of sensors (e.g., infra-red devices, active radars, sonars, photos, human eyes) from various sources (e.g., airplanes, drones, submarines, satellites) needs to be processed almost instantly so that it can be shared by the ships and planes in the squadron. More than that, cooperation needs to be maximized so that the ships and planes respond in the most efficient manner. It would not do to have three ships independently attacking one cruise missile while a second unattended missile strikes the targeted carrier.

What is true about the navy is also true about the army, only more so. In the 18th century soldiers would stand in tight formations in order to sustain a meaningful rate of fire with their cumbersome and slow-firing muskets. As rifles replaced muskets, and the rate of fire increased, it was only natural for soldiers to disperse and dig in. Those who stood together died together. Today and in the future, with weapons having awesome firepower, the need to disperse is even greater than before. But this makes gathering information about the conditions on the battlefield difficult. Scattering sensors of various sorts about the battlefield is one way to ease the difficulty. Another is to have direct radio communication with every small unit, perhaps with each soldier. Still another is to have helicopters and remotely unmanned air vehicles flying over the battlefield in order to survey the scene. Much of this will have to be real-time information. But, as with the navy, powerful computers are needed in order to process this incoming information, analyze it, and then suggest what courses of action should be taken. These computers together with a sophisticated communications system will give armies a cooperative engagement capability. Far more than in the past, they will have the capability of coordinating the activity of widely scattered troops, tanks, artillery, supply units, medical units, and so on to fight as if they were fighting shoulder to shoulder.

Understandably as a nation's military becomes increasingly dependent upon electronics, its enemies will seek to exploit that dependency. One of the crudest ways of accomplishing this is to generate an electromagnetic pulse (possibly with a nuclear explosion in near-space). Such a pulse destroys electronic equipment hundreds of miles around. Not only are computers thus made useless but, as a result, so are satellites, airplanes, helicopters, ships, tanks, trucks, artillery, communications headquarters, and everything else controlled by computer chips. A more subtle way to exploit this dependency to introduce viruses into the military's computer system. These viruses might shut down the system or they could introduce distortions in it so that the information disseminated is false or misleading.

Computers are not the only weak link in the electronics revolution. For quite some time radars have been attacked by radar-detection missiles that follow the radar signals down to their source and then explode. Radar-jamming has also been around for some time. More recently, radars have been challenged by stealth airplanes. These planes reflect back little of the radar signals that are used to "paint" them. As a result location is very difficult at best. Infrared sensors can similarly be defeated. The traditional way is to fire heat-generating rockets behind an airplane so that the attacking missiles chase the rocket rather than the airplane. But stealth can and will be used in the future by having airplane engines run "cool" so infrared guided missiles cannot find their targets easily. At sea, ships spray a cooling water mist around themselves to cool the gases emitted from their stacks and take other such measures so as not to send clear signals to the heat-seeking missiles attacking them. In these and other ways, the future promises that the next major war will be largely electronic. Both sides will use electronic equipment to gain an advantage and, at the same time, do what they can to counter the enemy's electronic attacks. Both sides will also try to counter the counters.

Electronics has become so important to modern warfare that in the future the winner might not be the side with the best and most airplanes, ships, and tanks, but the one that has created and kept an electronics gap in its favor. It seems somewhat fanciful, but still within the realm of serious thought, that a war in the future could be decided in favor of one side even before a major battle has been fought. If one side is crippled electronically it may be that it could have in its possession terribly expensive and highly sophisticated equipment that, nonetheless, is useless for military fighting purposes.

Because the trend to electronics is now, and promises in the future to be, revolutionary, other trends seem only evolutionary. But they too are bringing rapid changes that will forever make war different from what it was before. One such change has to do with the distance between opponents when a battle is fought. In ancient times the battle was at such close quarters that one literally had the blood of one's fallen opponent on one's hands. Spears, javelins, bows, and eventually guns gradually increased the distance between warriors at least on some occasions. In World Wars I and II air battles were still fought well within visual range and much of the artillery fired at an enemy was also within that range. The same is true for most naval battles. The one exception was when airplanes from carriers or land were sent out to find enemy shipping. But even here airplanes had to attack by visually locating the enemy and then pressing the attack to a few hundred feet or less. Bombing on land also involved bringing the bomber literally over the target, thus bringing it in harm's way. All that is changing. Airplanes are gradually being given missiles that can destroy the enemy beyond the visual field. Of course electronics comes into play here again. Several kinds of sensors will be needed to locate the enemy. Other kinds will check to see if the identified target is the enemy or a lost friendly airplane.

Other electronic black boxes will do the calculations that will tell the pilot which missile to fire and when to do it. Finally, the missile's reach and locating functions will be such as to guide it to the enemy plane in a "fire-and-forget" mode. This makes it possible for the attacking plane, if it wishes, to begin an assault on a second plane even before its first missile has hit the first. Bombing will be different, too. Bombers will not literally go over the target to drop their bombs, but fire missiles or bombs that will glide to the distant target while the bomber is already escaping. On the ground, artillery will use indirect fire more often, that is, fire on targets well beyond the visual field.

A third trend is robotic warfare. This trend probably will not be fully manifested for another 15 or 20 years. Robotic warfare takes the human factor of the attacking force out of harm's way. At present this trend is best represented by the cruise missile and the unmanned air vehicle. With the former the missile is autonomous once it is fired. It monitors its own path to the target and then makes adjustments so as to achieve a direct hit. With the latter, its surveillance functions are usually controlled by a "pilot" on the ground. In the future we likely will have unmanned fighter planes, tanks, missile launchers, ships, and even "unmanned" soldiers.

The need for robots is the result of a fourth trend in war. The battlefield is becoming increasingly lethal. With all the sensors available to the war participants, warriors will not be able to hide at night, in bad weather, or even underground. Once located, smart weapons will reach and destroy them with powerful explosives. In the air, when there is need for an attacking plane to fly directly over or near the target, as there might when the targets are moving, the attackers will pay a heavy price. Well-coordinated air defenses will destroy perhaps more than half their numbers. In such a setting it makes sense to have these missions performed by robotic planes and thereby keep air forces from suffering the loss of pilots and their very expensive aircraft. These robotic planes have other advantages. They will be launched not only from aircraft carriers and airports but from submarines, destroyers, and other ships; and, on land, launched from almost any position on the fighting front.

A fifth trend follows from those already described. Unit costs of weaponry will stay high and likely continue to rise. It is true that robotics may lead to lower unit costs in some cases. A robotic airplane will probably cost half of its manned counterpart since, without a cockpit, the plane will be smaller and simpler. It is also likely that computer prices will keep falling even as they become more powerful. But technology continues to advance and new sensors, countersensors, longer range missiles, and other weapons will come on line. The pressure to continue developing weapon systems promises to continue even in these post-Cold War days. Military leaders and their political masters know that technological leadership in the future is a very important factor determining whether wars are won or lost. So we are not likely to see very many lower unit costs for planes, helicopters, tanks, artillery, soldiers (personally carrying various sensors, communications equipment, as well as their guns and ammunition), and ships.

As unit costs stay high, or rise, a sixth trend will emerge. We can see this trend at work already today. Military forces will become smaller. No nation will be able to afford to keep large military forces with all the electronically laden military weaponry available. Fighter planes that cost tens of thousands of dollars in World War II came to cost several million dollars in the years immediately following that war. Costs then rose to tens of millions of dollars and in some cases hundreds of millions. Costs of training pilots went up. Aircraft carrier costs went into the billions. So it is with almost all equipment and training. With such costs, instead of buying thousands of airplanes (the U.S. built tens of thousands during 1944) now, at best, only a few hundred F-22 fighter planes (at a cost between 70 and 100 million dollars per plane) will be built over several years. Other planes will be delivered to various air and naval forces each year by the handful rather than by the hundreds or thousands.

But costs are not the only reason for the trend to smaller military forces. A second reason is that weapons have become so much more powerful that one airplane, one tank, one ship can today do the work that only many could do in the past. Whereas in World War II a half-dozen airplanes might be sent to destroy one target, today, and more so tomorrow, one airplane will be sent to destroy several targets. On land it is no longer necessary for a tank to fire shell after shell before hitting its target. Today, and more so in the future, the practice will be "fire one shell (or missile), destroy one, or more, enemy tank."

A third reason goes back to electronics. If sensors can be scattered all over the battlefield by planes and other means, fewer soldiers will be needed for patrol and other such duties. Similarly, electronics does much of the work in an airplane so only the pilot is needed to perform the mission. Ships are becoming "smart" so, again, many fewer sailors are needed to operate a destroyer, a submarine, and other vessels compared to the past.

III. WHAT MIGHT HAPPEN IN A HIGH-TECH WAR

Much of the discussion so far has been aimed at understanding what a war between high-tech nations will look like in the foreseeable future. One scenario says that the sum of all these trends would be a form of mutual destruction. It is generally recognized that mutual destruction would result if nuclear war were fought between two of these nations. But the power coming into the hands of high-tech military forces may be such as to lead to mutual destruction even if nuclear and other nonconventional (i.e., chemical and biological) weapons were not used. The destruction would not likely be the same as that coming from a series of nuclear exchanges. It would be extensive, nonetheless, since serious land and air war would range well beyond what we conceive of as "the front." The economic costs to both sides of fighting such a war would also likely constitute a form of mutual destruction. One needs to keep in mind the high costs of the equipment in a high-tech war. Losing one aircraft carrier with its planes and many of its personnel would cost roughly 10 billion dollars. The loss of one B-2 bomber would cost another 2 billion dollars. The cost of fighting the high-tech war would mount as thousands of missiles were fired, some of them costing hundreds of thousands of dollars each, others costing millions. Then there are the damage costs to both the military and civilian sectors on both sides.

But in truth no one knows what would happen if two high-tech nations met in war since such a war has never been fought. Here is another possible scenario. With this one the economic cost to everyone involved would be terribly high. Still, one side would prevail because it has the overall technological edge. Perhaps its cooperative engagement practices are more effective or its radar works more consistently at longer ranges so it can shoot enemy aircraft from the skies before they can return fire. Or perhaps its missiles have more range and are more difficult to evade or its people are better trained to manipulate the equipment put in their hands. Whatever the advantages might be, they create a magnifying effect. The small but significant technological advantages one side has leads to large differences in battlefield results. So one side wins and wins big.

A variation of this scenario presents another possibility. In the past, before the nuclear age, the losing side was at the complete mercy of the winner. If it wished, the winner could demand and receive unconditional surrender. But today's and the future's high-tech losers will likely have some remaining nuclear and other nonconventional (i.e., chemical and biological) weapons at their disposal. So even if they suffer a quick and humiliating loss in a conventional war, they will still be able to hold onto a strong negotiating stance by threatening the use of these weapons.

There is still another scenario to consider. This one might occur quite apart from whether one side has the capability to dominate the other. As the war begins, or soon after, one side resorts to the use of unconventional weapons. This could happen in a piecemeal fashion or systematically. If the former, there would likely be a response in kind at least equal to, and possibly greater than, the initial unconventional attacks. A counterresponse to the initial response would follow, and escalation to a full blown unconventional war would also quickly follow. If the latter, escalation would be immediate. Whatever the case, the result would be unqualified mutual assured destruction.

IV. TRENDS IN WAR WITH LOW-TECH NATIONS

If it is almost totally unclear what would happen were two powerful high-tech nations to meet in war, it is clearer what would happen if a high-tech nation fought one possessing a significantly inferior technology. The battle would be one sided. It would probably be quick and costly to both sides but especially for the loser. The loser could capitulate at this point or, if it too possessed nuclear and other nonconventional weapons, it could threaten their use.

This latter possibility needs to be taken seriously since in the future more nations will possess nonconventional weapons. It is clear even today that relatively small and poor nations such as Libya, Iraq, Iran, and North Korea can acquire the capacity to make chemical, biological, and even nuclear weapons. They can also develop the means to deliver them by building or buying fairly long-range missiles. These missiles need not be terribly accurate to achieve their purpose of threatening or destroying enemy cities. So these nations will soon have the negotiating power to prevent their more powerful foes from imposing heavy demands on them when they have suffered a military defeat by conventional means. They will also have negotiating power even to prevent being attacked in the first place. These nations might not be able to threaten their potential opponents with destruction quite in the complete sense that the major powers threaten each other. Nonetheless, they could threaten far greater destruction than they could using only conventional weapons by saying, for example, if you attack us we will drop one, two, or three nuclear weapons on your cities.

Even if a technologically inferior nation lost and did not have nonconventional weapons at its disposal, it has one other option short of capitulating. It could continue the war by resorting to guerrilla tactics. If this were to happen the technologically superior winner would lose most of its advantages since guerrilla war makes aircraft carriers, air-superiority fighters, tanks, and other heavy military equipment largely irrelevant. However, the high-tech nation might retain some advantages. More than in the past, electronic sensors will make it possible to track guerrillas in some of their favorite hiding places such as the jungle and mountains. Still, the guerrilla battles tomorrow will likely not be so different from what they are today and were a generation ago.

The same can be largely said for wars fought between low-tech or medium-tech nations. To some extent high-tech equipment will trickle down to less-wealthy nations. In the near future data gathered from satellites will be commercially available to everyone. Also, in small numbers, export versions of modern aircraft, tanks, artillery, submarines, and other war ships will be sold to second- and third-level nations. Still, these wars in the foreseeable future will be labor intensive. Low-tech nations will not be able to afford much of the exotic electronic equipment that will make a decisive difference in a war's outcome. So lacking these technologies they will have to maintain large military forces and thus try to win their wars "by the numbers." In the near future, then, there will be an enormous difference in how wars are fought. Those nations with an abundant source of human talent and money will fight wars in ways never fought before. They will employ a relatively small elite number of warriors to bring about enormous damage to their opponents. They will aim to win their wars quickly and decisively. Lacking the human and financial resources, the less high-tech nations will engage in slugfests that could go on for years. Their wars will be like many in the past.

V. TRENDS RESULTING FROM WAR AND WAR PREPARATION

Wars of the present and future will create trends in society beyond the effects caused by the war itself. One of the most obvious is the development of military–industrial complexes. These complexes developed partly as the result of the Cold War. Without that "war" there would undoubtedly be fewer nuclear weapons as well as fewer major naval ships, tanks, and other instruments of war on the planet. And without that war, these complexes would not possess the political power to maintain themselves. But the Cold War and its effects mask a reason why these complexes are not likely to go away in the foreseeable future. As should be clear by now, modern military weapons are terribly complex. They cannot be designed, produced, and deployed in a year or so as was the case even with the weapons of World War II. It will take close to 15 years, for example, to take the American F-22 air-superiority fighter from its design stage to deployment. Other weapons may not take that long, but the years required will range beyond 5 and often up to 10. These rough estimates of years between design and deployment assume that the skills and facilities needed to produce modern weapons are in place. Were military–industrial complexes allowed to "fade away," it would be impossible for a modern industrial/information-age society to present a potential enemy with a credible defense posture.

Couple these thoughts about the slow pace of weapons deployment in our electronic world with a potential enemy's military reach, and one can appreciate why nations suffer from security anxiety. Again, even as late as World War II, and for a time beyond that, military establishments did not have the reach to threaten potential enemies who were continents or oceans away. But today all nations are subject to quick and powerful attacks from far-away enemies. Tomorrow, more nations will have the capability to reach out and devastate someone if they so wish. Thus, so long as the world remains insecure, nations will not allow their military–industrial complexes to decay.

Another trend caused by modern war is the isolation of the military from the rest of society. This trend has already started. In the past, not only in the century but in the 18th and 19th centuries as well, large numbers of conscripts were employed to fight wars. This, as had been noted, is largely a consequence of modern industrial production that has made it possible to place guns in the hands of millions. Today as the costs of arming military personnel rise, nations can afford to arm only a few. They will also find it necessary to train these few to higher standards in order for them to properly operate the high-tech and expensive equipment they are asked to use. This means that the most feasible model for most nations is a professional military. The few will protect the many. Inevitably the few will be drawn from certain families and ethnic and racial groups and so on more than others. Some groups will have many relatives and close friends in the military;

many more will not. Some will contact the military for business reasons but, again, most will not. A few in government will have direct contact with the military; most will not. Along with the fact that military training takes place in segregated facilities both in country and abroad, the result will be a kind of social isolation of the military where it will be easy for the military and the rest of society to misunderstand and even be suspicious of one another.

To some extent there is a trend going in the opposite direction. This trend is not due to the military, directly or indirectly, but to factors found in a key segment of society. Curiously enough this trend, like so many in the military, is caused by technology. The technology in question is television—the videocam, video tapes, satellites, and television sets at home. Although, as just noted, the military operates in relative isolation in military camps at home and overseas, once the battle begins television will be there to record the battle or at least its blood-laden aftermath. For a generation now, people at home have seen and will in the future continue to see what war looks like. The shock of seeing death, injury, and damage in large doses will continue to put pressure on military forces to keep their own casualities as low as possible. Indeed, television may apply pressure on these forces in such ways as to make carrying out certain military missions impossible. It can do this as follows: Television first dramatizes the plight of some starving or oppressed people. These visions of suffering encourage politicians to send the troops to set things right. But once the troops are sent, they suffer casualties. Television dutifully records these tragic events and thus creates pressure on the military and the politicians to "bring the boys home" before they can possibly complete their mission.

Two additional present and future trends in war deserve attention. As will become evident shortly, the first is partly supported by television. This trend has to do with the influence of ethics on war and in particular with the influence of what has traditionally been called just war theory. Briefly, this theory says, first, that a nation should attempt to satisfy certain principles before it goes to war and, second, once it enters war, it should restrain its forces as to how they fight. The former principles, usually numbering six or so, fall under the heading of justice of the war (*jus ad bellum*). One such principle is that a nation should have a good reason (just cause) for entering a war such as that it or its ally is under attack. A war of aggression whose intent is to grab some land from a neighboring state does not count as a good reason under this theory. Another principle under the heading of justice of the war is last resort. It says that a nation should not plunge precipitiously into war, but should make all sorts of effort to settle whatever disputes there are between it and its potential enemy. A third principle is proper authorization. Only those in government who are legally charged to start a war can do so justly. Private citizens and groups may in fact get a nation involved in war by simply gathering an "army" together and starting an invasion. But they cannot do so justly. If these and the other principles are satisfied, then a nation is said to have justice on its side in entering a war.

Once in the war, however, just war theory says the war must be fought justly (ethically). The most important principle of this justice-in-the-war (jus in bello) portion of just war theory is that certain people are immune from attack. This is called the principle of discrimination. It can be stated in many ways. One is that those who are not actively involved in the war should not be attacked; those who are, can be.

Historically, interest in just war theory has waxed and waned. Usually it has waxed during and after particularly bloody wars such as the Thirty Years War in the 17th century. The horror of that war inspired Grotius to develop a version of just war theory independent of religious doctrine. There was a similar rise of interest after World War II and even more so during and after the VietNam War. At other times interest waned and the doctrine of Realism dominated as it did, perhaps as much as any time, prior to World War I. With its concern for national self-interest, the extreme form of this position had little time for talk of ethics before and during war.

Today, interest in guiding military politics in accordance with just war theory seems to be strong. Indeed, it has been institutionalized within the military so that it seems likely it will influence military behavior in the future. This institutionalization can be seen in the military ethics courses taught at military academies and war colleges in many "liberal" Western and Asian countries, in the lectures one hears about military ethics within and outside the military, and in the many books and articles written on the subject. In contrast with the past when ethical discussions focused mainly on "internal" military matters such as loyalty and obedience, nowadays both officers and enlisted personnel cannot plead that they did not know right from wrong when they acted immorally against an enemy. Today, again in contrast to the past, they have been exposed to too much talk about military ethics to plead ignorance.

Of course, courses taught and books read do not necessarily translate into good behavior on the battle-field. Under pressure, military personnel and their leaders will undoubtedly misbehave no matter how many ethics lessons they have digested. But there are at least two reasons for believing that just war theory will have some real influence in the future. One is television, once again. At least in liberal countries where the mass media have the power to tell their stories, it is increasingly going to be difficult for the military to encourage or even condone behavior counter to just war theory and get away with it. Once people see their soldiers acting like beasts they will be revolted and quickly withdraw whatever support the military has for its war efforts. In short, it is in the military's best interest these days to do all it can to control the behavior of its people so it is in accord with ethical principles.

The second reason for believing that just war theory will have a real influence returns the discussion to high-tech weapons. Modern weaponry makes it easier for high-tech military forces to fight in accordance with just war theory. To see why, it is useful, once again, to contrast the past with the present and future. World War II technology made it impossible for Allied air forces to attack Germany and Japan without violating the principle of discrimination. Airplanes dropped their "dumb" iron bombs in such a way as to kill military and civilians alike. But today, with "smart" bombs and missiles, discriminate bombing is a real possibility. Military and military related targets can be hit without hitting civilian homes, schools, hospitals, religious structures, or businesses that have little or nothing to do with the war.

The second, and final, trend in war to be discussed has to do primarily with the political sphere and only secondarily with technology. In the distant past the political unit that brought war to its neighbors was the city-state or some regional group of people headed by a powerful ruler. Eventually the unit became larger so that nations became the war-making political unit. With nations, war usually served as an instrument of national expansion but could also serve a political ideology, such as communism, or a religion, such as Christianity or Islam. Today and tomorrow it seems that nations can and will continue to bring wars to others. But in many regions of the world, nations are under internal pressure from ethnic and racial groups that constitute them. As each group makes claims to its own identity, wars often result. These wars are fairly low-tech in nature since at least one side usually has limited economic means and also lacks the know-how to deploy high-tech equipment. These wars also tend to diverge rather sharply from the principles of just war theory. Each participant group tends to demonize the opposition, thus making it easier to destroy and abuse it with impunity. This brutal behavior poses a challenge for those nations intent on acting in accordance with just war theory since one of the just causes for entering a war is to stop slaughters and their after-effects. If they have the power and ability to do so, it would seem that powerful nations have a duty to interfere.

However, it is not easy to adapt military forces trained to fight big high-tech wars with one another to the task of stopping ugly local ethnic and racial struggles. It requires certain changes in outlook. Occupying troops have to be more restrained in performing their peace-making and peacekeeping functions. To do this they need special training. They have to be equipped somewhat differently as well. Heavy tanks and air-superiority fighters are less needed than in a big high-tech wars. High-seas fleets are needed less as well. What is needed is high-tech equipment that enables the military to do its work decisively, but with great precision. There is a need also to keep the loss of life and the level of suffering to a minimum. Toward this end, navies have to prepare for littoral (i.e., close-into-shore and shallow-waters) warfare. One way to do this is to build "arsenal ships" armed with hundreds of precision missiles. Another is to convert submarines that in that past carried nuclear missiles to carry conventionally armed missiles. In effect, these submarines would become underwater arsenal ships. Either way, these ships will act as the mobile artillery for military forces intent on moving into an area in order to rescue the needy. Another way to prepare for these little wars is to have navies, armies, and air forces enhance their ability to move military personnel, equipment, food, and other supplies into the troubled areas quickly and in large numbers.

VI. SUMMARY

The fast pace of technological change and over a half-century of peace between major nations make it difficult to project what might happen were a major war to break out. No one knows which advanced weapons will succeed or fail, how much damage will be done, how long a war will last, and who, if anyone, will win. Although it is difficult to assess trends when it comes to the ends or results of war, assessing the means is not difficult. The means of war are largely affected by electronics. Electronics has given the military the means to locate enemies, reach them, and then, finally, destroy them no matter where they are. Electronics, along with other technological advances, make it possible to do these things in almost any environmental setting, and do them quickly, with great precision and devastating power. Quality of weaponry now counts, and in the future will increasingly count, far more than quantity. The days of military forces in the millions will soon be over. It is just as well, since high-technology weaponry has proved to be very costly. No nation, no matter how wealthy, can afford to arm millions of its people with high-tech equipment. The trend is to arm the few well and, concurrently, train them well. These few are and will be fully capable of doing more damage than the many could in the past. However, there are social pressures on these high-tech military forces to constrain their power in accord with the principles of just war theory. Unfortunately these same social pressures do not seem to be present in the small ethnic and racial wars that are common these days. These wars promise to be nasty, brutish, and long.

Also See the Following Articles

COMBAT • JUST-WAR CRITERIA • MILITARY-INDUSTRIAL COMPLEX, CONTEMPORARY SIGNIFICANCE • WAR CRIMES • WARFARE AND MILITARY STUDIES, OVERVIEW • WARFARE, MODERN • WARFARE, STRATEGIES AND TACTICS OF • WEAPONRY, EVOLUTION OF

Bibliography

Addington, L. H. (1984). *The patterns of war since the eighteenth century*. Bloomington: Indiana University Press.

Christopher, P. (1994). *The ethics of war and peace*. Englewood Cliffs, NJ: Prentice–Hall.

Cook, N. et al. (1997). Scenario 2015: How science shapes war. *Jane's Defence Weekly*, 47–66.

Dunnigan, J. F. (1993). *How to make war*. New York: William Morrow.

Fotion, N. G. (1990). *Military ethics: Looking toward the future*. Stanford, CA: Hoover Institution Press.

O'Connell, R. L. (1989). *Of arms and men: A history of war, weapons and aggression*. New York/Oxford: Oxford University Press.

Ropp, T. (1962). *War in the modern world*. New York: Macmillan.

Warriors, Anthropology of

Andrew Sanders

University of Ulster

I. Introduction
II. The Tribal Warrior
III. The Warrior in Centralized Polities

GLOSSARY

Age Set Formally organized group of persons of a common age range.

Genipa Bluish-black pigment of the fruit of the tree *Genipa americana.*

Mana Personal mystical power associated with Polynesians of high rank, causing them to be, to varying degrees, sacred.

Military Associations Men's social groups of the Native American tribes of the North American Great Plains, which carried out military activities.

Tipi Conical skin tent of the North American Plains Indians.

Tsantsa Shrunken human head trophy of the Jivaro Indians of Ecuador.

WARRIORS are persons whose vocation is warfare and who engage in the actual physical activity of fighting. In contrast to soldiers, and in particular to conscripts, they fight for personal glory. Consequently they often fight as individuals rather than as members of disciplined military formations. To warriors, warfare is a way of life and its values dominate much of their behavior. In contrast to modern soldiers, warriors supply their own weapons. With the development of the state, warriors (such as medieval knights) fought in a more disciplined way, but their lives continued to be dominated by values of personal and military glory. It is not possible to make an absolute distinction between the warrior whose vocation is warfare and the soldier whose profession is warfare, and today's professional soldiers still demonstrate some aspects of warriorhood. Personal honors are awarded for military deeds of outstanding bravery, and battle honors are given to successful military units and services. But personal glory and individual prowess have become subordinated to military strategy and technical efficiency.

I. INTRODUCTION

In discussions of "primitive" societies, the term "warrior" is often applied to any fighting man. This is particularly true in popular literature, where "warrior" and adult male are used as if they are synonymous. In most human societies all able-bodied men were at least potential fighters and engaged in military activity when necessary, but there are fewer examples of persons to whom warfare was a vocation and whose lives were dedicated to military pursuits.

In the great majority of human societies, the role of fighting with weapons was culturally restricted to men. There were notable exceptions, the Amazons of Dahomey being the most famous authenticated example. These were women soldiers in the service of the kings of Dahomey in the 18th and 19th centuries. In 1845 Dahomey had a standing army of 12,000 soldiers, of whom 5,000 were women. The Amazons were organized in brigades with their own female officers and were billeted in special apartments in the royal palace. They formed the king's bodyguard and were recruited by the king, to whom they were said to be devoted, from among both free Dahomeans and captives. They should remain celibate until middle age, when they could marry on receiving permission from the king. Their historical origins appear to have been the women employed to hunt for game for the royal table, and the élite corps among the 19th-century Amazon companies was the Fanti company, which was recruited from elephant huntresses. Amazon companies wore the uniform of Dahomean regular soldiers and were armed with muskets and bayonets, or bow and arrows in the case of young recruits.

Dahomey was a politically and socially complex precolonial West African state. In some tribal societies (see below) in which men's and women's activities were not strongly differentiated, such as the Ojibwa Indians of the North American Great Lakes region, women warriors were not unusual and their war exploits were accorded social recognition. Other nonindustrial societies have produced individual female warriors, such as Celtic warrior chieftainesses and Jeanne d'Arc, but either their warlike activities were an aspect of their special status (they belonged to cultural categories different from normal men and women) or they were regarded as abnormal and their exploits explained in supernatural—or similar—terms.

II. THE TRIBAL WARRIOR

A common anthropological classification of human societies is to divide them into four types on the basis of complexity of social organization and political structure. These are: bands, tribes, chiefdoms, and states. This is a useful classification for a general examination of warriors, as patterns of warfare are related to general types of political structure.

Bands and tribes are egalitarian forms of political organization that lack formalized political hierarchy or a social division into dominant and subordinate political groups. Leadership is based on achievement and is for limited purposes only. The power an individual can acquire depends on his ability and is influential rather than coercive. Because of this, bands and tribes are classed together as uncentralized structures, in contrast to chiefdoms and states, which are hierarchically organized.

Bands constitute the simplest form of political organization. They are associated with a hunting and foraging way of life and usually contain between 30 and 100 persons. They are of fluid composition: size and membership fluctuate with local and seasonal changes in the availability of natural resources. A band's members have relatives in many neighboring bands, may change their band of residence relatively frequently, and often marry persons from other bands. Consequently, important social and personal ties often link persons residing in different bands. Under these circumstances there is no formal organization for warfare and war is not an important activity, although actions such as homicide and wife-stealing may provoke retaliatory attacks between families. Bands do not produce fighting men who are warriors by our definition.

Tribes usually consist of a number of residential groups—villages, hamlets, or homesteads. These settlements are made up of close kinsmen and have a high degree of political autonomy. They are confederated through the operation of kinship groups, political and recreational associations, and ritual organizations, which are organized on a tribal basis. In some cases a tribe may constitute a single large village, but common residence is cemented through village-based organizations and activities. Tribal organization is associated with horticulture, the large-scale keeping of livestock, and with more complex patterns of hunting. (However, tribes are not the only forms of social organization to be based on these ways of life.)

Tribes were more effectively organized for warfare than were bands. The typical fighting unit was a small group of kinsmen mobilized to carry out a raid in retaliation for a perceived offense against one of its members. Recruited on the basis of obligations of mutual assistance between close kinsmen, it was a temporary unit, informally organized and lacking authoritative leadership. Raiding was the major form of military activity, but if hostility developed between communities or tribes over a long period it might culminate in a battle in which, at most, the victorious group could kill its opponents or drive them away. Men usually lacked extensive training in military activities and tended to act on their own initiatives during fighting. Although all able-bodied adult males fought as the occasion required, warfare was not usually a vocation. It was one of a man's several cultural roles and was not the principal means of attaining prestige.

A. Warrior Societies

However, some tribes placed a strong value upon warfare and war-like achievements. Warfare was a cultural value, exalted in itself, and assumed the character of a personal vocation. Outstanding fighting men received honor and prestige. Warfare was integrated with other aspects of culture, such as religious beliefs and ritual practices. Pierre Clastres terms these societies "warrior societies" because of the special place given to war and violence in their cultural ethos. Some warrior tribes had special organizations whose members carried out military activities. The equestrian Indians of the North American plains in the 18th and 19th centuries possessed men's social and recreational associations that competed with each other in military activities, and many East African pastoral tribes had age-based organizations that pursued warfare. However, the diagnostic characteristic of warrior tribes is a matter of cultural ethos and personal calling rather than the presence of specialist military organizations.

Keith Otterbein lists six possible goals of war: subjugation and tribute; acquisition of land; acquisition of plunder; trophies and honors; defense; and revenge. (To this we should perhaps add a further category, ritual goals—for example, acquiring heads for religious purposes or prisoners for human sacrifice.) Revenge or retaliation is generally regarded as the most common motive for the warfare of bands and tribes, as they lack the organization to subjugate a defeated foe, but there are also economic motives in some situations. For example, pastoral peoples in East Africa, Central Asia, and southern Siberia fought for control of pastures to graze their flocks and herds, and the Indians of the Gran Chaco in Paraguay fought for control of water. In warrior societies, personal glory (Otterbein's "acquisition of trophies and honors") was a particularly important motive for participating in warfare. Military activity continued to be an individualistic enterprise characterized by limited discipline, informal controls over individual warriors, and restricted powers of leaders.

Many anthropologists argue that underlying the individual motives and social goals of warfare are deeper influences. For example, Otterbein claims that changing patterns of warfare in southeastern Africa in the 19th century, and the associated political changes, resulted from pressure on land caused by population increase. In contemporary anthropology, the most influential of these explanations are material ones; patterns of warfare are the product of ecological influences or of (often hidden) economic factors. It may be argued that idealistic motives really mask more fundamental material ones. Or that warfare operates to maintain favorable ecological and demographic relations—by reducing the pressure of population on land or by producing a more ecologically efficient distribution of resources, for example—and that ecological and demographic problems generate particular patterns of warfare that serve to resolve them.

In some tribes a warrior ethic was associated with intergroup competition for scarce material resources. For example, pastoral tribes often fought for pasture, and some tribes of the New Guinea Highlands fought for land. But material causes do not appear universal. In the peripheral areas of the New Guinea Highlands, warfare was endemic in the precolonial period, but there was no shortage of land and acquisition of land was of little importance as a goal of warfare. A warrior ethic may not be simply a cultural response to material conditions. Competition for material resources may have been of little importance in the creation of a warrior ethos among the Jivaro Indians of Ecuador, the Indians of the North American plains, or the Indians of northeastern North America. Clastres argues that a society may develop a warrior ethic in a variety of ways. It may be a response to external social influences or be an internal cultural development. The transformation may not be permanent. He also suggests that warrior societies have the potential to become predatory, looting societies through raiding their neighbours for booty, and cites the North American Apache as an example.

However, anthropological accounts of many warrior societies describe them after they had been subjected to the influences of European colonial expansion, which may have stimulated warfare through dispossession and competition for land, demand for European commodities, or the development of more efficient weapons and military techniques. Warrior ideals were sometimes created by this process, while existing warrior ideals often came to be more strongly expressed. Seventeenth-century Iroquois militarism exemplifies the latter development. As a result of contact with Europeans, the Iroquois (a warrior society of the New York–Pennsylvania region) developed new military tactics that gave them a commanding position in the intertribal conflicts that were generated by European colonialism and gave new goals to warfare. Recent studies of South American warrior societies argue that Mundurucu militarism was intensified through their use as mercenaries by the Portuguese and that Euro-American colonial and commercial activities intensified Jivaro warfare.

B. The Integration of Warriors in Tribal Social Structures

In warrior societies, there was often a marked differentiation between the proper social role of the warrior and that of the elders, with the latter directing community policy-making. War was primarily a young man's occupation, and the warriors' passion for war often conflicted with more pragmatic policies advocated by their elders. Consequently, the elders sought to exercise some control over the activities of the warriors. In East African pastoral societies such as the Masai, male roles were allocated within a formal system of associations recruited on the principle of socially recognized age. Initiation into an age set created a common identity and a strong *esprit de corps* among its members. The members of the elder's age sets were expected to decide policies in matters vital to the well-being of the community. The warriors' age sets acted to defend land, cattle, and other resources and to raid enemies. The impulsive glory-seeking warriors should be under some control from their elders. Among North American Plains Indians such as the Crow, influential civil leaders, whose status in part depended on their war performance in the past, decided policy through consultation with their peers. They used the military associations of the tribe to implement their decisions. Within the tribe, competition for prestige between different military associations may have acted both as an outlet for the aggressive values of young men and as a mechanism to reduce the likelihood of conflict arising from the differing interests and values of the young and the old.

However, assaults from more powerful societies might promote an increase in the power of warriors and their leaders over the direction of community policy. This development occurred among many Native American societies during the European colonization of the Americas.

C. Training

In warrior societies, warfare was strongly integrated with religious and social values, and from childhood a male was socialized into warrior ideals and trained in military activities. Among South American tribal groups such as the Tupinamba and the Guarani, boys were taught that they must avenge warriors killed by enemies by capturing prisoners to sacrifice as compensation for their loss. The primary aim of a Jivaro boy's upbringing

was to make him a brave and skillful warrior. A father sought to inculcate his hatred of his enemies into his sons, and young boys were taken on war expeditions. At puberty a Jivaro boy drank a narcotic prepared from the bush *Datura arborea*, which caused him to hallucinate. Ancestral spirits appeared to him, to help him become a valiant and successful warrior. Throughout his life he would take narcotic drinks in order to consult the spirits for advice in military matters. Among the Indians of the North American plains in the 18th and 19th centuries, a boy was taught from infancy that bravery provided the route to social success and that old age was an evil and it was good to die young in battle. He was taught to admire and emulate eminent warriors. (Boys who showed no inclination toward this way of life might be allocated to a nonmasculine gender and allowed to pursue a lifestyle different from other men.)

In coastal Melanesia, boys were taught to regard allies and enemies as significantly different persons. The enemy were defined as external, negative objects against which one's self and one's group were defined. The successful taking of enemy life was associated with joy and prestige, and the torture and cannibalizing of enemy prisoners might be relished. In some tribal societies, adulthood was entered through initiation rituals, which might involve ordeals. In warrior societies successful passage of initiation might be necessary to qualify for warrior status, as in parts of East Africa and Melanesia.

D. War Honors

Where warfare was exalted and the warrior was an ideal, particular achievements often provided the criteria of personal success. They were demonstrations of worthiness. To become an important man, a Jivaro should have participated in successful war expeditions and killed at least one enemy. To be elected a war leader he had to be a renowned warrior who had taken part in many wars, killed many enemies, and taken at least one enemy head and participated in the subsequent *tsantsa* feast.

Accumulation of war honors increased social status. A Bagobo man of Mindanao in the Philippines who had killed two persons was entitled to wear a chocolate-colored kerchief as a symbol of his achievement and was believed to be protected by two great spirits. Four killings entitled him to wear blood-red trousers, and when he achieved six he was entitled to a suit of blood-red and could lead war parties and assist in annual ceremonies.

War achievements were ranked, and the highest might stress the bravery involved in the exploit. Warriors achieved prestige and became war leaders by performing the higher-ranked deeds. Among Plains Indians, the highest war achievement, the *coup,* involved touching the body of a living or dead foe with a special stick. This testified that the warrior had been at close quarters with the enemy. It was an expression of personal bravery, and counting *coup* on a foe usually ranked higher than killing him, which could be done from a distance. Achievements had to be socially recognized to be valid, which usually meant that they had to be witnessed. Consequently a man counting a *coup* in battle would call out his exploit aloud, and war exploits were recounted at public gatherings. The 19th-century Cheyenne Indians allowed three persons to count *coup* upon the same body, the first *coup* ranking highest. Other high-ranking deeds involved saving a wounded comrade, having a horse shot from under one, being the first to locate the enemy, and charging a body of enemies alone. The Crow allowed four *coups,* ranked according to the order in which they were struck. They recognized four categories of war honors: striking a foe, leading a war party, stealing a picketed horse from an enemy camp, and snatching a bow or gun from a foe in hand-to-hand combat. To be recognized as a distinguished warrior, a man had to have achieved at least one deed of each type. Honors were displayed in dress and personal decoration and painted on the warrior's *tipi.*

Ranking of military achievements engendered competition between warriors. War was fought as an individual activity, for personal glory. The successful warrior was driven continuously to seek greater achievements, so that he became an individual who invited death. Formal single combats between noted warriors or between champions of groups are reported from warrior societies around the world. They are frequently reported for 19th-century Plains Indians. Sometimes they involved behavior comparable to the medieval European idea of chivalry. A classic example is the American artist George Catlin's account of a duel between the noted Mandan leader Mato-Topé ("Four Bears") and a prominent Cheyenne warrior. When a party of Mandans met a much larger Cheyenne war party, Mato-Topé rode toward them and thrust his lance into the ground. He hung his sash (the insignia of his position in his military association) upon it as a sign that he would not retreat. The Cheyenne leader then challenged Mato-Topé to single combat by thrusting his ornate lance (the symbol of his office in his military association) into the ground next to that of Mato-Topé. The two men fought from horseback with guns until Mato-Topé's powder horn was destroyed. The Cheyenne then threw away his gun so that they remained evenly matched. They fought with bow and arrow until Mato-Topé's horse was killed, when the Cheyenne voluntarily dismounted and they fought on foot. When the Cheyenne's quiver was empty both men discarded bow and shield and closed to fight with knives. Mato-Topé then realized that he had left his knife at home, and a desperate struggle ensued for the Cheyenne's weapon. Although wounded badly in the hand and several times in the body, Mato-Topé succeeded in wresting the Cheyenne's knife from him and then killed him and took his scalp. Consequently, among his war honors Mato-Topé wore a red wooden knife in his hair to symbolize the deed, and the duel was one of the 11 war exploits painted on his buffalo robe. He also wore in his hair four small yellow sticks, one blue stick, and one red stick to symbolize wounds received in battle. His *coups* were indicated by yellow horizontal stripes on his arm and a yellow hand painted on his chest showed that he had taken prisoners (Fig. 1).

Although some war honors might exalt risk, others might not require it. War was not usually indulged in for risk: honors might be awarded for any homicide. Among the Bagobo of Mindanao, killing a sleeping enemy and killing from ambush ranked equal to homicide carried out in more dangerous circumstances, as did killing a faithless wife and her lover. The Jivaro tried to kill their enemies by ambush and surprise attack and avoid open fights, but a warrior was expected to show valor and contempt for death. He was taught not to run away or abandon his fellows. Melanesian warfare eulogized hit-and-run tactics, the killing of women and children, and deeds that entailed little risk. Plains Indian raiding and warfare gave the highest honors for risk-taking behavior, but Plains culture also regarded high loss of life on one's own side as an unacceptable price for success. A successful war leader who had never lost a follower ranked higher than one who, however successful in terms of other war honors, had done so. A Cheyenne's rank as a warrior was created by a combination of his score in personal war honors and his ability to lead successful raids in which Cheyenne losses were low.

E. Trophies

Warriors often had to obtain trophies to demonstrate their power and achievements and sometimes for ritual reasons. A famous example is the taking and shrinking of heads by Jivaro warriors. The Jivaro shrunken-head trophy (*tsantsa*) was not only a victory token, it was a repository of supernatural power for the slayer and it gratified his ancestors' desire for revenge and secured

FIGURE 1   Mandan warrior, Mato Topé ("Four Bears"), displaying his war honors. Watercolor sketch by Karl Bodmer (1834). (Salamander)

their good will. The more valiant the enemy, the greater the power of the *tsantsa* made from his head. Taking a head and celebrating a *tsantsa* feast brought honor to the slayer and was believed to promote his material success, future victory, and long life.

Head-taking was a common form of trophy acquisition. It often involved religious motives, as in Indonesia and Melanesia. For example, headhunting in the Purari delta of New Guinea was interpreted as taking the life force of other communities to augment the spiritual force of one's own clan spirit-ancestors. These were given the form of large wicker monsters that were fed enemy heads, which were placed in the mouth of the effigy and shaken into its stomach.

Like war honors, war trophies might be graded in importance and prestige. Among the South American equestrian tribes of the Gran Chaco there was a hierarchy of scalps. The Chulupi placed highest value upon scalps from their inveterate enemies, the Toba. (According to Clastres, the Chulupi claim that during the Chaco War of 1932–1935 between Bolivia and Paraguay, they killed so many Bolivian soldiers that their scalps depreciated in prestige to the point where warriors only bothered to scalp officers.)

Killing and the collecting of trophies might be accompanied by some degree of cannibalism, performed for ritual purposes and restricted to parts of the body considered to be the seat of particular virtues. The Bagobo ate the heart of a courageous foe in order to obtain his courage. Sometimes a more systematic form of cannibalism was carried out on war prisoners. The warrior societies of eastern North America often ate the remains of a prisoner in a cannibalistic feast after he had been killed by systematic prolonged torture. The Tupinamba Indian tribes of the Brazilian coast practiced the ceremonial killing and cannibalizing of war prisoners after they had enjoyed a period of freedom within their captors' community. (Prisoners did not attempt to escape. Their own communities rejected them and to be killed and ceremoniously eaten was an honored fate.) The executioner of a prisoner scarified himself in order to create upon his body a permanent mark of his prestige.

Although Tupinamba cannibalism was performed for religious purposes related to warfare and general cultural values, it also involved a genuine enjoyment of human flesh. In some Melanesian societies cannibalism had strong ritual and cosmological significance. It was believed that by incorporating the enemies' life-force the victors acquired strength, well-being, and spiritual rejuvenation. In others, cannibalism was more a culinary delicacy or a way of insulting an enemy.

F. Preparations for War

Going to war in warrior societies involved ritual preparations to promote a successful enterprise. Throughout native South America, omens were consulted to gauge the likely outcome of a proposed raid. If a Tupinamba warrior dreamed of a meat-rack full of enemy flesh, this was a good sign. Should he dream about corpses of his own people, this was a bad omen and the war party would be aborted. Rites were performed to protect the warriors and make their expedition a success. The Araucanian Indians of southern Chile, who became equestrian warriors through Spanish contact, observed strict chastity before going to war. They drew magic symbols on their weapons and inoculated themselves with magic powders to make themselves invulnerable. They rubbed

their horses with feathers or vicuña skins to make them swift. Shamans performed rituals and consulted oracles to discern the future. On the march, warriors continued to look for omens and would return home on sighting an inauspicious animal or hearing the call of an inauspicious bird.

When a Jivaro expedition was being planned the warriors, and particularly the war leader, repeatedly drank narcotic drinks in order to consult with ancestors and other spirits. They paid special attention to dreams. For several nights before the expedition the war party performed a ritual dance as an exhortation to war and an attempt to secure victory. Armed warriors were organized in two lines and they performed the ritual in pairs, each pair engaging in a stereotyped dialogue. While the party was away, the women assembled each night and danced. This was believed to protect their men and lull the enemy into a false sense of security. Before attacking an enemy household, the Jivaro warrior dressed for battle. Rafael Karsten describes the symbolism of the warrior's dress and armaments. To give him strength and valour, he wore a necklace of jaguar's teeth, long ear tubes, and a belt of boa's skin—or he might wear a belt of human hair, as it was believed to have supernatural properties, hair being the seat of the soul. He painted his face, limbs, and the exposed parts of the body black with *genipa*, to make him resemble a demon and give him the strength and ferocity of this spirit. His lance of chonta palm had special power, as the palm is the abode of a spirit; and his shield was decorated with paintings of spirits and animals intended to inspire him with strength and courage and strike fear into his foe.

Ritual preparation for war was not only a symbolic act to promote success. It created a frame of mind conducive to performing acts of violence, which often involved physical risk and required courage. Even in the most war-like cultures aggression and courage have to be fostered in the individual. The Yanomanö Indians of Venezuela and Brazil are noted for their fierceness. Violent responses to personal slights are lauded. Yet even here, fighting cannot rely upon the existence of a violent temperament. Young warriors practice simulating rage as a tactic in interpersonal confrontation, and men use drugs to put themselves in a fighting mood. The attitudes of warriorhood in coastal Melanesia involved intense anger projected onto a dehumanized enemy. This was accomplished through war cults that transformed the warrior into a virulent persona of enragement and aimed to reduce the enemy to fear. In Avatip, a community on the middle Sepik river in Papua-New Guinea, headhunting involved rituals associated with the village men's cult, intended to put warriors in a depersonalized state where their spirits were believed to act through them. Men were emotionally transformed so that they perceived others as quarry and were capable of killing anyone. They killed in order to become ritually significant individuals. A man went out to kill with an ornament in the form of a face clasped between his teeth. It went before him and obscured his real face. Simon Harrison argues that ritual transformation did more than create an attitude that enabled killing. It enabled men to break strongly held moral conventions that governed everyday behavior and social relationships. By attributing their actions to Spirit acting through a disassociated self, they were able to explain why they did so and to distance themselves from their "antisocial" behavior. This practice was common in warfare on the middle Sepik.

G. Avoiding the Demands of Warriorhood

In warrior societies, not everyone wished to pursue the demanding life of the ultimate warrior to its logical conclusion by constantly courting death in seeking to outdo his fellows. It was a way of life that appealed to relatively few. Consequently, there were institutionalized ways in which a warrior could avoid such a course without losing honor. The equestrian tribes of the Gran Chaco each had a warriors' association, membership of which was the ultimate recognition of warriorhood and conferred high social status. In late adolescence, boys underwent a painful rite of passage which entitled them to bear arms; but to attain full warrior status by entering the warriors' association a man had to bring back the scalp of an enemy killed in combat. Many men who could qualify did not wish to commit themselves to constant engagement in situations of personal danger, so when they killed an enemy they chose not to take the scalp. Provided they continued to fight bravely when the occasion demanded, they lost no honor thereby. Among the Crow Indians of Montana, men joined one of several named associations that operated as military and recreational clubs and competed with each other for military renown. Each club possessed its own insignia and songs and had a number of club offices to which eminent or aspiring warriors were appointed each year. Four officers were standard-bearers who carried special staffs and were pledged not to retreat in the face of the enemy. Because of the danger, many men refused to accept these offices. A reluctant candidate might be compelled to do so by having a ceremonial pipe forced against his lips.

III. THE WARRIOR IN CENTRALIZED POLITIES

Centralized polities are hierarchically organized, with administrative functionaries who act as agencies for the redistribution of goods. In states, this agency takes the form of an organized, centralized government that claims a monopoly over the use of force within the society. Centralized polities are inegalitarian, with marked differences in rank and with social strata that are differentiated from each other in terms of prestige and often of power.

A. Chiefdoms

A chiefdom is characterized by hereditary chiefs, drawn from high-ranking kinship groups, who are the foci for the redistribution of goods and services. In addition, they may direct cooperative labor. Chiefly status is sanctioned by ritual, and chiefs perform important religious duties affecting the whole polity.

Some anthropologists argue that warfare was an important factor in the evolution of tribes into chiefdoms, suggesting that ecological pressures intensified warfare between polities and produced centralization. Others argue that increased warfare may be a consequence of increased centralization and social stratification—centralized organization enabled the development of a more efficient military force. Whichever view is taken, it is usually argued that once chiefdoms have developed, they are likely to expand by incorporating territory—and often by subjugating its population—through warfare and that, consequently, neighboring polities are likely to adopt more centralized institutions in their own defence.

The immediate motives for conflict between chiefdoms were usually chiefs' desires to revenge what they perceived as slights against themselves. Within chiefdoms, hostilities involved grievances and clashes of interest between paramount chief and subchiefs. Warfare might result from, or be influenced by, economic considerations such as retaliation for trespass or seizure of territory when a chiefdom's land was no longer able to support its population.

Military practices in centralized political systems tended to be characterized by hand-to-hand combat, fortifications, and sieges, whereas in uncentralized political systems war was generally fought with projectiles. Chiefly armies averaged about 100 persons, but in larger, more strongly hierarchical chiefdoms they might be as large as 5000 individuals. Military encounters were battles rather than raids and resulted in much higher loss of life than was usual in the military activities of uncentralized peoples.

The military organization of chiefdoms was much more complex than that of tribes. It was based upon the hierarchical structure of the polity and had a permanent, hierarchical command structure where senior members could transmit orders to their subordinates. This situation contrasts with uncentralized societies, where involvement in fighting was an individual decision or a group decision in which the individual fighter participated. In chiefdoms, war was decided upon by leaders who had the power to compel subjects to participate. A chief's status was hereditary and sanctioned by his prestige and ritual position, including his association with rituals of war. But he also had at his command a retinue of personal retainers who would enforce his decisions.

War leaders were usually chiefs or their representatives (who were appointed from among their close kinsmen), and consequently the role of the warrior was to some degree hereditary. In a typical chiefdom, the paramount chief led his army and established military alliances with other chiefdoms. It was usual for the heir to the chieftainship to be trained from childhood in the martial arts. The chief not only led his forces; often he was expected to demonstrate his personal bravery in combat. Although he might command support, he led by example. Chiefs and renowned warriors might engage in single combats. For example, the leaders of Maori war parties were usually high-born chiefs and their military training, rank, and *mana* were supposed to make them brave men and successful leaders. If hostile Maori forces met in the open, renowned warriors might challenge each other to single combat. The fight was supposed to be conducted with some degree of chivalry. However, the ideal was not always followed, and a warrior might seek to disadvantage his opponent by tricking him. Although single combats might give individual renown, the military strategies of chiefdoms often involved trickery, treachery, and ambush.

Members of a chief's domain could be mustered for combat at the chief's demand, but personal bravery and individual military success (measured in terms of enemies killed and prisoners taken) were applauded and outstanding performance socially rewarded. In contrast to uncentralized polities, warfare was more organized, often with military campaigns aimed to restrict the power of other chiefdoms. But fighting was a personal action that required skill and bravery. The encouragement of these qualities meant that in many chiefdoms, particularly those where warfare was endemic,

fighting men, and not only those of high rank, were also warriors. A Fijian who clubbed an enemy to death was given an honorary title, and commoners who distinguished themselves in battle could be raised in rank to a position just below that of town chiefs and priests. However, genealogy was important in determining social status, and a man's war exploits only enabled him to elevate his rank within certain social limits. Among the Maori, a courageous and successful warrior was given the title of "*toa*." Among the Chibchan chiefdoms of the Cauca Valley in Colombia, where warfare was intense, the principal way a man could raise his status was by taking prisoners in war. Killing enemy warriors also merited prestige, and a brave and successful warrior could raise his rank and might achieve the position of war captain.

1. Trophies

Success in warfare increased the prestige of the chief; it could strengthen his power by increasing the number of his subjects and consequently the amount of tribute he received. War trophies gave prestige to the chieftainship. The Maori smoke-dried and preserved the heads of defeated enemy chiefs and publicly insulted them. In the Cauca Valley, skulls and dried heads were hung from the bamboo palisades and walls of temples and houses and heaped on platforms in village plazas. In at least one Cauca Valley chiefdom, enemy corpses were smoke-dried and preserved as trophies in a special house belonging to the paramount chief. Treatment of prisoners varied with culture and social circumstances. The Maori feasted on the flesh of dead enemies. The survivors might become slaves of chiefs and perform menial tasks. However, although they might be killed as human sacrifices or to provide part of a feast, the physical conditions of their servitude were not severe. In the Cauca Valley and in Fiji, obtaining prisoners to cannibalize became an increasing factor in promoting war. Robert Carneiro argues that in neither region was there any reason for large numbers of captives for economic exploitation, and consequently prisoners were usually killed and eaten.

2. Preparations for War

From his comparative analysis of Fiji and the Cauca Valley, Carneiro argues that courage-instilling rituals prior to war were more elaborate in chiefdoms. He considers this to be a consequence of the increased risk of death in battle. Presumably it was also related to the fact that participation in war was compulsory and no longer a matter of individual choice. Before going to war, the forces of a Fijian chiefdom would assemble to

FIGURE 2 Fijians performing war dance. Original photo: Henry King (Sydney, Australia).

undergo a review in which each man would boast of how he would kill the enemy (Fig. 2). The chief would encourage them by promising rich rewards for their valor.

B. States

The hierarchical organization of chiefdoms enables them to become larger and more complex by incorporating defeated populations. The evolution of early states was a development of processes and structures already present in chiefdoms. The importance of warfare in the creation of the first states is debated, but there is universal agreement that once they evolved, warfare was a major factor in their expansion, which generated new states.

The simplest states often did not contain warriors or professional soldiers. Waging war was only one of a man's cultural roles. The army was organized and mobilized on the basis of local divisions that incorporated all the able-bodied men of a district, often fighting under the command of their local chief. Other simple states had standing armies and made war into a young man's profession. The great Zulu king Shaka (d. 1828) organized his army on the basis of age regiments, each with its own name, leader, and barracks. Young men of equivalent age were initiated together to form a new regiment, whose members lived together until middle age, when the king gave them permission to marry.

Under these circumstances, each regiment developed a strong *esprit de corps*. While bravery was encouraged and rewarded, warfare was a disciplined activity and Zulu fighting men were more like professional soldiers than warriors. Such standing armies appear associated with expansionist warfare.

With the development of aristocratic states, an aristocratic class dominated the highest military offices. S. P. Reyna describes these states as organized on the basis of two major social classes, aristocracy and peasantry, with differential property ownership, occupations, and political rights. Often, the aristocracy was a military caste of professional warriors, as in the case of medieval knights and Japanese samurai. War was a major means by which the aristocratic class acquired land, tribute, and rents. It was carried out principally in pursuit of aristocratic interests, and it has been claimed that warfare was necessary to maintain an aristocratic ruling class.

In aristocratic states warriorhood was an occupation, closely associated with the ruling class and with a strong hereditary aspect. The Greek heroes of Homer were born of high rank. War was their main means of attaining wealth and their lives were given over to warfare, government, religious ceremonies, and sports—the only activities worthy of a warrior. Their personal qualities were those proper to the warrior—courage, strength, and skill. Similarly, to the medieval knight war was a noble profession and the main purpose of life. He fought because it was his legal obligation to his feudal lord and because war provided the opportunity for material gain, but also out of love of war and to defend his honor. European feudal nobility lauded the skills and characteristics of the warrior. Courage and contempt of death were valued. Unwarlike persons (*villeins*) were despised. The knight was driven to perform feats of arms, both in his military activities and in his private life. The only civil activities with which he was likely to concern himself involved the exercise of judicial responsibilities. Proper peacetime pursuits involved demonstration of skill and courage, such as hunting and participating in tournaments, and a prodigal and luxurious lifestyle was the ideal. During the second feudal age the ideal knightly qualities became defined in a code of chivalry, which from about 1100 was described by the word "*courtesie.*" A knight should use his sword in good causes and to defend the Holy Church. He should not slay a vanquished or defenseless enemy. He should eschew any part in false judgement or acts of treason and aid those in distress. Although the reality was far different, the ideal was supposed to set the noble class apart as a special category of persons, superior to other classes.

A trained warrior, the knight provided his own specialized equipment and fought in armor from horseback. The superiority of aristocratic armaments, their personal use, and skill in their use, enabled the operation of a warrior ethic as part of the aristocratic way of life. Knights formed the heavy cavalry core of shock troops of medieval armies, and with the invention of the stirrup in the 10th century their characteristic weapon became the long heavy lance. Armies consisted of a core of aristocratic warriors, with foot soldiers drawn from their feudal subjects. By 1250 knighthood had become hereditary, an aspect of the noble class of medieval European kingdoms. From the second half of the 11th century, a new knight formally received his vocation through a ritual in which he was given his weapons by an established knight, who struck him a blow with the flat of his hand. This ritual of "dubbing" became a Church service performed by a priest, in which the knight took an oath to abide by the knightly code, and there developed the concept of knighthood as an order to which all knights belonged and into which an initiate was religiously ordained.

Archaic or aristocratic empires created mercenary groups from conquered populations or from groups living on their borders, such as the barbarians who were settled within the later Roman Empire as *feodorati* and the Cossacks of Imperial Russia. They were recruited to form military units in imperial armies, often because they held warrior values. Now, however, they were fighting in disciplined formations under imperial command and were professional soldiers rather than warriors. In a similar manner, the recent Age of Imperial Expansion resulted in certain groups—such as Ghurkas, Senegalese, and Scottish Highlanders—becoming associated with war-like abilities and recruited for imperial armies, with a corresponding development of a tradition in military careerism.

With the development of industrialization and the nation-state, armies have become huge and intensely specialized with complex and sophisticated command hierarchies. Modern military personnel undergo intensive training to equip them with the skills and values of their occupation, which set them apart from the civilian population. Senior personnel are not exclusively drawn from ruling classes. Status within the military organization depends more on ability than birth. Women are recruited to military occupations. Material factors and class or national interests are the main causes of modern warfare. Combined with modern technology, this makes modern warfare a highly organized and disciplined activity and makes the true warrior, pursuing personal glory in battle, redundant.

However, there are elements in modern military life that are universal aspects of a military vocation and consequently are shared with the warriors of tribal societies and of simpler states. It is not possible to draw a clear line between warriors and professional service personnel. Courage remains valued within the military services and is given special honors. There are medals for personal valor. Honor is associated with regiments and services and symbolized in battle honors. Rituals, often of a secular nature, continue to be used to generate military values and promote *esprit de corps*. This is particularly the case with officers, and officer-recruits may have to prove themselves during a long, humiliating period of initiation which resocializes the apprentice officer and creates commitment to the values of the military profession and establishes a strong identity with fellows and loyalty to comrades, as well as instilling discipline and obedience to orders.

Also See the Following Articles

ANTHROPOLOGY OF VIOLENCE AND CONFLICT • ENEMY, CONCEPT AND IDENTITY OF • EVOLUTIONARY FACTORS • MILITARY CULTURE • WARFARE, TRENDS IN

Bibliography

Bloch, M. (1965). *Feudal society*. London: Routledge and Kegan Paul.
Carneiro, R. L. (1990). Chiefdom-level warfare as exemplified in

Fiji and the Cauca valley. In J. Haas (Ed.), *The anthropology of war*. (pp. 190–211). Cambridge, UK: Cambridge University Press.

Catlin, G. (1973). *Letters and notes on the manners, customs and conditions of North American Indians* (Vol. 1). New York: Dover.

Clastres, P. (1994). *Archaeology of violence*. New York: Semiotext(e).

Ferguson, R. B. (Ed.) (1984). *Warfare, culture and environment*. San Diego: Academic Press.

Ferguson, R. B., & Whitehead, N. (Eds.) (1992). *War in the tribal zone: Expanding states and indigenous warfare*. Santa Fe, NM: School of American Research Press.

Haas, J. (Ed.) (1990). *The anthropology of war*. Cambridge, UK: Cambridge University Press.

Harrison, S. (1989). The symbolic construction of aggression and war in a Sepik river society. *Man (N.S.), 24*, 583–599.

Jones, D. E. (1997). *Women warriors: A history*. Washington, DC: Brassey's.

Karsten, R. (1923). *Blood revenge, war, and victory feasts among the Jibaro Indians of eastern Ecuador*. Bureau of American Ethnology, Bull. No. 79.

Knauft, B. M. (1990). Melanesian warfare: A theoretical history. *Oceania, 60*, 250–311.

Lowie, R. H. (1956). *The Crow Indians*. New York: Holt, Rinehart and Winston.

Métraux, A. (1963). Warfare, cannibalism, and human trophies. In J. Steward (Ed.), *Handbook of South American Indians* (Vol. 5, pp. 383–409). New York: Cooper Square.

Otterbein, K. F. (1970). *The evolution of war*. New Haven, CT: HRAF Press.

Otterbein, K. F. (1973). The anthropology of war. In J. J. Honigmann (Ed.), *Handbook of social and cultural anthropology* (pp. 923–958). Chicago: Rand McNally.

Otterbein, K. F. (1994). *Feuding and warfare: Selected works of Keith F. Otterbein*. Langhorne, PA: Gordon and Breach.

Redmond, E. (1994). *Tribal and chiefly warfare in South America*. Ann Arbor: University of Michigan Museum of Anthropology Publications.

Reyna, S. P. (1994). A mode of domination approach to organized violence. In S. P. Reyna & R. E. Downs (Eds.), *Studying war: Anthropological perspectives*. (pp. 29–65). Langhorne, PA: Gordon and Breach.

Reyna, S. P., & Downs, R. E. (Eds.) (1994). *Studying war: Anthropological perspectives*. Langhorne, PA: Gordon and Breach.

Vayda, A. P. (1960). *Maori Warfare*. Polynesian Society Maori Monographs 2, Wellington.

Weaponry, Evolution of

Dave Grossman

Arkansas State University

GLOSSARY

Acquired Violence Immune Deficiency Syndrome (AVIDS) The "violence immune system" exists in the midbrain of all healthy creatures, causing them to be largely unable to kill members of their own species in territorial and mating battles. In human beings this resistance has existed historically in all close-range, interpersonal confrontations. "Conditioning" (particularly the conditioning of children through media violence and interactive video games) can create an "acquired deficiency" in this immune system, resulting in "Acquired Violence Immune Deficiency Syndrome." As a result of this weakened immune system, the victim becomes more vulnerable to violence–enabling factors such as poverty, discrimination, drugs, gangs, radical politics, and the availability of guns.

Conditioning A type of training that intensely and realistically simulates the actual conditions to be faced in a future situation. Effective conditioning enables an individual to respond in a precisely defined manner in spite of high states of anxiety or fear.

Chariot A two-wheeled platform pulled by horses (usually two) generally carrying a driver and a passenger. Of limited value for commerce due to its small capacity, the chariot was primarily an instrument of war and the hunt. Its greater mobility gave it a high degree of utility in the pursuit of a defeated enemy. The passenger was usually an archer who would fire from the platform while on the move or during brief halts.

Phalanx A mass of spearmen in tight ranks, carrying spears approximately 4 meters long and protecting themselves with overlapping shields, highly trained to move in a formation organized in depth (i.e., moving and fighting "in column" as opposed to "in line") and trained to strike the enemy as a coherent mass. First widely utilized by the ancient Greeks.

Physical Limitations The physical limitations of the human body which, when overcome, will assist in physically enabling killing. These can be broken down into force, mobility, distance, and protection.

Posturing: In the territorial and mating battles of every species the individual who puffs itself up the biggest or makes the loudest noise is most likely to win; this process is referred to as "posturing." Humans engaged in close-combat are invariably profoundly frightened, and in such individuals primitive, midbrain processing often causes the actual battle to be, from one perspective, a process of posturing until one side or another turns and runs, after which the real killing usually begins. Thus posturing is critical to warfare and victory can be achieved through superior posturing. Bagpipes, bugles, drums, shiny armor, tall hats, chariots, elephants, and cavalry have all been factors in successful posturing (convincing oneself of one's prowess while daunting ones enemy), but, ultimately, gunpowder proved to be the ultimate posturing tool.

Psychological Enabling Factors The processes that can be manipulated as a weapon to psychologically enable a human, or a group of humans, to kill. These can be broken down into posturing, mobility, distance, leaders, groups, and conditioning.

Weapon A device or system that is designed to permit humans to overcome natural physical and psychological limitations in order to enable the killing and domination of other creatures, particularly their fellow human beings.

Weapons Evolution The process of Darwinian natural selection in the development of a series of ever-more-effective weapons.

Weapons Lethality A factor of the effectiveness of the weapons used to kill and the ability of medical technology available to save lives. Thus, weapons lethality can be thought of as a contest between weapons effectiveness (the state of technology trying to kill you) and medical effectiveness (the state of technology trying to save you).

HUMANS HAVE PROVEN themselves to be infinitely ingenious at creating and using devices to overcome their limitations. From one perspective human history can be seen as a series of ever-more-efficient devices to help humans communicate, travel, trade, work, and even to think. Similarly, the history of violence, peace, and conflict can be seen as the history, or the evolution, of a series of ever-more-efficient devices to enable humans to kill and dominate their fellow human beings.

The concept of an "evolution" of weaponry is very appropriate, since the battlefield is the ultimate realm of Darwinian natural selection. With few exceptions, any weapon or system that survives for any length of time does so because of its utility. Nothing survives for long on the battlefield simply because of superstition. Anything that is effective is copied and perpetuated, anything ineffective results in death, defeat, and extinction. There are fads and remnants (the military equivalent of the appendix) but, over the long run, everything happens for a reason, and a valid theory of weapons evolution must make these reasons clear, explaining all extinctions and all survivals.

I. WEAPONS AS DEVICES TO OVERCOME PHYSICAL AND PSYCHOLOGICAL LIMITATIONS

Ultimately the nature of humans determines the nature of their weapons. There is the nature of the body *and* the nature of the mind; let us first examine the nature of humans' *physical* limitations and the evolution of weapons to overcome these limitations.

A. Overcoming Physical Limitations

The physical limitations of humans are a key factor in their search for weapons. The need for force, mobility, distance, and protection have been the key requirements in this realm.

1. The Need for Force

The physical strength limitations of humans led to a need for greater physical force in order to hit an opponent harder and more effectively, resulting in the development of more-effective methods to transfer kinetic energy to an opponent. This process evolved from hitting someone with a hand-held rock (providing the momentum energy of a greater mass than just a fist), to sharp rocks (focusing the energy in a smaller impact point), to a sharp rock on a stick (providing mechanical leverage combined with a cutting edge), to spears [using the latest material technology (flint, bronze, iron, steel) to focus energy into smaller and smaller penetration points], to swords (which permit the option of using a thrusting, spear-like penetration point or the mechanical leverage of a hacking, cutting edge), to the long bow (using stored mechanical energy and a refined penetration point), to firearms (transferring chemical energy to a projectile in order to deliver an extremely powerful dose of kinetic energy).

2. The Need for Mobility

Limited by the constraints of a bipedal body that could be outrun by a majority of ground-based creatures and recognizing that a human who has cast off weapons and armor is hard for a human carrying a weapon to catch and kill, humans' cross-country speed limitations created a need for a mobility advantage, resulting in a succession of weapons to provide more-efficient means to go around or to chase an enemy. These weapons evolved from the chariots of the Egyptians, Babylonians, and Persians [which were without horse collars (an invention of the Romans) and were thus quite inefficient since the mounting system choked the horse]; to the cavalry of the Greeks and Romans (which, without stirrups, limited but did not completely prevent the ability to strike from horseback); to the cavalry that dominated the battlefield throughout the age of the European knights (since the introduction of stirrups made it possible to deliver a powerful blow from horseback without danger of falling off) and continued to play a key (but ever-decreasing) role up to the beginning of the 20th century; to modern mechanized infantry; tanks; and (the ultimate form of mobility) aircraft. Simultaneously, a similar evolution of ever-more-effective forms of mobility took place with ships at sea until the introduction of aircraft [originally based on ships (aircraft carriers), but increasingly ground-based, long-range aircraft] came to dominate this realm.

3. The Need for Distance

Similarly, human limited reach created a need for a range advantage in an effort to attack more people than just those in immediate reach (i.e., to increase the zone of influence) and to do so without placing oneself in danger. This need resulted in increasingly more efficient means to kill at a distance, moving from the spear, to the long spear of the Greek phalanx, to the throwing spears of the Roman legionary, to the bow, the crossbow, the English long bow, firearms, artillery, missiles, and aircraft.

4. The Need for Protection

Physical vulnerability resulted in a continuous need for armor that would help to limit an enemy's ability to inflict harm (in the form of kinetic energy) upon one's own forces. This evolution generally followed the latest development of material technology, incorporating leather, bronze, iron, and steel, until the invention of firearms created a degree of force so great that the human body could not carry sufficient steel to stop a penetration, and the only remnant of armor was the helmet to stop fragmentation (grenade and artillery) wounds to the vulnerable and crucial brain area. Today this evolution continues in tank and ship armor. Interestingly, in recent years, human-made fiber technology (such as Kevlar) has again made body armor practical, and for the first time in centuries the average combatant, in both law enforcement and military realms, once again wears body armor.

B. Psychological Enabling Factors

These physical needs for force, mobility, distance, and protection interact with each other in the evolution of weapons, but man's psychological limitations are even more influential in this process. Lord Moran, the great military physician of World War I and World War II, called Napoleon the "greatest psychologist," and Napoleon said that, "In war the moral is to the physical as three is to one." Meaning that psychological advantage, or leverage, is three times more important than physical advantage, and modern studies supports Napoleon's contention.

1. The Resistance to Killing

At the heart of psychological processes on the battlefield is the resistance to killing one's own species, a resistance that exists in every healthy member of every species. To truly understand the nature of this resistance to killing we must first recognize that most participants in close combat are literally "frightened out of their wits." Once the arrows or bullets start flying, combatants stop thinking with the forebrain (which is the part of the brain that makes us human) and thought processes localize in the midbrain, or mammalian brain, which is the primitive part of the brain that is generally indistinguishable from that of an animal.

In conflict situations this primitive midbrain processing can be observed in the general, widespread existence of a powerful resistance to killing one's own kind and in particular the fellow adult males of one's own species. During territorial and mating battles, animals with antlers and horns slam together in a relatively harmless head-to-head fashion, rattlesnakes wrestle each other, and piranha fight their own kind with flicks of the tail, but against any other species these creatures unleash their horns, fangs, and teeth without restraint. This is an essential survival mechanism that prevents a species from destroying itself during territorial and mating rituals.

One major modern revelation in the field of military psychology is the observation that this resistance to killing one's own species is also a key factor in human combat. Brigadier General S. L. A. Marshall first observed this during his work as the Chief Historian of the European Theater of Operations in World War II. Based on his innovative new technique of postcombat interviews, Marshall concluded in his landmark book *Men Against Fire* that only 15 to 20% of the individual riflemen in World War II fired their weapons at an exposed enemy soldier.

Marshall's findings have been somewhat controversial, but every available, parallel, scholarly study validates his basic findings. Ardant du Picq's surveys of French officers in the 1860s and his observations on ancient battles, Keegan and Holmes' numerous accounts of ineffectual firing throughout history, Paddy Griffith's data on the extraordinarily low killing rate among Napoleonic and American Civil War regiments, Stouffer's extensive World War II and postwar research, Richard Holmes' assessment of Argentine firing rates in the Falklands War, the British Army's laser reenactments of historical battles, the FBI's studies of non-firing rates among law enforcement officers in the 1950s and 1960s, and countless other individual and anecdotal observations all confirm Marshall's fundamental conclusion that man is not, by nature, a close-range interpersonal killer.

The existence of this resistance can be observed in its marked absence in sociopaths who, by definition, feel no empathy or remorse for their fellow human beings. Pit bull dogs have been selectively bred for sociopathy, bred for the absence of the resistance to killing one's of kind in order to ensure that they will perform the unnatural act of killing another dog in battle. Breeding to overcome this limitation in humans is impractical, but humans are very adept at finding *mechanical* means to overcome natural limitations. Humans were born without the ability to fly, so we found mechanisms to overcome this limitation and enable flight. Humans also were born without the ability to kill our fellow humans, and so, throughout history, we have devoted great effort to finding a way to overcome this resistance. From a weapons evolution perspective, the history of warfare can be viewed as a series of successively more effective tactical and mechanical mechanisms to enable or force combatants to overcome their resistance to killing.

2. Posturing as a Psychological Weapon

The resistance to killing can be overcome, or at least bypassed, by a variety of techniques. One technique is to cause the enemy to run (often by getting in their flank or rear, which almost always causes a rout), and it is in the subsequent pursuit of a broken or defeated enemy that the vast majority of the killing happens.

It is widely known that most killing happens *after the battle*, in the pursuit phase (Clausewitz and Ardant du Picq both commented on this), and this is apparently due to two factors. First, the pursuer doesn't have to look in his victim's eyes, and it appears to be much easier to deny an opponent's humanity if you can stab or shoot them in the back and don't have to look into their eyes when you kill them. Second (and probably much more importantly), in the midbrain, during a pursuit, the opponent has changed from a fellow male engaged in a primitive, simplistic, ritualistic, head-to-head, territorial or mating battle to prey who must to

be pursued, pulled down, and killed. Anyone who has ever worked with dogs understands this process: you are generally safe if you face a dog down, and you should always back away from a dog (or almost any animal) in a threatening situation because if you turn around and run you are in great danger of being viciously attacked. The same is true of soldiers in combat.

Thus one key to the battle is simply to get the enemy to run. The battlefield is truly psychological in nature, and in this realm the individual who puffs himself up the biggest, or makes the loudest noise, is most likely to win. The actual battle is, from one perspective, a process of "posturing" until one side or another turns and runs, and then the real killing begins. Thus posturing is critical to warfare and victory can be achieved through superior posturing.

Bagpipes, bugles, drums, shiny armor, tall hats, chariots, elephants, and cavalry have all been factors in successful posturing (convincing oneself of ones' prowess while daunting one's enemy), but, ultimately, gunpowder proved to be the ultimate posturing tool. For example, the long bow was significantly more accurate and had a far greater rate of fire and a much greater accurate range than the muzzle-loading muskets used up to the early part of the American Civil War. Furthermore, the long bow did not need the industrial base (iron and gunpowder) required by muskets, and the training of a long bowman was not really all that difficult.

Thus, mechanically speaking there are few reasons why there should not have been regiments of long bowmen at Waterloo and the 1st Bull Run cutting vast swaths through the enemy. [Similarly there were highly efficient, air-pressure-powered weapons available as early as the Napoleonic era (similar to modern paintball guns), which had a far higher firing rate than the muskets of that era, but were never used.] But it must be constantly remembered that, to paraphrase Napoleon, in war, psychological factors are three times more important than mechanical factors. The reality is that, on the battlefield, if you are going "doink, doink," no matter how effectively, and the enemy is going "BANG!, BANG!," no matter how ineffectively, ultimately the "doinkers" lose. This phenomenon helps explain the effectiveness of high-noise-producing weapons ranging from Gustavus Adolphus' small, mobile cannons assigned to infantry units to the U.S. Army's M-60 machine gun in Vietnam, which fired large, very loud, 7.62-mm ammunition at a slow rate of fire vs the M-16's smaller (and comparatively much less noisy) 5.56-mm ammunition firing at a rapid rate of fire. (Note that both the machine gun and the cannon are also crew-served weapons, which is a key factor to be addressed shortly.)

3. Mobility as a Psychological Weapon

Once it is understood that most of the killing (and thereby the *true* destruction and defeat of an enemy) happens in the pursuit, then the true utility of weapons that provide a mobility advantage becomes clear. First, a mobility advantage often permits a force to get in the enemy's flank or rear. Combatants seem to have an intuitive understanding of their vulnerability (both psychological and physical) from an opponent in their rear, and this almost always results in a mass panic and rout. Second, it is during the pursuit of a defeated enemy that a mobility advantage is needed if a pursuing force is to kill the enemy. An opponent who has cast aside his weapons and armor can generally outrun an armed pursuer, but a man on foot cannot outrun chariots or cavalry, and it is here, in stabbing and shooting men in the back, that chariots and cavalry had their greatest utility.

4. Distance as a Psychological Weapon

Another key factor in overcoming the resistance to killing is distance, which has been partially addressed earlier. The utility of weapons that kill from a distance cannot be truly understood without understanding the psychological enabling aspect of distance, which, simply stated, means that the further away you are the easier it is to kill. Thus, dropping bombs from 20,000 feet or firing artillery from 2 miles away is, psychologically speaking, not at all difficult (and there is no indication of any noncompliance in these situations), but

firing a rifle from 20 feet is very difficult (with high incidence of nonfirers) and from a few feet away it is virtually impossible to stab an opponent. John Keegan's landmark book *The Face of Battle* makes a comparative study of Agincourt (1415), Waterloo (1815), and the Somme (1916). In his analysis of these three battles spanning over 500 years, Keegan repeatedly notes the amazing absence of bayonet wounds incurred during the massed bayonet attacks at Waterloo and the Somme. At Waterloo Keegan notes that "There were numbers of sword and lance wounds to be treated and some bayonet wounds, though these had usually been inflicted after the man had already been disabled, there being no evidence of the armies having crossed bayonets at Waterloo." By World War I edged-weapon combat had almost disappeared, and Keegan notes that in the Battle of the Somme, "edged-weapon wounds were a fraction of one per cent of all wounds inflicted in the First World War." Indeed, all evidence indicates that ancient battles were not much more than great shoving matches, until one side or the other fled. This can be observed in the battle record of Alexander the Great, who (according to Ardant du Picq's studies of ancient records) lost a *total* of approximately 700 men "to the sword" in all his battles put together, and this is simply because Alexander the Great always won, and the actual killing happened only to the losers *after* the battle (Fig. 1).

The only thing greater than the resistance to killing at close range is the resistance to *being* killed at close range. Close-range interpersonal aggression is the universal human phobia, which is why the initiation of midbrain processing is so powerful and intense in these

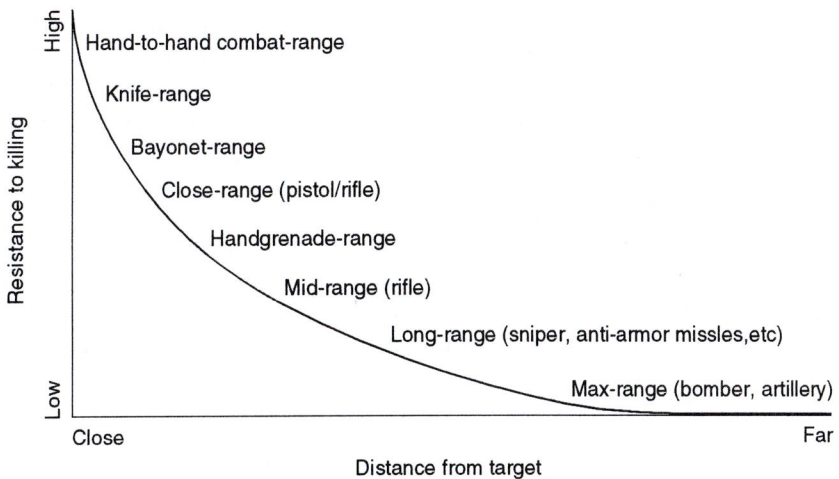

FIGURE 1 Distance vs. resistance (© D. Grossman, 1993).

situations. Thus, one limitation to killing at long range is that greater distance results in a reduced psychological effect on the enemy. This manifests itself in the constant thwarting of each new generation of air power advocates and other adherents of sterile, long-range, high tech warfare and a constant need for close combat troops to defeat an enemy.

5. Leaders as a Psychological Weapon

Milgram's famous obedience research demonstrated the tremendous influence that can be wielded by an unknown individual in a white labcoat in a laboratory situation, but on the battlefield the influence of a respected leader, with the trappings of true power, wielding authority over life and death, can far transcend Milgram's results. Marshall is one of many who have noted that soldiers will invariably fire if an officer stands over them and demands that they do so, but this firing will generally decrease as soon as the officer leaves.

The modern concept of a combat leader usually calls up visions of a hardened veteran moving behind a battle line of his men, exhorting, encouraging, punishing, rebuking, correcting, and rewarding them. But combat leadership has not always been like this. Armies have always had leaders, but the Romans were the first to take proven warriors and systematically develop them into professional leaders, starting at the lowest levels. Prior to this time leaders were usually expected to get into the battle and lead from the front, but the Romans were the first to place leaders *behind* their men in an open order of battle. The influence of this kind of leadership was one of the key factors in the success of the Roman way of war, and this process of having a respected, proven, small-unit leader, who moves behind his men and demands effective killing activity from them (but does not himself necessarily have to kill) continued to be a key factor in effective combat in the centuries that followed. This kind of leadership initially disappeared with the Roman Empire, but it appeared again sporadically in the firing lines of English long bowmen and then as a systematically applied factor in the firing lines of the successful armies of the gunpowder era and continued into the present.

6. Groups as a Psychological Weapon

Konrad Lorenz observed that "man is not a killer, but the group is." This fundamental observation of human nature has great utility in helping to understand the effectiveness of what are generally referred to as "crew-served" weapons. These are weapons that require more than one individual to use, which provides a form of mutual accountability and a diffusion of responsibility,

which is very effective in enabling killing. Marshall noted in World War II that the firing rates of individual soldiers was very low, but crew served weapons (primarily machine guns) almost always fired.

Such weapons have generally done the majority of the killing throughout the history of warfare, beginning with the chariot, which was the earliest crew-served weapon. The chariot often employed a driver and a "passenger" who generally fired a bow (which added the factor of distance in the killing-enabling equation) and was most effective in the pursuit, when their mobility advantage gave them the ability to shoot large numbers of fleeing enemy in the back. The powerful group dynamics of the chariot (along with its mobility) were to show up again, over 2 millennia later, in the tanks of the 20th century.

The Greek phalanx was a mass of spearmen in tight ranks, carrying spears approximately 4 meters long and protecting themselves with overlapping shields, highly trained to move in a formation organized in depth (i.e., moving and fighting "in column" as opposed to "in line") and trained to strike the enemy as a coherent mass. As such it was a form of crew-served weapon in which newer members were placed in the front and were thereby under direct observation and accountability by the veteran warriors behind them. The phalanx was of such utility that it has shown up repeatedly throughout history and around the world.

The first systematic military use of gunpowder was in cannons, and these crew-served weapons immediately began to dominate the battlefield. Unlike the early muskets, cannons were effective killers from the beginning. Not only did they provide the best form of posturing (i.e., noise making) ever to be seen on the battlefield, but they were also a highly effective crew-served weapon (being generally manned by numerous individuals and directly commanded by an officer or a sergeant with sole responsibility for that gun and its crew) whose crew members almost never showed any hesitation or mercy in killing the enemy. At close range the cannon fired "grape shot" into tightly packed enemy formations, thus becoming, in effect, a great shotgun capable of killing hundreds of men with a single shot. Napoleon, that "greatest psychologist," demonstrated his understanding of the true killing utility of the cannon (and the comparative ineffectiveness of infantry) by ensuring that his armies always had a higher percentage of cannons than his enemies and by massing those cannons at key points in the battle.

In the 20th century the cannon became an "indirect fire" system (i.e., firing over the heads of friendly combatants from a great distance away), and the machine gun (with its "gunner" and "assistant gunner" or "loader") came to replace the cannon in the crew-served, "direct fire" role on the battlefield. In World War I the machine gun was called the "distilled essence of the infantry," but it was really just a continuation of the cannon in its old, crew-served, mass-killing role.

The crew-served machine gun is still the key killer on the close-range battlefield, but the evolution of group-enabling processes can continue to be seen in tanks and armored personnel carriers. At sea the dynamics of the crew-served weapon have been in play since the beginning of the gunpowder era—i.e., crew-served weapons, distance, and the influence of leaders.

7. Conditioning as a Psychological Weapon

By 1946 the U.S. Army had completely accepted Marshall's World War II findings of a 15–20% firing rate among American riflemen, and the Human Resources Research Office of the U.S. Army subsequently pioneered a revolution in combat training that replaced the old method of firing at bulls-eye targets with that of deeply ingrained "conditioning" using realistic, human-shaped pop-up targets that fall when hit. Psychologists know that this kind of powerful "operant conditioning" is the only technique that reliably influences the primitive, midbrain processing of a frightened human being, just as fire drills condition terrified school children to respond properly during a fire, and repetitious, "stimulus–response" conditioning in flight simulators enables frightened pilots to respond reflexively to emergency situations.

Throughout history the ingredients of posturing, mobility, distance, leaders, and groups have been manipulated to enable and force combatants to kill, but the introduction of conditioning in modern training was a true revolution. The application and perfection of these basic conditioning techniques appear to have increased the rate of fire from near 20% in World War II to approximately 55% in Korea and around 95% in Vietnam. Similar high rates of fire resulting from modern conditioning techniques can be seen in FBI data on law enforcement firing rates since the nationwide introduction of modern conditioning techniques in the late 1960s.

One of the most dramatic examples of the value and power of this modern, psychological revolution in training can be seen in Richard Holmes' observations of the 1982 Falklands War. The superbly trained (i.e., "conditioned") British forces were without air or artillery superiority and consistently outnumbered 3-to-1 while attacking the poorly trained but well-equipped and carefully dug-in Argentine defenders. Superior Brit-

ish firing rates (which Holmes estimates to be well over 90%), resulting from modern training techniques, has been credited as a key factor in the series of British victories in that brief but bloody war. Any future army that attempts to go into battle without similar psychological preparation is likely to meet a fate similar to that of the Argentines.

II. A BRIEF SURVEY OF WEAPONS EVOLUTION

Having established an understanding of the physical factors required for effective weapons (force, mobility, distance, and protection) and the psychological enabling factors required to effectively employ these weapons (posturing, mobility, distance, leaders, groups, and conditioning), an overall survey of weapons evolution becomes possible. Although parallel evolutionary, weaponry processes have occurred around the world, the process is most easily observed in the west, and it is in western civilization that the evolutionary development of weaponry achieved a degree of ascendancy that permitted western domination of the globe starting as early as the 16th century and culminating in total western domination in the 19th and 20th centuries.

Combat throughout ancient history generally involved more and more effective applications of force, moving from rock, to sharp rock, to sharp rock on a stick, to swords and spears using the latest metal technology. This aspect of close-range, hand-to-hand combat remained the same until the late 19th century when reliable, repeating gunpowder weapons replaced swords and bayonets as the weapon of choice to kill repeatedly at close range. Some aspects of distance weapons have been present, in the form of archers and slingers, since ancient Egypt, but until the introduction of the long bow the available armor (generally just a shield) was sufficient to stop these weapons from becoming decisive.

A. The Chariot

The chariot was introduced to ancient Egypt early in the Second Millennium B.C., and subsequently it was to become the first major, evolutionary weapons innovation. As a system it was made possible by the domestication of the horse, the invention of the wheel, and the invention of the bow and arrow—particularly the compound bow. The chariot was a two-wheeled platform pulled by horses (usually two) generally carrying a driver and a passenger. It was of limited value for commerce due to its small cargo capacity and was primarily an instrument of war. Its mobility gave it a high degree of utility in attacking vulnerable flanks or in the pursuit of a defeated enemy, and the passenger was usually an archer who would fire from the platform while on the move or during brief halts.

The ascendancy of the chariot for well over a millennium has been called "inexplicable" by some historians, but an understanding of the chariot's powerful psychological contribution makes its role clear. The chariot undoubtedly had many limitations: the horses were very vulnerable to archers and slingers and if just one horse was disabled the whole chariot was out of action, and the absence of a horse collar meant that the mounting system choked the horse, thus making the chariot's effective range a fraction of that of the cavalry, which would later replace the chariot in its mobility role. And yet, in spite of these limitations, the mobility advantage of the chariot (useful primarily in the pursuit, when most of the killing occurred) combined with some group processes (driver plus archer) and some distance processes (archer firing from a mobile platform) made the chariot the dominant weapon of an era ranging from the Egyptian to the Persian Empires. Ultimately it would be defeated by the phalanx and replaced by cavalry.

B. The Phalanx

One limitation of the chariot (and later of cavalry) is that horses consistently refuse to hurl themselves into a hedge of sharp, projecting objects such as a phalanx, with its deep ranks of tightly packed men carrying 4-meter spears and protecting themselves with overlapping shields. The Greek phalanx required a high degree of training and organization, but starting around the 4th Century B.C., the Greek city-states were able to use it to negate the impact of the chariot in battle. The tightly packed ranks of the phalanx created a group process that apparently permitted it to act as a vast, crew-served weapon. This factor, along with some distance (through the long spears) and the simplicity and economic viability of the phalanx, made it the dominant weapon system of its era. These aspects of the phalanx *combined* with the later Greek mastery of horseback riding (albeit absent stirrups) in order to approach an enemy from vulnerable flanks and to exploit pursuits permitted the Greeks to conquer a vast portion of the world.

The Greeks were defeated by the Romans, but the inherent simplicity of the phalanx combined with its psychological fundamentals were so powerful that after the fall of the Roman Empire the phalanx again became ascendant, with the Swiss achieving the epitome of perfection of the phalanx in the Middle Ages and early Renaissance. The armies of the early gunpowder era continued to use phalanx formations of pikemen combined with formations of primitive, early muskets. The pikemen were replaced with the advent of the bayonet, which made every man a potential pikeman, and a remnant of the psychological dynamics of the phalanx could be seen in the great, column-based bayonet charges of Napoleon's armies.

C. The Roman System

It must be remembered that the Roman Empire lasted for approximately half a millennium (and longer if we count the Eastern Roman Empire) and that to say "the Romans did this" or "the Romans did that" would generally be inaccurate when referring to a military system that evolved and changed constantly across the centuries. But certain things did stay somewhat constant over the centuries in the Roman legions, and it was these constant factors that can be generally attributed to the extraordinary military success of the Roman Empire, starting in the 2nd and 1st Centuries B.C. and continuing for around 500 years.

The Greek phalanx required a high degree of training to be effective, but an efficient phalanx could still be achieved, for example, as the product of a local militia who trained in their free time. But the Roman system was a highly complex professional army that devoted itself full-time to the development of its skills and to the development of a leadership structure with systematic professional advancement based on merit, taking soldiers from the ranks and placing them in charge of larger and larger groups of men as they demonstrated competence at each level. The Roman open order of battle permitted their small-unit leaders to move behind the battle line, holding their men accountable and rewarding skill and valor with advancement and reward. Today most professional armies are designed around a professional small-unit leadership drawn from the ranks with advancement based on merit, and small-unit leaders who have proven themselves in combat (except in emergencies) are expected to stay behind their men in order to directly influence their actions in battle, but it must be remembered that the Romans were the first to truly, systematically introduce these factors to the battlefield on a large scale over a long period of time.

Another key aspect of the Roman way of war was the fact that each of their soldiers carried a variety of throwing spears (the number and type varied over the years) with which they were highly proficient. An approaching enemy was greeted with a series of volleys from these spears, which served to break up an enemy's ranks and often to strip them of their shields. These ingeniously designed distance weapons often included light javelins, which were thrown at a long range, followed by a standard heavy spear (or pilum), which was thrown at a medium range, followed by a lead-weighted pilum, which was hurled, with enormous force, as one final volley before closing with swords.

After shattering an approaching enemy force from a distance with a series of spear volleys, the Romans closed with short swords designed and intended for stabbing. These swords were often qualitatively no different from those of their opponents, but the Romans were systematically trained to use their swords to stab and thrust in a highly effective way that was largely unprecedented prior to this. Like the post-World War II training that was to be developed 2 millennia later to condition men to fire in combat, Roman training used constant, repetitive training, to the point where it could be accurately described as conditioning, in order to insure that their soldiers would thrust in combat rather than use the more natural hacking and slashing blows. This was a technique that was to be used in later centuries to train some elite warriors in fencing and swordsmanship, but never before, nor probably since, has an entire army been trained to this degree of perfection.

This combination of projectile weapons, intense training, and the presence of effective small-unit leaders who moved behind their men and demanded effective killing activities was a devastating force that smashed approaching enemy formations, including the phalanx. The final ingredient in a Roman battlefield victory was the organization of their forces into small units with reserves with dispassionate, highly trained, small-unit leaders operating behind their men, ready to maneuver their unit to exploit any exposed enemy flanks or penetrate deep into the enemy rear. Once the enemy was defeated, the final blow (and most of the killing) was executed by cavalry auxiliaries (which, still without stirrups, were little different from the cavalry of the Greeks), who would pursue and kill a broken, fleeing enemy.

The result of this complex process was the Pax Romana: hundreds of years of relative stability and peace in the western world. But it was a fragile strength, created through complexity and economic abundance, difficult to sustain in the best of times, and impossible to replicate (at least in western Europe) for almost a millennium after the Roman Empire collapsed.

D. The Mounted Knight

With the fall of Rome the complex Roman way of war collapsed, to be replaced by simpler systems, such as the phalanx, and one new system, which was the mounted knight. The introduction of the stirrup (coming to Europe from China and India around the 10th Century A.D.) made it possible for a man on horseback to strike an opponent with remarkable force without danger of being unseated. Furthermore, horse breeding had developed increasingly larger and more powerful mounts who could carry sufficient weight of armor to make both horse and man virtually invulnerable. A devastating blow could be delivered by a spear, or lance, which could be "couched" or semi-attached to the knight. Charging at full speed, the spear point would strike an opponent with the combined momentum and weight of horse, man, and armor approaching at full gallop. After the initial blow with the lance the knight could continue to plow into an enemy formation, delivering blows from above with heavy weapons (sword, mace, flail, or morning star) assisted by the force of gravity and downward momentum. A formation of such knights, striking together, was an extraordinarily frightening and almost overwhelming force, combining high degrees of posturing, force, and mobility, which could only be stopped by a hedge of spears and the horse's complete and consistent unwillingness to impale itself.

Thus, the answer to the knight was a phalanx, but the horse's mobility made it possible to maneuver around a phalanx, or any enemy formation, in order to attack from a vulnerable direction and to pursue the enemy after they have been broken. This created the need for spear- or bayonet-equipped ground troops to form a "square" that faced outward in all directions while keeping other units inside the protection of the square. This was an effective defensive maneuver as long as the infantry kept their nerve (if only a few men broke and ran the knights could move into that gap and break the entire formation), but until the introduction of the long bow and (later) gunpowder the forces inside the the square were completely neutralized and could often be held at bay by a small force of knights.

The long bow (and, later, gunpowder weapons) spelled the doom of the mounted knight and, ultimately, of all individual armor until the 20th century. Cavalry would continue to exist on the battlefield for centuries, but their economic cost and their increasing vulnerability to small arms fire meant that by the late 19th century the utility of cavalry had reverted to that of the Greek and Roman era: useful for reconnaissance, to move riflemen rapidly to key a location where they would dismount and fight, and for mobility in the pursuit. During the 20th century mechanization (trucks, tanks, etc.) would almost completely supersede the horse's mobility contribution to the battlefield.

E. The Age of Projectile Weapons

Humans had always thrown rocks or fired arrows, but usually these could be neutralized by armor. With the advent of the long bow (ca. 1400), for the first time the average combatant could single-handedly fire a weapon, from a distance, that would penetrate even the best of available, man-portable armor. This was a revolution that introduced a combination of distance and force that would continue in its basic format up until the present. The long bow began the process of rendering the knight extinct, but the advent of gunpowder introduced powerful posturing processes into the equation that quickly (in evolutionary terms) led to the extinction of both the knight and the long bow.

Once individual gunpowder weapons were introduced and widely distributed (ca. 1600), the evolution of close-range, interpersonal weaponry subsequently moved along a single, simple path of perfecting this weapon. The early, crude, primitive, smoothbore, muzzle-loading, gunpowder weapons were pathetically ineffective. They were almost impossible to aim, very slow to fire, and useless in any kind of damp conditions. And yet their posturing (i.e., their noise) combined with their absolutely overwhelming force (when they could hit something) was so great that they soon came to dominate the battlefield.

Gunpowder was invented in China, but China was under a comparatively centralized government that appears to have seen gunpowder weapons as a threat to the established order and made a conscious decision not to develop this weapon. (Over a millennium later the Japanese would do something similar.) A powerful argument can be made that this single decision in weapons development resulted in the eventual subjugation of the east and the inevitable domination and colonization of the world by western Europe. In Europe there were constant wars and turmoil and a complete absence of centralized authority, which created an environment that pursued a continuous development and refinement of gunpowder weapons. This process led to weapons that could be fired in wet weather (percussion caps), fired accurately (rifled barrels), loaded from a prone position (breech loaders), fired repeatedly without loading (repeaters), and fired repeatedly with no other action than pulling the trigger (automatics).

Almost all of this development of gunpowder weapons occurred in the 19th century. By the early 20th century this developmental process had reached its culmination. One common myth in this area involves the increasing "deadliness" of modern small arms, which is largely without foundation. For example, the high-velocity, small-caliber (5.56 mm/.223-caliber) ammunition used in most assault rifles today (e.g., the M-16 and the AK-74) was designed to wound rather than kill. The theory is that wounding an enemy soldier is better than killing him because a wounded soldier eliminates three people: the wounded man and two others to evacuate him. These weapons do inflict great (wounding) trauma, but they are illegal for hunting deer in much of the United States due to their ineffectiveness at quickly and effectively killing game.

Similarly, since World War I and until recently the U.S. military's weapon of choice in pistols was a .45 automatic (approximately 12 mm). In recent years the military weapon of choice has become the 9 mm, which has a smaller, faster round that many experts argue is considerably less effective at killing.

What these new, smaller ammunitions (5.56 mm for rifle and 9 mm for pistol) *do* make possible is greater magazine capacity, and this has increased the effectiveness of weapons in one way, while decreasing it in another.

The point is that there has *not* been any significant increase in the effectiveness of the weapons available today. The shotgun is still the single most effective weapon for killing at close range and it has been available and basically unchanged for over 100 years. Long-range killing technology (missiles, aircraft, and armored vehicles) have all evolved at quantum rates, but the basic technology of close-range killing through transferring kinetic energy has apparently achieved an evolutionary dead-end in this century.

F. Enabling the Mind to Kill

Thus the basic, close-range killing weapon has not changed fundamentally in nearly a century, but there *has* been a new, evolutionary leap in the conditioning of the *mind* that has to use that weapon to kill at close range. The development of a psychological conditioning process to enable an individual to overcome the average, healthy, deep-rooted aversion to close-range killing of one's own species is a true revolution. By changing from bulls-eye targets to pop-up, human-shaped targets that fall when hit, modern armies and police forces have learned to operantly condition their combatants to respond reflexively even when literally frightened out of their wits. This process has repeatedly demonstrated an ability to raise the firing rate among individual riflemen from a baseline of around 20% in World War II to over 90% today. This is a revolution on the battlefield, and it is a revolution that has also had an absolutely unprecedented influence on civilian violence and domestic violent crimes.

III. THE ROLE OF WEAPONS EVOLUTION IN DOMESTIC VIOLENT CRIME

Weapons play the same role in domestic violent crime as in war. The resistance to killing also exists in peacetime, and weapons provide psychological and mechanical leverage to enable killing in peace as well as in war.

A. Weapons Lethality

Weapons lethality (in peace *and* war) is a factor of the effectiveness of the weapons used to kill and of the ability of available medical technology to save lives. Thus, weapons lethality can be thought of as a contest between weapons effectiveness (the state of technology trying to kill you) and medical effectiveness (the state of technology trying to save you). Like weapons lethality, the difference between murder (killing someone) and aggravated assault (trying to kill someone) is also largely a factor of the effectiveness of available weapons vs the effectiveness of available medical life-saving technology.

B. Advances in Weapons Effectiveness

Throughout most of human history the effectiveness of weapons available for domestic violence was basically stable, a relative constant. The relative effectiveness of swords, axes, and blunt objects has been basically unchanged, and killing (as an act of passion vs a premeditated act like poisoning or leaving a bomb) was only possible at close-range by stabbing, hacking, and beating.

Bows were kept unstrung, not in a state of readiness for an act of passion. It required premeditation plus training plus strength to kill with a bow. Early, muzzle-loading, gunpowder weapons were also often not kept in a state of readiness. It required time, training, and premeditation to load and shoot such a weapon. Once loaded, the humidity in the air could seep into the gunpowder, and the load could become unreliable. Only in the late 19th century, with widespread introduction

of breech-loading, brass cartridges, was a true "act of passion" possible with state-of-the-art weapons technology. Powerful weapons could now be kept in state of readiness (i.e., loaded), and they now required minimal strength or training to use. This achievement in weapons effectiveness has been virtually unchanged since the 1870s. Colt's revolver or a double-barrel shotgun is basically equally effective to any small arms available today (Table I).

Thus, the effectiveness of weapons available for domestic violence has remained relatively stable throughout most of human history. It then made one huge

TABLE I

Landmarks in the Evolution of Weapons Effectiveness

ca. 1700 B.C.	Chariots provide key form of mobility advantage in ancient warfare
ca. 400 B.C.	Greek phalanx
ca. 100 B.C.	Roman system (pilum, swords, training, professionalism, leadership)
ca. 900 A.D.	Mounted knight (stirrup greatly enhances utility of mounted warfare)
ca. 1350	Gunpowder (cannon) in warfare (Battle of Crecy, 1346)
ca. 1400	Widespread application of long bow defeats mounted knights (Battle of Agincourt, 1415)
ca. 1600	Gunpowder (small arms) in warfare, defeats all body armor (30 Years War & English Civil War)
ca. 1800	Shrapnel (exploding artillery shells), ultimately creates renewed need for helmets (ca. 1915)
ca. 1850	Percussion caps permit all-weather use of small arms
ca. 1870	Breech loading, cartridge firing rifles, and pistols[a]
ca. 1915	Machine gun
ca. 1915	Gas warfare
ca. 1915	Tanks
ca. 1915	Aircraft
ca. 1915	Self-loading (automatic) rifles and pistols
ca. 1940	Strategic bombing of population centers
ca. 1945	Nuclear weapons
ca. 1960	Large scale introduction of operant conditioning in training to enable killing in soldiers
ca. 1960	Large-scale introduction of media violence begins to enable domestic violent crime[a]
ca. 1970	Precision guided munitions
ca. 1980	Kevlar provides first individual armor to defeat state-of-the-art projectiles in 300+ years

Note. Dates generally represent century or decade of first major, large-scale introduction.

[a] Represents developments influencing domestic violent crime.

quantum leap in the late 19th century and then has not moved since, with the sole exception of the psychological conditioning to enable killing.

C. Advances in Medical Effectiveness

Since 1957, in the U.S., the per capita aggravated assault rate (which is, essentially, the rate of *attempted* murder) has gone up nearly sevenfold, while the per capita murder rate has less than doubled. Vast progress in medical technology since 1957 to include everything from mouth-to-mouth resuscitation, to the national "911" emergency telephone system, to medical technology advances is the reason for this disparity. Otherwise murder would be going up at the same rate as attempted murder (Table II).

Furthermore, it has been noted that a hypothetical wound that 9 of 10 times would have killed a soldier in World War II would have been survived 9 of 10 times by U.S. soldiers in Vietnam. This is due to the great leaps in battlefield evacuation and medical care technology between 1940 and 1970. And we have made even greater progress since 1970. Thus it is probably a very conservative statement to say that *if* today we had 1930's level road networks, evacuation vehicles, communications, distribution of medical care, and medical technology (no penicillin, etc.), *then* we would have *10 times* the murder rate we currently do. That is, attempts to inflict bodily harm upon one another would result in death 10 times more often.

Consider, for instance, some of the quantum leaps in medical technology across the years. Just a century ago, *any* puncture of the abdomen, skull, or lungs created a high probability of death. As did any significant loss of blood (no transfusions) or most large wounds (no antibiotics or antiseptics) or most wounds requiring significant surgery (no anesthetics, resulting in death from surgery shock). Also consider the increasing impact of police methodology and technology (fingerprints, communications, DNA matching, video surveillance, etc.) in apprehending killers, preventing second offenses, and deterring crime.

Each of these technological developments, in their place and time, should have negated the effects of weapons evolution and saved the lives of victims of violence. When assessing violent crime across any length of time we could and should ask what proportion of trauma patients survive today and what proportion of those would have died if they had: 1940s-level technology (no penicillin), 1930s-level technology (no antibiotics), 1870s-level technology (no antiseptics), 1840s-level technology (no anesthetics), or 1600s-level technology (no doctors, no anatomical knowledge, etc.).

TABLE II

Landmarks in the Evolution of Medical Lifesaving

ca. 1690	French army institutes first scientific, systematic approach to surgery
ca. 1840	Introduction of anesthesia overcomes surgical shock
ca. 1840	Introduction in Hungary of washing hands and instruments in chlorinated lime solution reduces mortality due to "childbed fever" from 9.9 to .85%
ca. 1860	Introduction by Lister of carbolic acid as germicide reduced mortality rate after major operations from 45 to 15%
ca. 1880	Widespread acceptance and adaptation of germicides
ca. 1930	Sulfa drugs
ca. 1940	Penicillin discovered
ca. 1945	Penicillin in general use and ever-increasing explosion of antibiotics thereafter
ca. 1960	Penicillin synthesized on a large scale
ca. 1970	CPR introduced on wide scale
ca. 1990	911 centralized emergency response systems introduced in U.S. on wide scale

Note. Dates generally represent century or decade of major, large-scale introduction.

D. Increases in Worldwide Violent Crime

Thus, instead of murder, we have to assess attempted murder, or aggravated assault, or some other consistently defined attack as an indicator of violent crime, and the increase in this indicator is staggering.

Between 1957 and 1992 aggravated assault in the U.S., according to the FBI, went up from around 60 per 100,000 to over 440 per 100,000. Between 1977 and 1986 the "serious assault" rate, as reported to Interpol:

- Increased nearly fivefold in Norway and Greece, and the murder rate more than tripled in Norway and doubled in Greece.
- In Australia and New Zealand the "serious assault" rate increased approximately fourfold, and the murder rate approximately doubled in both nations.
- During the same period the assault rate tripled in Sweden and approximately doubled in Belgium, Canada, Denmark, England-Wales, France, Hungary, Netherlands, Scotland, and the U.S; while all these nations (with the exception of Canada) also had an associated (but smaller) increase in murder.

All of these increases in violent crime, in all of these nations, occurred during a period when medical and law enforcement technology should have been bringing murder and crime rates down. It is no accident that this has generally only been occurring in western, industrialized nations because the same factor that caused all of these increases is the same weapons factor that caused a revolution in close combat (Table III).

E. Military Conditioning as Entertainment for Children

The tremendous impact of psychological "conditioning" to overcome the resistance to killing has been observed in Vietnam and the Falklands, where it gave U.S. and British units a tremendous tactical advantage in close combat, increasing the firing rate from the World War II baseline of around 20% to over 90% in these wars.

Through violent programming on television and in movies, and through interactive point-and-shoot video games, western nations are indiscriminately introducing to their children the same weapons technology that major armies and law enforcement agencies around the world use to "turn off" the midbrain "safety catch" that Brigadier General S. L. A. Marshall discovered in World War II.

The U.S. Bureau of Justice Statistics research indicates that law enforcement officers and veterans (including Vietnam veterans) are statistically less likely to be incarcerated than a nonveteran of the same age. The key safeguard in this process appears to be the deeply ingrained discipline that the soldier and police officer

TABLE III

International Violent Crime Rates

	Serious assault			Murder		
	1977	1993	Increase	1977	1993	Increase
Australia[a]	21.9	81.3	+3.7	2.8	4.5	+1.6
Belgium	65.9	125.0	+1.9	2.2	3.1	+1.4
Canada[b]	447.0	916.0	+2.0	3.0	2.0	—
Denmark	78.7	179.0	+2.3	2.5	4.8	+1.9
England-Wales[a]	163.0	362.0	+2.2	1.4	2.5	+1.8
France	59.8	99.0	+1.7	3.4	4.9	+1.4
Greece	14.4	68.4	+4.8	1.2	2.5	+2.1
Hungary[c]	45.1	76.9	+1.7	3.5	4.5	+1.3
Netherlands[d]	101.1	196.0	+1.9	8.3	27.4	+3.3
New Zealand[a]	83.4	313.0	+3.8	1.8	4.0	+2.2
Norway	12.8	62.0	+4.8	.7	2.5	+3.6
Scotland[e]	53.0	123.0	+2.3	8.4	11.4	+1.4
Sweden	17.3	51.1	+3.0	4.8	8.8	+1.8
United States	241.0	440.0	+1.8	8.8	9.5	+1.1

Note. All data represents incidents per 100,000 population, as reported by each nation to Interpol and recorded in Interpol International Crime Statistics, Vols. 1977 to 1994. (Except for Canadian data, as stated below in footnote b). Different nations use different criteria to define "murder" and "serious assault," therefore ability to use this data to compare between nations is limited, but comparisons of increases within each nation across time is valid. This information was previously reported in a different format in *On Killing*, © 1996, Dave Grossman.

[a] Data is only through the following dates when the indicated nations stopped reporting to Interpol: Australia, 1988; England-Wales, 1991; India, 1991; New Zealand, 1992.

[b] Canada does not report crime data to Interpol; Canadian data is from Canadian Center for Justice.

[c] Data begins in 1980, when Hungary started reporting to Interpol.

[d] Netherlands did not begin reporting serious assault data to Interpol until 1981, but murder data begins in 1977.

[e] Scotland's serious assault data begins in 1977, but murder data begins in 1985 (when they apparently started reporting murder under a broader definition) and both murder and serious assault data only run through 1991 when Scotland stopped reporting to Interpol.

internalize with their training. However, by saturating children with media violence as entertainment and then exposing them to interactive "point-and-shoot" arcade and video games, it has become increasingly clear that society is aping military conditioning but without the vital safeguard of discipline.

The observation that violence in the media is causing violence in our streets is nothing new. The American Academy of Pediatrics, the American Psychiatric Association, the American Medical Association, and their equivalents in many other nations have all made unequivocable statements about the link between media violence and violence in our society. The APA, in their 1992 report *Big World, Small Screen*, concluded that the "scientific debate is over." And in 1993 the APA's commission on violence and youth concluded that "there is absolutely no doubt that higher levels of viewing violence on television are correlated with increased acceptance of aggressive attitudes and increased aggressive behavior." The evidence is quite simply overwhelming.

Dr. Brandon Centerwall, professor of epidemiology at the University of Washington, has summarized the overwhelming nature of this body of evidence. His research demonstrates that anywhere in the world that television is introduced, within 15 years the murder rate will double. (And remember, across 15 years, the murder rate will significantly underrepresent the problem because medical technology will be saving ever more lives each year.)

Centerwall concludes that *if* television technology had never been introduced in the U.S, *then* there would today be 10,000 fewer homicides each year in the United States; 70,000 fewer rapes; and 700,000 fewer injurious assaults. Overall violent crime would be half of what it is.

Centerwall notes that the net effect of television has been to increase the aggressive predisposition of approximately 8% of the population, which is all that is required to double the murder rate. Statistically speaking 8% is a very small increase. Anything less than 5% is not even considered to be statistically significant. But in human terms, the impact of doubling the homicide rate is enormous.

F. Acquired Violence Immune Deficiency Syndrome (AVIDS)

There are two filters that a human mind has to go through to kill at close range. The first filter is the forebrain. A hundred things can convince the forebrain to take gun in hand and go to a certain point: poverty,

drugs, gangs, leaders, radical politics, and the social learning of violence in the media—magnified when the child is from a broken home and is searching for a role model. But, traditionally, all of these influences slam into the resistance that a frightened, angry human being confronts in the midbrain. With the exception of sociopaths (who, by definition, do not have this resistance) the vast, vast majority of circumstances are not sufficient to overcome this midbrain safety net. But, if you are conditioned to overcome these midbrain inhibitions, then you are a walking time bomb, a pseudosociopath, just waiting for the random factors of social interaction and forebrain rationalization to put you at the wrong place at the wrong time.

An effective analogy can be made to AIDS in attempting to communicate the impact of this technology. AIDS does not kill people, it simply destroys the immune system and makes the victim vulnerable to death by other factors. The "violence immune system" exists in the midbrain, and conditioning in the media creates an "acquired deficiency" in this immune system, resulting in "Acquired Violence Immune Deficiency Syndrome" or AVIDS. As a result of this weakened immune system, the victim becomes more vulnerable to violence-enabling factors such as poverty, discrimination, drugs, gangs, radical politics, and the availability of guns.

In weapons technology terms this indiscriminate use of combat conditioning techniques on children is the moral equivalent of giving an assault weapon to every child in every industrialized nation in the world. If, hypothetically, this *were* done, the vast majority of children would almost certainly not kill anyone with their assault rifles; but if only a tiny percentage did, then the results would be tragic and unacceptable. But it is increasingly clear that this is not a hypothetical situation. Indiscriminate civilian application of combat conditioning techniques as entertainment has increasingly been identified as a key factor in the worldwide, skyrocketing violent crime rates outlined above. Thus, the influences of weapons technology can increasingly be observed on the streets of nations around the world.

IV. CONCLUSION: THE FUTURE OF WEAPONS EVOLUTION

Wars are fought by one group of humans to force another group to submit to their will. Weapons are tools to help humans overcome their physical and psychological limitations in order to inflict their will upon others. Democratic nations seldom, if ever, go to war against each other, choosing instead less destructive methods of influence.

Thus, with the coming of the age of democracies, the time of wars may be coming to an end, and the passing of war may also mark the passing of some of the instruments of war. Indeed, a precedence for an end to war can be found in weapons evolution.

It has become increasingly obvious that each act of violence breeds ever-greater levels of violence, and at some point the genie must be put back in the bottle. The study of killing in combat teaches us that soldiers who have had friends or relatives injured or killed in combat are much more likely to kill and commit war crimes.

The world is just now recovering from the most violent and bloody century in human history, and the streets of the western, industrialized nations are the scenes of a level of violence that is unprecedented in human history. Each individual who is injured or killed by violence provides a point of departure for further violence on the part of their friends and family. Every destructive act gnaws away at the restraint of human beings. Each act of violence eats away at the fabric of our society like a cancer, spreading and reproducing itself in ever-expanding cycles of horror and destruction. The genie of violence cannot really ever be stuffed back into the bottle. It can only be cut off here and now, and then the slow process of healing and resensitization can begin.

It can be done. It has been done in the past. As Richard Heckler has observed, there is a precedent for limiting violence-enabling technology. It started with the classical Greeks, who for 4 centuries refused to implement the bow and arrow even after being introduced to it in a most unpleasant way by Persian archers.

In *Giving Up The Gun*, Noel Perrin tells how the Japanese banned firearms after their introduction by the Portuguese in the 1500s. The Japanese quickly recognized that the military use of gunpowder threatened the very fabric of their society and culture, and they moved aggressively to defend their way of life. The feuding Japanese warlords destroyed all existing weapons and made the production or import of any new guns punishable by death. Three centuries later, when Commodore Perry forced the Japanese to open their ports, they did not even have the technology to make firearms. Similarly, the Chinese invented gunpowder but elected not to use it in warfare.

But the most encouraging examples of restraining killing technology have all occurred in this century. After the tragic experience of using poisonous gases in World War I the world has generally rejected its use ever since. The atmospheric nuclear test ban treaty continues after 3 decades, the ban on the deployment of antisatellite weapons is still going strong after 2 decades, the U.S. and the former USSR have been steadily reducing the quantity of nuclear weapons for the past 2 decades, and we have seen a Nobel Peace Prize awarded to a new movement to eliminate land mines. As we have deescalated instruments of indiscriminate mass *destruction*, so too can we deescalate instruments of indiscriminate mass *desensitization* as entertainment in the media.

Firearms probably will not go away any time soon, but their abuse will almost definitely be strongly influenced by technology that will make guns "keyed" so that they can only be fired by a designated individual and will thereby be useless to all others. Similarly, violence in the media will not go away as long as there is a market for it, but there will probably be movement *away* from indiscriminate violence-enabling of children through violent video games and violence in the media and *toward* protecting children from these things while still permitting their availability to adults, in much the same manner as alcohol, tobacco, prescription drugs, pornography, and guns.

Heckler points out that there has been "an almost unnoticed series of precedents for reducing military technology on moral grounds," precedents that show the way to understanding that we do have a *choice* about how we think about war, about killing, and about the value of human life in our society. In recent years we have exercised the choice to move ourselves from the brink of nuclear destruction. In the same way, our society can also take the evolutionary steps *away* from the technology that psychologically enables killing in children. Education and understanding is the first step. The end result may be for weapons evolution to take a considered step backward and for our civilization to come through the dark years of the 20th century and enter into a healthier, more self-aware society.

Also See the Following Articles

BEHAVIORAL PSYCHOLOGY • COMBAT • EVOLUTIONARY FACTORS • MILITARY CULTURE • PSYCHOLOGICAL EFFECTS OF COMBAT • RITUAL AND SYMBOLIC BEHAVIOR • TELEVISION PROGRAMMING AND VIOLENCE • WARFARE, STRATEGIES AND TACTICS OF • WARFARE, TRENDS IN • WARRIORS, ANTHROPOLOGY OF

Bibliography

Dyer, G. (1985). *War*. New York: Crown.
Griffith, P. (1989). *Battle tactics of the civil war*. New Haven, CT: Yale University Press.

Griffith, P. (1990). *Forward into battle*. Novato, CA: Presidio Press.

Grossman, D. (1995/1996). *On killing: The psychological cost of learning to kill in war and society*. New York: Little, Brown.

Holmes, R. (1985). *Acts of war: The behavior of men in battle*. New York: The Free Press.

Keegan, J. (1994). *A history of warfare*. New York: Knopf.

Keegan, J., & Holmes, R. (1985). *Soldiers*. London: Hamish Hamilton.

Marshal, S. L. A. (1978). *Men against fire*. Gloucester, MA: Peter Smith.

Stouffer, S. (1949). *The American soldier: Combat and its aftermath*. Princeton, NJ: Princeton.

Women and War

Jennifer Turpin

University of San Francisco

I. Introduction
II. The Impact of War on Women
III. Women's Responses to War
IV. Contemporary Debates
V. Research Questions
VI. Gendered Social Relations as a Cause of War

GLOSSARY

Essentialism The assumption that women and men, based on their gender, have an underlying universal nature that is more fundamental than any variations that may exist among them and that the essential nature of women differs from that of men. This nature is generally characterized as biological or genetic in origin and always present.

Ethnic Cleansing The use of mass rape, torture, and killing to inflict genocide or the expulsion of an ethnic group from a particular region.

Gender The socially assigned traits and social roles attributed to members of a biological sex category. These ascribed traits and roles may differ from culture to culture and play a powerful role in defining and shaping their members' lives.

Genocide The systematic killing of, or a program of action intended to destroy, an entire national or ethnic group.

Militarism The prevalence of military values in society. Militarism is reflected both structurally and cultur-

ally; in the allocation of human, economic, scientific, and ecological resources to military preparation, as well as in the popular culture of the society.

Structural Violence The violence experienced by people, not as a consequence of direct violence inflicted by other individuals, but because of the inequality or structural conditions embedded in the society. The violence may be a consequence, for example, of government policies eliminating health care or denying people access to safe water and food.

Total War The warfighting strategy that targets the enemy's homeland as well as the enemy's army. This strategy effectively eliminates the distinction between civilians and soldiers and aims at demoralizing the enemy by destroying their homes, families, communities, and entire social fabric. This strategy has advanced in use since World War II and has resulted in the widespread killing of civilians in wartime.

I. INTRODUCTION

Conventional views of the relationship between gender and war suggest that men make war; women make peace. Men, representing their nations or social groups, combat men of another group, while women remain outside the fighting, protected by "their" men. Women do remain invisible in military policy-making, reflecting taken-for-granted international assumptions about the maleness of war. But both feminist scholarship and empirical reality have challenged the prevailing assumptions about war's relationship to men and women. We have learned that war has profound and unique effects on women and that warmaking, rather than separate from women's lives, relies on women's participation. Even though women are more likely than men to become war's casualties or refugees, women have little or no say in military or security decisions.

This article examines the distinct impact that war has on women because of their gender, the various ways that women respond to war, the major debates within this field of study, and, finally, gender inequality as a cause of war.

II. THE IMPACT OF WAR ON WOMEN

Women suffer from war in many ways, including dying; experiencing sexual abuse and torture; and losing loved ones, homes, and communities. Many people assume that women are unlikely to die in wars, since so few women serve in the armed forces worldwide. But women, as civilians, are more likely to be killed in war than are soldiers.

A. Women as Direct Casualties

War's impact on women has changed with the development of increasingly efficient war-making technologies that make war and militarism increasingly deadly. Ingomar Hauchler and Paul Kennedy have documented the trends in war. The past century has witnessed the killing of about 104 million people in wars—more than three-quarters of all war dead recorded since the year 1500. Most people killed in war are civilians. The advent of high-altitude bombing, more powerful bombs, and a strategy of "total war" has ended the distinction between combatants and civilians as targets of war. While 50% of WW II's casualties were civilians, in the 1980s this figure rose to 80% and by 1990 it was a staggering 90%. Women and their children constitute the vast majority of these civilian casualties.

These deaths are not randomly distributed throughout the world—most of the wars since the 1960s have taken place in less-developed countries, particularly in Asia and sub-Saharan Africa (see Fig. 1). Military intervention, on the other hand, is perpetrated primarily by the former colonial powers, mostly by the United States, followed by Britain and then the USSR/Russia and Belgium. In addition to their direct interventions, the

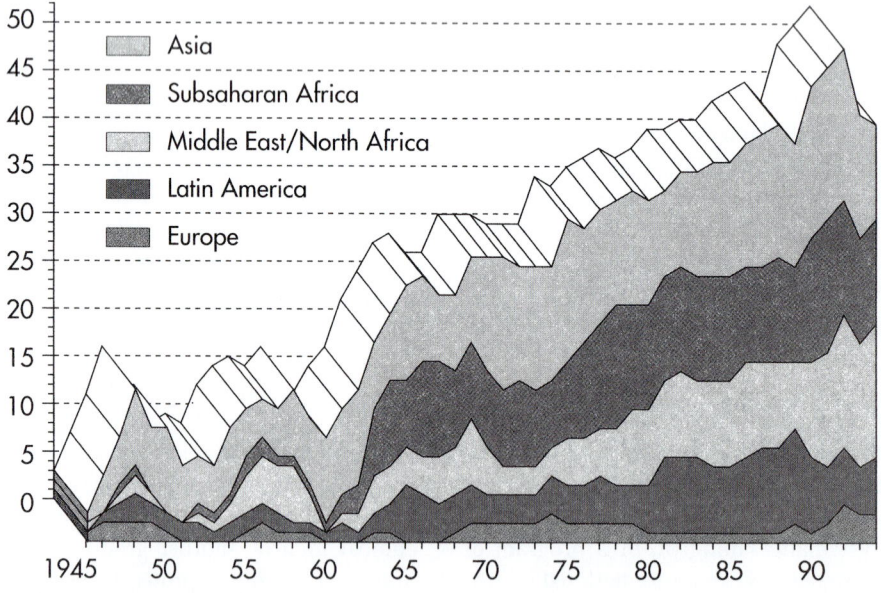

Wars per Year by Regions 1945–94

Asia
Subsaharan Africa
Middle East/North Africa
Latin America
Europe

Source: AKUF 1994 (as of May 15, 1994); own calculations.

FIGURE 1 Wars per year by regions, 1945–1994, from *Global Trends*, edited by Ingomar Hauchler and Paul Kennedy. Copyright 1994 by The Continuum Publishing Company.

United States and the former Soviet Union have also exported the most arms to the developing world.

Besides analyzing war through the lens of gender, we must also analyze the global intersections between gender and class, race, nation, and ethnicity. Women may be more or less vulnerable to the effects of war and militarization depending on their home society, their economic status, and their racial/ethnic identity. Women in developing countries are most likely to experience war and most likely to be driven from their homelands.

B. Women as War Refugees

Women are also most likely to be uprooted by war. More than four-fifths of war refugees are women and young girls, who also experience additional and often sexualized violence during their flight. By the end of 1992 more than 46 million people had lost their homes; about 36 million of these were women and girls. In Africa there were more than 23.6 million external and internal refugees; more than 12.6 people fled their homes in the Middle East and in South and Central Asia. There are 2 million displaced persons in Latin America and about 6 million refugees in Europe. About 2 million people fled the former Yugoslavia.

Refugee women often serve as their children's sole caretakers, as many of them are widows or separated from their spouses and other extended family. They must seek food and safety not only for themselves, but also for their children, who also need health care, housing, and an education. Refugee women in exile are often the supporters of an extended family network, playing a central economic role yet still lacking decision-making power in their societies.

C. Wartime Sexual Violence against Women

The United Nations High Commissioner on Refugees cites sexual attacks on women and girls by camp guards as a major problem. Even those women and girls stationed in camps and refugee settlements, as well as in new societies of residence, frequently suffer sexual abuse, abduction, and forced prostitution. History has demonstrated the link between war and control of women's sexuality and reproduction through rape, sexual harassment, and militarized prostitution.

1. Rape

John Tenhula relates the stories of women and children who fled Vietnam by boat and were the subjects of attacks by pirates during their flight. He quotes eyewitnesses of these attacks.

> Two of the young and pretty girls were taken to the front of the boat and raped. Everyone heard everything, all of the screams. That is what I remember, the screams. After a while the screams stopped, the crying stopped, and there was silence.

But being young and pretty has very little to do with becoming a victim of wartime rape. There are numerous accounts of very old women being brutally raped and murdered. These women, who often have limited mobility and live alone, are especially vulnerable to attack by soldiers.

As Lois Ann Lorentzen demonstrates, the torture of political prisoners is also gendered. Women imprisoned for their political activities are commonly raped repeatedly by different rapists. In the former Yugoslavia, thousands of Muslim women have been forced into camps and raped by Serbian soldiers, and Muslim and Croat soldiers have also committed mass rapes. Rape has been used as a weapon for ethnic cleansing, which uses attacks on women to humiliate and as an attempt to exterminate another ethnic group.

The idea that genocide could be accomplished through the mass rape of women of the enemy ethnic group derives from a patriarchal definition of ethnicity. The child is thought to inherit the ethnicity of her or his father, implying, for example, that if a Serb soldier rapes a Muslim woman and she becomes pregnant, her child would be a Serb. And because women are viewed as symbols of the family, and the family as the basis of society, the humiliation for women of giving birth to the enemy's children symbolizes the destruction of the community.

Vesna Nikolic-Ristanovic has interviewed many refugee women from different ethnic groups in the former Yugoslavia. Those women who became pregnant because of wartime rape expressed anguish over carrying a child who is both their own and the enemy's child. This form of psychological torture is incomparable to other forms of wartime torture. In addition, raped women are often stigmatized. Women may be shunned by their own families and communities, viewed as tainted, worthless "property."

The horrifying reports of mass, ethnically defined rape have attracted widespread public attention, but they are not unique to the war in former Yugoslavia. Soviet soldiers reportedly raped approximately 2 million women in eastern Germany in 1945. In 1971 Pakistani soldiers raped more than 200,000 Bengali women in the Bangladesh war of independence. Cynthia Enloe reports one estimate that during the war against Kuwait, Iraqi troops raped as many as 3,200 women between August, 1990 and February, 1991. The link between rape and war has been ignored by many policy-makers and scholars, but feminists have identified wartime rape as symptomatic of war's gendered nature.

Even the United Nations peacekeepers—the multilateral forces sent to protect civilian human rights in war-torn areas—have committed rape and sexual abuse against women and young girls. Such cases have been documented in Mozambique, Somalia, Cambodia, and other regions. This suggests that those trained to fight wars are not best suited to protect the human rights of women and children and that sexual violence is endemic to military culture.

Attitudes of military personnel often support the sexual abuse of women and girls. Carolyn Nordstrom states that when the head of the UN mission in Cambodia was questioned about the sexual abuse of women and girls by UN troops, he responded that he was "not a puritan: 18-year-old, hot-blooded soldiers had a right to drink a few beers and chase after young beautiful things of the opposite sex." And in 1995 when three U.S. Marines were charged with assaulting and raping a 12-year-old girl on the Japanese island of Okinawa, the commander of the U.S. Pacific Command told reporters: "I think it was absolutely stupid, as I've said several times. For the price they paid to rent the car, they could have had a girl." In addition to implicitly accepting rape as a part of military life, militaries around the world also support and may even enforce prostitution attached to their military installations.

2. Prostitution

Wartime prostitution may be either physically forced or economically coerced. During World War II the Japanese military set up brothels in East and Southern Asia, forcing between 100,000 and 200,000 women into prostitution. Cynthia Enloe has pointed out that prostitution relies not only on the "sex worker" and the "client," but rather involves a whole host of characters, mainly men, who contribute to the creation and maintenance of prostitution as an institution around any military base in the world. It includes husbands and lovers; bar and brothel owners; local public health officials; local police and mayors; national and foreign finance ministry and defense officials; male soldiers in the national, local, and foreign forces; and local civilian male prostitution customers.

Militaries may manage and control the lives of women working as prostitutes by implementing curfews, demanding regular checkups for sexually transmitted diseases, and even regulating which customers they have sex with. During World War II brothels linked to U.S. military bases generally had two separate entrances: one for men of color and another for Whites. Because militaries may provide huge infusions of capital into the societies where they establish bases, the local government has an incentive to cooperate with demands for women to have sex with the soldiers, and poor women may have little other choice in order to support themselves and their families.

These prostitutes are often young girls endeavoring to support their families or women who need to support their children. Stories are told of young girls coming down from the mountains around Subic Bay (the recently closed U.S. military base in the Philippines) when American military ships pull into the harbor. The girls, from poor rural families, come to serve as prostitutes for American servicemen. And girls who are orphaned by war may be sold into domestic and sexual slavery. In societies where women are valued for their virginity, these girls may be permanent outcasts, trapped in a life of prostitution, and, if they live to old age, poverty.

D. Wartime Domestic Violence

While battering of women is common in most societies in peacetime, recent research indicates that domestic violence increases in wartime. This suggests a link between gendered violence at the micro and macro levels and calls for an inquiry into the gendered dynamics of power from the household to the international arena. Among the findings of research conducted through a Belgrade agency for domestic violence are: an increase in the number of sons who commit violence against their mothers in wartime; an increase in the number of assaults involving weapons, including pistols, grenades, and other weapons from the war; an increase in violence in marriages where the husband and wife's ethnicity differ; an increase in alcohol consumption among men returning from combat; and a link between economic decline, especially refugee status, and wife battering and rape.

What wartime conditions would lead to an increase in woman battering and rape within the household? Several factors have been postulated. First, in wartime, there is an influx of weapons into the societies, and those weapons are often not controlled or limited to battlefield use. Research from both criminology and security studies demonstrates that the presence of weapons increases both the likelihood and lethality of violence. Second, former soldiers or soldiers who have contact with their families have been affected by their experiences in combat. They may be frustrated, nervous, intolerant, and aggressive.

State-produced media propaganda that endorses violence as an acceptable means of conflict resolution, combined with hate propaganda against members of other ethnic groups, may also be related to the escalation of domestic violence in wartime. All of these factors, along with a cultural acceptance of violence against women, even in peacetime, put women at greater risk.

E. Loss of Family

Loss of family members inflicts suffering on women and men alike, but women are affected in particular ways because of their family roles. Women may lose husbands and sons on the battlefield, and they may lose their daughters and young children as civilian casualties or witness their suffering as victims of assault and rape. As the primary caregivers to children in most societies, women arguably suffer the loss of their children in gender-specific ways. Although the relationship of motherhood to women's stance toward war is debated, women in many different historical and cultural contexts have argued that a mother's suffering is unique. Nationalist propaganda often calls on women to give up their sons at wartime and to take pride in a son's military service. Clearly, many women do respond to this call, and not every mother responds to the loss in the same way. As Nancy Scheper-Hughes points out, women living in conditions of scarcity and violence may more readily surrender their sons and husbands to potential death.

Losing husbands and sons may, for many women, mean not only emotional loss but also lost economic support and social legitimacy. Women's lack of economic power and opportunity may force them to rely on their male family members for economic survival. These women may become poor and homeless when they lose their husbands and sons. In some societies, women with no male family members lose all rights to protection, employment, benefits, or guarantees to security.

F. Loss of Work, Community, and Social Structure

Those women who are able to work outside the home may lose their jobs when war destroys the economic infrastructure. Indeed, with total war as the strategy of contemporary militaries, factories, hospitals, office buildings, agricultural fields, and civilian communities all become targets. Destruction of the economy, whether it be industrially or agriculturally based, affects women in unique ways because of their caretaking roles in the family and community. In conditions of food scarcity, women are more likely than men to give up their food so that children can eat. Women's caretaking roles become increasingly burdensome as they struggle to feed their children in adverse conditions created by war and to nurse wounded survivors when hospitals, medicine, and clean water are scarce.

G. War, Environmental Destruction, and Women

In addition to destroying the social and economic infrastructure, war destroys the natural environment. This has devastating consequences for women, again due to their roles as food providers and as caretakers. In most of the world, women grow the food; for example, in Africa, women produce 80% of the food. Women also gather most of the fuel and water and prepare the meals. When war destroys the vegetation, these tasks become difficult, if not impossible. For example, Lois Lorentzen and Jennifer Turpin have observed that in El Salvador, which has been devastated by war, 80% of the natural vegetation has been eliminated and 77% of the soil has eroded or lost its fertility. The militaries employed "scorched earth" tactics similar to those used by the U.S. in Vietnam, destroying huge tracts of land and forest. Peasant women there find it harder and harder to gather firewood and grow food.

Water pollution becomes a major problem for women, as they need it not only for themselves and their families to drink, but also to clean wounds. Illnesses caused by lack of potable water account for 34.6% of all child deaths in the developing world. And women, who often walk for hours to find potable water, must walk farther and farther in their search.

In the Gulf War, both the Iraqis and the Allies (primarily the U.S.) deliberately destroyed the natural environment of the region as a part of their war strategy. Iraq pumped oil into the sea, causing an oil slick about 80 miles long and 10 miles wide. About 600 oil wells were set afire in Kuwait. The U.S. deliberately bombed chemical and nuclear facilities, causing black rain to fall throughout the region. Hospitals and clinics were destroyed, and the water supply became contaminated. Basic health and sanitation levels dropped in the region, and the impact on the local economy made food prices

TABLE I

The Economy of Death[a]

Amount	Paid for	Could have paid for
$20 million	20 Patriot missiles	Vaccines to protect all the women in Africa from tetanus
$65 million	1 E-2C Hawkeye aircraft	The estimated total amount of external funds spent on AIDS in Africa in 1990
$350 million	Two days of air combat	UNICEF's 1990–1991 budgeted expenditures plus $48 million)
$12.3 billion	Noncombat costs, January–March	The total current annual amount of investment in water supply in the developing world
$500 million	One day of air and ground	Oxfam's operating combat budget—46 times over—for 1989–1990
$6.9 million	1 CH-47D army transport helicopter	All of Save the Children's refugee programs in Indonesia and Thailand, 1989–1990 (providing services for 25,000 people)
$20,000	1 Stinger missile	Basic medical equipment and building materials for a maternity center in Mali

[a] If you were to spend $1.2 million a day for 10 years you would spend $44 billion, the estimated amount spent on the Gulf War alone (not including long-term costs of operating a base in Saudi Arabia or reconstructing Kuwait).

Source: Reprinted by permission of *Ms. Magazine* © 1991.

soar. Women suffered in gender-specific ways as they struggled to provide for their children.

H. The Impact of Military Spending on Women

In spite of war's increasing destructiveness, huge amounts of resources continue to be spent on arms while displacing social spending. Military expenditures account for 5% of goods and services produced in the world, 5 times more than that allocated before World War II, representing 3 times the government expenditures for education and 15 times those for housing worldwide. Jeanne Vickers shows that governments are spending 30 times the amount of money allocated to each child in school on each member of the armed forces.

While governments are constantly decrying their lack of available funds to meet social needs, there seems to be an unending supply of capital for military spending, and many have observed a direct trade-off between the two (see Table I). For every dollar spent on research and development in the United States, 64 cents goes to the military while only 1 cent goes to protecting the environment.

V. Spike Peterson and Anne Sisson Runyan have shown that the huge military expenditures of the past few decades have produced social service cuts, where women worldwide are most likely to be employed. Although military spending does provide jobs for some women, they tend to be low-paying, assembly-line positions in defense factories. Women provide cheap labor for defense contractors, who, in the U.S., rely primarily on the labor of Asian, Black, and Latina women.

III. WOMEN'S RESPONSES TO WAR

A. Joining

Although women are stereotyped as pacifists or war resisters, they have fought in wars and now often seek equal status in the militaries of many countries. Other women support the war effort through their work in munitions factories or defense firms. Women tend to occupy the lowest ranks and to perform "women's roles" within those settings, although those roles are being challenged and debated.

1. Soldiers

Although women have reportedly fought in wars for centuries, they have routinely been relegated to second-class status in the military. Public resistance to women as warriors is rooted in traditional ideas about femininity and masculinity. These ideas become more flexible in certain political contexts. Women have been known to fight in wars of liberation and civil wars, including among the Chinese communists in the 1930s and 1940s, the African National Congress in South Africa in the 1970s and 1980s, in Vietnam in the 1960s and 1970s, and in El Salvador in the 1980s. Women have been voluntary and eager participants in recent conflicts such as the Gulf War, genocide in Rwanda, and ethnic cleansing in Bosnia, disproving the notion of women as essentially peaceful and nonviolent.

In recent decades we have witnessed a shift toward increasing, although not equal, numbers of women in the military along with expanded roles for women. Yet while some restrictions on women in combat have been removed, women are still excluded from ground combat by the U.S. military as well as from ground, naval, and air combat by most other militaries. Janet Beilstein demonstrates in her UN report that almost no women have served in the United Nations military peacekeeping operations. Only 5 of the 6,250 troops who served in military peacekeeping missions between 1957 and 1979 were women, and from 1957–1989, only 20 of the roughly 20,000 troops were women. Most of these women served in traditional roles as nurses in medical units. Women still comprise less than 2% of the troops in UN peacekeeping missions.

This trend is evident in national militaries as well: while a small percentage of women hold high-ranking positions, most women are relegated to traditionally feminine roles within the military as secretaries, nurses, and technicians. Militaries often emphasize differences between men and women rather than their equal abilities; for example, as Francine D'Amico points out, the Israeli military teaches women how to apply their makeup. These military roles are not only gendered; they are also race and class-based, as poor and working-class women from minority groups are disproportionately recruited.

Some feminists have argued for women's greater access to military jobs and benefits. This argument is based on the notion that citizenship derives in part from one's capacity to fight for one's country. Equal-rights feminists have argued that political power has been elusive for women because, in many countries, military service is a prerequisite for high political office. Western feminists such as Judith Hicks Stiehm have argued that increased military participation can emancipate women from their status as the weak and defended—women can instead be the defenders.

Critics of this approach charge that the military is not good for women or that women should reject the military because of its sexism. They point out that military indoctrination for men generally includes the systematic denigration of all that is "feminine." Male recruits are often called "girls" as a form of humiliation, and they often chant sexist lyrics as part of training. Women recruits report being sexually harassed and even raped by their fellow soldiers.

2. Military Production Workers

Another way women can support militarization is to work in the defense industry. During both World Wars, there was a huge influx of women into munitions factories. Recruitment propaganda called on women to do munitions work previously done by men. A British recruitment poster proclaimed, for example, that "These Women are Doing Their Part: Learn to Make Muni-

tions." According to Angela Woollacott, about a million British women worked in munitions factories during the First World War, making guns, shells, explosives, and aircraft. Women munitions makers in both world wars achieved more economic independence than before, and many expressed pride in contributing to the war effort.

In contrast, today's women defense workers are some of the worst-paid women in the labor force. As noted earlier, most women working in the defense industry occupy low-paying jobs as assembly workers, with few if any benefits. It is not clear that they feel linked to success in any particular war.

3. Sending, Supporting, and Reproducing Men

Militaries have not only conducted campaigns to bring women into munitions work; they have also generated propaganda that links motherhood, nationalism, and militarism.

Women and girls have also been called upon to urge their husbands and boyfriends to war. A British leaflet issued to "the young women of England" in 1917 asked:

> Is your "best boy" wearing khaki? If not, don't you think he should be? If he does not think that you and your country are worth fighting for, do you think he is worthy of you? If your young man neglects his duty to his king and country, the time will come when he will neglect YOU. Think it over—then ask him to JOIN THE ARMY.

Women and girls were told to "show a white feather," used as a symbol of cowardice, to any man they saw whom they suspected of having failed to enlist.

Lorraine Bayard de Volo has studied the ways mothers have been targeted by war propaganda in two very different countries: the U.S. and Nicaragua. Each government attempted to educate women as to what constitutes a "good mother" during wartime. Bayard de Volo finds the propaganda strategies to be remarkably similar, drawing on representations of the good (patriotic) mother as one who is willing to sacrifice her sons to war.

During the American Civil War, as well as during both world wars, the U.S. government established organizations whose aims were to stimulate feelings of motherly patriotism among women. Similar organizations, such as the Mothers of Heroes and Martyrs, were developed in Nicaragua during the war against the Contras. State propaganda has also been directed at mothers in Israel to prevent dissent against their sons' involvement in the Israeli Defense Forces. Women who protest the war are portrayed as disloyal to their children. Women are even called upon by many states to produce more sons for the military, and some states, such as Croatia in the former Yugoslavia, have outlawed abortion in wartime. Despite governments' efforts to the contrary, many women do protest their sons' being called to war and publicly mourn their deaths in ways that defy the state.

B. Mourning

While some wives, lovers, sisters, and mothers mourn the war-dead in private, others mourn publicly as a form of resistance. Some women's groups, such as Women in Black, rather than mourning the loss of particular family members, symbolically mourn the continuing deaths caused by the Israeli occupation of Palestine. Sara Ruddick writes that the figure of the *mater dolorosa*—the suffering mother—is the predominant image of women in war. Indeed, many mothers' groups have been formed who express their suffering, not only in private, but as a form of protest against the war

Mothers' groups may also organize to glorify their lost sons, providing support for revolutionary struggles against interventionist powers. Such was the case of the Mothers of the Heroes and Martyrs in Nicaragua, who not only honored their dead sons but also called for the Contras to stop their war.

C. Resisting

Some women's groups actively resisting war have also drawn on gender roles and employed stereotypic symbols in their activism. For example, at the Greenham Common women's peace camp in England, women hung diapers on the wire fence around the nuclear installation and wore pictures of their children around their necks. The members of Women Strike for Peace in the U.S. declared a "strike" on their domestic work, refusing to perform household work as a form of protest against nuclear war preparations. When they appeared in public spaces such as courthouses and parliaments, these women dressed up in traditionally feminine clothing to unsettle the men and appeal to them as might their sisters, wives, and mothers. The *Materinskoe Serdise*, Soviet mothers who drew attention to their killed sons in Afghanistan, organized demonstrations and hunger strikes and broke into official meetings. The women of Another Mother for Peace in the U.S. sent a Mother's Day card to members of the U.S. Congress during the Vietnam War. It said:

For my Mothers' Day gift this year
I don't want candy or flowers.
I want an end to killing.
We who have given life
Must be dedicated to preserving it.
Please, talk peace!

This group created a creed of *Pax Materna*, or mother's peace, and a logo that was translated into 20 languages and distributed worldwide. These groups demonstrated that feminine symbols often associated with passivity can be transformed into effective forms of political protest.

Women's association with peace is an ancient historical theme. Women have developed national organizations as well as transnational groups such as Women's International League for Peace and Freedom, World Women Parliamentarians for Peace, and the International Feminist Network. Women's involvement in the peace movement worldwide suggests that, although we may reject arguments that women are inherently peaceful, we must also ask why so many women are drawn to peace work.

IV. CONTEMPORARY DEBATES

Scholarship on women and war has generated a wealth of knowledge and challenged traditional approaches to studying war that typically ignore the role of gender and the impact of war on women. Within the subfield of women and war, a number of debates are underway.

A. Essentialism versus Difference

The debate over whether women have a feminine nature that is distinct from men's has raged both within conservative political circles and among feminists. Are women and men fundamentally different because of biology? While conservatives have answered "yes," their answer leads to the policy conclusion that men should fight wars and women should support them in distinctly feminine, maternal ways. Some feminists, including both cultural feminists in the West and radical non-Western feminists, have also answered "yes," but conclude that women, as natural peace-makers, should resist wars and that women should be accorded more power over world affairs so as to make the world less violent.

This debate has become more nuanced and complicated. Cross-cultural analyses have yielded evidence that neither men nor women have an "essential" nature: rather, gender is a fluid social category that people express differently in different cultural contexts and through diverse roles. Neither men nor women have proven to be inherently violent or peaceful; instead, humans have the capacity to be both. The fact that states produce so much propaganda to instruct men and women how to properly behave suggests that masculinity and femininity are learned rather than inherent traits. A group of internationally renowned scientists concluded in the Seville Statement on Violence that humans are not inherently violent and therefore that social and political factors more likely contribute to war and its gendered nature.

B. The Politics of Motherhood

A second debate within the field concerns the relationship between motherhood and war. As discussed earlier, mothers can respond in quite different ways to war, again, depending on the social and political context. Yet patterns emerge over time, with significant numbers of mothers' groups organizing to protest wars in different parts of the world. At the same time, many mothers support decisions to go to war and willingly send their sons to fight. Scholars continue to debate whether there is something universal about motherhood that predisposes women to one response over another.

C. Women in the Military

A third major debate, especially among feminists, centers on women's participation in the military. It includes a number of questions. Should women join the military? While some argue that women should be free to join whatever organizations they choose, others protest that the military is the most fundamentally sexist social institution and women should not participate in it. Some argue that women in greater numbers will change the military for the better, while others claim that it is more likely that the military will change women.

Should women serve in combat roles? Equal-rights/ liberal feminists argue for women's access to the same military jobs as men, claiming that women will also gain greater political power as a consequence. Conservatives and cultural feminists reject the notion of women in combat.

D. Women and Collective Organizing

A final debate that has emerged from women's multiple responses to war concerns whether women constitute a group for organizing in any unified fashion around issues of war and peace. Do women across cultures and social groups share the same concerns? Do women have a collective identity that can be mobilized? Elise Boulding points out that women have over time organized transnationally to oppose war, sexism, and inequality. She believes that women's collective sensibility stems not from some biological commonality, but rather from women's distinct social roles and knowledge. Women, she argues, can make a distinct contribution to peacemaking.

V. RESEARCH QUESTIONS

Some of the most fruitful areas for research draw on the previous debates. Among those areas are the following:

A. Factors That Determine Women's Responses to War

Scholarship that examines women's responses to war in different historical, cultural, and geopolitical contexts will help us to understand why and under what conditions women support war or peace; why some women respond to war by becoming prostitutes, while others are munitions workers, soldiers, or protesters. As a part of this analysis, we need to better understand the ways in which women's class status, race, ethnicity, sexuality, and nationality affect their experiences.

B. Militarism in Peacetime

Much of the research on women and war suggests that war magnifies already-existing gender inequality and women's subordination. We need more research that examines the ways that violence against women and women's lower social status in peacetime is connected to that in wartime. Sexual violence against women, for example, is routine in most contemporary societies and yet is magnified in wartime. And domestic militarism, such as internal policing, is also gendered. We need to understand how women's lives are militarized in times of "peace" in order to understand how their lives are transformed by war.

C. The State's Role in Mobilizing Women

Further research should examine the different strategies that states utilize to mobilize women to support war. Which states, for example, attempt to recruit women into military service and which attempt to mobilize mothers to support war? How do cross-cultural differences, historical circumstances, and dynamics of the war in question shape states' behavior? Which strategies are most effective for mobilizing which women? What resources do states invest in these efforts, and who makes decisions about mobilization campaigns? How do women's reactions figure into declarations of war and defense department press releases?

D. Women Making Security Policy

A final question that merits further research elaborates on the debate concerning women's and men's standpoints toward war, whether they be based in essential nature or acquired attitudes. Would women, if represented in greater numbers in policy-making positions, change security policy? Some maintain that if women were in key political and military positions, such as the Secretary of Defense or on the Joint Chiefs of Staff in the case of the U.S., nations would be less likely to go to war or would at least exercise greater attempts at diplomacy and conflict resolution. However, we have numerous examples of women political leaders who have pursued militaristic policies and led their nations to war. Another argument suggests that simply having a woman in a key position is not the issue; rather a "critical mass" of women would make a difference in decision-making. Since so few women make security policy around the world, this question remains unanswered.

VI. GENDERED SOCIAL RELATIONS AS A CAUSE OF WAR

Perhaps the most significant issue raised by the scholarship on women and war and by the women who have experienced war concerns the link between militarism and patriarchy. This relationship is dialectical: militarism relies on patriarchal patterns and patriarchy relies on militarization. First let us consider how militarism relies on patriarchy. Militaries rely on male privilege and female subordination in order to function. That privilege takes both structural and cultural forms. Structurally, because women have less political, social, and economic power in society, they also have less power to make security decisions and very little power in military institutions. Poor women are compelled by their economic need to occupy low-ranking positions in the defense industry or the military. Other poor

women are coerced into serving as prostitutes near military bases.

Cynthia Enloe has shown that these structural conditions are complemented by cultural ones: militaries need men and women to behave in gender-stereotypic ways. Women should behave in maternal fashion, they should need men to protect them, and their wartime experience should be sexualized. Men should feel that in order to prove their masculinity, they should fight and generally support their nation going to war. Men should take on exceptionally masculine behaviors and attitudes through their military training.

The complementary argument suggests that in order for societies to be patriarchal or male-dominated, military values must predominate—masculine values must be privileged over feminine values, and masculine values become equated with military ones. Those values become evident in various cultural forms, including gendered, militarized rhetoric, in popular culture, and in religious symbols. Gendered social relations encourage militarism, and militarism in turn relies on gendered social relations. As Betty Reardon has argued, without sexism, the "war system" cannot function, and sexism is based on militarized notions of masculinity. For persons concerned about war and about sexism, this suggests that these interlocking problems must be addressed simultaneously.

Also See the Following Articles

FEMINIST AND PEACE PERSPECTIVES ON WOMEN • GENDER STUDIES • MILITARISM • MILITARY CULTURE • SEXUAL ASSAULT • SOCIAL CONTROL AND VIOLENCE • STRUCTURAL VIOLENCE • TOTAL WAR, SOCIAL IMPACT OF • WARRIORS, ANTHROPOLOGY OF • WOMEN, VIOLENCE AGAINST

Bibliography

Adams, D. et al. (1992). The Seville statement on violence. *Peace Review, 4*(3), 20–22.
Beilstein, J. (1995). The role of women in United Nations peacekeeping. *Women 2000*, 1, 1–10. New York: United Nations Division for the Advancement of Women.
Boulding, E. (1995). "Feminist inventions in the art of peacemaking: A century overview." *Peace and Change, 20*(4), 408–439.
D'Amico, F. (1996). Feminist Perspectives on Women Warriors. *Peace Review, 3*(3), 379–384.
Elshtain, J. B. (1987). *Women and war*. New York: Basic Books.
Enloe, C. (1993). *The morning after: Sexual politics at the end of the cold war*. Berkeley: University of California Press.
Forbes Martin, S. (1992). *Refugee women*. London: Zed Books.
Fraser, A. (1988). *The warrior queens*. London: Mandarin.

Hauchler, I., & Kennedy, P. M. (1994). *Global trends*. New York: Continuum.

Holm, J. (1992). *Women in the military: An unfinished revolution*. Novato, CA: Presidio.

Lorentzen, L. A., & Turpin, J. (Eds.) (1998). *The women and war reader*. New York: New York University Press.

Nikolic-Ristanovic, V. "War and violence against women." In J. Turpin & L. A. Lorentzen (Eds.), *The gendered new world order: Militarism, development, and the environment*. New York: Routledge.

Nordstom, C. (1996). "Girls behind the (front) lines. *Peace Review*, 8(3), 403–410.

Peace Pledge Union (1997). "Women and peace resource guide. London: Peace Pledge Union.

Peterson, V. S., & Runyan, A. S. (1993). *Global gender issues*. Boulder, CO: Westview Press.

Reardon, B. (1993). *Women and peace*. Albany, NY: SUNY Press.

Ruddick, S. (1990). *Maternal thinking: Towards a politics of peace*. London: Women's Press.

Scheper-Hughes, N. (1992). *Death without weeping: The violence of everyday life in Brazil*. Berkeley: University of California Press.

Segal, M. (1995). Women's military roles cross-nationally: Past, present, and future. *Gender and Society*, 9(6), 757–775.

Stiehm, J. H. (1989). *Arms and the enlisted woman*. Philadelphia: Temple University Press.

Tenhula, J. (1991). *Voices From southeast Asia*. New York: Holmes and Meier.

Turpin, J. & Lorentzen, L. A. (Eds.) (1996). *The gendered new world order: Militarism, development, and the environment*. New York: Routledge.

Vickers, J. (1993). *Women and war*. London: Zed Books.

Woollacott, A. (1994). *On her their lives depend: Munitions workers in the great war*. Berkeley: University of California Press.

Women, Violence against

Mimi Ajzenstadt

The Hebrew University of Jerusalem

GLOSSARY

Continuum of Violence Violence against women as well as the societal response to it are seen as being located on a continuum of male power over women along with a variety of economic, psychological, and social mechanisms of control.

Contextualized Approaches to Violence against Women Violence against women is perceived not as a rare and deviant phenomenon, but as a predictable and common dimension of the combination of patriarchy and social structures that form the environment supporting and legitimizing violence.

Definition of Violence against Women as a Social Problem The recognition of this behavior as troublesome and thus as deserving of official response, which is expressed by its discussion in the public agenda and culture, the allocation of funds, and the establishment of programs addressing the behavior.

Medicalization of Violence against Women A process whereby violent behavior is given a medical meaning and is defined in terms of health and illness. Medical practice becomes a vehicle for eliminating or controlling the problem.

Social Control of Women Regulations and programs that intervene and monitor the lives of individuals, aiming to secure adherence to social norms.

State and Women's Role State's protection of women who were victimized is contingent upon their roles as mothers.

Victim Provocation The assumption that the rape victim should be blamed for the crime. Rape is considered to occur in situations where the victim's behavior is understood by the offender as inviting or signaling her readiness for sexual contact.

Victimization Surveys Empirical techniques attempting to measure the prevalence of a criminal phenomenon. Women are asked anonymously to indicate whether they became victims in the past period, e.g., 6 months.

Women's Responsibility for Violence against Them Perceptions that women must monitor their behavior since they are responsible for preventing their victimization. If they are unsuccessful, women are blamed for initiating the violence and their suffering is questioned, ignored, or trivialized.

VIOLENCE AGAINST WOMEN includes acts of verbal or physical force, coercion, or omission that cause physical, psychological, or other harm to girls and to women and that force them to remain in a subordinate position.

Violence against women takes numerous patterns and expressions, but they all share common modes of female victimization, making this behavior a distinct phenomenon. This behavior relates to all women in intimate relationships, including marriage, heterosexual common law marriage, and dating as well as lesbian relationships.

I. SCOPE OF THE PROBLEM

During the early 1970s, various social groups in North America, Europe, and Australia set out to attract public attention to the phenomenon of violence against women. Representing varying ideological beliefs and proposing a range of explanations and solutions to the problem, these groups promulgated a distinct discourse, which is continuously expanding. The discourse includes a wide range of behaviors defined as violent acts against women, theoretical explanations presenting psychological, biological, cultural, and social reasons for such behavior and a variety of legal, social, and professional programs, plans, and policies responding to the phenomenon.

Initial definitions of the behavior focused mainly on damaging physical violence directed toward women by their spouses, partners, and strangers. Later the focus of the discourse expanded from this limited perspective to look at a wider range of problems, from coercive sex and physical abuse to psychological abuse and nonviolent forms of sexual coercion in which women are assailed by a combination of cultural factors rather than by a specific individual. During the 1980s and 1990s, behaviors such as sexual abuse, marital rape, pornography, incest, battery, sexual harassment, obscene phone calls to women, date rape, flashing, courtship rape, stalking, and sexual murder were brought to the forefront of the concern of investigators, experts, and policy-makers. Moreover, wider cultural and social processes, such as economic coercion and general patriarchal relations, and professional practices, such as psychosurgery, lobotomy, abortion, forced cesarean sections, venereal diseases legislation, and sterilization, came to be considered violence against women.

This extension in the scope of the behavior reflects changes in theoretical approaches dealing with the cause of violent behavior. Until the 1970s, most explanations were grounded in the psychological and biological disciplines, focusing on traits of individuals. The 1980s and 1990s saw the development of new perspectives that contextualized behaviors and located them within wider social, cultural, and political circum-

stances. New feminist theories challenged the narrowness of early definitions associated solely with injury to the body and claimed that this very association reflects the way women are perceived in society—in a way that focuses on their bodies, leading to the definition of women as reproductive agents, lacking social context. They resisted the attribution of the behavior to both specific individual male abusers and female victims. Moreover, some feminist writers criticized the traditional separation between victims and nonvictims and claimed that violence against women should be seen as an actual threat relating to and endangering all women.

Drawing on social-Marxist perspectives, other scholars claimed that women of color were ignored and that their experiences were not included within the discourse relating to violence against women. They called upon researchers and policy-makers to develop new concepts that would enable these unique experiences to be accounted for within the discourse, thus widening the discourse and referring to the class and racial/ethnic dimensions as part of the social control over women in society (Table I).

Over the years, numerous studies have been conducted with the purpose of measuring the prevalence of various forms of violence against women. These studies faced methodological difficulties, since women avoid reporting their abuse to the official legal, medical, and welfare agencies due to shame, fear, sense of responsibility for their behavior, lack of confidence in state agencies to help their situation, and unwillingness to expose themselves and their private lives to public investigation and control. These studies led researchers

TABLE I

Social and Legal Approaches to Violence against Women

Period	Approaches
Prior to 1970	Early campaigns against domestic violence, mainly by members of women's rights movements
Since 1970	Campaigns to define violence against women as a social problem and initiatives of mainly women groups to assist women through organizations located outside the state
Mid-1970s	Law reforms and new regulations designed to change discrimination against women by the police and the courts
Mid-1980s	Evaluation of the new policies lead to a disappointment from legal changes and lead the search for other solutions such as community-based programs.

to estimate that in the U.S., for example, more women have been raped than is reflected in crime statistics.

In order to overcome this difficulty and to try to estimate the prevalence of the phenomenon, some studies administer victimization surveys and others rely on samples of women who seek help at battered women's shelters, hospitals, or other crisis services. Those scholars concluded that most violence against women can be considered as "hidden violence," which is not reflected in official crime statistics. For example, according to Koss, in the U.S. 38 women out of 1000 are raped at least once in their life. This rate is 10–15 times greater than the official criminal justice statistics.

The Canadian National Survey estimated that in the 1980s and 1990s 3 of 10 women who are married or had been married in the past experienced at least one incident of physical or sexual violence by their husbands or partners. This survey also confirms that a woman's abuse is rarely a one-time occurrence and that young women (18–24 years old) are at the highest risk of being abused or assaulted. In England scholars inferred that assault of women is the second most common form of violent crime in that country and that women's experiences of physical and sexual violence are most likely to be within intimate relationships with men, including family members, known to them. The Papua New Guinea Law Reform Committee found that 17% of wives in the urban areas needed hospital treatment for injuries related to battering. In Bangladesh, assassination of wives by husbands accounts for 50% of all murders. In Peru, one-third of women's visits to hospital emergency units are as victims of abuse. Over two-thirds of Korean women are beaten regularly by their husbands. It is estimated, further, that a substantial number of women from developing countries fall prey to sex trafficking in their efforts to find legitimate employment in other countries as overseas contract workers.

II. SOCIAL CONSTRUCTION OF THE DISCOURSE

During the late 19th and early 20th centuries, strong public campaigns against the abuse of women were led in western countries, mainly by the first wave of feminists, demanding to stop or at least control this behavior. The first societies established to confront family violence focused first on child abuse, but they soon were dealing with wife abuse. While such calls resulted in local legal and reform policies, the early waves of concern faded away, and the abuse of women became less visible for many decades during the 20th century.

The movement to define violence against women as a crime and as a "social problem" started in western Europe, North America, Australia, and New Zealand in the 1970s and became global during the 1980s. As a result of public and official activities, first rape and then other violent and abusive behaviors were beginning to be interpreted not as a private sorrow but as a public issue. The redefinition of violence against women as a matter for public concern was advanced mainly by various feminist groups who established consciousness-raising frameworks (through which the experiences of battered women were put on the public agenda), including rape crisis centers, refuges and shelters for battered women, counseling services, and women's aid groups. Chiswick Women's Aid, established in England in 1971, was the first widely publicized shelter.

Moreover, various movements calling upon their governments to reform rape laws were established, and as a result parliamentary committees investigating police policy and procedures and the existing laws regarding rape and domestic violence were formed. In addition, during the 1970s and the 1980s, a number of popular books were published describing the experiences of battered women in the family and later on in the workplace. The mass media played a major role in bringing the phenomenon to the knowledge of the public, and popular and special-interest magazines published reports on sexual coercion and sexual harassment. In her study of the role of the American mass media in the creation of public attention to violent behavior against women, Tierney concludes that until 1976, the media in the U.S. paid little attention to this issue. Ironically, "domestic violence" referred to riots and terrorism. During the mid-1970s, wife-beating became a "newsworthy" subject for the media as it was controversial, mixing elements of violence and social relations. It served as a point of departure for the discussion of such issues as feminism, inequality, and family life and at the same time was used as entertainment in the media industry.

During the process that led to the reconceptualization of violence against women, feminists created "coalitions of interests" with other social and political groups. Such a coalition, for example, was created in the campaign to change rape laws when feminist groups joined forces with human rights activists concerned with victims' rights and the victims' role in the trial process. In addition, during the 1970s, various groups called upon their governments to adopt "back to justice" policies to focus on the offense and not on extralegal considerations when imposing sentences. Sharing this approach, feminists called upon judges to focus on the offense and ignore psychological and social circumstances used in trials to legitimize the offense, which often led to light punishments.

The process that led to the interpretation of violence against women as a social problem was influenced by various professional, political, and ideological developments that took place during the 1960s and the 1970s. From the end of the 1960s, new social approaches to the family and relations within the family developed and the family was perceived as going through a "crisis." Familial violence was seen as a symptom of pathological relationships within the "disintegrating" family. This period is characterized by conservative attempts to maintain the family unit as a necessary factor within the social structure; women were encouraged to stay with their husbands for the sake of family unity, even when they experienced abuse from their partners. At the same time, during the post-World War II period, the parenting approach, which encouraged child-centered parenting, considered violent coercion in the family to be less tolerable than in the past. Also during this time the family was exposed to increasing professional intervention, which revealed "hidden" behavior to the public eye.

The 1950s and the 1960s witnessed a decline of ideas about modesty and privacy as well as support of a more "confessional" mode of behavior. Two decades later, within this new social mode and with the help of mental health professionals and others in the medical community, the abusers themselves were redefined as victims who required treatment, guidance, sympathy, and assistance. This approach helped to legitimize abusers' violence, which no longer had to be hidden. Medical practitioners looked for "new" areas for intervention. Violence against women became an arena for struggle for the ownership of such diverse areas as legal, financial, political, professional health, and welfare issues. Many providers of services began to "invest" in the problem—for which experts, it was believed, should be brought in to find solutions.

III. CONTENT OF THE DISCOURSE

A. Theoretical Perspectives

1. Psychological Approaches

Between the 1960s and the mid-1970s, the dominant academic and cultural approaches perceived violent behavior against women as originating in uncontrolled desires and drives of certain individuals. Those early investigations of wife-beating and physical abuse employed a psychodynamic model of abuse and violence and attempted to identify pathological personality traits and character disorders that caused people to physically attack their family members. Psychodynamic researchers focused on internal defense systems and the presence of mental illness or psychopathology leading to impaired ego functioning. Abusive men were thus labeled as passive–dependent, infantile, lacking impulse control, obsessive–compulsive, paranoid, having a borderline personality, passive–aggressive, and pathological. Other psychologists, who attempted to construct personality typologies to account for abusive and violent behavior, held the view that sexual aggression originated from having a strong, maternal mother and a weak father. Certain studies tried to find links between violent behavior and other deviant behaviors such as drug use, alcoholism, and involvement in criminal behavior or links between physical violence and lower levels of rational thinking and negative attitudes toward battered women.

From the end of the 1980s, this focus on abusers led to the proliferation of programs for batterers run by ex-batterers, the clergy, the military, and local men's or women's groups and sometimes even by shelters for abused wives. These programs used psychoeducation and psychotherapeutic approaches. Common to those approaches was the assumption that once the batterer resolved his past and current injuries, he would be able to control his behavior. In the U.S., Canada, and Australia abusive men were being "diverted" into treatment programs, and all criminal charges against them were dropped if they completed the treatment. Critics of these programs observed that the diversion option was allocated only to "privileged" offenders, those who belong to the middle class. They were generally diverted to private treatment facilities, such as alcoholism clinics or private psychiatrists where records of attendance are rarely kept, while lower-class batterers were either sent to jail or routed into state-run services. Other scholars who challenged these psychological perspectives claimed that psychological studies of convicted sex offenders, for example, uniformly failed to demonstrate any association between psychiatric diagnosis and sexually assaultive behavior. Some studies found that the great majority of convicted offenders did not suffer from psychiatric conditions, psychological disorders, or severe mental retardation, which were all used to explain their offenses and were invoked to diminish criminal responsibility.

While these explanations focused on male abusers, other theoretical approaches centered on female victims and their psychological traits and disorders. Attempting to understand why certain wives "choose" to stay in abusive marriages and/or seek assistance from outside institutions for a private problem that "normally" should be resolved between two "independent" adults, these approaches saw battered wives as suffering from a range of problems such as low self-esteem, emotional dependency, poor self-image, passivity, or oversubmissiveness. For some specialists, women who experience violence in their relationships are afflicted with relationship addiction and thus choose dangerous husbands and dangerous situations. Other experts used the term "learned helplessness" to describe the process through which women were socialized from their childhood not to be autonomous and to accept rape and abuse-supportive attitudes and beliefs. These women were represented as powerless and unable and unwilling to act or help themselves. Others compared the relations developed between the abused wife and her husband to the relations developed between hostages and hostage-takers, concluding that abused wives developed the "Stockholm syndrome," which includes positive feelings on the part of the hostage toward the captor. These approaches were institutionalized during the 1980s when new categories were added to the *International Classification of Disease:* "battered spouse" and "battered women" and, later on, the specific sociopsychological category "the battered woman syndrome." In this way, the phenomenon of battered women became an arena for intervention since it identified women experiencing persistent violence as having unique personality disorders and as deserving of public and expert concern, requiring specific therapeutic intervention.

This approach ignored the fact that most women are unable to leave battering marriages since they are economically dependent on their husbands and have neither the job skills nor the opportunities necessary for financial independence. Many scholars noticed, further, that battered women experience a range of posttraumatic psychological responses to abuse. They suffer from depression, irritation, and lack of sleep; experience difficulties in sustaining relationships; and become paranoid and frightened as a response to their condition. The impact of harassment at work leads as well to a variety of problems manifested in such areas as somatic health, decline in work productivity and quality, and low satisfaction and commitment. Those traits and patterns of behaviors developed as a response to the woman's abuse and did not exist before the battering.

Similarly it was found that in some cases when psychiatrists prescribed long-term psychiatric hospitalization, psychosurgical operations, electroconvulsive therapy, and lecotomy to women, these women had experienced some form of physical, sexual, or psychological abuse by men prior to their admission to the hospital. These conditions caused the women to be depressed and enabled some psychiatrists to label them as sick and thus their complaints about violence were ignored, as it was argued that sick women could not comprehend reality clearly. Being a victim led many women to isolate themselves from the wider community, restrict their lives, and confine themselves to a particular place or activity. They often retreated into their homes as safe places, where their resultant dependency on men made them even more vulnerable to abuse and thus they felt trapped and like failures. Since most women were socialized to believe that marital happiness and stability are the primary responsibility of women, many battered women felt shame and even responsible for their condition.

Some scholars, however, claim that women are not passive and that they adopt ways to enable them to make sense of their situation and resist it. Some women use various mental techniques to make it possible for them to neutralize violence against them; some appeal to the salvation ethic and identify with the role of the woman as serving others; others perceive the battering as an event beyond the control of the abuser. Women deny their own injury or victimization, some deny the existence of practical options to assist them, and, finally, some appeal to higher loyalties and see violence against them as being part of a religious or traditional commitment.

There are women who adopt various techniques and strategies to protect themselves. They learn from experience how to avoid the hitting or how to resolve the problem at the beginning. These survival techniques include such measures as nonactive response, physical or verbal resistance, screaming, crying, shouting, or escape. Most women try to reason with the abuser, others try to contact relatives, friends, and various legal, medical, and social agencies.

2. Institutional Explanations

During the 1980s, academic research focused on macrosocial elements and the dynamics of interrelations that were perceived as leading to violence against women. This was a functionalist system approach, which was used to explain violence as originating in sick, weak, and violence-prone family systems within which violence between the cohabitants existed. Using a Parsonian framework, those scholars claimed that intimate relationships that are systematically disequilibrated produce frustration, negatively affecting the future quality of the relationships. Individuals experiencing strained relationships in family life adapt to them in order to preserve the relationship or the self and may respond in violent behavior.

Straus and Gelles, who conducted numerous studies attempting to explain the nature of the relations between wife abuse and the family institution, assumed that the source of the violence is located within the family and occurs when tensions exist between its members. For them, wives and husbands behave very much alike in their mutual assaults. These findings, which attributed equal amounts of violence to both partners and considered violence as a problem of both sexes, became a locus of academic debate. Leading feminist scholars such as Dobash and Dobash claimed that there are large qualitative differences in the nature of the violence taking place between wives and husbands. For example, men usually initiate the attack and women respond. Women's violence often takes a drastic form of self-defense or escape.

Other scholars broadened their research beyond the family to include the community and attempted to identify the relations between wife abuse and the subsystems both within and outside the family institutions. They noted that violence is controlled to some extent by a social network of friends, neighbors, and relatives who can help control and discipline women by legitimizing the violent behavior. At the same time, however, such networks can set limits to violent behavior. In some communities, extended families are havens of care and concern and sometimes are in a better position to intervene against abuse than social and legal services. Finally, some researchers claim that wider social and political transformations affect intimate relations. They argue that the move toward a more sexually egalitarian society may be stressful for both men and women. Men may be responding to loss of dominance and privilege with violence.

In the 1970s, the prevalent model emphasized structural familial arrangements that produced stress and conflict and yielded numerous programs that attempted to prevent and treat family violence. In the various treatment techniques, couples were taught methods that would enable them to identify expressions of stress and anger and positive ways to control the relationship and express themselves. They were also shown strategies to interrupt and redirect the cycle of anger and ways to develop high-quality relationship feelings. Evaluative studies, attempting to estimate the impact of these programs, were impeded by a range of methodological problems, since most of them lacked comparison groups and a clear definition of what could be considered successful. Many studies considered a decrease in violence as a measure of success. However, it is important to note that while for some women this decrease might be an important change, for others it may not remove the constant fear generated by few but severe violent events.

3. Medicalization of Violence against Women

Previous theoretical perspectives defined violence against women in medical terms, thus leading to the *medicalization* of the behavior. The male abuser, the female victim, and the family structure were portrayed as suffering from pathological disorders and thus requiring treatment. Such medicalization is evident, for example, in the reaction to sex offenders who were considered to be sick and deviant and not criminals. The term "sexual psychopath," which was coined as early as the 1930s, was used to describe the violent male offender who was unable to control himself. Similarly, the definition of rape in medical terms reduced the rapists' responsibilities, and rape was reconceptualized from the perpetrator's point of view. He was described as a sexually ineffectual, reasonably hard-working, "mama's boy" with a tendency to drink excessively and thus should not bear full responsibility for his involvement in abusive behavior.

Medical rhetoric is not restricted to experts only, but is employed as well by other agents. Various studies have indicated that in cases brought before the court for violence committed by males toward women, judges used medical terminology to explain violence as due to a sickness of the accused or the complainant and thus to justify light punishment or acquittal.

Within the medical community, women's victimization was often attributed to her involvement in other criminal or deviant behaviors. Thus, abused women were portrayed as drug users, alcoholics, or, in more general terms as suffering from one of a myriad of "female disorders" such as depression, hysteria, or hypochondria. Moreover, they were represented as aggressive, masculine, sexually frigid, masochistic, castrators, or sadistic. These descriptions provided medical practitioners with labels they could use to "organize" a history of otherwise unrelated "accidents" to explain their injuries and their problems with husbands and cohabitants. In this way, battering was seen as a tragic but inevitable consequence of their more basic problems. In the same way, studies in the U.S. that looked at how physicians in public hospitals handled abuse victims, concluded that these physicians focused on the "mechanism of injury": how the blow impacted on the body, not on the person, and thus the entire battering event was reduced to an interaction between the male's hands and the female's body.

Other studies claimed that social workers defined the problem of marital violence in terms of child care. In this way, the welfare of the woman is subordinated to that of her children. Women are encouraged to sever their ties to their partner only in order to prevent child abuse. Sometimes, they are encouraged to seek reconciliation and to continue the relationship for the sake of the children. The maintenance of the marriage became a therapeutic end in itself. Moreover, battered women and their needs were assessed through a normative prism, examining their attitudes and performance in terms of traditional sex roles. Thus the woman's failure to behave according to the traditionally accepted norms, such as keeping the house clean, was regarded as the source of the violent reactions of the husband. In this way, social workers regarded women as adjuncts of their families and contributed to the maintaining of the gendered social order. This medicalization process led further to women's social powerlessness and to the neglect of wider social, ideological elements and contributed further to the silencing of women, since their valid accounts and justifications were obscured, redefined, or ignored.

B. Contextualized Explanations: Feminist Approaches

Beginning in the 1970s, feminist scholarship analyzing the phenomenon of violence against women shifted the focus of the inquiry from biology and psychology to society. Emphasizing the social and cultural factors involved and the societal reaction to it, feminists challenged the approaches that saw violence against women as manifestations of innate sexual drives, uncontrollable biological urges, crimes of frustrated attraction, or as acts originating in victim provocation. For feminist researchers, violence against women was conceived as part of socially structured hierarchy of power in a gendered society. These new approaches focused on the subordination of women in the realm of the social sphere where this condition was seen as part of a socially produced and reproduced gender asymmetry.

For early feminist theorists such as Brownmiller, rape was interconnected with the maintenance of power relations between men and women—relations which were part of a structure to keep men in a position of dominance over women. Rape was seen as a process of intimidation that kept all women wary of the power of men over women. They saw all sexual violence as hav-

ing a common characteristic since those behaviors involve men using a variety of forms of abuse, coercion, and force to control women, and as being part of the continuum of sexual violence—a continuum that links particular forms of sexual violence to more common male behaviors.

During the 1980s, feminist theorists criticized this line of inquiry, linking power, violence, and sexuality, claiming that it ignored cultural and historical variations in definitions and conditions related to gender, sexuality, and sexual behavior. Instead, feminists of this decade attempted to contextualize the conditions and forms of women's oppression within various institutional structures. Such an analysis saw sexual violence as entailing multiple, often hidden, power relations and of changing gender roles within the contexts of the family and institutions of the state to reinforce female dependency. MacKinnon, a key theorist in this stream of ideas, claimed that the social construction of "normal" male sexuality as being aggressive and that the assertion of dominance had to be central to the analysis of rape and violence against women. The state itself, through its cultural, social, and legal institutions prompted violence against women by institutionalizing male dominance and by avoiding punishing abusers. For MacKinnon, heterosexuality itself, not only sexual violence, should be interpreted as an example of what she calls the "eroticization of dominance," where violence against women is sexualized and legitimized.

Other scholars saw violence against women as originating and, at the same time, reinforcing social structural differences between males and females in terms of economic vulnerability, with norms and values favoring the husband's role as head of the household. In this way, violence against women was interpreted as one aspect of gender subordination and as one of many social phenomena characterizing the gender organization of the patriarchal society. This attitude toward women provided sexual scripts presenting sexual coercion as a culturally normative behavior and a source of sexual pleasure for men and, to some extent, for women.

For some researchers, the accounts and explanations given by batterers and rapists for their behavior reflect power structure relations and the dominance of males over females that further legitimize violence against women. Examining batterers' explanations for their activities, scholars pointed out that abusers neutralize their violence, excusing themselves from full responsibility, blaming the victims, and denying their wrongfulness and the physical or psychological harm caused to the victim. Some rapists even saw themselves as behaving nicely toward the victim and predicted that if they were not so nice, the attack could have been even worse. Those justifications are socially and culturally constructed and the same scripts that motivate "normal" sexual behavior also provide a potential vocabulary of motives for the rapist, who does not invent his explanations for his behavior, but derives them from generally accepted cultural norms.

Recently, the phenomenon of violence by women against other women in intimate relationships has challenged feminist theories about violence against women. Some scholars claim that male and female abusers suffer from pathological traits that are expressed by violence. Sex role theorists, however, see violence against women as a gendered activity. Women who batter other women have internalized the norms of heterosexism that underlie the sex role system and behave in socially constructed masculine ways. Various studies highlight the complex situation in which abused victims of intralesbian relationships are situated. They are doubly exposed to rigid negative social responses: first as battered women and second as lesbians. This victimization is evident, for example, in situations where they seek help from feminist groups established to help abused women. Sometimes, these groups refuse to help lesbian victims in order to avoid taking sides in a struggle between two women. At other times, these groups deny support services, such as access to safe houses, since these shelters rely on state support and do not want to support lesbian women, who are so negatively stigmatized by society. Some feminists thus call for the development of new theoretical explanations and practical solutions that would be able to coexist with current feminist theories and policy but be more sensitive to individualistic experiences.

IV. RACE AND CLASS DIMENSIONS OF THE DISCOURSE

During the 1980s and the 1990s, voices were heard criticizing the dominant feminist perspectives about violence against women, its origins, its results, and its cultural and social meaning. Various feminists have claimed that throughout the debate on domestic violence, race and ethnicity generally have been absent, due mainly to the exclusion of women of color in feminist leadership and scholarship. Moreover, only a limited empirical literature addressing the experiences of women of color exists and thus concepts relating to their specific cultural and political circumstances were not used in the explanations and policies addressing

violence against women. The discourse did not construct race as a factor and used a universal rhetoric that saw all women as oppressed, ignoring the unique differences of specific groups. This monolithic perspective did not recognize the diversity and complexity of women's experiences.

Claiming that the discourse should expand to examine the intersection of multiple structures of domination, various scholars suggested that while women from all backgrounds are exposed to abuse, membership in marginalized social or ethnic groups informs the responses to violence against women by the state, by professionals, and by the voluntary service sector. Such differences in women's positions in relation to the power structures of race, class, and sexuality can be found as early as in the colonial period in the U.S., when the rape cases most likely to come to court were those in which the perpetrator was from a social class lower than that of the victim. Black men who were accused of sexually attacking White women received the harshest penalties, often capital punishment or lynching. While the legislation was written in general terms, its general application was influenced by the power hierarchy: offenders or suspected persons arrested by the police were generally from the lower strata of society, mainly immigrants and members of marginalized ethnic groups. In the modern era, the class and race dimension of the societal reaction toward violence against women is evident in Canada, for example, where it was found that most offenders arrested for abusing their wives have low-level jobs, if employed at all, and little education. Some researchers concluded that in South Africa, working-class males abuse and assault girls and women as a result of their own economic and social subordination. Apartheid and capitalism limited the power of the Black male of the lower strata. Oppressed both in terms of race and of social class, their violent behavior toward family members was socially sanctioned and legitimized, as it was seen as being the only arena where they were able to express their masculinity and exercise any dominance.

Differing experiences of women members in marginalized groups is evident, for example, in the case of Israeli Arab women, battered by their husbands or relatives. They experience difficulties in requesting help from state institutions. Living in a traditional patriarchal society where women are subordinate to men, they are exposed to extreme abuse and isolation for daring to challenge family values by actively coping with the violence and leaving the home. Women who seek help from the judicial system are usually faced with religious court judges who encourage them to resolve "their" problems along the lines of "family honor," "family reputation," and family stability and unity. Similar approaches characterize other ethical and national minority groups.

Aboriginal women in Canada, who live in small communities, are reluctant to resist or report their abusers due to their fear of gossip, intimidation, and segregation from supporters of the abusers or their own families. This isolation cannot be solved through the connection with judicial, welfare, or medical authorities and services, which usually are staffed with nonnative practitioners who lack an understanding of the specific circumstances of the aboriginal women. Moreover, many of those in positions of power are influenced by stereotypes portraying aboriginal women as sexually promiscuous and not deserving of state protection. Thus, complaints are not taken seriously or the solution is not suited to the women's social and cultural circumstances. Finally, it was found that the police and the courts are lenient with aboriginal males who attack aboriginal women and thus when a complaint finally reaches the court it will usually be dismissed or the abuser will be punished in a way that allows him to return to the community and continue his violence.

Another manifestation of a specific ethnic experience can be found in the practice of genital mutilation which physically, psychologically, and socially affects more than 80 million women worldwide, mainly in Africa and in the near-eastern countries. It is estimated that at least 2 million girls are mutilated each year and the mutilations are often performed by other women. While some groups support legal sanctions prohibiting genital mutilation, other groups claim that such laws often punish only the women concerned: both the women who undergo the operation and those who perform them. Another group, supported by a growing number of feminists, condemns these practices and sees them as an expression of male power over women, but objects to penalizing women in support of their rights. They suggest, instead, using various techniques to increase awareness of the practice and discourage its use; for example, parents who refuse to expose their daughters to such practices or those who refuse to marry their sons to girls who have been sexually mutilated.

Another form of violence against women is brideburning, or dowry murder which is exercised mainly in India. In these cases, married women are being murdered—usually burned to death—by husbands or in-laws whose demands for a larger dowry from the bride's family were refused. Various studies indicate that though dowry murders are publicly condemned, this practice has not disappeared.

Historical studies show that in Europe, European colonies, and in countries such as China and Bermuda and the Alaskan territory, unwanted female children were killed during infancy. Among the Alaskan natives, the prevalence of female infanticide was indicated by demographic trends in which the childhood sex ratio was heavily biased in favor of males. In Alaska, family survival depended on hunting prowess and for this reason many female babies were killed. Currently these practices have been replaced by the abortion of female fetuses in some Chinese and Indian communities when the sex of the unborn child is determined through modern prenatal diagnostic techniques. Despite laws passed in India, for example, in 1988 against the misuse of sex determination tests, female infanticide continues.

Being members of a specific marginalized group often exposes women to sexual abuse by the sovereign males. Such harm is legitimized and seen as part of the prevailing relationship between rulers and subjects. During the colonial period in the U.S., White males raped Black girls and women. In some places, rape of Black women facilitated a financial gain since their babies were sold and the profits were collected by their masters. Only recently, the combination of gender and ethnic inferiority led to the rape of more than 20,000 Muslim women in Bosnia as part of the political conflict. Many women were held in "rape camps" where they were raped repeatedly and forced to bear Serbian children against their will (Table II).

TABLE II

The Source of the Problem and Proposed and Actual Resolution

Source of the problem	Resolution
Pathological problems of specific individuals and family relations	Physical, psychological treatment aiming to identify pathologies, offering counseling, medical care, and strategies to handle conflicts in marital relations
Male power and dominance	Assistance and help to specific female victims
	Demands for law reforms
	Equality between males and females
Wide social structure and patriarchal ideology	Questions about the transformative potential of laws and the state
	Empowerment of women
	Attempts at creating community-based programs
	Wider social change

V. INSTITUTIONALIZATION OF THE DISCOURSE

The activities of various groups, mainly feminists, who called upon their governments to change women's powerless positions led to reformist efforts, aiming to recognize the inherent criminality of male violence against women. In several countries, efforts led to changes in rape laws and legal procedures relating to domestic violence and sexual harassment at work as well as to changes in police practices. While these reforms differed from one society to the next, most of these legislative, policy, and procedural changes aimed to encourage police action against domestic violence and to enhance the protection available to women, convincing them to file charges against their abusers.

A. Police Response to Violence against Women

Most laws have expanded the power of the police to arrest abusers and have empowered their units to issue protective orders in cases where a potential victim reasonably fears violence or harassment. In some countries, mandatory arrests and procharge polices have been established. The police are authorized to bring a charge of assault whenever the evidence permits, thus removing the onus of action from women. Police training in the area of domestic violence has been expanded. In the Netherlands, for example, an active prosecution policy has been administrated, combined with attempts to improve police performance. In the U.S., various laws to enhance the power of police to arrest batterers have been passed. Such legislation allows officers to arrest persons for misdemeanor assaults on the basis of probable cause in domestic violence cases in spite of the fact that in all other misdemeanor assaults, officers must either witness the crime or have a signed complaint by a citizen in order to make an arrest. In Brazil, Colombia, Uruguay, Peru, Costa Rica, and Argentina women-only police units have been established to encourage women to complain about violence.

Various studies have been conducted in order to estimate the impact of these new policies. Most of these studies concluded that in various countries more women are being treated with greater sensitivity by police officers, and an atmosphere has been created in which more cases of violence against women were reported. The establishment of women-only units led to a sharp increase in complaints. However, at the same time, there was a high proportion (around 49% in some countries) of recorded cases that were categorized as "no crime" and so were not recorded as offenses. Other cases were frequently dropped between the time of the report and the trial. On many occasions police officers were reluctant to arrest the male partner. It was found that the police used inappropriate crisis intervention techniques and failed to refer victims to welfare or medical agencies providing aid.

It is important to note that in Canada, for example, an increase in complaints by women was shown after the introduction of new reforms and policies. However, this increase can be explained by the comparison to nonsexual crime arrests, which increased as well. In fact, such a comparison indicated that the number of all cases of sexual assault was actually lower than that of violent nonsexual crimes. This increase can thus be seen as reflecting the trend toward law-and-order policies that characterized Canadian society at the end of the 1980s. Studies that examined the processing of rape/sexual assault cases in the U.S. found that extralegal variables, such as the age of the abused woman, her ethnicity, and her social class, were interconnected with the investigators' judgments concerning victim credibility and consent. Assessing the "relative legitimacy" of rape and sexual assault complaints, police officers tended to see young women and teenagers as less credible. Moreover, investigators assumed that women from lower socio-economic strata are characterized by a generally low level of morality, and thus sexual assaults were perceived as an expected feature of their lives.

Studies found that many police officers often hold traditional views about women's roles and expectations—perceptions that affect their decisions about the criminal nature of the behavior. For example, many investigators believe that women must make efforts to stay with their husbands and that they must conform to their role as mothers and wives and continue to see themselves as being inferior to their partners. In cases of domestic violence, the police tend to emphasize reconciliation rather than arrest and prosecution. Thus, the police are reluctant to define violence between husband and wife or cohabitants as crime. Using rhetoric that emphasizes privacy and sanctity, police officers see the home and family as being located outside the public concern and thus choose not to interfere in many complaints. According to these beliefs, women are regarded as responsible for their own victimization and thus the violent male is seen as noncriminal. Such an approach furnishes the police with a rationale for nonintervention in many abusive situations.

B. Courts' Response to Violence against Women

Various groups have called upon their governments to change legislation that legitimizes violence against women. But legal attitudes differ from one place to another. In some countries, laws make it almost impossible to prosecute violence against women. In Pakistan, for example, four male Muslims must testify that they witnessed a rape. Moreover, since 1979, sexual relationships outside the family are considered as a crime against the state, and women who fail to prove that they were victims of rape are jailed for adultery or fornication. In Latin America assault of a woman is defined as a crime only when the injury incapacitates the victim for a week or more. In India, an arrest can be made only when the injury is considered to be a "grievous harm," which includes permanent injuries such as loss of sight or hearing. In Latin America and some parts of Asia, before entering a charge of rape, the victim must be examined by forensic doctors, who receive patients only during very limited times. They are usually located only in the larger cities and thus it is very difficult for rural women to be examined and consequently they usually cannot prosecute their attackers. In many places the punishments for violent acts against women are minimal and light. In Peru, for example, the stiffest sentence for wife abuse is 30 days of community service.

Until the 1970s, in most countries of the western world, legally women could be raped by their husbands and have their sexual history questioned in court when they appeared as witnesses in rape and assault trials. During the 1970s and the 1980s, many countries introduced reforms to change the laws. Aiming to bring harsher punishments on aggressors and abusers and thus to encourage women to come forward, the new laws canceled the prior requirement of corroboration for the complaint of rape in order to facilitate prosecution. They included stiffer penalties and protected women while appearing in court as witnesses. Countries such as the Bahamas, Barbados, Malaysia, and Puerto Rico reformed their penal codes and criminalized domestic violence. In some countries, judges are authorized to require a man to leave his home and make him provide financial support to his family.

Many studies set out to assess the effects of law reforms and found that, in general, women were treated with more sensitivity by the court than previously. However, it was clear that the possibility of gaining a conviction had diminished. More than 50% of the cases that appeared before the courts did not result in a conviction. In many cases, the court downgraded or dismissed cases of men who abused women. Assaults against wives or female cohabitants have been marginalized and trivialized and most of them were diverted to the civil or the lower courts. The criminal justice system remains slow and unable to provide long-term protection to women. More women are being subjected to the unnecessary ordeal of an intensive interrogation and an exhausting medical examination and are frequently intimidated by their attackers, who are demanding that they drop the charges. They are denied adequate legal and counseling support, only to see the case against their assailant abandoned. Sometimes women who refuse to testify against these men are charged with contempt of court. They are coerced to undergo the humiliation of the court appearance, which them culminates in the dismissal of charges.

Moreover, while the courts did not address these women's positions as victims, they served as mechanisms of social control, judging them according to traditional societal norms and expectations and reinforcing traditional patriarchal beliefs by differentiating between "good" and "bad" women. Female victims who adhere to the moral codes designed by society, such as having sexual relations while married, having children, and so on, are usually constructed as innocent victims. At the same time, women whose social position or behavior is not seen as modest or conventional and pristine are blamed or not believed. This differential attitude is evident in Brazil, Costa Rica, Ecuador, and Guatemala, where the law defines certain sexual offenses as crimes only when they are committed against "honest"—that is, virginal—girls or women. In this way, the criminal justice system maintains and reinforces traditional family structure, couching the criminalization of "domestic violence" in terms of the importance of the nuclear family and the danger battering presents to this institution, not to the female victim. Moreover, the courts often offered relief and protection to women from their batterer husbands not on the basis of the women's needs, but on their role as mothers. In this way, the response of the criminal justice system, through its form, language, and substance, mirrored and strengthened the patriarchal values of the dominant society.

VI. THE STATE AND VIOLENCE AGAINST WOMEN

Changes in laws, regulations, and policies relating to violence against women and the implementation of these reforms raised questions about their influence on the nature of relations between women and the state. Some writers who saw the political arena as the appropriate mechanism, able to protect and assist female victims, claimed that increasing legal sanctions against abusers would empower battered women and discourage male abuse. Others claimed that the new powers allocated to the police and other control agents are symbolically important, since the state would be seen as signaling its disapproval of this behavior.

In spite of this, many feminists perceived it as debatable whether the existing legal system could support women and empower them. Many activists agreed that reforms in legislation cannot change the structural conditions that perpetuate male violence and women's economic dependence on violent males. Some have argued that the legal system is designed to maintain women's subordinate status within the nuclear family and the economy. The Canadian scholar Snider, for example, points to the lack of transformative potential of the criminal justice system, whose primary role it is to enhance social control. In order to achieve this aim, the law and the state depoliticize and delegitimize complainers, mainly by making them voiceless and powerless.

The state, through its various institutions and agencies, uses discretionary state power, which intervenes in the lives of women, especially those of marginal social status, exposing them to legal, medical, and welfare controls and regulations. In this way, the law and service agencies widen the net of control over a population who are already vulnerable to state regulation and discipline. Moreover, the tendency of these agencies to prefer reconciliation and encourage women to remain in abusive relations in order to maintain the family confines women to their homes and to their traditional duties. This process strengthens the separation between the private and the public realms, excluding women from the public arena. At the same time, it opens the private arena to state regulations, stretching state activity and control into the private realm through an extended patriarchy. The new reforms thus created a new disciplinary system, controlling working-class and poor women through promoting a middle-class social order.

Moreover, women who seek assistance from legal, welfare, or medical institutions and do not leave their abusing husbands, or refuse to prosecute them, are defined as failing to take responsibility for themselves. Consequently, they are represented as unreasonable, incapable of making a choice, and are typically seen as less deserving of the help of the law. At the same time, women who cooperate with the authorities and agree to the arrest of their husbands are offered instead subordination to patriarchal authority within the family. In this way, the law offers these women, who are mainly drawn from marginalized social groups, a "self" that they are unable to claim, thus further victimizing them.

The laws blame abused women for their inability to take responsibility for themselves and ignore the economic structures that do not provide women with opportunities to become the breadwinner for themselves or their families. While the laws and various programs encourage women to take control over their lives, they are unable to provide them with the material means to assert this control. Thus, legal intervention is directed toward gender inequality, but it does not address the class and racial inequalities that constrain the lives of many women. Women who complain to the police or remain in the abusive relationship might be arrested or their children might be taken away by the child protection services. And in some ways this intervention increases the surveillance and control of both working-class and poor women and men by middle-class agencies and the legal system, and in practice even worsens the experience of the victims. In this way, the state reinforces the expected and desired conformity and subjection of women to men and their corresponding acquiescence with the appropriate gender roles.

For others, the very creation of laws penalizing violence against women was part of wider social and ideological processes and did not originate out of concern for abused women. In Mexico, for example, new legislation was introduced in the mid-19th century, criminalizing domestic violence. This legislation was part of the liberal vision of nation-state formation and capitalist development that legitimized state authority in both the public and private spheres. For the liberals, good citizenship, morality, the order of society, and the legitimacy of the authorities relied on the stability of the heterosexual, patriarchal, nuclear family, on the wife's subordination to the husband, and on his subordination to the state. The liberals did not question the husband's right to govern his wife, but they redefined the basis of his authority. The subjection of women to men in marriage was based on the new laws produced by the state that increased the husband's legal rights over his wife as opposed to the previous kind of authority, which arose from physical violence. This type of violence was now seen as a sign of barbarism that had to be abandoned in "modern" times, which were governed by free will, reason, and relations based on legal contracts. The goal of the new laws was the domestication and discipline of men whose violent behavior was seen as a threat to social order and civility.

In more recent times, according to some scholars, the nature of law reforms addressing the phenomenon of violence against women reflected the dominant patriarchal ideology that emphasized the significance of the gendered social order. State agencies criminalized violence against women and thus defined this behavior as a problem of individual abusers and specific victims and not as a reflection of problematic gender relations. In her analysis of this process, Morgan claims that in this way the state adopted the "social service" aspect of women's groups and not the feminist political agenda. The state, thus, strengthened its political and ideological legitimization in aspects of gender relations, but did not have to make wider changes in gender relations. The criminalization of abusers, however, threatened to burden the criminal justice system, which was already overloaded by increasing crime rates and limited resources. In order to solve this problem, abusers were diverted to welfare agencies. In this way, the state managed the problem while the radical political demands calling upon the government to wider social changes were minimized. The focus on increased policing of battering diverted attention away from the general source of the violence to its individual perpetrators and at times to individual victims. In this way, structural issues became isolated and segmented through a process of individualization. This therapeutic focus reduced the social problem of violence against women to the problem of specific deviant men or women. The individualization process in the U.S. involves the combination of the criminal justice, medical, and welfare institutions—an apparatus that isolates conflicts and inequalities from their structural origins and social and political contexts.

Moreover, this societal reaction to the phenomenon of violence against women, which became service oriented, changed the orientation of feminist groups. The early feminist orientation and the antirape movement was antistate and many activists saw themselves as an alternative to the services and control provided by the state, mainly by emphasizing a community network and community support. With the new reforms these groups were partially absorbed into the network of service organizations, the ideals giving way to preexisting social control and welfare service goals. The community base has been replaced largely by middle class, White professionals whose main interest in the organization is one of service delivery. As a result, many refuge houses were transformed into service centers aimed at family reunification. In this way, the focus was shifted to the management of the aftermath of rape or abuse rather than to making large-scale changes in social relationships in order to prevent it. The state, through professionalization and individualization, became enmeshed in gender relations and incorporated feminist goals only in limited ways.

Due to these conflicting ideas and perspectives, a range of suggestions for the "appropriate" societal response to the phenomenon exist. While some call for the increase of control of the state on batterers and the reform of the criminal justice system to give a voice to women, others suggest finding ways to deal with the phenomena outside of state agencies. The reasoning is that since legal institutions, which reinforce dominant patterns of gender, race, and class, treat victims and offenders as legal subjects and employ gendered legal thinking and practice, they cannot be seen as separate from the dominant culture, which supports and facilitates the subordination of women to men. For these other reformers, the aim in the long run is to enhance women's control over resources so they can live safe and independent lives. This can be achieved through the creation of plans and programs that deal with violence against women not as a separate issue, but as a sociopolitical phenomenon.

While scholars and practitioners hold different and sometimes conflicting ideas about the causes, the prevalence, and the "appropriate" response to violence against women, most of them share the belief that in order to prevent violent behavior there is a need to establish a social, cultural, and legal atmosphere in which males and females are valued equally. Moreover, there is a need to encourage greater equality within the family and to provide support for people in need within the family, the extended family, and the community. In some places, the disappointment with the legal system's inadequacy to bring about change led to the establishment of various community-based programs, aiming to empower women. In Canada and the U.S., coordinated community intervention policies are implemented, where battered women's groups, law enforcement agencies, the justice system, and other relevant groups coordinate the response to domestic violence.

Also See the Following Articles

FAMILY STRUCTURES, VIOLENCE AND NONVIOLENCE • FEMINIST AND PEACE PERSPECTIVES ON WOMEN • GENDER STUDIES • HOMOSEXUALS, VIOLENCE TOWARD • INSTITUTIONALIZATION OF VIOLENCE • NONVIOLENCE THEORY AND PRACTICE • SEXUAL ASSAULT • SOCIAL CONTROL AND VIOLENCE • STRUCTURAL VIOLENCE

Bibliography

Bart, P. B., & Moran, E. G. (Eds.) (1993). *Violence against women: The bloody footprints*. Newbury Park, CA: Sage.

Breines, W., & Gordon, L. (1983). The new scholarship on family violence. *Signs, 8*, 490–531.

Brownmiller, S. (1975). *Against our will: Men, women and rape*. London: Secker & Warburg.

Dobash, R. E., & Dobash, R. P. (1992). *Women, violence and social change*. London: Routledge.

Gordon, L. (1988). *Heroes of their own lives: The history and politics of family violence, Boston 1880–1960*. New York: Viking/Penguin.

Edelson, J. L., & Eisikovits, Z. C. (Eds.) (1996). *Future interventions with battered women and their families*. Thousand Oaks, CA: Sage.

Fineman, M., & Mykitiul, R. (Eds.) (1994) *The public nature of private violence*. New York: Routledge.

Hanmer, J., & Maynard, M. (Eds.) (1987). *Women, violence and social control*. London: Macmillan.

Hanmer, J., Radford, J., & Stanko, E. A. (Eds.) (1989). *Women, policing, and male violence: International perspectives*. London: Routledge.

Heise, L. L., Pitanguy, J., & Germain, A. (1994). *Violence against women: The hidden health burden*. Washington, DC: The World Bank.

Hester, M., Kelly, L., & Radford, J. (Eds.) (1996). *Women, violence and male power*. Buckingham, England: Open University Press.

Kelly, L. (1988). *Surviving sexual violence*. London: Sage.

Koss, M. (1988). Hidden rape: Sexual aggression and victimization in a national sample of students in higher education. In A. Burgess (Ed.), *Rape and sexual assault 2* (pp. 3–25). New York: Garland.

MacKinnon, C. (1987). *Feminism unmodified: Discourses on life and law*. Cambridge, MA: Harvard University Press.

Matthews, N. A. (1994). *Confronting rape: The feminist anti-rape movement and the state*. London: Routledge.

Morgan, P. A. (1985). Constructing images of deviance: A look at state intervention into the problem of wife-battery. In N. Johnson (Ed.), *Marital violence* (pp. 60–76). London: Routledge & Kegan Paul.

Roy, M. (Ed.) (1977). *Battered women: A psychological study of domestic violence*. New York: Van Nostrand Reinhold.

Searles, P., & Berger, R. (Eds.) (1995). *Rape and society: Readings on the problem of sexual assault*. Boulder, CO: Westview Press.

Snider, L. (1994). Feminism, punishment and the potential of empowerment. *Canadian Journal of Law and Society, 9*(1), 75–104.

Straus, M., & Gelles, R. (1990). *Physical violence in American families*. New Brunswick, NJ: Transactions.

Tierney, K. J. (1982). The battered women movement and the creation of the wife beating problem. *Social Problems, 29*(3), 207–221.

Valverde, M., MacLeod, L., & Johnson, K. (Eds.) (1995). *Wife assault and the Canadian criminal justice system*. Toronto: The Center of Criminology, University of Toronto.

World Government

Hanna Newcombe

Peace Research Institute—Dundas

GLOSSARY

Confederation A loose integration of two or more countries which retain their internal political structure while acquiring some common structures for the whole unit.

Federalism A system of government with more than one level, with citizens directly electing representatives at all levels.

Subsidiarity A system in which problems are solved at the lowest level possible, at which there are no significant effects at higher levels. Levels might range from neighborhood, to municipal, to provincial (state), to national, to continental, to global.

WORLD GOVERNMENT is a proposal to maintain world peace and solve global problems by providing a set of unifying institutions at the global level without abolishing nation-states. The concept has a long history and is embodied in several contemporary organizations. Various approaches exist: some would reform the United Nations, others would begin afresh outside the United Nations.

I. THE BASIC IDEA

There are three justifications for wanting to institute a world federal government:

1. The unity of humankind. This can be based both on biological grounds (we are a single species, *Homo sapiens*) and on religious grounds (we are the children of the one God). We have lived for a long time under the governments of various nations (186 at this time), sometimes regarding each other as strangers or even enemies. The time has come to recognize our essential unity and to embody this in global institutions.

2. The abolition of international war. This was always desirable through the ages, but has now become mandatory and urgent because of the invention of mass-destruction weapons (nuclear, chemical, biological); it has also become possible because of the modern means of communication and transport that have brought us into close and daily contact.

3. The need to solve global problems. These problems involve basic social justice and equity among nations (overcoming the gross disparity between the rich and the poor nations by properly regulating world trade, aid, and debt) and urgent global environmental problems [global warming through excessive carbon dioxide emissions, ozone depletion through chlorofluorocarbon (CFC) emissions, ocean pollution by dumping oil, toxic wastes, and radioactive wastes] and others. Gross violations of human rights (genocide, disappearances, torture), formerly considered to be domestic problems within nations, have also now come to be considered global problems for the whole human community.

II. PROBLEMS

Objections are sometimes voiced to the world government concept on several grounds:

1. It is said that it would homogenize the various cultures existing in the world, thus shrinking diversity, to the detriment of us all. National sovereignty is claimed to be vital to the preservation of national cultural identities. In fact, many ethnic nationalities that do not yet have (or have lost) a state of their own now claim to want to obtain a state and a territory in which they could govern themselves by the right of national self-determination. This contemporary trend runs counter to the need for a world government.

2. Even more dangerous, the critics claim, is the possibility that a world dictatorship would arise. Even if the world government were to be originally democratic, a dictator might seize power illegally, and there would then be no place to which persons persecuted under this regime could turn for asylum as refugees.

3. It is also pointed out that, while a world government would eliminate (almost by definition) all international wars, it would not necessarily prevent civil wars. It is noted that most recent wars have, in fact, been civil wars.

4. At the theoretical level, the critics point out that the world government concept is based on a Hobbesian view of the world. According to the philosopher Thomas Hobbes, people in a state of nature live in a "war of all against all," in which human life is "nasty, brutish, and short." Therefore people form a society and the rule of law to improve their lot. If this view is transferred to the international society,

which is still anarchic without a world government, it is seen that nations live in a situation of potential war of all against all, i.e. at each other's mercy (especially in the nuclear age). The critics say, however, that the Hobbesian view of human nature is obsolete and invalid: people naturally cooperate as well as fight, and nations obey most international laws and treaties to a large extent most of the time. Therefore, the present international system conforms to Grotius (the father of international law) more than to Hobbes, although it reverts to war occasionally.

III. SOLUTIONS

This section formulates the answers that proponents of world government would make to the objections of the critics.

1. Proponents of world government claim that world unification would not homogenize national cultures because the world government would not be highly centralized. In fact, the concept is usually called "world *federal* government," and its proponents call themselves "world federalists." Nations as its units would not be abolished, and would remain free to support and nourish national cultures as long as they would not fight each other and would contribute to the solution of global problems. Actually, wars are more destructive of national cultures (as well as of the environment) than global regulation would be. Cultural diversity would be protected and could flourish, especially if human rights were promoted under a world federal government. It is as philosopher John Stuart Mill said in his essay *On Liberty*: all nations (as all individuals) should be free to do as they please, as long as they do not encroach on the freedom of others. In the case of nations, this would constitute "*limited sovereignty*" as opposed to "absolute sovereignty." The latter is a fiction anyway in our age of economic globalization.

The concept of federalism is often further expanded into the concept of "subsidiarity," implying (a) more than two levels of government and (b) solving problems at the lowest level possible without significant external effects on the higher levels. There might be about six levels: neighborhood, municipal, provincial/state/cantonal, national, continental region, and world. Citizens would vote directly for their representatives at all six levels. The division of powers might remain controversial for a long time (since "significant external effects" are impossible to define exactly in a system in which everything depends on everything else), but gradual (and perhaps shifting) adjustments could be made in a gradual democratic manner without resorting to violence.

2. Against the danger of a world dictator usurping power, there could be three sets of safeguards: (a) checks and balances to maintain a democratic structure, as in the established democracies in the world; (b) citizenship education to foster a democratic political and civic culture; and (c) if all else fails, widespread popular practice of nonviolent civil disobedience. If these safeguards were securely in place, a potential dictator would not get very far. This is not an absolute guarantee, but few things in this world are.

3. Civil wars usually arise because of social, economic, and political tensions within a country, the oppression of a minority, or violations of human rights. If these underlying causes of discontent could be avoided, civil wars could be prevented. In any case, the situation would be no worse under a world federal government than it is under the present systems of unregulated multiple nations.

4. If the present international system is at least partly Grotian rather than wholly Hobbesian, this still leaves further room for improvement into a Kantian system of harmony and cooperation under an integrated world order. Philosopher Immanuel Kant wrote an essay, *On Perpetual Peace*, in which he advocated the integration of the world's states recognized at that time into at least a confederation of republics. A confederation is a looser structure than a federation, perhaps more like the present European Union. By "republics" (as opposed to monarchies), Kant meant something similar to the modern concept of "democracies." It is known from peace research that democratic states never fight wars with each other, as indeed Kant claimed would be the case for republics.

IV. HISTORICAL PROPOSALS

The idea of a world government is not new; in fact, it has deep roots in history. Only an abbreviated list with brief comments is given below.

Pierre Dubois' book, written between 1305 and 1307, advocates a union of Christian states to recover the Holy Land. Arbitration would replace war among Christian states.

Dante Alighieri, Italian poet in the 14th century, wrote *De Monarchia*, advocating a unitary world state under a powerful monarch. Motto: one God, one King.

George Podebrad, king of Bohemia, late 15th century, proposed an international parliament to unite Christian nations against the Turks.

Dutch philosopher Erasmus wrote *The Complaint of Peace* in 1517. It was a plea to European kings to stop waging war on humanistic grounds.

Emeric Cruce in France wrote *Le Nouveau Cynee* (*The New Cyneas*) in 1623, appealing to European kings to convene an assembly or congress.

Hugo Grotius (Dutch surname: van de Groot) wrote *De Jure Belli ac Pacis* in 1625. He is considered the father of international law.

King Henry IV of France (or perhaps his finance minister Duc de Sully) wrote *Le Grand Dessein* (*The Grand Design*) in 1638. European states would be unified under three great religions: Catholic, Lutheran, and Calvinist, with very clear borders. The alliance might include Russia and Turkey, but would be directed against the Habsburg empire and would try to conquer Asia and North Africa.

William Penn (later the founder of Pennsylvania and a Quaker) wrote *An Essay Toward the Present and Future Peace of Europe* in 1693. He saw justice as the foundation of peace and "wars as the duels of princes."

John Bellers, a British Quaker, wrote a similar proposal in 1710. Both Penn's and Bellers' proposals resemble that of Henry IV.

Saint-Pierre in France wrote *Project for Perpetual Peace in Europe* between 1712 and 1713. He wanted 24 specified states to form a perpetual congress or senate. War would be waged against any state not living up to its responsibilities (the beginnings of "collective security"). Secret treaties would be banned.

French philosopher Jean-Jacques Rousseau wrote *A Project for Perpetual Peace* in 1761. It proposed a constitution for the federation of 19 European states.

Jeremy Bentham in England wrote *A Plan for a Universal and Perpetual Peace*, which was published posthumously in 1843. His system was the first to include a world court.

German philosopher Immanuel Kant wrote the very well-known plan *On Perpetual Peace* (*Zum ewigen Frieden*) in 1795. It took the form of a treaty for a European confederation of republican states—not monarchies. He believed that monarchies were war prone, while republics would be peaceful.

Saint-Simon published a proposal for a Parliament of Europe in 1814, a year before the Congress of Vienna, which ended the Napoleonic wars. Perhaps the Holy Alliance formed there used this as a model at the behest of Czar Alexander of Russia. The alliance of Saint-Simon was the first to include the United States. However, the

Holy Alliance became identified with antidemocratic forces.

William Ladd in the U.S. founded the American Peace Society in 1828 and wrote his peace proposal in 1840. There was to be a congress of ambassadors of "civilized" nations and a separate court.

William Jay, also in the U.S., proposed a plan that also included a world court.

Johann Caspar Bluntschli in Switzerland advocated a federated Europe in 1876.

James Lorimer in Edinburgh in 1884 had a plan with a separate executive, senate, chamber of deputies, and a judicial tribunal. Annual elections would be held.

The 19th century closed with the two Peace Conferences in the Hague, convened by Czar Nicholas II of Russia in 1899 and 1907. The conferences established a Permanent Court of Arbitration.

In the 20th century, with the Hague Conferences and the Permanent Court, we enter the stage of actual world institutions, not only proposals. The League of Nations was formed after World War I in 1918 and the United Nations after World War II in 1945. The Permanent Court of Arbitration was transformed into the International Court of Justice, usually called the World Court.

Writers of world constitutions did not stop when some actual institutions were formed. Proposals for either reforming the United Nations or starting a new (presumably more perfect) world government abound in our century. Sixteen of these schemes (a small sample of existing ones) were listed in Hanna Newcombe's article "Comparison of World Order Schemes" in 1985 in *The Journal of World Peace*. Only five are mentioned here.

In 1946, Garry Davis, an early proponent of world government, staged a sit-down at the newly formed United Nations sited temporarily in Paris, publicly tore up his U.S. passport, and declared himself a world citizen. This gave an impetus to the Citoyens du Monde organization in France, long led by Guy Marchand (now deceased) and still headed by his wife, Renee Marchand. The Registry of World Citizens, headquartered in Paris, has spun off several organizations, the main one being the People's Congress, cumulatively being elected in transnational elections across the world. Meanwhile Garry Davis has become the head of the World Service Organization, claiming already to be the world government, issuing passports and other documents.

In the late 1940s a group of eminent scholars assembled at the University of Chicago under the leadership of Robert Maynard Hutchins, Giuseppe A. Borgese, and others to consider plans for a world government. This

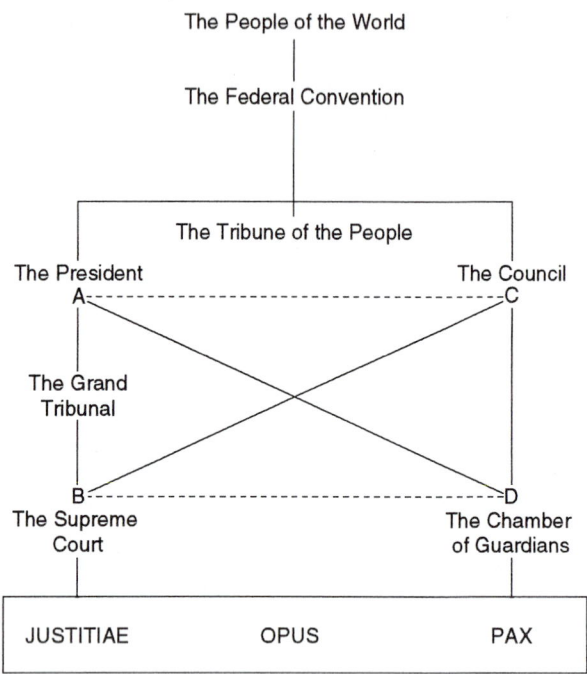

FIGURE 1 Organizational diagram of Chicago Constitution (from E. M. Borgese, p. 53).

effort resulted in the publication of the so-called *Chicago Constitution*, formally entitled *Preliminary Draft of a World Constitution*, published in 1948, and republished in 1965 by Elisabeth Mann Borgese, Giuseppe Borgese's daughter. It is 30 pages long. Unlike previous drafts, this constitution gathered ideas from many diverse cultures and historical eras (e.g., *Tribune of the People* from ancient Rome) and featured a division of the world into nine semicontinental regions, albeit still heavily slanted in favor of western democracies (Fig. 1).

United States international law experts Grenville Clark and Louis B. Sohn published an influential book, *World Peace Through World Law*, in 1958. Their plan took the form of a drastically revised United Nations Charter, paragraph by paragraph, accompanied by explanations of why these changes were necessary or beneficial. The plan included general and complete disarmament, a world police force, weighted voting in the General Assembly, a change of the Security Council into an Executive Council with no veto, a world development authority, and other far-reaching changes.

Aake Anker-Ording, Norwegian parliamentarian and scholar active in various United Nations organizations, formed a plan described in an article in the journal *International Associations* in March, 1973, entitled "Three Stages of Possible U.N. Development." Illustrated by three diagrams, this plan shows how representation of nations in the General Assembly could change over time from governments to parliaments to citizens, how nongovernmental organizations (NGOs) could gain more importance, and how the Specialized Agencies of the UN could become departments or ministries of a world government (Figs. 2a–2c).

In each chart of Fig. 2 rectangles at the bottom symbolize nations. Within them are indicated national NGOs, district organs, local organizations, and individual citizens. On top of the rectangles are the national parliaments and on top of them are national governments. Lines go up from the national governments to the UN General Assembly (at the top of Fig. 2a). The other UN bodies (Security Council, Economic and Social Council, Trusteeship Council, International Court of Justice, Secretariat, and the Specialized Agencies) are indicated in appropriate places. The international NGOs (INGOs), MNCs (multinational corporations), and regional intergovernmental organizations are also drawn in. The NGOs are linked in the Union of International Associations.

The following changes occur in going from Fig. 2a to 2b.

1. The lines around the nation rectangles grow fainter.
2. The lines to the UN General Assembly go from parliaments, not governments.
3. The Trusteeship Council has disappeared.
4. The Specialized Agencies have moved from the sidelines to center stage, some new ones have been added, and some names have been changed.
5. There is a World Congress of INGOs.
6. There is a Peace Security Force.
7. There is a World Ombudsman.

The following changes occur in going from Fig. 2b to 2c:

1. The lines around the nation rectangles have vanished, though the internal structures remain.
2. The UN General Assembly has become a Global Parliament with three chambers: the Chamber of Citizens directly elected by the people, the Chamber of Nations elected by national parliaments, and the World Production Chamber linked with the MNCs and the INGOs.
3. The International Court of Justice has become the World Supreme Court with district courts under it.
4. The Peace Security Force has become World Police Force.

5. The world functional bodies (originally UN Specialized Agencies) have become departments of the world government.

The "Constitutions for the Federation of Earth," a lengthy document (55 pages), was developed over 20 years by the World Constitution and Parliament Association led by Philip Isely and published and officially approved by the World Constitutional Assembly (nongovernmental) in Innsbruck, Austria, in 1979. It features three chambers (House of Nations, House of Peoples, and House of Counsellors). Direct popular elections would be held in 1000 equal-population world districts, which could overlap national borders. For some purposes, the 1000 districts would be grouped into 20 regions or 10 magnaregions or 5 continents. This constitution is being actively promoted, and several sessions of the Provisional World Parliament have already been held, but still with no participation of national governments (Fig. 3).

The early peace plans were not always world federations. Most were limited to Europe, or to Christian nations, and therefore not universal. Also some were alliances put together to defend against outsiders (e.g., Turks) or to conquer other parts of the world (the Holy Land, Asia, and Africa). Nevertheless, they were early attempts to go beyond nation-states, which is why they are mentioned here.

V. PRESENT ORGANIZATIONS

The largest organization promoting world government today is called the World Federalist Movement (WFM), with the main office at 777 U.N. Plaza, New York 10017. It has undergone several name changes since its founding in Montreux, Switzerland in 1947. The original name was World Association for a World Federal Government. The immediately previous name was World Association for a World Federation (WAWF); this name was considered to be too long and awkward, but was perhaps more descriptive. The previous head office was in Amsterdam.

The founding conference in Montreux (which celebrated its 50th anniversary in 1997) outlined four main paths to a world federal government:

1. Reform of the United Nations, probably through Charter revision as specified in the Charter (the Clark and Sohn model; see above).
2. Regional federations, like the (then) newly formed European Community, to be later merged

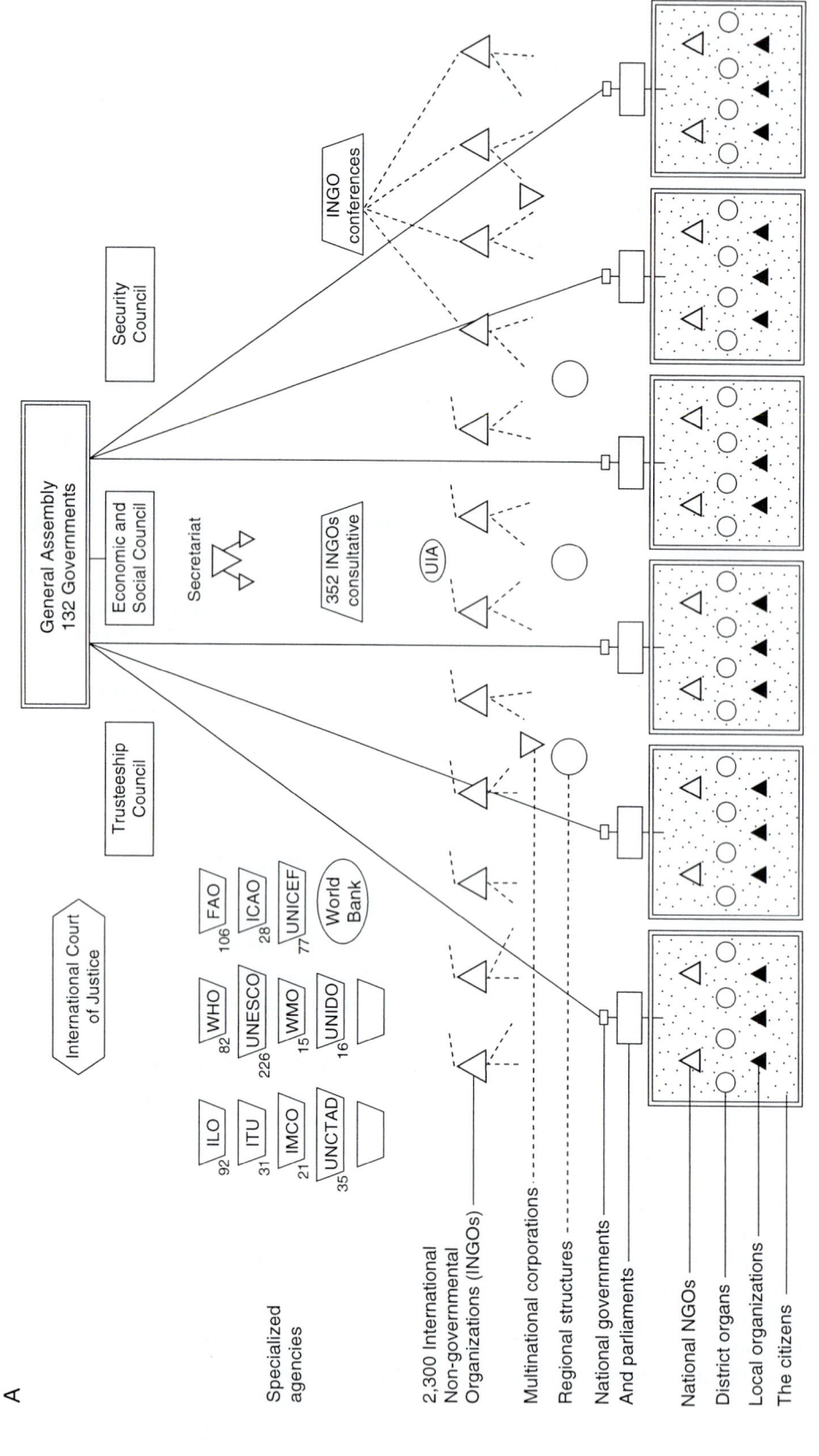

FIGURE 2 Anker-Ording's three stages of possible UN development. (a) The organization of the United Nations at present. (b) The proposed future organization of the UN. (c) The proposed organization of a world government.

A

Specialized agencies

ILO 92
ITU 31
IMCO 21
UNCTAD 35

WHO 82
UNESCO 226
WMO 15
UNIDO 16

FAO 106
ICAO 28
UNICEF 77

World Bank

2,300 International Non-governmental Organizations (INGOs)

Multinational corporations

Regional structures

National governments And parliaments

National NGOs

District organs

Local organizations

The citizens

International Court of Justice

Trusteeship Council

General Assembly 132 Governments

Security Council

Economic and Social Council

Secretariat

352 INGOs consultative

UIA

INGO conferences

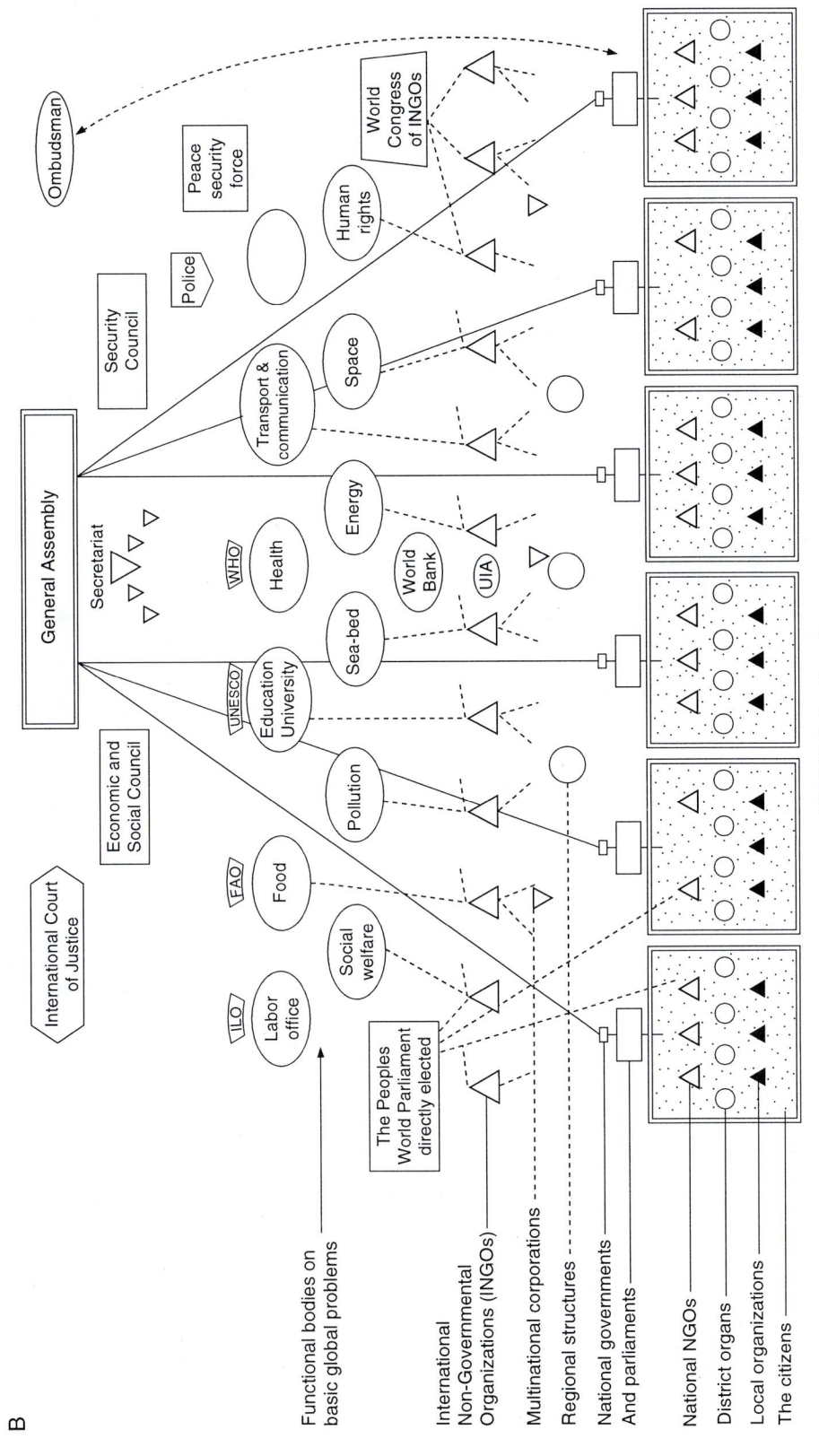

B

Ombudsman

Peace security force

Police

Security Council

General Assembly

Secretariat

International Court of Justice

Economic and Social Council

World Congress of INGOs

Human rights

Transport & communication

Space

WHO Health

Energy

World Bank

UIA

Sea-bed

UNESCO Education University

Pollution

FAO Food

Social welfare

ILO Labor office

The Peoples World Parliament directly elected

Functional bodies on basic global problems

International Non-Governmental Organizations (INGOs)

Multinational corporations

Regional structures

National governments And parliaments

National NGOs

District organs

Local organizations

The citizens

FIGURE 2 *(continued)*

833

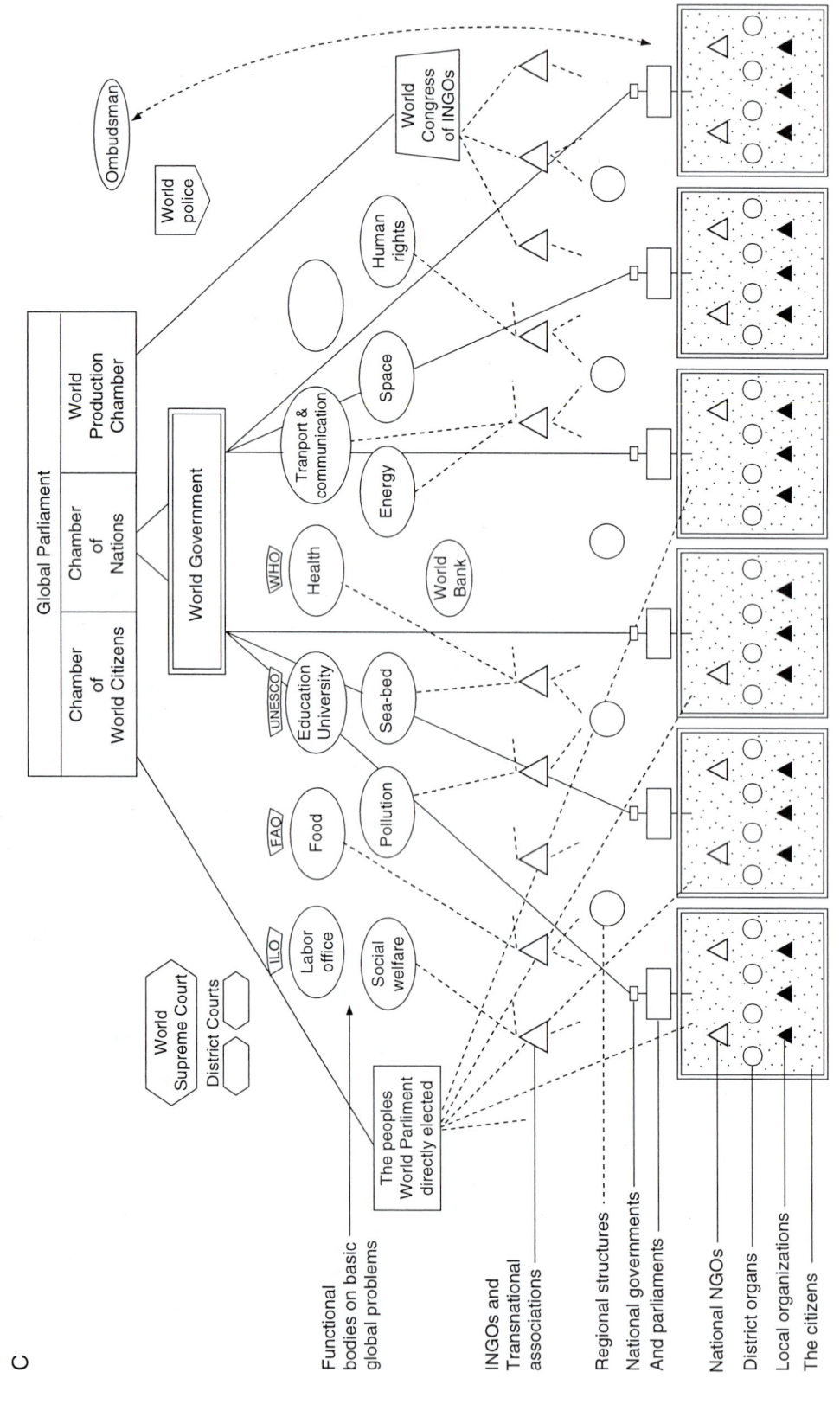

C

Global Parliament
Chamber of World Citizens | Chamber of Nations | World Production Chamber

World Government

World Supreme Court
District Courts

Ombudsman

World police

World Congress of INGOs

Human rights

Space

Energy

Transport & communication

WHO Health

World Bank

UNESCO Education University

Sea-bed

FAO Food

Pollution

ILO Labor office

Social welfare

The peoples World Parliment directly elected

Functional bodies on basic global problems

INGOs and Transnational associations

Regional structures

National governments And parliaments

National NGOs

District organs

Local organizations

The citizens

FIGURE 2 (continued)

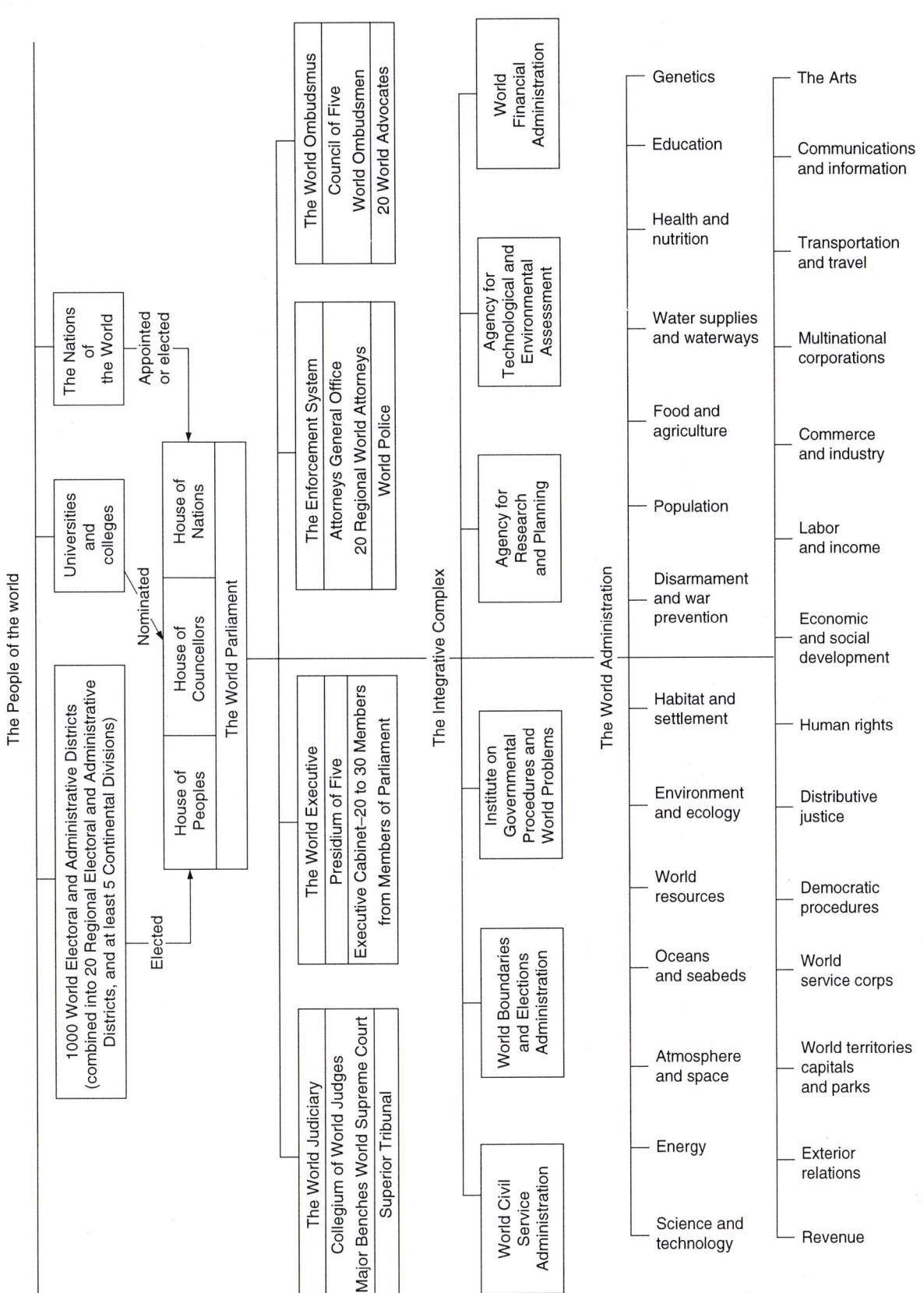

The People of the world

1000 World Electoral and Administrative Districts (combined into 20 Regional Electoral and Administrative Districts, and at least 5 Continental Divisions)

Universities and colleges

The Nations of the World

Appointed or elected

Nominated

Elected

The World Parliament

House of Peoples | House of Councellors | House of Nations

The World Executive
Presidium of Five
Executive Cabinet–20 to 30 Members from Members of Parliament

The Enforcement System
Attorneys General Office
20 Regional World Attorneys
World Police

The World Ombudsmus
Council of Five
World Ombudsmen
20 World Advocates

The World Judiciary
Collegium of World Judges
Major Benches World Supreme Court
Superior Tribunal

The Integrative Complex

World Civil Service Administration

World Boundaries and Elections Administration

Institute on Governmental Procedures and World Problems

Agency for Research and Planning

Agency for Technological and Environmental Assessment

World Financial Administration

The World Administration

- Genetics
- Education
- Health and nutrition
- Water supplies and waterways
- Food and agriculture
- Population
- Disarmament and war prevention
- Economic and social development
- Habitat and settlement
- Environment and ecology
- World resources
- Oceans and seabeds
- Atmosphere and space
- Energy
- Science and technology

- The Arts
- Communications and information
- Transportation and travel
- Multinational corporations
- Commerce and industry
- Labor and income
- Human rights
- Distributive justice
- Democratic procedures
- World service corps
- World territories capitals and parks
- Exterior relations
- Revenue

FIGURE 3 Diagram of world government under the Constitution for the Federation of Earth.

835

into one global federation ("Community of Communities," the European model).

3. A People's World Convention or a World Constituent Assembly to write a completely new World Constitution to replace the UN Charter (the American model).

4. Functional cooperation worldwide on economic problems, which would eventually "spill over" into political integration (The David Mitrany model, according to his book "A Working Peace System").

Over the years, WAWF–WFM has concentrated mainly on the first path, reform of the United Nations, leaving the other three alternative paths to be pursued by a dozen or so smaller organizations.

There is a separate organization of European federalists, especially active in Italy, with a very active youth wing, that promotes the second path. However, sometimes they lose sight of the final goal of a world federation, promoting a European federation only. Nevertheless, world federalists and European federalists have recently held a joint congress in Ventotene, Italy, and are now cooperating more closely.

The third path to a world federation, through a constitutional convention, has been pursued by several organizations. The People's Congress, fostered many years by Guy and Renee Marchand of the Citoyens du Monde in Paris, is one such organization and has already been mentioned. Also described above is the World Constitution and Parliament Association, with its Constitution for the Federation of Earth. The World Authority Committee, founded by Swiss international lawyer Max Habicht and Aake Anker Ording of Norway, was originally meant to be a research organization providing information to governments for the calling of a governmental world constitutional convention, but when governments did not respond, it produced some research and publications of its own, though not another world constitution. It has dwindled and now no longer exists, with both its founders deceased. John Logue, a prominent leader in the U.S. affiliate of WFM, has called for a wholly new constitution to replace the ineffective UN Charter, the way the founders of the U.S. constitution replaced the ineffective articles of confederation at the Philadelphia convention in 1793 (This is the "American" model). Other examples could be cited.

The fourth (functional) path is not explicitly promoted by any organization, but it is perhaps the way in which developments in world governance are actually occurring. There have been vast changes in international law in regard (at least verbally) to human rights, in discussions of development and elimination of poverty, in environmental treaties, in care for refugees, in humanitarian assistance, in health and education, in arms control and disarmament, and in peacekeeping and postwar peace-building. Many of these new agreements have not yet been properly implemented, and some of the new efforts have failed or gone sour, but the numerous changes, largely though not entirely under the UN, cannot be ignored. The Carlsson–Ramphal Independent Commission has called for "world governance," though explicitly not world government.

What is the difference between "world governance" and "world government"? Basically it is the "democratic deficit," often mentioned in connection with the European Union, but even more applicable to the world stage. There could be a whole network of global agencies regulating a whole range of world issues and problems, but to whom would they be accountable? To national governments, presumably, but not directly to the world's people. Actually, globalization policies, especially in trade matters, are increasingly more under the control of multinational corporations rather than national governments. Democratic accountability is even more lacking in this case.

Aiming at democratization of the United Nations has been the chosen task of several new organizations. The basic idea is to call for people to be represented at the UN, not only governments; that is, a People's Assembly parallel to the General Assembly should be formed. This could be done without a formal revision of the UN Charter by the General Assembly, creating "an auxiliary organ."

One organization promoting this idea is the Council for a More Democratic United Nations, led by Jeffrey Segall of England and Harry Lerner of the U.S., a physician and a psychologist, respectively. Several conferences have alreay been held and books issued. The supporting network of this group contains more than 100 other groups. Another group is calling for a United People's Assembly, originally nongovernmental and parallel to the UN General Assembly, but hoping to become eventually an official part of the UN system and perhaps be popularly elected as a House of Peoples. This group is led by teacher and philosopher Lucile Green from San Francisco. The WFM favors another model, a UN Parliamentary Assembly, to which delegates would be chosen by national legislatures in all countries.

All the organizations described, and over a dozen others, meet regularly under the World Government Organizations Council (WGOC) to exchange views and information. Since the organizations basically disagree on several points, WGOC has not been able to undertake joint projects, but it is useful as a clearing house. A newsletter helps this function.

VI. RELATION TO OTHER PEACE MOVEMENTS

Sometimes other peace movements do not consider world federalists as part of the overall peace movement, and sometimes world federalists, too, see themselves as separate from the peace movement. However, most of the time, most observers would regard world federalism as a particular strand of the peace movement, albeit with its own peculiar characteristics.

What are the similarities and differences? Both peace movements and world federalists strive for disarmament (conventional as well as nuclear), want to close the poverty gap, support human rights, want to protect the environment, believe in the unity of the human family, and abhor violent methods. However, peace movements are sometimes antagonistic to government in general, being more inclined toward philosophical anarchism, and therefore would not want government at the world level. Peace movements generally believe that "small is beautiful" and that both the means and the goals should be formulated and practiced at the local community level.

There is also a difference in emphasis on the various issues on which the two movements agree. Peace movements would put a greater emphasis on nonviolence, while world federalists would sometimes accept a small degree of military force, as in UN peacekeeping. Peace movements usually have separate groups working for disarmament, development, human rights, and environmental protection, while world federalists tend to subsume all of these issues under the heading of "world problems" that should be solved at the world level. Sometimes world federalists focus more on the institutions that would be charged with finding solutions to these issues than on the particular means by which the problems should be solved. World federalists put greater emphasis on law as a substitute for force, while peace movements would replace force by nonviolence.

There is also some difference—though not absolute—in the means used by the two movements. World federalists usually concentrate on trying to persuade national leaders through legal democratic means; for example, briefs, petitions, delegations, letters to governments or newspapers, participation in radio phone-ins, organizing meetings and conferences, and the like. Peace movements, while also employing all these means, tend to appeal more to the grassroots level and use, in addition, mass demonstrations, vigils and even civil disobedience (extra-legal means).

While the two streams remain separate, cooperation between them, at the UN and elsewhere, has been generally increasing and will probably continue to do so. Many individuals are actually participating in both streams, though some opposition is still sometimes expressed.

VII. A SPECTRUM OF ALTERNATIVE PROPOSALS

Proposals made at recent conferences or gleaned from the literature can be arranged approximately in the following continuum, from the most radical to the most moderate:

1. Declaring that world government already exists, and we are it. This is derived from the notion that only individual citizens possess sovereignty and they can delegate it to whomever they wish. Hence, the formation of a world government does not have to wait for the consent of national governments. As mentioned, this path is being followed by Garry Davis.
2. A world government in formation, under the same theory of sovereignty as above, but considered not yet completed. This is being pioneered by the People's Congress and by the Constitution of the Federation of Earth, as described above.
3. A wholly new UN Charter, though leaving the name "United Nations" and its universal membership unchanged. Here we have the proposal by John Logue and also a similar one by Don Kemner. While calling for a wholly new constitution, the advocates of this approach do not specify what the precise content of the new UN constitution should be, only that it should create a genuine world federation.
4. The call for convening a UN Charter revision conference, as specified in Article 109 of the present UN Charter. The conference participants would decide what the new Charter would contain. This is being advocated by Tad Daley.
5. Federation of the Democracies (FEDEM) has been proposed recently by Menko Rose, but has older roots in Clarence Streit's proposals for Atlantic Union. It is argued that the presence of totalitarian regimes would corrupt or make impossible a democratically operating world government

and that therefore these should be initially excluded. The UN with its universal membership should continue, as a debating forum, alongside FEDEM, with its limited membership but true governmental powers. Eventually, when all states become democratic, the UN and FEDEM would merge.

6. A comprehensive revision of the UN Charter, as envisioned, for example, by Grenville Clark and Louis B. Sohn in "World Peace Through World Law." This introduces some wholly new institutions and rules, as already described, but retains the basic structure of the old Charter and preserves some of the wording.

7. A moderate revision of the UN Charter, such as the proposals of the Campaign for Charter Reform in the U.S. This set of proposals features a permanent UN force, compulsory jurisdiction of the International Court of Justice, an international criminal court, weighted voting under Richard Hudson's Binding Triad formula, and so on. Most world federalist proposals are along this line.

8. Reinterpretation of the present UN Charter by introducing a series of enabling resolutions. This has been proposed in great detail by Benjamin Ferencz in his book *Global Survival*.

9. Work within the present UN Charter but add a Second (People's) Assembly, which could be done without formal Charter revision by the General Assembly, invoking Article 22 to form an auxiliary body. The alternatives within this framework have been described above.

10. Provide for "global governance," which is not world government. This approach has been used by the Independent Commission on Global Governance, chaired by Carlsson and Ramphal. As well, the role of the NGOs could be further upgraded, giving them accreditation not only to the Economic and Social Council as at present, but also to the General Assembly. They might be given the right to introduce resolutions, to speak in debates, or even to vote under some conditions. The Carlsson–Ramphal Commission proposed a Forum of Civil Society.

These 10 graduated reform and renewal proposals raise a series of questions: Where are the boundaries between the truly new and the old? Do we change only names or also institutions; maybe constitutions? Do we revise them somewhat or more than that or throw them out and start all over again? Do we have to evolve new

social species or merely metamorphose from a larva to a butterfly? Does the reorganization have to involve a step of partial planned destruction or abandonment of previously achieved institutions to clear the way for new growth, like a forest fire? Or can we adapt existing structures to new uses? Such questions, of course, are relevant for all social change.

VIII. FUTURE PROSPECTS

Some world federalist aims are being partly realized, e.g., the permanent International Criminal Court has been negotiated. It will realize a long-time plank in the world federalist platform, i.e., that individuals, not whole states, should be responsible for crimes against peace, war crimes, and crimes against humanity. Also, in the contest between national sovereignty and human rights, human rights have tended to gain ascendancy gradually over the years. Many disarmament treaties have been signed and ratified and are being implemented. And the UN is gradually recognizing the greater role of NGOs in their operations and at its conferences.

However, assertions are still made that "the UN is not a world government," which, of course, is true at the factual level; but the implication often is that it should not be or become a world government. Nationalism, both of the ethnic and the civic kind, is very strong today, even stronger than in past years. Countries tend to split rather than integrate. Yet this trend is not necessarily detrimental to the goal of uniting the world at the top. A world government as a union of smaller units could equally well exist as a union of larger ones.

Globalization is already happening in our world, but not everyone is happy about it. It concerns modern means of communication (the Internet), on the one hand, and international trade (groupings such as NAFTA) on the other. Economic nationalists everywhere see this type of globalization as a threat to national independence and self-determination. If the principle of subsidiarity requires an emphasis on the lower levels that are closer to the people, then undemocratic globalization is seen as a threat.

It could be said that the world already has a world government, but it is one of the wrong kind, i.e., undemocratic. Economically the world is ruled by the group of seven (now eight) industrialized nations and the World Trade Organization; politically the world is ruled by the five Permanent members of the UN Security Council, and most prominently by the United States, the one remaining superpower. This kind of globalization (concentration of power at the top) could become the wave of the future. The world federalist ideology of subsidiarity will have to actually counteract this trend by pressing for democratization of the UN and globalization from below.

The path to world government through creating a new world constitution apart from the United Nations does not seem to be a possibility at this time, but one never knows how situations may change, and it is therefore desirable for this activity to continue at some level so that this path would be available if needed.

It is probably counterproductive to speculate too much about the future. We have had too many surprises in world politics lately. Yet in the long run, the very fact that (as was said at the beginning of this article) world government is now not only desirable, but also urgent as well as possible augurs well for the future. But its democratic nature must be carefully guarded and preserved.

Also See the Following Articles

ALLIANCE SYSTEMS • CONFLICT TRANSFORMATION • ETHNIC CONFLICTS AND COOPERATION • PEACE MOVEMENTS

Bibliography

Anker-Ording, A. (1973). Three Stages of Possible UN Development. *International Associations*, 25(3), 3 pp.

Borgese, E. M. (1965). *A constitutions for the world.* Santa Barbara, CA: Center for the Study of Democratic Institutions. 112 pp.

Clark, G., & Sohn, L. B. (1958). *World peace through world law.* Cambridge, MA: Harvard University Press. 525 pp.

Ferencz, B. B. (1994). *The new legal foundations for global survival; security through the security council.* Dobbs Ferry, NY: Oceana.

Hemleben, S. J. (1972). Plans for world peace through six centuries. New York: Garland.

World Constituent Assembly (1977). *Constitution for the federation of earth.* Lakewood, CO: World Constitution and Parliament Association.

World War I

Daniel Segesser

University of Berne

GLOSSARY

Central Powers Alliance between Imperial Germany, Austria-Hungary, Bulgaria, and the Ottoman Empire.

Dominions Self-governing entities of the British Empire (i.e., in 1914): Australia, Canada, Newfoundland, New Zealand, and the Union of South Africa.

Entente Alliance between France, Russia, and the United Kingdom named after the "Entente Cordiale" of 1904 between France and the United Kingdom.

Great War Term by which World War I was known between 1918 and 1945. It was used to denote the new scale that warfare had reached in this conflict and the social, cultural, and demographic impact it had had.

July Crisis Term used to denote the critical phase in July, 1914 between the assassination of Austrian Archduke Franz Ferdinand in Sarajevo and the Austrian declaration of war on Serbia. It was marked by diplomatic activity to avoid a war and at the same time keep the alliances intact between France and Russia on the one hand and Austria-Hungary and Germany on the other.

League of Nations International organization for the maintenance of peace created after World War I according to the ideas of American President Woodrow Wilson and South African Defence Minister Jan Smuts.

Militarism Principle of maintaining a large military establishment; tendency to regard military efficiency as the supreme ideal of the state and to subordinate all other interests to those of the military, and the process of the reshaping of society according to military principles and values.

Mobile Warfare Method of fighting which characterized most of the fighting on the eastern front and in the Middle East. Its main characteristics were the high mobility of its operations and a tendency to try to outflank the enemy. On the western front there were only two phases of mobile warfare, in 1914 up to the Battle of the Marne and in 1918 after the black day of the German army.

Navalism Principle prevailing in the United Kingdom of maintaining a large naval force with a tendency to regard naval superiority as the most important to the survival of the country.

Schlieffenplan Operational plan originally conceived by field marshal Alfred Count von Schlieffen, Chief of the German General Staff from 1891 to 1905. It made provision for a two-front war by stipulating that the mass of the German army should move through Belgium to defeat the French army in the west first, while only small defensive forces should remain on the eastern front. Once the war had been won in the west—which was supposed to happen soon—the majority of the German forces should be committed against the Russians.

Total War There is no final definition as to what constitutes a total war. Certain elements have, however, been agreed upon. They are total mobilization (material and personal), total war aims, and total conduct of war, centrally managed and conducted by a professional political and military leadership with the help of a huge bureaucratic apparatus.

Trench Warfare Prevailing method of fighting on the western front in World War I. Once the front line stabilized at the end of 1914, the fighting parties dug trenches from where they continued to fight each other by artillery, machine gun, and/or rifle fire. A whole system of front-line and support trenches was built. Attacks were most of the time only conducted after a long preparation by artillery fire and were extremely costly.

World War There is no final definition of what constitutes a world war, but it can best be understood as a phenomenon that connects regional wars on different continents into the framework of a great conflict which has its roots in Europe and which includes europeanized and indigenous populations of non-European countries to a significant extent.

ALTHOUGH RECENT RESEARCH has assigned the term "world war" also to earlier wars like the French Wars of 1792–1815, it is used here to denote the first world war of the 20th century, which took place between 1914 and 1918 and was also called "The Great War" by contemporaries.

I. WORLD WAR I IN WORLD HISTORY

For British Prime Minister David Lloyd George, the bell of Big Ben echoed "Doom! Doom! Doom!" in his ears like the hammer of destiny and his colleague, Foreign Secretary Sir Edward Grey, saw the lamps going out all over Europe when World War I began. The two British statesmen did not stand alone in their analysis of the consequences of the war. Many observers agreed with them and after the war there was a growing desire in all countries and sections of society that war, with its enormous casualties, might become a thing of the past. A League of Nations was created to attempt to solve conflicts between nations by arbitration, so as to make sure that the Great War, as it was called at the time, would be the last war in the history of mankind.

The military analysis was quite different from the popular perception. Either they tried to prove how effective their measures had been or they criticized the ways in which the war had been conducted and offered alternatives for future war. A world without war was not a real possibility for them and they watched the League of Nations with deep mistrust. Many people in the Central Powers never accepted the verdict of the Peace Settlement and welcomed nationalist revisionism. After World War II it seemed that the Holocaust, Hiroshima, and the consequences of that war had made World War I and its outcome less relevant for the modern world, even though there was an enormous number of casualties. It was only in the 1960s that Fritz Fischer and Arthur Marwick rediscovered World War I as a relevant topic for historical analysis. While Fischer concentrated on the war guilt debate, Marwick analyzed the destructionist dimension of World War I and its impact on society. Most recent research has focused on the questions of whether World War I had really been a world war from the beginning and whether it had been a total war as many writers so far had assumed. World War I was now seen not only as a predecessor of World War II, but as the Great War it had been to those at that time.

II. PROTAGONISTS

The major powers involved in World War I were Austria-Hungary, also known as the Habsburg Monarchy or the Dual Monarchy; Imperial Germany; the United Kingdom of Great Britain and Ireland, with its worldwide empire; the French Republic; and Czarist Russia. The U.S., another major power, entered the war only in 1917. Minor powers involved included Belgium, Serbia, Italy, Rumania, Bulgaria, the Ottoman Empire, and Japan.

A. Austria-Hungary

The Habsburg Monarchy had been divided into two roughly equal halves, Austria, or Cisleithania, as it was called, and the Kingdom of Hungary, in 1867. Both had separate governments sharing only three ministries, the Foreign Ministry, the War Ministry, and the Finance Ministry. Recruiting and the organization of national militias did, however, not fall into the domain of the central war ministry, but was the responsibility of the respective governments of Austria and Hungary. This meant that in reality there was no united central government agency able to coordinate the policy of the whole monarchy except for external affairs. The separate economic arrangements hindered war mobilization considerably, much more than the nationalist movements of the large ethnic minorities in both parts of the monarchy. The army was recruited in both halves of the monarchy on the basis of conscription. About a quarter of its rank-and-file came from the German, the Hungarian, and the southern Slav part of the monarchy each, the rest coming from the Czech, the Rumanian, and the Italian part. The officers were predominantly German (76.1% of the regular officers and 56.8% of the reserve officers) and German was also the official language in the high command of the army.

B. Imperial Germany

The unification of Imperial Germany in 1871 had been the fulfillment of nationalist aspirations in Germany. Under the leadership of the Prussian king, who was at the same time emperor of Germany, and his ministers, the country became a major player, politically as well as economically, in Europe and throughout the world. Although its first chancellor (*Reichskanzler*), Otto von Bismarck, had been opposed to acquiring colonies, Imperial Germany became a colonial power by the end of the 19th century. Internally Germany was dominated by a ruling elite, mainly aristocrats and bureaucrats, who were dependent on the confidence of the Emperor and to a more restricted extent on the parliament. The military had an extraconstitutional status in the German political system and they saw themselves—and were seen by many—as the founders of the empire and the guarantor of its stability. The rise of new classes as a consequence of the industrial development of their country threatened their social privileges. Only a war, they believed, would give them the possibility to keep their position in German society. At the height of the July Crisis they therefore demanded a military solution to the conflict even though they knew that the war would not be quickly won. The German army was recruited by universal conscription with a duration of service of 3 years. Conscription was, however, not vigorously enforced for fear of giving military training to potentially politically unreliable persons. During the war the military were able to secure control not only over military affairs, but also of much of the interior organization of the country including the economy, mainly because the civilian administration was weak and the politicians unable to come to an agreement.

C. United Kingdom of Great Britain and Ireland

Up to the middle of the 19th century the United Kingdom had been the undisputed world power, controlling large parts of the world without having to do so directly. In the second half of the 19th century this position was challenged by the newly federated German Empire and the growing United States. Overtaken economically by both these powers in 1900, the United Kingdom retained its predominant position mainly through its dominance in world finance and the control that its navy exerted, at least potentially, in the whole world. The governments of the United Kingdom tried to meet the military and naval challenges with a series of agreements with Japan in 1902 and its main imperialist competitors, France and Russia, in 1904 and 1907, respectively. Domestically, the liberal government that came to power in 1905 tried to overcome the growing political and social tension with a series of social reforms and a form of local autonomy for Ireland. The latter, however, proved very difficult because of the strong opposition to it in the northern part and the island was on the brink of civil war in 1914. The small army—divided into the regular, the Indian, and the territorial army—as well as the Royal Navy were recruited by voluntary enlistment. The Dominions raised their own land and naval forces according to their own laws. The coordination was guaranteed by the Imperial General Staff and the Admiralty, respectively. The war not only put an end to strife in Ireland, but also halted all further projects for social reform, although the government of liberal Prime Minister H. H. Asquith tried to pursue a policy of "business as usual." Soon it became clear that it would be impossible to continue fighting the war on this footing, but Asquith and his cabinet refused major changes. In 1916 they were replaced by a coalition government headed by David Lloyd George, which tried to adapt the governmental structures to the war.

D. French Republic

After losing the war of 1870–1871, France had become a republic again; one of only three in Europe by 1914. Regaining the lost provinces of Alsace and Lorraine was one of the aims common to all of the many French governments, throughout the period from 1871 to 1914. Although France had a very high fluctuation rate in governments, many ministers and all the permanent heads of departments kept their offices for long periods and thereby provided the country with the necessary political stability. The parliamentary system in France continued to work throughout the war with the exception of two periods, one just after the outbreak of the war and one after the accession to government of Georges Clemenceau, when the French parliament voted extraordinary powers for the government. The governments continued to change rapidly in France, a fact that helped the military keep the great freedom from civilian control they had gained just after the outbreak of the war. In terms of global production, France ranked fourth before 1914. Its centers of industrial production were concentrated in the north and east of the country, close to the border of Imperial Germany and Belgium. Conscription was applied vigorously in France in order to keep pace with Germany in terms of wartime strength of the army. In 1913 the duration of compulsory military service had been raised to 3 years. The French high command, which lost a lot of its power only after the accession of Clemenceau to government, was committed to the offensive because it believed that France and Britain together would enjoy a decisive numerical superiority, permitting them to carry the war into enemy territory.

E. Czarist Russia

Russia was the fastest growing economy in the period between 1890 and 1914. Rapidly it was modernized from a completely agrarian society and economy into a country with a substantial industrial production and a much more urbanized society. Large parts of the country, however, remained underdeveloped and agrarian. These formed the economic base of the ruling elite, which lived in the Czarist capital of St. Petersburg and rarely traveled to their large properties in the country. Czar Alexander II had tried to pursue a policy of limited social reform, but it had remained incomplete and his successors did not continue it, not least because Alexander had been assassinated by radical anarchists in 1881. The rapid modernization of the Russian economy and the wanting social and political reforms led to a growing uneasiness among the country's small *intelligentsia* and working class. Most clearly this could be seen after the Russian defeat in the Russo-Japanese War of 1904–1905, when thousands of people took to the streets and Czar Nikolaj II was forced to accept some form of representation of the people. The newly formed parliament, however, had only restricted powers and, apart from a plan for an agrarian reform, it was not able to achieve much before the beginning of World War I. The Russian army was recruited by conscription, the soldiers serving between 3 and 4 years. As the Russo-Japanese War had shown, its training, leadership, and equipment were deficient, but no measures to remedy these problems were undertaken before 1914. Still, Russians armed forces were taken as a serious threat to national security by the German and Austrian general staffs and as a potentially great aid by the French, mainly because of its enormous manpower resources.

F. United States

The United States entered World War I with an army that was neither equipped nor trained to fight a modern war and had to rely on the support of the military establishments of the allies, especially of France. Economically, the United States, number one in terms of world production before the beginning of the war, had been involved in the delivery of arms and especially the procurement of capital mainly for the Entente since 1914. Still, most American politicians considered the war to be a European affair that the United States should keep out of. President Wilson therefore ran his campaign for reelection in 1916 under the motto "He kept us out of the war." His aim was to establish the United States as a mediator in order to achieve "a peace without victory." Wilson's attempts, however, did not succeed and finally he saw no other way to end the war than to enter it as an associated power on the side of Entente. The American society, multiethnic in its composition and with a large group of recent immigrants, was split between people who wanted to fight on the side of the democracies in danger and others who wanted the country to be kept out of the war because they believed it to be the consequence of German militarism and British navalism.

III. FEATURES OF WORLD WAR I

A. Trench Warfare

Trench warfare was the main characteristic of the war on the western front. The trench was in no way a new means of warfare—the Duke of Marlborough had used it at Malplaquet, Wellington at Torres Vedras, as well used by both parties in the American Civil War. Before 1914, however, only the Germans—to be able to withstand a Russian attack in the east and a French attack on some parts of the western front—had made any preparations for this contingency by stockpiling entrenching tools, various types of timber, hand and rifle grenades, searchlights, flares, periscopes, and trench mortars. By the end of September, 1914 both sides had dug themselves in as a consequence of the stabilization of the front line, building the trenches in a zig-zag to avoid enfilade fire and to limit the effects of shell bursts. Protective aprons of barbed-wire entanglements were used to check attempts to rush them and well-placed machine guns massacred attackers caught in the wire. Heavy artillery seemed the only way to make a successful attack on the enemy, but the ever-increasing complexity of the trench system made even this a gamble that was always paid for in heavy losses for the attacker. New weapons like flame-throwers or torpedoes to blow gaps in enemy wire were brought to the battlefield, but none of them were able to break the deadlock in the trenches. The reasons for the end of trench warfare in 1918 are a matter of debate among historians and military analysts. While some claim that it was only brute force that was responsible, others think that the use of new tactics—infiltration tactics—combined with the use of new weapons like tanks and airplanes were responsible for the return to mobile warfare. In the east the German breakthrough at Gorlice-Tarnow ended the stabilization of the front line by 1915 and even though there were attempts to return to a form a stabilized warfare, there was no return to trench warfare on this front.

B. Use of New Weapons and Technologies

New weapons such as gas, the tank, and the airplane were welcomed by all military high commands, as they seemed to offer a way out from trench warfare that for many high military officers was not a "real war." Gas was not an entirely new weapon in warfare, but World War I saw the first use of this weapon on a large scale. The debate concerning who started gas warfare already had begun during the war, with both parties accusing the other of having been the culprit. Today it seems fairly clear that both parties had not only made preparations for the use of gas, but were also prepared to make use of it. Neither of them, however, was sure of the effects that the use of gas would have on the operational level. On April 22, 1915, the Germans launched the first massive gas attack, with the release of 150 tons of chlorine from cylinders near Ypres. According to the most recent research a maximum of 800 to 1200 allied soldiers—the number is still a matter of debate—were killed. Many, however, simply fled their trenches in order to escape that fate. The German high command had, however, no reserves ready in the area to exploit the breakthrough they were able to achieve. So far no satisfactory answer has been given as to why not. Gas

was subsequently used by both parties on the western as well as the eastern front, but with no decisive success.

The tank made its reputation in the *Blitzkrieg* operations of the German generals in World War II and many who had been involved in its development during World War I later claimed that they had always aspired to such a strategic use of the new weapon. These stories have since been proved wrong. The tank was in reality developed as a trench warfare weapon, intended to break through the machine gun/barbed wire combination, which had led to the stabilization of the front-line by the end of 1914. It was first used by the British during the battle of the Somme in 1916, but with little success, mainly due to the little numbers, technical difficulties, and the fact that the troops did not know how to use them on the tactical level. Both the British and the French subsequently used tanks in several operations and achieved some success in breaking into enemy positions. They were, however, not able to break fully through enemy lines. Tank development on the side of the Central Powers was not substantial.

Of all new weapons of World War I, it was undoubtedly the airplane that established itself most brilliantly. Tens of thousands of army and navy officers and non-commissioned officers were trained as air crew and a substantial portion of ground artillery was adapted for antiaircraft defence. Air warfare not only brought a new dimension into the war, but for many also was the last refuge for honor and glory, as air fighting provided liberation from the horror of the trenches. A German pilot claimed that he was still fighting the honorable combat of man against man, which stood out like a thing of another age amid the din and shock of mass warfare. Air warfare was, however, much more than the fighting of two or more men in the skies, as planes and airships began to be used to drop bombs not only on the front-line, but also on civilian centers like London, Paris, Düsseldorf, Freiburg, or Cologne. Not only industrial areas, but also civilian marketplaces were targeted by the airforces of both sides. Overall, however, the war in the air had little impact on the outcome of the war, whether they were used over the battlefield or to bomb civilian and industrial areas.

Trench warfare also led to an enormous use of weapons and ammunition that had to be replaced at a pace never imagined before the war. Although the railway systems were expanded to a great extent, it was not possible to transport goods and troops by rail transport alone. Already in the first months of the war the military leaders therefore made use of improvised means of road transport by requisitioning private motorcars, taxis, and buses. The British army alone increased its number of motor vehicles from 1,485 in 1914 to 121,720 at the time of the armistice in 1918. At the peak of fighting in Verdun in 1916 12,000 vehicles used a makeshift road for 2 days to supply the French defenders and an entire division was permanently employed to maintain the vehicles.

C. Home Front Experiences

After the opening months of the war the development of military techniques and strategies brought about similar crises concerning munitions supplies for all waring parties. Comparable efforts were made to augment and rationalize production and similar measures were instituted to resolve the conflict between industry and the military in their competition for manpower. There were, of course, differences between the different belligerents and democratic countries like France or the United Kingdom took somewhat longer to adapt to the changing conditions the war brought about, but war collectivism was a feature in all countries involved in the war. Its elements were the collaboration between organized capital and the state, the accommodation of the patriotic labor movement, and the exclusion and prosecution of all groups that could not be integrated into the war effort. Economic mobilization for war placed enormous pressures on civilian society, including population movements to industrial centers; price and wage inflation; shortfalls of labor and industrial skills; shortages of accommodations, food, and fuel; labor militancy; and profiteering, with its accompanying popular discontent. Everyday life, with its rhythms, social patterns, and customary social sanctions, was profoundly disturbed in every country involved in the war, even if the front line was several thousand kilometers away, such as in the case of the Dominions of the British Empire.

D. Worldwide Warfare

World War I did not remain limited to the fighting in Europe, even though the major battles took place on this continent and the use of new weapons such as tanks and gas was limited to this part of the world. The first shot of British troops in the war was, for example, not fired in Europe, but at Port Philip Heads near Melbourne to stop a German ship from leaving the harbor on the morning of August 5, 1914. The Dominions did, however, not restrict their war efforts to guarding their harbors and protecting their coasts from an enemy attack, but raised large forces to contribute to the allied war effort. Australia, New Zealand, and South Africa, moreover, raised separate forces to occupy the German colonies in their neighborhood and even as far away as German East Africa, where the war only ended with the armistice in November, 1918. Their governments also refused to acquiesce to British leadership during the war, sending their prime ministers or Ministers of Defence to London to confer with British authorities about the conduct of the war and asserting their right to representation at the Versailles Peace Conference and to separate membership in the League of Nations. They were also involved in the naval war effort and responsible for the defence of their coastal shipping and the protection of adjacent waters. The ships of the Royal Australian Navy especially played an important role in driving the German East Asiatic Squadron to leave the Pacific.

The United States only entered the war militarily in April, 1917, but they had made a substantial contribution to the allied war effort before. Private firms had supported the allied governments in raising funds for their war effort and American productive capacities were used widely to increase allied war-related production. Even though the government officially pursued a policy of neutrality and even forced the British government to accept a loosening of its naval blockade of the Central Powers, it tolerated the open support to the allied war effort by private American enterprise. The sinking of the passenger ship *Lusitania* in 1915 led to the first wave of indignation against the Central Powers, but President Wilson remained firmly committed to a policy of neutrality and arbitration. Only after the renewed declaration of unrestricted submarine warfare did Wilson decide to break diplomatic relations with the Central Powers and to send American troops to Europe. He did this, however, not as an ally but as an associated power, thereby signaling that he was not prepared to fight for the war aims of the allied countries. The arrival of American troops in Europe did have a significant psychological impact, but, although not negligible, the use of American troops did not prove to be decisive militarily. The reasons were that they were not adapted to the new way of warfare and remained heavily dependant on the French for military equipment and modern weapons.

Two major Asian countries also played an important role, namely Japan and India. Whereas Japan entered the war on its own, India was involved in the war as a part of the British Empire. The Indian war effort was, however, far larger than the Japanese one, Japan restricting itself mainly to supporting the Royal Navy in the Pacific and later in the Indian Ocean and in the Mediterranean as well as occupying the German colonies in China and in the Pacific north of the equator.

India contributed a significant number of native troops not only to the campaign in Mesopotamia, but also in the Middle East and Europe. Large numbers of Indian troops were retained in India itself for fear of an Islamic uprising, which the Ottoman Sultan had called for as an Islamic leader. The Indian troops were not the only non-European soldiers on the western front. Moroccan and other indigenous units from the French African colonies also fought on the western front.

IV. COURSE OF EVENTS

World War I began on July 28, 1914 with the Austrian declaration of war on Serbia as a consequence of the assassination of Archduke Franz Ferdinand in Sarajevo by a Serb nationalist. Although the murder was the immediate cause of the declaration of war, the structural causes of the war lay much deeper. Among them were the development of national states and the rise of nationalism throughout the 19th century, the globalization of the world economy, the spreading of liberal and socialist ideas throughout the world, the imperialist expansion of all major European powers except Austria-Hungary, the complex structure of alliances that emerged around the turn of the century, and, as a consequence of the last two processes, the growing armaments race between the leading European powers. The German General Staff followed the adapted Schlieffen-plan and invaded Belgium and France on August 3, 1914 while leaving one-sixth of its forces in the east to resist a Russian attack on East Prussia. The German advance was only stopped at the Marne, where French commander-in-chief Joseph Joffre succeeded in counterattacking the spread-out German forces and driving them back about 50 kilometers. French and Russian offensive plans failed, the latter at the battle of Tannenberg at the end of August, 1914. A last attempt by the German high command to outflank the allied troops in western Belgium failed in October, 1914. Thereafter the front line stabilized and the period of trench warfare began on the western front. On the eastern front the same happened in December, 1914 and in the south Serbia had been able to withstand the Austrian offensive. Military operations were now characterized by massive firepower and the use of new weapons, but none of the waring parties were able to obtain any strategic success on the western front. Major allied offensives at the Somme in 1916 (60,000 casualties on the first day only) and at the Chemin des Dames and Ypres in 1917 were unsuccessful, as were German attempts to break the stalemate at Verdun in 1916 (about 695,000 casualties for the whole campaign). In the east, however, in 1915, the Central Powers were able to break up the deadlock and to force Russia to abandon Gallicia, Poland, and Kurland. In the south they were able to overrun Serbia. An attempt by Britain and France to come to its aid by landing troops in neutral Greece failed, as well as an attempt to knock the Ottoman Empire out of the war by attacking the Dardanelles. In 1916 Russia tried to regain the initiative with the so-called Brusilov offensive, but had to withdraw after some initial success. This failure contributed largely to the demoralization of the Russian army and to the beginning of the Russian Revolution, which finally, in March, 1918, forced the country out of the war. In 1915 Italy decided to join the Entente, but even though their activities bound up large amounts of Austrian troops in the border region no decision was reached in this new theater either. In March, 1918 the new German high command (Oberste Heeresleitung, OHL) tried to gain the upper hand by concentrating superior forces in the west before American troops would be able to join the allied war effort and thereby, they feared, tip the balance. Even though they were successful in the beginning, they failed for logistical reasons, however, because of the enormous amount of materials that the allied armies were able to mass against the German attack. In July, 1918 the allied forces counterattacked and succeeded in breaking the German front. The last months of the war saw a return to mobile warfare, which finally led to the demand of an armistice by the German government in November, 1918. The front in the Balkans broke in September, 1918 and Bulgaria and Austria-Hungary sought an armistice at the end of the month and in October, respectively. The Italian front was not pierced before the armistice.

The war was, however, not only fought in Europe, but also in the colonies and at sea. Most of the German colonies in Africa had been occupied by 1915 by French, British, Belgian, or Dominion troops. Only General Paul von Lettow-Vorbeck in German East Africa resisted until after the armistice and conducted a guerrilla war against British and South African troops. At sea the war was characterized by a similar stalemate as the land war. The British and German fleets only seldom came out from the safety of their bases and the only major sea-battle, the battle of Jutland, ended in a draw, which in effect meant a strategic success for the Royal Navy, as the German high seas fleet remained locked up in the North Sea. The Germans tried to break the impasse by attacking British and other commerce shipping with submarines, but after some initial success they finally failed to hit British food supplies and war

TABLE I

Course of Events[a]

	Western front	Eastern front	Italy and Balkans	War outside Europe	War at sea	Home front
July–September, 1914	8/3: G Attack on B & F 9/6–9/9: Battle of the Marne	8/26–8/30: Battle of Tannenberg	7/29: A-H attack on S	8/30: JP declaration of war 8/30–9/17: Aus and NZ forces occupy G Samoa and New Guinea 9/9: First USA mediation attempt	8/5: Beginning of the UK Blockade of G waters 9/22: G submarine sinks three UK armored cruisers	Solemn declarations of national unity in all countries 7/31: Assasination of F socialist leader Jean Jaurès
October–December, 1914	10/20–11/10: Battle of Ypres		12/6: Second A-H attack on S	10/3–10/21: JP occupation of G Micronesia 10/13: Boer Rebellion in SA 10/27: Occupation of G Togo by UK forces 11/2–11/5: Entente declarations of war on OE 11/7: Occupation of G Tsingtao by JP forces	11/1: UK squadron defeated by G Pacific squadron at Coronel (Chili) 12/8: Defeat of G Pacific squadron at the Falkland Islands	
January–March, 1915			2/3: OE attack on the Suez Canal		2/4: Beginning of the first phase of submarine warfare	1/19: First G air raid on London by zeppelin 3/20: First opposition against war credits in G
April–June, 1915	4/22: Second Battle of Ypres; first use of gas	5/1–5/3: Breakthrough of CP troops at Gorlice-Tarnow	5/23: I declaration of war on A-H	4/25: Landing of allied forces at Gallipoli	5/7: Sinking of the *Lusitania* by G submarine 5/13: Partial G suspension of submarine warfare.	5/26: Coalition government in the UK Asquith remains Prime Minister
July–September, 1915	9/22–11/11: F offensive in the Champagne	8/5: Occupation of Warsaw by CP		7/9: Occupation of G southwest Africa by SA forces	9/18: G stops submarine warfare against all neutral ships and passenger ships of all nations	8/19: War Aims Speech by G Reichskanzler Bethmann–Hollweg 9/5–9/8: Zimmerwald conference of the antiwar European left
October–December, 1915			10/5: Landing of allied forces in Salonika 10/14: Bu declaration of war on S 11/24: Occupation of S by CP	12/19–12/20: Allied withdrawal from Gallipoli		
January–March, 1916	2/21: Beginning of the Battle of Verdun			2/18: Occupation of G Cameroon by allied forces	2/29–5/4: Intensification of G submarine warfare	1/6: Introduction of conscription in the UK (exceptions for Ireland and married men) 1/29: Zeppelin raid on Paris

continues

continued

	Western front	Eastern front	Italy and Balkans	War outside Europe	War at sea	Home front
April–June, 1916		6/1: Beginning of the first Ru Brussilov Offensive		4/29: British capitulation at Kut-el-Amara	5/31–6/1: Battle of Jutland	4/24: Easter rising in Dublin 4/24–4/30: Kiental conference of antiwar European left
July–September, 1916	7/1: Beginning of the battle of the Somme 9/15: First use of tanks		8/27: Ro declaration of war on A-H			
October–December, 1916			12/6: Occupation of Bucarest by CP			11/7: Reelection of Woodrow Wilson as USA president 11/21: Death of A-H emperor Franz-Joseph 12/6: Asquith government replaced by war cabinet under the leadership of Lloyd George
January–March, 1917	3/14: G withdrawal to the Siegfried line	2/10–2/15: February Revolution in Russia		2/3: Breaking of diplomatic relations between the USA and G	2/1: G declaration of unrestricted submarine warfare	3/15: Abdication of Ru czar Nikolaj II
April–June, 1917	4/16: F offensive at the Chemin-des-Dames 5/20: Mutinies in the F army 6/26: Arrival of the first USA division in Europe	6/30–7/11: Second Brussilov Offensive		4/6: USA declaration of war on G		4/7: G emperor announces an electoral reform for Prussia after the war 4/16: Return of Lenin to Ru
July–September, 1917	7/31: Beginning of the third Battle of Ypres	9/3: Occupation of Riga by CP			8/1–8/2: Mutinies in the G high seas fleet	
October–December, 1917	11/20: First massive use of tanks at Cambrai	10/25: October revolution in Ru	10/24: I defeat at Caporetto	11/2: Balfour declaration in favor of a national home for Jews in Palestine 12/9: UK troops capture Jerusalem		
January–March, 1918	3/21: Beginning of G spring offensive	3/1: Occupation of Kiev by CP , 3/3: Peace Treaty of Brest-Litowsk between Ru & CP		1/8: Fourteen Points announced by USA President Wilson		1/8: War Aims Speech by Lloyd George January: Strike by A-H munitions workers
April–June, 1918						
July–September, 1918	8/8: Allied counteroffensive; black day of the G army	8/3: Landing of UK troops at Wladiwostok; beginning of allied intervention in Ru	9/15: Allied breakthrough in Macedonia	9/22: Collapse of G-OE front line in northern Palestine		9/29: G High Command demands immediate ceasefire and democratisation of G

continues

continued

	Western front	Eastern front	Italy and Balkans	War outside Europe	War at sea	Home front
October–December, 1918	11/11: Armistice with G	10/28: Czech declaration of independence	11/3: Armistice with A-H	10/30: Armistice with OE 11/14: Capitulation of G forces in east Africa	10/20: Formal end of submarine warfare 10/28: Mutinies in the G high seas fleet	10/28: Constitutional changes transform G into a constitutional monarchy 11/3: Seamen revolt in Kiel; beginning of revolutionary unrest in G 11/9: Abdication of German emperor Wilhelm II 11/11: Abdication of A-H emperor Charles I

^a Abbreviations: A-H = Austria-Hungary; Aus = Australia; B = Belgium; Bu = Bulgaria; CP = Central Powers; F = France; G = Germany; I = Italy; JP = Japan; NZ = New Zealand; OE = Ottoman Empire: Ro = Rumania; Ru = Russia; S = Serbia; SA = South Africa; UK = United Kingdom; USA = United States of America.

production in any significant manner. Commerce raiding was another way of attacking the resources of the allied nations, but most ships that had been transformed for that purpose were either destroyed by allied warships or interned in neutral countries. Rumors of new ships and the success of the few commerce raiders that were able to break the British naval blockade, however, kept naval authorities in Japan and the British dominions and colonies busy throughout the war.

V. PEACE SETTLEMENT AND WAR GUILT DEBATE

The war in military terms was over on November 11, 1918, but the decision as to what peace would look like still hung in the balance. The allied and associated powers decided to meet in Paris in January, 1919. United States President Woodrow Wilson had made clear in a statement in January, 1918 that his aim in fighting was not to help the Entente to reach their war aims, which had become more and more extreme—as did those of the Central Powers—the longer the war had lasted and had been set in secret negotiations throughout the war, but to construct a new world order. In his famous "Fourteen Points" Wilson had set out to end the period of secret diplomacy; to restore the sovereignty of Belgium, Serbia, and Rumania, as well as to achieve the restitution of the occupied parts of Russia and France, including Alsace-Lorraine; to win the right of self-determination for the nationalities in Austria-Hungary and the Ottoman Empire; to create a

League of Nations; and generally to make the world safe for democracy. The main European powers, however, did not share Wilson's enthusiasms for a new world order and were rather oriented toward securing the best terms possible for their respective countries. Especially French Prime Minister Georges Clemenceau, who at home was known as "the tiger," opposed Wilson at the peace conference, claiming that his country, as the main victim of the war, had a right to security and territorial integrity. It was only by threatening to leave the peace conference and with the diplomatic support of South African Defence Minister and member of the British War Cabinet Jan Smuts that Wilson finally succeeded in overcoming the French opposition to the League of Nations proposals. The French, however, insisted on strict military terms in the peace treaty so as to make future aggression by Germany impossible. They were supported at first by the British and Belgian delegations. British Prime Minister Lloyd George, however, returned to the traditional British policy of the balance-of-power as the conference progressed. In the

TABLE II

Peace Treaties

June 28, 1919	In Versailles with Germany
September 10, 1919	In St. Germain-en-Laye with Austria
November 27, 1919	In Neuilly with Bulgaria
June 4, 1920	In Trianon with Hungary
August 10, 1920	In Sévres with Turkey

final peace treaty Germany was declared solely responsible for the war, forced to abandon most of its fleet, forbidden to have an air force and tanks, and its armed forces were limited to a 100,000-man professional army serving long-term only. Moreover, it had to pay 269 billion Goldmark in reparations for the damages caused during the war, lost all its colonies, which were given to different allied countries as mandates by the League of Nations, and had to agree to occupation of the Rhineland (the western border area, including a large part of the country's economic capacities) for 15 years. The peace treaties also defined the new national borders of Germany, Austria, Hungary, and Bulgaria, the main profiteers being the newly founded states of Poland, Czechoslovakia, and Yugoslavia as well as Rumania. The delegations of the Central Powers were given no hearing at the conference and had either to accept or refuse the treaties, the latter signifying the resumption of military operations. All countries except the United States and Soviet Russia accepted the treaties, the former making a separate peace treaty with Germany in 1921, which excluded the paragraphs concerning the League of Nations and War Guilt from the original Versailles Peace Treaty.

Article 231 of the Versailles Peace Treaty stipulated that Imperial Germany had been the only power responsible for the outbreak of the war in 1914. Many in Germany viewed this as a humiliation of their nation and demanded a revision of the peace treaties. Nationalist parties took up their claim and brought it into the political arena, thereby weakening the traditional parties who were trying to bring stability to the newly democratic German nation. Hitler finally made a revision of the Versailles Peace Settlement one of his chief political aims. Allied politicians like Lloyd George agreed with those in Germany outraged by the accusation of war guilt. They were, however, not able to make the French government change its position, as France was very much afraid that a revision of the peace treaty would only be the first step toward renewed German aggression. After 1945 the Germans accepted the fact that they had been responsible for the outbreak, or, better, the unfettering of World War II very early on; they refused, however, to say the same about 1914. In 1961 Fritz Fischer was the first to challenge this position, claiming that France and Russia had only been passive in the July Crisis and that Germany had wanted the war. His book *Germany's Aims in the First World War* caused a general uproar in Germany and many other historians tried to prove that Fischer had been wrong. They claimed that the influence of the army had been strong in all countries, that Imperial Germany had acted out of a strategic necessity, and that generally the war had been unavoidable. Today Fischer's theses are mostly accepted by historians, especially after Stig Förster proved in 1995 that the German general staff had acted in exact knowledge of the fact that the coming war was not going to be a short and limited war. Even though they even did not expect to win it, they demanded their government give the order for the troops to march.

Also See the Following Articles

WARFARE, MODERN • WORLD WAR II

Bibliography

Burk, K. (1985). *Britain, America and the sinews of war 1914–1918.* Boston: George Allen & Unwin.

Chickering, R., & Förster, S. (Eds.) (1999). *Great War-Total War: Germany, France, Great Britain, and the United States, 1914–1918.* Cambridge, UK: Cambridge University Press.

Ferro, M. (1990). *La Grande Guerre 1914–1918.* Paris: Gallimard.

Fischer, F. (1967). *Germany's aims in the First World War.* London: Chatto & Windus.

Gilbert, M. (1994). *The First World War.* London: Weidenfeld and Nicholson.

Halpern, P. G. (1994). *A naval history of World War I.* London: UCL Press.

Harvey, A. D. (1992). *Collision of Empires: Britain in three world wars 1793–1945.* London: Hambledon Press.

Hiery, H. (1995). *The neglected war: The German South Pacific and the influence of World War I.* Honolulu: University of Hawai'i Press.

Lepick, O. (1998). *La grande guerre chimique, 1914–1918.* Paris: Presses Universitaires de France.

Marwick, A. (1991). *British society and the First World War* (2nd ed.). Basingstroke, UK: Macmillan.

Michalka, W. (Ed.) (1994). *Der Erste Weltkrieg: Wirkung, Wahrnehmung, Analyse.* Munich: Piper.

Robbins, K. (1993). *The First World War* (2nd ed.). Oxford, UK: Oxford University Press.

Terraine, J. (1992). *White heat: The new warfare 1914–18* (2nd ed.). London: Leo Cooper.

Trask, D. F. (1993). *The AEF and coalition warmaking, 1917–1918.* Lawrence: University Press of Kansas.

World War II

Charles S. Thomas

United States Naval War College/Georgia Southern University

GLOSSARY

Blitzkrieg Literally, German for "lightning war." Term coined by western journalists to describe the potent combination of armored and air power that Germany employed in the opening phases of World War II.

German–Soviet Nonaggression Pact Agreement signed on August 23, 1939, wherein Germany and the Soviet Union publicly promised not to aid each other's enemies in the event of war and privately drew up the plans for the partition of Poland.

Kamikaze Literally, "divine wind." Japanese term for the suicide pilots who crashed their aircraft into Allied ships in 1944 and 1945.

Lebensraum Literally, "living space." German term referring to territorial acquisitions necessary to provide mineral and especially agricultural resources to sustain a world power in its competition with other world powers.

Manchukuo Japanese name for the puppet state created by Japan in Manchuria in 1932.

Panzer Literally, "armored." German term for the ar-

mored divisions that formed the major ground component of the Blitzkrieg.

Peace of Paris Collective term for the five peace treaties that ended World War I between 1919 and 1920. The treaties were signed between the victorious Entente powers and individual members of the Central Powers: Germany, Treaty of Versailles; Austria, Treaty of St. Germain-en-Laye; Bulgaria, Treaty of Neuilly; Hungary, Treaty of Trianon; and Turkey, Treaty of Sèvres.

Tripartite Pact Pact signed between Germany, Japan, and Italy on September 27, 1940 promising mutual aid in the event that one of them was attacked by a power not currently involved in either the European or Asian wars. The pact sought to deter the United States from entering the war.

WORLD WAR II was the largest conflict in human history and devastated Europe, Asia, north Africa, and large portions of the Pacific. It began as two separate wars, one involving Japan against China in the 1930s, the other involving Germany against Poland, France, and Great Britain in 1939. With the entry of the United States into both wars in December, 1941, the two conflicts merged into a single global struggle during which a coalition of "Allied" powers (the United States, the Soviet Union, Great Britain, China, Free France, and a host of smaller nations) defeated a coalition of "Axis" states (Germany, Italy, Japan, and smaller satellites). This article uses a largely narrative approach, interspersed with a separate section on economic, psychological, and demographic aspects of the conflict, to describe the origins, course, and consequences of the war.

I. THE ORIGINS OF WORLD WAR II

The Peace of Paris (1919–1920) left an assortment of states dissatisfied with the outcome of World War I. All of the vanquished Central Powers (Germany, Austria, Bulgaria, Hungary, and Turkey) endured territorial losses, reparations, and quantitative or qualitative limitations on their armed forces. Although not a signatory of the Peace, the newly founded Soviet Union likewise lost territory to a tier of successor states in eastern Europe (Finland, the Baltic States, Poland, and Romania) that were either reestablished as states or enlarged following the collapse of Tsarist Russia. Even minor members of the victorious Entente complained that their wartime sacrifices far outweighed their gains and that the interests of the major victors—France, Great Britain, and the United States—had taken precedence over theirs. Italian patriots, for example, decried the "mutilated" peace that failed to bring Italy all of the territorial acquisitions promised by Entente statesmen in 1915. Similarly, although Japan fell heir to Germany's forfeited island holdings north of the equator in the Pacific, Japanese expansionists lamented their country's failure to gain additional territory on the Asian mainland at the expense of China.

Dissatisfaction over newly redrawn frontiers sparked a host of smaller conflicts in the immediate aftermath of the Great War. Between 1919 and 1921 Poland engaged in border struggles with Germany over Silesia, with Lithuania over the city of Vilna, and with Czechoslovakia over the region surrounding Teschen. Similarly, disputes over Poland's eastern border with the Ukraine (briefly independent after 1918) and the Soviet Union led to prolonged struggle, culminating in a full-scale Polish–Soviet war that only ended with the Treaty of Riga in 1921. Elsewhere, Italian irregulars skirmished with Yugoslav partisans over the city of Trieste in 1919, and in 1923 the new Italian dictator, Benito Mussolini, sent forces to bombard and briefly occupy the Greek island of Corfu following a boundary dispute between Greece and Italy's client state, Albania. Greek forces also waged a bitter war with Turkey between 1920 and 1922 that produced approximately 1,400,000 Greek and 400,000 Turkish refugees. Elsewhere in eastern and central Europe, the presence of significant unassimilated national minorities continued to complicate inter-

national relations. Nevertheless, by 1924, with the peaceful resolution of the Franco-Belgian dispute with Germany over war reparations and the Ruhr, it appeared that a tenuous peace had at last returned to Europe.

Developments in the mid- to late 1920s reinforced the appearance of normality. At the Locarno Conference of 1925 Germany voluntarily recognized its western frontiers with France and Belgium, and the following year Germany entered the League of Nations. Although the absence of the United States and the Soviet Union from membership in the League weakened the effectiveness of that organization, both countries became signatories (along with Britain, France, Germany, Italy, Japan, China, and 52 other states) of the Kellogg–Briand Pact of 1928, renouncing offensive war as an instrument of national policy.

The coming of the Great Depression in 1929–1930 altered this picture of international harmony. Most industrialized countries reacted to the Depression by adopting protectionist policies and emphasizing national solutions to the world economic crisis; gone was the spirit of international cooperation that had characterized the mid-1920s. The effects of the Depression also undercut both the military capability and the resolve of the major status quo powers, Great Britain and France, to uphold the Peace of Paris. The greatest impact of the Depression, however, was in those countries that would challenge the international status quo in 1930s. In Germany, economic catastrophe dramatically eroded public support for the Weimar Republic and immeasurably aided in the assumption of power by Adolf Hitler's aggressive and expansionist National Socialist (Nazi) Party. In Japan, the reduction in international trade occasioned by the Depression highlighted the Japanese home islands' paucity of natural resources and reawakened interest in expansion on the Asian mainland as a means of achieving autarky and reestablishing economic prosperity.

The first evidence of the changed international circumstances occurred in the Far East, where ultranationalist Japanese army officers initiated the conquest of Manchuria from China following a staged incident at Mukden in September, 1931. Chinese military resistance was ineffective, and League of Nations condemnation of Japanese action merely resulted in Japan's withdrawal from the League in 1933. That same year a truce left the Japanese in de facto control of "Manchukuo," as they now termed Manchuria.

The year 1933 brought changes in Europe as well, where on January 30, Hitler became chancellor of Germany. Hitler immediately began laying the foundations for a program of aggressive continental expansion, which he had outlined in his autobiography, *Mein Kampf* (1925/1927). On February 3 he met with leading generals and admirals to accelerate the small and secret rearmament program that the Weimar Republic had undertaken in violation of the Treaty of Versailles, that portion of the Peace of Paris pertaining to Germany. At the same meeting he revealed the underlying purpose of rearmament—the seizure of living space (*Lebensraum*) in the east and its "ruthless Germanization." In October, 1933 Germany withdrew from both the world disarmament conference and the League of Nations. In March, 1935, with rearmament already under way, Hitler announced the resumption of conscription and the reestablishment of an air force (*Luftwaffe*), both violations of the Treaty of Versailles.

For a time it appeared that Hitler's measures would meet with a firm international response. In April, 1935, at a meeting in Stresa, Italy, leaders of Britain, France, and Italy formally expressed their misgivings over Germany's action reestablishing conscription. They also reaffirmed the independence of the most likely target of German aggression, Austria, which was a fellow German speaking nation and the land of Hitler's birth. Two months later, however, on June 18, Britain concluded a separate agreement approving the expansion of Germany's navy, the one branch of the Reich's armed forces that still labored under restrictions imposed by Versailles. All remnants of the so-called "Stresa Front" disappeared the following October, when Britain and France condemned Italy's invasion of Ethiopia. The resulting rift between the two western democracies and Italy resulted in Italy's withdrawal from the League of Nations. It also distracted international attention from the continuing process of German rearmament, including Hitler's remilitarization of the Rhineland in March, 1936, and helped to pave the way for an Italo-German rapprochement that same year.

The Spanish Civil War, which broke out in July, 1936, had much the same effect. While France and a decidedly more reluctant Britain provided marginal support for the established Spanish republic, Germany and Italy furnished substantial economic and military aid for Francisco Franco's insurgents, who would ultimately secure power after a 3-year struggle. Mussolini's pronouncement of a Rome–Berlin "Axis" on November 1, 1936 provided further evidence of closer Italo-German relations. That same month Germany and Japan signed the Anti-Comintern Pact, pledging mutual cooperation against the machinations of the Communist International, a Soviet-sponsored organization that had loudly championed world revolution since its foundation in 1919. Not to be left behind, Italy joined the Anti-Comintern Pact in January, 1937. Although neither the Rome–Berlin Axis nor the Anti-Comintern Pact represented formal military alliances, the increasing community of interest between Germany, Italy, and Japan was evident.

In July, 1937 renewed fighting broke out between Japan and China. During the ensuing struggle, which lasted until the end of World War II 8 years later, the nominal leader of China, Chiang Kai-shek, was unable or unwilling to forge an effective united front against the Japanese invaders. Instead, Chiang's Kuomintang (Nationalist) Party, Mao Tse-tung's Chinese Communist Party, and a host of independent warlords pursued largely distinct policies that were aimed as much at each other as they were at the Japanese. Coupled with China's notorious backwardness, these internal divisions facilitated Japanese efforts to occupy vast areas of China, including most of its major industrial centers and ports. Another feature of the war was its exceptional brutality. Both sides routinely slaughtered each other's wounded and prisoners, and Japan's greater arsenal of aircraft enabled it to launch terror raids on those cities that remained beyond Japanese control. Perhaps the most horrible atrocity of the Sino-Japanese War, however, was the so-called Rape of Nanking in December, 1937, during which Japanese soldiers ran amuck in the former Nationalist capital and murdered between 200,000 and 300,000 Chinese civilians. Perhaps because of this event and others like it, public and official opinion in Britain and the United States gradually tilted in favor of Chiang, whose government relocated from Nanking to Chungking, in the interior of China. Most support from the Western democracies was initially moral rather than material. Eventually, though, small amounts of military and economic aid would begin trickling into China via French Indochina or, after March, 1939, the famous Burma Road.

While Japanese troops engaged in bloody fighting in China, Hitler's Germany enjoyed a series of bloodless triumphs in central Europe. In March, 1938 German troops occupied Austria without opposition. Many within both countries saw this as the logical reunion of kindred people who had been wrongly separated by Otto von Bismarck's exclusion of Austria from German affairs in 1866. Despite some reservations, the governments of Britain and France found it difficult to deny the logic of this argument, and Mussolini, who had earlier opposed union (*Anschluss*) between Germany and Austria, now gave his blessings to Hitler's action.

The German dictator wasted little time in moving toward his next objective. Throughout the summer of 1938, Hitler encouraged the largely German-speaking populace of the Sudetenland, the frontier region of Czechoslovakia, to demand union with Germany. Czechoslovakia's international standing was outwardly more secure than Austria's had been; it was allied with France and had recently negotiated a defensive pact with the Soviet Union that was conditional upon activation of the French alliance. Unfortunately for Czechoslovakia, French action was unlikely without British support. In September, 1938, at meetings at Berchtesgaden and Bad Godesberg with Neville Chamberlain, the British prime minister, Hitler delineated the stark choice between international acquiescence to German demands on Czechoslovakia, or war. On September 29 and 30, at a four-power conference at Munich, which included Germany, Italy, Britain, and France and which excluded both Czechoslovakia and the Soviet Union, Britain and France approved of German acquisition of the Sudetenland in exchange for Hitler's guarantee of the integrity of the remainder of Czechoslovakia. Abandoned by the western democracies, Czechoslovakia reluctantly implemented the provisions of the Munich Pact in October.

Munich represented the high point of the western democracies' strategy of "appeasement"—that is, the attempt to maintain peace by making concessions to aggrieved states such as Germany. Hitler kept the promises he made there for less than 6 months, for on March 15, 1939 German forces occupied Bohemia and Moravia, the Czech-speaking portions of Czechoslovakia. The following day Hitler announced their conversion into a German "Protectorate." Although Slovakia remained nominally independent, its status as a German puppet state was equally evident. On March 23, Germany reannexed Memel from Lithuania, which had occupied it in 1923. Any thoughts that Hitler's appetite for territory was sated now disappeared, and on March 31, Britain and France guaranteed the independence of Poland, a state which German diplomats had already begun seeking to cajole into concessions and which, like the recently dismembered Czechoslovakia, contained a large German minority.

Hitler's demands on Poland concerned two vital issues: reacquisition of the Free City of Danzig, a largely German port city on the Baltic that had been separated from Germany and placed under League of Nations supervision in 1919, and Polish cession of extraterritorial transit rights across the "Polish Corridor" separating German-controlled East Prussia from the rest of the Reich. Polish leaders, including Foreign Minister Josef Beck, feared that any alteration of the status of the Corridor or Danzig would be the first step in transforming Poland into a Nazi satellite.

Consequently, during the winter, spring, and summer of 1939, Poland politely but firmly rejected German approaches.

Hitler responded by accusing the Poles of atrocities against the German minority in Poland and by solidifying his own alliances. On May 22, Hitler and Mussolini concluded the "Pact of Steel," an offensive alliance that outwardly cemented the Rome–Berlin Axis. Far more surprising, however, was the signing of a German–Soviet Nonaggression Pact on August 23, wherein the two countries publicly pledged not to aid each other's enemies in the event of war. A secret annex to the agreement stipulated the partition of Poland between Germany and the Soviet Union in the event of German–Polish hostilities. Hitler clearly intended that the public rapprochement between the Soviet Union and Germany, bitter ideological enemies since 1933, would discourage British and French intervention on Poland's behalf. On August 25, however, Britain and Poland concluded a formal treaty of alliance, thus complementing the preexisting Franco-Polish alliance; that same day Hitler's own ally, Mussolini, privately informed him that Italy was not yet prepared for war. These latest developments notwithstanding, Hitler initiated the invasion of Poland on September 1, 1939. In contrast to the experiences in Austria and Czechoslovakia in 1938 and 1939, the Poles resisted, and on September 3, Britain and France declared war upon Germany.

II. THE EXPANSION OF THE AXIS (1939–1942)

The German invasion of Poland revealed many of the features that were to become hallmarks of the war. Although only 16 of 55 German combat divisions employed in Poland were heavily mechanized (6 *Panzer* and 10 motorized infantry), their level of training and ability to coordinate closely with units of the *Luftwaffe* gave the German army huge advantages over the Polish army, which relied primarily on traditional infantry and cavalry formations. Exploiting a potent combination of firepower and mobility that western journalists subsequently styled *Blitzkrieg* ("lightning war"), German forces reached Warsaw on September 15. The indiscriminate aerial bombing of the Polish capital during the ensuing siege foreshadowed the fate of many cities, great and small, European and Asian, during the war. Likewise, isolated acts of violence against civilians, including the murder of Jews at places such as Lukow and Czestochowa, anticipated Hitler's more radical measures in 1941 and 1942. The war's tendency to make strange partners became evident on September 17, when, in accordance with the secret provisions of the German–Soviet Nonaggression Pact, Soviet forces swept over the lightly defended eastern border of Poland and began the occupation of the eastern half of that unfortunate country. On September 27, Warsaw surrendered to German forces, and by October 6 all organized resistance within Poland had ceased, leaving the Germans and the Soviets in de facto control of the country. A Polish government in exile ultimately settled in London, the first of many refugee governments that would locate there during the war.

While German and Soviet forces completed the conquest of Poland, Britain and France sought to mobilize for a longer and more deliberate struggle. Although Hitler pressed for an immediate offensive against France, the onset of winter forced the postponement of major action in the west until the following spring. In Scandinavia, however, conflict broke out in two separate arenas. In November, 1939, the Soviet Union initiated a brief but costly war with Finland in order to secure a more defensible frontier in the northeast. The Soviet Union's aggression resulted in its expulsion from the League of Nations, a unique event in the history of that organization, but on March 12 the Finns signed the Treaty of Moscow, thereby relinquishing more than a tenth of their territory to the Soviets. Then, on April 9, 1940, German forces invaded Denmark and Norway in order to protect German access to Swedish iron ore and to gain bases for expanded naval operations against the British. Danish forces capitulated within a day, after which the Danish government continued to hold office under a German "Reich Plenipotentiary." Abetted by Allied expeditionary forces, formal Norwegian resistance continued until the country was overwhelmed in June, 1940, after which a Norwegian government in exile formed around King Haakon VII in Britain.

Allied failure in Norway prompted the fall of the Chamberlain Cabinet in Britain and its replacement by one headed by Winston Churchill on May 10. That same day Hitler began his long-awaited offensive in the west. German troops rapidly overran Luxembourg, the Netherlands, and Belgium. On May 20, German tanks reached the English Channel, thereby cutting off the British Expeditionary Force (BEF) and much of the French army, which failed to use its own substantial armored force effectively. In the air the *Luftwaffe* provided effective close support for ground troops and, on May 14, leveled the center of the undefended city of Rotterdam. By May 26, the Allied position in the Low Countries was hopeless, prompting the British to evacuate approximately 340,000 Allied troops, roughly two-thirds of whom were British, from the port of Dunkirk (Operation Dynamo). Although the BEF would live to fight another day, virtually all of its heavy equipment had to be abandoned on the continent.

Buoyed by its recent successes, the German army then turned on France, whose forces had already suffered severely during the campaign through the Low Countries. French attempts to restore the situation by replacing Maurice Gamelin with Maxime Weygand as supreme military commander proved unavailing. The French debacle prompted Mussolini's Italy to declare war on Britain and France on June 10 in a belated effort to share some of the spoils of the anticipated Allied collapse. Italy's underequipped and poorly led ground forces made no significant difference to the campaign. Nevertheless, the Wehrmacht's continued successes in the north resulted in the occupation of Paris on June 14 and Premier Paul Reynaud's resignation and his replacement by the aged World War I marshal, Philippe Pétain, 2 days later. Pétain sought and received an armistice, which was signed on June 22 and which went into effect on June 25. By its terms, German forces occupied three-fifths of metropolitan France, including Paris, the Channel coast, and the Bay of Biscay coast. The remaining two-fifths of France remained under the control of the Pétain government, which relocated to Vichy. From that small spa, the Pétain regime retained control over a small army, a substantial fleet, and the greater part of France's overseas empire, whose garrisons generally chose to follow the lead of Vichy rather than the small Free French movement that was forming under Charles de Gaulle.

Germany's stunning victory had taken scarcely 6 weeks. Many observers, including Pétain, now anticipated British entreaties for a negotiated settlement with the Axis powers, and on June 28, Pope Pius XII made offers to Britain, Germany, and Italy to mediate between the warring parties. The Churchill government, however, proceeded with its own plans for continuing the war. On the same day as the Pope's mediation effort, Britain officially recognized de Gaulle as the leader of Free France, and on July 3 the Royal Navy launched a destructive attack on Vichy French naval forces at the port of Mers-el-Kébir in North Africa to preclude their use by the Axis. Despite Britain's show of resolution, Hitler evidently still anticipated peace overtures. Thus, although he approved limited air raids on British ports and convoys in July and issued a directive on July 16 for the armed forces to prepare for the eventual invasion of Britain (Operation Sealion), in a speech on July 19 he also hinted at a compromise peace that would allow Britain to retain its empire in return for recognition of

Germany's gains on the continent. When the British government rebuffed this overture on July 22, Hitler ordered the *Luftwaffe* to accelerate its campaign to achieve air supremacy preparatory to a cross-Channel invasion of Britain in the early fall.

The resulting air campaign, known as the Battle of Britain, proved noteworthy for a number of reasons. In the first place, the Royal Air Force (RAF) was able to deny the Luftwaffe air supremacy, ultimately prompting Hitler to postpone Sealion indefinitely on September 17. The cost in men and material in this first major German setback was significant for both sides; between July 10 and October 31, the *Luftwaffe* lost over 1300 aircraft, while the RAF sustained almost 800 aircraft destroyed and over 500 aircrew killed.

Losses to aviators, however, paled in comparison to civilian losses, for after an initial period in which each side avoided densely populated targets, the *Luftwaffe* and RAF Bomber Command engaged in bombing strategies that knew fewer and fewer restraints. The two national capitals figured prominently in the mutual escalation of terror. Accidental German bombing of London on August 24, for example, prompted a British retaliatory strike on Berlin on the night of August 25. Hitler responded with a series of attacks on London, initially by day and later, as *Luftwaffe* losses mounted, by night. Between September 7 and November 12, the *Luftwaffe* undertook 58 major raids on London. The *Luftwaffe* also attacked Birmingham, Manchester, Liverpool, Clydebank, Plymouth, Coventry, and a host of other industrial centers and ports, in the process killing approximately 42,000 British civilians and seriously wounding another 50,000. Most German cities were initially spared major British raids, partly because the RAF was busy trying to disrupt preparations for Sealion by bombing invasion craft in the Channel ports in France and the Low Countries, partly because of the RAF's initial difficulties in finding even city-sized targets at night. The ordeal of the German cities would come later.

In the meantime, the other powers of the world sought to adjust to the changed circumstances occasioned by France's fall. In spite of the German–Soviet Nonaggression Pact, the ease with which the Wehrmacht had crushed the French army caused deep concern for the Soviet Union. Although Josef Stalin continued to seek good relations with Germany, during the summer of 1940 Soviet forces annexed Bessarabia and northern Bukovina from Romania and formally integrated Estonia, Latvia, and Lithuania, which had been occupied the year before, into the Soviet Union. Coupled with the earlier seizure of eastern Poland, it was hoped that these annexations would form an advanced bastion against a potential German invasion.

The United States also took precautions. In July President Franklin Roosevelt signed the Two-Ocean Navy Expansion Act, which, when completed, would give the United States a navy that would dwarf any potential competitor. In August the United States began transferring 50 overage destroyers to the British in exchange for long-term leases on bases in the western hemisphere. Nor were American preparations confined to naval matters, for on September 16, 1940, the United States Congress enacted limited conscription. Clearly, the German conquest of western Europe had sent alarming signals across the Atlantic.

If Germany's success threatened the United States and the Soviet Union, it seemed to offer opportunity to Japan, which by 1940 was mired in a seemingly endless war with China. The German conquest of the Netherlands and France meant that those countries could deploy only weak forces to defend their holdings in the Far East, the Netherlands' East Indies and France's Indochina. Britain's navy, long a bulwark of western influence in the Far East, was likewise stretched to the limit by the fall of France and the addition of a significant Italian fleet as an adversary in the Mediterranean. Particularly within the Imperial Japanese Navy, expansionists hoped that the conquest of southeast Asia and Indonesia would simultaneously give Japan the resources necessary to finish the war in China and allow it to withstand any pressure by Britain and the United States to relinquish its gains. In September, 1940 Japanese forces occupied northern Indochina as a first step in the acquisition of the so-called Southern Resources Area. On September 27, Japan signed the Tripartite Pact with Germany and Italy, wherein each party pledged to come to the aid of the other should one of them be attacked by a power not currently engaged in either the Sino-Japanese War or the war in Europe. Since a special clause of the agreement excluded the Soviet Union as a possible adversary, the Tripartite Pact was an obvious warning to the United States to stay out of the conflicts in Asia and Europe.

For a time, in the fall of 1940, German leaders contemplated luring the Soviet Union into the Tripartite Pact as well. In November, 1940, the German Foreign Minister, Joachim von Ribbentrop, sought to persuade his Soviet counterpart, Vyacheslav Molotov, to join an anti-British bloc consisting of Germany, Japan, Italy, and the Soviet Union. Hitler's and Stalin's suspicions over each other's designs in eastern Europe as well as continued signs of British resilience precluded such an arrangement. By early winter Hitler had returned to earlier plans to attack the Soviet Union. Conquest of the Soviet Union, he reasoned, would destroy British hope of a continental ally (thereby encouraging a victorious peace with Britain), gain the *Lebensraum* that National Socialist ideology claimed was indispensable for Germany's survival as a great power, and, by removing the Soviet threat to Japan in the Far East, free Japan to menace the United States. On December 18, 1940, Hitler ordered completion of preparations for the invasion of the Soviet Union, codenamed Operation Barbarossa, by the following May.

By spring 1941, however, the strategic situation was changing rapidly. During the winter Hungary, Romania, and Bulgaria had tilted toward the Axis by signing the Tripartite Pact. On the other hand, Italian offensives from Libya into Egypt (September, 1940) and from Albania into Greece (October, 1940) had been turned back by British and Greek counteroffensives during the winter. In March, 1941, Yugoslavian army officers balked at their country's adherence to the Tripartite Pact, and, after a coup d'etat on March 27, Yugoslavia signed a treaty of friendship with the Soviet Union the following month. Although the vast seas of mud resulting from the spring thaw would probably have delayed the start of Barbarossa in any case, the deteriorating Axis position in the Balkans and in the Mediterranean necessitated German action to shore up the southern flank before the invasion of the Soviet Union. In February, 1941 Hitler dispatched General Erwin Rommel's Afrika Korps to bolster Italian forces in north Africa. In April and May, German forces overran first Yugoslavia and then Greece. The monarchs of both nations joined a lengthening list of refugees in London; meanwhile, their two countries became the scene of some of the most ferocious guerrilla activity of the war.

All previous campaigns of the war, however, were dwarfed in size and ferocity by the implementation of Operation Barbarossa on June 22, 1941. On that day over 3,000,000 German soldiers and 500,000 soldiers from an array of allies that would ultimately include Finland, Slovakia, Romania, Hungary, and Italy (plus a volunteer division from Franco's Spain) began the largest offensive thus far seen in European history. Aided by the element of surprise and the employment of huge armored encirclement battles, Axis forces inflicted massive losses on the Red Army. By mid-September, German forces had taken Kiev in the Ukraine and were besieging Leningrad in the north; by December 5, amid rapidly deteriorating weather conditions, the German army had driven to within 19 miles of Moscow. That same day, however, the Red Army began a series of counterattacks which, over the next 2 months, would drive the German army back from the gates of Moscow and ensure that the Soviet Union would remain in the war, at least for another year.

The campaign on the eastern front reached levels of savagery that, with isolated exceptions, had not been seen elsewhere in the European war. Excluding the sick, casualties in the German army during the first year of war with the Soviet Union totaled almost 1,300,000; Soviet losses were vastly larger. In addition, both sides used the age-old policy of "scorched earth" to deny resources and shelter to the enemy. The impact of modern ideological training was also more evident on the eastern front than it had been in the western campaigns. In 1941, the German army encouraged its soldiers to make free and easy use of a series of "Commissar Orders" to execute Red Army political leaders on the spot. Depending on the circumstances and the proximity of SS *Einsatzgruppen* ("Action Squads"), other categories of Soviet citizens—members of the Communist party, intellectuals, common soldiers, civilians, and especially Jews—risked falling victim to a similar fate. Maltreatment, starvation, and overwork awaited even those "lucky" soldiers of the Red Army who managed to attain the status of "normal" prisoners of war; of approximately 5,700,000 Soviet soldiers captured during the war, 3,300,000 died in captivity. In 1941, the advancing German army lost far fewer prisoners to the Red Army. Nevertheless, the initiation of partisan warfare behind German lines guaranteed an endless cycle of atrocities by both sides.

In December, 1941, the war took another major turn with the entry of the United States into both the war in Europe and the war in the Far East. Since the signing of the Tripartite Pact in September, 1940, United States relations with the Axis powers had deteriorated markedly. In March, 1941, the Roosevelt administration had shepherded through a Lend-Lease bill, a formal extention of military and economic aid to Britain and China. Following the German invasion of the Soviet Union, the United States had included the Soviets in Lend-Lease as well. In the fall of 1941, as United States naval forces began assisting in convoying war material to Great Britain, an undeclared war had broken out at sea between the United States and Germany.

It was Japan, however, that initiated formal hostilities with the United States. This decision came after the United States had frozen Japanese assets and imposed an oil embargo following Japanese occupation of southern Indochina in July, 1941, a measure that American diplomats correctly saw as a preparatory step toward further Japanese expansion into southeast Asia. After successive Japanese and American negotiations revealed the fundamental incompatibility of the two countries' aims, Japan's government decided on war rather than retreat. Although Japanese planners intended for the declaration of war to be delivered minutes before the scheduled carrier air strikes on Pearl Harbor, delays in decrypting the wording of the announcement at the Japanese embassy in Washington meant that formal notification of war occurred after the devastating attack on United States forces in Hawaii. That same day Japan also declared war on Great Britain. In view of the brazen nature of the Japanese attack, the other signatories of the Tripartite Pact were not technically bound to come to Japan's aid; nevertheless, on December 11, both Germany and Italy declared war on the United States, thus transforming what had been two parallel regional wars into a true world war.

The next 6 months brought a string of Japanese successes. Between December, 1941 and May, 1942, Japanese army and naval forces conquered Guam, Hong Kong, Wake Island, Malaya, the Netherlands' East Indies, most of Burma, the Philippines, and a host of smaller islands in the Pacific. In the process the Japanese army inflicted a stunning defeat on the British army at Singapore, taking over 100,000 British and Commonwealth prisoners. The Japanese also captured large numbers of American prisoners at Bataan and Corregidor in the Philippines. Allied prisoners would suffer terrible privations over the next 3 years, in forced marches to POW camps (such as the Bataan Death March), in forced labor, or simply in the camps themselves.

Japan's remarkable successes in the Pacific and southeast Asia coincided with the renewal of offensive action by Axis forces in north Africa and Russia. In June, 1942, German and Italian forces recaptured the Libyan fortress of Tobruk from the British. Rommel's subsequent advance into Egypt was halted later that summer at El Alamein by logistical difficulties and determined British resistance. In Russia German forces sought to capture the Caucasus, at that time the main oil producing region of the Soviet Union, and the city of Stalingrad, a major industrial and transportation center on the Volga. Although the Red Army resisted doggedly, by November, 1942 much of the Caucasus and approximately 90% of Stalingrad were in German hands. Anticipating the fall of the city, Hitler assured the German public that Stalingrad was his.

III. THE TURNING OF THE TIDE (1942–1943)

In fact, Axis claims to final victory were premature. The first faint signs of this became evident in the Pacific where, at the Battle of the Coral Sea in May, 1942, an American carrier task force, forewarned by decrypted enemy radio transmissions, compelled a Japanese invasion fleet to turn back from its intended target, Port Moresby, New Guinea. Although tactically a draw, the battle represented the first significant strategic setback for the Japanese in the Pacific war; it was also noteworthy as the first fleet engagement on the high seas in which all offensive action was undertaken by carrier-based or land-based air units rather than surface vessels. In June, 1942, American carrier forces again exploited Allied code-breaking abilities and inflicted a devastating defeat upon the Japanese at the battle of Midway in the central Pacific, sinking four irreplaceable Japanese fleet carriers at a cost of one of their own. In August, United States marines began the invasion of Guadalcanal in the Solomon Islands, initiating a bitter 6-month campaign of attrition that imposed further losses on the Imperial Navy and culminated in American conquest of the island in February, 1943. By the end of 1942, the United States had clearly wrested the initiative from the Japanese in the Pacific.

The Axis also sustained setbacks in north Africa. On October 23, General (later Field Marshal) Bernard Montgomery's British 8th Army began an offensive to drive Rommel's German and Italian forces from their positions at El Alamein. When Axis troops finally began to retreat on November 4, Montgomery pursued cautiously but relentlessly, bringing his army to the gates of Tripoli by the end of the year. Moreover, Allied exploitation of the success of Operation TORCH, the Anglo-American invasion of the Vichy French colonies of Morocco and Algeria on November 8, 1942, would confine Axis forces in north Africa to a narrow bridgehead in Tunisia by the following spring. In the Mediterranean as in the Pacific, the initiative now rested with the Allies.

The winter of 1942–1943 brought a devastating blow to the Axis in Russia. On November 19, 1942, Soviet-mechanized forces undertook a massive pincer movement (Operation Uranus) against the German forces besieging Stalingrad. When Soviet formations linked up with one another 4 days later, they isolated over 200,000 German soldiers in the Stalingrad pocket. Partly because of the symbolic value he attached to a city bearing the name of Stalin, Hitler refused to approve a German withdrawal. Bolstered by *Luftwaffe* assurances that the pocket could be resupplied by air, he ordered the German commander at Stalingrad, Friedrich Paulus, to maintain his position at all costs. By late January, 1943, the situation was clearly hopeless. On January 30, Paulus received notification of his promotion to the rank of field marshal, along with Hitler's pointed reminder that no one holding such an exalted rank in the Prusso-German pantheon had ever been captured. The following day, Paulus surrendered those portions of the Stalingrad force that were still under his effective command, and by February 2 all resistance at Stalingrad had ceased. In the course of the battle, over 100,000 German soldiers had fallen prisoner to the Red Army; the overwhelming majority of these would never see Germany again, succumbing instead to exposure, a devastating typhus epidemic in the summer of 1943, or persistent overwork in Soviet prison camps.

Stalingrad was perhaps the most dramatic and highly publicized turning point of World War II. It was, however, a different victory—the defeat of the German submarine threat after a much less visible but even more prolonged campaign—that marked the final step in the _annus mirabilis_ of the war. In late 1940 and again from 1942 until early 1943, Allied merchant ship losses to German submarines severely threatened Great Britain's economic survival. Yet even as the "Battle of the Atlantic" reached its climax in the spring of 1943, developments were underway that would doom Axis efforts. Buoyed by a 10-fold increase in cargo ship construction in the United States and Canada, available Allied shipping capacity had begun to outpace continued heavy losses to German wolfpacks in the winter of 1942–1943. In the spring of 1943, moreover, Allied countermeasures, including the use of escort carriers, long-range patrol aircraft, airborne radar, and improved search-and-destroy techniques by surface escorts, began to inflict heavy damage on Germany's submarines. In May, 1943 Germany lost 47 U-boats while Allied shipping losses dropped dramatically. Confronted with such losses, the head of the German navy, Grand Admiral Karl Dönitz, reluctantly withdrew his submarines from the vital north Atlantic convoy routes to safer but less crucial areas. Thenceforth, the sustenance of Britain and the transatlantic mobilization of men and material for the liberation of western Europe could proceed without major impediment.

IV. NATIONS AT WAR

Allied victory in the Battle of the Atlantic was partly the result of the vast disparity between the economic power of the Atlantic Allies—the United States, Britain, and Canada—and that of Germany. This disparity was evident in the land and air campaigns in Europe and in the Allied war against Japan as well. Indeed, it was in the economic sector of warfare that the shortcomings

of the Axis vis-à-vis the Allies were most glaringly evident.

A comparison of national consumption of modern energy sources—coal, petroleum, natural gas, and hydroelectricity—offers a rough indication of the disparity in the opposing coalitions' potential for waging an industrialized war. Expressed in equivalents of million metric tons of coal, approximate energy consumption in 1938 for the three major partners of the Axis were Germany (228), Japan (96.5), and Italy (27.8), a coalition total of 352.3 million metric tons. Equivalent figures for the future Allied coalition were the Soviet Union (177), Great Britain (196), and the United States (697), a coalition total of 1070 million metric tons of coal equivalent.

These figures, however, tell only part of the story. Because of the lingering effects of the Great Depression, much of the United States' industrial work force and infrastructure was underutilized in 1938. Nevertheless, in that same year, with two-thirds of its steel mills idle, the United States produced almost as much steel (26.4 million tons) as Germany and Japan combined (26.7 million tons) and with German and Japanese mills working near their full capacity. Once war production began, the United States could exploit its reserve capacity to achieve far greater levels of production. German conquest of France and the Low Countries in 1940 and of the western part of the Soviet Union in 1941 should have partially offset this imbalance by bringing new resources to the Axis in Europe, but Axis gains in the Soviet Union were partially offset by a number of factors. By utilizing draconian evacuation measures, the Soviets were able to relocate many skilled workers and large amounts of industrial equipment farther to the east, beyond the reach of German forces. Moreover, "scorched earth" policies and partisan activities severely hampered industrial production in German occupied territories. A final factor, however, was the nature of German rule in Russia, for wasteful looting of resources, mass deportations, and maltreatment of the remaining work force also took their toll. As a result, in 1943, the German-occupied portions of the Soviet Union produced only one-tenth of their prewar industrial yield.

Decisions as to what to produce and when to produce it also dramatically impacted the war-making capabilities of the two coalitions. Early in the war, Hitler's conviction that the collapse of the home front had caused German defeat in World War I prompted him to allow considerable consumer spending in Germany. Similarly, his confidence that the war would be short resulted in cutbacks or time-consuming shifts in armaments production in 1940, after the fall of France, and again in the fall of 1941, when the success of BARBA-ROSSA seemed certain. It was only in January, 1942, after his failure to take Moscow, that Hitler yielded to the prodding of Fritz Todt, his Minister of Armaments and Production, and ordered massive increases in war production. Thereafter, by shifting production priorities, eliminating overlapping agencies, and transferring millions of German and foreign workers into key industries, Todt's successor, Albert Speer, achieved noticeable armaments increases, even as the Allied strategic bombing campaign reached its crescendo. Taking the combined production of tanks, assault guns, and self-propelled guns as a measure, Germany's total rose from 5,200 in 1941 to 19,800 in 1943 and peaked at 27,300 in 1944.

Britain's war mobilization offers an interesting contrast with the German experience. Fully a year and a half before his initial setbacks in Russia drove home the same lesson to Hitler, the fall of France in 1940 shattered the illusion that the Allies could win the war without undue disruption of civilian life. In the wake of Dunkirk British men and women were subjected to more stringent rationing, greater taxation, and more extreme demands on their labor than their German counterparts endured. As a result, British war production compared favorably with that of Germany, despite Britain's smaller population and its aging industrial plant. British vulnerability to air attack had prompted crash programs in fighter production even before the outbreak of war, and by the time of the Battle of Britain in 1940, Britain's annual production of aircraft already outstripped that of Germany (15,049 to 10,826). Britain's ascendancy in this sector continued until 1944, when Speer's belated efforts resulted in 39,275 German aircraft (mostly less expensive single-engine interceptors) to balance Britain's annual production of 26,461, including many four-engine bombers. By that time large numbers of Soviet and American aircraft were deployed in Europe to keep the balance firmly tilted in favor of the Allies.

Soviet war production suffered severely from the German conquest of heavily industrialized regions in western Russia and the Ukraine. Nevertheless, the relocation of capital goods and workers beyond the reach of the Germans and the prewar industrial development of areas east of the Urals meant that Soviet production of basic armaments remained formidable. Soviet tank production exceeded that of Germany in every year of the war, as did Soviet aircraft production in all years except 1940. Perhaps more threatening to Soviet survival was the loss of fertile agricultural land and farm workers to German control. In 1942 and 1943, Soviet

agricultural production fell to less than 40% of the level in 1940. In view of this, it was in the delivery of foodstuffs as well as over 400,000 trucks and jeeps that United States Lend-Lease aid to the Soviet Union proved most vital.

That the United States could provide enormous amounts of military and economic aid to its allies while equipping its own forces was testimony to American economic muscle. Nevertheless, although early British and French purchases, prewar naval expansion, and Lend-Lease all helped to "jump start" American mobilization, it was not until mid-1943 that United States production began to reach peak efficiency. Once underway, however, the flood of American war material was spectacular. One measure of this may be seen in the wartime production of aircraft carriers, the key to the gigantic naval engagements between the United States and Japan in the Pacific. Between 1941 and 1945 the United States built 18 fleet carriers and 116 light carriers compared to 6 fleet carriers and 14 light carriers for Japan. Such an overwhelming disparity radically narrowed Japanese options. Indeed, to many Japanese, by late 1944 and 1945, the only viable alternatives open to their country appeared to be surrender or the suicide tactics of the *Kamikaze* pilots.

The *Kamikaze* represented an extreme and, to western observers, unfathomable example of the attempt to redress material weakness with psychological or spiritual strength. Yet what the *Kamikaze* pilots attempted at the individual level was paralleled throughout the war in a much more general way by the propaganda efforts of all belligerents. Indeed, despite the negative connotation now associated with propaganda, Allied and Axis leaders recognized that winning the war meant exploiting the psychological resources of their nation and targeting those of their enemies. Propaganda efforts naturally differed according to available resources, sophistication of the media, national traditions, and how the war was going at the time in question. Although it is difficult to generalize, the propaganda campaigns of Germany and Britain offer instructive examples of both the possibilities and limits of propaganda.

Germany's initial propaganda efforts benefitted both from its Propaganda Minister, Joseph Goebbels', long experience in the field and from Germany's early military successes. Goebbels' exaggerated "*Blitzpropaganda*" brought domestic support for the National Socialist regime to an all-time high following the conquest of France, while the carefully cultivated image of an invincible Wehrmacht was a powerful deterrent to neutrals who were contemplating joining the Allies. After the tide of war turned against Germany, Goebbels' manipulation of popular fear of "Bolshevism" and of the unforeseeable consequences of the Allied demand for Germany's unconditional surrender meant that the National Socialist regime retained an astonishing amount of domestic support until the closing days of the war. On the other hand, premature assertions of final German victory and implausible claims of success in the face of obvious failure meant that German propaganda ultimately lost most of its effectiveness among Allied and neutral citizens.

Given the early failures of British arms, Britain's propaganda effort faced initially greater challenges than Germany's did. Britain's domestic propaganda, however, benefitted from Churchill's inspiring rhetoric and his projection of bulldog tenacity. Moreover, by insisting that British pronouncements adhere as closely to the truth as was possible in wartime, the director of the British Political Warfare Executive, R. H. Bruce Lockhart, ensured that BBC broadcasts generally retained a greater degree of credibility among listeners in neutral and Axis-occupied countries than Axis broadcasts did. Whether this British advantage also held true for many Axis citizens and whether concrete advantages accrued from it is debatable.

One feature common to both sides' propaganda efforts was the tendency to dehumanize the enemy. Although the consequences of this were felt on all fighting fronts, they were most evident in the German–Soviet and Japanese–Allied conflicts, where both sides presented their enemies in racist or demonic terms and adopted combat measures to suit their rhetoric. Perhaps because of this, the Pacific war and the eastern front also witnessed the disturbing spectacle of mass deportations of suspect civilians. In the United States and Canada, fear of Japanese military successes in the Pacific and prewar resentment against Japanese immigration led to forcible deportation of over 100,000 Japanese-Americans and Japanese-Canadians from the west coast to relocation camps in the interior in 1942. Although the circumstances of Japanese deportation were reasonably humane, they were nevertheless accompanied by considerable losses of property and needless assaults on human dignity. Paradoxically, perhaps because they were indispensable to that territory's economy, only about 1% of the 150,000 Japanese-Americans living in Hawaii were deported.

Soviet authorities also undertook mass deportations of suspect populations, beginning with the forcible resettlement of Poles during the period of German–Soviet cooperation between 1939 and 1941. Later, suspected or actual collaboration with the Axis led to the removal of dozens of groups of ethnic minorities, including Kalmyks, Chechens, and Crimean Tatars, from vulnerable areas to regions further east in 1943 and 1944. Supervised by the Soviet secret police, these migrations were usually chaotic and accompanied by substantial loss of life due to overexertion, maltreatment, and exposure.

All deportation measures paled in comparison, however, with the actions that the German government undertook against the Jews of Europe. Initial German wartime measures ran the gamut between policies designed to expel the Jews from Europe (to Madagascar, according to one unlikely scheme), forcible resettlement in ghettos such as Warsaw and Lódz, and sporadic killings by *Einsatzgruppen* in Poland in 1939. Germany's invasion of the Soviet Union in June, 1941 brought a marked increase in the mass murder of Jews; at Babi Yar in September, 1941, for example, approximately 33,000 people of all ages were shot with machine guns. *Einsatzgruppen* figured prominently in most atrocities, but they were sometimes aided by other Germans, Lithuanians, Ukrainians, and Romanians. By the end of 1941, roughly one million Jews had been killed in the German-occupied portions of the Soviet Union.

During the winter of 1941–1942, German authorities began implementing a more systematic extermination policy via the "Final Solution." At a conference in the Berlin suburb of Wannsee on January 20, 1942, Reich officials adopted a series of measures aimed at relocating all European Jews, including those residing in neutral countries and in the as-yet unconquered British Isles, to death camps in Poland and the Ukraine. By the time of the Wannsee conference, one such camp at Chelmno was already in operation, and within months additional ones went into operation at Sobibor, Belzec, Treblinka, and Auschwitz-Birkenau. Between 1942 and 1944, the systematic killings of most of the Jews of occupied Europe took place, either in gas chambers at the camps, in mobile gas vans, or through chronic overwork. Some governments were able to protect their Jewish citizens, either in full (Bulgaria, Finland, and, to a large degree, Denmark) or in part (Italy). Elsewhere, in Croatia, Slovakia, and Vichy France, collaborationist governments cooperated willingly in delivering Jews to their murderers.

In 1944 the Soviet liberation of Poland prompted German authorities to begin shunting surviving Jewish captives to older concentration camps in Germany. Even then the killing continued as emaciated prisoners succumbed to forced marches, abuse, and disease. By war's end, approximately 6 million Jews had died at the hands of the Nazis; only the complete collapse of the Third Reich had prevented the total destruction of European Jewry.

V. THE DEFEAT OF THE AXIS
(1943–1945)

Hitler's defeat—and that of his coalition partners—was due primarily to the combined efforts of the three main powers of the Grand Alliance, Great Britain, the Soviet Union, and the United States. Between 1943 and 1945, the Soviet Union continued to bear the lion's share of the land war against Germany. At Kursk in July, 1943, in the largest tank battle of the war, the Red Army thwarted a German attempt to regain the initiative on the eastern front, and in the fall of 1943 the Soviets began the reconquest of the Ukraine. In June, 1944 Soviet troops began the destruction of German Army Group Center (Operation Bagration), while supplementary offensives drove Romania and Finland out of the war in August and September, respectively. In January, 1945, Russian and Polish forces at last liberated Warsaw, which had been devastated by German suppression of uprisings by Jews in the Ghetto in 1943 and by the Polish Home Army in 1944. By March, 1945, Russian troops under Marshals Georgi Zhukov and Ivan Konev were poised on the Oder River for the final assault on Berlin.

Until June, 1944, American and British land operations against the Axis in Europe remained confined to the Mediterranean. In May, 1943 Allied troops drove the Axis out of their north African bridgehead in Tunisia. That summer, the Allied invasion of Sicily prompted the fall of Mussolini's government and its replacement by one headed by Marshal Pietro Badoglio. Although Italy surrendered to the Allies in September, German forces successfully disarmed most of the Italian army, occupied much of the mainland, and reestablished Mussolini as a puppet in northern Italy. Allied landings in southern Italy in September, 1943 and at Anzio in January, 1944 eventually led to American entry into Rome on June 4, but German resistance in Italy continued unabated. Meanwhile, Allied solidarity threatened to founder on Soviet impatience over Britain's and the United States' delay in opening a more effective "Second Front" in western Europe.

One response to Soviet complaints was the western Allies' combined bomber offensive. Initiated by Churchill and Roosevelt at the Casablanca Conference in January, 1943, the campaign combined nighttime "area" attacks on German cities by RAF Bomber Command with supposedly more precise daylight attacks on industrial sites by American bombers. For a time, in late 1943 and early 1944, heavy Allied aircraft losses and the apparent resilience of German morale and Ger-

man industry called into question the efficacy of Allied bombing strategies. By spring 1944, however, newly introduced long-range fighters such as the P-51 "Mustang" were beginning to destroy the *Luftwaffe* in the skies over Germany and compel its withdrawal from tactical missions in Russia, Italy, and western Europe.

The United States' and Britain's hard won air superiority paid huge dividends during Operation Overlord, the Allied invasion of Normandy. There, on June 6, 1944, 12,000 Allied aircraft and 6,000 Allied merchant and naval vessels overwhelmed German coastal defenses, and by day's end over 150,000 British, Canadian, and American combat soldiers had established the long-awaited "Second Front" in France. Tenacious German resistance initially limited expansion of the beachhead to a narrow front. In late July, however, Allied troops began to break out from Normandy. During the late summer and early fall, Allied troops liberated Paris (August 25), linked up with Free French and United States forces that had launched a supplementary invasion of southern France (Operation Anvil/Dragoon), and pushed to the German and Dutch frontiers. There in mid-September, stiffening German resistance thwarted Operation Market Garden, a daring Allied attempt to end the war by a narrow thrust into Germany's industrial heartland in the Ruhr.

The last winter of the war in Europe brought continued fierce struggle. On December 16, 1944, Hitler attempted to divide Allied forces in western Europe via a desperate armored thrust through the Ardennes. The resulting "Battle of the Bulge" ended with the bloody repulse of German forces and the exhaustion of most of Germany's mobile reserves. In March, 1945 Allied forces breached the Rhine River barrier in a number of places. While British, Canadian, and Free Polish forces fanned out onto the north German plain, United States troops encircled the Ruhr and invaded Bavaria. On April 25, American troops met up with Soviet forces at Torgau on the Elbe, thus severing the Reich in two. Hitler committed suicide in Berlin 5 days later, as Red Army soldiers battled their way into the capital. With German resistance crumbling, Hitler's successor, Grand Admiral Dönitz, accepted Allied demands for unconditional surrender, and at ceremonies at Rheims (May 7) and Berlin (May 8) the war in Europe came to an end.

By spring 1945, Japan was also in desperate straits. Japanese troops continued to occupy substantial parts of China, but many had been reduced to conducting "rice offensives" in order to sustain their presence there. Elsewhere, in southeast Asia, a Japanese thrust into India in 1944 had been repulsed with heavy losses, and in 1944–1945 General William Slim's British 14th Army had reconquered much of Burma. During the same period, American submarines and aircraft had virtually destroyed the Japanese merchant marine.

These difficulties, however, paled in comparison with the threat posed by two American offensives across the Pacific. In the southwest Pacific by the end of 1944, General Douglas MacArthur's United States and Australian forces had recaptured New Guinea and begun the liberation of the Philippines, thus threatening Japan's already tenuous connection with the Southern Resources Area. In the central Pacific, Admiral Chester Nimitz's forces had advanced across the Gilbert, Marshall, and Mariana island chains. During the two-pronged offensive, the American navy had virtually destroyed the Japanese navy at battles in the Philippine Sea (June, 1944) and Leyte Gulf (October, 1944).

Nimitz's conquest of Saipan and Tinian in the Marianas brought the Japanese home islands within effective range of American aircraft, which began using incendiary bombs to systematically destroy Japanese cities in March, 1945. Nevertheless, desperate Japanese resistance in fighting on outlying islands such as Iwo Jima and Okinawa as well as suicide missions by *Kamikaze* pilots testified to the Japanese military's willingness to continue the war and to the losses the Allies could expect in an invasion of the home islands. The United States' use of atomic bombs on Hiroshima (August 6) and Nagasaki (August 9), coupled with the Soviet Union's declaration of war on Japan (August 8), at last brought home the futility of further struggle. Prompted by the intervention of Emperor Hirohito, Japan surrendered on September 2, 1945, bringing World War II to a close.

VI. AFTERMATH

It is difficult to exaggerate the impact of World War II on the modern world. First and foremost an exercise in human misery, the war claimed approximately 55 million dead and approximately 35 million wounded. Passions and political changes stirred by the war resulted in a further 20 to 30 million postwar refugees and deportees, as states in Europe and Asia sought to make nationality lines conform with international boundaries; the westward movement of the Soviet Union's border, for example, displaced over 4 million Poles, while as many as 12 million ethnic Germans were driven from eastern Europe and the Balkans into a divided and geographically reduced Germany. The economic costs of wartime destruction, taxes, debts,

lost opportunities, and postwar resettlement are incalculable.

It is easier to assess the political impact of the conflict. The war left the Axis powers defeated, physically devastated, and psychologically traumatized. In addition, Italy and Japan were shorn of their colonial holdings in Libya, east Africa, east Asia, and the Pacific. Although nominally a victor, China had likewise suffered immense destruction and was ripe for the renewal of a civil war that culminated in the triumph of Mao Tse-tung's Communist Party 4 years later. The war also severely strained the economies, societies, and political systems of France and Great Britain. One manifestation of this was both countries' retreat from empire in the postwar era. Decolonization came in various ways, with a measure of good grace, as in India in 1947, or after a bitter war, as in Vietnam in 1954 and Algeria in 1962; whatever the case, the British and French examples were followed by the Dutch, the Belgians, and, belatedly, the Spanish and Portuguese.

The war affected international and intranational relations in other ways as well. The explosion of European anti-Semitism in the form of the Holocaust convinced many Jews that a Jewish national state was the only alternative to extinction, and Jewish suffering during the war played an immense role in rallying international support for Israel's establishment in 1948. Bitter Arab resentment against Israel would help to fuel a succession of wars in the latter half of the 20th century. The Allies' wartime crusade against Nazi racism also revealed profound contradictions in American society, as the United States' military had campaigned against the supposed Nazi "master race" with racially segregated units and racially segregated blood supplies of its own. It was no accident that many of the local leaders of the postwar civil rights movement in the United States were returning African-American servicemen whose awareness of their second-class status had been sharpened by their experiences abroad.

Changes in the United States were not, however, confined to domestic matters. One of only two of the world's powers to emerge from the war with its strength enhanced, the United States benefited from its gigantic and intact economy, its enormous military strength, and its leadership in science (enhanced by the infusion of European and Asian refugees) to become a superpower. Half a world away, despite catastrophic human and economic losses, the Soviet Union also emerged as a global power. For the next two generations, the relative decline of its neighbors, its retention of powerful military forces, its occupation and exploitation of a tier of states extending from Poland to the Black Sea, and the legitimizing effect that victory over Nazi Germany conveyed upon communist ideology, both domestically and abroad, would sustain Soviet power. Given the bipolar configuration of the postwar world, the profound ideological differences between communism and capitalism, and both countries' access to nuclear weapons after the Soviet Union acquired nuclear capability in 1949, the emergence of a "Cold War" between the Soviet Union and the United States was, if not inevitable, at least not surprising. That both states would seek allies, even among former enemies, and that Europe would soon be divided by the North Atlantic Treaty Organization (NATO, 1949) and the Warsaw Pact (1955) was equally unsurprising.

Yet curiously, the memory of World War II may have also helped to play a major role in defusing the Soviet–American confrontation that it had helped to create. Unwilling to repeat the sacrifices of the world wars, statesmen from both superpowers sought alternatives to war when confronting one another directly. Universal revulsion over the immense human and economic cost of the wars formed the bedrock for the United Nations and for regional associations that sought to achieve peace through mutual consultation or economic interdependence. Perhaps the most successful of the latter was the experiment in European economic and political integration which stemmed from its founders' conviction that Europe could not sustain another fratricidal war and which culminated in the formation of the European Community between 1957 and 1992. In time, the spectacle of reconciliation and shared prosperity between former members of the Allies and the Axis in western and central Europe, most notably France, Great Britain, and West Germany, would be a major factor in the voluntary retreat of the Soviet Union from eastern Europe and in the peaceful dissolution of the Warsaw Pact.

Also See the Following Articles

WARFARE, MODERN • WORLD WAR I

Bibliography

Bartov, O. (1992). *Hitler's army: Soldiers, Nazis, and war in the Third Reich.* New York: Oxford University Press.

Bell, P. M. H. (1986). *The origins of the Second World War in Europe.* New York: Longman.

Dear, I. C. B. (1995). *The oxford companion to World War II.* New York: Oxford University Press.

Dower, J. W. (1986). *War without mercy: Race and power in the Pacific war.* New York: Pantheon.

Dreyer, E. L. (1995). *China at war, 1901–1949.* New York: Longman.

Ellis, J. (1990). *Brute force: Allied strategy and tactics in the Second World War.* London: Andre Deutsch.

Ellis, J. (1993). *World War II: A statistical survey.* New York: Facts on File.

Kennedy, P. (1987). *The rise and fall of the Great Powers: Economic change and military conflict from 1500 to 2000.* New York: Random House.

Messenger, C. (1989). *The chronological atlas of World War II.* New York: Macmillan.

Parker, R. A. C. (1989). *Struggle for survival: The history of the Second World War.* Oxford, UK: Oxford University Press.

Spector, R. (1985). *Eagle against the sun: The American war against Japan.* New York: The Free Press.

Weinberg, G. (1994). *A world at arms: A global history of World War II.* New York: Cambridge University Press.

Wright, G. (1968). *The ordeal of total war, 1939–1945.* New York: Harper & Row.

Youth Violence

James F. Short, Jr.

Washington State University

I. Youth and Violent Crime
II. The Age/Crime Connection
III. The Social Distribution of Violent Youth Crime
IV. Youth Gangs and Other Collectivities Associated with Violence
V. Explaining Youth Violence
VI. Understanding and Controlling Youth Violence

GLOSSARY

Communal Violence Interracial violence occurring in response to expansion of a minority population into a majority population community. In the United States, communal violence characterized many large cities during and after World War I, involving clashes between African Americans and Whites. During and after World War II, urban rioting most often occurred within African-American commuties, taking the form of property destruction and looting, striking out against the agents and symbols of the larger society.

Drug Crews Small groups organized solely for the purpose of marketing illegal drugs on the street or in designated buildings, e.g., "crack houses."

Drug Gang vs Street Gang Like the typically smaller drug crews, drug gangs are focused on drug sales. Unlike street gangs, drug gangs tend to have well defined and hierarchical leadership, strong cohesiveness, and a code of loyalty and secrecy. Drug gangs also avoid involvement in crimes other than those that are drug sales related, as a means of avoiding unnecessary contact with law enforcement authorities.

Hazing The practice of subjecting initiates to embarrassing, and sometimes painful, treatment as part of, or prior to, initiation ceremonies.

Human Capital vs Social Capital Human capital consists of education, skills, and experiences possessed by individuals; social capital consists of qualities associated with interpersonal relationships and networks, e.g., the extent to which they involve trust, and their emotional and intellectural content.

Index Crimes These eight crimes, so designated by the U.S. Federal Bureau of Investigation because they are the most serious and the most likely to be known to the police, include murder and nonnegligent manslaughter, forcible rape, robbery, aggravaged assault, burglary, larceny-theft, motor vehicle theft, and arson.

Marginalization The process of withholding full membership rights and privileges from a person or class of persons based often on such statuses as race, ethnicity, gender, age, sexual orientation, and economic position.

YOUTH VIOLENCE takes many forms, which often overlap with one another. Consider the many forms of violent crime. The U.S.'s Federal Bureau of Investigation's four "index," or most serious, violent crimes include homicide (murder and nonnegligent manslaughter), forcible rape, aggravated assault (defined as attack for the purpose of inflicting severe or aggravated bodily injury), and robbery. None of these is specific or homogeneous with respect either to behavior or to the circumstances of their occurrence.

This article begins by noting strengths and weaknesses of official data concerning violent crime, followed by a discussion of what those data have to say about the involvement of young people in violent behavior, both as offenders and as victims. The social distribution of violent youth crime, by gender, race and ethnicity, and other marginalized categories of persons, is then described. Because most youth crime involves companions, the participation of young people in youth gangs is given special attention. Poverty, low social cohesion, and ineffective social institutions in communities are then identified as important correlates of youth violence.

Other forms of youth violence, also involving collectivities of young people, are then discussed, including drug crews, "wilding," and other hate-motivated gatherings. Similarities and differences in the nature of the international and community contexts within which these forms of youth violence occur are noted.

The final two sections seek to explain youth violence, reviewing what is known about its causes, and to point the way toward better understanding and control of youth violence.

I. YOUTH AND VIOLENT CRIME

Arrests of juveniles (persons under the age of 18) for the U.S. Federal Bureau of Investigation (FBI) categories of serious violent offenses totaled 117,200 in the United States in 1994. Arrests of juveniles for the index *property* crime of arson, plus those for less serious crimes involving violence or its threat (other assaults, vandalism, and weapons violations) totaled more than 325,000.

Note that these data reflect numbers of *individuals* arrested. Accordingly, they obscure one of the fundamental characteristics of most crimes commited by young people, that is, that most such acts are committed in the company of others, usually other young people. Most youth violence tends to involve cooffenders and is, in this sense, *collective*.

With some exceptions, the criminal law, particularly as it concerns common crime, defines criminal acts as behavior engaged in by individuals. One of these exceptions concerns special legislation aimed at youth gangs, a common context for youth violence in the U.S. Law enforcement actions taken in support of laws aimed at collective violence poorly reflect its prevalence and frequency of occurrence. For this reason, official statistics of crime often are of limited value to the understanding of much youth violence. Statistics on homicide, a crime that is so serious that it virtually always comes to the attention of authorities, are useful for understanding general trends, but they, too, fail to capture the varied contexts in which homicides take place.

II. THE AGE/CRIME CONNECTION

Another way of assessing the juvenile contribution to crime is provided by the perecentages of crimes known to the police that are cleared by arrests of juveniles. By this measure, in 1994 juveniles were involved in 14% of all violent crimes and 25% of all property crimes cleared. For index violent crimes these figures were: murders (10%), aggravated assaults (13%), forcible rapes (14%), and robberies (20%).

Juvenile arrest rates vary over time and by specific crimes. Rates for murder/nonnegligent manslaughter varied little between 1975 and 1987, for example, but increased by 84% between 1987 and 1991, then remained relatively constant through 1994. Similar recent rises were recorded for aggravated assault and robbery, but juvenile arrest rates for forcible rape, after rising significantly between 1975 and 1987, experienced little change through 1994.

Since few violent crimes are commited by juveniles below the age of 10, it is important to focus primarily on juveniles above that age, and to examine *rates* of involvement, rather than raw numbers. Figure 1 presents total violent crime index arrests for juveniles ages 10–17 beginning in 1980 and projected to the year 2010 under two conditions: (1) assuming continuation of trends in *arrest rates* since 1980 and (2) assuming that the *arrest rate* remains unchanged after 1992. The most recent data suggest that the first assumption may be more realistic and may even be conservative.

A National Research Council report on violent crime documents considerable fluctuation in violent crime rates in the United States throughout the 20th century. It is clear, however, that despite recent declines in vio-

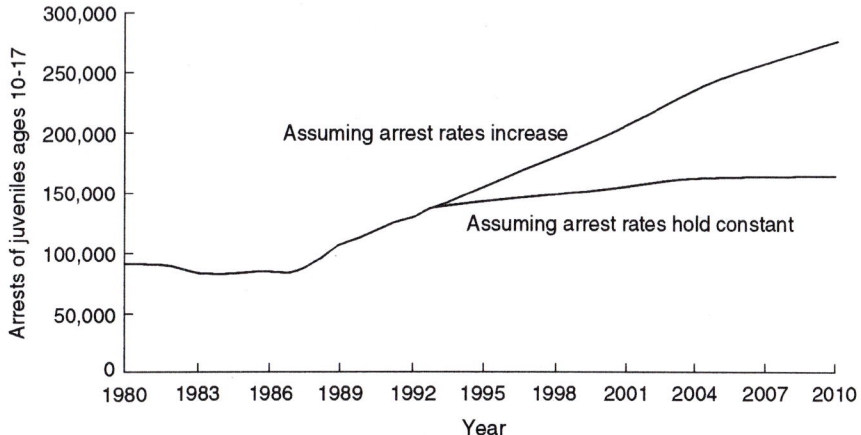

FIGURE 1 If violent crime index arrest rates for juveniles ages 10–17 increase in the future as they did from 1983–1992, arrests will more than double by 2010. Data sources: FBI (1994). Age-Specific Arrest Rates and Race-Specific Arrest Rates for Selected Offenses 1965–1992; Bureau of the Census (1993). Current Population Reports, U.S. Population Estimates by Age, Sex, Race and Hispanic Origin: 1980 to 1991; (1995). Current Population Reports, U.S. Population Estimates by Age, Sex, Race and Hispanic Origin: 1992 to 2050. In Snyder et al. (1996). Juvenile Offenders and Victims: 1996; Update on Violence. Washington, DC: National Center for Juvenile Justice, Office of Juvenile Justice and Delinquency Prevention, p. 15.

lent crimes, the United States has by far the highest homicide rate of all modern countries. The U.S. homicide rates are more than double those of most countries. Because homicide is the most serious and reliably reported violent crime, homicide data are of special importance in assessing the level of violence in any country.

Homicide rates in all countries fluctuate over time. In the U.S. the homicide rate rose sharply after 1985, to 9.4 per 100,000 population in 1990, a level slightly below that of the two previous peaks, in 1931–1934 and in 1979–1981. The *age-specific homicide rate*—a more accurate reflection of trends, since it takes into account the varying age distribution of the population—was relatively flat during the 15 inclusive years (1980–1994). Even this rate is deceptive, however, because it masks a dramatic rise in the homicide rate among younger age groups (ages 14–17 and 18–24), which began in 1985. In contrast, the homicide rate for persons aged 25 and older declined fairly steadily between 1980 and 1994. Almost 30% of juvenile homicide offenders had adult accomplices (when more than one offender was involved in the killings this figure is nearly 60%). It is likely that the vast majority of adult accomplices were young adults, between the ages of 18 and 24, for these are the ages at which homicide offending occurs most often.

Figure 2 depicts changes in age-specific murder rates between 1965 and 1992. The National Center for Juvenile Justice notes that the number of juvenile homicide offenders tripled between 1984 and 1994 and that virtually all of this increase is accounted for by the increasing use of firearms in homicides. Although the number of "nongun homicides" commited by juvenile offenders decreased slightly between the late 1970s and 1991, the number of "gun homicides" increased rapidly, beginning in the mid-1980s (see Figure 3).

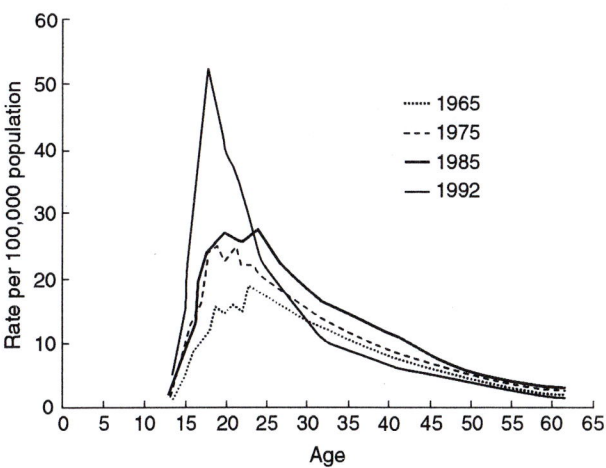

FIGURE 2 Age-specific murder rate: 1965–1992. Source: Age-Specific Arrest Rates and Race-Specific Arrest Rates for Selected Offenses, 1965–1992, Uniform Crime Reporting Program, Federal Bureau of Investigation, Washington, DC: December 1993. In Blumenstein (1995). Violence by Young People: Why the Deadly Nexus? *National Institute of Justice Journal*, August, p. 4.

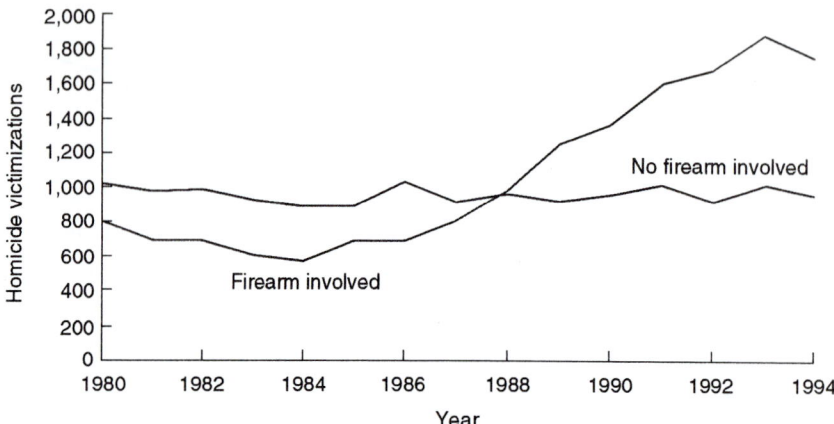

FIGURE 3 While juvenile homicide victimizations not involving firearms remained constant, those involving firearms nearly tripled from 1984 to 1994. Data source: Fox, J. (1996). Supplementary Homicide Reports 1976–1994 [machine-readable data file]. In Snyder et al. (1996). Juvenile Offenders and Victims: 1996; Update on Violence. Washington, DC: National Center for Juvenile Justice, Office of Juvenile Justice and Delinquency Prevention, p. 3.

III. THE SOCIAL DISTRIBUTION OF VIOLENT YOUTH CRIME

In addition to age, official crime data contain a great deal of information about the social distribution of violent crime, ecologically, and by gender, race, ethnicity, and (when combined with other data sources) socioeconomic status. Regrettably, data that would permit international comparisons among such categories are not available.

A. Gender

The National Center for Juvenile Justice notes that, until they become teenagers, boys and girls are about equally likely to be murdered. Throughout their teen years, however, the gap between male and female homicide victimizations widens dramatically, with late teen male victims outnumbering female victims by about 5 to 1. Males also account for the great majority of violent crimes commited by juveniles. Homicide arrests of males typically outnumber female arrests by about 6 to 1. Recent data suggest, however, that female juveniles have become increasingly involved in serious violent crimes, since arrests of juvenile females for homicide have increased by more than double the increase in male arrests. Female arrests for index property crimes rose even more rapidly, compared to male arrests, during this period, and female arrests for nonindex offenses also rose more rapidly, but by a smaller margin.

B. Race and Ethnicity

Data concerning the race and ethnicity of young violent crime offenders are problematic for several reasons: they exhibit great variation over time and from place to place; rates of violent crime typically vary more *within* than *between* racial and ethnic groupings; categories used to distinguish race and ethnicity mask a great deal of variation in the living conditions of persons in different racial and ethnic categories; and classification of persons as "Hispanic" or "Latino," "Asian" or "Oriental," "Black" or "African-American," "White," or "Native American" is not based on rigorous scientific criteria, but on general and often erroneous and confusing social criteria. Finally, race- and ethnic-specific data on violent offenders and victims—particularly on variables and processes related to the etiology of such behavior and its control—often are lacking or of poor quality.

Nonetheless, such data as are available tell us a great deal about the social distribution of violent crime among youths in various racial and ethnic categories and, in combination with other relationships, about the etiology of violent crime.

Historically, with few exceptions (such as Jews and eastern Europeans) youths from immigrant minorities in the United States have had high violent crime rates, relative to the native-born. Early in the history of the country, Irish and German, and later Italian and Polish, youths accounted for relatively higher proportions of violent crime than did youths from other nationality groups. Once these immigrants and their descendants became integrated into family, community, economic, and political life, their rates of interpersonal violence declined.

Long-term trends for African Americans in the U.S., however, are sharply and tragically different. Young African Americans are both victims and perpetrators of violent crimes to a far greater extent than are white youths. The ratio of non-White to White homicide arrest rates in the U.S. varied between 2 or 3 to 1 during the latter part of the 19th century, but increased early in the 20th century to between 4 and 5 to 1, only to increase to more than 8 to 1 by 1994. Figure 4 presents numbers of Black, White, and "other race" homicide victimizations from 1980 to 1994. The disparity between black and white youths is even more dramatic than the figure suggests, inasmuch as Blacks comprise only about 15% of the juvenile population.

Juvenile court data confirm that Black youths commit higher rates of "person offenses" (index violent crimes plus simple assault, other violent sex offenses, and other person offenses) than do White or "other race" youths. The ratio of person offense case rates for Blacks is about 4 to 1, compared to both White and other-race youths, at every age from 10 to 17.

Note that these data are quite incomplete with respect to both race and ethnicity. Neither the race (mostly Whites, but with a large percentage of Blacks) nor the ethnicity (mostly from Mexico, Central, and South America, and the Carribean, but including Spanish speaking persons of European countries) of Hispanics is distinguished, nor are they included in the "other race" category. Yet Latinos (the term does not include those from European backgrounds) constitute approximately 10.5% of the total U.S. population and that percentage is increasing. The law enforcement data on which Figs. 1 to 4 are based also do not include Native American (Indian) and various oriental or Asian categories. Native American Indians and Asians are included in the juvenile court data noted above, however.

Crime data on these other racial and ethnic categories are hard to come by. Studies of violence among young American Indians are especially rare. Additionally, the American Indian population is extremely diverse and it is not clear how such diversity relates to youth violence. Moreover, even homicide rates for American Indians are suspect because the Bureau of the Census has increasingly, but inconsistently, relied on self-identification of respondents' race and ethnic identity. Between 1980 and 1990 the American Indian population increased in all reporting states and the District of Columbia, in some cases by large percentages, but changing (more favorable) attitudes toward American Indians and affirmative action policies may have increased self-identification as Native American. How this may have influenced homicide rates of American Indians is unknown. Federal Bureau of Investigation reports, however, consistently report higher homicide

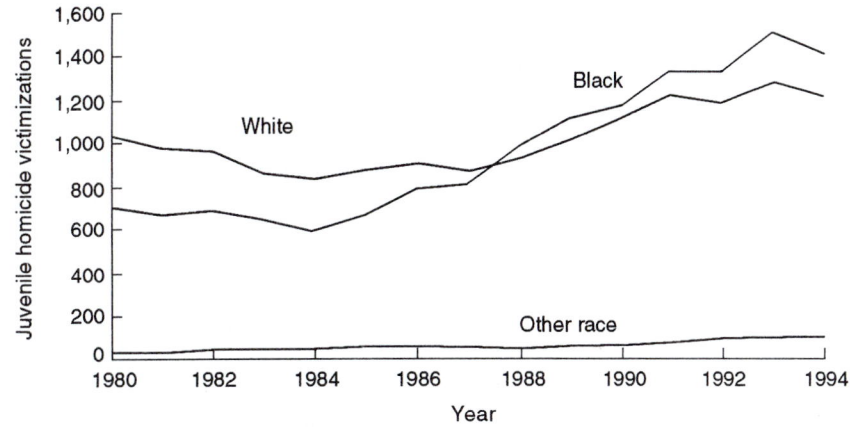

FIGURE 4 Blacks make up 15% of the juvenile population, yet Black juvenile homicide victims have outnumbered white victims since 1988. In 1994 1380 murdered victims were Black (52%) and 1180 were White (44%). Between 1980 and 1994 the number of White juveniles killed rose 15% while the number of Black juveniles killed rose 97%. In 1980 the rate of homicide victimizations for Blacks was 4 times greater than the rate for Whites; by 1994 the Black rate was 6 times greater than the White rate. Data source: Fox, J. (1996). Supplementary Homicide Reports 1976–1994 [machine-readable data file]. In Snyder et al. (1994). Juvenile Offenders and Victims: 1996; Update on Violence. Washington, DC: National Center for Juvenile Justice, Office of Juvenile Justice and Deliquency Prevention, p. 4.

rates among American Indians than among Whites, but lower rates than among Blacks.

Homicide rates for individual states and counties with Native American populations vary enormously. With respect to age at the state level for the years 1980–1984, the percentage of the American Indian population ages 15–24 was positively related to the homicide rate among those so classified, but this relationship failed to attain statistical significance when American Indian *unemployment* and the percentage of American Indians living in poverty were controlled.

It is equally difficult to obtain reliable and valid information concerning violence among Latino youths. A California study found that age-adjusted death rates involving firearms were 40% lower for Latinos than those for African Americans and 10% lower than rates for non-Latino whites. Yet, *gang-related* homicide rates appear to be especially high among Latinos, according to studies conducted in Chicago and Los Angeles. Similarly, data concerning youth violence among various Asian nationalities in the U.S. is based primarily on studies focused on gangs in particular cities. For this reason, it is necessary to discuss violent cooffending among youths before conclusions can be reached concerning race and ethnicity.

IV. YOUTH GANGS AND OTHER COLLECTIVITIES ASSOCIATED WITH VIOLENCE

Gangs (and cliques within them) are only one of several collective forms in which youth violence takes place. Others include drug crews, "wilding" groups, free-floating crowds, goal-directed crowds, and rioting mobs, all of which may be associated with violent behavior by some or all of their members. Additionally, youths participate in a variety of groups with distinct subcultural themes that sometimes promote violence. Examples include "skinheads," "bikers," "punks," and sports-related hooliganism, each of which may involve violent behavior.

It is not clear how all these variations relate to one another, but we know that individuals and groups often are participants in more than one of them. Moreover, terms designating youth collectivities involved in violent behavior lack precise or consistent definitions, either in law enforcement terms or in scholarly discourse. *The absence of a viable typology of youth collectivities, from twosomes to gangs to crowds, is a major impediment to understanding youth violence and to its control.*

A. Street Gangs

In spite of serious definitional problems, we know more about street gangs—the major subspecies of the phenomenon—than we do about most other collective forms of youth violence because of the very large research literature devoted to them, and because police and sherif departments—the front lines of law enforcement—collect large amounts of data concerning gangs. Law enforcement officials have become more sophisticated in gathering gang intelligence.

Common to all definitions of street gangs is the fact that they are unsupervised youth groups that meet together with some regularity, over time, and that they are nonadult-sponsored and self-determining with respect to membership criteria, organizational structure, and acceptable behavior. For understandable reasons (that is their business) law enforcement agencies include criminal behavior in defining gangs. Some scholars include a "criminal orientation" as well. Quite aside from the logical problem that is created by including either criminal behavior or orientation in defining gangs (that is, including in the definition phenomena one wishes to explain), doing so necessarily takes as given, rather than to be explained, the behavior of interest.

Most studies of street gangs report that they are loosely organized and that changes in their structures and in the behaviors in which they take part occur frequently. Gangs that are involved in or oriented to criminal behavior are similar in these respects to most other unsupervised youth groups. There is ample evidence that delinquent behavior often is regarded as play by youth groups and that some of those groups later become more seriously involved in crime. There is evidence, as well, that street gangs that are involved in serious criminal behavior, and/or that are oriented toward criminality, often evolve from essentially nondelinquent play groups.

Gang researchers note large differences in the behavior of individual members and smaller cliques within gangs. These differences include involvement in violent crime and in other forms of violence, such as fighting. Street gangs often merge with other gangs, and shifting alliances among gangs are, in fact, often implicated in gang fighting.

Despite such differences and changes, violence clearly is a common feature of street gang life. Violence has been described as the "currency" of gang life and a "central feature" of it. Yet, serious violence is relatively rare even among the most violent gangs. Studies of gangs over many years and in many places report great variability in the levels of violence within, as well as between, gangs. The task, then, is to determine the conditions under which violence occurs and why it occurs when it does. Clues are found in law enforcement data.

Law enforcement agencies differ widely in their definitions of gangs and in their attribution of crime to gang members. Cheryl Maxson and her associates compared homicides attributed to gangs in Chicago and Los Angeles. Chicago police restrict gang attribution to *gang motivation*, while Los Angeles authorities classify as gang-related any homicide in which a gang member *participates*. Not surprisingly, the more restricted Chicago definition produced many fewer gang homicides than did the Los Angeles definition. Importantly, however, characteristics of gang homicides were similar in the two cities. In both, for example, gang homicides occurred more often in the street (about one-half versus a third or less of nongang homicides) and were more likely to involve unidentified assailants and to involve victims with no prior contact with their assailants. Gang homicide suspects and victims tended to be younger than nongang suspects and victims, and gang homicides were more often attributed to fear of retaliation.

1. The Spread of Street Gangs in the U.S. and Elsewhere

Evidence from a variety of sources suggests that street gangs have proliferated rapidly in the United States since about 1980 and that they are increasingly found in cities where previously they did not exist. Not surprisingly, large cities (over 150,000 population) have more and larger gangs than do smaller cities. Moreover, gangs in smaller cities tend to be autonomous and to lack the pattern of generational transmission of gang culture and ties to neighborhood traditions that are found in some larger cities.

While numbers of gangs, and numbers of gang members, reported in cities are subject to large reporting errors and to significant changes over time, numbers of gang-related crimes at least reflect violations of laws, with real victims. Estimates that more than 40,000 gang-related crimes occur in the U.S. annually must therefore be regarded as an indication of the seriousness of gang-related crime.

2. Studies of General Populations

Longitudinal studies of more general populations in Denver, Colorado and Rochester, New York yield unique information on the prevalence of gangs in those cities and on the relationship of gang membership to delinquency. Both studies focus on "high risk" populations of the two cities; that is, areas characterized by high crime rates, which in both cities also tended to be areas of lower socioeconomic status with high percentages of racial and ethnic minorities. Differences in sampling procedures make some comparisons between the two studies difficult. Finn-Aage Esbensen and David Huizinga found that the percentage of youth who indicated they were gang members in a given year was about 7% of youths ages 12 to 18 in Denver, while Terrence Thornberry and his associates reported that 20% of those ages 13 to 15 in Rochester were gang members. In both cities gang membership was characterized by frequent changes in the membership status of individuals and by limited gang cohesion. Over a 4-year period, two-thirds of the Denver gang members were members only one year, about one quarter belonged for 2 years, and only 3% belonged for all 4 years.

The relationship between gang membership and involvement in delinquent behavior also was similar in the two cities in that prevalence rates of all types of self-reported delinquency were much higher for both male and female gang members than for nongang members. Differences were especially great for more serious "street" and violent offenses. Both studies found that gang members were not uniformly delinquent and that individual youths were more delinquent when they were in gangs than when they were not.

Although gang members frequently invoke family relationships to describe what gang membership means to them, careful observations suggest that for many members the gang is a context in which violent events are more likely to occur within the gang than between members of rival gangs. Status threats are often played out in violent episodes involving fellow gang members. Fighting prowess is a valued comodity among gang members, within the gang as well as in confrontations between rival gangs. Ironies abound. Youth, especially males, join gangs "for protection," yet gang membership exposes them to additional dangers. Some join for companionship, yet gang friends often are undependable and sometimes become combatants. They join gangs for excitement, yet gangs spend most of their time together "hanging" and waiting for something to happen. Gang members face the same sorts of problems faced by all young people (relationships with peers, including members of the opposite sex, getting along in school, preparation for employment, getting and keeping jobs, family relationships, "growing up," etc.), yet the evidence strongly suggests that gang life is an impediment to finding solutions to such problems. Most gang members realize that the gang is not "forever." When the Denver researchers asked respondents about their future involvement in gangs, more than 60% indicated that they did not expect to be, nor did they want to be, gang members in the future.

The picture of gangs, and the consequences of gang membership, yielded by both surveys of more general populations and most studies of particular gangs are similar. In most gangs, membership tends to be unstable. Members can leave from time to time without severe penalty. Many gangs exist for only short periods, and their behavior patterns also change frequently. Yet, both surveys and studies of particular gangs fail fully to capture important features of gang behavior, including the relevance of race, ethnicity, and poverty. For this it is necessary to triangulate the findings of the varied approaches to the study of gangs.

3. Gang Homicides

A series of studies using Chicago police data inform both the racial and ethnic character and a number of other characteristics of gang-related homicides in that city. By the Chicago police criterion of gang related as gang motivated, gangs do not account for a majority of teenage homicides. The percentage of Chicago homicides accounted for by youth gangs tripled between 1965 and 1981, however. Virtually all of these gang homicides involved an assault situation rather than being instrumental in character, as in theft, robbery, or related to the sale or acquisition of drugs.

Later Chicago studies reveal further rapid increases in gang homicides and in gang involvement in instrumental violence, much of it related to drugs. Observed increases in gang homicides appear to follow a pattern of episodic peaks and troughs rather than a linear pattern. Peaks occur primarily in "turf hot spots," but there are also "drug hotspots" and some hot spots that involve both conflicts over territory (turf) and drug markets. Most gang homicides, it appears, result from expressive confrontations between friends, acquaintances, neighbors, and partners in (often) illicit enterprises. Although many gang members use and sell drugs, and some gangs control drug sales in their "turf," the connection between street gangs, as such, and drugs is weak and clearly cannot explain the rapid increase in youth homicide rates.

The highest levels of gang homicides occur in neighborhoods in which gangs contend over territory rather than over drug markets. Street gang assaults did not increase during the 1980s rise in gang homicides, but weapons used in such assaults increased in lethality, chiefly in the form of high-caliber automatic or semiautomatic weapons.

Most street gangs are racially homogenous, a function largely of racial segregation. Gangs tend, also, to be ethnically homogenous in terms of such categories as "Latino," "non-Latino White, "and "Asian." Much variation is also evident within these categories, however. The importance of race and ethnicity for youth violence is not clear, though significant variation is evident in different localities. Chicago data indicate higher rates of homicide offending among Latino male gang members, with black rates falling between Latino and non-Latino White rates. Los Angeles data indicate higher homicide rates and more rapid increases among young Black males than among Hispanics. Note that the latter do not refer to gang membership status and that the broader classification of Hispanic, rather than Latino, is employed. Reported differences are large. In both cities homicide offending and victimization tend to be racially and ethnically homogenous. As is true in virtually all reporting areas, these studies suggest that homicide among all racial and ethnic groups is associated with poverty. That is, the combination of poverty, race, and ethnicity characteristic of gangs and their communities characterizes youth violence more generally.

B. Drug Crews, Gangs, and Violence

It is important to distinguish between street gangs and gangs that are organized primarily (or only) for criminal purposes. The latter include drug selling "crews" and gangs that sell stolen goods or engage in systematic theft. Although some gangs control, or seek to conrol, drug traffic in local communities, most do not.

Drug use and selling are common activities among many street gangs, but street gangs should not be equated with drug gangs. The stereotype that gang violence is closely associated with violent drug marketing appears to be valid for some gangs in some cities, but most drug selling by gang members tends to be small scale. Malcolm Klein found that drug motives for *homicide* increased among nongang youths but not among gang members. Police reports suggest that the gang–drug marketing connection is relatively rare. Similarly, many gang members become involved in other petty hustles, but these also tend to characterize individuals or small cliques rather than entire gangs.

The connection between drug trafficking and violence, however, is well established, and much of that trafficking involves young people. Studies suggest that *drug gangs* are smaller and more cohesive than street gangs, and they command more group loyalty. Members of drug gangs tend to be older, on average, and to come from a more restricted age range than do street gang members. They also have more centralized leadership and market-defined gang roles. Group turf is defined by market considerations rather than the residence of members, and market competition is controlled more effectively than is the case with street gang members' involvement in drug selling.

"The Cocaine Kids," an exception to the general picture of older drug gang members in that they were all teenagers, were a drug selling "crew" studied by Terry Williams. They were rationally organized, and their sole purpose was to make money. They depended a great deal on the highly intelligent and "streetwise" leadership of their dealer–entrepreneur leader. Success in dealing cocaine was demanding and dangerous, requiring organizational skills, long and unpredictable hours, and constant vigilance. In a business based largely on trust, both partners and connections often proved untrustworthy. Official discovery and armed competitors and/or customers were constant threats. Money and status were the common denominators in the "cocaine culture." At the end of nearly 5 years of observation, the crew leader was burned out. The crew broke up, and only one former member continued to sell cocaine.

The association of violence with drug marketing is common knowledge among children in high-risk areas. A 1988 Urban Institute survey of 9th- and 10th-grade boys in Washington, DC found that drug selling was more common than using. High percentages of both frequent sellers and others perceived the risk of severe injury or death in a year of drug dealing to be very likely, but frequent dealers viewed selling as more profitable.

C. Other Types of Youth Collectivities and Violence

Much gang behavior is imitative of other gangs, especially of gangs with notorious reputations. Gang "wannabes" are also common in many localities, particularly among young males, and these also may turn to violence as a means of validation of themselves as youth with gang credentials.

Less frequent, but extremely violent, are so-called "wilding" groups. The research literature is largely silent on the phenomenon, with the notable exception of a study of a group of young African-American males in Texas by Scott Cummings. This group engaged in exceptionally brutal attacks on elderly Whites who had been effectively isolated in a largely Black community. Interviews with these young men suggested that they were socially marginal in the community, had unstable personality qualities, and that they were motivated by racial antagonism.

Another form of hate-motivated violence takes the form of crowds of (mainly) young people in White communities who attack "outsiders." Typically, the latter are members of minority groups who, often innocently or inadvertently, come into white communities that feel threatened by invasion of people from minority populations. "Communal" violence of this type, common throughout the history of the United States, is similar to violence in other countries with histories of conflict between members of different ethnic groups. The large-scale riots that occurred in U.S. cities during the 1960s and later during the 1980s and 1990s in Miami and in Los Angeles in 1992 were but the most recent examples of this type of violence. Although young people are not the only participants in such violent episodes, young people are always involved. Actions by law enforcement personnel often are involved in precipitating this type of collective violence. A unique feature of the most recent such episodes in the U.S. is the violence occurs *between members of different minority groups*.

Little systematic evidence is available concerning several other youth collectivities that occasionally engage in violence. These include sports-related crowds and riots such as occur when important games are won (or lost) and ideologically motivated groups such as skinheads, bikers, and cult groups organized loosely around musical preferences or satanic rituals. In each case, however, young people appear to be the main participants in such crowds and groups. Such evidence as exists suggests that participants in each of these types of collectivities are less concentrated in lower socioeconomic strata than are street gangs and more often include middle- and even upper-class youths. "Soccer hooliganism," often involving major episodes of vandalism and assault, has been a problem in Great Britain for many years, spilling over at times into several other European countries, including Madrid and Barcelona in Spain and Stuttgart in Germany. Most participants are young men who feel themselves to be politically and socially marginalized. Teenagers also take part in such episodes, however.

Systematic information regarding street gangs and other youth groups in other countries is extremely rare. Informal surveys suggest that street gangs similar to those in the U.S. are found in a few large cities in other countries and that the pattern may be spreading. Malcolm Klein's on-site and literature surveys note the presence of a wide variety of youth groups and subcultures in many cities throughout the developed world over the past 4 decades and, more recently, in several less developed countries.

Klein identifies "American style" street gangs in Berlin, Brussels, Mexico City, Port Moresby, Australia, and several South African and Russian cities. A pattern of "commuting to turf," rather than defending groups' home turf, also appears in several European cities, including Stockholm, Zurich, Frankfurt, Stuttgart, Slovenia, as well as in Melbourne. This pattern is characterized by loosely structured groups in which young people, mostly males, use public transportation to travel to areas in the city in search of entertainment and in some cases criminal enterprise. Violence tends to be episodic rather than the results of sustained rivalries between groups with histories of meeting together over time. Drug-using and -trading groups, rather than American-style street gangs, are found in a wide range of cities, including London and Manchester and perhaps in some mainland Chinese cities. Other cities report the presence of such youth culture patterns as bikers, punks, heavy metal groups, and right-wing political groups, similar to those found in the United States.

It is difficult to generalize about such groups, so varied are they in cultural context. The most common elements among them appear to be minority status and economic deprivation and, in many cases, social and political alienation. Also common are the sorts of weak institutional and community controls found in the U.S.

D. Homeless Youths and Violence

A final type of youth violence to be considered is violence defined by a specific context, namely, violence by homeless youths. John Hagan and his colleagues compared youths who were homeless and living on the streets of two cities (Toronto and Vancouver) with youths in those cities who were in school. They found that street life exposes young people to criminal networks and is especially violent. Peer pressure was less important to the explanation of both violent and nonviolent crime committed by these youths, however, than is the case with most other forms of youth violence. Street life operates as a mediating variable between other more traditionally emphasized variables associated with violence, such as family structure and relationships and unemployment. Such basic needs as food and shelter and protection from predation were especially important.

V. EXPLAINING YOUTH VIOLENCE

A. The Macro-Social Level of Explanation

Aside from violence by "wannabe" youth groups and such silliness as hazing, most forms of youth violence

have in common disproportionate involvement of youths who have been marginalized by disadvantaged socioeconomic status, race, or ethnicity. Some youths become marginalized by virtue of alienation from values represented by their families and communities. This was the case with many so-called "hippies" and with children from affluent families who ran away from home and took to the streets. Nevertheless, it is clear that street youths—whether in gangs or among the homeless—come disproportionately from families that are disadvantaged by their "surplus" status; that is, children of unemployed single-parent families or two-parent families in which both parents are unemployed. Surplus status, in turn, is heavily concentrated in minority groups and lower socioeconomic status White populations.

Marginalization is a powerful factor in the explanation of youth violence because it isolates those affected (youth and adults) from institutional and community processes that protect and support families and individuals as well as control criminal and other forms of disapproved behavior.

1. Economic, Community, and Institutional Contexts of Youth Violence

Studies of the socioeconomic status (SES) of violent offenders suggest that relatively minor forms of violence are common throughout the socioeconomic spectrum, but that more serious violence occurs more often, at younger ages and more persistently, among young people in the "new urban poor," the lowest SES category. In this respect the socioeconomic, community, and institutional contexts of youth violence are virtually the same for gang and nongang members. Data come from a variety of sources.

Early ecological studies identified structural characteristics of communities that were associated with high rates of crime and delinquency, including violent crime: low economic status of community residents, ethnic heterogeneity, and high residential mobility. These were taken as indications of low social cohesion and ineffective social institutions, resulting in weakened social control of violence and other types of crime.

Recent studies add other social indicators to this picture, confirming the importance of community factors in both the production of violence and the lack of effective social control. Among these factors are family disruption and weak community institutions, the lack of strong friendship and acquaintance networks, the inability to supervise and control teenage peer groups, and low rates of local participation in voluntary associations. Poverty, combined with joblessness, exacerbates and may be the primary cause of social disorganization.

Studies demonstrate that urban minorities who are concentrated in inner-city areas are especially vulnerable to social and economic change. Of particular importance, William Julius Wilson and others argue, are the shift from goods-producing to service-producing industries, increasing segmentation of the labor force into low-skill and low-wage jobs versus high-skill and high-wage jobs, technological changes, and the relocation of manufacturing industries out of central cities. The result of such changes, it is argued, is the emergence of the new urban poor, for whom work has virtually disappeared. The nature and the extent to which this development is a permanent fixture in the U.S. is a matter of import and much debate. The economic changes noted clearly are important, however, as is their impact, especially among young African-American males.

A major factor contributing to weakened social control at the community or neighborhood level under ghetto poverty conditions is social isolation from mainstream institutions, values, and role models. During the 1970s and 1980s many African-American working-class families, and the growing middle-class, found it possible to move out of the ghetto into areas with more desirable housing and other neighborhood conditions, leaving behind the ghetto poor. An important "social buffer" that might have mitigated the impact of prolonged and increasing joblessness thus was removed. Without the buffer of economically stable and secure families, basic institutions such as churches, schools, stores, and recreational facilities were no longer viable. The absence of such families also removed mainstream role models for young people, models that might help persuade young people of the importance of education and job preparation as a viable alternative to welfare or to participation in street gangs and illegal drug and stolen goods markets. As a result, in some communities it has been impossible to sustain the basic institutions of socialization and social control.

Recent studies also confirm the association of violence with public health problems such as high rates of infant mortality, low birth weight, tuberculosis, child abuse, and other detrimental aspects of child development. Researchers note, for example, that rates of violent death in local communities in New York City, and perhaps in other cities, are closely related to rates of low birth weight and infant mortality. These same communities also experience high levels of family disruption (divorce, desertion, and female-headed families). Community structure and the mediating processes of community social organization thus are important determinants of variations in the accessibility and quality of prenatal care, child health services, and general child care as well as of community networks of informal social control. Accessibility and quality of prenatal care, child health services, and general health care are poorest in lower-income, minority and/or racially/ethnically heterogeneous communities and in communities with high population turnover. A finding with particularly important implications for social policy is that "planned shrinkage," such as occurs when existing housing is destroyed for the construction of large housing projects or major institutional construction, typically leads to reductions in municipal services, arson, vandalism, general urban decay, and the loss of social integration and networks, all processes associated with increases in behavior patterns associated both with these public health deficits and with violence.

Conditions such as those discussed in this section have had devastating effects on many individuals, families, and communities. One of these effects has been the increase of gangs among minorities, while at the same time traditional White ethnic gangs, which often were transitional to adulthood via marriage, jobs, and social club membership, have decreased. Another has been extension of the influence of street gangs on both individual gang members and communities. Several gang researchers have noted the "stretching" of gang members' ages, particularly among minorities, as young men have found good jobs unavailable and marriage prospects unattractive. Expansion of illicit sources of income, including drug markets, has been a frequent result. In some instances "gang wars" become "drug wars," resulting in greater exposure of bystanders, including children, to violence. A participant observer study of a large housing project in Chicago concluded that, while most residents did not participate in illicit activities and were resentful and fearful of gang violence, the role of gangs in the community was enhanced when law enforcement (police and housing authorities) failed to protect the community. Some gangs reportedly assumed the role of "vigilante" groups, who provided security and protective services, such as nightly escorts for young women.

2. International Comparisons

Although these developments have been especially consequential for minority populations in the United States, data from other countries suggest that a more general principle may be at work, beyond the specific U.S. economic, community, and institutional context. Studies of German and French data, for example, report that arrest rates of foreign-born minorities, the vast majority of whom are White, are much higher than are those of native-born French and German citizens. These minorities originate in many other countries. Many have fled their home countries for economic reasons. Many have been actively recruited to the French and German labor forces. Their common experience, however, is that they have been marginalized in their adopted countries. Marginalization takes many forms, including law enforcement and economic discrimination. As noted, above, other youth collectivities at risk as victims/perpetrators of violence also share experiences of marginalization.

3. Family Structure, Family Relationships, and Youth Violence

The link between socioeconomic status and youth violence occurs via many social institutions, including especially schools and other youth serving agencies, institutions of employment, and institutions of government, including law enforcement agencies. In all of these respects marginalized populations fare poorly. The most significant direct linkage between socioeconomic status and youth violence, however, lies in the family. Out-of-wedlock births are more common among lower SES groups, as are single-parent families in general. So, also, are family disruptions in the form of unemployment. Studies indicate that there is a positive association between parental unemployment and harsh, inconsistent, coercive, and abusive parental discipline of children. Extreme forms of parental rejection, abuse, and neglect, in turn, have a long history of association with youth violence, drug use, and other forms of delinquency.

B. The Individual Level of Explanation

There is no reason to believe that the processes of learning differ among youths who are violent and those who are not. Learning occurs by observing what goes on around us and by reinforcing mechanisms of rewards and punishments. The most important contexts within which these processes occur are intimate groups such as the family and peer groups. The social nature of learning is not simply imitative because human beings possess certain distinctive capabilities that enable us to be active agents in our own behavior. Among these are the capacity to use symbols—fundamental to the capability of forethought—as well as self-regulatory and self-reflective capabilities. Self regulation is more difficult for some children than for others, however. For children who are impulsive, and for gang members and homeless street youths, for example, self-reflection and self-regulation are especially difficult, either because they lack sufficient internal controls over their own behavior or because of peer pressures and group processes. For street children, whether members of gangs or homeless, constraints that operate in conventional institutional settings are weak or absent, giving freer rein to temptations on the street and to group processes. Similarly, opportunities for learning and doing violence are more available in areas frequented by homeless youths and by street gangs.

The most common form of youth violence, fighting with age peers, is ubiquitous among young males in lower SES strata for whom socialization into violence begins early in life. Violence between parents and toward children, as well as assaultive behavior involving others, also are more common in lower SES communities. Violent role models are readily available, even for very young children. Increasingly, such violence involves adolescents attacking other adolescents.

In the ghettos and barrios of the inner city a major source of socialization into violence are the streets and other public areas of cities where teenagers learn to establish their identity in part by learning to behave violently. Crowded housing conditions push young people into public spaces where networks of similarly situated peers compete for status and for material possessions, often by violent means. Among gang members, intragang fighting is even more common than either intergang fighting or other violent behavior directed outside the gang.

Violence often is quite functional. The experience gained by fighting may later be applied to the systematic pursuit of income. While most fighting among boys in their early and middle teens is about status, for some, the scarcity of resources, the symbolic significance acquired by some types of property, and the lack of access to legitimate means of acquiring these symbols translate into violence at an early age as the "code of the streets" leads to confrontation over seemingly trivial matters.

C. Social Capital and Youth Violence

Social capital reflects the quality of personal relationships in families and communities, particularly intergenerational relationships. Social capital, like physical capital (wealth and other economic assets) and human capital (education and personal networks), is both a personal and a community resource. Though it is not always conceptualized as such, traditional forms of social capital produced by conventional intergenerational relationships in families and communities are reported in many studies of violent youths to have changed dramatically. The potential for development of human capital among the young, even for those who are initially advantaged by virtue of family wealth and education, may be severely limited if adequate social capital is lacking—if, for example, the human capital of parents is employed primarily outside the home to the neglect of children.

Again, however, minority children of the poor clearly are especially disadvantaged. Studies find that White children, particularly those in stable neighborhoods, are more likely to secure jobs, and better jobs, than are their minority counterparts. Moreover, White youths are better able to hold onto jobs because they have had the opportunity to become familiar with workplace discipline (an important type of *human capital*). Acquisition of familiarity with, and acquiescence to, workplace discipline, however, is enhanced by an important type of social capital, namely superior personal networks that connect White youths to better jobs.

The reciprocal nature of social capital, human capital, and crime is suggested further by data from a longitudinal study of London youths. Adult employment is hindered, and adult criminality made more likely, by early involvement in delinquent behavior with delinquent friends and with criminal parents. So concentrated is delinquent and criminal behavior among poor, minority youths that it has been suggested that *criminal capital* has become a major influence in some communities. In turn, possession of criminal capital is a serious impediment to participation in conventional society.

To the extent that they exist, conventional families—the most important source of social capital—serve for both males and females as an important buffer against the pattern of youth pregnancy and single parenting that is associated with the poverty/ethnicity/violence cycle. Studies support the importance of family relationships to crime and delinquency in general as well as to violence among young people. The most violent young people are those for whom deficits in both human and social capital are greatest. In many communies among the new urban poor the declining presence and influence of "old heads" and other attractive, conventional role models is a further indication of deficits in social capital in underclass communities. Many "old heads"—respectable, and respected, middle- and working-class adults who made it a point to advise young people as to acceptable conduct—have left these communities. Those who remain often find themselves ignored, disparaged, or threatened. Younger, flashier, and apparently successful drug dealers become role models who appeal to many who are even younger. For many such youths gangs and the homeless become agents and con-

texts of street socialization and barriers to integration of young people into conventional community life.

D. Youth Culture, Subcultures, and Violence

Young people are influenced by a variety of subcultures, some of which promote violence. Street gang culture has diffused widely across the United States and in some other countries, for example. Items of clothing, graffiti, and hand signals associated with gangs have become widely known via media portrayals. Youth who know little beyond such symbolism may use them, and affect behaviors associated with them, in a "wannabe" fashion. They may identify themselves as gangs, and become identified as gangs by others, thus enhancing their gang status. This is but one form of the cycle of gang formation and perpetuation and its influence on young people.

But more than gang culture is diffused. An even more general cultural phenomenon—youth culture—has been widely diffused throughout much of the world. Macroeconomic and social forces that fail to provide meaningful roles for young people in the adult world separate them from participation in that world. The inevitable result has been a vast gap between generations, and cultural differentiation among the young and between them and their elders. Because conditions of life vary greatly among young people, a variety of youth cultures have emerged and continue to evolve. These subcultures influence and are influenced by the broader youth culture that contains elements common to many such varieties, such as youth-oriented preferences in music, interactive media, distinctive types of clothing, and differences in life styles. Together with media advertising that caters to youthful appetites, fads, and currency, youth culture and its many variants become major influences in the lives of young people. The seductions of commercial products among less affluent youth, and the thefts and assaults that often are associated with their acquisition have been documented by a number of observers.

Observers of youth groups everywhere also note that status differences within and between them tend to be highly refined. They are also extremely variable. The criteria for status within a group, or between one group and another, may be based on relative economic affluence, skills in valued activities, public appearance, school performance, or perhaps most importantly, on life style differences. These bases of stratification typically also become criteria of inclusiveness and exclusiveness which, in turn, create opportunities for both friendship and rejection.

Adolescence is a period of especially intense relationships and shared feelings of friendship, acceptance, and respect. The converse is also true. Feelings of rejection and disrespect also are especially intense among adolescents, and often the basis for group and subcultural formation.

Next to families, schools are perhaps the most important contexts for adolescent friendship, achievement, and recognition. Because of this, school contexts (including the journey to and from schools) are the settings for much adolescent behavior, including delinquent and criminal behavior. On occasion they have also been the setting for the most extreme forms of violence (e.g., mass killings by students or others alienated from their fellows or from mainstream institutions in general). The specific causes of such extreme alienation are complex, but it is clear that schools have been especially targeted precisely because of their importance in the lives of adolescents, as symbols of rejection by both peers and an adult world that seems far removed from adolescent concerns. The ready availability of guns at times transforms normal adolescent turmoil and conflict into deadly confrontation.

VI. UNDERSTANDING AND CONTROLLING YOUTH VIOLENCE

A. Gang Members and Other Violent Youths

Except for their higher levels of involvement in violence and drug use, gang members look very much like youths who do not belong to gangs. Gangs are conducive to violence, however, because they provide a context in which violence-producing processes occur. Intervention in such group processes may prevent violence from occurring. Because provision of adult supervision is necessarily limited, however, such intervention can never be entirely successful. Most students of gangs agree that prevention of violence by gang members is best accomplished by weaning young people from gang participation. Programs that have this as their primary goal, while also providing an adult presence whenever possible, are more likely to succeed than are programs that rely solely on adult supervision.

At the individual level, most youths who become involved in violence—gang members and nongang youths alike—need individual therapy less than they need education, job skills, opportunities that will enable them to break away from peer influences, and encouragement to do so. Although males are perpetrators of violence more often than females, this generalization applies to both. Females appear to be especially vulnerable to family or domestic violence and to perpetuate such violence when they, too, become mothers, often as single teenagers. Intervention in the form of preventing unwanted pregnancies thus may be an important way to control domestic violence as well as a major factor in countering the cycle of poverty.

Studies conducted under the auspices of governmental agencies and private foundations have identified a variety of interventions that offer promise of preventing violent behavior among youths. Although they are designed with more specific goals in mind, many of these programs seem likely to increase social capital at both community and family levels. Community policing, for example, involves close cooperation between police and community residents and institutions in directing and reinforcing law enforcement. Family-oriented programs that provide much needed pre- and postnatal care for infants and their mothers can better prepare the very young for learning, and involve their parents in education and other community affairs. Economic development programs can provide jobs and job training for both youths and adults. A variety of school programs have been evaluated. Some seek to provide better security for all students and teachers. Some are aimed at teacher training and skills development and at greater involvement of students in the learning process. Still others bring other community programs and agencies into school properties so as to promote greater citizen participation in community affairs and in developing community integration.

There is general consensus that no single approach can effectively prevent violence among either young people or adults. Instead, successful programs require coordination of efforts by law enforcement and other agencies directed toward individuals, families, and community institutions. Schools and other youth-serving agencies, for example, must be both participants in and targets of violence prevention efforts. Above all, all young people, but especially those who are at risk for violent behavior, need more involvement in their lives by adults. Law enforcement agencies are both the targets and instigators of change as must be youths themselves.

B. Future Projections

Over the last quarter of the 20th century, poverty rates in the United States have been higher for juveniles than for the elderly, reversing the long-time relationship of the relative affluence of the young and the aged. Over this period, however, poverty has not been equally dis-

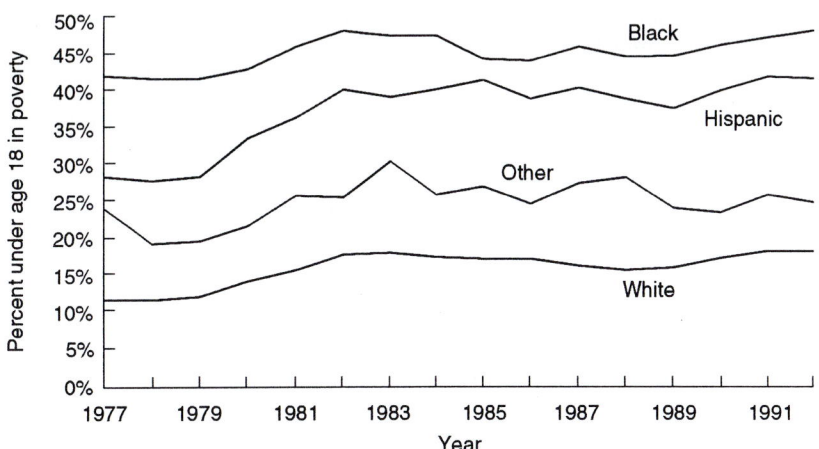

FIGURE 5 Between 1977 and 1992 increases in the proportion of juveniles living in poverty was greatest among those of Hispanic origin. In 1992, 9 million White juveniles, 5 million Black juveniles, 0.7 million juveniles of other races, and 3 million juveniles of Hispanic origin were living in poverty. (Note: Race proportions include persons of Hispanic origin. Persons of Hispanic origin can be of any race.) Source: Bureau of the Census. (1993). Poverty in the United States: 1992. Current Population Reports: Consumer Income. In Snyder and Sickmund (1885). Juvenile Offenders and Victims: A National Report. Washington, DC: National Center for Juvenile Justice, Office of Juvenile Justice and Deliquency Prevention, p. 7.

tributed among racial and ethnic populations. As can be seen in Fig. 5, the highest percentage of juveniles living in poverty is among African Americans. Hispanic juveniles, however, have experienced the largest increase in poverty, while poverty rates among "other" juveniles have fluctuated between Hispanics and Whites.

The data in Fig. 5 take on added significance in view of population projections that juveniles of Hispanic origin will increase by 71% between 1990 and 2010. This figure for African Americans is 26% and for Whites, 8%. Unless the economic and social conditions associated with youth violence change, therefore, future prospects for reductions in youth violence do not appear to be bright.

Also See the Following Articles

CHILDREARING, NONVIOLENT AND VIOLENT • DRUGS AND VIOLENCE • ETHNICITY AND IDENTITY POLITICS • GANGS • JUVENILE CRIME • MINORITIES AS PERPETRATORS AND VICTIMS OF CRIME

Bibliography

Anderson, E. (1994). The code of the streets. *Atlantic Monthly*, May, 81–94.

Bachman, R. (1992). *Death and violence on the reservation: Homicide, family violence, and suicide in American Indian populations*. New York: Auburn House.

Baldassare, M. (Ed.) (1995). The Los Angeles riots: Lessons for the urban future. Boulder, Westview.

Blumstein, A. (1995). Violence by young people: Why the deadly nexus? National Institute of Justice Journal, August, 2–9.

Bufford, B. (1991). *Among the thugs*. New York: Vintage Books.

Butts, J., Snyder, H., Finnegan, T., Aughenbaugh, A., & Poole, R. (1996). *Juvenile court statistics, 1993*. Washington, DC: National Center for Juvenile Justice, Office of Juvenile Justice and Delinquency Prevention.

Cummings, S., & Monti, D. (Eds.) (1993). *Gangs: The origin and impact of contemporary youth gangs in the United States*. Albany, NY: State University of New York Press.

Hagan, J., & McCarthy, B. (1997). *Mean streets: Youth crime and homelessness*. New York: Cambridge University Press.

Hagan, J., & Peterson, R. D. (Eds.) (1995). *Crime and inequality*. Stanford, CA: Stanford University Press.

Hawkins, D. F. (Ed.) (1995). *Ethnicity, race, and crime: Perspectives across time and place*. Albany: State Universiy of New York Press.

Huff, R. (Ed.) (1996). *Gangs in America* (2nd ed.). Newbury Park, CA: Sage.

Klein, M. (1995). *The American street gang*. New York: Oxford.

Reiss, A., & Roth, J. (Eds.) (1993). *Understanding and preventing violence*. Washington, DC: National Academy Press.

Sanchez-Jankowski, M. (1991). *Islands in the street: Gangs in American urban society*. Berkeley: University of California Press.

Sanders, W. (1994). *Gangbangs and drive-bys: Grounded culture and juvenile gang violence*. New York: Aldine de Gruyter.

Schwendinger, H., & Schwendinger, J. (1985). *Adolescent subcultures and delinquency*. New York: Praeger.

Short, J. (1997). *Poverty, ethnicity and violent crime*. Boulder, CO: Westview.

Snyder, H., Sickmund, M., & Poe-Yamagata, E. (1996). *Juvenile offenders and victims: 1996 update on violence.* Washington, DC: National Center for Juvenile Justice, Office of Juvenile Justice and Delinquency Prevention.

Snyder, H., & Sickmund, M. (1995). *Juveile offenders and victims A national report.* Washington, DC: National Center for Juvenile Justice, Office of Juvenile Justice and Delinquency Prevention.

Spergel, I. (1995). *The youth gang problem: A community approach.* New York: Oxford.

Williams, T. (1989). *The cocaine kids: The inside story of a teenage drug ring.* Menlo Park, CA: Addison–Wesley.

Wilson, W. J. (1996). *When work disappears: The world of the new urban poor.* New York: Knopf.

Wilson, W. J. (Ed.) (1993). *Sociology and the public agenda.* Newbury Park, CA: Sage.

Index